DISCARDED

S 1.1: 969-76/V.26

Foreign Relations of the
United States, 1969–1976

Volume XXVI

Arab-Israeli
Dispute,
1974–1976

Editor   Adam M. Howard

General Editor   Edward C. Keefer

United States Government Printing Office
Washington
2012

0872-B

DEPARTMENT OF STATE

Office of the Historian

Bureau of Public Affairs

For sale by the Superintendent of Documents, U.S. Government Printing Office
Internet: bookstore.gpo.gov   Phone: toll free (866) 512-1800;   DC area (202) 512-1800
Fax: (202) 512-2104 Mail: Stop IDCC, Washington, DC 20402-0001

ISBN 978-0-16-082998-7

Preface

The *Foreign Relations of the United States* series presents the official documentary historical record of major foreign policy decisions and significant diplomatic activity of the United States Government. The Historian of the Department of State is charged with the responsibility for the preparation of the *Foreign Relations* series. The staff of the Office of the Historian, Bureau of Public Affairs, under the direction of the General Editor of the *Foreign Relations* series, plans, researches, compiles, and edits the volumes in the series. Secretary of State Frank B. Kellogg first promulgated official regulations codifying specific standards for the selection and editing of documents for the series on March 26, 1925. These regulations, with minor modifications, guided the series through 1991.

Public Law 102–138, the Foreign Relations Authorization Act, established a new statutory charter for the preparation of the series which was signed by President George H.W. Bush on October 28, 1991. Section 198 of P.L. 102–138 added a new Title IV to the Department of State's Basic Authorities Act of 1956 (22 USC 4351, et seq.). The statute requires that the *Foreign Relations* series be a thorough, accurate, and reliable record of major United States foreign policy decisions and significant United States diplomatic activity. The volumes of the series should include all records needed to provide comprehensive documentation of major foreign policy decisions and actions of the United States Government. The statute also confirms the editing principles established by Secretary Kellogg: the *Foreign Relations* series is guided by the principles of historical objectivity and accuracy; records should not be altered or deletions made without indicating in the published text that a deletion has been made; the published record should omit no facts that were of major importance in reaching a decision; and nothing should be omitted for the purposes of concealing a defect in policy. The statute also requires that the *Foreign Relations* series be published not more than 30 years after the events recorded. The editor is convinced that this volume meets all regulatory, statutory, and scholarly standards of selection and editing.

Structure and Scope of the Foreign Relations *Series*

This volume is part of a subseries of volumes of the *Foreign Relations of the United States* series that documents the most important issues in the foreign policy of the administrations of Richard M. Nixon and Gerald R. Ford. Three volumes in this subseries, volume XXIII,

Arab-Israeli Dispute, 1969–1972, volume XXV, Arab-Israeli Crisis and War, 1973, and volume XXVI, Arab-Israeli Dispute, 1974–1976, cover U.S. foreign policy as it relates to the Arab-Israeli dispute. This volume begins at the start of 1974, during the aftermath of the October 1973 Arab-Israeli War and the final months of Richard Nixon's presidency. The first chapter focuses on U.S.-led negotiations between Egypt and Israel that culminated in a historic disengagement agreement between the two countries. The second chapter focuses on U.S.-led negotiations between Syria and Israel, which also resulted in a historic disengagement agreement between those two countries. The third and fourth chapters cover the U.S.-led negotiations between Egypt and Israel after Gerald Ford became president in August 1974, which ultimately led to a second disengagement agreement between Egypt and Israel. The fifth chapter concentrates on the U.S. reaction to the outbreak of Lebanon's civil war beginning in 1975.

Focus of Research and Principles of Selection for Foreign Relations, *1969–1976, Volume XXVI*

The focus of this volume is the negotiations leading to the two disengagement agreements between Egypt and Israel and the one disengagement agreement between Syria and Israel. The end of the October 1973 War left the Egyptian and Israeli armies interlocked in the Sinai and Israeli and Syrian armies interlocked in the Golan Heights. This stalemate provided Secretary of State Henry Kissinger, who had taken the lead role in negotiations concerning the Arab-Israeli dispute after the October 1973 War, the opportunity to negotiate landmark agreements between Israel and two of its Arab neighbors in the months following the war. Initial discussions between Kissinger and Arab leaders began in November 1973 (coverage of this is found in *Foreign Relations, 1969–1976*, volume XXV, Arab-Israeli Crisis and War, 1973) and culminated in formal disengagement agreements beginning in 1974. Kissinger preferred these disengagement agreements instead of a comprehensive agreement as a way to create a relationship between the Israelis and Egyptians and Syrians that could lead to a future comprehensive settlement of the Arab-Israeli dispute. Additionally, he argued that this more modest step-by-step approach would prevent individual crises, such as terrorist attacks, to sidetrack negotiations. Accordingly, this volume documents the development of this step-by-step approach beginning with the first disengagement agreement between the Israelis and Egyptians in January 1974, the only disengagement agreement between the Israelis and Syrians in May 1974, and the second disengagement agreement between the Israelis and Egyptians in September 1975.

This volume also documents the U.S. response to the outbreak of civil war in Lebanon. This final chapter begins with the U.S. Government's observation of the war in the fall of 1975, but focuses primarily on the period after the disintegration of the Lebanese army in March 1976, followed by the evacuation of U.S. embassy personnel, and concludes in August 1976 with a strategy session between Kissinger and U.S. ambassadors to the Middle East.

Since Jordan had not fought in the October 1973 War, it had no armies interlocked with the Israelis, thus leaving the Israelis little incentive to negotiate an agreement with Jordan. Due to page limitations, therefore, this volume does not cover the attempts by Jordan to engage the Israelis through U.S. mediation efforts. Additionally, this volume includes coverage of the U.S. response to the Rabat Conference in October 1974 at which the Arab League named the Palestine Liberation Organization (PLO) as the sole representative of the Palestinian people. This replaced Jordan as the representative entity to negotiate any agreements relating to the Palestinians in the West Bank and East Jerusalem.

It is worth noting that there are several memoranda of conversation between King Hussein of Jordan and Kissinger, all of which are located in the Records of Henry Kissinger at the National Archives in College Park, Maryland. They provide insight into the Jordanian government's desire to negotiate with the Israelis, observations of the Egyptian and Syrian engagement with Israel, and discussion of bilateral relations between the United States and Jordan.

Due to the intensive negotiations documented in this volume, memoranda of conversation and summaries of meetings between Kissinger and Arab and Israeli leaders dominate the documentation selected for this volume. The large number of verbatim memoranda of conversation made it necessary to use summaries from Kissinger to Nixon or Ford at different points throughout the volume. When summaries were used instead of memoranda of conversation, the memoranda of conversation have been cited to provide readers with the location of the original conversations in the archives.

In the wake of the Watergate scandal, Congress played a growing role in U.S. foreign policy and this volume includes several memoranda of conversation of congressmen meeting with Kissinger, Nixon, and Ford. The American Jewish community also expressed a strong interest in U.S. policy towards Israel during this period. Leaders of the American Jewish community met with Kissinger on numerous occasions and this volume includes a few memoranda of conversation of those meetings. Among these American Jewish leaders, Max Fisher had unique access to both Kissinger and Ford, and several of his meetings with them are documented in this volume.

Editorial Methodology

The documents are presented chronologically according to Washington time. Memoranda of conversation are placed according to the time and date of the conversation, rather than the date the memorandum was drafted.

Editorial treatment of the documents published in the *Foreign Relations* series follows Office style guidelines, supplemented by guidance from the General Editor and the chief technical editor. The documents are reproduced as exactly as possible, including marginalia or other notations, which are described in the footnotes. Texts are transcribed and printed according to accepted conventions for the publication of historical documents within the limitations of modern typography. A heading has been supplied by the editor for each document included in the volume. Spelling, capitalization, and punctuation are retained as found in the original text, except that obvious typographical errors are silently corrected. Other mistakes and omissions in the documents are corrected by bracketed insertions: a correction is set in italic type; an addition in roman type. Words or phrases underlined in the source text are printed in italics. Abbreviations and contractions are preserved as found in the original text, and a list of abbreviations is included in the front matter of each volume. In telegrams, the telegram number (including special designators such as Secto) is printed at the start of the text of the telegram.

Bracketed insertions are also used to indicate omitted text that deals with an unrelated subject (in roman type) or that remains classified after declassification review (in italic type). The amount and, where possible, the nature of the material not declassified has been noted by indicating the number of lines or pages of text that were omitted. Entire documents withheld for declassification purposes have been accounted for and are listed with headings, source notes, and number of pages not declassified in their chronological place. All brackets that appear in the original text are so identified in footnotes. All ellipses are in the original documents.

The first footnote to each document indicates the source of the document, original classification, distribution, and drafting information. This note also provides the background of important documents and policies and indicates whether the President or his major policy advisers read the document.

Editorial notes and additional annotation summarize pertinent material not printed in the volume, indicate the location of additional documentary sources, provide references to important related documents printed in other volumes, describe key events, and provide summaries of and citations to public statements that supplement and elucidate the printed documents. Information derived from memoirs and other first-hand accounts has been used when appropriate to supplement or explicate the official record.

The numbers in the index refer to document numbers rather than to page numbers.

Advisory Committee on Historical Diplomatic Documentation

The Advisory Committee on Historical Diplomatic Documentation, established under the Foreign Relations statute, reviews records, advises, and makes recommendations concerning the *Foreign Relations* series. The Advisory Committee monitors the overall compilation and editorial process of the series and advises on all aspects of the preparation and declassification of the series. The Advisory Committee does not necessarily review the contents of individual volumes in the series, but it makes recommendations on issues that come to its attention and reviews volumes, as it deems necessary to fulfill its advisory and statutory obligations.

Presidential Recordings and Materials Preservation Act Review

Under the terms of the Presidential Recordings and Materials Preservation Act (PRMPA) of 1974 (44 USC 2111 note), the Nixon Presidential Library in Yorba Linda, California has custody of the Nixon Presidential historical materials. The requirements of the PRMPA and implementing regulations govern access to the Nixon Presidential historical materials. The PRMPA and implementing public access regulations require the Nixon Library to review for additional restrictions in order to ensure the protection of the privacy rights of former Nixon White House officials, since these officials were not given the opportunity to separate their personal materials from public papers. Thus, the PRMPA and implementing public access regulations require the Nixon Library formally to notify the Nixon estate and former Nixon White House staff members that the agency is scheduling for public release Nixon White House historical materials. The Nixon estate and former White House staff members have 30 days to contest the release of Nixon historical materials in which they were a participant or are mentioned. Further, the PRMPA and implementing regulations require the Nixon Library to segregate and return to the creator of files private and personal materials. All *Foreign Relations* volumes that include materials from the Nixon Library's Nixon Presidential Materials Staff are processed and released in accordance with the PRMPA.

Declassification Review

The Office of Information Programs and Services, Bureau of Administration, conducted the declassification review for the Department of State of the documents published in this volume. The review was conducted in accordance with the standards set forth in Executive Order 12958 on Classified National Security Information, as amended, and applicable laws.

The principle guiding declassification review is to release all information, subject only to the current requirements of national security as embodied in law and regulation. Declassification decisions entailed concurrence of the appropriate geographic and functional bureaus in the Department of State, other concerned agencies of the U.S. Government, and the appropriate foreign governments regarding specific documents of those governments. The declassification review of this volume, which began in 2007 and was completed in 2010, resulted in the decision to withhold no documents in full, excisions of a paragraph or more in 5 documents, and minor excisions of less than a paragraph in 9 documents.

The Office of the Historian is confident, on the basis of the research conducted in preparing this volume and as a result of the declassification review process described above, that the record presented in this volume here provides an accurate and comprehensive account of U.S. foreign policy as it relates to the Arab-Israeli dispute and Lebanon from 1974 to 1976.

Acknowledgments

The editor wishes to acknowledge the assistance of officials at the Nixon Presidential Materials Project of the National Archives and Records Administration (Archives II), at College Park, Maryland. Additionally, the editor wishes to acknowledge the Richard Nixon Estate for allowing access to the Nixon presidential recordings and the Richard Nixon Library & Birthplace for facilitating that access. The editor also wishes to acknowledge the invaluable assistance of the archivists at the Gerald R. Ford Presidential Library in Ann Arbor, Michigan, in particular Donna Lehman, Helmi Raaska, and Geir Gundersen. John Haynes of the Library of Congress was responsible for expediting access to the Kissinger Papers. The editor was able to use the Kissinger Papers with the kind permission of Henry Kissinger. The editor would also like to thank Sandra Meagher at the Department of Defense.

Adam M. Howard collected the documentation for this volume and selected and edited it under the supervision of Edward C. Keefer, the General Editor of the *Foreign Relations* series. Dean Weatherhead coordinated the declassification review under the supervision of Susan C. Weetman, Chief of the Declassification and Publishing Division. Mandy A. Chalou did the copy editing. Do Mi Stauber prepared the index.

Bureau of Public Affairs	**Dr. Stephen Randolph**
August 2012	*The Historian*

Contents

Preface	III
Sources	XI
Abbreviations and Terms	XVII
Persons	XXI
Arab-Israeli Dispute, 1974–1976	
First Egyptian-Israeli Disengagement Agreement, January 1974	1
Syrian-Israeli Disengagement Agreement, January–May 1974	105
Negotiations and Reassessment, June 1974–June 1975	381
Second Egyptian-Israeli Disengagement Agreement, June 1975–March 1976	690
Lebanese Civil War, September 1975–August 1976	930
Appendix A	1067
Appendix B	1071
Index	1075

Sources

Sources for the Foreign Relations *Series*

The 1991 *Foreign Relations* statute requires that the published record in the *Foreign Relations* series include all records needed to provide comprehensive documentation on major U.S. foreign policy decisions and significant U.S. diplomatic activity. It further requires that government agencies, departments, and other entities of the U.S. Government engaged in foreign policy formulation, execution, or support cooperate with the Department of State Historian by providing full and complete access to records pertinent to foreign policy decisions and actions and by providing copies of selected records. Most of the sources consulted in the preparation of this volume have been declassified and are available for review at the National Archives and Records Administration.

The editors of the *Foreign Relations* series have complete access to all the retired records and papers of the Department of State: the central files of the Department; the special decentralized files ("lot files") of the Department at the bureau, office, and division levels; the files of the Department's Executive Secretariat, which contain the records of international conferences and high-level official visits, correspondence with foreign leaders by the President and Secretary of State, and memoranda of conversations between the President and Secretary of State and foreign officials; and the files of overseas diplomatic posts. All the Department's indexed central files through July 1973 have been permanently transferred to the National Archives and Records Administration at College Park, Maryland (Archives II). Many of the Department's decentralized office files covering the 1969–1976 period, which the National Archives deems worthy of permanent retention, have been transferred or are in the process of being transferred from the Department's custody to Archives II.

The editors of the *Foreign Relations* series also have full access to the papers of Presidents Nixon and Ford as well as other White House foreign policy records. Presidential papers maintained and preserved at the Presidential libraries include some of the most significant foreign affairs-related documentation from the Department of State and other Federal agencies including the National Security Council, the Central Intelligence Agency, the Department of Defense, and the Joint Chiefs of Staff. Dr. Henry Kissinger has approved access to his papers at the Library of Congress. These papers are a key source for the Nixon-Ford subseries of the *Foreign Relations* series.

XII Sources

Research for this volume was completed through special access to restricted documents at the Nixon Presidential Materials Project, the Ford Presidential Library, the Library of Congress, and other agencies. While all the material printed in this volume has been declassified, some of it is extracted from still classified documents. In the time since the research for this volume was completed, the Nixon Presidential Materials have been transferred to the Nixon Presidential Library and Museum in Yorba Linda, California. The Nixon Presidential Library staff is processing and declassifying many of the documents used in this volume, but they may not be available in their entirety at the time of publication.

Sources for Foreign Relations, *1969–1976, Volume XXVI*

The holdings of the Nixon Presidential Materials Staff at the National Archives and Records Administration (NARA), specifically the National Security Council (NSC) Files are the most valuable resources for Nixon administration foreign policy at the highest level. Within the NSC Files, the NSC Institutional Files or (H-Files), are of particular importance. These contain the relevant National Security Study Memoranda, the resulting National Security Decision Memoranda, supporting study and policy papers, other background material, and memoranda of note. They contain documents prepared for the National Security Council, Senior Review Group meetings, and Washington Special Action Group meetings, and the minutes of those meetings.

Also held by the Nixon Presidential Materials Staff as part of the NSC Files, are the Agency Files, the Country Files, the Saunders Files, Kissinger's Office Files, Presidential/HAK Memcons, and Subject Files. For this volume, the Presidential/HAK Memcons provided crucial memoranda of conversation that included many verbatim discussions between Kissinger and leaders of the countries involved in shuttle diplomacy, especially Israel, Egypt, and Syria, but also including Jordan, Saudi Arabia, and Lebanon. The Country Files hold valuable material for researching bilateral relations. Although much of the material in the Country Files can be found in Record Group 59, the Department of State Central Files, the Country Files contain cable traffic on topics deemed most significant by the White House. The Country Files also include memoranda of conversation involving various Middle Eastern leaders, and White House, State Department, and NSC assessments of each country's importance to the United States in terms of Middle East negotiations. The Country Files, the Presidential Trip Files, and VIP Visits Files (which include important briefing material) provide comprehensive documentation on high-level meetings, which are crucial to the makeup of this volume. The most critical Country Files for this volume include Israel, Egypt, Syria, Jordan, and Lebanon. Kissinger's

Office Files, particularly his Country Files on Egypt, and the Middle East, are an important source of material. Although significant for researching Middle East issues during this period, the Harold H. Saunders Files include lower level material during this era of U.S. diplomacy in the Arab-Israeli dispute. Saunders regularly maintained copies of critical cable traffic, most NSC internal memoranda, study papers, background and briefing material prepared for Kissinger, and letters to Kissinger for Nixon.

The most significant material for this volume found in the Ford Library derived from the National Security Adviser file. Since this volume includes a large number of memoranda of conversation relating to the various negotiations during Ford's presidency, the Memoranda of Conversation section of this file proved especially rich with verbatim memoranda of conversation between Kissinger and various foreign and domestic leaders. Also within the National Security Adviser file, the Trip Briefing Books for Henry Kissinger held helpful documentation for Kissinger's shuttles that took place in the Middle East from 1974 to 1975.

For the chapter on Lebanon, the Record Group 59 Lot Files, held at NARA, were of primary importance for Secretary of State Kissinger's Staff Meetings, which included memoranda of conversation between Kissinger and high level officers within the Department. At these meetings Kissinger and his staff observed the situation in Lebanon between 1975 and 1976 and debated what U.S. actions needed to be implemented. Many of these conversations include Kissinger's take not only on Lebanon but also asides about his views regarding the Department of State's bureaucracy and general current affairs of that time. Additionally, the Country Files for Lebanon provide some relevant cable traffic between the Department of State and the U.S. embassy in Lebanon.

The Henry A. Kissinger Papers at the Library of Congress were essential for this volume although these papers are closed to the public. The Kissinger Papers contain copies of telegrams and memoranda of conversation not available in any other repositories. The Geopolitical Files and Subject Files proved most helpful in finding telegrams and memoranda of conversation that were not available elsewhere. Additionally, within the Geopolitical Files and the Chronological Files for Egypt, Israel, Syria, and the Middle East, there are many documents either not found in other repositories or found in more complete form.

Documentation from Record Group 330, Records of the Office of the Secretary of Defense at the Washington National Records Center in Suitland, Maryland, which are also closed to the general public, proved of minimal use as the Department of Defense played no significant role in diplomatic negotiations. However, material relating to arms sales are plentiful there, especially memoranda of conversation between Israeli leaders and the Secretary of Defense as well as some Arab leaders and DOD officials.

For those who wish to see conversations between King Hussein and Kissinger as well as a meeting between King Hussein and President Ford, several memoranda of conversation are listed below. They provide insight into various subjects of interest to both sides during this period. For 1974, there are memoranda of conversation for January 19 (National Archives, S/S Files, Lot 91D414, Box 3, Folder–Nodis Memcons September–December Folder 7 cont'd), March 3 (National Archives, S/S Files, Lot 91D414, Box 7, Folder–Nodis Memcons March 1974 Folder 6), March 15 (National Archives, S/S Files, Lot 91D414, Box 7, Folder–Nodis Memcons March 1974 Folder 7), May 5 (National Archives, S/S Files, Lot 91D414, Box 8, Folder–Nodis Memcons May 1974 Folder 3), August 16 (National Archives, S/S Files, Lot 91D414, Box 9, Folder–Nodis Memcons August 1974 Folder 4), and October 12 (National Archives, S/S Files, Lot 91D414, Box 25, Folder–CATC Nodis Memcons). On April 29, 1975, King Hussein met with President Ford for the first time and discussed the Egyptian-Israeli negotiations as well as bilateral relations between Jordan and the United States (National Archives, S/S Files, Lot 91D414, Box 22, Folder–Classified External Memcons, December 1974–April 1975 Folder 7).

Almost all of this documentation has been made available for use in the *Foreign Relations* series thanks to the consent of the agencies mentioned, the assistance of their staffs, and especially the cooperation and support of the National Archives and Records Administration.

The following list identifies the particular files and collections used in the preparation of this volume. In addition to the paper files cited below, a growing number of documents are available on the Internet. The Office of the Historian maintains a list of these Internet resources on its website and suggests that readers refer to that site on a regular basis.

Unpublished Sources

Department of State

Central Files. *See* Record Group 59 under National Archives and Records Administration below

Lot Files. *See* Record Group 59 under National Archives and Records Administration Below

National Archives and Records Administration, College Park, Maryland

Record Group 59, General Records of the Department of State

Central Foreign Policy Files, 1973–1976

Part of the online Access to Archival Databases; Electronic Telegrams, P-Reel Index, P-Reel microfilm

Lot Files

S/S Files, Lot 78D443
>Transcripts of Secretary of State Kissinger's Staff Meetings, 1973–1977

S/S Files, Lot 91D414
>Records of Secretary of State Henry Kissinger, 1973–1977

S/S Files, Lot 74D131
>Records of Assistant Secretary of State Joseph Sisco, 1973–77

Nixon Presidential Materials Project, National Archives and Records Administration, College Park, Maryland (now at the Nixon Presidential Library and Museum, Yorba Linda, California)

National Security Council (NSC) Files
>Agency Files
>Backchannel Files
>Country Files
>>Europe
>
>Kissinger Office Files
>Country Files
>>Middle East
>
>HAK Trip Files
>Name Files
>NSC Institutional Materials (H-Files)
>>Meeting Files, Senior Review Group Meetings
>>Minutes of Meetings, NSC Meeting Minutes
>>Minutes of Meetings, Senior Review Group
>>Miscellaneous Institutional Files of the Nixon Administration
>>Policy Papers, National Security Decision Memorandums
>>Study Memorandums, National Security Study Memorandums
>
>NSC Unfiled Material
>Presidential Correspondence
>Presidential/HAK Memcons
>Harold H. Saunders Files, Middle East Negotiations Files Subject Files
>VIP Visits

White House Central Files
>President's Daily Diary

Gerald R. Ford Presidential Library, Ann Arbor, Michigan

>National Security Adviser Files
>>Backchannel Messages
>>Kissinger Reports on the USSR, China, and Middle East Discussions
>>Kissinger-Scowcroft West Wing Office Files
>>Memoranda of Conversations
>>National Security Decision Memoranda and National Security Study Memoranda

NSC Staff for Middle East and South Asia, Convenience Files
NSC Meeting Minutes
Presidential Country Files for the Middle East and South Asia
Presidential Name File
Presidential Subject File
Scowcroft Daily Work Files
National Security Council Institutional Files
President's Daily Diary

Library of Congress, Washington, DC

Papers of Henry A. Kissinger
Cables
Chronological File
Department of State
Geopolitical File
Memoranda of Conversations
National Security Council

Washington National Records Center, Suitland, Maryland

RG 330, Records of the Office of the Secretary of Defense
OSD Files: FRC 330–79–0050
Top Secret Records of the Secretary of Defense and the Special Assistant to the Secretary and Deputy Secretary of Defense
OSD Files: FRC 330–79–0058
Secret Records of the Secretary of Defense, the Deputy Secretary of Defense, and the Special Assistant to the Secretary and Deputy Secretary of Defense

Published Sources

Kissinger, Henry. *Years of Upheaval*. Boston: Little, Brown, 1982.
———. *Years of Renewal*. New York: Simon & Schuster, 1999.
United Nations. *Yearbook of the United Nations, 1973*. New York: Office of Public Information, United Nations, 1976.
United States. Department of State. *Bulletin*. 1973–1976.
———. National Archives and Records Administration. *Public Papers of the Presidents of the United States: Richard M. Nixon, 1971, 1972, 1973*. Washington: Government Printing Office, 1972, 1974, 1975.
———. National Archives and Records Administration. *Public Papers of the Presidents of the United States: Gerald R. Ford, 1974, 1975, 1976–1977*. Washington: Government Printing Office, 1975, 1977, 1979.

Abbreviations and Terms

addee, addressee
AF, Bureau of African Affairs, Department of State
AID, Agency for International Development
Amb, Ambassador
APC, Armored Personnel Carrier

backchannel, a method of communication outside normal bureaucratic procedure; the Nixon White House, for instance, used backchannel messages to bypass the Department of State
BBC, British Broadcasting Corporation

C–5A, military transport aircraft designed to carry troops and heavy cargo
CA, circular airgram
CBU, Cluster Bomb Unit
CENTO, Central Treaty Organization
CIA, Central Intelligence Agency
COMINT, Communications Intelligence
COMSEC, Communications Security
CRA, Continuing Resolution Authority
CSCE, Commission on Security and Cooperation in Europe

Del, Delegation
DIA, Defense Intelligence Agency
Dissem, dissemination
DOD, Department of Defense

E and E, emergency and evacuation
ECM, electronic countermeasures
EEC, European Economic Community
ELINT, Electronic Signals Intelligence
EOB, Executive Office Building
ERDA, Energy Research and Development Administration
EXCOM, Executive Committee
Exdis, Exclusive Distribution (extremely limited distribution)

F–4, Phantom II Fighter Bomber
FLIR, Forward Looking Infrared Radiometer
Foxbat, NATO codename for the Soviet MIG–25 fighter jet
FROG, Free Rocket over Ground, Soviet artillery rocket
FMS, Foreign Military Sales

GNP, Gross National Product
GOE, Government of Egypt
GOI, Government of Israel
GOJ, Government of Jordan
GOL, Government of Lebanon
GOS, Government of Syria

XVII

XVIII Abbreviations and Terms

Hakto, series indicator for telegrams sent by Henry Kissinger
Hawk, surface-to-air missile

ICAO, International Civil Aviation Organization
ICRC, International Committee of the Red Cross
IDF, Israel Defense Force
IMF, International Monetary Fund
INR, Bureau of Intelligence and Research, Department of State
INR/RNA/NE, Office of Research and Analysis for Near East and South Asia, Near East Division, Bureau of Intelligence and Research, Department of State

J, Under Secretary of State for Political Affairs
JCS, Joint Chiefs of Staff

Lance, mobile field artillery tactical missile
Limdis, Limited Distribution
LGB, laser guided bomb
LOU, Limited Official Use
LST, Tank Landing Ship (formally defined as Landing Ship, Tank)

M–48, U.S. Army tank used extensively in Vietnam
M–60, machine gun
MEPC, Middle East Peace Conference
MFA, Ministry of Foreign Affairs
MFN, Most Favored Nation
ME, Middle East
MEPC, Middle East Peace Conference
MIG–23, Soviet fighter jet

NATO, North Atlantic Treaty Organization
NEA, Bureau of Near Eastern and South Asian Affairs, Department of State; after April 27, 1974, Bureau of Near Eastern Affairs
NEA/ARN, Country Director for Lebanon, Jordan, Syrian Arab Republic, and Iraq Affairs, Bureau of Near Eastern and South Asian Affairs, Department of State
NEA/ARP, Country Director for Saudi Arabia, Kuwait, Yemen, and Aden Affairs, Bureau of Near Eastern and South Asian Affairs, Department of State
NEA/EGY, Country Director for Egyptian Affairs, Bureau of Near Eastern and South Asian Affairs, Department of State
NEA/IAI, Country Director for Israel and Arab-Israeli Affairs, Bureau of Near Eastern and South Asian Affairs, Department of State
NEA/RA, Office of Regional Affairs, Bureau of Near Eastern and South Asian Affairs, Department of State
NEA/SYR, Country Director for Syian Affairs, Bureau of Near Eastern and South Asian Affairs, Department of State
NIE, National Intelligence Estimate
Nodis, no distribution (other than to persons indicated)
Noforn, no foreign dissemination
NSA, National Security Agency
NSC, National Security Council
NSDM, National Security Decision Memorandum
NSSM, National Security Study Memorandum

OAPEC, Organization of Arab Petroleum Exporting Countries
OAU, Organization of African Unity

OPEC, Organization of Petroleum Exporting Countries
OV–1D, surveillance airplane

PFLP, Popular Front for the Liberation of Palestine
PL–480, Public Law 480
PLA, Palestine Liberation Army
PLO, Palestine Liberation Organization
PM, Prime Minister
PNG, persona non grata
POW, prisoner of war
PRC, People's Republic of China

reftel, reference telegram
Rep(s), Representative(s)
Res, Resolution
RG, Record Group
RN, Richard Nixon
rpt, repeat

S, Office of the Secretary of State
SA–7, Soviet portable and shoulder-fired surface to air missile
SALT, Strategic Arms Limitation Treaty
SAM, surface-to-air missile
SCUD, surface-to-surface missile system
SG, Secretary General
Secto, series indicator for telegrams sent by the Secretary of State
septel, separate telegram
SFRC, Senate Foreign Relations Committee
SIGINT, Signals Intelligence
SNIE, Special National Intelligence Estimate
SR–71, U.S. Air Force jet known as the Blackbird; a successor to the U–2, gathering intelligence at high altitude
SRG, Senior Review Group; Special Review Group
S/S, Executive Secretariat, Department of State
S/S–O, Operations Center, Executive Secretariat, Department of State

TASS, Soviet news agency
Tohak, series indicator for telegrams to Henry Kissinger
Tosec, series indicator for telegrams to the Secretary of State
TOW, Tube-launched, Optically Tracked, Wire Guided (Anti-Tank Missile System)

U, Office of the Under Secretary of State
UJA, United Jewish Appeal
UK, United Kingdom
UN, United Nations
UNDOF, United Nations Disengagement Observer Force
UNEF, United Nations Emergency Force
UNESCO, United Nations Educational, Scientific, and Cultural Organization
UNGA, United Nations General Assembly
UNRWA, United Nations Relief and Works Agency for Palestine Refugees in the Near East
UNTSO, United Nations Truce Supervision Organization
USIS, United States Information Service
USNATO, United States Mission to the North Atlantic Treaty Organization

USSR, Union of Soviet Socialist Republics
USUN, United States Mission to the United Nations

VOA, Voice of America

WH, White House
WSAG, Washington Special Actions Group

Persons

Albert, Carl, member, U.S. House of Representatives (D-Oklahoma); Speaker of the House of Representatives
Alireza, H.E. Ali, Saudi Ambassador to the United States from 1975
Allon, Yigal, Israeli Deputy Prime Minister until March 1974; Israeli Foreign Minister from June 1974
Anderson, John B., member, U.S. House of Representatives (R-Illinois)
Anderson, Glenn M., member, U.S. House of Representatives (D-California)
Anderson, Robert, Special Assistant to the Secretary of State for Press Relations
Arafat, Yassir, Chairman, Palestine Liberation Organization's Central Committee
al-Asad (Assad), Hafez, President of Syria
Atherton, Alfred L., Jr. "Roy," Deputy Assistant Secretary of State for Near Eastern and South Asian Affairs until April 27, 1974; thereafter Assistant Secretary of State for Near Eastern Affairs

Ball, George, Under Secretary of State from January 1962 until September 1966; Representative to the United Nations from June 1968 until September 1968
Bar-On, Aryeh, Colonel, aide to General Dayan
Begin, Menachem, leader, Likud party of Israel
Bentsen, Lloyd, Senator (D-Texas)
Bhutto, Zulfika Ali, Pakistani Prime Minister
Bitsios, Dimitrios, Greek Foreign Minister from October 1974
Boumediene, Houari, President of Algeria
Bouteflika, Abdelaziz, Algerian Foreign Minister
Bremer, L. Paul "Jerry," Special Assistant to the Secretary of State from May 1973
Brezhnev, Leonid, General Secretary of the Communist Party of the Soviet Union
Brooke, Edward W., Senator (R-Massachusetts)
Brown, George S., General, USAF, Chairman of the Joint Chiefs of Staff from July 1, 1974
Brown, L. Dean, Ambassador to Jordan until November 1973; Deputy Under Secretary of State for Management until February 1975; Special Envoy to Lebanon from April 1976 until May 1976
Brzezinski, Zbigniew, Director of the Trilateral Commission
Buffum, William B., Ambassador to Lebanon until January 17, 1974; Assistant Secretary of State for International Organizations from February 4, 1975, until December 18, 1975
Bunker, Ellsworth, Ambassador at Large; chief of the U.S. delegation to the Geneva Middle East Peace Conference
Burton, Phillip, member, U.S. House of Representatives (D-California)
Bush, George H.W., Director of Central Intelligence from January 30, 1976
Butz, Earl, Secretary of Agriculture until October 4, 1976

Callaghan, James, British Foreign Minister from March 5, 1974, until April 8, 1976
Carter, Jimmy, Governor of Georgia; Democratic Presidential candidate in 1976
Case, Clifford P., II, Senator (R-New Jersey)
Chamoun, Camille, President of Lebanon from 1952 until 1958; leader, Lebanese National Liberal Party, which joined the Lebanese Front in 1976
Cheney, Richard, White House Chief of Staff from November 21, 1975
Clark, Richard, Senator (D-Iowa)

XXII Persons

Clements, William P., Jr., Deputy Secretary of Defense
Colby, William E., Director of Central Intelligence until January 30, 1976

Daoudi, Riad, legal adviser to Syrian President Hafez al-Asad
Davis, Jeanne W., member, National Security Council staff
Day, Arthur R., Deputy Assistant Secretary of State for Near Eastern and South Asian Affairs from 1975
Dayan, Moshe, Israeli Defense Minister until June 1974; Knesset member from 1959
Dinitz, Simcha, Israeli Ambassador to the United States
Dobrynin, Anatoliy, Soviet Ambassador to the United States
Dominick, Peter, Senator (R-Colorado)
Draper, Morris, Country Director, Lebanon, Jordan, Syria, Iraq, Bureau of Near Eastern and South Asian Affairs, Department of State

Eagleburger, Lawrence S., Executive Assistant to the Secretary of State until February 1975; thereafter Deputy Under Secretary of State for Management
Eban, Abba, Israeli Foreign Minister until June 1974
Eilts, Hermann F., Ambassador to Egypt from March 1974
Elazar, David, General, Chief of Staff of the Israel Defense Forces until April 1974
Elias, Asad, Syrian Press Secretary
Ellsworth, Robert F., Assistant Secretary of Defense for International Security Affairs from June 1974 until December 1975; Deputy Secretary of Defense from December 1975
Evron, Ephraim, Deputy Director General, Israeli Ministry of Foreign Affairs

Fahd bin Abdul Aziz al Saud, Prince, Saudi Minister of the Interior; Second Deputy Prime Minister
Fahmy (Fahmi), Ismail, Egyptian Foreign Minister; Deputy Prime Minister from April 1975
Faisal ibn Abd al-Aziz al Saud, King of Saudi Arabia until his death on March 25, 1975
Fisher, Max, Special Adviser to President Ford
Ford, Gerald R., Vice President of the United States until August 8, 1974; President of the United States from August 9, 1974
Frangieh, Suleiman, Lebanese President until September 1976
Frelinghuysen, Peter, Jr., member, U.S. House of Representatives (R-New Jersey)
Fulbright, J. William, Senator (D-Arkansas) until 1974; Chairman of the Senate Foreign Relations Committee until 1974

al-Gamasy, Mohammed Abdel Ghani, General, Egyptian Chief of Staff; Deputy Prime Minister from April 1975
Gazit, Mordechai, Director General, Israeli Prime Minister's Office
Giscard d'Estaing, Valéry, President of France from May 1974
Godley, G. McMurtrie, Ambassador to Lebanon from February 1974 until January 1976
Goldmann, Nahum, Zionist and President of the World Jewish Congress
Goldwater, Barry S., Senator (R-Arizona)
Greenspan, Alan, Chairman, Council of Economic Advisers
Gromyko, Andrei, Soviet Foreign Minister
Gur, Mordechai, Lieutenant General, Chief of Staff of the Israel Defense Force from 1974

Haig, Alexander M., Jr., Brigadier General, USA, White House Chief of Staff until September 1974; Supreme Allied Commander Europe from December 1974
Hamilton, Lee H., member, U.S. House of Representatives (D-Indiana)
Hassan II, King of Morocco

Hays, Wayne, member, U.S. House of Representatives (D-Ohio); Chairman of the House Administration Committee
Hébert, Felix E., member, U.S. House of Representatives (D-Louisiana)
Humphrey, Hubert H., Senator (D-Minnesota)
Hussein bin Talal, King of Jordan
Hyland, William G., Director, Bureau of Intelligence and Research, Department of State, from January 1974 until November 1975; Deputy Assistant to the President for National Security Affairs from 1975

Iklé, Fred, Director of the Arms Control and Disarmament Agency
Ingersoll, Robert S., Assistant Secretary of State for East Asian and Pacific Affairs until July 1974; Deputy Secretary of State from July 1974 until March 1976
Inouye, Daniel, Senator (D-Hawaii)

Jackson, Henry "Scoop," Senator (D-Washington)
Javits, Jacob K., Senator (R-New York)
Jumblatt, Kamal, leader of anti-government forces in Lebanon

Karame (Karami), Rashid, Lebanese Prime Minister from July 1, 1975, until December 8, 1976
Katzir, Ephraim, President of Israel
Keating, Kenneth B., Ambassador to Israel from August 1973 until May 1975
Kennedy, Edward M., Senator (D-Massachusetts)
Khaddam, Abdul Halim, Syrian Foreign Minister
Khalid bin Abdul Aziz, King of Saudi Arabia from March 25, 1975
Kidron, Avraham, Director, Israeli Ministry of Foreign Affairs
Kissinger, Henry A., Assistant to the President for National Security Affairs until October 1975; Secretary of State from September 1973
Koch, Edward, member, U.S. House of Representatives (D-New York)
Kollek, Teddy, Mayor of Jerusalem
Korologos, Tom C., Deputy Assistant to the President for Legislative Affairs (Senate) until 1974
Kosygin, Aleksei, Soviet Premier

Lambrakis, George B., Chargé d'Affaires of the Embassy in Beirut
Leor, David, Brigadier General, Military Assistant to Prime Minister Meir
Lord, Winston, Director, Policy Planning Staff, Department of State
Lynn, James T., Director of the Office of Management and Budget from 1975

Mahon, George H., member, U.S. House of Representatives (D-Texas)
Malik, Charles H., former Lebanese Foreign Minister; former President of the U.N. General Assembly
Malik, Yakov A., Soviet Representative to the United Nations
Mansfield, Michael, Senator (D-Montana)
Mathias, Charles, Senator (R-Maryland)
Maw, Carlyle E., Department of State Legal Adviser until July 1974
McClellan, John, Senator (R-Arkansas)
McCloskey, Robert J., Ambassador at Large until February 1975; Assistant Secretary of State for Congressional Relations from February 1975 until September 1976; thereafter Ambassador to the Netherlands
McCloy, John J., adviser to Presidents John F. Kennedy, Lyndon B. Johnson, and Richard Nixon
McFall, John J., member, U.S. House of Representatives (D-California)
McGovern, George S., Senator (D-South Dakota)

XXIV   Persons

McNamara, Robert S., President of the World Bank
Meir, Golda, Israeli Prime Minister until April 11, 1974
Meloy, Francis E., Jr., Ambassador to Lebanon from May 1, 1976, until his assassination in Beirut on June 16, 1976
Moorer, Thomas H., Admiral, USN, Chairman of the Joint Chiefs of Staff until July 1974
Morgan, Thomas E., member, U.S. House of Representatives (D-Pennsylvania)
Morton, Rogers B., Secretary of Commerce
Moynihan, Daniel P., Representative to the United Nations from June 1975 until February 1976
Mubarak, Hosni, Major General; Egyptian Vice President
Mulcahy, Edward W., Deputy Assistant Secretary of State for African Affairs from 1974
Murphy, Richard W., Ambassador to Syria from September 1974
Muskie, Edmund S., Senator (D-Maine)

Nasser, Gamal Abdel, President of Egypt from June 1956 until September 1970
Nessen, Ronald H. "Ron," Press Secretary for President Ford
Nixon, Richard M., President of the United States until August 9, 1974

Oakley, Robert B., Area Director for Middle East and South Asian Affairs, National Security Council staff
O'Neill, Thomas P. "Tip," member, U.S. House of Representatives (D-Massachusetts); House Majority Leader

Pahlavi, Mohammed Reza, Shah of Iran
Passman, Otto, member, U.S. House of Representatives (D-Louisiana)
Pell, Claiborne, Senator (D-Rhode Island)
Percy, Charles H., Senator (R-Illinois)
Peres, Shimon, Israeli Defense Minister from June 3, 1974
Pickering, Thomas R., Ambassador to Jordan from February 1974
Porter, William J., Ambassador to Saudi Arabia from December 1975

al-Qadhafi, Mu'ammar, Chairman of the Libyan Revolutionary Command Council and Commander-in-Chief of the Libyan Armed Forces

Rabin, Yitzhak, Israeli Minister of Labor from March 10 until June 3, 1974; thereafter Prime Minister
Ramsbotham, Peter, British Ambassador to the United States
Reagan, Ronald, Governor of California; Republican Presidential candidate in 1976
Rhodes, John, member, U.S. House of Representatives (R-Arizona)
Ribicoff, Abraham A., Senator (D-Connecticut)
Richardson, Elliot L., Ambassador to the United Kingdom from February 1975 until January 1976; Secretary of Commerce from February 1976
Rifai, Zaid, Jordanian Prime Minister until July 1976
Robinson, Charles W., Under Secretary of State for Economic, Energy, and Agricultural Affairs from December 1974 until April 1976; thereafter Deputy Secretary of State
Rockefeller, Nelson, Vice President of the United States from December 19, 1974
Rodman, Peter W., member, National Security Council staff; Special Assistant to Henry Kissinger
Rosenthal, Benjamin S., member, U.S. House of Representatives (D-New York)
Rumsfeld, Donald H., Permanent Representative to the North Atlantic Treaty Organization until August 1974; Assistant to President Ford until September 1974; White House Chief of Staff until October 1975; thereafter Secretary of Defense
Rush, Kenneth, Deputy Secretary of State from February 1973 to May 1974; Ambassador to France from September 1974

al-Sadat, Anwar, Egyptian President
Salim, Mamdouh, Egyptian Prime Minister from April 1975
Sapir, Pinchas, Israeli Finance Minister
Saqqaf, Omar, Saudi Arabian Foreign Minister
Sarkis, Elias, Lebanese President from May 1976
Saunders, Harold H., member, National Security Council staff until 1974; Deputy Assistant Secretary of State for Near Eastern and South Asian Affairs from 1974 to December 1975; thereafter Director, Bureau of Intelligence and Research, Department of State
Scali, John, Representative to the United Nations from February 1973 until June 1975
Schlesinger, James R., Secretary of Defense until October 1975
Schmidt, Helmut, German Minister of Finance until May 1974; German Chancellor from May 1974
Schweid, Barry, Associated Press reporter
Scotes, Thomas J., Principal Officer, U.S. Interests Section in Syria from February 1974; Charge d'Affaires ad interim from June 1974 until August 1974
Scott, Hugh D., Jr., Senator (R-Pennsylvania); Senate Minority Leader
Scowcroft, Brent, General, USAF, Deputy Assistant to the President for National Security Affairs until October 1975; Assistant to the President for National Security Affairs from October 1975
Scranton, William W., Representative to the United Nations from March 1976
Seelye, Talcott W., Special Representative to Lebanon after Ambassador Meloy's assassination
Shalev, Mordechai, Chargé d'Affaires of the Israeli Embassy in the United States
al-Shihabi, Hikmat, Brigadier General, Syrian Chief of Intelligence and Reconnaissance
Siilasvuo, Ensio, General, Finnish Commander of the UN Emergency Force until August 1975
Simon, William E., Secretary of the Treasury
Sisco, Joseph J., Assistant Secretary of State for Near Eastern and South Asian Affairs until February 1974; Under Secretary of State for Political Affairs from February 1974 until July 1976
Sparkman, John J., Senator (D-Alabama); Chairman of the Senate Foreign Relations Committee from 1975
Stennis, John C., Senator (D-Mississippi); Chairman of the Senate Armed Services Committee
Stevenson, Adlai, III, Senator (D-Illinois)

Takla, Philippe, Lebanese Foreign Minister from 1974 until 1975 and from 1975 until 1976
Timmons, William, Assistant to the President for Legislative Affairs until 1974
Toon, Malcolm "Mac," Ambassador to Israel from June 1975 until December 1976
Tower, John, Senator (D-Texas)

Vest, George, Special Assistant to the Secretary of State for Press Relations until April 1974; thereafter Director, Bureau of Politico-Military Affairs, Department of State
Vinogradov, Sergei, Soviet Ambassador to Egypt; Soviet Representative to the Geneva Middle East Peace Conference from December 1973 until January 1974

Waldheim, Kurt, Secretary General of the United Nations
Wiesel, Elie, Author; Distinguished Professor at City University of New York
Winter, Elmer L., President, American Jewish Committee

Yamani, Ahmed Z., Saudi Oil Minister
Yariv, Aharon, Major General, Israeli Transport Minister and Information Minister

Yost, Charles W., Representative to the United Nations from January 1969 until February 1971

Zablocki, Clement, member, U.S. House of Representatives (D-Wisconsin)
Ziegler, Ron, White House Press Secretary

Arab-Israeli Dispute, 1974–1976

First Egyptian-Israeli Disengagement Agreement, January 1974

1. Memorandum From the President's Assistant for National Security Affairs (Kissinger) to President Nixon[1]

Washington, January 6, 1974.

Following seven hours of discussions with Defense Minister Dayan,[2] focused principally on the question of disengagement of forces along the Egyptian-Israeli front, I can report good progress and a substantial evolution in Israeli thinking. I want to give you the essence of these talks and describe as well the potential pitfalls ahead.

You will recall that when Prime Minister Meir was here in November,[3] the word "withdrawal" was, in effect, taboo. Over the last two days, however, Dayan, backed by a Cabinet decision, outlined a pullback plan designed to reduce the likelihood of renewed war and to return a part of the Sinai to normal Egyptian peace-time activity, including the opening of the Suez Canal. Dayan is reporting to the Cabinet today, and I expect to hear from him tomorrow. They have urged me to take the plan to Cairo immediately.

The principal features of the plan, many details of which, on your instructions, I had discussed or suggested to Mrs. Meir in our December talks,[4] are as follows: Israel would withdraw all of its forces

---

[1] Source: National Archives, Nixon Presidential Materials, NSC Files, Kissinger Office Files, Box 136, Country Files, Middle East, Dinitz, 1/1–7/1, 1974, (2). Secret; Nodis.

[2] On January 4, Kissinger met with Dayan and others between 12:20 and 2:40 p.m., and on January 5, Kissinger met again with Dayan and other U.S. and Israeli officials between 10:30 a.m. and 1:40 p.m. Both meetings were held at the Department of State. (Memoranda of conversation; ibid., RG 59, Records of Henry Kissinger, 1973–77, Box 6, Nodis Memcons, August 1974)

[3] See *Foreign Relations,* 1969–1976, volume XXV, Arab-Israeli Crisis and War, 1973, Documents 305, 306, and 312.

[4] For documentation on Kissinger's December 1973 trip to Jerusalem, see ibid., Documents 398–401.

presently west of the Suez Canal behind a main Israeli defense line which would be about 30 kilometers east of the Canal approximately at the western end of the Mitla and Gidi Passes; the Egyptian second and third armies would retain, with slight modification, the line they presently hold, which runs about 8 to 10 kilometers east of the Canal; the armies would be substantially thinned out east of the Canal to create an additional 6–10 kilometer wide forward zone containing only light Egyptian weapons; moving eastward, there would be about a 10 kilometer demilitarized buffer zone supervised by the UN force; next, there would be a comparably lightly armed 6–10 kilometer Israeli forward zone up to the main Israeli defense line. In addition, the Israelis would be willing to move their artillery and anti-aircraft weapons far enough eastward so that only their own forces are covered, provided the Egyptians are willing to move their own artillery and anti-aircraft back far enough west of the Canal to accomplish the same purpose.

The fact that the Israelis have been willing to put forward such a plan means that they have now come 85 percent of the way to the Egyptian position on disengagement, and this without any demands for reciprocity. Nevertheless, while the plan has a sensible inner logic and is a major step forward, there is hard bargaining ahead which could lead to a very serious delay. The principal points at issue are likely to be:

(a) Dayan was firm that the main defense line must be no more than 30 kilometers east of the Canal so that the Israelis retain full control of the two strategic passes, this despite the fact their representative at Geneva pulled a major blunder yesterday when he spoke of a "model" plan envisioning a line 35 kilometers east of the Canal and in the passes themselves. Sadat will be very tough on this since he wants the main Israeli defense line to be east of the passes.

(b) A second serious point relates to the number and types of arms Egypt would retain in its forward zone east of the Canal. Dayan has said no more than 2 or 3 battalions could be allowed and no tanks. In my last talk with Sadat,[5] I was able to get him down from the present 5 divisions to 2 divisions and a minimum of 200 tanks.

(c) A third concern relates to the positioning of the main artillery and anti-aircraft weapons in the rear security zones. Because the disengagement, in Sadat's eyes, is all taking place on Egyptian sovereign territory, he will find it very difficult to accept any limitations in the territory west of the Suez Canal and he will want to keep his artillery and anti-aircraft close to the Canal.

In addition, the Israelis lay considerable stress on certain bilateral assurances from us which, on the whole, should not prove insurmount-

---

[5] See ibid., Document 390.

able. In particular, they want: (a) assurance from the U.S. that free passage through the Red Sea at Bab Al Mandeb will be assured; and (b) that the U.S. would veto any unilateral withdrawal of the UN force that might be attempted in the UN Security Council. They also stressed heavily that the ceasefire must be of a permanent character and that everything possible should be done to build up peaceful activities in the Canal area as a further psychological deterrent to a renewal of war.

In addition to the above main substantive issues, we have a critical timing problem. My judgment is that unless we can avoid an impasse resulting from the substantive differences and break the back of this thing in the next ten days, matters could get out of control. Any of a number of unfortunate developments could take place. For example, if resolution of the differences is put into the Geneva forum,[6] the Egyptians are likely to have to prove their manhood, regardless of the proximity of the Israeli plan to their own proposals. This could result in the prestige of both sides becoming involved, with consequent deadlock or at best substantial delay. Another possibility is that if there is no rapid movement, the Soviets may decide to run with the ball. Other Arab nations, such as Syria and Libya, could try to inject themselves into the issue, creating further delay and confusion. Conversely, if we do not move very quickly and the radical Arabs perceive that an agreement is shaping up, they could go to war to prevent its consummation. Finally, of course, a quick agreement is essential to get the oil embargo and production restrictions lifted.[7]

The need for speed to avert these pitfalls is apparent and I am giving urgent consideration to the best means for bringing these matters to a rapid conclusion.

---

[6] A reference to the Middle East Peace Conference, which began on December 21, 1973, in Geneva, Switzerland, under the auspices of the United States and Soviet Union. Foreign Ministers from Israel, Egypt, and Jordan attended the conference to negotiate a settlement of the Arab-Israeli dispute, but Syria refused to send a representative. See ibid., Document 408.

[7] In October 1973, the Arab members of OPEC cut the production of oil and embargoed the sale of oil to the United States and Western Europe in response to their support of Israel in the October war. See ibid., volume XXXVI, Energy Crisis, 1969–1974, Document 223.

---

2. Editorial Note

According to his memoirs, in early January 1974, the President's Assistant for National Security Affairs Henry A. Kissinger sent a message to Egyptian President Anwar al-Sadat offering to visit Egypt and discuss what Sadat considered the appropriate approach to the disengagement process with Israel. Concurrently, Israeli Defense Minister Moshe Dayan would discuss Kissinger's views on Dayan's proposal with the Israeli Cabinet. On January 8, Sadat contacted Kissinger and implored him to visit Egypt immediately. (*Years of Upheaval*, page 804) Kissinger replied on January 9 in a message transmitted in telegram 4086 to Cairo that he would fly to Egypt on January 11 with the intention of then visiting Israel and getting a concrete proposal from the Israelis that he was "confident will contain the basic principles and concepts previously discussed between us, though not necessarily in conformity with every detail." He also noted that he believed "an agreement should be attainable during the course of this trip." (National Archives, Nixon Presidential Materials, NSC Files, Kissinger Office Files, Box 133, Country Files, Middle East, Egypt/Ismail, Volume 9, January 1974) According to Kissinger's Record of Schedule, Kissinger first flew to Spain on the afternoon of January 11, meeting with Spanish Foreign Minister Pedro Cortona for approximately two hours. He then departed Spain at 2:25 p.m. and arrived in Aswan, Egypt at 8:30 p.m., heading immediately to President Sadat's rest house for a meeting. The next day, January 12, he traveled to Jerusalem. (Library of Congress, Manuscript Division, Kissinger Papers, Box 438, Miscellany, 1968–76)

3. Memorandum From the President's Deputy Assistant for National Security Affairs (Scowcroft) to President Nixon[1]

Washington, January 13, 1974.

Dr. Kissinger has sent you the following report on his conversations in Egypt and his initial talks in Israel.

"I met with President Sadat for two hours on Friday night and an additional four hours on Saturday.[2] He asked that I convey to you his

---

[1] Source: National Archives, Nixon Presidential Materials, NSC Files, Kissinger Office Files, Box 140, Country Files, Middle East, Secretary Kissinger's Middle East Trip, January 11–20, 1974, Memcons and Reports. Top Secret. Sent for information. A handwritten notation reads: "President has seen."

[2] No other record of these January 11 and 12 conversations has been found. According to Kissinger's memoirs, Sadat called in his associates to join him and Kissinger only once during the shuttle for a meeting on Monday, January 14, and it was the only time Kissinger's notetaker, Peter Rodman, was in attendance. (*Years of Upheaval*, p. 822) This is the only meeting that an actual memorandum of conversation between Sadat and Kissinger has been found for the entire first shuttle, which took place between January 11 and January 19. See Document 5.

warm regards, and talked at length about his desire to normalize Egyptian-U.S. relations.

"Sadat made it clear that he is anxious that an agreement on disengagement be accomplished within one week, and urged that I personally engage myself in developing an agreement that can be signed at kilometer 101, rather than sending the negotiations back to Geneva, with the inevitable delays that would entail.

"We had a long discussion on oil. Sadat told me that if a disengagement agreement can be reached this week he will use his personal influence—particularly with King Faisal and President Boumediene—to see that the oil embargo is brought to an end shortly after agreement is reached. He also said that while it would be necessary publicly to maintain the fifteen percent production cut, he is prepared to see that total production is restored for the U.S. through the Bahrain refineries once we have a disengagement agreement. Thus, we would receive fifteen percent more oil than anyone else. He emphasized, however, that if any word of this concession should leak the Arabs will be forced to disavow it.

"On disengagement Sadat added little new on Egypt's substantive position. He wants a detailed agreement, leaving as little to the military representatives to work out later as possible. He agreed to some form of undertaking (not yet specified) on free transit through the straits south of Israel, but is standing firm in opposition to agreeing to any limitations on the size of Egyptian forces on the eastern side of the Suez Canal.

"Following my talks with Sadat I flew to Jerusalem where I met briefly with Mrs. Meir[3] (who is ill) and then had a long business dinner with Deputy Prime Minister Allon, Dayan, and Eban.[4] I reported on Sadat's views, and discussed in detail an Israeli plan for disengagement which Dayan had foreshadowed in his talks in Washington on Friday and Saturday of last week.[5]

"The Israelis find themselves ham-strung by the lack of a new government, but indicated they were prepared to sign an agreement this week if outstanding issues can be compromised—subject to ratification

---

[3] The conversation between Meir and Kissinger took place on January 12 between 8:15 and 9 a.m. at Meir's residence in Jerusalem. A memorandum of conversation is in the National Archives, Nixon Presidential Materials, NSC Files, Kissinger Office Files, Box 140, Country Files, Middle East, Secretary Kissinger's Middle East Trip, January 11–20, 1974, Memcons and Reports.

[4] According to Kissinger's Record of Schedule, Kissinger met with these Israeli Cabinet members on January 12 at 9:30 p.m. for 2½ hours. (Library of Congress, Manuscript Division, Kissinger Papers, Box 438, Miscellany, 1968–76) No other record has been found.

[5] See footnote 2, Document 1.

by their parliament (which they expect could be achieved without difficulty) when it meets next week.

"We meet again on Sunday,[6] when we will continue discussions of the Israeli plan. At the moment I am hopeful that reasonable accommodations can be reached; the two most difficult outstanding areas seem to be:

—The distance eastward the Israelis will withdraw their forces. The Israelis want to keep their forces along a line just west of the mountain passes, and Sadat is talking about leaving Israel in control only of the eastern end of the passes.

—The number and character of Egyptian troops on the east side of the Canal. Sadat is talking about two divisions while Dayan is talking about two to three battalions.

"I will report to you Sunday evening on the outcome of the second round of talks with the Israelis. I plan to return to Egypt late in the evening to present the Israeli plan to Sadat Monday. When I have an Egyptian proposal in writing, which I should now be in a position to shape, I will bring it back to Jerusalem."

---

[6] Janaury 13.

---

4. Memorandum of Conversation[1]

Jerusalem, January 13, 1974, noon–1:15 p.m.

PARTICIPANTS

    Yigal Allon, Deputy Prime Minister
    Abba Eban, Minister for Foreign Affairs
    Moshe Dayan, Minister of Defense
    Simcha Dinitz, Ambassador to U.S.
    General David Elazar, Chief of Staff
    Mordechai Gazit, Prime Minister's Office
    Avraham Kidron, Director General, MFA
    Ephraim Evron, Deputy Director General, MFA
    General Eliahu Zaira, Chief of Intelligence

---

[1] Source: National Archives, Nixon Presidential Materials, NSC Files, Kissinger Office Files, Box 140, Country Files, Middle East, Secretary Kissinger's Middle East Trip, January 11–20, 1974, Memcons and Reports. Top Secret. The meeting was held in the Prime Minister's office. Brackets are in the original.

General Leor, Military Adviser to Prime Minister
Eytan Bentsur, Aide to Eban
Col. Bar-On, Aide to Dayan

Dr. Henry A. Kissinger, Secretary of State
Ambassador Kenneth Keating
Ellsworth Bunker, Ambassador at Large
Joseph J. Sisco, Assistant Secretary for Near Eastern and South Asian Affairs
Carlyle Maw, Legal Advisor, Department of State
Alfred L. Atherton, Deputy Assistant Secretary of State
George Vest, Special Assistant to the Secretary for Press Relations
Harold Saunders, Senior NSC Staff
Peter W. Rodman, NSC Staff

Dayan: Eli will start. Inform the Secretary about the Egyptians.

Zaira: [Standing at map easel] I will begin with the Egyptian deployment. The total strength from Cairo to the front line is about 2,200 tanks, 1,700 artillery pieces and 1,300 APCs. They are deployed with three main forces: the Second Army from here up [indicating on map], the Third Army from here down, a special force which is called the "Badr" force composed of two divisions is here, on the East side of the Canal, and a certain force which defends Cairo.

The total order of battle is, in three numbers: On the 5th of October, the Egyptians had 2,650 tanks; they lost during the war 1,100; now the order of battle is again 2,650. They received 750 tanks from Russia, 200 from Libya, and the rest is composed of Algerian forces. So basically they are back to the same order of battle.

In aircraft, they began the war with about 600 airplanes. They lost 220, and have received about 115. So they are a little bit below the prewar order of battle.

The important point is the additional SCUD missile launchers. Before the war they had 10 SCUD launchers and now they have 20.

This is in rough numbers the order of battle. I have more details if they are needed.

Kissinger: I would like to know where their artillery and SAMs are deployed specifically.

Zaira: I will begin with artillery. Artillery pieces from here down to here, they have 994 artillery pieces and 720 tanks and 325 APCs. From here down.

Kissinger: That is on all the East Bank?

Zaira: Yes.

Kissinger: [to General Dayan] Does everyone here know the plan?

Dayan: Yes.

Kissinger: So, just to translate it into what we are talking about: They would have to withdraw all their artillery and tanks on the East Bank.

Dayan: Yes.

Kissinger: That includes the Third Army. The tanks would have to go to the West Bank.

Elazar: That is what we estimate. It might not be accurate because that is from air photos, etc. That is approximate.

Kissinger: But still it's in the hundreds in each case. So what we are asking of them is not a minor move.

Dayan: What we move is not a minor move either. You will hear in a minute about the number of tanks we have on the Western side.

Kissinger: Have they any artillery on the West Bank?

Zaira: Yes, a lot. Now, here on this side of the Canal, totally on the West side, they have about 1,100 tanks and 384 artillery pieces. About half as much as they have here. Because most of the artillery is deployed with the infantry divisions which they have here, five of which are on the East side. And here we have mostly tanks and mechanized divisions. So totally on the West side, they have more than 1,000 tanks, nearly 400 artillery pieces and about 600 APCs.

Kissinger: How many artillery pieces would they have to move on the West bank?

Zaira: [pointing to northern part of West side] Only from here up, which is about 112.

Kissinger: 112 artillery pieces within the zone, in that 30-kilometer zone?

Zaira: Yes.

Kissinger: How many SAMs?

Zaira: Generally in this area they have 15 battalions.

Kissinger: Within the 30 kilometers?

Zaira: Yes.

Kissinger: And they are located specifically where?

Elazar: Only here [pointing to northern part of West side].

Zaira: This I can show you here [hands Dr. Kissinger a paper].

Kissinger: Does one of you want to come with me to Aswan and see how easy it will be to tell them they have to move a thousand tanks and 700 artillery pieces across the Canal?

Dayan: Can you say something about the number of tanks we have to move?

Kissinger: We will get to that. Can I keep this?

Zaira: [hesitates] Yes. [he hands it over] For you! [Zaira's map at Tab A.][2]

---

[2] Tab A attached but not printed.

Kissinger: I don't think it will improve my standing there to hand over a map written in Hebrew.

Zaira: They can translate it.

Kissinger: Let me get it straight again: There are about 900 tanks and 720 artillery pieces that have to be moved?

Zaira: Just the opposite—720 tanks and 994 artillery pieces from here to here.

Kissinger: On the East Bank. Then on the West Bank they would have to move an additional 100-plus artillery pieces.

Elazar: I am not sure if they have to move all these. Because of the 112 pieces that are in the area, some of them I suppose will not be in the 30-kilometer area. So I don't know if it is 50% or 60% but some of that artillery they will have to move.

Kissinger: Unless they don't want the 30 kilometers zone behind your line. But we will have to see.

Elazar: That depends on the artillery line, if there is another artillery line.

Keating: Do they know what you have on the West Bank?

Zaira: Well, they take photos of our dispositions and also the Russian Foxbats which take off from Cairo West fly over our area and take pictures. They look at our pictures and we look at theirs. So I believe they know.

Keating: My point, Mr. Secretary, was that perhaps for your argument purposes you would like to know what Israel would have to move.

Kissinger: But they don't accept the symmetry anyway, so . . .

Keating: I know they don't.

Kissinger: This is not a negotiation we can settle by symmetrical withdrawal.

Keating: I realize that.

Kissinger: Alright. I understand. I just wanted you to understand what will be in their minds when we discuss it. It's not going to be trivial. I was hoping their artillery would be on the West Bank. I didn't realize they had most of it on the East Bank.

Dayan: As far as the artillery is concerned, I still believe this is in their interest. If they say they want each party to keep its artillery in position, which I doubt—of course if they always want only us to withdraw I can see their point.

Kissinger: But if they want to keep their artillery on the East Bank . . .

Dayan: And if we keep ours where it is, there won't be any cease-fire, there won't be any opening of the Canal or anything. The artillery is close to one another, so if someone opens fire and the other replies, before you know it the whole area is on fire. You can see what is going on now. I cannot imagine that they will start working on the Suez Canal or anything else if our artillery is not withdrawn, and to ask us to do it as a one-sided move, this I can imagine, but it is unacceptable to us. Well, anyway, this is the picture.

Allon: I would like only to inform you that the Cabinet was very tough on this matter, heavy equipment and tanks as far as the East zone is concerned.

Kissinger: They can be tough, but at some point they have to face their real alternatives.

Allon: Of course. But the same applies to the other side.

Kissinger: The tanks I think is a manageable problem. I think, I hope; I don't know.

Allon: What is the difficulty with the artillery?

Kissinger: The difficulty is the psychological problem of his having to move major forces from territory he considers his own. There is no sense arguing it now because this is not the time.

Allon: I am asking what is the difference between tanks and artillery from this point of view.

Kissinger: I am giving you my assessment, based on many conversations, of his probable reaction. He has to consider what orders he has to give to his military, and how he will look to his military, if he makes certain types of agreements. And I am concerned. We will see.

Allon: Any more questions about Egypt, or can we move to Syria?

Kissinger: Just a minute. Could I hear what you have on the West Bank?

Elazar: By the way, I would like to mention that they have about 50% of their artillery on the Eastern Bank. Because 900 is out of 1,900 artillery pieces.

Kissinger: But that means it is a massive artillery deployment on the East Bank.

Elazar: Yes, 50%.

Kissinger: I just hadn't realized. I somehow thought they had it on the West Bank. I am just thinking about the orders that have to be given. It is a massive movement, and hard to justify as a unilateral decision. Once you have put 50% of your forces on the East Bank it is hard to say that you came to the conclusion unilaterally that you are better off having them on the West Bank. But let's see what his reactions are.

Elazar: Well, we have now on the West Bank 3 armored divisions—actually two armored divisions and one is a mechanized division. That is to say, about 600 tanks, a little more, about 630. We have about 15 battalions of artillery, that is to say in pieces, about 200 artillery pieces. We have on the Eastern Bank another 3 divisions. That is to say, we have now 50% of our troops on the Egyptian front on the Western Bank.

Actually we managed during the last months to make some fortifications there in spite of the constant fire on our fortification works. And we feel that this force on the Western Bank is quite sufficient if there are some hostilities. What I mean is that we don't feel we are trapped on the West Bank. That is what we have there.

Dayan: Perhaps there is one more point that should be made, that is about the mountain there. We think that there is a dominating high ground there, Jebel Ataka, in the South, which cannot be appreciated just by number of tanks or artillery, but by the fact that our forces that are holding it are only infantry troops there, with light weapons. But I think if they get back that mountain, although it will not be calculated by artillery or tank pieces, it is a very important strong point. And I think they should appreciate it.

Kissinger: But why is it that you feel you are not in a trap there when you have only 200 artillery pieces against about 1,000 and 600 tanks against so many more?

Elazar: That results from the ratio of forces between us and all the Arab armies. That is the normal ratio. And we don't feel trapped in the Middle East in spite of this ratio of forces. We have the same ratio of forces on the West Bank.

Kissinger: What is facing you on the West Bank? How many tanks?

Dayan: If I may say one thing [gets up and goes over to map]. The only way they can really try to put us in a trap is by cutting from here, cutting the bridgehead we have there. Let's say in this area, not across the lake, but here. They cannot do it with their forces on the Western side. They can press with those forces but we can fight it out. It is only pressure but it will not cut us off. To cut us off they have to link their Second and Third Armies. Then they will come against the forces that we have here, not inside the trap. In order to link the Second Army with the Third Army and to cut our bridge, they have to come against the forces that we have here. And I think they absolutely cannot do it.

There is another thing. The Third Army, which should do part of the job, hasn't got a missile umbrella, because this is out of range because we are sitting here [on the West Bank]. This area is under our control, and their missiles are here. That is to say, our Air Force is free to act against the Third Army.

Now, I mentioned the mountain that we have here which dominates all the area around here. It is very important, not only topographically but as a military position. So I cannot see how they can cut us off and put us in a trap. I should say that if war starts they will find the weakness of their Third Army earlier than we would feel some difficulties in our position here. They have a lot of forces here. They can press on us, but . . .

Kissinger: Sadat said to me that his estimate is that you could destroy his Third Army if a war started, but you would take very heavy casualties doing it.

Dayan: Well, let's say that if something like that will take place, once we destroy the whole or even part of the Third Army, then our bridgehead will not be only here but will be extended here too, so there won't be any question of being trapped. Besides that we have the Navy here, with the LSTs. So I think the general idea that we are trapped is just because of misinformation or people do not realize the position of the Third Army, and the Navy possibility. And it is almost impossible for them now to link the Third Army and the Second Army.

Keating: They will also drive in force near Cairo.

Dayan: They will press us but they will not cut.

Allon: Maybe the Egyptians underestimate our strength on the West Bank of the Suez Canal, but I don't want you to be a victim of their trap about the assessment of our strength. I am not boasting too much; we know our weaknesses as well. To my judgment they cannot push us back. We may suffer casualties, of course, but we are not trapped.

Kissinger: That is my judgment, but . . .

Allon: We shall suffer casualties but we shall destroy a great deal of their army, more than he can afford politically.

Kissinger: My estimate is that even if you win, the political world pressures would become such that . . .

Allon: [interrupts] This is a different problem.

Kissinger: From the military aspect, I grant you that you would probably win; the cost you can assess better than I can.

Allon: The battle cannot be decided by artillery. That is very helpful and very important, but it will be decided by tank warfare, armor, and the Air Force. In these two cases I think he may be surprised.

Kissinger: My assessment is—and we have talked about it on other occasions and again yesterday[3]—that Israel is diplomatically and internationally very badly placed for a resumption of the war on the West Bank. And that is not based on my assessment of the strategic situation. I would assume that if you tell me you will win, as the Defense Minister

---

[3] See footnote 4, Document 3.

has said yesterday,[4] I believe that. In any event, you would be a much better judge of that, but we went over that yesterday.

Allon: We would like to avert a war, no question about that. Even if the diplomatic situation would be better.

Kissinger: The major information I wanted was what he would have to remove if he accepts your plan, so I can understand what is in his mind when I am talking to him. Let me understand: The APCs can stay, if I understand correctly. I thought that was what you said to me in Washington.

Dayan: I think those attached to the battalions, to the infantry battalions, can. The way I see it is all defensive weapons, if they go on mining the area, anti-tank guns and APCs and armored cars—but those that belong to the respective units, not just if they artificially stuck in hundreds of thousands of them. But when we speak about policing battalions, or they can do it with APCs, from my point of view it is all right.

Kissinger: I understand. I think I have a sufficient idea of your plan now so we don't have to go over it. Because the tough part of it will come when we get a reaction. For presentation purposes I understand it well enough. If they accept it, the tough part will come in spelling out all the details.

Atherton: Could we have the number of personnel they have?

Kissinger: Five divisions is how much?

Zaira: About 60–70,000.

Allon: You mean the two armies East of the Suez Canal?

Alazar: Yes.

Kissinger: You drive a hard bargain.

Dayan: Either he wants to fight or he wants peace.

Elazar: We have about 50,000 men on the West Bank.

Dayan: I suppose the best thing to convince somebody from Egypt is to take him for a guided tour along our forces there and to tell him the number of people we have there and the fortifications and this business of the mountain—I really don't know whether Sadat is acquainted with the area and knows the meaning of that mountain—and the naval business and all these things.

Kissinger: That is not his problem. His problem is what orders he has to give to his military and how he will look to his military. And that is going to be quite a problem.

---

[4] According to Kissinger's Record of Schedule, Kissinger met with Dayan on January 12 around midnight for approximately one hour. (Library of Congress, Manuscript Division, Kissinger Papers, Box 438, Miscellany, 1968–76) No other record has been found.

Dayan: To get us out of there is also a problem.

Kissinger: He may think world pressure will get you out. There is no sense discussing the plan any further. Let's see what his reaction is; then we have something to discuss. If he accepts it. If he rejects it, we will see again. Okay, let's see the Syrian front.

Zaira: The Syrians had 2,100 tanks on October 5th; they lost about 1,100, then got from Russia 800. Today they have about 1,800 tanks, out of which they have between Damascus and the front line about 1,360. They do not include the Jordanian forces.

Kissinger: They just evacuated.

Allon: Nor the Iraqis.

Zaira: They have here four divisions on the front line—the 5th, 8th, 7th and 3rd. And they have the First Division behind the lines. They have a lot of artillery, about more than 900, and all of them along the front line; about 1,300 APCs, all of them along the front line; some Moroccan forces here, Iraqis, some Saudis here and some Kuwaitis probably somewhere here. We don't count them yet. They also have missiles.

Dayan: We're very popular.

Kissinger: Are the Saudis finally there? It took them about three weeks to get there.

Zaira: But we have patience. [laughter]

Kissinger: Once during the war their unit was lost somewhere in Jordan.

Zaira: Purposely.

Now, I have to add that there is a difference in the capability of using surface-to-surface missiles by the Syrians. They used the FROGs during the war; we understand that now they have the SCUDs.

Kissinger: Did the Egyptians have FROGs?

Zaira: Yes, a lot. They used a lot and they also used SCUDs. We found some fragments of SCUDs which were sent to the Pentagon already, I believe. But if the Syrians have the SCUDs, they can cover even Pafah and El Arish, can even destroy Gaza if they want to. I believe the Syrians having SCUDs is something different, because they will not be very scrupulous about using them. And I believe the fact that the Syrians and the Egyptians have the SCUDs and the FROGs will bring a new dimension to the war here if it resumes, and I speak about using surface-to-surface missiles against cities.

Kissinger: Why didn't they use them in the war?

Zaira: They used what they had. They only had the FROGs; the Syrians did not have the SCUD.

Kissinger: Why not the Egyptians?

Zaira: The Egyptians I believe had the SCUDs to be used only if we attacked cities in Egypt. At the same time also the only people who could really fire the SCUDs were the Russians; now I believe that the Egyptians can use them. But during the war only the Russians could fire them, and according to our information it was the Russians who fired the missiles that were fired.

Kissinger: But at what were they fired?

Zaira: At the Fayid area, not at cities.

Elazar: In the bridgehead area.

Zaira: A few minutes before five o'clock on the 22nd of October on the West side of the Canal.

As to airplanes, the Syrians lost about 200 airplanes. They have received back by airlift about 140, all of them from either Russia or the satellites. They were all assembled and tested by Russians or East Germans.

Kissinger: Do you think the Russians delivered such massive numbers of tanks from existing units? They couldn't have had them in store.

Zaira: Either existing units or reserve units. I tend to think they were taken out of reserve units.

Kissinger: But certainly not out of current production?

Zaira: Because we know some of the tanks that were shipped to Syria were used tanks, so they just took out the tanks from the stores of reserve units or maybe even active units.

Kissinger: Our intelligence had the impression that some were taken from active units.

Maw: How many aircraft do they have now?

Zaira: Today about 300.

Kissinger: How many do you have there? What was the old line?

Elazar: [referring to map] Here is the 1967 line. There is a no-man's land of about two kilometers. Here is the new line.

Kissinger: I see. No, I mean the line on the day the 1967 war broke out, the June 5th line.

Dinitz: It doesn't exist on our map!

Elazar: Oh, you mean the 1949 line. It is somewhere here.

Allon: It is too close to my kibbutz.

Elazar: Here is the Jordan River, so it was approximately here.

Kissinger: What is the deepest point of your penetration from the pre-1967 war line? What is the deepest penetration on the Golan Heights? Altogether, from what you call the 1949 line to the deepest penetration you have now.

Zaira: It depends on where you take the axis. From here to here along the road [pointing], it is about 60 kilometers. From here to here [pointing] about 40.

Kissinger: And what is the deepest point of your penetration in the last war?

Elazar: About 30 kilometers.

Allon: About 30 kilometers each war.

Kissinger: One more war for Damascus [laughter]. Your Defense Minister said during the war, "We are on the road to Damascus." The Russians went crazy and I complained. So your Defense Minister very helpfully pointed out in his next public statement that the road from Tel Aviv to Damascus is also the road from Damascus to Tel Aviv. [laughter]

Elazar: What we have here now is about two armored divisions, approximately 500 tanks.

Kissinger: You think you can hold this line now?

Elazar: Yes.

Kissinger: Easily?

Elazar: Easily. It is much better because of the topographical advantages.

Kissinger: They can't pinch off the salient?

Elazar: I would say that as a main line of defense it is much better. This area here is a great advantage. I have no doubt that we can defend it with two divisions, two armored divisions, 500 tanks.

Kissinger: Can you defend it without mobilization?

Elazar: No, we have to mobilize.

Allon: It depends on how many fronts we have.

Elazar: We can have altogether a little more than two armored divisions unmobilized. But usually even in peacetime we always have a certain part of our reserves mobilized in training periods and so on. So to have an additional armored division as a reserve armored division which is on training, that is quite a normal procedure.

Kissinger: What is the length of military service here?

Elazar: Three years compulsory service and 30 days for reserve units every year, and three days every two months. For commanders it is 40 days.

Kissinger: So it is 48 days. Six times three plus 30.

Elazar: Sometimes more. For officers it is 42, plus 12 days, so it is almost two months every year.

Keating: And for women?

Elazar: 20 months compulsory service.

Kissinger: And then reserve service.

Elazar: They have reserve service of 30 days.

Kissinger: It is a big chunk out of people's lives.

Elazar: We used to say they are soldiers on 11 months leave every year.

Allon: It is more a citizens' army than it is a people. But it is a burden, no question about it.

Kissinger: Jordan. The Jordanians were about two weeks ago telling us you had two and a half armored divisions concentrated against them and you were getting ready to start against Saudi Arabia. Fortunately they also told this to Saudi Arabia.

Elazar: We didn't have actually armored divisions but we had several infantry brigades.

Kissinger: Why?

Elazar: Well, in any case, to give him an excuse at least.

Kissinger: So he could pull out his armored divisions. Oh, I see.

Allon: I understand he is improving his forces now, thanks to two American shipments of arms.

Kissinger: I know of only one shipment. What are you talking about?

Allon: A new deal for supplies.

Kissinger: I will tell you, we are sending some TOW missiles, but except for that I don't know of anything now. They have asked for a lot more, but nothing was agreed to.

Allon: This is out of context now, but during the war he did his best to avoid direct confrontation on the Eastern front.

Kissinger: We know.

Allon: But in certain hours he was on the edge of intervening directly because he was under great pressure from other Arab countries, and I don't know how much he can resist in case of another war.

Kissinger: There is no question that that is true, and we were in daily contact with him and daily asked him not to do anything. And he is paying a price for it, because his present position in the peace negotiations is weak because he did not enter the war.

Eban: At Algiers, when they said they took part in the war, the Egyptians smiled derisively.[5]

Kissinger: We made a major effort to keep him out of the war. He sent us messages twice a day. He is under great pressure.

Shall we talk about Syrian disengagement?

---

[5] The Arab League Summit was held in Algiers November 26–28, 1973.

Allon: The only thing I am authorized to say today as a result of the Cabinet meeting is that we are ready in principle to enter negotiations with the Syrians about a disengagement or separation of forces agreement, provided that they will hand over first the list of the prisoners of war to the Red Cross and permit the Red Cross personnel to visit the prisoners and report on their conditions. Once we start, of course, we will get moving.

Kissinger: I understand. Let me say this. If the Egyptians are receptive to your proposal, then Sadat wants me to go to Damascus—for his reasons. If I go to Damascus, Asad will undoubtedly raise this issue. I don't have to have a plan approved by the Cabinet; in fact, I would rather not have a plan. But I would like to have something to talk about. Now I understand your original proposition that they must give the list of prisoners and Red Cross visits. I have already said this to Sadat and he said he would write a letter to Asad to urge him to make this concession.

Allon: It is very important, emotionally and humanly.

Kissinger: You have no problem with us on this point. There are two issues, one procedural and one substantive. Procedurally, Sadat has suggested that one way of breaking the log-jam on Syrian participation in the Conference would be that if they were willing to give lists and permit Red Cross visits that they join the Egyptian delegation to discuss disengagement with you. I have told him, (a), I don't know whether it would be acceptable to you, and secondly . . .

Allon: It is not good for him either.

Kissinger: You can't tell him what is good for him when he is proposing it. On the condition that they give the lists and permit Red Cross visits, would you then talk to them in the framework of the Egyptian-Israeli discussions on disengagement? The lists are the sine qua non.

Allon: I would prefer not. I don't know what would be the last answer, but as far as my first reaction is concerned, it isn't good to link together the Egyptians and the Syrians. It will start by having joint talks; it will end up by an Egyptian refusal to reach an agreement over disengagement unless and until we reach a similar agreement with the Syrians. We will have more difficulties with the Syrians than the Egyptians.

Kissinger: That is an incorrect analysis. What will block an agreement with the Egyptians may be your plan, but there is no doubt in my mind that Sadat will not wait for the Syrians to accept a plan he considers domestically bearable for himself. And my recommendation to Sadat would be that this issue would not be raised until the agreement with you is already signed and in the process of being implemented. They made the proposal to me three weeks ago that Syrian officers join the Egyptian delegation in Geneva. I mentioned it to you, or maybe I didn't even mention it, because I told Fahmi. He called me from Geneva, and I told him this would so totally confuse the issue that no progress would be made and I didn't even bother to pass it on because I thought I knew what your answer would be. But now he has resurrected it. It will come up only in the context of an already-signed agreement which has begun to be implemented. And it is his way of getting them pregnant so that they cannot attack his disengagement agreement. And it is in that context that you should consider it.

Allon: You mean that the negotiations with the Syrians would take place in Geneva?

Dinitz: I think the confusing sentence was your phrase, "within the framework of the Egyptian negotiations."

Kissinger: What he has in mind, in order to avoid a Syrian Central Committee argument, is that Asad can send officers to sit with the Egyptians in Geneva on his own, but he cannot take a formal decision to join the Geneva peace talks. So he thought that we'd say the disengagement group which is now discussing Egyptian disengagement will then discuss Syrian disengagement, without an additional decision of Syria about joining the peace talks. It is, however, clearly understood that they must give the prisoner lists and Red Cross visits before that can take place, even as part of the Egyptian group. And I would not recommend it unless the disengagement plan with Egypt were already signed and in the process of implementation. The advantage of this tactically, frankly, is that it would avoid a consideration of the second phase of the Geneva Conference, since the second phase would then be Syrian disengagement and it would give Syria a vested interest not to raise the ultimate issues because its own disengagement scheme would be considered. In that framework I would frankly recommend it.

Allon: Just to find out whether I understood correctly; Sadat thinks that it is too difficult for the Syrian regime to adopt a resolution in the Central Committee to start direct negotiations with us over the disengagement, and it would be easier . . .

Kissinger: Or to join formally the Geneva Conference.

Allon: And they think it would be easier for them to join the Egyptian team and to negotiate together the Syrian points after we conclude the agreement with Egypt?

Kissinger: And the implementation had started.

Allon: And they don't want to have it somewhere in the field between the two fronts?

Kissinger: No.

[Mr. Saunders and Mr. Sisco join the group.]

Allon: I personally would recommend the Cabinet accept it. If you come back from Egypt and say this is the only way to meet with the

Syrians. But I will recommend, if possible, that we should discuss the Syrian problem when you come back from Egypt again.

Kissinger: I agree with you.

Allon: You will know better and we shall know more. We didn't go into details on this in the Cabinet. There is a great sensitiveness on Syria.

Kissinger: If I go to Syria it will probably be Wednesday.[6] I would have been here once again. And it would be a day, if things go well, in which drafting would be going on. It would help me. With Sadat, you have given me a bit that will help me. By the time I go to Syria it would help me, not to know what your plan is, but the way the Defense Minister talked, which gave me a sense of what is inadmissible and what is possible to think about. The last time he [Asad] pulled out a map and said, "If we do disengagement with the Israelis, what are you talking about?" And I frankly didn't have a clue as to what I was talking about and I didn't dare say anything. And at least I want to know, not a plan, but what is totally inadmissible, so I can narrow the area of consideration.

Allon: Frankly speaking, I don't think that any one of us is authorized to commit ourselves.

Kissinger: Not to commit yourselves, but can we think out loud?

Allon: What is inadmissible—I would say that no retreat will take place from any of the old demarcation lines, under any circumstances.

Kissinger: Alright. That is helpful to know.

Allon: And of course we could also not give up the entire new territory. But this is really my very personal view. I can hardly commit myself, let alone the Prime Minister or the Cabinet.

Kissinger: Asad has said, incidentally—he volunteered this—the one thing he said about disengagement was that he recognized that no Syrian forces could move into areas from which the Israelis withdrew. So you have no problem of thinning of forces or anything, if he still maintains that. We are not talking about any particular territory. Because on the Sinai, when Sadat talked to me in November,[7] I had a sense of what was feasible from our many discussions on the interim agreement and my discussions with the Foreign Minister and the Prime Minister. On the Golan Heights, I had no sense at all. So when I come here on Tuesday—you don't have to settle it now—if we could just sit together privately and give me the thinking out loud. I would give him nothing.

---

[6] Wednesday, January 16.

[7] See *Foreign Relations, 1969–1976*, volume XXV, Arab-Israeli Crisis and War, 1973, Document 324.

Allon: I understand.

Kissinger: But at least in giving him nothing I won't be sitting there like an idiot. What you said now is already very helpful. If you say you could give up nothing of the old territories, that is one limitation that is useful for me to have.

Allon: I prefer that we discuss Syria when you come back, but we did adopt a decision that ...

Kissinger: I saw that; that is very useful.

Eban: One difference between their joining the Egyptian delegation or coming themselves in their own capacity to Geneva—it might not make a practical difference but there is a political difference. I think it should be sold as a concession. By coming to the Conference, they accept a certain ideology of recognition.

Kissinger: I think Sadat thinks—it is obviously helpful to Sadat that he is not the only Arab who makes a disengagement plan.

Allon: May I go back to Egypt for a minute? It has been mentioned last night about the frequent violations of the ceasefire—on both fronts, but I am speaking about Egypt now because you are going to Egypt. From midnight to this hour there have been already ten incidents, and two casualties, wounded, one officer and one soldier. This can't go on. We shall give them hell, but ... And this is one of the signs of goodwill from tonight on.

Kissinger: Just a minute, from tonight on nothing will happen, Yigal. Let's be realistic. Tonight I am not going to see Sadat. I want to start early in the morning. If he accepts your plan in principle, then I can insist that he stop the ceasefire violations as a sign of good faith. If he rejects your plan in principle, I guarantee you the number of violations will increase. So I cannot very well tell him ...

Allon: We shall not confine ourselves to hit back only in the place where we are being attacked. It is a wide front. I must convince him that we mean business.

Kissinger: Yigal ...

Allon: The war of attrition will not be renewed. With all my respect for Field Marshal Sadat and his victorious army, if the violations continue, there might be a retaliation in a way that even you might not like.

Kissinger: It depends entirely on the context in which it occurs. If he accepts it in principle, I can insist that there be an end to ceasefire violations. If he does not accept it in principle, there will be increased ceasefire violations. This you will then have to consider, not on the basis of abstract rhetoric and toughness, but on the situation in which you will find yourselves if all hell breaks loose internationally, but there is no sense debating that now.

Allon: Henry, we are not going to pay the price that the international community is expecting of us. We learned something. Everybody will be happy at our expense. It won't happen.

Kissinger: The most important thing about history is to learn the right lessons. Usually people learn a lesson and then apply it in a different period when it is no longer valid. You know my advice about 1956. There it was not necessary. In 1973 it may have been necessary, but let's not discuss it now because it is not the concrete issue. I would recommend strongly that before you take any retaliation, you wait until I get back here, which is, after all, hopefully within 24 hours of my leaving.

Allon: You will be back tomorrow night?

Kissinger: I hope I can get enough of a beginning reaction during the day tomorrow so I can leave Egypt late in the day and arrive here no later than during the night Monday, so we can work together starting Tuesday morning. So I hope that at 10 o'clock Tuesday morning we shall start working. But until then you should not do any drastic retaliation, because you have to hear what his reaction is.

I'll see the museum Tuesday at 8:30.

Allon: You didn't see it today?

Kissinger: No.

Allon: You saw Teddy [Kollek]?

Kissinger: Yes. For five minutes.

Allon: So you know what he feels about Jerusalem.

Kissinger: [pause] If he accepts it in principle, the first demand I will make is that he stop the pressure. If he accepts it in principle there will be no problem. The real problem we will have is if he rejects it in principle. Even then I will urge him to step down his activity to see what that news produces here. But let's not get the situation out of hand while I am in the area here. I think that would be extremely dangerous and foolish.

Allon: I want to make it clear, because you are going to see him, because I won't see him. He should understand that we shall not tolerate a war of attrition. We may regret it too, but we will retaliate.

Kissinger: Yigal, please.

Allon: If he wants a war then we have no alternative, and if he rejects in principle our proposal it means he wants war.

Kissinger: It may not mean this. We are running into the danger of talking slogans. If he rejects it, from my judgment of what I have seen, it is because of his own domestic position. Just as you have a domestic position, he has one. And you are asking him to give the army, which he has finally got under control, a lot of orders that will be extraordinarily unpalatable to them. I do not know whether he can do it or not. I have no question in my mind, having spent these many hours with him, that he genuinely wants a settlement and that he almost certainly wants peace in the Canal zone. Whether his domestic situation permits him to do what you think you require for your domestic situation, that I don't know, and we will now find out within the next 36 hours. No sense debating it. But it is not as simple as "does he want peace" or "does he not want peace."

Allon: Without using slogans, we are not asking you to help us in our domestic situation. We are undertaking all the calculated risks involved with open eyes because we believe this is a responsible decision we are taking, and you know how difficult it is to explain, because we can't boast of an advantage of such an agreement until after it has been signed.

Kissinger: Even then you can't.

Allon: I mean to say we lost nothing militarily if we are here or there. Some explanation will be given, not to boast, not to make it an Israeli victory. It is not a victory but it is not a defeat. Since I know this argument which goes on with us for 26 years about the domestic problems of each Arab country and the whole Arab world all together, so to some extent an enlightened people can take it into consideration. But we are not going to pay the price for his domestic affairs. If he can't control the army for a disengagement agreement, then he can't control the army but by going to war. So let him come.

Kissinger: I have to explain to you what the realities are internationally or domestically in America. Before you take drastic decisions you have to consider that this is a different world now from the late 1950's. I suggest, however, we do not debate it now. It is not a current issue.

Allon: No, but deliver the message in the spirit and letter, because it is very serious.

Kissinger: I will deliver it but you have to rely on me as to how to handle him. I do not happen to believe that your particular formulation is the exact way for me to deliver it to him, but I will get across to him that you are not to be played with.

Allon: The second problem is the problem of the bodies of the dead soldiers. This is a thing which I can't understand.

Kissinger: Dayan has raised that and it is a reasonable demand.

Allon: It is high time he let us search for the bodies and bring them for burial and inform the families, and this should be one of the signs of goodwill.

Kissinger: No question. If he agrees to it in principle, there should be no problem.

Dinitz: And this goes for Mizrachi.[8]

Kissinger: He has also agreed to give back Mizrachi when you're on the final line. If you will keep quiet about it—and the Soviets too—and just let us ask for him, he will give him to us for you. If you and the others keep quiet about it, if we ask for him, we will get him back. He took it particularly ill that the Soviets raised it too. Levy[9] I have never raised with him, because I understand he is crazy.

Dinitz: That is a simple case of a human being who is sick, was in an asylum.

Kissinger: Mizrachi I can assure you about, and he gave me the exact reason why he is not so interested to release him. Levy I have never raised with him, but if the facts are what you have described, I can't imagine any problem.

Allon: Now, we adopted a decision today about authorizing you to put forward a plan which we negotiated last night and this morning, and we shall make the announcement today as you asked it.

Kissinger: But you will say that you adopted it "learning and taking into account the Egyptian position." That makes it easier for him not to demand too much in return.

Sisco: When will that be announced?

Eban: Within a couple of hours.

Kissinger: It is very helpful, extremely helpful. And I must say that the talks this morning, going over the map, brought very useful clarifications. I do not just say this for the record, but I say it genuinely.

Allon: And, just to give you my impression from the discussion we had at the Cabinet, as far as their forces or the presence of offensive type of weapons on the East bank would create a great problem in our parliament, and quite rightly so. This is not a matter of domestic problems. We can overcome all sorts of problems. Therefore, do not concede—

Kissinger: Let me explain exactly what my position has to be, for the preservation of my own position. I cannot be in Egypt as Israel's lawyer. I cannot be in Egypt to start with one position and then say to him, well, I will accept another one. The position that I will bring to him is the only position I will discuss. The only thing I can do is, acting as an interpreter of what I take to be your views, I can tell him if the line may be five kilometers more or less, or I can say to him it is a waste of time for me to bring it here. If he says, "I need two more battalions," I cannot say I accept it. But I can say I will take it to Israel and see what they say.

---

[8] Baruch Mizrachi was an accused Israeli spy in Egyptian custody.

[9] Levy was an accused Israeli spy in Egyptian custody.

I in no case will go further than telling him that I will take certain things to Israel for your consideration. You will have the perfect freedom when I arrive to reject what I bring to you. I must do that, for my own sake, because I do not want to be in a position where I have plenipotentiary powers from you and say I agree to four battalions rather than three battalions. That puts me into a bad position because it makes me look vis-à-vis him that I am trying to strike the best possible bargain for Israel. So it would destroy my usefulness even with Egypt. So the use I am as your intermediary is to give him my interpretation of your thinking and steer him away from some things altogether; others I bring here and you can still reject them.

Allon: I understand, but I felt it my obligation to tell you what was the spirit of the discussion, because people take the problem of the limitation of forces in the security zones very seriously.

Kissinger: But steer your press away from any discussion that I am going to Aswan and then I will return here with a finished product that I have agreed to with Sadat. Because if I could get away with that, it would destroy—strangely enough—my usefulness with Egypt.

Allon: I think we have earned our lunch already. Have a good lunch.

[The meeting adjourned at 1:15 p.m.]

5. Memorandum of Conversation[1]

Aswan, January 14, 1974, 10:30 a.m.–2 p.m.

PARTICIPANTS

    Anwar al-Sadat, President of the Arab Republic of Egypt
    Ismail Fahmi, Minister of Foreign Affairs
    Maj. General Mohammed Abdel Ghany el-Gamasy, Egyptian Chief of Staff

    Henry A. Kissinger, Secretary of State
    Ambassador Ellsworth Bunker, Ambassador-at-Large, Head of U.S. Delegation to Geneva Peace Conference
    Joseph J. Sisco, Assistant Secretary for Near Eastern and South Asian Affairs
    Peter W. Rodman, NSC Staff

[Secretary Kissinger and President Sadat conferred privately from about 10:30 to 10:45 a.m., discussing a map which the Secretary had carried with him from Israel.[2] About 10:45, General Gamasy was summoned to join the discussion. At 11:15 a.m., Ambassador Bunker, Assistant Secretary Sisco, and Peter Rodman were brought into the meeting.]

Secretary Kissinger: Sisco was up until 4:00 a.m. Saturday night. We did it in turns. I started at 7:30.

President Sadat: They said in the papers that a working committee was set up [between the U.S. and Israel].

Secretary Kissinger: Yes, working groups.

[Photographers were admitted, for a brief photo opportunity.]

Secretary Kissinger: I told the press that by tonight we would know whether it was a Kissinger plan or a Sisco plan. [Laughter]

Minister Fahmi: It depends on its success. [Laughter]

I told Joe that if it is a Joe plan, we'd send him to the Valley of the Queens. We'd preserve him.

Secretary Kissinger: Why preserve him? [Laughter]

I have presented to the President the evolution of my knowledge of Israeli thinking and also the political situation in Israel as we see it—which is a divided Cabinet trying to form a new Cabinet, in which factions have this idea or that idea but it is difficult to get together. We insisted, on this visit, that there had to be a plan, and that they couldn't play the game with us of offering models and then taking them back.

---

[1] Source: National Archives, Nixon Presidential Materials, NSC Files, Kissinger Office Files, Box 133, Country Files, Middle East, Egypt, Volume 9, January 1974. Top Secret; Sensitive; Exclusively Eyes Only. The meeting was held in the President's House. Brackets are in the original.

[2] Presumably the map given to Kissinger by General Zaira. See footnote 2, Document 4.

First they suggested to replace Israeli forces with UN forces—which I rejected. Then I showed the President a map they gave us Saturday, which was official—they would leave the West Bank, you would stay in the Second and Third Army areas, and the UN takes this area, and there would be forward zones on both sides, and then the main lines. We rejected this, on the ground that the Egyptian presence on the Canal had to be unbroken and I couldn't face President Sadat with this proposal. Also, I didn't think it right that Egypt had to give up this territory. [See map at Tab A][3]

They wanted me to present this and come back to them. I said no.

Now their proposal is this: that there would be an Egyptian line, a UN line, and the Israeli line. This they say—and I believe it—is absolutely their final main line. They will not go off this road. I told the President, although I have no authority to do this, that I believe morally it is not possible or easy to ask Egypt to give up any territory they conquered. So I told the President I would be prepared to go back to Israel to ask that it go to Egypt, not the UN. [See map at Tab B][4]

So it is an unbroken line to the furthest extent of your present line plus the unbroken line.

I have no authority but I will strongly urge it.

President Sadat: I told Dr. Kissinger to push the UN line forward in front of our line.

Secretary Kissinger: I am positive they won't go back further here.

President Sadat: The main line.

Secretary Kissinger: Yes. Your President wanted me to discuss it. I think—and my associates were present at all my meetings—that their original idea was like the Yariv[5] idea, ten to twelve kilometers and no more. But I think they will go as far as this road. In the south I haven't discussed with them with the same intensity.

Here [the artillery line further back] is another line I haven't discussed with the President. They are willing to withdraw their artillery to this line if you are willing to withdraw your artillery.

President Sadat: From the East or West Bank?

Secretary Kissinger: From the East Bank.

Let's go through it all. In their view, in the Egyptian area on the East Bank they say there should be in the whole area two to three battalions. I told them this is impossible.

---

[3] Tab A attached but not printed.

[4] Tab B attached but not printed.

[5] A reference to Israeli General Aharon Yariv, the chief Israeli negotiator at Kilometer 101 on the Cairo-Suez Road, where Israeli and Egyptian military officials negotiated between October 28 and November 29, 1973.

President Sadat: That's right.

Secretary Kissinger: I am a lousy negotiator on their behalf, but I want to tell you my idea of what is possible and what is not. The zone is with no tanks, no artillery; APC's are possible, and anti-tank guns are possible. They want this whole withdrawal to take three months—then they said two months. I said it has to be shorter.

They have agreed to open the two roads to Suez City and the road to Kabrit within 48 hours of the first withdrawal. I promised you this.

President Sadat: Yes.

Secretary Kissinger: Their basic theory is that the artillery of each side should be such that it does not cover more than the forward zone. Theirs would be back here, thirty kilometers.

They also are willing in this zone of thirty kilometers to have any limit of deployments that you are willing to have in your zone.

President Sadat: In the Western Bank.

Secretary Kissinger: Yes. So if you have, say, 300 tanks, they will do the same. They don't insist on it. But if you are willing.

They also want a line of 18 kilometers here with no artillery, then only 155 mm in the zone between 18–30 kilometers, and then 175 mm beyond the thirty kilometers.

If you want this, it can be done. I personally think it will be impossible to distinguish by photography between 155 and 175 mm, and I believe the practical consequence is that it means unrestricted artillery.

General Gamasy: Impossible.

Secretary Kissinger: In my judgment, yes.

President Sadat: Quite right.

Secretary Kissinger: They also want that anti-aircraft missiles be placed in such a way that they can't reach beyond the forward edge of your forward zone. Again I had a long argument with them about this, and they are willing to do the following—which shows that the argument is heavily political. They don't mind that you can build emplacements for them as long as you don't move missiles in. But they say you can do it in 24 hours.

President Sadat: All our sites now are in this range on the West Bank. Beyond Qantara.

Secretary Kissinger: Your range is about 40 kilometers.

President Sadat: The maximum is 35 kilometers.

Secretary Kissinger: Unless you have better ones than the North Vietnamese, they don't hit much at the maximum range. Our experience in Vietnam is they are easy to avoid at the maximum range.

President Sadat: Quite right.

Secretary Kissinger: Now, I've presented to you their full plan, which caused us unbelievable anguish to produce—even though you won't like it.

My judgment is this: I believe the number of battalions should be increased. I've already told them this is an unreasonable proposal. I don't know what they are willing to accept.

President Sadat: That depends on how many they put on the main line. I can't do it unless they tell me what they will have.

Secretary Kissinger: Their theory is your main line is the Canal and theirs is here. They will put symmetrical forces in their forward zones. I have told you there will be no tanks, no artillery in the forward zone. So this would be symmetrical.

Behind this main line they are willing, if you have only, say, 300 tanks between the main line and thirty kilometers, they'll do the same. We haven't discussed it all, but I believe it has to be a simple line.

President Sadat: It must be simplified at this stage.

Secretary Kissinger: I have given you the worst now.

Let me now go through it. I'll give you my assessment later.

President Sadat: Please.

Secretary Kissinger: There are seven essential conditions they said they had to have: [reads from memo at Tab C][6] The first is that the Agreement must renew the commitment to the ceasefire. I see no problem here.

President Sadat: No.

Secretary Kissinger: The second is the blockade of Bab El-Mandeb. We have agreed on that.

The third is that if Egypt opens the Canal, Israeli ships must go through.

President Sadat: These are political issues!

Secretary Kissinger: I'm just telling you.

The fourth is that "all foreign troops and volunteers must be removed from Egypt."

President Sadat: Ridiculous.

Secretary Kissinger: Then there are "provisions for supervision, control and verification." That's automatic.

Then there are provisions I don't understand:

"The parties undertake not to interfere in any manner whatsoever, directly or indirectly, with scheduled or non-scheduled civil flights currently operating to or from territory of the other party."

---

[6] Tab C attached but not printed. Entitled "Points to be Included in the Agreement with Egypt on the Disengagement and Separation of Forces in Addition to the Technical Provisions," it included seven points for inclusion in the agreement.

Secretary Sisco: They told me something about interference with their flights to Africa.

Secretary Kissinger: My judgment is that these should be part of the peace negotiations.

President Sadat: It has to do with the boycott. It is purely political.[7]

Secretary Kissinger: I'll tell you what I think is attainable and what is not attainable. So we can use this week efficiently.

If you agree, Mr. President.

President Sadat: Certainly; certainly. [The Egyptian side confers.] Can we form a working committee from both sides here?

Secretary Kissinger: Certainly.

Would you like us to leave you alone now?

President Sadat: No, because we first have to agree, you and I, on the principles on which they will work.

Secretary Kissinger: I think we should form a working committee but we have to tell them what to do in this working committee.

President Sadat: Exactly.

[At 11:50 Kissinger and Sadat go out to discuss alone. While waiting, Gamasy, Fahmi, and Sisco go over the map:]

General Gamasy: Here is our main line now. We can't consider moving our main line here.

Minister Fahmi: Reciprocity is illogical. If they want us to put only 300 tanks here, it is defending the whole country. Their tanks aren't defending anything, and they are on Egyptian territory.

General Gamasy: [Opens up his own map] This is what we expected you would bring.

Minister Fahmi: We can't keep only 300 tanks to defend against a shock attack. If they change their mind and try to kick us out of the East Bank.

General Gamasy: We have our anti-aircraft on our main line. There are very few artillery pieces of ours that can hit their forces in their forward zone. We have very few 122 mm pieces.

Ambassador Bunker: What about 130 mm? With 27-kilometer range?

General Gamasy: We have very few. And they have very few 175 mm that can hit our forces. The concept of their plan is to draw their

---

[7] On December 2, 1945, the Arab League imposed a boycott prohibiting trade between Arab countries and Israel. By 1948, the boycott had evolved into three components: a continuation of the primary boycott imposed in 1945, a secondary boycott against any companies that operated in Israel, and a tertiary boycott aimed at those companies that had relationahips with companies that operated in Israel.

forces back a little and behind this line to do whatever they like. And ask us to draw our main forces back.

Minister Fahmi: To take our forces back from the East Bank. And all of this is on our own territory.

Assistant Secretary Sisco: I understand you reject symmetry.

Minister Fahmi: Politically what they are doing is redeploying their own forces and diminishing our defensive forces on our own territory, to guarantee their safety and diminish our safety. This is what they are doing.

Before we crossed the Canal we were much stronger. If we remove the rockets and keep only 300 tanks ... We were much stronger even before October 6. We had 2,000 tanks.

General Gamasy: This [the Egyptian artillery line] is a very important line. Why do they have this?

Assistant Secretary Sisco: It's the parallel of their line here. They'd accept whatever limits you would accept.

Minister Fahmi: You see, they pick and choose. One time they ask for reciprocity and similarity; on other points they don't. They give themselves a security zone but not one for us. And they keep the main [north-south] road. The UN zone has no road in it; it's useless.

General Gamasy: That means the UN has to work inside our troops.

Then if we have two–three battalions, about 1,800 men, for the 180 kilometers, that means we can do better with police than with these three battalions.

Minister Fahmi: This shows what is in the back of their minds. This is meant to undo the effects of October 6, not only politically but militarily.

We have a special corps, of Nubians, to control the frontiers. They would be better than the 1,500 men they would give us. They want to reduce the Second and Third Armies to 1,500 men.

General Gamasy: We heard all this from Yariv.

Assistant Secretary Sisco: But we have Cabinet approval for this.

General Gamasy: The Cabinet approved this?

Assistant Secretary Sisco: Yes. There are many factions in Israel.

General Gamasy: I think they proposed this just to have us reject it.

Before the war, we had five infantry divisions on the West Bank. Now they are on the East Bank. They [the Israelis] know this. They [our troops] were working—and are—under the security of the air defense system we have. Now under this proposal we have to have these five divisions back on the West Bank, without the air defense system, and with only 300 tanks.

Mr. Rodman: There was no figure for tanks. It was just a symmetrical limit: whatever you have, they will have.

Assistant Secretary Sisco: It's a mutual limitation.

General Gamasy: With the permission of my Foreign Minister, we still have prisoners of war with Israel and they won't hand them back. I think they should, and it would be a good attitude.

Assistant Secretary Sisco: I am sure if this is agreed on, something can be worked out.

They expressed concern to us about the number of ceasefire violations. This is what they say to us. They say: "Make it clear to the Egyptians that we have been very restrained and if these violations continue it will be very difficult to continue this restraint." They say you're shooting at their boys when they are improving their positions. They say there is no prohibition of improving positions and you are doing the same.

I just feel under an obligation to convey what they said.

Minister Fahmi: They say this in Geneva. If they continue, we may have to react.

Assistant Secretary Sisco: They say the violations are on your side. They say you're fortifying positions, too.

Minister Fahmi: But it's Egyptian territory.

Assistant Secretary Sisco: You can't use that argument for everything, Ismail.

Minister Fahmi: They want to link 60 prisoners to this agreement when it is part of the Six Points.[8]

General Gamasy: I gave Yariv our word of honor that Mizrachi and Levi, the two spies, along with other agents, will be exchanged at a later date. There was one prisoner they were especially interested in, Dan Avidan, who was held for four years, whom I brought with me to 101. This was a hint.

Assistant Secretary Sisco: They give you 100 percent credit for treatment of their prisoners. But they expressed the view to us about the pattern of ceasefire violations.

General Gamasy: Siilasvuo mentioned that to us, but our Minister said one thing: If they stop the engineering works, we'll stop shooting.

---

[8] Reference to the Six-Point Agreement, signed on November 11, 1973, between Israel and Egypt and sponsored by the United States. The agreement secured a cease-fire that had been violated several times since the formal end of hostilities in October. See *Foreign Relations*, 1969–1976, volume XXV, Arab-Israeli Crisis and War, 1973, Document 330.

We don't mind their improving the works, but they are making a new Bar-Lev line.[9] It means they are staying there forever.

Assistant Secretary Sisco: That's helpful to know.

Minister Fahmi: They also have to respect the other points of the Six Point agreement.

For example, there are sick people in the Suez City who are dying because the medical facilities there are inadequate. They are dying. If we did this to them, they would be crying and screaming.

General Gamasy: We have an isolated position in Kabrit. They refuse to allow supplies to them. It's only a company. They said, "Evacuate them." We said no. Siilasvuo raised this with Dayan and he said no. Not to allow supplies for 100 soldiers while allowing supplies for thousands makes no sense.

We have three points:

—the prisoners of war;
—the wounded and sick civilians in Suez City;
—the supply of Kabrit.

Minister Fahmi: The Minister of War said it was so serious in Suez City that it was going to be an epidemic. He was going to make a speech and I told him not to. There were very few, now there are 200.

Assistant Secretary Sisco: They say to us: "Yes, we are building these positions, which is not prohibited. If they stop shooting at us we will allow convoys in." They talk about dead bodies. What about this from your point of view?

General Gamasy: The minute they made difficulties on these points—refusing to evacuate the sick and wounded and to allow us to supply Kabrit—we refused to give the dead bodies. We gave some but we stopped. I tell you this frankly. Especially when we came to a deadlock at 101.

I am sure if we announce that we have one prisoner of war, they will cry, and we will get our prisoners on the second day.

We took some of their prisoners to visit Jewish families and a synagogue in Cairo. They were amazed to see they were well-treated.

Assistant Secretary Sisco: I know from the time of the Six-Day War you have never mistreated Jews in Egypt.

General Gamasy: Another funny thing. We spent two weeks with Yariv to get him to allow newspapers into Suez. Then he agreed. We

---

[9] The Bar-Lev line, named for Israeli Chief of Staff Chaim Bar-Lev, was created by Israel soon after it captured the Sinai in the 1967 Arab-Israeli War. The defensive line relied on a chain of fortifications along the East Bank of the Suez Canal to repel any attempts by Egyptian forces to cross the canal.

sent in newspapers and magazines; they let in the newspapers but not the magazines. I don't like to raise these minor points but it shows their attitude.

Minister Fahmi: The Agreement Henry drafted says, for the Third Army, "non-military equipment" but for Suez City it says "food, medicine, and water."

General Gamasy: So they don't allow razors for shaving. It's not "food."

Minister Fahmi: They won't allow the citizens, civilians, in Suez City to go to Cairo for registering, or for errands. You know in our country everything is centralized in Cairo.

We are ready to respect the Six Points in their entirety, every point.

Assistant Secretary Sisco: The danger is that once it breaks down, you may not be able to limit it to tit-for-tat.

Minister Fahmi: They want us to influence the Syrians to do everything. But if you compare what they do to what the Syrians do, it is identical.

[At 1:30 p.m., Dr. Kissinger and President Sadat returned.]

Secretary Kissinger: [to General Gamasy] I have already told your President: We thought you would be defeated in 48 hours. On the Tuesday after the war started, the Israelis came to us and said they had lost 400 tanks.

Should I sum up our understanding of our conversation?

President Sadat: Please. You're much cleverer.

Secretary Kissinger: But not as wise.

The President and I had discussions not only of the technical provisions but also of the pros and cons of moving quickly against moving slowly at Geneva. The technical provisions might be better if done at Geneva, but we assessed the advantages of moving quickly.

That is our assessment.

The Egyptian line defends Egypt; the Israeli line doesn't defend Israel. So for the Egyptians to move back their own defense line on Egyptian territory is politically unacceptable. I must say I find this a very persuasive argument.

So I am prepared to go back to Israel with something I had never heard—to abandon all these distinctions between zones. The Israeli forces will move back to this line, and the Egyptian line is defined here—so there is no Egyptian withdrawal required. So we'll describe any limits not in terms of withdrawal but in terms of distance between the Egyptian line and the Canal and the Israeli line.

The second point President Sadat said is that it is very difficult for Egypt to sign in a document limitations of forces on their own territory.

President Sadat: Quite right.

Secretary Kissinger: So we thought of various possibilities, such as letters to the Presidents, etc. Then the President had an idea, that should be explored—that we should write a letter to both President Sadat and the Israeli Prime Minister proposing certain limitations. So it is not an obligation to each other.

President Sadat: It's an American proposal.

Secretary Kissinger: And there is no suggestion of who imposed what upon whom.

The working group should prepare two documents—an agreement to be signed at 101 and an American proposal to the two sides which would spell out some of the limitations. With the proviso that I have no idea what the Israeli reaction will be. It can say in the Egyptian-Israeli document that there will be limitations—which are not spelled out—in the two zones, and that all other limitations can be described in terms of distances to and from the Egyptian line.

On limitations, the President thought the number of forces on the East Bank should be increased substantially from what the Israelis suggested. It should be left blank in the document; I know what he has in mind but I know I won't make the decision. He is not now prepared to accept no tanks.

President Sadat: Quite right.

Secretary Kissinger: Then the President and I agreed on the proposition that in these zones, which are described geographically, neither should deploy weapons that can reach the other's line.

Up to thirty kilometers from the Egyptian line and thirty kilometers from the Israeli line, there should be no artillery and no surface-to-air missiles. This should be written in the document as a blank, not as a line.

Secretary Kissinger: Do you want that? Are there any airfields there?

President Sadat: Yes.

Secretary Kissinger: I'll look into that. It doesn't seem unreasonable to me.

That we then ask the drafters to do two documents:

—the Agreement to be signed by Israel and Egypt;
—the American proposal to Israel and Egypt on limitations.

President Sadat: Right.

Secretary Kissinger: I warned the President that to my certain knowledge this proposal would almost certainly be published.

President Sadat: Not from the American side.

Secretary Kissinger: I don't want to put Egypt in an embarrassing position. But there is no way Israel will not publish it somehow, in their Parliament, etc.

The distances of where forces can be deployed should be left blank. I know the President's thinking on tanks and missiles. But I don't think we should go there with these numbers.

Then I told the President that of the Israeli demands . . .

President Sadat: Political ones.

Secretary Kissinger: Political ones. We drop the one on foreign troops and volunteers.

We drop the one on passage of Israeli ships through the Canal, and we drop the one on civil flights.

On Bab Al-Mandeb, we agreed that the President will write me a letter as to the actions of Egyptian forces.

That leaves one point that I didn't raise with you, about the withdrawal of United Nations forces. They say "the parties will undertake not to demand unilaterally the withdrawal of the UNEF. The withdrawal of the UNEF will require the consent of both parties." What is your view on that?

President Sadat: Indefinitely?

Secretary Kissinger: That withdrawal requires the consent of both sides.

Minister Fahmi: Its place is not in the disengagement agreement; it should be in the final agreement.

Secretary Kissinger: I've told the Israelis, "How can you put something permanent in the disengagement proposal which is not a final agreement?"

Minister Fahmi: That is right.

And if you look at this paragraph, it treats the Sinai as a part of Israel. "The evacuation of UNEF from Egypt and Israel." There is no UNEF in Israel. It shows they treat Sinai as part of Israel. It is a mistake but it shows their mentality.

Secretary Kissinger: I would recommend we defer this issue. I don't think the agreement will fail on this issue. I'll tell them you refused it and maybe they will have another idea.

I have told President Sadat that we do not want to put you in an embarrassing position, to weaken the position of the most moderate Arab leader we've had the pleasure of working with. We know you don't want to make a separate peace.

We agreed that now that we are working, it would make no sense to interrupt it by going to other places now. So you could inform your brethren. I will go to Damascus. Maybe I can go to Jordan.

Minister Fahmi: If you do, Damascus will be furious.

Secretary Kissinger: But I will be going there.

[President Sadat and Minister Fahmi confer.]

President Sadat: He has a point. It will seem as if there is an axis—Cairo–Amman—and Syria is forgotten.

Secretary Kissinger: We'll do whatever you suggest. We will go to both later.

I also have in mind the President's view on the south here.

May I make a practical suggestion?

President Sadat: Yes.

Secretary Kissinger: That I meet now with my colleagues and we do two documents, then present them to you at 4:30, and then plan to leave here at 8:30, and that I notify Israel now that I plan to arrive at 10:45 and return here tomorrow night.

They will probably need more than a day to consider it; they will need a Cabinet meeting.

So I will probably be back Wednesday. There is no day that is inconvenient for you?

President Sadat: No, no.

Secretary Kissinger: Probably I will have to go back once more to Israel, and once more here will do it. Because the tank issue and the line issue will be unresolved.

Assistant Secretary Sisco: What do we say to the press?

Secretary Kissinger: I don't think we should say anything now.

But we agreed that at some point we should say it is a complex issue, a difficult negotiation. "I have an Egyptian map that I am now taking to Israel. Nevertheless, good progress was made today, and I am optimistic that progress will be achieved."

So those who oppose the agreement won't think it is on the verge of breaking down.

My worry is that the General here hasn't solved the problem of communicating with the North Koreans who are here, and they will shoot me down. [Laughter]

President Sadat: They are very near. [Laughter]

Secretary Kissinger: In what language do you communicate?

General Gamasy: Korean. [Laughter]

President Sadat: I have an idea. We will send Sisco as a test. [Laughter]

Secretary Kissinger: Good idea.

6. Memorandum of Conversation[1]

Jerusalem, January 15, 1974, 2–3:50 p.m.

PARTICIPANTS

Yigal Allon, Israeli Deputy Prime Minister
Abba Eban, Minister of Foreign Affairs
Moshe Dayan, Minister of Defense
Simcha Dinitz, Ambassador to the U.S.
Lt. Gen. David Elazar, Chief of Staff
Abraham Kidron, Director General, MFA
Ephraim Evron, Dep. Director General, MFA
Mordechai Gazit, Director General of Prime Minister's Office
Colonel Bar-On, Aide to Dayan

Henry A. Kissinger, Secretary of State
Joseph J. Sisco, Asst. Secretary of State for Near Eastern and S. Asian Affairs
Ellsworth Bunker, Ambassador-at-Large
Kenneth Keating, Ambassador to Israel
Carlyle E. Maw, Legal Advisor, Dept. of State
Alfred L. Atherton, Jr., Dep. Asst Secretary for Near Eastern & S. Asian Affairs
Harold H. Saunders, NSC Senior Staff
Peter W. Rodman, NSC Staff

Dep. Prime Minister Allon: Gentlemen, since the soup is very hot, we can start business.

We had time to see the Prime Minister and showed her the documents and the draft.[2]

She agreed to participate in the Cabinet meeting, which will be at her home. And she wants to see you before the Cabinet meeting.[3] She is not too well, so don't exhaust her.

Secretary Kissinger: There is no evidence I can do that. [Laughter]

Every time you give me proposals which I consider totally outrageous, they accept them. [Laughter]

---

[1] Source: National Archives, Nixon Presidential Materials, NSC Files, Kissinger Office Files, Box 140, Country Files, Middle East, Secretary Kissinger's Middle East Trip, January 11–20, 1974, Memcons and Reports. Top Secret; Sensitive; Exclusively Eyes Only. The luncheon meeting was held in the Foreign Minister's residence. Brackets are in the original. Kissinger and Allon and their parties met earlier in the day at 9:40 a.m. to review Kissinger's meeting with Sadat on the previous day. (Memorandum of conversation; ibid.)

[2] Apparently a draft of the Egyptian-Israeli Agreement on the Disengagement of Forces attached to memorandum of conversation of the 9:40 a.m. meeting.

[3] Kissinger met with Meir later that day between 4 and 5:30 p.m. at her residence and discussed the Egyptian proposals. (Memorandum of conversation; National Archives, Nixon Presidential Materials, NSC Files, Kissinger Office Files, Box 140, Country Files, Middle East, Secretary Kissinger's Middle East Trip, January 11–20, 1974, Memcons and Reports)

First Egyptian-Israeli Disengagement Agreement 39

Dep. Prime Minister Allon: We should continue that way.

Secretary Kissinger: So my standing as an expert is declining.

Dep. Prime Minister Allon: Mr. Gazit is still working on changes [laughter]—minor ones, ones which the Prime Minister is concerned about.

Secretary Kissinger: Now for the good news.

Dep. Prime Minister Allon: By and large we must say you achieved great progress in your visits in Jerusalem and Aswan. We will give you some changes which we think you will consider logical. And we see no reason why there cannot be a signing at Kilometer 101 Friday.[4]

What we accept is, we accept the geographic concept. [Laughter]

Secretary Kissinger: It is a great victory, to get Israel to accept its own proposal. [Laughter]

Dep. Prime Minister Allon: But on the southern zone, our Chief of Staff is considering, and we will try to be forthcoming.

Secretary Kissinger: Good.

Ambassador Dinitz: But not southcoming. [Laughter]

Minister Dayan: Suppose we do move on the main line southward—which I think we will do—but the area evacuated by us should be kept by the UN, not by them, and they will maintain all the area they have.

Ambassador Dinitz: They will also move.

Secretary Kissinger: No.

Minister Dayan: They will stay where they are—which is the change in our map. If we didn't move back, there would be no room for the UN.

Secretary Kissinger: Given their mentality, first of all, this will help. Psychologically, if there is one kilometer you can give them, it will help.

Dep. Prime Minister Allon: Our General Elazar went to headquarters and he is studying it.

Secretary Kissinger: Good.

Dep. Prime Minister Allon: In most drafts there are references to "weapons and armaments," not forces. So Gazit will change the wording.

Secretary Kissinger: They are extremely allergic to it for political reasons, not as substance.

Dep. Prime Minister Allon: Can you say "armed forces," or "forces and armaments"?

---

[4] January 18.

Secretary Kissinger: If you give me that choice.

Dep. Prime Minister Allon: On the number of battalions, we had an argument among ourselves, because when we said two–three battalions, we meant it. If you can settle it on 5 or 6, you will be awarded the Ben-Gurion prize.[5]

Secretary Kissinger: Six is impossible.

Dep. Prime Minister Allon: If they stick to 10 and we stick to six, maybe 8.

Secretary Kissinger: Maybe. Well, maybe 9.

Dep. Prime Minister Allon. No.

Ambassador Dinitz: Yigal was not supposed to say that.

Secretary Kissinger: We can't do it, because if it takes too long, his advisers will turn against it.

Minister Dayan: Battalions have 900.

Ambassador Bunker: Gamasy told me 600.

Secretary Kissinger: We can get a definition.

Dep. Prime Minister Allon: So, officially six, unofficially seven to eight. The word "reinforced" worries us a little bit; it needs clarification. It can mean anything.

Minister Eban: Tanks.

Dep. Prime Minister Allon: No, not tanks because they are covered.

Secretary Kissinger: His argument was, if you don't put it in, it will be said that it is only the men and not the support units.

Minister Eban: If it means engineers, let's be specific.

Secretary Kissinger: So we don't waste time, have your Chief of Staff come up with a definition of "reinforced" as "such organic units," etc. He said it would be infantry battalions. But I said he could have APC's. You never told me . . .

Minister Dayan: I would rather have them define it as not exceeding a certain number of men and not exceeding light arms, or something like that. Not whether or not they have medical corps, etc.

Secretary Kissinger: We have to have precise procedures.

Dep. Prime Minister Allon: Now we accept the number of thirty tanks, and not one more.

Secretary Kissinger: You think you can handle that?

Dep. Prime Minister Allon: It will be public in the Cabinet. And not concentrated. Only for support.

---

[5] The Ben-Gurion Prize was awarded by the Ben-Gurion University of the Negev to those who had worked to help humanity.

On artillery: the guiding principle is that we would like their artillery to confine itself to covering and support of their own units but not to be able to hit either the UN or Israeli area. I think it should include also the UN zone.

Secretary Kissinger: It is difficult for them because it means they can't have it on the East Bank.

My view is they will find it extremely difficult to move back more than thirty kilometers.

Ambassador Dinitz: There are different types of artillery ranges and missiles. Each has its own range. We would like to talk about the principle.

Secretary Kissinger: If you get into that, you would have to inspect every piece. It is an almost hopeless exercise. Gamasy will be delighted with it.

Dep. Prime Minister Allon: But the principle is important.

Secretary Kissinger: You will get the principle but no substance.

Dep. Prime Minister Allon: With regard to surface-to-air missiles, the principle is they can protect the Egyptian-held areas, but neither the UN zone nor the Israel area should be covered. By the same logic.

Secretary Kissinger: They won't do it.

Dep. Prime Minister Allon: But add ... We say thirty, you say twenty-five.

Secretary Kissinger: I will try it.

Dep. Prime Minister Allon: Since we have great faith in you, you will get it.

Secretary Kissinger: No. I will raise anything you want. But I would counsel you as a friend—right now if I get into a negotiation that gets into the artillery and missile situation, it reopens it. Now I can tell him he already accepted it. He will be in the grip of his advisers. Gamasy was furious.

Dep. Prime Minister Allon: It makes no difference for the protection of his own forces. It makes a lot of difference for us.

Secretary Kissinger: Why?

Dep. Prime Minister Allon: With the new type of missiles they will hit the new types of aircraft flying over our own zone.

Secretary Kissinger: On surface-to-air missiles there is a chance. Because it is not so reciprocal. With the artillery, once you start specifying distances, you are on Gamasy's territory.

I think there is a thirty percent chance of getting five kilometers more on surface-to-air missiles.

Dep. Prime Minister Allon: He won't retreat from the whole idea because of five kilometers.

Secretary Kissinger: Well, there is always a point when . . .

Dep. Prime Minister Allon: He didn't concede an inch.

Secretary Kissinger: Yigal, if you stay on the West Bank and the embargo stays and while the whole world starts up again, you are in an impossible position. Even if you win, which I am sure you will win.

Dep. Prime Minister Allon: Of course. It will be useful for both.

Secretary Kissinger: Of course. Even if it goes badly, you are not risking much.

Gamasy, when he saw it, was outraged. He says, "That means all my artillery has to go back."

Dep. Prime Minister Allon: It is safer for his artillery!

Secretary Kissinger: He said the President agreed only on the basis of his own map.

Dep. Prime Minister Allon: The UN line should be covered.

Secretary Kissinger: I don't think I can do that.

Minister Dayan: The key is the distinction between offensive and defensive weapons. If they say, "We want the artillery to take care of our own people," it is one thing. But if they say they want to cover a further kilometer . . .

Secretary Kissinger: They say you will attack.

Minister Dayan: Then there will be a buffer zone or not? If so, it means the no-man's land in between will not be covered by the other party. I am not worried for protecting the UN but it means advancing our artillery, and no buffer zone.

Mr. Sisco: But it doesn't reach the other . . .

Minister Dayan: But he will ask the Finns out.[6]

Secretary Kissinger: But if he is going to do that, he will move his artillery up.

Minister Dayan: A buffer means they are out of range of the artillery.

Secretary Kissinger: My problem is I have to raise a whole new concept. Given the attitude of Gamasy and Fahmi to this whole limitation scheme, we run a major risk of losing what you have got. I am scared of this artillery problem.

There is no risk in asking for fewer battalions, or a wider zone for SAM's, but to change the whole concept of the artillery may lose the whole thing.

Dep. Prime Minister Allon: Whatever limits we ask, we accept for ourselves.

---

[6] A reference to the Finnish soldiers who served with the United Nations Emergency Force in the Sinai.

First Egyptian-Israeli Disengagement Agreement   43

Secretary Kissinger: But they don't accept symmetry.

Ambassador Dinitz: It is not a new concept really, because it was in our original position.

Secretary Kissinger: It is not new for you!

Dep. Prime Minister Allon: The next problem is the composition of the UN Security Force. Against our wish, this includes many who don't have relations with Israel, not to mention those who are hostile. So we want that the elements of the force observing our positions should be composed only of those who have relations.

I am consulting with you. Can we change the composition?

Secretary Kissinger: No. The UN would never do it, and you can't do it without getting into a brawl in the UN and not getting it anyway. The best way is to let us work with Waldheim.

Mr. Sisco: We have done well this way.

Secretary Kissinger: True, he did well in the Geneva meetings.

I sent him a report.

Ambassador Dinitz: We have a practical problem. The inspection will be as it is now, with the UN and liaison officers; then we can face a situation in which we can be inspected by a country that does not have relations with us.

Secretary Kissinger: Wait a minute. I haven't raised it with him, but I am not sure he doesn't think it will be done by aerial photography.

Minister Dayan: I think now it is only by the friendly countries. They inspect the posts, etc. The document says the same procedure.

Mr. Sisco: We can work this out with Waldheim, I am sure.

Minister Eban: It can only be done empirically—but it can be done empirically because he is a pragmatist. In fact, the Security Council does not take any interest in it. It is mostly done by the Secretary-General.

Secretary Kissinger: I am 99 percent certain we can handle it.

Dep. Prime Minister Allon: On inspection, we do accept that direct photography will be done by the United States Air Force. They suggest once in a fortnight, you say. We will accept more often.

Secretary Kissinger: Particularly if it is done at irregular intervals.

Dep. Prime Minister Allon: And the photographs are given to each side. But each side should be entitled to have flights on its own side.

Secretary Kissinger: It is in the agreement.

Dep. Prime Minister Allon: You say the Egyptians didn't know what we meant by interference with civilian flights. I can tell you what this means. Our regular flights from Ben-Gurion at Lod to Capetown, Nairobi, Johannesburg, go down the Red Sea. We must be assured—or you must be assured by them—that they will never interfere with this. It is important that they know you know this.

Mr. Sisco: Have they ever been interrupted?

Dep. Director General Evron: There is ever the permanent threat of forbidden "defense zones", and more importantly, of getting the ICAO and its bodies to cancel flight routes along these lines. They are using these threats. So when we fly there we are doing so "illegally." We are asking that they desist from that practice too.

Secretary Kissinger: They will take the position that this is a disengagement agreement and not a settlement of all outstanding issues. Fahmi will reject it. Sadat may do something. Now I understand your position and can raise it. I will raise it seriously.

Mr. Sisco: When was the last time you have evidence that such a thing happened?

Dep. Director General Evron: Six months ago.

Dep. Prime Minister Allon: Now a serious problem—the Egyptian prisoners. How many are there? Seventy?

Minister Dayan: Eighty by now. There are new ones every day.

Dep. Prime Minister Allon: Now we are facing a most complicated internal problem, which you can sense when you met the families Sunday.[7] I hate to say it, but it is almost inconceivable that we let the Egyptians go back before we get our prisoners from Syria.

Secretary Kissinger: Then you won't get an agreement.

Dep. Prime Minister Allon: It is not that we want to link them, but we need the lists.

Secretary Kissinger: Look, he wrote a letter to Asad, and failed, and he said, you do it. To ask him to raise it is easy. But he cannot agree to leave his here. To link his with Syria I think is a massive mistake.

Dep. Prime Minister Allon: The problem is we misled our people, saying Brezhnev gave his word of honor.

Secretary Kissinger: Which is true.

Dep. Prime Minister Allon: We said we had an assurance from you.

Secretary Kissinger: If he can't get the prisoners because it is linked with Syria, he might as well pursue Syrian policy.

Dep. Prime Minister Allon: If we could do something in our memorandum of understanding.

Secretary Kissinger: Maybe.

---

[7] On January 13 in Jerusalem, Kissinger met with representatives of the relatives of Israelis captured or missing in Syria.

Minister Dayan: The one thing is that we are responsible for eighty Egyptian prisoners. Such as the mood in the country is, we can't explain to our people why there is no progress with Syria. Nobody believes us when we say Soviet Russia tried. We did sign an agreement on the exchange of prisoners before, so we fulfill it. This isn't an exchange but one-sided. In this agreement there is no clause about release.

Secretary Kissinger: We can do it as an understanding. I don't see how it is in your interest to link them, when the advantage is to split Egypt and Syria, and the result is to break off the agreement. Then he might as well pursue Syrian policy.

Minister Dayan: We do want to release them but we can't do it now in the agreement on disengagement. That is our situation, not our stand.

Secretary Kissinger: If you give me your assurance you will do it—in March, when disengagement is completed—I can explain it to him. It is not mentioned in the agreement.

Minister Dayan: We don't want to keep them or feed them. But we can't commit ourselves now to a blank date.

Secretary Kissinger: He can't commit himself to this unless I can assure him he will get them at the end of the process. He will say he wants them now, and then I will explain your position to him. For years you have complained that the Egyptians don't care about prisoners; now you get an Egyptian leader who does care, and you won't do it.

He won't sign the agreement without it.

Minister Dayan: Parliament won't accept it.

Secretary Kissinger: Then it will fail. For two months he has been harassing me and I have transmitted them to you. I believe he has written to Asad because he has got an answer that is consistent with what I have seen elsewhere.

Dep. Prime Minister Allon: All we need is the lists.

Secretary Kissinger: But I have to explain it will be done de facto.

Minister Dayan: Explain it to the Prime Minister, because she will have to defend it to Parliament.

Dep. Prime Minister Allon: On length, we think 45 days is enough.

Secretary Kissinger: He says 23.

Dep. Prime Minister Allon: He doesn't have to move as far as we do. We need six weeks. It is a big army there.

Secretary Kissinger: All right. It is like the five kilometers. I will do my damnedest. I think I can probably get very close to 45 days if not 45.

Dep. Prime Minister Allon: In the paper there is always reference to what we have to do, not what he has to do. You explained his problem. Can we have it rewritten "it should be implemented"?

Secretary Kissinger: All right, we will look at this.

Dep. Prime Minister Allon: Gazit will look at it.

Minister Dayan: On the schedule, Gamasy's proposal is unaccepted. Only the maximum time should be in there. In 48 hours the roads to Suez will be open, and the same time for getting the bodies of the soldiers.

Secretary Kissinger: You want that in the document?

Minister Dayan: I don't care about the document, but it should be done.

And the third point I want you to know—we allow you to tell Sadat—that we will not remove any civilian installations because most are already removed. [Laughter] Like the port there, the cranes. We were there for two months, bombing and shelling already.

Minister Eban: The scorched earth will be scorched no further!

Minister Dayan: A UN observer can see that after signing, there is nothing else that will be done.

Secretary Kissinger: Let me see if I can delete that paragraph, because it will be more trouble than it is worth. If I say this to Sadat, it will be better to remove the whole paragraph.

Dep. Prime Minister Allon: Yes.

Secretary Kissinger: I will do my best.

Minister Dayan: The problem is the way the situation is, not the way the paragraph is. The paragraph is no problem.

Secretary Kissinger: If there is any crane left, someone will get courtmartialed. [Laughter]

Minister Dayan: The 48 hours for Suez City is 48 hours after the beginning of evacuation, not after the signing.

Secretary Kissinger: You meet 48 hours after signature, probably at Kilometer 101, to work out the technical means. This is done within five days after that. Then withdrawal starts 48 hours after that. Forty-eight hours after that, the roads will be open. So eleven days after Friday.

The Egyptians will interpret this as a formal obligation to complete the technical negotiations.

Minister Dayan: No, you can give them our word we won't drag it on.

Dep. Prime Minister Allon: It should be understood, in case you forget, [to mean] after the Cabinet approves after you come back with the final clarification. We have to get the Cabinet approval and get it ratified in the Knesset next week.

Secretary Kissinger: I am guiding myself by you gentlemen's assumption that the Knesset will approve it.

Dep. Prime Minister Allon: I hope so.

Secretary Kissinger: No time is lost by the ratification process because the talks will be going on.

Dep. Prime Minister Allon: Now we have the problem of how to notify our people, and the Knesset. Including the Committee which meets today. We will do our best to hold back the substantive information before the agreement is signed. If you don't take the *New York Times* man on the plane.

Secretary Kissinger: Who?

Dep. Prime Minister Allon: Terrence Smith said it had to be a massive Egyptian force.

Mr. Sisco: He is the one in Jerusalem.

Secretary Kissinger: Our press complain that I am giving them nothing.

Dep. Prime Minister Allon: Most of the stories are not true.

We must explain to the Knesset as soon as possible, not earlier than the signing of the agreement.

Minister Dayan: You are too optimistic. I go to the Foreign Affairs Committee tonight. If I tell them, it will be in the press tomorrow. What is more, once we tell the Cabinet today, it is the same thing. Because it is a new proposal, not the same as before. Each one has to go to his own party and tell it to the entire party.

I don't see how we can get the support of our people without telling them, and it will be leaked.

Secretary Kissinger: It will blow up.

Mr. Sisco: It will be a disaster, I tell you.

Minister Eban: We can't do it without telling them the advantages for Israel.

Minister Dayan: The critics are saying there are no limitations, that it is one-sided.

Secretary Kissinger: Sadat says that disclosure before the signature is a disaster; and after the signing it is only an embarrassment.

Mr. Sisco: Can you give the general principles without mentioning the figures at all?

Dep. Prime Minister Allon: Yes. I am just warning ourselves.

Minister Dayan: The papers say it is a one-sided withdrawal.

It is not a question of dragging it out. We have to have the approval of our Cabinet.

Secretary Kissinger: But it is a fact. If it now blows up so close to success and if your people don't understand this... As far as this group is concerned, it has been an enterprise among friends. Our problem now is the maddening domestic situation you have. It must be more maddening for you than for us. But I am convinced that Sadat has gone beyond the outer edge of what he feels is safe. He has gone further towards us and you. He has got a long trip planned, which he wants to do as an Arab leader, one way or the other.

Minister Dayan: Can you sign Thursday?

Secretary Kissinger: We could do it. I don't want to go there and give him the sense that you are so eager for it.

Minister Dayan: The only way to handle it is we shall put censorship on it, and if anything is printed, it is not official and can be denied.

Dep. Director General Evron: But they can fly to Cyprus and print it.

Secretary Kissinger: He figures he can subsume the limitations in the glory of getting the territory back. If he has to defend the limitations before he gets the agreement, he is in trouble.

Minister Eban: What can we say to the Cabinet?

Secretary Kissinger: Not that parallel letter of the President's, but that there are mutual limitations.

Minister Dayan: I won't even mention that.

Secretary Kissinger: I asked how will you justify the thinning out? He said he will just say he needs to clear the Canal and needs room to put the people in.

Any Israeli crowing that this thing is a great victory . . . In a way you are better off if the press keeps saying you are betraying your country.

Minister Eban: That is normal.

Ambassador Dinitz: You won't meet the same government here!

Secretary Kissinger: Avoid saying it is Dayan's proposal, because that means it is all a game.

Dep. Prime Minister Allon: Get us a list of the spies they want back.

Secretary Kissinger: I will try for that.

Dep. Prime Minister Allon: It would be beautiful if it could be done at the same time.

Ambassador Keating: At Kilometer 101 with Henry.

Mr. Sisco: We will bring them in the back of the plane with the press.

Secretary Kissinger: They won't give Mizrachi unless you release the prisoners when the agreement is consummated. Even that is hard, but I can explain it.

Minister Dayan: Once we give a pledge, we might as well give them tomorrow. There is no point in keeping them.

Secretary Kissinger: If the Syrians and Egyptians get linked together by your action, there is no hope of getting the prisoners back.

The only hope is if Sadat emerges with an agreement and enhances the Syrian covetousness for an agreement. If he fails, the Syrians will be vindicated. Then we will lose any possibility of influence and will never get the prisoners back. Maybe the families are not rational enough to understand this.

Dep. Prime Minister Allon: The last item is the Memorandum of Understanding.

Secretary Kissinger: I don't think Thursday is possible. I want to leave with a document, of which you have approved every word. I want a map which we can use as an official map. I want a memorandum of understanding. I want to go over again what we have agreed. Then we have to agree what my authority is. Will I have to come back?

We must aim for Friday. There are just too many things to do.

Minister Eban: It would be better for you to come back.

Secretary Kissinger: I will come back.

Dep. Director General Evron: Since the Cabinet meeting is at 5:30, and before that the Secretary will meet with the Prime Minister, I suggest immediately after that, a working group should put into shape all the documents, with the changes.

Secretary Kissinger: Keeping your changes to a minimum. For example, "forces and armaments" may be attainable.

Dep. Director General Evron: We should get together at 9:00 or 9:30.

Minister Dayan: The Chief of Staff will be here at 5:30. I can call on him and tell him.

Secretary Kissinger: Do a map for me which we can append to this document which shows the zones and all the areas turned over to the UN. Adjust the UN zone so there will be some buffer in a few areas. And give us the best you can in the south.

Mr. Sisco: It will be an official map.

Minister Dayan: There will be three zones—the UN, Egyptian and Israeli.

Secretary Kissinger: Yes.

Minister Dayan: The Egyptian area will include the areas they now hold.

Secretary Kissinger: A kilometer for me here or there.

Minister Dayan: A kilometer for you on the Gulf of Suez will be a pleasure. Come with me, and I will show you Egypt!

Secretary Kissinger: On the Egyptian side, you can define it with the Suez Canal. On the Israeli side, you need a dotted line for your line

200 meters west of the road. Because the letter refers to the Israeli line and "a line as indicated on the attached map."

So draw a dotted line and say the "zones of limited armaments" or "area." You don't mind "zone."

Mr. Sisco: Don't use the word "zones."

Mr. Saunders: There is a partial description in the paper.

Secretary Kissinger: Call it the "line described in Paragraph X of the Agreement." So it can be published.

Minister Dayan: We will be careful on the Egyptian side because it is defined by the Suez Canal and the Egyptian line.

Secretary Kissinger: Right.

Minister Dayan: "UN forces"?

Secretary Kissinger: Use the language of the agreement. "UNEF."

Dayan: The map will be ready today.

Secretary Kissinger: Let's agree on a schedule.

Minister Eban: We will have by now a formulation of the changes on which we would like you to do your utmost. It will be ready. Then there is the problem of the memorandum of understanding.

While the Cabinet meets, the working group will redraft the documents to take into account your comments. Then the documents will be presented again to this group after the Cabinet meeting.

Secretary Kissinger: Then we will do a list of all the things I am to take up and in what manner.

Mr. Sisco: A checklist.

Secretary Kissinger: That we will finish tonight. Notify the Egyptians that I will leave tomorrow at 11:00, and get in at 1:15. I will be back here Thursday.

How do we get all these documents typed? Who is going to bring them? Joe?

Next to no communication is possible. Once I leave Aswan, it will be almost impossible to communicate.

Dep. Director General Evron: I thought this working group would meet immediately following the Cabinet. Around 7:30. At 10:00, a plenary meeting. We will try to prepare all the documents in the meantime.

Mr. Sisco: There is no need to duplicate in the memorandum of understanding points covered in the agreement.

Ambassador Dinitz: Two points: One, the undertaking to reopen the Canal and rehabilitate the cities is between us in the memorandum of understanding. Second, there will be no further Israeli withdrawal until the opening of the Canal.

Mr. Sisco: Impossible.

Ambassador Dinitz: The Prime Minister is convinced that two weeks later there will be massive pressure to go to the next phase. We have intelligence information that the Russians will be pressing immediately for the next step.

Secretary Kissinger: We will do our best on that.

Minister Eban: What we want is an American assurance.

Secretary Kissinger: We can discuss it in general terms of strategy, but a flat commitment, no. You couldn't hold us to it anyway.

This is in too absolute terms. We will try to find what we can responsibly do. Certainly it is our intention to go at as leisurely a pace as possible until you can see whether there is an improvement in the situation on the ground.

I told you privately this morning: If you can get the Senators and those intellectuals to ease off on MFN[8] so I can use it with Dobrynin . . . Because if they all gang up on Soviet tyranny, etc., and I am supposed to go to the Russians and say "Be moderate towards Israel . . ." So we can use MFN with Russia as we always intended—just to give them enough to keep their appetite whetted. If we can dangle it as a carrot, we have enough to moderate their conduct. If you can do it, this will do you more good than a clause in this memorandum.

If Gromyko reconvenes the Geneva Conference and makes a wild speech, and forces Fahmi and Rifai to imitate him, there is nothing we can do except not go along.

We will use MFN in a coldblooded way, but we need it to whet their appetite. I really want to tell you if we had MFN and the credits to play with, it would do you more good than a clause here.

We will give you some statement anyway.

We will add a sentence, not just communicate the Egyptian assurance [on the blockade].

The sentence [on the arms requests] we will delete. The memorandum of understanding won't get you one rifle.

Ambassador Dinitz: We don't mean a specific list of arms, but an understanding that we are undertaking a redeployment that puts us into certain positions, and the U.S. will take this into account in considering the arms requests.

Secretary Kissinger: That is fair enough. It will be helpful, in fact, with our bureaucracy.

---

[8] A reference to Kissinger's concern that Israeli officials were encouraging American intellectuals and Senators to delay Most-Favored-Nation status for the Soviet Union until it allowed more Soviet Jews to emigrate from the Soviet Union.

7. **Memorandum of Conversation**[1]

Jerusalem, January 16, 1974, 8:30–10:20 a.m.

PARTICIPANTS

Yigal Allon, Deputy Prime Minister of Israel
Abba Eban, Minister of Foreign Affairs
Moshe Dayan, Minister of Defense
Simcha Dinitz, Ambassador to United States
Mordechai Gazit, Director General, Prime Minister's Office
Avraham Kidron, Director General, MFA
Ephraim Evron, Deputy Director General, MFA
Eytan Bentsur, Aide to Eban
Col. Bar-On, Aide to Dayan

Dr. Henry A. Kissinger, Sec. of State, Asst. to President
Ellsworth Bunker, Amb. at Large
Kenneth Keating, Amb. to Israel
Joseph J. Sisco, Asst. Sec. for Near Eastern and South Asian Affairs
Carlyle Maw, Legal Adviser, Dept. of State
Alfred L. Atherton, Jr., Dep. Asst. Sec for Near Eastern and South Asian Affairs
Harold Saunders, NSC Senior Staff
Peter W. Rodman, NSC Staff

Allon: How is the American-Israeli war of attrition proceeding?

Kissinger: I am afraid to say we are making progress.

Allon: I am happy with the Israeli press for attacking us for giving in.

Kissinger: Do they attack you?

Eban: They say it is a one-sided retreat, there is no limitation on Egyptian forces, there is linkage, etc.

Allon: All right, Henry, let's start.

Let me say for the record that any memorandum of understanding reached between the U.S. and Israel is binding on both parties.

Kissinger: Let's say "henceforth" it is binding, so it scraps all the previous ones. [laughter]

Let's go through the agreement.

Dayan: [shows a new map Tab A][2] The Chief of Staff didn't like it, but I overruled him, so we are redoing it. The important point is this one, this promontory [in the south]. Here we have a fortified position. I

---

[1] Source: National Archives, Nixon Presidential Materials, NSC Files, Kissinger Office Files, Box 140, Country Files, Middle East, Secretary Kissinger's Middle East Trip, January 11–20, 1974, Memcons and Reports. Top Secret; Sensitive; Exclusively Eyes Only. The meeting was held in the Prime Minister's office. Brackets, with the exception of ones noted, are in the original. All blank underscores are omissions in the original.

[2] Tab A attached but not printed.

said we would go two kilometers south of that, so that the piece will be not only not in our control, but our forces will be south of it. We are giving it . . .

Kissinger: . . . to the U.N.

Dayan: To the U.N. Our forces will not be in sight of Suez City. In substance, this is the main thing, to go off this dominating point.

Kissinger: You have only one map now?

Dayan: They will prepare it and bring it to the airport. [See second map, Tab B][3]

Kissinger: No, last night we were going to have two maps, one like this and one that takes you substantially further south.

Dayan: We are going ten kilometers more [in the other map].

Kissinger: What you are doing is widening the U.N. zone here.

Dayan: And adding one kilometer.

Kissinger: And adding one kilometer.

Dayan: Because of this road junction, we couldn't go more than two kilometers off.

Kissinger: Where is the road junction?

Dayan: [shows it] It doesn't show here but we need to keep it.

Kissinger: This is the map I took to Israel [*Egypt*?].[4]

Dayan: No, this is the corrected map.

Kissinger: You are making two maps, with overlays, so I can show him what you first gave him?

Bar-On: Yes.

Kissinger: So all they have to give up is one little corner here; and if he complains about it I can give it back to him.

Dayan: The importance of that is that we go off this fortification, so we shall practically not be in sight of Suez.

Kissinger: Right. Let's go over the document now. Will you come to the airport with me to go over the map with me?

Dayan: If you want, I will be.

Kissinger: Good.

Dinitz: [reads Agreement at Tab C][5] "Egyptian-Israeli Agreement on Disengagement of Forces.

"Egypt and Israel will scrupulously observe the ceasefire on land, sea, and air called for by the U.N. Security Council and will refrain

---

[3] Tab B attached but not printed.
[4] Bracketed correction added by the editor.
[5] Tab C attached but not printed. Entitled "Egyptian-Israeli Agreement on Disengagement of Forces," it is a draft of the disengagement agreement.

from the time of the signing of this document from all military and hostile actions against each other."

Kissinger: My prediction is "and hostile" will probably go.

Allon: What about violating the ceasefire not by action but by moving forces?

Kissinger: That is covered elsewhere.

Sisco: And that is an action.

Dinitz: [continues reading] "B. The military forces of Egypt and Israel will be separated in accordance with the following principles:

"1. All Egyptian forces on the east side of the Canal will be deployed west of the line designated as Line A on the attached map. All Israeli forces, including those west of the Suez Canal and the Bitter Lakes, will be deployed to the line designated as Line B on the attached map."

Kissinger: If anyone can figure out what is happening just from this document, it will be an accident.

Maw: It should be "east of the line."

Kissinger: Carl is right. It should be "deployed east of the line," instead of "deployed to the line."

Allon: "And south."

Kissinger: Should we say "east and south?"

Allon: If there is a map attached, it will be clear.

Dinitz: [continues reading] "2. The area between the Egyptian and Israeli lines will be a zone of disengagement in which the United Nations Emergency Force (UNEF) will be stationed. The UNEF will consist of units from countries that are not permanent members of the Security Council. Existing procedures of the UNEF, including the attaching of Egyptian and Israeli liaison officers to UNEF, will be continued."

Allon: This is with the understanding that in the other document there will be a reference to the fact that countries without relations with us will not be inspecting our forces.

Kissinger: A reference to UNEF and only non-permanent members. We already do that.

Sisco: Say "will continue to consist."

Kissinger: Right.

Dinitz: [reading] "3. The area between the Egyptian line and the Suez Canal will be limited in armament and forces.

"4. The area (as indicated in the attached map) between the Israeli line and the line designated as Line C on the attached map ... "

Maw: Why not define the Israeli line [in Paragraph B(4)] as Line B?

Kissinger: For clarity. Take out the parenthesis on "(as indicated in the attached map)," because it is a reference to an earlier draft.

Dinitz: "4. The area between the Israeli line (Line B on the attached map) and the line designated as Line C on the attached map, which runs along the western base of the mountains where the Gidi and Mitla Passes are located, will be limited in armament and forces.

"5. The limitations referred to in paragraphs 3 and 4 will be inspected by UNEF with officers of Egypt and Israel acting as liaison officers attached to UNEF."

Kissinger: You realize that no single paragraph in this document stands on its own. Every one refers to something else!

Dinitz: Should we make it clearer that inspection by liaison officers will be only on our own territory?

Kissinger: You can't say your "own territory?"

I think this paragraph won't survive.

Dinitz: [reads] "Air forces of the two sides will be permitted to operate up to their respective lines without interference from the other side."

Allon: All right.

Saunders: Something was left out in typing of paragraph C. Let me read it. [Saunders reads the full text] "C. The detailed implementation of the disengagement of forces will be worked out by military representatives of Egypt and Israel, who will agree on the stages of this process. These representatives will meet no later than 48 hours after the signature of this agreement at Kilometer 101 for this purpose. They will complete this task within five days. Disengagement will begin within 48 hours after the completion of the work of the military representatives and in no event later than seven days after the signature of this agreement. The process of disengagement will be completed not later than 45 days after it begins."

Dinitz: "D. This agreement is not regarded by Egypt and Israel as a final peace agreement. It constitutes a first step toward a final, just and durable peace according to the provision of Security Council Resolution 338[6] and within the framework of the Geneva Conference."—Should be "provisions."

---

[6] UN Security Council Resolution 338 was adopted on October 22, 1973, and called for a cease-fire between forces fighting in the October War within 12 hours of its adoption. Additionally, the resolution called for the parties to immediately work toward the implementation of Security Council Resolution 242. For text of Resolution 338, see *Yearbook of the United Nations, 1973*, page 213. Resolution 242 was adopted on November 22, 1967, and contained two key principles: first, the withdrawal of Israeli forces "from territories occupied" in the June 1967 war, and second, the end "of all claims or states of belligerency and respect for and acknowledgment of the sovereignty, territorial integrity and political independence of every State in the area." See *Foreign Relations*, 1964–1968, volume XIX, Arab-Israeli Crisis and War, 1967, Document 542.

Eban: Plural.

Dinitz: "... of Security Council Resolution 338 and within the framework of the Geneva Conference."

Kissinger: We should put two lines on it at the end. This is the agreement. This will be signed by both sides. Sadat never said anything other than that both will sign it together. The U.S. proposal is different. There was some confusion.

Allon: Mrs. Meir had the impression ...

Kissinger: She was wrong.

Is there a list of things I must raise?

Saunders: Yes. [hands over checklist drafted the night before by the working group, Tab D][7]

Kissinger: This is a commentary and exegesis. Can someone do a simple checklist? Let Hal and Gazit get together in the next room and do an agreed checklist. [Mr. Saunders and Mr. Gazit go out.]

Allon: So you just add under here a line, "for Egypt" and another line "for Israel."

Eban: On the next page, there is a paragraph B(7) which we don't want.

Kissinger: If you staple it together, I will give it to Sadat. [to Sisco] Can you make sure that when I see Sadat this is on a separate paper and not stapled together?

Dinitz: [reads] "7. In order to facilitate the transition in the areas involved in the separation of forces, from the beginning of disengagement all industrial, administrative, infrastructure and other civilian properties and facilities will be left complete and intact in all areas over which control is relinquished by one party to the other."

Allon: This will mislead him to say "left intact and complete." It is not intact now; it is all broken.

Kissinger: "Will be left in the condition existing at the time of signing."

Allon: Right.

Kissinger: That's the truth.

Let's go over it [Agreement at Tab C] so you know, because when I come back, that is it.

They may drop "and hostile" [in paragraph A].

They may want to put Israeli forces before Egyptian forces in paragraph 1. In that case we may have to renumber the lines.

---

[7] Tab D attached but not printed. Entitled "Talking Paper," it is a checklist of points Kissinger should review with Sadat.

Paragraph 2 may be unchanged.

Allon: If we put Israel first, we should put Egypt first in the other.

Kissinger: They will probably want two separate paragraphs again. I am assuming you will accept that.

Dinitz: The Prime Minister suggests that to give it a more even-handed look.

Kissinger: But that was when the writing of the paragraph was less even-handed.

Dinitz: "Hostile" is important because we wanted non-belligerency.

Allon: But the problem is the movement of arms without hostilities. Maybe just to add a word.

Kissinger: They have already rejected "belligerent." I can't go back and forth. If they want to drop one of them, you would prefer to keep "and hostile," and drop "military." Because we already have a "scrupulous observance of the ceasefire."

Allon: What about "qualitative and quantitative changes in armaments?"

Kissinger: That is implicit in the other document, which spells out the limitations. We have the document approved by Sadat.

It depends in what forum Sadat negotiates with me. If Sadat is alone, you have a good chance; if Fahmi and Gamasy are in every session, it will be like here.

Paragraph 1 may be written in two separate paragraphs.

Paragraph 2 I don't foresee any problem with.

Paragraph 3 I don't foresee any problem with.

Paragraph 4 I don't foresee any problem.

Paragraph 5 probably will not survive in this form.

Allon: Why not? There is nothing new in it.

Kissinger: Maybe it will. But it calls attention to the inspection of Egyptian forces.

Sisco: If it is nothing new, why do you insist on it?

Kissinger: One of the two of them will go.

Dinitz: What we are interested in is not to have a new paragraph but that the UNEF continues its practice.

Kissinger: If they start raising hell, I will drop the sentence about "existing procedures" because that is the way it is done.

Dayan: If they don't want it this way, they have to suggest something else.

Kissinger: I don't think you need "existing procedures" for UNEF if you have paragraph 5. You don't need the last sentence of paragraph 2 now. I will keep it in but be prepared to concede it.

On the detailed implementation, they want in the opening of the road to Kabrit and Suez within 48 hours of disengagement. If I get something for it, can I concede this?

Allon: Can this be parallel to something on the bodies and Mizrachi?

Kissinger: Mizrachi, no. He has told me he will do it in response to a request from us but not in an agreement with you. It is totally out of the question. You want him mentioned?

I need a little maneuvering room.

If I come back with an uncompleted agreement, I am going home Thursday[8] night and you can finish it with them.

Allon: We should put it in with bodies and the location of absentees.

Kissinger: I recommend you stay away from absentees unless you want a reference to the 80 prisoners in it.

Dayan: Unless we give them the two roads, they can't get out.

Kissinger: He wants your posts off that road.

Dayan: But we could get the bodies.

Kissinger: That is reasonable. How do I write it? "The two sides will help each other . . ." or "will place no obstacle."?

Dayan: They should turn them over, and should have them all prepared by the time we turn the roads over.

Allon: They should do it without the agreement anyway.

Kissinger: I have six hours, and there is no time for a substantive discussion. How do I write it?

Dayan: It is for them to do.

Kissinger: But we can say it symmetrically.

Dayan: They are taking the area and don't need us to do it for them. They will be able to get their bodies. At the same time, they should hand over ours.

Kissinger: "Israel agrees within 48 hours of the agreement to open the two roads from Suez City to Cairo. During the same period Egypt will turn over the dead bodies of the Israeli soldiers to the UN." Something like that.

There is a strong probability that it won't come up that way, but by assurances. But I want to be ready.

Allon: Whichever way you choose, in the agreement or in the Memorandum of Understanding.

---

[8] January 17.

Dayan: And it should say, "The details will be worked out by the military representatives."

Kissinger: Yes.

Allon: On Mizrachi, we can't get him in return for access?

Kissinger: No. But you can get him within 45 days. But I can assure you, Sadat will not sign the agreement unless I can assure him he will get his 86 prisoners back.

Dayan: Ninety.

Allon: It grows every day!

Kissinger: As I told the Prime Minister yesterday, I am prepared to explain to Mr. Avriel why I persuaded you to do this and why it is in your interest, and why the other course will lead to exactly the opposite.

Allon: We will get Levi and Mizrachi?

Kissinger: Yes. Levi he had never heard of.

Allon: He is just an insane man.

Kissinger: He [Sadat] didn't reject it; he just hadn't heard of him. We are through with this.

Allon: What document now?

Kissinger: Joe, make sure when I get off the plane, I don't have the document with B–7 attached to it?

Maw: The next paper is the U.S. letter [Tab E].[9] It begins: "Dear Mr. President: I am transmitting the attached . . ."

Kissinger: It is the U.S. proposal.

Maw: I will read it: "Dear Mr. President: I am transmitting the attached proposal as part of the agreement between Egypt and Israel on the disengagement of their forces. I am also transmitting the attached proposal to the Prime Minister of Israel.

"Receipt of your signature on the attached proposal will constitute acceptance, subject to the signature of the same proposal by the Prime Minister of Israel."

Allon: Are there two separate documents to the two sides?

Maw: Yes. "In order to facilitate agreement between Egypt and Israel and as part of that agreement, and to assist in maintaining scrupulous observance of the ceasefire on land, air, and sea the United States proposes the following:

Kissinger: Does Gazit want to say "or any other medium that may exist?"

---

[9] Tab E attached but not printed.

Maw: "That within the areas of limited armaments and forces described in the agreement, there will be: (a) no more than ____ reinforced battalions of armed forces and no more than 30 tanks; (b) no artillery except anti-tank guns; (c) no weapons capable of interfering with the other party's flights over its own territory; (d) no permanent, fixed installations for missile sites. The entire force of each party shall not exceed 7,000 men." Should we say "within the area?"

Eban: "Within their areas?"

Maw: "Within its area of limited armaments."

Dinitz: There is no need for it. It is describing the area of limited armaments.

Allon: Simcha's right.

Maw: Yes. [reads] "2. That in areas 30 kilometers west of the Egyptian line and east of the Israeli line, there will be no weapons in areas from which they can reach the other line."

Kissinger: Do we need "in areas" twice? Why not substitute "at a distance?"

Sisco: "To a distance."

Kissinger: Right.

Maw: "3. That to a distance of 30 kilometers west of the Egyptian line and east of the Israeli line, there will be no surface-to-air missiles.

"4. That the above limitations will apply as from the time the agreement on disengagement between Egypt and Israel is signed by the parties and will be implemented in accordance with the schedule of implementation of the basic agreement."

Kissinger: No one knows what this paragraph means but it looks very legalistic.

May I raise one point with General Dayan?

The phrase "no artillery except anti-tank guns" may be too wounding. I would like to be able to substitute in (b) as a fall back, "no weapons which can reach beyond the UNEF line." That is what you originally proposed.

I will start with what we agree on.

Maw: "No weapon that can reach beyond its own line."

Kissinger: That's right.

May I give you my exegesis of this document, so we will know what I will be doing?

We will have massive problems with Paragraph 1, and Paragraph 3. The difficulty with Paragraph 3 is that at the request of Gamasy he moved it back from 30 to 25, and therefore he would have to overrule Gamasy again. Gamasy wanted nothing. He may not want to overrule Gamasy again.

On Paragraph 1, the "no artillery" point will be massive. "No weapons capable of reaching the other line" he may accept. We will have to see.

Allon: Yesterday you said the no-missiles point wouldn't be a problem.

Kissinger: No, I said that having accepted it once he may do so again.

I just want you to know I may not come back with exactly this document. I want you to be prepared mentally.

Dayan: I don't want it to break off, but I can't see what flexibility there can be.

Kissinger: Don't make a decision now; but I just want you to know.

Allon: Some mad commander may misjudge the distances.

Kissinger: I won't raise it, so you don't have to convince me.

Allon: The Cabinet spent an hour on this.

Kissinger: Your Cabinet reminds me of the JCS. While negotiating, we never hear from them, but after an agreement is reached you hear a lot about what they would have gotten.

I am not asking for a decision today.

Since we can't argue tomorrow, you should think about it today.

We won't have good communication.

Dayan: On the 7,000 man force, the Cabinet felt about the expression "reinforced battalions" that there had to be a ceiling.

Kissinger: I understand. But as a man of the world, you know that some time you have to agree to something so the other fellow can go to his colleagues and say he got something. If we say 7,500 men, you won't break off.

Dayan: I don't see why you don't start with 5,000.

Kissinger: That is a good idea.

Does it translate right? If I start with 5,000, that makes about 800 as a battalion.

Dayan: "Reinforced battalion"—you don't know what it means.

Kissinger: All right.

I want my Israeli friends to know that when I say "I understand," it doesn't mean it will happen.

The next document. [Tab F][10]

Maw: [reads] "Letter from President Sadat to President Nixon— Dear Mr. President: In connection with the agreement on the disen-

---

[10] Tab F attached but not printed.

gagement of Egyptian and Israeli forces, the Government of Egypt confirms that it regards the Straits of Bab el-Mandab as an international waterway for ships of all flags and that it will not interfere with the free passage through those straits of Israeli ships or cargoes.

"Upon the opening of the Suez Canal, the principle of free passage will likewise be observed and that principle will be extended to Israel when a final peace agreement has been concluded between Egypt and Israel. As a first step, all cargoes destined for and coming from Israel or owned by Israel will be permitted through the Canal from the time of its opening."

Now we left out of this document the words we agreed to try for: "whether by blockade or otherwise," at the end of the first paragraph.

Kissinger: That is impossible.

Allon: It means boycotts, etc.

Kissinger: He has already told me that.

Eban: Now the Memorandum of Understanding [Tab G].[11]

Maw: This parallels the letter.

Kissinger: We have to consider how to get the typing done. How do we get authentic copies?

Allon: You want us to send Phantoms to Aswan to pick it up?

Dinitz: [reads] "Memorandum of Understanding between the United States Government and the Government of Israel.

"1. The United States informs Israel that Egypt's intentions are to clear and open the Suez Canal for normal operations, and to rehabilitate the cities and towns along the Canal and resume normal peacetime economic activities in that area, beginning as quickly as possible after the Disengagement Agreement is implemented.

"2. The United States has received assurances from Egypt of its intention, upon completion of the implementation of the Agreement, to start reducing significantly its forces under mobilization if Israel gives a like indication to Egypt through the United States."

Kissinger: And this I will now do. I will inform Sadat officially that Israel will carry out a significant demobilization during the process of disengagement.

Eban: On the basis of reciprocity.

Kissinger: Yes. I will do this today.

Dinitz: [reads] "3. It is the policy of the United States that implementation of the Disengagement Agreement and substantial steps by Egypt to implement its intentions in Paragraph 1 above should take

---

[11] Tab G attached but not printed.

precedence over the undertaking of new commitments by the parties related to subsequent phases of the Geneva Conference. The United States will do its best to help facilitate the Conference proceeding at a pace commensurate with this view.

Eban: Right.

Dinitz: [reads] "4. The United States position is that withdrawal of United Nations Emergency Forces during the duration of the Disengagement Agreement requires the consent of both sides. Should the matter of the withdrawal come before the United Nations Security Council without the consent of Israel, the United States will vote against such withdrawal.

"5. The United States will oppose supervision of Israeli-held areas by United Nations Observers from the Soviet Union, from other communist countries or from other countries which have no diplomatic relations with Israel. With respect to the deployment of forces in the United Nations Emergency Forces zone, the United States will approach the United Nations Secretary General with a view to working out arrangements whereby no units or personnel of nations which do not have diplomatic relations with Israel will (a) be deployed adjacent to the Israeli line, or (b) participate in the inspection of the Israeli area of limited forces and armaments.

Eban: The reference to other Communist forces should mean Communist forces now in the force, because we told the Romanians we wouldn't object to them.

Kissinger: But that is not needed.

Dinitz: [reads] "6. The United States has informed the Governments of Israel and Egypt that it will perform aerial reconnaissance missions over the areas covered by the Disengagement Agreement at a frequency of about one mission every ten days or two weeks, and will make the photographs available to both Israel and Egypt."

Dayan: Can you let us know what the date is of these photographs?

Kissinger: So you can move your artillery? [Laughter] You will see the damnedest Israeli movement. [Laughter]

Dinitz: [reads] "7. The United States regards the Straits of Bab el-Mandeb as an international waterway and will support and join with others to secure general recognition of the right of free and innocent passage through those Straits. The United States will do what it deems feasible to maintain free passage of Israeli ships and cargoes through the Straits. In the event of interference with such passage, the United States will consult with Israel on how best to assure the maintenance and exercise of such rights."

Eban: The first sentence isn't just for us but is a statement of your international position. But to say, "do what it deems feasible" sounds very skeptical. I prefer "will strongly support."

Sisco: Yes.

Kissinger: That we can do.

Dinitz: [reads] "8. Recognizing the defense responsibilities of the Government of Israel following redeployment of its forces under the Disengagement Agreement, the United States will make every effort to be fully responsive on a continuing and long-term basis to Israel's military equipment requirements."

Kissinger: I will send this to Secretary Schlesinger.

Dinitz: We have a cable from Washington.

Kissinger: I have a cable too,[12] and I want to talk about this. I was told the Defense Department agreed to the whole $500 million and the only thing is the delivery dates.

Dinitz: No, they haven't finished going over the whole list yet and General Sumner is ill in bed and only back today.

Kissinger: I am told the whole list is gone over and approved. And any additional, the $700 million, will require a Presidential determination, and I have given instructions to start that process.

Dinitz: Scowcroft said to Shalev that the Pentagon was dragging their feet.

Kissinger: I have a later word. I am told that they approved the whole list. They agreed to 400 tanks and 800 APCs, and some artillery. The only item outstanding on the $500 million list were certain advanced weapons. The further items will require a Presidential determination, and if I return with this agreement I am sure I can get this Presidential determination.

Dayan: One set is the Presidential determination, but the other problem is they are holding up advanced equipment.

Kissinger: They are instructed not to use the phrase "political decision."

Dinitz: [reads] "9. In case of an Egyptian violation of any of the provisions of the Agreement, the United States Government and the Government of Israel will consult regarding the necessary reaction."

I suggest adding "and any of its attachments or annexes."

Kissinger: Certainly.

Where is the checklist?

---

[12] Cable not further identified.

Let me repeat again, because there is a typist here: Sadat has repeated to me so often that he will clear and reopen the Canal, but it will not happen if Israel continues to make it as a condition. If you can restrain your press from claiming an Israeli victory, it may happen. Let him claim it as his own achievement. As of three weeks ago I was convinced this was one of the first things he would do.

Eban: "Restrain the press"—I don't know how to do it. We will make no official comment. The Prime Minister won't mention it in her speech.

Kissinger: [goes over the new checklist prepared by Gazit and Saunders, Tab H,[13] reads the items]

—sea minefield map.

Gazit: This was mentioned by the Chief of Staff last night.

Kissinger: This he won't agree to.

All right. [finishes reading]

Allon: One last point. How long will clearing of the Canal last?

Kissinger: He already told me: Six months to open it, eight months to have it in full operation, and he wants to deepen it.

Can we talk procedures? I will try to finish the document with him today and return here tonight. We will have to agree with him on a simultaneous announcement here, in Cairo, and Washington that the agreement will be signed the next day.

I will try for 7:00 p.m. here.

Dayan: Friday morning.

Kissinger: It will be midnight in Washington.

Dayan: Or midnight here.

Keating: Six o'clock p.m. will make the morning papers.

Kissinger: That will miss all the networks. How about 9:00 here?

Dayan: I can't go to the Foreign Affairs Committee and say here are the documents, and it is already agreed.

Allon: The signing will be at 2:00 in the afternoon at Kilometer 101?

Kissinger: My colleagues in Washington will want it on the evening news on Thursday and on Friday. It has to be announced at 3:00 p.m. Thursday in Washington which is 9:00 here.

Dayan: 5 o'clock is better.

Kissinger: Our experience is that it is too late. What difference will it make if it is in the papers the next morning?

---

[13] Tab H attached but not printed.

Dayan: If I see them in the evening, even if it is in the morning papers, Gamasy won't read it. We should shorten the time between the announcement and the signing.

Kissinger: All right. The signing will be at 11:00 a.m. Friday and the announcement at 9:00 in the evening.

Dayan: I don't want the announcement of the signing before I meet with them.

Kissinger: Can you meet with them at 4:00 or 5:00?

The Egyptians don't care whether the agreement is leaked. But the U.S. proposal, the limitations, should not be leaked before the signature.

Dayan: That is what will be leaked. If I meet at 4:00 or 5:00, it will be over by 6:00 or 7:00.

Sisco: If you meet at 8:00, and the announcement comes out at 9:00.

Kissinger: Meet at 6:00, finish at 8:00, and the announcement at 9:00.

Allon: Nine o'clock local time here.

Kissinger: Yes.

Dinitz: There is also an aspect we have to consider: It is not very good from the public point of view to announce it just before the signing. It looks like we are rushing it.

Eban: It must be the day before.

Dayan: If we can't say the details, the tanks, etc. what can we tell the people?

Kissinger: You can say there are severe limitations.

Dayan: In the morning there will be the details, but Gamasy won't read it.

Kissinger: We won't confirm it.

Dayan: We can't sign it and leave the people in the dark.

Kissinger: Can't you sign it and reveal the details later?

Dayan: We have to do it on Friday because there are no papers on Saturday.

Kissinger: I think you are very sensitive to the Egyptian feeling, so I think you will bear this in mind.

Dayan: I have to put the papers before them.

Kissinger: If the fact of a U.S. proposal leaks, they may not go. He has told me he will not sign.

Sisco: Can't you describe it and say a formal U.S. proposal is coming later?

Dayan: They [the Knesset Committee] have the right to ask for all the papers.

Sisco: Can you meet later?

Dayan: Late at night.

Kissinger: Could you meet after the announcement? It is a safer course.

Dayan: The announcement is: "Egypt and Israel are about to sign."

Kissinger: "Have agreed to sign."

Dayan: The Committee should have the option to take a decision not to sign, theoretically.

Kissinger: Believe me, I won't explain this to Sadat.

Allon: Are you going to the Prime Minister?

Kissinger: Should I?

Dinitz: She said she would like to if you had the time.

Kissinger: I had better leave.

How do we get all these letters signed? Do we have all this stationery?

Sisco: We have got it on the plane.

Kissinger: On the Presidential letters, I will have to initial them.

Sisco: Right. Is there a U.N. man in Jerusalem?

Dayan: Of course. He has good communications.

Kissinger: We will do it tomorrow. If Ken [Keating] goes to the U.N. to ask for Kilometer 101 tomorrow, it will be in the newspapers. The U.N. will notify Waldheim and he will hold a press conference.

There is a massive typing problem to get all these typed.

Eban: "Egypt and Israel have reached agreement on the separation of forces. The time for signature has been set for _____," or "has been scheduled for _____."

Kissinger: Yes. You must get yourself geared for rapid decisions tomorrow.

Eban: Yes. We have scheduled the meetings already.

Kissinger: I will do my utmost to come back tonight.

Allon: I hope there will be no need for another Cabinet meeting because there will be no substantive changes.

8. Memorandum From the President's Deputy Assistant for National Security Affairs (Scowcroft) to President Nixon[1]

Washington, January 16, 1974

Secretary Kissinger has asked that you be passed the following report on his latest meetings with President Sadat:

"1. After two meetings with Sadat today,[2] I can report that we are on the verge of an agreement between Egypt and Israel on disengagement.

"2. In essence the agreement calls for:

"—Israeli withdrawal of its forces from the west and east of the Canal to a line no more than 20 kilometers east of the Canal;
"—Egyptian forces maintain roughly their present line east of the Canal;
"—A UN buffer zone between the two forces.

"3. Sadat has accepted most of the limitations on his forces which Israel has suggested; the few exceptions relate to numerical strength and types of weaponry. I should be able to get Israel's agreement to the Egyptian exceptions tomorrow. I shall also have to get Mrs. Meir's agreement to release about 90 Egyptian POW's when disengagement has been accomplished.

"4. In order to make all this possible Sadat has agreed to:

"—A public document describing the three areas outlined above.
"—A classified letter from you to Sadat and Meir describing the limitations on Israeli and Egyptian forces and personnel. Both leaders will sign this proposal on separate copies, thereby incorporating it in the basic agreement.
"—A classified letter to you from Sadat stating that Egypt will not interfere with free passage of Israeli ships and cargoes through the straits south of Israel, and that, after the Canal is opened, Egypt will allow Israeli cargoes through immediately. Sadat promises to permit free passage for Israeli ships through the Canal when the state of belligerency has ended.

"5. We will also be providing Sadat and Meir with letters from you expressing satisfaction at the signing of the agreement, and assuring

---

[1] Source: National Archives, Nixon Presidential Materials, NSC Files, Kissinger Office Files, Box 44, HAK Trip Files, January 10–20, 1974, Europe and Mid East State Cables, Memos, Misc. Top Secret; Sensitive; Exclusively Eyes Only. A handwritten notation reads: "Back from President."

[2] No memoranda of conversation have been found. See footnote 2, Document 3. According to Kissinger's Record of Schedule, he met with Sadat on January 16 from approximately 2:30 to 4:30 p.m. and approximately 8:15 to 9 p.m. (Library of Congress, Manuscript Division, Kissinger Papers, Box 438, Miscellany, 1968–76)

them that we will do our utmost to see to it that it is fully implemented. Finally, we will be transmitting to Sadat, in a classified letter from you, the Prime Minister's assurance that Israel will not attack the civilian areas to be established by Sadat in the Sinai.

"6. The existence of the classified documents listed in the two preceding paragraphs is extremely sensitive. Public knowledge of their existence could ruin the whole deal.

"7. Assuming I get Meir's concurrence to the remaining changes suggested by Sadat, the plan is for a simultaneous announcement on Thursday[3] in Jerusalem, Cairo and Washington at 9:00 p.m. Cairo/Tel Aviv time (3:00 p.m. Washington time).

"8. The announcement which Sadat has cleared and which we will be clearing with the Israelis tomorrow reads as follows:

'In accordance with the decision of the Geneva Conference, the Governments of Egypt and Israel, with the assistance of the Government of the United States, have reached agreement on the disengagement and separation of their military forces. The agreement will be signed by the Chiefs of Staff of Egypt and Israel at noon Egypt–Israel time, Friday, January 18, at Kilometer 101 on the Cairo–Suez road. The Commander of the United Nations Emergency Force, General Siilasvuo, has been asked by the parties to witness the signing.'

"9. We will be sending you a suggested draft statement you may wish to make in Washington at the same time.

"10. President Sadat has asked me to defer my visit to Damascus until after he, himself, has visited there. He argues that if he first sets the stage for my visit with Asad, my own visit may make it possible for us to get things moving with the Syrians. Thus, Sadat has rearranged his own travel plans so that he can be in Damascus on Saturday. I will follow him on Sunday, and then return to Washington late Sunday evening."

---

[3] January 17.

9. Memorandum of Conversation[1]

Jerusalem, January 17, 1974, 9:30 a.m.–12:30 p.m.

PARTICIPANTS

    Yigal Allon, Deputy Prime Minister
    Abba Eban, Minister of Foreign Affairs
    Moshe Dayan, Minister of Defense
    Simcha Dinitz, Ambassador to the U.S.
    Mordechai Gazit, Prime Minister's Office
    Avraham Kidron, Director General, MFA
    Ephraim Evron, Deputy Director General, MFA
    Lt. General David Elazar, Chief of Staff
    Colonel Bar-On, Aide to Dayan

    Dr. Henry A. Kissinger, Secretary of State
    Ellsworth Bunker, Ambassador at Large
    Joseph J. Sisco, Assistant Secretary for Near Eastern and South Asian Affairs
    Carlyle Maw, Legal Adviser, Department of State
    Alfred L. Atherton, Jr., Deputy Assistant Secretary for Near Eastern and South Asian Affairs
    Peter W. Rodman, NSC Staff

Secretary Kissinger: I promised Sadat I would let him know by two or three o'clock where we stand.[2]

Deputy P.M. Allon: There will be a Cabinet meeting today.

Secretary Kissinger: I went over the list of your concerns, which I will go over.

He suggests the best way to deal with the pressures is to adjourn the Geneva Conference until April. Then the Russians can't do anything and the other Arabs can't do anything.

I won't go to Kilometer 101.

Deputy P.M. Allon: You will be flying over Kilometer 101.

Secretary Kissinger: And shot at by both sides.

Minister Dayan: One side hitting and the other side missing. American weapons are superior! [Laughter]

Secretary Kissinger: His Chief of Staff said the Hawk's are better than SAM's except for the altitude.

---

[1] Source: National Archives, Nixon Presidential Materials, NSC Files, Kissinger Office Files, Box 140, Country Files, Middle East, Secretary Kissinger's Middle East Trip, January 11–20, 1974, Memcons and Reports, Folder 2. Top Secret; Sensitive; Exclusively Eyes Only. The meeting was held in Secretary Kissinger's suite at the King David Hotel. Brackets, with the exception of ones describing omitted material, are in the original.

[2] A reference to one of the January 16 meetings between Sadat, Fahmi, and Kissinger. See Document 8.

Minister Dayan: Have they placed their orders yet?

Secretary Kissinger: It could be arranged.

It was an emotional meeting. Gamasy walked out.

Sadat will go to Syria, so (1) it is his agreement, not an American agreement. Second, he said it is essential to see him without Khaddam, and (3), he said he will raise the matter of the lists of your prisoners.

Deputy P.M. Allon: We want Red Cross visits, too.

Secretary Kissinger: I know. You are getting it for nothing.

He showed me a message which Asad sent to him yesterday which said he could conduct disengagement talks with Israel. The question cannot be raised without the lists. He said he had tried, but Asad would not promise the lists. But the combination of him and me was the best chance of getting them.

He is going to leave Damascus by 10:00; I will arrive by 11:00.

Should we wait for your Chief of Staff?

I told Keating that if he cannot plan a military coup secretly, he can't do the job. [Referring to a report in this morning's Israeli press that the U.S. Embassy was plotting with the Israeli military against the Government.]

Deputy P.M. Allon: Our press, until now, has been very good. Moshe will see the editors today to warn them about tomorrow.

Secretary Kissinger: One thing you should watch for is, I saw in the *Jerusalem Post* that this is the same as the interim agreement you offered in 1971.[3] This you have to watch.

I went through the agreement and the military provisions with him, and he accepted 90 percent again. He said, "There is only one issue: Do we want to make peace or not? If we want war, we can get 1,000 tanks across in two days." He said you both should begin with the attitude that both sides want peace.

He said, "Tell the Israelis that as a sign of my good faith I will keep no tanks on the East Bank. If they say anything about it I will send them across. I will keep thirty there until the disengagement is completed, then remove them."

He said he had to take a trip through the Arab world because he has certain necessities.

Then I had a meeting with Gamasy and Fahmi. Gamasy was furious; he said he would not sign. He said you can fool the people but not the army; the army knows what it means.

---

[3] Apparently a reference to a February 9, 1971, response by Prime Minister Meir to a February 4 proposal by President Sadat offering to open the Suez Canal in return for a partial withdrawal of Israeli forces from the East Bank of the Suez Canal. Documentation on this is scheduled to be published in *Foreign Relations,* 1969–1976, volume XXIII, Arab-Israeli Dispute, 1969–1972.

He said now he has five divisions, 800 tanks, and 700 artillery pieces there, which he now has to remove. "The Army will know what we are doing."

So I went back to Sadat. There are two points he wants, which I will mention. I said, "Are we hurting you?" He said, "Yes, but the army first did not want to go to war, and now they don't want peace. I will take the responsibility."

Let me take care of the collateral things. [He looks over Israeli checklist from the previous day, Tab A.][4]

—"The Canal cleared and open within a specific period."

He told me it would start on the day disengagement is completed from the West Bank. He will deny it if you speak of it. He says he will begin at the southern end, where he doesn't need so much equipment. And will clear the Bitter Lakes. As for the opening, he could do it in four to six months, but he could stretch it out, if we wanted, from the American point of view vis-à-vis the Russians.

He also wants to build another Canal.

Minister Dayan: A practical project, or a scheme?

Secretary Kissinger: He will give me the papers tomorrow. He says a Peruvian firm gave it to him.

Deputy P.M. Allon: East or west of the Canal?

Secretary Kissinger: East of the Canal.

Deputy P.M. Allon: At the expense of the UN zone or the Israeli zone?

Secretary Kissinger: That will be an argument, I am sure. And whether he can dump the dirt on your side.

He will declare Port Said a free port.

"Substantial demobilization"—He will do it if you do it. Again, with respect to the other Arabs, he won't do it if you talk about it.

Minister Dayan: Can we interpret "significant" into something practical? Say, half?

Deputy P.M. Allon: Can he be more specific?

Secretary Kissinger: I can try it tomorrow.

It is not an exact comparison, because you can mobilize faster.

Minister Dayan: It is not symmetric, because half for us is 70,000 and for him 400,000.

What will be the ratio of regulars as opposed to reserves to be demobilized?

---

[4] Tab A has not been found. The checklist is presumably the one prepared the previous day and attached at Tab H to Document 7.

Secretary Kissinger: He didn't say.

Minister Dayan: I ask, more for curiosity.

Secretary Kissinger: If you tell me what you intend, I can—if I have a social conversation—mention it to him and see what he says.

"Information on missing Israeli soldiers."—He said he didn't understand the question; he had no Israeli prisoners left, but if you addressed specific questions he would see what he could do.

Minister Dayan: We could give a list of the missing, mostly pilots.

Secretary Kissinger: He assures me he has no prisoners. He said in an earlier period they held some.

Deputy P.M. Allon: Maybe they are held in the hands of other units—Iraqis, Palestinians.

Secretary Kissinger: I didn't ask. I will try that.

Minister Dayan: The Iraqis asked for some prisoners from the Syrians so that the Iraqis could ask for an exchange for Israeli pilots: Maybe Egypt did the same.

Secretary Kissinger: I will raise that.

[Elazar comes in]

"UNEF composition."—This is taken care of by the Agreement.

Oh, Mizrachi and Levy.—Levy he says he has not yet found the facts on, but he is looking. Mizrachi will be released when you are back on the line. But he absolutely insists his prisoners must be released at the end of the process. I explained your Parliamentary process; I said it couldn't be this week. He said okay, but it had to be done.

Gamasy later said that if this keeps up they will kidnap some Israelis. You will force him. He raised it several times. There was a debate on how many it had to be. Gamasy said thirty; Fahmi said five would do.

Minister Dayan: When we get the lists from Syria, we would release his right away, and it would be linked with Mizrachi in the package.

Secretary Kissinger: If you don't get the lists, you still have to release them.

Even if you make the most treacherous interpretation, it will be hard for him to explain why you get your prisoners and he doesn't.

Deputy P.M. Allon: It has to be simultaneous.

Secretary Kissinger: Yes, it will be. I more or less determine when Mizrachi gets released because I have to request it.

Deputy P.M. Allon: And Levy?

Secretary Kissinger: Levy couldn't be a problem, Sadat said. He didn't know he had him.

They will be released no later than when the forces are back at the disengagement line.

Minister Dayan: We will give the Egyptian prisoners as part of the disengagement agreement, so it is simple. But if we can get a list earlier, it would make it much easier for us to release them earlier.

Secretary Kissinger: That is a good argument. I will make that argument in Damascus.

Deputy P.M. Allon: I have got a point about opening access between Suez and Cairo. Maybe connect this with Mizrachi.

Secretary Kissinger: No, I will explain that.

"Aerial reconnaissance"—he again confirmed. I said it would be at irregular intervals, so he couldn't move it all in one day!

"UNEF composition."—I explained your position, and he said that would be no problem. That is the way it is now. On liaison officers, their concern was that Israelis didn't inspect their positions. It is the same as yours.

On "UNEF withdrawal"—they said it won't arise.

On Bab El-Mandeb, there was a tremendous fight with Fahmi who wanted not to mention Israeli ships but only free passage.

Minister Eban: They have said that for twenty years.

Secretary Kissinger: On the Canal, we had [omission in the original] allowing ships at the end of the state of belligerency. Fahmi said it was intolerable, that it had to be in the final peace agreement. When I said this to Sadat, he said "Tell the Israelis I mean what I said—at the end of belligerency."

Ambassador Dinitz: We received a cable from Washington about notifying them in advance of ships coming through.

Secretary Kissinger: That will end. He knows it. I will raise it again. He told me his military wanted them to stop every tenth ship; he rejected it because he would go through hell over every ship. We'll put it in the memorandum of understanding.

—On civil air flights to Africa: He promises if you don't fly over Egyptian territory, and stay over the Red Sea, he won't interfere. He promises you no Egyptian interference.

Deputy P.M. Allon: Good.

Secretary Kissinger: On the specifics of the U.S. proposal you both sign, he says we can say tonight that the U.S. has made a proposal on limitations which has been agreed to by both sides. So we don't have to keep it secret. He says it would be an extraordinary sign of good faith on your side if you have a secret session of the Knesset from which it would leak. I have convinced him it will leak.

Deputy P.M. Allon: There are no secret sessions.

Secretary Kissinger: He is going through the Arab world and wants this help.

Minister Dayan: We can meet him half way. We will inform the Knesset that the details will go to the Security and Foreign Affairs Committee.

Deputy P.M. Allon: What would you prefer to have, a good press or a bad press? [Laughter]

Secretary Kissinger: A moderately good press.

Deputy P.M. Allon: Whichever would help you in America.

Secretary Kissinger: As long as you don't say I got a tremendous victory.

Deputy P.M. Allon: We couldn't get that if we tried.

Secretary Kissinger: This is a good agreement.

Deputy P.M. Allon: It is not a bad agreement. [Laughter]

Minister Eban: "Good agreement" in Israeli translates into "not a bad agreement."

Secretary Kissinger: On the schedule, he agreed to 28 days. You told me thirty, and I took the liberty of saying 28.

General Elazar: Fourteen days for the first phase and fourteen for the second.

Secretary Kissinger: Gamasy—unless he is an extraordinarily good actor—I had several meetings with them—his problem is what orders he has to give. On SAM's he said he will have to go through weeks of complicated maneuvers around and then stop them at some point. I believe this.

Minister Dayan: He will have tanks on the East side and we will have no forces on the west.

Secretary Kissinger: The tanks won't be a problem. Gamasy has the opposite argument. He wants you to let him move the Third Army—he thinks you will either force him where to move because your forces still are there, or you will keep them trapped until the last phase. It is not enough to open the roads, he says, but there has to be some territory where he can put them. You know what he means.

General Elazar: Yes.

Minister Dayan: That we will not quarrel with, if he means it.

Secretary Kissinger: He says he wants to thin out the Second and Third Army symmetrically. He doesn't want the Third Army kept bottled up until the last phase.

General Elazar: That is not a problem.

Secretary Kissinger: And he wants to be able to move to his territory. He gave us a description. I cannot judge it, but you could do a different description which achieves the same objective.

Assistant Secretary Sisco: May I say I think how you enter this in the next ten days, your attitude, will make a tremendous difference.

Secretary Kissinger: I agree.

General Elazar: Symmetrical thinning of the Second and Third Armies I can accept, provided it is symmetrical to ours.

Secretary Kissinger: Yes. I will do it. Can I tell them today that you agree in principle that the Second and Third Armies could be thinned out symmetrically, and you will give him the room he needs behind him? And that you will go into details at Kilometer 101? He did not want me to confirm the details, but the principle.

[Dr. Kissinger gives Elazar Tab B, the Gamasy proposal.][5]

The "first seven days" I wouldn't pay any attention to.

He says by Thursday[6] the two roads to Suez should be open; he will on that day give you the dead bodies.

General Elazar: [Reads the Gamasy proposal] It is exaggerated.

Secretary Kissinger: I am sure it is negotiable. His concern is not to have the Third Army trapped until the last day.

General Elazar: We agree to it in principle.

Secretary Kissinger: I am sure it can be worked out if you are reasonable.

Deputy P.M. Allon: Can you be reasonable, Dado?

General Elazar: Yes.

Secretary Kissinger: He [Sadat] will give back the dead bodies by then, and he also said—this is sentimental—it is the wedding day of his daughter and it would make a terrific impact.

Deputy P.M. Allon: We are not invited?

Secretary Kissinger: I knew you would make a cynical comment.

Thirdly, I said if we didn't get the oil embargo lifted we would not encourage you to withdraw. He needs some act to justify it—a signature is not enough. But the opening of the two roads would be enough.

Minister Dayan: I think soon after the meeting of the Knesset we can do it.

Secretary Kissinger: That is why he said Thursday.

Minister Dayan: And at the same time we get the bodies.

Secretary Kissinger: He says he has quite a few. I spoke of the bodies in the Third Army area; he corrected me and said the Second Army, too. He said you would get all of them in the same time frame.

General Elazar: When?

---

[5] Tab B has not been found.

[6] January 24.

Secretary Kissinger: Thursday, I don't know whether it is possible in one day. But he said so.

Deputy Director General Evron: Can you ask him tomorrow morning?[7]

Minister Dayan: Suppose we get the bodies. We shall take off the check posts.

Secretary Kissinger: That is his definition of opening the roads.

Minister Dayan: Every population can go in or go out. The same thing with supply, it is all right. But let them not bring in any military supply. Suez City is theoretically a city.

Secretary Kissinger: Let's get that clear. You don't mind convoys of trucks, but not artillery, and tanks.

Minister Dayan: And ammunition, and shells.

Secretary Kissinger: I am confident that he wanted the road open in order to get his troops back.

Deputy P.M. Allon: And some guests to the wedding will be coming from Suez. It will be symbolic.

Minister Dayan: We have thousands of troops and equipment there on the roads, and need it to move ourselves.

Secretary Kissinger: Good point. But as long as you don't block the roads.

Minister Dayan: No, we will be straightforward.

Deputy P.M. Allon: Is there any hint about the number of dead soldiers?

Secretary Kissinger: No, but I got the impression it was larger than I thought.

Deputy P.M. Allon: It is not small.

Minister Dayan: We don't object to vacating the Second and Third Army areas simultaneously but his proposal is unacceptable.

Secretary Kissinger: But if I can tell him you accept in principle and will work it out. I don't want to get into details.

Assistant Secretary Sisco: Could we understand what your problem is?

Secretary Kissinger: I don't want to get into it.

General Elazar: They want us to leave 60 to 70 percent of the West Bank in the first seven days.

Minister Dayan: You can assure President Sadat that even though we don't accept Gamasy's specific details, we accept the principle. There is no problem.

---

[7] Kissinger was scheduled to meet with Sadat on January 18.

Secretary Kissinger: The Israeli forces would be across the Canal in 28 days instead of 30 days.

Now, the Agreement. They want to call it "The Egyptian-Israeli Agreement in Pursuance of the Geneva Conference."

Deputy P.M. Allon: We have no objection to it.

General Elazar: It is a strange, "in pursuance of a conference."

Secretary Kissinger: On paragraph A, they do not accept "hostile," but they agree to all "military or paramilitary."

Deputy P.M. Allon: There is no objection, gentlemen.

Minister Dayan: It is better than nothing.

Secretary Kissinger: On paragraph B, there was some heartache about the Egyptians being mentioned first, and some about the fact there is no way to tell what is going on. But they accepted. It stays as it is.

[He hands over copies of the Agreement at Tab C and the Proposal at Tab D.][8]

On paragraph 2, they accept it but they wanted to delete the sentence about liaison officers and move it to paragraph 5 where it makes sense.

Minister Dayan: There is no problem. They are right.

Secretary Kissinger: Paragraph 3 they accept.

Paragraph 4 they accept.

We got them to drop the paragraph on no dismantling of installations.

Minister Dayan: You didn't tell them what was happening?

Secretary Kissinger: No, I said it would avoid contention about what was destroyed in the war.

Minister Dayan: That is a good argument.

Secretary Kissinger: In this paragraph [5] they wanted to take out the sentence from paragraph 2 and put it here.

Paragraph 6 they accept.

Paragraph C they accept with 30 days and put in "aegis of the UN," for the Kilometer 101 talks.

Deputy P.M. Allon: It is a military arm of the UN, not a civilian one.

Secretary Kissinger: The same procedure as now.

They have already got Siilasvuo in Cairo now.

---

[8] Tabs C and D have not been found.

They took another run at putting in 242[9] but we didn't accept it.

Deputy P.M. Allon: What about B–7?

Secretary Kissinger: It is dropped.

Deputy P.M. Allon: Are there two lines for the signature?

Secretary Kissinger: Yes, it is the same document.

Ambassador Keating: Speaking as a lawyer, may I suggest that we not have the last two lines on a separate page?

Secretary Kissinger: Very good point. We should have some text on the signature page.

On the Proposal [Tab D]: we settled on eight battalions and 7,000 men. This is what produced an absolute uproar from Gamasy. He says you are asking him to have the Egyptian infantry left there without any anti-aircraft, without tanks, and without artillery, in a way that is humiliating, in a way that is demoralizing for his soldiers who have never seen anything like this.

He wanted to drop 1 (b), because he said it was covered elsewhere. I rejected it. On (b) he said he had to have an exception for mortars or howitzers. He suggested "mortars and howitzers of a calibre up to 122mm (M–3)." Sadat said "howitzers of a calibre which cannot reach the opposing lines."

Minister Dayan: The opposing line is the Israeli line? At twenty kilometers?

Secretary Kissinger: That depends on where you put them. Gamasy says if you have 6,000 men, with 30 tanks, that means four men in a tank and a Headquarters. Some are in engineering units. So how many batteries would he put in anywhere, protected by only 7,000 men and thirty tanks? He asked me to ask the Chief of Staff.

Minister Dayan: He speaks about eight battalions, and wants artillery.

Secretary Kissinger: Artillery he yielded on. "Antitank missiles" he wants too. He said they are on vehicles with rubber tires.

Minister Dayan: And are very good.

Secretary Kissinger: The M–3 he says has a range of 11.8 kilometers, and there is one model D–3, which has a range of 15 to 18 kilometers. I asked, "Can you tell from the air?" He said no. But he said the UN could inspect it.

Minister Dayan: Can I suggest something constructive? We agree to howitzers but specify a range of 11.8 kilometers.

---

[9] A reference to UN Security Council Resolution 242; See footnote 6, Document 7.

Secretary Kissinger: Let's say a "range no more than 12 kilometers." People would ask where we got 11.8; 12 we can justify by distance.

Minister Dayan: And secondly, there should be a limitation of numbers. He says he doesn't want a number of supporting arms. But there can't be an unlimited number. And mortars, there is a question of distance.

General Elazar: It is a question of the calibre.

Minister Dayan: In principle, if he speaks about supporting weapons, they must be limited by number. Mortars and howitzers.

Secretary Kissinger: They are very angry also about the anti-aircraft restrictions.

Deputy P.M. Allon: Which angered them more, the anti-aircraft or the artillery restrictions?

Secretary Kissinger: I think if they have to choose, they will take the SAM's.

General Elazar: About the artillery, we are talking about forces defending the Canal. There is no possibility for defending forces by artillery there. They would have to place them across the Canal.

Secretary Kissinger: But it is a moral question.

General Elazar: They will be able to reach our forward line.

Secretary Kissinger: I said this, and they said you have few forces there.

Ambassador Keating: Why not the second alternative?

Secretary Kissinger: "No howitzers which can reach the other line."

My theory is that it is better to give it to Gamasy than to Sadat. Keep it closer to what Gamasy wants.

Minister Dayan: There are parts there, near the lakes, where they can't push the artillery back. About one-third or more of the area; they have to be on the other side of the lake.

Secretary Kissinger: Gamasy wanted all this out.

Incidentally, I didn't tell them you would accept eight battalions and 7,000 men. I told them I would take it to you.

Deputy P.M. Allon: It doesn't serve the Egyptian interest either, except for their morale.

Secretary Kissinger: Gamasy said he would be crazy to put anything across under these restrictions.

On air forces [paragraph 6], they wanted "up to their respective lines," instead of "over their respective territory."

On "no permanent fixed installation for missile sites," he said, "This I am accepting for Begin."[10] [Laughter]

On surface-to-air missiles, Gamasy says their experience with the SAM–2 is that at a low level, thirty kilometers is the effective range. Second, you don't drop your bombs right over the line; you have airplanes drop your bombs about five kilometers back.

Deputy P.M. Allon: That depends on the supplies from America.

Secretary Kissinger: No, we are not talking about standoff, but you have to do it five kilometers back anyway. He says 25 kilometers is the effective range; he will give you 30.

General Elazar: The question is low-level, which is for attacking—but we are not attacking. We are worried about high-level reconnaissance.

Minister Dayan: We will consider the range, and howitzers.

It is a fact that there are parts there where they cannot keep artillery on the other side. Near the lakes.

Secretary Kissinger: One point Fahmi made is that if you are brutal about any point of this agreement, you give them the maximum incentive to break it. It is a lousy agreement for them.

Minister Dayan: There should be a limitation on howitzers.

Secretary Kissinger: You are better off giving them no artillery. He can't accept so many restrictions by numbers. He says he wants artillery that is "organic."

I frankly think that the humiliation already of 30 tanks is so great that he will say "forget the howitzers."

Minister Dayan: Suppose they agree to eight battalions each that have four howitzers, that is 32. How it will appear in the agreement, that is another thing. You know part of the UN zone is only 4 kilometers wide.

Secretary Kissinger: Can we express it in a number other than a restrictive number of howitzers?

Deputy P.M. Allon: Dayan's proposal, "on the coast of the lakes and not the Canal."

Secretary Kissinger: That is worse. It tells them where they can put them.

Ambassador Bunker: There is a normal number.

General Elazar: No, there isn't a normal number of artillery in an infantry battalion.

Usually it is six in a battery.

---

[10] Menachem Begin, a leader of the Israeli Likud Party, founded in 1973.

Secretary Kissinger: Since there are eight battalions, we should say no more than X batteries of howitzers. I think 32 guns look pathetic. No one knows how many in a battery.

Deputy P.M. Allon: Four or five batteries?

Secretary Kissinger: That is twenty.

Minister Dayan: There are batteries of four and batteries of six.

Deputy P.M. Allon: Five batteries means 30 guns.

Secretary Kissinger: If there are eight battalions, could you have eight batteries?

General Elazar: Not necessarily, because the artillery have a bigger range and one battery can support two battalions.

Secretary Kissinger: Thirty guns won't change the course of history.

Minister Dayan: But we can't explain it to the Cabinet.

Deputy P.M. Allon: There are two problems—they may not be military but psychological—the distance for the anti-aircraft missiles, and . . .

Minister Dayan: You have to spell out the range, too.

Secretary Kissinger: I don't think we should put into the agreement how many guns there are in a battery. We have to consider when it appears in the Beirut newspapers, how we will look.

Deputy P.M. Allon: Can you get them back to thirty kilometers? Maybe we could do a package deal.

Secretary Kissinger: If I am there, I can do things. But now we have to do it by cable. It is certainly easier to drop the howitzers if you give them the missiles. If you give them five kilometers on SAM's, he will drop the howitzers.

Deputy P.M. Allon: He would prefer howitzers?

Secretary Kissinger: I think he would prefer the SAM's. He says it required redeployment of the first line in any case, and if you made it thirty kilometers, it required a redeployment of the second line. He has the same problem with SAM's as you do.

You are telling me your security depends on thirty howitzers.

Deputy P.M. Allon: I think the howitzer is more effective because of its ballistic effect.

Secretary Kissinger: If it were more effective, he would have more of them.

Minister Dayan: What I said was a good thing.

Deputy P.M. Allon: As usual.

Minister Dayan: On the lake, I don't want them to be in the position that they think they are really out of danger.

On howitzers, we should say a range of 12 kilometers.

Secretary Kissinger: That I can do.

Minister Dayan: That would go well together; eight battalions and six batteries of six guns—without specifying the number in a battery, or eight battalions and eight batteries, with a limit of four. Six batteries of guns with a range not more than 12 kilometers.

Secretary Kissinger: I will send it to our Ambassador.

If the number of individual howitzers is reduced, I will explain it to Sadat. I told him I would take it back to the Israelis.

I now can tell him you agree to eight battalions and 7,000 men.

Deputy P.M. Allon: We accept those certain number of batteries of howitzers, and he should accept the thirty kilometers with missiles. It is a package.

Secretary Kissinger: But you drop bombs from five kilometers away.

Deputy P.M. Allon: But we are not dropping bombs; we are worried about reconnaissance.

Secretary Kissinger: Your biggest problem is not Sadat. The experience they have with you is that you really try to squeeze everything out of them. Next week, I really think it makes a difference. Try giving them ten percent more than they ask for, on one occasion.

If this is a big con game, we will know by April. And then you will not have lost much, because he will have broken so many pledges to us that we will have an additional moral obligation to be on your side. I think he is genuinely interested in making peace. He never raised the question of the 1967 borders.

This is just a question of your attitude. I have nothing specific in mind.

Minister Dayan: You said about Port Said.

Secretary Kissinger: Yes, he said you have a strong point built there. Under the agreement you have to pull back your artillery, etc. from there.

Deputy P.M. Allon: Inevitable.

Secretary Kissinger: He would consider it a sign of good will if you did something with that strong point, like turn it over to the UN. You can't do anything with it anyway.

Sadat hasn't accepted it; it was Gamasy who raised it.

Minister Dayan: They can't ask us not to put heavy howitzers in this strong point.

Secretary Kissinger: I would strongly urge you not to.

Minister Dayan: But we will have anti-tank guns.

Secretary Kissinger: At a minimum he wants assurance that you are not going to shell Port Said. I gave them the assurance. He wants assurance that it is not an offensive post.

Minister Dayan: It is not an offensive post.

Deputy P.M. Allon: We can't have artillery there.

General Elazar: We can, if it is symmetrical.

Minister Dayan: You can give him your word and my word that we won't shell Port Said.

Deputy P.M. Allon: We won't keep howitzers there.

Secretary Kissinger: When can I communicate with him?

Deputy P. M. Allon: Immediately after the Cabinet meeting. It will be over by 3:30.

Secretary Kissinger: Joe, get a message to Egypt that the Israelis feel they must have another Cabinet meeting—that makes it look tougher—and we can't answer until about 5:00. But tell Fahmi I am reasonably optimistic, so he doesn't panic.

Ambassador Dinitz: On the other documents.

Secretary Kissinger: He didn't like your Memorandum of Understanding.[11] [Laughter]

General Elazar: Who is in charge of the logistics of signing?

Minister Dayan: Who will be . . .

Deputy P.M. Allon: Would they consider, as a part of the agreement, an open bridge for foreign tourists between Israel and Egypt?

Secretary Kissinger: Now?

In the letter on waterways, [Tab E][12] the only thing they wanted is to take out "owned by Israel," because they didn't want to raise the question of ownership. It has "cargoes destined for and coming from Israel."

Deputy P.M. Allon: It is better for us.

Secretary Kissinger: Do we have a text of the announcement? [Tab F].[13]

Deputy P.M. Allon: [reads it] Wonderful wording.

Minister Dayan: It should say, "signature is scheduled to be signed . . ." We are in the position now that it has not yet gone to the Cabinet."

---

[11] Apparently a reference to the draft of the Memorandum of Understanding between the United States Government and the Government of Israel, attached at Tab G to Document 7.

[12] Tab E has not been found. The final text is Document 12.

[13] Tab F has not been found. The text is in telegram Secto 72/129 from Jerusalem, January 17. (National Archives, RG 59, Central Foreign Policy Files)

Deputy P.M. Allon: You mean we need the approval of the Knesset?

Minister Dayan: It makes no difference, but it would be better to say "scheduled to be signed."

Secretary Kissinger: Can I tell them that on your radio it will say "scheduled" and that they can say "will be signed." [They nod]

Mr. Maw will take it to Cyprus. The Agreement is ready to be typed.

Minister Dayan: Will he sign in Arabic and English? The last time he signed in Arabic only.

Assistant Secretary Sisco: Why do you raise this? It is not important.

[The meeting ended at 12:30 p.m. Dr. Kissinger and Mr. Rodman then went to meet the Prime Minister at her residence.][14]

---

[14] Kissinger met with Prime Minister Meir from 12:45–1:45 p.m. A memorandum of conversation is ibid., Nixon Presidential Materials, NSC Files, Kissinger Office Files, Box 140, Country Files, Middle East, Secretary Kissinger's Middle East Trip, January 11–20, 1974, Memcons and Reports.

---

10. Telegram From Secretary of State Kissinger to the Mission to the United Nations[1]

Jerusalem, January 17, 1974, 0131Z.

Secto 74/131. Subject: Disengagement Agreement Between Israel and Egypt.

1. Text follows subject agreement referred to in instruction telegram previously sent.[2]

2. *Begin text. Quote* A. Egypt and Israel will scrupulously observe the ceasefire on land, sea, and air called for by the UN Security Council

---

[1] Source: National Archives, Nixon Presidential Materials, NSC Files, Kissinger Office Files, Box 133, Country Files, Middle East, Egypt, Volume 9, January 1974. Secret; Niact Immediate; Exdis (Distribute as Nodis Cherokee). Also sent Niact Immediate to USNATO. Repeated Immediate to Tel Aviv, Geneva for MEPC Del, and Cairo. According to Kissinger's Record of Schedule, he was in Jerusalem until 8:30 a.m. and then left by train for Lod Airport in Tel Aviv. (Library of Congress, Manuscript Division, Kissinger Papers, Box 438, Miscellany, 1968–76)

[2] Not further identified

and will refrain from the time of the signing of this document from all military or para-military actions against each other.

B. The military forces of Egypt and Israel will be separated in accordance with the following principles:

1. All Egyptian forces on the east side of the Canal will be deployed west of the line designated as Line A on the attached map.[3] All Israeli forces, including those west of the Suez Canal and the Bitter Lakes, will be deployed east of the line designated as Line B on the attached map.

2. The area between the Egyptian and Israeli lines will be a zone of disengagement in which the United Nations Emergency Force (UNEF) will be stationed. The UNEF will continue to consist of units from countries that are not permanent members of the Security Council.

3. The area between the Egyptian line and the Suez Canal will be limited in armament and forces.

4. The area between the Israeli line (Line B on the attached map) and the line designated as Line C on the attached map, which runs along the western base of the mountains where the Gidi and Mitla Passes are located, will be limited in armament and forces.

5. The limitations referred to in paragraphs 3 and 4 will be inspected by UNEF. Existing procedures of the UNEF, including the attaching of Egyptian and Israeli Liaison officers to UNEF, will be continued.

6. Air forces of the two sides will be permitted to operate up to their respective lines without interference from the other side.

C. The detailed implementation of the disengagement of forces will be worked out by military representatives of Egypt and Israel, who will agree on the stages of this process. These representatives will meet no later than 48 hours after the signature of this agreement at Kilometer 101 under the aegis of the United Nations for this purpose. They will complete this task within five days. Disengagement will begin within 48 hours after the completion of the work of the military representatives and in no event later than seven days after the signature of this agreement. The process of disengagement will be completed not later than 40 days after it begins.

D. This agreement is not regarded by Egypt and Israel as a final peace agreement. It constitutes a first step toward a final, just and durable peace according to the provisions of Security Council Resolution 338 and within the framework of the Geneva Conference. *End text.*

---

[3] Map is not attached, but see the final disengagement map, Appendix B, Map 1.

3. Agreement will not be public until it is signed at noon Middle East time January 18. It is terribly sensitive and it must rpt must not leak.

Kissinger

---

11. Letter From President Nixon to Egyptian President Sadat[1]

Washington, January 17, 1974.

Dear Mr. President:

I am transmitting the attached proposal as part of the agreement between Egypt and Israel on the disengagement of their forces. I am also transmitting the attached proposal to the Prime Minister of Israel.[2]

Receipt of your signature on the attached proposal will constitute acceptance, subject to the signature of the same proposal by the Prime Minister of Israel.

Sincerely,

Richard Nixon

Attachment

In order to facilitate agreement between Egypt and Israel and as part of that agreement, and to assist in maintaining scrupulous observance of the ceasefire on land, air, and sea the United States proposes the following:

1. That within the areas of limited armament and forces described in the agreement there will be: (a) no more than eight reinforced battalions of armed forces and 30 tanks; (b) no artillery except anti-tank guns, anti-tank missiles, mortars and 6 batteries of howitzers of a caliber up to 122 mm (M–3) with a range not to exceed 12 kilometers; (c)

---

[1] Source: National Archives, Nixon Presidential Materials, NSC Files, Box 1180, Harold H. Saunders Files, Middle East Peace Negotiations, January 10–17, 1974. Secret. According to Kissinger's memoirs, the text of the letter was drafted by Kissinger's negotiating team. (*Years of Upheaval*, p. 833)

[2] The letter to Prime Minister Meir and the attached proposal is identical to the letter sent to President Sadat. (National Archives, Nixon Presidential Materials, NSC Files, Box 1180, Harold H. Saunders Files, Middle East Peace Negotiations, January 10–17, 1974)

no weapons capable of interfering with the other party's flights over its own forces; (d) no permanent, fixed installations for missile sites. The entire force of each party shall not exceed 7,000 men.

2. That to a distance 30 kilometers west of the Egyptian line and east of the Israeli line, there will be no weapons in areas from which they can reach the other line.

3. That to a distance 30 kilometers west of the Egyptian line and east of the Israeli line, there will be no surface-to-air missiles.

4. That the above limitations will apply as from the time the agreement on disengagement between Egypt and Israel is signed[3] by the parties and will be implemented in accordance with the schedule of the basic agreement.

---

[3] The agreement was signed at Kilometer 101 on January 18 at 12:25 p.m.; see Document 16.

---

12. Letter From President Nixon to Israeli Prime Minister Meir[1]

Washington, January 17, 1974.

Dear Madame Prime Minister:

I want to inform you that the Government of the United States has received from the Government of Egypt assurances to the effect that, in connection with the agreement on the disengagement of Egyptian and Israeli forces, the Government of Egypt confirms that it regards the Straits of Bab el-Mandeb as an international waterway for ships of all flags and that it will not interfere with the free passage of Israeli ships or cargoes.[2]

Further assurances have been received from Egypt that upon the opening of the Suez Canal, the principle of free passage will likewise be observed and that principle will be extended to Israel when the state of belligerency between Egypt and Israel has ended.[3] As a first step, all

---

[1] Source: National Archives, Nixon Presidential Materials, NSC Files, Box 1180, Harold H. Saunders Files, Middle East Peace Negotiations, January 10–17, 1974. Secret.

[2] These assurances were expressed in a letter from President Sadat to President Nixon, January 17. (Ibid., Kissinger Office Files, Box 133, Country Files, Middle East, Egypt, Volume 9, January 1974)

[3] The assurance of free passage was included in the same letter that confirmed the Straits of Bab el-Mandeb as an international waterway.

cargoes destined for and coming from Israel will be permitted through the Canal from the time of its opening.
Sincerely,

Richard Nixon

13. Letter From President Nixon to Egyptian President Sadat[1]

Washington, January 17, 1974.

Dear Mr. President:

I understand that once the agreement between Egypt and Israel on disengagement of forces is in effect, you intend to begin work looking toward an early return of the Suez Canal to full operation and toward the rehabilitation of the cities and towns along the Canal and the resumption of normal economic activities in that area. I want you to know that if you proceed in this way the United States gives you its assurance that Israel will refrain from taking any military action against those civilian centers, installations and populations.
Sincerely,

Richard Nixon

---

[1] Source: National Archives, Nixon Presidential Materials, NSC Files, Kissinger Office Files, Box 133, Country Files, Middle East, Egypt, Volume 10, February 1974. Secret. According to Kissinger's memoirs, Kissinger drafted the letter himself. (*Years of Upheaval*, pp. 834–835)

14. Memorandum of Understanding[1]

January 18, 1974.

MEMORANDUM OF UNDERSTANDING BETWEEN
THE UNITED STATES GOVERNMENT AND
THE GOVERNMENT OF ISRAEL

1. The United States informs Israel that Egypt's intentions are to clear and open the Suez Canal for normal operations, and to rehabilitate the cities and towns along the Canal and resume normal peacetime economic activities in that area, beginning as quickly as possible after the Disengagement Agreement is implemented.

2. The United States has received assurances from Egypt of its intention, upon completion of the implementation of the Agreement, to start reducing significantly its forces under mobilization if Israel gives a like indication to Egypt through the United States.

3. It is the policy of the United States that implementation of the Disengagement Agreement and substantial steps by Egypt to implement its intentions in Paragraph 1 above should take precedence over the undertaking of new commitments by the parties related to subsequent phases of the Geneva Conference. The United States will do its best to help facilitate the Conference proceeding at a pace commensurate with this view.

4. The United States position is that withdrawal of United Nations Emergency Forces during the duration of the Disengagement Agreement requires the consent of both sides. Should the matter of the withdrawal come before the United Nations Security Council without the consent of Israel, the United States will vote against such withdrawal.

5. The United States will oppose supervision of Israeli-held areas by United Nations Observers from the Soviet Union, from other communist countries or from other countries which have no diplomatic relations with Israel. With respect to the deployment of forces in the United Nations Emergency Forces zone, the United States will approach the United Nations Secretary General with a view to working out arrangements whereby no units or personnel of nations which do

---

[1] Source: National Archives, Nixon Presidential Materials, NSC Files, Kissinger Office Files, Box 136, Country Files, Middle East, Dinitz, 1/1–7/1, 1974 (2). Secret. According to Kissinger's memoirs, the Israelis on several occasions sought Memoranda of Understanding between the United States and Israel. He attributed this to Israeli "consciousness of having only one friend among the nations of the world," which produced "an endless quest for reassurance in the form of additional concessions or side letters on the interpretation of existing agreements." (*Years of Upheaval*, p. 652)

not have diplomatic relations with Israel will (a) be deployed adjacent to the Israeli line, or (b) participate in the inspection of the Israeli area of limited forces and armaments.

6. The United States has informed the Governments of Israel and Egypt that it will perform aerial reconnaissance missions over the areas covered by the Disengagement Agreement at a frequency of about one mission every ten days or two weeks, and will make the photographs available to both Israel and Egypt.

7. The United States regards the Straits of Bab el-Mandeb as an international waterway and will support and join with others to secure general recognition of the right of free and innocent passage through those Straits. The United States will strongly support free passage of Israeli ships and cargoes through the Straits. In the event of interference with such passage, the United States will consult with Israel on how best to assure the maintenance and exercise of such rights.

8. With regard to the Egyptian undertaking not to interfere with the free passage of Israeli ships or cargoes through the Straits of Bab el-Mandeb, the United States informs the Government of Israel that it is the United States position that no notification in advance of the names of vessels passing through the Straits or any other prior communication to Egypt is required. The United States will immediately seek confirmation that this is also the Egyptian position.

9. Recognizing the defense responsibilities of the Government of Israel following redeployment of its forces under the Disengagement Agreement, the United States will make every effort to be fully responsive on a continuing and long-term basis to Israel's military equipment requirements.

10. In case of an Egyptian violation of any of the provisions of the Agreement or any of its attachments, the United States Government and the Government of Israel will consult regarding the necessary reaction.

15. Telegram From Secretary of State Kissinger to the President's Deputy Assistant for National Security Affairs (Scowcroft)[1]

January 19, 1974, 1814Z.

Hakto 56. Ref: Tohak 112.[2]

1. You may pass to the President that I have Sadat's assurance that the oil embargo will be lifted no later than a week from Monday.[3] You should also tell him that Sadat has promised to make a statement giving credit to the President for lifting of the embargo,[4] that I have given Sadat a suggested text of what he should say in that statement; and that Sadat has promised to use the statement I have given him.

2. You should emphasize to the President that our best hope is Sadat, and that we must keep our oil men out of this affair, their interests are parochial and they clearly do not have the ear of the King.

3. Admittedly, even with Sadat's assurances nothing may happen, but who else can we bet on. My own belief is that we can count on Sadat to produce what he has promised to produce.

4. You should emphasize to the President my deep belief we must stay with the game plan which has brought us this far. If we attempt to play with the program we have worked out we are likely to fail, and in the process may set our entire timetable back immeasurably. Should Sadat fail to perform on the firm assurances he has given us we can then turn to another course such as that suggested in Tohak 112.

---

[1] Source: National Archives, Nixon Presidential Materials, NSC Files, Kissinger Office Files, Box 43, HAK Trip Files, January 10–20, 1974. Top Secret; Sensitive; Flash. According to Kissinger's Record of Schedule, he was in Egypt on January 19 until 3 p.m. at which point he departed for Aqaba, Jordan, where he spent the rest of the day. (Library of Congress, Manuscript Division, Kissinger Papers, Box 438, Miscellany, 1968–76)

[2] Tohak 112 has not been found.

[3] On January 27, Sadat wrote Nixon that he had communicated with King Faisal about lifting the embargo and that Faisal had agreed to lift it. (Telegram 422 from Cairo; National Archives, Nixon Presidential Materials, NSC Files, Kissinger Office Files, Box 133, Country Files, Middle East, Egypt, Volume 9, January 1974)

[4] That same day, Scowcroft replied to Kissinger that President Nixon believed he would be announcing the lifting of the oil embargo in his January 30 State of the Union address. (Telegram WH 40308; ibid., Box 43, HAK Trip Files, January 10–20, 1974) See *Foreign Relations*, 1969–1976, volume XXXVI, Energy Crisis, 1969–1974, Document 292.

16. Telegram From Secretary of State Kissinger to the Department of State[1]

January 19, 1974, 2131Z.

Secto 115. Subj: KM 101 Signing of Egypt-Israel Disengagement Agreement.

1. Egyptian-Israeli Agreement on Disengagement of Forces was signed at Kilometer 101 at 12:25 p.m. January 18 by Chiefs of Staff Gamasy for Egypt and Elazar for Israel. UNEF Commander Siilasvuo signed as witness. Maw of State Department and Saunders of NSC staff were present in capacity of turning over to UNEF Commander four copies of agreement to be signed, one each for Egypt, Israel, UN and U.S. Others present in tent at table were: for UN, Political Adviser Gorge, Chief of Staff Col. Hogansk, Capt. Fallon; for Egypt, Gen. Magodub and Col. Howaidy, who represented Egypt at Geneva Military Working Group and Fawzy el Ibrashi of MFA who had attended earlier Kilometer 101 talks; for Israel, Gen. Adan, new Southern Front Commander, Col. Sion from Geneva Working Group, Col. Levran and Meir Rosenne, MFA Legal Adviser.

2. In twenty minutes before delegates entered tent, Gorge shuttled back and forth between Egyptian and Israeli tents which flanked meeting tent confirming arrangements for size of each group at table and procedures for signing. Israel wanted a larger group. Both sides also agreed that substance should be discussed after signing and that the U.S. representatives should remain through whole meeting. Neither side wanted to be difficult and problems were settled quickly. Egyptian side entered tent first. Salutes and simple greetings were exchanged when the Israelis entered. Atmosphere at this point was correct and polite, but no more.

3. Siilasvou welcomed those present in one sentence and suggested proceeding immediately to signing. Each of four copies was signed by each of the three signers and initialed on each page, including map attached.[2]

4. When signing was completed and each copy checked by Siilasvuo and Maw, signed copies were distributed among four groups at table. Signed copies, each in red binder, had been brought by Maw from Jerusalem to Cairo night before. Copies had been verified by Evron for Israel in Jerusalem. Maw and Saunders took copies to Ga-

---

[1] Source: National Archives, Nixon Presidential Materials, NSC Files, Kissinger Office Files, Box 133, Country Files, Middle East, Egypt, Volume 9, January 1974. Secret; Nodis; Immediate. Repeated to Cairo, Tel Aviv, and USUN.

[2] Map is not attached, but see the final disengagement map, Appendix B, Map 1.

masy's office in Cairo for verification before driving to Kilometer 101. Following signing, Siilasvuo suggested that next item on agenda be setting a date for the next meeting. Gamasy said he was prepared to meet at any time. Elazar suggested 11:00 a.m. January 20, and it was agreed.

6. Siilasvuo asked whether other questions should be discussed such as procedures for the next meeting. Gamasy said he would like to discuss principles which might guide the technical discussions, and Elazar agreed this would be helpful.

7. Gamasy then laid out following five principles, speaking briefly and precisely from notes scribbled in what seemed to be some sort of daily diary:

A. Each side would agree strictly to observe ceasefire on land, sea, and air. He had given order to start at 6:00 a.m. and so far, for first time, there had been no violations. Siilasvuo interjected that Elazar had given similar order and no violations had been reported.

B. Disengagement would be carried out in three phases: (1) In first 15 days, redeployment of Israeli forces from West to East Bank and redeployment over area between two sides. (2) In next 15 days, Israeli forces would be redeployed to lines on map attached to the agreement. Second Egyptian Army would be redeployed. (3) Final 10 days would be used to check positions and armaments on ground and establish procedures for UNEF.

C. Evacuation of Israeli troops from West Bank will start from south and move north so as to hand over Suez–Cairo road during first three days. Gamasy explained that sooner road was free, sooner redeployment of Third Army could begin. It would be difficult for Egypt to begin redeployment of Second Army before Third was taken care of.

D. UNEF should operate between two sides through all phases of disengagement with five kilometers between.

E. There should be no destruction of factories or other installations in the Suez area. It would improve the atmosphere for both sides if Egypt found no such destruction.

8. Gamasy concluded that he was prepared to continue meeting at the Chief of Staff level or at any other level Elazar preferred. He thought it might be useful if he and Elazar attended next meeting to assure that decisions could be taken on spot.

9. Elazar began his response by saying with a smile that maybe it was a good omen that the two sides had very similar ideas about implementing agreement. Generally, he said, Israel accepted the principles Gamasy outlined. Specifically:

A. Israel is prepared for implementation in three stages. He had in mind 14, 14, and 12 days in order to evacuate Western Bank within 28 days.

B. Starting Israeli evacuation in south and moving north is accepted. Israel understands Egyptian interest in problems of the Third Army and is prepared to cooperate.

C. Israel has similar idea on UN forces, though different in detail. Israel would like to have UNEF move in behind Israeli forces so evacuation areas could be turned over to UNEF and then be transferred to Egypt. Israel had thought of more than five kilometers between the two forces, but this could be discussed.

D. With regard to installations and other property in Suez, Elazar said he would give very strict orders not to change anything from this moment on. But he pointed out that unfortunately war had been fought over this area and there had been a great deal of damage.

10. Elazar concluded by agreeing that the Chiefs of Staff both attend the next meeting and decide there on attendance at future meetings. He agreed that it was important to start the talks well and said Israel has no other interest than to honor the agreement in spirit and letter in order to improve atmosphere for future agreements.

11. Gamasy thanked Elazar for his comments and asked whether he saw the first 28 days as divided into two phases. At this point, Elazar produced map with overlay indicating steps in which evacuation might proceed, emphasizing that map had been prepared only as a basis for discussion, not as a final solution. Elazar said if Gamasy had initial comments Israel would try to adapt its proposal before Sunday.[3]

12. Gamasy suggested that perhaps Israeli evacuation of the West Bank could be completed in less than 28 days. Elazar said he had no objection in principle and only problem was whether it was logistically possible to finish in a shorter time. He would look at it.

13. Gamasy said he hoped that road to Suez City might be opened even before disengagement began. Elazar said he would not suggest opening the road until after the Israelis had withdrawn north of it so as to avoid both forces on the road at the same time. Gamasy accepted point with regard to military traffic, but said he was talking only at this stage about civilian traffic moving in convoys under UNEF supervision. Elazar said he would come Sunday with an answer.

14. Elazar said he would like arrangements as soon as possible for collecting bodies of dead Israeli soldiers and for trying to locate missing. Gamassy said he was ready to discuss this. Gamasy said he would not raise the question of Egyptian prisoners because he already had answer. With regard to Kabrit, Egypt would like to treat it as part of Third Army for food and supply if Israel did not object. Elazar said

---

[3] January 20, the date of the next meeting.

there would be no objection. He said Israel would like a map of sea mines in the Gulf of Suez.

15. Siilasvuo asked desires of the parties on briefing the press. Elazar said he would say simply that agreement has benefits for both sides and represents a first step toward a better future. Gamasy indicated he would not comment. Both sides indicated they would leave release of agreement to political levels of their governments.

16. In closing, Siilasvuo indicated an interest in how mine fields would be cleared since UNEF taking over evacuated areas. Elazar said mines would be left, but Israel would provide maps. Gamasy said if Egypt had maps it would concentrate all its engineer efforts on clearing the fields.

17. Siilasvuo askied whether photographers should be invited in. Gamasy preferred photos be limited to delegations leaving tent. Coffee was served, and there was small talk. The meeting ended at 1:15 pm.

18. After the signing, the atmosphere relaxed from correct to cooperative and even cordial as Generals began discussing their business. Setting was combination of desert simplicity and efforts to recognize what everyone present felt to be historic moment. UNEF Honor Guard in field uniforms lined two paths leading from Egyptian and Israeli tents to signing tent. About 150 members of press stationed 150 feet away. Inside dirt-floored signing tent was battered U-shaped table covered with old gray felt and surrounded by slatted wood folding chairs of some other era.

19. Readiness on both sides to get on with implementation quickly and to deal with disagreements as practical problems to be solved characterized approach of both sides. Siilasvuo and Gorge were quick to recognize obvious preparatory work done by Secretary Kissinger to assure parallel thinking on both sides about mechanics of implementation. Both expressed deep gratitude for U.S. contribution, and Siilasvuo asked that his congratulations and thanks be extended to the Secretary.

Kissinger

17. Memorandum of Conversation[1]

Washington, January 21, 1974, 10–11:40 a.m.

PARTICIPANTS

President Nixon
Dr. Henry A. Kissinger, Secretary of State and Assistant to the President for National Security Affairs
Lt. General Brent Scowcroft, Deputy Assistant to the President for National Security Affairs
Bipartisan Congressional Leadership

SUBJECT

Bipartisan Leadership Meeting on the Egyptian-Israeli Disengagement Agreement

President: Welcome back to the new session. Welcome back, John Scali. There will be two meetings this week—one on the Middle East today and one on energy on Wednesday. We moved the State of the Union to the 30th because of the Women's National Press Club.

We don't know when the oil embargo might be lifted. Henry will cover that, plus the Egyptian agreement.

Kissinger: First, let me go over what our strategy has been. The conflict at the end of October had found us on one side, the Arabs with Soviet backing on the other side, and the oil embargo. We were a potential enemy to the Arabs; Israel was in a trauma digging in on the new lines they had taken. The debate in the UN was whether Israel should withdraw five kilometers, and Israel refused. Even had they done it, the situation would not have been substantially changed. The military situation was very unstable and the possibility of renewed war was high.

At this point, the President decided we should cooperate with the Soviet Union and set up the Geneva Conference.

Resolution 242 means different things to different parties. The problem with a general conference is that the Soviet Union would take an intransigent position which the Arabs would have to support and there would be a deadlock. Instead, we decided to move by stages within a comprehensive framework. None of this could have been done without President Sadat. He is a wise leader. He was willing to talk with Israel at Kilometer 101 and to trust us.

---

[1] Source: Ford Library, National Security Adviser, Memoranda of Conversations, Box 3, January 21, 1974, Nixon, Bipartisan Leadership. Secret; Nodis. The meeting was held in the Cabinet Room of the White House. Brackets are in the original. A list of attendees is in President Nixon's Daily Diary. (National Archives, Nixon Presidential Materials, White House Central Files)

President: Compare Nasser and Sadat. Nasser had a mystique but he was persona non grata with conservative Arabs. He had to take radical positions on Israel, and after the Aswan Dam, with the United States. We underestimated Sadat—because he didn't have the charisma. But he didn't have the debt to the radicals, the utter hatred of Israel, etc. Egypt is a non-oil state, yet he can lead the Arabs.

Kissinger: Nasser was a pan-Arabist; Sadat is an Egyptian nationalist, yet Sadat is better able to lead the Arabs. Nasser scared the Saudis silly. There are three levels of Arab problems: the Arab-Israeli problem itself; the internal political conditions in each country; and the relations to other Arab countries. For example, Asad described the internal problems he had moving in directions like Sadat was going—they are enormous. Without Sadat having moved, there would be no chance.

In November I told Sadat that if he wanted enforcement of Resolution 339,[2] he could get it with a great deal of pain; but if he would work with us, we thought we could get a major move; with some effort, a real disengagement. To Sadat's credit, he didn't know whether he could pull it off—neither did I. Golda had been tough here. We had 2:00 a.m. meetings at the Blair House.[3]

President: Henry usually doesn't mind that.

Kissinger: [Joke about making love to Golda and her having shingles.] We told Sadat that we wanted to get this major movement with the consent of Israel, not by raping her—and nothing could be done prior to the Israeli elections. So we needed time to convert Israel. Also we needed it to educate Egypt as to what was possible. For six weeks we engaged in academic debates with both sides. Israel said they would win another war. We said, even so, where are you? And for us, it was a dead end street. We finally convinced them to develop a plan of their own. Dayan then came over with a plan[4]—this was done willingly. We kept both sides fully informed.

The present Israeli political situation is bad. Her coalition must include parties opposed to each other and to withdrawal. The Geneva talks were working themselves into a deadlock. The President decided we needed to get things moving. Dayan said he had two problems: to get the plan approved by the Cabinet and to get it considered at a level in Egypt where it wouldn't be rejected as a test of manhood.

---

[2] See *Foreign Relations, 1969–1976*, volume XXV, Arab-Israeli Dispute and War, 1973, Document 324. UN Security Resolution 339, adopted on October 23 after the fighting in the Middle East continued, reiterated the terms of Resolution 338, calling again for a cease-fire (see footnote 6, Document 7). For the text of Resolution 339, see *Yearbook of the United Nations, 1973*, p. 213.

[3] Kissinger is referring to the November 1973 meetings in Washington with Meir; see footnote 3, Document 1.

[4] See Document 7.

There was a big risk in my going; we didn't know it would work. The original plan was to get a plan first and present it to Egypt and finalize it at Geneva. But Sadat said: "Why not finish it now so it won't bog down?" He said he was willing to give more to get it done faster.

I won't go into the details, but at some point in the negotiations they stopped being enemies and became collaborators in a common objective. One other point was that when political leaders agreed on a point, they asked me to take these points to their respective military. They exploded in each case, and were overruled by Golda and Sadat.

There was no way this agreement could have been reached bilaterally. Each could say things to us to pass that they couldn't say directly.

[Secretary Kissinger went to the map on the easel and described the agreement.]

There is a zone of limited armaments. Each side refused to discuss its deployments with the other side. We decided that the United States would make a proposal to each, which they would sign. Neither of them had to say they had accepted limitations proposed by the other. The legal status of this is not that we are guarantors; we just generated the paper and it is attached to the agreement. It should be kept secret for the moment. The key is that the limitations remove any offensive capability—please do not reveal this—but neither can reach the other side with weapons. So, neither one can attack the other without warning, and each war in this area has started with a surprise attack.

Next, both wanted assurances they were reluctant to get directly. We have, however, made each party aware of the understandings with the other. None of these are obligations of the United States. For example: Bab el Mandeb [he described how it went]. Another was on how the UN would inspect. Each side wanted the UN forces to have liaison officers of the side being inspected. We also said we opposed any unilateral removal of UN forces. Another was: informal assurances of no howitzers which could reach Port Said. Another—please keep this secret—we told both of them we would give them reconnaissance photos of the lines. Flights will be made with the acquiescence of each.

One could almost feel the change in attitude between the sides as the talks went on. For example, Kabrit, and the Israeli dead. Five days were set aside for technical discussions—they were all settled yesterday. This mood is very significant.

The next moves relate to Syria and Jordan. The Syrians were beside themselves that Egypt would make a separate agreement, and appealed to other Arabs. They said this would freeze the situation. Sadat asked to let him go to Syria before me. There was an enormous difference between my first and second visits. It was a painful meeting,[5] but they did produce a plan—it was unacceptable, but at least it was a plan. We also worked out a face-saving way they could start talks with Israel. Asad asked me to stop in Israel to give them the plan. It is a start. I believe if we can get disengagement schemes worked out, the sides can't get at each other, and we will have changed the psychological climate. After this is done, we will go to Egypt to move toward a final settlement and let them be the pacesetters. We must be careful not to push out the Soviet Union—we will use Geneva to get their involvement and we have kept them partially informed.

An overall settlement will be a painful process—with much emotion, but this is a start. Both the Israeli and Egyptian press have been positive.

Now on energy—we should say nothing publicly. That would prevent movement. The problem now is that Arab disunity makes it hard to get an agreement among them to lift the embargo. But Sadat is on a trip now to get the lifting. We hope he will succeed but we don't know when. We are optimistic but we must not predict it. It can't be lifted as a favor to the U.S. but for their own motives.

President: Without the disengagement, there is no chance of lifting of the embargo. With it, there is a chance, but we can make no prediction as to when and how. The Arabs must make the decision—and not as the result of an American pressure ploy. The embargo has been on our minds in these negotiations. The disengagement is more important in the long term, but I know the concerns of your constituents. We have removed the major impediment, and we are in contact with all of them, but we have no predictions.

Albert: Is the problem an objection because we provided arms to Israel?

Kissinger: That is now overcome.

President: The fact that we brought about the disengagement tends to wash out the arms thing. The radical Arabs could say there can be no lifting of the embargo before a final settlement is reached, or at least until further movement. That was a major point.

Kissinger: That is no longer a major point. The President's position was that we wanted to move in the Middle East but not in a way to give in to Arab blackmail. The difference between the U.S. and others, is that they can only give arms and only we can deliver.

Fulbright: It's a remarkable job.

---

[5] Kissinger met with Asad in Damascus on January 20. See Document 19.

President: I want to leave you with no illusions about anything. This is a big step. I knew the fact that three months ago that Syria would receive Kissinger was unthinkable—only Iraq is more radical.

Kissinger: Asad jokes about pursuing an anti-Soviet policy.

President: On energy, we hope we have made constructive progress, but there is nothing to predict. On the long-term settlement—it will involve Jerusalem, the question of the '67 lines, etc. The U.S. will use its constructive influence toward a long-term settlement. We will continue to use our influence with all the states in the area.

Kissinger: I would not use the word "interim agreement." "Separation of forces," okay, "preliminary"—just not "interim," because it has special connotation.

President: Another point regards the Soviet Union. It is not useful to brag about the Soviet Union being cut out. Had the Soviet Union moved to prevent this agreement, we would have had a problem. The line is the Soviet Union has been kept informed. We think their interest as well as ours is served by this.

One other point—not only will peace take time but the American presence, and capability, are of great substance. Lots of people have ideas for a settlement, but only we can do it—so our strength and diplomacy is very important.

Peace doesn't come because men of goodwill want it, but only when both sides have more to gain by moving peacefully than by war. We have demonstrated that another war would be dangerous to world peace—both sides know they suffered badly. We also demonstrated that the U.S. wants nothing in the way of territory and domination over any one. We are respected and we amount to something. That is why we got what we now have. I look forward to good relations with every Arab state. The Middle East is the Balkans for the 1970s and very dangerous. We need a constructive relationship with all of the parties. But we don't want to irritate the Soviet Union; we just want to play a constructive role.

Kissinger: If the Soviet Union wants peace, peace in the Middle East is not directed against the Soviet Union—only if they want turmoil in the Middle East.

President: We have had long talks with the Soviet Union on the Middle East. Both of us know it is important to each, but neither side wants a confrontation there.

18. Memorandum of Conversation[1]

Washington, January 23, 1974, 10 a.m.

SUBJECT

Secretary Kissinger's Report on Egyptian-Israeli Disengagement Agreement

CABINET MEETING
(Excerpt on Foreign Policy)

Kissinger: I want to underline what the President and Vice President said. When something works it looks easy, but one has to look at what other things might have happened. It would be difficult now if we had a crisis on autobahn, or something, while we were working on the Middle East. It is easy for Jackson to posture against the Soviets because we have them all quieted down.[2] The fact is the President has quieted the world down. In 1970 we had four crises going on.

In the Middle East last October, the Europeans and Japanese panicked and started to compete for Arab favor. At the middle of the month it looked as if we were isolated in support of Israel and the Soviet Union could keep the turmoil going by escalating its demands. We got a ceasefire, and then it blew up. We had a momentary crisis with the Soviet Union and an alert—which even the Arabs thought was essential. The Arab moderates felt themselves trapped by the radicals, the Soviets, and the Europeans.

What we had to get across is that everyone else could posture but only we could deliver. Only the United States had the leverage on Israel.

The President, therefore, sent me to the Middle East with a message that we won't promise what we can't deliver, but we will deliver what we promise. Sadat's wisdom though was indispensable. His willingness and his patience gave us time to get things turned around.

The stalemate stemmed from the tendency of the Arabs to confuse great proclamations with achievement. And the Israelis equate security with military force.

---

[1] Source: Ford Library, National Security Adviser, Memoranda of Conversations, Box 3, January 23, 1974, Cabinet Meeting. Confidential. The meeting was held in the Cabinet Room of the White House. A list of attendees is in President Nixon's Daily Diary. (National Archives, Nixon Presidential Materials, White House Central Files)

[2] A reference to Senator Jackson's efforts to link Most-Favored-Nation status for the Soviet Union to the liberalization of Soviet emigration policies, especially regarding Jews.

We had to break the international front—a coalescence of the Arabs, the Soviet Union, the Europeans, and Japanese, but do this without antagonizing the Soviet Union. So we developed the Geneva framework to keep the Soviet Union involved. Geneva brought the parties together for the first time.

The moral force of the United States in the world is overwhelming. After billions of Soviet expenditures and effort in the Middle East, it was the United States which they all turned to. Sadat couldn't accept the Israeli proposal for force limitations but could accept the President's proposal in the interest of peace in the world. It could only have been done with us. The negotiations were direct, but we provided the essential catalyst.

This is the first time Israel has ever moved back of her own accord. We have now disengaged the military forces of the two sides and averted a possible resumption of the war and a possible great power confrontation. The achievement of surprise is now impossible. With forces that are at all equal, victory in a desert war comes only with surprise.

One of the most encouraging developments was to see the two sides changed from looking at each other as devils to a recognition they had a common problem. Problems which had been deadlocked, after the agreement were settled almost immediately.

We still face enormous problems in the future. Our first need is to help prevent Sadat's isolation in the Arab world. That was the reason for my visit to Syria.[3] They are wacky but it was an enormous step for them to send a disengagement proposal to Israel, which they did. It was unacceptable, but we can get a negotiation going and Sadat is no longer isolated. If we can get a Syrian disengagement, we can then move with Sadat for a permanent settlement. Then we can work on the Palestinians. The Israeli problem is that there is the Religious Party[4] in the Cabinet which regards the West Bank as part of Biblical Israel.

None of this could have happened without Soviet acquiescence. All they had to do was to put out proposals that were more Egyptian than Sadat put out. They are not happy, but it was crucial they did not interfere. Without détente it couldn't have happened.

President: On embargo, you can say that without disengagement, no lifting of the embargo would take place—but don't predict that it will. Just say we are working on it.

---

[3] Kissinger met with Asad in Damascus on January 20. See Document 19.

[4] The National Religious Party, an orthodox Jewish political party that formed in 1956.

One political point—Golda has always told me that she doesn't need our men there—that with our arms they can beat the Arabs every time. But even if that is true, it is possible only if we hold the ring against the Soviet Union. If the Soviet presence had moved into the Middle East, we would have had a serious problem. If that had happened, it wouldn't matter how much Congress appropriated.

We are not trying to freeze out the Soviet Union. It's just that we intend to play a role in the Middle East.

With regard to Arab moderates, it is essential they side with us because the Soviet Union could support the revolutionaries. Even the radicals, who are anti-Israel and because of that anti-U.S., are not pro-Soviet but pro-themselves. We have to play this carefully. The Soviet Union is close and we are far away. If the Soviet Union didn't have other fish to fry with us, we would have a bigger problem in the Middle East.

Israel is totally dependent on us, the moderate Arabs partly. The radicals even need us in a way.

Without détente, the Soviet Union could have opposed our initiative and blown it sky high. Why did they play the role they did? It was in their interest—which would not have been served by confrontation with us because it would have hurt with respect to Europe, SALT, China. This is why détente is right and will continue.

Kissinger: This is why the constant Congressional pressure against the Soviet Union can destroy détente. If the Soviet Union gets nothing from it, they won't continue this posture.

President: That is right. The military will react against SALT, the Congress against MFN. But we must do what is right for détente. We must recognize that the Soviet leadership could change. The same with the PRC. They could be a tremendous nuclear power in 15–20 years. When you hear the nitpickers remember it is not done with mirrors nor is it accidental. It is not because Brezhnev loves us—but because his alternatives are worse.

Syrian-Israeli Disengagement Agreement, January–May 1974

19. Memorandum From the President's Deputy Assistant for National Security Affairs (Scowcroft) to President Nixon[1]

Washington, January 20, 1974.

The following is a report from Secretary Kissinger's discussions this morning with President Asad of Syria:

"1. I have just completed a five hour discussion with President Asad of Syria.[2] Given the Egyptian-Israeli disengagement agreement, he now appears ready—in a very gingerly way—to try for a disengagement agreement of his own.

"2. During my first meeting with Asad a few weeks ago[3] he insisted that a Syrian-Israeli disengagement agreement had to be fully buttoned down before he was willing to commit himself to the Geneva Conference.[4] Today he softened his position somewhat, emphasizing that he must know where he is going and have some indication of the possibilities for disengagement before he fully commits himself to negotiations.

"3. Asad gave me some concrete indications of the kind of disengagement agreement he would accept.[5] Although they are no more than a starting point, I made it clear to him that the substantial pull back he has in mind will certainly be rejected by the Israelis. But he has now at least given us a concrete proposal which he said I could give the

---

[1] Source: National Archives, Nixon Presidential Materials, NSC Files, Kissinger Office Files, Box 44, HAK Trip Files, January 10–20, 1974, Europe and Mid East State Cables, Memos, Miscellaneous. Secret; Sensitive; Exclusively Eyes Only. A stamped notation reads: "The President has seen."

[2] The meeting between Asad and Kissinger took place on January 20 in President Asad's office. (Memorandum of conversation; ibid., Box 1028, Presidential/HAK Memcons, January 1–February 28, 1974, Folder 2) According to Kissinger's Record of Schedule, the meeting took place from 12:30 to 4:45 p.m. (Library of Congress, Manuscript Division, Kissinger Papers, Box 438, Miscellany, 1968–76)

[3] Kissinger first met Asad on December 15, 1973. See *Foreign Relations*, 1969–1976, volume XXV, Arab-Israeli Crisis and War, 1973, Document 393.

[4] Asad told Kissinger in their first meeting that Syria would not participate in the opening of the Geneva Conference in December 1973.

[5] Asad presented Kissinger with three options: first, an Israeli withdrawal from the Golan Heights with a demilitarized area; second, an Israeli withdrawal that would leave the Israelis with a five kilometer area of control in the Heights; or, third, an Israeli withdrawal approximately halfway between the October 6, 1973, line and the original June 5, 1967 line.

Israelis and indicated that he knew he would have 'to make a further proposal' if the Israelis reject this one.

"4. I shall make a brief airport stop in Israel on the way home to give them a report of the conversation with Asad.[6] This is a good move, not only because Asad wanted me to do so, but also because as thin a reed as it is it helps relieve pressure on Sadat (who is presently under attack for having agreed to a disengagement scheme without waiting for the Syrians). The fact that the Syrian-Israeli disengagement talks can be said to have begun today will be helpful to Sadat and buy time for all concerned. With this Syrian-Israeli process started it also helps reduce the amount of trouble that the Soviets can cause.

"5. My plan is to describe briefly the Syrian proposal to the Israelis, ask them to study it and come up with concrete ideas of their own which perhaps Dayan can bring to us in ten days or two weeks in Washington. I want the U.S. role to be the same as that we played on the Egyptian-Israeli disengagement negotiation."

---

[6] The meeting between the Israeli negotiating team and Kissinger took place on January 20 from 6:55 to 8:04 p.m. at Ben-Gurion (Lod) Airport in Tel Aviv. (Memorandum of conversation; Library of Congress, Manuscript Division, Kissinger Papers, TS 34, Peace Negotiations, Memcons and Telegram Book, Volume 1, December 1973 to January 1974, Folder 1)

---

20. **Telegram From the Department of State to the Embassy in Lebanon**[1]

Washington, January 29, 1974, 2353Z.

19342. Subject: Message From the Secretary to President Assad. Beirut pass Damascus for Scotes.

1. Scotes should convey following oral message from the Secretary to President Assad in manner he deems most appropriate.

2. *Begin text:*

As Secretary Kissinger informed President Assad in his last message, he conveyed to the Israeli Government on January 20 President Assad's proposal with respect to the disengagement of forces on the

---

[1] Source: National Archives, Nixon Presidential Materials, NSC Files, Box 1181, Harold H. Saunders Files, Middle East Peace Negotiations, January 26–31, 1974. Secret; Cherokee; Nodis; Immediate. Drafted by Atherton; approved by Sisco.

Syrian front.[2] The Secretary has been in further communication with the Israeli Government following his return to Washington and wants to bring President Assad up to date on where matters now stand.

We have succeeded in persuading the Israelis, despite initial resistance on their part, to agree in principle to enter disengagement talks with Syria. We have also obtained their agreement to the idea of carrying out such talks in the context of the Egyptian-Israeli Military Working Group to which Syrian representatives would be attached. At the same time, the Israelis have reiterated the great importance they attach to the POW issue, as the Secretary indicated to President Assad would be the case. Nevertheless, the Secretary wants President Assad to know that he is confident that, following the pattern developed in pursuing Egyptian-Israeli disengagement, he can persuade the Israelis to send General Dayan to Washington with a response to President Assad's proposal once Syria has provided a list of POW's and has agreed to Red Cross visits.

In keeping with his undertaking to deal with President Assad in full candor, the Secretary wants to give the President his judgment that, in the absence of Syrian willingness to make the prisoner list available and to permit Red Cross visits, there will be a delay in getting Syrian-Israeli disengagement negotiations started. The Secretary reiterates his personal commitment to assist in every way possible in facilitating such negotiations as a step toward a just and durable peace.

Secretary Kissinger will look forward to receiving President Assad's views with respect to this message and meanwhile conveys to the President his warm personal regards. *End text.*

Kissinger

---

[2] See footnote 6, Document 19.

21. Telegram From the Department of State to the U.S. Interests Section in Syria[1]

Washington, February 5, 1974, 0059Z.

23475. Subject: Message for President Assad from Secretary. Beirut not Addee, pass Scotes in Damascus.

1. Scotes should convey following letter from Secretary to President Assad by most expeditious means possible.

2. *Begin message*:

Dear Mr. President:

We have been having great difficulties with the Israelis in moving matters along on the question of Syrian-Israeli disengagement. As you know, the recent Israeli Cabinet statement reaffirmed Israel's interest in a disengagement agreement with Syria. However, the Israelis insist that before they engage in any negotiations on this matter with Syria, the POW list must be provided and Red Cross visits permitted.

I have been giving considerable thought to how in these circumstances progress can be made. I am willing to try out the following formula on the Israelis and would like to have your reaction before doing so. In conveying the following thoughts to you, I want to make clear that they have not been previously discussed with the Israelis. My thoughts are along the following lines:

1. We would convey to the Israeli Government the number of POW's Syria holds.

2. The Syrian Government would send the list of POW's to its Interests Section here in Washington.

3. We would insist with the Israelis that they come up with a concrete proposal on disengagement which they would make available to me, in exchange for the list of POW's.

4. As soon as the visit of the Red Cross takes place, I would transmit Israel's concrete disengagement proposal to you and at the same time would insist with the Israelis that they send a high-level official to Washington with a view to discussing further modifications in whatever proposal the Israelis had made available.

5. A negotiating process would then begin perhaps in the framework of the Israeli-Egyptian Military Working Group.

---

[1] Source: National Archives, Nixon Presidential Materials, NSC Files, Box 1181, Harold H. Saunders Files, Middle East Peace Negotiations, February 1–8, 1974. Secret; Cherokee; Nodis; Niact Immediate. Repeated Niact Immediate to Cairo and Beirut. Drafted by Sisco and Atherton; approved by Kissinger.

I want to stress once again that none of the above has been discussed with the Israelis. I also want to point out that the difficulties we are experiencing with the Israelis presently are akin to those which we experienced in the early stages of the Egyptian-Israeli disengagement discussions. I urge, Mr. President, that you not be deflected or diverted as a result of the procedural difficulties, as important as they are, which presently exist. I remain confident that, if we can get over these procedural hurdles, with the United States playing a role similar to that which it played in the Egyptian-Israeli disengagement discussions, an agreement acceptable to both sides can be achieved. It is important, Mr. President, that you stay on the course we have discussed and not be deflected by Israeli maneuvers.

However, an even more serious difficulty has now arisen. I have just been informed by the Government of Saudi Arabia that, following your visit to Riyadh, and in response to your request, the Saudi Government has taken the position that the oil embargo against the U.S. will not be lifted unless a disengagement agreement has been reached between Syria and Israel and is being implemented.[2] We are informing the Saudi Government that, unless the embargo is lifted promptly, President Nixon will not authorize further efforts by the United States Government to achieve Syrian-Israeli disengagement.[3]

The United States had earlier expressed understanding of the decision that was made to impose an embargo in the heat of the recent war. Since then, however, the situation has fundamentally changed. The United States undertook to engage its prestige and influence fully in the search for an overall just and durable peace between Israel and all of its neighbors. We have given evidence of our commitment to that goal and have achieved Egyptian-Israeli disengagement as a first step. This was done in spite of, and not as a result of, the embargo.

This new development places President Nixon and me in an impossible position. Congressional and public opinion in the United States will not support continuing United States efforts, which will be both difficult and time-consuming, to bring about Syrian-Israeli disengagement, to say nothing of the further steps required to achieve the final settlement the Arab countries seek, while those countries continue their discriminatory measures against the United States. Continuation of the embargo will thus work against the objectives which you and I have discussed. We would very much regret having to discontinue our efforts, which as I have indicated, are going forward intensively with Israel and which we believe hold out hope of progress over the weeks

---

[2] See *Foreign Relations*, 1969–1976, volume XXXVI, Energy Crisis, 1969–1974, Document 298.

[3] See ibid., Document 300.

ahead. This will, however, be the inevitable consequence of a continuation of the embargo. As for the effects of the embargo, you are undoubtedly aware that the United States is taking measures at home which will enable us to manage economically even if the embargo continues.

I value the relationship I have established with you, Mr. President, which must continue to be based on complete frankness and honesty between us. In this spirit, I have conveyed the foregoing full statement of our position, as we are explaining it to the Saudi Government, for your confidential information. While awaiting a successful resolution of the embargo issue, I would welcome your reaction to the procedural ideas outlined at the beginning of this message with respect to the Syrian-Israeli disengagement question.

I want to make clear, however, that I will only be able to initiate with Israel such efforts to solve the immediate problem of getting Syrian-Israeli disengagement moving after the oil embargo has been lifted. At the same time, I want to reaffirm to you my strong commitment, including my personal participation, to work for a disengagement of Syrian and Israeli forces as a further initial step toward a just and durable peace in the Middle East.

With warm regards,

Henry A. Kissinger

End message.

3. For Cairo: Ambassador Eilts should see Fahmy and fill him in fully on text of foregoing letter to Assad.

Kissinger

---

22. Telegram From the Department of State to the U.S. Interests Section in Syria[1]

Washington, February 6, 1974, 0219Z.

24425. Subject: Message to President Assad re Secretary's Talks With Soviets.

1. You should convey following oral message from the Secretary to President Assad in most expeditious way possible:

---

[1] Source: National Archives, Nixon Presidential Materials, NSC Files, Box 1181, Harold H. Saunders Files, Middle East Peace Negotiations, February 1–8, 1974. Secret; Cherokee; Nodis; Niact Immediate. Drafted by Atherton; approved by Kissinger.

2. Secretary wants to inform President Assad of his discussions with the Soviets about the Middle East during Gromyko's visit to Washington.[2] Main point Soviets made was that in future all our Middle East diplomatic activities should be carried out on a joint U.S.-Soviet basis and that modalities should be joint. They also want all activities to be carried out in Geneva and to have U.S. and Soviet participation in all Geneva meetings between the parties. We have for the moment simply said that we agree in principle that we and Soviets should coordinate our efforts, because Secretary first wanted to get President Assad's views. He would appreciate any suggestions President may have as to whether U.S.-Soviet coordination is desirable and how U.S.-Soviet coordination might work in practice, particularly as regards efforts to achieve Syrian-Israeli disengagement. Meanwhile, Secretary wants President Assad to know that he has not revealed to Soviets any of the matters discussed in confidence between President and himself and to express hope that President Assad will keep him informed of anything he might tell Soviets about these matters so that no misunderstandings arise. Secretary would appreciate receiving President Assad's views with regard to these matters.[3]

Kissinger

---

[2] Documentation on Gromyko's visit is printed in *Foreign Relations,* 1969–1976, volume XV, Soviet Union, June 1972–August 1974.

[3] Telegram 57 from Damascus, February 9, 1710Z, transmitted President Asad's reply that Syria had "no objection to a U.S./Soviet coordination." Asad concluded by stating that Syria lacked "the data which may enable us to suggest a practical plan for such co-ordination." (National Archives, Nixon Presidential Materials, NSC Files, Box 1181, Harold H. Saunders Files, Middle East Peace Negotiations, February 9–15, 1974)

23. Memorandum of Conversation[1]

Washington, February 8, 1974, 4:20–5:40 p.m.

PARTICIPANTS

    Paul Ziffren
    Sol Linowitz
    Simon Rifkind
    Elmer Winter
    Lawrence Tisch
    Albert List
    Morris Abram
    [See biographies at end]

    Henry A. Kissinger, Secretary of State
    Peter W. Rodman, NSC Staff

Ziffren: Judge Rifkind can start out and give you a fill-in on how we all got started.

Secretary Kissinger: Good. I appreciate the paper you left the last time.[2]

Rifkind: It is simple, Mr. Secretary. In the fall of last year, almost by spontaneous combustion, many of us began to worry about developments in this country—all the Arab propaganda on the scene, with Madison Avenue methods, the oil companies activity with their ads, an anticipated scarcity of fuel—which has now become a reality—meaning travel restrictions and shortages.

We thought all these might combine and pose a threat to the Jewish community in the United States. We thought we would address ourselves to this problem. We would form a low-key, low-profile group to follow the true situation in the Middle East and the oil situation, and try to persuade that our interest in the Near East was an American interest, not a Jewish interest, and that American strategy was for American interest not Israeli interest, and that the fuel situation was a long-term problem. We tried to put ideas down on paper and see if it could be fed into the American media stream and try to keep a protective cover over the situation. We were not too hasty. An ad in the *Wall Street Journal* yesterday—by Alfred Lilienthal, who has long been an Arab sympathizer and, I believe, an anti-Semite—reads: "Do arms

---

[1] Source: National Archives, RG 59, Records of Henry Kissinger, 1973–77, Box 1, Nodis Memcons, September–December, Folder 3. Confidential. The meeting was held in the Conference Room on the Seventh Floor of the Department of State. Brackets are in the original. A list of the attendees, which includes their positions in the business community, is attached but not printed.

[2] Not further identified.

for Israel mean no fuel for Americans?" The answer is supposed to be yes.

This is the situation we are trying to gain control of. Therefore, I am delighted to have the opportunity to speak with you.

Secretary Kissinger: I appreciate it. That effort is in no way inconsistent with our policy. On the contrary. Apart from the merits of the dispute, American policy cannot be affected by the withholding of raw materials by raw material countries. For example, on Israeli-Syrian disengagement, we favor it, but it is my intention to halt all our efforts if they don't lift the embargo. Because we can't be in the position where they say they forced us to do it—even if we would have done it otherwise. We cannot be forced to curry the favor of the raw material countries, because once we start it, it is an endless process.

In 1955 I believed that the first country to take Soviet arms should be made to pay for it. Because otherwise it would start a trend.

Rifkind: It was true.

Secretary Kissinger: It turned out to be true. If we do it now, it is the same with the Energy Conference.[3] But given the cravenness, cowardice and cupidity of the Europeans, we won't do what we should. We can use it as a pretext for disassociation.

I am assuming this is entirely off the record.

Rifkind: Of course.

Ziffren: If the question comes up, we will say that any comment should come from you.

Secretary Kissinger: I don't object to your acknowledging you met with me. And you can tell the Israeli Embassy of anything we discuss.

It is good that this is happening when there is no real issue. There is nothing I want, except on MFN, which I mentioned.

I want to give you my analysis of the situation.

The problem you are addressing in your committee hasn't been acute, partly because the Arabs are not too skillful and partly because we are somewhat skillful here. But the problem could become serious. I must say that the Israelis themselves were in no position to help themselves without our active intervention.

The situation is this. At the end of October, Israel was in a desperate situation. Technically she won some victories but lost the war strategically. Prior to October 6, Israel's security was assured by the conviction of everyone that Israel could win any war and would win

---

[3] The Washington Energy Conference was scheduled to convene on February 11. See *Foreign Relations*, 1969–1976, volume XXXVI, Energy Crisis, 1969–1974, Document 318.

quickly, overwhelmingly, without the problem of resupply except after the war. Therefore she didn't have to negotiate. I met with Eban on October 4 at the UN.[4] I said: "Is there anything to discuss?" He said: "We never had it so good. The best thing you can do for us is to leave us alone."

That was the valid Israeli assessment. It was completely shattered by the war. By the end of the week Israel was in desperate straits because of the exhaustion of supplies. Without the airlift, they would have lost. Starting the airlift was an unusual decision, and absolutely cannot be counted on as normal procedure of American policy—and so quickly. And it depended on the accident that we could blackmail the Portuguese into letting us use their islands. Third, we had a leader in Egypt whom we could keep quiet while we did it, and fourth, the oil situation was not yet perceived here.

It needs an extremely well-disposed Secretary of State and a President willing to do it. This is a fact that has to be faced—we simply cannot expect an airlift during combat, and this is a new fact.

The Arabs don't have to win; they only have to survive as a fighting force and they can impose a dangerous attrition on Israel. Such a level of casualties as they took in October cannot be sustained at that level at regular intervals.

Moreover, the political situation has changed because of the oil situation. Israel faces the United Arabs, the Europeans, Japan, and the Soviet Union in total opposition to them, and only the U.S. with them, in a UN forum with only two votes for them. They would face an unending series of resolutions which Israel wouldn't carry out, and then there would be sanctions. It is an irony that Israel, conceived as an escape from the ghetto, would become a ghetto itself. This is the situation as it is.

And the peculiar qualities that made Israel what it is would have hastened Israel's doom. To go to Israel 50 years ago, when it was only a dream—this is something achieved by extraordinary endurance, not by flexibility. It required an almost peasant-like doggedness and an almost provincialism that is not usually associated with the Jewish people. These qualities served them well until they are now faced with this international situation where they need flexibility and maneuver—indeed, the qualities of the ghetto. But their instinct was to dig in. If it led to a new crisis, the whole world would turn on them. The reason they needed disengagement was to create belts so that any attack couldn't take place without attacking the UN. Of course they can't trust them. It

---

[4] According to Kissinger's memoirs, Kissinger spoke with Eban in New York on October 4, 1973, and received assurances that Egyptian and Syrian military movements were routine. (*Years of Upheaval*, p. 464)

is not based on trust. But there is no way they can do it without breaking solemn international agreements. That the American people understand, and it even gives some standing in the international community.

And we sought to break the coalition of the Europeans and the Arabs. Why did we attack the Europeans at the end of October?[5] First, to show the Arabs they couldn't bring pressure on us by putting pressure on the Europeans, and second, to show the Europeans we didn't want their free advice. Otherwise we would have been pressed to heed them in the name of Atlantic unity. It was essential for what came later. This is why we were so brutal to the Europeans—not that they didn't deserve it on other grounds!

The other reason is that Sadat is by far the most moderate Arab leader. He is an Egyptian nationalist rather than a pan-Arabist, and he probably wants to make peace with the Israelis. Whether he can do it on terms the Israelis can accept, I don't know.

With the Syrians, it is much harder. Then there is the problem of the Palestinians and then Jerusalem.

So each success only gets you to a harder problem.

The strategy is to keep the Arabs in some disunity and to keep the issue out of international forums. This is why we need some Soviet cooperation, and why we set up the Geneva Conference. The Soviets could have wrecked it by providing the propagandistic forum and military muscle for a radical policy.

First, it is essential to get some progress on the Syrian-Israeli front, primarily because if the most radical Arab state bordering Israel has made an agreement, whatever it is, it will change the moral pattern, separate Syria from Iraq, and make it easier for Sadat to take the next step. An Egyptian territorial settlement will take them out of the war.

This is why a Syrian settlement is essential, and some Soviet cooperation is needed.

The American Jewish Community is now quiescent, but in my experience it is volatile. The problem is that they seek to prove their manhood by total acquiescence in whatever Jerusalem wants. The second problem is in Jerusalem. They couldn't in a million years have led the way to the settlement which brought them temporary salvation—given their Parliamentary situation, their Cabinet distrust, etc. At the end, they were grateful. Yet time and again they ran incredible risks, making proposals that were outrageous.

---

[5] A reference to forceful statements made by the Nixon administration against NATO allies after tensions arose between them over U.S. support for Israel during the October war. See *Foreign Relations, 1969–1976*, volume XXXVI, Energy Crisis, 1969–1974, Document 236, footnote 3.

They can't risk a negotiation like this on the issue of 30 versus 50 tanks, at a time when they had 1,000, and it made no difference because even 100 couldn't give the Egyptians the capacity to launch an attack.

Sadat, for his reasons, didn't rise to the bait. He asked me "Could I do better?" I said "Yes, if you want three weeks of haggling and the risk of a blow-up." It worked with Sadat—but it won't with Syria because Asad is a madman. It would be suicide. Basically, the Syrian assessment of Israel's position is better than Sadat's. He first said: "Don't talk to me about disengagement. Sooner or later you'll get tired of them. Then we will kill Israel." Asad wants to kill Israel. Faisal wouldn't object to the destruction of Israel. So Sadat and Hussein are only two forces on which you can build a settlement.

The tactics with Syria should be entirely different than with Egypt. The fact of Syria's signature on a piece of paper makes it possible to get a settlement with Egypt. That is all they should want from Syria.

At the moment, it is hung up on prisoner lists, and we won't do any more if they don't lift the embargo. So I don't need anything from you now, but I may later. It is essential we keep close ties to Egypt because they legitimize the whole thing. I want you to understand.

The second problem is: I predict that if the Israelis don't make some sort of arrangement with Hussein on the West Bank in six months, Arafat will become internationally recognized and the world will be in a chaos. But at the moment in Israel the balance of power is held by the religious party. Hussein wants only a foothold on the West Bank so he can claim he speaks for somebody. But no one has an interest in pushing it, and this will enable Israel to ignore it for six months, maybe a year—at the price that at the end of the year, the terrorists will dominate. If I were an advisor to the Israeli Government, I would tell the Prime Minister: "For God's sake do something with Hussein while he is still one of the players." But it is not an American interest, because we don't care if Israel keeps the West Bank if it can get away with it. So we won't push it.

The third issue is the Soviet Union. What I have done is a tightrope act to break up the coalition of Europeans and Japanese, to keep it out of international forums, and for this we need the cooperation of the Soviet Union. If you look at the record, it is a myth that we sold anything for détente. The wheat deal was the product of election-year politics and bureaucratic bungling.[6] What we do from the White House—like credits—we dole out in driblets. The wheat deal is not the result of

---

[6] A reference to the 1972 U.S.-Soviet grain deal in which the Soviet Union used credits provided by the U.S. Government to purchase nearly a billion dollars worth of grain. With the Soviets buying so much U.S. grain, the price of grain inflated in the United States, leading to criticism concerning the lack of government oversight.

détente. Aside from this, Brezhnev's colleagues can say he was taken to the cleaners. We settled the Vietnam war on substantially our terms—we kept the government there in power and got out with our prisoners and beat on a Soviet ally. And we got a Berlin settlement,[7] and pushed their naval base out of Cuba, and pushed them out of the Middle East.

Winter: Could we have gotten more for the wheat? Not in dollars.

Secretary Kissinger: Yes. We could have gotten more in political benefits. It was bureaucratic bungling. But now we have, for prestige reasons, to get MFN. I was present at [during] Politburo meetings where it was clear that MFN was in return for Vietnam. That was the debate. Now at the end of three years of détente they've got nothing. If they lose credits too, they will take a more intransigent course.

We are more than willing to work it out so Jackson can take the lead in reformulating it. I have a good personal relationship with him, too.

This is one area where a group like this could help us.

Tisch: When did you last speak to Jackson?

Secretary Kissinger: I deliberately speak with him when the environment is right. I have waited until, say, some group comes to us. I know we can settle it amicably and in a way that he gets credit. If he is interested.

Rifkind: Would it be helpful that he be made aware that if he settles it in a compromise, he won't get flak?

Secretary Kissinger: Even more, that his standing in the Jewish Community would be enhanced. I am afraid that if I approach him prematurely, it will be an issue between him and me. Sol, you are more of an expert on Washington.

Linowitz: Jackson sincerely thinks he has succeeded with his amendment and his policy, and he is right.

Secretary Kissinger: The fact that these guys are brutal bastards is irrelevant.

Linowitz: Yes.

Secretary Kissinger: The fact is that these brutal bastards have thousands of megatons and we have to reduce the danger of nuclear war and they have the power to prevent a Middle East settlement. And they have let out 35,000 Soviets Jews last year—even during the war—and we have it in writing that it will continue at this rate. Our policy signifies no moral approbation whatever. Twenty years ago Solzhen-

---

[7] The Berlin settlement was an agreement, signed in September 1971, among France, the United Kingdom, the Soviet Union, and the United States to normalize trade and travel between West Germany and West Berlin. It also aimed to improve communication between East and West Berlin.

itsyn and Sakharov would have been killed.[8] So in their peculiar way it is an amelioration.

Abram: Right.

Secretary Kissinger: Given the nuclear danger, it is essential. Given the vulnerability of Israel, we must keep the Soviets from mobilizing anti-Israel pressures. For this we need MFN.

Up to now I have been able, at great cost in emotional wear and tear, to get the Israelis to go along with saving themselves. When the disengagement with Egypt was done, they agreed it was good for Israel. I don't exclude that when we get to the much more emotionally difficult issue of Syria, it will be more difficult.

As long as I am here, we will not knowingly do anything that injures the possibility of the survival of Israel. We can make an error of judgment. If so, this office is open to those with whom I have always been willing to speak.

It is important, if it happens, that the Israelis don't think they can automatically count on mobilizing support here.

It hasn't happened yet. I thought it would happen over Egyptian disengagement. They, because of domestic reasons, lived dangerously in the negotiations.

Tisch: What is the timing on the oil embargo?

Secretary Kissinger: My position on the oil embargo—which I may not be able to hold—is that if no lifting takes place, we will stop. The Syrians can't do it [go to war] without Egypt, and I don't think Egypt will go to war. They will see if they can get anything. But it will be a rough period.

Tisch: You are on the right course.

Secretary Kissinger: We are not doing it for Israel but for the United States. We will pursue Syrian disengagement regardless. If we can get an Egyptian territorial settlement, then we are out of the Middle East problem.

Ziffren: Then Jerusalem, the West Bank, and Syria.

Secretary Kissinger: Yes, but who will be the spokesman? If the Israelis can get a settlement with Jordan—which will only take giving him Jericho, which is three kilometers from the line—if we get a settlement in Jordan, we won't hear about Jerusalem for three years.

Ziffren: What about Faisal?

Secretary Kissinger: But what can he do?

---

[8] Aleksandr Solzhenitsyn, a Russian novelist and historian, was deported from the Soviet Union on February 13. Andrei Dimitrievich Sakharov was a Russian nuclear physicist and dissident.

Ziffren: You are right.

Secretary Kissinger: The problem is the religious party.

Tisch: Golda is negotiating with the Likud.

Secretary Kissinger: Really? That is a problem. If we hadn't had disengagement, the issue would have gone to the UN ...

Tisch: The problem is personal animosity between Golda, Begin, Tamir.[9]

Secretary Kissinger: Begin is intelligent. I have never dealt with a government in which any change in negotiations has to be a Cabinet decision.

Tisch: Government by committee.

Rifkind: It is a coalition situation.

Secretary Kissinger: But the British, who have a Cabinet system, start with a position and go back to the Cabinet later, just before concluding it.

Abram: What signals do you get from the Israeli Government on MFN?

Tisch: None. I had a discussion with General Yariv. He is happy with disengagement.

Secretary Kissinger: That they like.

Linowitz: They don't think it [MFN] is their issue. But they are somewhat concerned that we are using up credits that might affect their situation.

Secretary Kissinger: With MFN we can moderate Soviet behavior while MFN is being considered.

Tisch: Do you see a possible détente between Israel and the Soviet Union?

Secretary Kissinger: If there is a Syrian disengagement, the Soviets will be driven to that.

List: If you back out of the Syrian negotiations over the embargo, that leaves Israel in a difficult position.

Secretary Kissinger: I haven't stopped yet. But I will. Golda will be glad if they don't have to decide.

Tisch: They are nowhere near forming a government.

Secretary Kissinger: That shows they have no sense of the tragic. As soon as there is a deadlock, the Europeans will pour in there and show that they are better friends of the Arabs. They [the Israelis] don't have all that time. We have kept up the illusion by our momentum.

---

[9] Shmuel Tamir was a founding member of the Free Centre Party, which joined the alliance of right-wing parties that formed Likud prior to the 1973 Israeli elections.

It is impossible for the Europeans to pay for the oil they need by trade, at the current prices. They would have to sell 200,000 Mirages to pay for one year's oil bill—if a Mirage costs three-and-a-half million dollars.

The shortsightedness of the Europeans now is pathological.

We called a conference for next week which is almost unilaterally in Europe's interest and with nothing in it for us except a cooperative international system—and the Europeans are determined to commit suicide. We have so much more to offer them [the Arabs]—not only resources but assistance against Arab radicals. Saudi Arabia and Iran couldn't survive without American good will. And third, only we can get progress in the Arab-Israeli area.

List: When Paul and I met with you, we brought up the idea of counter-measures, what effective means there are throughout the world. Can we move in that direction, through legislative or other means? In view of your view on blackmail, what does this mean?

Secretary Kissinger: We will get it lifted, though it will be a few rough weeks. If the newspapers keep screaming it was deception by the President, the Arabs will get tough. But they don't have the nerve for a prolonged confrontation. If we have a moderate amount of public support . . .

Rifkind: I think we know where we can be helpful.

Secretary Kissinger: Can you let me know if you do something on MFN?

Ziffren: Can we talk about that for a minute?

Secretary Kissinger: I have refrained from doing anything because I don't want to force a confrontation.

Linowitz: Next step should be discussed without the Secretary.

Secretary Kissinger: Yes. I talked with a group headed by Klutznick,[10] who shared the sense of this group.

Linowitz: We should coordinate [with him].

Rifkind: Our job is to make Jackson feel he won't be left out in the cold if he makes an accommodation, or that it will be to his credit.

Secretary Kissinger: And I will do it in a way that it doesn't look like he retreated.

Everything I have said to you I have said to Dinitz. This is not to maneuver around Israel.

---

[10] Philip Klutznik was Chairman of the Governing Council of the World Jewish Congress. The "Klutznik Group" was comprised of a number of prominent American Jewish academics, businessmen, and community leaders. For a list of these men, see "Conversation with Kissinger," *Journal of Palestine Studies*, Vol. 10, No. 3 (Spring, 1981), pp. 194–195. See also Document 189.

Tisch: It is to help Israel.

Secretary Kissinger: That is the intention.

Ziffren: Does Dinitz agree with this?

Secretary Kissinger: He and key members of the Cabinet share this analysis. But even so, they can't generate the moves. It is ironic for Jewish leaders not to know how to maneuver.

So there is no disagreement now. Maybe down the road there will be, when we get to an Egyptian territorial settlement. It will be hard.

Ziffren: What about the Syrian POWs?

Secretary Kissinger: The Syrians made a move which I can't tell you, because only the Prime Minister knows. It puts a floor under Israel's list.[11] I think I can get the lists. The problem now is that the Israeli Cabinet now decided it needs Red Cross visits too. You know, you are dealing with a bunch of maniacs in Syria, who worry about their own position.

I have put a very complicated proposition to Golda, which she says her Cabinet will approve if she can tell them Syria has accepted it.

Ziffren: [Laughs] It sounds like a typical Kissinger proposal.

Secretary Kissinger: It is very complicated.

My prediction is: the way to sell any scheme to the Syrians is to tell them they are getting exactly what the Egyptians got; i.e. something more than the October 6 line. Even if it is three kilometers. Even if they put the UN there. So I could easily dream up a proposal. But in the present composition of the Israeli Cabinet, they won't agree to 100 yards beyond the October 6 line. Even though it makes no conceivable difference.

But it hasn't happened yet because there are no negotiations going on.

The mere fact of the Syrians negotiating with Israel is a change in the Middle East situation.

All I am asking is that the Israelis don't think they can count on automatic support from you everytime some junior Cabinet member there cries we are anti-Semitic.

I think the Israeli Government exaggerates the support they have in this country. It is one thing to vote $2.2 billion;[12] it is another for a Congressman to vote for another war, after Vietnam, and have the energy crisis pinned on Israel.

---

[11] According to Kissinger's memoirs, Kissinger received word on February 7 that the Syrians held 65 Israeli prisoners. (*Years of Upheaval*, p. 940)

[12] In December 1973, Congress approved $2.2 billion in emergency aid for Israel.

[The meeting broke up at 5:40 p.m. with effusive expressions of appreciation for the Secretary.]

---

24. Telegram From the Department of State to the Embassy in Lebanon[1]

Washington, February 11, 1974, 0105Z.

27121. Subj: Response to Message From President Assad to the Secretary. Ref: Damascus 97.[2] Beirut pass Damascus.

1. Scotes should convey the following oral message from the Secretary to President Assad in most expeditious manner.

2. *Begin message:*

The Secretary wants to thank President Assad for the message conveyed to him through Mr. Scotes the evening of February 9. The Secretary is confident that on the basis of President Assad's acceptance of the procedural proposal set forth in his letter of February 5,[3] it will be possible to initiate negotiations looking toward a Syrian-Israeli disengagement agreement. Specifically, he is confident he can elicit a concrete proposal from the Israelis and, as soon as Red Cross visits begin, get them to send a senior official to Washington for intensive discussions with the Secretary. As the Secretary indicated in his February 5 letter to President Assad, as soon as the oil embargo question has been resolved he will initiate with the Israelis the steps outlined in our procedural proposal.

The Secretary understands that discussions are now under way among the Arab leaders concerned on the question of lifting the embargo.[4] He welcomes this development and looks forward to hearing the results in the very near future so that he can get things moving with regard to disengagement on the Syrian front. In this connection, the

---

[1] Source: National Archives, Nixon Presidential Materials, NSC Files, Box 1181, Harold H. Saunders Files, Middle East Peace Negotiations, February 9–15, 1974. Secret; Cherokee; Nodis; Immediate. Repeated Immediate to Cairo and Jidda. Drafted by Atherton; cleared in S/S; and approved by Kissinger.

[2] This reference is incorrect. It should be telegram 57 from Damascus, which transmitted Asad's agreement to Kissinger's procedural formula. See footnote 3, Document 22.

[3] See Document 21.

[4] A reference to a meeting of Arab leaders in Algiers taking place that week to discuss the oil embargo.

Secretary reiterates what he has said before—further steps on our part must await a solution of the embargo question.

The Secretary wants President Assad to know that he is communicating also with President Sadat, King Faisal, and President Boumediene in the above sense.[5] Meanwhile, he wants again, on behalf of President Nixon and on his own behalf, to assure President Assad of our determination and commitment to make a major effort to achieve Syrian-Israeli disengagement as rapidly as possible as a further initial step toward a just and durable peace settlement in the Middle East. *End message.*

Kissinger

---

[5] Documentation on the linkage between lifting the oil embargo and achieving a Syrian-Israeli disengagement agreement is in *Foreign Relations,* 1969–1976, volume XXXVI, Energy Crisis, 1969–1974.

---

25. Memorandum From the President's Deputy Assistant for National Security Affairs (Scowcroft) to President Nixon[1]

Washington, February 27, 1974.

Secretary Kissinger asked that I pass the following report to you:

"I met with President Assad for four hours last night;[2] it was a long, complicated but basically friendly discussion which I think is moving us toward the successful initiation of Israeli-Syrian talks. At the conclusion of the discussion President Assad and I agreed on the following:

"1) The Syrians have authorized me to transmit a list of the total number of Israeli Prisoners of War now held by the Syrians to the Israelis. The list contains 65 names.

"2) Assad has also agreed that Red Cross visits to the Israeli POW's held by Syria can begin on March 1.

---

[1] Source: National Archives, Nixon Presidential Materials, NSC Files, Kissinger Office Files, Box 129, Country Files, Middle East, Middle East, Folder 1. Secret; Sensitive; Exclusively Eyes Only. Sent for information. Nixon wrote "good!" at the end of the memorandum.

[2] The conversation between Asad and Kissinger took place on February 26 from 12:10 to 3:25 a.m. at the Presidency in Damascus. (Memorandum of conversation; ibid., Box 1028, Presidential/HAK Memcons, January 1–February 28, 1974, Folder 1)

"3) The Israelis are expected to give me ideas on March 1 on Syrian disengagement for transmission to Syria. I will personally deliver those ideas to the Syrians in Damascus.

"I will be sending Brent Scowcroft a draft press release covering the three points above which I hope to be able to sell to the Israelis when I arrive in Jerusalem this afternoon. If I am successful with the Israelis, the press release can be issued by Ziegler at 2:30 p.m. today (February 27) Washington time. I will be in direct touch with Brent on this as soon as I have further word from the Israelis."

26. Memorandum From the President's Deputy Assistant for National Security Affairs (Scowcroft) to President Nixon[1]

Washington, February 27, 1974.

Secretary Kissinger asked that I pass the following report to you:

"I have completed a second meeting with Asad.[2] As I indicated to you in my previous report, Asad has agreed to let me hand over the POW list, and to authorize Red Cross visits. But he is taking a very tough position on the overall issue of disengagement. He has told me that if the Israelis come forward with a disengagement scheme that does no more than return the sides to the 1967 lines he will break off the talks. On the basis of past performance I am forced to believe that he means it and will do precisely that. Also on the basis of past performance, I expect it will be extremely difficult to obtain an opening position from the Israelis that will not run afoul of Asad's prescription. Thus, I plan to work for the development and presentation to the Syrians of a proposal that is vague enough in its details to avoid the pitfalls possible on both sides while serving to get negotiations started. I will know more on this after I finish my meetings with the Israelis tonight.

---

[1] Source: National Archives, Nixon Presidential Materials, NSC Files, Kissinger Office Files, Box 129, Country Files, Middle East, Folder 1. Secret; Sensitive; Exclusively Eyes Only. Sent for information. A notation at the top of the page reads, "The President has seen."

[2] The conversation between Asad and Kissinger took place on February 27 from 9:40 a.m. to 12:30 p.m. at the Presidency in Damascus. (Memorandum of conversation; ibid., Box 1028, Presidential/HAK Memcons, January 1–February 28, 1974, Folder 1)

"In my first meeting with PM Meir this afternoon[3] I turned over the POW list. She was grateful, and asked that she be given time to notify the families before we made any public announcement, thus the slight delay in the release time in Washington.[4]

"I will finish my first round of talks with the Israelis this evening and go on to Cairo tomorrow. I will report to you from there."

---

[3] The conversation between Meir and Kissinger took place on February 27 from 4:20 to 5:45 p.m. at the Prime Minister's office in Jerusalem. (Memorandum of conversation; ibid., RG 59, Records of Henry Kissinger, 1973–77, Box 4, Nodis Memcons, January 1974, Folder 4) That conversation was immediately followed by a meeting between Kissinger's negotiating team and the Israeli negotiating team, which lasted from 6 to 7:50 p.m. at the Prime Minister's office in Jerusalem. Kissinger and the Israelis focused on various expectations for the upcoming negotiations with Syria. (Memorandum of conversation; ibid., Nixon Presidential Materials, NSC Files, Box 1028, Presidential/HAK Memcons, January 1–February 28, 1974, Folder 1)

[4] The White House released a statement on February 27, before Meir announced to the Israeli public that she had received the POW list. On March 1, Red Cross inspectors visited the Israeli prisoners of war held by Syria.

---

27. Memorandum From the President's Deputy Assistant for National Security Affairs (Scowcroft) to President Nixon[1]

Washington, February 28, 1974.

Secretary Kissinger asked that I pass the following report to you:

"I met with President Sadat for some four hours today;[2] it was an extremely fruitful session.

"I went over with Sadat the results of my earlier meeting with Assad, and told him I foresaw real problems in getting the Syrians and Israelis to the negotiating table. After hearing me out, Sadat offered to send his Chief-of-Staff, and a senior political advisor to Syria to urge a reasonable posture on Assad. Gamassy has already left, and should have completed his talks with Assad before I get to Damascus tomorrow evening.

---

[1] Source: National Archives, Nixon Presidential Materials, NSC Files, Kissinger Office Files, Box 133, Country Files, Middle East, Egypt, Vol. X, February 1974. Top Secret; Sensitive; Exclusively Eyes Only. Sent for information.

[2] The conversation between Sadat and Kissinger took place on February 28 in President Sadat's rest house near the pyramids of Giza. No time is indicated on the memorandum of conversation. (Memorandum of conversation; ibid.)

"Sadat said he would urge the October 6 line on Assad as a reasonable disengagement line, but doubted that the Syrians would accept it. He promised, however, that if we can get the Israelis to offer a few kilometers beyond the October 6 line, plus the town of Kinetra, he will be prepared to back the U.S. publicly should Syria refuse to accept the offer.

"We talked about your trip here; Sadat says you will receive a tumultuous reception. We also had a lengthy talk on a whole range of fundamental Middle East issues. I will need to talk to you personally on what we went over.

"The announcement of a resumption of diplomatic relations[3] has played well here, and was met with enthusiasm. I plan to attend, accompanied by the Egyptian Foreign Minister, a flag raising ceremony at our Embassy here tomorrow morning. I will leave immediately thereafter for a day of talks with Mrs. Meir in Tel Aviv, and an overnight in Damascus. I shall report to you from there."

---

[3] Egypt and the United States restored full diplomatic relations on February 28, 1974.

---

28. Memorandum of Conversation[1]

Herzliyya, March 1, 1974, 1:15–2 p.m.

PARTICIPANTS

    Mrs. Golda Meir, Prime Minister of Israel
    Yigal Allon, Deputy Prime Minister
    Abba Eban, Minister for Foreign Affairs
    Moshe Dayan, Minister of Defense
    Simcha Dinitz, Ambassador to the United States
    Lt. Gen. David Elazar, Chief of Staff
    Mordechai Gazit, Prime Minister's Office
    Ephraim Evron, Deputy Director General, MFA
    Brig. Gen. David Leor, Military Assistant to the Prime Minister
    Eytan Ben-Zur, Private Secretary to Eban

---

[1] Source: National Archives, RG 59, Records of Henry Kissinger, 1973–77, Box 7, Nodis Memcons, March 1974, Folder 7. Top Secret; Sensitive; Nodis. The meeting was held at the Guest House in Herzliyya near Tel Aviv. Brackets are in the original. Kissinger met with Meir prior to this meeting from noon to 1 p.m. and also after this meeting from 2 to 3:15 p.m. The memoranda of conversation are ibid.

Mr. Mizrachi, Aide to Eban
Colonel Bar-On, Aide to Dayan
Dr. Henry A. Kissinger, Secretary of State
Joseph Sisco, Under Secretary of State for Political Affairs
Kenneth Keating, Ambassador to Israel
Ellsworth Bunker, Ambassador-at-Large
Robert McCloskey, Ambassador-at-Large
Winston Lord, Director, Policy Planning
Alfred L. Atherton, Deputy Assistant Secretary of State, NEA
Harold H. Saunders, NSC Senior Staff
George Vest, Special Assistant to the Secretary for Press Relations
Peter W. Rodman, NSC Staff

Mrs. Meir: Dr. Kissinger.

Dr. Kissinger: Madame Prime Minister. I spent the afternoon with Sadat yesterday[2] and we reviewed the negotiations with the Syrians.

Incidentally, would it be possible to get an English translation of that newspaper account you read to me?

Mrs. Meir: Yes, surely. [Mr. Gazit goes out to get it. See Tab A.][3]

Dr. Kissinger: I will find it very helpful for my meeting this evening. [To Sisco] Apparently Sadat called in the Egyptian press after we met in which he advocated a four-stage process of negotiations, including the 6-point agreement, initial contacts at Kilometer 101, Geneva Conference and Aswan, and that Syria, too, must be prepared to go through them.

So I reviewed the situation with him. I misrepresented your positions somewhat, by saying that the plan you suggested to me included only about half of the new territories, but I said maybe with great effort we could talk about the October 6 line, but I was not authorized to mention that yet. And then I told him I was not at all clear whether the Syrians are playing for a settlement or for a reason to break matters up. Also I told him that what the Syrians wanted from me was something he had never asked for, namely that the Syrian proposal has never changed from my first visit there, which is that I should give them a final line which they would negotiate with me, and only after it was agreed on would they be prepared to discuss any of the other things. Since I was in no position to discuss a final line without a negotiating process that previously had taken place between the Israelis and the Syrians, we were already in a procedural stalemate. To hold me responsible for whatever the initial Israeli position was was nonsense, and I said that if he had the willingness and courage to go into negotiations with you without a prior assurance from me, therefore it wasn't pos-

---

[2] See Document 27.
[3] Tab A has not been found.

sible to do more for the Syrians. And therefore it was a procedural question, not just a substantive problem. They had a right to ask for my assistance, participation, mediation, whatever you want to call it, once some process was going on, but to demand from me to draw a line which they did as a condition for Geneva, which they did again Wednesday morning[4] as a condition for disengagement talks, that was an impossibility.

Sadat took a very positive position. He said he wanted Syrian disengagement primarily because it would prevent, for many of the reasons which independent of him I had given to you Wednesday night: He wanted a Syrian disengagement because it prevented once and for all the Syrian capacity to make mischief in the Arab world; because it would then be possible to pursue constructive policies without the interferences; because it would eliminate a risk of war started by the Syrians into which he would be organically triggered. And he said he would do his best.

I said to him also that it was premature for me to present a concrete Israeli plan in these circumstances in Damascus and maximize the risk of an immediate confrontation. I told him roughly what I had thought of suggesting to you, that I would present concepts in Damascus not tied to any particular line, and say that because of the formation of the government and because of the difficulty of the subject, Israel would send a senior official to Washington within two weeks of forming the government to present a formal proposal, after which Syria would send someone, and then there would be some talks about it.

He agreed with all of this. Then he described his own position as follows: He had no fixed views on where the line should be. He would do his best to present to the other Arab countries the October 6 line as a significant Syrian achievement—if I could get that from Israel. He personally thought that Syria had to get some kilometers beyond the October 6 line. If Israel made such a proposal, then he would be prepared to agree that he would not go to war if Syria rejected it and went to war. He could not make that commitment on the October 6 line. He didn't pursue the subject, and I didn't pursue the subject with him.

He agreed we had to prevent a blowup. He agreed with me that the immediate problem was to keep this negotiating process going and not face an ultimate line. For this purpose, he sent Gamasy to Damascus today to explain. I told him it was my impression in any event, wherever the line was in the new territories, that you were prepared as part of that settlement to permit civilians to return to the territories. And he said he was sending Gamasy to stress some of their experiences

---

[4] February 27. See Document 26.

in the negotiations, first of all. And he is doing it in the capacity of Chief of Staff of the Joint Command—and you remember he stressed that when he was on television with me. Secondly, he would also send letters to Faisal, to Kuwait and other Arabs, all of whom received letters from Assad that I had brought nothing—saying that the process was well-launched and the Syrians would be unwise to break it up. And he has sent an emissary to these countries. He is sending a Foreign Office emissary to Assad this afternoon. He is prepared either for concurrent talks in Washington or also in the Egyptian military commission with Syrian officers in Geneva. He said he would offer it immediately to the Syrians so they would be in the wrong if they turn down either venue. And that is essentially the substance of my talk with him on the Syrian disengagement.

I gained the impression that he is sincere about what he is saying. He certainly put himself, on TV when I was there, very much on record by saying—someone asked him: would you recommend patience to the Syrians? And he said: Yes, to be patient. They asked him: Is progress being made? And he said: Yes, as much progress as could be expected is being made.

So if the Syrians blow it up tonight—which I don't exclude—they will certainly do it in opposition to his public statement, and to the emissaries he is sending around.

Mr. Eban: How would they blow it up—by refusing to have a further procedural stage?

Dr. Kissinger: Well, Assad has said to me—and that is basically a position he has never deviated from in any of my meetings—that if I bring a position that is confined to the new territories, he will not talk further. I won't bring him such a position; I won't bring him any position that is tied to any line, so he can't blow it up on that ground. I will draw from the presentation that the Minister of Defense and the Chief of Staff made, concepts that can be applied in any place.

Mr. Eban: And procedural proposals.

Dr. Kissinger: Yes. But you see, your questions are more rational than the discussion is going to be. Since the only procedure he has ever been willing to discuss with me is a procedure that follows an agreement, not a procedure to get an agreement, since he believes that he is paying a heavy price to talk to Israel at all in any form. He feels that he must have an assurance of something worthwhile before he talks. This was essentially his position on the Geneva talks. And when all is said and done, when all the verbiage is stripped away from what he said to me on Wednesday, that is what he was saying to me on Wednesday.

The reason he and I always talk for four hours is because we always talk past each other. I talk procedure and he is perfectly rational about the procedure, and I keep forgetting that he never budged from what he said three months ago. So if I don't immediately ask him: now when does this procedure start?, we are in a never-never land in which we have a perfectly rational discussion about procedure but in his mind it starts afterward, after the agreement, and in our mind of course it is a way of getting an agreement. And basically we have never really broken the logjam. I thought on Tuesday night when I saw him for four hours[5] that we were operating from the premise that there would be a negotiation parallel to the Egyptian-Israeli style, and it wasn't until Wednesday morning that I understood this wasn't so. Therefore the public statement of Sadat yesterday really puts him squarely on your side, and ours, that the procedure had to precede the negotiations.

Mrs. Meir: [to Mr. Dayan] You see, in the four stages Sadat spoke of, there was the 6-point agreement, the Kilometer 101, Geneva, then it was Aswan. So he took us through the four stages.

Dr. Kissinger: Now you see why we all treasure Joe Sisco so much. He just turned to me and said: You are going to have a tough time tonight! Now, I won't go, you go. [laughter].

So Sadat is backing our procedure one hundred per cent. He is backing it moreover with Faisal, and wherever else he is sending his emissaries. And he is putting himself on record with the Syrians, and for that matter he is also putting himself on public record that what I have achieved this week is satisfactory.

Secondly, he showed me a map that the Syrians have given him of their minimum line, which I will not share with you, for your emotional stability. You know it anyway.

Mr. Dinitz: Is it the same map?

Dr. Kissinger: Yes, the same map I brought [on January 20].[6] What is interesting to me is he doesn't know it. And he asked his generals, and General Ismail, the War Minister, to come and show us what they knew, and they had the two Syrian lines, and he agreed that that was out of the question, that he would not support that.

But, we have two problems now. The first is the procedure, the second is substantive. I frankly don't want a substantive position right now. It is not to anybody's advantage to have to take a substantive position. I want to maintain a position that I don't have a substantive position. I want to go to Damascus and discuss procedures, concepts, like thinning out, return of civilians, . . .

Mr. Dayan: And release of prisoners.

---

[5] Presumably the meeting in the early morning hours of February 27. See Document 25.

[6] The map has not been found. Presumably Asad gave it to Kissinger on January 20. See footnote 5, Document 19.

Dr. Kissinger: Yes, release of prisoners.

[Mr. Allon arrives and joins the group].

I've never seen Yigal and the Defense Minister both wearing neckties.

Mrs. Meir: You see the American influence, as our opposition says.

Dr. Kissinger: They say Israel is a satellite of the United States. [laughter]

So tonight I will keep it confused on substance and precise on procedure, with an Israeli commitment that a senior official will come to Washington in two weeks, and let's play it from there.

Mr. Dayan: From what you know—and perhaps Sadat said something about Assad's position in Damascus—is it something like Sadat in Egypt, that is to say, that he is the only one that can make decisions and concessions or changes in something, or perhaps he doesn't hold the same position that Sadat enjoys in Egypt?

Dr. Kissinger: Well, I have the impression . . . How these two ever got together is now beyond my understanding, how these Arabs ever agreed on the same time, I mean. Forgetting now about Sadat and Assad—Fahmi and Saqqaf, the two who were in Washington. Never do I see Fahmi that he doesn't warn me against Saqqaf. Sadat has said to me previously that he has two problems—actually, three slightly contradictory problems: In Damascus everyone is bought by someone in the Baath Central Committee: some belong to the Iraqis, some to the Soviets, some belong to local groups, but everyone is bought by someone, according to him. So it is a precarious situation. Secondly, especially today, he spoke extremely ill of Assad personally. He said, "You have to remember, these are traders, merchants." He spoke much more ill of the Syrians than of Israel yesterday. And thirdly, he says that still Assad is the best one to deal with. He said that again yesterday. He is making an effort now to bring Assad to his knees, and that is why he wants to present the October 6 line as reasonable although not enough—I mean reasonable enough to get talks started but not sufficient.

But I am not going to give them a line. So that is an assessment. That is why he is saying it. He of course would also like Assad to be split off from Boumedienne. But he feels that at this stage the Syrians are totally unreasonable. He spoke worse of the Syrians than of you.

And I have said to him—since I take the position that you haven't agreed to the October 6 line—I of course had to take the position that no line beyond the October 6 line had ever entered our conversation, and that I was certain of one thing—that no Israeli settlement would ever be given up as part of the agreement. You know that puts an automatic limit. He said he agreed with that.

This is the full extent of what I know of Sadat in terms of a final settlement with Israel. He never raised it at all. And I felt I'd better not have the record show that I was in the Middle East talking to him and—so after we had been on TV, where he had already said the time was not appropriate to discuss it, I took him aside and said, "I just want you to know, Mr. President, I am prepared to discuss it, now or at some other time, and I don't want you to think that I avoid the subject." But the cars were already lined up, and he said: "I don't want to talk about it now, this is not the right time to discuss it, it requires careful thought." So we never discussed anything about the ultimate settlement at all.

[General Elazar arrives]

Mr. Eban: Have you changed your views about what the effect would be if we were not to get a settlement?

Dr. Kissinger: I have the impression that he believes that if you get no settlement because of the refusal to give up any of the old territory that he would probably be forced into a war even if he thinks the Syrians are unreasonable. That is what I derived from it. My conclusions are essentially the ones of the other night: in fact they are reinforced. I had no sense before yesterday of how much there was any limit beyond which he could fail to support Syria. At least we have some sense now of that. He has given me flat assurance that beyond a certain point he would not go to war if Syria went to war.

That, for God's sake, must remain absolutely confidential.

Again, I committed nothing to anybody. And he agrees; moreover he said tactically it would be a mistake to offer them now any line, even if it were beyond the October 6 line, because they'd just pocket it and ask for more. So on the immediate procedure, he is in total agreement with us. In fact, in my presence he specifically instructed Gamasy not to raise any line in Damascus and not to discuss any line. Our Ambassador, who understands Arabic, said that while he was instructing Gamasy he was giving a summary of what in fact I said here.

Madame Prime Minister, I am in for one hell of an evening, because the last thing he wants is to discuss the procedure. He thinks it is irrelevant.

My basic objective has to be to get out of Damascus without this thing being blown up. His basic objective may be quite the opposite—to show that he did everything that his brothers asked and that he was deceived and got nothing for it. His basic analysis—which is correct—is that the basic fact of talking to Israel in any shape creates an illusion of some kind of compromise which is in itself a liability for him, and unless he knows what is the outcome he has paid too high a price just for the talks.

My own judgment is that he would not accept a line even across the October 6 line which did not at least go half way or some distance towards what he calls his minimum line. I am just giving you my assessment. I have never heard him say anything that would indicate that he would be content with 3 to 5 kilometers. He certainly wouldn't accept if I offered it to him without any process.

So that is not our issue today at all. Our issue today is whether I can give him enough substance drawn from what the Defense Minister said the other day, as amended by the Chief of Staff, in which I will be very flexible about deployment patterns as long as they are reciprocal.

Mr. Eban: There was a statement from Damascus that you gave assurances of the final line.

Mrs. Meir: In the Cabinet someone asked me would I today ask you whether this statement that came out was made by you. I said I wouldn't even ask it; it's just inconceivable. But the statement that came out said that Dr. Kissinger promised Assad that he would get us off the Golan Heights.

Dr. Kissinger: I think the answer you should give is the one I have always given, which is that in Egypt I told the Egyptians I would discuss nothing but disengagement, and since I have promised Syria to do exactly for them what I did for Egypt, I am discussing only disengagement and no final lines. As it turns out, I have never expressed any view about the final line. He has, of course, expressed vehement views on the final line; I didn't. I am taking rigidly the line I took with the Egyptians, with whom I have never had a substantive talk of even the most superficial kind about a final solution. That didn't even come up. He expressed himself vehemently. I didn't even reply in a noncommittal way; I didn't reply at all, but just treated it as a non-subject. Moreover, Sadat showed me the message Assad sent him, which was that Kissinger brought nothing. That would certainly not be nothing. So you can flatly deny and I will flatly deny; it is inconsistent with my whole concept of how these disengagement talks should be handled. But do it not on the ground of what the position on the ground is but that it is not part of the disengagement talks.

Mrs. Meir: I understand that concretely, if he agrees, it boils down to this: that in about two weeks after we have a government, we will send someone to Washington and discuss things with you. Subsequently the Syrians will send someone to you.

Dr. Kissinger: I can't stop them from having someone there concurrently if they wish, so that within a day of hearing your idea I can give it to them. But ideally I'd like to stage it so that your representative comes and then I will summon the Syrian representative. Only if those two get within range of each other do we start the negotiations.

Mr. Dinitz: How are we supposed to proceed now with the Mizrachi affair,[7] through the committee in the area?

Dr. Kissinger: Sadat gave orders in my presence to release Mizrachi immediately, so I did not ask for the time. But I have the impression that it would be today or at the latest tomorrow. And I told him you would release all of the 73 that you could still find except the Russian.[8]

Mr. Allon: Was it difficult to persuade him to leave the Russian with us?

Dr. Kissinger: [laughs] Since he created such happy auspices for Gromyko's visit[9] by staging a flag raising ceremony at the American Embassy this morning.

Mr. Allon: Did you raise with him the possibility of keeping this joint tent or staff together even after the disengagement is implemented?

Dr. Kissinger: I mentioned it but he laughed. He didn't say yes or no. We didn't discuss it.

Mr. Dayan: About Syria, if the question of return of civilians comes up, there is a point about it: If this is done within the general agreement, then of course the area will be handed over to the UN. But if for some reason they say, "All right, let's start with the return of the civilians," so it is still under our positions there, which I am almost sure the Syrians wouldn't accept—he wouldn't want their civilians to go and be under Israeli occupation. So, on the one hand at least I am for starting with something—of course with the idea that our prisoners of war will be handed back—but besides that, on the other hand, I would have liked to see some movement, let's say the beginning of return of civilians, and anyway, why keep them in refugee camps? On the other hand, I realize that there is a problem because if we are there they won't like it. And I am sure we won't feel like withdrawing some of our positions unless it will be reached within a general agreement. So that is another problem that I just wanted to mention.

Dr. Kissinger: If we could ever get them into a negotiation on the return of the civilians separated from the final line, we'd already be in good shape.

Mrs. Meir: When I read the statement by Sadat,[10] I saw hope in it. Because he really went out of his way.

---

[7] See footnote 8, Document 4.

[8] The Russian POW is not further identified.

[9] Gromyko visited Damascus and Cairo February 28–March 1.

[10] Apparent reference to a statement made by Sadat at the flag-raising ceremony in Cairo to mark the reopening of the U.S. Embassy. Sadat mentioned the four stages of the Israeli-Egyptian disengagement and said it should be a model for Syrian-Israeli disen-

Dr. Kissinger: He is trying to keep the procedure going.

Mrs. Meir: He went out of his way to say: "Look, we didn't get it in one step; we went through various steps before we reached this stage where we are." And I thought maybe this would have some influence on Assad if he wants something.

Dr. Kissinger: Madame Prime Minister, you are absolutely right. Sadat's strategy is to isolate Assad. I mean after all, he could have made my position hellish by just saying, "This is between Syria and Israel and we wish you well, but we won't get involved in the nuances of this." It would have made it hell. Instead, his joint appearance with me—and what I didn't know until I got here, his separate statement afterwards—is in effect putting the onus on the Syrians if it breaks up at this point. And he is also sending a message to Faisal, Kuwait and others. Moreover, his demands, which may be politically unbearable here, are not wild, and he is willing to back them up with some very specific assurance, all of which I think will be a constructive attitude. But that is the last problem we have to face now, even though it is a problem.

He, himself, says no discussion should go beyond the October 6 line right now. And I wouldn't even go that far. I think it would be a grave mistake for me to take the risk that Assad didn't mean what he said the other day—since every time we found him to mean what he says. Therefore I can't run the risk. It is definitely in his interest to blow this thing up while I am out here, if he is going to blow it up at all. For the very reason that I want it to blow up, if it does, at the subordinate level, he wants to blow it up on a high level.

Mr. Eban: Is there any information on the prisoners we think are alive?

Dr. Kissinger: No, he has no information.

Mr. Eban: Do you have any impression of what the Soviets and Syrians might have talked about?

Dr. Kissinger: We have no information whatsoever and the Egyptians have been given no information whatsoever, nor have the Egyptians asked Assad what the Soviets are saying to him.

Incidentally, he says they replenished not one airplane of his since the war.

Mrs. Meir: Really?

Dr. Kissinger: Sadat says they have given some tanks but no airplanes. But you will know that better than I do.

---

gagement. (Summarized in the memorandum of conversation between Meir and Kissinger, March 1, noon–1 p.m. National Archives, RG 59, Records of Henry Kissinger, 1973–77, Box 7, Nodis Memcons, March 1974, folder 7) See also the *New York Times*, March 1, 1974, p. 1.

Mrs. Meir: We will see what we have on that.

Dr. Kissinger: He claims they have not replenished planes. He says they got tanks.

Mrs. Meir: And missiles?

Dr. Kissinger: I didn't go into the details. He said they got about two-thirds of the tanks replaced, but with better tanks, so he is not complaining about the tanks.

Mr. Allon: Did he mention the Scuds?

Dr. Kissinger: No, not at this meeting. At a previous meeting he did, but he said he wants to assure me that every missile on Egyptian territory is operated by Egyptians.

Mr. Eban: His air losses were less heavy than his tank losses though.

Mr. Keating: But the Israeli papers said he has been supplied.

Mr. Dayan: The Egyptians owe a lot of money to the Russians. Do they pester them to pay it back? And could it be due to their financial difficulties?

Dr. Kissinger: When I was there, McNamara from the World Bank was also in Egypt. He gave me a breakdown of their financial situation, which you probably have too. He hasn't mentioned that to me. But his behavior to the Soviets is provocative beyond a point that is conceivable according to that double-track theory we heard the other day. He is putting himself in a position where it will be very difficult for him to cross tracks simultaneously. Switching back to the Soviets would require him to pay a very heavy price politically, and vice-versa. I think his behavior to the Soviets has been really gratuitous. They showed me the schedule they have for Gromyko. It was really very minimum, very little protocol.

Mr. Sisco: I don't see how he could go back to the Russian alternative and stay top man in the country. You would really have to think in terms of an alternative for Sadat with that kind of reversal.

Dr. Kissinger: He is imploring us to let him know what we are telling the Soviets so he doesn't get embarrassed. It is either a game of unbelievable deviousness, which I don't see the benefit in, or he must be paying the price. I don't know what the Russians have done for him.

I have no idea what I will face tonight in Damascus. I think there is a fifty-fifty chance that I will face there what I faced before. There is nothing you can do to change it, so I am not even asking.

It could well be that the Syrian domestic situation is such that the only final line they can accept is the line they gave you, and in their mind it is already such a huge concession. In that case we will have this negotiation blow up no matter what line you will talk about.

Mrs. Meir: Shall we go to lunch?

---

29. Memorandum of Conversation[1]

Damascus, March 1, 1974, 7:30–11:30 p.m.

PARTICIPANTS

    Hafiz al-Asad, President of Syria
    Asad Elias, Press Secretary

    Henry A. Kissinger, Secretary of State
    Isa Sabbagh, Interpreter
    Alfred L. Atherton, Jr., Department of State (NEA)

Secretary Kissinger: (After introducing Mr. Atherton) Working for me requires a special kind of masochism. Anyone who stays with me for six months becomes devoted.

President Asad: Why six months?

Secretary Kissinger: It takes that long. He has to work 18 hours a day. They tell a story about me that when I was at the White House I had one of my staff prepare a draft which I sent back 12 times to be rewritten. After the twelfth draft, I asked him if this was the best he could do. When he said yes, I said "then I will now read it."

President Asad: You say they tell this story. Is it not true?

Secretary Kissinger: Almost. When I give a speech, it goes through 12 or 14 drafts.

President Asad: I find that natural.

Secretary Kissinger: You are a great speaker Mr. President.

President Asad: When I deliver a written speech, it also requires great effort and much paper is torn.

Secretary Kissinger: I do the same.

President Asad: Speaking extemporaneously is easier.

Secretary Kissinger: It is too dangerous for me to give extemporaneous speeches. My press conferences are extemporaneous, however.

---

[1] Source: National Archives, RG 59, Records of Henry Kissinger, 1973–77, Box 4, Nodis Memcons, January 1974, Folder 4. Secret; Sensitive; Nodis. The meeting was held at the Presidency in Damascus. Brackets are in the original.

President Asad: Ninety-five percent of my press conferences are extemporaneous. But extemporaneous speeches cause problems for persons in positions of responsibility. It is easy to make mistakes.

Secretary Kissinger: Sometimes what one says in the context of a crowd sounds alright but is terrible when you read it afterwards.

You know the President speaks English perfectly. He is taking advantage of the interpreter to have time to think.

President Asad: If my time permitted, I would like six months to study English. That would give me the same confidence as Secretary Kissinger has in his associates.

Secretary Kissinger: In six months we won't be talking any more of disengagement. We will be in the second phase. That is my certainty.

Asad Elias: I recall a book by Harry Hopkins[2] about Franklin Roosevelt, who also required many drafts of his speeches.

Secretary Kissinger: He was a great President, but I am not sure he understood foreign policy.

President Asad: Policies change with circumstances.

Secretary Kissinger: I agree. Great leaders in some circumstances are not great in others. Roosevelt was a great leader in wartime, but he did not understand how to build the world after the war. He did not understand that the location of military forces importantly determines the political outcome. (Asad laughs.) I do not think President Asad needs a lesson on this point. Roosevelt made a mistake in putting our military forces into Southern France instead of the Balkans.

President Asad: Why was that?

Secretary Kissinger: He saw this as purely a military problem. He was looking at how to beat Germany. But in the end the problem was not to beat Germany but to acquire strategic position. Don't repeat this to Gromyko, but the problem was to achieve a position vis-à-vis the Soviet Union. For that purpose, an invasion of the Balkans would have done more good than putting forces into Southern France.

President Asad: Do you mean to suggest that you are taking this aspect into consideration in the Middle East?

Secretary Kissinger: No. In the Middle East we recognize that the Soviets have vital interests. We are not conducting an anti-Soviet policy. We are ready to cooperate for peace. We don't want Middle Eastern states to be clients of the United States or the USSR. We want them to follow independent policies. I have formed the opinion of President Asad that he is not good material for a client.

---

[2] Harry Hopkins, a close adviser to President Franklin Roosevelt during his entire presidency.

President Asad: That is right. I will be frank; we want to be friendly with all others, and we want them to respect us. We base our policy on what is good for us.

Secretary Kissinger: That is all we ask. The best nations to cooperate with are those that have self-respect.

President Asad: That is true. A leader who is not good for his own country is not good for any other.

Secretary Kissinger: A leader who is the client of one country will be the client of others.

President Asad: This is our firm policy.

Secretary Kissinger: I must tell you the truth. Until I started dealing with Syria, I considered it a satellite of the Soviet Union.

President Asad: Why?

Secretary Kissinger: During the war, we went to the Soviets when we wanted something from the Arabs. Since Arab military equipment came from the Soviets, we thought you would do what the Soviets said. Now that I know President Asad, I think he is not easy for the Soviets to deal with. I am convinced you go your own way. That is all we ask. Therefore, we have no difficulties in our bilateral relations.

President Asad: I agree.

Secretary Kissinger: You know we want to improve relations. We don't want to add to Syria's difficulties, but we are prepared to increase our representation in Damascus and to send more senior people.

President Asad: We also desire to expedite the improvement in our relations. There are no bilateral difficulties. Your visits have helped. The first visit was a bit strange, the second less so, and the third time seems natural.[3] Some people are talking to us about it. We talk right back to them.

There are no problems between us except the occupation of our land. When people discuss U.S.-Syrian relations, they always come to this. Without American help, our land would not be occupied today. This is a fact. There are those who say things must move slowly, that things must first move in the United States.

But these difficulties will gradually disappear. As a first step, send more senior people if you wish.

Secretary Kissinger: With Egypt, at the start of disengagement talks, we sent an Ambassador even without formal relations. In other words, in November we raised our Interests Section to Ambassadorial-rank.

President Asad: At the start you had an Interests Section?

---

[3] Asad previously met with Kissinger on December 15, 1973, and January 20, 1974.

Secretary Kissinger: We had a junior officer there.

President Asad: Here in Damascus you had no one. At the present stage, send a higher ranking person if you wish. We have sent a Minister to Washington.

Secretary Kissinger: We have sent you a good man.[4] Unless we want to do so for symbolic reasons, there is no need to send a more senior person now.

President Asad: I have no objections to the man you have here now. He is doing his work well. Rank is not always the most important thing. All I meant to say was that if you wished to send a man of higher rank, it is alright. Mr. Scotes has the added distinction of knowing Arabic.

Secretary Kissinger: The choice is between doing something symbolic and just looking for the best person.

President Asad: At this stage the proper person is the one who can work to improve relations. If you send a new man of higher rank who is less attentive to our relations, that would not be good.

Secretary Kissinger: In the United States, Syria has the image of being an unfriendly country. It is a problem for us to take Syria's side. At some point we need to do something which the American people will see as symbolically more friendly. We do not have to do it on this trip. We can do it on the next trip.

President Asad: When the disengagement agreement is signed, we could raise the level of our representatives and relate it to the signing. Later we could do what you did in Egypt.

We have good relations with President Boumediene.

Secretary Kissinger: He is a great admirer of yours.

President Asad: We have discussed the resumption of relations. He sent me word of his desire to do so.

Secretary Kissinger: President Boumediene is a fine man. I write to him often. It is not that Algeria is so important to the United States but Boumediene is a great person.

President Asad: He was looking forward to seeing you, but his trip to China interfered.

Secretary Kissinger: I know China and admire Chou En-Lai very much. Don't tell that to Gromyko when he comes back on the 5th. I don't think he likes Chou.

---

[4] A reference to Thomas J. Scotes who served as the Principal Officer of the U.S. Interests Section, which was established in the Italian Embassy on February 8, 1974. The Embassy in Damascus was re-established on June 16, and Scotes became the Chargé d'Affaires ad interim until the appointment of Ambassador Richard W. Murphy on August 9.

President Asad: If you gave Gromyko a choice of Chou En-Lai or Henry Kissinger, whom would he choose?

Secretary Kissinger: He would choose me. But I have a great regard for Gromyko.

President Asad: As you requested, I gave Gromyko your regards. You charged me with this trust and I carried it out.

Secretary Kissinger: What did Gromyko have to say?

President Asad: We reviewed the Middle East situation and how we see disengagement. We gave our views on what is happening. I told him exactly what we had agreed with respect to the POW list and Red Cross visits, that you were returning to Damascus and that we had agreed on nothing during your last visit. Gromyko asked how I viewed disengagement. I said I see it as a step toward full Israeli withdrawal and that this had been made clear to Secretary Kissinger from the start.

Secretary Kissinger: I have always understood that disengagement is not the last step. It is not a peace settlement.

President Asad: We also discussed bilateral matters, including economic matters. When Gromyko returns, he will discuss these matters with the Ministries.

Secretary Kissinger: Gromyko is always well-prepared.

President Asad: I saw him the day after he arrived, at 11:00 in the morning. He left this morning.

Secretary Kissinger: With regard to a peace settlement, the United States is not competing with the Soviets. We are ready to cooperate. You are free to say to Gromyko that our only concern is how to bring this about most effectively. Syrian policy will not be affected by who makes peace but by what is in Syria's interest.

President Asad: That is true. We will do all possible for peace.

Secretary Kissinger: If the President is willing, perhaps we can discuss disengagement.

President Asad: I have received a message from Fahmy which gives me some idea.

Secretary Kissinger: I have not seen it.

President Asad: It came from President Sadat. You know about it.

Secretary Kissinger: I have not seen the message.

President Asad has good insights. He said to me before that we should give the Arabs U.S. arms to defeat U.S. arms in Israel since we can't let U.S. arms be defeated by Soviet arms. I want the President to know that I do not forget his words.

It is not impossible that our relations will change fundamentally, so this would no longer sound like such a revolutionary idea. There is no reason for the United States and Syria to be enemies.

President Asad: Absolutely.

Secretary Kissinger: You can count on this. Besides, you are such a tenacious negotiator that our nerves could not stand having you as an opponent all the time.

President Asad: When will we reach the point where Zionism does not spoil our relationship?

Secretary Kissinger: When there is peace. I do not want U.S. relations disturbed for reasons that are not American reasons.

President Asad: The Arabs only seek justice. I believe that is what all people seek.

Secretary Kissinger: That is correct. But sometimes there are different concepts of justice.

President Asad: Perhaps—but justice is generally clear, especially when it touches on land and tangible things. I believe where large causes are involved, the path of justice is clear. In the Middle East, for example, does not he who seeks to recover usurped land have right on his side? I cannot imagine any objective person disagreeing or asking that we give up territory.

Secretary Kissinger: I understand the Arab viewpoint.

President Asad: It is not reasonable that this problem not be solved. If the problem of the Palestinian people is not solved, there will be no peace. Any Arab who says otherwise is doing us an injustice. It is not possible for any Arab leader to make peace without solving the Palestinian problem. Even if some leader would agree, he could not do so. If Sadat, Hussein and I agree to solve the Palestine problem without solving the problem of the Palestinians, we could not make it stick.

Secretary Kissinger: The question is how to define a solution.

President Asad: At the next stage you need better contacts with the Palestinians.

Secretary Kissinger: You know we have had some contact with the Arafat group. As I said before, we will not play the game of dividing the Arabs. We let every Arab leader know what we do with other Arab leaders. We tell each one the same thing.

President Asad: That is good.

Secretary Kissinger: In the second phase we will increase our contacts with the Palestinians. Can you advise which Palestinians we should deal with?

President Asad: At present, you have contacts with Fatah. That will not be adequate after awhile, though it is perhaps alright at this stage.

Secretary Kissinger: In the next stage we will consult with you, but we must keep this confidential.

President Asad: Our relations with Fatah are quite strong. We established them before others did.

Secretary Kissinger: Which group is trying to shoot down my airplane?

President Asad: In Syria?

Secretary Kissinger: In Beirut. I don't want to deal with them. I don't know who they are.

President Asad: The Palestinian movement is based on Fatah and Saiqa.[5] Saiqa is also strong militarily. Perhaps others are more interested in formulations. As concerns training, Saiqa is the best. The relations between Saiqa and Fatah are good. They decide jointly on Palestinian policy.

Secretary Kissinger: It is our impression that Syria controls Saiqa.

President Asad: We are in the same party and have good relations. But Fatah grew up here. We certainly help them. In times of crises, we defend them.

In his 1972 State of the Union Message, President Nixon referred to the 1970 Jordanian crisis as the most dangerous to world peace.

Secretary Kissinger: I remember, we were not on your side then.

President Asad: I ordered the intervention and was there.

Secretary Kissinger: Our concern was not Fatah but Jordan and our conception of Soviet influence.

President Asad: The Soviets had no hand in our intervention.

Secretary Kissinger: I believe that now.

President Asad: They learned about it from the radio.

Secretary Kissinger: How is that possible when the Soviets had advisors in your military units?

President Asad: It was not the business of the Soviets. After we went into Jordan, everyone knew about it.

Secretary Kissinger: The Soviet advisors could have informed their headquarters.

President Asad: They didn't know about it until we reached the border.

Secretary Kissinger: We misinterpreted Syria, but we were concerned about the Soviets and confrontation. That was our concern, not Syria. We also feared that the Israelis would attack.

President Asad: The French wanted Syria to pull out of Jordan.

---

[5] Al-Saiqa was a Palestinian Baathist political and military organization created by the Syrian Baath Party in 1966.

Secretary Kissinger: Did you do so because of what the French wanted?

President Asad: No, we did so when the Arab Committee arrived.

Secretary Kissinger: We did not understand Syria at that time.

Shall we now talk about disengagement? I do not want to press you.

President Asad: Yes.

Secretary Kissinger: I don't know what Sadat has said to you.

President Asad: He sent disturbing news. I saw General Gamasy.

Secretary Kissinger: I knew about Gamasy's coming to Damascus.

President Asad: Sadat's letter was full of verbiage, telling things we both know. There was no justification for indulging in all of this. But the important thing is Sadat's conversation with you. According to Sadat, you said it would be possible to guarantee the October 6 lines and then it might develop that it would be possible for us to get back Quneitra. Sadat said time would be needed and described the stages and time required for the Egyptian agreement but disengagement on the Syrian front need not take so much time.

Secretary Kissinger: I agree.

President Asad: But Sadat said time was needed.

Secretary Kissinger: I did not know Sadat was writing to you.

President Asad: Sadat said you promised to continue your efforts.

Secretary Kissinger: True.

President Asad: Gamasy described the history of the Egyptian disengagement. I explained that the Syrian situation was different—for example, with regard to POW's, Suez, etc.

Secretary Kissinger: In essence what you have described is correct. The phrase "guaranteeing the October 6 lines" is an overstatement, but it is not worth arguing about.

The problem is that Syria sees Israel as monolithic and purposeful. I see it as divided, especially while it is forming a new Government. After its Government is formed, it can reach decisions more easily.

I took seriously what you said about not submitting an Israeli plan to you which would be dead from the start. I spent six hours with the Israelis today and ten hours on Wednesday,[6] meeting them in small groups. I want to be honest and not mislead you. They have not yet agreed to the October 6 lines. What I said to Sadat was that if President Asad wants to settle quickly and I use pressure, we can perhaps convince Israel to accept the October 6 line in a few weeks. The Israelis

---

[6] See Document 28 and footnote 3, Document 26.

have some ideas about the location of forces that are not so different from what you said to me in December.[7] For example, Israel agrees to accept any limitations which Syria accepts on the Golan Heights. If there is a zone of light forces on the Syrian side, there would be the same on the Israeli side. This can include the greatest part of the Golan Heights. I recall how you explained this, and then you sent a telegram with further clarifications. This idea is accepted as an idea. The details will need to be discussed but that is not worthwhile until there is an agreed concept.

President Asad: The limitations will be linked to the disengagement line.

Secretary Kissinger: Yes, the Israelis accept this.

Next, I want to stress the following: your idea that there must first be an agreement before you negotiate would make me Syria's negotiator with the Israelis. I am flattered by this, since I am told that Syrians are good negotiators. But this is not the best way to help you. Eventually there must be an Israeli-U.S. confrontation. Their views and ours are probably not the same. It is best for everyone to defer this confrontation to the second stage and not to exhaust the American domestic structure in the first phase, by seeking to move Israel through the use of great pressure in this phase. Sapir told me today that the American decision on financial assistance is taking a long time.

President Asad: Sadat told me this.

Secretary Kissinger: This is not visible, however. I must proceed according to our methods. To do that I need a Syrian-Israeli negotiating process.

I have an Israeli assurance, which I can make public, that within two weeks, after an Israeli Government is formed, they will send a senior official to Washington to work on this problem. You might also send someone with whom I could work—not for meetings with the Israelis. After some weeks I could return here and conclude the agreement. The details could then be worked out in the military working group. But there is no need for you to now announce a decision on the negotiating forum, which I understand is one of your concerns.

President Asad: I have full confidence in you. The question is the objective we may be able to reach by these means and whether the repercussions of that objective will be positive or negative. I am increasingly convinced that the Israelis do not want to reach this objective, and popular and military sentiments in Israel seem to support my view. The latest Israeli statements indicate that what Mrs. Meir has said about Golan is not just for domestic consumption.

---

[7] See footnote 3, Document 19.

Secretary Kissinger: Those statements may reflect some Israeli intentions, but the idea of dealing with Syria is so unusual for the Israelis that it will take them awhile to get used to it.

President Asad: In Syria, it has not been our habit in the past to talk about peace. Now we are clear; we want a just peace. I said this during the war. Efforts will be required to achieve peace.

It still remains for us to imagine where these steps will lead. I know you do not represent Israel, but it is a fact that without the United States there would be no Israel. Given this fact, Israel cannot remain adamant. If we accepted the October 6 line, what do you imagine would be the view of the Syrian Army and people?

Secretary Kissinger: I am not asking you to accept that line. I recognize the disengagement line must be across the October 6 line.

President Asad: I would like your views. I have the strong conviction that what you are convinced of is achievable. Do you have an idea about the line? What is feasible? It is not that I am against disengagement, but I am against its having nothing good in it. It could even be harmful.

Secretary Kissinger: How could it be harmful?

President Asad: If it has no meaning. For example, there is the Israeli pocket.[8] The people and the army know what the war cost and they know that war is a back-and-forth affair. Our people think Syria was victorious despite the pocket. There is hardly a home in Syria without a son in the army. The people know that the ceasefire prevented our retaking the pocket. We assumed there would be another fighting front.

I believe Egypt should have continued fighting. Sadat sent me a pessimistic telegram during the war when the Israeli penetration occurred on the Egyptian front. I sent him a telegram after he had accepted the ceasefire saying there was no cause for concern. I said the penetration on the Syrian front was in Syria's favor and that he could wipe out the Suez pocket.

Secretary Kissinger: You didn't have an army encircled.

President Asad: It [the Egyptian Third Army] should not have been surrounded.

Secretary Kissinger: Why was it?

President Asad: I don't know. A few mistakes were made.

But we are deviating. Our people feel we fought honorably and that circumstances stopped us. Now the battle is political. Disengage-

---

[8] A reference to the Israel Defense Force penetration into Syria beyond the June 1967 cease-fire line.

ment falls within the political battle. If it takes place on the October 6 line, the people will ask why we went to war. We say this is disengagement, not Security Council Resolution 242. The people will say why not wait to carry out Resolution 242. If there is a meaningful disengagement line, then we can get support. The refugees must return home. The people must see that Israel did not win.

Secretary Kissinger: Of course the population will return where Israel withdraws.

President Asad: The human problem is on the Golan Heights. Return of the population would create satisfaction and then the people would begin to understand peace. Even Sadat has spoken in this vein.

Secretary Kissinger: You are the leader of Syria and will make this judgment.

President Asad: I have put my cards face up. I described to you the possibilities as I see them. Can we realize these views?

Secretary Kissinger: My view is that you can realize some distance behind the October 6 line, but not the minimum line you gave me.

President Asad: That's a problem.

Secretary Kissinger: That is my honest feeling. I did not spend 18 hours with the Israeli Cabinet because they can visualize giving up anything behind the October 6 line. The Israelis say to me that they lost no territory to Syria but gained territory from Syria. They think the present line is better than the line of October 6. They see any withdrawal as a unilateral concession. They know there will be a second phase. There could be the same clause as in the Egyptian agreement about disengagement being only a step toward implementation of Resolutions 242 and 338.

I find it nervewracking; both of you say the same thing to me. I would like to see you and Prime Minister Meir face-to-face. When I say to the Israelis they must go beyond the October 6 lines, it is a shock to them. They say why—we won—why go back? What is my answer if they start a propaganda campaign against me in the United States, saying I am asking for unilateral withdrawal from which Israel gets nothing.

I say to you, after they have withdrawn, it will be clear who has withdrawn. If I am any judge, you will not be less determined to achieve your objective than before. Wherever the line, you will say this is the first stage. The people will know you have gained. It is the first phase in a political process.

Now for the question about why disengagement, why not wait for full withdrawal? My answer is that I think any withdrawal changes Israeli attitudes. Their change in attitude with respect to Egypt is great since they agreed to withdraw. Before the war, many said that the

Arabs could not make an agreement until their dignity was restored. I understand that. Now, from the Israeli viewpoint, it is better to get withdrawal by agreement without humiliation. If they are forced to withdraw to your minimum line, there will be less chance of further withdrawal. It is more likely to become the final line than if the withdrawal is limited.

President Asad: What will they seek if they are forced to the minimum line?

Secretary Kissinger: They will seek a U.S. commitment not to press for further withdrawal for two years, plus $700 million for arms.

President Asad: Circumstances may change. Once the Geneva Conference machinery starts, they cannot stall for two years.

The line we propose is close to the October 6 line, West of the Quneitra hills. No one could live in Quneitra if we did not hold the hills.

Secretary Kissinger: I have not looked at the topography or at where the Quneitra hills are. I am not yet ready to discuss it in this detail. The purpose of your getting back Quneitra would be to permit people to live there?

President Asad: For this reason, we need the hills.

Secretary Kissinger: I did not say that Israel should hold the hills.

President Asad: Our minimum line is 3–4 kilometers West of the hills.

Secretary Kissinger: How far are the hills from Quneitra?

President Asad: About 1½ kilometers.

Secretary Kissinger: To make sure I understand: Your minimum line is 3 kilometers from the hills, the hills are 2 kilometers from Quneitra and Quneitra is 3–4 kilometers from the October 6 line. Hence, you are discussing a distance of 8–10 kilometers West of the October 6 line.

President Asad: Yes. Remember the map I gave you.

Secretary Kissinger: Is that the present Syrian minimum line?

President Asad: Yes—in the North. It is probably about the same in the South. These were our considerations when we delineated the line—so that most of the inhabitants could return and those villages overlooked by high ground would not be so vulnerable. This is the reason for our line. It is about halfway [between the October 6, 1973 and pre-June 5, 1967 lines].

Secretary Kissinger: I do not think it possible to get Israel back that far as part of a disengagement agreement. That is my honest judgment. There is no sense lying to you. How far back is hard to judge—six kilometers?—I don't know, I will have to see. Right now I am expending my energies getting Israel used to the idea of some withdrawal.

President Asad: That's a problem. If they cannot be moved to a greater distance, there is no point in discussing this again.

Disengagement on the Egyptian front ends March 5?[9]

Secretary Kissinger: Yes.

President Asad: There are no Israelis on the West Bank. Then Egypt's military situation is now better.

Secretary Kissinger: There is no question about that.

President Asad: Are the Israelis thinking of a further war—do they want that?

Secretary Kissinger: I don't think they want another war.

President Asad: What is in their minds? Do they believe it possible that the occupation can continue?

Secretary Kissinger: I think the October War was an unbelievable shock to Israel. The consequences have not fully sunk in. People in shock tend to freeze their positions.

In November, when I talked of returning to the October 22 line at a dinner in Washington—and I was the guest of honor—Golda Meir would not even speak to me.[10] Now they are accustomed to the idea on the Egyptian side. The first thing is to get a transition in their minds, from hostility to the possibility of peace. This is the importance of disengagement on the Syrian side. If three months ago I had spoken to the Israelis of peace with Egypt, they would have said I was crazy. Now they can talk rationally with Egypt, and they know Egypt wants the same thing as Syria.

With Syria they are not to that point yet. They are fearful; they don't know your mild nature.

President Asad: If we can't get them back ten kilometers, our nature is indeed mild.

How far back are they on the Egyptian side?

Secretary Kissinger: It is a different situation. From the Egyptian forward line, perhaps 10–12 kilometers, but this must be related to the depth; there is great depth in Sinai and they evacuated the pocket they held as they would in Syria. Things must be in perspective. All distances are greater in Sinai.

President Asad: Although the Israelis evacuated a sizable amount of territory in Egypt, perhaps the Egyptians found it easier. Gamasy said it was rough dealing with the Israelis.

---

[9] The disengagement actually ended on March 4, a day ahead of schedule. (*New York Times*, March 5, 1974, p. 3)

[10] In fact, Kissinger spoke with Meir at the dinner in Washington on November 1, 1973, and again the following day on November 2. See *Foreign Relations, 1969–1976*, volume XXV, Arab-Israeli Crisis and War, 1973, Documents 305, 306, and 312.

Secretary Kissinger: Exactly. Therefore they must be given some time. I never gave a final line to the Egyptians.

There is one thing we can do before you commit yourself. Let them send a representative to Washington in two weeks. After he returns to Israel, you can send a representative so they will not be in Washington at the same time. After that I can return to the area. Then it will be easier to judge.

President Asad: But the line is ten kilometers. I agree time is needed, but everything depends on the line. Their pocket is part of the front; it is 10–18 kilometers deep, but it is not a problem. But if the line is not ten kilometers back, I won't consider disengagement.

Secretary Kissinger: I never made a commitment to Egypt. If I wanted to gain time, I could say yes to you and then in three weeks say I couldn't achieve it. But what is at stake is more important. I want Syria's friendship and trust, so you will know our word counts.

President Asad: I agree. I am telling you things that are inherently harmful to me. Without confidence in you, I would not say them.

Secretary Kissinger: We want to help you. You know the length to which we have gone to contribute to Sadat's international position. We want to do the same for Syria. We would like Syria to emerge stronger from the negotiations.

I am not asking you for another line. Before you gave the POW list, Israel would not even discuss disengagement. I have spent 18 hours with them, and they are just as tough as you but less pleasant. Since they don't trust each other, they have eight people in the room at once.

May I ask you frankly, is there anyone you trust enough to send to Washington for frank talks with me after the Israelis leave?

President Asad: Yes.

Secretary Kissinger: I propose to have long talks with the Israelis. There will probably be a new Defense Minister—General Rabin, who is intelligent and one of the few Israelis who thinks conceptually. Most of them speak of hills and roads and of all the things that are not important. When I negotiated the Egyptian disengagement, they had a Cabinet meeting over 30 howitzers.

President Asad: Will it be Rabin?

Secretary Kissinger: Unless Dayan changes his mind.

President Asad: From Sadat I hear that Dayan is a practical man.

Secretary Kissinger: Yes. Before October I thought he was stupid and tough but in the Egyptian negotiations where the Israelis treated me as a traitor (they had demonstrations against me in December), I spent 15 hours with Dayan and others. Three to four weeks later they began to change. I think we are at December in the Syrian negotiations.

Today I gave the Israelis my reasoning. I told them I don't want to hear their views now; I wanted them to think for two weeks and then send a senior representative to Washington.

Dayan has become practical. Rabin is also, but he thinks like a Frenchman. He puts forth absurd propositions before drawing correct conclusions.

President Asad: Rabin may be better. He has been a diplomat.

Secretary Kissinger: Remember there was a history behind withdrawal from the Canal. They had considered it in 1971.[11] They have never considered withdrawal from the October 6 line, so it is a tough intellectual problem for the Israelis.

President Asad: I remember in 1971 Golda Meir said something about withdrawal from Golan.

Secretary Kissinger: With effort and wisdom, I think we can manage.

President Asad: You said you would call a senior Israeli to Washington?

Secretary Kissinger: Yes. After he leaves, perhaps you will agree to send someone you trust to me. May I ask who it will be?

President Asad: If it is a military man, General Midhat Shihabi, Chief of Intelligence and Reconnaissance.

Secretary Kissinger: It is up to you. It should be someone you trust.

President Asad: Absolutely.

Secretary Kissinger: I will tell you what I think. Your representative will return, and about then I will be ready to come back to the Middle East—or perhaps I will first ask the Israeli to return to Washington. I will decide with your representative what to do. This might be the best procedure. Then there is no need to negotiate in the working group.

President Asad: That is better.

Secretary Kissinger: I will go to Moscow the second half of March. Before or after Moscow, I will come back to Damascus. We will keep you informed of our significant contacts with others. If others tell you something we haven't told you, check with us as you did from Lahore.[12] I may disappoint you but I won't deceive you. We must have confidence.

---

[11] See footnote 3, Document 9.
[12] A meeting of Islamic leaders was held in Lahore, Pakistan, February 22–24.

I see Faisal tomorrow. Do you object if I tell him in general terms of our talk?[13]

President Asad: No objection.

Secretary Kissinger: I also have no objection if you tell him.

President Asad: I tell President Boumediene everything, and he tells me everything.

Secretary Kissinger: Do you know how to reach him? I believe he is in North Korea.

President Asad: During the Lahore meeting, I urged Boumediene to see you when he returns.

Secretary Kissinger: I had a good talk with Boumediene a month ago.[14] I wanted to stop in Algeria this time on my way to Damascus. I will write him and tell him I have no objections if he shows you my letters.

President Asad: There still remains the question of the disengagement line.

Secretary Kissinger: This is what must be determined after the visits of Israel's and your representatives to Washington.

President Asad: What is now envisaged will do us no good. Yet what we want does not seem achievable. What is the solution?

Secretary Kissinger: First, I must get Israel accustomed to the idea of withdrawal beyond the October 6 line. Once they accept the principle, it may be easier to discuss the exact number of kilometers. Also, it may then be possible for us to see if some adjustments are possible in your position. Right now with Israel, the problem is the principle. Once the principle is accepted, it will be eaiser.

President Asad: The line I mentioned was not decided by me. It was arrived at by a number of experts in our Armed Forces.

Secretary Kissinger: It is one thing to devise a line when you are thinking of only your own position. When you know the other side's views, you can have another look at it.

President Asad: Our first meeting was very formal, and we discussed the whole Golan. But what I said at the first meeting still holds, namely, that disengagement discussions should be held on a technical basis. My point was that neither side should gain an advantage. But this does not appear to be the case.

---

[13] A portion of the memorandum of conversation between Kissinger and King Faisal is printed in *Foreign Relations, 1969–1976*, volume XXXVI, Energy Crisis, 1969–1974, Document 332.

[14] Kissinger last met with Boumediene in person on December 13, 1973, in Algiers. See ibid., volume XXV, Arab-Israeli Crisis and War, 1973, footnote 2, Document 393.

Secretary Kissinger: There must be a combination of political, psychological and technical considerations.

President Asad: That is true. We can adjust specific points—a hill here or there. But do you envisage any specific depth for the line?

Secretary Kissinger: I don't have a map here. I have thought that some kilometers beyond Quneitra might be possible, but I was just thinking out loud. As of now, Israel hasn't accepted the October 6 line. I do not want to create confusion, and I therefore have not asked Israel.

President Asad: I have confidence in you and therefore I am asking you. I proceed from the premise that if withdrawal beyond the October 6 line is conceptually feasible, it can be done.

Secretary Kissinger: And if there is some flexibility on your side.

President Asad: You have never seen such flexibility. We started talking about all of the Golan, and now we are talking about 10 kilometers. These meetings with you are responsible.

Secretary Kissinger: Israel's negotiating tactic is to move from the intolerable to the impossible and call it a concession.

President Asad: (laughing) I hope we are not that way.

Secretary Kissinger: If this is the end of your flexibility, I would not want to meet you when you were inflexible. But seriously, considering the history of U.S.-Syrian relations, I consider these meetings with you very special. I appreciate them. I hope, since I am not the Assistant Secretary for the Middle East but the Secretary of State, that you appreciate the time I am spending here.

President Asad: You will hardly find an area of bigger problems of such importance to the world.

Secretary Kissinger: I have spent two-thirds of my time since October 6 on this problem. If your Foreign Minister had answered the phone on October 6 when I tried to reach him to stop the war, I am sure that he would have taken my advice.

President Asad: Really?

Secretary Kissinger: I doubt it.

President Asad: I insisted on going to war.

Secretary Kissinger: I totally underestimated your capabilities. I also thought we should limit the extent of your certain defeat and not create a problem as in 1967. I have learned much since October 6. But I did not expect to be sitting in Damascus with President Asad three months after the war. This is an important chance—historically more important than the number of kilometers. Wherever the disengagement line is, it will not be final.

President Asad: I am confident of that.

To return to the question of the line, we must discuss it since it will have repercussions both positive and negative. I am not ill at ease with the present line. I do not agree with some of Sadat's remarks. Specifically, I do not agree with him that Israeli withdrawal from the salient will lessen the pressure on Damascus. From the point of view of our people, I find the salient an advantage. I am surprised our brothers in Egypt do not understand us.

Secretary Kissinger: The major reasons for disengagement are political and psychological, not military. I have never used the military argument.

President Asad: You mentioned "some" kilometers West of Quneitra. What does that mean? In Arabic, this has the precise meaning of between three and nine.

Secretary Kissinger: I would think it would be nearer three than nine.

President Asad: You do not want to define things precisely.

Secretary Kissinger: I don't want to say something that I cannot deliver. I can deliver the October 6 line even if Israel has not yet agreed. West of that they have conceptual difficulties. I have spent my energy convincing Israel to accept the October 6 line, since I did not want to confuse matters. Once a principle is accepted, it will be easier. It is like the October 22 line in Egypt. At the beginning, even eight to ten kilometers seemed impossible to the Israelis.

This is why I am hesitating. I am not trying to be clever. I am not bargaining. My interest is to try to get the maximum for you, not the minimum. But I don't know what that is.

President Asad: I believe you. I have been pressing you because I must give some idea of what is feasible to people close to me with whom I discuss this question.

Secretary Kissinger: I understand. I do not think you are being unreasonable.

President Asad: Please don't think I am putting you through the third degree.

Secretary Kissinger: I think you are extremely persistent.

President Asad: To the extent that we agree conceptually, this will help. I am not saying we must form a single front.

Can I hope that you will expend all possible efforts to realize the minimum I am seeking?

Secretary Kissinger: You can count on that. I will make a maximum effort to get all that is attainable. That is a promise, not a hope. You can call me back to Damascus after a reasonable interlude.

President Asad: I have no more questions.

Secretary Kissinger: Let me be sure I understand. First, I will invite a senior Israeli official to Washington to pursue the objective we have just agreed on. After he has left, you will send a trusted representative to Washington. We will give you a week's notice. He will have full security protection. After he returns to Damascus, I will contact you or you will contact me, to discuss the next step. In any case, when I go to Moscow, I will stop here either on my way there or on my return.

I will not concert with the Soviets. I will tell them only what you and I agree. But I need to know what you will tell the Soviets—about our discussions, not about bilateral matters.

President Asad: We can agree on this at the end of our discussion.

Secretary Kissinger: In an emergency, I am prepared to come to Damascus apart from my Moscow trip. In any event, this will be in about a month, give or take a week.

President Asad: You mean after you have invited Israeli and Syrian representatives to Washington?

Secretary Kissinger: Yes.

President Asad: Do you think it will be possible to have disengagement during your Moscow trip?

Secretary Kissinger: I will make a major effort, at least to get agreement on a line. We can then give the matter to military representatives to work out the details. I estimate this will take about five weeks.

President Asad: Do you mean that the Military Committee will be Egyptian, with Syrian officers attending?

Secretary Kissinger: Yes.

President Asad: That will be good for the Geneva Conference.

Secretary Kissinger: There are many peculiarities in the Middle East. Historically, wars start between countries that are at peace. Here they start between countries that are already at war.

Let me give you another example. At the opening of the Geneva Conference, Israel said it would not accept UN auspices, and Syria said it would not go to Geneva. Now Israel wants only UN auspices and Syria wants to negotiate only in Geneva.

The final document must be signed by Syrians, however.

President Asad: The Working Group will be headed by an Egyptian.

Secretary Kissinger: Then both Egypt and Syria must sign. I doubt that Israel will accept only an Egyptian signature.

President Asad: Let them both sign.

Secretary Kissinger: Compared with the Vietnamese, you are not the most difficult person I have negotiated with.

President Asad: We are more flexible.

Secretary Kissinger: And more human. However matters turn out, I am touched by the humanity of the Arabs with whom I have talked.

President Asad: This is something we learn from childhood. We are not vindictive. For example, we have one custom—more common in rural areas—that when two tribes are enemies and one kills a number of members of the other, if he then goes to the camp of the bereaved, they cannot harm him.

Secretary Kissinger: Is that because he is a guest?

President Asad: Yes.

Secretary Kissinger: If he leaves the camp, is he in trouble?

President Asad: No. Once he has entered the camp or the home of the other, there must be reconciliation. (SOLH!)

We also have the custom of vengeance. If a person is seen outside his territorial limit, he must then be killed.

So you see, your idea of having Mrs. Meir come to Damascus is not so bad.

Secretary Kissinger: This is one of the rewards of these meetings. If the American people learn to know the Arabs better, they will understand them better.

President Asad: We are our own worst enemies.

Secretary Kissinger: After 1967, the Arab mistake was to try to achieve your goals through hostility toward the United States. Friendship will help not only bilaterally but to achieve peace.

I have told you President Nixon plans to come to the Middle East in May, and you said he might come to Damascus. If he is received with the same warmth I have been, the publicity will help in the United States.

President Asad: He will be warmly received.

Secretary Kissinger: I can assure him of this on the basis of my own experience.

President Asad: Egypt has announced his trip.

Secretary Kissinger: No. They announced they have invited him.

President Asad: They said it would be April.

Secretary Kissinger: That is wrong. When he comes, it will be on the same trip—in mid-May. We will agree jointly on an announcement, but we do not have to do this until April. All visits will be at the same time. We have no special favorites.

President Asad: It will be an opportunity for establishing relations with Arab countries.

Secretary Kissinger: It will have a profound impact on relations.

President Asad: Unfortunately, we lack accommodations in Syria. Egypt has the former Kings' palaces. It is our bad luck that Syria never accepted a King.

Secretary Kissinger: You have a proud people as a result. The Guest House is very comfortable. The President has simple taste. He does not judge hospitality by luxury. He will want frank and open discussions with you. You and he will find that you can speak frankly and in a common language. I will have the pleasure of seeing you in April before the President's visit.

I want you to know that we plan to budget some money for cultural exchanges with Syria, for students. It is up to you if you want to take advantage of this.

President Asad: Everyone wants to go to the United States. Our most famous professional people have specialized in the United States.

Secretary Kissinger: I will tell Mr. Scotes to discuss this with the Foreign Ministry.

President Asad: I notice that people who study in a given place return with their attitudes changed. Those who study in America return with high standards.

Secretary Kissinger: And as radicals, whereas those who study in the Soviet Union return as conservatives.

President Asad: What shall we tell the Soviets of our discussions?

Secretary Kissinger: It would not be useful to discuss specific lines with them.

President Asad: I agree.

Secretary Kissinger: We can tell them of the evolution we foresee—namely, that Israel, and later Syria, will send representatives to Washington, and then I will make a return trip to the area. Then Gromyko will come back here again. But that's your problem. I promise that if Gromyko comes first, I will not follow him around.

President Asad: What if Gromyko expresses the wish to be here?

Secretary Kissinger: Perhaps it would be better not to mention that I will be returning.

President Asad: This time, the Soviets requested that Gromyko be here at the same time with you.

Secretary Kissinger: What if they do so again?

President Asad: We will find a way.

Secretary Kissinger: With the press, I suggest that we say our discussions will continue here and in Washington, and that Syria will send a representative to Washington when this is necessary. Will you say the same?

President Asad: It is up to you to do.

Secretary Kissinger: I will say we had good constructive talks. The matter will now proceed with Israel sending a representative to Washington. After that Syria may be prepared to send a representative. I will say I am optimistic about the evolution of the matter and that I will make a great effort to bring about disengagement. I will say only that I brought ideas here from Israel, and will add informally that anyone who has dealt with the Syrians knows that they do not accept the ideas of others. You can say that you presented your ideas and insisted on them and that the discussions will continue.

President Asad: The press will speculate about specific disengagement lines.

Secretary Kissinger: I will discuss no lines.

President Asad: What if I say you brought ideas and we did not agree with them.

Secretary Kissinger: All right, but don't be too antagonistic. Make it sound as though there is the possibility of progress so our press does not report a failure.

President Asad: A White House statement referred to your bringing an Israeli plan. It would be better to say we had received the plan and did not agree with it.

Secretary Kissinger: We have not said "plan." It is better to use the word "ideas." If you say plan, the Israeli Cabinet will ask "what plan?"

President Asad: Right, we'll say "ideas."

Secretary Kissinger: I will say that I brought Israeli ideas, that Syria did not accept them, that you gave me your own ideas, that the discussions will continue, and I will describe how they will continue. On background, I will tell the press the two sides are still far apart.

Israel has given me the names of a number of its soldiers missing in action and wonders if you have any information about them.

President Asad: A number of bodies were buried. We brought a rabbi from Damascus for the ceremony. Perhaps they are some of the missing. You can be sure that the number of living is as I have given to you.

Secretary Kissinger: I trust you. The question is whether you have any information about those who were buried?

President Asad: I will tell Mr. Scotes if we find any of the missing on this list among the buried.

Secretary Kissinger: The Israelis have also given me two other names on whom they seek information. They were seen parachuting and Israel thought they had been captured. We appreciate how meticulously you have kept your word about the Red Cross visits.

President Asad: Given the intensity of the battle, there is no doubt that some who parachuted, including Syrians, were hit.

Secretary Kissinger: This is not an accusation that prisoners-of-war were killed. It is a serious attempt to find out about missing-in-action. I will see that no accusations are made.

President Asad: I would like to talk longer, but I know you must get up early for your visit to the mosque. After that you will not be received in Israel.

Secretary Kissinger: I will take my chances.

(After amenities, the meeting adjourned.)

---

30. **Backchannel Message From the Deputy Director of Central Intelligence (Walters) to the President's Assistant for National Security Affairs (Kissinger)**[1]

Rabat, March 8, 1974, 1327Z.

To: The White House for Dr. Henry A. Kissinger, eyes only. From: Lt. Gen. Vernon A. Walters.

On March 7 I saw PLO representatives at King Hassan's guest house in Fes in real Arabian nights environment. Present as at previous meeting in November[2] were Khalid el Hassan and Mujid Abu Sharawa. Also present this time was Abu Marwan, PLO representative in Rabat, but as he spoke no English he might as well not have been there.

I opened by saying that we realized that Palestinians were a factor in any Middle East settlement but that for us it was essential that disengagement begin on the Syrian front before we could go any further. Khalid who did all of the talking for them seemed a little disappointed that I had not come with an invitation, a date for a meeting, and an agenda. As we talked, his understanding of our position grew. Finally he said that for them too disengagement on the Syrian front was vital. He did hope that after this occurred I could talk to them more precisely. He felt that in about four or six weeks this could be appropriate. If such a meeting took place in Washington their level of representation would

---

[1] Source: National Archives, Nixon Presidential Materials, NSC Files, Kissinger Office Files, Box 139, Country Files, Middle East, Palestinians, Folder 1. Secret; Sensitive; Eyes Only. Walters first met with PLO officials on November 3, 1973. See *Foreign Relations,* volume XXV, Arab-Israeli Crisis and War, 1973, Document 318. On February 12, PLO officials relayed word through the Moroccan Government that they wished to meet again in Morocco as preparation for an eventual meeting in Washington, DC. (Library of Congress, Manuscript Division, Kissinger Papers, CL 189, Geopolitical File, Middle East, Palestinians Contact Messages Book, 1973–1975) According to Kissinger's memoirs, the U.S. Government agreed on February 16 to a meeting in Morocco between Walters and PLO representatives in March. (*Years of Upheaval,* p. 1037)

[2] A reference to the first meeting between Walters and PLO representatives on November 3, 1973.

depend on the circumstances at the time. I asked if secrecy could be maintained if such a meeting did take place. The Secretary felt very strongly that if secrecy is lost in delicate negotiations then propaganda would follow and this was not conducive to success. He acknowledged that your tactics had scored many successes and said that they would confine such knowledge to their central committee.

Very significant to me was the fact that unlike what took place at our first meeting, not only did they not inveigh against King Hussein but they never once mentioned his name or their sufferings at his hands. I draw from this that they were impressed by our telling them in November that he was our friend and are keeping their options open with him.

Khalid said that Gromyko had received Arafat officially in Cairo and had told him that the Soviets were prepared to recognize the PLO as the government of a state. In the past all of their dealings with the Soviets had been with the CPSU rather than with the Foreign Minister. Khalid said that they realized that their relationship with the Soviets and the U.S. could not be exactly the same but they hoped that their relationship with us could change. They could not remake their public opinion toward the U.S. overnight. Khalid spoke well of Sadat and Assad and somewhat dubiously of the Iraqi regime. He asked about the Zarqa Mutiny[3] and I said that my information was that it involved pay and in some measure corruption but did not involve their loyalty to King Hussein. He said that their information agreed with this. At this point he could easily have made some derogatory remark about Hussein or Zaid Rifai but did not do so.

Khalid also asked about Iranian-Iraqi relations, particularly about the border clashes. I said I knew little other than that such clashes had occurred. The Iraqis had bad relations with almost all of their neighbors such as Iran, Saudi Arabia, Kuwait and Jordan but they did have good relations with the Soviets. Khalid commented that King Faysal was very firm on Jerusalem. I said the oil weapon should be used carefully. It was important to know when to turn it off before it did more damage than good.

Khalid noted the high educational level of the Palestinians and the major contribution they had made to other Arab states in administrative and technical competence. He said immense amounts of capital would soon be available to the Arabs because of the new oil prices. He

---

[3] On February 3, a garrison of Jordanian troops in the town of Zarqa, 15 miles northeast of Amman, attempted an uprising against the Jordanian Government over a lack of pay raises to keep up with the cost of living and over the perceived corruption of several Jordanian officials. The uprising was suppressed by February 6. (*New York Times*, February 7, 1974, p. 7)

wondered if we had given any thought to these funds and how they should be used. I assured him that you had given much thought to this. I noted that such wealth brought responsibility as well as advantages. This seems a very important point. Playing the role of intellectual mentors to the rich Arabs would not displease the Palestinians. In fact I think they would relish the prospect of playing a key role in the use of the great funds soon to be available to the Arabs (particularly in the context of a Saudi-American agreement on such matters). This could provide an outlet for the Palestinians that would relieve some of their pressures for resettlement in Palestine for all Palestinians and soothe some of their hangups.

The Palestinians feel that they rendered you a great service by warning President Franjiyeh through the Kuwaitis about the plot against you in Beirut.[4] When I mentioned that you had not appreciated the Damascus caper[5] Khalid replied that the Beirut plot had been much more dangerous.

Khalid harped a little on the U.S. special relationship with Israel which he said had been a dagger in the heart of the Palestinians and hoped this would change. I said I could not tell him that the U.S. would abandon Israel but we had such special relationships with a number of countries and they were not exclusive of others.

Khalid said that the Palestinians had been somewhat troubled by a number of people offering to act as intermediaries for them with the U.S. President Ceaucescu in particular had harrassed them on this point, claiming credit for your initial contacts with the Chinese. I said we too had had a number of people make approaches to us claiming to be acting for PLO. Khalid with Shawara nodding agreement said they wished to use this as the only channel.

Khalid complained that the Palestinians got very bad treatment in the U.S. media. I said that this was the fault of the terrorists who had given the Palestinians a bad name. He said scornfully that it was easy to be a terrorist, all one needed was a hand grenade. I said that if our channel is to continue there must be no act of terrorism against the U.S. He agreed.

The Palestinians accepted before the end of our talk the fact that we were not prepared to go further until after the beginning of disen-

---

[4] In December 1973 Kissinger received a report that Palestinians planned to shoot down his plane as he flew into Beirut for talks with President Frangieh. (*Years of Upheaval*, p. 788)

[5] According to Kissinger's memoirs, on February 27, 1974, Palestinian militants planted mines in the road that led to the Omayed Mosque in Damascus with the intention of detonating them under Kissinger's car. Since a morning meeting with President Asad had finished later than planned, Kissinger postponed the visit to the mosque and avoided the assassination attempt. (*Years of Upheaval*, p. 958)

gagement on the Syrian front. They did not like it but they accepted it. They are clearly hopeful that once this has begun that I will bring them something more precise.

This talk lasted two hours and in addition to the above we talked economics, philosophy as well as black Africa and agreed on the existence of God.

I will be in Washington Sunday afternoon and will call you then. King Hassan did not attend the talk but I saw him both before and after my discussions with the PLO representatives.[6] I will send a second message on my talks with him.

On meeting and leaving the Palestinians I was kissed. (It was only on the cheeks and I know you will understand.)[7]

---

[6] In telegram (*text not declassified*) March 8, Walters described his meetings with King Hassan both before and after his meeting with the Palestinians. (National Archives, Nixon Presidential Materials, NSC Files, Kissinger Office Files, Box 139, Country Files, Middle East, Palestinians, Folder 1)

[7] According to a summary of U.S. contacts with the PLO from 1973 to 1974, a Palestinian made an approach to U.S. officials in Beirut on April 20 with a message from Arafat requesting that the U.S. Government provide encouragement regarding PLO aspirations for "national authority" and participation in Geneva. On May 6, the U.S. Government offered an informal reply through Beirut, which noted that the United States will consider the Palestinian role in a settlement and Palestinian "legitimate interests." It also noted that the U.S. government had not excluded in advance any possible arrangement. (Ibid.)

31. Memorandum of Conversation[1]

Washington, March 8, 1974.

PARTICIPANTS

    President Nixon
    Secretary Kissinger
    GOP Congressional Leadership
    Lt. General Brent Scowcroft, Deputy Assistant to the President for National Security Affairs

SUBJECT

    Middle East

President: It is very important not to talk about linkage. I don't know how Henry has stood it. He has been out there talking to everyone. There is movement on an agreement between Syria and Israel. It is more difficult than the Egyptian one, and we don't know when it'll be done. Don't predict. The Egyptian disengagement was an enormous achievement. Henry?

Kissinger: It might be helpful to summarize your basic strategy, Mr. President.

In October and November of last year we found a united front of the Soviet Union, Europe, Japan—most of the world—supporting the Arabs and then following generally the Soviet line. All of the issues were lumped together in one big ball. We were the only supporter of Israel, and everything we advanced the Soviet Union would block.

Our objective was (1) to break up this coalition, (2) to change the situation where the Soviet Union was the supporter of the Arabs and we were the supporter of Israel, and (3) to break out the issues into separate items.

We demonstrated to the Arabs that the Soviet Union could give them arms, but only the U.S. could give them political progress. The Jordanian crisis of 1970 and all our other actions were parts of this policy, to demonstrate that the Arabs would have to come to us.

President: At the time of the '67 war, the U.S. ended up on the Israeli side. This time, we saved Israel with an airlift; we stopped a possible Soviet intervention—both of these looked pro-Israel. We saved Is-

---

[1] Source: Ford Library, National Security Adviser, Memoranda of Conversations, Box 3, March 8, 1974, Nixon, GOP Congressional Leadership. Secret; Nodis. The meeting was held at the White House. Brackets are in the original. A list of attendees is in President Nixon's Daily Diary. (National Archives, Nixon Presidential Materials, White House Central Files)

rael. But we did this in a way which enhanced our role with the Arabs and did not posture us as anti-Soviet.

Kissinger: The paradox of the situation is that it is in our interest to have Israel so strong the Arabs can't defeat it, so they must come to us for progress. We must keep the Soviet Union out but not frustrate them so that they actively oppose negotiations. Asad of Syria said he wanted U.S. equipment because I told him we wouldn't let Soviet equipment defeat U.S. equipment.

Sadat is a wise, moderate leader who permitted a reduction of tensions by agreeing to disengagement. He ran the risk of separating himself from the other Arabs; Asad immediately started a campaign against Egyptian disengagement. A Syrian disengagement is tougher. Egypt acts as an independent country and not as part of a pan-Arab movement; the Sinai is not close to Israel. But the Syrians are at the front of the movement of pan-Arabism; much of Israel used to belong to Syria, and the domestic situation in Syria is more complicated.

President: Tell us about Asad. Sadat turned out to be more able than Nasser.

Kissinger: Sadat is able. He is not mesmerized by exhortation or tactics. Asad is very intelligent, perhaps more intelligent than Sadat. Also there is a difference in background—Egypt was British, Syria was French.

Syria doesn't want to be the first one to have made an agreement with Israel—whatever the content. This is the reason we have adopted the procedure we did. We had planned to do it like Egypt and Israel at Kilometer 101.[2] It became apparent to me, though, that this would just produce a situation where each side would constantly have to prove its manhood. The way we ended up was a way we could get things moving and lead into it gradually. The Syrians would reject anything I brought back, so I brought something very vague. Now they have said they have rejected it—whatever that can mean—and made a counter-proposal publicly—thus getting that public element out of the way.

President: The point is we won't get an instant settlement.

Kissinger: And they may attack—to prove they can't win and must negotiate; to prod Israel back into the conflict; to force Soviet support; or even egged on by the Soviets.

---

[2] At Kilometer 101 on the Cairo–Suez Road, Israeli and Egyptian military officials negotiated between October 28 and November 29, 1973, in an attempt to disengage their forces. The Egyptians broke the talks off on November 29, but negotiations continued at the Geneva Conference in December 1973. See *Foreign Relations, 1969–1976*, volume XXV, Arab-Israeli Crisis and War, 1973.

President: There is no indication of the latter, and we don't want any anti-Soviet coloration to our policies.

Kissinger: The President is right. Soviet influence is down drastically. And they must be asking: what have they gotten from their aid?

President: You should know that we are prepared to help clear the Suez Canal. It is the right thing to do.

Burleson: What is the significance of the Iran-Iraq dispute?[3]

Kissinger: We have no relationship to it. But if the Iranians tie down Iraq, they can't go to Syria. Iraq is a radical element in Syria. Syria can't fight back by itself.

President: What can the leadership say on the embargo?

Kissinger: As little as possible.

President: Why not say we are making progress—apart from the embargo—and hope to avoid rationing? We are working on negotiations and that will have a favorable effect—but the embargo is a matter for the Arabs to decide. We are seeking peace as an end in itself—the fact of the embargo makes it more difficult. They should lift the embargo as an end in itself because a positive American role in their countries is in their interest.

On the other point. Israel is saying: Between '67 and '74 you were our friend; now you are renewing relations with the Arabs, etc. The answer is this is not at the expense of Israel. We always will stand by Israel, but we are seeking better relations with the Arabs in Israel's own interest, and also to keep the Soviets out and not have Israel surrounded by countries either radicalized or under Soviet influence.

Kissinger: In fact, after the Syrian disengagement we plan to go back to the Egyptian part and seek a territorial settlement. Also with Jordan. Jordan is difficult because of Israeli domestic politics. Israel hasn't realized their choice is between dealing with Jordan and dealing with Arafat. They can't deal with neither.

We must deal with the situation one item at a time. This process has been very painful for the Soviet Union. Before, even we dealt with the Soviet Union as the spokesman for the Arabs. Now everyone is coming to us. We are not trying to force them out—but their negotiating style is too legalistic for this situation—and they also tend to push more extreme views.

---

[3] According to a White House note prepared for the President's Daily Briefing on March 7, continued border disputes between Iran and Iraq had led to sporadic fighting during the first week of March. (National Archives, Nixon Presidential Materials, NSC Files, Box 1230, Harold H. Saunders Files, March 1–10, 1974, Folder 3)

But the Soviet Union has the capability of going public, stirring up trouble, etc.

President: The Arabs are very emotional.

Kissinger: A moderate Soviet policy is important—therefore the President's relationship with Brezhnev is important—and MFN. We can't put it to them in every area and expect them to continue to take it.

President: Remember, if the Soviet Union and China had wanted the Vietnam War to go on, it would have, and the POW's would still be there. Our interests are opposed to those of the Soviet Union in most areas of the world—but we discuss with them our differences and we seek to avoid any of these issues from provoking nuclear war.

Rhodes: Do we have a promise of the embargo lifting?

Kissinger: The President's language in the State of the Union was Arab language. The problem is Arab unity. They have to have unity to lift the embargo. We have to decouple the embargo or we will be blackmailed at every step if they think we need it.

President: We can't link the two.

Kissinger: Take Faisal. He wants to lift the embargo, but by having it, he is at the head of the radicals—for free.

Rhodes: We'll be playing the same game until Jerusalem?

Kissinger: No, he is not blackmailing now.

Bob [omission in the original]: This tells me we ought to get off our duff and get going so the embargo doesn't matter.

President: Right.

Kissinger: One point on the MFN and credits.

President: Yes, this is very important to the world.

Kissinger: This is a case where an action produces the opposite reaction to what was intended. Cutting off MFN will push emigration back to what it was in the Johnson times, not increase it. It will radicalize their Middle East policy. We can't frustrate them in every area. The result of an MFN cutoff would be that after three years of détente they would be worse off than when détente started.

The story is we have been taken to the cleaners in détente. We got our way in Vietnam, solved Berlin, prevented war in Cuba, and got the Soviets moderated in the Middle East.

Until 1972 we were attacked for not making increased trade an end in itself.

President: I will veto if the credits are not passed. Our relations with the Soviet Union were cool during the '50s and '60s. We didn't trade; there was little communication. The new policy doesn't mean a change in attitudes—I despise what they did about Solzhenitsyn,[4] but he is in Paris, not in Siberia, or dead.

The question is how do you get the Communists to change? Not through the Glassboro technique[5]—a little of that is helpful. But great nations consult their interests, not their emotions. The primary U.S.-Soviet interest is that we are both nuclear powers, and I can push a button to kill 20 million Soviets and he can kill 20 million Americans, and we are in consultation to find common points of interest, and the basic point is we are not interested in destroying each other. There is a gradual change which we can anticipate in a very long term. But in getting there we must avoid a holocaust. If détente breaks down, we will have an arms race, no trade—that's not very important—confrontation in the Middle East and elsewhere, and they will go right on repressing their people and even more so. The only alternative is a $100 billion increase in the defense budget and that might not do it. I don't think that is viable, because they can keep up an arms race.

Kissinger: One other point: Our careful détente policy prevents a wild European détente policy toward the Soviet Union. They can't do it now, because they fear we could outbid them.

President: We are trying to build a new world—not to change human nature, but to break the ice which prevented peaceful settlements of disputes. That is where we are now, and we must build now on this. People like Jackson think I have gone soft—I know them and they know me.

Our options are very clear. We can follow our present track, build up our defenses, or bug out of the world.

Beall: Can we get this to the Jewish community?

President: Henry and I are trying to. They are worse than Jackson. Isn't it better for the U.S. to have influence with its enemies than the Soviet Union? Israel says all it needs is weapons. But even if they can hold off the Arabs, there is the Soviet Union. Who can keep the Soviet Union at bay? It is in Israel's interest to have us on good terms with the Soviet Union.

Kissinger: We are making progress. The leaders are receptive now and I think they are working on Jackson. But labor and others are running with this ball.

President: There is also a partisan interest that this diplomatic effort would fail.

---

[4] See footnote 8, Document 23.
[5] A reference to the June 1967 Summit between President Johnson and Soviet Premier Alexei Kosygin in Glassboro, New Jersey.

Scott: The worse case may be a vetoed bill, and we would have to try then for a bill with MFN.

32. Memorandum of Conversation[1]

Washington, March 29, 1974, 12:05–2:45 p.m.

PARTICIPANTS

    General Moshe Dayan, Minister of Defense
    Simcha Dinitz, Israeli Ambassador to the United States
    Colonel Aryeh Bar-On, Aide to Minister Dayan
    Mordechai Shalev, Minister, Israeli Embassy
    Moshe Raviv, Counselor, Israeli Embassy

    Dr. Henry A. Kissinger, Secretary of State and Assistant to the President for National Security Affairs
    General Brent Scowcroft, Deputy Assistant to the President for National Security Affairs
    Joseph J. Sisco, Under Secretary of State for Political Affairs
    Ellsworth Bunker, Ambassador at Large
    Alfred L. Atherton, Assistant Secretary-designate for Near Eastern and South Asian Affairs
    Harold H. Saunders, Senior Staff Member, NSC
    Peter W. Rodman, NSC Staff

[The Secretary, Minister Dayan and General Scowcroft conferred alone from 12:05 to 12:45 p.m. in the Secretary's Office. The meeting then began in the Conference Room.]

Secretary Kissinger: I have already welcomed you here. I am delighted you are here. The last time I saw you I was afraid I wouldn't see you in an official capacity. [Laughter] Without interfering in Israeli politics, I want to say it is a great pleasure for us.

General Dayan: Thank you very much.

Secretary Kissinger: We will meet again tomorrow. The principal reason we are here is to discuss Syrian disengagement. I will talk to you also about my talks in Moscow, which were very tough, and in a way quite worrisome. Which way should we do it?

---

[1] Source: National Archives, RG 59, Records of Henry Kissinger, 1973–77, Box 7, Nodis Memcons, March 1974, Folder 5. Secret; Nodis. The meeting began in the Conference Room on the Seventh Floor of the Department of State, then moved to the Dining Room on the Eighth Floor. Brackets are in the original.

General Dayan: There are four subjects: One is our plan, the other one is the present situation on the Syrian front, which is something to make us worry too. Then if you could tell us about Moscow and the future of Geneva, and then our requests for armaments, which we will discuss tomorrow probably.

Secretary Kissinger: Right.

General Dayan: Should we present our plan?

Secretary Kissinger: Let me talk to you five minutes about Moscow. It was the roughest conversation I have ever had with the Soviets on any subject, including Vietnam.[2] On Vietnam they were tough, but since it didn't affect their interests they gave up easily.

The main thrust was we had squeezed them out of the Middle East and violated our understanding—that understanding which we showed you the text of.[3] The understanding of course was premised on the fact that we needed these auspices in order to get the sides together. It never occurred to us it should mean they could insist they had to be there.

They insisted on immediately reconvening the Geneva Conference and that the Syrian disengagement talks be held there. They refused any proposal that I consult with Gromyko before or after a trip.

They were much tougher generally. On U.S.-Soviet things we made good progress except on SALT, where, between us, our position is as crazy as theirs.

They said the Syrians wanted them present. We checked with the Syrians and fortunately it was not true. But it is clear they won't accept any settlement in which they don't participate, and they want the Geneva Conference, and they want the Palestinians present.

I think nothing would please them more than a breakdown of the negotiations with Syria. Nothing would please them more than to be able to say to the Syrians we couldn't produce progress. They may prevent the Syrians from making an agreement, and then the problem will be whether we can separate the other Arabs from Syria.

It was a very brutal talk. They didn't come back to it. We left it that I would see Gromyko again when he comes to New York.

Ambassador Dinitz: To the special General Assembly.

Secretary Kissinger: Yes. Let's see your plan.

---

[2] Kissinger discussed the Middle East with Soviet leaders in Moscow on March 26 and 27. The memoranda of conversations are printed in *Foreign Relations*, 1969–1976, volume XV, Soviet Union, June 1972–August 1974, Documents 167 and 170.

[3] A reference to the understanding that Kissinger and Gromyko initialed on October 22, 1973, in Moscow that Middle East peace negotiations would begin "under appropiate auspices." See ibid., Document 144.

[Dayan unfolds a map on the table. See Tab A.][4]

General Dayan: Let me explain. These are our settlements on this side. It is important to bear it in mind. These are Arab villages. Some are still inhabited, those in red. The ones in green are evacuated. So you see there are some Arab villages empty. All except one in the new area are empty now.

Secretary Kissinger: I should have known you would place your settlements right on the road!

General Dayan: This is the map. That is where they are. [Laughter]

If the Syrians want the people to go back to villages, here they are.

I think it is important both in principle and as a practical matter that as many as possible go back.

Secretary Kissinger: I agree. They have said this to me.

General Dayan: It used to be no man's land before, where no one could go. I think now the status should be different—the people should go back and it should be Syrian administration. The civilians should go back even to the area under UNEF administration.

The blue line is our line, the red line is the Syrian line. So it is the same as in the old area except UNEF goes between and the civilians go back.

Here [in the north] we won't want to go back to the old line. We would divide it in three parts—our area, the UNEF zone, and the bigger part to go back to Syrian forces without any restrictions, except some I will mention that are mutual.

There are two [overlay] maps here, one with the villages and one with the lines.

We've followed the model of the Egyptian agreement on limitation of forces: There will be ten kilometers with limited forces, and an additional 15 kilometers with some limitation, and then 30 kilometers.

There will be two infantry battalions, with 60 tanks, 3,000 men, within the ten kilometers. Then, within the 25 kilometers, one infantry division, 300 tanks, and 100 guns. Then the 30 kilometers is without anti-aircraft missiles, on both sides.

Secretary Kissinger: It is like Admiral Moorer presenting a SALT plan. It is probably exactly what you have got there now. Our military have discovered that arms control is a way to expand armaments; you build up to a compulsory ceiling.

General Dayan: At least I am in good company.

Secretary Kissinger: Do you have that much there now?

---

[4] Tab A, a map entitled "Separation of Forces Plan," is Appendix A, Map 1.

General Dayan: We don't have that much there now. [Laughter] That is why we want more tanks.

Now we have about 350 tanks now along the Syrian line. I don't like it because the war might break out now. We have more than 300.

Secretary Kissinger: You want more?

General Dayan: No, I don't want so many there, so close to Damascus.

We don't want this kind of war of attrition. If we strike back, they will say we are undermining the situation on the Egyptian front. This can't go on every day.

Of what we have heard of the Egyptian [Syrian] position, besides that they want to ask us to get off the Golan Heights, they also want no buffer zone.

Secretary Kissinger: We never raised it formally but it is my impression too.

General Dayan: They told Kreisky.[5]

Secretary Kissinger: That is nonsense, what they told Kreisky. We heard that they told him about the '67 borders and the Palestinians. That was Asad's maximum position.

General Dayan: The buffer zone is very important for two reasons. It is a real buffer. There is no demilitarized zone, like on the Egyptian side. The question is whether there is something like that on the Syrian front too, something to make war less likely. So the question is whether this is an obstacle to offensive operations. Of course, everyone can overrun a UN force.

Secretary Kissinger: But it would be a moral barrier.

General Dayan: It would make things more difficult.

Secretary Kissinger: No, we would support a UN zone, and I think the Egyptians would.

General Dayan: With civilians returning, it will be Syrian administration.

But here it is too narrow and if they agree, it will have to be widened.

The question is whether they want a UN zone.

Secretary Kissinger: I have never raised it formally, and my impression is if I raised it now, they would reject it.

General Dayan: So the question is whether they want it and what the conditions would be—like how wide, and the status of the civilians.

---

[5] Bruno Kreisky, the Austrian Chancellor, led a mission of the Socialist International through the Middle East in mid-March 1974.

The second question is whether they want a limited-forces zone.

Secretary Kissinger: It depends on whether they have enough forces! [Laughter]

General Dayan: The main question is anti-aircraft missiles. We would have to take ours back.

Secretary Kissinger: How many artillery do you have there?

General Dayan: About 120 guns.

Secretary Kissinger: Will you make sure, while we are negotiating, that you put more there than you want to leave? Quite seriously.

General Dayan: We have 300 tanks there and want only 60.

Secretary Kissinger: You said you have 360 on the Golan Heights.

General Dayan: It depends on what you mean by the Golan Heights. This is all the Golan Heights. We would have to take them further back behind the 1967 line.

Secretary Kissinger: Looking at the Syrian line, if you put your tanks—the 300—behind the old line, that is something they can understand.

General Dayan: Whatever they are willing to do, we will do.

Secretary Kissinger: That is fair enough.

General Dayan: The number of tanks and the distances are the same for both parties.

Secretary Kissinger: Let me give you my view. As a plan of disengagement of forces, I can't argue with it. What are the arguments for Syrian disengagement? The arguments are not as militarily compelling as on the Egyptian front. Second, you are dealing with a country that will be even less reliable than Egypt. Third, you are dealing with a leadership that is less stable.

The argument is a temporary neutralization of the most radical elements; it gives the opportunity to take the Egyptians out of the negotiations altogether. Third, while it can't prevent a war, it permits a war to start under conditions that help keep the others out. Fourth, the Soviets want this to fail to bring about a disintegration of our role in the Middle East.

If this happens, the Soviets will accomplish not only the end of the American role but also the destruction of Sadat, which I think they are interested in. Second, the French are determined to see our role fail because that is an obstacle to their policy in the Middle East. Third, Callaghan, whom I saw yesterday,[6] I could see was under pressure from the

---

[6] Kissinger met with James Callaghan on March 28. On March 5, Callaghan had been appointed British Foreign Minister after the Labour Party took power in the United Kingdom.

experts in the room. They [the new Labour Government] are well-intentioned but their ignorance is a problem. You saw their endorsement of the November 6 declaration on the Middle East.[7]

So we can't afford a failure. And if the oil embargo is reimposed . . .

This plan—I have to consider whether even to present it. From abstract logic, you are reasonable. The civilians returning is reasonable. But these lines are impossible. We can present it only on the basis that something else can be done with you. I will be frank with you. The war may break out anyway, if the Soviets give a blank check, no matter what you do. But if I present this, war will break out. We will be discredited; Egypt will be discredited.

I have told your Ambassador, some slice of the Golan Heights, including Quneitra, will have to be part of this arrangement. I know you're not authorized to discuss it here. You don't have to discuss it. But one reason I am going in so leisurely a pace is to let Israel reflect on it.

As to the other aspects: I think it should include a UNEF zone. If they totally reject it, we have another problem. But it is to our advantage to have it as close to the Egyptian model as possible. Sadat can support it more easily.

On first look, I like this idea of the zones. I think these numbers are much too high. But if you accept the principle that anything they will accept you'll accept, . . .

General Dayan: No, on Egypt, we agree to 60 tanks.

Secretary Kissinger: You are giving me your fallback position on Egypt. When I was in Israel, Golda said she would die if there were any tanks.

General Dayan: No, it is double the Egyptian.

Secretary Kissinger: If you accept that principle, it is fine. If it is flexible, not a ceiling, I think we are fine. I have no reason to haggle with these figures. We will support symmetrical limits.

We are back to the problem of where the line is.

Asad has told me in innumerable conversations that the October 6 line was unacceptable. All our intelligence indicates this is his position. Sadat took this position too. The Soviets told me their impression is what is needed is a small line beyond the October 6 line, and didn't say they objected to that.

General Dayan: Did the Soviets tell you they want the final lines?

---

[7] The November 6 declaration was a European Community declaration calling for Israel to withdraw immediately to the October 22 cease-fire line.

Secretary Kissinger: No, they didn't mention it. We have to discuss, before Gromyko gets here, what we can give them. They mentioned only the Palestinians in connection with the Geneva Conference. They might pay a price for it.

You have to report to your Cabinet my strong conviction that it is very dangerous for me to present this line even to the man that comes here. I don't say give him your final position, because if you do, he will have to reject it, to show how tough he is.

General Dayan: One point: We are now keeping the old Syrian positions on Mt. Hermon and we suggest we will hand them over to UNEF.

Secretary Kissinger: To present this line will produce a war. It will certainly produce a war. What do you think, Joe?

Mr. Sisco: That is what worries me the most.

Secretary Kissinger: It will produce a war and almost certainly eliminate us from the negotiation.

We have an urgent request from Sadat for food grains which the Russians have cut off. Someone told me he made an anti-Soviet statement.

Mr. Sisco: In a Beirut interview, he said that the Soviets told him a lie during the war, that the Syrians had agreed to a ceasefire.

Minister Shalev: October 13.

Mr. Sisco: He cabled to Asad who said no, they hadn't. So he accused the Soviets and Vinogradov of double-dealing.

General Dayan: On the Syrian front, we are very worried. We hear the Egyptians will send 3–4,000 troops, commandos, there. This information repeated itself several times. There are Cubans there, out front, manning tanks there with others. There are some pilots from Pakistan, from Saudi Arabia, and Kuwait. So there is quite a mixture of international brigades—mostly from Arab countries, and they all came to fight, not to be stationed there. What worries us is the ones from Communist countries who are not Arabs—this is new: North Korea, Cuba, Poland, East Germany.

Secretary Kissinger: But this strengthens my argument, really, that it is essential we make a major effort to keep this from being stirred up. I have told you this. What I have said is, it has to include Quneitra and some line parallel. There will be no American pressure to give up settlements. I think it is 60–40 Asad will accept it, but whether his Government will is another problem.

The problem is how to deal with the Soviets. With Jackson and the Congress, we can't say to them they will lose détente if they don't behave, because our Congress is wrecking it anyway. On SALT, we are giving up nothing; we are offering them nothing. All Dinitz's brigade is writing profound articles on SALT. I am not blaming you. And we are squeezing them in the Middle East. So if I tell them they are threatening détente, they will say, what? I am very worried about the Soviets.

Can we do something to get them to cooperate if we give them the line as I suggest? I think we can do it if we get Boumedienne lined up. If I gave this line to Asad, he would switch completely to a destructive line.

I know you have no possibility to change it now, but you should report to the Cabinet what I am saying.

General Dayan: I want to say one thing about the timetable: It has been going on for a month now. If we have an intensive negotiation, it is at the end of April.

Secretary Kissinger: We don't want an intensive negotiation now before Asad goes to Moscow. I will write to Sadat tomorrow;[8] I won't present details but an attitude. I will tell him to use his influence to get the military activity to stop.

General Dayan: Will it affect the Egyptian front?

Secretary Kissinger: I will tell him (a) to use his influence on the Syrian front, and (b) not to join a war, provided Israel doesn't do anything wild.

We will talk about it again tomorrow. Because if we get squeezed out of the negotiations now, we have an unfortunate combination of circumstances—the Russians, the French, the British Foreign Office, and the Germans, who are shaky. We are keeping them out only by the illusion of success. And Dinitz's brigade, who want now to undermine our foreign policy ... If on top of that the Middle East blows up next month, you will have a combination of desperate men, infuriated Soviets, French eager for our failure, the British civil servants, who are already pushing Callaghan in a certain direction ...

General Dayan: I am scheduled to be on "Meet the Press" Sunday. Is there any objection if I mention the Cubans there? Because it is a fact.

Secretary Kissinger: Bebe Rebozo[9] will love you. Let's have lunch.

[The party moved to the Eighth Floor and continued the conversation at lunch]

Ambassador Dinitz: The General's problem is that we have to give Siilasvuo an answer.

Secretary Kissinger: You will have the photos next week. We will fly at the very end of the period the Egyptians gave us.

---

[8] Apparently a reference to a message transmitted in telegram 64526 to Cairo, March 30. (National Archives, RG 59, Central Foreign Policy Files, P850038–2011)

[9] Bebe Rebozo was the son of Cuban immigrants who became a wealthy banker and close friend of President Nixon.

General Dayan: I will be challenged very hard in the Parliament. One aspect is the promise; the other is the finding.

I will have to go Tuesday afternoon to say something and we will have to rely on our own checking.

Secretary Kissinger: On Wednesday, the photographs will show, and you will be okay.

I think it would be suicidal for you at this complex point to take on the Egyptians, when we have these assurances. Over an issue that is essentially trivial. It is not like 1970.

General Dayan: It is not the Government; it is the opposition!

Secretary Kissinger: Then they will have to be faced down.

General Dayan: I will have to say I believe that by the end of next week they [the extra Egyptian guns] will be removed.

Secretary Kissinger: That is all right.

General Dayan: But I would have to mention Siilasvuo.

Secretary Kissinger: I will get in touch with Sadat. I am extremely reluctant to make an American statement on this without checking with the Egyptians.

Maybe they will have removed it by then. Although this doesn't quite solve your problem.

I am sure I can get a formal assurance that they will be out by next week. We already have the formal assurance from [War Minister] Ismail, who has been more of a problem than Sadat.

General Dayan: On the prisoners, I wonder if we can get an immediate exchange of wounded in accordance with the Geneva Convention. We just got a report from the Red Cross that two are in hospital and are getting operations. We don't think they have the best surgeons.

Secretary Kissinger: The Red Cross knows how many wounded you have?

General Dayan: Yes. About 30–40 wounded in Israel, in the class that should be returned right away. And could they give us the names of about 18 who were killed there, and let us recover the bodies? And we would give them three Syrians killed in Israel.

And if the Syrian civilians come back, it will have to include the exchange of prisoners.

Secretary Kissinger: Yes, that will have to.

General Dayan: And the Jews in Syria—if they can let them out . . .

Secretary Kissinger: He has told me so many times they were well treated, he would be offended. I didn't realize why they didn't leave until you told me they weren't allowed to leave.

Frankly, I should raise this at the end of the negotiation, not during it.

General Dayan: Would the Russians get involved, or wouldn't they touch it?

Secretary Kissinger: The Russians will pay a heavy price to get involved, and for that they might even support the line I am proposing—not your line. But I am not eager to let the Russians into the room. Because I am not sure what Israel and Syria will do in a room together that won't be disastrous.

General Dayan: I was negotiating with a Syrian in 1948—and another Syrian came over and said, "What are you two Jews conspiring about?" Because he was Jewish; I hadn't known it.

We have word the Russians are delaying the return of their civilians to Syria.

Secretary Kissinger: I am uneasy because the last time Brezhnev yielded so easily was after June [1973] in San Clemente[10] when it was followed by massive arms shipment to the Middle East and no real restraint. So maybe I faced him down; but maybe they are about to do something.

General Dayan: Did the Russians promise to help?

Secretary Kissinger: I don't know. For letting a Russian into the Conference, we could get quite a few concessions. On Syrian Jews, I don't know. For the line I suggested, it is almost certain.

Brezhnev had a map of the disengagement things once—which he never produced. When he was showing me other maps, I saw it. From a quick glimpse, it looked like the October 6 line plus the salient.

Ambassador Dinitz: Do you have any information about Egyptian contingents being sent to Syria?

Secretary Kissinger: No. It strikes me as improbable. And if it is so, they are being sent there to restrain them.

Mr. Sisco: They would have informed you.

Ambassador Dinitz: It seems improbable too, but we have repeated intelligence.

General Dayan: The rationale would be he wants to keep his own line quiet and show solidarity with Syria. He doesn't want his own front flared up.

Secretary Kissinger: No.

General Dayan: They have opened up the Morgan oil field.[11]

---

[10] Brezhnev visited the United States for a nine-day trip from June 16 to June 24, 1973, which concluded with a meeting at Nixon's home in San Clemente, California. Documentation on the talks, which included lengthy discussions of the Middle East, is in *Foreign Relations, 1969–1976*, volume XV, Soviet Union, June 1972–August 1974.

[11] The Morgan oil field is in the Gulf of Suez.

Ambassador Dinitz: You will have, in addition to minesweeping, other units of the Sixth Fleet there?

Secretary Kissinger: No.

Ambassador Dinitz: Zumwalt[12] will say he has not enough ships to put there!

General Dayan: I saw a letter in the *Washington Post* asking if you are getting money from the Europeans for opening the Canal, since they get the benefit.

Secretary Kissinger: The Russians don't get all that much benefit from it, and we can send carriers through too. This is one of the cheap insanities the intellectual community is now engaged in. This isn't a great period to conduct American foreign policy.

Do you as a military man think it makes any difference?

General Dayan: If it shortens the lines for ships in the Indian Ocean. As an infantry man, I don't take the navy very seriously anyway. [Laughter]

Do they have an aircraft carrier?

Secretary Kissinger: They have a helicopter carrier.

General Dayan: What kind of helicopter do they have? Like the Cobra,[13] of course.

Secretary Kissinger: I don't know.

General Dayan: The *New York Times* said the Russian equipment was better than American in the October war. Our people didn't like that.

Secretary Kissinger: Is that true?

General Dayan: Regarding anti-aircraft missiles, yes.

Secretary Kissinger: We were too busy designing planes which play the national anthem of the country over which they are flying.

Ambassador Dinitz: How about the armored personnel carrier?

General Dayan: The American ones are better—there is such a variety of missiles attached, it is not a simple personnel carrier.

We don't think very much of the new Russian tank, by the way.

Secretary Kissinger: Really?

General Dayan: We were expecting something more efficient and with better armor. There is not much difference between the T–62 and the earlier one. Not basically. We thought it would be of a new genera-

---

[12] Admiral Elmo R. Zumwalt, Jr. was Chief of Naval Operations from July 1970 until July 1974.

[13] The Cobra is an attack helicopter made by Bell Helicopter Textron.

tion that would cause new problems. Not that it is not a good tank, but it is nothing special.

Secretary Kissinger: Why does it require special training?

General Dayan: It has night-aiming, and anti-infrared, and a lot of new devices.

Ambassador Dinitz: Is there any progress on Soviet Jewry?

Secretary Kissinger: I want to discuss that with you.

We are now in a suicidal period of American foreign policy. In Vietnam, $200 million stands between us and guaranteeing South Vietnamese survival. $200 million caused by inflation and oil. We fought there for ten years, with a loss of 50,000 men—and now we can't get it.

On MFN—if we get that, then we have the problem of credits. I must say, negotiating with the Russians as American Secretary of State, we really have nothing to offer.

No sooner will détente end than they will all switch to the left of us. Once they have the assurance there will be no SALT agreement, they will point out that we have 15,000 warheads overkill.

General Dayan: Is the oil embargo lifted completely?

Secretary Kissinger: Yes.[14]

General Dayan: Sadat got his way on the postponement of the Arab summit.[15]

Secretary Kissinger: Yes. That is why we have to get something on the Syrian front.

Mr. Sisco: Our Israeli friends can be helpful there, in your interest as well as ours.

General Dayan: We don't want escalation on the Syrian front; but if it increases ... So far, they are not shelling settlements, only military positions. But if one commander some day decides to shell a settlement, there will be an outcry. Everything might happen.

Mr. Atherton: What have your casualties been?

General Dayan: Last night there was one dead and one wounded. In a month, not many—five killed and five wounded in a month.

Ambassador Dinitz: But there is growing sentiment to retaliate.

Secretary Kissinger: I understand the situation. In many ways the Syrians are the hinge. That is why the Soviets are so nervous. Once the Syrians reach an agreement ...

Ambassador Dinitz: Then they will work on the Palestinians.

---

[14] The embargo ended on March 17.
[15] Apparently a reference to the Seventh Arab League Summit Conference at Rabat, Morocco, which was held in October 1974. See Document 112.

Secretary Kissinger: But there is no obvious confrontation aspect. The Saudis and the Egyptians will have a good alibi to keep things quiet; they will have a vested interest.

Ambassador Dinitz: If the Russians tell the Syrians: "Accept that line but in a month we will be behind you on the '67 line."

Secretary Kissinger: That will be true on any line.

General Dayan: The Russians asked for immediate opening of the Geneva Conference?

Secretary Kissinger: Yes, and to have the Syrian disengagement discussions there, and in a room with the United States and the Soviets, the Egyptians and Syrians and Israelis. It has a number of advantages: It puts the Egyptians on the spot. If the Egyptians don't back the Syrians, or if they do.

The only possibility for us is to tell the Syrians, "If you play with us you will get something; if you don't you will get nothing." The only other possibility is, if there is an agreement, to let them ratify it. But letting them in will be too dangerous.

Ambassador Dinitz: Did they raise the question of resuming diplomatic relations with us?

Secretary Kissinger: Not in Moscow. But Dobrynin did in the week before. I found him, in the week before, somewhat misleading. Some of the press problem is from briefings by him.

Has your Foreign Minister decided to come to the UN?

Ambassador Dinitz: He has not decided yet. It depends on who else is coming.

Secretary Kissinger: What *Time* said [about Eban's low standing] won't help.

Ambassador Dinitz: That came from an Israeli source. That article [about Kissinger] came out all right.

Secretary Kissinger: Yes.

Ambassador Dinitz: There is another one coming in the *New Republic*.

Secretary Kissinger: That won't come out so well.

Ambassador Dinitz: Not as well, but not bad.

Secretary Kissinger: Really?

General Dayan: Is there anyone in America who is not a newspaperman? [to Dinitz:] Not that you know. [Laughter]

Ambassador Dinitz: After we spoke to you about the need to play down Egyptian violations, you know Marilyn Berger[16] physically

---

[16] Marilyn Berger was a staff writer for the *Washington Post*.

changed the headline from "Gross Egyptian Violations" to "Diplomatic sources play down violations."

That is because I told her.

Secretary Kissinger: That is more than I could do.

Ambassador Dinitz: You should have had me in Moscow with you.

Secretary Kissinger: Yes. The situation is not so gloomy, or it is gloomy but not because of what happened there but because of the stupidities here. They constantly altered the schedule, and so on, but that is no different from the way it has been on previous pre-summit meetings there.

The underlying reality is gloomy because we are facing these brutal bastards with nothing to offer them.

Ambassador Dinitz: What do you think is Brezhnev's situation with respect to the war party there?

Secretary Kissinger: The only thing different was that he stuck religiously to a talking paper. Either he will be replaced by the right or he will shift to the right.

Mr. Sisco: What will determine the situation? SALT?

Secretary Kissinger: On SALT we will have nothing. Given Jackson and our Armed Services Committee. Economic things would help. On the Middle East they need a little face-saver. Well, more than a face-saver. They want a dominant position in Syria.

Ambassador Dinitz: Is it hurt pride, or are they afraid of you getting a position in Syria like in Egypt?

Secretary Kissinger: They should see, if they are intelligent, that we will be in much more difficult negotiations a year from now. So part of it is hurt pride.

General Dayan: Egypt is more important to them than Syria.

Secretary Kissinger: Egypt they have already lost. Unless they can get rid of Sadat.

General Dayan: They might try it.

Secretary Kissinger: That is why they want the Syrian thing to fail; it discredits both the U.S. and Sadat.

It is unfortunate this happens at a time when China is paralyzed. We can't use China to scare them. We have no moves to make to China.

Ambassador Dinitz: Fahmi is the big man now.

Secretary Kissinger: Hafiz Ismail will be sent to Moscow.

General Dayan: If there is anything Sadat wants us to do to avoid embarrassing him, I suppose we should do it.

Secretary Kissinger: Military trainees!

Mr. Sisco: What would you recommend, Mr. Secretary, to the Minister to say on "Meet the Press?" He will get asked, "Are there violations?" "If so, what are you going to do?"

General Dayan: I will say we had a dispute about the number that should have been left, because it was expressed in units rather than in numbers, but we think it will be corrected.

Secretary Kissinger: Good. On disengagement, you can say you brought a plan.

General Dayan: And we will meet tomorrow.

Secretary Kissinger: Yes. We should say it was a constructive talk, and we are hopeful.

Can I say you accepted my offer to return as Defense Minister? [Laughter]

General Dayan: Can you find out about the Egyptian troops in Syria?

Secretary Kissinger: Yes, I will. I don't want to deal with the people who are in Egypt now; I want to send our Ambassador to see Sadat.

Ambassador Dinitz: He [Sadat] is in Yugoslavia now.

Secretary Kissinger: Yes.

I don't know whether I need to propose a toast to someone who is a friend as well as an ally. But I want to express our hope we can bring this to a successful conclusion.

General Dayan: Yes. Thank you.

We will be asked whether these Egyptian guns were discussed today.

Secretary Kissinger: You can say it was discussed.

General Dayan: And if you can, by the time I am home, give me some formula I can use.

Secretary Kissinger: Yes. We won't have an answer until Monday.[17]

Sisco will be at the throttle. He was last week.

Mr. Sisco: I must say, Mr. Secretary, I didn't really feel you were ever away!

Secretary Kissinger: Ellsworth, we really have to send you to Geneva. Vinogradov was there in Moscow. You really have to keep him company there, doing nothing with him.

Mr. Sisco: That is the only job he has now.

Secretary Kissinger: Because Sadat would not let him back.

---

[17] April 1.

When we put in for economic aid for Egypt, we may need your help.

Ambassador Dinitz: That presupposes our economic aid will be solved by then. [Laughter]

Secretary Kissinger: Before I leave, I am going to get you declared PNG.

General Dayan: Will we get the full $1.5 billion in grant?

Secretary Kissinger: That will be settled in the next week.

General Dayan: After Sadat comes back. [Laughter]

Secretary Kissinger: He hasn't approved it yet!

The question is a presentational one. The determination made is not final. If we said all of the $1.5 is to be a loan, he would have the right to retroactively make it grant even if the initial determination is loan.

Ambassador Dinitz: But we hope it won't be this way.

Secretary Kissinger: No.

Ambassador Dinitz: We don't want our credits made into a grant. Because our policy is to pay all our loans. It would look like forgiving a loan.

Has the President finalized his Middle East trip plans? Because we get many reports.

Secretary Kissinger: No. You will be the first to know. It depends on many domestic things, and he can't go while Syrian disengagement is unsettled. It would put him under too many pressures.

Ambassador Dinitz: *Al-Ahram*[18] keeps saying May.

Secretary Kissinger: That is the intention. If we get a Syrian disengagement done, we can aim at the last third of May.

General Dayan: Will we meet tomorrow?

Secretary Kissinger: Make it 9:30.[19]

[The luncheon then ended. Kissinger and Dinitz meet alone in the Secretary's office from 2:45–3:00. The Secretary and the Minister then went down to the Main Lobby together to face the press.]

---

[18] *Al-Ahram* is a daily Arab newspaper based in Cairo.

[19] Kissinger met with Dayan on March 30 from 9:50 until 11:05 a.m. in the Secretary's office at the Department of State. (National Archives, RG 59, Records of Henry Kissinger, 1973–77, Box 7, Nodis Memcons, March 1974, Folder 5)

33. Letter From Secretary of State Kissinger to Israeli Prime Minister Meir[1]

Washington, April 3, 1974.

Dear Madame Prime Minister:

I have just completed detailed discussions with Defense Minister Dayan[2] who presented the views of your government on the question of Israeli-Syrian disengagement. I know that Minister Dayan will be reporting to you and members of the Cabinet fully regarding our talks, but I feel that it is essential that I communicate with you directly on how I see the situation which faces Israel and the United States at this critical juncture. You know from our previous discussions that I believe that if a disengagement agreement is achieved between Syria and Israel, it is likely to last for some time, provided military restraint is maintained on both sides.

I understand fully from my talks with Minister Dayan the considerations that went into the development of the current Israeli proposal on Syrian-Israeli disengagement. I appreciate that it represents a further evolution in the Israeli thinking on this matter and contains a number of positive features.

However, in the spirit of friendship and candor which has been characteristic of our discussions, as well as the intimate and special relationship that exists between Israel and the United States, I must convey to you my deepest concern over a number of important aspects of the Israeli proposal, particularly as it relates to the line to which Israel would withdraw.

As presently formulated, I believe the plan has no chance of being accepted by the Syrians and is likely to result in a break in the talks with a possibility—and in my honest judgment—a probability, that war again would break out, at least between Syria and Israel. I express this judgment with a heavy heart.

In addition, such a break in the talks would take place on conditions most difficult for Israel and the United States. The efforts of the U.S. would be largely discredited; the Soviets would be provided with an unparalleled opportunity to recoup their losses in the area and to reconvene the Geneva Conference and through it establish for themselves a role of the kind which they have to date been denied by the Arabs themselves. The Europeans would be strengthened in their

---

[1] Source: National Archives, Nixon Presidential Materials, NSC Files, Kissinger Office Files, Box 136, Country Files, Middle East, Dinitz, January 1–July 1, 1974. Secret.
[2] See Document 32.

pro-Arab course. The oil embargo would probably be reinstated. Egypt would be isolated and weakened in its resolve to stay out of future conflict. The positive trend which the Egyptian-Israeli disengagement agreement has brought about would be reversed, and much of what has been accomplished over the past months fundamentally undermined.

You will recall that in my conversations with you I outlined what I believe is needed in order to give hope that an agreement can be achieved[3]—an agreement which would protect the security interests of Israel, would leave untouched Israeli settlements, and would provide the only sensible alternative to war. I explained to Minister Dayan as I did to you in my talks in Jerusalem, that what is required is an Israeli proposal that provides for Israeli withdrawal along the lines I explained to General Dayan but not to include any Israeli settlements. This will enable us to obtain support from other Arab countries. I do not know whether Syria would find this acceptable, but I am confident that with such an Israeli proposal, put forward on the basis of agreed tactics between us, the capacity of the Soviet Union to be successfully troublesome would be reduced. It would provide President Assad with an alternative to war while placing whatever territory Israel gives up under the control of UNEF, it would sustain our mutual efforts, and it would avoid giving additional ammunition to those European countries who seem poised today to inject themselves unhelpfully into the situation should present efforts fail to achieve agreement.

Madame Prime Minister, I am writing to you in all solemnity because I am convinced that we are now reaching a very critical point. I know there are varying views in Israel on this matter. I believe I understand the concerns, the worries, the anguish which all Israelis feel that nothing should be done which could affect adversely Israel's security. It is a grave and awesome responsibility—a responsibility which you have long carried with great courage and distinction. I know your fervent desire for peace, your fervent hope that not one more Israeli ever be lost in another war. Because I know that you fully realize this, I am writing to you at this point to urge you to reconsider on an urgent basis the proposal that has been conveyed to us and to consider seriously and give weight to the views I have expressed in this letter. In doing so, I would ask that your government look at the totality of the strategic and political considerations I have outlined and not the military aspects alone.

As you know, I will be seeing the Syrian representative about April 11 or 12. I do not ask you to formulate a new Israeli proposal for

---

[3] See Document 28.

these meetings. However, I am most fearful that presenting your current ideas will have the serious results which I have described in this letter unless I can at least offer in the talks some hope that we can expect a further progression of your views by the time I come to the area, in the latter part of April.

I would appreciate hearing from you before my talks with the Syrians here in Washington.[4]

With warm regards and respect,

Henry A. Kissinger[5]

---

[4] Prime Minister Meir replied to Kissinger's letter on April 9, stating that the proposal presented by Dayan during his visit to Washington "reflects the position of the Israel Government." (National Archives, Nixon Presidential Materials, NSC Files, Kissinger Office Files, Box 136, Country Files, Middle East, Dinitz, January 1–July 1, 1974)

[5] Printed from a copy that bears this typed signature.

---

34. Editorial Note

On April 11, 1974, three members of the Popular Front for the Liberation of Palestine-General Command attacked the Israeli town of Kiryat Shmona near the border with Lebanon. The PFLP–GC members killed eighteen Israeli civilians in an apartment building, and all three attackers were later killed that day by Israeli forces in a shootout. (*New York Times*, April 12, 1974, p. 65) On April 12, Israel launched retaliatory attacks against six Lebanese villages bordering Israel and destroyed the houses of residents suspected of sheltering Arab guerrillas. (Ibid., April 13, 1974, p. 1)

35. Memorandum of Conversation[1]

Washington, April 13, 1974, 10:40 a.m.–12:23 p.m.

PARTICIPANTS

    Brigadier Hikmat al-Shihabi, Syrian Army, Chief of Staff for Intelligence
    Dr. Sabah Kabbani, Chief of Syrian Interests Section

    Dr. Henry A. Kissinger, Secretary of State
    Joseph J. Sisco, Under Secretary of State for Political Affairs
    Ellsworth Bunker, Ambassador at Large
    Alfred L. Atherton, Jr., Assistant Secretary-Designate for Near Eastern and South Asian Affairs
    Harold S. Saunders, NSC Senior Staff
    Camille Nowfel, Interpreter
    Peter W. Rodman, NSC Staff

[Photographers were admitted briefly as Secretary Kissinger greeted Brigadier Shihabi in his office.]

[After the photographers departed, the Secretary introduced the members of the American side. The reasons for the large number, he said, were two: First, his own colleagues did not fully trust him. Second, decisions in this conversation would be taken by majority vote. "I'll probably lose," he added.]

Secretary Kissinger: What I thought we should do is review the evolution of where we are with the Israelis, and where we should go, with great precision.

Brigadier Shihabi: Yes.

Secretary Kissinger: There are a number of things to keep in mind about the Israelis. In the Arab world I know there is the view that the Israelis are terribly clever and everything is thought out. Our experience with the Israelis is that it is a very divided government, with about ten Cabinet members who think they should be Prime Minister. In fact Israel is one of the few countries in the world where you insult a man by offering him a Cabinet position—because he usually thinks he is entitled to more. It is the opposite of the State Department, where all my State Department friends know I am unqualified for the Foreign Service and the only way I could get a job in this building is as Secretary of State. [Laughter]

What this means is that on almost any issue in Israel it is almost impossible to have a rational debate on the overall strategy. The more

---

[1] Source: National Archives, Nixon Presidential Materials, NSC Files, Box 1028, Presidential/HAK Memcons, March 1–May 8, 1974, Folder 2. Secret; Nodis. The meeting took place in the Secretary's office. Brackets are in the original.

general your idea is, the more you unite all the factions against it. Secondly—I want to give you an explanation of our strategy, then we can get into specifics—it is no secret that there are pressure groups in this country who work together with the Israelis. What we have to prevent is a coalescence of all these forces.

Therefore our strategy with these negotiations is to move one step at a time. We ask the Israelis to make one decision; then we ask them to make another decision; then we move them step by step towards the objective.

Let me explain the Egyptian case, as I began to do yesterday.[2] We had no contact with the Syrians at all at that time. We asked Israel to discuss with us the October 22 line. They absolutely refused, and I received on one weekend thirty phone calls from Members of Congress who—at that time they said we were doing it with the Russians. And also a newspaper campaign started. So I decided not to fight that issue right away, and to get myself organized first. By the end of November they were willing to discuss disengagement. By mid-December they were willing to leave the West Bank of the Canal—you remember they had a bridgehead—but only if all the territory they left were turned over to the UN. We rejected that. Then they said half the territory could go to Egypt. As late as when I went to Aswan the first time, they said they were willing to give Egypt two-thirds of the territory on the West Bank but they had to have the bridgehead across the Canal.

So it was not until the last three days of the negotiation that we got them to go back to where they did.

It is the same with Syria. This you have to understand.

Brigadier Shihabi: As you have pointed out, Mr. Secretary, moving forward towards the objective step by step may be the best way.

Secretary Kissinger: I will show you the latest proposal; I will first explain their first proposal.

Brigadier Shihabi: I would like to point out that time is of the essence in this respect.

Secretary Kissinger: I agree with you. And our intention is that I plan to come to the Middle East during the last days of April. I will fix a date after you have left. Then within a week ... I hope on my next trip to come to a final settlement. By May 10th. Maybe earlier. At any rate, when I go to the Middle East, I hope we will come to a conclusion. And I would travel back and forth between Damascus and Israel for as long as is necessary. Unless President Asad wants to meet in Palmyra.

---

[2] According to Kissinger's Record of Schedule, there was no meeting with Shihabi the previous day. (Library of Congress, Manuscript Division, Kissinger Papers, Box 438, Miscellany, 1968–76)

Brigadier Shihabi: Any place you would like to meet, we would be pleased to arrange for you, Mr. Secretary.

What I wanted to point out with respect to time is, if we keep the situation as frozen as it has been, we are likely to bring about that what has been achieved might be misconstrued in a way jeopardizing to all that has been achieved.

Secretary Kissinger: But in two weeks? I plan to leave two weeks from today or tomorrow.

Brigadier Shihabi: This is good, Mr. Secretary. But I wanted to point it out because of the importance of time.

Secretary Kissinger: We need two weeks. I would like to have the situation prepared once I am out there. I do not want them to have me sitting in Jerusalem looking impotent. We will leave during the weekend two weeks from now. And I will go certainly to Israel before Damascus, to get their [proposals].

I will of course keep you closely informed. Also I will keep you informed of any conversations we have with anybody bearing on this subject. And we will not discuss anything with any Arab country that you do not know about—concerning Syria. Because it is not in our interest to create any misunderstandings in the Arab world.

Let me explain where we were in the Israeli position.

When I was in Israel—when was it?—in the first part of March,[3] their proposal was that they would give up half of the salient, and the other half was to be put under the United Nations. And that no civilians could return into the area. So we did not even present this to President Asad, because I did not want to insult him.

We then said that, one, whatever territory they withdraw from, the civilians should return. So that is a condition as far as we are concerned, and I assume it is a condition as far as you are concerned.

Second, we could not ask you to accept restrictions on your side that they would not accept on their side. In other words, there had to be an equitable arrangement.

Thirdly, we told them they had to make a much more substantial withdrawal than just part of the salient.

Then they sent Dayan over here, and presented a plan that accepted two of our proposals.[4] So I am just showing you there is progress. One, they agreed that civilians can return to whatever area they withdrew from, and Syrian civil administration can return. And second, the restrictions on their side of the line would be the same as on

---

[3] Kissinger met with Israeli leaders in Israel on March 1. See Document 28.
[4] See Document 32.

your side. And they gave us a line further back than the first one. In fact, it is almost the October 6 line, not exactly. I will show it to you in a minute.

I then had a private talk with Dayan—what I say, you know, should go only to the President, because it would be very unfortunate if it got into the newspapers—and I told him in my judgment it was impossible for President Asad to settle for the October 6 line, and there had to be some change beyond the October 6 line. And I told him we would be quite sympathetic to this point of view, but others, like Rabin, are opposed.

So after I returned I wrote a letter to the Prime Minister in which I made this point very strongly. And she replied and did not reject it. She did not accept it either.[5] But they know that when I go out there I am not going to accept this line.

We have to move these things [the line] further over. But the civilians returning, Syrian civil administration, and symmetrical restrictions—that we have achieved.

You know the problem for them is very difficult. Because for them the Golan is a much more emotional issue than the Sinai. So maybe if I get blown up in the Middle East, it will be in Jerusalem, not in Damascus. [Laughter]

Brigadier Shihabi: We are aware of the fact that security measures have to be . . .

Secretary Kissinger: I meant it as a joke.

Brigadier Shihabi: You may not be concerned about your safety as a person, but in view of your importance to the world at large, every measure will be taken.

Secretary Kissinger: I will have a difficult time. Because the person whom we relied on, Dayan, has been severely weakened. And the Prime Minister—she is not very imaginative, but once she makes up her mind, she can be quite courageous—has also been weakened. Eban has no influence. Allon lives in a settlement near the Syrian border, so he is . . . not very fond of Syria. [They smile.] I want to be realistic. The Chief of Staff, who was very helpful on the Egyptian side, has just been dismissed.

But that is my problem. I am determined to produce a settlement. I have always told your President that I do not think I can achieve the line he proposed. But I will achieve the maximum line that is possible. And it will have to be beyond the October 6 line. And it has to include Quneitra.

---

[5] See Document 33 and footnote 4 thereto.

So let me show you what they have given us. You should not get too upset [laughter] because ...

[They get up and go over to the table to examine the Israeli map brought by Dayan on March 29. Tab A][6]

They did not tell me I could pass this over to you, so we will just use it for discussion.

[Pointing out on the map:] This is the October 6 line. They want to make this the UN zone. Civilians can return up to this line [including the UN zone] and Syrian civil administration can be introduced here.

Then they accepted the same basic principle as with the Egyptians, that is, various zones, with limited forces. For example, in this zone there will be two infantry battalions, 60 tanks, and 3,000 men. And the same here [on the opposite side]. In this zone—which is the same distance on both sides—there can be that many [indicates numbers in table at the bottom of the map].

I told them these forces seemed very large to me for up there. They told me they were prepared to negotiate. They do not insist on these figures. At any rate, they accept the principle that the figures should be the same on both sides.

As I said, this zone will have to be moved here, and that, of course, would move the separation zones over here [westward]. What they did here [in the southern sector] is to take the old demilitarized zone; they want to put the UN into the old demilitarized zone, but Syrian civil administration.

I have the impression that President Asad would not accept this—or am I wrong? [Laughter]

I am not even going to present this.

Brigadier Shihabi: I believe it would be preferable not to present this to him.

Secretary Kissinger: I won't present it to him. The thing to remember about this is not whether it is acceptable—it is not acceptable—but that it is the first proposal that one can even discuss, in terms of ideas, for example, the symmetry of limitations. Now the problem is to move the line over here [to the west]. Then the size of forces, and so forth, we should discuss later.

President Asad told me he agreed to the idea that forces should be limited on both sides of the line. Or did I misunderstand him?

Brigadier Shihabi: In principle, the question is discussable and negotiable, and some settlement along these lines can be reached.

---

[6] Tab A is Appendix A, Map 1.

Secretary Kissinger: I agree. I think these figures are ridiculous. But it is up to you. I personally do not think they need one infantry division and one armor division in this zone. And I said this to Dayan, and I had the impression that he is prepared to lower this.

Your problem is that you scared them so much on October 6 that they are no longer so self-confident. [Laughter]

In that week—it was my first week here—the intelligence people in the State Department, the Sunday before October 6, told me about your deployment of tanks. To me the deployment of your tanks looked like you were getting ready to attack. So I asked the Israelis, and they said, "Impossible. The Syrians can never attack. It is impossible." I asked them three more times that week, and each time they told me it could not happen.

So that was quite a shocking event. This is their present concept, but I will not present this concept in Damascus.

Brigadier Shihabi: As much as this plan will not be presented, I see no need to go into a detailed discussion of it. But my first impression is that it does not represent a real disengagement between the forces of both sides. It does not indicate a desire on the other side for real withdrawal and consequently a real move in the direction of peace.

In addition, this plan seems to impose a relinquishing of sovereignty over more areas of our own territory. The defense of Damascus would be weakened. [He points to the limitation line farthest to the east.]

Secretary Kissinger: This line has to do with missiles. This line [the other] refers to forces.

Brigadier Shihabi: A plan like this can by no manner or means be acceptable. And you are right, Mr. Secretary, it would be pointless to present it to the Syrian Government.

Secretary Kissinger: I understand the line is unacceptable too.

Brigadier Shihabi: Yes, it is not acceptable in any respect—because it is not disengagement, it is relinquishing sovereignty and it is not a real move to peace.

Secretary Kissinger: But there are two problems—one is the line and the other is these zones.

Brigadier Shihabi: Also, the lines are very far from being acceptable.

Secretary Kissinger: What I want to understand is this concept—even if the lines are moved over here—of limited armament like on the Egyptian side—whether that concept is acceptable.

Brigadier Shihabi: Yes, the concept of defining areas on both sides equal in size and limiting the numbers of forces in these parallel areas is acceptable.

Secretary Kissinger: It is acceptable.

Brigadier Shihabi: It is acceptable in so far as negotiating this point is concerned.

Secretary Kissinger: Yes, we are not talking about numbers. And this concept of two zones, with light and limited forces, on the Egyptian model?

Brigadier Shihabi: It would be better, rather than two zones, [to have] one zone, in which there would be a reduction of forces on the two sides.

Secretary Kissinger: I would have to discuss this with the Israelis. They think more along the Egyptian lines. You think more in terms of one zone.

Brigadier Shihabi: Yes.

Secretary Kissinger: The next question is what is your view about a UN force? With the understanding that Syria would administer the civil administration in that area. It would be Syrian sovereignty but a UN force.

Brigadier Shihabi: As you realize, Mr. Secretary, the best guarantee of peace is to have a real desire and move in the direction of peace.

Secretary Kissinger: Right.

Brigadier Shihabi: The Golan area differs in many respects from the Sinai area.

[Everyone is seated.]

Secretary Kissinger: I don't think looking at the map will improve his disposition. [Laughter]

Brigadier Shihabi: It differs in terms of terrain. And Golan is a populated area. There are 273 populated towns there. The population is between 170,000 and 180,000. It is small in terms of area. All these factors make it necessary to look at it differently from the Sinai with regard to the presence of an international force. In our estimate, the presence of UN observers would be more appropriate as far as the Golan is concerned.

Secretary Kissinger: It would ease matters greatly if we could have a UN force there. But it need not be extremely large.

[To Sisco:] Have we ever made an estimate of what is needed? There are 8,000 people in the Sinai, but that is a much longer line.

Under Secretary Sisco: No, we have not.

Brigadier Shihabi: In our opinion, Mr. Secretary, as long as either of the parties does not have a desire for peace, the presence of any emergency force, whatever the size, is useless.

Secretary Kissinger: I agree that if either side wants to go to war, it can go to war.

Brigadier Shihabi: The nature of the area, the fact it is populated, and third, the fact that the Syrian people are raised in such a way that they are not willing to have a foreign force on their territory, make them unwilling to accept a foreign force there. Our view is that our desire for peace is the best guarantee, and the presence of an international force would, I believe, in our country create a complication that would be unnecessary. As far as observers are concerned, we might increase their numbers, increase their effectiveness.

Secretary Kissinger: Everything is a problem, believe me. I have negotiated with the Israelis. At one point they had a five-hour Cabinet meeting over thirty guns. And you are not exactly easy to deal with, either. [They smile.] You did not survive for 2,000 years with various foreign pressures on you, by being easy to get along with. [Laughter]

But I respect a fierce sense of independence. That is a good guarantee of stability in the long term. [Shihabi nods yes.] Because countries that have a strong sense of independence towards one side have it towards everybody.

Honestly, I have to tell you, I used to think of Syria as a Soviet satellite. [Laughter] I am serious. I don't think you are good satellite material.

Brigadier Shihabi: As I pointed out last night, it has always been our desire that our relations with all peoples, particularly with the big nations, the United States and the Soviet Union, should be based on friendship and mutual respect. During the period when we had no bilateral relations between us, we always felt that was an abnormal situation. During the period when we had relations with the Soviet Union, and there were people who were not really aware of the situation as it was in Syria, we sought to make it known to everyone that Syria was very concerned about its sovereignty and self-respect. It is no secret to you, Mr. Secretary, and to your colleagues who are aware of what was going on, it was a period when we were under a great deal of pressure. But in spite of all the pressure and all the difficulties we have had, we have never lost sight of our independence and our sovereignty. Just as fiercely and strongly as we resisted such alliances as the Baghdad Pact, we just as strongly resisted the creation of other pacts.

Secretary Kissinger: I am aware of this. We recognize Syria is conducting its own policy. We also recognize that it is no accident that Damascus has through so many centuries been the center of Arab nationalism, and that is not without its meaning to us. And basically, the only long-term basis for a long-term relationship is with people who have their own self-respect. They are more difficult to deal with, but they are more reliable.

Our own view on the Syrian-American relationship is that if we now succeed in this disengagement, we are prepared, at whatever pace you wish to set, to accelerate normalization of our relationship. And I frankly believe it will help the further evolution of the peace efforts if in the American mind the view of Syria is improved as a country with which we have better relations.

Brigadier Shihabi: On the basis of my personal desire, as well as on my experience and knowledge, there is such a desire on the part of our Government at all levels.

Secretary Kissinger: President Asad has said this to me.

Brigadier Shihabi: There is a real desire to further relations between us, to further cooperation between our two countries. As far as a desire to accelerate this is concerned, I am going to convey what you just said to the President.

Secretary Kissinger: We won't press you; we just want you to know we are prepared to accept whatever initiative you wish to make.

Brigadier Shihabi: We appreciate your position in this respect, Mr. Secretary. But as you appreciate, any move in this direction would have to be the outcome of the evolution of a new set of circumstances that our people could understand as appropriate.

Secretary Kissinger: We understand you have your domestic necessities. We just want you to know we are willing. We also want you to know we have no special favorites among the Arab countries, and we are prepared to do with any Arab country what we are prepared to do with any other. So President Asad can assume, observing what we do with other Arab countries, that the same is true in principle with Syria. And you will see we will be improving our economic relations with Egypt over the next few months, and we are prepared, whenever you are ready, to do the same with you—but you determine the pace—and be helpful in your economic development. Because in the long term, that is where the hope of the area resides, to fulfill the aspirations of your people. My colleagues told me of the very interesting talk you had last night of the possibilities of the economic development of Syria. Once peace is achieved in the area, there are really good projects.

Brigadier Shihabi: This is very true.

Secretary Kissinger: Now, I am having lunch with Gromyko.[7] I just want to tell you what I am telling him—with your approval. Actually it is social; his wife will be there, and my wife, so not much business will be done. But social conversation is not a Soviet specialty. [Laughter] So we will probably get to business eventually.

---

[7] Gromyko was in Washington for talks with U.S. officials. He and Kissinger discussed the Middle East on April 12. See *Foreign Relations*, 1969–1976, volume XV, Soviet Union, June 1972–August 1974, Document 173.

I will say I presented certain Israeli ideas, which we do not support. And that I will continue efforts with Israel to produce a line more in keeping with Syrian necessities. I will not discuss the problem of limited armaments or the problem of the return of the Syrian population. I don't object to your saying this to them if you want to. But I, if you agree, would like to know what you tell them, because I would like to tell them more or less the same thing.

You have not been in contact with them here.

Brigadier Shihabi: There has been no such contact and I have no intention to make any such contact. Inasmuch as you have pointed out you do not support the Israeli plan which has been presented, and you will not present it to President Asad on your visit to Syria, therefore I feel there is no need to enter into a detailed discussion of this subject with the Soviets.

Secretary Kissinger: My idea, though, if you agree, is to leave the idea that we are making some progress, so they do not start a propaganda campaign. [Shihabi nods agreement.]

Let me give you an honest judgment of what the progress is—this is for you, not for the Soviets. The progress is return of the Syrian civil administration and population. Second, that Syrian forces can return to the areas vacated, except perhaps to the demilitarized zone between the two sides. And that Israeli forces will be thinned out in the same proportion as the Syrian forces. But since there are no Syrian forces now in the areas being vacated, the objective result is an augmentation of your forces and a thinning out of theirs.

So the three components will be: a movement forward of Syrian forces, a withdrawal of Israeli forces, a thinning out of Israeli forces beyond the line of withdrawal, and return of Syrian civilians to the vacated territories. Those are the positive elements that have already been achieved. What has not yet been satisfactorily achieved is the line. And the United States agrees it should be beyond the October 6 line. And we are putting great pressure on the Israeli Government to go along with it.

So this would be where we are now. Therefore what remains to be done when I come to the Middle East is to move the line. And to agree on the disposition of forces. On both sides.

I hope I am not like the man who during the war said the way to deal with the submarine menace is to heat the oceans and boil the submarines to the surface. Someone said, how do you do that? He said: I have given you the idea; the technical execution is up to you. [Laughter]

This is what we have to achieve.

I would not come out if I did not think it could be achieved. What will be necessary when I come out, quite frankly, is this: I do not think extreme flexibility is the characteristic of Syrian negotiators. [Laughter]

Brigadier Shihabi: Thanks for the compliment. [Laughter]

Secretary Kissinger: So we should not let the details stand in the way of the accomplishment. I don't have anything specific in mind.

Brigadier Shihabi: As a result of your contacts with Syrian officials, and particularly with the President, I am sure you are aware of our desire to move objectively in the direction of peace.

Secretary Kissinger: I am a great admirer of your President.

Brigadier Shihabi: Our desire for a just peace is an objective and durable desire. Whatever discussions we have are based on this desire and on our capability of moving in this direction.

Secretary Kissinger: Let me deal with two other problems, with regard to Soviet relations. President Asad said we should reach an agreement in principle first, and the details could be worked out in the military committee. Frankly, I believe when we work out the principles we will also work out the details. Because it is hard to separate them.

But we can work out a ceremony in which the Soviets can have standing, and so forth.

I think once we have discussed the line and size of forces, there is not much more to negotiate. But I will follow your wishes on this. But it may not be so easy to split this in two parts. You do not have to make a decision now.

Brigadier Shihabi: I will convey this to the President.

Secretary Kissinger: If we reach that point, it will be a happy problem!

Second, as you know, the Soviet Union is eager to have it appear as if there is Soviet participation. I may agree to meet with Gromyko in Geneva on my way to the Middle East. I want you—I want your President—to know that this will be a symbolic meeting, done for Soviet self-respect. Nothing will be discussed there beyond what I have told you I will discuss. We will negotiate with President Asad directly, not through another country.

I do not suppose you would object to a meeting in Geneva?

Brigadier Shihabi: I do not think so but in any case I will convey this to the President. But I do not think there is any objection.

Secretary Kissinger: We have informed your President after every meeting and we will be very meticulous about this. And in fact I will send him a letter tonight thanking him for sending you and about some of our discussions.[8] And I hope you will convey to him my warm per-

---

[8] Apparently a reference to messages transmitted to Asad in telegram 75900 to Damascus, April 14. (National Archives, RG 59, Central Foreign Policy Files, P850023–2017)

sonal regards, as well as my gratitude for sending you. [Brigadier Shihabi nods yes.]

Will I see you in Damascus?

Brigadier Shihabi: I hope I will have the privilege of seeing you. It has been an honor for me to be sent here as the representative of my Government. I am happy to return to the United States, after a long absence. I am pleased to have the opportunity to discuss these things with you.

Secretary Kissinger: I hope we can look back on these meetings as the beginning of peace.

When do you return to Syria?

Brigadier Shihabi: Immediately upon completion of my mission.

Secretary Kissinger: Is there anything we can do? [to Sisco:] Are we taking care of him? Theater, and so on?

[to Shihabi:] I will be taking you downstairs. There are many press there. How do you think we should handle this?

Brigadier Shihabi: Before I answer your question, I would like to mention that I have with me a map which shows the lines to which withdrawal should go. I would like to present it to you.

Secretary Kissinger: Oh, yes. Let us discuss it. We should discuss it. [They get up to the table again.] Can I keep it here?

Brigadier Shihabi: Yes.

[They spread out the map on the table. Tab B][9]

The orange line represents the international boundary. The blue line represents the line to which we would want the Israelis to withdraw as a preliminary step towards disengagement [sic].

Secretary Kissinger: That is the line the President gave me [on January 20]?[10]

Brigadier Shihabi: It is almost the same line. It varies in that it takes into consideration areas that are populated. The previous line went between two populated villages up in the north; the present line has the two villages on this [the Syrian] side of the line.

At the southern part, the line takes in a rather sizable village, Fiq, which has a population of about 10,000.

[Indicating:] This is the October 6 line. This is the salient area.

The red line is the line to which we want our forces to move.

For practical purposes, on this map, the occupied territory is divided into three parts:

---

[9] Tab B is Appendix A, Map 2.
[10] See Document 19 and footnote 2 thereto.

The blue area falls between the international boundary and the line to which the Israelis should withdraw. This is the area where the Israelis are to remain only on a temporary basis.

The green area is the buffer zone between Israeli and Syrian forces. Naturally the civilians are to return to this area and it is to be under Syrian civil administration. And the international observers can move freely throughout here. The width varies, between three and six kilometers.

The red area is the area in which there would be Syrian forces.

As you know, Mr. Secretary, our ability and maneuvering in presenting our point of view is extremely limited. As you know from your talks with the President, we have given you our final opinions with respect to this subject.

The details on this map are an indication of a number of positive steps on our part:

First, it shows appropriate withdrawal as the first step in the direction of peace and as an expression of a desire for peace. It will give us a chance to make the plan acceptable to our people.

It has an adequate buffer zone which will make impossible daily clashes, and which would make possible the removal of the state of tension. And this plan will make it possible for us to repatriate a large portion of the population of the area, and that in itself will have a great positive effect, first on the people of the area and on the population at large.

The positioning of our forces, their going beyond some important centers like Quneitra, will be a positive step and give a feeling of security, particularly to the population in this area.

Mr. Saunders: Is there any concept of limitation in this area?

Secretary Kissinger: As I understand the General, he has agreed to the principle of limitations for both sides.

Brigadier Shihabi: In principle this is negotiable, and . . .

Secretary Kissinger: Why don't you make some studies, for your own use, so we can discuss them when I come? Because it will be valid wherever the line is.

Brigadier Shihabi: Yes, we will.

Secretary Kissinger: I recognize this represents a further evolution of your thinking—this line, and the creation of a buffer zone.

I think you should present it to the Israelis. [Laughter]

Brigadier Shihabi: Mr. Kabbani pointed out that this map is larger, clearer, and much more specific than the Israeli map they presented, so it represents a clearer, more positive desire for peace.

Secretary Kissinger: I recognize the Syrian Government made much evolution in their thinking, and it shows a desire for peace. There are many constructive elements in here.

What do we do with the press?

Brigadier Shihabi: What do you suggest?

Secretary Kissinger: We can step in front of the television for two minutes. We can say we had very full and very frank talks. I presented some of the Israeli ideas and he presented very detailed Syrian ideas. That we will continue our efforts to bring these two positions together, and the United States will do its utmost to bring about disengagement between Israel and Syria, and we consider that these talks have been very helpful. I can say it, or you can say it and I can confirm it.

Brigadier Shihabi: [in English] I prefer you will say it. [Laughter]

Secretary Kissinger: Then you will say "You are a liar." [Laughter] You should say a few words too.

[The Secretary and Brigadier Shihabi thereupon went down in the Secretary's elevator to the main lobby where they spoke briefly to the press. Their remarks are at Tab C.][11]

[11] Tab C attached but not printed.

36. Memorandum of Conversation[1]

Washington, April 25, 1974, 5:08–6:35 p.m.

PARTICIPANTS

Mr. Max Fisher
Rabbi Israel Miller, President, Conference of Presidents of Major American Jewish Organizations
Mr. Jacob Stein, Former President, Conference of Presidents of Major American Jewish Organizations
Mr. Yehudah Hellman, Executive Director, Conference of Presidents of Major American Jewish Organizations
Mr. Stanley Lowell, President, Conference of Soviet Jewry
Rabbi Arthur Hertzberg, President, American Jewish Congress

[1] Source: Library of Congress, Manuscript Division, Kissinger Papers, CL 155, Geopolitical File, Israel, April 1974. No classification marking. The meeting was held in the Conference Room on the Seventh Floor of the Department of State. Brackets are in the original.

Mr. I. L. Kenen, Chairman, American-Israeli Public Affairs Committee
Mr. David Blumberg, President, B'nai-B'rith
Mrs. Rose Matzkin, President, Hadassah
Mr. David Sheinkman, President, Jewish Labor Council
Mr. Louis Cole, President, National Jewish Community Relations Advisory Council
Mrs. Charlotte Jacobson, President, World Zionist Organization
Mr. Herman Rosenberg, Young Israel
Mr. Paul Zuckerman, United Jewish Appeal
Mr. Edward Ginsburg, United Jewish Appeal
Mr. Raymond Epstein, Council of Jewish Federations and Welfare Funds

Dr. Henry A. Kissinger, Secretary of State and Assistant to the President
Mr. Leonard Garment, Counsel to the President
Mr. Joseph J. Sisco, Under Secretary of State for Political Affairs
Mr. Peter W. Rodman, NSC Staff

[The Secretary conferred with Max Fisher privately in his office from 5:00–5:06 and with Garment and Fisher from 5:06–5:08.]

Kissinger: I appreciate this opportunity to see you. Going off to the Middle East, I wanted to talk to you about what we are trying to do there, and what might come out, so you have a feel when you read the newspapers of what our basic strategy is.

Nothing that I tell you is behind the back of the Israeli Government. Everything I tell you I have told them. In fact, I have told them more than I am telling you. [Laughter]

No, there is a 100 percent agreement on the basic strategy. On tactics, there will be 100 percent agreement by the time I leave Jerusalem. There may be tactical differences sometimes.

Now, why do we want a Syrian disengagement?

It is important there be confidence in the Jewish community in what we are doing. There are a lot of dangerous people spreading around dangerous things. For example, that we are in cahoots with the Soviet Union, that we are doing all this for détente, and that Israel is the victim of détente. Any serious person knows what we are doing is of profound damage to the Soviet Union. On my last trip to Moscow, there was a four-hour brawl with Brezhnev on the Middle East.[2] Our whole strategy for four years was to create a situation where the Arabs become frustrated with the Soviet Union and turn away from the Soviet Union. So it is crucial that the Jewish community understand what is going on.

The second crucial point is that if the Arabs turn from the Soviet Union, that they have the option of turning closer to the United States. This is vital to the security of Israel. Let us say, in a horrendous case—which will never happen—if the United States replaced all Soviet mili-

---

[2] See footnote 2, Document 32.

tary equipment in Egypt with American equipment, one-for-one, Israel's security would increase by 500 percent. Because you know that in a war, we would never resupply Egypt by airlift in the middle of a war the way we did with Israel. But it is an absurd case, and it will never happen. There will be economic aid. If we supply any weapons, it will be a symbolic trickle.

So I hope the Jewish community does not fall for this Jackson amendment on the economic aid bill that no Soviet military ships can go through the Suez Canal. Reconstruction of the Canal was one of the conditions that Israel put on the disengagement agreement. Because every dollar spent there is a hostage to Israel because they are only 15 kilometers away. So don't fall for easy answers in a complicated situation.

Some Jewish leaders get upset when I am seen with Arab leaders. [Some laughter] But this is essential to the success of our strategy.

What were the issues last year? Jerusalem, the 1967 borders, the rights of the Palestinians. What are the issues now? Disengagement. Because every Arab leader has learned, painfully, that they have to deal with us, and if they deal with us they have to deal with us on one issue at a time, and this is Israel's interest.

The alternative to the present course is not to do nothing; the alternative is that the United States will not be the mediator, but it will be in international forums in which the Soviets, Europeans and Japanese will be influential, and all the issues will be lumped together, and the Arabs will turn back to the Soviets.

It is easy to make heroic speeches.

In October, I prohibited for two weeks any discussion on energy in our government. So all our decisions were taken in absence of consideration of energy. The embargo was put on on the last day of the war.[3]

I tell you frankly: I consider it highly improbable that the largest airfield in the Azores will be available to us for an airlift again. It took massive blackmail and agreement on support for Portuguese policy in Africa. [Murmuring in the group.]

Third, you don't have to take my judgment on the domestic situation, but I think it will be harder to get $2.2 billion from the Congress next time.[4]

So I agree, Israel is in danger, in fact in greater danger than is generally recognized. This is why we have moved slowly, with painstaking agreement on the very last detail with the Israeli Government. This is the only course with the possibility of success.

---

[3] The oil embargo was imposed on October 19, 1973.
[4] See footnote 12, Document 23.

We have to have the capacity to maneuver. We have to maintain the confidence of the Arabs; we have to keep the Soviets from disrupting everything. This is complicated.

This is the strategy: To go from Syrian disengagement to either another negotiation with Egypt or a negotiation with Jordan. It depends on the preference of Jerusalem. I think probably it will be with Egypt. There is a chance for very major progress on the Egyptian side.

That is why everything depends on Syrian disengagement. We are in a very uncertain situation. There is uncertainty about the [Israeli] domestic situation.

I am counting on your excellent discretion here.

We are in a situation where Dayan, and Golda, who put over the Egyptian disengagement, are on the way out. Even Eban is reported on his way out. On the other hand, Rabin I know well, and he was a close friend of mine among Ambassadors. He is one of the few in Israel with a geopolitical sense. I often called him in to chat about areas unrelated to Israel. This is not generally known. We used to sit in the Map Room of the White House and just chat. Because I respected his judgment.

It is a complicated situation in Syria now, too. There is an Iraqi faction, a Syrian nationalist faction. Compared to other Syrians—when I compare the messages I get from him [Asad] today with the first talk Joe and I had with him in January, there is an enormous change.

And the Soviet situation. Here is a situation in which they put in $15 billion, or, depending on how you measure it, maybe $20 billion in aid, and their Foreign Minister cannot even get into the country. It is something pathetic for me to see him in Geneva on the way in and to pretend we are consulting.[5] I saw him barely two weeks ago. Nothing could have happened in these last two weeks. And to see him on the way in—I couldn't have talked to anybody yet. They are being put through a humiliating show of impotence.

On one hand this is good, but on the other hand it is dangerous. If they become obnoxious, they can make it impossible for the Syrian Government to settle. If they do what they haven't done, they could insist on the 1967 lines or on a positive linkage to them. In our first talk with Asad, he insisted on the 1967 borders, which was a concession for them because never before had Syria agreed that Israel had a right to any borders. Now they don't even discuss the 1967 borders because my answer is that we should deal with one issue at a time.

So we have to consider how to conduct the negotiations, and then how to give the Soviets a pretense of participation. It is even more hu-

---

[5] Kissinger and Gromyko met in Geneva on April 28 and 29. They discussed the Middle East on April 29; see *Foreign Relations,* 1969–1976, volume XV, Soviet Union, June 1972–August 1974, Documents 175 and 176.

miliating, because no one is fooled. Again, I am counting on your discretion here. The hardest problem in fact is the Syrians, who insist that I do the negotiation. It is in our interest to maintain that position, because the maximum price we would pay to the Arabs would still make them more dependent on us than on a move with Russian backing.

You know the map. Israel is willing to return about three quarters of the bulge, and to divide what they return between a UN zone and a Syrian zone. The Syrian position is that they first asked for the 1967 line, then they asked for about half of the Golan. The Israelis cannot accept that because of the settlements, but you have to remember it is an enormous concession for the Syrians to agree to any line on the Golan.

What we have to prevent is a breakdown of the negotiations in which other Arabs have to support Syria. We have to get a situation where other Arabs like Boumediene support it, and where if the war starts they fight alone. A breakdown of the negotiations I guarantee will lead to an outbreak of the war with Syria. The only question is whether Egypt will join.

Our maximum objective now is a disengagement agreement, which will be a situation in which the resumption of hostilities will be physically difficult. Our minimum position should be to create a situation where if Syria fights it will be fighting alone. The worst situation is with the others joining in, and the Europeans too. The Europeans, especially the French, are just waiting for it to break down. The only way we keep them under control is to keep our negotiations going.

What is the issue? The Syrians asked for one half of the Golan. Maybe 15 kilometers. Both Sadat and Boumediene have told us that if Syria can get Quneitra and a line south, they will feel that Israel has made a reasonable proposition.

Boumediene took me aside before he left and said to me: "Please see that Sadat doesn't get totally demonized."[6]

If we can't produce Quneitra, which is three kilometers from the old line, how can we promise to get a full settlement? And if we can't do that, how can we conduct our diplomacy? Then they have to shop around again.

We are talking about four to five miles, at the most. With this, we are practically certain of achieving our minimum objective, and we have four out of five chances of achieving the maximum objective of a disengagement agreement.

---

[6] Boumediene met with President Nixon and Kissinger on April 11 in Washington. A memorandum of conversation of their meeting is in the Ford Library, National Security Adviser, Memoranda of Conversations, Box 3, April 11, 1974, Nixon, Algerian President Boumediene. There is no record of a private conversation between Kissinger and Boumediene.

There are other subsidiary issues. You don't have to get into this. Of course, you can ask me anything you want. But one issue is whether we have a UN emergency force or only UN observers. My feeling of the way we will solve this is to triple the number of observers, or put a UN emergency force in and call them observers. [Laughter]

Another issue is that they will want to give the territory back to the UN and not to Syria.

But, if we can agree on a line with them, we can settle the other issues. Not that they are a joy to negotiate with where territory is involved. [Laughter] They are tough negotiators. Sometimes their domestic situation creates incredibly petty situations. But if they were easy to deal with, the Arabs wouldn't be coming to us, and the pressures would start again. But though they are a pain in the neck, we understand their situation.

This group is always concerned about: Do we do enough for Israel? It is important that you understand that we understand that our strategy depends on Israel being so strong that it can defend itself and that they have to come to us. If Israel was so weak the Arabs could impose their will on them, our strategy couldn't work.

The Israeli Ambassador knows that they have gotten seven times more equipment than in any comparable period in the history of Israel-Arab relations. It was more than the Berlin airlift in terms of tonnages. But we did this with no peep out of the Arabs—precisely because of our diplomacy. When Joe was Assistant Secretary, whenever we shipped two Phantoms, we got cables from everywhere in the Arab world that riots would start and American lives were at stake.

Every problem you solve gets you to a harder one. Though the Egyptian one I think may be easier. It is not as explosive. I don't think Egypt will go to war.

I don't know whether the present Israeli Government can make this move beyond Quneitra. They haven't refused it. The Prime Minister knows exactly what we think is necessary. She is not a fool: If she is going to turn it down, she knows it is better for her to do it now than when I have already begun to go through Algiers, Cairo. So I am reasonably optimistic. You know them. So if problems develop, you will know the area of debate. They are right not to decide now before it is absolutely necessary. Because if the Arabs knew, they would just add on more demands.

But on the Soviet issue and the Arab issue, it is important that you understand, so you don't fall for the easy litanies from different people.

Rabbi Miller: First, we want to thank you for your candor. This is a significant date to be discussing Israel—it is Independence Day—but I want you to know that if we raise issues, it is not because of pettiness but because of concern.

Kissinger: Oh no, I know.

Rabbi Miller: But many of us last night expressed concern about the UN vote. Maybe the UN isn't the most important organization, but we just didn't understand the second vote of the U.S. in voting for the resolution.[7]

Kissinger: On the United Nations, we faced this problem. Last week, all of those Arabs whose interests at least on this step are parallel to Israel, that is, who are advising Syria to be moderate, advised us that a U.S. veto would be a disaster. I know you aren't talking about a U.S. veto, but I just want to show the evolution. There was the non-aligned resolution that we would have vetoed. We then called the Lebanese Foreign Minister down here. We were told it was in his hands what resolution would pass. We worked with the Lebanese Foreign Minister, who was adamant. We worked out a resolution which he was willing to support, which included at least a condemnation of any act of violence. We didn't say we would support it but left him with that impression to get him off the non-aligned resolution. Then we introduced the amendment. We decided if we could get any other government to go along with us, we would abstain. But we couldn't leave any of those governments who would have been left in a painful position—so we took the lesser of two evils and voted for the resolution.

But today we made a statement [reading the text:] "It condemns equally . . . all acts of violence, especially those resulting in the loss of innocent civilian lives, which covers the wanton and criminal massacre at the village of Qiryat Shmona." [Tab A][8]

Moreover, we made it clear that in our view paragraph three means what the amendment meant. We have distributed this to the press. So we have made it clear that as far as the U.S. is concerned, we condemn the massacre. This was not perfect, but given the conflicting pressures we felt this was the lesser evil.

Rabbi Miller: We understand what you have said about rapprochement with the Arabs. But where does the line go?

Kissinger: Remember that this is the best resolution the Security Council has ever voted. It always used to condemn Israel unilaterally. This condemns all acts of violence, and in addition, it calls for all governments not to do anything to interfere with the peace efforts. We got this far through the rapprochement.

---

[7] UN Security Council Resolution 347 was adopted on April 25 after a Lebanese complaint to the UN that Israel had raided Palestinian refugee camps on Lebanese territory. The resolution condemned Israeli violation of Lebanese sovereignty. For the debate in the Security Council and the text of the resolution, see *Yearbook of the United Nations, 1974*, pp. 207–211.

[8] Tab A, entitled "Transcript of Press, Radio and Television News Briefing Thursday April 25, 1974, 12:57 p.m.," attached but not printed.

Questioner: In the past, whenever I was feeling gloomy, we used to have to go to Israel to find reassurance. Now I can come here.

Secretary Kissinger: You are nice.

Questioner: I understand this strategy, to draw them from the UN and the Soviets. It seems to be working. But there is still apprehension. As Heinrich Heine said, "I have a toothache in my heart." I can understand where the economic aid fits in, but on military aid to them ...

Kissinger: That was an absurd scenario I gave you.

Questioner: Yes, but you told us before about the resistance to the airlift at the lower levels of the Pentagon. And today we see in the *New York Times* what we had feared—all this Arab wealth coming into the United States.[9] Where does it end?

Kissinger: We won't rearm the Arabs. It could never happen with Syria under any conditions. If anything happened with Egypt, it would only be in the context of further progress toward Israel and drawing away from the Soviets.

We have to maneuver this very carefully. I must say that Israel's position is enormously difficult. I must say as a friend, we are mitigating the dangers, not removing them. I have never denied it. On military aid to the Arabs, this is not a realistic danger at this moment.

If Arab influence in this country becomes so great that there is an airlift to the Arabs in an Arab-Israel war, Israel would be finished. Because then they could also block an airlift to Israel, and this could then happen without a U.S. airlift to them.

We will never become an arms supplier to the Arabs, because one lesson we have learned is that you can never buy enough. The Arab view—unlike ours—is that the Soviets didn't give enough and withheld it.

Questioner: If the Soviets don't do it, where will he get the arms?

Kissinger: The Yugoslavs, the Indians, the French—there are many suppliers. It is better for Israel that the Arabs not be on the end of a Soviet supply line.

The Soviets stripped their armored divisions; the French don't have any armored divisions. I find French policy totally malicious. The Soviets at least gain something for themselves; the French gain nothing except to cut up the United States.

Questioner: Just six months ago Egypt was close to the Soviets. Now, at a bewildering pace, all this has changed—on the political level, on the military level, and on the economic level, with the President's

---

[9] A *New York Times* article entitled, "Arabs Starting to Invest New Oil Money in West." (*New York Times*, April 25, 1974, p. 1)

bill for $250 million for Egypt.[10] The test of the intentions of Egypt becomes terribly important. We still read statements by the Egyptians that they'll go back to 1956 and then to 1947. There was a statement by a high-level Egyptian in Beirut.

Kissinger: [to Sisco] Did you see that?

Mr. Sisco: No.

Questioner: This money for rebuilding cities and the Canal. And trade too. Commodities.

Kissinger: I think the greater the stake in economic progress, greater is his stake in a peaceful evolution. For a while, Egypt approached us but we fended him off because Israel wasn't ready for negotiations, because frankly we felt he was a clown and we underestimated him. The Israelis thought they never had it so good. I was impressed with him first during the war. When we started the airlift, we sent him a message. We said: "We are doing this but you should remember that your hopes for progress depend on us. So try to restrain your reaction." And he did.

When I first came to Egypt on November 7, I had never been in an Arab country. I had never dealt with a high-level Arab leader. The European Community had submitted a resolution to the United Nations to return to the October 22 lines. Japan was for it. Israel was totally isolated—and was in the wrong on that issue, technically.

I said to Sadat, "You can have a brawl on this, or you can let me work out something both sides can live with." He agreed. And I didn't offer him economic aid as an inducement at any stage. If you can imagine where we would be if the embargo were still on now and blamed on Israel ... For him to turn, which is not inconceivable—well, it is inconceivable: The only way he could turn is if the negotiations failed totally or if we kicked him in the teeth. We have to gamble on him. We have to use this period. If we played with him the way we play with the Soviets, keeping adding on concessions ... If you saw how he gives us information on the situation in the Arab countries, you would see that $250 million is cheap.

Jacobson: The last time we raised the matter of the $2.2 billion and we expressed our concern. At that time you indicated you knew of no problem. Israel was counting on it. Now there is a tremendous disap-

---

[10] In a foreign aid request sent to Congress on April 24, President Nixon requested $350 million for Israel, $50 million in security support and $300 million in military credits; $250 million in supporting assistance for Egypt; $207.5 million for Jordan, $77.5 million in security support and $130 million in military grants and credits; and a $100 million Special Requirements Fund for any new needs that might arise. For text of President Nixon's message to Congress, see *Public Papers: Nixon, 1974*, pp. 373–379.

pointment when we read that there would be only $1 billion in grant. Maybe more will come later, but you know their economic condition.

Kissinger: First, this decision was worked out with the Israeli Government. Second, one decision was whether it would be declared necessary, which was not an automatic decision. And third, the terms of the credit were an issue. We had the problem of not starting a Congressional brawl and not doing something disruptive of the diplomatic situation. Sapir is not spending sleepless nights on this. [Laughter] He may be spending sleepless nights but not on whether the other $500 million will ultimately be granted. The credit will be on concessional terms, and will be grant.

Mr. Kenen: Sadat is moving cautiously. We are giving him $250 million. Is there any possibility that he can renounce belligerency at this stage?

Kissinger: He doesn't need the $250 million all that badly. The Soviets would gladly give him $500 million if he would only shut up about them. He wants $250 to show he has a western option. The best way to deal with him, the best strategy is to tie no strings and to count on what the evolution will be, as it must.

Zuckerman: From my circles, labor circles, the issue has never been Congressional support for Israel. The blame has never been put on Israel for the embargo but in another direction.

Kissinger: Right.

Zuckerman: You have raised this concern in the future, if the embargo were imposed again. But in the meantime why do the Soviets sit back and take this? And not try to create a belligerent state.

Kissinger: First, their leadership now is not the most able, so they may not know how to do it. Second, if they create a belligerent state, it could end up like 1967 and 1973 and a stalemate. We would let them know they would sacrifice détente. Except that this time, there would be great temptation to escalate and try to face us down. In October, we had to spend three weeks explaining our alert.

So the incentives are pretty evenly divided. One reason we are concerned about MFN is not, as some of your labor friends think, that we are soft in the head about the Soviets, but we are using détente to regulate Soviet behavior.

Sadat is not going at our pace. In fact we would probably prefer him to go slower.

Hertzberg: The criticism of you in the Jewish Community isn't the details on strategy, which you argue so brilliantly, but that you misunderstand American interests versus the Soviet Union. Letting them into the Suez Canal, letting them turn the flank of the Middle East, and insufficient pressure on the totality of Soviet policy, that is, generally giving them their head. My colleagues here know I don't have this view, but these issues must be posed.

Kissinger: Yes.

Hertzberg: The Soviets must be getting something, to be good boys; what is it? QED, it is not in the American interest. That is the argument.

Kissinger: When you play chess, it doesn't follow that the loser gets something out of it. Talk to Rabin; we had a deliberate strategy to create such frustration in the Arab world that they would turn against the Soviets. For five years we worked on this. In 1970 I said publicly that our objective was to expel the Soviets from Egypt. Every liberal newspaper jumped on me for that, for "returning to the Cold War."

In the [October] war, in spite of what you read, on the airlift, our strategy required that Israel not lose—because we would not let the Arabs win with Soviet arms. So we are reaping the benefits of five years of the strategy. To think this is being done in collusion with the Soviet Union is absolute insanity.

Geneva for Gromyko is a damage-limitation situation. At least for the yokels it looks good, but it fools no one.

Are we so committed to détente that we will pay any price? You know the argument. It is interesting that this debate started during the Vietnam war, when we were attacked as war criminals by the very people who now say we are soft on Communism. Mondale[11]—who is a friend of mine—every year submitted a resolution demanding that we trade with the Communists. I have told this group that if I were an opponent of Brezhnev in the Politburo I could make an overwhelming case against him: The Vietnam war was ended on our terms. You may not like the terms, but they were our terms. We got a settlement in Berlin. We got rid of a naval base in Cuba.

What about the Suez Canal? First, if we succeed there will be no flank to turn, because we will squeeze them out from Iran to Saudi Arabia. And if we succeed with Syria, we will work on Iraq. Second, there is no law that says when a Soviet ship goes through, it can't be followed by an American ship. Every Soviet ship that goes through the Canal can be followed by an American ship, and we have more ships there.

What have they got? The wheat deal.[12] The wheat deal was done by bureaucrats. It was done for politics. It was done on the assumption that we couldn't sell enough wheat. That had nothing to do with foreign policy.

---

[11] Senator Walter Mondale.
[12] See footnote 6, Document 23.

I am seeing Meany[13] when I get back.

Fisher: We really appreciate this. Our talks here are based on frankness. We would be remiss if you didn't know our concerns.

Kissinger: No, I knew them anyway. [Laughter] But I think they should be put on the table.

Fisher: They should be based on confidence. We are wishing you well on this visit and praying for you.

On foreign aid, we are concerned about Israel. No one I have talked to is concerned about aid to Egypt; we think it is a master stroke. But when Israel is in such dire straits, to ask for only $300 million in grant aid looks bad.

Kissinger: I am counting on Dinitz' troops to work on that. [Laughter] We won't veto an increase, I can tell you that. [Laughter]

Fisher: It is important that you know what we are thinking about. But we wish you success. It has been tremendously useful. I only hope when you get back from Syria there is a smile on your face, because you look unhappy today.

Kissinger: I am not certain how it is going to go. If it fails, everything I have said is in severe jeopardy. But I am going to act on the trip as if it is certain to succeed. I hope the Jewish Community can support it as much as its conscience permits.

You shouldn't be pessimistic. I think we have a good chance to get our minimum objective, and a better than even chance to get our maximum objective, that is, a disengagement agreement. Syria would be the first radical state to sign on a line. We wouldn't have these incidents over Mt. Hermon because there will be demilitarized zones all around.

Fisher: Well, we understand you have a time problem.

Kissinger: Yes.

All: Thank you.

[The meeting then broke up with thanks and handshakes—and some wedding congratulations—to the Secretary.

[Secretary Kissinger then conferred in his office privately with Mr. Fisher, Len Garment, and Rabbi Miller, who introduced him to Stanley Lowell, the President of the Conference on Soviet Jewry.]

---

[13] George Meany, President of the AFL–CIO.

37. Letter From President Nixon to Israeli Prime Minister Meir[1]

Washington, April 30, 1974.

Dear Madame Prime Minister:

I am writing to you regarding Secretary Kissinger's mission to the Middle East and on the eve of his arrival in Israel. I received yesterday a full report of his conversations with Mr. Gromyko[2] in which, as he has reported to you, he successfully resisted Soviet proposals which in our judgment would have been enormously complicating and prejudicial to the common efforts of Israel and the United States to achieve a satisfactory separation of forces in the Golan Heights.

In my talks with Secretary Kissinger before he left, we discussed and reflected on the immediate days ahead, their crucial character, and their decisive impact on future developments. Simply stated, Madame Prime Minister, if a Syrian-Israeli disengagement can be achieved, it could build further on the foundation of confidence which has begun to develop as a result of the scrupulous implementation by Egypt and Israel of the disengagement agreement. It could also open new avenues for additional steps towards peace and a further strengthening in Israel's security.

On the other hand, if we fail in this endeavor, I am convinced that Israel will face a situation fraught with risks. It would mean the reversal of the trend towards reduced Soviet influence in the area, the injection of the views of others who neither appreciate nor seem interested in helping to maintain Israel's security, a situation in which the capacity of the United States for constructive purposes will have been effectively neutralized, and the likelihood of another war in the Middle East under conditions in which both domestically and internationally American actions would be much more difficult than in October.

Madame Prime Minister, you have often said, and I have appreciated it, that my Administration has given more support to Israel—material and political—than perhaps any other Administration. This is not said, I know, in any partisan way, but I believe this judgment to be ac-

---

[1] Source: National Archives, Nixon Presidential Materials, NSC Files, Kissinger Office Files, Box 136, Country Files, Middle East, Dinitz, January 1–July 1, 1974. No classification marking. Kissinger wrote Meir a letter on April 29, urging Meir to make the compromises necessary for disengagement with Syria. He warned that "if our present diplomacy fails in the critical period ahead, it will be beyond our power to prevent a resumption of hostilities, a return of diplomatic efforts to unmanageable international forums, a restoration of Soviet dominance in the area, and extreme jeopardy to the progress that has been so painfully achieved in recent months." (Ibid.)

[2] See footnote 5, Document 36.

curate. We have pursued a policy of protecting and strengthening Israel's security both with material support and diplomatic efforts.

I therefore find it profoundly disturbing to see reports from Israel which are casting doubt on the U.S. role and describe our policy as one which is pursuing détente without full regard and understanding of Israel's interests. I cannot overemphasize what a fundamental mistake I believe it would be for Israel to approach the critical days ahead and Secretary Kissinger's mission in this frame of mind.

Israel is going through a period of readjustment. You have suffered pain and anguish from a recent war which was neither your desire nor your choosing. But I find it painful, Madame Prime Minister, to see developing in Israel an attitude of gloom and distrust regarding the U.S. efforts. A vote on a Security Council resolution,[3] which in our judgment was not as balanced as we would have liked but was more balanced than any in the past, cannot erase the magnitude of the timely airlift in Israel's hour of peril, nor the achievement of an Egyptian-Israeli disengagement agreement which you yourself characterized as a very favorable result for Israel. It is difficult for me to understand how such an atmosphere could develop in the week in which I authorized a generous apportionment of the $2.2 billion commitment,[4] and sent to the Congress a foreign assistance program for 1975 which provides equally generously for your future needs.[5] It is perplexing to me that our steadfast support for Israel could be seriously doubted at this critical hour as Secretary Kissinger is arriving in your country on his vital mission.

I know and understand your worries and fears. Difficult decisions lie ahead, but the risks of failure are so great and the consequences are so profound that I felt it incumbent upon me to share with you my concerns and hopes regarding the coming weeks. I can assure you that it is not our intention to ask of you and your government concessions that would be prejudicial to the survival of Israel.

I hope therefore, Madame Prime Minister, that you and your government approach the talks with Secretary Kissinger in a mood of opportunity as Israel faces one of the most fateful weeks in its history.

Sincerely,

Richard Nixon

---

[3] See footnote 7, Document 36.
[4] See footnote 12, Document 23.
[5] See footnote 10, Document 36.

38. Memorandum From the President's Deputy Assistant for National Security Affairs (Scowcroft) to President Nixon[1]

Washington, May 1, 1974.

Secretary Kissinger asked that I pass on to you this report of his meeting with President Sadat:

"Sadat and I continued our talks for four hours tonight[2] in the same cordial and constructive spirit. We worked out in great detail a position for the Israeli-Syrian talks which is extremely reasonable. If Israel rejects it, I may have to ask you for and am counting on your all out support in influencing the Israelis.

"Sadat again said that he looks forward to your visit, which we went on to discuss at length. He wants you to make your first stop in Cairo and to spend two and a half days in Egypt. He hopes to take you with him on a special train from Cairo to Alexandria through the thickly-populated Delta region. He estimates at least eight million people will line the route. Sadat proposes that your trip start around May 30 so that you are in Egypt at about the time the oil ministers are meeting June 1 to consider the embargo.

"In sum the talks here reconfirmed Sadat's willingness to play a responsible and forthcoming role at this delicate stage of the Middle East talks. His high esteem for you and your approach to these problems was apparent throughout our discussions.

"I leave for Jerusalem in the morning and will report on my first round of talks with the Israelis tomorrow night."

---

[1] Source: Ford Library, National Security Adviser, Kissinger-Scowcroft West Wing Office Files, Box 12, Egypt CO, April 24–May 15, 1974. Secret; Sensitive. Sent for information. A stamped notation at the top of the page reads, "The President has seen."

[2] The conversation between Sadat and Kissinger took place on May 1 in Alexandria, Egypt. (Memorandum of conversation; National Archives, RG 59, Records of Henry Kissinger, 1973–77, Box 1, Folder 10)

39. Memorandum From the President's Deputy Assistant for National Security Affairs (Scowcroft) to President Nixon[1]

Washington, May 2, 1974.

Secretary Kissinger has asked me to transmit the following message to you:

"I am reporting to you promptly on my private meeting with Prime Minister Meir and subsequently another meeting with her and all her principal colleagues[2] because the Israeli position presented to me today foreshadows, in my judgment, a possible break in the negotiations at an early stage.

"Before I came, I made clear to both sides my assessment of what would be required in order to achieve a Syrian-Israeli disengagement. I said specifically that there would have to be Israeli withdrawal to a point roughly 2–3 kilometers west of the October 6 line, including a line west of the town of Kineitra. As you know, for the past several weeks both the Israelis and the Syrians have encouraged me strongly to come to the area once again to see whether the disengagement agreement could be concluded and in the knowledge of my judgment as to what was required in order to achieve agreement. Despite the internal crises in Israel, both publicly and officially, the Israelis have been insistent that I pursue the negotiations in the area.

"Both in my private meeting with the Prime Minister and subsequently with the Cabinet, at which the Chief of Staff made a detailed presentation, the line to which Israel indicated it would be willing to withdraw was one several kilometers east of the October 6 line with the Israelis occupying the high ground throughout. The new Chief of Staff, Gur, used the specious argument that there was no other line further west to which Israel could withdraw which it would consider defensible. The line was essentially the same line which Dayan gave me four weeks ago[3] with some slight change favorable to the Syrians in the south but with a more important change in the north on Mount Hermon in favor of the Israelis. In short, the line I received today can be

---

[1] Source: National Archives, Nixon Presidential Materials, NSC Files, Kissinger Office Files, Box 45, HAK Trip Files, Middle East Memos and Security, April 28–May 31, 1974. Top Secret; Sensitive; Eyes Only. A notation at the top of the page reads, "The President has seen."

[2] The conversation between Meir and Kissinger took place on May 2 from 1:20 to 3:55 p.m. (Memorandum of conversation; ibid., RG 59, Records of Henry Kissinger, 1973–77, Box 1, Folder 10) Another meeting took place with the Israeli Cabinet from 4:10 to 6:05 p.m. (Memorandum of conversation; ibid., Box 6, Nodis Memcons, March 1974, Folder 3)

[3] See Document 32.

considered, if anything, a retrogression from the line given to me by Dayan four weeks ago which I told him then would prove unacceptable. If I were to present this line to the Syrians, there would be a blowup in the negotiations and the likelihood of a renewal of war greatly increased. Once again, the Israelis have continued to view the disengagement line in narrow military terms—and even in these terms, it is not wholly defensible since there is a high ground on which a line could be drawn roughly 3 kilometers west of the October 6 line which in our judgment would be defensible. I am therefore playing for time and will discuss secondary issues when I go to Damascus to give Israel an opportunity to reconsider.

"I pointed out to the Israelis that disengagement could not be viewed only on the basis of these narrow military considerations. I stressed that Israel faces two choices: to stick with the present very unsatisfactory position which in my judgment would have the following consequences—it would break the negotiations with the onus on Israeli shoulders; it would reverse the trend in the Arab world towards moderation; it would weaken the Sadat leadership in the Arab world; it would offer both the Soviets as well as the West Europeans an opportunity to inject themselves into the picture in a most unfavorable way; it would throw the whole matter into international forums, i.e., the United Nations Security Council and the Geneva Conference; it would result in a loss of control by the United States in both the negotiations and the trend of developments in the area; it would probably result in the reinstituting of the embargo since the Oil Ministers are again scheduled to meet to review the situation on June 1—it is likely to result in Syria starting another war against Israel, a war of attrition in which even the moderate Arabs would be under pressure to come to Syria's support, where the Soviets would see an opportunity to regain influence by all-out military support of Syria and in circumstances where the United States would be isolated and in the likelihood that the kind of support necessary would be dependent on a most uncertain public and Congressional opinion.

"At the same time, I openly acknowledged that there was a risk for Israel in going forward on the kind of line which has been previously discussed as one that is within reason. I agreed with Mrs. Meir that there could be no absolute guarantee that if they withdrew to this point a war would not result eventually, but I felt that time is on the side of Israel. If an agreement is achieved, this would permit Sadat to continue to take the lead toward a peaceful settlement, and there was less risk, in my judgment, in this course than the one which the Israelis seem stuck on.

"I am, therefore, meeting with Mrs. Meir this evening to consider together the consequences of the failure of my mission and how one could proceed in these circumstances.

"It is, of course, possible that what we have heard today is tactical, for the Israelis have asked us to go to Damascus tomorrow and to take up a number of specific elements in the disengagement agreement other than the question on the line. I will do this and I will be able to get by for this one round with Asad, but in the absence of anything more from the Israelis, it cannot be strung out much beyond early next week.

"I, therefore, would like you to consider on an urgent basis the consequences which will face us should this mission be terminated in the circumstances that I have described. I believe a letter from you which lays out frankly the consequences which would ensue, particularly with respect to U.S. policy, would be most helpful at this juncture.[4] If you agree, I would like it sent soonest and I could have the opportunity to review it before it is transmitted. You will wish to weigh, Mr. President, what specifically you would want to tell Mrs. Meir regarding American policy in these circumstances. What would the reaction of the American people be to a course which is likely to result in not only the maintenance of the high prices of oil but the reimposition of the embargo? Could Israel expect American support for an airlift of the kind which would be required in order to prevent an Israeli defeat? What could Israel expect by way of changes in our ongoing arms policy? These are very fundamental questions and I would hope that your letter would deal with these matters. Finally, could Israel expect the consistent and steadfast political and diplomatic support we have given in circumstances where the United States would be isolated? I do not wish to prejudge your answers—my own idea is that we may have to take some very painful decisions.

"I would appreciate your consideration of the above on a most urgent basis."

Secretary Kissinger plans now to return to Jerusalem on Saturday evening.[5] If it is your wish to send a letter to Prime Minister Meir, I will draft it, check it with Kissinger, and get it to you on your trip for approval before dispatch to Mrs. Meir.

---

[4] Printed as Document 41.
[5] May 4.

40. Telegram From Secretary of State Kissinger to the President's Deputy Assistant for National Security Affairs (Scowcroft)[1]

May 3, 1974, 1232Z.

Hakto 29. Since my last report to you I have had an additional meeting with Prime Minister Meir and her colleagues last evening and another one with the Prime Minister alone this morning.[2] As a result of this effort, there has been a bit of movement in the Israeli attitude and they indicated they now would be willing to withdraw to a line slightly behind the pre-October line, which would (1) put most of Quneitra in the UN zone so that Syrian civilians could return and (2) permit Israel to retain the main defensive positions which it relied on before the October war. This line would thus return to Syria a small area which Israel conquered in 1967, and Syrian civilians could return to all the areas Israel vacated.

In light of this, I want to hold the kind of letter which I recommended last evening[3] and which I am confident will be needed at a subsequent stage of the discussion. However, it is essential to keep the Israeli feet to the fire and therefore I recommend that the following brief letter from the President to the Prime Minister be sent on Saturday:[4]

[Omitted here is the text of Document 41.]

For Scowcroft:

Scowcroft should make arrangements to have it delivered to Shalev Saturday stressing that it was sent by the President from the plane.

Advise by flash cable time of delivery.

Warm regards.

---

[1] Source: National Archives, Nixon Presidential Materials, NSC Files, Kissinger Office Files, Box 45, HAK Trip Files, Middle East Memos and Security, April 28–May 31, 1974. Secret; Sensitive; Eyes Only; Flash.

[2] Kissinger met with the Israeli negotiating team on May 2 at the Foreign Minister's Residence in Jerusalem. The memorandum of conversation lists the time as "After Dinner." (Ibid., RG 59, Records of Henry Kissinger, 1973–77, Box 7, Nodis Memcons, March 1974, Folder 6) Kissinger then met with Dayan from 11:40 p.m. to 1:30 a.m. at the King David Hotel in Jerusalem. (Memorandum of conversation; Library of Congress, Manuscript Division, Kissinger Papers, CL 192, Geopolitical File, Middle East, Peace Negotiations, Israeli-Syrian Relations, Negotiation Books, Volume I, March–May 1974) Kissinger met with Meir on May 3 from 9:05 to 10:25 a.m. in the Prime Minister's Residence in Jerusalem. (Memorandum of conversation; National Archives, RG 59, Records of Henry Kissinger, 1973–77, Box 7, Nodis Memcons, March 1974, Folder 3)

[3] See Document 39.

[4] May 4.

41. Letter From President Nixon to Israeli Prime Minister Meir[1]

May 4, 1974.

Dear Madame Prime Minister:

I am writing to you as I am flying in Air Force One to Spokane, Washington.[2]

I have read detailed reports from Secretary Kissinger on his talks with you and your colleagues. I understand from his reports that your discussions are continuing and that today he leaves for Damascus with your latest ideas.

I wish only to convey to you at this time a few brief observations. I believe that the arguments which Secretary Kissinger made regarding the consequences that would ensue if the negotiations failed as a result of the Israeli position on this matter were, if anything, understated. The present peace-making effort is crucial to Israel's future and the ability of the United States to go on helping as it has.

There are positive trends in the area which we believe it is essential to encourage because they serve both the short and long range interests of Israel and the United States. You cannot take for granted that the patterns of the past will be automatically repeated. These patterns of the past, as you may recall, required a worldwide alert and a massive airlift which I personally ordered over strong objections from elements of the Congress.

Madame Prime Minister, I have been Israel's friend for a long time. I understand the heavy responsibilities you and your colleagues bear for Israel's present and future security, and I believe you know there are few others in the world who know as I do what responsibility is. It is in this spirit that I underscore how essential it is for Israel in its own interest to grasp the opportunity which exists in the present situation.

Sincerely,

Richard Nixon[3]

---

[1] Source: National Archives, Nixon Presidential Materials, NSC Files, Kissinger Office Files, Box 136, Country Files, Middle East, Dinitz, January 1–July 1, 1974. No classification marking. A handwritten notation at the top of the first page reads, "Hand delivered to Min Shalev, 12:40, 5/4/74."

[2] According to the President's Daily Diary, Nixon departed Phoenix, Arizona, on May 4 at 8:03 a.m. Mountain Standard Time and arrived in Spokane, Washington, at 10:37 Pacific Daylight Time. (Ibid., White House Central Files)

[3] Printed from a copy that indicates Nixon signed the original.

42. Memorandum From the President's Deputy Assistant for National Security Affairs (Scowcroft) to President Nixon[1]

Washington, May 4, 1974.

Secretary Kissinger has asked me to transmit the following message to you:

"I have completed six hours of intensive discussion with Asad[2] based on the strategy that I would focus in Damascus on issues other than the disengagement line. On these some progress was made and most, if not all, would probably not prove irreconcilable after considerable further effort if we can eventually achieve agreement between the two sides on a line of disengagement.

"On these specific issues:

A. Syria agrees that the ceasefire should be an integral part of the disengagement agreement. While I am in the area Asad has agreed to reduce Syria's shelling and stop raids;

B. He agrees that there should be a buffer zone and his ideas are sufficiently flexible to bridge the gap between Israel's insistence on a UN force and Syria's strong preference for an observation corps;

C. He agrees that there should be an exchange of POWs and missing in action as part of the disengagement agreement;

D. It is unclear at this point whether he will agree to mutual limitations of arms and forces which was a key element in the Egyptian-Israeli disengagement agreement but I think it is likely;

E. On the disengagement line, both sides are still far apart. If Israel does not move beyond the October 6 line, no settlement is possible. Even it it does, Asad's objectives may be more ambitious than the negotiations can sustain.

"Asad was very positive about improvement in relations and said again you are very welcome to come to Damascus during your Middle East trip.

"I will go next to Alexandria for a few hours to fill in Sadat and return to Israel Saturday night to renew my talks with Mrs. Meir and her colleagues prior to a Sunday afternoon Cabinet meeting. It will be es-

---

[1] Source: National Archives, Nixon Presidential Materials, NSC Files, Kissinger Office Files, Box 144, Country Files, Middle East, President's Trip to Middle East, June 1974. Secret; Sensitive; Eyes Only. A notation at the top of the first page reads, "The President has seen."

[2] The conversation between Asad and Kissinger took place on May 3 at 5 p.m. in Damascus. (Memorandum of conversation; ibid., Box 1028, Presidential/HAK Memcons, March 1–May 8, 1974)

sential that I bring to Damascus on Monday night a line within negotiating range."

---

43. Memorandum From the President's Deputy Assistant for National Security Affairs (Scowcroft) to President Nixon[1]

Washington, May 5, 1974.

Secretary Kissinger has sent you the following report from Jerusalem:

"We have reached the crucial stage in the negotiations. The Israeli Cabinet meeting Sunday afternoon will be critical in determining in large measure the direction in which things will take. In my meeting with Mrs. Meir and her closest Cabinet colleagues (Allon, Dayan and Eban) and in a 1:00 A.M. private meeting with her subsequently,[2] I once again reviewed the considerations which make it essential that the Cabinet decide on a position that is within negotiating range and that I can present to Asad as such.

"Prior to these meetings, I had spent the entire day with Sadat[3] reviewing where matters stand. He was displeased both with the Syrian and the Israeli position. Sadat has a vital stake in the achievement of a Syrian-Israeli disengagement agreement since he fully realizes that to fail at this juncture would not only reverse all the positive trends in the area but would in fact expose him to the radical tendencies in the area which he would be forced to join in one way or another. He believes that if it is possible to secure Israeli agreement to a line that includes some modest modifications in the October 6 line including all of Quenitra he can help mobilize key Arab support and will himself exercise influence also to get Syrian agreement. I suggested that to help achieve

---

[1] Source: Library of Congress, Manuscript Division, Kissinger Papers, CL 192, Geopolitical File, Middle East, Peace Negotiations, Israeli-Syrian Relations, Negotiation Books, Volume I, Folder 2. Secret; Sensitive; Eyes Only. A notation at the top of the first page reads, "The President has seen."

[2] The conversation between Meir and her colleagues and Kissinger took place on May 4 from 9:30 p.m. to 1:10 a.m. at the Prime Minister's Residence in Jerusalem. (Memorandum of conversation; National Archives, RG 59, Records of Henry Kissinger, 1973–77, Box 7, Nodis Memcons, March 1974, Folder 4) No record of the subsequent private meeting between Kissinger and Meir has been found.

[3] The conversation between Sadat and Kissinger took place on May 4 from 11:35 a.m. to 3 p.m. at the Maamura Rest House in Alexandria. (Memorandum of conversation; ibid., Box 21, Classified External Memcons, May–November 1974, Folder 1)

this that I send a member of my party, Harold Saunders, to Jidda and Algiers to talk to Faisal and Boumediene. Sadat agreed and made available a close assistant of his, Ashraf Marwan, who will make parallel efforts in these two capitals.

"Sadat made clear that if the Israelis would accept this proposal he would not only support it privately with the principal key Arabs but he would also agree to support it publicly. Moreover, Sadat said that once Syrian-Israeli disengagement is achieved, he is prepared to embark on a serious negotiation with the Israelis on a second phase.

"I described this strategy fully to the Israelis last night as well as Asad's reactions to other elements of a disengagement agreement, most of which I pointed out are negotiable but would involve a very heavy struggle indeed.

"The decision the Israeli Cabinet must make today is whether I can take an Israeli position to Damascus late Monday night or Tuesday morning[4] as close as possible to the above proposition. My impression is that the Israelis will be willing to draw the line so that the Eastern part of Quneitra will be under Syrian Civil Administration with the Western part under the UN. This is insufficient in my judgment. It will even be considered an insult by Asad. If this proves to be the final word at this juncture we will then have to develop a course of action which minimizes the adverse impact on us and at least slows down the probable adverse trend inimicable to our interests. I would then return home fairly quickly.

"Your letter arrived Saturday evening[5] as I was meeting with Mrs. Meir and I believe helped immensely in bringing to Mrs. Meir and her colleagues the reality of the situation Israel faces.

"I meet with Mrs. Meir and a larger number of Cabinet members this morning before I go on to Amman, returning to Israel once again on Monday.

"Warm regards."

---

[4] May 6–7.
[5] Document 41.

44. Memorandum From the President's Deputy Assistant for National Security Affairs (Scowcroft) to President Nixon[1]

Washington, May 6, 1974.

Secretary Kissinger has asked that I provide you with the following report.

"I have just completed over four hours of intensive discussions with Mrs. Meir, alone in the first instance, and subsequently with her key Cabinet colleagues.[2] I appreciate your telegram of support for the line I intended to take with the Israelis and which, I believe, has now produced some positive results.[3]

"The Israelis have agreed to drawing a new map which reflects two major improvements over their past position:

a) They have agreed to draw their defensive line west of the entire city of Quneitra; and

b) They have agreed to make certain minor modifications in other parts of the line which would have them withdrawing at certain points a small symbolic distance west of the October 6 line.

"There are a number of other serious problems which remain, such as whether there is a zone of limitation; a buffer zone, and to what point Syrian civil administration will extend. Nevertheless, Israeli willingness to withdraw to a line west of Quneitra and the October 6 line is a step forward. I can represent it with Sadat, Faisal, the Amir of Kuwait and Boumediene as a line meritorious of their support. We are by no means out of the woods because Asad will almost certainly reject this proposal. It then depends on Arab pressures on him. It ought to be possible to get some or all of the above four to weigh in with Asad. Even though it is probably a less than 50–50 chance that the Syrians will accept this line, we will have made important gains with key Arabs which should help reduce the adverse impact should the negotiations reach an impasse.

---

[1] Source: National Archives, Nixon Presidential Materials, NSC Files, Kissinger Office Files, Box 136, Country Files, Middle East, Dinitz, January 1–July 1, 1974. Secret; Sensitive; Exclusively Eyes Only. Sent for information. Nixon wrote at the bottom of the first page, "Personal Message to H from RN—'You are doing a superb job against great odds—regardless of the outcome. But let us hope and work for the best.'"

[2] No record of Kissinger's private discussion with Meir has been found. The subsequent conversation took place on May 5 from 10:15 a.m. to 1:20 p.m. at the Prime Minister's office in Jerusalem. (Memorandum of conversation; ibid., RG 59, Records of Henry Kissinger, 1973–77, Box 8, Nodis Memcons, May 1974, Folder 2)

[3] See Documents 40 and 41.

"I will meet with Gromyko tomorrow,[4] and I plan to say as little as possible to him regarding where matters stand on the Middle East in order to reduce the possibility that he can involve himself directly in the negotiations in an unhelpful manner. After returning to Israel tomorrow night, at which I hope to receive the new map as described above, with the support of the Cabinet, I will proceed to Damascus on Wednesday morning to make a major effort with Asad."

---

[4] The report of the meeting between Kissinger and Gromyko in Nicosia on May 7 printed in *Foreign Relations, 1969–1976*, volume XV, Soviet Union, June 1972–August 1974, Document 179.

---

45. Memorandum From the President's Deputy Assistant for National Security Affairs (Scowcroft) to President Nixon[1]

Washington, May 6, 1974.

Secretary Kissinger has asked that I provide you with the following report.

"In a few hours I will be returning to Jerusalem from Amman[2] to receive the views of the Israeli Government following its Cabinet meeting of yesterday. I am concerned that at best they will present me with a proposal which draws the line of disengagement through East Kuneitra and that my pleas and arguments that the line must be drawn to include all of Kuneitra will basically have gone unheeded. My concern has increased because I have now received clear-cut reports that in response to the emissaries which President Sadat and I sent to see Faisal,[3] we have the full support of Egypt, Saudi Arabia, and Kuwait and a willingness on their part to apply pressure on Asad provided we can get Israel to agree to a disengagement proposal which draws the line to include all of Kuneitra as well as a small area in certain parts

---

[1] Source: National Archives, Nixon Presidential Materials, NSC Files, Kissinger Office Files, Box 136, Country Files, Middle East, Dinitz, January 1–July 1, 1974. Top Secret; Sensitive; Exclusively Eyes Only. Sent for information. A handwritten notation at the top of the page reads, "The President has seen."

[2] Kissinger met with Hussein on May 5 from 5:10 to 7:17 p.m. at the Royal Diwan in Amman. (Memorandum of Conversation, RG 59, Records of Henry Kissinger, Box 8, Nodis Memcons, May 1974, Folder 3)

[3] Kissinger had sent Harold Saunders and Sadat had sent Ashraf Marwan as emissaries to see Faisal and Boumediene. See Document 43.

west of the October 6 line. I expect a similar reaction from Boumedienne whom the emissaries will see tonight. In short, my judgment is that the negotiation can succeed or fail with all of its implications over a kilometer or so in and around Kuneitra and a similar distance west of the October 6 line.

"The situation in which all Arab States will support us against Syria will not return. I shall therefore insist tonight that Israel yield in Kuneitra at the risk of public dissociation by the United States. I do this based on the conviction that I will have your full support. Later tonight a letter from you may be essential.

"If you disagree, please have Scowcroft flash me."

Henry will be meeting briefly with Gromyko tomorrow on Cyprus. Gromyko is concluding his visit to Syria, and Henry felt that a meeting with him at this time before firm positions on the Syrian/Israeli disengagement had been developed would avoid the possibility that the Soviets could become involved in the substance of the discussions.

46. Memorandum of Conversation[1]

Jerusalem, May 6, 1974, 5:55–6:40 p.m.

PARTICIPANTS

    Mrs. Golda Meir, Prime Minister of Israel
    Simcha Dinitz, Ambassador to the United States

    Dr. Henry A. Kissinger, Secretary of State and Assistant to the President for National Security Affairs
    Peter W. Rodman, NSC Staff

Meir: How was the King? [Hussein][2]

Kissinger: All right. There was not much to discuss with him.

Meir: Was he in a bad mood?

Kissinger: No.

---

[1] Source: National Archives, RG 59, Records of Henry Kissinger, 1973–77, Box 7, Nodis Memcons, March 1974, Folder 5. Secret; Nodis. The meeting was held at the Prime Minister's office in Jerusalem. A meeting with the rest of the Israeli negotiating team followed this one from 6:45 to 9:10 p.m. (Memorandum of conversation; ibid., Folder 4) Brackets are in the original.

[2] See footnote 2, Document 45.

Meir: Did your friend [Gromyko] leave Damascus for good?[3]

Kissinger: If not, I won't go. I think he's leaving for good. I told you I had proposed the 9th, but for the reasons I gave you I'll see him on the 7th. So if you'll oblige with some governmental activity ...

Meir: There is a hunger strike outside my house.

Kissinger: On what?

Meir: That we shouldn't sell out. That we shouldn't give up Kuneitra. That we shouldn't do anything dangerous.

Kissinger: Every course is dangerous. I've never told you different.

Meir: And the shooting yesterday was awful.

Kissinger: I'll take this up.

Meir: The Russians are bringing in equipment.

Kissinger: That's our information as well.

Meir: And there is an international force there—Kuwaitis, Pakistanis ...

Kissinger: All this is true.

Let me tell you about the Saunders mission. Here is a new report: [paraphrases from cable]:[4]

"I met Sunday with Saqqaf, Rashid Pharaon, and Adham." All this is in the context of what I presented as my idea. "I met with Adham. The key point in his position was that it would be a good first step." This is the first-step argument which I use in Saudi Arabia and in the area that it creates a good situation for getting the shooting to stop and going ahead. "Adham and Pharaon are regarded here as the men most likely to reflect the King's thinking. Pharaon reiterated his question of Saturday night of whether Kuneitra would be under UN or Syrian administration. I replied that it depended on the position that Israel would finally adopt but under the proposal we were discussing it would be under Syrian administration. Pharaon made two points. It was essential that a way be found to put Kuneitra entirely within Syrian administration. I explained the great difficulty in doing this and explained the problem created by Israeli settlements so close there.

"Pharaon stressed that it was important to present a position which Saudi Arabia, Egypt, and Algeria could support ... He said it was a good position especially if Kuneitra could be under Syrian administration and the Syrians would be isolated if they did not accept it. He asked whether Boumedienne would accept ... I told him I would be going to brief Boumedienne."

---

[3] Gromyko arrived in Damascus on May 5 and left the morning of May 7.

[4] A reference to telegram 965 from Algiers, May 6. (National Archives, RG 59, Central Foreign Policy Files, P850067–2495)

Now since then I have seen both Marwan and Saunders. Marwan claims the Kuwaitis took the same position as the Saudis, and according to him, the Kuwaitis even said they'd cut off the subsidy to Syria if they rejected it.

So, if we look at the positive side, what started as a discussion of the 1967 frontier is now down to a narrow strip. Sure, they'll say it's the first step, but they'll say the 1967 borders anyway. My strategy is to leave Syria to last.

It was almost unanimous in our group that the Israelis should not be asked to give up Golan. That will not be a contentious issue between Israel and the United States. Now we're down to the absolute minimum that's needed.

Meir: Yesterday there was a long Cabinet meeting and the consensus was—there was a map, you'll see it soon[5]—and Kuneitra is divided. And we can't move the entire border. You'll see the map. And in some places where we move we have to ask them to move to widen the buffer strip. We didn't say the army would stay.

Dinitz: Our military line will be west of Kuneitra.

Kissinger: That's not the problem.

Dinitz: But what's important for presentation purposes is that the military line is west.

Kissinger: Every Arab leader agrees they can support giving Kuneitra. I did my best with Marwan—showing him the map, and the dividing line, and I gave him all the arguments. He says the only way they can support it is if he can say Kuneitra even if it doesn't mean anything. The rest of it depends only on whether the line moves west.

Dinitz: You'll see the map.

Kissinger: Let's see what it looks like.

Meir: My Party is up in arms. I wish it could be, but I can't.

Kissinger: What is your alternative?

Meir: I agree, you've never said there is no danger. So that's all in your favor. I certainly can't say to my people there is no risk.

Kissinger: No. If you asked me to defend it before your Committees, I'd say it is the lesser of two dangers. In October if Syria had attacked alone, you would have totally defeated them.

Meir: Yes.

Kissinger: If we can keep the Arabs divided. If we can keep the currents going ... if I had been Secretary of State three months earlier

---

[5] The map was shown to Kissinger in the plenary meeting that began at 6:45 p.m. The map is not attached but see Appendix B, Map 3 for a map of Kuneitra and its surroundings.

maybe I could have begun maneuvering. Being united is not their natural state. Morgenthau[6] can say I'm taken in by Sadat, but look at the price he's paid. And we've paid him nothing. As I said to Morgenthau, the Munich nightmare for Israel is not this slow process which you can partly control; the Munich disaster for Israel is the 1967 frontier imposed by foreign decision. I remember when we came here right after the October war, the first question you asked me was, "Did you agree with the Russians on the 1967 frontiers?"

Meir: The danger is a war in which we're in a worse position.

Kissinger: No, if Syria is alone. As I've said, from my point of view it's better if this fails, because if something goes wrong I could say I had warned you against it. This way, if you agree, I'm forever paying the price.

The danger is a united Arab world. One piece of intelligence from Saunders is that Faisal told me Faisal is trying to change Syrian policy by changing the government structure—getting rid of that party. Faisal says the civilians in Syria are the worst, and the military aren't. Hussein told me this independently. Khaddam would go, and Shihabi might be Prime Minister.

Meir: Asad would stay?

Kissinger: Yes. Asad is no Sadat but it's clear they are anti-Soviet and want to be pro-Western. This is the impression I also got from Shihabi.

Meir: The reports we get from Cairo are even more serious—coming from Moslem fanatics.

Kissinger: My present plan is to come back here from Cyprus tomorrow evening, about 7:00 or 8:00.

Meir: Of course.

Kissinger: And I'll report to you immediately. I won't tell him any details of the plans. I'll tell him they're still meeting.

Meir: I can't believe the Russians, with all the equipment they've been putting in, will just step out.

Kissinger: No, they won't step out.

Meir: They'll do everything possible to stop the agreement. They have nothing to lose.

Kissinger: The risk for them is if it breaks up in circumstances in which there is total U.S. support for the Israeli position, they face a situation in which their client will lose.

---

[6] Hans Morgenthau was an international relations specialist.

Dinitz: If the Arab world lines up behind your plan, there is little risk the Syrians will want to be alone.

Kissinger: If we succeed in getting Boumedienne, I think Syria will yield. Marwan says if Asad rejects it, he should think about it for two days, and Faisal and he would send emissaries. I can't speak about Boumedienne. But I've promised him a Joint Economic Commission and diplomatic relations, but only after diplomatic relations. I don't know why he needs it. He'll get some EX-IM credits for a natural gas line. But there won't be any economic aid.

Meir: He doesn't need it.

Kissinger: But I held that up because of the embargo. There is no new plan. In any case, he knows he can't get it without disengagement. So I think he'll come.

Dinitz: In the Cabinet there was a consensus for a list of requests we had, on economic aid and military equipment.

Kissinger: We have to work it out differently from the last one. We can work out the understandings but not tie them to the agreement.

Dinitz: What she said is we have to sit together and concretize those needs, possibly by sending a delegation to the United States.

Kissinger: You should have a long-term arms agreement whatever you do, because you shouldn't have to do it every six months. You should do it in the time frame of disengagement because we can use that explanation to the Arabs. On economic aid, I don't know how to do it.

Dinitz: We should have experts meet.

Kissinger: What I should do is get a formal Presidential authorization to promise long-term arms aid, and send a mission, and send you a letter saying the President has authorized this. What you need is not just a mission.

Dinitz: A decision in principle on long-term arms aid.

Kissinger: That's right.

Meir: And something that we shouldn't be asked to come down from the Golan Heights. The Cabinet was unanimous.

Kissinger: This we have to work out...

Dinitz: Yes, if it leaks...

Kissinger: It'll kill us.

Dinitz: It would be better if it's a Presidential letter to the Prime Minister.

Meir: [to Dinitz] There was a letter; which you didn't think much of.

Dinitz: [to Kissinger] When you were in Mexico, he sent a letter, with Sisco, that "no Israeli soldier would be asked to leave territory until there was peace." I didn't think much of it.[7]

Meir: You said, Mr. Secretary, to Rabin, that if you had been there it wouldn't have been sent, because it couldn't be implemented.

Kissinger: Yes.

Meir: One more thing the Cabinet wanted: If there is another war, we shouldn't go through such agony as in October before the airlift. There should be contingency planning.

Dinitz: The Pentagon asked us for lists of what we'd need if there was a new war. We weren't sure we wanted to give it to the Pentagon, but . . .

Kissinger: I'm in favor of contingency planning.

Dinitz: With the Azores and the Europeans, could we have some planning?

Kissinger: It is a mistake to approach European Governments. Contingency planning I have no objection to.

The immediate [Pentagon] political game is clear. It's such a total change in their orientation that I'm not sure what they're up to. Never mind, I have no problem agreeing to contingency planning.

If this story gets out, all hell will break loose. But it shouldn't be at a military attaché level. So officers?

Dinitz: Yes.

Kissinger: Let me talk to Haig and Scowcroft about how to do it. I have no problem giving you an understanding on it since the Pentagon has already offered it.

I'd be wary of giving your detailed supply situation; can't you give just your needs?

Dinitz: Just how soon we'll need certain items. I have no trouble giving it to Scowcroft.

Kissinger: If the Arabs find out they'll play it more cleverly. Scowcroft can discuss it but it has to get into the Pentagon machinery.

Dinitz: Yes.

Kissinger: First you give me a list of what you want. Second, I'll send a letter to the President tonight saying this is what we should promise the Israelis and why. Third, I'll give a letter to you saying the President is prepared to work out the following things.

Meir: There is the issue of military equipment. Then the promise that the U.S. will not ask us to go down from the Golan Heights.

---

[7] Not found.

Kissinger: This I have to think about. In this Administration it won't happen.

Meir: Then we have to consider what will happen if someone wants to remove UNEF.

Kissinger: That we can easily have.

Dinitz: You don't need to bother the President with it.

Kissinger: We can have some understanding like on the Egyptian one. Because the Senate Foreign Relations Committee will never believe we didn't have understandings. We could show them those. Like the Egyptian things.

I can leave somebody here tomorrow.

Dinitz: Not for sensitive things.

Kissinger: No, but for other things.

Dinitz: For a Memorandum of Understanding.

Kissinger: Yes, because I don't want to create the impression this [the Gromyko meeting] is a U.S.-Soviet agreement. We should leave someone here to be working with you.

[The Prime Minister and Secretary Kissinger went into the larger Conference Room for the plenary meeting.]

---

47. Memorandum of Conversation[1]

Jerusalem, May 7, 1974, 9:07–11:15 p.m.

PARTICIPANTS

Mrs. Golda Meir, Prime Minister of Israel
Moshe Dayan, Minister of Defense
Simcha Dinitz, Ambassador to the United States
Lt. Gen. Mordechai Gur, Chief of Staff
Col. Aryeh Bar-On, Aide to Dayan

Dr. Henry A. Kissinger, Secretary of State and Assistant to the President for National Security Affairs
Peter W. Rodman, NSC Staff

Meir: I called a Cabinet meeting thinking it would be short. It took two and a half hours.

---

[1] Source: National Archives, RG 59, Records of Henry Kissinger, 1973–77, Box 7, Nodis Memcons, March 1974, Folder 1. Secret; Nodis. The meeting was held at the Prime Minister's office in Jerusalem.

Dayan: I want to say I was happy last night when you came back about having these enclaves. I felt bad because I thought I had misled you. Actually Israel doesn't have troops in between there. So all these lines would turn out to be ridiculous.

Let's get to business. I hope you will be happy—though I have never seen you happy. (Laughter)

Kissinger: My happiness consists on having something that has a maximum chance of being accepted.

(Looks over the map on the Prime Minister's desk.)[2]

Gur: Here on Mount Hermon we didn't include the Syrian position.

So we start the red line in no-man's land. We go down—you know that line.

Here, in the northern side of Kuneitra, you can see we moved not only in Kuneitra but in the whole northern valley there.

Kissinger: Any populated area there?

Gur: There is a big village there.

Kissinger: Any village they could move people back into?

Gur: That is a political question

Kissinger: He has an obsession about populated areas.

Gur: The village of Akhmadia. We can move the line a few hundred yards.

Kissinger: We don't need that for tomorrow.

Gur: So all this area we give back.

Dayan: Here is the first stronghold we really pull back. No monkey business.

Kissinger: The wriggly line is of no value if there are no villages there. It would create more problems.

Gur: There are two considerations—the villages and the road.

Dayan: We shall not break it on this village.

Gur: We tried to make enclaves between the strongholds. This is an area where I can't remove strongholds. But here are two villages in no-man's land where I don't mind if they come in.

Kissinger: You can't designate a specific village; you have to allow them into all villages.

Dayan: No, there are only two there.

Kissinger: Fine. But it makes a difference if I can say they can come into all villages.

---

[2] The map is not attached.

Gur: Here, the Rafid area. Here (in the southern bulge) we gave up a stronghold. In Rafid area we will give up a stronghold. Here is the village of Rafid where I understand they can come.

Kissinger: I haven't mentioned it.

Gur: Here (in the southern bulge) is the third stronghold we'll pull back. To the south we can't pull back because it is plains; I don't know of any village. And here I would not recommend to bring back civilians. Here the terrain is such—voluntarily I wouldn't give up that stronghold, but that picture was too sophisticated.

Kissinger: My worry was . . .

Dayan: They would have thought we had cheated them and it was meaningless.

Kissinger: You are absolutely right.

Dayan: Now you can point to three strongholds and can point to return of civilians there. I don't think you should say anything about the south, because there are no villages there.

Kissinger: It would be a mistake to speak about any exclusions.

Dayan: When it comes to that, we will speak of that later. There are insignificant villages there. South of Rafid I don't think they will initiate anything but you don't have to discuss it.

Kissinger: This village will help. The northern half.

Dayan: It would look ridiculous.

Kissinger: Can't you do something here (along thin part of the strip in the middle section)?

Dayan: I don't think so.

I was a bit worried. On the map I brought to Washington (he takes it out), south of Rafid, there are no Syrian villages. We took an old Syrian map and wanted to see what happened at any time. But they have some villages where the farms go up to our line. It was no-man's land. It is abandoned now.

They can go back there, three villages south of Rafid.

Meir: The question is where is the line they compensated?

Dayan: It is all rocks. Perhaps there is grazing in the summer, but it is not settled now.

Kissinger: It would be of maximum help to be able to say civilian authority can move into any area. I am not blaming you—it is a common problem. Because if I know the Arab mind, the Egyptians moved forward all along the line and he and Boumediene say it is important. This gap won't help.

Dayan: We always talked about "all along the line" with Egypt, but it is really ten percent of the line. There is all the area south—Abu

Rudeis. (Points to wall map—the whole western coast of Sinai.) This is the whole Egyptian line.

Kissinger: I'll have trouble for this whole area (the southernmost part) and I will have trouble up here. The problem is what happens if they reject it. The Egyptian Marwan said today—I misled him a bit, because I told him you would withdraw along the whole line. I remembered we had prepared a false map for Sadat and then got a better one. So they all think I can do better than the first one I presented. So Marwan urged me not to give it all at once. Here (the southernmost part), I am not arguing, nor in the north.

My question is whether there is anything at all that can be done in this stretch of line (the center).

Meir: When we move military installations, we move them out.

Dayan: I honestly think nothing more can be done. There is a limit and we have reached the limit.

Gur: There is such a thing as this village (in the middle sector) which doesn't bother me. I won't speak about strongholds because I am against it completely.

Dayan: You know when we had the Egyptian agreement, there were no demonstrations against the Foreign Minister's house.[3]

Meir: A woman I have known for many years, the widow of Ben Zvi (Yitzhak Ben Zvi, the first President of Israel)—who is no demagogue—joined them. That really bothered me.

Kissinger: The question is whether if it fails they won't be demonstrating against worse things. I thought before the question was if it fails; now I think there is a chance of it succeeding.

Dinitz: How should it be titled?

Kissinger: "Zone of separation" is better. All Arabs have a thing about the UN.

Dayan: We have to go into it later.

Kissinger: The Egyptian thinks we shouldn't offer him the Mount Hermon thing tomorrow.

Dinitz: So we can make a worse map, easily.

Kissinger: I am sure!

There are two schools of thought: We can either say this is absolutely all we can get, or . . .

Dayan: Can we use the old map where we asked for mutual withdrawal?

---

[3] Demonstrations against a U.S.-brokered disengagement agreement between Israel and Syria began upon Kissinger's arrival in Israel on May 2 (*Washington Post*, May 3, 1974, p. A26) and continued over the next few days (*Years of Upheaval*, p. 1062).

Kissinger: Let's wait until we have the big group. These villages will help.

(Gur leaves.)

Gromyko started out with all-out support of the Syrian position. He said basically disengagement isn't a Soviet idea anyway; they believe in the 1967 frontiers. But if there is a disengagement, it has to be extensive enough so that visibly it looks like going to 1967. He said, "Do you support the Israeli position?" I said "There is no Israeli position. You have a strategic decision to make. I assume when I go to Syria, we will have a common position and our support. Our assessment is that if it fails there will be another war, and Syria will lose. And you will have a difficult decision to make."

From that point he started backtracking. He said it must include all of Kuneitra. I said I don't know. He said, "Are the Israelis withdrawing from the 1967 line?"

Basically, he left me the view not that they would necessarily support it but they wouldn't necessarily support Syria if if breaks down. That is at the end of the meeting.

I took him aside and said, "Look at Germany. Bahr will go. Schmidt is my friend, and if you start a harassing game, we can do it too. We could work together in Central Europe."

After I said these two things, his attitude changed. He said there had to be an organic link to 1967. I argued with him. He said, "You are willing to make reference to the fact that this is the first step toward an overall settlement without reference to what it is?" I said I didn't know but I could discuss it with the Israelis. So he thinks he got a great victory.

Marwan and Saunders came back from Boumediene. He'll support it but it isn't clear how. Marwan thinks it means he will send an emissary. It could be true. Boumediene is very cautious. Boumediene asked specifically about Mount Hermon.

Marwan's view—though predicated on the view that you'll pull back all along the line—is that I should just show him Rafid and Kuneitra tomorrow. Because all Arabs think when Kissinger says he can't get more, it's not true.

Dinitz: Jews too!

Kissinger: I will show him Kuneitra and then throw in the rest later. It sort of makes me believe something is possible. Apparently the Syrians have not shown the Russians the map I showed them—which is interesting.

But I have to tell you, every Arab that I have seen places emphasis on a continuous line. Since I don't need it tomorrow, maybe you can take another look. Let's see what his reaction is.

Dayan: What time do you meet him tomorrow?

Kissinger: I will arrive there at 1:00. So I could leave there in the evening and come back here. If I leave at 6:30 I will be back at 6:30. Thursday[4] I am going to Riyadh and Cairo. Though it is very risky to leave here for Riyadh.

Meir: Why?

Kissinger: Because the King of Saudi Arabia is very pained when somebody comes from Jerusalem.

Meir: But he has nothing against Jews!

Kissinger: But he does about Israel. But that is my problem. I think I should go to the King. Sadat later. Then back to Syria on Saturday.

The major problem is it looks like a series of pockets.

Dayan: A pocket?

Kissinger: A pocket in the north, and a pocket in the south. I am talking about how it looks.

Dayan: It depends on the physical terrain. Every military line must follow the physical terrain.

Kissinger: I don't think we can get any further in arguing before we even have his reaction.

Dayan: The present Chief of Staff was chief of the Northern Command and he knows every inch there. He has good experience in Washington as Attaché. He is really stretching himself.

Meir: We don't even have Cabinet approval on this (previous) map.

Dayan: But it is our internal affair. But it will be impossible to move back a little more.

Kissinger: What do they think the alternatives are?

Meir: They don't think. Some are demagogues; some are really anxious.

Kissinger: But what are alternatives? So everything doesn't fall on Israel internationally. Rabin asks me, "What do we gain time for?" To gain time, we gain having Heath replaced by Wilson, Brandt by Schmidt and Pompidou by Giscard.[5] I am not claiming credit for it, but Europe's view is a little different now.

Meir: I know Schmidt, he is a friend of ours.

(They confer in Hebrew.)

---

[4] May 9.

[5] In 1974, Harold Wilson succeeded Edward Heath as British Prime Minister, Helmut Schmidt succeeded Willy Brandt as West German Chancellor, and Valéry Giscard d'Estaing succeeded Georges Pompidou as French President.

Kissinger: The strategic problem for you is, unless there is agreement, the argument will be increasingly "if you can't force them to go two kilometers, how can you ...?"

Dinitz: But it is not two kilometers, because of the salient.

Kissinger: Maybe he will accept it.

Meir: What Gur explained, it is a question of ridges. And we can't lose sight of who the Syrians are. They have never kept any agreement. Once we move back from the ridges.

Dayan: It was the same with the Mitla Pass.

Kissinger: You convinced me of that, because I felt if he really wanted an agreement, it wouldn't make such a difference whether he had Mitla. There were many factors. And we were dealing with Sadat.

Meir: Look at the area he is getting back.

Dayan: They are there because this is terrain of land, not because of an accident. So we could take one or two back and make up for it by making two new ones on either side. That is one thing. But to move the whole line ...

I can't resign because I already have! But the Chief of Staff says he has gone to the limit.

Nobody will support it.

Meir: (to Dayan) Last night in our Parliamentary party group you didn't come. I was there until 12:30.

Kissinger: You don't have to convince me. We have a common problem. If nothing can occur to us, maybe we will go with what we have got. Maybe it gives Sadat a way out.

Meir: I was at the Parliament party; Yigal was before the Committee. We can't do it unless we are convinced.

Dinitz: I strongly recommend you take first another map which doesn't include Hermon because they are bound to reject it.

Meir: Yesterday's map, for instance.

Kissinger: That will infuriate them.

Dinitz: But the Hermon thing is psychological, and you can say the Israelis don't want to withdraw from an area you have attacked and killed so many men.

Kissinger: Anyway I need two maps, military and civilian.

Dinitz: Talk to Moshe; he has a problem with it. Because the civilians don't go to all the area where the military withdrew.

Kissinger: That is a presentational point. I need a less-good map than the one we have. They are very interested in the Hermon area.

Dayan: They are suffering very heavy casualties there; they don't announce it. Maybe you can say half of Kuneitra.

Kissinger: No, that would inflame them. Maybe drop Rafid and Hermon.

Dayan: And maybe say we insist on mutual withdrawal.

Kissinger: My instinct is, that would be too inflaming.

Dayan: Why not say a buffer zone with no civilians returning?

Kissinger: He seems extremely concerned with what his military think. If we could give him the north and not fool around in the south.

Dinitz: Maybe he will accept the first map.

Kissinger: You have produced a permanent stomach upset for me. Between you and the Syrians. Not the food, but the state of tension.

(Dayan brings in yesterday's map.)[6]

Dayan: It went way up to Hermon (the UN zone). Today we cut it to here (to give Syrians more).

Kissinger: You could just put your line up here somewhere. They are obsessed with bloody Hermon.

Dayan: It is not bloody, but it snows.

Meir: A lot of blood is shed there too.

Kissinger: You are opposed to showing two maps, one for civilians and one for military? For tomorrow it is too complicated.

Dayan: You can just tell him about the civilians going back.

Kissinger: There is a pathetic quality to these Arabs, a sort of machismo. I think Asad's problem is to get something not as bad as Sadat got.

Meir: It is a fact of life he didn't do as well.

Kissinger: I tell that to all the other Arabs.

Dayan: I will get you another map tomorrow. One that keeps Hermon, and also Rafid, if you think it . . .

Kissinger: My basic instinct is . . .

Dayan: He probably heard about Rafid from Sadat and others.

Kissinger: But all he heard was that I would try to do it, not that I would succeed. Tomorrow I will sell him this salient (north of Kuneitra) which seems in my mind to connect with Kuneitra. If you can throw in this village. That is a sort of coherent slice.

I have got two problems tomorrow—to give him enough to keep it going and to give him hope for a little more. I could say you insist now on holding Hermon but I have given you an ultimatum—if you don't mind.

Dayan: You can say months back we offered Hermon but now, with all this fighting . . .

---

[6] See Document 44. The map has not been found.

Kissinger: I will give him a strong impression he will get Hermon.

Dinitz: And Kuneitra.

Kissinger: As a certainty.

Dinitz: And then you go back and get also Rafid.

Meir: He shouldn't think he is getting all his civilians back.

Kissinger: I will tell him Israel has left Kuneitra. The civilian administration will be an enormous negotiation anyway. Once he has accepted the line he is in a different psychological position—because it means he has convinced the Ba'ath party and the Russians acquiesced.

I know your view. You know I think it is wrong. There may be another brawl about it, but there won't be a trick.

I am going to be slightly misleading to him on the civilians, because all he is going to be able to tell his colleagues is he has gotten Kuneitra. It is a little dishonest. But once he has accepted the line, he has talked to his Knesset or whatever he's got, and he has more a vested interest.

Meir: The Hermon for him is a great thing. We just heard he has a field hospital there.

Dinitz: Because of the casualties.

Meir: We have had some too, but he has had tens of casualties.

Kissinger: The key is to keep the Arabs divided.

Meir: I know Kuneitra has become a symbol to them, but Hermon's a reality.

Kissinger: Boumediene raised Hermon. I have written a letter to him.[7]

You know these babies—these Arabs—have let it be known they are hurt that I am not taking Nancy[8] there.

Dinitz: As it is, she is spending too much time in Egypt.

Kissinger: It'll be finished here.

Dinitz: But as of now, we are upset. (Laughter)

Kissinger: Let's be clear! What map is he shown?

Dayan: Without Hermon and Rafid. And say you will try to get something in the south.

Meir: You said Sadat wouldn't be impressed with Rafid.

Dinitz: He knows you got Rafid.

Kissinger: No, I told him I would try.

Meir: There is no muezzin outside.

---

[7] Not found.
[8] Nancy Kissinger.

Kissinger: Sadat you can handle.

I wish you direct negotiations with the Syrians!

Meir: There are some things for tomorrow.

Kissinger: Why don't I call on you tomorrow before I go?

Meir: Good.

Rodman: You want to know the number of square kilometers being given up?

Kissinger: Yes. Gromyko asked me how many.

Meir: East of the purple line?

Kissinger: Yes.

Dayan: I will get it for you.

Meir: Here there is one thing. This is a summary on our friends, the Kurds (Tab A).[9]

Kissinger: We have approved several million.

Meir: They are in trouble.

Kissinger: I can't believe it. The Egyptians asked us to ask the Shah to put pressure on Iraq so Iraqi troops all leave Syria. That is why there was trouble in February between Iran and Iraq.

Meir: Are they (the Jordanians) participating and intending to move towards Syria?

Kissinger: I am certain he is not. He has checked with us every day.

Meir: We have awful reports of what the terrorists plan. May is a bad month, the month of Independence for Israel.

Kissinger: They don't want us to go to Kuwait, the Jordanians. They think it's too dangerous.

---

[9] Tab A attached but not printed. Entitled "The Situation in Kurdistan," the paper assesses the fighting in Iraqi Kurdistan between Kurds and Iraqi forces with an emphasis on Soviet support for the Iraqis against the Kurds.

48. Memorandum of Conversation[1]

Damascus, May 8, 1974, 12:15 p.m.

PARTICIPANTS

Hafez al-Asad, President of Syria
Abdel Khalim Khaddam, Deputy Prime Minister and Minister of Foreign Affairs
Maj. General Hikmat Shihabi, Chief of Staff
Mr. Daboul, Presidential Adviser

Dr. Henry A. Kissinger, Secretary of State and Assistant to the President for National Security Affairs
Joseph J. Sisco, Under Secretary for Political Affairs
Harold H. Saunders, NSC Staff
Isa K. Sabbagh, American Embassy, Jidda (Interpreter)

[Omitted here is discussion unrelated to the Arab-Israeli dispute.]

Kissinger: On the disengagement negotiations, I wanted to review the difference between the Egyptian and the Syrian negotiations, and the Israeli and American domestic situations, so we can make a common assessment, if that is all right with you. Then you can understand the pressures on me and on the situation rather than talk about abstract lines.

In Israel demonstrators are now showing signs with my name in Arabic. I can't call on the Prime Minister because her house is surrounded by demonstrators.

My assessment is as follows:

First, the Syrian negotiation is much more difficult than the Egyptian negotiation for many reasons. For one thing, the territory involved is much smaller. Also, there is a civilian population. The territory is much closer to the security centers of each country. It raises an emotional and psychological response in Israel.

And the military situation is different: The "pocket" that Israel had across the Canal had a narrow supply route in a corridor 15–20 kilometers wide. It was pinched by two Egyptian armies. It was in flat country at the end of a very long supply line. They had a great sense of vulnerability. In the Syrian pocket, they don't feel as vulnerable. I am just assessing the situation, not defending it. They have a line of hills behind it and Mount Hermon beside it. They are not eager to give it up.

If you study the Egyptian agreement, they (the Israelis) didn't withdraw from any place where there were not Egyptian troops. There

---

[1] Source: National Archives, RG 59, Records of Henry Kissinger, 1973–77, Box 8, Nodis Memcons, May 1974, Folder 1. Secret; Nodis. The meeting was held at the Presidential Palace in Damascus.

were five Egyptian divisions across the Canal. In Egypt, we established a line on the existing line of control and the withdrawal of the pocket. There was a UN zone in a flat place with no population.

In Syria, we are doing separate things: One, to restore Syrian civilian administration. And secondly, we are talking about Israeli withdrawal from newly-acquired territories. In Egypt, they withdrew from no new territories.

Asad: What is the area of the pocket?

Kissinger: We will check that.

Asad: On the West Bank, the Israelis said it was 1700 square kilometers.

Kissinger: We will send you a message. That adds a particular complexity to the negotiation.

Secondly, the problem of the Syrian-Israeli negotiation also has to be seen on one hand as a geographic issue and on the other as an issue of political orientation.

I repeat, I say this analytically.

I have thought a lot about where we are. I must admit that it is very difficult for me to work in this atmosphere. This part of Syria we are talking about is seen in Israel as an extension of Israel. They never thought of the Sinai this way.

What is involved now is the basic question His Excellency raised the other day: Whether Israel will live in peace with its neighbors or behave like the Americans toward the American Indians.

There is a tremendous psychological battle in Israel which the older generation cannot understand.

I have met them on three separate visits for seven hours each. The older generation is in tears. In Israel, which is friendly, the atmosphere is much tenser than here, where we have no relations.

The reason is that what we are trying to bring about is to move the body politic in Israel from war towards peace and from a military to a political conception. I believe it is the policy we have pursued since October that has removed the present government. If Israel had had our support, it would and could have stayed in the occupied territories whatever the USSR did, as it did for six years.

Now your courage and the heroism of your soldiers has made possible the change in Israel which now realizes that peace cannot come from a policy of strength alone.

It is important now to keep in mind what is the first step. I have been an admirer of what deGaulle did in Algeria. I believe the independence of Algeria became inevitable the day deGaulle gave independence to the black African nations. It was inconceivable he could deny independence to Algeria. That was the crucial decision. In any political process, you have to understand the crucial issue. The crucial decision now is for Israel to decide to come back.

Let me tell you what a senior minister told me Sunday:[2] "The worst things you are doing to us are: (1) after every war so far, we have extended our territory and you are asking us to contract it; (2) after every war we created a new permanent situation for a reasonably long period. You are wishing us to take a step you say is only a first step toward implementing Resolution 338."

So this is the problem in Israel.

It is compounded by the fact there is an old government that is daily losing authority but a new group is not yet established. The new group is more realistic, less emotional, less wedded to a policy of colonization. They will be no easier to deal with.

I was thinking of bringing the Prime Minister today.

We will reach a point in the talks with the Israelis where we will have to judge, one, whether there will be a total political immobility, or two, adoption of a stance of total militancy. Out of this chaos there will be a victory of the right wing military.

I believe a disengagement agreement brought about by the kind of pressures we are using will bring about a change in Israel in a favorable direction.

Let me talk analytically about the American political situation.

In the past any Secretary of State who tried to do anything on the Arab-Israeli problem has been either destroyed or immobilized.

The reason is this. I know no situation in the United States where a Secretary of State had a political following of his own. Therefore, Israeli strategy has always been to attack the Secretary of State who was more vulnerable. Right now the opposite is true as a political fact. Secondly, in the past, our policy has not been conducted in an intelligent adaptation to the American scene. The Arab tendency has always asked for so much it was easy to mobilize pressures against the policy. We have succeeded in splitting the issues so much that it was harder for Israel's friends to use the media to focus pressures on us. We have also always moved so fast that something was finished before it could be criticized. We have, therefore, been able to move step by step. For example, yesterday both the Senate majority and minority leaders made speeches in support of my policies. Honestly, I don't think the minority leader knew what he was saying; he wanted to benefit from my popularity, not from the negotiation.

---

[2] May 5. See Documents 43 and 44.

In terms of the American political situation, the strategy is to push the Israelis as far as possible without raising a general uproar. If we push it too far, given the situation the President faces, we could face months of paralysis. We have to use my prestige to put this over. If we fail, a campaign will say that the Secretary of State is colluding with the USSR to impair Israeli security. It is already starting. Joe Kraft[3] says I got the Soviets to have Syria to attack Israel so I could score a success by stopping the war I started.

Asad: Kraft?

Kissinger: He was here. His point is: For my own purposes, I worked with the Soviets to start a war so I could get it stopped diplomatically. But that is only the beginning. If we could succeed, all this we could sweep away.

What is important is whether we can keep the momentum of Israel going backward or whether we are going to have another stalemate.

There cannot be another military change. In a political situation where Israel is going back, a point will be reached as in Algeria where a decision will be inevitable.

Gromyko wants to put a solution into the context of an agreement with me. It isn't that kind of a problem.

The big change in the last six months is in political mobility. The Israelis can no longer count on U.S. support on all issues. The American Secretary of State is urging Israel to move back.

This is the general assessment I wanted to share. After lunch we can go into details.

From my own selfish viewpoint the best thing for me would be for the negotiations to fail. I would be criticized for three weeks, but then I could withdraw. If I succeed and continue—as I will—I will suffer great attacks. But if we succeed, we can generate political support for what we are doing.

(The party moved to lunch.)

Kissinger: Sisco is the only individual who is a conspiracy all by himself.

Asad: He is a phenomenon!

Kissinger: I have studied the purges in the USSR in the 1930's. Stalin developed a definition that had a curious aspect: A person didn't have to have done something; he just had to have the potential to harm Stalin. On that basis, I would have to purge my whole staff.

Sisco: I am still here. I must be not so bad, or else I'm inefficient!

---

[3] Joseph Kraft was an American columnist.

Kissinger: Did you see an article by Prof. Morgenthau? He compared me to Chamberlain. The campaign being made against me is that I am working with the Soviets and Arabs to destroy Israel.

Asad: Does he work in political science?

Kissinger: Yes.

Asad: Is he a good American if he makes enemies of the Arabs?

Kissinger: No. He is wrong. We each pursue our own interests. I believe it can't be in the U.S. interest to have Arab enmity, especially for a third country.

Saunders used to press me to be more friendly to the Arabs. I told him the time wasn't right yet. Without the war it would not have been possible yet.

Asad: In order to make a judgment, these professors should make an assessment of the losses and gains for the U.S.

Kissinger: Next time, I am planning to bring Mrs. Kissinger.

Asad: Yes, we are planning on it . . .

Khaddam expected that on Cyprus you would agree with Gromyko to postpone discussion of disengagement until Moscow.[4] Does Gromyko want to discuss this in Moscow?

Kissinger: If I go to Moscow, it will not be to discuss the Middle East.

I think the situation by early next week will be: We will either know whether we can agree, and then we should move very quickly. We will know by Saturday or Sunday[5] what is the maximum I can achieve. Then you will have to decide whether it is enough. If it is enough, we will have to move very fast before they can organize against us. If I can return with a success, I can explain it as a movement toward peace. If I come back with a stalemate, I will have to explain who is at fault. Gromyko couldn't help one iota. The worst thing I could do would be to make an agreement with Gromyko and sell it in America. Why should I make concessions to the Soviets and not to you? We want friendlier relations with Syria.

So if we have a stalemate and if I go to Moscow, I will not talk with them about the Middle East. If they told you they could do better in Moscow, that is wrong. They tried this at two summits and failed.

Asad: We are aware of these things.

Kissinger: I think it is unlikely I will go to Moscow in two weeks. But if I do, no matter what you are told, the subject will be SALT. In Moscow at the end of March, they were discussing their participation,

---

[4] A reference to the Moscow Summit scheduled for late June.
[5] May 11–12.

not the substance of a disengagement.[6] That was the argument with Brezhnev. I told him if he could settle the disengagement, I would not ask to participate. I am not trying to talk against the USSR because we know you have to get your military equipment there.

Asad: If you started giving arms to the Arabs, you would be better able to control the arms.

Kissinger: Just in this room, we are starting with Saudi Arabia. They are sending a mission to Washington in June on general cooperation. We will have a military section to that.

Asad: The nations here need arms. The need, of course, would be lessened, given peace.

Kissinger: What we want to do is establish a pattern. We are starting on economic cooperation, including technical and scientific cooperation. And that can expand. We may do it with Egypt next. After the disengagement or after a reestablishment of relations, we would be prepared to do it with Syria.

Asad: We are anxious that, as fast as possible, things go back to normal. But sometimes, one lets go emotionally sometimes. One sees certain proposals that make me angry. We are in earnest, Dr. Kissinger. For your own ears, if you are worried about 1–2000 demonstrators in Israel, there are many more in Syria who would march against us for cooperating with you.

The Syrian difficulty is that people here who have been nurtured over 26 years on hatred, can't be swayed overnight by our changing courses. We would never take one step except in the interests of our own people. We are all human—we all have our impulsive reaction to things. But in leadership, we have to restrain ourselves and analyze and take steps in our own interest. A just peace is in the interest of our people.

Kissinger: And of Israel and of all people in this area.

Asad: Wars waged for aims other than to establish justice should not be waged.

Kissinger: The extraordinary thing last October was that people who were bold enough to make a war against all odds were moderate enough to follow a restrained policy in peace.

Asad: On the first day—October 6—I made a speech saying we are entering a war to stop bloodshed. We want peace. So, of course, we have to bend every effort for peace.

Kissinger: I agree. That is why I tried to explain the framework.

---

[6] Kissinger went to Moscow at the end of March for talks with Soviet officials, including General Secretary Brezhnev. See *Foreign Relations, 1969–1976*, volume XV, Soviet Union, June 1972–August 1974, Documents 167–170.

Last November, we thought Damascus was physically dangerous for an American to visit and we didn't even propose a visit. That was before I knew the Foreign Minister. I have invited him to come to Washington when he comes to the U.S. next. Our hospitality is not as advanced as Syria's.

Shihabi: I protest.

Kissinger: We know what tremendous efforts you have made to entertain such large parties. You'd be less well equipped if you hadn't had 2000 years of barbarian invasions. Our security people operate; arrest them.

Asad: Relations are improving.

Kissinger: Whatever happens on disengagement, we are prepared to try to continue improving relations.

Asad: We too. Will Rabin form a Cabinet?[7]

Kissinger: Yes. I think they're waiting for these negotiations. If they succeed, they'll speed the transition to a more political position.

The best one in Israel is Dayan.

Asad: Will Eban be in the Cabinet?

Kissinger: The present Cabinet will almost certainly not be in the Cabinet—but not for this reason. They're looking for a scapegoat. Eban will probably be in the Cabinet.

Shihabi: Dayan may come back later. He is still young.

Kissinger: If we do not succeed, the right wing will gain more and more the upper hand. In a year or two, Dayan may come back.

Asad: I heard Eban make a good statement after the war that wars aren't going to help. They should follow a policy of making the Arabs desirous of not going to war any more.

Kissinger: That is the overwhelming issue. That is why this is such an important phase.

(At 5:15 p. m. everyone rose from the table. While the group reassembled, Dr. Kissinger noted a reviewer's comment on his first book "Nuclear Weapons and Foreign Policy." The reviewer said he could not tell if Dr. Kissinger was a great writer but anyone finishing the book was a great reader. Seriously, some of the considerations in that book were dated and some were coming back. It pre-dated the era of missiles.)

---

[7] After Golda Meir's resignation as Prime Minister on April 11, Yitzhak Rabin was nominated to be Prime Minister. He negotiated with various Israeli factions to form a new Cabinet while Meir continued to head a caretaker government. On June 2, the Knesset approved his new government.

Asad: Seriously, we wish that peace will reign all over the world, and that competition will be peaceful. It is one of the traits of this world that conflict remains.

Kissinger: I think we have an important opportunity for peace.

Let me show you now where we stand in our talks with the Israelis—if you won't get too angry. I think I can get some more, but the objective situation is difficult unless you want to accept this. Let me show you, and then I'll tell you what I'll try to do. When I come back Saturday or Sunday we can take stock. You should make your decisions in terms of the overall analysis I gave you.

(Showing a map.)[8] Israel has now agreed to go back to the October 6 line everywhere but Mt. Hermon.

Asad: This is the October 6 line?

Kissinger: No, this. They agreed to leave October. We will not show anything as a UN zone. They want a zone with no military forces but it will be Syrian. I'm saying they have to go back on Mt. Hermon and they must find some other stretch along the line where they can go back.

They haven't agreed.

Asad: (Followed the line.)

Kissinger: They want all points on top of Mt. Hermon. I've told them they must reconsider this.

Asad: This configuration is creating a dovetailing. Last time we asked for a straighter line—irrespective of the terrain. We would decide on a line and then discuss adjustments one way or another. They're not going back behind the October 6 line generally.

So I make these observations: Observation # 1: There is no return behind the October 6 line. Observation # 2: There is no straight parallel line. Thus complicates the situation. Observation # 3: They keep points they occupied after October 22. For example, on Mount Hermon, where they had no positions. The only observer post they had was on the October 6 line. Observation # 4: There is no significant area of land from which they are withdrawing. There is no withdrawal of any substance.

Kissinger: The pocket and Quneitra.

Asad: They are not giving back Quneitra. They have just split Quneitra.

Kissinger: That's what they started out doing. Now the line is just on the Western edge of Quneitra. They started dividing the city. We refused the idea.

---

[8] The map has not been found. It is presumably one the Israelis gave Kissinger the day before. See Document 47.

Asad: The city is important because we want to return the civilians. We can't do it unless the military situation is good. As it stands now, it is not good.

Kissinger: I'll report every point you make. It took a letter from our President[9] to move them from the middle of Quneitra. The United States is interested in return of civilians to Quneitra and would do everything it could to assure a return of civilians and its rehabilitation. We would be prepared to say we would give strong support if the civilians are harassed.

Asad: The civilians will be up in arms against us.

Kissinger: This we would not permit.

Asad: I hope this is clear to Dr. Kissinger: We cannot agree to a disengagement of this kind. This indicates the Israelis are insisting on war. We would not take Quneitra back in this form. We would only agree to a line near the line we have indicated. If we agreed to this kind of disengagement, we could not return to civilian life. This does not suggest Israeli seriousness. First, we want a straight line. We could say let's go back to the October 22 line (in the north?). Of course, Dr. Kissinger knows we can't possibly accept.

Kissinger: Let me give my personal view. I know you can't accept. I think we should ask Israel to withdraw some other distances along the line and in Mt. Hermon. Even Qunietra—it was first just a little corner.

Asad: I believe you.

Kissinger: I agree they must do more. I've already told them my thinking.

I believe in addition that, if they were very wise, they would make it much easier for you because I believe you have been very reasonable. However, you should keep in mind that whenever I say I've pressed them to the maximum, we will have to consider where we are.

Even this brings the line very close to their settlements and will create great insecurity. It will create a tremendous political situation there.

Asad: I'm with you. Your thoughts are clear. Yes, but look at it from our point of view. It doesn't inspire a belief that they are earnest. It would not help us continue. I could not send the civilians back. The situation there is worse.

Kissinger: Why?

Asad: We would have to redeploy. It would cost us money. It is weak on some political points like a recognition of the October 22 line. It would be as though we were projecting an untruth on our people.

---

[9] Document 41.

Kissinger: I understand.

Asad: I hope you will understand my remarks are directed at Israelis. We want a just peace. We say this to everybody around the Arab area. We don't want to fall into traps. We can't understand peace as a realization of gains for the Israeli people. We don't want to deceive our people.

Kissinger: This I understand. On the other hand, leaving aside details, look at the concept. Once the 1967 line is broken, for the first time, the Israelis would have withdrawn from strongpoints and territory which they did not lose in conflict. Therefore, Syria would have achieved an actual Israeli withdrawal under political pressure under the pressure of Syria and the United States. Particularly with some more territory. In the pocket—you will know—the Israelis claim the present line is easier to defend.

I will go back and explain your considerations and your attitude. I will try to continue the strategy that I'm pursuing—to use maximum political pressure short of a political explosion in the United States. I'm not yet under full-scale attack. The way the Israelis present it in the U.S., they treat Syria as part of USSR and say I'm making concessions to the USSR and what am I getting in return. So why do I want Israel to withdraw?

You have your own political requirements and maybe we cannot succeed. I will make an effort to improve the map. The significance for the Israelis is that this is an encroachment on their settlements for the first time.

Asad: My retort is that their settlements can be shelled by us now.

Kissinger: The best way to get them off the Golan Heights is to put pressure on the settlements in Golan.

Asad: I am suggesting point counter point.

Kissinger: The Egyptians are not emotional. The most useful thing is for me to go back to Israel. There is no sense in discussing secondary issues—UN, etc.—until we have a line.

My job is to see whether I can improve the line.

May I bring Mrs. Meir here?

Asad: We'll be occupied twice!

Kissinger: You want to come with me tonight?

Asad: It would be a strange historic event.

Kissinger: What is maddening about negotiating with her, is the emotion. She thinks an injustice has been done to her. She says: You started the war therefore you have to lose territory.

They say "You started the war, you get the pocket back and some territory behind the '67 lines."

Asad: You may keep the map.

Kissinger: Never give away a free map. Is that the motto of the Director of Intelligence? I'll make a maximum effort. I'll give them two days. I'll come back Saturday or Sunday, depending on what I can achieve. You know how long it took me to get this.

Asad: We could have demonstrations. I fear our people.

Kissinger: If it turns into a contest between demonstrators, I'll just leave the area, go to Washington and lead my own demonstrations. I'm losing.

What I said to you about the Israeli domestic situation is not based on the demonstrations but on the basis of what is going on there. If they lose this battle—and lose the pocket—they will be discouraged. If they keep the pocket, their strategy will be justified. They want to make it a U.S.-Soviet dispute. We want to decouple it. Success cannot be measured in territory. We've spent days and weeks bringing pressure on Israel.

Now what should we say to the press?

Asad: We cannot say we've reached agreements with regard to certain elements. We could say we discussed certain elements.

Kissinger: I'll say we've discussed some elements, and made some progress, but we should avoid an impression of a rupture.

Asad: Neither this nor that. Neither cause them to be optimistic nor pessimistic. Not create an overexpectation.

Kissinger: Your brothers in Egypt always predict total success for me without being told anything by me.

Asad: I've had contacts with Sadat.

Kissinger: While the Israelis are deliberating, I may go to Riyadh and stop in Cairo to pick up my wife for a few hours. I won't show maps to the Arab leaders but I will talk in a general way of what I'm trying to do in pushing the Israelis back. I'll say what I did before lunch but with less precision.

Asad: I sent them summaries. They said the Israeli plan is confined to the pocket and that Dr. Kissinger is going back to Israel.

Kissinger: What we discussed after lunch, I won't say. The details are your business. I have to leave time for King Faisal who always gives me religious instruction for half an hour.

Asad: Communism and Zionism. You never know. There may be a relationship.

Kissinger: He thinks Moscow is controlled by Tel Aviv.

Asad: Isn't Mrs. Meir Russian?

Kissinger: Can we say to the press that we brought some Israeli considerations to Damascus? We're now going back with some of your considerations. I'll return here Saturday or Sunday. For my press, I'll say we're making some progress, but we're not near an agreement.

Asad: Yes. We are not near an agreement. You have to say there is progress. You give same nuance.

Kissinger: Let's agree on something else. If they say, "Did you bring a map?"

Asad: Yes.

Kissinger: I'll say I brought some geographic considerations. In all seriousness, I appreciate your spirit. This is painful for you. We are talking about your territory.

49. Memorandum of Conversation[1]

Herzliyya, May 8, 1974, 9:45–10:55 p.m.

PARTICIPANTS

    Mrs. Golda Meir, Prime Minister of Israel
    Yitzhak Rabin, Minister of Labor and Prime Minister-designate
    Yigal Allon, Deputy Prime Minister
    Abba Eban, Minister of Foreign Affairs
    Moshe Dayan, Minister of Defense
    Shimon Peres, Minister of Information
    Simcha Dinitz, Ambassador to the U.S.
    Mordechai Gazit, Director, Prime Minister's Office
    Lt. Gen. Mordechai Gur, Army Chief of Staff
    Avraham Kidron, Director General, Ministry of Foreign Affairs
    Ephraim Evron, Deputy Director General, Ministry of Foreign Affairs
    Col. Aryeh Bar-On, Aide to Dayan
    Lt. Gen. David Leor, Military Assistant to the Prime Minister

    Dr. Henry A. Kissinger, Secretary of State and Assistant to the President for National Security Affairs
    Ambassador Kenneth B. Keating, U.S. Ambassador to Israel
    Mr. Joseph J. Sisco, Under Secretary of State for Political Affairs
    Ambassador Ellsworth Bunker, Ambassador at Large & Chief U.S. Delegate to Geneva Peace Conference on the Middle East
    Mr. Alfred L. Atherton, Jr., Assistant Secretary of State for Near Eastern and South Asian Affairs
    Mr. Carlyle E. Maw, Legal Adviser

---

[1] Source: National Archives, RG 59, Records of Henry Kissinger, 1973–77, Box 8, Nodis Memcons, May 1974, Folder 2. Secret; Nodis. The meeting was held at the Guest House in Herzliyya. All brackets, except those indicating omitted material, are in the original.

Mr. Harold H. Saunders, National Security Council Senior Staff
Mr. Peter W. Rodman, National Security Council Staff

Dr. Kissinger: Let me give you a brief summary of what happened. Given again the delicacy of what we are doing, if we can maintain the discretion that has characterized all our meetings for a week. I just would like to keep re-emphasizing it, because it has helped to get us here.

It was the best meeting we have had.[2] For the first time I believe we have a chance of getting an agreement. For the last week I have thought that the best thing that we could do would be to elaborate a cause of break-up that would not isolate Israel and would not lead to an explosion in the Middle East. My major concern had been to keep the Arabs divided on the issue of break-up rather than to produce a solution.

I still do not say the chances are better than 50/50, and maybe not even quite 50/50, but it was the first rational discussion I have had with the Syrians about the possibility of a disengagement.

As I am accompanied by the press, I always have the problem of making sure that the meeting doesn't end prematurely or they'll scare the world half to death. The meeting took what?, about four and one-half hours. And the first hour or so I spent on describing U.S.-Soviet relations to him, on the theory that whatever I told him was probably more than the Soviets had told him. Secondly, on the theory that if he saw that the Soviets were working with us on a lot of agreements, he might estimate their willingness to run risks for him that would jeopardize our relationship.

I did it in the form of giving him a report of what happened in Cyprus.[3] I de-emphasized the key discussion in Cyprus and gave him a lot of the discussions on other matters, having to do with the Summit. And that also gave me the opportunity, in the guise of describing the SALT negotiations, of telling him about the strategic relationship between the United States and the Soviet Union and the superiority in numbers of warheads we had. Again, I repeated this in the guise of telling him what the issues were in SALT, and why it was hard to frame an equitable proposal, since for the Soviets to catch up we would have to stand still for five years.

This he enjoyed hugely, and he asked many clarifying questions and made a very helpful suggestion. I said to him that the Soviet proposal sounded reasonable, but since we were already at the limit of what the Soviets proposed for us and the Soviets hadn't even started on their program, it would take them five years to reach their limit while

---

[2] See Document 48.
[3] See footnote 4, Document 44.

for five years we do nothing. He said, "Why don't you propose that both sides stop building these missiles now?" [Laughter]

Mrs. Meir: You never thought of it!

Dr. Kissinger: General Gur's friends—that is exactly the program of the JCS. That's what the Joint Chiefs of Staff want us to propose, that both sides now stop deploying multiple warheads, since we already have over 1,000 missiles and the Soviets have yet to build one. That's a fair enough proposal!

Well, at any rate, I just give you this to describe the mood. With respect to the Middle East, apparently the Soviets, in their inexhaustible tawdriness, have tried to use with them a remark that Gromyko made to me at the end of the meeting yesterday, to try to make some money with the Syrians. At the end of the meeting, Gromyko invited me to come to Moscow in a few weeks. He repeated an invitation, that they have extended to me ever since March, that I should come once more before the Summit, and I replied, as I did since March, that if the SALT discussions warranted it, I would come. If the SALT discussions did not warrant it, there was no purpose in my coming and it had absolutely nothing to do with me.

Apparently the Soviets told him that if the disengagement did not succeed, they would be prepared to take it up when I visited Moscow in two weeks. So Assad asked me whether I agreed to that with Gromyko, and I said absolutely not, that we were in no position to negotiate disengagement in Moscow with the Soviets, that we didn't think it was a bilateral matter between the Soviet Union and the United States. That we were talking to him, and that all our discussions would be between Syria and Israel and under no circumstances would we work out a solution with the Soviet Union.

All of which pleased him enormously. He made an approving comment about this approach.

Well, then we turned to the substance, and I made a very long analysis to him of the situation as I saw it, beginning with the difference between the Egyptian and the Syrian negotiation, the difference in the position of the salient, the difference in the position of the location of the armies, the proximity to vital centers, the fact that the area was populated, and pointing out that in effect in the Egyptian disengagement the Egyptians did not ask the Israelis to withdraw from lines that the Egyptian armies did not occupy. And that, therefore, the negotiating problem for us in the Syrian-Israel one was infinitely more complex and that the terms in which he had posed it were unfulfillable.

I then analyzed the Israeli domestic situation, and pointed out to him that there was a limit beyond which it could be stretched. He said if demonstrations impress me, what I needed is that he would be glad to organize one for me in Damascus.

Mr. Allon: A very organized society.

Dr. Kissinger: He said he had read there were several hundred demonstrators against me in Jerusalem. He said it would be no problem to get tens of thousands into the streets of Damascus.

Then I explained the American domestic situation, as I saw it. And I told him my view that if he relied on a stalemate and superpower pressure, the results were more likely to be similar to the 1967–73 period than anything else. And I said therefore the time has come to see whether we can have a reasonable discussion about disengagement. I said all this before I showed him the map. I said the major thing we have to settle is the attitude with which we are going to work. I can't stay out here much longer. We should settle it within the next few meetings. We have to see whether we can get into an agreement in principle. If we can get to an agreement in principle, we should then work very hard to get it settled as rapidly as possible before outside influences start confusing things. If we can't get an agreement in principle, then we should analyze where we are and where we go from there.

And I told him we were prepared to have friendly relations with them under conditions of peace in the Middle East, and so forth.

He replied in a very rational way, and not emotionally, and said that he wanted to point out that we had made a very good analysis from the Israeli point of view, but he too had his problems, that for 26 years the Syrian people had been taught that the Israelis were devils and that for him to make peace required some tangible results that he could show. And even under those conditions it was extremely difficult. And he said he was prepared to make a genuine effort towards peace.

General Shihabi was there, whom we know from his visit in Washington,[4] and who is rather impressive, and to our view a rather pro-American Syrian—I mentioned him to you once or twice—and I am inclined to believe this, because none of us really took him to be a man of consequence when he arrived, so we didn't give him any special treatment. We thought he had a message to deliver and we would take the message and send him home. It was only due to the accident that Gromyko was in Washington that weekend he was there, and I asked General Shihabi how to get in touch with Assad who was in Moscow. It was then I discovered that he was really extremely anti-Soviet and extremely worried that the Soviets might tell Assad something about their meetings in Washington, and he was trying to work out all sorts of ways by which he could get to Assad and keep him from being misled.

---

[4] See Document 35.

At any rate, Shihabi was there. And I then said to him their line just couldn't be done, and I presented, shall we say, the modified map. That is, the map which showed only the Kuneitra salient, not the Hermon, not Rafid. So, if I could implore the people here to keep this discussion out of the newspapers—I don't know whether you can censor them—but really . . .

He looked at that and said it is totally out of the question. But he made a very—it was not like on Saturday, or whenever I was there last, Friday;[5] on Friday he exploded. And this time he made a very rational analysis. He pointed out that the Hermon range was acquired after October 22nd and therefore he could not accept that. He said that what he needed was some movement over of the October 6th line in a straight line. He kept repeating that over and over again. He didn't really object too much to the depth of the salient, but he kept stressing over and over again that it had to go in a straight line, a more or less straight line, south.

With respect to Kuneitra, with respect to what he did see, he made two observations. He found the Chief of Staff's village. He and Shihabi went very carefully over the map to look for villages to which they could go back. He said he is very eager to re-settle. They looked for the village; they found that village and showed it to me. He said, "There are the Israelis; don't they understand? They don't understand how to make peace. How can I be asked to resettle half of a village?"

I am just reporting this to you so that you can make your assessment.

Then he went at Kuneitra. Actually, I gave him a slightly misleading representation of your position. Not misleading; I didn't give him a full exposition. I wish you [to Mr. Dayan] wouldn't stare at me like that. I know what you think.

Mr. Dayan: You don't know!

Dr. Kissinger: You know I have my heart set on Kuneitra. It's my birthday on May 27th. Will you give it? All my life I wanted it. [Laughter] Ever since you took me there in 1967.

Mrs. Meir: Especially when you saw the hills. [Laughter]

Dr. Kissinger: I frankly—you built the hills afterwards.

Mrs. Meir: After the 22nd of October?

Dr. Kissinger: That's it. You built the hills after . . . [Laughter] Well, then with respect to Kuneitra, he said: "It ought to be in the Israelis' interest that I settle this area. I cannot settle a town that has an Israeli military line running through it." He said, "I cannot do this." He said, "If I

---

[5] Kissinger had previously met with Asad on Friday, May 3 at 5 p.m. See Document 42.

want a town called Kuneitra, I can build a town called Kuneitra and I can place it anywhere."

Mrs. Meir: Good idea!

Dr. Kissinger: He said, "But the importance of the town would be if I could settle it," and for the rest, he said, "Of course the line had to go down." He clearly abandoned his plan. He agreed that if we can agree on a line, he would make a major effort to settle all other issues. I showed him zones of limited armament; I didn't go into any details. I said the other things had to be demilitarized. I don't say he accepted but he also didn't reject it. None of this—wouldn't you agree, Joe?—none of this caused . . . It still certainly is going to be a nuisance when we negotiate it. On the demilitarized line, maybe he didn't understand it properly, but I could see him trying to line it up. There is a town in the southern end of your pocket, which is a road junction. You know what I am talking about?

General Gur: Yes.

Dr. Kissinger: I don't know what's the name of it.

General Gur: It's a hill they built after the last war—that *they* built!

Dr. Kissinger: He was trying to line up the red line to see whether the village was on the demilitarized side or was not on the demilitarized side, but he didn't raise the point.

Mr. Rabin: Is it [omission in the original]?

Dr. Kissinger: He didn't mention. I just saw, when he and Shihabi went over the map, they were trying to line up the red line to see where that town was.

General Gur: It is in their hands.

Dr. Kissinger: Is it in their hands also militarily?

General Gur: I think so.

Dr. Kissinger: I have the impression that if it isn't, he will raise it, but I can't be sure.

General Gur: It is below the hill, so I didn't mind exactly where the line was.

Dr. Kissinger: I have never heard of such a hill obsession. He needs psychiatric treatment!

General Gur: I think I left it in their hands.

Dr. Kissinger: I am not saying it is going to be raised; I am indicating that he must have known what that red line was there for, because he was lining it up.

There was much more desultory talk. I finally said to him, I said, "Look, I understand what you are saying. I will go back to Israel. I will report exactly what you have said about the line. I will see what we can get, and come back to you Saturday or Sunday." He was very fulsome in his praise for my efforts. He said he wanted us to know that he really wanted to make an effort, but you had to make it possible for him. You could not put him into an impossible position which wouldn't enable him to do it.

And then we discussed what to say to the press. He said he recognized we had to show some progress, so that people wouldn't think there was no hope, but we shouldn't give the impression that there was an agreement, because if we gave that impression, then the consequences would be very drastic if it failed.

I give you all this detail because it is the first nonemotional discussion I have had with him.

I told him I was going to visit other Arab leaders, because he was going to find it out anyway, and that I would like to give them the same analysis I had given to him as to why disengagement agreement was desirable. He said, "Please do that; that would help me." But, he said, "Don't give them the details of the map. Just give them the general theory."

But he said again: the line has to move in a straight line. That was the theme he kept repeating.

Then I drove out to the airport, and as I was entering the plane I was intercepted and taken into a reception room and I was told that General Shihabi wanted to say a word. Khaddam was talking to Assad. Shihabi said to me, in English, that we should understand their problems, that he was an old friend of Assad's, that they wanted to come to a conclusion but it had to be one that they could defend domestically. That they would make a big effort with the line if I could bring them something that they could accept.

Khaddam then came back and said he talked to Assad who wanted to impress on me that his only interest in Kuneitra was the ability to settle it, and for that he needed the hills. I told him right away that this was a subject that I had already discussed with the Israelis, and that seemed to be undo-able, and I didn't want them to expect me to come back with the hills.

That's the essence of where we stand. But both in the language they used—and at no point did they threaten what they would do with the Russians. Now, on the plane I got a cable from Fahmy[6] saying that we should try to avoid a summit meeting—asking what we knew of Assad's plan for a summit meeting—and that we should try to avoid it

---

[6] Telegram 2962 from Cairo, May 8. (National Archives, Nixon Presidential Materials, NSC Files, Box 1183, Harold H. Saunders Files, Middle East Peace Negotiations, May 1–May 12, 1974)

at all cost, and that he thought that it was important to get a disengagement agreement. He didn't have any specific ideas. He was more concerned with heading off the summit tactically.

Mrs. Meir: Did Assad mention the summit meeting to you?

Dr. Kissinger: No.

Mr. Peres: There's been a lot of talk on the Arabic radio announcing it.

Dr. Kissinger: The only way the summit came up at all was when we were discussing the EC-Arab summit and I told him I was opposed. The EC Foreign Ministers meeting, the dialogue with the Arabs. I told him I was opposed. I told him I was opposed. I said any non-Arab that gets 20 Arab ministers together in one room is crazy. I said, "Any European would sit there and write down everything you people said, and it is going to turn into a mad-house." And he laughed and he said, "That's absolutely right." He said, "At any rate, foreign ministers' meetings are not how the Arabs decide; we decide them at summits." That's the only time he mentioned the summit.

Otherwise, I do not believe he will do anything to rock the boat until he knows whether the thing will succeed or fail.

Mr. Allon: You didn't discuss with him the problem of ceasefire so long as the talks were continuing?

Dr. Kissinger: I think it would have been a grave tactical mistake to start nit-picking. I got your point.

Mr. Allon: He gave you a promise in a previous meeting.

Dr. Kissinger: I didn't raise it. I didn't raise any other points because I didn't want him to raise any other points.

Now I will go to Faisal—that will be fairly easy—and to Sadat, with whom I will discuss candidly what the position is. The two big sticking points, as I see them now, will be Kuneitra—not in terms of hills, but what one can do about civilians there and what assurances can be achieved. And the second is to make the line go as consistent as possible.

Mr. Allon: But for that townlet there, did he agree to the red line east of the old demarcation line?

Dr. Kissinger: He raised no objection to it. That doesn't mean he won't raise it. I have said this to him one hundred times and I said it again, and I said, "This will be a demilitarized area." He didn't say, "Yes, I agree to it." But actually, when we showed where his army can go, when he was rejecting it, he said, "Look, this requires a lot of redisposition. Our army has to move from there." And he pointed to the red line.

Mr. Dayan: When you said, "straight line", what exactly do you mean? Where did they have this straight line? [He unfolds a map on the table.][7]

Dr. Kissinger: This you moved up a bit this morning. I think the generals moved this a little bit. Or is this the way we had it?

General Gur: The paper moved a little bit. [Laughter]

Dr. Kissinger: This is the village.

General Gur: Ahmadiya. He didn't see that village for quite a long time. Nothing exists, and if he wants to build the village . . .

Dr. Kissinger: This is the problem we keep going over and over. To them it is a symbolic thing. If he wants to rebuild the village, he can do it here. I am just pointing out that he called special attention to this. And then this whole area he called attention to—this one he doesn't know—he called attention to this whole area, of course. And when he said straight line—what was your interpretation? [They study the map.]

The town he was trying to place was this one [near the red line in the center]. That they were pointing to and moving the red line.

This [Mt. Hermon] he violently objected to, but we don't have to spend enormous time on.

He didn't make a specific proposal. But if you compare his original scheme to this, we are now in the area at least of rationality. It may be undo-able, but it is not any more an irrational discussion.

My plan, as I said, is to see Faisal. All I have to tell Faisal is that I agreed with Assad that I will try to get him more. And I know that I can get him more. So it is easy to deal with Faisal. I will then report to Faisal that I did get him more. So that's not a major problem. The Saudis are not distinguished by heroism anyway. Although it would help to keep them quiet for two weeks if the thing breaks up. It is one thing for them to change their position. It is another right away to go and—

Second, I will go to Sadat. I think I should discuss with Sadat and the private secretary of the President, Marwan, who is the one who was sent around, their assessment of what can be done. I would try to get Sadat—Sadat has already sent two messages to Assad, and Boumedienne has sent one—whether we can get them to send another one. That's why I am going to stay here on Saturday. At any rate, I will not go to Syria until I can see whether I can get some Arab pressure generated, and depending on Sadat's view, I may or may not send somebody to Boumedienne again.

---

[7] The Israeli map is not attached.

So then I will be back here Friday early afternoon.[8] Perhaps we could meet then. I mean, there's nothing you don't know that I know, and we still will then have about 36 hours to discuss strategy. Certainly it depends on what we want to do Sunday. We have those two additional things we have already agreed to that I can get him.

Mrs. Meir: What map will you show to Sadat?

Dr. Kissinger: The Rafid map.[9]

Mrs. Meir: And he will not notify Assad?

Dr. Kissinger: No. It is in Sadat's interest to have these negotiations succeed. Or I will describe—I will think about it—I will describe it orally in terms of something that I can get but have not yet got and therefore they'd better keep quiet. After all, it was Sadat's idea that we not show everything at once. So he has no interest in destroying the strategy he himself recommended.

My original idea was to bring every concession to Syria yesterday. It was his private secretary, it was Marwan in Cyprus: I didn't have a map to show him; I told him I was going to get a map from Israel that evening. He said, "Whatever you do, don't give them everything." I told that to you yesterday. So it was the Egyptian idea not to give everything. So I don't believe that they will now destroy the strategy they themselves have recommended.

Whatever their long-term motives, their short-term interest has to be in an agreement. Their position at the summit, at the oil conference, will be extremely embarrassing. Vis-à-vis the Soviets, it will be extremely difficult. My judgment is that whatever their long-term strategy, they now want an agreement.

Mrs. Meir: There is one thing that I fear, and I want to get your reaction to that. For instance, you will report to Sadat what has happened in Syria and he will be encouraged. Like it is encouraging when you say that he speaks rationally and didn't react emotionally and didn't go back to some wild ideas. But if, for instance, it is stressed that the line he wants is a straight line, and if Sadat accepts it, he will support him in that. The thing that I fear is that to the best of my knowledge we have actually gone to the limit.

Dr. Kissinger: I will tell him that you have told me that you have gone to the limit. First of all, I think what Sadat's judgment will be worthwhile for, and Gamasy's . . . I don't think that this negotiation is a question of whether he will support to the limit, because he has had many opportunities to support to the limit; his approach will be to see

---

[8] May 10.

[9] The Rafid map refers to a map that revealed Israeli concessions in the Rafid area of the southern Golan Heights and on Mount Hermon in the northern Golan Heights.

what he thinks he can sell to other Arabs if it comes to a blow-up, or he may ask Gamasy's opinion whether based on his knowledge of the Syrians they can be brought to accept it. Now, I must say that Sadat was more optimistic on Saturday than I was.[10] He turned out to be right as to the possibilities of a settlement, and his pressures so far have not been in the direction to see what he could bleed out of Israel but rather to define the minimum that he thought was necessary.

I will make clear to him that this is considered by Israel the maximum position.

Mrs. Meir: Because Sadat will also see the part of Rafid; he will see the picture. What I am afraid of is that we shouldn't be faced with a position on Friday—I don't want to be misunderstood—but it will probably be easier for Sadat to take the stand he has taken when Assad was speaking a wild language. But now that he is speaking more or less like a normal person, then Sadat can say to himself: "Well, this is an accomplishment." And I agree that this is an accomplishment, something encouraging for us too if he is becoming rational. But then the outcome may be that he may say: "Well, after all, Assad has made this wonderful evolution and now it is a question of drawing a straight line and going a bit west, and something like that." As you say, you will tell him as far as we are concerned, this is the map we gave you. We are not playing tricks with you. You saw how we measured things out.

Dr. Kissinger: I have no possible interest in arousing in Sadat expectations that cannot be fulfilled. That is totally contrary to his experience with me. I have no interest whatsoever in showing that. On the other hand, if I tell him: "This is what the Israelis assert, and I have reason to believe that is their maximum position," if he then tells me: "Look, this will not be sustainable in the Arab world, you have got to know that," you can still maintain your position. We will not necessarily be guided by Sadat's views, but you have to know them. In my judgment, he in this negotiation will make every effort to make it succeed. Because if he wants a blow-up, he will do it for his own reasons, not for Syria's reasons. And he wouldn't run a risk of war for Syria if he can possibly avoid it.

Mrs. Meir: Because he, probably, and Gamasy, certainly, will understand why we say this is the line and not here. He may not agree with us but he will understand the reasons. It isn't a question of prestige.

Dr. Kissinger: It won't be at all an emotional discussion with the Egyptians. The discussion with the Egyptians will be purely tactical,

---

[10] May 4. See Document 43 and footnote 3 thereto.

and he will give me his tactical assessment. And I have no incentive to get him to raise demands that then may not be fulfillable. But if he makes them, you have to know them. And then you make your decision in the light of what you know.

Mr. Allon: I understand that Assad didn't want you to show the map to any Arab leaders. So you can describe it orally to Faisal and—

Dr. Kissinger: With Faisal, I wouldn't even get into it. What Faisal wants to hear I can give him. I will tell him a simpleminded version of it. I will tell him first of all why it will be necessary to have an agreement, because a stalemate will bring the Russians right back into the area. I will give him a simpleminded version that Israel after long hesitation has agreed to this salient around Kuneitra, that I am now going back to Israel and will produce additional things. That is all he wants to hear. Whether it is along the whole line or not, I don't think he would analyze so carefully. His Foreign Minister has also taken the same position as Assad. You just have to accept the fact that this is a symbolic thing in the Arab world. Saqqaf wrote me a letter last night making that same point.[11] But the map will not be shown in Saudi Arabia.

Mr. Allon: Now, if I am not wrong, in your last meeting with Sadat, you showed him the Rafid area, but not Kuneitra, if I am not wrong. Now you will come back to him, and you have Kuneitra as an additional—

Dr. Kissinger: It is senseless, whether I say that; it is not a horse trade. It is not between me and Sadat. What we have, what is additional to what Sadat has seen, is that the Rafid area is extended beyond that little—

Mr. Eban: Assad may have told Sadat about our Kuneitra proposal.

Dr. Kissinger: My impression is that all he told the other Arab leaders is that your first proposal concerned only a part of the salient and therefore he rejected it. I don't think he has given anybody a precise definition of any plan, and I think that is a good sign, because if he wanted to break it up he would have described your iniquity in eloquent terms.

The judgment is not whether I bought a hundred dollars worth or a thousand dollars worth. The judgment he will have to make is whether he can justify it in his conception of the Arab world. He may have a totally different idea of what should be handled, which hasn't

---

[11] No letter from Saqqaf has been found, but a letter from Faisal is in telegram 2485 from Jidda, May 7. (National Archives, RG 59, Central Foreign Policy Files, P850071–2027)

occurred to me, and all I can do is bring it to you. I can't negotiate with Sadat as to what is reasonable.

Mr. Allon: I am sure you know how to deal with Sadat better than I do; I never met him. But what I want to say is that from the little you showed him on your last visit to Alexandria, you bring a great change on behalf of the Israelis.

Dr. Kissinger: I know that.

Mr. Allon: So maybe as you do your tactics, you can say: "I got already this little bit, I hope I will get something else." And not show him the whole thing at once, to develop the achievement, if possible.

Dr. Kissinger: That is the strategy with Assad. With Sadat I have to find out what he in fact is willing to support if it blows up.

Mr. Allon: So you have to tell him.

Dr. Kissinger: More or less.

Mr. Allon: So it is essential, really, to say, as the Prime Minister has said, that we have reached the limit, both on the ground and with the people.

Dr. Kissinger: His desire will be to wind it up. Judging by Fahmi's cable, I think their earnest desire is to wind it up as fast as possible. So I don't think he is looking for any complications.

Mrs. Meir: When are you leaving tomorrow?

Dr. Kissinger: Very early. I don't need any decisions tonight for this trip. I think after I come back we ought to make an unemotional, cold-blooded assessment of where we stand. We are not bargaining with you. If I can build a little house at the entrance of East Kuneitra, that is all I need.

Mrs. Meir: You can build a house on the hill. One of the hills around Jerusalem.

Mr. Allon: I am sure one of the kibbutzim will offer you an honorary citizenship.

Mr. Dayan: If you take a map to Sadat, I suggest it will be an accurate one. I am very sorry about this small one, even with an explanation. I would rather have a precise map. Why have the wrong map with the right explanation when you can have the right map? It is a map drawn by our people. I am terribly unhappy with it. Had I been there, they wouldn't have done it. This is not a way, to have a wrong map with the right explanation. Let's have the right map. The map must be a hundred per cent accurate. Let me have the five maps back and change it, so you have the map expressing exactly how our position is. And then you can have any kind of confusion you want, but a thing extended and drawn by us, that is how to express our views about it.

Mrs. Meir: You mean the map that the Chief of Staff drew?[12]

Mr. Dayan: Nobody was there. We were all away, and then our people were asked to—

Mrs. Meir: You are not speaking about the small map.

Mr. Dayan: We should work all the night through and give you an accurate map exactly according to what we agreed about last night.

Mr. Allon: I think the Secretary's tactics with the Syrians were good.

Mrs. Meir: But that is what he intended to do with Sadat anyway.

Dr. Kissinger: Yes. You cannot play through all the refinements of your domestic position; there is a lot more at stake. You have to play through the consequences of a break-up over any period of time against the consequences of an agreement and see where you are, and where we are, and where everyone is. No one is going to sneak civilians into Kuneitra without anyone noticing it. There are going to be a thousand discussions before it happens. He has said he doesn't want to put civilians into Kuneitra under the present circumstances.

Mr. Allon: Not even if we sign a . . .

Dr. Kissinger: I wouldn't leave a map with Sadat anyway.

Mr. Allon: No, I mean about what you said about the population. Not even if we sign an agreement?

Dr. Kissinger: No, not with the present line. That is what he said today. He may change his mind by Sunday.

Mr. Eban: What is the motivation of the straight line? Is it cosmetic, symbolic, or does he want something on the ground?

Dr. Kissinger: I think it would prove that they succeeded in obtaining a change in the October 5 line. But maybe we can think of some other way of straightening the line. I have explained to you every objection he made. Another way of looking at the thing is to look for the maximum number of villages one can put under his control, which seems to be a thing which is very much on his mind. Maybe other things occur to people at this table.

Mr. Dayan: I know there is no point to argue with you about Assad's position. But he is not here, so what I understand is . . .

Dr. Kissinger: He has his pride. The Prime Minister wouldn't come here; I offered him a ride here.

Mr. Dayan: But under the circumstances, on the one hand I understand that he wants the maximum of refugees or farmers to come back to their places. The way I see it, I am very much for that. I don't know

---

[12] A map drawn up by Lieutenant General Mordechai Gur.

what everyone in our country thinks, if they agree with me, or even in the Cabinet, but I am for that. Secondly, of course it doesn't matter where the village was, he can rebuild it anywhere, because nothing is left there. So if he really wants people to be resettled, it can really be built anywhere. I am not trying to make excuses why they shouldn't go there, but I am just saying—I said it from the beginning—he can build a Kuneitra wherever he wants. It is nonsense to say this. But then he said that he can't have his people going somewhere very close to our military line. So what that means is, for instance, this village, Ahmadiya: How can we cut it into two? Supposing we move our military line to the end of the village. He will say, "How can our people live close to your military line?" If I understand correctly, that is what he said about Kuneitra, that he can't bring the people back because our military line is there.

So what does all this mean? We are there at that line because of the features of the ground. It is not because of a straight or a curved line. We can't move the hills. You can move the village if he won't want his people there, or if we don't want our people to live close to the Syrian military line, we can build the village somewhere else. But you cannot move the hills. So I don't know. If we don't want to mislead ourselves, to deceive ourselves, I really think that there is no chance whatsoever, whatever the arguments or the alternatives will be, I see no chance for any changes, not significant, but even non-significant changes in the line of the map that we drew last night. Not because we were at our best, but this is the kind of ground features it is.

Dr. Kissinger: After the next round, we, the United States group will make a decision whether there is any sense in going on. If we decide not to go on, whatever else happens, the next round will not be discussed with yardsticks and with measuring centimeters and all these fine points that we have spent every night patiently discussing. But the judgments will be made on a much cruder basis in a much more absolute way.

But let's face that when it comes up. Maybe your final line will be accepted. Believe me, I do not urge Arabs not to accept the Israeli positions. And there have been innumerable occasions where the Arabs have accepted Israeli positions which I thought might not be accepted.

For your own contingency planning, you ought to consider the possibility when they don't accept it, what can be done. I am not asking you to do it now; you have three days before you have to make a decision. But you are now enjoying the luxury of being able to massage this problem, ten yards at a time. That is not inherent in the situation. And many problems that are profound security concerns wouldn't look all that absolute when they get discussed elsewhere.

You can be sure that I will do my best to get it settled on this basis. If we can, we can.

I can certainly not go on. If we don't have an agreement in principle say by Monday, I am going to end my efforts. If I don't see by Sunday that it is very close, there is no sense returning back and forth, debating the theology of security that both sides have. I think we have got to the point where both sides are close. Either they are going to accept your position or you are going to have to change your position, and if neither of them is achievable, we have to have a hiatus. I see nothing that can happen. I do believe they now want to strive for a settlement. If that judgment is right, it is quite possible that your map is enough. I am not saying it isn't. I have reported to you what Assad said. Since I haven't presented them the southern part of the map, it may be that he feels about Rafid the way I feel about Kuneitra. [Laughter] Maybe his mother comes from there.

Mrs. Meir: I know you don't have to be told this, but the simple analysis is: I am sure that Assad, but at any rate you are convinced that no matter where we are, no matter where their civilians are, that one bright morning we won't get up and attack them. So if you speak of theology of security, his theology is good if he thinks in these terms, and he has no reason to think in these terms. Whereas with us, this is the matter that we have to take into consideration. And therefore beyond a certain limit—we laugh over hills, but it isn't because we like hills. These hills are not high enough; it is not the Hermon; but it is these hills upon which the security of our people depends. So I know that we are not always very popular when we speak so much about security.

Dr. Kissinger: It is not a question of popularity.

Mrs. Meir: But I am sorry that this is a major problem of our life.

Dr. Kissinger: It is a question of what the alternative will be, given certain conditions. I am not raising this now. I am saying if on Sunday night I come back and if then you have 12 hours or 24 hours to make up your minds, it is less good than if you can start thinking from now what you might say on Sunday night. At any rate, I will tell you now: If by Monday night there isn't either an agreement in principle, or an imminent agreement in principle, I am going home. I have to. And you will then have to evaluate where we will all be in the light of that situation. But it may not arise. There is no magic whether it is Monday or Tuesday.

Mr. Peres: Do you intend to go to Damascus again before you come here on Sunday?

Dr. Kissinger: No, I don't think I should go to Damascus until I have—nothing would be served. I am going to see whether Faisal and Sadat will send emissaries to Assad. Assad right now is in a rather benign mood. He knows I am travelling to the others. He knows what I am going to say. I have told him what I am going to say. I think he is trying to make an agreement or he wouldn't let me run around giving them the theory why an agreement should be made. Isn't that your interpretation, Joe? [Mr. Sisco nods yes.] So what his final conclusion will be, I have no way of knowing. He is certainly not happy with what I brought him today. I think there is a better than 50–50 chance that Sadat will urge him to do it.

Mrs. Meir: Look, I want to tell you. All our friends here understand. We have an internal problem, but I am not making that point at all. Because if the Likud and all the others, and those sitting opposite my house, if they want something that I am convinced and all of us are convinced is wrong, then the internal problem has no part in it whatsoever. The trouble begins when we begin to think that on certain points, not that they are right—I don't care what speeches Begin makes or Sharon or Tamir,[13] any of them, as long as they are wrong.

Mr. Allon: They're wrong.

Mrs. Meir: But I want to be right with myself. So the last thing I would want you people to think is that we are concerned about our internal problems. Sure, we have internal problems. But that is not the point. There isn't any of us Israelis around this table that would say to himself: "Well, really we can do this, but what will happen internally?" That isn't the question at all. That isn't the problem. The problem is that we have to be convinced that what we do is right.

Mr. Allon: I think Henry and his friends could see for themselves how painstakingly we tried to move each little bit where we could, the Minister of Defense, the Chief of Staff—in fact, all of us.

Dr. Kissinger: I believe we have had a very good discussion. I believe you have been very serious. I don't think we ought to debate it tonight, because there is no decision you can make tonight even if you had the best will in the world and there were maneuvering room, because we have no concrete basis on which to make a decision. After I have talked to Sadat, we will have a preliminary view of considerations that you might want to consider or not want to consider. The next time you have a decision to make is after I have talked to Assad. Because then you will know exactly what your range of choices is. The only reason I insist on it tonight is so that you can start thinking.

Your choice is not between absolute security and no security. Your choice will be to weigh the alternatives of the various courses of action.

---

[13] Menachem Begin, Ariel Sharon, and Shmuel Tamir were founding members of the Likud Party.

But that is a debate I recommend we have later. There is no sense debating it now, since there is no concrete proposal I can make to you.

Mr. Allon: Maybe Sadat will be satisfied with the map you show.

Dr. Kissinger: That is a distinct possibility.

Mrs. Meir: I told the Secretary of State to take the small map with him and he will be surprised that Sadat will say, "Fine, it's wonderful." He almost said it, I understand.

Dr. Kissinger: It was the location of my house that called attention to it. Because I wanted my house in the Syrian part and that's flat; there was no elevation.

Mrs. Meir: I think we should allow our American friends to go to sleep for a while.

Mr. Eban: I don't know why the Israeli side shouldn't be included in that.

[The meeting then adjourned.]

---

50. **Telegram From Secretary of State Kissinger to the President's Deputy Assistant for National Security Affairs (Scowcroft)**[1]

May 9, 1974, 0748Z.

Hakto 64. 1. Please tell Haig that I will use every available opportunity to mention the President's role in the current negotiations. I will continue to stress the importance of his involvement in our overall effort to seek a lasting peace.

2. Ask Haig to be sure the President understands that these negotiations may not succeed entirely. Ideally, I would hope to see an agreement concluded while I am in the area. Realistically, however, this may not be possible though I hope to keep the negotiating process alive. If these conditions are met, there is a good chance that the President's trip can take place and that he will be warmly welcomed wherever he visits.

3. Warm regards.

---

[1] Source: National Archives, Nixon Presidential Materials, NSC Files, Kissinger Office Files, Box 45, HAK Trip Files, Middle East HAKTO 1–179, April 28–May 31, 1974. Secret; Sensitive; Exclusively Eyes Only; Immediate.

51. Memorandum From the President's Deputy Assistant for National Security Affairs (Scowcroft) to President Nixon[1]

Washington, May 9, 1974.

Secretary Kissinger has asked me to provide you with the following report:

"I am in the process of organizing various forces for what I believe will be my climactic meeting with President Asad on Sunday.[2] Yesterday I brought the Israeli position to Asad[3] which represented an advance over the past Israeli proposals. I informed Asad of Israel's willingness to draw its defense line west of the entire city of Kuneitra. While this represents improvement, the fact is that when one analyzes the current Israeli withdrawal proposal, for all practical purposes it is not much more than a symbolic pullback from the line that existed just before the war of October 1973. Moreover, under the Israeli proposal Asad could not return his civilians to Kuneitra and the Israeli defense line would be at the edge of the city—in fact along one of the city streets. Thus some further Israeli concessions are clearly necessary. All this would be far short of Syrian demands.

"I had further discussions with Mrs. Meir and the key Members of her Cabinet last night,[4] and the current Israeli mood is resistant to any additional concessions.

"I will be meeting with them again on Friday evening[5] to review the situation, and on the basis of the Cabinet-approved position I will be presenting the Syrians on Sunday with a few additional modifications that draw the line west of the October line in a couple of places. For example, the Israelis are willing for the U.N. to take over their positions on the highest peaks on Mount Hermon. Whether I can get something more from the Israelis on Friday is doubtful.

"I will, of course, make a major effort with Asad. If the above Israeli position proves insufficient, the Israelis will then face a critical choice: to permit the negotiations to reach an impasse and thereby face the probability of an escalated attritional resumption of hostilities on the Golan Heights, or to face up to giving up another kilometer or so of territory which would not affect their security adversely but would re-

---

[1] Source: Library of Congress, Manuscript Division, Kissinger Papers, CL 192, Geopolitical File, Middle East, Peace Negotiations, Israeli-Syrian Relations, Negotiation Books, Volume I, Folder 4. Secret; Sensitive; Exclusively Eyes Only.

[2] May 12.

[3] See Document 48.

[4] See Document 49.

[5] May 10.

quire giving up some of the cultivated fields attached to settlements they established near Kuneitra in 1968. Again, I am struck with the lack of flexibility which the domestic situation in Israel causes, and with the lack of responsibility which stakes the American position in the Middle East and risks an enhanced role for the Soviet Union on a kilometer here and there and on the vagaries of Israeli domestic politics. At the same time, Asad, who seems to want a disengagement agreement, also has internal pressures which concern him. He stressed repeatedly that he must have the kind of disengagement agreement which he can explain to his people after 26 years of struggle and not provide the opponents of his regime an opportunity to upset him.

"My efforts in the last 48 hours have been designed to keep the Russians essentially neutralized and non-involved—this was the principal result of my meeting with Gromyko in Cyprus[6]—and preparing the groundwork for Saudi intervention in Damascus in support of the position I will be presenting to Asad on Sunday. My conversation with Faisal today[7] indicated that the Saudis are prepared to be helpful. Saqqaf, the Foreign Minister, publicly endorsed your foreign policy and our stand on disengagement. Faisal could not have been more flattering. There is a good chance that the Saudis will send an emissary to Damascus to weigh in on the side of moderation. I was also able to announce at the conclusion of my Saudi visit here today, the visit of Prince Fahd to Washington on May 24, which reflects the progress we are making in establishing a basis for long-term economic, scientific, technical and military supply cooperation between Saudi Arabia and the United States.

"Tonight I will be going to Cairo for further talks with Sadat and concerting with the Egyptians on ways in which they will exercise their influence in Damascus.

"There is still a chance for an agreement but it is tough going.

"Warm regards."

---

[6] See footnote 4, Document 44.
[7] No memorandum of conversation has been found.

52. Memorandum From the President's Deputy Assistant for National Security Affairs (Scowcroft) to President Nixon[1]

Washington, May 10, 1974.

Following is Secretary Kissinger's report of his meeting with President Sadat.

"In three hours with President Sadat today,[2] I explained exactly where the evolution of Israel's position stands and what I think I can achieve in my next talks in Jerusalem.

"President Sadat feels that the proposal which I expect to take to Damascus with me Sunday[3] could be justified to the Arab world. Indeed, from his recent contacts with other moderate Arab leaders, he feels reasonably certain that Saudi Arabia, Kuwait, and Algeria are already prepared to support this approach. However, he is uncertain that President Asad will be able to accept it as it is. He feels it will be necessary to persuade the Israelis to give a little more space around the city of Quneitra, and he is not sure Asad will have the courage. But he recommends that I present the Israeli map as it is since it reflects two significant gains over the last map I took to him: (1) it removes Israeli forces from Mount Hermon and (2) it gives Syria two slices of territory behind the 1967 line. The thought is that, if Asad is willing to accept this concept in principle, I would be able to come back to Israel and say that the agreement hinges entirely on a buffer zone around Quneitra. I shall see Prime Minister Meir Friday afternoon[4] to report on my soundings in Riyadh and Cairo. Then I will take the latest map to Damascus Sunday. Meanwhile, President Sadat will send a strong message to Asad stating that this is a moment of decision and urging him to seize it. If further Arab pressure is needed, he is prepared to send his War Minister and Chief of Staff to Damascus after I see Asad Sunday.

"I am encouraged by Sadat's attitude but would caution that Asad is still an uncertainty."

---

[1] Source: National Archives, Nixon Presidential Materials, NSC Files, Kissinger Office Files, Box 45, HAK Trip Files, Middle East, HAKTO 1–179, April 28–May 31, 1974. Secret; Sensitive; Exclusively Eyes Only. Sent for information.

[2] The conversation between Sadat and Kissinger took place on May 10 from 11:05 a.m. to 1:34 p.m. at the President's Giza Residence in Cairo. (Memorandum of conversation; ibid., RG 59, Records of Henry Kissinger, 1973–77, Box 8, Nodis Memcons, May 1974, Folder 3)

[3] May 12.

[4] Kissinger met with Meir and members of the Israeli Cabinet on Friday, May 10, at 4:30 p.m. at the Prime Minister's office in Jerusalem to brief them on his meetings in Saudi Arabia and Egypt. (Memorandum of conversation; RG 59, Records of Henry Kissinger, 1973–77, Box 8, Nodis Memcons, May 1974, Folder 2)

53. Telegram From Secretary of State Kissinger to the President's Deputy Assistant for National Security Affairs (Scowcroft)[1]

May 12, 1974, 0820Z.

Hakto 79. Please pass following report to the President.

Begin text:

I have had two meetings since returning to Israel Friday night, one with Mrs. Meir and her key Cabinet members, and a second one with Dayan chairing it because PM Meir was ill.[2]

These sessions helped refine our tactics for my key meetings with Assad today, and I now have Israel's specific views of all the key elements of an agreement.

The map I will present today represents two important advances over the previous map I left in Damascus: (1) it removes Israeli forces from Mount Hermon and would replace them with the UN; and (2) it would return to Syria two slices of territory behind the 1967 line, which Assad can make much of politically. The key issue remains the line of disengagement—and the agreement is likely to be made or broken on: (A) Israel's willingness to give up all of Kuneitra with perhaps a one kilometer UN buffer zone around it separating Syrians and Israelis; and (B) Syrian willingness to agree to continued Israeli control of three major hills west of Kuneitra.

Internally in Israel, it is now likely that Rabin will be able to form a government by the end of this week. Internally in Syria, Assad seems to be preparing the groundwork for an agreement. He is, of course, still an uncertainty, and the prospect of an agreement will be much clearer by tonight.

End text.

Warm regards.

---

[1] Source: National Archives, Nixon Presidential Materials, NSC Files, Kissinger Office Files, Box 45, HAK Trip Files, Middle East, HAKTO 1–179, April 28–May 31, 1974. Secret; Sensitive; Immediate.

[2] For the meeting with Meir and key Cabinet members, see footnote 4, Document 52. Kissinger met with Dayan and the Israeli negotiating team on May 11 from 9:15 until 11:10 p.m. at the Prime Minister's office in Jerusalem. (Memorandum of conversation; Library of Congress, Manuscript Division, Kissinger Papers, CL 343, Department of State Memcons, External, May 1974, Folder 1)

54. Telegram From Secretary of State Kissinger to the President's Deputy Assistant for National Security Affairs (Scowcroft)[1]

May 13, 1974, 0009Z.

Hakto 81. Please pass following message to President:

1. I presented today to Asad[2] the latest Israeli map which draws the defense line around Kuneitra and includes two slices west of the line that existed at the time of the October 1973 war. While Asad did not reject the proposal, he took strong exception to it and asked for adjustments in the line which go beyond the symbolic moves of at least one kilometer west of the October line which were embraced in the Israeli plan. Asad stressed in particular that with the Israeli defense line running through Kuneitra he could not send in any Syrian civilians since they would be under threat of Israeli guns and positions in the surrounding hills, and he needed more lands where he could settle his people in various villages in the north and south.

2. Two things impressed me in particular about the Asad meeting: A) I had the impression that he wants an agreement but has a problem bringing along people who had thought of Israelis as devils for 26 years; and (B) he used the meeting to bring in key leaders in his administration—the Minister of Defense, the Chief of the Air Force and the Chief of Intelligence in addition to the Foreign Minister—for obvious way to build a consensus.

3. I met for three hours this evening with Prime Minister Meir and her colleagues[3] and gave them a full report of the Asad meeting. In particular I stressed the positive benefits that would result from successful disengagement agreement to Israel, to the U.S. diplomatic efforts, the resultant decoupling of Soviet support of the Arabs, and all of the positive trends that have developed in the Middle East over the past six months. By the same token I painted the realistically stark situation that will face the Israelis—and U.S.—if the disengagement agreement fails, and we lose control over the diplomacy as well as a number of the key developments in the area. Again I impressed the theme, which I have

---

[1] Source: Library of Congress, Manuscript Division, Kissinger Papers, CL 193, Peace Negotiations, Israeli-Syrian Relations, Negotiation Books, Volume II, May 1974, Folder 1. Secret; Sensitive; Exclusively Eyes Only; Immediate.

[2] The meeting between Asad and Kissinger took place on May 12 from 1:30 to 6:15 p.m. at the Presidential Palace in Damascus. (Memorandum of conversation; National Archives, RG 59, Records of Henry Kissinger, 1973–77, Box 8, Nodis Memcons, May 1974, Folder 4)

[3] The meeting between the Israeli negotiating team and Kissinger took place on May 12 from 9 to 11:45 p.m. at the Prime Minister's office in Jerusalem. (Memorandum of conversation; ibid.)

reported to you in some detail in past messages, of how essential it is for the Israelis to look at the disengagement agreement in a broad political context rather than the marginal and narrow tactical consideration and quibbles over one or two kilometers here and there. I doubt that made much of an impression.

4. I have asked for a further meeting with Mrs. Meir and her key Cabinet members for 10:00 A.M. tomorrow morning before she convenes her full Cabinet. I plan in very strong terms to insist that they consider some change in and around the Kuneitra area while holding on to the hills. We have in mind a UN buffer belt of a kilometer or so around the city. Secondly, I have asked the Israelis to reexamine their present line of disengagement, both north and south, to see whether further adjustments can be made so that the Syrians can have returned to them a number of villages for resettlement purposes. Neither of the above changes would in any way affect adversely the strategic position of the Israelis on the Golan Heights. I am not at all certain that this would be sufficient to meet Asad's needs, but I believe it is important that I take something along these lines back to Damascus on Tuesday.[4] If it fails, we will have to suspend the talks in the least damaging way.

5. I do not ask you to do anything more on this matter at this time since I believe your messages over the recent days have been most helpful. I hope the Israelis will take a broad view.

Warm regards.

---

[4] May 14.

---

55. Memorandum From the President's Deputy Assistant for National Security Affairs (Scowcroft) to President Nixon[1]

Washington, May 14, 1974.

Following is the report of Secretary Kissinger's meeting yesterday with Prime Minister Meir.

---

[1] Source: National Archives, Nixon Presidential Materials, NSC Files, Kissinger Office Files, Box 45, HAK Trip Files, Middle East Memos and Security, April 28–May 31, 1974. Top Secret; Sensitive; Exclusively Eyes Only. Sent for information.

"I met with Mrs. Meir and her colleagues this evening[2] to receive the results of today's Cabinet consideration. The results were disappointing and my judgment, shared by my whole team, is that the very modest concessions given to us today will prove inadequate to achieve an agreement.

"The Cabinet decided that it would not agree to straighten the line, as asked by the Syrians, nor would they alter the Israeli line to provide some additional villages for resettlement of civilians.

"The Cabinet did agree:

(1) That the division between East and West Kuneitra would be eliminated;
(2) The division in a small village called Ahmadiya in the north would also be eliminated; and
(3) That a small UN zone behind the Israeli defense line around Kuneitra could be established.

"The weakness in this position is:

(1) That the Israeli defense line is still right up against the edges of Kuneitra and, therefore, Assad will feel that it is not possible for Syrian civilians to live in this town; and
(2) That the line was not drawn to include small hills within a couple hundred yards of Kuneitra where anybody living in town would be doing so in the shadow of the Israeli position.

"I once again repeated all the considerations in the broadest sense that were involved, including your message[3] about how much the United States has riding on all this in terms of our future relationships in the area and positive trends which failure of this negotiation will negate and then reverse.

"Nevertheless, I will present this Israeli position in the most effective way I know how in Damascus tomorrow. There is a slight chance that after tomorrow Asad will decide that he is so deeply committed to an agreement that he will go through with it anyway."

---

[2] The evening meeting between the Israeli negotiating team and Kissinger took place on May 13 from 6:15 to 8:30 p.m. at the Prime Minister's office in Jerusalem. (Memorandum of conversation; ibid., RG 59, Records of Henry Kissinger, 1973–77, Box 6, Nodis Memos, March 1974, Folder 2) There had also been a morning meeting on May 13 between the Israeli negotiating team and Kissinger which took place from 10:10 to 11 at the Prime Minister's office in Jerusalem. (Memorandum of conversation; ibid., Nixon Presidential Materials, NSC Files, Box 1029, Presidential/HAK Memcons, May 8–31, 1974, Folder 3)

[3] Document 41.

56. Telegram From Secretary of State Kissinger to the President's Deputy Assistant for National Security Affairs (Scowcroft)[1]

May 14, 1974, 0840Z.

Hakto 87. Sit room deliver at 008. Israeli intransigence is in my view due to these factors:

(1) Domestic divisions in Israel (2) a deliberate attempt to wreck our Arab policy (3) Israeli assessment of Presidential paralysis—the last message from the President[2] was brushed off with disdain by the PM (4) Israeli apparent belief that they have established a direct pipeline to the Pentagon.

We must deal with the first three factors after my return. It is imperative however that DOD be brought into line. Please have Haig call Schlesinger and hold up all new commitments. Also delay administratively all pipeline items. We can then review the entire situation after my return.

Please confirm.

Warm regards.

---

[1] Source: National Archives, Nixon Presidential Materials, NSC Files, Kissinger Office Files, Box 45, HAK Trip Files, Middle East, HAKTO 1–179, April 28–May 31, 1974. Top Secret; Sensitive; Exclusively Eyes Only; Immediate.

[2] See Document 41.

---

57. Memorandum From the President's Deputy Assistant for National Security Affairs (Scowcroft) to President Nixon[1]

Washington, May 14, 1974.

Secretary Kissinger has asked that I forward to you the following report.

"I have just completed four hours of discussion with President Asad[2] in which I conveyed the latest Israeli proposal with the three new

---

[1] Source: National Archives, Nixon Presidential Materials, NSC Files, Kissinger Office Files, Box 45, HAK Trip Files, Middle East Memos and Security, April 28–May 31, 1974. Secret; Sensitive.

[2] No memorandum of conversation of this meeting has been found.

elements of flexibility which the Israelis provided me with after my consultations yesterday. You will recall that these were: (1) Israel is prepared to cede Syrian civilian control and presence in all of Kuneitra; (2) Israel will turn over the high ground which abuts directly on Kuneitra on the north to a UN presence; and (3) Israel will return all of the town of Ahmadiya just north of Kuneitra to Syrian civilian control and presence, rather than one-half as previously offered.

"As I expected, President Asad rejected these proposals and he continues to insist that the Israelis must be out of the large hills west of Kuneitra, that there must be further movement westward in the Israeli line, about 1–2 kilometers and that there must be Israeli withdrawal from the one key remaining position on Mount Hermon. This position, from the Israeli point of view, is essential as an electronic listening post. Asad did suggest that he would be willing for the Israeli defense lines to be drawn through the peaks of the high hills north of Kuneitra with neither side occupying them, but I am confident that the Israelis will reject this since they would see it as affecting adversely their strategic position and it would involve giving up a number of cultivated fields.

"While I will have a further discussion with Prime Minister Meir and her colleagues tonight and tomorrow morning and will return to Damascus for a concluding session tomorrow afternoon, I do not expect the situation to change in any basic way.

"However, I am now convinced that major progress has indeed been made, particularly in our overall relationships with Syria and the other Arab states. The end of this mission will not result in a termination of the talks between the two sides. Asad has agreed that if the mission is wound up tomorrow as expected, he will issue a public statement: (a) praising the efforts of the United States; (b) indicating that progress has been made in the talks; (c) agreeing that the talks should be suspended to give the parties an opportunity to review the situation; (d) agreeing to resume these talks in a few weeks. This will have a profound impact on the attitude of other Arab states. Sadat will undoubtedly take the same line and Faisal will be under heavy pressure to do the same. Most significantly, this kind of a positive statement by Asad assures that there will be no new oil embargo imposed on June 1 when the Oil Ministers convene. And, finally, the atmosphere will be such in this area that it will be propitious for you to take your trip to the Middle East.

"You will recall that we had two objectives in undertaking this mission. The second was to at least make substantial progress. This we have done and in a way in which our overall relationships with the Arabs have been improved and our overall interests both protected and strengthened.

"Warm regards."

58. Telegram From Secretary of State Kissinger to the U.S. Interests Section in Syria[1]

Jerusalem, May 15, 1974, 1058Z.

Secto 419/867. Subject: Message for President Assad.

For Scotes from the Secretary. Please convey following message from me to President Asad:

Begin message:

As President Asad knows, I have been meeting with the Israeli Government[2] in a major effort to get it to revise its position to take account of the considerations you outlined to me yesterday.[3] I hope to be able to return to Damascus quickly for a continuation of our negotiations. The President should know, however, that all of Israel is currently and emotionally preoccupied with the incident in the Galilee area involving a threat to the lives of 85 Israeli children.[4] The President will remember how often I have talked with him about my hopes of improving Arab-American relations and bringing to Americans a better understanding of Arab policy and aspirations. Nothing could be more destructive of my efforts in this regard than incidents such as that now taking place.

American public opinion will never understand the holding of children as hostages and threatening their lives. The Secretary appeals to President Asad on a personal basis to use all his influence to bring about a satisfactory end to the current incident.[5] The Secretary is certain that President Asad and the Syrian people, with their strong sense of humanity which the President has often described to him, in no way

---

[1] Source: National Archives, Nixon Presidential Materials, NSC Files, Box 1183, Harold H. Saunders Files, Middle East Peace Negotiations, May 1–12, 1974. Secret; Exdis (Distribute as Nodis/Cherokee); Flash. Repeated Immediate to the Department of State.

[2] The meeting between Kissinger and the Israeli negotiating team took place on May 14 from 8:15 until 10:27 p.m. at the Prime Minister's office in Jerusalem. (Memorandum of conversation; ibid., Box 1029, Presidential/HAK Memcons, May 8–31, 1974, Folder 3)

[3] See Document 57.

[4] In the early morning hours of May 15, three members of the Democratic Front for the Liberation of Palestine crossed from Lebanon into Israel dressed in Israeli Defense Force uniforms. They first attacked a van carrying Arab women returning from work, killing two women and wounding one. The DFLP members then entered the Israeli town of Maalot, killing a husband, wife, and child in their apartment. They seized control of a school and took approximately 90 students and 4 teachers hostage. On the morning of May 16, the DFLP members demanded Israeli officials release 26 Palestinian prisoners in Israeli jails in exchange for the hostages.

[5] Around 5:45 p.m. on May 16, after hours of negotiations, Israeli commandos stormed the school and killed the 3 DFLP members, but not before 21 students were killed and 68 were wounded.

condone incidents such as this. He wants to say to the President with all sincerity that anything the President can do to disassociate Syria in the public mind from this incident would help the cause of the Arabs and of Syrian-American relations in the United States more than anything else he can think of.[6]

End message.

Kissinger

---

[6] According to Kissinger's memoirs, Asad never replied to this message. (*Years of Upheaval*, p. 1078)

---

59. Memorandum From the President's Deputy Assistant for National Security Affairs (Scowcroft) to President Nixon[1]

Washington, May 15, 1974.

I thought you should have the following analysis which Secretary Kissinger has sent me regarding the current situation and a cutoff of aid to Israel. He now plans to spend all day today in Israel and to go back to Damascus tomorrow.

"With respect to your recent message on cutting off Israel's aid,[2] I must tell you as strongly as I can that such a course would be disastrous in terms of the immediate negotiation, the long-term evolution and the U.S. position in the Middle East.

"On an immediate tactical level an ultimatum such as you describe would lead to an explosion here. With 85 Israeli children held by terrorists and three Katyusha rockets found at the outskirts of Jerusalem this morning a cutoff of U.S. aid would produce hysteria and maybe a military outburst.

---

[1] Source: National Archives, Nixon Presidential Materials, NSC Files, Kissinger Office Files, Box 45, HAK Trip Files, Middle East Memos and Security, April 28–May 31, 1974. Secret; Sensitive, Exclusively Eyes Only. Sent for information.

[2] According to Kissinger's memoirs, Nixon phoned Scowcroft twice on May 15, before hearing of the Maalot hostage crisis, and ordered Scowcroft to cease U.S. aid to Israel unless it altered its negotiating position, without specifying what he expected Israel to change in its stance. (*Years of Upheaval*, p. 1078)

"Moreover, the situation has improved in the last ten hours. After meeting with the Israeli negotiation team until the early hours[3] they agreed to review their position and are meeting now. The change they contemplate will not meet all Syrian demands but it is a significant step forward. I shall take it to Damascus as soon as we have the details worked out. It should prevent a break-up today.

"The Israeli position, while tough and shortsighted, falls short of the intransigence that would warrant the contemplated step. There are many issues of which the line is only one: disengagement zone, thinning out, UN status, etc. On all of them there are disagreements of various sorts. The Syrians while being more moderate than four months ago are far from being helpful. It would be a grotesque error to put all the blame on Israel. It would be unjust and contrary to facts.

"A public disassociation from Israel would have the following consequences:

"(A) Despair might provoke a suicidal Israeli move.
"(B) Syrian demands would immediately escalate so that we would be back in another stalemate.
"(C) Sadat would suffer because he would appear as having settled too easily. A radical Arab Government would have achieved more U.S. support than Egypt.
"(D) The Soviet Union—as in 1956—would enter the arena full-face with heavy-handed pressure both diplomatic and military.

"I do not exclude pressure on Israel—indeed you will recall that I have proposed certain steps even prior to the President's messages. However, it must be carefully prepared, discussed in the Government and based on Congressional support. Above all it must be related to actions which can be taken and decisions which can be made by the Israeli Government.

"For all these reasons I must request that the actions contemplated not be undertaken. It is essential also that Washington maintain an attitude of public and private calm. A crisis atmosphere of meetings, leaks and innuendoes will ruin the last chance we have to bring this off."

---

[3] No record of a meeting between the Israeli negotiating team and Kissinger on May 15 has been found. According to Kissinger's memoirs, he only spoke with Israeli Ambassador Simcha Dinitz and Golda Meir in private conversations that day. (*Years of Upheaval*, pp. 1076–1079)

60. Memorandum From the President's Deputy Assistant for National Security Affairs (Scowcroft) to President Nixon[1]

Washington, May 16, 1974.

The following is a report of Secretary Kissinger's latest discussions in Israel.

"This has been a difficult day for the Israelis which wound up with forces having to storm a schoolroom to kill three terrorists, but not until after twenty children had been killed by them and about fifty wounded.[2]

"However, despite this tragic event, I had several talks with the Prime Minister.[3] The Israeli Cabinet is meeting in a very late night session with a view to making a further adjustment in their position on disengagement to meet in a substantial way the latest Syrian views. My understanding is that there is a good chance that the Cabinet will agree to a new Israeli defensive line around Quneitra, both north and south, which will go close to 9/10ths of the way to meeting the Syrian proposals for this area.

"You will recall that the latest Syrian position was that the line should be drawn through the peaks of the hills west of Quneitra. The Israeli leadership is making a major effort tonight within the Cabinet to alter their defensive line so that it will be drawn close to the base of these hills and embracing some of the smaller hills north of Quneitra.

"You will recall also from my previous messages that in Asad's latest proposal he would like to see the Israelis make some further adjustment in the southern part of the line so as to include a number of Syrian villages. I do not expect that the Israelis will be able to make this change, and I believe the reasons they give are both logical and understanding. The Israelis have explained that if they move the line in the south so as to turn over a number of the villages to the Syrians, there is great danger that these villages will become populated with Saiqa Fedayeen. These villages are located on the plains close to a number of Israeli settlements. This would be a made-to-order situation for guaranteeing terrorist incidents of the kind which would place in jeopardy any disengagement agreement achieved.

---

[1] Source: National Archives, Nixon Presidential Materials, NSC Files, Kissinger Office Files, Box 136, Country Files, Middle East, Dinitz, January 1–July 1, 1974. Secret; Sensitive; Exclusively Eyes Only. Sent for information.

[2] See footnote 5, Document 58.

[3] See footnote 2, Document 58, and footnote 3, Document 59.

"I am encouraged by these developments. I will be meeting with Prime Minister Meir and her colleagues early Thursday[4] morning to receive the definitive views of the Cabinet. If the above position is approved, as I hope, I believe I will be carrying a reasonable Israeli proposition to Asad and it will then be up to him to show flexibility and compromise. If we can achieve agreement on the line, I would hope then to make a major effort to try to resolve the remaining issues—zones of limitation, buffer zone, UN presence, etc.

"I will be going to Damascus Thursday afternoon and be returning to Jerusalem Thursday night to bring back the Syrian response."

---

[4] May 16.

---

61. Telegram From the President's Deputy Assistant for National Security Affairs (Scowcroft) to Secretary of State Kissinger[1]

Washington, May 16, 1974, 1352Z.

Tohak 212/WH 41358. Deliver immediately upon receipt.

1. The President called me in after reading your latest report (Hakto 97).[2] He said to pass to you the following thoughts which you could use as you see fit.

2. The President said that, while no one believed that Syria was involved in the latest terrorist incident,[3] he foresaw enormous sympathy for the Israeli position as a result. The President's analysis is that Congress would now be fully supportive of Israel in the event a disengagement is not worked out, whereas previously there was great sympathy for the Arabs in the face of Israeli reluctance to compromise.

3. It is the President's personal opinion that in view of these latest developments, failure to achieve a disengagement will now be blamed on Syria and that this would reduce the ability of the United States to be usefully involved in efforts toward a permanent peace.

---

[1] Source: National Archives, Nixon Presidential Materials, NSC Files, Kissinger Office Files, Box 45, HAK Trip Files, Middle East, TOHAK 161–245, April 28–May 31, 1974. Top Secret; Sensitive; Exclusively Eyes Only; Flash.

[2] The text of Hakto 97 is in Document 60.

[3] See footnotes 4 and 5, Document 58.

4. The President also suggests reemphasizing that the disengagement arrangements in our eyes represent only a temporary arrangement, a beginning toward a permanent just settlement in the area.

5. Once again, the President said to use these thoughts if, and in any manner, you think they would be useful in your discussions with Asad.

Warm regards.

---

62. Telegram From Secretary of State Kissinger to the President's Deputy Assistant for National Security Affairs (Scowcroft)[1]

May 17, 1974, 0115Z.

Hakto 99. Please pass the following message to the President:

1. It is clear from my four hour discussion today with Mrs. Meir and her Cabinet and eight hours of talks with Asad[2] that neither side wants to break off the talks; indeed, whenever a recess is mentioned, they plead with me to persevere. At the same time, while there has been some give by each side, it has not been enough to bridge the remaining gap.

2. Based on my informal consultations with various Israeli Ministers and in conversation alone with Mrs. Meir, I was encouraged to introduce some new proposal of my own even though the Israeli Cabinet had not been able to come to any agreement in a formal way on modifying its position.

3. I therefore put the following proposal to Asad today making it clear that it was an American proposal and reflected my judgement of what might be possible to achieve with the Israelis. I said to him I thought there was a chance of getting something along the following lines if he were in a position to accept:

---

[1] Source: National Archives, Nixon Presidential Materials, NSC Files, Kissinger Office Files, Box 45, HAK Trip Files, Middle East, HAKTO 1–179, April 28–May 31, 1974. Secret; Sensitive; Immediate.

[2] Kissinger met with the Israeli negotiating team on May 16 from 9:45 until 11:30 a.m. at the Foreign Minister's Residence in Jerusalem. (Memorandum of conversation; ibid., Box 1029, Presidential/HAK Memcons, May 8–31, 1974, Folder 3) He also met privately that day with Meir from 12:05 until 1:30 p.m. at the Prime Minister's Residence in Jerusalem. (Memorandum of conversation; ibid., RG 59, Records of Henry Kissinger, 1973–77, Box 8, Nodis Memcons, June 1974) No memorandum of conversation with Asad on May 16 has been found.

A. The line around Kuneitra would move about 200 meters west with the distance between this line and the western hills (about one and a half kilometers) demilitarized under UN supervision.

B. The hills themselves would be under Israeli control with strict limitations on their military dispositions which the United States would guarantee bilaterally to Syria.

C. The Israeli line of control would be moved one kilometer back to the north and south of Kuneitra so as to meet Asad's concern about returning civilian population to Kuneitra while the city was enclosed too closely on three sides by Israeli forces.

4. While doing everything possible to prevent a break in the talks, Asad nevertheless continued to insist that at a minimum the line of control should run along the ridge of hills west of Kuneitra, with UN observers on top and Israelis and Syrians in control of the western and eastern slopes respectively. He later modified this somewhat by saying that the western side of the hill could be Israeli, the eastern side under the UN as well as the slope, and he added that neither Israelis nor Syrians should expect to cultivate the fields between the western hills and the outer edge of Kuneitra.

5. My judgement is that there is a chance that I might prevail on the Israelis to accept my proposal but there is little or no chance that the Israelis will accept Asad's formulation.

6. I will spend all day Friday[3] discussing the matter with the Israelis who undoubtedly will have to convene another Cabinet meeting. I will then take whatever I get to Damascus on Saturday with possibility of agreement on my proposal but more likely a suspension of talks for a few weeks.

7. While I naturally would like very much to get agreement on the line and then make an all out effort over the next few days to get agreement on all other related matters, I am convinced that even if there is a suspension we will have gained great ground in our overall Syrian-American relationships, and have preserved our position in the Arab world without affecting adversely our relationships with Israel.

8. I could stay over a few more days if there is a real prospect for an agreement. Otherwise, I will overnight Saturday in Cairo and be back in Washington Sunday evening.

End message
Warm regards.

---

[3] May 17.

63. Telegram From Secretary of State Kissinger to the President's Deputy Assistant for National Security Affairs (Scowcroft)[1]

May 18, 1974, 0925Z.

Hakto 102. Please pass the following message to the President:

1. I had a four hour discussion with Prime Minister Meir and her Cabinet colleagues on Friday[2] which produced some further Israeli flexibility which I will be taking to Damascus Saturday morning for what will probably prove to be a final effort resulting in either a break in the impasse on the question of the line of disengagement or agreement on a pause in the negotiations which would resume in a few weeks.

2. As you know, the principal focus of difficulty remains the line of disengagement as it relates to the area of Kuneitra. Yesterday I went over in detail with Mrs. Meir and her key Cabinet members some American ideas on how to loosen the situation around Kuneitra to ease some of Asad's concerns that he could not return Syrian civilians there with Israeli forces so closely hemming the city. I had explored in a general way these ideas with Asad on the previous evening,[3] and I have now been authorized by the key Cabinet members to put forward an American proposal on the understanding that if Asad accepts it, Mrs. Meir will make a major effort to push it formally through her Cabinet.

3. In substance, the proposal I will put to Asad this morning is the movement of the Israeli line of control west of Kuneitra a few hundred meters outside the city limits, with a demilitarized zone under UN supervision between this line and the big hills west of Kuneitra. On the hills themselves, the Israelis have agreed to limit themselves to light arms designed to meet air attacks but none that could shoot straight into Kuneitra. In addition, in order to give the Syrians more assurance that its civilians in Kuneitra would not be under Israeli guns, the Israelis have agreed to move the line of control one kilometer north and south of the line of Kuneitra.

4. I am not sanguine that Asad will accept this proposal since in a variety of ways in my previous talks with him he concentrated on proposals designed to get Israelis off the big hills west of Kuneitra.

---

[1] Source: National Archives, Nixon Presidential Materials, NSC Files, Kissinger Office Files, Box 45, HAK Trip Files, Middle East, HAKTO 1–179, April 28–May 31, 1974. Top Secret; Sensitive; Eyes Only; Immediate.

[2] Kissinger met with the Israeli negotiating team on May 17 from 1:25 until 3:55 p.m. at the Foreign Minister's Residence in Jerusalem. (Memorandum of conversation; ibid., RG 59, Records of Henry Kissinger, 1973–77, Box 8, Nodis Memcons, May 1974, Folder 1)

[3] May 16. No memorandum of conversation was found.

5. Of course, I hope he will accept this, and I would then press intensively over the next couple of days to complete the agreement. However, if as far more likely, he decides on a breathing period in the negotiations, I will work out with him a statement on suspension of talks which will protect our position in the area, keep manageable for a period of time any Arab buildup of pressures on us, hopefully assure that the June 1 Oil Ministers meeting will not reimpose the embargo, and provide the basis for an early resumption of the talks.

End text.

6. Warm regards.

64. Memorandum From the President's Deputy Assistant for National Security Affairs (Scowcroft) to President Nixon[1]

Washington, May 18, 1974.

Following is Secretary Kissinger's report of his Saturday meeting with President Assad:[2]

"In my message yesterday,[3] I described to you the proposal which I planned on making as an American proposal in order to break the impasse over the differences relating to the Kuneitra area. You will recall my proposal was designed to give the Syrians some assurance that the Israeli defense line could be drawn in such a way that Assad would not feel that civilians in the town were completely hemmed in. The proposal would also require Assad to agree that the Israelis would retain control of the big hills west of Kuneitra.

"I presented this proposal to Assad and I am pleased to report that he has accepted it and we have therefore achieved a significant breakthrough on the question of the line which now gives me hope that an agreement can be achieved. In accepting this proposal, Assad made it clear that he was doing so almost exclusively because of his confidence

---

[1] Source: National Archives, Nixon Presidential Materials, NSC Files, Kissinger Office Files, Box 45, HAK Trip Files, Middle East Memos and Security, April 28–May 31, 1974. Secret; Sensitive; Exclusively Eyes Only.

[2] Kissinger met with Asad on May 18 from 4:05 until 6:50 p.m. at the Presidential Palace in Damascus. (Memorandum of conversation; ibid., RG 59, Records of Henry Kissinger, 1973–77, Box 8, Nodis Memcons, May 1974, Folder 5)

[3] Document 63.

in the United States and the role that it is playing in the Middle East to achieve permanent peace.

"At the urging of Assad, I have decided to extend my stay in the area in order to try to conclude the agreement during the course of next week. While there are a number of other issues which will cause serious difficulties, I am of the view that if I can get the Israelis to accept the American proposal on the line that this should be possible with major effort. If it is, it will give further impetus to the trends in the Middle East which we have been developing. Assad clearly made this decision in the hopes that this will bring further developments in the new trends in the area and closer relationships with the United States. To use his words, 'it is not for Israel but for the U.S. that I am doing this.'

"I will make a major effort with Prime Minister Meir and her colleagues tonight and tomorrow, and I intend to be as firm as is necessary now that Assad has made what I consider to be a courageous decision.

"I have deferred my Cairo stop and will be cancelling a number of appointments with various Foreign Ministers in Washington next week, and I am asking Rush to lead the delegation at the CENTO meeting which convenes on Tuesday and Wednesday."

65. Memorandum From the President's Deputy Assistant for National Security Affairs (Scowcroft) to President Nixon[1]

Washington, May 20, 1974.

Following is a report from Secretary Kissinger of his Sunday discussions in Jerusalem.

"The stage is set for a climactic effort over the next several days to bring to a successful fruition the Syrian-Israeli disengagement agreement. After long, tedious and difficult discussions with Prime Minister Meir and her key Cabinet colleagues,[2] I will be bringing to Damascus

---

[1] Source: National Archives, Nixon Presidential Materials, NSC Files, Kissinger Office Files, Box 45, HAK Trip Files, Middle East Memos and Security, April 28–May 31, 1974. Secret; Sensitive; Exclusively Eyes Only. Sent for information.

[2] Kissinger's discussions with the Israeli negotiating team occurred over the course of three meetings. Kissinger met with the negotiating team on May 18–19 from 10:30 p.m. to 12:15 a.m. at the Foreign Minister's Residence in Jerusalem (Memorandum of conversation; ibid., RG 59, Records of Henry Kissinger, 1973–77, Box 8, Nodis Memcons, May 1974, Folder 5); on May 19 from 3:30 until 6:30 p.m. (Memorandum of conversation; ibid., Nixon Presidential Materials, NSC Files, Box 1029, Presidential/HAK Memcons, May 8–31, 1974, Folder 2); and finally on May 19 from 9:50 until 11:30 p.m. (Memorandum of

Monday[3] an Israeli map which reflects the American proposal relating to the Quneitra area which has broken the impasse.

"Today we had lengthy talks on all the key elements of the agreement including the area of separation, the area of limitations, the nature and mandate of the UN presence, the prisoner of war issue, the timing relationship between various segments of the agreement, and the scenario for signing the agreement within the framework of the military working group at Geneva, hopefully early next week.

"We are, of course, not entirely out of the woods since I can foresee at least several issues on which it will be difficult to achieve common ground. The Israelis and the Syrians have rather marked differences, which I hope can be bridged, on the zones of limitation and the UN presence. Nevertheless, I believe each side has now decided that an intensive effort should be made over the next several days to conclude this negotiation successfully and I am, therefore, hopeful of the results.

"I am assuming, Mr. President, that as an integral part of the overall agreement I can proceed along the lines of your instructions to develop certain written assurances in the form of letters from you to President Asad and Prime Minister Meir in the same way in which you provided assurances in the context of the Egyptian-Israeli agreement. The following letters will be necessary:

"(A) A letter would spell out the Israeli assurance to us as to the nature of the limitation of its forces on the big hills west of Quneitra.

"(B) An assurance to Asad that we will continue our efforts in the next stage to achieve a durable and stable peace in the area.

"(C) An assurance to Israel regarding long-term military supply along the lines of your various messages to me.

"For the next several days I will be shuttling between Jerusalem and Damascus. I am keeping the other key Arabs as well as the Shah informed as well as both the Soviets and the Chinese. I am pleased to report that both the Syrians and the Israelis agree that at any signing ceremony in Geneva within the framework of the military working group there are no objections to the US and Soviets observing the signing. There will also be some technical details on implementation of this agreement that the Israelis and Syrians will have to work out within the military working group at Geneva, but this will not afford the Soviets an opportunity to inject themselves in a harmful manner.

"I would appreciate confirmation regarding the various letters of assurance."

---

conversation; ibid., RG 59, Records of Henry Kissinger, 1973–77, Box 8, Nodis Memcons, May 1974, Folder 5).

[3] May 20.

66. Telegram From the President's Deputy Assistant for National Security Affairs (Scowcroft) to Secretary of State Kissinger[1]

Washington, May 21, 1974, 1431Z.

Tohak 263/WH 41432. The President called me out of staff meeting this morning.[2] He has a message for you, which he had written out longhand and which he half read and half ad-libbed to me. The message is as follows:

"As I am returning to Washington from Florida I am writing this personal message for Brent to transmit to you.

"Of all your superb accomplishments since we have worked together, the Syrian/Israeli breakthrough, regardless of what comes out in the odds and ends of bargaining which still lies ahead, must be considered one of the greatest diplomatic negotiations of all time. I know well how hard you have worked, how discouraged you must have been at times, and I just wanted you to know how personally grateful I am for this example of diplomatic service far beyond the call of duty, which has become your trademark.

"I believe we should follow up this development with a trip to the Middle East at the earliest possible time. We will thereby be able to seal in concrete those new relationships which are essential if we are to be successful in building a permanent structure of peace in the area.

"It is of course vital to constantly reassure our Israeli friends. The hardware-software analogy plus the implied U.S. commitment to hold the ring against great powers should they ever threaten Israel's existence should be conclusive to a realist like Rabin.

"On a personal note, I thought you would be interested to know that nowhere in the transcripts or the tapes, and I had Len Garment listen to the three in question, did I ever use the terms 'Jew boy' or 'wop.'[3] The *New York Times* following its usual practice nevertheless refuses to retract.

---

[1] Source: National Archives, Nixon Presidential Materials, NSC Files, Kissinger Office Files, Box 45, HAK Trip Files, Middle East, TOHAK 246–310, April 28–May 31, 1974. Top Secret; Sensitive; Exclusively Eyes Only; Black Patch; Immediate.

[2] According to the President's Daily Diary, Nixon met with Scowcroft on May 21 from 8:50 until 9:13 a.m. in the Oval Office. (Ibid., White House Central Files)

[3] In a May 12 article in the *New York Times,* Seymour Hersh wrote that in secret taped conversations, Nixon called Judge John J. Sirica a "wop" and referred to "Jew boys" in the Securities and Exchange Commission. (*New York Times,* May 12, 1974, p. 1)

"When you return I would like to have a long conference with you, if convenient for both of us at Camp David this weekend, before we have a briefing of the leadership next week.[4]

"Pat joins me in sending Nancy and you our warmest personal regards."

After reading-dictating the above, the President commented further on your fantastic ability to glean the framework of agreement from seemingly unreconcilable positions. He asked again for your views about a trip. I told him you would want to make a discussion of that a first order of business following your return. He said he understood and he wanted no discussion of a trip with anyone but he wanted, in order to get his own thoughts in order, your ideas for him alone on timing and itinerary in the event a trip should take place. He asked me, working alone, to start thinking about what a schedule might look like. While he stresses the tentative nature of the trip situation and the need to keep discussion confined to the three of us, it seems apparent where his inclination lies. Any tentative thoughts that you could give me just for him would greatly facilitate maintaining the present relaxed and composed atmosphere. I would continue, as I have thus far, to stress the tentative nature of any thinking along these lines until you return and discuss it thoroughly with him.

Warm regards.

[4] See Document 91.

---

67. Telegram From Secretary of State Kissinger to the President's Deputy Assistant for National Security Affairs (Scowcroft)[1]

May 21, 1974, 2115Z.

Hakto 124. Please pass the following message to the President:

1. I have just completed a five hour meeting with Assad[2] which was the most difficult of any that I have had with him. While some

[1] Source: National Archives, Nixon Presidential Materials, NSC Files, Kissinger Office Files, Box 45, HAK Trip Files, Middle East, HAKTO 1–179, April 28–May 31, 1974. Secret; Sensitive; Immediate.

[2] The meeting between Asad and Kissinger took place on May 21 from 5:45 until 9:45 p.m. at the Presidential Palace in Damascus. (Memorandum of conversation; ibid., RG 59, Records of Henry Kissinger, 1973–77, Box 8, Nodis Memcons, May 1974, Folder 7)

progress was made in certain areas, the remaining differences are serious enough to lead me to believe that an agreement may not be achievable.

2. The Syrians and Israelis are agreed on the line of demarcation. They are agreed with the arrangements in and around Kuneitra which gives Assad some breathing room so that he can bring in civilians. There is agreement in principle between the two sides that there should be zones of limitation and a buffer zone between the two main defense lines. There is also agreement in principle that there should be a UN role to help keep the cease fire and check on the agreement.

3. However, there are serious remaining differences. These are:

A. Syria insisted on taking over the positions in the Mount Hermon area; Israel is willing to give up all the positions on Mount Hermon to the UN except the one it maintains it took prior to the cease-fire going into effect.

B. Syria is insisting that its forward defense line more or less coincide with the October 6 line. Israel has been holding to the position that this line should be six to eight kilometers eastward, though it has made clear it is willing to consider advancing it provided it is satisfied with the arrangements regarding the zones of limitations.

C. Syria and Israel have different conceptions regarding the zones of limitations. Assad is thinking in terms of a narrow five kilometer zone east and west of the respective defense lines with only limited restrictions. Israel wants much more far reaching restrictions which the Syrians insist would require an actual pullback of a substantial part of their armed forces. Israel is also insisting that in a twenty five kilometer zone there be no weapons placed that can reach the defense line of the other side. Up to this point, Assad has not been willing to agree to any such restrictions. His Foreign Minister told me that to accede to these requests would lead to Assad's overthrow.

D. While the nature of the mandate for the UN presence can be compromised to meet the essential needs of both sides there is a large gap in the numbers with Israel insisting on about three thousand and Syria talking in terms of no more than three hundred observers. We know there is some give in these positions but whether there is enough flexibility cannot be determined too clearly at this point.

4. Apart from the aforementioned details there is a more fundamental consideration which seems involved in the current negotiations. Assad has underscored frequently that if he goes beyond his present position that he will not be able to sell the disengagement agreement internally. We have no real way of judging this since if he decides to go ahead, he can certainly point to a substantial Israeli withdrawal as a first step towards an eventual settlement. Israel is deeply suspicious and with the transition from the outgoing to the incoming

government few of the leaders, if any, seem able to take a broader view of matters.

5. Regardless of whether we achieve the agreement or not, I believe we have made sufficient progress that the talks could be suspended in such a way that no seriously adverse repercussions on our overall position would take place in the short-run, though the long-range implications of failing to achieve an agreement now are worrisome.

6. My judgment would continue to be that a trip by you to the Middle East would be favorably received. I expect to pass through Cairo on the way home and I would want to get President Sadat's judgment on this so that you and I can discuss it fully upon my return.

Warm regards.

68. Memorandum From the President's Deputy Assistant for National Security Affairs (Scowcroft) to President Nixon[1]

Washington, May 22, 1974.

Following is Secretary Kissinger's report of his discussions this morning in Jerusalem.

"The Israeli negotiating group this morning rejected completely the latest Syrian proposal on thinning out of zones.[2] The Syrians propose a 6–10 kilometer belt on each side with strictly limited forces. The Israelis insist that all artillery and surface to air missiles be moved back twenty-five kilometers out of range of Israeli forward positions. This would require a massive redeployment of Syrian forces which Asad feels he would not survive politically.

"My assessment is that the Israelis are asking the Syrians to protect Israeli settlements on the Golan Heights established in violation of existing resolutions and never recognized by the US. No Syrian president can accept this. The settlements under the Syrian scheme would be no

---

[1] Source: National Archives, Nixon Presidential Materials, NSC Files, Kissinger Office Files, Box 45, HAK Trip Files, Middle East Memos and Security, April 28–May 31, 1974. Secret; Sensitive; Exclusively Eyes Only. Sent for action.

[2] The meeting between the Israeli negotiating team and Kissinger took place on May 22 from 10:30 a.m. until 12:50 p.m. at the Prime Minister's office in Jerusalem. (Memorandum of conversation; ibid., RG 59, Records of Henry Kissinger, 1973–77, Box 8, Nodis Memcons, May 1974, Folder 8)

more vulnerable than they were before October 6 or for that matter than they are today.

"Unless the Syrians cave today I shall therefore recess the talks tomorrow.

"There is a slight chance that the Israelis may reconsider but it would require a stiff Presidential message delivered in Washington before the end of business today in Washington."

Dr. Kissinger thought you may wish to draft such a letter yourself.[3] A letter could appropriately state that you have studied Kissinger's reports of the remaining issues and that these do not seem to outweigh in importance the drastic consequences of a failure or a recess in his mission. You could outline those consequences in terms of our ability to play an active and constructive role in the Middle East and of our continuing ability to support Israel's needs, concluding with a request to Mrs. Meir to make one more maximum effort to seek a compromise which would permit an agreement. Should you wish me to draft such a letter, I will be pleased to do so.

---

[3] Document 69.

---

69. Letter From President Nixon to Israeli Prime Minister Meir[1]

Washington, May 22, 1974.

Dear Madame Prime Minister:

Since the beginning of Secretary Kissinger's current mission to assist in bringing about a disengagement of forces on the northern front, I have studied carefully the many complex elements of this difficult problem. It is clear that compromise involves terribly difficult decisions—the antagonisms on both sides are deep and are based upon years of mistrust that are not easily overcome. Continued violence makes more difficult the requirement to view this moment in perspective and to recognize how heavily the future peace and security of Israel turns on decisions taken now.

---

[1] Source: National Archives, Nixon Presidential Materials, NSC Files, Kissinger Office Files, Box 136, Country Files, Middle East, Dinitz, January 1–July 1, 1974. No classification marking. A covering letter from Scowcroft to Minister Shalev notes that the letter was delivered to Shalev at 6:15 p.m.

As you know, Madame Prime Minister, the United States has been Israel's closest friend and ally. Our relationship has endured for more than a generation in a spirit of mutual trust, understanding and concern. It is in this spirit that I read with deepest concern the recent report by Secretary Kissinger that the disengagement talks are in danger of breaking down over the thinning out of zones along the disengagement line as well as other issues which, however important, cannot but seem minor in relation to the severe consequences of such a breakdown.

I am therefore writing this personal message to you in order to insure that you and your Cabinet fully comprehend the detrimental effect of a breakdown or recess of the talks for which public opinion might judge Israel to be responsible. As a very long time personal and official friend of Israel, I urge in the strongest terms the modification of your position so as to avert a cessation or recess of the talks under these circumstances.

After these long and difficult negotiations which you and your colleagues have so wisely pursued and the hopes which have been raised of progress toward a settlement, a setback would indeed be a tragedy. Besides the thwarting of hopes for a major move towards peace, I fear it would lead inevitably to a deterioration of Congressional support, renewed opportunities for Soviet intervention, and massive pressure for a reassessment of United States policy toward Israel. That is an outcome which neither you nor I wish, jeopardizing as it would the ability of the United States to play an active and constructive role in the Middle East and to continue to assist in meeting Israel's needs.

Madame Prime Minister, in the conviction that we stand at a historic threshold in the search for a just and lasting peace in the Middle East, I urge that you and your Cabinet make a supreme effort to seek a compromise which would permit an agreement on the disengagement of forces on the Golan Heights and enable us to move another step away from strife and bloodshed and toward that peace to which we are both dedicated.

Sincerely,

Richard Nixon

70. Memorandum From the President's Deputy Assistant for National Security Affairs (Scowcroft) to President Nixon[1]

Washington, May 23, 1974.

Following is Secretary Kissinger's report of his Thursday morning talks with the Israelis.

"I have just completed a three-hour session with the Israeli Cabinet.[2] They have now moved to a slightly more flexible position on the issue of the thinned out forces. I hope this may enable me to make some further progress in Damascus.

"I am now flying to Damascus where I will make one more major effort with Asad. I will report again this evening."

---

[1] Source: National Archives, Nixon Presidential Materials, NSC Files, Kissinger Office Files, Box 45, HAK Trip Files, Middle East Memos and Security, April 28–May 31, 1974. Secret; Sensitive; Exclusively Eyes Only. Sent for information.

[2] The meeting between the Israeli negotiating team and Kissinger took place on May 23 from 9:05 to 11:50 a.m. at the Prime Minister's office in Jerusalem. (Memorandum of conversation; ibid., Nixon Presidential Materials, NSC Files, Box 1029, Presidential/HAK Memcons, May 8–31, 1974, Folder 1)

---

71. Memorandum From the President's Deputy Assistant for National Security Affairs (Scowcroft) to President Nixon[1]

Washington, May 24, 1974.

The following is the report of Secretary Kissinger's meeting with President Assad on Thursday.

"I have just completed another five-hour meeting with President Assad.[2] Enough progress was made to justify another round of talks, so

---

[1] Source: National Archives, Nixon Presidential Materials, NSC Files, Kissinger Office Files, Box 144, Country Files, Middle East, President's Trip to Middle East, June 1974. Secret; Sensitive. A handwritten notation at the top of the page reads, "The President has seen."

[2] The meeting between Asad and Kissinger took place on May 23 from 6 until 11:30 p.m. at the Presidential Palace in Damascus. (Memorandum of conversation; ibid., RG 59, Records of Henry Kissinger, 1973–77, Box 8, Nodis Memcons, May 1974, Folder 9)

I will spend most if not all of Friday in Israel and probably return to Damascus early Saturday.

"Tonight's meeting produced an understanding of a concept of limitations on armament behind the disengagement lines that I think can now provide a realistic basis of negotiation on this subject. Specifically, we now have Assad's agreement to put SAMs and the longest range (130 mm) artillery 25 kilometers from the disengagement line. This is an important achievement, but we still have to get agreement to limit the medium range (122 mm) artillery and tanks.

"My approach will be to try Friday in Israel to formulate what can be presented in Damascus as a U.S. proposal on limitations. This, you will recall, was the approach we used in the Egyptian-Israeli disengagement. In addition to major problems in reaching agreement with the key leaders in Israel on numbers of weapons and men in the limitations area, there will have to be a cabinet meeting.

"Besides the issue of limitations on which we are now concentrating, there seems to be tentative agreement on how to handle the separation of forces in the strategic Mount Hermon area. But on the size of the UN force, Israel is holding out for at least 2,000 and the Syrians want less than 1,000. Each of these items could take considerable time because a major problem in conducting these negotiations is that each issue becomes the subject of intensive bargaining over every detail. It is very different from the Egyptian negotiations when Sadat laid aside details in the interest of quick agreement. In order to put an end to this bargaining, I have tried to tell Assad that I must return to Washington.

"My plan is to return Monday evening at the latest."

---

72. **Memorandum From the President's Deputy Assistant for National Security Affairs (Scowcroft) to President Nixon**[1]

Washington, May 25, 1974.

The following is Secretary Kissinger's report of his discussions Friday in Israel:

---

[1] Source: Library of Congress, Manuscript Division, Kissinger Papers, CL 155, Geopolitical File, Israel, May 1974. Secret; Sensitive; Eyes only.

"I have completed hours of discussions here in Israel with Prime Minister Meir and her key cabinet members[2] as a prelude to my final effort tomorrow in Damascus to bring about an agreement. I remain doubtful that the remaining issues can be resolved. For one thing, this situation is different than the Egyptian-Israeli disengagement agreement. In that instance Sadat in particular had made a fundamental decision not to permit marginal details to sidetrack the agreement. In this particular negotiation, both sides are negotiating hard and tenaciously on every principal specific point, a reflection of the deep suspicion that exists between them.

"Assad sees disengagement as a pause that will retain for him either the war or the peace option and therefore is negotiating doggedly to give him an agreement with as much flexibility as possible to move either way.

"The discussions now are focusing on individual specific details, no one of which should be a breaking point, but when taken together as a group could require weeks more of negotiations unless more flexibility will develop in the next 24 hours. Without getting too technical, here are some examples: In the ten kilometer disengagement zone Israel is insisting on no artillery while Syria insists on 54 short-range artillery pieces. The numbers are also at issue. In the 10 to 25 kilometer area Assad refuses to agree to any limitation on military personnel or tanks which the Israelis want. We have his agreement to position SAMs and long-range artillery outside the zone. Assad is insisting that his defense line be advanced more westward than where it is presently placed. Israel is giving us a new map tonight moving the line westward, but whether this will be enough for Assad or not is problematical. Ironically, with all of the difficulties the Israelis have had in the past with the UN, it is pressing for a much more effective UN presence both in numbers and in mandate than Assad seems willing to allow at the present.

"There are a number of other similar issues which I will also seek to sort out in a climactic effort tomorrow. I will report promptly after my meeting with Assad."

---

[2] On Friday, May 24, Kissinger met with the Israeli negotiating team from 9:50 a.m. until 12:40 p.m. at the Prime Minister's office in Jerusalem (memorandum of conversation; National Archives, RG 59, Records of Henry Kissinger, 1973–77, Box 8, Nodis Memcons, May 1974, Folder 9) and with Prime Minister Meir from 5:25 until 7:30 p.m. at the Prime Minister's Residence in Jerusalem (memorandum of conversation; ibid.).

73. Telegram From Secretary of State Kissinger to the President's Deputy Assistant for National Security Affairs (Scowcroft)[1]

May 25, 1974, 2045Z.

Hakto 150. Please pass the following message to the President:
Begin message:

1. Both sides gave evidence today of a small amount of give in their respective positions which has provided the opportunity to keep the negotiation alive.[2] We are approaching an agreement on thinned out zones but the going is tough. There was some progress on other issues.

2. The critical difference which I will try to bridge in the next twenty-four hours is the question of how far forward the Syrian defense line should be. Assad is insisting that it be moved up anywhere between four to six kilometers to coincide with the October 6 line, while Israel has resisted this on the understandable ground that it will leave only a small two kilometer buffer and bring Syrian guns close to Israeli guns. I told Assad that I would make one more effort, that he will have to make a final decision tomorrow when I return on the assumption that I will be able to bring back Israeli agreement to some movement forward on the part of his defense line but not as far as he wants. I am meeting with Mrs. Meir and her Cabinet colleagues tomorrow morning and will return to Damascus late tomorrow afternoon.

3. There are still issues to be resolved regarding the size of the UN force and the nature of limitations in the zone beyond the ten kilometer zone.

4. This negotiation could go either way in the next twenty-four hours. I would feel more confident if I was not faced with an outgoing Cabinet in Israel in the last twenty-four hours of its life and an Assad who, while being very intelligent, is negotiating tenaciously every point as if he had a record to make—very much unlike Sadat who didn't bother with many of the marginal points.

End message
Warm regards.

---

[1] Source: National Archives, Nixon Presidential Materials, NSC Files, Kissinger Office Files, Box 45, HAK Trip Files, Middle East, HAKTO 1–179, April 28–May 31, 1974. Secret; Sensitive; Exclusively Eyes Only; Immediate.

[2] No records of conversations on May 25 between Asad and Kissinger or the Israeli negotiating team and Kissinger have been found.

74. Memorandum of Conversation[1]

Damascus, May 27, 1974, 12:15–2:22 a.m.

PARTICIPANTS

President Hafez al-Asad
Dr. Henry A. Kissinger, Secretary of State and Assistant to the President for National Security Affairs
Isa Sabbagh, Interpreter
Peter W. Rodman, NSC Staff

Kissinger: Well, we have had a long night, Mr. President. I shall miss our almost daily chats. [Laughter] But I respect the way you have conducted the negotiations. It is a very difficult step for you.

Asad: While we have reached [something], particularly with regard to the red line, we have not really solved the complicated question. Because this agreement will be published. Even the map will be published. Some papers have already published it.

Kissinger: In Israel?

Asad: No, even Arab ones. Lebanese papers and magazines. Of course, as I mentioned before, we have to present it to everybody. Apart from this subject . . .

Kissinger: Yes, I know.

Asad: Is there an American letter or not?

Kissinger: Yes.

Asad: Because three days ago you said you would have one.

Kissinger: About what?

Asad: About the second phase.

Kissinger: First, I told the President it would be sent two weeks after. I would leave him a draft, but the actual letter would be sent two-to-three weeks after. For the reasons which I gave.

Asad: You said it would be about a week after your appearance before Congress. About a week.

---

[1] Source: National Archives, RG 59, Records of Henry Kissinger, 1973–77, Box 21, Classified External Memcons, November 1974, Folder 2. Secret; Nodis. The meeting was held in the Presidential Palace and occurred on May 27, not May 26–27 as indicated on the original. Brackets are in the original. Previously, on May 26, Kissinger met with the Israeli negotiating team from 9:15 a.m. until noon at the Prime Minister's office in Jerusalem (memorandum of conversation; ibid., Box 8, Nodis Memcons, May 1974, Folder 10) and with Asad from 9 p.m. to midnight in Damascus (memorandum of conversation; Library of Congress, Manuscript Division, Kissinger Papers, CL 193, Peace Negotiations, Israeli-Syrian Relations, Negotiation Books, Volume III, May 1974, Folder 2). In these meetings, the final details of the agreement were discussed.

Kissinger: That is fine. That amounts to about two to three weeks.

Asad: Then we started discussing the content, and you never completed it.

Kissinger: Let me say, first, especially if the agreement is completed, there is a good chance the President will personally come to this area, and I believe the two Presidents will probably reach a rather satisfactory understanding about the second phase.

Asad: Of course, this is apart from the letter.

Kissinger: Yes. In letter, what we have in mind is something along the lines I discussed with the President yesterday: that within the year, we will engage ourselves to an active sustained effort to bring about the implementation of Security Council Resolution 338.[2]

Asad: We will start within the year?

Kissinger: Yes. And that this will include the legitimate interests of the Palestinian people.

Asad: You think things will remain so stable for a year? If within twelve months from now we will start this, when will it be carried out?

Kissinger: No, it will be started well before. I gave the President my estimate. We can have a preliminary discussion during the summer, and the start of active pressure in December, January.

Asad: In your estimate, when do you think Resolution 338 will be carried out?

Kissinger: I have to give you an estimate?

Asad: Yes.

Kissinger: Sometime during 1975.

Asad: Don't you think developments that would have come about in the area—psychological, military, social—would create different circumstances in the area?

Kissinger: Different from what?

Asad: You think things will remain stable in the area for a long time?

Kissinger: No, absolutely not.

Asad: I do not believe the situation in the area will remain for a period of a year if Israeli occupation is not ended. This is my own analysis.

Kissinger: It is my own analysis too. I can tell the President that I told the Israeli Prime Minister I thought there would be a war within a year if there is not progress towards a solution.

Asad: Yes, you are right.

---

[2] See footnote 6, Document 7.

So a letter along these general lines would not solve our problem, I think. Sure, I know the United States does not want any change in the area; a letter, of course, would have implied therein a moral commitment.

Kissinger: But if we did not want a change, we wouldn't be here. Why should the United States care about disengagement? Why should we care about Line A, Line B? This is nonsense from the American point of view—unless we wanted to start a movement toward a resolution.

Asad: That is true.

Kissinger: If we wanted to protect Israel, we could give it military protection on its present line.

Asad: You are protecting Israel.

Kissinger: But if we did not have a larger objective in mind . . .

Asad: We have to speak frankly. This kind of action by itself is capable of various interpretations and could be seen from various points of view. For instance, I evaluate this action as not necessarily in the interests of the Arabs. Maybe.

Kissinger: But this was always the President's view.

Asad: That is why I cannot from it alone or from it per se derive an indelible conclusion that America is moving in that direction.

Kissinger: I think if we put all the actions together . . .

Asad: I want to go a step further and say this is the way it looks: With this action you have somehow contributed to removing pressure from Israel. I do not mean Syrian disengagement, but the whole picture of disengagement, including Egypt and Syria. Of course, it has other facets, but I am talking about it from this point. The disengagement concept itself, as seen from the Arab point of view, has been like deflating various balloons, taking away the certainty of the preparedness, the readiness, the unison of the Arabs. We know the Israelis could come to this point. But this is a difficult point of the Arabs—military, political. What the Arabs were beginning to achieve by not having disengagement, by having them alert—this concept of disengagement would cause them to slacken.

That is why we can in summary say that acts of disengagement now could be explained as not being in the interests of the Arabs, could be explained from a certain angle as in the interests of Israel, and in any case need not be taken as an exclusive indication of America's intention for the future.

We have to separate these things when speaking of it. I for one am optimistic about the new trend we discern in the United States, but not necessarily based on that. Because perhaps it is the result derived from the consensus of our discussions, discussions which touched on other subjects wider than disengagement. But were I to shut my mind off from those positive indications I got from those discussions, and wider considerations, and concentrate on disengagement, I must say I feel in an uneasy mood, neither optimism nor pessimism.

Now we have gotten used to each other and have to speak frankly.

Kissinger: No, I appreciate it. I consider it a sign of confidence.

Asad: Therefore, I say this subject itself remains inadequate. And on this basis, I as the leader in this country cannot help but to continue to prepare militarily, economically, and look for friends, supporters, because this is not an adequate indication, (a) for me, and (b) for me to prepare my people for the new trend in America's intentions. This is the way I frankly evaluate the thing. I would like to go back to that point so you will rest assured that my personal result of these discussions is optimism. But who can guarantee? Because Israel is strong in America. She might turn things up side down.

Frankly speaking, our discussions here on disengagement have strengthened that belief that I have, and strengthened my conviction that Israel is as far away from wanting to pursue the path of peace as ever. For instance, Israel is standing firm on a few points as if that territory belonged to her from the start of creation. With all due respect for what Dr. Kissinger has said about if the United States wanted to give protection, if every country in the world gave that protection, unless Israel learns to live as a Middle East country, it will not work. The Arabs are an ancient nation in this area. They are the first nation to present civilization to the world—the sciences, writing—whereas Israel as a political event is a new development here. There is no historic nation called Israel in the area. There are Jews, yes. It is not a question of a nation I am talking about. The Arabs have among them the Christian, the Jew, the Moslem. But to these Arabs, to them belongs this ancient civilization. But Zionism does not have this ancient civilization.

Religion is not the basis for a nation. Christians do not form a nation; Moslems do not form a nation; and the Jews in the world are not one nation. Moslem nations fight one another. A Syrian Jew is different from a Soviet Jew, from an American Jew. It is true that Zionism is trying to form a nation from religion, but this is a view which is contrary to logic and history and will never prevail. Especially when formed against the interests of other people. I do not mean the Arabs, I mean at the expense of all other people. For example, when Zionism tries to extricate a French Jew from his country, France, that is a loss to France and to him.

Zionism is not just an offense to Arabs alone but to others. In my evaluation, Zionism will not triumph. And this is a fact which in my opinion as an Arab and as an Arab individual, will not be changed, as I said before, by Israel being protected by the Soviet Union or the United States.

Circumstances do change, and Dr. Kissinger as a political scientist knows there have been historic circumstances when the United States did not support Israel. Eisenhower did not; the Soviet Union once did, and now is not. There was a period when France was supporting Israel very deeply, and has now changed.

Kissinger: France is still the second largest weapon supplier to Israel.

Asad: At one time, there was one organic union between France and Israel—witness the 1956 invasion of Egypt. Is this circumstance still obtaining? No. Arab citizens, I don't think it will be possible to sway them by temporary considerations. That is why it is in the interest of Israel, the deep interest of Israel, to rush to follow the path of peace when the opportunity presents itself.

Kissinger: Let me make a few observations on what the President has said. First, I agree essentially with your analysis. I agree Israel must learn to live in the Arab world or it cannot live at all. I agree it is not possible to pursue a colonial policy, at all, but especially among a people as intellectually advanced as the Arab people. I agree it is absolutely imperative for Israel to seek the road of peace. And I have said so at every occasion, in Israel and publicly.

Now, in terms of the evolution of American policy: Of course both Zionism and Israel are strong in America, or America would never have started supporting Israel. That is a reality with which we must live, and with which I as a political leader must cope.

The President in his own experience must have come up against times when the least effective way to achieve something is a frontal assault on the pattern that is to be changed. And sometimes it is necessary to surround the problem rather than make a frontal attack. I do not think I have to give lessons in political leadership to the man who has led Syria the longest in its recent history.

Now, with respect to the current situation, I had made the current conclusion I gave to the President before October 6 war, that is to say, on the necessity of peace. I said that to the Arab Foreign Ministers to whom I spoke in New York.[3] But it is also clear we would almost certainly have failed, without the October 6 war. I have considered the October 6 war a strategic defeat for Israel. They achieved some tactical successes, but no strategic successes. I concluded from the very begin-

---

[3] Secretary Kissinger hosted a lunch for Arab Foreign Ministers and Permanent Representatives to the UN in New York on September 25. A report is in telegram 3416 from USUN, September 26, 1973. (National Archives, RG 59, Central Foreign Policy Files)

ning of the war that the war should be used as an opportunity to move towards peace. And therefore I have given much of my energy to bringing about a crucial first step towards peace.

The President is absolutely right about the long-term trends. But many things can happen before long-term trends express themselves. And therefore it has been the intention of our policy to accelerate this process by American pressure and to bring about a reorientation of Israeli thinking and an alteration in American attitudes.

I believe we have been quite successful in this. If the President's analysis is correct, and I believe it is, then no new line can be permanent. Because the same factors that produced the October 6 war are certain to produce other confrontations, and nations that were ready to go to war when the impression was that Israel was invincible will certainly go to war when they have gained their military self-respect. And it is for this reason that the United States has embarked on this process and is determined to pursue it.

Now there are many other forces in the world, and to the degree they have no direct responsibility or ability to do anything, they can afford to make big pronouncements. But we are engaged on a course we consider inexorable, the early stages of which will be painful and difficult, but which will gain its own momentum after a certain point.

It is, of course, entirely up to the President to conclude what he will do about United States intentions. It is entirely up to him what he wants to tell his people about it. We believe it is in the interest of [solutions to] the problems we discussed to create the best possible relations between Syria and the United States. But the pace of this progress has to be left to the President.

So I think a thoughtful analysis of the totality of our action can leave no doubt about our intention.

Asad: That is precisely what I meant when I said when I look at the total picture of American interests and actions, I am optimistic.

Kissinger: What have I done in the last four weeks? I have, every time I went to Israel, asked for more concessions. I have sometimes told His Excellency I thought I had reached the limit of what could be done. But never once have I proposed something whose trend went the other way. This is the first time the United States has done this systematically.

And I have done it in a period of extraordinary domestic difficulty for the United States. Some of our newsmen were told by some low-level Syrian officials that it was the Syrian Government's assessment that our present domestic difficulties made it easier for us to press Israel. The argument of these Syrians was that I needed to come home with a success.

Asad: That complicated formula, I rarely understood it myself. The situation is exactly opposite of what you just said—[in] the responsible Syrian analysis. Not only I, but I mean by responsible Syrian circles the political leaders working in this, the political current in this country: The Syrian analysis is that Israel is taking advantage of the comparatively weak domestic situation in the United States to intimidate the United States into freezing its efforts and energies so that it would not show its new intentions in the area. This is my analysis. Yesterday at Headquarters I said this. I said it was my feeling that the United States was wishing to do more but that—and that is what I added—the internal situation in the United States does not allow the United States to exercise more pressure up to what you call the explosive point. Plus the pressure of the Zionist movement in the United States.

Kissinger: This is fair enough. I think the President may not sufficiently understand and give credit for the enormous change we have already produced in American public attitudes in the last six months. We have in the public mind ended the polarization in the Middle East. Americans are no longer uncritical supporters of Israel but they take pride in the way the United States is participating and taking the lead in the move towards peace in the Middle East. And this is gaining more and more momentum. Very soon a point will be reached where Americans would feel if we did not contribute toward peace in the Middle East, we would not be doing our national duty.

When I started, there were very few Americans—politically active Americans—who believed we should engage ourselves in what they thought was a hopeless enterprise. And today in America it is quite different. And this is a big defeat for the extreme Zionism in America. Because to the extent that America engages itself for peace, it must be in the direction of removal of the occupied territories. It must bring about conditions in which the process will accelerate very dramatically. And whenever the President [Nixon] comes here—whether in two or three weeks or two or three months—this will give tremendous momentum to this public consciousness. [Asad nods yes].

So I would say His Excellency should appreciate this totality of events. The American people simply would not understand any more if, having gone this far, we would go no further. [Asad nods yes.]

Asad: I am going to give instructions to the Foreign Minister to tell Gromyko to come later at night. [He presses button to summon aide.]

Kissinger: Monday night.[4]

---

[4] Gromyko arrived in Damascus on Monday, May 27.

Asad: I told him to come Monday. We will tell him to arrive about 10 o'clock. Of course I will then not be so free to see him, because I will be busy. He will arrive at night but I will not be able to see him.

Kissinger: Let me explain our relationship with the Soviet Union. We cooperate with them in many areas. First, if I were the Syrian President, I would take as many arms from them as I could get.

[The aide comes in, and the President gives instructions concerning Gromyko. He then turns to Kissinger.]

Asad: About 10 o'clock.

Kissinger: That way I can meet him at the airport. I can come from Israel. [Laughter]. I am joking. I do not think I will come back. Unless there is an overwhelming emergency. It would not be good if I were here and did not meet him. But I will not be here.

Asad: If you come, you can go to Palmyra.[5] [Laughter]

Kissinger: It is not necessary. It is not necessary. Under no conceivable improvement of U.S.-Syrian relations could we give you the quantity of arms that the Soviet Union gives you. So I don't want to mislead the President. We realize it creates certain political realities also. Our concern with the Soviet Union has been that they seem to us to be more interested in form than in substance. And especially about their own participation. In an almost childish way. And in terms of strategic positions, as far as we are concerned, we have no strategic objective in the Middle East. We do not want any military bases and we do not want any military participation with us in any Middle East country. We do have an interest in better relations with the Arab countries for a variety of reasons. But we are not in a position of confrontation with the Soviet Union. We just do not like to be pushed when there is no practical objective. We do not see why we should talk to Brezhnev when we can talk to you or Sadat or Faisal. That is our only occasional difference. I mean, occasionally they ask us "what is your policy?" My view is: If we tell them our views, they have two choices: They can make an agreement with us without telling you and impose it on you, or they can go to you and ask your opinion. We do not have much confidence in imposed solutions. We think Syria is a lousy candidate for it anyway. [Laughter]. And if we wanted to ask your opinion, we can ask it directly.

And some of these travels, I frankly consider them irrelevant. They do not help anything and they do not hurt anything. I do not oppose them; I do not support them. And when the President [Nixon] and Brezhnev meet at the summit, they will have an irrelevant discussion about the Middle East but Brezhnev will make a lot of noise.

---

[5] An ancient city in Syria.

So that is our relationship, as far as the Middle East is concerned, with the Soviet Union. In many other areas, we have close cooperation. In the Middle East, we have a certain measure of cooperation but mainly on procedural issues.

Asad: You are in agreement on the Geneva Conference?

Kissinger: Yes.

Asad: When?

Kissinger: Oh, about a month after disengagement is completed. But do you think much is going to happen in Geneva?

Asad: The cause must be moved somehow.

Kissinger: And it is useful for that.

Asad: It doesn't mean that people will go to Geneva only to have their pictures taken. I believe, mark my word, if there is no solution, there will be a war within a year.

Kissinger: I agree.

Asad: So how do we move our energies in the direction of peace?

Kissinger: No, I believe Geneva is not bad. I am not opposed to Geneva. I believe we should talk privately, and have it come together at Geneva. I have told Gromyko privately that I am in favor of Geneva.

Asad: It is useful. And your utterances are convincing.

Let us go back now to the subject of the letter, therefore. Have you drafted it? Have you given it some thought?

Kissinger: I have drafted something along the lines of what I have told the President.

Asad: Where are your views on withdrawal? Is it limited by "secure borders?"

Kissinger: My personal view on withdrawal is, no Arab state will accept a peace settlement short of the '67 frontiers.

Asad: That is true.

Kissinger: And I consider that a reality. I do not know any Arab state that would settle for less.

Asad: Does the United States, is it its view that a solution should come about for less than this, the '67 frontiers?

Kissinger: No.

Asad: These questions are not just thrown at you academically.

Kissinger: No, I know.

Asad: This is important to evaluate the present trend of American thinking. It is very important to us. Why can't this sense be incorporated in the letter?

Kissinger: Because we cannot have the President sign a letter that he cannot politically live with if it is published. Whatever the assurances. When we reach the position of negotiation for final borders, then a new situation arises.

Asad: Then the original subject of the letter will be about 338 and the interests of the Palestinians.

Kissinger: And within a year . . .

Asad: Full implementation of 338.

Kissinger: In all its parts. And a U.S. commitment to engage itself in that within a year.

Sabbagh [explains]: Within a year—between one month and 12 months.

Asad: If the language could be made clearer, something like this: The United States commits itself to the full implementation of Resolution 338 within 12 months. In this sense there would be nothing harmful to the United States. Then there would be some moral commitment on the part of the United States.

Kissinger: Let me check this tonight. And I will let you know tomorrow morning.

Asad: I will jot down His Excellency's specific language so I can study it.

About the rights of the Palestinians, have you any specific language?

Kissinger: I have told His Excellency: We should take fully into account the legitimate interests of the Palestinian people. A settlement should.

Asad: What is the difference between "rights" and "interests" in this particular context? I understand some, but . . .

Kissinger: "Interests" means we have an obligation to consult the views of the Palestinians. "Rights" means we know what their interests are. But "legitimate," in any event, implies the notion of rights. And "legitimate rights" is a tautology.

Asad: And what I think is an advance of it.

Kissinger: No, it is "legitimate interests." I checked it last night.

Asad: In actual fact, the word "interests" could go in various directions. It could be interpreted as money, compensation. Of course, the Arabs are not looking in this direction.

Kissinger: No, in my view, the Arabs are looking for a Palestinian political entity, in one way or another.

Asad: Yes, the Palestinians themselves, this is what they want. In various ways. So this is where the meaning of rights fits in, in this concept. But "interests" would be a bit more confused.

You have not started any new contacts with the Palestinians?

Kissinger: No, but I have told the President that after this disengagement we will establish contact at a political level. We have sent them a message, which you may know, in Beirut, about two weeks ago, that we took seriously their legitimate concerns.[6] But we have not followed it up. But I think they understand us. When we reach this point, we would appreciate the advice of His Excellency [about] with whom we deal.

Asad [nods yes]: But my question is, do you insist on having the word "interests" and not "rights" included in the letter?

Kissinger: Yes.

Asad: Number one, I want to say the Palestinians cannot believe that in all our discussions we are not discussing them. Of course, I am telling them, wherever the occasion presents itself, that we always use the expression "Palestinian rights." We are not guardians over the Palestinians, but they cannot believe we are not discussing them.

Kissinger: I have no objection to His Excellency telling them some of our discussions here.

Asad: Does the United States have a specific concept of Palestinian rights? This is not for publication or announcement.

Kissinger: We are speaking personally and not officially: I have always thought there could be a Palestinian entity, on the West Bank, which could be connected with Gaza.

Asad: But Israel is hanging on tenaciously to parts of the West Bank. They want the river, they want . . .

Kissinger: This is one of the problems in the second phase.

Asad: You think the Israelis would agree to give the Palestinians a corridor between the West Bank and Gaza?

Kissinger: If you want my opinion on how to do it—which you will not like—my idea would be to let the Jordanians deal with Israel about the West Bank, and then let the Palestinians deal with Jordan.

Asad: On the West Bank?

Kissinger: Yes.

Asad: How about Gaza and the corridor?

Kissinger: And on that basis one could have Gaza and the corridor.

Asad: Because we have not expressed any view on the subject, whether to King Hussein or to the Palestinians. A lot has gone on between the King and the Palestinians.

---

[6] Telegram 89704 to Beirut, May 12, transmitted a message from Acting Secretary of State Kenneth Rush reported that the Palestinian role in the settling of the Arab-Israeli dispute "has been and remains very much on our mind." (Library of Congress, Manuscript Division, Kissinger Papers, CL 189, Geopolitical File, Middle East, Palestinians Contact Message Book, 1973–75)

Kissinger: I noticed that!

Asad: How can they solve it when they are estranged and there is a lot of resentment?

Kissinger: Maybe the Syrians could play a role there.

Asad: They seem to have unanimity not to be back under King Hussein's rule. There has been a massacre, and it is like milk curdling between them. We tried before the war. And the one responsible for this estrangement is King Hussein. Because he used to take one step forward and pull back. So we have come to a very complicated pass.

Kissinger: What is His Excellency's view on how to solve the problem?

Asad: Honestly, we haven't come to any clearly defined concept.

Kissinger: That is our problem. We haven't either.

Asad: There are many concepts in the works. But I have advised them not to quarrel about anything. Because in any case, Israel is still having the West Bank. My advice is, let us first get that which we have lost and then sort things out. It is sort of ridiculous to quarrel with King Hussein about the West Bank when Israel still has it.

Kissinger: That is my view.

Asad: Back to the letter. Do you think it is not useful, or is it possible, to mention the United States recognizes there will be no real solution to the Middle East unless going back to the borders of 1967, from the point of view of the Arabs?

Kissinger: This I have pointed out would be a problem. But when the President comes here, you will find you have a useful discussion.

Asad: Is there anything else you would like to discuss? When we have finished discussing these other things, we could go back to that.

Kissinger: Yes.

Asad: Of course you should rest a little too!

Kissinger: But this is important. It is also important because it will be impossible to explain, having spent four weeks in the Middle East, why it failed at the last moment.

[An aide comes in.]

Asad: The maps are here. The maps of scale 1:25,000.

Kissinger: Good. How does His Excellency visualize proceeding concretely in U.S.-Syrian relations? Because that is part of the strategy.

Asad: What I have in mind is that, within a period, we should restore relations. Without graduation; not gradually, but straightforward.

Kissinger: In what period?

Asad: Not before the carrying out of disengagement, but after.

Kissinger: That is a good idea.

Asad: Of course restoration of relations will help to increase our contacts, to have occasional exchange of visits. Personal contact is very important. These are my views on the subject, how we can start going about things.

Kissinger: Yes. We will establish, as President Boumediene may have told you, a Cooperation Commission with Algeria. For economic and technical cooperation. And we will do it also, as you know, with Saudi Arabia. And probably with Egypt. We would be prepared to do the same with Syria whenever the President [Asad] was ready. It should not be the first thing; it should be in some months. And the President can in general assume that whatever we do with any Arab country we would be prepared to do with Syria. We may not propose it specifically because we do not want to seem to have an unending desire to make proposals.

Asad: This is fine. As long as we have the intent to develop relations in the right direction.

Now back to the disengagement subject. There are three points, as I understand it.

The question of Kuneitra is finished as far as I am concerned. About tanks, etc. Although I knew they knew I have asked for this and am insisting on it, they have broadcast it.

Kissinger: I am embarrassed.

Asad: My thought is, it is natural from their point of view to know I have asked for it. Because it is absurd for people to exist between two enemies. Of course, within this context, I do not think we will expend a great effort in returning people to their places. I do not think they themselves [the Israelis] would go back under such conditions. Because no one would send their family there. The Israelis, whose homes are behind them, want *us* to pull *our* guns back. In spite of the fact that we have similar villagers ourselves. So the position of the villagers in Kuneitra will be a very bad one.

The two points are: The United Nations, and (2), the red line.

On the question of the United Nations—okay, it too, we can give and take on it. But on the question of the red line, once again I say it is impossible. Because this map is going to be published and the inhabitants whose villages are going to be in front of the red line have an untenable position too. Apart from everything else, it would look like something that is imposed on us by force. It has no clear justification we can use. So that is why I believe this subject must be discussed further and something must be done about it.

Kissinger: But how can something be done about it?

Asad: You said you expected their Council of Ministers [Cabinet] to meet. For them, it is not a very important thing, but for us it is important. Why this adamance on their part? Because we have really given in on a lot of things, things we have insisted on in the past.

Kissinger: Their adamance, as you say, derives from the fact that they think they are pulling their forces back 37 kilometers.

[They get up and look at the map.][7]

Asad: Their original defensive lines are here [October 6 lines].

Because all their defense lines here [in the salient] are temporary. Because there was not enough stability to establish defense lines in the bulge. This is their defense line [the October 6 line]. They worked hard on it, and established it.

Kissinger: And you penetrated it.

Asad: There is no defense line in the world that cannot be penetrated.

Kissinger: Exactly.

Asad: Every man knows it. It is a mistake if they think they are impregnable, because no matter how strong they make it, an enemy can put together a sufficient force and break it.

Kissinger: That is the lesson of military history. Their Council of Ministers will meet, but they will never agree. This Cabinet will not. They might change a kilometer in here, but it does not change your basic problem.

The only other thing that has occurred to me, Mr. President, was the point General Shihabi made. Because it had occurred to me also that we count the artillery line from here [the October 6 line] and not from here [the red line]. And for that we would have to get the approval of the Israeli Cabinet. I have no basis for it.

Asad: Of course, this is a positive point.

Kissinger: Why should I bargain with the President? I am like a doctor; I am trying to gauge what is possible without breaking it. I can tell you, at the end of the meeting today I did not get a satisfactory change in the red line. I went to Rabin, and Allon, and Eban, and said to them: It does not seem absolutely fair to me to count the artillery from here. If I come back from Damascus and say the artillery has to be from here, from 20 kilometers—the 10 kilometers has to be from here [the red line]—would you agree with it? And they said they cannot say yes. But I am assuming they would do it. So if we want to get it concluded tomorrow, and we have to be realistic, I could probably on my authority

---

[7] The map is not attached, but a final status map is printed in Appendix B, map 2.

get that done. And I could probably, based on the same sort of conversation, get another kilometer in here.

Asad: I really cannot explain this line away. What do I say about it? I have already told my people we are going back to the October 6 line. I explained it on the map, even, to the leadership of the party, the day before yesterday. The zone of limitation, the thinning-out zone, 6-plus kilometers, plus 10 kilometers here, and here of course it will stretch along.

Kissinger: But then the second 10 would be only 4 kilometers here, if they accept my theory.

Asad: Then that would be the advantage to the Syrian side? It would be a very limited advantage.

Kissinger: You would save these six kilometers.

Asad: The net result. For all. I imagine if you applied a little more pressure . . .

Kissinger: No, I have tried it, believe me. They will not do it. I know they will not do it. The mistake I made was, they wanted to do it all the way down here [in the south] and I refused.

Sabbagh: The Syrians want it all the way up here. The reverse. The red line.

Asad: I do not really know how to express it. Because I know very definitely you spent four weeks. I certainly appreciate all you have done. This is an imposition by force, so to speak.

Kissinger: Not by force.

Sabbagh: Not by physical force, but an enforced result.

Asad: It is very difficult that the ceasefire would remain stable in this kind of condition.

Kissinger: Why?

Asad: Because neither people nor officers would put up with seeing this kind of line, arrangement.

Sabbagh [to Kissinger]: I was wondering if there could be some sort of time frame, a bilateral understanding.

Kissinger: [to Sabbagh:] His problem is he has to publish this map.

Asad: It is inescapable.

Kissinger: If he doesn't, the Israelis will.

This has not been published yet?

Asad: The same concept, but not line by line.

A number of factors are accumulating which would not be helpful to stabilizing the ceasefire. The major factor is we have not defined a limited distance between us. So from a practical point of view, when they move one step forward, we will hit them, and if we move one step forward they will shoot at us. That is one important factor: that they do not have a defined distance between.

Normally when two armies face one another, there is a certain distance defined in which they cannot move. 100, 200 meters. As the case used to be before October 6. For instance, our authority stretches to the blue line. Can we really go up to the blue line where they happen to be? I believe our people will find some excuse to go to the blue line, because it is in the agreement. But they [the Israelis] will not permit this. This is a kind of irritation-type situation. For instance, around Kuneitra, they will establish themselves on the blue line, and already the border is the blue line. You can imagine this. This is clear?

Kissinger: Yes.

Asad: There is no belt: a soldier here, a soldier here.

These things as they can appear have confirmed rather than dismissed the aggressive intentions of Israel.

Kissinger: I do not think this is quite fair, Mr. President, because many of these confusions resulted from our pressure, and our pressure in turn was to give the maximum civilian authority to Syria.

Asad [thinks]: Yes, but of course it should be known that we will have to establish points—if we are not going to establish a defense line, we are bound to establish military anchors and observation posts.

Kissinger: Yes. Mr. President, I do not think you are unreasonable. I have told you from the beginning, I would do it differently, if I were to negotiate. I might not negotiate; I might decide on war. But if I were to negotiate, I would do it generously. And not grudgingly.

It depends on what line one publishes. If one publishes the line of civilian control, it is a forward movement of Syrian authority. I am thinking of the presentation.

Asad: No, the people on the lines—because these are military lines. When people think of lines, administrative lines, they immediately think of soldiers on that line.

Maybe you should rest up. And tomorrow we will discuss.

Kissinger: All right. What time should we meet tomorrow?

Asad: At your convenience.

Kissinger: What time is it now? 2:15?

Sabbagh: Yes, sir. 2:15.

Kissinger: 9:30? In fact, let us say 9:00, so I can get back. 9:00, 9:30.

Asad: 9:30.

Kissinger: Tomorrow is my birthday, Mr. President. I am going to debate the hills of Kuneitra. But it is worthwhile. I understand the President's problem. I really understand it.

Asad: There is not one of the military people who likes this.

Let us sleep on it.

[Dr. Kissinger and President Asad get up]

Kissinger: Where are my people?

Sabbagh: With Khaddam.

Kissinger: Tell them to meet me in the Guest House in 5–10 minutes.

[Before the Secretary left, the two maps of scale 1:25,000 were given over. Asad asked to look at them first. He and the Secretary spread them out on the table and examined them. They were then folded up again and given to Mr. Rodman to carry back to Israel.]

75. Memorandum of Conversation[1]

Damascus, May 27, 1974, 9:50 a.m.–1:15 p.m.

PARTICIPANTS

Hafiz al-Asad, President of Syrian Arab Republic
Press Counsellor Elias

Dr. Henry A. Kissinger, Secretary of State and Assistant to the President for National Security Affairs
Isa Sabbagh, Interpreter
Peter W. Rodman, NSC Staff

(Photographers were admitted briefly at the opening of the meeting.)

Asad: I saw the negotiating team after you left.

Kissinger: And I saw the negotiating team on our side also.

Asad: The Syrian side told me they were given documents for surrender. This is how they described them.

Kissinger: We talked among ourselves. It is a ... see, the difficulty is, we started out this negotiation with a gap that was too wide. And perhaps I should not have come out here until the conditions were a little more propitious, or until I understood a little better what the problems were. So I blame myself largely for having started this whole

---

[1] Source: National Archives, RG 59, Records of Henry Kissinger, 1973–77, Box 21, Classified External Memcons, November 1974, Folder 2. Secret; Sensitive; Nodis. The meeting was held at the Presidential Palace in Damascus.

process. See, some of the documents we show you are about a tenth of what the Israelis ask us to show you.

Asad: Why should we be obliged to agree to them?

Kissinger: No, we are not bringing you Israeli documents.

Asad: We are not dealing with human beings if those are their demands. There is no historic precedent to our agreeing to any of this kind of language.

Kissinger: What in particular?

Asad: Everything that occurred in the documents. We never in the past agreed to this kind of an arrangement. Nor would we ever agree in the future to anything we had not agreed to in the past. No, they seem to be real enemies.

Last night and this morning, their radio said we were discussing the question of the fedayeen—though we had refused to discuss it. Those who want to discuss the question of the fedayeen should discuss it with their organizations. Any Arab leader who thinks he is the guardian of the fedayeen is the worst type of leader, and anyone who does it will be smashed and deserves to be smashed. They are a deprived people and entitled to defend themselves.

Kissinger: Well, I do not know what Israeli radio reported.

Asad: We were forced—I ordered a denial to be issued. Because the people must know the facts. Because, as you know, we have refused to discuss it.

Kissinger: I have tried for four weeks to get the Israelis to control their radio. I was specifically assured yesterday that there would be no problems while I am here. But they may have a different definition of "problems."

I must tell you honestly that in my judgment there is really no basis at this time to conclude the relatively few things that remain to be done.

Asad: Yes, that may be the case.

Kissinger: It's a tragedy to come this close and fail. And it's an experience to which I am not used to in these negotiations. I have told His Excellency—and I know he agrees—why it would have been a very important step had we succeeded. But I also understand there are limits beyond which either side cannot go.

Asad: Yes, of course.

Kissinger: So what is His Excellency's view on what should happen now?

Asad: Our position is clear. The remaining points were: the red line—the question of the United Nations can be sorted out; differences in the positions.

Kissinger: I am not worried about that.

Asad: The question of Kuneitra, which I do not consider simple, but which could be settled. The question of the red line is the basic thing. And our attitude in this regard is not new, as you well know.

Kissinger: And there are some aspects in the documents.

Asad: We discussed the documents in the past, but yesterday I was presented with new things in the documents which were not there in the past. We did not think they would be incorporated in the documents that were brought to me yesterday. We agreed on one document, the basic agreement. There were not important differences.

Kissinger: I agree.

Asad: We discussed the American proposal,[2] and there were not important differences there. And we agreed the American proposal should only be about the restricted zone. Whereas yesterday, I was told there are new things in the American proposal.

The agreement, the American proposal, and the map—those were the three things we discussed in the past. We had no serious difficulties.

Kissinger: On the American proposal, the part that concerned His Excellency was the part that described what would happen in the demilitarized area.

Asad: No, several other points.

Kissinger: Like what?

Asad: Like the fedayeen crossing the line.

Kissinger: But all those are in the section on the demilitarized zone.

Asad: When it comes to the fedayeen, it would not be limited to one segment. It belongs to the people.

Kissinger: I am trying to isolate in the document. On the thinning-out zone in the American proposal, no disagreement.

Asad: Some textual questions.

Kissinger: But no problem. The problem arises in the other document, on the demilitarized zone.

Asad: There are eight points. Three we discussed before; five new points. Maybe they all belong to the demilitarized zone.

Kissinger: They belong to the demilitarized zone. I have looked it over. Of those five, several are not important—like who gets the fortifications which the Israelis abandon. I mean, that is not a major point.

But let me first explain to the President why we put it into that section, rather than into some other.

---

[2] Kissinger introduced an American proposal on May 16. See Document 62.

We first thought there might be a separate protocol on the demilitarized area, and that the Foreign Minister refused, and I understand why.

Asad: Never did it occur in our discussions, nor were we given to understand that the area was to be treated separately. All we knew was there would not be major forces in that area, specifically, artillery and tanks—this is what I myself said—and that our authority over it would be complete. Yesterday what I saw was new.

Kissinger: We had taken the idea of the buffer zone—maybe we never understood what a buffer zone is—but a demilitarized area under Syrian civil administration.

Asad: Why should we take it when it is going to be demilitarized? We agree it was just that one and a half kilometers.

Kissinger: But what was the idea when His Excellency sent me the idea of the buffer zone? What was his idea?

Asad: It was to have been west of the southern part of the front, the line which we agreed on, and to a distance one-to-three kilometers, devoid of people, which it is. Even so, with people in it, to the west of southern Golan.

Elias: The western half of Golan.

Kissinger: I think, Mr. President, what we should need is a few weeks to restudy this problem. Because we think we are close enough to a solution to be able to do something, although it is impossible to do something today, in time I have left. And I do not think we can do it with this present (Israeli) government. And what we should do is either ask two or three of the leaders to come to Washington or if the President should come to the Middle East, on that occasion to attempt another discussion on the subject.

Asad: That is possible,

Kissinger: Because I think it is primarily a problem of the red line, and for the other issues the President raises, we could probably find a compromise solution.

(Elias says something to Asad, goes out.)

Kissinger: I hope this does not declare me persona non grata while I am in the country.

Asad: No, this is the statement about the fedayeen, denying the Israeli report and saying we never entered into it and whoever wants to discuss the fedayeen should go to their organizations. This is necessary.

Kissinger: I understand.

Asad: None of it touches you.

Kissinger: No, of course.

Asad: We have never made such statements.

Kissinger: No, it is a great disappointment to both of us that this negotiation has not succeeded.

Asad: The fedayeen?

Kissinger: No, both of us. But I want the President to know we believe he has behaved in a decent, honorable, and constructive way. We have no complaints about the conduct of the Syrian side, nor shall we make any criticism of the Syrian side.

Asad: For our part, we will never say anything but good about Dr. Kissinger's work and efforts and energy. Because this is a fact. The Israelis have not left much of a breathing space.

Kissinger: The Syrians will surely say something about the Israelis. But if some space, a month, could be left before all-out criticism starts, it would help the negotiations.

Asad: Generally speaking, our information media will remain pragmatic and objective.

Kissinger: Now, what should we say?

I have some ideas on the red line, but there is no sense negotiating with you, going back to Israel, and having a three-day Cabinet crisis. When we start again, we will start from a new position. I would rather make a fresh start with the new Israeli Cabinet in two weeks' time.

Asad: How will you start?

Kissinger: To resolve these few remaining issues.

Asad: I agree with that.

Kissinger: I will try to do two things: I will have the Prime Minister, Defense Minister, and Foreign Minister come to Washington and talk with the President and me, or conceivably use the occasion if the President comes to the Middle East, if he now comes to the Middle East, to make further progress.

Can I ask the President, as a friend? What is his idea of the President's trip to the Middle East under these circumstances? Honestly.

Asad: I myself welcome it. But I think, in the circumstances—and that is the key sentence—a visit would be complicated. And I think, as the President of the United States of America, he should come in more auspicious circumstances, for his own dignity and that of the United States. This is the way I look at it.

Kissinger: No, I speak to you as a friend.

Asad: Of course, personally, I welcome seeing him anytime.

Kissinger: May I ask, again as a friend, this question? If, on the advice of the other Arabs or for other reasons, he should decide to come anyway, should he include Syria?

Asad: This is left entirely up to his own inclination and desire. I would welcome him any time.

Kissinger: Even in the absence of an agreement?

Asad: Yes.

Kissinger: Let me sum up, so I can reflect views I will give only orally: The President feels that, as a friend, he would recommend it would not be fully consistent with the dignity of the President of the United States to visit the area under these circumstances.

Asad: Yes.

Kissinger: And to wait for more auspicious time. However, if the President (Nixon) should decide, because he makes a different judgment or on the advice of other Arab leaders, then he (Asad) would be delighted to receive him in Damascus.

Asad: (nods): Yes.

Kissinger: This is a fair statement. And I will add on my account that I know Syrian hospitality. You do not have to say that; that goes with being in Damascus. Is that a fair statement?

Asad: Yes. Exactly. This is my thinking.

Kissinger: May I see whether a statement, which is similar to what we drafted the other day, would be appropriate to issue?

Asad: Okay.

Kissinger (reads from draft at Tab A).[3] "President Hafez Asad and Secretary of State Henry Kissinger today concluded a series of talks on the separation of forces between Syria and Israel." That is a fact. (Laughter) "They agreed to recess the talks for a few weeks and allow both sides to study the problems involved. President Asad expressed his deep appreciation for the efforts of the United States and for the initiative and determination of the Secretary of State. He believes the talks have been conducted in a cordial, friendly and impartial manner. Secretary Kissinger in turn has expressed his thanks to President Asad and his government for the positive spirit in which these talks have been pursued." His only complaint is the 5 kilos he put on while in Damascus. (Laughter) That I added. "He also thanked the President on behalf of his colleagues for the warm hospitality extended to them in Syria.

"President Asad and Secretary Kissinger agreed that very considerable progress has been made toward an agreement on disengagement of forces, including the matter of the disengagement line. However, a number of other complex and related issues remain, which will require further time to resolve.

---

[3] Tab A attached but not printed.

"They therefore agreed that during the period in which the talks will be briefly recessed, diplomatic contact designed to bridge the remaining differences will continue."

I've added a sentence at the end, but it is up to the President: "To this end President Asad plans to send a personal emissary to Washington soon to continue the discussions with Secretary Kissinger."

Asad: This last one wouldn't be very useful.

Kissinger: All right.

Asad: One person in Washington. We could say we could send someone to Washington for any other purpose. If we here couldn't do it, one person in Washington couldn't do it.

Kissinger: We could have a sentence: "President Asad agreed these talks have helped Syrian-U.S. relations, and to further these, he will send an emissary to Washington." Or "both agree."

Asad: The thoughts I agree with in principle, although I may have one or two adjustments in the text. I suggest a recess for a half hour; I will talk to the Syrian side and maybe come up with a statement.

Kissinger: Add that sentence, Mr. Elias: "Both sides agreed that these talks have contributed to U.S.-Syrian relations. In order to further develop these, the Syrian side will send an emissary to Washington."

We have two dangers, Mr. President: (1), that the American people shouldn't get discouraged with this effort. Because I am determined to continue and I need public support. Secondly, it is important that the American people retain the improving attitude towards Syria. And therefore, if, independent of a joint communiqué, the President could find it possible to say something friendly about our mission . . .

Asad: Yes.

Kissinger: It would ease the attacks which are going inevitably to start on me now. I want to tell the President now: For the next three weeks, you will see many attacks on me. Because all the Israeli supporters, who feel I've tormented them in recent weeks, will now take their revenge. You've seen it already this weekend: There are ten articles saying I'm neglecting my duties in Washington. And that can't be an accident. Nevertheless, I do not fight stupid domestic battles. And I will overcome them. And I—speaking to you as a friend—am not in the same position as the President. So I can mobilize my support. I am just saying this to the President so he doesn't get nervous.

Asad: That is the one point that is paramount in my thoughts. Because after having established this nice human personal contact, then out of loyalty, out of fondness, when we look at the imperative of Syrian-American relations, I'm particularly looking at the need not to harm you.

In your views, how far could the red line be moved? When it can be moved. Let's speak openly.

Kissinger: I'm in Never-Never Land, Mr. President. I'll tell you what I thought last night—for which I have no authority. I think the President and I went through the same process last night; we concluded it was extremely difficult if not impossible. So I tried to see what could I imagine—without any authority.

And let me say one other thing, again speaking personally and as friends: I don't want to do anything that would hurt President Asad. If the President accepted something that was extremely difficult for him and caused complications later for him, we would have defeated an important American purpose. So I don't want to be responsible for having made the President—through persuasiveness—do something that will later on hurt him. Because that would be a tactical success but a strategic defeat.

I want to say this about my view.

Asad: I appreciate this. The sincerity of this.

Kissinger: The President will see, in the context of our other discussions, that we'll give concrete proof of this. Within our limited capabilities.

But let me tell you what occurred to me. But I have no knowledge whatever whether the Israelis would accept it.

(They get up to look at the map.)[4]

One is, I think we can get another kilometer here (in the north). But that's not the key issue. But what I think—absolutely without authorization—just like the 20-kilometer thing, but that I discussed with three Israelis and have some support. What I discuss now I've never discussed with any Israelis. I give my personal word of honor. If we measure ten kilometers from each side of the October 6 line, but within the Syrian 10-kilometer zone, the area forward of the red line would be—whatever we call it—demilitarized, no tanks, whatever. So one would have this only as a dotted line, like this dotted line.

Asad: I didn't quite understand this. You mean ten kilometers from this?

Kissinger: There are two problems with the red line. One is, it starts the ten-kilometer zone from a point further back from the Syrian line of control. The second is the symbolic aspect of Syria just leaving this territory in an undefined nature, and the problem of explaining this to the public.

---

[4] The map is not attached, but a final status map is printed in Appendix B, map 2.

Practically I don't think it is so decisive because Syria could still defend this area from here. (Indicates) But symbolically . . .

Asad: Your analysis is correct.

Kissinger: I'm just giving the President my analysis.

When I couldn't sleep last night (Laughter), I was thinking what conceivably could be done in a matter of weeks. Suppose we say in the agreement that an area ten kilometers west of the blue line will be thinned out and an area ten kilometers east of the purple line will be thinned out. With 6,000 men, 75 tanks, 36 artillery pieces.

Asad: Yes.

Kissinger: However, in a separate understanding, the Syrian side agrees not to station forces forward of this line—or whatever line we finally agree to as the red line. (Asad studies the map.) For example, I could not get that accepted today, I can tell you that. (Asad studies the map.)

Asad: As to there being three to four kilometers east of the red line, the new zone.

Kissinger: Yes. Instead of ten kilometers. And down here there is no problem. It's my imagination, Mr. President.

Asad: Would it be possible to agree to something like this: Out of two brigades we were thinking of . . . (Sabbagh, in translating, intending to say "the President says," says by mistake "the Ambassador says," and then corrects himself.)

Kissinger: (to Sabbagh) Tell the President what you demoted him to! (to Asad) I certainly will not take responsibility. I need a victim. Sisco looks like a victim. Bunker is respectable. But I have a theory: Sabbagh and you were carrying on a conversation unrelated to our negotiation.

Sabbagh: There is an Arabic saying "Wipe it in my beard," meaning a scapegoat.

Kissinger: It's a new theory.

Asad: Out of two brigades, we would position a small proportion—say no more than half of these two brigades, in front of that red line. We could probably position them in certain locations. And from a practical point of view, our positioning them in certain locations would have more of a moral, psychological impact than anything else.

Kissinger: The whole thing is crazy. Even if you put 6,000 men here (on the October 6 line) you'd either attack with 100,000 men or not at all.

Asad: Yes.

Kissinger: So we're talking politics.

Asad: This kind of suggestion they might crack into their thick skulls and realize its importance that is moral, psychological, that no attack is designed. Because one brigade is ...

Another suggestion: Cut this distance in half, a little bit (between the October 6 line and the red line).

Kissinger: Then you would accept the red line?

Asad: If they could make some kind of pockets around these three villages.

Kissinger: I'll bet 100 to 1 those three villages are on hilltops.

Asad: Yes, there is a hill.

Kissinger: Here, they're indented.

Asad: As far as the hills are concerned, they're not gaining anything. We want it for observation purposes. We use hills for observation. Whether the line be here or there, we'll still be observing. We have our people there. They're not going to prevent our observing. These hills will be used in our interest. We have these hills at our disposal. From this point of view, we're not gaining anything.

Kissinger: Suppose the line went here. (Closer to the Oct. 6 line)

Asad: Yes. With two pockets.

Kissinger: How about this road in between? They'll certainly want to keep it non-military.

Asad: Line or no line, the road should be in the middle, civilian.

Kissinger: Suppose here.

Asad: Yes.

Kissinger: You talk about hills to the Israelis! Well, assuming it can be done.

Asad: I will bear the brunt of the other side. If this can be done, I will take it upon myself to do the other. This line will do us injury; if not on the October 6 line, but with this new suggestion, if the red line could be as you pointed out, I will myself take the responsibility. We'll find a justification for why the red line has to be where it is.

Kissinger: But then everything has to be counted from the red line, because my suggestion couldn't be done.

Asad: Okay.

Kissinger: But then the Israelis won't agree to it. I'd like nothing better than an agreement the President is happy with. Now we're down to 1,000 meters again.

Asad: You could present this as an American compromise proposal. Because it really is a problem. For only this, to balk and throw the rest down the drain ...

Kissinger: But what happens to the documents?

Asad: I understood from you those problems could be sorted out.

Kissinger: But both of us have to do something. (Laughter) The President's idea is that I sort everything out!

Asad: They amount to obligations on the part of Syria to the United States.

Kissinger: The remaining.

Asad: Yes. Because there are certain topics which touch inextricably on a radical solution to the entire problem. The problem with the Palestinians is separate unto themselves.

Kissinger: The problem of the Palestinians is this—I'm speaking openly. There were periods when the demarcation line was quiet between Syria and Israel. And that could not have been an accident.

Asad: That was the will of both sides; that is what I imagine. The question of the fedayeen. In those days there were no fedayeen.

Kissinger: This is a huge political problem in Israel. They're asking 10,000, 20,000 Syrians to come here. Supposing they're all Saiqa?

Asad: They have the Israeli army there, and observers must be closer to the blue line.

Kissinger: What we need, as a minimum, is some vague language. Then we're prepared to say something privately to the Israelis about helping them patrol this line. I mean, giving them mines—I don't know what we can say to them. They have them anyway.

Asad: They can put all they want. It might sober them (the fedayeen) up. It's up to them (the Israelis) to defend it. How can we assure their security and defense? They claim not to be able to defend themselves? Frankly speaking, the question is not dependent on our desire. Even if we had agreed to this.

Kissinger: Why not compromise? You need ten brigades to protect the fedayeen, and if you give ten brigades you'll keep the fedayeen out—Why can we not use the phrase that . . .

Asad: Even if we'd lined them up, 6,000 soldiers, along the 80 kilometers, even those wouldn't be adequate prevention.

Kissinger: If we said something like, "Syria will refrain from hostile action." Not "paramilitary," but "hostile." Not "prevent," but "refrain." If it's "prevent," then Syria has to keep the others from doing. When it is "refrain," then it is what is under the political, governmental control of Syria.

Asad: The word "hostile" is wider and has a wider application than "military."

Kissinger: That is true.

Asad: This applies to anything pertaining to the state of belligerency, the state of war. This expression pertains even to information policy.

Kissinger: Let's forget that now. If we can find a phrase, an adjective ...

Asad: Then it would go in the direction of the fedayeen. It would be very serious. Very serious.

Kissinger: Then the President could maintain the position that he has agreed to only stop things which are under the governmental control of Syria.

Asad: We could say something like, in Article A–1, that Syrian armed forces will scrupulously observe the ceasefire, or something like that. My desire is that the thinking of the average citizen not to go off on a tangent in the direction of something not in our authority, that is, in the direction of the fedayeen.

Kissinger: Let me ask the President this: I'm trying to see if a solution is possible. He won't like it. Something like this paragraph, and the United States then said we understand Israel's desire to protect itself against fedayeen attacks as a part of the cease-fire.

Asad: As a statement.

Kissinger: As an American statement.

Asad: No problem.

Kissinger: What if we made it publicly?

Asad: In America?

Kissinger: And they would want to tell it to their Parliament.

Asad: As long as there is no connection to us.

Kissinger: And you won't attack us for it.

Asad: (Laughing) Future American performance could really create a good impression with the fedayeen. There are some who are interested.

Kissinger: How about some who want to shoot down my airplane?

Asad: Some of them do. But not only yours!

Kissinger: I just want to be sure that if they capture me, the President will put in a good word for me.

Asad: No, because then they won't have a good word for me!

Kissinger: No, I know the responsible ones won't.

Asad: And inside our country I can't imagine anything happening because they know the penalty, and it would be catastrophic for them individually and for the organizations.

Kissinger: No, I've felt absolutely secure in your country.

Asad: (Laughing) I'm going to meet Arafat today.

Kissinger: I expect to meet Arafat eventually.

Asad: It's independent of our discussions.

Kissinger: You can speak to him of my views.

Asad: Maybe on King Hussein, Arafat has a different view from yours.

Kissinger: Yes.

Asad: Although there was once a time when they had contact.

Kissinger: Arafat and Hussein?

Let me sum up. If we can redraw the line and loop it around these villages, the President will accept it.

Asad: Yes. Yes.

Kissinger: Advancing the red line a little bit.

Asad: Yes.

Kissinger: All I need is a coup d'etat in Israel! And on the Palestinians, you would accept an American public statement saying it is the American interpretation that as part of the cease-fire Israel has the right to protect itself against fedayeen attacks and to take measures to defeat them, or whatever.

Asad: On the basis that this is an American view, not ours.

Kissinger: No, it is an American view. The implication would be that America would support Israel against fedayeen attacks from Syria. As an American statement. You don't have to say anything.

Asad: On the basis that this is an American opinion and that it was not discussed with us.

Kissinger: We will not say we discussed it with you. But we don't want to do it if it ruins Syrian-American relations.

Asad: It won't.

Kissinger: That is a possibility: If we make a public statement to that effect.

Asad: Any statement expressing an American opinion would not adversely affect Syrian-American relations.

Kissinger: All right.

Asad: Since it would not bear any relation to the agreement.

Kissinger: We would say the agreement doesn't prevent that, in our interpretation. It is no Syrian obligation.

Asad: No problem. Of course, Israel naturally has the right to defend itself.

Kissinger: Can we take a half-hour break while I discuss it with my colleagues?

Asad: Yes. At the Guest House?

Kissinger: Where they are. They are there. Can I just come back anytime I'm ready?

Asad: Oh yes.

Kissinger: I'll call you.

Asad: Of course, American forces won't take part against the fedayeen.

Kissinger: Oh no. (Laughter)

Asad: I was joking.

Kissinger: No, I will make a statement publicly there will be no American forces in the Middle East. I will do it within two weeks after I return to America.

Sabbagh: You have great courage.

Kissinger: No, I will volunteer it.

There will be no American troops in the Middle East—except to fight Russian troops. We won't fight Arab troops!

Asad: If there is peace, there is no need for Russian troops.

Kissinger: We are here to disengage, not to engage!

(At 11:25 a.m. Secretary Kissinger departed the Presidential Palace for the Residence, where he conferred with the staff. At 12:35 his private conversation resumed at the Palace with the President:)

Kissinger: I want to have a discussion in principle of what perhaps can be done.

Asad: Yes.

Kissinger: What you are asking for is two very fundamental changes in two very fundamental Israeli positions. One is the red line; the other is—especially in light of recent weeks—the problem of the fedayeen, or however you call it. Now, to sum up my understanding of what the President is saying: If we move the red line some distance towards the blue line—I have to tell him right away that half way will be impossible.

Asad: And the pockets.

Kissinger: And make two pockets, sausages, to include the villages, then the President will accept the red line.

Asad: Yes.

Kissinger: Secondly, if we drop the disguised reference to the fedayeen in the first paragraph, the President will oppose—or to put it another way—it will not affect Syrian-U.S. relations if the United States makes a very strong public—not secret—statement, that it understands that Israel as part of the cease-fire will take measures to protect itself against fedayeen attack.

Asad: "Has the right to."

Kissinger: "Has the right to." And that the United States will support such measures. Politically. We're not talking about militarily.

Asad: On the basis that this subject is not a common stand, and has not been discussed with you.

Kissinger: No, it is a U.S. statement. But we have to have an understanding that the President will not agitate among other Arabs against such a U.S. statement. Obviously you won't agree with it.

Honestly, I have the gravest doubts whether it is possible to succeed with the Israeli Cabinet. But I'm prepared to ask for a meeting of the Israeli Cabinet for 7:00 tonight. But, the only way this can succeed, the only way this can succeed, is that we finish all the documents in a satisfactory manner and that I take all the documents to Israel and say: "This is it; the Syrians accept all this here except the red line."

Asad: There are no other points.

Kissinger: What I would then propose to the President, if he accepts this procedure, is that I leave him again for an hour, then I go over the documents with my colleagues and then I go over them with him.

Asad: There are no big issues. The fortifications.

Kissinger: I want to be absolutely sure there are no disagreements except the red line and the first paragraph. I've already ordered a plane from the U.S. I will have the Israelis put the new lines on a map. I'll have Sisco come up here with the map.

Asad: Taking into account the differences we discussed yesterday.

Kissinger: No, the blue line will be adjusted so it is consistent with the overlay. 500 yards here. (in the Southern sector).

Asad: These three. And here (in the north).

Kissinger: Those three things will be changed in the blue line.

Asad: Four things, as I remember.

Kissinger: Yes, four things. Peter, will you write these down? (He and Asad point them out on the map.) The Kuneitra area. Rafid; five hundred yards. And two points to the south on the blue line.

Sabbagh: Meters.

Kissinger: So there is no misunderstanding, the ten-kilometer zone and the twenty-kilometer zone would be counted from this red line, I mean moved forward a bit.

Asad: Yes.

Kissinger: Good.

Asad: But explain it to them that it's more than ten and more than twenty.

Kissinger: Yes, but I don't want to complicate it. I now propose we take an hour recess. I'll go over the documents with my colleagues. I will then come here with my colleagues. And I agree with you, there shouldn't be much. But let's just get every detail one hundred percent. (Asad nods yes.) Then I can go to the Israelis and say: "It's all concluded; these are the documents, except for those two points." I'll send

Sisco here. Then we can announce tomorrow that it's agreed. Sisco unfortunately won't have the authority to negotiate. It won't be necessary.

Maybe I'll send him in the middle of the night. So he can reach me.

Asad: It is better.

Kissinger: You won't shoot him down!

Asad: We only need thirty minutes.

Kissinger: Then I'll stay in Israel overnight.

Asad: That is better.

Kissinger: That way is best.

Asad: Because after all this time and effort, it shouldn't fail. It would be very bad. Very bad.

Kissinger: I agree. Let me ask one more question. I'm trying to think of everything. Supposing there are hills there, in these two villages. (Laughter) I'm just ...

Asad: I understand.

Kissinger: Would the President authorize me, as a last resort, just as we did with the two hills behind Kuneitra, to give a personal letter to the Israelis that the Syrians will not station guns on top of these hills that will fire into Israeli civilians?

Asad: Yes. Direct?

Kissinger: Yes.

Asad: If there is a hill in front of a village, for instance?

Kissinger: I mean from the top of hills you don't shoot into the settlements. Direct.

Sabbagh: Direct at populated areas.

Kissinger: You can use artillery to shoot from behind.

Asad: Yes.

Kissinger: No weapons that can shoot in a direct line at populated areas.

Asad: Yes.

Kissinger: All right. Now then ...

Asad: This is not necessary to be included in the American proposal to us in writing.

Kissinger: No, no. I write it in a personal letter to the Israelis. "President Asad has assured me ..."

I have two other problems, then I'll take a recess. One, which may be embarrassing to the President, is the Gromyko problem. It would be easier in Israel if it were not presented in Israel as if Gromyko had anything to do with it. I don't care; I really don't care. If he could be delayed until tomorrow, it would be easier. But I don't want to embarrass the President. I won't make an issue of it.

Asad: He may be on his way.

Kissinger: It takes only three hours.

Asad: Now, it would be very embarrassing. It would even appear impolite.

Kissinger: Then don't do it.

Asad: From the point of view of character.

Kissinger: Character. What I want to avoid in America—again I'm speaking as a friend—is if the Israelis are able to make the Syrians appear as a Soviet tool, the second phase will be more difficult. My strategy in America is to say that Syria is difficult, very proud, very independent; it certainly takes Soviet weapons for its own purposes pursuing its own policy; and we cooperate with Syria when Syrian and American interests coincide. And where Syrian and Soviet interests coincide, obviously they cooperate. But it's not a matter of principle with the Syrians.

Asad: This is my opinion too.

Kissinger: That's why I'd like not to have it appear as a concession to the Soviet Union.

Asad: An American concession to the Soviet Union?

Kissinger: What happens tonight. Whatever happens with Gromyko, whatever is discussed, it would be better if it was related to the second phase. You will handle it. If the meetings could take place after Sisco is here, it would be better.

Asad: After Sisco is come and gone.

Kissinger: I'll make him come tonight.

Asad: Sisco must come tonight. If he comes in the morning, what time can he come?

Kissinger: There is a one-hour difference. It may take a little time to prepare the maps.

Asad: If he can't come tonight and if he can only come in the morning, I'd rather he arrive at our airport at 7:30 so he arrives here at 8:00.

Sabbagh: The President will receive him at 8:00.

Kissinger: The trouble is he'd have to leave Jerusalem at 5:30. I'll send him as soon as humanly possible.

Asad: I'll be receiving Gromyko after 10:00 in the morning. If you could make it as early as possible.

Kissinger: If you make it at 11:00, I'll make sure he has come and gone.

Asad: There is no hiding Dr. Kissinger's intense efforts. Every day I'm following your news anyway.

Kissinger: It's a stupid publicity problem. I'm not worried. Anyone who knows the reality . . .

Asad: Even babies.

Kissinger: Babies?

Asad: You're a household name.

Sabbagh: I swear, a friend of mine was telling me, there is a certain sour plum here. His daughter said, get me a couple of Dr. Kissinger's. (Laughter)

Asad: This whole business goes beyond this.

Kissinger: Mr. Scotes has a favorite taxi driver who calls me a prophet, wonderworker. You should introduce him to our press.

Asad: Because these piddly little things won't have any effect.

Kissinger: One other question. When we restore diplomatic relations—whenever that is, one month from now, two months—I want the President's judgment about the choice of Ambassador. My problem is, I could appoint a more senior person, a better known person, or I could appoint Scotes who is a more junior person but is known here. It is not usual to ask the President of another country whom to appoint, but I wanted our relations to be good.

Asad: Number one, the person should have your confidence. Number two, such a person should be objective. In other words, if he's not with us, he shouldn't be against us. He shouldn't be pro-Israel. If he arrives and his emotions are against us from the start, he won't work for an improvement in our relations, and his information will be different from the facts. These are my two qualifications.

Kissinger: How does Scotes fit this?

Asad: Scotes has been in touch with Mr. Elias, with my secretary, with General Shihabi, and with the Foreign Minister, and of course he may be competent.

Kissinger: I will repeat nothing that is said here. I'd like a person who has the confidence of the President. It will certainly be somebody who has my full confidence, because we'll have very sensitive things to discuss.

Asad: Yes.

Kissinger: And it will certainly be somebody who, while representing the American point of view, will be sympathetic to the policy I've outlined.

Asad: That will be better. I only saw Scotes once before yesterday. The impression I got is good. It is good.

Kissinger: I will review all the candidates. If I conclude that he, while junior, is really the best man, you will not consider that an offense to the President?

Asad: No.

Kissinger: I may send somebody else.

Asad: It doesn't really matter to us.

Kissinger: I don't have to exclude Scotes from consideration, in the President's judgment.

Asad: Yes. He gave me the impression he is good.

Kissinger: I can't judge his personal relations, but he writes brilliant reports about Syria. Seriously. The best reports of any Ambassador in an Arab country. Why? Every Ambassador sends reports on what he's told. But he sends me reports every two days—every day when I'm here—about the mood in Damascus: When Arabs say something, what they mean. He did one once—I'll show it to you sometime—about, when Arabs use a mediator, what they expect of him. It proved to be true.

Asad: He'd be the Ambassador.

Kissinger: He'd be called Ambassador. We'd promote him fast. There may be a delay because of regulations, but . . .

Asad: The one we're sending, do you have any requirements?

Kissinger: I want someone who has the President's personal confidence. I thought yesterday that you would want to send somebody anyway for a general exchange. He will see all the exchanges with the Soviets and the Egyptians during the October 6 war. Because we will deal with you honestly. You won't like everything we said. But you knew our strategy.

Why don't we meet in one hour? Then we plan to arrive in Israel at 6:00.

The President understands I haven't any idea Israel will accept this.

Asad: I know. I know.

Kissinger: I don't want to mislead him.

Asad: I know. But the statement about the fedayeen we issued, I trust Dr. Kissinger has seen it.

Kissinger: Yes. It wasn't bad. You had no choice.

(The meeting broke at 1:15 p.m.)

76. Memorandum of Conversation[1]

Jerusalem, May 28, 1974, 12:40–2:30 a.m.

PARTICIPANTS

    Mrs. Golda Meir, Prime Minister of Israel
    Yitzhak Rabin, Minister of Labor and Prime Minister-Designate
    Yigal Allon, Deputy Prime Minister
    Abba Eban, Minister of Foreign Affairs
    Moshe Dayan, Minister of Defense
    Shimon Peres, Minister of Information
    Simcha Dinitz, Ambassador to the United States
    Mordechai Gazit, Director, Prime Minister's Office
    Lt. General Mordechai Gur, Army Chief of Staff
    Avraham Kidron, Director General, Ministry of Foreign Affairs
    Ephraim Evron, Deputy Director General, Ministry of Foreign Affairs
    Col. Aryeh Bar-On, Aide to Dayan
    Eli Mizrachi, Assistant Director, Prime Minister's Office
    Col. Dov Sion
    Lt. General David Leor, Military Assistant to the Prime Minister

    Dr. Henry A. Kissinger, Secretary of State and Assistant to the President for National Security Affairs
    Amb. Kenneth B. Keating, U.S. Ambassador to Israel
    Mr. Joseph J. Sisco, Under Secretary of State for Political Affairs
    Amb. Ellsworth Bunker, Ambassador at Large and Chief U.S. Delegate to Geneva Peace Conference on the Middle East
    Amb. Robert J. McCloskey, Ambassador at Large
    Mr. Alfred L. Atherton, Jr., Assistant Secretary of State for Near Eastern and South Asian Affairs
    Mr. Carlyle E. Maw, Legal Adviser
    Mr. Harold H. Saunders, NSC Senior Staff
    Amb. Robert Anderson, Special Assistant to Secretary for Press Relations
    Mr. Peter W. Rodman, NSC Staff

Secretary Kissinger: The best thing to do is to give you a report chronologically, and what the issues are as they now present themselves.

---

[1] Source: National Archives, RG 59, Records of Henry Kissinger, 1973–77, Box 8, Nodis Memcons, May 1974, Folder 10. Secret; Nodis. The meeting was held at the Prime Minister's office and took place on May 28, not May 27–28 as indicated on the original. Brackets are in the original. Meir and members of the Israeli negotiating team also met with Kissinger on May 28 from 2 until 4 p.m. at the Prime Minister's office after the Israeli Cabinet met and agreed to the text of the agreement with the same minor modifications. However, the Israeli cabinet wanted Kissinger to get an assurance from Asad that Syria would not allow paramilitary groups to operate in Syrian territory and attack Israel. Kissinger agreed to raise the issue with Asad that evening. (Memorandum of conversation; ibid.)

First, last evening I spent about 5½ hours altogether with him, until about 3:00 in the morning.[2] It concerned mostly the Palestinians and the lines and the thinning out. On thinning out—you can't really say "no problem" because that doesn't exist—but it went roughly along the lines we had discussed.

Then we went into the blue line, and he found four discrepancies in your blue line, from the overlay. I told them there was no cheating, and we both had the same overlay. They just put the overlay over your map and it does show some slight discrepancies. Also it doesn't show those 500 yards in the Rafid area. That's one of the four. The other three are just discrepancies produced by the overlay.

Then, on the red line. That produced a horrendous argument. It just wouldn't stop. He called in his military commanders and they went over the red line and wouldn't stop either. They seemed to be arguing with Asad. The basic problem is how can they publish in their newspapers something that has a demilitarized zone in Syrian territory.

Then, the two villages: How could those two villages be forward of the red line.

Then there was an hour's brawl about the Palestinians, and he argued that it was impossible to say anything about the Palestinians. He asked to see me alone, and the others went off with Khaddam to draft the basic documents. I spent two and one half hours with him alone, all designed to get me to sign a private statement that I supported the 1967 borders and the legitimate rights of the Palestinians. I went into a stall and explained why the most we could do was a statement of support for Resolution 338—I didn't mention 242. By that time it was three o'clock in the morning. I met my colleagues who had had a session with Khaddam, who were hung up on every point. There was no issue they weren't hung up on.

So we decided among ourselves that it was finished. We left it at night that we would meet again with Asad at 9:30 a.m. I was so certain we were finished that I told you we could meet at noon.

He called and said he wanted to meet alone. He explained he had a domestic situation as you did. He had told his military commanders he'd get the salient back. It was impossible for them to say anything about the Palestinians. He said this with some eloquence and some emotion. He said he really wanted an agreement.[3]

---

[2] See Document 74.
[3] See Document 75.

So we started drafting—it's my best weapon—my departure statement. It was more or less agreed. We were discussing the President's visit.

Then he said if we really both make an extra effort, could anything be done about the red line? I said I didn't think so. I didn't give him that extra kilometer, because I didn't think it would make any difference.

I did mention, at night, the idea—as my idea—of measuring the distances from the blue line. He said it would help, but not enough.

On the Palestinians, he said he had kept the front quiet in the past and this wasn't his method of fighting. He couldn't do it in a statement. I said that after Ma'alot no American could say anything to the Israelis about terrorism. I said the only thing we could do is leave out the references to "hostile" in the first paragraph, and make a U.S. statement—publicly, not secret—that Israel has a right to take measures against terrorists. And we would support it politically, and by other means. I told him, "We don't have to say you agree to it, but just don't agitate about it."

I'm getting the actual protocol typed up so you can see it.

He said he wouldn't agitate against it. If on the day the agreement is announced, if we could permit the Israeli Government to state the U.S. interpretation of it. I'm not recommending it to you. He only expects me to present it. He said he'd accept this.

He said, "Our basic decision is whether we want to go to war or not. If we do, none of this is going to make any difference."

I said I wanted to consult my colleagues for a half hour. I said, "You tell me what you must have. Then I want to finish the documents. Then I will take the documents to the Israelis, whatever state they're in. Tomorrow I will send Sisco, with no authority, with an Israeli answer. If the Israelis agree, we have an agreement. If the Israelis don't agree, we don't have an agreement. So we should spend the afternoon finishing the documents so we know what Syria will do—not what it might do—and is prepared to sign provided these various adjustments are made." He agreed to this procedure.

His first proposal was to split the difference between the October 6 line and the present red line in the part north of those two bulges. Knowing I had your agreement to that one kilometer, I said I didn't think it was doable. I said some movement west and some "sausages" that would include these two villages. And he would agree I could give you a letter of assurance of his—if the villages were on the hilltops—that no weapons would be there that could fire on a direct line on the settlements, on populated areas. I would get as much movement as possible, plus two fingers to include these two villages.

We then went through the documents. On the basic agreement . . . You would have to read it. I don't think there is a problem, except the first paragraph which doesn't include "paramilitary." But it would go with a public—not secret—assurance. It's basically the agreement we've been working on.

There are a few points left open. They would like to shorten the time of withdrawal, but they left it to me to put in the figure I thought. If you could shave a day or two, it would be good psychology. But Sisco will take it.

He didn't want to phrase the release of prisoners as if disengagement was conditional on release of prisoners. We found this formula: "The prisoners will be released the morning after the conclusion of the work of the Working Group." It's actually less than twenty-four hours. And twenty-four hours after the conclusion of work of the Working Group, disengagement begins. It was 48 hours. We said the major reason for 48 and 24 was so disengagement began afterwards. And he proposed this.

Mrs. Meir: All of them?

Secretary Kissinger: The wounded will be released 24 hours after the signing. If it works out, the signing will be by the 30th. Then by Friday afternoon,[4] the wounded are released. All the remaining prisoners, including the three captured during subsequent events, would be released the morning after signature of the Working Group agreement.

Mrs. Meir: Including the Lebanese?

Secretary Kissinger: The Lebanese we have to do separately. I didn't want him to raise again all the Palestinians imprisoned here. He had said he'd give us a list and hasn't done it yet.

On the Working Group agreement, he wants five days, and will settle for seven. I told him it's up to him to speed it up. From what I've seen, it will take seven months.

Otherwise, I think there are only drafting problems.

Incidentally, they're very sensitive about the word "initialing". Can you avoid saying that on the radio? Can we say "agreement has been reached?" They want, I think, to avoid saying they signed something in the capitals. But they're perfectly happy to say an agreement was reached and will be signed. They're perfectly happy to initial it.

On the United Nations, they agree to a United Nations Disengagement Observer Force.

Mr. Sisco: You remember they had objected to the word "Force;" but they accepted it.

Mrs. Meir: Did they agree to the terms of reference?

---

[4] May 31.

Mr. Sisco: I think you'll find . . .

Mrs. Meir: Now we have UNEF, UNTSO, and UNDOF.

Secretary Kissinger: They wanted to add something about that UNDOF couldn't operate in the towns and villages, which took an hour and a half to get rid of. They did agree to mobile . . .

Mr. Allon: And the right to defend themselves?

Secretary Kissinger: Yes. They agree to 1250.

Ambassador Dinitz: The 50 is for your father!

Secretary Kissinger: Wise guys. I wanted to get 1286, so you would go into a frenzy trying to figure out how I arrived at it.

The UN mandate—there are no policy problems. We'll leave them with you. If there are any policy problems . . .

Now we come to the most difficult one, limitation of forces.

They agree to have it as a U.S. Proposal.

Incidentally, their treatment of Gromyko was unbelievable. Unbelievable. He was supposed to come at 1:00. Then Asad at midnight switched it to 10:00, on the theory that I would be out by then. I told him I didn't want the Soviet plane photographed with my plane. And I didn't want anything to do with him. So they had the Deputy Foreign Minister meet him, and towed his plane way out. And kept him there until my motorcade went. And said Asad won't see him until Joe has left.

Mrs. Meir: TASS says he's going at the request of Asad.

Secretary Kissinger: We don't know what's true. But he's said Gromyko asked.

On the military provisions, we have no problem. They're very good. On the ten-kilometer zone it's precisely described, and will be inspected by the United Nations Disengagement Observer Force. One thing I said—if there is any monkeying with the red line, then the twenty kilometers could not be counted from the October 6 line but everything had to be counted from the red line. And that is now in the agreement. Both the ten- and twenty-kilometer zones are counted from the red line in the agreement. The twenty-kilometer zone is accurately described and there will be no 162 mm. artillery, no SAMs, and so on. This is what we agreed to.

They agreed to put into writing that the United States can do aerial inspection of the provisions of the agreement.

Where we get into massive problems—and what cost me three hours—were the civilians on Mount Hermon and the police in the demilitarized zone. They say they cannot accept anything that implies they don't have jurisdiction over their civilians.

Mrs. Meir: Civilians on Mount Hermon?

Secretary Kissinger: Anything that puts restrictions on what the civilians will do. The maximum they're willing to say on Mount Hermon is, first, that the UNDOF takes over the Mount Hermon area, and no military observation of any kind can be conducted there, and the UN can inspect it. I said what about a shepherd? He said, if the UN thinks he's engaged in observation, it's prohibited.

On the number of police—on the assumption that this document, although secret, will become public—they don't want restrictions on civilian authority. They're willing to say "no police except comparable to those in comparable cities and towns in Syria." They won't put in the number, but they would give me a number for six months, after which if there are more civilians in Kuneitra, it may have to be adjusted. They said I should give them a number.

So there are four policy issues I can identify . . .

Minister Dayan: Did they accept the character of vehicles?

Secretary Kissinger: No armored cars. Not in writing.

You have no idea how long it took to do all of this.

Minister Dayan: What do you mean we have no idea? It's 1:30. [Laughter] We all have watches.

Secretary Kissinger: There are four issues: On "paramilitary," the American public assurance released on the day of the agreement can substitute. Second, what can be done about the red line.

Mrs. Meir: What can be done about the red line *after* the one kilometer?

Secretary Kissinger: Yes. I will show you what he asked for, and what might conceivably work. In my view if he got one kilometer and sausages, that would work.

Mrs. Meir: You offered him the one kilometer?

Secretary Kissinger: No. I think the one kilometer and sausages . . . He asked for half the distance, so I think a little more than one kilometer. We should calibrate what can carry it, and I'd give you my best judgment.

Terrorism, the red line, Mount Hermon, and police.

Mrs. Meir: What does he want with civilians on Mount Hermon?

Secretary Kissinger: He doesn't want civilians on Mount Hermon; he doesn't want to say the United Nations is the only and exclusive presence on Mount Hermon. That would take Mount Hermon away from Syria. He said, "what is it that worries the Israelis?" I said, "observation from there." So he said there will be no military observation and the UN can inspect.

So where we are is this: What will gain acceptance is these documents and whatever we can work out.

Mrs. Meir: Is the language on "first step" the same as in the Egyptian agreement?

Secretary Kissinger: Yes.

Minister Eban: Except the "Geneva Conference."

Secretary Kissinger: I didn't think we needed that.

Minister Eban: It's their business to ask for it.

Secretary Kissinger: My view is it's Gromyko's strategy to go back to Geneva, to raise the Palestinian issue, to raise the most comprehensive issues. My strategy—of course with your agreement, which we should discuss—is to turn Geneva into a talkfest.

The UN charter and the basic agreement—you make the judgment on "paramilitary"—are in my judgment signable.

We have to discuss the red line.

Minister Dayan: Why did they agree for Kuneitra to be in the demilitarized zone, but in two villages, to have forces there? What is the reasoning?

Secretary Kissinger: The first is, Kuneitra is a new acquisition and that he can explain. The other two villages, he says: It is one thing to lose control from 1967 on, everyone is used to it. Now when the people look at the map, they'll say he's given up more territory. He wants some military there. "Sausages" is his word.

Mrs. Meir: What is his concept of military forces in the villages?

Secretary Kissinger: They would be under the 6,000-man ceiling. He did agree not to station weapons in these villages that have a direct line to your settlements.

Mrs. Meir: Are they on the hills?

General Gur: Yes. The trouble is they're both very close to our positions. Eight hundred yards. Between these villages and our positions. That's why I don't think ...

Secretary Kissinger: He says if you're worried about observation ...

General Gur: The observations he can do with civilians.

Secretary Kissinger: Yes.

[Gur shows on the map.][5]

General Gur: The last houses to the west are 800 yards from our positions. To make the sausage like that is very complicated.

Secretary Kissinger: My own estimation is this: If we can straighten this a little bit and say this is it, he'll take it.

General Gur: That's a political matter.

---

[5] The map is not attached, but a final status map is printed in Appendix B, map 2.

Secretary Kissinger: I can't go up there again, and Joe can't negotiate.

Mr. Sisco: I'm glad.

Secretary Kissinger: I don't think it's in our interest to get into another haggle. We should go up and say this is it.

I'm assuming on the overlay there is no problem.

He also asked for a 1:25,000 map.

General Gur: We have one.

Secretary Kissinger: We also need one of the old kind, but the official map will be 1:25,000.

I think we should check the overlay now. I told them there was no attempt to cheat them.

Mrs. Meir: Especially since they caught on.

Secretary Kissinger: I don't think it's a substantive point. We're talking about 200 yards here and there.

General Gur: In favor of whom?

Secretary Kissinger: They say it's all in your favor. Then there were the 500 yards. They're haggling also for a few hundred meters also on the Mount Hermon red line, saying you'd drawn it where they already are.

Mrs. Meir: Mr. Sisco tomorrow can go to Mount Hermon.

Mr. Sisco: She's suggesting I go to Hermon.

Mrs. Meir: It's beautiful.

Secretary Kissinger: This is where we stand. If we change the red line, we can send Sisco up and show it to them. One kilometer here—that's the minimum we can show them.

Minister Dayan: It may be too late. If there is a question of interpretation of the agreement, can there be an agreement on who is authorized to interpret the agreement?

Mrs. Meir: Interpretation of what?

Minister Dayan: Any paragraph of the agreement. If there are differences of opinion, there used to be in the Armistice Agreements that the Chairman of the Mixed Armistice Commission would do it.

Secretary Kissinger: There is no provision in the Egyptian agreement. Seeing these people work, we have this choice. If there is a clause that's manageable, we can risk it.

My judgment is, if we can give them one of these sausages, the other might go.

On the text of the agreement, I'd under no circumstances, unless it was overwhelmingly important, raise a new paragraph. And they would raise a new paragraph. And Joe can't negotiate it, or shouldn't negotiate it. And we'd go on forever.

It seems to me the basic decision is to go ahead.

Let me say, first of all: You've gone a long way. If you decide against it, no one on the American side will feel you were unreasonable, so that shouldn't enter into it. What should enter into it is the basic merits of the consequences of an agreement against the consequences of no agreement, with a country whose basic reliability is uncertain but whose reliability is no more certain without the agreement.

Minister Eban: What is the nature of the American undertaking on terrorism?

Secretary Kissinger: The United States will declare that the first paragraph of the agreement gives Israel the right to take measures in self-defense against irregular attacks across the demarcation line, that if Israel takes such measures, the United States will support Israel. He asked me "militarily?" I said politically, but the U.S. will support Israel. And publicly, because you'll say it in the Knesset. If this is breached by the fedayeen and Israel retaliates, the United States would feel obliged to veto a resolution in the UN that condemns Israel.

Minister Dayan: You mentioned before that your interpretation of the first clause would include also paramilitary. It's your interpretation but not his.

Secretary Kissinger: I would say we interpret the first paragraph to mean that it in no way precludes Israel's right of self-defense against irregular attacks.

Minister Dayan: But you don't interpret it as binding the Syrians against letting terrorists across but you do interpret it as allowing Israel to fight it. It's a cease-fire but ...

Secretary Kissinger: I think it's in our interest to do something that the Syrians will not do a rejoinder to. We have a promise that the Syrians will not rejoinder.

Mr. Allon: Otherwise it allows the guerrillas to fight and us to fight. That we don't want.

Minister Eban: If self-defense is legitimate, the thing against which you defend yourself is illegitimate.

Mrs. Meir: There will be some reference to Article 1.

Secretary Kissinger: What we have is what I read to you.

Mr. Allon: This could be read as permission to the guerrillas.

Ambassador Dinitz: You say you don't consider the Israeli action a violation, but you don't say you consider the Syrian action a violation of the ceasefire.

Mrs. Meir: The reason we held your lunch up one hour on Sunday[6] was for Cabinet discussion of this. None of us can change this final position of the Cabinet. So, tomorrow we will have a Cabinet meeting at 9:00.

Secretary Kissinger: Could it be earlier?

Mrs. Meir: Eight-thirty.

Minister Dayan: The question is not when it begins but when it ends!

Secretary Kissinger: We have a concrete problem, which is that Asad promised not to see Gromyko until Sisco has been there—but that won't hold the whole day.

[They discuss notifying the Cabinet members now of a change in the time of the meeting.]

Secretary Kissinger: Should we reformulate the assurance now? So you'll have it.

Mrs. Meir: Yes.

Mr. Allon: I wonder if a few sentences excluded from the agreement could be in the American assurance?

Secretary Kissinger: I agree it should be expressed positively.

Minister Eban: There is no need to use euphemisms in the American statement.

Secretary Kissinger: We shouldn't use "paramilitary" because that caused ... Can you say "raids by armed groups or individuals across the cease-fire line are violations, and Israeli action in self-defense ..."?

Minister Eban: The words "self-defense" are terribly important in our context.

Secretary Kissinger: I told him that a private assurance was not enough.

Mrs. Meir: We've committed ourselves to the Knesset. They wanted us to bring it before any signing. We refused, because under our law we have the right to negotiate. But between the initialing and signing, we committed ourself. Does he know this?

Secretary Kissinger: He knows this. Your radio has said ... Can you do anything about the radio?

Mrs. Meir: We can change the red line, the blue line, but not the radio.

Minister Rabin: Not the radio line.

---

[6] May 26.

Secretary Kissinger: Can you stop discussing what the issues are? Radio Israel broadcast four times that I went there to discuss the fedayeen issue. This cost us one hour.

Minister Peres: For twenty-four hours we can do something.

Secretary Kissinger: They don't insist on initialing. They're willing to make an announcement tomorrow or Wednesday that agreement has been reached and will be signed. I told them you needed a day for the Knesset.

Assuming we can get the red line accepted and get Sisco off, then tomorrow we can have an announcement. How long would the Cabinet take? With Gromyko there.

Mrs. Meir: I've cut people off.

Secretary Kissinger: I suggest letting Sisco leave at noon at Ben-Gurion. That means not seeing Asad until 2:30, but that's all we can do.

Minister Dayan: The BBC says there will be 70,000 going back to Kuneitra.

Secretary Kissinger: He says he wants 20–30,000 there but first he has to send people there to clear the rubble. Seventy-thousand looks very high to me.

Minister Rabin: What is the number of policemen there?

Secretary Kissinger: I have to give him a figure. When I said 75, they had a heart attack.

Mr. Allon: A positive result anyway.

Secretary Kissinger: They said they'd accept the same number you had in Tiberias.

Minister Dayan: And the same class too.

Mrs. Meir: Unless they sleep in the street, he can't bring 25,000 people into Kuneitra.

Secretary Kissinger: He's expected some figure other than 75. I don't think 25 more or less, or 50 more or less, will determine the fate of this agreement. If he goes to war, he won't do it with policemen. Please be a little generous, since he invited me to give the figure.

I'll give Dinitz the American resolution.

Ambassador Dinitz: We need the documents, the points.

Secretary Kissinger: If you think these documents aren't satisfactory, you can reject them. But these are the best that could be achieved. No one who hasn't experienced it knows what it's like. To the extent that the defects can be solved by American assurances, assume they can be done.

Minister Dayan: The definition of what they want on Mount Hermon.

Secretary Kissinger: "No military observation of any kind will be permitted." "Of any kind."

Mr. Allon: And the UN will determine.

Secretary Kissinger: Yes.

Minister Dayan: What is demilitarization?

Mr. Sisco: There is a sentence, that also refers to Mount Hermon.

Secretary Kissinger: "The area of separation between line A and line B will be demilitarized." Then there is a separate paragraph which reads, "The United Nations Disengagement Observer Force will take over the positions in the Mount Hermon area. No military observation . . ."

Minister Dayan: Observation and personnel.

Secretary Kissinger: No observation of any kind, not just military personnel. They wanted "no military observation posts." We rejected that. It doesn't say by whom. It's the best we could get. On Mount Hermon their normal frenzy is heightened.

May I suggest my feel for what they want on the red line.

[They get up and look at the maps.]

Since he made a number of these points in front of his military commanders, whether he wins or loses has some significance.

If you can shave anything here, two hundred yards.

He claims his forces are 300 yards from the peak; that you're cheating him, and he says to write into the agreement that the UN will determine the red line by military positions. I didn't accept that because it would start the damnedest brawl on top of Mount Hermon.

Mrs. Meir: It's a dangerous place!

Secretary Kissinger: Shave a few hundred yards here.

Mrs. Meir: Did you ever see the 1947 map with the kissing points?

Secretary Kissinger: Yes.

Mrs. Meir: Three people were killed there yesterday.

Secretary Kissinger: It will certainly stop with the signing.

I can send a message. But I'm not going there again.

Mrs. Meir: But it is possible that the Cabinet will not accept the sausage.

Mr. Allon: It's not Kosher.

Secretary Kissinger: Then it may fail.

Mrs. Meir: But can I say to the Cabinet—what drives people mad is, we are on the way to Geneva, and with the shooting going on.

Mr. Allon: While debating in the Cabinet, with the shooting going on.

Secretary Kissinger: Please give Sisco a minimum of messages. I believe it will probably be agreeable. I didn't mention it today. I'll have Sisco mention it tomorrow. It is a reasonable proposal.

Mr. Gazit: It's what the Egyptians did.

Secretary Kissinger: That's the worst possible argument.

Minister Peres: In the American declaration, will it say "military and paramilitary?"

Secretary Kissinger: I don't think we should use the word "paramilitary."

Minister Eban: I think "paramilitary" is bad.

Minister Peres: What do you have?

Secretary Kissinger: "Crossing by armed groups or individuals..."

Minister Peres: Yes.

Secretary Kissinger: I think that is the way it should be phrased. It shouldn't mention fedayeen or paramilitary. Use Aubrey's phrase.

Minister Eban: "Crossing by armed groups or individuals." "Crossings and armed attacks."

Secretary Kissinger: "Armed attacks across the demarcation line by groups or individuals." For whatever it's worth, this one kilometer will not do it on the red line. A little more than that one kilometer, and if at all possible, a very thin sausage.

[Sisco and Kissinger show the overlay and blue line to Gur.]

Secretary Kissinger: On their map it didn't touch the old blue line.

General Gur: They're right.

Secretary Kissinger: What should we say to the press? At Damascus I said President Asad and I discussed all aspects of disengagement and I would send Sisco back to Damascus.

Minister Rabin: You didn't say the specific issues.

Secretary Kissinger: On the plane, on background, I did say that the thinning out and the UN are essentially settled—which is true—but I gave no figures.

Minister Peres: That is a problem, because they'll speculate.

Minister Rabin: Let them speculate.

Mrs. Meir: The Secretary brought us considerations from Damascus, the Cabinet will meet tomorrow for a final decision, and we will give you an answer.

Secretary Kissinger: I did say that some drafts exist with disagreed points.

Minister Peres: That is a problem. Because our press will speculate on the Palestinian issue. Here we must deviate.

Secretary Kissinger: Can't you have your press shut up about the Palestinian issue for 24 hours?

Minister Peres: I can try and ask them to not speculate about the Palestinian issue.

[The meeting then ended.]

---

77. Memorandum of Conversation[1]

Damascus, May 28, 1974, 8:15 p.m.–midnight.

PARTICIPANTS

    Hafiz al-Asad, President of Syria
    'Abd al-Halim Khaddam, Deputy Prime Minister and Minister of Foreign Affairs
    General Mustafa Tlas, Minister of Defense
    General Najd Tamil, Air Force Chief of Staff
    Brigadier Hikmat Shihabi, Chief of Army Intelligence
    Press Adviser Elias

    Dr. Henry A. Kissinger, Secretary of State and Assistant to the President for National Security Affairs
    Joseph J. Sisco, Under Secretary of State for Political Affairs
    Alfred L. Atherton, Jr., Assistant Secretary of State for Near Eastern and South Asian Affairs
    Harold H. Saunders, NSC Senior Staff
    Robert Anderson, Special Assistant to the Secretary for Press Relations
    Isa Sabbagh, Interpreter
    Peter W. Rodman, NSC Staff

[The Secretary and President Asad conferred alone from 8:15–10:50 p.m. At this point, the larger group was admitted and introduced.]

Kissinger: Our two Syrian friends, while Gromyko was here,[2] were waiting for the love call of the Siberian woodbird. They have never heard it.

Asad: He only sings it in your presence. [Laughter]

Kissinger: Wait for his departure statement! [Laughter]

---

[1] Source: Library of Congress, Manuscript Division, Kissinger Papers, CL 194, Geopolitical File; Middle East, Peace Negotiations, Israeli-Syrian Relations, Negotiation Books, Volume III, March–May 1974. The meeting was held at the Presidential Palace in Damascus. Brackets are in the original.

[2] Gromyko arrived in Damascus on May 27.

Khaddam: They have a draft joint Syrian-Soviet communiqué all ready. It will have to depend: I have waited to see how this goes before I decide what it will be.

Kissinger: Are you trying to blackmail me?

Asad: Not at all. [Laughter]

Kissinger: Does it mention imperialism?

Khaddam: Imperialism, Zionism, and reaction. [Laughter]

Kissinger: What do you do when Saqqaf comes here?

Khaddam: The one who attacks imperialism and reactionaries the most at meetings is Saqqaf! [Laughter] I will show you the memcons.

Kissinger: I thought the Foreign Minister has an all-purpose communiqué, and he just fills in the blanks.

Asad: The question of prisoners remains. They haven't sent a complete list of prisoners.

Kissinger: I'll take care of that tonight.

Asad: Including the PLA.

Kissinger: I'll talk to them tonight.

Asad: And about those in the Israeli jails? There are four or five.

Kissinger: You were going to give me a list.

[Asad summons an aide.]

I'm getting worried about getting back to Israel.

Asad: We can sit down. I'm worried about your lover Gromyko.

Kissinger: We'll depart the airport in an hour and fifteen minutes. [Sisco goes out to make these arrangements.] I need an hour or two in Israel. I'll just skip Gromyko. I don't have the time.

[The group goes in to dinner. They are joined at dinner by Minister of Defense Mustafa Tlas, Air Force Chief of Staff Najd Tamil, Press Adviser Elias, and Chief of Army Intelligence Brigadier Hikmat Shihabi.]

Kissinger: The Foreign Minister planned this dinner so I would miss Gromyko.

Asad: There is a phenomenon today that warrants attention—that Dr. Kissinger didn't want Mr. Sisco to come here alone!

Kissinger: I wasn't afraid he'd fail—I was afraid he'd succeed. [Laughter]

Asad: We're witnessing an historic fact. Sisco is born for achievement. Perhaps if you would let him, he would do great things.

Kissinger: It's an epic poem. [Laughter] He got it from the Defense Minister. As long as this group lives, it will know it has done something that has not been done in 6,000 years of recorded history: There has never been an organization called UNDOF. [Laughter]

Asad: These were my sentiments yesterday.

Kissinger: I've never heard the Defense Minister's poetry.

Shihabi: I have; the difference in comprehension is the same. [Laughter]

Sisco: The Israeli Chief of Staff writes children's books.

Tlas: He's planting in the minds of children hatred of the Arabs.

Asad: They are not military?

Shihabi: I have read it.

Kissinger: I have not. General Tlas recites his own, or others' poetry?

Asad: He knows very much poetry. But he's the author of a book on guerrilla warfare. The trouble is the fedayeen are attempting to apply his book. [Laughter]

Kissinger: On the Lebanese front.

Khaddam: The Israelis in 1969 in a raid in southern Lebanon captured 50 copies of General Tlas's book. They said they'd captured General Tlas! They'd captured only his book. [Laughter] This reveals their evil intentions! We should have his name on our list of prisoners they hold.

Sisco: The press says you and Gromyko met last night at the airport.

Khaddam: How often have you met him?

Kissinger: Five to six times a year. I make jokes about him but he is very able.

Tlas: There is a story about a Khalif whose court poets were sticklers for meter and dividing up meter precisely. That's why Dr. Kissinger wanted the poem in the agreement!

[The Defense Minister then recited a nonsense poem in Arabic which Isa Sabbagh insisted was impossible to translate.]

Sisco: It sounds like the chirping of birds.

Kissinger: Then Khaddam should recite it to Gromyko. [Laughter]

[At 11:45 the group reconvenes in the meeting room and Asad shows the map to his generals. The Army Chief of Staff Shakkour, and other generals come in. The generals take a copy of the map across the room to another table and study it. Secretary Kissinger, President Asad, Minister Khaddam and Under Secretary Sisco confer on the procedural details.]

[The President and Secretary Kissinger then agreed on the text of the following announcement:

"The discussions conducted by U.S. Secretary of State Dr. Henry A. Kissinger with the Syrians and the Israelis have led to an agreement on the disengagement of Syrian and Israeli forces. The agreement will be signed in the Egyptian-Israeli Military Working Group of the Geneva Conference on Friday, May 31, 1974 in Geneva."]

[They agreed it would be released at 7:00 p.m. Damascus time, 6:00 p.m. Jerusalem time, and at 12:00 noon Washington time.]

[President Asad gives Secretary Kissinger the names of the PLA prisoners held in Israel.]

Kissinger: I will raise it as a personal question.

Asad: Some time ago we released the people who had been in jail accused of cooperating with the Israelis. Those are some accused of cooperation with us. They are a mixture of Syrians and Druzes.

Kissinger: I will raise it with them.

The announcement of the fact of the agreement will be made tomorrow in Washington, and you can pick it up. [Asad nods yes.]

If there is no way of stopping publication, then the agreement, the protocol, and the map will be public at 8:00 a.m. Thursday Damascus time. The U.S. proposal will not be published.

Asad: No, it will not.

Kissinger: It will remain secret.

Asad: It will not even be referred to.

Kissinger: I will send you tomorrow the map.

Asad: 1/25000.

Kissinger: Yes, late in the afternoon, and one of the letters, broken down into two. I'll say "These are the letters, and we will get you the original." And if there are any questions about the other, send it back and we will rewrite it. It will be done in a way that strengthens our relations.

And there is a good chance the President will be coming here and that will be a good time to discuss it. It may be the best time to give it to you.

Asad: When will it be?

Kissinger: In about two weeks.

I have to get back to Israel. I may not be able to convince them. There is one consideration we discussed. But I am hopeful. The texts we don't have to worry about.

I'd better see Gromyko for ten minutes. I'll meet the Foreign Minister at the Guest House afterwards. Or I'll sing out a love call. [Laughter]

[The Secretary and Mr. Sisco thereupon departed for a courtesy call on Soviet Foreign Minister Gromyko.]

78. Memorandum of Conversation[1]

Jerusalem, May 29, 1974, 2:45–3:45 a.m.

PARTICIPANTS

Mrs. Golda Meir, Prime Minister of Israel
Yitzhak Rabin, Minister of Labor and Prime-Minister-designate
Yigal Allon, Deputy Prime Minister
Abba Eban, Minister of Foreign Affairs
Moshe Dayan, Minister of Defense
Shimon Peres, Minister of Information
Simcha Dinitz, Ambassador to the United States
Mordechai Gazit, Director, Prime Minister's Office
Lt. Gen. Mordechai Gur, Army Chief of Staff
Avraham Kidron, Director General, Ministry of Foreign Affairs
Ephraim Evron, Deputy Director General, Ministry of Foreign Affairs
Col. Aryeh Bar-On, Aide to Dayan
Eli Mizrachi, Assistant Director, Prime Minister's Office
Col. Dov Sion
Lt. Gen. David Leor, Military Assistant to the Prime Minister

Dr. Henry A. Kissinger, Secretary of State and Assistant to the President for National Security Affairs
Ambassador Kenneth B. Keating, U.S. Ambassador to Israel
Mr. Joseph J. Sisco, Under Secretary of State for Political Affairs
Ambassador Ellsworth Bunker, Ambassador at Large and Chief U.S. Delegate to Geneva Peace Conference on the Middle East
Ambassador Robert J. McCloskey, Ambassador at Large
Mr. Carlyle E. Maw, Legal Adviser
Mr. Harold H. Saunders, National Security Council Senior Staff
Ambassador Robert Anderson, Special Assistant to the Secretary for Press Relations
Mr. Peter W. Rodman, National Security Council Staff

Kissinger: Let me report on my meeting with Asad.[2] It took 4½ hours. I won't go into all the issues but just the central issues.

There was an endless discussion about the red line. He took violent exception to the fact what he said about foreign troops appeared in *Ha'aretz* and the Arabic service of Kol Yisrael.[3] He said it was impossible to have confidence in Israel.

---

[1] Source: National Archives, RG 59, Records of Henry Kissinger, 1973–77, Box 8, Nodis Memcons, May 1974, Folder 10. Secret; Nodis. The meeting was held at the Prime Minister's office in Jerusalem, and took place on May 29, not May 28–29 as indicated on the original. Brackets are in the original. Kissinger met with Meir right before this meeting from 2:10 until 2:45 a.m. at the Prime Minister's office. (Memorandum of conversation; ibid.)

[2] See Document 77.

[3] *Ha'aretz* is an Israeli daily newspaper and Kol Yisrael is an Israeli public radio service.

Let me talk about the fedayeen. I told him, first, ... frankly, I went there in order to be able to construct a letter to you saying that I told him what Israel's concerns were and that he understood them. I told the Prime Minister before I went what I thought was attainable.

I told him first what I was going to say publicly: If there are attacks across the line, the ceasefire can't survive. If the line turns into a fedayeen front, I, as the one who took the responsibility for getting Israel this far, couldn't ask them to take the last step unless I knew what his intentions were.

I talked to him only with my interpreter; there was no one else there. I asked my interpreter to write down the essence of the conversation as he understood it, and I made some notes as he was talking. And I also told him I couldn't allow 25,000 civilians returning to Kuneitra and then have it turn into a fedayeen base.

First, he made a long explanation of why the question of the Palestinians is a particular problem for Syria. First, as a people without a country, without identity, without support from the world community—Damascus as the center of Arab nationalism couldn't dissociate itself publicly from them.

"There is a feeling of despair among them which leads to certain radical actions, some of which can be tempered by moderate elements with whom Syria is in contact." I said I had to repeat again that it was not consistent with the cease-fire. He said, "We have committed ourselves to the cease-fire; we will be extremely careful about border areas. Specifically, there will be no firing across the lines by anyone. There is no possibility for organized armed bands to cross into Israel. No fedayeen can be stationed in the front areas. We can't guarantee against individuals sneaking through, but we can insure they won't start from the border areas." He said these are assurances he gives me.

This is from my interpreter's notes. I checked it with my own notes, that said the same thing. "Crossing won't happen." "Groups will not cross." "Individuals might cross—they are harder to stop."

Mrs. Meir: I understand you told him you'd convey it to us.

Kissinger: Yes, but he cannot. This is what he tells me. If it becomes public, it will be very difficult.

Allon: This is going to be in a letter from Asad to you. This is part of the protocol.

Kissinger: No. That's all it is.

Allon: It was an oral conversation of which minutes were taken?

Kissinger: Yes.

Mrs. Meir: That you'll convey to us, in addition to a public statement.

[Silence]

Mrs. Meir: Israelis don't talk?

Allon: A change!

Eban: That is obviously the maximum we're going to get on this issue, and we're going to meet and decide tomorrow.

[Silence]

Kissinger: The thing I find amazing is yesterday I was asked to bring back a paper saying I told him and he understood it.[4] Now I bring back that he spells it out in great detail and more than I ever expected.

Peres: You asked us to keep quiet, and we have. [Laughter]

Keating [to Peres]: You did very skillfully avoiding the details on TV.

Peres: That's my profession.

Allon: Of course, when one compares this to what we were given yesterday, there is progress. The only problem is, if eventually—as is bound to happen—this sort of thing leaks out, he will deny it. This is an open security.

Kissinger: I would have thought if a responsible Israeli cared about substance rather than publicity, he'd keep it secret. Unless it's violated, which is a different problem.

I was told this agreement was legitimizing terrorism—the stranger it seemed as I thought about it. You won't take this position; you'll have an American public statement; and third, you have these assurances in infinitely more detail than expected.

Dayan: Can we get a letter from you that you have reason to believe the Syrians so and so? The Syrian understanding of the cease-fire has no crossing, etc.

Kissinger: I'm prepared to put what I have here in a letter to the Prime Minister, and to add that if there is a violation, the U.S. would feel an obligation to call it to account. But as a secret letter.

Dayan: The Prime Minister will be asked what is the Syrian attitude. Can she say in public she has reason to believe Syrians understand the cease-fire means no crossing?

Kissinger: They've promised not to rebut my public statement. They're very sensitive to seem to have colluded with you against the Palestinians.

If you can omit the Syrians. Say "assurances" as if it is additional American assurances.

Mrs. Meir: I will say in rebuttal to Begin and Sharon that it is inconceivable the U.S. will say this to us without having reason to believe it.

---

[4] See Document 76.

Kissinger: You can say it's inconceivable they would say these to us without saying this to others as well. Because it's a public statement. You can say there are assurances as long as you don't mention Syria.

Dayan: Can she say she has assurances that it is the only interpretation of the cease-fire?

Mrs. Meir: It is inconceivable you would authorize us to read out such a statement without a basis for it.

Kissinger: You want to say you've been given additional assurances?

Mrs. Meir: Can we say that to the Knesset? That would be good.

Kissinger: They promise not to rebut. Maybe they won't keep their promise.

Mrs. Meir [to Dayan]: Moshe, to the Foreign Affairs Committee we have to get all the details.

Kissinger: If it leaks before signing, it will blow skyhigh.

Dayan: On TV last night they had the whole agreement—numbers, forces, everything.

Peres: It was from *Ha'aretz*. They left out only the Palestinians.

Dayan: But if it leaks it won't be an official leak.

Eban: Suppose it is signed Friday afternoon.[5]

Dayan: The Prime Minister can say further details were given to the Committee.

Mrs. Meir: Oh yes, I wouldn't say any more.

Dayan: If you said that besides the American letter further details will be given to the Foreign Affairs Committee ...

Kissinger: That would be by far the best.

Dayan: See what happens to me at 3:00!

Kissinger: You have a good idea.

Keating: That doesn't solve the problem of a leak from the Committee.

Kissinger: That you have anyway.

Dayan: No one from the Committee will do it officially.

Mrs. Meir: Because this is security, pure security, can't there be censorship?

Gur: I was discussing this just before with the spokesman and the official censor. The answer is no. Especially if it will be published abroad.

Kissinger: But the secret letter never will.

---

[5] May 31.

Allon: Other foreign papers print it and the next morning ours pretend to copy it.

Mrs. Meir: We will do everything possible.

Kissinger: That's all you can do.

Mrs. Meir: And will say further details will be given to the Committee.

Dayan: Last time we did eventually give them documents, so we can manage it.

Mrs. Meir: We'll think it over. One thing you can be sure is that we'll do everything possible.

Kissinger: I am confident.

Allon: Once you say there are further details, the entire public and press will search for what they are.

Mrs. Meir: "All details have been brought to the Foreign Affairs Committee."

Dinitz: I value very much if we move the signature to Thursday.

Mrs. Meir: We discussed that before.

Kissinger: The first problem is, when will we know when the Cabinet has decided?

Mrs. Meir: We meet at 7:30 in the morning.

Gur: In four hours.

Kissinger: What will the Cabinet announce? It can't say an agreement has been reached. Unless you want to be killed in Washington, and in Damascus.

Allon: What do you want us to say?

Kissinger: That we will convey the answer to Damascus and await their reply, and there will be a later announcement.

Dayan: There was an announcement from Damascus that an agreement was reached on the principles, but someone was left behind to complete the work.

Kissinger: I made no statement.

Dayan: This was a Syrian statement.

Kissinger: That was not unhelpful.

Allon: Let's say "we are very close to a successful conclusion to the negotiations and are expecting further clarification, and in a few hours we will make an announcement."

Kissinger: On the signing, if we are going to consider signing Thursday, we have got to get a lot of things moving fast.

Sisco: It is technically possible.

Kissinger: Asad would welcome it because he was very unhappy to publish the documents a day and a half before the signing. He didn't want a debate in Syria before it was signed. Therefore, he implored me to implore you to have the Knesset session secret. [Laughter]

His concerns are to get the documents—the Agreement, the UN protocol and map—published only on the day of the signing. Second, he wishes not to have the U.S. proposal published. Third, he has the difficulties I have read to you. So these are his concerns.

If we are thinking of signing Thursday, we had better get a cable off to him today. Then the documents will be public.

When you bring something to the Knesset, how do you do it?

Mrs. Meir: A speech.

Kissinger: You don't hand it? I think he would most prefer to get them published after the signature.

Mrs. Meir: That is impossible. We could send our delegation to Geneva Thursday, with instructions that they don't sign until they get the signal after the Knesset debate. The debate will be . . .

Peres: 10 hours. [All say no]

Mrs. Meir: If it is a four-hour debate, it means six hours. I have to introduce the debate, and someone has to close it, and that is not included. Then there is a vote.

We can start at 11:00.

Peres: Even 10:00.

Mrs. Meir: If it starts at 11:00, it will finish at 5:00 p.m.

Dinitz: Which is 4:00 Geneva time.

Mrs. Meir: Our people will be there, so they don't have to travel.

Kissinger: Then we'd better get a cable off to Asad tonight that in view of his great concern that the documents will be published the same day, we should have it Thursday. It should help his concerns.

Mrs. Meir: When do we get the wounded?

Kissinger: Twenty-four hours after. The other prisoners are released the morning after.

Mrs. Meir: I got permission from Burg [the NRP Minister][6] for even doing it Saturday.

Five o'clock Geneva time, 6 o'clock here.

Gazit: That is too tight.

Kissinger: Six o'clock Geneva time.

Joe, you realize none of this can be set in motion until tomorrow afternoon. Can we do it?

Sisco: Yes.

---

[6] Yosef Burg was a founding member of the National Religious Party (NRP).

Maw: We can have the mechanics done.

Dinitz: It will be a secret covenant openly arrived at.

Sisco: You'll have to send a cable shortly before the announcement.

Mrs. Meir: Do the UN people go from New York?

Sisco: They have people there.

Kissinger: What worries me is . . .

Eban: What difference is it if there is a flurry in Geneva on a contingency basis?

Kissinger: It is a concern to people I have to worry about. Simcha can explain.

Mrs. Meir: It is only Wednesday.

Kissinger: I'll send a cable to Asad tonight. We'll have an answer by the time a Cabinet decision is made.

Sisco is a national hero in Syria since I made the joke that he is out to get my job.

They postponed the dinner for Gromyko every two hours, then they cancelled.

Dinitz: That is why Gromyko was so unpleasant.

Kissinger: Gromyko was . . . very worrisome. He made a violent speech on the Palestinians, worse than anything Asad has made at his worst. On the other hand, he was playing a very pathetic role there.

Allon: According to the press, he had a meeting with Arafat there.

Kissinger: Yes.

Allon: This may explain his interest in that.

Kissinger: No, the Russian strategy is to get everything to Geneva, to lump everything together, to pick an issue on which the U.S. can't do anything for the Arabs and on which other Arabs have to support them, in order to push us out of our role. That is the Russian strategy.

Mrs. Meir: I want to tell you, since we are exchanging compliments around the table, I feel terribly guilty, since we urged you to go to Damascus.

Kissinger: It was worth it. I was dubious but it was the right thing to do.

Keating: Asad kissed Sisco tonight.

Kissinger: You will then make an announcement that at least leaves the final decision open.

Gur: There should be a working group tomorrow about the maps.

Kissinger: Oh yes. I promised I would send up your map with 1:25000 [scale].

Gur: It is done already. There is a difference between the Syrian map and our map. So there should be a working group. Sisco and

Motta Mottke [Gazit] should sit with Dovele [Sion]. There is a difference in the old purple line. This is a difference we had before. But it has no importance regarding the changes we did now.

Kissinger: They are eager to get the map. I told him any discussions about it should take place in the Military Working Group. But he said he would appreciate having it in Damascus—not in Geneva—before his Generals left.

Sisco: These copies are different?

Gur: Because it is on our map.

Kissinger: But I understand this doesn't affect areas affected by this negotiation. It is between you and the Syrians. As long as the Rafid salient doesn't disappear.

Dinitz: There was one sentence in the U.S. Proposal.

Kissinger: They wanted the same language in the Agreement as in the U. S. Proposal. It should say, "will not have any military forces" instead of "demilitarized." One, to have the same language, and second, because they say it translates badly. Everything else remains exactly the same.

The Syrians are sending a General and a Colonel.

The U. S. Proposal will be signed by their Chief of Staff, the U. S. Proposal about the thinning out. Their Chief of Staff will sign it in Damascus. Our Chief of our Interests Section will deliver the signed document to him.

Mrs. Meir: All documents will be signed by military. Is that right?

Kissinger: Yes. The one in Geneva will be signed by a General. The thinning-out agreement, the U.S. Proposal, will be signed by the Chief of Staff in Damascus.

Dinitz: In the Egyptian agreement, the President signed it.

Kissinger: They want to treat it as a military document. I had it at the Foreign Minister's level but Khaddam protested so violently that he wasn't the competent official on thinning out.

Dayan: The Red Cross should be alerted.

Kissinger: The wounded will be exchanged 24 hours after the signing. I've got the names of four Arabs he wants released. They look like hard cases.

Dayan: I have four Arabs I want to give him. Maybe the same ones!

Kissinger: They have not exactly short sentences. [He reads from a paper]: Twenty years, 10 years—a bicycle thief. [He hands it over] I have now transmitted it.

He said he doesn't know them but there was an appeal published in a Beirut paper.

Can I see you five seconds alone?

Mrs. Meir: Sure. The young people want to go to sleep.

Should we move the Knesset forward an hour, so we can get the prisoners back?

Dayan: Nine o'clock is all right.

Kissinger: Then make the signing at 5:00 p.m. in Geneva?

[Mrs. Meir and Secretary Kissinger conferred alone from 3:45–4:00 a.m. The rest of the party departed for the hotel at 3:45 a.m.]

79. Memorandum From the President's Deputy Assistant for National Security Affairs (Scowcroft) to President Nixon[1]

Washington, May 29, 1974.

Secretary Kissinger asked that I pass you the following report.

"I have just received word that the Israeli Cabinet has approved the agreement.[2] The Cabinet will reconvene at 9:00 a.m. Washington time today to give the impression that it is still considering the question in order to prevent any leaks. That session will run until shortly after 10:00 a.m. Washington time. To meet this timing I believe it is essential that you make the announcement of the agreement a few minutes before 10:00 a.m. Washington time but in no case later than 10:00 a.m.

"The text of the announcement which has been agreed upon reads as follows:

'The discussions conducted by United States Secretary of State Dr. Henry Kissinger with Syria and Israel have led to an agreement on the disengagement of Syrian and Israeli forces. The agreement will be signed by Syrian and Israeli military representatives in the Egyptian-Israeli Military Working Group of the Geneva Conference on Thursday, May 30, 1974 in Geneva.'"[3]

---

[1] Source: Library of Congress, Manuscript Division, Kissinger Papers, CL 155, Geopolitical File, Israel, May 1974. Secret; Sensitive; Exclusively Eyes Only. Sent for information.

[2] Kissinger met with Meir on May 29 from 1:10 until 2:30 p.m. at the Prime Minister's Residence. (Memorandum of conversation; National Archives, RG 59, Records of Henry Kissinger, 1973–77, Box 8, Nodis Memcons, May 1974, Folder 10)

[3] The President read the statement on nationwide radio and television at 1:02 p.m. on May 31. For text of his remarks about the significance of the agreement, see *Public Papers: Nixon, 1974*, pp. 463–464.

80. Letter From Secretary of State Kissinger to Syrian President Asad[1]

Washington, May 29, 1974.

Dear Mr. President:

I have the honor to transmit the following text of a letter from President Nixon:

Dear Mr. President:

As you begin to rebuild and repopulate Quneitra, I want you to know that the United States is prepared to consider how it might assist in the rehabilitation of that area. One important objective we share in seeking a lasting peace in the Middle East is to help people return to normal lives. It is a source of great satisfaction to me to know that the agreement on the disengagement of Syrian and Israeli forces will make it possible for some of the people displaced by war to return to their homes.

Sincerely,

(Richard Nixon)

The signed original of this letter will be forwarded to you.

Sincerely,

Henry A. Kissinger

---

[1] Source: National Archives, RG 59, Records of Joseph Sisco, Box 32, Briefing Book: Syrian-Israeli Disengagement Documents, Under Secretary Sisco. Secret.

81. Letter From President Nixon to Syrian President Asad[1]

Washington, undated.

Dear Mr. President:

I want to express to you my gratification at the conclusion of the agreement for the disengagement of Syrian and Israeli forces, and to af-

---

[1] Source: National Archives, RG 59, Records of Joseph Sisco, Box 32, Briefing Book: Syrian-Israeli Disengagement Documents, Under Secretary Sisco. Secret. According to Kissinger's memoirs, all documents associated with the agreement had to be complete by May 29. (*Years of Upheaval*, p. 1106)

firm that the United States considers this agreement only a first step toward a just and durable peace. You have my assurance that the United States will give full, and continuing support, including our active involvement within the year in the next stages of the negotiations, to the achievement of the full implementation of Security Council Resolution 338 in all of its parts.

In our view, the peace settlement should be in accordance with the interests of all the states in the area, consistent with their independence and sovereignty, and should take fully into account the legitimate interests of the Palestinian people.

Sincerely,

Richard Nixon[2]

[2] Printed from a copy that bears this typed signature.

82. Letter From Secretary of State Kissinger to Syrian President Asad[1]

Washington, undated.

Dear Mr. President:

I have the honor to transmit the text of a letter from President Nixon. The signed original will be forwarded to you.

Dear Mr. President:

In connection with the agreement between Syria and Israel on the disengagement of their forces, the Government of the United States has received the assurances below from the Government of Israel with respect to the Israeli presence on Tell abou Nida and Tell el Aaram, the two hills just to the west of Quneitra.

First, Israel will scrupulously observe the ceasefire, including observance with respect to the people and city of Quneitra.

Second, there will be no Israeli forces or weapons on the eastern slopes of the two hills.

[1] Source: National Archives, RG 59, Records of Joseph Sisco, Box 33, Briefing Book: Syrian-Israeli Disengagement, 1974, Folder 2. No classification marking. According to Kissinger's memoirs, all documents associated with the agreement had to be complete by May 29. (*Years of Upheaval*, p. 1106)

Third, there will be no weapons on top of these hills which can fire into Quneitra.

I want to assure you, Mr. President, that the United States will do its utmost to assure that these conditions are scrupulously observed.

As you begin to rebuild and repopulate Quneitra, I want you to know also that the United States is prepared to consider how it might assist in the rehabilitation of that area.

Sincerely,

(Richard Nixon)

Sincerely,

Henry A. Kissinger[2]

---

[2] Printed from a copy that bears this typed signature.

---

83. U.S. Proposal[1]

Jerusalem, May 29, 1974.

U.S. PROPOSAL

In order to facilitate agreement between Israel and Syria and in implementation of that agreement, and to assist in maintaining scrupulous observance of the ceasefire on land, air and sea, the United States proposes the following provisions:

(1) That the area of limitation in armament and forces west of Line A and east of Line B will be 10 kilometers in width. In each area, respectively, the following are permitted: (a) two brigades of armed forces, including 75 tanks and 36 pieces of short-range 122-mm artillery; and (b) the entire force of each party shall not exceed 6,000 men. The United Nations Disengagement Observer Force will inspect these provisions in the 10 kilometer zone.

(2) That in the area between 10 and 20 kilometers west of Line A and east of Line B: (a) there will be no artillery pieces whose range ex-

---

[1] Source: National Archives, RG 59, Records of Joseph Sisco, Box 32, Briefing Book: Syrian-Israeli Disengagement Documents, Under Secretary Sisco. Secret. Eban wrote the city and date by hand to the left of his signature. Another copy of the U.S. Proposal, sent to Syria, is signed by Lieutenant General Youssef Shakkut, Chief of Staff of the Syrian Arab Army. (Ibid.)

ceeds 20 kilometers; and (b) the total number of artillery pieces permitted is 162 with a range of not exceeding 20 kilometers; and (c) surface-to-air missiles will be stationed no closer than 25 kilometers west of Line A and east of Line B.

(3) Inspection of the provisions in paragraph 2 above will be performed by the U. S. aerial reconnaissance and the results will be provided to both sides.

(4) The area of separation between Lines A and B will not have any military forces. In the towns and villages in the area there will be stationed police forces of a size and character similar to those stationed in other Syrian towns and villages of comparable size.

(5) The United Nations Disengagement Observer Force will take over the positions in the area of separation on Mount Hermon. No military observation of any kind may be conducted in that area.

Abba Eban
Minister of Foreign Affairs

84. Memorandum of Understanding[1]

Undated.

MEMORANDUM OF UNDERSTANDING BETWEEN THE UNITED STATES GOVERNMENT AND THE GOVERNMENT OF ISRAEL

(1) The United States position is that withdrawal of the United Nations Disengagement Observer Forces agreed upon under the Israeli-Syrian Disengagement Agreement will require the consent of both sides. Should the matter of the withdrawal of the United Nations Disengagement Observer Forces or a change in its mandate be proposed before the United Nations Security Council without the consent of Israel or the United States, the United States will vote against such withdrawal or any change of mandate which would, in our mutual judgment, affect adversely the present operation of the Force.

---

[1] Source: Library of Congress, Manuscript Division, Kissinger Papers, CL 192, Geopolitical File, Middle East, Peace Negotiations, Israeli-Syrian Relations, Disengagement Agreement, May to September 1974. Secret. Initialed by Henry Kissinger and Simcha Dinitz, apparently on May 29 or 30 in Israel before Kissinger departed for Egypt on May 30.

(2) The United States will oppose supervision of Israeli held areas by U.N. personnel from the Soviet Union, from other communist countries, or from countries which have no diplomatic relations with Israel. With respect to the deployment of forces in the area of separation, the United States will approach the United Nations Secretary General or directly Syria with a view to working out arrangements whereunder no units or personnel of nations which do not have diplomatic relations with Israel will (a) be deployed adjacent to the Israeli line, or (b) participate in the inspection of the Israeli area of limited forces and armaments.

(3) The United States has informed the Governments of Israel and Syria that it will perform aerial reconnaissance missions over the areas covered by the Disengagement Agreement at a frequency of about one mission every ten days or two weeks, including special missions on request, and will forward the photographs to both Israel and Syria as soon as they are ready. In the event aerial reconnaissance detects violations, the United States will take this up diplomatically with Syria to bring about a rectification.

(4) The United States informs Israel that Egypt has informed the United States that it will support the disengagement agreement with Syria and that it is a fair agreement. It is the United States' understanding, from its discussions with Egypt, that Egypt has not committed itself to participate militarily in support of Syria if Syria violates the agreement by reopening hostilities or beginning a war against Israel.

(5) Recognizing the defense responsibilities of the Government of Israel following redeployment of its forces under the Disengagement Agreement the United States reaffirms that it will make every effort to be fully responsive on a continuing and long-term basis to Israel's military equipment requirements.

(6) It is the policy of the United States that implementation of the Disengagement Agreement should take precedence over the undertaking of new commitments by the parties related to subsequent phases of the Geneva Conference. The United States will do its best to help facilitate the Conference proceeding at a pace agreed upon by Israel and the United States.

(7) In case of a meaningful Syrian violation of any of the provisions of the Disengagement Agreement, or any of its attachments, the United States Government will immediately consult Israel regarding the necessary reaction and with a view to giving appropriate diplomatic support to Israel.

HK

S.D.

85. Letter from Secretary of State Kissinger to Israeli Prime Minister Meir[1]

Washington, May 30, 1974.

Dear Madame Prime Minister:

This is to inform you that the assurances with respect to guerilla action from Syria conveyed to the Israeli Government[2] have the following characteristics:

1. They were made to the Secretary of State by President Asad on the condition that there would be no publicity whatsoever.

2. President Asad emphasized that any publicity would force him to make a public statement contradicting the assurances and perhaps make it impossible for him to maintain them.

Best wishes,

Henry A. Kissinger

---

[1] Source: Library of Congress, Manuscript Division, Kissinger Papers, CL 155, Geopolitical File, Israel, May 1974. No classification marking.

[2] These assurances were presented as a U.S. text provided to the Israeli Government. The text reads, "The position of the United States with respect to the first paragraph of the Agreement between Israel and Syria on Military Disengagement is as follows: Raids by armed groups or individuals across the demarcation line are contrary to the ceasefire. Israel in the exercise of its right of self-defense may act to prevent such actions by all available means. The United States will not consider such actions by Israel as violations of the ceasefire and will support them politically." (National Archives, RG 59, Records of Joseph Sisco, Box 32, Briefing Book: Syrian-Israeli Disengagement Documents, Under Secretary Sisco)

86. Memorandum From the President's Deputy Assistant for National Security Affairs (Scowcroft) to President Nixon[1]

Washington, May 30, 1974.

Secretary Kissinger asked me to pass the following message to you regarding his meeting with President Sadat:

"I had an extremely warm and satisfying talk with President Sadat this afternoon in Cairo including a private luncheon and a two-and a-half hour meeting afterward.[2]

"I presented him with a copy of the Syria-Israeli disengagement agreement,[3] with a large map and related documents. I explained to him the arrangement we had reached with Assad for Mrs. Meir to refer publicly to a U.S. view that terrorist attacks across the line were violations of the ceasefire. Sadat believed this was a good way to handle the issue and would not unduly provoke the Palestinians.

"He recommended that we establish covert medium-level contact with the Palestinians soon, in order to encourage the moderate element—Arafat—whom he was trying to build into the main force of the movement. I stressed how politically damaging the terrorist attacks were in both Israel and America. He agreed completely, and assured me these were the work of dissident fringe elements. He would do his best to put a stop to terrorism.

"We then discussed your trip, U.S.-Egyptian relations, and the idea of a joint cooperation commission, on which I have already reported to you. We agreed to prepare as soon as possible an agenda of bilateral issues and projects that could be finalized on the occasion of your visit.

"Sadat was very eager for our assessment of the new Israeli Government and the prospects for the next phase of Israeli-Egyptian negotiations. We agreed the time was not yet ripe for beginning a negotiation, but that we should use the next few months to think ourselves about possible approaches. This will be one of the major topics he wants to discuss with you on your visit.

---

[1] Source: National Archives, Nixon Presidential Materials, NSC Files, Kissinger Office Files, Box 45, HAK Trip Files, Middle East Memos and Security, April 28–May 31, 1974. Secret; Sensitive; Exclusively Eyes Only.

[2] The meeting between Sadat and Kissinger took place on May 30 from 3 until 5:30 p.m. at the President's Giza Residence in Cairo. (Memorandum of conversation; ibid., RG 59, Records of Henry Kissinger, 1973–77, Box 21, Classified External Memcons, May–November 1974, Folder 2)

[3] Document 88.

"Sadat had no desire to accommodate the Soviets by reconvening the Geneva Conference. In any case, he himself would not be ready for it until September. He suggested—and then said to the press afterward—that the Arabs would need much time for mutual consultations, etc., before proposing resumption of Geneva.

"Sadat also wants to discuss the Soviet problem with you when you come to Cairo.

"When our meeting ended, he invited in the press and made some extremely warm statements about you, and about the American role in the achievement of disengagement and the search for a just peace in the Middle East. Comments have been sent to Scowcroft and Ziegler."

---

87. Letter From President Nixon to Israeli Prime Minister Meir[1]

Washington, May 31, 1974.

Dear Madame Prime Minister:

The Secretary of State has brought to my attention your letter dated May 12,[2] in which you have outlined your country's major concerns. Let me assure you, Madame Prime Minister, that I read it with great attention and understanding, for you know that during my entire Administration I have given concrete evidence of my own feelings for and commitment to Israel's continued survival in peace and security. I would like now to refer to those items which you raised.

With regard to your request to enter with the United States into a long-range military arrangement which will assure Israel the supply of the necessary military equipment for the next ten years, you have my full backing. I have noted the figures that you have quoted, and I understand your basic needs. With respect to modern aircraft, I understand that preliminary talks have already been held with Secretary Schlesinger, and I recognize your need to move into the new generation of aircraft. With respect to ground-to-ground missiles, I agree that Israel should be equipped with weapons similar to those supplied by the

---

[1] Source: National Archives, Nixon Presidential Materials, NSC Files, Kissinger Office Files, Box 136, Country Files, Middle East, Dinitz, January 1–July 1, 1974. Secret. A handwritten notation at the top of the first page reads, "Peter Rodman hand delivered to Min. Shalev 6/9/74, 5:00 p.m." A handwritten notation at the bottom of the second page reads, "I shall look forward to seeing you in a few days."

[2] The letter has not been found.

Russians to both the Egyptians and the Syrians. I assure you of my support in this program.

I suggest that a mission from your country come to Washington in the month of June to work out all concrete details. This will give me the opportunity to review the specifics sympathetically and within the framework of the aforementioned principles.

I realize that such a long-range military program will entail a heavy financial burden. I was mindful of this fact when I proposed special emergency assistance of $2.2 billion subsequent to the October war. I fully realize that substantial U.S. financial assistance will be needed to support this program, and I intend to ask Congress to provide such support.

I fully understand your concern for working out a contingency plan to provide Israel with military supplies, both ammunition and replacement of major equipment, in case of emergency. I have authorized our appropriate agencies to work with your officials to devise such a plan.

I noted your particular concern with regard to the continued supply of oil to Israel, in case any interruption occurs resulting from change of circumstances or other development. I suggest that appropriate representatives of our two countries meet in order to devise a plan whose objective would be to assure uninterrupted oil supply to Israel.

Madame Prime Minister, as you leave office, I want to pay tribute to the strong and effective leadership which you have given to Israel and its people.

Warmest regards,

Richard Nixon

88. Syrian-Israeli Disengagement Agreement[1]

Geneva, May 31, 1974.

AGREEMENT ON DISENGAGEMENT BETWEEN ISRAELI AND SYRIAN FORCES

A. Israel and Syria will scrupulously observe the ceasefire on land, sea and air and will refrain from all military actions against each other, from the time of the signing of this document, in implementation of United Nations Security Council Resolution 338 dated October 22, 1973.

B. The military forces of Israel and Syria will be separated in accordance with the following principles:

1. All Israeli military forces will be west of the line designated as Line A on the map attached hereto, except in the Quneitra area, where they will be west of Line A–1.

2. All territory east of Line A will be under Syrian administration, and Syrian civilians will return to this territory.

3. The area between Line A and the line designated as Line B on the attached map will be an area of separation. In this area will be stationed the United Nations Disengagement Observer Force established in accordance with the accompanying protocol.

4. All Syrian military forces will be east of the line designated as Line B on the attached map.

5. There will be two equal areas of limitation in armament and forces, one west of Line A and one east of Line B as agreed upon.

6. Air Forces of the two sides will be permitted to operate up to their respective lines without interference from the other side.

C. In the area between Line A and Line A–1 on the attached map there shall be no military forces.

D. This agreement and the attached map will be signed by the military representatives of Israel and Syria in Geneva not later than May 31, 1974, in the Egyptian-Israeli Military Working Group of the Geneva Peace Conference under the aegis of the United Nations, after that group has been joined by a Syrian military representative, and with the

---

[1] Source: National Archives, RG 59, Records of Joseph Sisco, Box 32, Briefing Book: Syrian-Israeli Disengagement Documents, Under Secretary Sisco. No classification marking. All three signers, Shafir, Shihabi, Siilasvuo, initialed each page. The agreement, accompanying protocol (Document 89), and attached map (Document 90) were published in the *New York Times*, May 31, 1974. For the final map agreed to by the Syrians and the Israelis, see Appendix B, Map 2.

participation of representatives of the United States and the Soviet Union. The precise delineation of a detailed map and a plan for the implementation of the disengagement of forces will be worked out by military representatives of Israel and Syria in the Egyptian-Israeli Military Working Group who will agree on the stages of this process. The Military Working Group described above will start their work for this purpose in Geneva under the aegis of the United Nations within 24 hours after the signing of this agreement. They will complete this task within five days. Disengagement will begin within 24 hours after the completion of the task of the Military Working Group. The process of disengagement will be completed not later than twenty days after it begins.

E. The provisions of paragraphs A, B and C shall be inspected by personnel of the United Nations comprising the United Nations Disengagement Observer Force under this agreement.

F. Within 24 hours after the signing of this agreement in Geneva all wounded prisoners of war which each side holds of the other as certified by the ICRC will be repatriated. The morning after the completion of the task of the Military Working Group, all remaining prisoners of war will be repatriated.

G. The bodies of all dead soldiers held by either side will be returned for burial in their respective countries within ten days after the signing of this agreement.

H. This agreement is not a peace agreement. It is a step toward a just and durable peace on the basis of Security Council Resolution 338 dated October 22, 1973.

For Israel:

Herzl Shafir
Maj. Gen.

For Syria:

Hikmat al-Shibabi

Witness for the United Nations:
Ensio Siilasvuo[2]

---

[2] General Siilasvuo wrote "Geneva 31 May 1974" after his signature, and General Shihabi's signature is is Arabic.

89. Protocol to the Syrian-Israeli Disengagement Agreement[1]

Geneva, May 31, 1974.

PROTOCOL TO AGREEMENT ON DISENGAGEMENT BETWEEN ISRAELI AND SYRIAN FORCES

Concerning the United Nations Disengagement Observer Force

Israel and Syria agree that:

The function of the United Nations Disengagement Observer Force (UNDOF) under the Agreement will be to use its best efforts to maintain the ceasefire and to see that it is scrupulously observed. It will supervise the Agreement and protocol thereto with regard to the areas of separation and limitation. In carrying out its mission, it will comply with generally applicable Syrian laws and regulations and will not hamper the functioning of local civil administration. It will enjoy freedom of movement and communication and other facilities that are necessary for its mission. It will be mobile and provided with personal weapons of a defensive character and shall use such weapons only in self-defense. The number of the UNDOF shall be about 1,250, who will be selected by the Secretary General of the United Nations in consultation with the parties from members of the United Nations who are not permanent members of the Security Council.

The UNDOF will be under the command of the United Nations, vested in the Secretary General, under the authority of the Security Council.

The UNDOF shall carry out inspections under the Agreement, and report thereon to the parties, on a regular basis, not less often than once every fifteen days, and, in addition, when requested by either party. It shall mark on the ground the respective lines shown on the map attached to the Agreement.

Israel and Syria will support a resolution of the United Nations Security Council which will provide for the UNDOF contemplated by the

---

[1] Source: National Archives, RG 59, Records of Joseph Sisco, Box 32, Briefing Book: Syrian-Israeli Disengagement Documents, Under Secretary Sisco. No classification marking. All three signers, Shafir, Shihabi, and Siilasvuo, initialed each page. There is an addendum to the protocol sent from President Nixon to Prime Minister Meir that states "the Government of Syria agrees to the following on a reciprocal and identical basis: 1. It will refrain from placing any weapons, including SAM's, which can reach the defense line of the other side in an additional ten-kilometer zone beyond the western edge of the agreed zone of limitation. 2. It agrees that the UNP shall conduct regular inspections to assure compliance with this provision." There is no signature. (Ibid., Box 33, Briefing Book: Syrian-Israeli Disengagement, 1974, Folder 2)

Syrian-Israeli Disengagement Agreement 373

Agreement. The initial authorization will be for six months subject to renewal by further resolution of the Security Council.[2]

Herzl Shafiz

Ensio Siilasvuo

Hikmat al-Shahabi[3]

---

[2] UN Security Council Resolution 350 establishing the UNDOF was adopted on May 31. For text, see *Yearbook of the United Nations, 1974*, p. 205.

[3] General Siilasvuo wrote "Geneva 31 May 1974" after his signature, and General Shihabi's signature is in Arabic.

---

90. Map of the Syrian-Israeli Disengagement Lines[1]

Undated.

[See Appendix A, map 3.]

---

[1] Source: National Archives, RG 59, Records of Joseph Sisco, Box 32, Briefing Book: Syrian-Israeli Disengagement Documents, Under Secretary Sisco. Secret; No Foreign Dissem. The map accompanying the May 31 Syrian-Israeli Disengagement Agreement contained only lines A, A–1, and B. The additional lines—the dots, dots and dashes, and dashes on the west and east sides of the area of separation—represent the zones of troops and armament limitations.

91. Memorandum of Conversation[1]

Washington, May 31, 1974, 10:30 a.m.

PARTICIPANTS

President Richard M. Nixon
Bipartisan Congressional Leadership
Dr. Henry A. Kissinger, Secretary of State and Assistant to the President for National Security Affairs
Major General Brent Scowcroft, Deputy Assistant to the President for National Security Affairs

SUBJECT

Dr. Kissinger's Middle East Briefing

President: Before the briefing, I would like to make one comment about the difficulty of these negotiations. I told Henry I thought that next to the Vietnamese negotiations, these were the toughest. He said that is a tough call.

He spent over 30 days out there. Several times it appeared to be about to break down. Through perseverance and some assurances, we finally made it. As Kissinger will say, the last point was cosmetic—an Israeli insistence against terrorist action across the zone and the Syrian refusal. As late as Monday[2] it was 75–25 against agreement on that point.

As Henry will point out, the Egyptian-Israeli disengagement and Syrian-Israeli disengagement agreements are important diplomatic achievements but they only open the long road toward a permanent settlement. No one should have any illusion that that won't take a long, long time. We owe to Henry and his team for 30 days of excruciating negotiations—our Arab friends can talk well into the night, and Henry went to bed at 5:00 a.m. many times. Henry—

Kissinger: Let me first explain the setting and then the details. Then where do we go from here.

In October, all the Arabs were united against the United States, supported by Europe, with the Soviet Union as their principal spokesman. We were pushed into unilateral support of Israel and faced with an oil embargo. Had that continued, Europe and Japan would

---

[1] Source: National Archives, Nixon Presidential Materials, NSC Files, Box 1029, Presidential/HAK Memcons, May 8–31, 1974, Folder 1. Secret. The meeting was held at the White House. Brackets are in the original. A list of attendees is in the President's Daily Diary. (Ibid., White House Central Files)

[2] May 27.

have been hostage to the Arabs and the radicals would have triumphed.

The first breakthrough was with Sadat in November.[3] He decided to go piece by piece, in diplomatic rather than military moves, and to rely on the U.S. rather than the Soviet Union. This produced an Israeli-Egyptian disengagement.[4] It was a diplomatic revolution. Egypt embraced the U.S. and reduced Soviet influence. It was a triumph for the moderates. But this brought Sadat under radical pressure. Since then, there has been a contest between the radicals and Sadat. The question was, would the situation move carefully? Or in one great move by the radicals supported by the Soviet Union, which would result in war?

Syria was the most radical of the Arab states. In November, I didn't even think of visiting Syria. The Syrian Ba'athists, the governing group, are somewhat left of Soviet Communism. Their hatred of Israel is proverbial. When I first went there their newspapers said "Kissinger arrived from occupied territory"—meaning Israel. Now the headlines spoke of "Syrian-Israeli disengagement"—which is the first mention of Israel's existence. They are the most militant of the Arab states. If there was no settlement, the war would have resumed. Egypt couldn't have stayed out, and the Soviets would have had to help. Sadat has been a great help in this process. In February, Syria first indicated it would talk.

There is a big difference between the situation on the Suez Canal and the Golan. The Suez is desert; the Golan is populated by Israeli villagers. It is a more constricted area, and there is the problem of Mount Hermon. There is a complex domestic situation in both countries. In Syria, there is division between the civilians and the military—with the civilians more militant, with Soviet wings, Iraqi and Palestinian wings. They are not sophisticated in military planning. Egyptian military experts had to educate them.

In Israel, the Cabinet was changing. The old Cabinet didn't want to go out under a cloud and the new one didn't want to come in under a burden.

Much of my technique was a seminar explaining to each what the others thought. One of the most moving things at the end was to see some appreciation of each other's concerns.

In Syria, the government hadn't made a formulated decision to agree, and was not under firm control.

---

[3] See footnote 7, Document 4.
[4] See Document 10.

On Monday I had given up.[5] Asad and I were alone and we were drawing up my farewell statement. He said it was a shame; couldn't we do something?

Then another hang up, as the President said, was on terrorism. There was great emotion coming from Maalot.[6] We solved it by assuring Israel that we would regard terrorist attacks as violations of the ceasefire.

[Dr. Kissinger gets up to the map.]

In March the Israelis grabbed Mount Hermon which dominated the area. In Suez, Egypt had seized Israeli-held territory; here there is no Syrian-held territory, and Israeli settlements had been built near the line and Mount Hermon was crucial. The Syrians wouldn't discuss it because it was seized in March. The Syrians are obsessive about foreigners on their soil—they won't even allow Russians in Damascus—so to have a UN force there was to them an insult. They were hung up on issues of sovereignty and wouldn't accept limitations of police.

The initial positions were far apart. The Syrians originally wanted the whole Golan back, or two-thirds of it. The other Arabs said they would be satisfied with Kuneitra. But there are Israeli settlements right near it, and the Israelis were reluctant to move out of Kuneitra.

The President authorized me to make a U.S. proposal—so that each side would accept a U.S.—not an enemy—proposal. The Israelis were allowed to keep the hills they needed outside of Kuneitra, but Israeli forces won't be visible to the Syrians in Kuneitra.

President: You may ask, why couldn't we start with a U.S. proposal? Because each would have said we were favoring the other and they would snipe at us. We had to move slowly.

Kissinger: Here is the final red line. The squiggles are to keep some Syrian villages under Syrian control. On Hermon, two-thirds went to the Syrians and one-third to the UN. The Syrians wanted 80 UN observers and Israel a force of 3,000. We came out with an "observer force"—so each got its name in—and with the same charter as the force on Suez.

Then we got into a wrangle on limitation of forces. Again the President authorized a U.S. proposal. There are two zones of 10 kilometers. The first zone is limitation of personnel and the second is limitation of equipment. There is a limit of 6,000 troops, 75 tanks and 36 artillery. In the second zone there can be 162 artillery pieces with a range of 20 kilometers and no SAMs. (This is all classified, by the way.)

The result is that it is harder for them to go to war. A surprise attack now is impossible.

---

[5] See Document 75.
[6] See footnote 4, Document 58.

Syrian-Israeli Disengagement Agreement 377

President: There may be incidents. The leaders will have to understand that. But it will be less than in Vietnam.

Kissinger: I think there will be few incidents. The Syrians haven't let the terrorists loose. They have come mostly from Lebanon.[7]

This is an important first step, but we have monumental problems ahead of us—Jerusalem, Palestine. If there is no movement, this front could erupt again, because the Syrians are unstable. However, failure would have meant immediate hostilities, Syrian pressure for a new oil embargo, and international pressures against us. Now the Arabs know that only the U.S. can bring a solution. It was very important to Sadat, because it meant a radical regime did the same as he did, and it ratified U.S. participation in the process. One reason Sadat wants the President to visit is to symbolize the American presence and participation and to begin movement to peace.

It could blow up in six-to-nine months. But we now have maneuvering room. We have completed the military phase and can move into a phase of political advance. And we did it with Israeli blessing.

President: And the U.S. commitment to Israeli security.

Kissinger: But that is in the U.S. interest, because only a strong Israel makes the Arabs turn to us.

President: Our relationship with the Soviet Union in the Middle East is a pragmatic one. We don't want a confrontation with the Soviet Union like we had last October.[8] The only thing the Soviet Union can promise is arms and war. As for us, we are not imposing a settlement on Israel, but the Arabs now see that a settlement without war can only come through the U.S. Soviet help could work only through war.

Kissinger: That is right. The only way to achieve objectives through the Soviet Union was conflict. We are moving the Soviet Union out of the Middle East but pragmatically cooperating. It is détente ...

President: Expand that—the Soviet Union could prevent a settlement, but at cost of other fish they fry with us. We shouldn't knock the Soviet Union.

Kissinger: What has happened is a major defeat for the Soviet Union. Take what happened to Gromyko in Damascus on Monday. He was to come in the morning. They delayed him 'til two, then kept him circling until he ran out of gas, and then he was met by their Deputy Foreign Minister. Then on Tuesday, Asad wouldn't meet with Gro-

---

[7] In both the Kiryat Shmona and Maalot episodes, the Palestinian guerrillas infiltrated Israel from Lebanon. See Document 34 and footnote 4, Document 58.

[8] During the October 1973 Arab-Israeli war, tensions between the United States and Soviet Union led the Nixon administration to raise the U.S. Defense Condition from level 4 to level 3. See *Foreign Relations*, 1969–1976, volume XXV, Arab-Israeli Crisis and War, 1973, Document 269.

myko because he was waiting for Sisco. Then when I came instead, Asad cancelled the dinner he had prepared for Gromyko and served it to me!

President: It is not the purpose and intent of U.S. policy. The Soviet presence hangs over the Middle East, and they can prevent progress if they have no other fish to fry. So don't characterize this as a Soviet defeat.

Kissinger: To carry this off requires détente. Why were they restrained? Because of their commitment to détente. We need MFN and credits to give them something to show. We could do this precisely because of détente.

A word about commitments. It's the same as on the Suez agreement. It doesn't imply a continuing military commitment on limitation because it's part of the agreement. There is also an Israeli commitment about stationing arms on the hills. The only U.S. commitment is to continue two-week reconnaissance flights over the area.

Every U.S. assurance—I have given them orally and they will be given to the Foreign Affairs Committees to look at. They are U.S. proposals which they signed with us which will be appended to the agreement.

Scott: What nations are in the UN force?

Kissinger: Permanent members are excluded. Probably it will be Nepal, Austria and Peru—because of the mountains there.

O'Neill: Do you now have to move to the Palestinian issue?

Kissinger: There are three issues: frontiers, the Palestinians, and Jerusalem. We would like to stay with the frontiers a bit more. The Palestinian issue is related to the Jerusalem issue—if Jordan could represent the Palestinians, that would help. But somewhere we must face the Palestinian issue.

Fulbright: Where, in Amman?

President: That is what you should say publicly. But nothing will be done in a public forum. The Soviet Union is pushing for a Palestinian state. There must be much quiet discussion.

Kissinger: The Soviets and Romanians want a Palestinian state—each is playing its own game. We will try to handle it so it doesn't blow up the negotiations yet still gives them some hope.

President: Our relations with the others were of great help—Boumediene, Sadat, Feisal each sent emissaries to Asad.

Kissinger: Boumediene, being a radical himself, was a big help.

O'Neill: How many terrorists?

Kissinger: The numbers aren't the issue. And there has been little activity across the Syrian borders since 1967. It was a symbolic issue in Israel.

President: Tell them about the Economic Commissions.

Kissinger: Sadat thought it was important to move our relations away from technical military affairs. He wanted the President to visit and not only due to the disengagement. Also there will be an Oil Ministers meeting coming up and we want to give them some incentive for moderation. This cooperation is for a commission to explore maximum cooperation in the economic, scientific and cultural areas. The purpose is plan long-range cooperation between Egypt and the United States. It is part of Sadat's attempt to reorient away from the Soviet Union and to establish the U.S. as a force in the Middle East for progress and moderation. We wanted to wait, but he wanted the President to visit there to symbolize the line in terms of U.S.-Egyptian relations rather than Israeli-Egyptian relations.

President: We will have to furnish Israel with items they feel essential to their security, or else they will think the territory essential. We can't move if Israel feels insecure. The other side of the coin is more difficult. I have heard grumbles from some of you Israeli supporters. If we can exercise a leavening influence, we can't do it just by talk, but by economic and other means which gives them a stake in relations with the U.S.

If your goal is peace in the Middle East and the survival of Israel, we have to have some stake with Israeli neighbors.

Kissinger: For Sadat to move to the U.S. as he has took enormous courage, in the face of the Soviets and the radicals. If we attach too many conditions, Sadat will be undercut. We have an enormous opportunity now. It is better not to break the fabric through onerous conditions. For example, Israeli flags through the Canal—he can't quite do it yet but he'll let cargoes through if we shut up about it.

Albert: Some of our Jewish friends will have to stop the publicity on this.

Frelinghuysen: I will do everything I can for a balanced program.

Kissinger: You know there is this $100 million fund in the budget. If Syria behaves, if we could commit something for the reconstruction of Kuneitra, it would have great symbolism. They get plenty of Soviet money, but if we don't do this, we could force them to turn only to the Soviets.

Stennis: Was there a manpower commitment?

Kissinger: No manpower commitment. Only that we would view their long-term military needs sympathetically.

Frelinghuysen: How about M–60's from NATO?

Kissinger: The Soviet Union has poured equipment in. Israel has to be so strong that the Arabs can't defeat it. The M–60's were a previous commitment.

President: We must maintain the balance. Weapons for Israel and PL 480 for Egypt are an investment for peace.

Hebert: We have manpower there for the Canal now. What if one gets killed?

Kissinger: That is not for military purposes.

President: It is the U.S. interest to have influences in the area.

Hebert: I'd like to get our boys out of there.

Mahon: This is an impressive picture. How can we convey this to our colleagues to get their support and votes?

Zablocki: We hope the President will go to the public and explain.

Hebert: The only way to get votes is to ring the bell and knock heads.

President: Sadat has recommended my trip. There is nothing to announce today. We have to examine what activities there will be, when and where to go. I'll make a decision early next week. We are also announcing my 27 June arrival in Moscow.

Aiken: From the discussion, one might think the Suez clearing only benefited Egypt.[9] I thought it benefited the world, and shouldn't we say so?

Kissinger: The Suez is an investment in peace. It is a physical barrier to conflict and an economic help to Egypt. It does help Soviet ships, but we can follow them. And our work has so influenced the moderates that the Soviet Union may not have any ports.

Tower: Say a word about Diego Garcia.

Kissinger: We need a presence in the Indian Ocean and a better means of operating there.

President: The Soviet Union is all over the area.

Question: It is cost-effective if we have ships there.

President: Thank you for coming. Both the disengagement agreements are interim settlements. They are essential to working out a permanent settlement over a long time.

The momentum must continue—whether clearing the Suez, economic measures, my visit, etc. If we don't the hatred and the radical forces will come slipping back. It is an enormous accomplishment by Kissinger, but this is only the first step. We have done about ten percent.

---

[9] A reference to the mine clearing process, begun in April by an international task force that included the U.S. Navy, in an effort to clear ordnance left in the canal after the October 1973 war.

Negotiations and Reassessment, June 1974–June 1975

92. Editorial Note

On June 12, 1974, President Nixon embarked on a tour of the Middle East, visiting Egypt, Saudi Arabia, Syria, Israel, and Jordan. He flew to Cairo on June 12 and met with President Sadat on June 12, 13, and 14. On June 14, President Nixon and President Sadat signed an accord, "Principles of Relations and Cooperation Between Egypt and the United States," that included agreement on establishment of the Joint Cooperation Commission and a U.S. promise to provide Egypt with nuclear technology that Egypt would use for peaceful purposes. (*Public Papers: Nixon, 1974*, pages 503–506) That same day, Nixon flew to Jidda, Saudi Arabia, and met with King Faisal. He continued his tour with a trip to Damascus on June 15. Nixon met with President Asad on June 16 at 10:30 a.m. in the Presidential Palace at Damascus. (Memorandum of conversation, June 16; Library of Congress, Manuscript Division, Kissinger Papers, TS 42, Geopolitical File, Syria, November 1973–July 1976) Later that day, Nixon made a joint announcement with President Asad re-establishing relations between the United States and Syria. (*Public Papers: Nixon, 1974*, pages 515–516) That same day, he continued his Middle East trip with a two-day stop in Israel, the first time a U.S. President had visited Israel. President Nixon met with Prime Minister Rabin on June 16 at 4:50 p.m. at the King David Hotel in Jerusalem (Memorandum of conversation, June 16; National Archives, Nixon Presidential Materials, NSC Files, Kissinger Office Files, Box 135, Country Files, Middle East, Dinitz, July 1–December 31, 1974) and on June 17 at 11 a.m. at the Knesset in Jerusalem. (Memorandum of conversation, June 17; ibid.) Also on June 17, Nixon held a private meeting with Rabin to discuss Israel's long-term arms needs. (Ibid., Box 1029, Presidential/HAK Memcons, June 1–August 8, 1974, Folder 3) On June 17, Nixon continued on to Jordan and met with King Hussein on June 18 at 9:30 a.m. to discuss the Palestinian situation and the West Bank. (Memorandum for the record, June 18; Ford Library, National Security Adviser, Memoranda of Conversations, Box 4, June 18, 1974, Nixon, Jordan's King Hussein) Nixon returned to the United States on June 19.

93. Memorandum of Conversation[1]

Washington, July 30, 1974, 3:20–5 p.m.

PARTICIPANTS

    Yigal Allon, Deputy Prime Minister and Minister for Foreign Affairs of Israel
    Simcha Dinitz, Ambassador to the United States
    Ephraim Evron, Deputy Director General, Ministry of Foreign Affairs
    Mordechai Shalev, Minister, Embassy of Israel
    Moshe Raviv, Counselor, Embassy of Israel
    Eliyahu Chasin, Adviser to Allon
    Eytan Ben-Tsur, Aide to Allon

    Dr. Henry A. Kissinger, Secretary of State and Assistant to the President for National Security Affairs
    Ambassador Robert S. Ingersoll, Deputy Secretary of State
    Joseph J. Sisco, Under Secretary of State for Political Affairs
    Ambassador Ellsworth Bunker, Ambassador at Large and Chief of U.S. Delegation to Geneva Peace Conference on the Middle East
    Alfred L. Atherton, Jr., Assistant Secretary of State for Near Eastern and South Asian Affairs
    Harold H. Saunders, Deputy Assistant Secretary of State for Near Eastern and South Asian Affairs
    Walter B. Smith, II, Director, Israel and Arab-Israel Affairs
    Peter W. Rodman, NSC Staff

[Sisco hands Secretary Kissinger a paper.][2]

Dr. Kissinger: If you will just sign this. [Laughter]

Well, Mr. Foreign Minister, it is a great pleasure to welcome you here. We have worked together for so long so many years, that this is not a negotiation between two governments but a discussion among friends. We all recognize that we have an extremely complicated situation. As I see it, the purpose of your visit is not to see if we can come to any agreements, but to have a common strategy. So we don't keep asking who's doing what to whom, but so we understand what we're doing. This is the spirit of my colleagues and myself here. And this is the spirit of what we are doing.

---

[1] Source: National Archives, RG 59, Records of Henry Kissinger, 1973–77, Box 9, Nodis Memcons, July 1974, Folder 2. Secret; Nodis. The meeting was held in the Seventh Floor Conference Room at the Department of State. Brackets are in the original. A second meeting took place between Allon and Kissinger the next day from 1:20 until 3:40 p.m. in the Madison Room at the Department of State. (Memorandum of conversation, July 30; ibid., Folder 1) Their discussion focused on military supplies for Israel, the next negotiating phase, Soviet Jewry, Syrian Jewry, missing bodies in Egypt, Law of the Sea, an Egyptian nuclear reactor, and the European Community's dialogue with Arab countries.

[2] Not further identified, but the paper was apparently used as a prop for a joke between Kissinger and Allon.

Minister Allon: Well, I consider it a privilege to open the pilgrimage month of Foreign Ministers from the Middle East to Washington. The very fact that Washington has become the world center where one can seek help, help to come to agreement, is itself a major development. Thanks to the President of the United States, and thanks to the gifted Secretary of State.

Dr. Kissinger: You will give my junior colleagues some time to rebut that last remark. [Laughter]

Minister Allon: I consider it more a consultation among friends rather than a negotiation, because it's not with the United States we have to sign a peace agreement. Sometimes the choice isn't between the best and the worst, but to find the least evil.

Of course no one regrets the signing of the disengagement agreements.[3] Those agreements served the interests of both sides, and only agreements that serve the interests of both sides have a chance to survive. But we all know it is only the first step. We remember the last article of those agreements—that they were "only the first step to a final, just and lasting peace." We have to think what now to do to achieve peace.

This is now the proper time to thank you, you and your colleagues, for your help to Israel in the last year. It was a difficult year, with the war. We are glad, too, that our neighbors think you helped them to achieve some of their targets.

We now have to consider the next steps.

We now have to consider that our neighbors are now building up their military option, a very powerful one. Whether they are using it to back up the political option, or, when the moment comes, to use it as a military force—we don't know.

There were times when we thought your intelligence services played it down too much and you thought we played it up too much for our own purposes. I'm glad in the last week there is now agreement.

Dr. Kissinger: I'm not on the distribution for that.

Minister Allon: It was yesterday's development.

Dr. Kissinger: I am not aware there is a fundamental disagreement, but I frankly haven't seen this.

Mr. Saunders: It has not been put on paper yet. We're doing it for you.

---

[3] A reference to the first Egyptian-Israeli disengagement agreement of January 18 (Documents 10–13) and the Syrian-Israeli disengagement agreement signed on May 31 (Document 88).

Amb. Dinitz: We checked the figures, and there is no real disagreement. On projections, there was some disagreement, but not fundamental.

Dr. Kissinger: [to Saunders and Atherton]: I would like to see the old differences, too, and the reconciled [assessments].

Minister Allon: Whether we are right or not, we take into account the possibility that if and when—and in certain circumstances the Jordanians will join, and the Iraqis—when they decide to go to war, they will be capable as far as armament is concerned. Our job is to see that it doesn't happen, by two means—politically, and by trying to maintain the balance of military strength. I'm not certain a strong Israel will deter them from attacking; if not, it will insure our survival. You all know from Shimon Peres what the ratio is. One to three.

I know that by overstressing the military aspect I may damage the political argument.

Dr. Kissinger: So far you haven't.

Minister Allon: Because if war is a threat, then we'd better make more concessions. I am representing a government that is very keen on making peace. It would be a great achievement for this government if we could achieve a peace agreement with our neighbors. This is the desire of all our people, though we may differ on the terms.

The problem now is all our neighbors now believe they can get anything they want. They all believe—I hope wrongly—that America will give them what they want.

Dr. Kissinger: I don't know how anyone who has dealt with you can think they will get everything they want. They'll be happy to get anything they want.

Minister Allon: Hm, that's true. When I left for the airport, they—journalists—asked me if our requests for future aid were an ultimatum to the United States. I said our relations were so good that there could be no ultimatums. I will add a sentence—I'll make an ultimatum to myself: I shall not go to Geneva, and I shall not budge one inch, until the bilateral understandings with America are beginning to be implemented.

We are watching the Soviet airlift to our neighbors. We are lagging a bit behind. And, as Foreign Minister, I don't feel I can go to Geneva until the understandings we arrived at when we negotiated the Syrian thing and when the President spoke to the Prime Minister, and when Peres was here, and we had very good talks when Simon was in Israel,[4]

---

[4] Secretary of the Treasury William Simon visited Israel July 16–18. He met with several Israeli officials, including Rabin on July 17; telegram 4080 from Tel Aviv, July 19, transmitted a report of that meeting. The joint communiqué issued at the end of Simon's

[are fulfilled]. Something has got to show. Bureaucracy is heavy and slow, maybe on both sides.

I don't have to tell you we don't see the present arrangements as a new status quo. We are prepared to go ahead—not run amok, but to contribute our share. Because everybody wants to use the momentum. So do we.

So we have to agree among ourselves on what kind of Geneva Conference, how to hold it, which Arab country should come first, and what generally to expect from it.

So I will be very brief.

I am very unhappy that every six months the two UN emergency forces have to renew their mandate on what we call the north and south. I am very afraid that the Egyptians and the Syrians will use these as pressure either to concede faster or more than practical politics allow. So I don't know if it is possible to see if it can be more than a year.

You are in a better position to judge. I won't make it as an ultimative statement.

Dr. Kissinger: Not even to yourself? [Laughter]

The Foreign Minister will be a nervous wreck if he keeps making ultimatums to himself. Unless he is more schizophrenic a personality than I am.

Minister Allon: If possible, not to convene the Conference until it's renewed.

Amb. Dinitz: The Egyptian one comes up the 25th of October. The Syrian one, the 31st of November. [Laughter]

Dr. Kissinger: Notice how Atherton spotted it? The best Foreign Service in the world. [Laughter] There won't be a 31st of November.

Mr. Evron: America can do anything! You're a superpower.

Minister Allon: Incidentally, this will help the Arabs postpone their summit. I know Hussein, and Hassan, are very anxious to postpone it. For their own reasons. So they also could postpone it, November, December.

This is a very serious matter. I don't want to labor under the threat of a date: "Unless there is progress before the 24th of October, Egypt will walk out."

If you can work on your friends, the Soviets, the Arabs, not to have debates in the UN on the Middle East. We need a relaxed atmosphere. Nothing good comes out of these debates. It is, how do you say, counterproductive. We managed this last year.

---

visit is in telegram 4044 from Tel Aviv, July 18. (Both in the National Archives, RG 59, Central Foreign Policy Files)

Now you probably read the latest resolution of the Cabinet on Jordan and the Palestinians. [Tab A][5] I should explain. I disregard what the papers said, that State Department was unhappy. Even Simcha does.

Amb. Dinitz: We weren't informed either.

Dr. Kissinger: That isn't something I am informed about.

Mr. Atherton [to Dinitz] I gave you the text of what we would say if asked. It certainly did not show unhappiness.

Dr. Kissinger: The Office of the Secretary of State certainly didn't express unhappiness.

Minister Allon: It was a very good resolution, in two ways. First, if there was the impression in the world or America that the Government of Israel thought only Egypt should be subject of the negotiations and Jordan should be left to last, they see now this is not so. Those of us who thought that Egypt should be first, it was because we thought it made things easier for Jordan. We thought it helped the King if Egypt were going ahead first. Second, there is more space in Egypt, between the lines; Jordan is more complicated. We thought it would give Jordan more time. It had also a negative effect. Jordan thought we were punishing them for not opening the third front in the war.

Now the Government decided that we, if I may translate the exact decision, the Government, will do its best to open negotiations with Jordan on a peace agreement. It coincides with our decision on the Palestinians. The Palestinian question is not taboo. You can see already in the program of the Labour Alignment, mention of the Palestinian identity which can find expression in a Jordanian-Palestinian State. Of course, Jerusalem should remain the capital of Israel, but the border between the two states can be negotiated. So if we approach the next steps we can think about Jordan as about Egypt. We just have to think about how best to serve the common cause, what can be done. We're not saying Jordan should come first; we should discuss it.

When we say the Palestinians, we refer to those Palestinians who will be represented by the delegation of the Kingdom of Jordan. This isn't very different from the Hussein-Sadat agreement, when Hussein got the concession from Egypt that Hussein should be the representative of the Palestinians within Jordan,[6] and the implication that this includes those on the West Bank.

---

[5] Tab A, telegram 4109 from Tel Aviv, is attached but not printed. The July 21 Israeli Cabinet statement expressed Israeli readiness to work toward peace negotiations with Jordan.

[6] On July 18, after two days of meetings, King Hussein and President Sadat issued a communiqué that recognized King Hussein as the representative of Palestinians inside Jordan and the Palestine Liberation Organization as their representative outside of

According to the statistics, most Jordanian citizens are Palestinians, and most Palestinians have Jordanian citizenship. This is important if we're discussing who should represent the Palestinians. Of course, not the PLO. The PLO is doing its best to stay out. If you read their 1963 platform, Israel doesn't have the right of existence. So this is for left-wing romantics to think about, not a practical thing.

So you see we've left it open. I don't want any negotiations, either with Egypt or Jordan, before Geneva. Any negotiations should be the result of Geneva.

We thought from the Secretary of State that the reopening of the Suez Canal would be done by the end of this year. But now we see it won't be done until next March, April, maybe May. The resettling is slow. We won't say anything; it's their domestic affair. But it is not yet normalized, and we both attached importance to it. In Syria, nothing is being done yet—neither your estate [in Kuneitra], nor anything else. I won't say anything publicly, to invite an answer: "It's none of your business."

But since you played the major role, I thought you should know it is slow. Maybe he will use the opening of the Canal to ask for more.

So, no negotiations before Geneva. Maybe it's a good idea to give the Geneva Conference something to decide about. So maybe the Conference could decide the next step is with Egypt, or with Jordan.

Finally, the Geneva Conference should be more a framework than a sitting. Maybe ceremonial. I am inclined to prefer at the ambassadorial level. I am not a keen traveler. I will do it if you want. But the real negotiation should be elsewhere. Have a nice ceremonial opening session, a cordial one, and go back to the talks.

Whether the next negotiation should be by shuttle diplomacy on the Kissinger level, it depends on your burdens, your work.

We would like to have movement but cautiously, carefully, because movement should be in a careful way.

Dr. Kissinger: My nerves aren't up to it. If I gave ultimatums to myself, I couldn't stand it.

Let me make a few observations.

First, on the necessity of a strong Israel. There is no debate between us, and on any thing of our motives—friendship, self-interest, or Machiavellian maneuvering—there always has to be a strong Israel. Because our ability to act between parties presupposes a strong Israel. Otherwise the Arabs will attack it and will have no need to ask for our assistance.

Jordan and expressed agreement that the Palestinians should have a separate delegation at the Geneva Conference. (*New York Times*, July 19, 1974)

So there is no need to give ultimatums to yourself. You can. It's entirely a domestic affair. [Laughter]

Minister Allon: There is a kibbutz saying, self-labor.

Dr. Kissinger: So within our domestic possibilities, we need a strong Israel. Since Dinitz controls our domestic possibilities, you have a check. [Laughter]

Let me discuss another aspect. Don't think you're doing us a favor going to Geneva. If you don't want to go, don't. I'm no particular fan of Geneva. I assume you're negotiating for your own reasons, not as a favor to us.

I don't think the Arabs think they're going to get everything they want. In fact, I think the Arabs think they may not get anything, and this is a more realistic sense, no matter what they tell their publics. The moderates are under increased pressure from the others, and fear they're getting nothing.

Second, there is the anomaly that it requires strength on both sides. It is necessary to create the impression that their demands, while not being met, may not be foreclosed. So you think—I'll be frank—that it's salami tactics and that sooner or later you'll be met with unacceptable demands. The only way is to discuss what we're doing. It is not so wise to make statements on what you will never do. Because that will only accelerate the pressures you fear. Not to want to go down from Golan is one thing; but to announce it now only accelerates diplomatic pressures we're trying to avoid. So a measure of ambiguity in the public stance is essential. This is important for the Jewish Community here as well as for Israel.

The problem as I see it is this. Dinitz will give me hell for saying this later but I must give my honest conviction. I have said many times that I consider the position of Israel is precarious. A coalescence of all Arabs must be avoided. If there is another war, coupled with an oil boycott, it may lead to an economic collapse all over the West in the present precarious situation, and it will be a combination of the whole world—the Europeans, the Soviets. I don't know what Portugal's attitude on Lajes will be the next time.[7]

If your nightmare is being forced back to '67, my conviction is that this will bring it about. This is my conviction. Therefore, it is necessary to have a process to deal with the problems piecemeal, and one at a time. It means one Arab country should be making some progress and no Arab country should be foreclosed. It doesn't mean there should be progress, just that it is not foreclosed.

---

[7] A reference to Lajes airbase in the Azores, which the U.S. Government received permission from Portugal to use to resupply Israel during the October 1973 Arab-Israeli War.

Since you say you will talk with Egypt and Jordan, that is substantially met.

The procedure you outline is suicidal. Under these conditions.

Minister Allon: Under these conditions?

Dr. Kissinger: Where the [Geneva] Conference meets when no country has an incentive to keep it on. With nothing prepared in advance, the next time it won't be so easy. The last time we got away with it because the Russians didn't know what was happening; the next time it's convened, they won't let it be closed so fast. I have less interest than you in it, but that's incompatible with your other proposition that you can't do anything until then. Without a timetable for at least one Arab country, you will get the Russians leading an abstract discussion of Jerusalem, the frontiers, everything. Tactically, the procedure you outlined is the worst possible way. Either work out something beforehand, or have Geneva as early as possible.

No one is pressing now because they are all waiting to see what happens in August.

Often I have said it won't happen and it does. But our position now in the Arab world is much more precarious than in May. There is a malaise there.

Second, will they repopulate the Canal Zone? I think they will. You know why they haven't: the area is devastated, no money has been appropriated here. I don't consider it a substantive argument. You can't hinge it all on that. If you want to make implementation of the next stage dependent on the opening, that is reasonable.

You could tell that to Senator Jackson this evening on the Suez Canal, so he would get off my back.

You have to give the Egyptians the same vista in December. I don't think it will work otherwise at Geneva. It is much too dangerous to have an unstructured Geneva. If there is some progress with Egypt beforehand, then they have incentive to abort Geneva.

But we have to talk about what the second phase is, because I and probably you have trouble coming up with a good package.

Minister Allon: May I interrupt? Since we think it's good to start with Egypt ...

Dr. Kissinger: It should start by September.

Minister Allon: So you tell Fahmy that we are ready to start negotiating, and he will agree to stop Geneva.

Dr. Kissinger: We don't want the Geneva Conference; we start with that. If you start at the ambassadorial level, that makes it easy for the immediate problems, but then they will make it a permanent organ. The Egyptians don't want it to be a permanent organ.

Minister Allon: Nor do I.

Dr. Kissinger: If you start it low key, at the ambassadorial level, it will go fairly well for a month, then they will escalate it to the Foreign Minister level and it will be difficult to refuse. The Soviets won't be pushed out so easily and will maneuver so as to make it extremely difficult to settle separately. Particularly because the Syrians will back them.

Minister Allon: Why have Geneva?

Dr. Kissinger: Because we are committed to it. [To Sisco:] You want to go to Geneva? You look wounded.

Mr. Sisco: Without negotiations already, it is very dangerous to have Geneva and nothing else.

Dr. Kissinger: Yes. It will lead to immediate pressure by the Arabs to start Geneva as rapidly as possible; it will make Geneva unmanageable. Thirdly, we should use the other negotiations to delay Geneva. If you do it with more than one, you will have allies in delaying it. So I strongly disagree with your strategy.

On tactics, I strongly disagree with shuttle diplomacy. It should be some other way. This too will delay it. It doesn't mean I may not go in at some point, but the basic pattern can't be shuttle.

We can't long delay some talks with Egypt or Jordan.

As to the content of these talks, it is very hard to see.

I am attracted to the idea of not opening Geneva until UNEF and UNDOF is renewed. If Geneva is never opened, you won't hear any complaint from me. It is manageable only if we agree on what to talk about with Egypt.

The Egyptian is coming here with his economic ministers,[8] so he will not only be discussing Israel.

On the problems Israel faces, there is one other point, our domestic situation. There is no question that in our domestic situation as it is, systematic pressure on Israel is less likely. I might as well state it, because you know it anyway. We haven't engaged in systematic pressure anyway. But it also makes it much less likely that in a crisis situation we can act with the ruthlessness and decisiveness that we have done in the past.

I don't think Geneva can be delayed until December; but I am not sure. Syria in any case will be a massive problem.

Geneva was going to be in July; we've pushed it back to September and October. But that doesn't avoid the problem of how to handle it.

---

[8] Foreign Minister Fahmy and a team of Egyptian economic officials visited Washington August 12–19.

On UN debate on the Middle East, it won't be encouraged by us and you.

So the questions we have to face are: What would be the package one wants to discuss with Egypt and Jordan? Second, what is the timing? And third, how do we get it started?

[Sisco goes out to release a statement on Cyprus.]

Minister Allon: Let me start with the self-inflicted ultimatum. I am very pleased with what you had to say about America's position vis-à-vis Israel's strength.

Dr. Kissinger: All of this is on the assumption that this new Government is immune to leaks.

Minister Allon: This is a responsible group.

But we know you mean it, and the President repeated it in June. But we are now trying to translate it into deliveries, concrete things. And we want you, as a friend, to mobilize your great influence on the other agencies, so the difficulties will be removed.

I don't want to go into the details of the long list, but I must convince you if you are not already convinced: We are bound to lose too many people. America should consider Israel's defense forces as really a most reliable army, which by its very existence and ability and efficiency serves a common interest. This wasn't the reason for its founding, but I am glad it serves a common interest and we couldn't have found a more reliable partner.

Since Peres was here . . . but time is a very crucial factor.[9] We are in a hurry because we would like to avert a possible war or at least win it safely if it happens.

So I would like to see that, when our military mission comes in a few weeks, it will have your assistance.

Dr. Kissinger: I have a list of deliveries you want to have speeded up. I don't know definitely, but I will certainly take it up in a favorable way with the Defense Department.

Minister Allon: Thank you.

Amb. Dinitz: There are two categories.

Dr. Kissinger: There are two categories: one is speeding up of the old items, and the second is the seven items that are new.

Amb. Dinitz: Or problematical.

Minister Allon: These seven items are really crucial.

Dr. Kissinger: We have the decision to make whether to do it or not do it. You will have to use it responsibly.

---

[9] Shimon Peres arrived in Washington on June 24 and met with Schlesinger on June 25 to discuss arms purchases. (*New York Times*, June 24, 1974, p. 1)

Minister Allon: This will be good news when I go back and tell the Prime Minister and my colleagues.

Dr. Kissinger: I haven't said . . . I told your Ambassador I would look into it.

Minister Allon: If you put your weight into it. You've put some weight on, so . . .

Amb. Dinitz: If I may, Mr. Secretary. It is difficult for every army to part with equipment, particularly when it's in short supply. But it takes a decision on a very high level to send it. It is not a question that the Secretary of Defense says he's for it; he has to be impressed that this is part and parcel of our ability to carry on the political dialogue.

Dr. Kissinger: I understand the point. It's not the first time I have heard it. I've told you what I can do. I can only repeat that you're not doing us a favor by continuing the political dialogue.

Minister Allon: About financing, we have already discussed with Secretary Simon. There are no problems of principle but, again, we feel the urgency is not felt.

Dr. Kissinger: I'm seeing Simon again today and I'll discuss it with him. I have also had discussions with Burns about it.

Minister Allon: The figures—

Dr. Kissinger: The figures I know. $4.5 billion.

Amb. Dinitz: I checked on that, Mr. Secretary: If the process of legislation is passed in both Houses, it automatically continues [in a new Congress]. If it is passed only in one House, it has to start over again in the new Congress.

Minister Allon: I don't have to tell you about the relationship between politics and economics.

Amb. Dinitz: Your lesson is coming back to haunt you!

Minister Allon: We placed before Simon a number of ideas, and if you can help . . .

Dr. Kissinger: Is there one Cabinet member who doesn't blame me for his troubles?

Minister Allon: But we need your help.

Dr. Kissinger: No, I understand. I agree with you. After I see the Secretary of Defense, on Friday, I can give you some idea of how influence from the White House can accelerate your deliveries. I am certain some acceleration is possible. On the other list, I will look it over. I'll take it up with the Secretary of Defense on Friday.

On the economics, I discussed it with the Appropriations Committee today. But they are obsessed with cutting expenditures across the board.

Amb. Dinitz: The State Department budget.

Dr. Kissinger: Thank God they didn't ask about that; I didn't know anything about it. They're looking for substantial cuts to make, for example, in the Defense budget, which affects a lot of things, including SALT. So one would really have to consider when the best time is to submit an authorization request. The first I heard of this scheme was yesterday.

In principle, I understand your concern. I have already indicated to some of your lobbyists that if they can get Congress to increase it we won't veto it.

Amb. Dinitz: That's on Supporting Assistance.

Minister Allon: It's amazing: my economists tell me the same money last year would have tripled the amount.

Amb. Dinitz: In agricultural products.

Dr. Kissinger: PL–480.

Amb. Dinitz: The same amount, just the price has gone up so.

Dr. Kissinger: You are seeing Simon?

Minister Allon: Thursday.

The idea on authorization was a substitute for the idea we discussed with the President in Jerusalem. The President thought it too difficult—long-term appropriation.

Dr. Kissinger: A long-term appropriation is impossible.

Minister Allon: But a White House request, and long-term authorization . . .

Dr. Kissinger: Joe Sisco and I for five years have always favored getting it out of the way once and for all so we don't have to go through it every year. If we can wrap it up in one negotiation, it's easier.

You can't look at it in conditional terms. You don't want the Arabs to coalesce. We can face these questions without blackmailing each other.

Minister Allon: Of course.

I can't help hearing what you say about if another war breaks out. We hope it won't. Militarily, we're confident. I have to say: if there is another war that is imposed upon us, we shall win it. And therefore those who will have to deal with the political aspect of it will face a more stubborn people. With Europe, without Europe. Because the people think that after every war we concede too much.

I learned my military lessons too well. I know what would have happened to the great President Sadat if the war had gone on two or three more days. Unless the Russians invaded, which is another problem.

So we want to avoid it by political movement—not gimmicks, but real movement—and strengthening Israel.

What movement is, I would like to discuss.

Dr. Kissinger: I'd like to hear your ideas because we don't have concrete ideas.

Why don't I give you ideas after Rifai is here.[10] On Jordan, we're not doctrinaire. On Jordan, the pressure isn't from other Arabs. The question is how long we can keep him in it before all the others commit themselves to the PLO.

Minister Allon: On negotiations with the Arabs, it's our problem but it's not only ours; it's a world problem. You're a super power, with interests in the Middle East. Therefore, we're consulting each other about the future. When I say we're not going to Geneva, it's just on the bilateral relationship between us. But you've given us an answer.

On Geneva, I don't need Geneva. We all understand it's part of the proceedings. We know we'll have to go at some point. But if the Arabs don't want it, we won't want it.

Thirdly, at the ambassadorial level: I meant only that someone would go just to watch the situation. With all due respect to the Ambassadors here, I meant it to give less importance to Geneva.

Dr. Kissinger: When Gromyko first suggested it, I was attracted to it. And I told him I was attracted to it. Fahmy saw it more clearly than I did. We can't make it an issue or principle. But with them, it's harder to end it because . . .

Ambassador Dinitz: Because of less busy people!

Dr. Kissinger: And it's worse if it escalates into the Foreign Minister level than if it started with the Foreign Ministers.

Ambassador Dinitz: Fahmy said he didn't have anybody he could trust.

Minister Allon: My problem is I have so many people I trust that I'd have a hard time choosing.

Dr. Kissinger: We're having lunch tomorrow? And a meeting? Make it longer.

Minister Allon: About the Geneva thing, dates: frankly speaking I'd like a little time.

Dr. Kissinger: I understand your problem. Rabin explained it to me when we met. We've cooperated with you.

Minister Allon: I remember in the first Geneva Conference, what was the practical outcome? There was a decision to go into negotiations with Egypt.

Dr. Kissinger: The reason it worked was we had started disengagement negotiations with the Egyptians. While there was no final posi-

---

[10] Prime Minister Rifai visited Washington August 5–8.

tion, we had told the Egyptians that if they left you alone until the elections, we'd get a disengagement.

You could send someone here, if you want a procedure. And we could tell the Egyptians the nature of the package. If they tell us it must be done by a certain date ...

Minister Allon: Why are they in a hurry?

Dr. Kissinger: I don't know if they're in a hurry. They don't want Geneva to get out of hand. I don't know how great a hurry they are in. I think they are in more of a hurry than your schedule indicates. If we agree to go at as slow a pace sufficient to keep the Egyptians on a moderate course, it is no problem.

You should come back, or Rabin should come.

Minister Allon: Yes.

Dr. Kissinger: Or you and Rabin. We don't need to decide now for December 1. We won't force you at all. We won't go faster than we think the minimum requirements are for the Egyptians, and maybe the Jordanians. We'll put it before you. Fahmy suggested he wanted the whole process completed by October; I said it was out of the question. I didn't have to consult with you. We'll give you the deadlines they give us.

And I want to talk to you privately for a minute.

Minister Allon: What should we tell the press?

Dr. Kissinger: What we should tell the press is we reviewed the whole process of the negotiation and agreed on the necessity of a negotiation. There was complete agreement.

Ambassador Dinitz: And we reviewed bilateral relations.

Minister Allon: Yes, we reviewed bilateral relations. And we discussed future steps.

Dr. Kissinger: I think it helps with the Arabs if we give a positive impression. A positive meeting.

[The Secretary escorted the Minister downstairs to the lobby where they both spoke briefly to the press. Text at Tab B.][11]

---

[11] Tab B, entitled "Remarks by Foreign Minister Yigal Allon and Secretary of State Henry A. Kissinger following their meeting in the Department of State, July 30, 1974," is attached but not printed.

94. Memorandum of Conversation[1]

Camp David, August 1, 1974, 8:10–11:10 p.m.

PARTICIPANTS

Yigal Allon, Minister of Foreign Affairs and Deputy Prime Minister of Israel
Simcha Dinitz, Israeli Ambassador to the United States
Eliyahu Chasin, Adviser to Minister Allon

Dr. Henry A. Kissinger, Secretary of State and Assistant to the President for National Security Affairs
Major General Brent Scowcroft, Deputy Assistant to the President for National Security Affairs
Peter W. Rodman, National Security Council Staff

SUBJECT

The Future Map of Israel

Allon: Can you try and tell me how would you envisage Israel's map within the context of peace and security arrangements, so any responsible Government can satisfy its people that this is an arrangement not for a decade, but forever?

Kissinger: There is no United States opinion. Do you want my personal opinion?

Allon: Yes.

Kissinger: My personal opinion is that—and I haven't thought it through—if we do it in terms of the 1967 frontiers, I don't think it is impossible to do it with the 1967 frontiers with Egypt; I do think it is impossible to accept the 1967 frontiers with Syria, and I think it is impossible with Jordan.

Allon: Impossible?

Kissinger: Yes. That is my conception on frontiers. On the West Bank where the frontiers should be. I don't know.

On the Syrian side it can't be 1967 but it can't be the present line—because I think it may be necessary to go one more move with Syria. But it will be some clear distance from 1967.

On the West Bank, I haven't thought it through.

With Egypt, it seems not incompatible with Israel's security, particularly if some special arrangements could be worked out—I don't understand the obsession with Sharm el-Sheikh—but for some stra-

---

[1] Source: National Archives, RG 59, Records of Henry Kissinger, 1973–77, Box 9, Nodis Memcons, August 1974, Folder 3. Secret; Nodis. The dinner meeting was held in the Laurel Cabin at Camp David, Maryland. Brackets are in the original.

tegic points. But it would be in the context of the substantial demilitarization of the Sinai.

But I have never discussed it with any of my colleagues—or with any Arab.

Nor with Sadat. I admit I sometimes talk in an ambiguous way that doesn't exclude it.

Allon: What do you foresee with Jordan?

Kissinger: Jordan is a special problem. One reason I think you shouldn't go to the final frontier question with Jordan is because you are not ready to discuss Jerusalem.

Allon: If there are these arrangements, what is the American idea of how it can act as a responsible body to oversee them?

Kissinger: In the context of peace, there should be some long-term supply arrangements even more than now.

Allon: The U.S. and Israel?

Kissinger: Yes. And I would be prepared to give an American guarantee.

Allon: A pact or a long-term understanding?

Kissinger: Either. But you should think it through, because I wouldn't recommend it. You almost have it now in fact, and it would start a violent debate. The Arabs might want one.

Allon: With you? Against whom? The Jordanians would want one?

Kissinger: No. The Egyptians would want one.

[At 8:20 the group moved to the diner table.]

Allon: Did you make any inquiry to be made by your experts: What is the meaning of demilitarized areas—legally, militarily, and practically? It would help.

Kissinger: I have not asked such a study to be made. It would be a good idea.

Allon: There is a basic mistrust in public opinion about demilitarized zones. We had a difficult experience with the Egyptians and Syrians. And we remember 1967. And we know the demilitarized zone between North and South Vietnam. And we remember the Rhine [the Rhineland].

Kissinger: Actually the demilitarized zone between North and South Vietnam served very well until 1972. And when they violated it in 1972, we reacted violently. The American public understood it. It was absurd.

They never really violated it seriously. All their major roads went through Laos. When we went into Laos in 1971, we used our forces to protect the flank, and it never came.

Allon: I would like to hear more of your view.

Kissinger: I don't think we should talk now about final borders.

Allon: So you understand that until now terrain plays a major role.

Kissinger: I understand.

Allon: In the defense of the country.

Kissinger: And also in the perception of itself of the country.

Allon: Yesterday to the Senators I had to explain why defensible borders are so important, without saying specifically what these borders are. I was prepared for a question by Fulbright; he never asked.

I'll explain my position. Starting with Egypt. You asked what is the importance of Sharm el-Sheikh. It's a legitimate question, particularly because in the October war, when Egypt imposed a blockade . . .

Kissinger: She did it at Bab el-Mandeb.

Allon: She did it at Bab el-Mandeb. But when we reach the next phase of the overall settlement, or interim, we may raise with the Egyptians and Americans: what are the guarantees of freedom of passage of Bab el-Mandeb?

Kissinger: I agree.

Allon: Even the unilateral guarantee of America couldn't do it.

Kissinger: It couldn't be done.

Allon: This is one of the questions I will raise: How can you guarantee freedom of passage through Bab el-Mandeb? Now Sharm el-Sheikh is important not only because it doesn't provide the Egyptians with the temptation to do it again. You may tell me Sadat is a wonderful man; but he's not immortal.

Dinitz: The Secretary said he was less impressed with Sadat than with Asad.

Kissinger: Because he played cutely with the President.

Allon: Now we are very close to the entrance of the Gulf of Suez. Maybe this is why they oppose it. Maybe it doesn't need Israeli sovereignty; maybe a lease of 60, 90 years.

Kissinger: This they will not do.

Part of my job is to tell you what is possible. Sometimes I am wrong. But it is not possible to get a final settlement now. You should draw a line that doesn't include Sharm el-Sheikh.

Allon: Now? I'm talking about a final settlement. I think in a permanent solution we should control Sharm el-Sheikh, not necessarily by extending Israel's sovereignty to Sharm el-Sheikh but by agreement with Egypt to lease it to us X number of years. But Israeli control.

We need there a military base, an airstrip for Phantoms, and of course military services. The Navy is there. To give us control of the

Red Sea and prevent the Egyptians from controlling it—the future leaders, or even Sadat himself.

As far as the Navy is concerned, this is the only place from which we can reach Bab el-Mandeb.

Scowcroft: With ships, not air cover.

Dinitz: We can with refueling. With F–14s and F–15s can we do it?

Scowcroft: Maybe with F–15s.

Allon: One other sensitive spot is Eilat. Where we've developed a beautiful air base near Eilat, to the west, on Egyptian soil, which is essential to the defense of the southern half of Israel.

Kissinger: That is conceivable. I'm not saying attainable, but conceivable.

Allon: So we must have breathing space. It is vital.

Kissinger: I understand.

Allon: Number three is Oudjah al-Haffir. It is a road juncture, on our side, but we need an extended area to make this juncture safer.

Kissinger: What is an extended area?

Allon: Forty kilometers, 35 kilometers, 30 kilometers. [Laughter]

Kissinger: Where is the airstrip near Eilat? Fifty kilometers away? [Laughter] Because I can understand one or two.

Allon: The third critical area is south of Rafah.

Kissinger: Where?

Allon: The Gaza strip. We must have a protected area. Not all the way to El Arish.

These are the four vital areas. [See map at Tab A.]

Kissinger: A 20-kilometer strip!

Allon: Four, five—I didn't bring maps.

Kissinger: But if I'm any judge, the places where it's 40 are more frequent than where it's five.

Dinitz: Mr. Secretary, you forget we're dealing here with Sinai. The last time you were with us it was [dealing with] 500 meters. But Sinai is a vast area. Three times the size of Israel.

Kissinger: I don't think Sadat will ever agree to give up an inch of Egyptian territory. Without another war.

Allon: What about another war?

Kissinger: With what result?

Allon: I know the military result.

Kissinger: But you cannot have a war in 1975 without being pushed back. There will be an economic collapse. I saw John McCloy today—he was discussing something else—he said there is no capital market anymore in New York. It wouldn't take much to push it over the cliff. And there would be a violent reaction. A time-wasting strategy now would . . .

Allon: That's what I wanted to talk about.

Kissinger: In 1976 everyone understands the limits of the American process. In a Presidential election year.

Another idea I was kicking around—whether it's possible to get those four items into some status other than Israeli possession of Egyptian territory. But keeping control. That conceptually I could understand.

Allon: What I tried to draw here is the minimum.

Kissinger: I understand.

Allon: The minimum that I could get a majority for.

Kissinger: I know. It's the minimum that any Israeli has ever described to me. It is not the same as just drawing the military line down.

Allon: Much less. Much less.

Kissinger: I try never to get into a position where I offer any plan.

Allon: All right. This is of course conditioned on wide areas of demilitarized area, and control, which I think should include the passes.

Kissinger: I agree with you.

Allon: This way could cover those points.

Kissinger: The Egyptians could advance militarily to the existing Israeli line—another ten kilometers—but everything else is demilitarized.

Allon: Yes. And the passes are very important. And they should be controlled by someone.

Kissinger: Some international force.

Scowcroft: How about a joint force?

Allon: This is the best.

Kissinger: That would put Israelis on Egyptian territory.

Allon: All three of them together!

Kissinger: We thought we could make some of the Syrian lessons work for us. We thought when we had a line, the rest would be easy; it took two and a half weeks, but it did defuse the situation. If on the Egyptian side we first got agreement on the line, we could spend lots of time on the other details. Which would be easy if I'm not there.

I like the idea of doing it in Washington.

Kissinger: And give me a line with Egypt, for the long term.

Allon: There are two possibilities: One is to move somewhere on the eastern end of the passes while the passes are controlled by UNEF.

Kissinger: What's the other?

Allon: The other is to go further east. But this should be accompanied by the measures we discussed in your office.

Kissinger: What would you want in return?

Allon: Peace de facto. If we give him less, then he may insist it will be limited for a shorter period. But peace de facto in any case. This is particularly if he gets back the oil. Because Abu Rudeis is very big. Maybe he shouldn't get the oil in the first stage; it would give him the incentive.

Kissinger: I'm not Sisco; I won't have a plan. [Laughter] But I have to have a concept. In November he had a plan to move to El Arish as part of disengagement.

Allon: If we move to a line: El Arish to somewhere west of Sharm el-Sheikh, we shall expect something substantial.

Kissinger: My feel for the Egyptians is, a decade is out of the question.

I know enough to get through August now, and I'll do no more until the UN. We'll have to decide now the tactics after I talk to Fahmi.

Tab A[2]

August 1, 1974.

[See Appendix A, map 4]

---

[2] Written across the top of the map at Tab A is the notation, "Allon's Strategic Points, 8/1/74." The handwriting is not identified.

95. Memorandum of Conversation[1]

Washington, August 12, 1974, 9 a.m.

PARTICIPANTS

    President Ford
    Dr. Henry A. Kissinger, Secretary of State and Assistant to the President for National Security Affairs
    Major General Brent Scowcroft, Deputy Assistant to the President for National Security Affairs

[Omitted here is discussion of Ford's speaking engagements.]

[Kissinger:] On the Middle East problem—you will be seeing a number of Middle East ministers over the coming weeks. The actors: Israel, Egypt, Syria, Jordan are the principals. Then other Arabs. Then the Soviet Union. Then the Europeans and Japan. Our job is to find a policy which relates all those problems to each other.

First, after 1967 I operated on the basis of the historical illusion that the Arabs were militarily impotent, and U.S. support was firm. Rabin told me, "We never had it so good." That was true as long as they could defeat the Arabs and we supported them. I had a misconception of our strategy. Between 1967 and 1974, Egypt and Syria were essentially Soviet satellites. In Egypt we had a low-level Interests Section and in Syria we had nothing. Our strategy during this period was . . . we always try to have a simple strategy but complicated tactics. We like complicated tactics, not for their own sake because we want the other parties committed first so we can sell our support to keep things fluid. We try to create a need for an American role before we give it—to ensure that both parties are ready. That we changed last spring. This was good strategy except with the Soviet Union, where we have to be simple, direct, and clear. In the Mideast before the October War, we tried to create such frustrations that the Arabs would leave the Soviet Union and come to us. We didn't want the impression that Soviet pressure produces results—that it had to be us. The Soviets could give only arms.

We didn't expect the October War.

The President: But wasn't it helpful?

Kissinger: We couldn't have done better if we had set the scenario.

The President: Even the heavy Israeli losses helped, didn't they?

---

[1] Source: Ford Library, National Security Adviser, Memoranda of Conversations, Box 4, August 12, 1974, Ford, Kissinger. Secret; Nodis. The meeting was held in the Oval Office at the White House. President Nixon resigned as President of the United States on August 9, and Gerald Ford was sworn in as President that same day at 12:03 p.m.

Kissinger: Once the war started, we helped Israel stabilize the situation. But it was not without a cost they couldn't sustain. Their casualties were enormous and had enormous impact. But they restored the situation and reversed some Arab cockiness—but the Arabs know Israel can't stand attrition.

The most moderate Arabs are the Jordanians. The most consistently moderate are the Egyptians. They almost broke with the Soviet Union and will be bellwethers to future progress. The most erratic are the Syrians. For them—radicals—to sign a document with Israel was a monumental event.

The other players—Saudi Arabia. Faisal is a kook but a shrewd cookie. He is in a position where all Arabs come to him.

The President: Is it him or his advisors?

Kissinger: It is him. He used to be the Foreign Minister. He has a standard pitch on Jews. The first time I went, his speech to me was that all Jews are bad. They are cowards, who are mentioned unfavorably in the Koran. The second time I went, he pointed out he recognized the difference between Jews and Zionists. The third time, the Foreign Minister said he didn't consider me a Jew but a human being. [Laughter] You might consider inviting him next year.

The President: Has he ever been here?

Kissinger: The second time over. With Nixon. On the left, there is Libya and Iraq. Algeria is a key. We will try to use your accession to restore diplomatic relations.

Then the Soviet Union. They lost Egypt and they are in trouble in Syria. It is becoming a movement in Iraq. Egypt was an enormous commitment of prestige and they have suffered badly.

It is not true that they started the October War—they opposed it but didn't try to stop it. The problem was they supported the Arabs but not enough. They tried to work a line between supporting the Arabs and not antagonizing us. We can't let Israel win the next war too heavily. Soviet intervention would be almost inevitable.

Europe is fearful of oil pressures and is eager to restore their former position in the Middle East. Right now they are in check because they are afraid if they interfere with American policy things will go bad and the embargo will be imposed again.

The Arabs' demand is for the 1967 frontiers. Israel considers that these would be the end of Israel. The country was only 12 kilometers wide in some places. Almost all of Israel would be under SAM coverage.

The Palestinians' rights are undefined and Jerusalem very complicated.

The basic strategy has been this: Israel can't stand and we can't handle dealing with all these issues at once. That is what the Soviet Union wants. That would guarantee a stalemate and a war. We must move step by step, which will make further steps possible. Israel says another Golan move is the last one. That is impossible but it is very difficult. To keep that last, we must move with Jordan or Egypt.

I have the instinct Rabin wanted to pull with Nixon what he did in 1971—produce a stalemate with abstract proposals and rely on American public opinion. They don't mind the Arabs being with the Soviet Union as long as it is not extreme. From 1967 to 1973 the situation was ideal for Israel. The Arabs can't make peace because they don't know how to settle the Palestinian issue. Israel can't either, because Jerusalem would burst their domestic structure. But they would like Sadat to formally end belligerency. Egypt can't do it, but maybe they can take the appropriate steps without a formal statement.

The President: Such as?

Kissinger: No blockade; Israeli cargo permitted through the Suez Canal.

The President: How is the Suez clearance going?

Kissinger: It can be completed by the end of the year. Sadat wants our advice on whether to hurry or delay. A delay is not worth it.

The Soviets want Geneva to open quickly. We don't because the Soviet Union will try to maneuver us into being Israel's lawyer. The last time, we opened and closed quickly, but it will be tougher the next time. So we want to set something up beforehand. But we can't humiliate the Soviet Union. We have to open Geneva by November, but keep it in a low key.

I told Dinitz that Rabin should ask to see you. They don't want to, because they are afraid you will pressure them to move and they don't want to. We can't stall till hell freezes over, like Israel wants.

The President: What is your timetable?

Kissinger: If Sadat knows what he will get, he will wait. Your talks with Sadat will be important.

The President: Should I see Rabin before or after I see Sadat?

Kissinger: Israel wants after, but that's tougher. We wanted to complete Jordan first, but a cable today[2] showed that is not possible. The problem in Jordan is the Palestinians backed by the radical states. Israel is afraid that a Palestinian state would be radical. Yet the Israeli Government needs the Religious Party to govern and their religion says they must have all of Israel to govern. So a new election must be held if

---

[2] Cable is not further identified.

any territory is to be given up, and the government is afraid of the results.

We are trying to get Israel to negotiate with Jordan and give back some of the West Bank. Then we can say the issue is between Jordan and the PLO. Then we can stay out of the triangle—Jordan, Israel and Arafat.

I made progress with Allon on a scheme which might work. If Egypt will wait, we are in grand shape. If Egypt has to go first, we are okay, if Egypt will keep the Palestinians quiet. If they want simultaneous negotiations, we are in trouble.

If there is a blow-up, Europe and Japan would support the Arabs. There should be no illusions about that.

If you could go with Jordan first, the negotiations would give us a 3–4 months breather.

On Syria, Israel can't give up all the Golan, but it can be more flexible. The problem is the settlements they have right up to the line. We use your newness to delay.

This is the context of Israeli supply. Defense can't use the Israel-Arab process to put the monkey on your and my back.

The President: It is better if the problem is logistics rather than political.

Kissinger: Yes. You can control the taps.

The President: Allon told me about their shortage of military equipment. Is that true?

Kissinger: Yes. But we have tanks in storage in Europe. Supply is our big card now.

They have a $5 billion authorization they would like you to put in all at once to draw on over the next three years.

The President: I think we should hold them off until we see their attitude. That is a hole card we control. I'm not sure Congress would jump at something like this with the current inflation.

Kissinger: There would be an explosion in the Arab world with the $5 billion they proposed. It should be done in the context of ongoing negotiations and getting back Arab territory. We got the FMS to go through that way.

The critical issue is Egyptian military equipment. The Soviet Union is turning them off. If that continues, the military will have to turn out Sadat or go back to the Soviet Union. We are trying to get others to give parts to Egypt, but sooner or later we have to face up to it. We have had talks on equipping them through Saudi Arabia. The first step would be to send it to Saudi Arabia and let Egyptian troops train in it. The legal problem would come up if equipment filtered to Egypt.

Saudi Arabia is willing to use 200 million for Egypt and DOD has broken out a package which makes sense.

The President: What are they talking about?

Scowcroft: F–4s, TOWs. I will bring a list tomorrow.

Kissinger: The thing we have going with the Arabs is that we deliver and we treat them gentler than the Soviet Union.

With Fahmy you can avoid getting into this or talk. If you talk, I recommend a sympathetic approach, but point out that it presents bureaucratic problems and you need to get control first. At present, DOD would leak.

The President: I agree. What would be the DOD position?

Kissinger: Clements would agree. Schlesinger would agree on the surface but his actual position would depend on his political assessment. Brown is okay. Ellsworth I can't assess.

The President: Ellsworth is a team player—first class.

Kissinger: There is no philosophical objection by Schlesinger but he would try to shift responsibility out of DOD.

If you could indicate sympathy, but say we have a big problem with the bureaucracy and Congress.

First, the sales to Saudi Arabia are no problem. But before they give it to Egypt you would have to tell Congress.

Even Israel should be willing to go along, because we could control resupply.

The President: I would think it would be better for us than the Soviet Union to control their resupply.

Kissinger: Yes, but it will be traumatic for them and all hell will break loose here.

To cut Egypt off will certainly force Egypt back to the Soviet Union.

The President: Domestically, it will depend on Egypt's willingness to make a reasonable settlement with Israel.

Kissinger: Sadat is wise. He has to make tough statements because he has his own constituency. We have a fine relationship with him. Israel has had exercises to scare them. The Egyptian Chief of Staff got intemperate with me and Sadat calmed him down. He is relaxed about it now.

The President: Is he a good leader?

Kissinger: Egyptians aren't great soldiers like the Israeli soldiers. But he is a decent, competent military leader.

The Middle East is the worst problem we face. The oil situation is the worst we face. We talk again. But we can't afford another embargo. If we are faced with that, we may have to take some oil fields.

The President: Like the Gulf and Iran.

Kissinger: Not Iran. I oppose Simon because Iran wouldn't join an embargo.

The President: How do we do it without contingency plans?

Kissinger: DOD is doing that along with other contingency plans. It would be helpful if you said to Fahmy that an oil embargo would face you with a difficult situation.

The President: Let's talk Wednesday morning about Fahmy's strategy.

Kissinger: Great, and I'll talk oil strategy then.

Our energy actions are going well. The key elements of our proposal—even oil sharing—are being accepted. I'll brief on this Wednesday also.

In October we should get the key producers together to talk next steps—not military action. One thing would be to get Europe not to buy beyond a certain price and have a sharing program to help out in case of any selective boycott. The key element is Project Independence.[3]

The President: It seems to have languished.

Kissinger: Sawhill doesn't have the power to push it. The best way to get a handle on all this is through Project Independence. You are in a great position to get allied cooperation which is unprecedented since the 40's.

The President: I want an updating on Project Independence. Part of the problem is Congress.

Kissinger: There is too much bureaucracy involved.

The President: Also Scoop and ERDA and getting all the agencies working together. We are playing a funny game.

[Omitted here is discussion unrelated to the Arab-Israeli dispute.]

---

[3] Project Independence was President Nixon's domestic response to the energy crisis brought on by the Arab oil embargo.

96. National Security Study Memorandum 207[1]

Washington, August 12, 1974.

TO

The Secretary of Defense
The Deputy Secretary of State
The Director of Central Intelligence

SUBJECT

Israeli Future Military Requirements

The President has directed a study of the proposals of the Government of Israel included in its paper "The Defense Requirements of the Israeli Defense Forces for the Next Ten Years (1974–1983)," known as "Matmon B."[2] The purpose of the study is to review and assess the Israeli plan in the context of its implications for the situation in the Middle East, the peace settlement process, U.S. foreign policy, U.S. military readiness posture including international security interests, and defense production. The study should consider, but not be limited to the following:

Military factors:

—Assessment of the threat as projected by the Israelis, and the rationale and reasons for differences in U.S. and Israeli perceptions of the threat.
—Assessment of the force structure which the Israelis consider necessary to meet the threat.
—Military strategy which the projected Israeli force structure is designed to implement.
—Implications of Matmon for U.S. defense planning, i.e., impact on U.S. defense production as it affects the readiness of U.S. forces and the ability of DOD to meet military assistance and sales commitments to other nations.

Political and economic factors:

—An assessment of the political strategy which the projected Israeli force structure is designed to implement, both in terms of Israeli interests and U.S. interests;
—the effect of approval of Matmon in whole or in part on the

---

[1] Source: Ford Library, NSC Institutional Files (H-Files), Box 31, NSSMs, NSSM 207, Israeli Future Military Requirements, Folder 1. Secret; Sensitive. Copies were sent to the Chairman of the Joint Chiefs of Staff and to the Director of the Office of Management and Budget.

[2] Matmon is the Hebrew word for "treasure." Matmon B was a list of military equipment Israel requested from the United States after the October 1973 Arab-Israeli war.

Middle East peace settlement process, possible Soviet reaction, and U.S. long-term interests in the Arab world;

—budgeting and funding requirements to support the Matmon proposal.

Based on the foregoing assessment, the study should present alternative U.S. responses to the Matmon proposal. Each option should include specific implementing actions relevant to the peace-making process, funding and production capabilities, and actions required for obtaining Congressional approval for the necessary multi-year programming and funding. The advantages and disadvantages of each option should be thoroughly assessed.

The study should be prepared by an NSC ad hoc group comprising representatives of the addressees and the NSC staff, and chaired by the representative of the Secretary of Defense. The completed study should be submitted by August 26, 1974, for review by the NSC Senior Review Group prior to its consideration by the President.

The study should be conducted on a most close-hold, need-to-know basis.

Henry A. Kissinger

97. Memorandum of Conversation[1]

Washington, August 14, 1974, 11:45 a.m.

PARTICIPANTS

President Ford
Dr. Henry A. Kissinger, Secretary of State and Assistant to the President for National Security Affairs
Lt. General Brent Scowcroft, Deputy Assistant to the President for National Security Affairs

Kissinger: The overall situation: Sadat courageously bet on the U.S. last winter. The Soviets had poured equipment on and they are getting little from us. The nuclear plant is held up on an Israeli technicality. We are trying to get Butz to make a year's commitment of PL–480.

President: He signed 100,000 tons.

---

[1] Source: Library of Congress, Manuscript Division, Kissinger Papers, CL 280, Presidential File, August 1974. The meeting was held in the Oval Office at the White House. All brackets, except those that describe omitted material, are in the original.

Kissinger: That is the first quarter. Tell him you will do the utmost.

On negotiations: The Jordanians want to go first. Egypt feels they can't wait. They want something by October 6.

[Wilson calls]

[Omitted here are Ford's side of a telephone call to British Prime Minister Wilson on Cyprus and discussion of British leaders.]

Kissinger: Back to Fahmy: He is afraid we will push for Jordan rather than Egypt. We should, but we need Egypt. You should tell him we will put Egypt first. That problem with Hussein—but we discussed that. You should get a promise he will help you with Jordan. Also you need 4–6 weeks to get control of the government before you move. You really should.

President: Before or after Moscow?[2]

Kissinger: We should start before but complete it after. I may have to go consecutively to Cairo and Jerusalem the end of September. If I go to Moscow in October and you go to Vladivostok in December, I should go to China the middle of September—about the 10th. I would stop in Tokyo on the basis of preparing your trip—a total of 6–7 days. I don't want to, but I am worried about the Chinese seeing all this Soviet activity.

Israel wants to wait until next year. No way. The Syrians might not wait. You should tell Dobrynin you won't meet Brezhnev if the Syrian buildup turns into something.

Tell Fahmy another oil embargo will have dire consequences—you don't have to spell it out. Allon promised ideas in three or four days for a Sinai move. But we have heard nothing yet. Fahmy says, "How can we believe you?"

We are doing a paper for you on Israeli aid.[3] There is no small dispute within the bureaucracy. The big issue is with Congress—how much to ask for. I could confirm the shopping list.

The Saudi purchasing mission came here to buy it for their account. I would tell Clements to do it.

President: How is that bureaucratically?

Kissinger: I'm afraid of leaks. You could tell Schlesinger and insure him to secrecy.

President: How about getting both of them over here? I think that is best. We want it implemented with total security in Defense.

Kissinger: Good. Maybe meet early next week. If you could assure Fahmy of this.

---

[2] A reference to Kissinger's October 23–27 trip to Moscow where he met with General Secretary Brezhnev, Foreign Minister Gromyko, and other Soviet officials.

[3] See Document 96.

President: It would be part of the Saudi sale.

Kissinger: Yes, it should be part of a larger package.

President: What are we agreeing to?

Kissinger: Tell him you signed for 100,000 but the year total will be higher. You're going to work with Congress to get the $250 million. You've approved the supply arrangement and the list Nixon gave Sadat—with strict security. We will have to get Congress involved, but deliveries can't start before the first of the year.

I will write Sadat again.

98. Minutes of Senior Review Group Meeting[1]

Washington, August 30, 1974, 9:41 a.m.–10:33 a.m.

SUBJECT

Israeli Resupply (NSSM 207)

PARTICIPANTS

Chairman
Henry A. Kissinger

State
Robert Ingersoll
Sidney Sober
Thomas Stern

DOD
William Clements
Robert Ellsworth
James H. Noyes

CIA
LTG Vernon A. Walters
[name not declassified]

JCS
LTG John W. Pauly

NSC
LTG Brent Scowcroft
Harold Saunders
Col. Clinton Granger
James Barnum

SUMMARY OF CONCLUSIONS

It was agreed that:

—CIA would do an estimate of French capabilities to supply arms to the Arab countries over the next five years;
—Defense would determine what the maximum amount of equipment the U.S. could provide under the Israeli "Urgent List", the strategic implications thereof; and how such a list is to be funded.

---

[1] Source: Ford Library, NSC Institutional Files (H Files), Box 23, Meeting Minutes—SRG Originals, August 1974. Top Secret; Sensitive; Eyes Only. The meeting was held in the White House Situation Room. All brackets, with the exception of ones describing omitted material, are in the original.

Secretary Kissinger: The subject of today's meeting is Israeli Resupply.[2] I want to follow this meeting with a short discussion on SALT. I want to give you some idea of what the President wants on SALT. Dick (General Walters), you look like you have a briefing ready to go.

Gen. Walters: began to brief from the attached.[3]

Secretary Kissinger: Are you going to talk about Matmon A[4] also?

Gen. Walters: No, we are looking only at Matmon B.

Secretary Kissinger: Then history will never know what Matmon A is.

Gen. Walters: That's right. (continued to brief).

Secretary Kissinger: What does that assessment have to do with Matmon B? (in reference to a statement in the briefing that the Israelis claim that any withdrawal from the occupied Arab lands would be regarded as a sign of Israeli weakness, inviting further pressures or attacks.)

Gen. Walters: Well, that they would need the weapons.

Secretary Kissinger: If they withdraw, they will want more than what is provided for in Matmon B.

Amb. Ellsworth: Actually, withdrawal has not been discussed. This is just an assumption of why they are asking for so much in Matmon B.

Gen. Walters: Yes, this is their assumption, that if they would withdraw, that would be perceived in the Arab world as a sign of weakness. (continued to brief.)

Secretary Kissinger: On all four fronts? (in reference to a statement that the next Middle East war will be fought simultaneously on all fronts with all the Arab states.) You mean Lebanon, Syria, and Jordan would join in? What is your projection of Jordan's contribution?

Gen. Walters: They would join in, probably after it started. (continued to brief.)

Secretary Kissinger: Are they assuming that Jordan would be getting additional military deliveries?

[2 lines not declassified]

Secretary Kissinger: I'm just testing the assumptions. Can France really supply weapons of that scale? [2 lines not declassified]

---

[2] The SRG was considering the interagency NSSM 207 response, entitled "Israeli Future Military Requirements," dated August 26, which presented options for the U.S. response to Matmon B, Israel's request for military equipment. (Ibid., Box 31, NSSMs, NSSM 207, Israeli Future Military Requirements) NSSM 207 is Document 96.

[3] Briefing not attached.

[4] A reference to a previous Israeli military aid request.

Mr. Clements: Yes, Henry, I think they can. Whether they will or not is a question, but my point is that they could devise a program where they could build more, if they wanted to.

Secretary Kissinger: There must be some give-way in the French program. There must be an upper limit to what they can produce and supply. Can we get a paper done on French arms capability?

Gen. Walters: Sure, we can do a paper.

Secretary Kissinger: I want to know the limits of what they can do.

Gen. Walters: We'll do the paper. (finished the briefing.)

[4 *lines not declassified*]

Secretary Kissinger: Well, we'll have an NSC Meeting on this a week from tomorrow:[5] Dick (Gen. Walters) in your briefing, present first what the Israelis are asking for, [*less than 1 line not declassified*]. The President does not know what the Israelis are asking for. Keep it simple so that he can understand it. [2 *lines not declassified*] Also state that that has the following financial implications. Do this in about a five or ten minute briefing. I don't want to make it a long briefing.

Mr. Clements: Dick (Gen. Walters) I think it has to be done in broad terms, not a lot of detail.

Secretary Kissinger: Yes, that's right. Do it in division levels, the number of tanks, etc. On the chart, show what the balance of forces was as of October 6, 1973, and then the balance as of today. Then, show what the Israeli request is and an analysis of its validity. The decision that we want to get out of the NSC Meeting is not specific approval of each little item, but the overall concept. The President has to focus on the magnitude of the overall request, not on every little item.

Mr. Clements: Henry, I think you also need a third chart that would put the balance of payments problem in perspective. We need to put a dollar sign on those items.

Secretary Kissinger: Yes, that should also be part of the presentation. I don't want to pick the Israeli's case apart, just show what is involved. You (Gen. Walters) can present their case, and then what it means financially.

Gen. Walters: Treasury will want to present the impact of the request on the Israeli economy at the NSC Meeting.

Amb. Ellsworth: That program represents 40% of their GNP!

Secretary Kissinger: I don't want endless nit-picking on the request. I just want to be helpful to the President so that he will understand it. I think we should present as good a case for the Israelis as we can. That doesn't change the conclusions.

---

[5] September 7. The NSC met on September 6. See footnote 3, Document 101.

Gen. Walters: Treasury will make their point at the NSC Meeting.

Amb. Ellsworth: We still have made no reference in the interagency study to the fiscal impact this will have on our own budget process.

Secretary Kissinger: We'll (Gen. Scowcroft) work with you on the briefing, Dick. Even if the President goes along with all of Matmon B, we'll face some difficult decision in the future. If we announce today that we are giving $40 billion to the Israelis, (King) Faisal would stop asking me to visit him.

Let's talk substance now. What I want to do is get a manageable program forwarded to the President for decision. What is our estimate of the situation? Can we, and do we want to, underwrite the whole Matmon B package? What are the implications of the $1 billion Urgent List?[6] Suppose we don't underwrite anything? What is our concept of the diplomatic processes involved? How can we implement the package diplomatically?

Mr. Clements: Henry, I understand your problem. But, we need to know what you want to do. We need some guidance from you on this thing. If you'll tell us what you want to do, then we can go from there. We intend to back you to the hilt—do everything we can to help you, but we need to know first what you want to do.

Secretary Kissinger: I need to get the package first. What are the strategic implications of opposing the $1 billion package now? What will this do to the $1 billion package now? What will this do to the Israeli forces?

Mr. Clements: Well, it can do two or three things. They need that priority list first. But, it's impossible to get it to them by April as they have asked. It's just impossible.

Secretary Kissinger: You can if you want to take it away from our own forces.

Mr. Clements: No you can't, because some of it doesn't even exist.

Secretary Kissinger: Then we need to know what is the maximum you can do for them. We need to know: (1) what is the maximum under the $1 billion package you could deliver; (2) what is the strategic impact of $1 billion of equipment if delivered by April and what are the future implications? Say, for example we approve a package of $750 million. How are they going to pay for it? Will this mean another grant?

Mr. Stern: Their assumption is that is has already begun under foreign military assistance.

Mr. Noyes: Some of the equipment included in the "Urgent List" has already been funded.

---

[6] Not found. Presumably it was part of the Matmon B request.

Secretary Kissinger: Well, what we need is this: (1) what is the maximum amount of equipment we could deliver under the "Urgent List"; (2) what are the strategic implications of such a list; and (3) how is it going to be funded? If we can't supply what they want, will they ask for $300 million more? $500 million more? If it takes $500 million, that's a fact we'll have to face.

Amb. Ellsworth: You already have a break down on the "Urgent List." (reads from the "Urgent List.")

Secretary Kissinger: My question is, what will the impact of these items be versus the Arab forces by next April?

Mr. Clements: Henry, the way I read this—what comes out of this in the short term—is that the Israelis are trying to relieve themselves from the logistical supply problems like we had in the October war. I think they really want a stockpile, and don't want to have to depend on us for logistic supply the next time.

Secretary Kissinger: Well, if this is true, it has profound political implications.

Mr. Clements: I think that is exactly what they are trying to do. They want to relieve themselves of logistical supply problems.

Secretary Kissinger: I also want to know what effect such a decision would have on Israeli forces.

Gen. Pauly: Under Option 1D in the interagency paper it tells what the "Urgent List" would do. It tells in gross terms what that would do to the Israeli force structure.

Mr. Clements: There is just no question in my mind that the Israelis are trying to relieve themselves of supply problems in the event of another war. Granting them the "Urgent List" would also reduce your leverage in another conflict.

Secretary Kissinger: That's true.

Mr. Clements: There is no question in my mind but that is what they want to do.

Secretary Kissinger: The question is, can we make an assessment of Israeli motives for the "Urgent List." Is the military balance of power shifting? Do they believe they will need that equipment in 1975, or do they have some other purpose in mind? If there is a real, immediate threat, that requires one decision. If they want the equipment only for stockpiling, that requires another decision.

Amb. Ellsworth: You (Sec. Kissinger) need to tell us. How do you perceive the threat?

Secretary Kissinger: I think we can get through the rest of 1974. I think there is a 50–50 chance of renewed hostilities in 1975. I think there is a high potential for Syrian action by the middle of 1975. One thing we can do is tie the $1 billion package to the negotiations.

Mr. Clements: Absolutely!

Secretary Kissinger: That would be the only way it would be palatable to the Arabs. We would tell them we are trading arms in return for territory. That can probably be managed.

Amb. Ellsworth: Then what you want is strictly an assessment of the impact on the Israelis of a full delivery by April, and you want that broken down into discrete increments. We're clearer on the $1 billion package than the whole package.

Secretary Kissinger: Do we have a Working Group on this?

Mr. Clements: Yes, and a damn fine one, too.

Secretary Kissinger: I'm wondering what we are going to have to ask the President to approve. We'll probably have to break it down into five and ten-year programs. Also, what is the long-term implication, and what can a smaller package do.

Is anybody here in favor of the full package? (No). Is anybody in favor of the full Matmon B package? (No). Matmon B on a five-year term? (No). Okay, what the President needs to know is, does he want to do any of it. Give him some idea of the increments and the diplomatic scenario to implement it.

Mr. Clements: Henry, I think all of us here favor implementation of the plan in one form or another to help you in your diplomatic efforts. We want to back up your diplomatic efforts. We also want to do the most we can for the Israelis without putting our own forces in jeopardy.

Secretary Kissinger: One firm impression I have is that the President is not in favor of abandoning Israel. He is committed to the security and integrity of the Israeli State. If the $1 billion package improves Israeli stocks, and the strategic balance is not affected, then we have some flexibility for diplomatic purposes. I have not found the Israelis willing to do things for services already rendered.

Your view Bill (Mr. Clements) is that if in the President's judgement the Israelis need the equipment increments, you'll break your back to see that they get it.

Mr. Clements: Absolutely!

Secretary Kissinger: Brent (Gen. Scowcroft) work with them on the briefing.

Gen. Scowcroft: Right.

Mr. Clements: One last thing. I think it important that the President understand that as you move into this thing, our production facilities may not be able to cope. The amount of aid we can give to Israel may be dependent upon our ability to produce. That has to be made clear.

Secretary Kissinger: Yes. CIA will do the factual briefing (for the NSC Meeting). I will do the diplomatic framework and then outline the next steps.

Negotiations and Reassessment 417

Gen. Walters: You want only a presentation of facts?
Secretary Kissinger: Yes, as I asked for earlier.

99. Memorandum of Conversation[1]

Washington, September 10, 1974, 3:40–4:08 p.m.

PARTICIPANTS

Yitzhak Rabin, Prime Minister of Israel
Simcha Dinitz, Ambassador of Israel
Mordechai Gazit, Director General, Office of the Prime Minister
President Ford
Dr. Henry A. Kissinger, Secretary of State and Assistant to the President for National Security Affairs
Lt. General Brent Scowcroft, Deputy Assistant to the President for National Security Affairs

President: We are most grateful that you have come. It is nice to have this chance of renewing old friendships. It means much to have an old friend come back to help solve some of the problems which we both have an interest in.

Rabin: Thank you very much. I am very glad to be here and see you. I want to discuss our problems with you frankly. I am coming from a country which has had a traumatic experience. We went through a war in which we were caught by surprise. There was no one to blame but ourselves. The war ended in a way which left many questions. In retrospect many thought the war should have continued. This was the only war in which we didn't gain years of tranquility through destruction of the enemy. After the war we cooperated because we thought there might be some more to gain. Before, people said you succeeded too well; it destroyed their self-respect. So this time it was thought it might be different. The disengagement agreements are a beginning. We took the risk with the Syrians on the chance that it would lead to peace.

---

[1] Source: Ford Library, National Security Adviser, Memoranda of Conversations, Box 5, September 10, 1974, Ford, Kissinger. Secret; Nodis. The meeting was held in the Oval Office at the White House. Brackets are in the original. Kissinger and Rabin met the following day without President Ford from 11:30 a.m. until 2:45 p.m. at the Department of State to continue the discussion. (Memorandum of conversation; National Archives, RG 59, Records of Henry Kissinger, 1973–77, Box 10, Nodis Memcons, September 1974)

We are watching closely. There is a difference between Egypt and Syria in the way the disengagement is carried out. Egypt obeys both in letter and in spirit.

President: I am glad to hear it.

Rabin: Basically Egypt keeps the military part and the civilian part of the agreement. They are trying to reconstruct the cities and reopen the Canal. I can't fault them.

But Syria is completely different. They didn't like UNDOF and now they are making a real effort to bring about a change in its role. Instead of having a buffer zone, they are trying to do something different.

As a result of the disengagement, Israel was ready to take risks with its security for peace. We were promised by President Nixon and Dr. Kissinger arms for these risks so we could defend ourselves. It's a real problem. I hope we will find a solution. Golda gave it as one of the reasons for the disengagement agreement, and now what have we got?

President: I thought it was an impressive story of the disengagement negotiation. Dr. Kissinger brought back a favorable reaction of the Israeli role.

In our talks, let's lay our cards on the table. We hope to meet these military demands which are part of the commitment. We don't want another war—as you don't. We want Israel to be strong and capable of defending itself. Israel has the backing of the United States. It is a matter of how much you need and how much we can make available. We have constraints but we will keep the commitment that was made about your strength and your survival.

I have enjoyed working with your Ambassador. He has been very helpful. He told you of the commitment for the M–48's. That was done to clear the decks for our talk.

Rabin: Thank you.

Dinitz: We appreciate your clearing the decks.

President: It was partly a bureaucratic confusion.

Rabin: Let me tell you what we face. Egypt doesn't get major items, but Syria gets an unlimited supply. It has over 30 MIG–23s, the best in the Middle East. The A–3, with 90 mm. guns, is the lowest-grade tank in the Middle East. We destroyed 1100 Syrian tanks—now they have more. Egypt is about back to its pre-war level. Their forces are bigger than NATO. We are not talking about matching them, but enough to enable us to meet an attack.

The stronger Israel is the better the chance for peace, and we are ready to move toward peace.

The Arabs believe that with this threat, diplomacy, and the oil thing, they can achieve what they want. We don't seek a war. As long as disengagement holds we will obey it, but we will not stand for violations. We thought the purpose of disengagement was to give an opportunity to move to peace. But none but Jordan talk to us. We offered Hussein four options; he didn't seem ready for any of them. It showed that since the disengagement he felt there should be unilateral withdrawal, and he had hardened his position. I can't say we have found common ground to move ahead. On certain grounds we have found common grounds. We both see the same way on the PLO and on having no third state between us. Both are opposed to terrorism. But beyond that, there is no common ground.

We offered an overall settlement. But he said he couldn't be the first. We offered principles of a settlement to carry out in stages. No withdrawal from the Jordan River. Leave Jerusalem open. We offered a functional division of responsibility. We offered condominium.

Kissinger: He was worried he might have left a favorable impression.

Rabin: We spent three hours on it. He wasn't negative.

Kissinger: He was afraid he might have done that. He didn't want that impression.

Rabin: We at least can sit and talk. It shows that on our side we are willing to work things out. With Egypt there may be something possible. With Syria I am more than doubtful.

President: We all know Syria is the toughest.

Kissinger: The Prime Minister and I will have breakfast together and will be together most of the day. We will review and narrow things down for you. He is seeing Schlesinger.

Rabin: The trouble with Schlesinger is he always has to get a new instruction before he can move. We haven't even asked for anything new. I wouldn't deny we are disappointed with him.

President: Our people are committed to the survival and security of Israel. We can talk frankly: Look at the diplomatic and military situation.

Kissinger: The Prime Minister has planned every one of the Prime Minister's visits here. They came out all right.

Rabin: That is when *I* do the planning.

President: I am looking forward to meeting Thursday[2] and to greeting Mrs. Rabin for dinner Thursday night.

---

[2] September 13.

100. Memorandum of Conversation[1]

Washington, September 13, 1974, 12:15 p.m.

PARTICIPANTS

Yitzhak Rabin, Prime Minister of Israel
Ambassador Simcha Dinitz, Ambassador to the U.S.

President Gerald R. Ford
Dr. Henry A. Kissinger, Secretary of State and Assistant to the President for National Security Affairs
Lt. General Brent Scowcroft, Deputy Assistant to the President for National Security Affairs

Rabin: I want to give you a letter from those people who have relatives in the Soviet Union. I was asked to do this.

President: We are working hard and are making headway.

Rabin: Presidents Taft and Teddy Roosevelt visited Tsarist Russia about the stories about discrimination there.

President: I notice here the Zalmonson case. She has been released. We would like help on the Trade Bill.

Rabin: I had a meeting with the Senators. I kept out of it, and said we couldn't speak to the trade bill.

Kissinger: The Soviet Union won't accept a positive renewal each year.

President: If Dinitz could help. We want a bill.

Rabin: Jackson and Javits said they were on the verge of agreement.

President: Not exactly. We need some help.

I understand that you and Secretary Kissinger have discussed the [military aid] list I proposed.[2] It is because I feel so strongly about your security that I have your higher items of priority here and the money wanted. It is a reflection of my attitude.

Rabin: We all appreciate the time you have taken. Without your decision we wouldn't have gotten this. There were certain other items . . .

---

[1] Source: Ford Library, National Security Adviser, Kissinger–Scowcroft West Wing Office Files, Box 15, Israel, Items 8–14, September 3–15, 1974. Secret; Nodis. The meeting was held in the Oval Office at the White House. Brackets are in the original.

[2] A meeting between Rabin and Kissinger to discuss the list took place on September 13 at Blair House. Tab B to the memorandum of conversation contains the proposed list. (National Archives, RG 59, Records of Henry Kissinger, 1973–77, Box 20, Classified External Memcons, September 1973–April 1974, Folder 2)

President: Henry is going to check it out. We will do what we can.

Rabin: We didn't stress the F-4's, the big difficult items. It is mostly ammunition and other general equipment. We face very sophisticated systems—much more than in Vietnam. We think we need your advanced technology to offset the advanced technology of the Soviet Union, which is going to our neighbors.

President: There is the laser item which you consider high-priority. One item caught my eye—50 additional tanks. I will make that without further reference. We will check out the report.

Rabin: It is difficult to find the right words to express our need for the right weapons to defend ourselves.

Dinitz: We really appreciate it. We have been working for years on this.

President: We think it is essential that we affirm progress with respect both to Egypt and Jordan.

Rabin: We are ready to enter every effort to move toward a political settlement, which would not be just a military settlement but a step toward peace. We are ready—vis-à-vis Egypt or Jordan. We prefer Egypt. The difference between Egypt and Jordan is we haven't found a basis with Jordan on which we can move. I believe the preferred move is with Egypt. Egypt is the Arab leader and it is good to go there first. But Egypt can't be alone, and we understand it would be immediately followed by Jordan. What we seek from them is non-belligerency, demilitarization, and time to change the infrastructure, so we can defend on the new line.

Kissinger: I don't think non-belligerency is attainable. But you can ask for it.

President: Kissinger will be there from about October 8–14. If he could get something.

Rabin: We will do our best to work with Secretary Kissinger.

President: Can I have a good, strong commitment that you will work with him? We both have a strong interest to keep the momentum going.

Rabin: We will do our best to move at that time.

I understand the issue of the final borders won't be discussed.

Kissinger: We have not discussed final borders at all [with the Arabs]. They have not raised it. And we haven't. We have discussed interim steps, but neither I nor the President have talked final steps. At the time of the Syrian disengagement, I said we would not push Israel off the Golan.

President: I reaffirm that commitment.

Rabin: Thank you very much. I commanded at the Golan for three years; it was an intolerable situation.

Kissinger: For us to keep this process going, we need some ambiguity, you know. We take the position that it is unrealistic to discuss final borders. If Israel could avoid saying what they will never do with the Syrians, we would be better off.

Rabin: I never mentioned a line, just that we wouldn't leave.

Kissinger: Even that . . .

President: My feeling is we have made progress, and I appreciate the opportunity to meet with you. It has been fruitful.

Rabin: Thank you. We appreciate it and know that without you we wouldn't have gotten this decision.

Kissinger: What do we say to the press? The less said about quantities the better.

Dinitz: We can just say the principle of our ongoing relationship has been reaffirmed.

Kissinger: The ongoing relationship was reaffirmed.

Dinitz: In a concrete way.

Kissinger: It was continued with concrete decisions.

President: The ongoing relationship was reaffirmed with concrete results . . .

101. National Security Decision Memorandum 270[1]

Washington, September 24, 1974.

TO

The Secretary of Defense
The Deputy Secretary of State

SUBJECT

Military Assistance for Israel

The President has reviewed the NSSM 207 response[2] and the options for military assistance for Israel which were discussed at the National Security Council meeting of September 6, 1974.[3]

The President has decided to provide the Government of Israel with the military equipment listed in the attachment to this memorandum. The list consists of the items in 1(a), 1(b), and 1(c) of the options discussed at the National Security Council meeting, plus certain additional items.

The President has directed that all items on the attached list be delivered by April 1, 1975.

U. S. government credit guarantees are authorized to provide necessary funding.

Henry A. Kissinger[4]

---

[1] Source: Ford Library, National Security Adviser, NSDMs, Box 1, NSDM 270. Top Secret; Sensitive. A copy was sent to the Chairman of the Joint Chiefs of Staff.

[2] See footnote 2, Document 98.

[3] No minutes of the September 6 NSC meeting have been found. According to Kissinger's Record of Schedule, the meeting took place from 2:06 to 4 p.m. (Library of Congress, Manuscript Division, Kissinger Papers, Box 438, Miscellany, 1968–76) On the morning of September 6, Kissinger briefed President Ford and Vice President Rockefeller for the meeting. The memorandum of conversation is in the Ford Library, National Security Adviser, Memoranda of Conversations, Box 5, September 6, 1974, Ford, Rockefeller, Kissinger.

[4] Scowcroft signed for Kissinger above Kissinger's typed signature.

Attachment

MILITARY EQUIPMENT FOR ISRAEL

Searchlight, Artillery	30
Carrier, Tracked Cargo M548	60
Cartridge 105mm, Anti-personnel M–49E3	6,000
Proximity Fuze	20,000
LAW	20,000
Propelled Charge for Breaching Minefields	176
Trucks, utility ¼ ton (Jeep)	2,450
M725 Ambulance, 1½ ton	120
Cartridge, 106mm, Anti-personnel	2,000
Cartridge, 5.56mm	100 million
Maverick AGM–65	200
Chaff RR 150/160	192,000
Hobo, MK 84	280
Chaff Bomb, MJU 1/B	2,600
Doppler Navigation System	10
Searchlight, Naval Mercury-Xenon	10
Sonar, Variable Depth	12
DST Mines	200
Torpedo MK 46	50
Field Cable, spiral	1,000
Switchboard, Field SB 22	300
Wire, Field WD 110	10,000 miles
Battery, BA 4386	100,000
Generator, D. C. 1.5 KW	570
175 Self-Propelled Gun	13
Redeye Air Defense Missile	1,082
M88 Tank Recovery Vehicles	5
TOW Launchers	72
TOW Missiles	2,757
M60A1 Tanks	100
M113A1 Armored Personnel Carrier	300
M577A1 Command Post Carrier	48
155mm Self-Propelled Howitzer (M109A1)	92
M578 Armored Recovery Vehicle	4
M16A1 Rifles	80,000
Shrike missiles (AGM 45–3A and 45–4)	200

102. Memorandum of Conversation[1]

Washington, October 5, 1974, 7:30–8:51 a.m.

PARTICIPANTS

    President Gerald Ford
    Ismail Fahmi, Minister of Foreign Affairs of Arab Republic of Egypt
    Dr. Henry A. Kissinger, Secretary of State and Assistant to the President for National Security Affairs
    Lt. General Brent Scowcroft, Deputy Assistant to the President for National Security Affairs

Fahmi: We need some concrete progress on the Sinai front. This is a must. If Kissinger can do it in not more than two months, that is good. It is necessary. We are working with the extremists, to change the image of the United States. It can be done, but it is tricky and could go either way now.

Kissinger: Can you make a Sinai move alone?

Fahmi: Sure. Not to a peace. We must proceed slowly. We must get some equipment from the Soviet Union, but I can make it sweeping or just enough to get by.

Kissinger: You must do what you want, but a sweeping deal would cause an outcry that you are a Soviet stooge. The next move will be tough, because in the Sinai the next move will interrupt a decade of infrastructure. I told the President when he came in that there would be an attack on me and an attempt to split me and the President.

But we can't move before November 5. You didn't notice, but the President got additional aid to Israel taken out of the Continuing Resolution—for the first time ever.

The next step in the Sinai is much more important than the first, because now there is no logical stopping place.

Fahmi: No one can accuse us of being a Soviet satellite. We get nothing from the Soviet Union now and we need something. But if we get nothing from the Soviet Union and nothing from you, and are asked to make more concessions, my army will think I am foolish. We have to get some equipment, but the issue is whether it will be a lot or a little. If we can get something from you early next year, we can get by with only a little [from the Soviet Union].

---

[1] Source: National Archives, RG 59, Records of Henry Kissinger, 1973–77, Box 5, Nodis Memcons, November 1974, Folder 1. Secret; Nodis. The breakfast meeting was held in the First Floor Private Dining Room at the White House. Brackets are in the original.

The oil people are the biggest political amateurs—nice to us internally but with loudspeakers outside.

Kissinger: The reason I arranged this appointment is because I agree with Fahmi's appraisal. I think Sadat is very exposed. Last November he made a big gamble. There is no doubt he is anti-Soviet. But the radicals are using his moves against him, and if he gets no progress for his efforts and no help from us, he is in trouble.

Fahmi: What he needs is movement in the Middle East more than arms. We are diversifying our arms supply now—your allies are selling to us.

President: We must push Israel into the arena to participate.

Kissinger: What Israel is asking for is an end of belligerency. We have to find a formulation—you can't give that—something which looks like progress toward peace without giving up your principles.

Fahmi: Sadat can give nothing more than military disengagement. It has to be described that way. Non-belligerency is out of the question. We could not sign anything like that. Politically he couldn't survive. He can sign a military agreement and some other things. But for him to make another big move in Sinai without a move on the Syrian and Jordanian fronts would be a big political move: It would get us out of the conflict, and what more could they want?

Kissinger: I had a brutal meeting with Allon yesterday[2] because he said he would discuss only non-belligerency.

Fahmi: Khaddam came to Cairo only to block any separate move by Cairo. We agreed there would be no separate political move. So it must look like a military one.

Kissinger: So Israel will try to force the next move to be a political one. Israel likes to make offers which look reasonable and which the Arabs can't make.

The radicals want to make Egypt look like it is betraying the Arabs; Israel wants Egypt to look like it is resisting progress to peace.

The Soviet Union is pushing for a total solution in order to freeze the situation and make progress impossible. If there is no progress in the next six months we are in bad trouble.

---

[2] No memorandum of conversation has been found. According to Kissinger's Record of Schedule, no meeting took place between Allon and Kissinger on October 3 or October 4. (Library of Congress, Manuscript Division, Kissinger Papers, Box 438, Miscellany, 1968–76)

103. Memorandum From the President's Deputy Assistant for National Security Affairs (Scowcroft) to President Ford[1]

Washington, October 10, 1974.

Secretary Kissinger asked that you be provided with the following report of his first meeting with President Sadat:

"Shortly after I arrived in Cairo Tuesday night, I held an 80-minute initial meeting with President Sadat[2] to lay the groundwork for a longer and more detailed discussion with him today. I found Sadat sober in mood, preoccupied with the present delicate position in which Egypt finds itself in the Arab world, and anxious to hear precisely how progress can be made towards a second-stage disengagement on the Egyptian/Israeli front. Having taken the lead over the past year in negotiations under U.S. auspices with the Israelis, and anxious that he be able to demonstrate that the resumption of diplomatic relations with the U.S. benefits his people and the Arab world generally, Sadat feels he must show more progress towards a negotiated settlement in order to defend himself against those who are against the closer Egyptian/American connection. (He believes that he has at most three months to retain control of events.) You will recall that Fahmy underscored this basic concern and orientation in his recent meeting with you.[3]

"At the same time, we must not be under any illusions, since if he cannot find a way to build on the trends and momentum developed in the past, he will come under increasing pressure to re-establish some of the closer ties with the USSR, a development which I do not believe he desires but he would, in my judgment, move to if he concluded that it was the only course he had available to promote the national interests of Egypt. He is eager to meet with you and lays great stress on the U.S. connection. We discussed the possibility of such a meeting in late January sometime after your State of the Union speech, and he thought that would be a good time.

"My strategy last night was to avoid getting into specific details but rather to paint the picture in the area with all its complexities. I indicated that I would be going to Israel to seek specific proposals from Rabin which I can take back to Sadat on Monday.[4] I said he should not

---

[1] Source: Ford Library, National Security Adviser, Trip Briefing Books of Henry Kissinger, Box 1, October 8–13, 1974, Middle East, HAK Messages for President, October 10, 1974. Secret; Sensitive. A handwritten notation at the top of the page reads, "The President has seen."

[2] No memorandum of conversation has been found. Kissinger arrived in Cairo on Tuesday, October 8.

[3] See Document 102.

[4] October 14.

expect any such initial Israeli proposal to be very far-reaching, but I hoped it could provide the basis for a beginning of a negotiating process under our auspices between Egypt and Israel. I added it would also be necessary for there to be Egyptian political quid pro quos if Israel could be expected to withdraw to a new line in the Sinai. While I am sure that it contributed to his sobriety, I told him candidly that he could not expect a successful conclusion of such negotiations before the end of next January. If I can get something in Israel to start the process, Sadat can use it to moderate action at the upcoming Arab summit meeting at the end of the month. I asked for his cooperation at this meeting to help assure that the Arabs will not peg out an unrealistic overall posture—particularly on the Palestinian issue—which could sidetrack meaningful negotiations.

"I also described to him briefly the kind of pressures that we are under at home from certain quarters on this whole issue, and I sought to reassure him that under your leadership we intend to make a further determined effort on a step-by-step basis towards an ultimate overall settlement.

"I will report to you again after my next conversation with Sadat tonight which is likely to be extended.

"I saw Fahmy for two hours this morning[5] to go over essentially the same ground as well as our attitude on the PLO vote in New York."

---

[5] No memorandum of conversation has been found, but Kissinger sent a memorandum to Scowcroft for President Ford summarizing the meeting on October 10. (Ford Library, National Security Adviser, Trip Briefing Books of Henry Kissinger, Box 1, October 8–13, 1974, Middle East, HAK Messages for President, October 10, 1974)

---

104. Memorandum From the President's Deputy Assistant for National Security Affairs (Scowcroft) to President Ford[1]

Washington, October 11, 1974.

Secretary Kissinger has asked that I pass to you the following report of his second meeting with President Sadat:

---

[1] Source: National Archives, RG 59, Records of Henry Kissinger, 1973–77, Box 25, CATC NATURAL 1974, Arab-Israeli War. Secret; Sensitive; Eyes Only. A handwritten notation at the top of the page reads, "The President has seen."

"I had a detailed and very satisfactory three-hour talk with Sadat,[2] and I can report that we achieved more than I expected for this round. Sadat has agreed to engage in direct political negotiations with Israel, with a U.N. representative present, looking towards a second-stage agreement on the Egyptian-Israeli front. This is the first time any Arab leader has agreed to bilateral direct talks. The talks would be held in the U.N. zone in the Sinai between the Israeli and Egyptian lines. Of equal significance, he has also agreed that these talks will have a political character as the Israelis insist, rather than a purely military one. In order to de-emphasize cosmetically his willingness to engage in direct negotiations of a political character, he will send a top military man to head his delegation, but he will be flanked by a high-ranking political adviser so that Egypt can discuss both political and military questions.

"At the same time, he stressed that while he cannot agree to a formal declaration of non-belligerency as the Israelis insist, he is prepared to consider and agree to specific elements of non-belligerency in return for a further substantial second stage withdrawal of Israeli forces from the Sinai. He still has in mind a line of withdrawal which Israel will resist very strongly, and I therefore avoided pressing the specifics of this at this stage since it is better strategy for the differences over the line to be raised in the first instance between the Egyptians and Israelis themselves when the talks begin. I mentioned to him several specifics Israel wants, such as cargoes through the Canal, no Red Sea blockage, and he agreed.

"While he would strongly prefer a disengagement agreement before the end of the year, he has accepted the target of late January for conclusion of the agreement.

"He apparently seems ready to go ahead on such an agreement if he can get the kind of withdrawal he wants, whatever the objections of other Arabs; and he seems prepared to deal with Arab charges that he is headed for a separate agreement with Israel contrary to the general Arab view that there needs to be an overall settlement involving all three fronts—Jordan, Syria and Egypt.

"The major immediate problem he faces is the upcoming Arab summit meeting beginning on October 24. He apparently does not intend to tell his Arab colleagues of the above understanding that has been achieved between us, since he does not want it known at this point that he is ready to move ahead in political-military talks with the Israelis. Therefore, he wants no announcement of the above during my current trip, and we agreed that we would be very general with the

---

[2] The memorandum of conversation of the meeting between Sadat and Kissinger, which took place on October 10 from 9:02 until 11:50 p.m. at the President's Giza Residence in Cairo, is ibid., Box 5, Nodis Memcons, November 1974, Folder 1.

press, avoiding specifics; otherwise, he would have to give specific details of our understanding to his Arab brothers at the summit, thereby opening himself to attacks. Also, I will not tell the details to the Israelis who will certainly leak them. This means that we may have some characterization of my mission in our press as either unproductive or a failure, but it is essential that we play the press in this way in order to help Sadat meet the difficult tactical problem at the Arab summit. We agreed that I should return to the area about November 3 or 4 in connection with the India trip. The announcement of the beginning of negotiations will be made then. This will require some adjustment of my schedule, probably dropping my planned stops to Romania and Yugoslavia.

"All of the above is very sensitive, and I am not reporting this in any other channel. It is imperative therefore that the above understandings between Sadat and myself not be revealed in any way or hinted at or Sadat will be in an impossible position. I will have to be most circumspect in what I tell the Israelis and other Arab leaders.

"Finally, I discussed the Palestinian issue at great length and explained our strong view that it has been a mistake for the Arabs to press this matter at the U.N. so prematurely.[3] Sadat understood that if we did anything but vote against hearing the Palestinian Liberation Organization as the representative of the Palestinian people, it would make our position completely untenable in Israel. He agreed to help explain our position in as positive light as possible at the Arab summit though it would cause us difficulties. I believe he has taken a farsighted view on this point. He is more interested in our influencing the Israelis to move constructively towards negotiations rather than a tactical victory at the U.N.

"I leave for Damascus in the morning where my main purpose will be to convince the Syrians that we are determined to continue our efforts, and that progress is possible on one of the other fronts within the kind of January timetable we have in mind. The most difficult pill for Assad to swallow will be my reiteration that no concrete progress is possible in the foreseeable future on the Syrian front. I will, however, give him your commitment to another stage on the Golan."

---

[3] On September 11, all 20 Arab states represented at the United Nations and 23 non-Arab states formally requested that the UN General Assembly consider Palestine as a separate item on its agenda. During the previous three decades, the General Assembly had discussed Palestine as part of an overall Arab-Israeli settlement, but never as a separate item. (*Yearbook of the United Nations, 1974,* pp. 218–219) General Assembly Resolution 3210, adopted on October 14, invited the PLO, as the representative of the Palestinian people, to participate in General Assembly deliberations on the Palestinian issue. The United States voted against the resolution. For text of the resolution, see ibid., p. 226.

105. Memorandum From the President's Deputy Assistant for National Security Affairs (Scowcroft) to President Ford[1]

Washington, October 11, 1974.

Secretary Kissinger has asked that I pass to you the following report of his conversation with President Asad:

"I have just completed almost five hours of conversation with President Asad[2] whom I found, not unexpectedly—firm in his determination against separate deals between the Arabs and the Israelis; doubtful that the road to peace can be achieved by political means, yet willing to continue the diplomatic track for the time being, at least. In Asad's words, 'We deeply desire that the United States not undertake any separate efforts. U.S. efforts must proceed on all fronts.' I quote this literally to emphasize several points: Asad's insistence that he will make this view against partial steps prevail at the Arab summit; as a reflection of Syria's deep concern that it does not wish to be isolated and left out; as his conviction that through a united Arab front there is strength; and that the goal must be total Israeli withdrawal to the '67 borders, and the rights of the Palestinians restored through the PLO. All of the above illustrates cogently and dramatically the tough job that Sadat will have on his hands when he goes to the Arab summit to get support for his efforts to move ahead in a second stage Egyptian-Israeli negotiation, or at least to neutralize the opposition.

"This strong statement of Asad's came after I had carefully explained our 'step at a time' approach as the only feasible way to proceed. I stressed on your behalf, your firm intention to support further negotiations on the Syrian-Israeli front 'at the right time' in the future; I indicated that progress on the Egyptian and Jordanian fronts was probably more feasible in the immediate future, and I maintained that progress on any one front was in the interest of all the Arabs. As is evident from Asad's thrust, he has not accepted this view as of now, though he was careful not to say that he was giving up on diplomacy and going to war.

"Reflecting deep Syrian suspicion of the Egyptians, Asad probed to find out whether Sadat had indicated a willingness to go ahead with

---

[1] Source: Ford Library, National Security Adviser, Trip Briefing Books of Henry Kissinger, Box 1, October 8–13, 1974, Middle East, HAK Messages for President, October 11, 1974. Secret; Sensitive; Eyes Only. Ford initialed the memorandum.

[2] According to the memorandum of conversation of the meeting between Asad and Kissinger, the meeting took place on October 11 from 6:30 to 9:15 p.m. at the Presidential Palace in Damascus. They also discussed Cyprus. (National Archives, RG 59, Records of Henry Kissinger, 1973–77, Box 21, Classified External Memcons, November 1974, Folder 5)

the Israelis on his own. I responded carefully that our discussions in Cairo had been general, that Sadat wants to first listen to what I bring back to him on Monday[3] from Israel, and that the matter will come up for discussion at the Arab summit.

"I then asked whether or not we should press for Jordanian-Israeli negotiations regarding the West Bank. His response was, whether or not there was such a negotiation, the net result would have to be determined by what the Palestinians think or want; he said he had no problem with a Jordanian-Israeli negotiation, provided 'the West Bank is relinquished to the PLO via Jordan.' He threw cold water on the procedures which Hussein has in mind: a negotiation between him and Israel with the ultimate fate of the West Bank to be determined by some act of self-determination.

"I concluded by underscoring that we are prepared to be helpful to the parties if this is their desire, and that it was up to the Arabs themselves to decide in which direction they might move. In response to his statement that separate efforts by the United States will be interpreted in the Arab world as a U.S. attempt to put splinters between the Arab parties, particularly between Egypt and Syria, I responded that our aim is not separatism, and that we believe that progress should be made wherever possible, in the interest of both sides, including all of the Arabs. It was left that, in addition to returning to Cairo on Monday after talks with the Jordanians and the Israelis, I would also return to Damascus for a few hours. I did this to gain some time and avoid a blow-up now. Asad also thought it was a good idea that I return to the area about November 3 or 4 after the Arab summit, at which time we would know the results of the summit meeting and be able to determine whether negotiations on one or more fronts can proceed.

"Asad expressed himself passionately, while being as personable as ever. He reiterated a serious desire to maintain and strengthen good relations with the U.S. He made no direct threats about going to war, tempering his doubts about a political solution with reiteration of his serious willingness to pursue peaceful negotiating efforts towards a settlement. He obviously does not want a situation created in which at some point he will be left negotiating alone with the Israelis on the question of the Golan Heights. In many respects, the Arabs face fateful decisions at the upcoming summit since a prescription to move on all negotiating fronts is a prescription for impasse and stalemate.

"For the Israelis too, there are hard and important decisions: it is in their interest to adopt the kind of flexible posture which can help bring about the successful Egyptian-Israeli negotiation if not one with Jordan

---

[3] October 14.

as well. Otherwise, they face an impasse which is likely to lead to a more united Arab alignment, spearheaded by the radicals, and leading away from the path of diplomacy towards eventual resumption of hostilities.

"This is being written enroute to Amman, having spent part of the morning in Cairo and most of the afternoon and early evening in Damascus. I expect to have a brief talk with Hussein tonight and a much fuller one Saturday morning."[4]

---

[4] October 12.

---

106. Memorandum From the President's Deputy Assistant for National Security Affairs (Scowcroft) to President Ford[1]

Washington, October 13, 1974.

The following is Secretary Kissinger's report of his first meeting in Israel:

I had a two and one half hour initial session with the Israeli leadership—a cautious questioning, somber Rabin, flanked by Foreign Minister Allon, Defense Minister Peres, and Chief of Staff Gur.[2] I carried away the impression of three relative equals—of a collegium—Allon and Peres, rather than the Prime Minister carrying the discussion in a decisive way and in a definitive direction. At one point they had to suspend the meeting to concert their responses to my inquiries regarding next steps in negotiations.

The first half of the meeting was spent on giving them impressions of the mood and temperament I found in the three Arab capitals already visited. I described the nervousness and tenseness I found in each Arab leader—a Sadat trying to figure out how he can manage the upcoming October 26 Arab summit so that he is free to undertake Egyptian-Israeli negotiations if he wishes; a volatile and passionate Asad, firm against piecemeal agreements and seeking to prevent a separate Egyptian-Israeli negotiation; and worried Hussein who will insist

---

[1] Source: Ford Library, National Security Adviser, Trip Briefing Books of Henry Kissinger, Box 1, October 8–13, 1974, Middle East, HAK Messages for President, October 13, 1974. Secret; Sensitive. Ford initialed the memorandum.

[2] No memoranda for these two meetings have been found.

he, and not the PLO, be supported at the summit by his Arab colleagues as the negotiator for the return of the West Bank, but ready to remain aloof from the negotiating process if the Arabs support the PLO.

I did not press the Israelis at this time either to give me a specific line of withdrawal in the Sinai or a map. I asked for a personal assurance (rather than a cabinet decision which would leak) from the three cabinet members that they would agree to a political-meeting type negotiation involving a second stage Israeli withdrawal from the Sinai if I could get Sadat's assent; these talks to take place in the U.N. buffer zone in the Sinai; the announcement of which would come about November 3 or 4 if I decided to return to the area. I stressed, however, that before I pressed Sadat to this end I had to have a rough idea at least as to what the Israeli essential requirements were. If these requirements were out of the ball park, I would be foolish to press Sadat into something which would perhaps weaken him irreparably and thereby undermine fundamentally overall interests of the U.S. in the Middle East.

I got something from them—far less than a more farsighted Israeli Government would have provided, but perhaps barely enough to at least carry forward my talks with Sadat and give him some glimmer of hope that something reasonable could come out of a negotiation with Israel. Sadat will need to be fortified in this way if he is to proceed in a reasonably bold fashion at the Arab summit. You can get an idea of the magnitude of the Israeli starting demands when I tell you that for withdrawal of somewhere between 30 and 50 kilometers from their present line on the Sinai, they want not only a commitment of Egyptian non-belligerency, but they want assurance there will not be a third phase negotiation for at least five years. In other words, a defacto separate peace with Egypt for what will be considered by the Arabs a modest withdrawal. This will be impossible to achieve, but the Israeli ideas can be used to begin a process during which there will and must be grudging and inevitable give on their part.

We meet again early Sunday[3] morning at which time I will focus more on the Jordanian aspect of the negotiations.

---

[3] October 13.

107. Memorandum From the President's Deputy Assistant for National Security Affairs (Scowcroft) to President Ford[1]

Washington, October 14, 1974.

Following is a report of Secretary Kissinger's second meeting with the Israelis.

"In a three-hour session with Rabin and Cabinet colleagues,[2] Israel has agreed in principle to open negotiations with Egypt looking towards a second stage agreement. My session this morning had been preceded by an Israeli Cabinet meeting which concluded in the middle of the night. Since it is essential none of the above be revealed, I am not reporting this in any other channel.

"The mood was still reserved and cautious, but more relaxed than Saturday night[3]—a reaction in part, I believe, to the fact that I did not ask Israel to produce a map or line of withdrawal in the Sinai at this time, since I was afraid it would leak and it is not what is needed anyway at this stage. The understanding with Rabin, Allon and Peres is that I will return to the area in early November to try to fix the date, place and modalities of negotiations between Egypt and Israel, but none of this can be final, of course, depending on the results of the October 26th Arab summit. The question is whether Sadat will feel free to engage in such a negotiation as he has told me, or will Syria be able to build up enough pressure at the summit to make Sadat cool on the idea. I told the Israelis that if Sadat agreed to a separate negotiation, we will have achieved a tremendous step forward in reducing the danger of war. In these circumstances they must make a substantial withdrawal including the oil fields. In response, they made some excessive demands but on the whole we have achieved what we came for: an Arab-Israeli negotiation provided Sadat holds through the Arab summit.

---

[1] Source: Ford Library, National Security Adviser, Kissinger-Scowcroft West Wing Office Files, Box 15, Israel Items 16–24, September 17–November 6, 1974. Secret; Sensitive. Ford initialed the memorandum.

[2] According to the memorandum of conversation, the meeting between the Israelis and Kissinger took place on October 13 from 9:45 until 11:55 a.m. at the Prime Minister's Residence in Jerusalem. They also discussed immediate Israeli defense needs, U.S.-Soviet détente, negotiating strategy, long-term arms supply, and the PLO vote in the UN General Assembly. (National Archives, RG 59, Records of Henry Kissinger, 1973–77, Box 22, Classified External Memcons, December 1974 to April 1975) The meeting was preceded by a breakfast meeting between Rabin and Kissinger from 8:45 to 9:30 a.m. They discussed next steps in the negotiations, military supply, Europe, and the Kurds. (Memorandum of conversation, October 13; ibid., Box 25, CATC Nodis Memos, July to December 1974)

[3] October 12. See Document 106.

"Israel has set no preconditions to entering these negotiations which they insist cannot be limited only to a military withdrawal, but must be political in content, i. e. there must be an Egyptian commitment to non-belligerency. I told them this was impossible as a formal statement but that some of the content of non-belligerency was achievable by specific steps.

"The Israelis are clearly in no hurry to enter into negotiations with Jordan. They have left open this option, however, and seem disposed to consider negotiations on this front as well if Hussein decides he wants them in the aftermath of the Arab summit. Such talks could proceed at a slower pace than those with Egypt. Again, however, any final decision in this regard must await the results of the Arab summit. Sisco went to Amman Sunday to brief Hussein on the Israeli talks. Hussein confirmed that he will make an all out effort to get support that he, and not the PLO, should be the negotiator with Israel. He told Sisco that he has modified his approach somewhat to the Arab summit in the last 24 hours. If he is not supported he will not tell his Arab colleagues, as previously planned, that he has given up entirely any future plans to regain the West Bank by political means, but rather he will retain his option and will limit himself to a statement pinning the responsibility for continued Israeli occupation of the West Bank on the Arabs supporting the PLO—for everybody knows Israel will not negotiate the West Bank with the PLO nor anyone else other than Hussein.

"Finally, some time was spent on bilateral matters particularly Israeli preoccupation with long term arms procurement. I reaffirmed your support for such a program, and that as a matter of principle the U.S. is committed to a long term supply of arms. However, I also made clear that no final decisions had been made as to when and in what form the authorization will be submitted, that no specific amount had been committed, and that the timing of submission has to be phased into an overall strategy for making progress towards peace in the area. I said the arms question was not linked to negotiations, but it was related to it.

"Monday is perhaps our longest and most arduous day—Cairo in the morning, Damascus at mid-day, and Algiers at night."

108. Memorandum From the President's Deputy Assistant for National Security Affairs (Scowcroft) to President Ford[1]

Washington, October 14, 1974.

The following is Secretary Kissinger's report of his final conversation with President Sadat:[2]

"I have just finished my final talk with President Sadat which culminated with a brief announcement to the press that we have made progress towards the beginning of negotiations between Israel and Egypt and that I will return to the area in early November. The final decisions on the time, place and modalities of course, will have to be determined in early November and after President Sadat has met with other Arab leaders at the October 26 summit.[3]

"Obviously under some strain from the fasting during Ramadan which comes to an end in about 48 hours, and dry of mouth as the conversation extended into the second hour, President Sadat nevertheless remained quietly determined throughout the discussion with me to move towards negotiations with Israel and not be deflected by what he hears at the summit. I reported this morning to him the results of my discussions in Israel, including the kind of terms which the Israelis could be expected to open with at any negotiation involving a second stage withdrawal from the Sinai. As expected he rejected the notion of a formal declaration of non-belligerency once again, while leaving open finding ways to give the essential content of such a declaration. He will not accept the kind of 30–50 kilometer withdrawal the Israelis have in mind which would exclude among other things the oil fields in the southern part of Sinai, nor would he accept the notion of a five-year agreement pointing out that the present disengagement agreement is openended. He did not seem surprised at these far-reaching terms and what I find significant is that this did not seem to deter him from his intention to begin a negotiating progress some time after the summit.

"His philosophy seems to be rather simple and straight-forward: He says he will face trouble and problems at the summit but Egypt will face even more troubles and difficulties if there is no progress towards a settlement. He goes on to say if there is an impasse, there is likely to be war and Egypt is apt to end up with nothing. This is a sensible view.

---

[1] Source: Ford Library, National Security Adviser, Trip Briefing Books of Henry Kissinger, Box 1, October 8–13, 1974, Middle East, HAK Messages for President, October 14, 1974. Secret; Sensitive. Ford initialed the memorandum.

[2] No memorandum of conversation has been found.

[3] A reference to the Arab League Summit in Rabat; see Document 112.

"I also briefed him on King Hussein's dilemma and I came away with the impression that he intends to support King Hussein on the question of a Jordanian negotiation with Israel over the West Bank. I believe he was fortified somewhat by the positive results of my discussion with King Faisal[4] who also, hopefully, can be expected to support the kind of line the Egyptians will pursue at the summit. I promised him that once negotiations get started he can expect that we will do everything possible to achieve what we consider to be a reasonable result for him. Looking ahead to my meeting with President Asad in a few hours he advised me to lay it on the line; in other words, not shrink from explaining to him how we evaluate the relative difficulties of an Egyptian, Jordanian, and Syrian negotiations with Israel respectively—drawing the conclusion that at this juncture, the Egyptian and Jordanian fronts offer more opportunities for progress. He is not entirely comfortable over our no vote on the PLO resolution at the UN,[5] expressing concern that it might give too much ammunition to America's enemies, but he nevertheless reiterated his intention to explain our decision on this question in proper perspective to the other Arabs.

"Finally, in this brief observation, I have become convinced that one of the most positive outcomes of my trip this week will be to have encouraged each of the friendly Arab leaders to stay on the course of moderation and hopefully to reflect this view in the face of radical pressures at the upcoming summit. I believe too, we have helped dispel some of the gloom and doubt and nervousness we found in various Arab capitals. While I was aware of the pressures which the Arab governments felt themselves to be under, I did not fully appreciate the depth of the dilemma they are experiencing until these discussions. They are concerned about how they are to relate to one another; how to resolve the dilemma that if they bend towards the public outcry in support of the PLO instead of King Hussein the West Bank will remain with the Israelis indefinitely; they are asking themselves how to get the Israelis to adopt a reasonable posture—all of those concerns help explain the anxiety, nervousness and tenseness we have found—not because of any fear on their part of an immediate war, but rather the thrashing about that is characteristic in trying to determine how to make the tough decisions ahead. In short, had the mission not taken place, the situation in the area might well have taken a sharp and irreparable nosedive. In these circumstances, President Sadat's decision and outlook is a courageous one."

---

[4] A draft memorandum of conversation of the meeting between King Faisal and Kissinger, which took place on October 13 in Riyadh, is in the Library of Congress, Manuscript Division, Kissinger Papers, CL 208, Geopolitical File, Saudi Arabia, August 10–October 28, 1974, Folder 2.

[5] See footnote 3, Document 104.

109. Memorandum From the President's Deputy Assistant for National Security Affairs (Scowcroft) to President Ford[1]

Washington, October 14, 1974.

Secretary Kissinger asked that the following message be passed to you regarding his meeting with President Asad:

"In a spirited three-hour session with President Asad,[2] in which I reported generally on my conversations in Israel, Saudi Arabia, Jordan and Egypt, I made clear that we are ready to continue to assist the Arabs and the Israelis to agree on the next step in the negotiating process, and that I will be returning to the area in early November for this purpose. At the same time, however, I made clear that the U.S. would not inject itself into the consultations that will soon take place between Arabs at the summit, and that the choice between support of the PLO and a resultant impasse or opting for a realistic piecemeal step-by-step process is one for the Arabs to make.

"President Asad knows we feel that simultaneous negotiations on all fronts is unfeasible; that pressing for an early Geneva Conference in which all aspects of the overall settlement will be aired will result in lofty rhetoric but no practical results; and that it is up to the Arabs, either individually or collectively, to decide how and whether they will proceed to the next state. I had adopted this strategy in my talk with him because I had concluded that to put ourselves in the position of appearing to press for separate negotiations on the Egyptian and Jordanian fronts to the exclusion of Syria would only strengthen President Asad's resolve to resist the step-by-step approach at the summit and make both President Sadat's and King Hussein's job at the meeting more difficult. It would also run the risk of all Arabs combining against us.

"The situation is this: If President Sadat at the summit remains firmly committed in face of opposition to the Egyptian/Israeli negotiation, we will be able to achieve the breakthrough we seek in early November—a serious start in the negotiating process with a fair chance of a reasonable outcome. For King Hussein too, the summit will be a watershed. If the summit, in effect, tells King Hussein to go ahead with ne-

---

[1] Source: Ford Library, National Security Adviser, Trip Briefing Books of Henry Kissinger, Box 1, October 8–13, 1974, Middle East, HAK Messages for President, October 14, 1974. Secret; Sensitive. Ford initialed the memorandum.

[2] The memorandum of conversation of the meeting between Asad and Kissinger, which took place on October 14 from 2 until 4:45 p.m. at the Presidential Palace in Damascus, is in the National Archives, RG 59, Records of Henry Kissinger, 1973–77, Box 21, Classified External Memcons, November 1974, Folder 5.

gotiations—it will be possible to pursue the Jordanian track as well. If the summit supports the PLO, he will keep his negotiating posture in deep freeze and continue to cooperate informally with the Israelis to maintain quiet on the West Bank.

"President Asad's strategy at the summit is clear. He will press for a decision calling for an early convening of the Geneva Conference in which all aspects of the overall settlement—Egypt, Jordan and Syria—will be discussed and in which the PLO would be participants. It is this proposal that President Sadat, King Hussein and King Faisal will have to deflect or finesse—a difficult talk in view of the fact that Syria will make an all out effort and will get the firm support of Algeria, Iraq, and Libya. Weak states, like Lebanon, may very well go along out of fear of repercussions from the Palestinians, as well as Kuwait, which has a large size Palestinian minority. Sudan and the small sheikdoms will follow the Saudi lead. The best result we can hope for from the summit is that there will be no consensus, and that this will free Egypt and Jordan to pursue the course they believe most desirable.

"President Asad today was personable, reasonably relaxed, a spirited promulgator of the PLO view and listening intently for any hint that one of his Arab brothers was bent on a separate negotiation which would leave him out. I believe I took him aback when I said that we are ready to help, but we will remain inactive unless the Arabs want us to help. I had the distinct impression that this veiled hint that we would opt out has given him reason to pause.

"I gave as my judgment that it is very desirable, and it ought to be possible, for there to be a move in early November opening negotiations. I assured him there would be no move on our part between now and then. He took our negative vote on the PLO issue,[3] I thought, with understanding, though he clearly forewarned that the PLO reaction would be strong. What came out clearly also was his view that oil and the Middle Eastern settlement were inextricably linked.

"I am sure that he will ponder for some time as the summit approaches, one of my concluding statements: 'If we can't be helpful, then we are prepared to let events take their course. There is no historic law that says that the United States can solve every problem in the world.' The last thing that President Asad wants is for the United States to move from its role of activist to benign bystander."

---

[3] See footnote 3, Document 104.

110. Draft Telegram From Secretary of State Kissinger to the President's Deputy Assistant for National Security Affairs (Scowcroft)[1]

Undated.

Please pass following message to the President.

1. Having just completed my seventh mission to the Middle East during this past year, I want to report to you my overall conclusions and suggestions as to how we should next proceed.

2. I am convinced that the Middle East today remains the most dangerous trouble spot in the world; the seeds of war between Arabs and Israelis remain, as does the potential for a dangerous confrontation between ourselves and the USSR. But it goes beyond this; in view of our overall economic interests—indeed the world's interest in the Middle East and the Arabian and Persian Gulf—the interdependence between producer and consumer, and the need for developing a stable economic and monetary system based on cooperation, the settlement of the Arab-Israeli dispute is even more crucial to our national interests today than at any time in its history. Our involvement therefore is imperative and inevitable; and we are the only ones who can do it—if it can be done at all. If we can succeed, it will put us far ahead of the Soviets in the Middle East for some time to come.

3. My trip accomplished what we expected—and perhaps something more. We have given the leaders in the area a necessary psychological shot in the arm by reaffirming your intention that the U.S. will remain directly and actively involved. This is most welcome by both sides. This has helped assure the central role of the U.S. in the negotiations for the time being at least, and will help keep in check Soviet and European opportunities to inject themselves in the negotiating process in an unhelpful way. We defused the adverse impact of our no vote at the UN on the Palestinian issue[2]—all the Arab leaders showed understanding of our rationale and reasoning and it did not divert Boumediene from agreeing to announce resumption of US-Algerian diplomatic relations on November 12. We were able to add to Arab appreciation of America's serious intention to organize the consumers for hard-headed, no-nonsense talks with producers on oil and monetary policies. We have affected in a positive way the views and positions of the Arab leaders (in particular Sadat, Faisal, Hussein and Has-

---

[1] Source: National Archives, RG 59, Records of Joseph Sisco, Box 33, Briefing Book: Mr. Sisco's Outgoing. Secret; Sensitive; Eyes Only. There is no indication that this telegram was sent, but a handwritten notation at the top of the page reads, "Oct 74."

[2] See footnote 3, Document 104.

san) will take at the October 26 summit. And above all and most important, we have laid the groundwork for an announcement in early November of the opening of negotiations between Egypt and Israel and possibly Jordan as well unless the summit deflects Sadat and Hussein. It is at this meeting that the Arabs must choose between meaningless, empty and ineffectual pie in the sky declarations regarding the Palestinians and the reality of practical progress through piecemeal negotiations relating to the Sinai and possibly to the West Bank.

4. A special word is necessary regarding Israel. Rabin and the other leaders are grappling with the dilemma of history and logic—the history has been one of pain, anguish, suffering, suspicion and four costly wars—the logic is that the risks of stand-patism are far greater than realistically facing up to the necessary step-by-step compromises essential for progress towards a settlement, because the choices they will face a year from now if they let the situation drift will be much worse than those they face now. I hope Rabin is the leader to do this, but I must candidly tell you I doubt it, even taking into account the weakness of any Israeli government operating in Parliament with a majority of one vote. I am also deeply disturbed by the trend developing in Israeli politics towards the right, reflecting itself in a more hawkish and more intransigent posture regarding negotiations and territorial concessions. We have an abiding interest to support Israel's security, but our interests in the area go beyond any one country—strategically, politically, and economically. The period ahead, Mr. President, will inevitably be a period of strain in our relations with Israel for we alone can bring—indeed force—them to pursue the path of serious negotiations on the basis of compromises which protect Israel's security and serve our own interests. The alternative is likely to be another war in the Middle East which would not only affect vital U.S. strategic and political interests, but also our economic and monetary interests and those of the Western world. We must begin soon after our November elections to educate the American people and Congress to these realities.

5. In the next stage in early November, I am hopeful we will get the breakthrough start on negotiations we have carefully advanced during this mission. Our strategy of segmenting the issues which divide Israel and its neighbors into negotiating units which are politically manageable for us and the parties remains sound. This is based on the belief that a progressive series of limited agreements could create new situations which in turn will make further agreements possible. I am hopeful because I found on this mission that: there is continuing confidence in the indispensable role of the U.S. to help make progress towards a settlement; that there is continuing broad support for the step by step approach, notwithstanding the fact some elements in the area will seek to undercut negotiations; that there is general agreement

that the next stage of negotiations can and should begin in the near future. In short, the issues have been sharpened, the choices have been discussed, and the course of action has begun to take shape. However, we must not be over-optimistic because the political situation in the Arab world as well as in Israel is extremely complex, and the makings of a stalemate are always present. This could be the result of the Arab summit, but for the moment we have done everything possible to assure against this.

111. Minutes of a National Security Council Meeting[1]

Washington, October 18, 1974, 3:40–5:45 p.m.

SUBJECT

Mid East Status, SALT

PRINCIPALS

The President
Secretary of State Henry A. Kissinger
Secretary of Defense James R. Schlesinger
Director of Arms Control and Disarmament Agency Fred Ikle
Acting Chairman of the Joint Chiefs of Staff General David C. Jones
Director of Central Intelligence William E. Colby

OTHER ATTENDEES

State
Deputy Secretary Robert Ingersoll

Defense
Deputy Secretary William Clements

CIA
Mr. Carl Duckett

White House
Mr. Donald Rumsfeld, Assistant to the President
Lt Gen Brent Scowcroft

NSC
Jan M. Lodal

---

[1] Source: Ford Library, National Security Adviser, Box 1, NSC Meetings File, NSC Meeting, October 18, 1974. Top Secret; Sensitive. The meeting was held in the Cabinet Room at the White House.

MIDDLE EAST

President Ford: It is nice to have you here. In the last day or so, Henry has filled me in on the results of his trip to the Mid East, but he might not have had a chance to do the same with the rest of you. I thought I might ask him to take ten minutes and give this group the benefit of what his trip brought.

Secretary Kissinger: The trip was arranged at the urgent request of Sadat who wanted to try to bring about a cooling off in the area. He made several approaches to the President; Asad finally joined in the request. We had no precise idea where we would go. But it quickly became apparent that Sadat knew what he was talking about—the Mid East was extremely tense and uncertain. There were many factors—the Mid East Summit next week; the unanticipated change of Presidents here, and the question of whether this change meant a change in U.S. policy; pressures from the radicals; and the oil problem.

The major purpose of the trip was to try to get a new round of negotiations started.

I might add that the Israelis also face considerable uncertainty. They have a new government with a small majority and events seem to be closing in on them.

As I said, the major purpose was to get a new round of negotiations started. The secondary purpose was the oil problem, which I raised only quietly. I didn't want to be seen as being there primarily because of the oil problem.

In the Mid East, there are three categories of problems:

—Territorial.
—The Palestinians.
—Jerusalem.

I have always told everyone that Jerusalem would have to come last, that to raise it now would tie up the talks. So it never came up.

On the territorial problems, there is Egypt, which is the easiest; the West Bank, which is the next easiest; and Syria, which is the most impossible. The West Bank is next easiest only if Jordan is the one negotiating. If the PLO negotiates, the West Bank becomes by far the most difficult problem. Of course, while we were there, the PLO issue came up in the UN.

President Ford: We were a very small minority—something like 4 out of 110.

Secretary Kissinger: That was expected. I told everyone we would be in a very small minority because we were not killing ourselves over the issue. Faisal understood this. We paid no price with the Arabs for our PLO vote in the UN.[2]

The easiest thing to do next is to get negotiations underway between Egypt and Israel, if the other Arabs will tolerate it, and if others don't make demands which undermine the position of Sadat. Israel wants a political settlement. For Sadat to negotiate with Israel alone is an unbelievable political act in itself. But if he has to certify that the talks are political, the situation becomes impossible.

Sadat has to go to the Summit[3] next week and say there is no set position yet.

Asad is determined that there not be separate negotiations. He says this three times a week in his local newspapers. He says there will not be any movement with Egypt alone if there is nothing for Syria. His position is that only all Arabs can negotiate. He believes that all Arabs should negotiate all territorial problems, that all Arabs should negotiate the Palestinian problem, and then all the Arabs should negotiate the Jerusalem problem. He and the Soviets have pushed for reconvening the Geneva Conference. The Soviets know that in separate negotiations they will be excluded. In a large conference, they can maximize their influence.

This is the minefield we have to run through. It is essential that no impression be given that any particular negotiating approach has been agreed. All of those who want separate negotiations have to go to the Summit portraying an open mind. This is especially true of those taking a moderate line—Egypt, Faisal, and Morocco.

Syria and Jordan constitute a separate problem. Syria is trying to line up other Arab support for its position against separate negotiations.

If we can hold Faisal with Sadat, we have practically got it wrapped up. Saqqaf made a statement at the airport in which he said he used to have doubts about Kissinger's negotiating approach, but he was now convinced that this was the only route—to take a step-by-step approach. This is even somewhat further than Sadat has gone.

I am not concerned about Sadat inviting Brezhnev to Egypt. This will let him look like he is making a slight move to the Soviets.

We face a difficult week next week with the Summit in Rabat. Once that is over, we will have to move fast. It is crucial that before then, we give no indication that we have any agreed outline or approach. Once Sadat moves out, he must not look ridiculous in the face of the other Arabs.

---

[2] See footnote 3, Document 104.
[3] See Document 112.

President Ford: Dayan seems to be going off on a tangent.

Secretary Kissinger: In Israel, the domestic politics are absolutely disgusting. A year ago, Dayan was the leading dove; he has now moved totally to the right. The Defense Minister of the present government is the second man in the Rafi faction[4] which Dayan heads, and it is important that the seven from this group stay in power. If he is out, the government falls.

Secretary Schlesinger: They also have the religious group.[5]

Secretary Kissinger: That's right, but assuming Egypt and Israel get negotiations started, talks on the West Bank must follow shortly. It is important that Sadat is not isolated. But the religious group opposes any West Bank talks. If it holds a balance in the Israeli cabinet, the government will be out. Therefore, the Rafi group is necessary for progress. Rafi seems more interested in the Sinai than the West Bank.

We are making good progress, but it will require a hell of a lot of work to keep it together. Last year, I thought we were playing for time. Now, we have the opportunity for serious progress, if the Israelis can recognize the realities of the situation. Some people think the split between Egypt and Syria is a game and that they are just faking it. But the Arabs are too undisciplined to pull that off. You cannot sit with Asad one half hour and think that he could possibly be playing a game. All the Arabs see this rivalry—even Boumediene, who is usually considered one of the most radical, was saying to me, "I know how it will end up—they will go back to the 1967 borders with a few changes, and everyone will quit." If the Israelis were only smart enough to realize this, I think even Faisal would go along.

Deputy Secretary Clements: Isn't Faisal's backing of Sadat a must?

Secretary Kissinger: Yes. Faisal, who is in some respects the most reactionary, makes it legitimate for the radicals. He can keep Syria in line.

With respect to oil, despite what the media here are saying, I think the speech you gave, Mr. President, has led to a massive reaction.[6] I received two assurances—that there will be no increase in prices, so that with inflation, this would mean a decrease in the real price. Second, that there would be no use of the oil weapon during negotiations, although it would be used if there were a general Arab-Israeli war.

Finally, I think that at the right moment, there is a possibility that we would get some reduction in price. Even Boumediene said some po-

---

[4] The Rafi faction of the Israeli Labor Party.

[5] Apparently a reference to the National Religious Party.

[6] A reference to President Ford's October 8 address to Congress on the economy, which was broadcast on nationwide TV and radio. For text, see *Public Papers: Ford, 1974*, pp. 228–238.

litical reduction in price might be possible. We have to analyze this. I believe we can almost certainly hold the line at the present prices, and maybe get a small reduction. But the kind of reduction we are talking about, from $9.60 to perhaps $8.00, will slow down the producers' accumulation of funds, but it does not change our fundamental problem. Our conservation program and the approach discussed at Camp David remain important.

Above all, it is essential that the Israelis do not humiliate Egypt. The Israelis can pretend that a political negotiation is underway, but it cannot be set up so that it is called a political negotiation.

We will try again in early November to get the talks set up. I believe that once Egypt moves, the other Arabs will come along. Syria may try to impose its tough position, but not if they are all alone.

Director Colby: The Israelis will probably want some kind of early warning system. They have a thing about that.

Secretary Kissinger: The Israelis have a thing about so many things. They want an Israeli electronic station in the Sinai.

Director Colby: Presumably, it would be a demilitarized zone.

Secretary Kissinger: I don't believe they will be able to get an electronic station on what will, in effect, be Egyptian territory.

Deputy Secretary Clements: With respect to the matériel we have been sending to Israel, we need to bring into the foreground what has been done and how much they have. There is no question but that the capability of the Israelis to preempt already exists. We cannot squeeze them to their limit.

Secretary Kissinger: The crucial period will be from November through January. During that period, there will be a need for pressure.

President Ford: Are you talking about what is on hand now, or what we have agreed to as a package?

Deputy Secretary Clements: What is on hand now. This has come as something of a surprise to us. We have sent the JCS task force out there, and they found that what the Israelis have exceeds what they had before the October war.

President Ford: How long can they sustain an offensive operation?

Deputy Secretary Clements: Eighteen days.

President Ford: On two fronts?

Deputy Secretary Clements: On the same basis as last year, which was two fronts. To put it another way, they have three times the capability they had last fall, which was only six days.

President Ford: Perhaps we should move now to our other subject—

Director Colby: One last point on oil prices. One of the keys is the Shah. Any influence we can use there is critical.

President Ford: If we could get a reduction from $9.60 to $8.00 or $7.00, it would be a real shot in the arm for the domestic economy.

Secretary Kissinger: I think a reduction to $7.00 is very improbable.

Director Colby: They are talking about compensation for inflation, so if the price just stays where it is, we are ahead.

Secretary Kissinger: I am confident it will stay where it is. On whether we can bring it down, I am not sure.

[Omitted here is discussion of SALT.]

112. Memorandum From the President's Deputy Assistant for National Security Affairs (Scowcroft) to President Ford[1]

Washington, October 30, 1974.

Secretary Kissinger has asked that I pass you the following message:

"My principal judgment in the wake of the Rabat conference[2] is identical with what you have already told the American people in your press conference: continued movement toward a just peace in the Middle East is essential.[3] The alternative will be a deterioration of the situation over the months ahead—militarily, politically and on the oil front—that could bring a major catastrophe, not only for the Middle East but for the U.S. and the world as a whole. The strength of Arab determination to oblige Israel to begin to move toward a settlement on all fronts, and to deal with the Palestinians as part of that process, could

---

[1] Source: Library of Congress, Manuscript Division, Kissinger Papers, CL 156, Geopolitical File, Israel, October 1974. Secret; Sensitive. Sent for information. A handwritten notation by Ford on the first page reads, "See note at end, GRF." Kissinger was traveling in South Asia.

[2] The Arab League Summit Conference, held at Rabat, Morocco October 26–29, 1974, was attended by leaders from 20 Arab countries. On October 28, the conference voted unanimously for the creation of an independent Palestinian state anywhere "on Palestinian land that is liberated" from Israeli control. Additionally, the conference recognized the PLO as the "sole legitimate representative of the Palestinian people." (*New York Times*, October 28, 1974, p. 1) The Embassy's preliminary appraisal of the summit is in telegram 5290 from Rabat, October 30. (National Archives, RG 59, Central Foreign Policy Files)

[3] The President held a press conference on October 29; see *Public Papers: Ford, 1974*, pp. 481–493.

not be more evident. This includes King Faisal and the other Arab oil producers as well as the negotiating parties.

"Unlike the Arab summit following the 1967 war,[4] which took a position of no peace, no recognition of Israel, and no negotiations, the Rabat summit was devoted to forging a United Arab Front for negotiations on peace settlement. This historic transformation of the Arab position since 1967 should not be lost sight of. On the other hand, in the 1974 context, Israel is much less ready than it was in 1967 to give up territories occupied in that war and is adamantly opposed to dealing with the PLO, which has become a major factor on the Arab side. While all the returns on Rabat are not yet in, there is no question that the decisions reached there have greatly complicated the task of engaging Israel in negotiations.

"Nevertheless, our only real option is to continue our efforts to get movement started toward an eventual overall settlement. No other country has the capability of doing this, and the Arabs and Israel are absolutely unable to negotiate without outside help.

"The tragedy is that Israel could have prevented this situation from developing had it heeded our repeated urgings of the past six months and offered Sadat or Hussein enough to make possible for them to move along together. We warned Israel it should move diplomatically before the Arab summit. As it was, Sadat and Hussein went to Rabat with no precise or meaningful offer, merely a vague promise to negotiate the surrender of some relatively minor amounts of territory in exchange for a binding long-term agreement on non-belligerency. This was impossible for them to accept and survive politically. Israel also made clear publicly and privately its refusal to move at all with Syria or the PLO, two points of great importance even to friendly Arab leaders such as Kings Faisal and Hussein. Our domestic situation also had a negative impact on Rabat. Congress' failure to pass the aid bill and its negative views on the nuclear reactor for Egypt[5] gave the impression we were reneging on our commitments to Sadat and Asad. This and the public attacks on me in the United States and elsewhere, combined with Israel's failure to move diplomatically, raised doubts among Arab leaders about whether the U.S. was able to continue to play an effective role as peacemaker.

"With respect to specifics of the Rabat summit, the initial reports are discouraging. On the face of it, both Sadat and Hussein appear to have had to surrender their freedom to negotiate alone, and the issue of

---

[4] The Khartoum conference, which met from August 29 to September 1, 1967. See *Foreign Relations*, 1964–1968, volume XIX, Arab-Israeli Crisis and War, 1967, Document 434, footnote 3.

[5] See Document 92.

the Palestinians and the PLO has assumed a more central role. But initial appearances are often deceiving in the Arab world. It may be that there is still room to maneuver and get separated or phased negotiations underway behind a facade of Arab unity. It may also be that it is still possible for Jordan instead of the PLO to negotiate with Israel provided there is an assured role for the Palestinians (with PLO leadership) in any outcome and they have a voice in helping determine Jordan's negotiation policy. The decision with Jordan, Syria, Egypt and the PLO to meet to work out the details of their negotiating relationship means that everything is not yet pinned down. Just how much flexibility Sadat and Hussein retain remains to be determined. Sadat in any event has urged me to come to Cairo.

"I believe that only by making my planned trip to the area can we determine the effects of Rabat on the prospects for negotiation. After talking with the Arabs and Israelis I will have a much clearer idea as to what possibilities exist for continuing the movement toward a peaceful settlement. Moreover, should I not go it would be interpreted by the Arabs and Israelis that the U.S. has abandoned—not merely postponed—its peacemaking efforts and there is no other recourse than force. Meanwhile, I have urged Israel in the strongest terms to dampen public reactions to Rabat and not lock itself into flexible positions.

"Unless you think otherwise, I will proceed to see Sadat, Hussein, Faisal, Asad and the Israeli leaders after the Rome Conference, probably returning to Washington late Saturday, November 9."[6]

---

[6] In the margin next to this paragraph, Ford wrote "OK" and his initials.

113. Telegram From Secretary of State Kissinger to the Department of State[1]

Dacca, October 31, 1974, 0130Z.

Secto 264/4975. For Eagleburger only from the Secretary.

1. I want you to tell Dinitz that I am absolutely outraged by Allon's letter and Dinitz' oral message.[2] I want you to convey this to him with some heat, pointing out that I had to push through a negative vote over the recommendations and protests of our entire bureaucracy. It is entirely false to say we were ambiguous with the Europeans. We went to every single country Allon suggested. In each case the reply was exactly the opposite of what Allon predicted. If the Israelis believe the Europeans on this, a confidential relationship between us becomes impossible.

2. Tell Dinitz I will not put up with this kind of ingratitude and shortsightedness any longer. He should know that our foreign policy is made in Washington not Jerusalem and I do not appreciate his government's constant harassament any longer.

3. I am sending Scowcroft a message on military equipment.[3]

4. With respect to my forthcoming trip, Dinitz should not tell me the obvious. It is clear that no final decisions can be made after the Rabat summit. We will obviously not brief the press in an unproductive direction.

5. My schedule prohibits me from doing the Weizmann Institute before next March as I have said at least five times.[4]

Kissinger

---

[1] Source: Library of Congress, Manuscript Division, Kissinger Papers, CL 156, Geopolitical File, Israel, October 1974. Secret; Cherokee; Nodis, Immediate.

[2] Dinitz's oral message, conveyed to Eagleburger, expressed a number of concerns, especially the Israeli Government's fear of Arab attempts to "translate decisions taken in Rabat into a new UNGA Resolution aimed at upsetting U.N. Resolutions 242 and 338." (Telegram Tosec 332/238082 to Dacca, October 30; ibid.) Dinitz also presented Allon's letter to Eagleburger. In the letter, Allon applauded the U.S. vote against the UN General Assembly's invitation to the PLO, but he criticized the United States for not making a greater effort "to obtain the support of other countries for its position." Allon concluded that "firm opposition by the U.S. to the Arab initiative which, if vigorously pursued, will no doubt secure the support of other like-minded nations," and he sought assurance from Kissinger "that this will indeed be the course to be taken by the United States." (Telegram Tosec 333/238083 to Dacca, October 30; ibid.)

[3] In telegram Tosec 332/238082 to Dacca, Dinitz expressed his hope that the U.S. Government would respond positively to Israeli requests for military equipment. (Ibid.)

[4] Dinitz also asked if Kissinger would be accepting an honorary degree from the Weizmann Institute. (Ibid.)

114. Memorandum From the President's Deputy Assistant for National Security Affairs (Scowcroft) to President Ford[1]

Washington, November 3, 1974.

Secretary Kissinger has asked that I discuss personally with you the following:

"While I do not yet have a full picture of what happened at the Rabat Summit,[2] everything we have heard since then bears out the initial assessment I sent you. That assessment is also shared by such perceptive observers of the Middle East scene as Bhutto and the Shah of Iran. They agree that the best opportunity for progress in the Middle East was during the past summer when the various Arab leaders were visiting Washington. They also agree that the Israelis' stonewalling of the negotiation process prevented us from making progress.

"I am not at all certain that it will be possible to get this delicate process moving again. However, it is clear that the Israelis must get from us a sober appraisal of the situation and it is equally clear that they must hear it from you. Therefore, I think it would be a tremendous assistance to my trip if prior to my arrival in Israel you would agree to call in Dinitz, or in his absence Minister Shalev, and speak to him very sternly. This will be worth doing only if you are prepared to take a very stern line with the Israelis.

"If you agree, I would suggest you talk to Dinitz or Shalev along the following lines:

—Secretary Kissinger is in the Middle East at my instruction to determine the situation in the aftermath of the Rabat Summit and prior to our own policy review. Pending his return we obviously cannot make judgments on how the situation will develop.

—However, it is clear that the present situation has the enormous danger of leading to precisely the kind of United Arab-European-Soviet front which we have worked with Israel so hard to avoid over the past year.

—This could have been avoided if Israel had taken our advice. We urged Israel repeatedly, beginning last year and again as recently as August, to make a viable proposal to King Hussein that would enable him to preempt the PLO before a pro PLO bandwagon developed in the Arab world. We also urged Israel to make a further proposal to Sadat,

---

[1] Source: Library of Congress, Manuscript Division, Kissinger Papers, CL 156, Geopolitical File, Israel, October 1974. Secret; Sensitive; Exclusively Eyes Only. Sent for information. Ford initialed the memorandum.

[2] See Document 112.

but instead Israel dragged matters out and Sadat went empty-handed to the summit. Furthermore, Israel's public statements about never giving up any more of the Golan Heights left the Syrians with no hope and certainly contributed to their hard line position at the summit. Finally, Israel's stonewalling of the nuclear agreement with Egypt,[3] the slow progress of aid legislation in Congress all left Sadat with no viable options.

—Therefore, I have called you in to tell you that while the United States remains a steadfast friend of Israel and is prepared to listen seriously to Israeli concerns, we cannot permit our policy to become a prisoner of domestic Israeli politics. Israel simply cannot hold the entire world at ransom.

—A continued stalemate in the negotiations will pose serious dangers. I hope your government will, therefore, talk to Secretary Kissinger with an open mind and not in the nagging tone so characteristic of our recent exchanges.

—We must be given an opportunity to make a reasonable examination of the options facing us and to conduct our policy in the period ahead on the basis of the new realities created by Rabat. We will want to examine all of this together with Israel.

Meanwhile it is absolutely essential that Israel avoid actions and statements that would limit their and our maneuvering room, and begin to examine seriously what it can do to prevent a stalemate from developing."

---

[3] See Document 92.

---

115. Memorandum From the President's Deputy Assistant for National Security Affairs (Scowcroft) to President Ford[1]

Washington, November 6, 1974.

Secretary Kissinger has asked that I pass you the following report of his meetings in Cairo:

---

[1] Source: National Archives, RG 59, Records of Henry Kissinger, 1973–77, Box 5, Nodis Memcons, November 1974, Folder 6. Secret; Sensitive; Exclusively Eyes Only. Sent for information. Ford initialed the memorandum.

"I have just concluded my Cairo stop which consisted of one and a half hour discussion with Sadat last night and another one this morning as well as a meeting with Foreign Minister Fahmy.[2] The principal result of the meeting is that Sadat continues to attach great importance to finding a way to continue the step-by-step approach which he would hope would lead to a further Israeli withdrawal in the Sinai placing the strategic passes in his own hands and returning the oil fields in the south to Egypt. These talks culminated in a prepared statement by Sadat which strongly endorsed our approach and continued confidence in the U.S., stated flatly Egypt's strong desire for continued active American diplomacy, and insisting that the Rabat summit has not closed all doors.

"Despite the fact that he was suffering from a very heavy cold, Sadat insisted on this full exchange and he took the time to meet with the press so that the aforementioned positive message could be gotten through publicly. He intends the above statement to be a counter to the attack on our policy which he has noted in our press and particularly stories emanating from Israeli sources that Rabat was a major diplomatic surprise and defeat for the United States.

"While Sadat has once again reaffirmed in strong terms the step-by-step approach, he is particularly anxious that some negotiating process be in train by the time Brezhnev arrives in Cairo in mid-January. He wants it conducted through diplomatic channels until the outline of an outcome appears. At that point he is prepared to move to formal negotiations. He is not sure he can carry the whole process on his own because it will make him very vulnerable. He would like something to be going on with either the Syrians or the PLO in the same time frame of Egyptian-Israeli negotiations though it can be dragged out. I made clear to him that he should not expect that Israel will agree to negotiations with the Syrians or the PLO at this juncture.

"A good part of the talk was spent by Sadat and Fahmy filling us in on the details of the discussions of the Rabat summit. The Egyptian version is that all was going reasonably well until Jordanian Prime Minister Rifai and King Hussein told the other Arabs that we had pressed Jordan to make a disengagement agreement with Israel that would constitute a final peace. I made clear that at no time did we ever do this, and that there is no satisfactory explanation for the statements being attributed to Rifai and Hussein by the Egyptians. I will be interested in

---

[2] The November 5 meeting between Sadat and Kissinger took place at 9:30 p.m. in President Sadat's bedroom at the Giza Residence. An uncleared draft memorandum of conversation is ibid., Box 4, Nodis Memcons, January 1974, Folder 2. No memoranda of conversation of meetings between Sadat and Kissinger or Fahmy and Kissinger on November 6 have been found.

Hussein's version of these events when I see him in the next twenty-four hours.

"I made no proposals and no decisions were taken. Sadat indicated that he is prepared in the immediate days ahead to have further talks with us on negotiating possibilities quietly through diplomatic channels rather than in a more formal setting which he does not feel he can undertake at this time unless Israel also agrees to negotiate either with the Syrians or the PLO.

"I do not want to overemphasize the result of my meetings with Sadat but once again I am struck with the fact that he has taken the high road of statesmanship and that he is looking for ways to create some breathing space for us and to continue an effective role by the United States. We have a little breathing space. His public statement will help to put to rest the notion that U.S. diplomatic efforts in the Middle East have ended. It will be a setback for the USSR. The fact remains that if nothing is going on by mid-January he will be under unbearable pressure from the Russians and from his own people. Moreover, he has reiterated that he is very much looking forward to his visit with you, and we discussed the possibilities of its beginning about January 20."

116. Memorandum From the President's Deputy Assistant for National Security Affairs (Scowcroft) to President Ford[1]

Washington, November 6, 1974.

The Secretary has asked me to provide you with the following report of his meeting with King Faisal.

"I flew from Cairo to Riyadh, the desert capital of Saudi Arabia, for an hour and a half audience this evening with King Faisal[2] before going on to Amman tonight. With his wealth and prestige, the King carries great weight in those Arab countries which are important to our peace efforts, and I again sought his support in urging moderation on the Syrians and PLO during the period ahead.

---

[1] Source: Ford Library, National Security Adviser, Trip Briefing Books of Henry Kissinger, Box 2, Europe, South Asia, Middle East, Kissinger Messages to President Ford, Folder 2, November 6, 1974. Secret; Sensitive. Sent for information. Ford initialed the memorandum.

[2] No memorandum of conversation has been found.

"I explained generally to the King, and in greater detail to his Foreign Minister, the problems the Rabat Summit decisions will cause us with the Israelis and at home. While I do not expect to change Faisal's strong commitment to the Palestinian cause, I am hopeful that through his Foreign Minister, whom he is sending to New York, the Saudis will seek to exercise a moderating influence during the Palestinian debate in the General Assembly next week.

"Faisal continues to take an oversimplified view of the Israeli side. The important thing, however, is that he reaffirmed his support for our peace efforts and authorized his Foreign Minister to make a statement at the airport strongly supporting our step-by-step approach. He also authorized Foreign Minister Saqqaf to reiterate Saudi Arabia's policy of working to stabilize and ultimately bring down oil prices.

"In addition, the meeting with Faisal gave me an opportunity to relieve Saudi suspicions that had been aroused by recent Israeli-inspired press stories about our military supply to Israel, and to counter suspicions shown at the Rabat Summit about our policy toward a Middle East peace settlement.

"We continue to face a difficult road ahead, and I do not want to over-estimate the Saudi will or capacity to stand up alone to pressures from extremist elements in the Arab world. There is no doubt, however, that Faisal wants to continue to work with us, both bilaterally and in the Arab world and can be helpful in cooperation with other moderates, particularly Sadat. That the two continue to work closely together was evident from the fact that Sadat sent his special emissary, Ashraf Marwan, from Cairo to Riyadh after my meetings in Cairo this morning to brief the King before my audience with him. To sum up: we defused the situation and created an opening for negotiations. A lot now depends on the Israelis.

"I will meet with King Hussein tomorrow morning before going on to Damascus and Tel Aviv, after which we should have a clearer picture of where the Rabat Summit leaves us. At a minimum, however, I am hopeful that my current trip has defused the post-Rabat situation in the area and may possibly have opened up the opportunity for a further negotiations."

117. Telegram From the President's Deputy Assistant for National Security Affairs (Scowcroft) to Secretary of State Kissinger[1]

Washington, November 7, 1974.

Tohak 180. The President met with Shalev.[2] I spoke with the President briefly beforehand and reviewed your points. He was quite nervous in his presentation but basically did a good job—tougher than he has been on some other occasions.

The President started by saying that the whole situation for your talks with Rabin is different from what we had hoped. He said he was very concerned that we could find ourselves faced by a united front of Arabs, the Soviet Union, and the Europeans against us. As he looked back to October and November of last year, there was simultaneously a very tough conflict, an oil embargo and a fairly close confrontation with the Soviet Union. It was not in either of our interests to have that happen again or perhaps even worse. We had hoped that negotiations could be undertaken with Sadat and Hussein and eventually even with Syria. It is our judgment that had negotiations been under way, the Rabat outcome could have been avoided. Our concern is that if a stalemate is allowed to develop we will face the danger of a united front which would be perilous for us both. He asked that Shalev communicate with Rabin his grave concern that there be a serious and open exploration of the situation with you resulting in quick movement on the substantive issues. He said his past record of support for Israel was well-known. He thought we could have avoided Rabat and he thinks now we can perhaps avoid the consequences of Rabat if Rabin would seriously face with you on the situation which confronts us.

Shalev answered that Rabin had made a statement to the Knesset that Israel was willing to negotiate with Egypt and Jordan but not with the PLO and he thought that that was in accordance with our wishes. Israel could not negotiate with the PLO because they seek to destroy Israel.

The President said he understood the Israeli concern about the PLO but reiterated the imperative to move. Shalev responded by saying he was not aware of any difference with the U.S. on the steps fol-

---

[1] Source: Library of Congress, Manuscript Division, Kissinger Papers, TS 29, Geopolitical File, Israel, May 6–November 28, 1974. Top Secret; Sensitive; Exclusively Eyes Only. The original is the text as approved for transmission.

[2] The memorandum of conversation of the meeting between Ford and Shalev on November 6 at 3 p.m. in the Oval Office at the White House is in the Ford Library, National Security Adviser, Memoranda of Conversations, Box 7, November 6, 1974, Ford, Israeli Minister and Chargé Mordechai Shalev.

lowing the disengagement and he felt that Rabat would have happened in any event.

The President responded by saying that while he, of course, had not been in on all the discussions, his understanding was that we urged early movement, and that the Israelis had insisted their domestic situation required some delay. Had there been negotiations under way, the Rabat outcome would have been different. Shalev responded that their confidence in Sadat's wishes for peace had been seriously shaken and they thought he was at least keeping all his options open. He pointed out that Egypt is now starting to build anti-aircraft bunkers on the Egyptian side of the Canal, in violation of the disengagement agreement. He pointed out that on your last visit with Sadat you told him the Israelis would be prepared to negotiate and he (Shalev) did not think that a few weeks would have made any difference.

The point seemed in danger of being lost, so I interjected at that point to say that the record of our bilateral discussions was quite clear. We had been strongly urging early negotiations ever since President Nixon's Middle East trip. You had told Allon in July that Egypt wanted the next stage completed in September, and we had for many months stated that if Israel would not negotiate with Hussein while the opportunity existed, they would at some point be faced with negotiating with the PLO. I said that it was only under strong pleas by the Israelis that their domestic situation would not permit such fast movement, that we reluctantly receded on our timetable demands. That had been wrong and what the President was pointing out was that that could not be allowed to happen again. We could not tolerate it.

The President said he wanted to sum up the discussions by saying that a stalemate must be avoided and in order to do that the Israelis had to examine the options in the light of current realities and be willing to move. He wanted this communicated clearly to the Prime Minister. Shalev said that nothing was further from their minds than a delay of negotiations but they had their security to think about. The President concluded by saying we will maintain our guarantees for Israel's existence and security but that could in no way be used as an excuse to avoid making the hard decisions that would produce movement.

I talked briefly with Shalev afterwards to summarize in somewhat harsher terms what the President had said. I think there is no question that he got the message.[3]

Warm regards.

---

[3] See Document 117.

118. Telegram From Secretary of State Kissinger to the President's Deputy Assistant for National Security Affairs (Scowcroft)[1]

November 7, 1974.

Please convey the following message to the President:
Begin text:

1. My three-hour conversation with President Asad today[2] confirmed that his strategy at Rabat in support of the PLO was intended to block any negotiations on either the Jordanian-Israeli or the Egyptian-Israeli fronts in the absence of any immediate possibilities for practical progress on the Golan Heights. Several times during the conversation, however, I detected anxiety on the part of Asad as to how now to proceed in light of Rabat. He punctuated this by several times asking: how do you see the next step; why can we not move commonly on all fronts? I sensed therefore both relief on his part that it was unlikely some negotiation would be going on that would exclude Syria, while at the same time concern over the probable impasse he has helped create as a result of the support he gave to the PLO at Rabat. I am coming more to the view therefore that a period of time in which all concerned, particularly the Arabs at this moment, will be needed in which the full implications of Rabat can make themselves felt.

2. I took the posture with Asad that I intended to make no new move, but that I am available to be helpful if either the Arabs or the Israelis want my assistance. I advised the desirability of moderation in the upcoming debate on the Palestinian issue at the UN General Assembly when it opens on the 13th. I also in a very low key asked Asad to reflect on whether it is in his interests to hold back on the extension of the United Nations Observer Force in the buffer zone between Syria and Israel when this matter comes up in the UN Security Council in late November. I believe he now sees that if they decide against renewing the mandate of the UN Force for another 6 months that this will only feed the Israeli contention that negotiations with the Syrians are neither feasible or worthwhile. I do not know, however, what he will decide.

3. I spent a good deal of my time making clear again what we mean by a step-by-step approach, that its objective is not to divide the Arabs, nor to exclude the Syrians but rather my belief that basically it is the only manageable way to proceed. It is clear that Asad is looking for

---

[1] Source: National Archives, RG 59, Records of Joseph Sisco, Box 33, Briefing Book: Mr. Sisco's Outgoing. Secret; Sensitive. The original is not initialed by Kissinger and does not have a Hakto number, but apparently the telegram was sent.

[2] No memorandum of conversation has been found.

some way for negotiations to take place more or less simultaneously between the Egyptians and the Israelis and the Syrians and the Israelis.

4. Finally, I think it is noteworthy that Asad went out of his way to stress that whatever differences there may be between us regarding how next to proceed that he wants to maintain the improved relations which exist between the United States and Syria. He apparently attached sufficient importance to this to have Foreign Minister Khaddam make this point publicly at the airport as I left Damascus.

End text.

Warm regards.

---

119. Memorandum From the President's Deputy Assistant for National Security Affairs (Scowcroft) to President Ford[1]

Washington, November 8, 1974.

Secretary Kissinger asked that I pass you the following report of his meeting with Prime Minister Rabin.

"I arrived tonight in Jerusalem after talks earlier today in Amman and Damascus, and went immediately to a two and one-half hour working dinner with Prime Minister Rabin and his inner circle of key Cabinet Ministers and Advisers.[2]

"At Rabin's request, I gave them a full report on the mood and attitudes I found in the Arab capitals I have just visited. I painted a somber picture of the prospects for negotiations in the situation on the Arab side resulting from the Rabat summit conference, and of the consequences of a stalemate which would write the Soviets, Europeans, Japanese and Arabs against Israel and the United States. In particular, I stressed the opportunity that had been lost to preempt the PLO by earlier giving King Hussein a viable West Bank offer and made clear that

---

[1] Source: Library of Congress, Manuscript Division, Kissinger Papers, CL 156, Geopolitical File, Israel, October 1974. Secret; Sensitive. Sent for information. Ford initialed the memorandum.

[2] The memorandum of conversation of the meeting between the Israeli negotiating team and Kissinger, which took place on November 7 from 9:45 until 11:26 p.m. at the Prime Minister's Residence in Jerusalem, is in the National Archives, RG 59, Records of Henry Kissinger, 1973–77, Box 25, CATC Nodis Memos, July–December 1974. There was another meeting between the Israeli negotiating team and Kissinger on November 8 from 10:45 a.m. until 12:10 p.m. Their discussion focused on the PLO and Jordan and military equipment for Israel. (Ibid.)

Israel bears the main responsibility for this. So far as the future is concerned, I said we had not made up our minds whether further efforts at this stage were feasible. I told them the only possibility I saw would be if procedures could be devised whereby a next stage agreement could be worked out with Sadat, before Brezhnev visits Cairo in January, that would not surface publicly until it was close to completion; even then, there was a large question whether Sadat would be able politically to go it alone in the new atmosphere of Arab solidarity resulting from Rabat. I told them that some sort of negotiations with Syria might be necessary if Egypt were to be able to move.

"Rabin took a confident and tough line at the dinner meeting, arguing that a firm stand would bring the Arabs back to reality.

"So far as the PLO is concerned, the Israelis were united in their adamant and emotional opposition to making any bow in its direction. Although there may be more serious reflection within the Government of Israel than meets the eye, they displayed a state of high anxiety that we may make some move toward the PLO, despite my making clear that we had left no doubt in Arab minds that we would not press Israel to negotiate with it. This question touches the most sensitive nerves in Israel.

"After the working dinner, I had an hour's discussion with Rabin alone.[3] I found him more understanding and more disposed to consider in a positive spirit ways to move things ahead. I will report personally to you on the specifics of this talk. I believe your talk with Shalev[4] helped and Rabin assured me he would cooperate in making practical progress.

"All in all, with luck and discipline, we may be able to bring off a successful Egyptian-Israeli negotiation by the end of February."

---

[3] No memorandum of conversation has been found.
[4] See Document 117.

120. Letter From President Ford to Israeli Prime Minister Rabin[1]

Washington, November 26, 1974.

Dear Mr. Prime Minister:

We are looking forward to the visit of Foreign Minister Allon and regard it as of major importance.

After the long pause in the negotiations since the Syrian disengagement agreement, it is absolutely essential that another step be taken soon. The Soviets are obviously moving into position to regain some of the ground they have lost, and Brezhnev's visit to Cairo appears to have been timed to coincide with the time when they judge our negotiating effort will have lost momentum.

If we cannot give realistic promise of progress very soon, we risk losing all control over the situation. Coming on the heels of the failure to start Jordan negotiations on time, this would have the most serious consequences for Israel and for the United States. A stalemate on all fronts, therefore, cannot be accepted.

Foreign Minister Allon should come prepared to develop a proposal that can promptly become the basis for a realistic negotiation with Egypt. Secretary Kissinger has told you enough about President Sadat's views that it should be possible for you now to know what the issues will be and how they might be dealt with in ways that will protect the interests of both sides. Recalling our conversation in Washington[2] and the discussions you and Secretary Kissinger have had since then, I am counting on substantial progress during the Foreign Minister's visit.

I am pleased that it has been possible to work out an extension of the UNDOF mandate. I did not want to raise this subject while the UNDOF issue was still unsettled, but now as I look back over the past two weeks, I want to say, so that there will be no misunderstanding later, that Israel's sudden call-up of reservists[3] at that tense moment

---

[1] Source: Ford Library, National Security Adviser, Kissinger-Scowcroft West Wing Office Files, Box 15, Israel, Items 25–31, November 15–December 4, 1974. Secret. A handwritten notation at the top of the first page reads, "Hand delivered to Min. Shalev by General Scowcroft, 11/26/74, 5:30 p.m." Kissinger's covering memorandum to Ford, November 26, recommended that before Allon's arrival in Washington on December 9 for a meeting with Ford, the President should write a letter to Rabin to convince him of the need to send Allon with "a proposal we can work with and not just some more preliminary ideas."

[2] See Documents 99 and 100.

[3] On November 15, Israel called up approximately one-third of its reservists and increased its guard on the Golan Heights. Reportedly, some Israeli leaders claimed the call-up was in response to provocative military moves made by Syria coordinated with

without prior discussion with us is something that cannot be risked again.

There may be some in Israel who feel it helped bring the Syrians around. I know from our efforts in Damascus that it did not and would be a serious mistake to follow that reasoning in the future.

In any case, it is essential that we work together closely. We cannot be responsible for the consequences and cannot play the role you look to us to play—and which we wish to play—if we are again taken by surprise by a move of this kind.

As you know from our conversation, I want us to cooperate closely and effectively, and I believe Israel's interests have been fully taken into account in our every move. This will continue to be the case in my Administration, and I will look to you to assure that our common interests are taken into account in each of your moves.

Sincerely,

Gerald R. Ford

---

the Soviet Union. (*Washington Post*, November 18, 1974, p. A14) The UNDOF mandate was renewed for another six months on November 29.

---

121. Memorandum From the President's Assistant for National Security Affairs (Kissinger) to President Ford[1]

Washington, December 5, 1974.

SUBJECT

Premier Rabin's Reply to You on Mideast Negotiation

On November 26 you wrote to Israeli Premier Rabin to urge that Foreign Minister Allon, when he comes here December 9, "should come prepared to develop a proposal that can promptly become the basis for a realistic negotiation with Egypt." (Your letter is at Tab B.)[2] You warned that Soviet attempts to regain lost ground in the Middle East required that we maintain the momentum of our negotiating ef-

---

[1] Source: Ford Library, National Security Adviser, Kissinger/Scowcroft West Wing Office Files, Box 15, Israel, Items 32–37, December 5, 1974–January 12, 1975. Secret; Sensitive. Sent for information. Ford initialed the memorandum.

[2] Tab B is Document 120.

fort. You also urged that there be no repetition of the sudden call-up of Israeli reservists, which added to the tension in mid-November.

Premier Rabin's reply to you is at Tab A.[3] He makes the following points:

—He says that the Soviets can always be blocked by a "firm steadfast" U.S. position.

—He reiterates the standard Israeli position that the next agreement with Egypt must involve "political" concessions from Egypt in return for any Israeli territorial concessions. Unless Egypt engages itself in a "conscious progression towards peace," Israel is gaining only a temporary prolongation of a ceasefire, "i.e., a mere postponement of the resumption of hostilities."

—Rabin comments that Israel had had frequent contacts with King Hussein but that the King's proposals were always unacceptable. Thus Israel does not feel itself responsible for the failure to achieve a successful negotiation with Jordan before Rabat. Israel remains ready to reach agreement and peace with Jordan.

—On the reserve call-up, Rabin asserts that he informed us immediately when the decision was taken.[4] He attributes the call-up to Israel's natural need to avoid being caught by surprise again. He expresses gratitude for our military assistance but reminds us that "in the final analysis" Israel bears the "awesome responsibility" for its own security.

The main point of your letter was the need for Allon to come with proposals enabling us to make substantial progress with Egypt. Rabin's reply repeats a number of basic Israeli points but gives no indication of what Allon will bring.

---

[3] Tab A is Rabin's letter as enclosed in a letter from Dinitz to Ford, December 1, attached but not printed.

[4] Telegram 6618 from Tel Aviv, November 15, summarized reports by the Defense Attaché of a briefing on the alert he had received from the Israeli Chief of Intelligence. (National Archives, RG 59, Central Foreign Policy Files)

122. Memorandum of Conversation[1]

Washington, December 9, 1974.

PARTICIPANTS

President Ford
Dr. Henry A. Kissinger, Secretary of State and Assistant to the President for National Security Affairs
Lt. General Brent Scowcroft, Deputy Assistant to the President for National Security Affairs

Kissinger: [Discussed Ray Cline piece on the October war.][2]

On Allon: At the dinner on the last night it should be only Max Fisher from the Jewish community and no trained seals from the press.

You got a letter from Sadat.[3]

President: I thought it a statesmanlike letter.

Kissinger: He followed it up with an oral message.

President: What does Sadat need?

Kissinger: Israel has to give up the passes. Maybe just give Egypt a Western toehold and put the passes themselves under the UN. Israel is willing to give up the northern oil field, but I think they would give up the southern field too. If they gave up all the oilfields and maybe 50 kilometers in the north, we could play around with the passes.

A quick agreement carried out over nine months with a one-year extension of UNEF should take Egypt out of it.

If we get an agreement, I think we should give military aid to Egypt. The Egyptian military establishment can't run down without the Egyptian military doing something about it.

President: I have an open mind about it.

Kissinger: It would be useful to tell Sadat we are turning in that direction.

President: How about covert aid?

Kissinger: That is not worth the risk. Three years ago it would have been easy—not now.

President: Do we need Congressional approval for cash subsidies?

---

[1] Source: Ford Library, National Security Adviser, Memoranda of Conversations, Box 7, December 9, 1974, Ford, Kissinger. Secret; Nodis. The meeting was held in the Oval Office at the White House. All brackets, except ones that describe omitted material, are in the original.

[2] A reference to Ray Cline's article in *Foreign Policy* entitled "Policy Without Intelligence." (*Foreign Policy*, No. 17 (Winter 1974–1975), p. 128)

[3] The letter has not been found.

Scowcroft: Only if there is some prohibition on Egyptian aid.

Kissinger: If not, I would just announce it.

[Omitted here is discussion unrelated to the Arab-Israeli dispute.]

[Kissinger:] Back to Allon—

If he has reasonable proposals, you can be conciliatory. If not, say we can't underwrite them under these conditions. If there is no settlement, there will be a war and I don't know how we would conduct ourselves in that situation.

[There was a discussion of laser-guided bombs.]

President: I told Jim[4] I recognize the April 1st target but I had to be cognizant of our own units and we wouldn't strip our units until we had full cooperation from Israel.

Kissinger: I think it is dangerous to put them in that strong a military position; then they are sorely tempted to tell us to go to hell.

A confrontation sometime down the road is inevitable. If they had moved on the West Bank, we could have avoided Rabat. Now Hussein is knocked out. If we can get something on Egypt, we can go to Geneva—Syria wants to—and let it get stalemated there. If there is another war I think—cost what may—you have to get a final settlement.

President: How shortsighted they are!

Kissinger: Three million people can't stand against 120 million with unlimited resources. With Soviet backing. Winning is as dangerous as losing.

If the Israelis march on Damascus and the Soviets put in two divisions and announce they are just going to the '67 borders, and call on us and the Europeans and Japanese to join in guaranteeing the '67 borders . . .

[Omitted here is discussion of the Oval Office, Lyndon Johnson, Richard Nixon, and Golda Meir.]

---

[4] Secretary of Defense James Schlesinger.

123. Memorandum of Conversation[1]

Washington, December 9, 1974, 12:57–2:15 p.m.

PARTICIPANTS

    Yigal Allon, Deputy Prime Minister and Minister of Foreign Affairs of Israel
    Simcha Dinitz, Ambassador of Israel
    Mordechai Shalev, Minister, Embassy of Israel

    President Gerald R. Ford
    Dr. Henry A. Kissinger, Secretary of State and Assistant to the President for National Security Affairs
    Lt. Gen. Brent Scowcroft, Deputy Assistant to the President for National Security Affairs
    Amb. Kenneth Keating, U.S. Ambassador to Israel

[Omitted here is discussion about Cyprus and European issues.]

[President:] Let me welcome you. I'm glad to have you here. I remember our conversation when I was Vice President [August 1, 1974].[2] I am glad to talk with you now because we are faced with some tough decisions.

Secretary Kissinger has just described your conversation with him.[3] He told me that your proposals were unattainable. I don't know the details, but I agree. I will take time going over them because of their importance and because the commitment to Israel's security is of utmost importance to me. I have spent a great deal of time on this since I came into office. We have worked hard to keep things moving, because momentum is vital. I have talked to no one who doesn't think the prospects of war are high if something is not done—and most of these are people who are friendly to Israel.

I think it is wise to look at what happens if we don't have results. We always used to do this on the Hill. "Think of the worst. The best will

---

[1] Source: Ford Library, National Security Adviser, Memoranda of Conversations, Box 7, December 9, 1974, Ford, Kissinger, Israeli Deputy Prime Minister Yigal Allon. Secret; Nodis. The meeting was held in the Oval Office at the White House. All brackets, with the exception of ones describing omitted material, are in the original.

[2] No memorandum of conversation has been found.

[3] The memorandum of conversation of the meeting between Allon and Kissinger, which took place on December 9 from 10:35 a.m. until 12:25 p.m. in the Secretary's office at the Department of State, is in the Library of Congress, Manuscript Division, Kissinger Papers, CL 156, Geopolitical File, Israel, December 9–31, 1974. Two meetings between Allon and Kissinger followed the meeting with Ford. The first meeting took place took place from 2:45 to 3:55 p.m. Their discussion covered several issues, including the Soviet Union, long-term arms aid authorization, a Middle East aid package, P.L. 480, Soviet and Syrian Jewry, and a nuclear reactor for Egypt. (Ibid.) The second meeting took place from 4:10 until 5:25 p.m. in the Secretary's office at the Department of State. Their discussion focused on the disengagement talks between Israel and Egypt. (Ibid.)

take care of itself." A potential confrontation in the Middle East—I don't know where that would go with the Soviet Union. We made headway at Vladivostok,[4] but we had a potential confrontation last October. If there is a war, there will be another oil embargo. Last year we were in fairly good economic shape—today, it could have dire consequences. Israel and the U.S. would be pretty well isolated as far as Europe and the rest of the world are concerned. No one helped us in '73. And Japan also would be the same. I'm just pointing to alternatives which could happen.

We want Israel to be strong, and we have done a good economic and military job on that. Supposing the worst happens—a war—and Israel is successful. The odds are you would be. Suppose the Soviet Union goes further and doesn't back down as they did under President Nixon. It would be a tough decision for the President to go to the people for military action in the Middle East. Attitudes are different than, for example, in 1950. I don't like it. I want Americans to think they have a role and a strong role. But look at the last years of Vietnam. The aftermath of that doesn't indicate that a President would get public support. I want to say as a friend—and my record supports I am a friend—that the consequences of the worst lead me to the hope that we can change things somehow so we can say it *is* attainable. That is the way it is.

Kissinger: We have the problem of what is realistic and the problem of what do we tell Egypt. We haven't discussed it yet, and we will this afternoon. I am grateful to Allon for getting me out of the House hearing meeting.

Allon: Thank you for the way you introduced your views. First I want to convey the greetings of Yitzhak Rabin.

President: Please reciprocate for me.

Allon: He is making a good Prime Minister. We are a highly political people. There is no doubt the United States and Israel have common interests in the Middle East. We may appear to disagree tactically, but basically we agree. I am glad of that. We come to you frequently for military and economic support, but in the last analysis I think we are an asset, not a liability. It would be different if we were weak. Looking at a wider prospective—at the soft underbelly of Europe—we can be useful if we coordinate together more.

The last thing we want is another war—although we would win it quickly, because we are better prepared. And we won't get caught again. We learned bitter lessons and the morale is high.

---

[4] Ford met with General Secretary Brezhnev at Vladivostok on November 23 and 24.

We would have preferred an overall settlement which would have brought peace to the area. Secretary Kissinger said that it is not possible and we accepted the necessity of interim agreements, over serious domestic opposition. We are determined to overcome the opposition and to sign an interim agreement. We understand that Egypt is the only chance, that Jordan is out for now, but we hope not forever. Syria wants an overall agreement, and if we do that we don't need interim measures.

Dr. Kissinger always used to stress on principle—never negotiate while under a threat. If the Arabs realize—and the Soviet Union—that they can get what they want by threat of war or an oil embargo, there is no limit to what they will go after. If they know there is a logical limit that is different. If they know you can be backed into a corner . . .

Kissinger: The President has said, with the Arabs he has talked to, that if there is a new embargo we would not accept it. He is talking to you about . . .

Allon: But any war would be over in days, and most of the West has enough oil for months, so this threat doesn't hold. The West can get through the winter. So we shouldn't overestimate the immediate effect of an oil embargo.

We are prepared to take substantial territorial steps in return for an end to acts of belligerency. It can be an end to acts of belligerency, not to the state of belligerency.

The next question is, what should be the duration of an agreement? In 1949 it was unlimited.[5] It didn't work. We had another war. If there is a time limit it must be longer than what they need to get ready for another war. If only a few years, that is just what they need to prepare for war. The Arabs are good on defense, bad on offense. They are not rushing into war, but the situation could be created where they would have to—even against their wishes. If it could be a longer-term agreement, and a longer-term for UNEF, we could give more. Egypt says everything must be kept secret. But we have our problems, too.

I think Secretary Kissinger can tell Egypt we are prepared for a considerable withdrawal, to negotiate after—not before—the Brezhnev visit to Egypt.[6] If we do it before, it will look like we did it because of Brezhnev's visit.

So the matter is how deep the withdrawal, how solid the observers, and how long the agreement.

---

[5] The 1949 Armistice Agreements, brokered by the United Nations, ended the 1948 Arab-Israeli war between Israel and Egypt, Syria, Jordan, and Lebanon.

[6] On December 30, the Soviet government announced the postponement of Brezhnev's visit to the Middle East due to poor health. (*New York Times*, December 31, 1974, p. 1)

I am thinking of a decade—Kissinger thinks it is too long. We could give more for that. At a minimum it should be five years, plus one year for the redeployment of our line. Then we can go to the Knesset with something.

Dinitz: We have spent a billion and a half dollars fortifying this line.

Allon: Kissinger can say to Sadat that we are well disposed.

Kissinger: I have done that too much. I have to show him some specifics—at least orders of magnitude of kilometers, and so on.

Allon: Can't you say I am thinking of a 30-to-50 kilometer withdrawal? In certain areas 30, in others, 50.

Kissinger: There are some principal points—the passes and the oil fields. He doesn't care about lines in the sand.

Allon: What is his alternative? To stay where he is?

President: One is the resumption of Soviet supplies to Egypt. That is not good for either.

Allon: I agree, but he will do it anyway.

Kissinger: He hasn't yet.

Allon: It is not possible to reach a point where he will cut off relations with the Soviet Union.

Kissinger: One alternative is heating up the international situation to bring pressure on us. If he needs two or three years, he can use that to escalate an anti-American crusade.

Allon: We are offering something substantial.

President: Dr. Kissinger says it is unattainable. I haven't looked at the details. But if that is true it means we are therefore risking disaster.

Maybe Europe is fixed for an oil embargo, but here, while we have plans for belt-tightening, the impact would be serious. Also, on the PLO resolution[7] you saw the United States and four others were the only ones against it. We were glad to stand on that, but that ought to be a signal that it is not the most wholesome situation in the UN. Every head of state I talked to I told that we were pursuing a step-by-step process. I think it is therefore essential that we move and get something of substance. You and Dr. Kissinger are experts, and I give it my personal attention. But I have said frankly what we might face if there is no movement.

Allon: If we give up the passes and the oil field—which give us half of all our oil—we will take away all the Egyptian incentive to take another step and will encourage them to begin agitating. It could prove

---

[7] See footnote 3, Document 104.

to be a mistake, and then it would be too late. They could agitate with the Soviet Union, get the UNEF withdrawal, and then we will be in the same war situation.

I don't think Egypt wants subjugation by the Soviet Union. Why not give my proposal a chance? Why not? Henry can find the right words to make it sound good. Why give up beforehand? If we have to fight, we are better off on this line. Why do you want it today? Why not talk the oil field and passes after Brezhnev has departed? If we give him everything at first, they will ask for more.

The last thing we want is a misunderstanding between Israel and the United States. Let's be patient.

Dinitz: Egypt will have to think carefully about going back to the Soviet Union, because only the United States can help them.

Allon: They know only the United States can give them territory.

Kissinger: They can get 90% of their economic needs from Europe, and from Europe with the Soviet Union on the character of peace. We are holding Europe off by saying "Give our efforts a chance." If we visibly fail, there will be no holding them back. The Europeans can give economic help and can add political pressure to the Arabs.

We don't have to have your final concessions today, and I am not saying we can't turn these into something. We need to discuss how to approach the Egyptians. We need a strategy which includes a concept including the oil fields and the passes.

There are two problems—to see where this can go, and how should it be presented to the Egyptians. How to give Sadat enough to support him for the Brezhnev visit. To give him courage.

Allon: How about the length?

Kissinger: There is only one issue on duration. The disengagement has no time limit. Why not assume it is unlimited?

Allon: Is it true that Fahmy said one more disengagement would take Egypt out of the war?

Kissinger: Fahmy said it. Sadat maybe said it. We will check.[8] Fahmy said the next step had to be in the context of taking Egypt out of the war.

Allon: Can U.S. troops be in the UNEF? I don't trust these small countries. That, I guess, would permit Soviet forces.

Kissinger: Never do you want to legitimize Soviet presence.

Allon: You can't rely on these little countries.

President: What about Canada?

---

[8] Fahmy said it to President Ford on October 5, 1974. [Footnote in the original. See Document 102.]

Allon: Canada is fine.

Kissinger: We could examine the question of Soviet forces. They would jump at the chance, but I don't think Sadat would like it and I doubt the Congress would.

Allon: But we need to find some stability for the UNEF forces.

Kissinger: All the Egyptians now tell me of the error Nasser made in 1967. The Egyptian appetite is not as great as the Syrian appetite.

Allon: If we have no time limit for the agreement, except for the UNEF . . .

President: Let me say I appreciate the opportunity to meet again. We have the same objective. We want Israel secure and its integrity maintained. That is what we both want.

Allon: Thank you very much, Mr. President. May I raise one other thing?

President: Sure.

Allon: We raised the question last summer of a long-term authorization. We mentioned $4.5 billion for an unspecified period. You said maybe the most important complication would be with the Congress. But the Congressional people I speak to are ready to consider it if the Administration proposes it.

President: When your Prime Minister was here, we discussed the immediate and the long-range military programs.[9] I went farther than my advisers wanted on the short-range program. We now are in the throes of a bitter fight in the Congress on foreign aid. We barely won in the Senate on a crucial vote, by 46–45. Even that bill is not all good. The House debate starts tomorrow. Rosenthal has been very difficult. He has collaborated with the Greeks.

Allon: I thought he had changed. He promised.

President: He hasn't gotten the word. The House vote seems to have gone down about 20 votes—from a combination of right-wing Republicans and liberal Democrats. This is the background. I can't go for long-term authorization for Israel if we don't get support for our foreign policy as a whole. That is asking too much.

Allon: If you don't get a majority for the aid in the Congress, maybe you can get a Middle East package.

President: We need a world program.

Dinitz: In the Senate, we were as helpful as possible. We got some votes changed—as Dr. Kissinger knows. We believe in the foreign aid program and we will continue. What we have in mind with long-range

---

[9] See Documents 99 and 100.

economic aid—we may need a specific bill, because the amounts are out of proportion to the rest of the aid.

President: I don't rule that out, but I have to take one step at a time. I can't look down the road if we don't get the tools we need now. There are several—Rosenthal, Dupont, Fraser—who have to get the word. It doesn't do any good to get the Middle East package if we lose our whole foreign policy.

[After warm farewells the conversation concluded. Minister Allon, Secretary Kissinger, Ambassadors Dinitz and Keating, General Scowcroft and Minister Shalev proceeded to the State Department for the luncheon hosted by the Secretary.]

124. Memorandum of Conversation[1]

Washington, December 17, 1974.

PARTICIPANTS

President Ford
Dr. Henry A. Kissinger, Sec. of State and Assistant to the President
Lt. General Brent Scowcroft, Deputy Assistant to the President

The President: Tell Mahon and Passman that I want the CRA on basis of the authorization. I would be happy to call Passman.

Kissinger: I promised Hays 15 minutes with you.

The President: Okay.

Kissinger: I think we are facing a major crisis with Sadat. Nixon promised to sell him arms. He doesn't have anything we promised. We have two problems with him: The Israeli negotiation and his general perception of us. I think you should send him a letter saying we would like to open our hearts with them. He could send Fahmy or his personal aide, Marwan, or as a last resort I could go.

If we could hold it to January until he goes to France, I could maybe meet quietly. We must get to him with someone he trusts.

---

[1] Source: Ford Library, National Security Adviser, Memoranda of Conversations, Box 8, December 18, 1974, Ford, Kissinger. Secret; Nodis. The meeting was held in the Oval Office at the White House. The original is incorrectly dated December 18. According to the President's Daily Diary, Ford met with Kissinger and Scowcroft on the morning of December 17 after the 9 a.m. meeting with the congressional leadership (see footnote 2 below). (Ibid., Staff Secretary's Office Files, President's Daily Diary)

The President: Can't we get something between Israel and Egypt within the next few weeks? Can't we act quickly on the Middle East package?

Kissinger: Yes. He said publicly yesterday that he would give us only a bit more time on step-by-step before turning to Geneva.

The President: You got the consensus in the leadership meeting.[2] It is not at all solid.

Kissinger: I will talk to Dinitz today. Tomorrow we talk with Golda,[3] and you talk to her at the end alone. If it blows up and gets to a war, you can't guarantee American support. Their constant nitpicking has brought us to the edge of disaster. You don't want to say this officially, but she should tell the leaders.

Six months ago the U.S. was a dominant figure in the Middle East, and a visit by me would quiet things. It's not so now. This stuff about cooperation with the Soviet Union—They insist on the '67 borders. If you are willing to do that, there is no reason to do it with the Soviet Union.

We have got to tell Israel we need their maximum position. I am not sure the Israeli-Egyptian negotiation will succeed. Sadat seems to be posturing himself.

There are two alternatives: Let Geneva fail and at the blow up impose a settlement that is close to the 67 borders. The other way is to do it without provocation, but that will be tougher.

[Omitted here is a brief discussion of administrative matters.]

---

[2] The memorandum of conversation of the meeting with the bipartisan congressional leadership is ibid., National Security Adviser, Memoranda of Conversations, Box 8, December 17, 1974, Ford, Kissinger, Bipartisan Congressional Leadership)

[3] See footnote 3, Document 125.

125. Memorandum of Conversation[1]

Washington, December 18, 1974, 9:40–10:20 a.m.

PARTICIPANTS

The President
Dr. Henry A. Kissinger
Lt. General Brent Scowcroft

Kissinger: Mahon is worried that we will load up the Senate bill. Sadat's problem may be that we aren't giving him an agreement before Brezhnev comes.

The President: How can we? I saw Israel released its proposals yesterday.[2]

Kissinger: Tell Golda[3] that if the Israeli Government doesn't improve its procedures, you don't see how we can continue its relationship. Dinitz said Sadat wants an excuse for going back to the Soviet Union. He said we are making it tough by saying that another war would be a tragedy and the whole world would gang up on Israel. Tell her about leaking in the strongest possible terms.

Wayne Hays said he gave a Chamber of Commerce speech and after it a banker stood up and said George Brown[4] is one of the greatest Americans and is right and got a three-minute ovation.

I believe Israel is insane for not taking what they can get in a Sinai settlement.

If this negotiation blows up, we should move quickly to Geneva. We should either get a settlement fast or diffuse the responsibility by going to Geneva.

The President: What is the Israeli reaction to going to Geneva?

---

[1] Source: Ford Library, National Security Adviser, Memoranda of Conversations, Box 8, December 18, 1974, Ford, Kissinger. Secret; Nodis. The meeting was held in the Oval Office at the White House. All brackets, with the exception of ones describing omitted material, are in the original.

[2] The *New York Times* reported accounts in Tel Aviv newspapers on December 15 of the Israeli withdrawal proposals that Allon made in Washington the previous week. (*New York Times*, December 16, 1974, p. 14)

[3] The memorandum of conversation of Ford's meeting with Meir on December 18 at 3:30 p.m. is in the Ford Library, National Security Adviser, Memoranda of Conversations, Box 8, December 18, 1974, Ford, Kissinger, Former Israeli Prime Minister Golda Meir. The memorandum of conversation of a December 19 meeting from 8 until 9:25 a.m. is in the Library of Congress, Manuscript Division, Kissinger Papers, CL 156, Geopolitical File, Israel, December 9–31, 1974.

[4] Apparently a reference to General George S. Brown, Chairman of the Joint Chiefs of Staff.

Kissinger: They don't like that either. The first issue there would be the PLO.

George Ball hurts us by saying we should work it out with the Soviet Union.[5] That means the '67 borders. If we are willing to do that, we don't need to do it with the Soviet Union.

Sadat is pissed off because we let him go naked into Rabat and now into a Brezhnev meeting.

Keep Golda to 45 minutes—30 minutes with us and 15 alone. She will be very emotional.

The Israelis told Rockefeller the three indispensables in the Cabinet are me, Schlesinger and Simon.

[Omitted here is discussion unrelated to the Arab-Israeli dispute.]

---

[5] Former Under Secretary of State George Ball reportedly warned of a future preemptive Israeli military strike and stated that Kissinger's shuttle diplomacy had shut out the Soviet Union from the peace process. (*New York Times*, December 15, 1974, p. 30)

---

126. Minutes of Washington Special Actions Group Meeting[1]

Washington, January 14, 1975, 10:42 a.m.–noon.

SUBJECT

Middle East

PARTICIPANTS

Chairman
Henry A. Kissinger

State
Robert Ingersoll

DOD
William Clements

JCS
Gen. George S. Brown

CIA
William Colby

NSC
Lt. Gen. Brent Scowcroft
Jeanne W. Davis

Secretary Kissinger: I thought we would use this occasion for a review of where we stand on our planning and what our expectations are

---

[1] Source: Ford Library, NSC Institutional Files (H-Files), Box 24, Meeting Minutes, WSAG-Originals, January 1975. Top Secret; Sensitive; Codeword. This meeting was held in the White House Situation Room.

with regard to another Arab-Israeli war as well as the gravest emergency that I have described. Incidentally, someone is not letting that *Business Week* story die.[2] Also, you should know that the President is extremely interested in this and we may want to have an NSC meeting primarily for briefing purposes.

Mr. Clements: That would be a very good idea.

Secretary Kissinger: (to Mr. Colby) Bill, what are your expectations?

Mr. Colby: Over the next two or three months we believe there will be no incentive for either side to start a fight. After that, we're not so sure.

Secretary Kissinger: Even if we get a second-phase Sinai agreement?

Mr. Colby: If we get a second-phase Sinai agreement, that may stall a war. The problem will come in Syria when the UN Force renewal issue comes up.[3] Even then, Damascus may not opt immediately for a fight. In this event, the danger will be on the Lebanese-Israeli border where events might escalate and get out of control. Any Israeli decision to opt for a first strike will depend on Israel's perception of what Syria might do. We do not believe Israel will move on its own unless they believe it is clear that Syria plans to move. This would be particularly true if negotiations were underway. If there is no Sinai disengagement....

(Secretary Kissinger left the room)

Gen. Brown: (to Mr. Colby) Your people had a report that a unit had been formed in Syria and moved into Lebanon. DIA has some more information on that. They say they are armed with SA–7s and are a mixture of Syrian military with Palestinians, controlled from Damascus.

Mr. Colby: We think there are Syrian advisors with the group but that is a little different from units.

(Secretary Kissinger returned)

Mr. Colby: If there is no Sinai disengagement, the Arabs will probably start planning an attack, probably by Syria and Egypt. We believe they will hold up on implementation until they are sure the negotiations have gotten nowhere. If Israel attacks Syria, Cairo would probably go to war. However, Israel probably assumes that they could knock out Syria before help could arrive and, under those circumstances, they hope Egypt would stay out.

---

[2] See "Kissinger on Oil, Food, and Trade" in *Business Week*, January 13, 1975, p. 66.
[3] A reference to the renewal of the UNEF mandate, which was due to expire in April.

Secretary Kissinger: Unless the Egyptians are very carefully prepared, they have little or no offensive capability. By the time the Egyptians get going ...

Gen. Brown: I agree. I have never understood why, once they had established themselves on the East Bank, they didn't push out—they just sat there.

Secretary Kissinger: I think that is a correct estimate of their capabilities. If they hadn't put an armored division across, they would have been in good shape. They moved out and lost 300 tanks in one day.

Mr. Colby: We believe Israel could knock out Syria in five to seven days, and remain south of Damascus.

Secretary Kissinger: Knock them out or push them back?

Mr. Colby: Knock them out as a fighting force.

Secretary Kissinger: The Syrians might withdraw north of Damascus. They wouldn't fight Israel frontally. They would withdraw and try to bleed the Israelis.

Mr. Colby: That's not in their character.

Mr. Clements: They would stand and fight.

Gen. Brown: They would have to be pretty sophisticated to withdraw.

Mr. Colby: In any event, they couldn't move fast enough to get away from the Israelis.

Secretary Kissinger: But they don't have most of their army south of Damascus now, do they?

Mr. Colby: A fair chunk of it.

Mr. Clements: They have lots of armor and artillery and lots of prepared positions.

Gen. Brown: They have 85,000 troops plus air defense.

Secretary Kissinger: Colby believes Israel could knock them out in five days. Do you expect that the Russians would do nothing for five days? Is that based on the last war?

Mr. Colby: They would provide support to the Syrians but would try not to get directly involved.

Secretary Kissinger: Based on what?

Mr. Colby: Their disinclination to get involved, provided Israel stopped south of Damascus. That is based on the détente strategy.

Secretary Kissinger: Which is weakening considerably.

Mr. Colby: What can they do?

Secretary Kissinger: That's my question. If this goes on much longer, the Turks will build highways for them through Turkey. Do they have enough equipment to airlift an air-borne division?

Mr. Colby: It would take them a couple of weeks to make the decision and do it.

Gen. Brown: That's a pretty leisurely schedule. It depends on how much they want to do it.

Mr. Colby: Let's say a week or two.

Mr. Clements: They have enough equipment in Syria.

Secretary Kissinger: It's very dangerous to judge them by previous performances. In 1970 they were surprised. In 1973 they assumed the Arabs would lose. I think from the beginning they had planned to come in after five days. But they were badly wounded in Egypt and Syria. They may think that this was one reason for their impotence during the war. One reason Brezhnev is in trouble may be because of the Middle East—that along with trade. They may not be so restrained this time. They may try to demonstrate our impotence. I don't exclude that strategy. In 1973 I was confident they wouldn't come in for five days, if then.

Mr. Colby: The NIE isn't finished yet but it estimates a couple of weeks.

Secretary Kissinger: Let's look at what the Soviets would do if there is a Politbureau decision to take the risk.[4]

Mr. Clements: You don't mean after five days?

Secretary Kissinger: Would it be mostly air resupply?

Mr. Colby: If Israel stays out of Damascus, we believe the Russians would stay out and negotiate for moves backwards.

Secretary Kissinger: That would mean that for the fourth time a Soviet-backed army gets shellacked and the Soviets do no more than resupply them. That means, in effect, that the Soviets are supplying Israel.

Gen. Brown: If the Soviets believe that, why don't they put forces into Syria now?

Secretary Kissinger: The Syrians are highly nationalistic. They may not be willing to take Soviet forces. They don't like the Russians.

Mr. Clements: They don't like anybody.

Secretary Kissinger: I agree.

Mr. Colby: Asad is trying to keep his independence.

Secretary Kissinger: I like the Syrians; they are very reliable. They may not let the Soviets in except in an extremity.

---

[4] SNIE 11/30–1–75, entitled "Possible Soviet Military Intervention in a Syrian-Israeli War," was issued on January 30. (Central Intelligence Agency, NIC Files, Job 79–R01012A)

Gen. Brown: If there is movement with Egypt in the Sinai, the Syrians would be in a different position in the north.

Secretary Kissinger: The Syrians would settle for 5–8 kilometers in the Golan; not necessarily permanent, but for two or three years. Asad lost 50,000 men in the war and has nothing to show for it. He got one kilometer around Kuneitra, but the Israelis had leveled it. That is the reason for his intransigence. Some of the Israeli settlements on the Golan would have to go.

Mr. Clements: Was Dayan clued in when he made his statement?[5]

Secretary Kissinger: No. For five or six kilometers in Jordan and five or ten kilometers on the Golan Heights we could have kept the process going. That's the tragedy of it. The Egyptians could move and the Syrians could move and we could have gone to Geneva and kept it going until 1977. Even now, we could do something if Israel gave us five kilometers on the Golan Heights.

Mr. Clements: Aren't they moving that way?

Secretary Kissinger: No. They're not moving on the Sinai. They want to drag us into 1976.

Mr. Clements: I'm surprised. I thought there would be some movement in Sinai within 90 days.

Secretary Kissinger: Not voluntarily.

Mr. Clements: The Arabs are hearing this from somewhere.

Secretary Kissinger: They're hearing it from me.

Mr. Colby: The Israelis are saying it to split the Arabs.

Secretary Kissinger: They're saying it publicly. Of course we are doing our best to promote something in the Sinai in the next 90 days.

Mr. Colby: Our estimate of a war in Sinai is that it would last about 10 days, with the Israelis winning more or less along the current lines.

Secretary Kissinger: What if they got to the other side of the passes?

Mr. Colby: It would be the same thing. If they were neutralized, the Israelis could get in before the passes were closed up.

Secretary Kissinger: I don't see the Egyptians dashing for anywhere.

Gen. Brown: There's no indication of that.

Secretary Kissinger: Would it take them longer to knock out Egypt than Syria?

---

[5] Possibly a reference to a lecture Dayan delivered in Jerusalem on January 2 or to his subsequent comments on January 3. (Telegram 58 from Tel Aviv, January 4; National Archives, RG 59, Central Foreign Policy Files)

Gen. Brown: Why is that—geography?

Mr. Colby: We assume it would be both Egypt and Syria.

Secretary Kissinger: Oh, you mean five days for each but with Syria first. Let's look at the Soviet contingency. What would they do if they want to go all-out from the beginning? Do they have enough equipment in Syria so that all the Soviets would have to do would be to airlift bodies?

Mr. Colby: They would have to take the equipment from the Syrians.

Secretary Kissinger: Are there no depots?

Mr. Clements: There is a lot of surplus equipment in Syria, but not in depots in the regular sense.

Mr. Colby: We don't know if they have clandestinely developed the capability to move in and operate.

Secretary Kissinger: Suppose they mounted an infantry division on the second day. How long would it take them to go in and become effective? Would it take more than a division? How many would it take to push the Israelis back to the 1967 border?

Mr. Clements: It would be a helluva fuss.

Gen. Brown: What do we do if the Soviets come in?

Gen. Scowcroft: Could they do it with air power?

Mr. Colby: How would they get the air in?

Gen. Brown: The MIGs are there. It would be a question of displacing Syrian pilots with Soviet pilots.

Secretary Kissinger: Would they have enough to handle the Israeli Air Force with Soviet pilots?

Gen. Brown: We don't know how good the Soviet Air Force is, but we don't think they are as good as the Israelis. All of their training has been under close control. This downplays initiative.

Secretary Kissinger: They would need a lot of command and control.

Gen. Brown: Exactly. The Israeli Air Force would clean up unless the Soviets were very well established.

Secretary Kissinger: How long would it take them to get established?

Gen. Brown: Quite a while. They would have to get their radar in. Remember, the Soviet Air Force has never fought. The Israelis would be more than a match for the Soviets for several months. And the Soviet Air Force would be attrited during that period. They don't have a large reserve—not enough pilots.

Secretary Kissinger: They ran out of pilots in the last war. (to Mr. Colby) Do you assume that for three weeks the Israelis would not require resupply?

Mr. Colby: Yes, they have 18 days worth of combat supplies.

Secretary Kissinger: They wouldn't need anything?

Mr. Clements: You mean they would leave us alone for 18 days?

Mr. Colby: Hell, no! They'd be all over us in 10 minutes.

Mr. Ingersoll: There would be some critical ammunition shortages.

Gen. Brown: We got a new list from the Israelis last week.[6] They described them as consumables that they would need by air. It was mainly ammunition.

Secretary Kissinger: What are you doing with the list?

Gen. Brown: We're seeing what we could do for them. They might be able to buy some of the things from us and come and get it now.

Mr. Colby: I couldn't agree more.

Secretary Kissinger: That's absolutely right. Will we get a crack at the list before you do anything with it?

Gen. Brown: Of course. The whole government will.

Secretary Kissinger: We would like to avoid the situation where the Israelis come to Scowcroft and say that the White House is being obstructionist.

Mr. Clements: Neither George (Brown) nor I is telling them anything like that. We're not telling them anything at all. We're not even talking to (Ambassador) Dinitz.

Secretary Kissinger: The President got a letter from Rabin[7] complaining that he was not issuing the right instructions to the Defense Department. We have to know before you plan any large shipments.

Mr. Clements: Absolutely.

Gen. Brown: We want to avoid a situation where we are using our whole C–5A force plus tankers. We want to try to identify what stocks we have here.

Secretary Kissinger: When you identify them, will you tell us?

Gen. Brown: We won't tell anyone but your office.

Mr. Clements: We don't want to have to use all our C–5As.

Secretary Kissinger: There are two separate problems with this. If war is unavoidable, the Israelis would be better off to come get the material now. But if war is not unavoidable, we don't want to do anything that would make it less avoidable.

---

[6] List has not been found.

[7] In his January 12 letter to Ford, Rabin urged Ford to ensure the delivery of weapons requested in Matmon B (see Documents 96, 98, and 101). Rabin specifically cited laser guided weapons and Lance missiles as military supplies owed to Israel based on his discussions with Ford in September 1974 (see Documents 99 and 100). The letter is attached to Document 127 at Tab A.

Mr. Clements: I have an alternative. We could put it on a ship and preposition it somewhere. We don't even have to tell the Israelis where.

Mr. Colby: Israel will only preempt with a first strike if they think the other side will.

Mr. Ingersoll: If they are in a strong position, they won't move diplomatically.

Secretary Kissinger: The only way to get Israel to move is to give them something to enhance their military security. If they have military security anyway, they won't move.

Mr. Colby: Even if they have security, they have to move eventually. They can't face the attrition of a war every year or two.

Secretary Kissinger: They don't understand that. You say 7500 casualties. Do you mean killed?

Mr. Colby: Killed and wounded.

Secretary Kissinger: That's more than the last war. You mean against Syria alone? That's pretty heavy. That's 750,000 by American standards.

Mr. Colby: That's what I mean. They can't do it. It would be pretty traumatic. That's what's impressing them. That's why they will preempt if they fear the other side will jump them. They claim they would have preempted them last time . . .

Secretary Kissinger: No—they weren't organized. We didn't keep them from preempting. That's a myth.

Mr. Colby: That's right, but they are determined that the other side will never have the jump on them again.

Secretary Kissinger: (to Mr. Clements) Are you saying that you will undertake no aerial resupply of Israel?

Mr. Clements: We hope we won't have to.

Gen. Brown: We want to identify what they want and whether we have the items.

Secretary Kissinger: When you have identified them, who will take the responsibility for not delivering them? There is a limit to what you can pile on the President.

Gen. Brown: The only things that will be delivered are the things the President has approved. This is a new list, brought into the Defense Department by their attaché.

Secretary Kissinger: You have no authority to deal with such a list. The only valid list is that which was approved by the President when Rabin was here.[8]

---

[8] See Document 100.

Gen. Brown: But if we tell them to come in through the White House, that will put pressure on the President.

Gen. Scowcroft: That's routine for them to come in this way.

Secretary Kissinger: What quantities are they talking about? What will you tell them?

Mr. Clements: We will tell them nothing until we talk about the matter here. There are some medical supplies on the list. After we look at the list we will table it here and talk about it. We will do anything you want us to; you know that.

Secretary Kissinger: I don't want every Jewish leader heading for the President and accusing him of undermining the security of Israel.

Mr. Colby: If we have to resupply Israel, we will get an embargo. If we don't have to resupply Israel, it may be less than a total embargo.

Secretary Kissinger: Our objective is to prevent a war from starting.

Mr. Colby: Some ammunition won't push Israel into war.

Secretary Kissinger: All Rabin thinks about and talks about is military equipment. He has the mind of a quartermaster-general.

Mr. Clements: When we have looked at the list, we will bring it over here. Then we can say 'no' or Scowcroft can say 'no'. It's the same thing.

Gen. Brown: They said: "These are our consumption rates. These might help you in your planning for resupply." Our logistic planner just took the list. There was no conversation.

Secretary Kissinger: (to Mr. Colby) Your judgment is that we won't face a substantial Soviet military presence if there is another war.

Mr. Colby: I would like to hold my final judgment until the next National Estimate is out, but that's my present thinking.

Mr. Clements: You've changed your estimate.

Mr. Colby: It's a different thing. If war breaks out and the Israelis stop at Damascus, there will probably not be active Soviet involvement. If Israel goes beyond Damascus and there is total humiliation, the Soviet will have a tough problem.

Secretary Kissinger: What would they do if they decide to go? It's the same problem. If they can do it, they might decide to do it whether the Israelis are in the south or the north.

Mr. Colby: They won't be pushed into it if the Israelis stay below Damascus.

Secretary Kissinger: If they can do it effectively, they might do it in any event. That's a political decision.

Mr. Colby: If you mean effective enough to throw the Israelis back, that's a hard problem. If they get Soviet troops in you would have a political schamozzle. You might have a symbolic confrontation. This raises the whole question of an East-West confrontation. They wouldn't accomplish it with their defense forces or with a few Air Force pilots, but an air-borne division is different.

Gen. Brown: (to Secretary Kissinger) You asked if there was sufficient equipment in Syria for a Soviet movement if they flew in the man-power. If the Syrians have stocks for 27 days, including tanks, artillery, etc., they have enough equipment for Soviet troops.

Mr. Clements: Right. There's a lot of stuff there.

Mr. Colby: It's a question of their plan.

Gen. Brown: Right. They have enough to fight with.

Secretary Kissinger: Two Soviet air-borne divisions could step up the attrition rate substantially.

Mr. Colby: Yes. We figured 7000 Israeli casualties during the whole period against Syria.

Secretary Kissinger: Presumably the Soviets would fight better than the Syrians.

Mr. Colby: Possibly.

Secretary Kissinger: Why do we consider the Soviets so fierce in Europe and so impotent in the Middle East?

Mr. Colby: Because they are all structured for Europe.

Gen. Brown: And they have their command and control in being. In this regard, our estimate of Soviet forces in Europe has changed. They are no longer ten feet tall.

Mr. Colby: Yes, we've cut it down a lot.

Secretary Kissinger: If we can't increase our forces at least we can lower our intelligence estimates! We have to increase our security somewhere! The Europeans will never mobilize. They won't even get to the railroad station. They will find a way to cop out.

Mr. Colby: Absolutely.

Secretary Kissinger: The Turks and the Greeks will fight; maybe the Germans. But the Danes and the Dutch and the French will surrender. The British won't have to.

Mr. Clements: That's a dismal assessment.

Secretary Kissinger: I may be wrong, but that's my personal judgment.

Gen. Brown: In NATO only the US and the Germans are worth counting.

Mr. Colby: The nuclear factor is such a big thing.

Gen. Brown: Maybe the French would move.

Secretary Kissinger: The standing army, maybe, but you wouldn't even get the reserves to the Gare du Nord. It would be a political impossibility. I may be wrong, but that's my personal view.

Mr. Colby: Because of the nuclear factor, everyone would say they should stay out.

Secretary Kissinger: We can't go much further in the Middle East until we know what the Russians will do. What are our capabilities?

Gen. Brown: We could get some forces in. We could land C–5As in Israel.

Secretary Kissinger: Suppose the Soviets put forces into Syria, saying they want a return to the 1967 borders. They ask the Europeans to join them and warn them that they will be in physical jeopardy if they refuse.

Gen. Brown: Then we're on the losing side. The Russians would be doing what we have wanted to do.

Secretary Kissinger: Would the Europeans let us use bases in those circumstances? I think it would be 50–50 in Germany, but with no chance anywhere else. Where would you move troops if the Russians landed? Do you have a plan?

Gen. Brown: No. We have a few Marines in the Mediterranean—one brigade afloat. And we could move ground units from Europe.

Mr. Colby: If we could get the transits.

Gen. Brown: We would ignore the transits—just go.

Secretary Kissinger: If the Russians put forces into Syria to push the Israelis back to the 1967 border, and then guarantee the 1967 border, we would have an impossible problem in Europe. If we let the Russians claim that they pushed the Israelis back by force, our position in the Middle East is dead. That's why we want to avoid war. If the Arabs win, with Soviet support, and we do nothing, we've had it.

Gen. Brown: We should beat the Russians to the game.

Secretary Kissinger: You mean push Israel back to the 1967 boundary? By a political solution, you mean. But suppose we can't get a political solution? If not, what do we do then?

Mr. Colby: Can you blockade the Soviet troops from going in? We might blockade anything unless they go straight over Turkey. Possibly by airpower.

Secretary Kissinger: Suppose we then wanted to move American forces.

Mr. Colby: You mean send in American forces to keep the Russians out?

Gen. Scowcroft: You could prevent them from going in by using the Sixth Fleet.

Mr. Colby: Yes. We wouldn't be getting into the Arab-Israeli fight; we would be saying "Russians, stay out."

Secretary Kissinger: Can it be done?

Mr. Colby: If we send US ground forces into Israel, we could write off the whole Arab world.

Mr. Clements: That would be impossible.

Secretary Kissinger: Not in New York.

Gen. Brown: It would tear the country apart.

Secretary Kissinger: That's exactly my nightmare. If war breaks out, and if I were the Russians, I would put forces into Syria. They can't afford to go through this every two years—resupply their friends and have the Israelis pick up two divisions of Soviet equipment.

Mr. Colby: Don't forget the Soviets are very cautious.

Secretary Kissinger: And they have lost. It's my judgment that détente is on its last legs.

Mr. Colby: It's shaky.

Secretary Kissinger: They are going to turn down the trade bill.[9] We have no more leverage. In a crisis, what do we tell them? That we are mad at them? We told them that after Hungary and Czechoslovakia and it lasted about three months. Or are we going to use force? They can read our papers—they know what's going on. I'm not talking about the next six months.

Mr. Colby: Possibly with the next generation of leaders.

Secretary Kissinger: They have lost three times. We have beaten them by moving more skillfully diplomatically. But it's unrealistic to believe this will continue.

Mr. Colby: The Soviets are poorly structured for something like this.

Secretary Kissinger: If you're right, I would be delighted. But we have to plan for the worst case. My nightmare is the scenario that I have described.

Mr. Colby: You're right.

Gen. Brown: I share your nightmare.

Mr. Colby: Could we establish some sort of barrier in the Black Sea—over Greece or Turkey?

Gen. Brown: Let's look at the next step. What happens if the Israelis are pushed back to the 1967 border with a Soviet guarantee of that border?

Secretary Kissinger: We'd be dead.

---

[9] Kissinger announced on January 14 that the Soviet Union had nullified the 1972 U.S.–USSR trade agreement because of Soviet objections to conditions imposed by the 1974 Trade Act on granting MFN status, specifically the Jackson–Vanik amendment. President Ford signed the Trade Act on January 3. (*New York Times*, January 15, 1975, p. 1)

Gen. Brown: We simply have to educate the Jewish community in the US.

Secretary Kissinger: Look, I meet with the Jewish leaders regularly. It's a very complicated problem. You may assume that we will do our utmost to prevent this from happening. That is exactly why we are pressing so hard to prevent it from happening. It's not because of Arab blackmail. But in our contingency planning, we have to be prepared to prevent the Soviets from getting in. I'm more attracted to interception by US aircraft.

Gen. Brown: Then you have started World War III. We would have no great problem in disrupting their airlift, but that would mean bare, naked US-Soviet combat.

Mr. Colby: It would be a "blink" thing. The question is whether we could limit it to a blockade.

Secretary Kissinger: The problem is the same either way. I've learned one thing, and that is if you are going to move with force, you should move massively. There are no awards for moving elegantly. We can't start shooting down Soviet planes and not be prepared to go to war.

Gen. Brown: Then we will have to dust off the nuclear option.

Secretary Kissinger: That shows where we are. We have to prepare some contingency plans for the scenario I have outlined. In Colby's judgment, the Soviets won't operate that daringly. If he's right, we have the resupply problem. We need a systematic analysis of how the Soviets would go in—by air, navy, air-borne. And what they would need to do now to plan for it.

Mr. Colby: We will do it.

Gen. Brown: If we stop them, will they accept it?

Secretary Kissinger: There's a great possibility that if they think we will stop them, they won't come.

Mr. Clements: I have an idea. We have been in Saudi Arabia twice before militarily. There is a beautiful airport at Dhahran. I think there is a 50–50 chance of getting the Saudis to ask us into Dhahran.

Secretary Kissinger: When?

Mr. Clements: Right now. It would show everyone we mean business. We could protect what is most important economically, and it would be a clear signal to the Russians that we mean business and they shouldn't get involved. I think we should discuss this, and George (Brown) agrees. We might sell it to the Saudis if we go about it right. A year ago we talked about selling F–4s to the Saudis. We agreed to do so then, but when the Saudis learned we were willing to sell them, they decided they didn't want them. George (Brown) and I could go over there very quietly for about five days. We could sell it to them. We could reinstitute the F–4 sales case. The Saudis could say they have decided they want them, and the day after tomorrow we could fly in two squadrons of F–4s with full equipment. They could become a training aid for the Saudis.

Secretary Kissinger: You would have a lot of Egyptians taking on Saudi Arabian nationality. How many in a squadron?

Gen. Brown: Eighteen. But we're flexible—it can be anything you like.

Mr. Clements: It's worth a try. We could make it work. It would be a signal.

Secretary Kissinger: To whom?

Mr. Clements: The Russians.

Gen. Brown: To everyone.

Secretary Kissinger: And you would use the two squadrons against the Russians in Syria?

Gen. Scowcroft: It's too far away.

Gen. Brown: Yes, but they would be there.

Mr. Clements: It's a helluva signal. How would the Israelis look at it?

Secretary Kissinger: They would look at the two squadrons in Saudi Arabia as a subterfuge for our arming the Egyptians. They would say that F–4s in Saudi Arabia mean that they will wind up in Egypt.

Mr. Clements: That might be their first reaction.

Secretary Kissinger: And their second and third and fourth and fifth reaction. They are afraid of F–4s in Arab hands. We may want to do it, but we will never sell it to the Israelis.

Mr. Ingersoll: We might want to give a signal to the Israelis.

Secretary Kissinger: The Israelis will think only that the Arabs have F–4s. Any sensible Israeli would want to have the whole Egyptian army equipped by the US so that there would be no resupply in case of war. But I guarantee that if we try to sell 50 tanks to the Egyptians the Israelis would be after us like maniacs. If we could have sold 20 F–4s to Sadat over the last year, it wouldn't have made any difference. We may decide to do it against the Israelis, nevertheless. We need a contingency assessment of what happens in an Israeli-Arab war if the Russians want to play it rough. Have the Russians the capability of launching missiles with high explosive warheads from Syrian territory? Suppose they wanted to raise the ante during a war?

Mr. Colby: They could.

Secretary Kissinger: The Russians have never played up to their full capability in a crisis. Suppose they do.

Mr. Clements: The Israelis, after they have had time to think about it, wouldn't be too excited about F–4s in Saudi Arabia. They would be a stabilizing influence. It's possible the Russians would move into Iraq. The most excited person would be the Shah.

Secretary Kissinger: The Shah may not like it, but he is manageable. He's nothing like the Israelis.

Mr. Clements: I think the Shah would go up the wall.

Mr. Colby: The Shah would think he could control the situation through us.

Secretary Kissinger: Bill's (Clements) argument might carry weight with the Shah but not the Israelis. There would be no chance of selling it to them, but that doesn't mean we shouldn't consider doing it. If we face the total oil embargo of the West, we have to have a plan to use force. I'm not saying we have to take over Saudi Arabia. How about Abu Dhabi, or Libya?

Mr. Clements: We want to get you over to the JCS think tank. We can show you conclusively why Libya, Abu Dhabi, Dubai won't serve the purpose. Saudi Arabia is the only country that would serve our purpose.

[Omitted here is discussion unrelated to the Arab-Israeli dispute.]

127. Memorandum of Conversation[1]

Washington, January 16, 1975, 5:10–6:40 p.m.

PARTICIPANTS

    Yigal Allon, Deputy Prime Minister and Minister of Foreign Affairs of Israel
    Simcha Dinitz, Ambassador of Israel
    Mordechai Shalev, Minister, Embassy of Israel

    President Ford
    Dr. Henry A. Kissinger, Secretary of State and Assistant to the President for National Security Affairs
    Lt. Gen. Brent Scowcroft, Deputy Assistant to the President for National Security Affairs

[The press was admitted for photographs. There were a few minutes of light conversation about the President's State of the Union Message, the size of the Knesset, and a Presidential visit to Israel. The press then departed.]

Allon: This is the room where the President works?

President: Yes, but I have one down the hall also. Every President has a separate working office. President Nixon's was across the street; mine is just 20 feet down the hall.

It's good to see you again. This must be the third or fourth time we've met. I have always thought that we could sit and talk frankly and in friendship. I hope we can talk about some headway we can make toward peace in the area.

I have been pushing Henry to some extent. I feel we have to make progress. I understand you were somewhat disturbed about my com-

---

[1] Source: Library of Congress, Manuscript Division, Kissinger Papers, CL 156, Geopolitical File, Israel, January 1975. Secret; Nodis. The meeting was held in the Oval Office at the White House. Brackets are in the original. Allon also met with Kissinger on January 15 from 4 to 4:30 p.m. (Memorandum of conversation, January 15; ibid.) and on January 16 from 11:25 a.m. to 12:55 p.m. (Memorandum of conversation, January 16; National Archives, RG 59, Records of Henry Kissinger, 1973–77, Box 25, CATC, Kissinger Shuttle, Israel-Egypt). They discussed U.S. military assistance to Israel, the Jackson–Vanik amendment, Europe, and the PLO. Allon also met on January 16 with Schlesinger at 9:30 a.m. in Schlesinger's office at the Pentagon. (Memorandum of conversation., January 16; Washington National Records Center, OSD, FRC 330–79–0058, Israel, January 1975) They discussed Soviet General Secretary Brezhnev's poor health, the Middle East peace process, and Matmon B. Finally, Allon met with Rockefeller on January 17 from 5:10 p.m. until 6:40 p.m. (Ford Library, National Security Adviser, Memoranda of Conversations, Box 8, January 17, 1975, Rockefeller, Kissinger, Israeli Deputy Prime Minister Yigal Allon) They discussed oil.

ment the other day.[2] You shouldn't be—our relationship is such that there is no reason why we should differ. I predicate everything on the basis that we can work together.

I want Henry to go to Egypt. But he has to have something more tangible to bring there than what came from our previous talk.[3] I think we need another settlement by the end of February. We need stability for the next year and a half to two years, to recover our economy, our energy situation, and our position in the world. We need time, and a settlement will give that. But Henry has to have more for Sadat than you brought before.

Allon: First, Mr. President, I want to thank you for seeing me. I like the way we talk to each other. Dinitz said the Hebrew press says, when they heard I was seeing you and the Vice President, that Kissinger mobilized the heavy artillery of the Administration against me.

President: You have only friends here.

Allon: I told the [UJA] people on the West Coast that I heard you say a strong Israel is in the interest of the United States. I drew strength from your State of the Union speech.[4]

Kissinger: Schmidt made a statement, Mr. President, that your speech was a great contribution to trans-Atlantic solidarity. That is very unusual.

Allon: I was very comfortable after hearing your speech. It was reassuring.

Kissinger: The European press reaction has been favorable.

Allon: We, in Israel, trust the intentions of the United States government, the President and Secretary Kissinger. We may sometimes disagree about points, but it is among friends. Let me say this: We want an agreement. We need it. We think Egypt needs it. It would be good for both parties. This is what I believe. Frankly, we have to face a bitter opposition in Israel.

Strategically, whoever controls the passes controls the Sinai. They are extremely important. The oil is not so much a matter of the money but mainly: First, once they get the oil back without important conces-

---

[2] Apparently a reference to comments made by Ford that were published in a January *Time* Magazine interview about the Middle East, which included the remark that the United States has "to judge what is in our national interest above any and all other considerations." (*New York Times*, January 13, 1975, p. 14)

[3] See Document 123.

[4] President Ford delivered his State of the Union address on January 15. For text, see *Public Papers: Ford, 1974*, Book I, pp. 36–46.

sions they have no incentive for taking further steps. And second, the fields are so close to the straits that they are a strategic problem.[5]

Kissinger: Since you don't want a third step, that is a small loss.

Allon: But because we are all mortal, things change and people change.

When I was here before, I said to you that the depth of our withdrawal will be highly influenced by what Egypt offers. I fear that once Egypt knows about the passes and the oil, it would be all over with Egypt.

I am glad we adopted a wait-and-see position on my last trip before the Brezhnev trip to Cairo. It was good for Brezhnev, too, because he knew we knew how to play our part.

We want to know with whom will we sign an agreement? With Egypt, or the United States? Will the land to be given up be turned over to Egypt, or will it be demilitarized? Fahmy commented on that.

Kissinger: Fahmy has made several statements which don't help. His problem is he is so pro-American that if this doesn't work out he will be out and maybe in prison. He therefore is compelled to make strong statements.

Allon: The question last is the stability of the peacekeeping force. Four of the contingents have left since the last agreements. Nepal, Panama . . .

Kissinger: That is a legitimate concern. We must look into it.

Allon: Sadat made a statement recently that any agreement should have an American guarantee. It was the first time he ever said that.

President: Did he say what he meant?

Kissinger: No. He said it. To President Nixon he said he wanted us to guarantee Israel. It solved his problem, and in that case he wanted Egypt to be guaranteed by the U.S. also.

Allon: I don't know how, but if we could get American troops in UNEF without the Soviets, that would be a tremendous contribution. I am trying to figure out how we can add to the stability of the peacekeeping force. I think Egypt would like it, and if so, what can the Soviets do?

Kissinger: They would veto it unless Soviet forces were included, and inclusion of Soviet forces I think would be a grave mistake.

Allon: So the problem is how to make UNEF more stable. This would give Sadat one excuse not to follow an adventurous policy. Sa-

---

[5] Specifically, the Abu Rudeis oil fields in the Sinai, which were under Israeli control.

dat the other day said that the U.S. would not allow the Arabs to destroy Israel.

Now the most crucial problem—the duration of the agreement. If it is short—two to four years—I don't think I could recommend it to the Knesset because this is just the time required to reorganize the Egyptian forces.

Sadat is probably planning for one or two years after the American elections. What is three or four years in return for the passes and the oil? Sadat knows he can get nothing by force; through negotiations he can get a lot. I gave Henry an idea which is a personal idea of mine, not the Cabinet's: Why not have an agreement that has no time limit, but to give Egypt an incentive we would agree that after a certain number of years we would negotiate a third step? The U.S. would have to agree not to pressure us to move earlier than that—unless there is a good chance and then we would be happy to move.

I think Sadat accepted my earlier proposals better than Henry thinks.

Kissinger: He hid it well.

Allon: Except for the 10-year duration, what could he object to, except for the leaking to the press?

President: Those leaks are a deterrent to what we are trying to achieve. I know we ourselves are the leakiest government—even my speech leaked out. But when we are talking peace and war, we just can't have it. I don't know how to stop it, but we must.

Allon: We both live in democracies. We just have to live with it and not to lose our tempers.

Kissinger: Leaking something against us is one thing; leaking something which has a tendency to make agreement more difficult can be disastrous.

Allon: And many times it is the wrong information. For example, about your pressuring us—they don't believe you aren't doing it.

Kissinger: I don't believe it is possible to get a fixed term from Egypt. If Sadat were to agree in writing that a negotiation for a final peace wouldn't start for six years, he couldn't survive. You must at least address the contingency that he will reject it. It is not unreasonable, but we have to consider the consequences if this fails. Egypt could be driven into a war with Syria; people here are already saying we should settle it with the Soviet Union. You are better off, also, not linking any step to a final peace, but to focus on step-by-step.

There is no linkage between the Sinai and the Golan. If Sadat demands that, we will probably have to go to Geneva. Our fear is a massive blow-up caused by the frustration of the Arabs. What we want is that the Arabs see that they make progress only through us and that radical demands get nowhere.

Allon: We don't want a stalemate. But in addition to no fixed term, the UNEF mandate has to be given permanently. The Security Council should be able only to terminate, not to renew, the mandate.

President: We have never linked Egyptian and Syrian settlements. Do I understand that the passes and the oil fields can be settled if we can get something on time and UNEF?

Allon: That's a good question. I deliberately avoided a Cabinet debate. I felt the Cabinet was not well disposed when I left because of the Arab statements, so I have no authorization. But there is a direct relation between what we can give and what we can get.

Kissinger: If what you want can be achieved from Egypt, we are okay, but suppose we can't. Sadat has not been willing to talk frankly to Eilts. What we need to achieve is a concrete understanding on this trip, because if we keep talking along inconclusively, we may find one day that Sadat will blow up. We have to make a basic plan for contingencies. Even if his proposals are reasonable they may not be achievable. But all the problems must be weighed against the alternatives we will face.

Allon: But remember Damascus in May. You went to tell them you were breaking off and I said you would come back with something.[6]

Kissinger: Just because you win a few times at roulette, you can't turn it into an assumption of your policy that you will win every time. If Sadat accepts, fine, but if I go there and fail, we have a monumental problem.

President: If Henry goes there with an inadequate package which is rejected, there will be an adverse impact in the United States. Under these conditions, it would be a terrible jolt in this country.

Kissinger: Also, thus far we have had no adverse European reaction. We would get a bad one and the Soviet Union would profit.

Allon: I suggested to Henry that he take a quick trip—spend one day in each place. He should call it exploratory. That way it is riskless.

Kissinger: Sadat can't see me before the 3rd of February. If I got there on the 10th, I would have to promise a settlement within two weeks. Nothing new will be learned after I have left, through diplomatic channels. So unless I can give him a firm assurance that I will be back with an agreement in two weeks, it won't work.

---

[6] A reference to Kissinger's meeting with Asad on May 27; see Document 75.

Allon: We want to know what he is willing to give.

Kissinger: I proposed this to Sadat—a meeting in Europe. He rejected it and said "Come when you can settle."

Dinitz: What concerns us is if you give him ten days or so, you give him leverage.

President: Can Henry go to Egypt and talk in terms of the passes and the oil fields and see what he can get on time and UNEF?

Allon: I think he should come to Israel first.

Kissinger: Tactically, if I know that the Prime Minister, Foreign Minister and Peres will back me, I would rather go with that than have a Cabinet meeting. If it leaks, the Egyptians are likely to quit. I would rather take my chances on the top two or three leaders.

President: So you would go to Israel first and then ...

Kissinger: I'd have to go to Amman, to Damascus, and to Riyadh also. I could do it in 3–4 days. I only need three hours in the other capitals.

Allon: Let me make one point. To concede more than the last time requires a Cabinet meeting. I think we should start out without knowing where we end up.

Kissinger: We must face the fact we can't have an endless delay. We have to move.

Allon: I said yesterday the time had come.

President: I have read the letter from Prime Minister Rabin on the arms. [Tab A].[7] I can assure you that the commitment for April 1 will be adhered to. On Matmon–B, you can send people here ...

Kissinger: Better not send too many.

Dinitz: The Pentagon needs to talk with us on availability and delivery times.

President: On the LGB, the Lance, and the emergency list—it will be delivered.

Dinitz: On Lance there is no real problem. On LGB ...

President: We will deliver. On Matmon–B, I said I couldn't go to the Congress without results. If I can go to the Congress with results in Egypt, I can do better. That is not pressure, just the facts of the situation today.

Allon: But Matmon–B was promised at the end of the last disengagement.

---

[7] Tab A is attached but not printed. See footnote 7, Document 126.

Kissinger: A long-term relationship, not a plan.

Allon: Okay, but I was pleased when I read the record of Rabin's meeting with you [the President],[8] and the reaffirmation of it. But if the Pentagon can't get our orders, the deliveries get later and later.

President: But they can't order without the money.

Allon: So until the climate gets better, let's go with the first year.

President: But at a time when I am telling the American people there are no new domestic programs, if I go to Congress for money, I have to be able to justify it.

Allon: But I fear that delay will be interpreted by Israel as indirect pressure. I know it isn't, but if I could go to Rabin and say we can start working out the techniques so that we don't lose time when the proper time comes.

Dinitz: We need delivery times, costs, and so forth.

President: I will talk to Henry tonight and we will figure out how we can start the process. It is a delicate situation—how to proceed in a technical way to protect us and you. Henry can tell you tomorrow.

Allon: When Simon visited Israel,[9] we agreed on setting up joint committees. Last month I thought everything was okay. Now I feel everything is not right.

President: I am not familiar with it.

Allon: We gave a paper on this to the State Department.[10] If I can go back with some good news ... If we could take back that you are considering our FY–76 requests favorably ...

I am afraid that as a result of the Trade Bill, the Soviet Union will punish the Jews there. We can't take it—nor the Jews elsewhere. We know you will know how to pass the word.

President: We will do what we can. That would be the worst that could happen.

Kissinger: But you shouldn't get statements out about fear of a holocaust before something happens.

Allon: Whenever you want to visit the Middle East, you are most welcome.

President: I would like to whenever I have the opportunity. I think this meeting was very useful.

Allon: What should we tell the press?

---

[8] See Document 100.
[9] See footnote 4, Document 93.
[10] Paper is not further identified.

Kissinger: We can say we continued detailed discussions in a friendly atmosphere.

[The statement issued to the press after the meeting is at Tab B][11]

---

[11] Tab B is attached but not printed.

---

128. Memorandum of Conversation[1]

Washington, January 22, 1975, 5:15 p.m.

PARTICIPANTS

President Ford
Max Fisher
Lt. Gen. Brent Scowcroft, Deputy Assistant to the President for National Security Affairs

Fisher: I haven't seen the new decorations in this office before.

President: That's right. We just finished it recently, while I was in Colorado.

Fisher: I am leaving tomorrow for Israel. I was telling Brent that my first appointment is lunch with Rabin. I just need to have a chance to get a feel for the situation. I will hold what you tell me in confidence, but I want to do what I can for peace. We must do this.

President: I agree. My sense of what is the consensus of everyone in the area is that we have to move if the situation is not to deteriorate.

We think there is a unique opportunity to move. I have talked to Allon[2] and I am in communication with Sadat. Henry is going to Jerusalem about the 10th, and if the situation develops properly, he'll go to Cairo briefly. If we can get a breakthrough, we should be guaranteed peace there for at least a year or two.

Fisher: What will it take?

President: I'm convinced Israel has to give up the passes and the oil fields—not to Egypt, but to make it a demilitarized zone. You will be asked what is the time duration of the truce commitment; this must be

---

[1] Source: Ford Library, National Security Adviser, Memoranda of Conversations, Box 8, January 22, 1975, Ford, Kissinger. Confidential. The meeting was held in the Oval Office at the White House.

[2] See Document 127.

negotiated. Israel wants a big one—Egypt has offered nothing. Unless there is an agreement along this line, there will be a stalemate and the chance of conflict is greatly increased.

Fisher: Will Egypt be able to make an agreement by itself?

President: We think yes.

Fisher: If they give up the oil, what are the chances for a guaranteed supply of oil?

President: I haven't heard that it was mentioned. Was it, Brent?

Scowcroft: Allon did not mention it, as far as I know.

Fisher: That may come up, and I just wanted to know how to deal with it.

Scowcroft: I certainly think we would be willing to discuss arrangements.

Fisher: I can play a useful role if I speak to them frankly. I can't speak for you, but I can give them my honest appraisal.

President: They are very interested in military and economic aid. I talked about this and about the oil and passes to Allon. He made no commitment. I told him that it shouldn't be thought of in terms of a quid pro quo, but that if there is no progress, Congress wouldn't be receptive to an aid request and I couldn't propose it. If there is an Israeli/Egyptian agreement, it creates a totally different environment. The Congress and I are both interested in peace. A new outbreak of conflict, with another possible embargo, would ruin our influence with the Arabs and would be far bloodier than the last war. We want to keep the Soviets out and have friendship with the Arabs.

Fisher: You don't have to put it on a quid pro quo basis; it is just reality. Is Egypt willing to give concessions?

President: Israel wants non-belligerency. Egypt can't do that, but they can give much of the substance without the fact of it.

Fisher: A piece of paper doesn't mean much anyway. I think I now have a feel for it and I will convey your thoughts.

President: I had a good meeting with Allon. He is impressive—he has a tough job. Sadat is in a tough spot—he turned down Brezhnev and could use a settlement. Rabin could be a statesman and make an agreement which would help us all.

Fisher: I will talk with the opposition too, but I can't be so frank with them. Has there been any discussion of the Syrian situation?

President: There has been no discussion by us that Israel has to give up the Golan. There is no tying-in of Syria with a Sinai agreement.

Fisher: Is there anything else?

Scowcroft: Stress the need for movement now, as the President said. Allon may have a more relaxed view.

President: Absolutely. That is the key to it.

Fisher: When does the UN thing come up?

Scowcroft: The UNEF renewal is April.

Fisher: That fact that you and I talked will be useful with Rabin. I will give you a report of how it goes.

President: Henry and I would both like to see your report.

Fisher: I will see Rabin, Allon and Peres—each alone.

[Omitted here is discussion of Jewish emigration and trade and the U.S. domestic economy.]

129. Memorandum of Conversation[1]

Washington, February 5, 1975, noon.

PARTICIPANTS

President Ford
Mr. Max Fisher
Dr. Henry A. Kissinger, Secretary of State and Assistant to the President for National Security Affairs
Amb. Donald Rumsfeld, Assistant to the President
Lt. Gen. Brent Scowcroft, Deputy Assistant to the President for National Security Affairs

SUBJECT

Mr. Fisher's Report on His Talks in Israel

Fisher: Let me give you a feeling for my visit. I met with Rabin, Peres, Allon, Rabinovitch and Dayan. (He will be a power again, I know). All of them have a great deal of confidence in Henry. [to Kissinger:] I know you get aggravated, but you should know that.

This feeling of urgency—Rabin is committed to the step-by-step approach, but he was badly shaken by Percy's statement on the PLO.[2] Something should be done about that.

---

[1] Source: Ford Library, National Security Adviser, Memoranda of Conversations, Box 9, February 5, 1975, Ford, Kissinger, Max Fisher. Secret; Nodis. The meeting was held in the White House. Brackets are in the original.

[2] On January 25, Senator Charles H. Percy, having just returned from a trip to the Middle East, stated that Israeli leaders were not realistic if they believed they could avoid contact with the PLO. He also asserted that there were limits to how much the United States could support Israel. (*New York Times*, January 29, 1975, p. 3)

Kissinger: They are stupid to make us keep reaffirming that. Our position is firm. To repeat it makes us look insecure. But I'll do it again.

Fisher: You don't have to convince me.

Kissinger: Percy was totally on his own. None of us even talked to him.

President: We didn't even know he was going.

Rumsfeld: This problem comes from Percy's comments to the Jewish group that the Administration supports him.

Fisher: There is no doubt in my mind about your policy. Rabin is still worried about Golda and Dayan in the background.

He does feel that Egypt will keep its word. That is an important confidence factor.

If you would see Golda ... I didn't. I told Dayan that in 1970 he asked me to convey a step-by-step proposal to you [Kissinger].

Kissinger: Three or four months ago he felt strongly that way. He is changing now that he is going back into politics.

Fisher: The issue is the quid pro quo. They desperately need time. I told them on the oil thing they should look for an assured supply from the U.S. They mentioned the Shah. If it is possible to break the economic boycott by having Egypt keep selling the oil to Israel after the return of the fields, that would be a big move. They feel this boycott badly.

On the issue of aid and the letter from Nixon,[3] I told them that there is a much better chance to get it, with the present Congressional attitude, in the euphoria of a settlement. I expressed the urgency to move. And they are shaken by the economic circumstances in the U.S.

Rabin is playing his cards close to the vest but he is okay. Peres is a tough nut to crack. He won't back Rabin. He said he would be willing to go all the way with Egypt if Israel could get what it wants. He won't oppose a move but he will put himself into a position where if it fails, he will look good.

Allon is fine.

Kissinger: Will Dayan oppose it?

Fisher: He wants to get back into power. But I told him this program was his idea in '70. I wish he was in the government.

Kissinger: He would be terrific in the Cabinet. He was before.

Fisher: The opposition is not too bad because the Sinai doesn't involve the religious problems.

Kissinger: I will see Dayan and Golda in Israel.

---

[3] See Document 87.

Fisher: They are very sensitive on several things: One is Percy; two is the need for continued aid.

President: There is no question that if there is no movement, selling aid to the Congress will be difficult if not impossible.

Kissinger: Dupont[4] told me the first thing he wants is to cut Israeli aid in half.

Fisher: I think it is important that the arms promised be delivered on time. That confidence is important.

Kissinger: Everything has been.

Fisher: On Geneva, it is those out of government or those who want to gain time who are pushing it.

They have confidence in the President. They are reluctant to show their hand. I said both of you are friends, but that they better grab any opening.

President: You are convinced that all of them but Peres are convinced something has to be done and they are willing to move?

Fisher: Yes. They understand. They will be tough bargainers but they feel the U.S. is their friend.

President: Do you think they may just be trying to create a favorable attitude but then they won't move and say they tried?

Fisher: No. They are defensive. But the people are now more willing to follow Rabin.

Kissinger: That depends on what Dayan does. Golda I can get under control. I can strengthen Dayan too.

Fisher: With this, there is a feeling that Egypt has kept its word. I don't know what you can do with Dayan, but he is key.

Kissinger: I better see him before he gets set. If he were Prime Minister, we would be all set.

President: Is he in the Knesset?

Kissinger: Yes. But he is the leader of the Rafi, which is the right wing of the governing party. If it hadn't been for '73, he would have replaced Golda. He has great imagination and courage. But he's mercurial and wild—like the others in their domestic politics. He said to me last fall that Israel had to do whatever was necessary in the Sinai to get Egypt off its back.

Fisher: They feel they made a mistake on the West Bank. Now they are hoping the situation will drop back toward Jordan. If you could see Dayan ...

Kissinger: I will.

---

[4] Apparently Pierre "Pete" Du Pont, Republican Congressman from Delaware.

Fisher: The American Jewish community is more tense than the Israeli community. Henry needs to meet with the leaders after his trip. But the Israeli leaders know it is important; they have an economic problem ...

Kissinger: Whatever you can do with the American Jewish leaders. If we go to Geneva, the first question we face will be the PLO. If we go to Geneva with a success behind us, the Arabs will look to us. If we go after a defeat, it will be a bear-baiting exercise.

Fisher: I am getting a group together to do what I can. Do the Egyptians show signs of willingness to move?

Kissinger: Yes. But the key is the facts that another settlement produces; that is the real progress. We can get some other details, but a fixed time will be difficult for Sadat to accept. I haven't sat down with Sadat. I have to ask him what is the best he can do.

130. Memorandum of Conversation[1]

Washington, February 7, 1975, 9:22–10:05 a.m.

PARTICIPANTS

President Ford
Dr. Henry A. Kissinger, Secretary of State and Assistant to the President for National Security Affairs
Lt. General Brent Scowcroft, Deputy Assistant to the President for National Security Affairs

[Omitted here is a brief discussion of unrelated matters.]

[Kissinger:] On my trip, we have pretty well reviewed the Egyptian-Israeli situation. If there is no progress, we will have to go to Geneva under the worst circumstances. Sadat will be lined up with the radicals, and probably even Faisal will be. Israel has to understand their specific terms are less important than continuation of this process—and they will have to take what they can get. But I will tell Sadat he must give all he can so as to not upset our domestic situation too badly.

President: Would the passes be demilitarized?

---

[1] Source: Ford Library, National Security Adviser, Memoranda of Conversations, Box 9, February 7, 1975, Ford, Kissinger. Secret; Nodis. The meeting was held in the Oval Office at the White House.

Kissinger: I haven't really thought that through because I haven't talked to Sadat. On my first stop in Israel I will be very tame, so there will be no newspaper campaign while I am in Egypt. I will tell Rabin we are not ready to move ahead on aid if there is no progress.

President: Tell him cold.

Kissinger: He must know it is one thing to sneak things through Congress when we connive at it; it's another to do it with Administration opposition. You can't be willing to pay $3 billion for a stalemate.

President: What are you thinking about the oil fields?

Kissinger: They can be demilitarized, with Egypt running the oil fields. We may have to make some compensatory arrangement—and may have to pay for a new Israeli defense line.

President: That is O.K., but we won't pay for a stalemate.

Kissinger: Nahum Goldmann is now attacking me. He wants a drastic settlement and a return to Geneva. What you have is a coalition of those who want rapid movement and those who want none.

President: How could we get a partial settlement at Geneva?

Kissinger: Impossible, except as stages toward a settlement which is already defined.

President: It will be interesting to see your meeting with Gromyko.[2]

Kissinger: Egypt wants to buy non-lethal equipment. It requires a Presidential Determination. I would recommend, for now, telling Sadat that we would sell a Presidential Determination for training only.

President: Could we do it as part of a settlement?

[Omitted here is discussion about Panama.]

---

[2] Kissinger met with Gromyko in Geneva on February 17 after his Middle East shuttle.

131. Memorandum From the President's Deputy Assistant for National Security Affairs (Scowcroft) to President Ford[1]

Washington, February 11, 1975.

The following is a report of Secretary Kissinger's initial discussions with the Israelis:

"1. I have just completed intensive discussions with Prime Minister Rabin and his two key members of the Israeli negotiating team, Allon and Peres. After a three-hour dinner meeting last night, I met with Rabin alone at breakfast for an hour this morning, followed by three hours with the Prime Minister and his entire negotiating team, followed by a two-hour work lunch at which Rabin included most of the other key cabinet members, and concluding with an additional two hour session in the afternoon.[2] I capped off the day with a brief courtesy call on President Katzir[3] who is scheduled to see you in Washington on March 3.

"2. I found a rather curious, and in my judgment, somewhat contrived surface calm both in public opinion as reflected in the Israeli press and in Rabin, Allon and Peres. I have the impression that below the surface there is a deep concern particularly regarding the long range situation that confronts Israel in the area. There seems also to be uncertainty among the leadership, in the aftermath of several recent Congressional visits here, as to how much support for Israel in the U.S. has eroded.

"3. In one way I was encouraged, in another way less so. I was impressed with the manner in which Rabin handled the work luncheon with the key cabinet members. It was obvious that he was using me during the extensive question and answer period to make the arguments in favor of a second stage agreement with Egypt. There seem to

---

[1] Source: Library of Congress, Manuscript Division, Kissinger Papers, CL 157, Geopolitical File, Israel, February 1–11, 1975. Secret. Sent for information.

[2] No memorandum of conversation has been found of a February 10 dinner meeting or a February 11 breakfast meeting between Rabin and Kissinger. There is a memorandum of conversation of the meeting between the Israeli negotiating team and Kissinger, which took place on February 11 from 10:15 a.m. until 12:45 p.m. at the Prime Minister's office in Jerusalem. (National Archives, RG 59, Records of Henry Kissinger, 1973–77, Box 22, Classified External Memcons, December 1974 to April 1975, Folder 5) There is also a memorandum of conversation of a luncheon between Israeli Cabinet members and Kissinger that took place on February 11 at the Prime Minister's Residence in Jerusalem. (Ibid., Box 10, Nodis Memcons, February 1975, Folder 4) The memorandum of conversation of the concluding session between Kissinger and the Israeli negotiating team, which took place on February 11 from 4:10 until 6:05 p.m. at the Prime Minister's office in Jerusalem, is ibid., Box 22, Classified External Memcons, December 1974–April 1975, Folder 5.

[3] No memorandum of conversation of this meeting has been found.

be differences of view in the cabinet; some contending that the step-by-step approach subjects Israel to an unacceptable salami tactic. In a sense, it almost seems that the Israeli Government is in a state of indecision and is looking to us to help crystallize opinion here. Nevertheless, just twenty-four hours before I arrived, the Israeli cabinet took a decision endorsing the step-by-step approach, but I have the distinct impression that some here see in the Geneva Conference an opportunity to maintain the present impasse. This view I believe underestimates seriously the kinds of pressures which Israel would be put under at any Geneva conference, particularly should our present effort fail. To avoid being put in a position where the prospect of going to Geneva could be used as pressure on us, I made clear Geneva holds no terrors for us and we are prepared to go either way.

"4. As you know, it is not my intention during this current week's trip to press for definitive decisions on the elements of an agreement either from Israel or from Egypt. While Rabin has given me the impression at the cabinet luncheon that he was preparing the groundwork for an agreement, I am less encouraged by the specific positions taken by the Israelis. Rabin adhered tenaciously to the view that in the absence of more specific indications from Egypt as to what it is willing to give for withdrawal, he was unable and unwilling to go beyond the 30–50 kilometer withdrawal decided upon by the cabinet some weeks ago and which would exclude the Gidi and Mitla passes and the Abu Rudeis oil fields.

"5. Rabin said in an ABC interview a few days ago that Israeli willingness to withdraw east of the passes and out of the oil fields is conditioned upon Egyptian commitment to end all acts of belligerency. To put it in Israeli words, 'We want in an exchange for such a withdrawal, that Egypt effectively is taken out of the war.' Not only are the Israelis continuing to insist upon an Egyptian commitment to non-belligerency, but also are pressing for an agreement of at least ten years in duration. I made clear that the kind of time frame they have in mind is unattainable since Sadat would not be able to agree to put the Sinai on ice for a decade without being vulnerable to the charge in the Arab world that he made a de facto peace with Israel.

"6. While I did not indicate this to the Israelis, there are some other quid pro quos which they mentioned which may prove achievable. To give you a little fuller flavor of the points which the Israelis emphasized I cite the following. They want the interim agreement linked to future negotiations for an overall settlement with Egypt; they insist that there can be no linking of the Egyptian-Israeli agreement to negotiations with other Arab countries, meaning Syria in particular. They want the document containing the agreement signed by both sides which should cause no real difficulty; they want the political dimensions of the agreement clearly in the public domain as reflected, for example, in their desire to have civilians sign it rather than military. They insist that there must be no recognition or negotiations with the PLO and on this point I reassured them.

"7. As to the Geneva Conference, Rabin said that regardless of the fact that they adopted a positive public posture 'of not being afraid of Geneva,' they are really against such a conference unless the present stage with Egypt can be successfully achieved. Peres and some others seem more disposed to go to Geneva in lieu of the present step-by-step approach. The Israelis want it to be a prolonged conference which would not achieve results but would become an instrumentality of deterrence against renewal of hostilities.

"8. It is clear from what I have reported to you that the Israelis are taking a hard line and some of their views were ambiguous and contradictory. I am inclined to feel that Rabin and Allon would like to get the agreement, but they are trying to exact the highest possible price from Sadat which raises the serious question as to whether Sadat can meet the principal Israeli considerations.

"9. I made clear that we will continue to be helpful in the step-by-step approach but if these negotiations fail, we are prepared to go to Geneva even in the difficult climate that will exist after such a failure. I pointed out that it would likely prove necessary for the U.S. to make its substantive position clear at such a Geneva Conference—possibly in the form of some disassociation from the Israeli position—in order to protect our overall interests—i.e., not being totally isolated from our western allies; avoiding a serious deterioration in relationships between the U.S. and USSR, and avoiding jeopardizing our economic and financial interests in the Arab world. I believe I have given the Israelis a good deal to think about. I go to Cairo tomorrow to meet with Sadat and then to Damascus, following which I will return to Israel on Thursday[4] to report the results of the discussion in these two Arab capitals.

"10. Upon my return and in light of the full discussions with the Israelis and Egyptians, we will have to decide on just what elements we should insist upon for inclusion in the agreement. Recalling our conversation on this whole matter, I made it very clear to the Israelis that in our view a stalemate is unacceptable."

---

[4] February 13.

132. Memorandum From the President's Deputy Assistant for National Security Affairs (Scowcroft) to President Ford[1]

Washington, February 13, 1975.

Secretary Kissinger asked that I pass you the following report:

"I have just completed about nine hours of talks with President Sadat and Foreign Minister Fahmy,[2] which I believe have achieved reasonably satisfactory results and which could set the stage for more decisive progress during my next mission to the Middle East in early March.

"During these talks we discussed not only the question of withdrawal of Israeli forces out of the strategic passes and the oil fields, but we explored possible quid pro quos which the Egyptians might give in return. The points discussed are so sensitive that I strongly prefer to brief you fully upon my return.

"My intention now is to give the Israelis only a general picture of what I found here in Cairo, pointing out to them that a number of ideas discussed were being given further study by the Egyptians. I want them to ponder awhile longer the situation they face, and I am concerned that if I discuss with them at this stage some of Sadat's concrete ideas they will leak to the Israeli press. What we must avoid now is any sort of public disclosure. I suggest that you maintain the same public line which you have been expressing on the Middle East publicly in recent days. I think it would be best, for tactical reasons, that you not indicate that you have received hopeful reports from me, but rather that the White House limit itself to indicating, without characterizing the talks, that I am keeping you fully informed. In the remainder of my stops in the Middle East as well as in Europe, I intend to keep my discussions on the Middle East in very general terms.

"I found the atmosphere warm and friendly. The Egyptians are considerably more relaxed than the Israelis, and I have the impression that Sadat will try to do his best—within the limits of his own political situation in Egypt and in the Arab world—to meet some of the quid pro quos to which Israel attached importance. Foreign Minister Fahmy, while continuing to be most friendly, is approaching the matter somewhat more cautiously than President Sadat, who still seems able to take a broad view of the matter.

---

[1] Source: Ford Library, National Security Adviser, Trip Briefing Books of Henry Kissinger, Box 5, February 10–18, 1975, Middle East and Europe, HAK Messages for President, February 13, 1975. Secret; Sensitive. Sent for information. Ford initialed the memorandum.

[2] No memorandum of conversation has been found of either meeting.

"I have committed myself to return to the area starting with Cairo on March 7. We will make a definite announcement of this at the conclusion of my visit here Thursday morning."

133. Memorandum From the President's Deputy Assistant for National Security Affairs (Scowcroft) to President Ford[1]

Washington, February 14, 1975.

Secretary Kissinger asked that I pass the following report to you:

"I met for four hours today with President Asad in Damascus.[2] The entire conversation was relaxed and extremely friendly, but Asad left no doubt about his concern that Egypt will enter into a separate agreement with Israel. Despite my explaining to him in detail the difficulties it would cause to inject the Golan Heights into the negotiations, he was firm in insisting that the next step should be a simultaneous one involving both Egypt and Syria. There was an explicit threat that Syria would cause problems for Egypt both internally and in the Arab world if Egypt went it alone.

"I assured Asad that Sadat has always made clear he will not enter into a separate peace settlement with Israel, but I avoided any commitment to include Syria in the present round and I gave him no details about Sadat's present thinking. At the same time I assured him that we recognized the need to make an effort on the Syrian front, once a next-stage Egyptian-Israeli agreement had been concluded.

"I probed Asad's ideas about what a new Golan agreement might look like. I found that the Syrians have clearly been giving some thought to this, although their ideas are non-starters so far as Israel is concerned. Asad made no effort to press the idea of going to Geneva or bringing the Soviets in; he left no doubt that he would prefer to work through us. He made a largely pro forma pitch for the Palestinians, but did not argue the point when I explained why we cannot deal with this issue at the present time.

---

[1] Source: Ford Library, National Security Adviser, Trip Briefing Books of Henry Kissinger, Box 5, February 10–18, 1975, Middle East and Europe, HAK Messages for President, February 14, 1975. Secret; Sensitive; Eyes Only. Sent for information. Ford initialed the memorandum.

[2] No memorandum of conversation has been found.

"I stressed to Asad the importance of there being some political concessions to Israel in the direction of non-belligerency in any future agreement. I asked that he give some thought to this prior to my next trip.

"By leaving matters with him that we would defer any decisions about how to proceed until my next visit, I believe we have at least bought some time with the Syrians. Hopefully they will remain manageable long enough for us to make a major effort on the Egyptian front, although I cannot be entirely sure of this. I understand Sadat's concern much better now."

---

134. Memorandum From the President's Deputy Assistant for National Security Affairs (Scowcroft) to President Ford[1]

Washington, February 14, 1975.

Secretary Kissinger asked that I pass the following report to you on his second meeting with the Israelis:

I have just completed my last session with the Israelis,[2] and I wanted to give you my judgment as to where I believe matters stand. In short, I believe the ground work has been set for my second mission in early March, but I still cannot be sure where the Israelis will come out.

The principal change which has resulted from my current trip is that the main focus of the Israeli leadership is no longer on the limited 30–50 kilometer withdrawal, in which Sadat, understandably, has no interest. I believe they now understand this would be insufficient and that the Israeli leaders may be willing to consider a withdrawal east of the passes and out of the Abu Rudeis oil fields, provided Sadat is able to provide certain political quid pro quos. This is a meaningful shift in perception. Rabin and Allon seem disposed to bring this proposition to the Cabinet if we can bring back from Cairo during my next mission the

---

[1] Source: Ford Library, National Security Adviser, Trip Briefing Books of Henry Kissinger, Box 5, February 10–18, 1975, Middle East and Europe, HAK Messages for President, February 14, 1975. Secret; Sensitive. Sent for information. Ford initialed the memorandum.

[2] A memorandum of conversation of the meeting between the Israeli negotiating team and Kissinger, which took place on February 13 from 9:35 until 11:35 p.m. at the Prime Minister's Residence in Jerusalem, is in the National Archives, RG 59, Records of Henry Kissinger, 1973–77, Box 22, Classified External Memcons, December 1974–April 1975, Folder 5.

kind of political quids which can help develop broad support in the country and of other political leaders.

I also believe that Sadat has made meaningful political concessions though I have held on to them for fear of leaks.

Therefore, it is important that none of us be confused by the kind of ambiguous and conflicting public reports which will be emanating from the various Middle Eastern capitals between now and early March. For example, Rabin gave a backgrounder today saying that I had brought nothing new to him from Cairo. Taken literally, this in fact is quite accurate. This public line is being taken purposely by Rabin since at this juncture he wants to avoid stirring up speculation among and between the Cabinet members, which could build up prematurely all sorts of opposition to a possible agreement. In a sense, Sadat is also doing the same thing publicly, by coming out with a strong line that he cannot give to the Israelis the kind of quids they want. The public line being taken by the Israelis will not come as a surprise to Sadat since we had previously agreed that I would not discuss with the Israelis any specific quids Sadat may have in mind.

The Syrian aspect is also complicating. I believe Asad will make an all-out effort to cause difficulty for Sadat if he concluded that Egypt intends to enter into a separate arrangement which leaves Syria out. For this reason, I was careful to avoid giving Asad the impression he was being kept on the sideline, but he is already deeply suspicious. Sadat will have to face up to that difficulty if we get to the point where common ground has been achieved between Egypt and Israel. This will also be of great concern to King Faisal, whom I see tomorrow.

I wanted you to have a picture of the current situation, as I see it, and the reason why the public manifestation of where matters stand will tend to give a conflicting picture. For my part, I plan to continue to take the line that we have no concrete proposals and decisions have been left for the next trip.

I had an interesting two hour lunch with Mrs. Meir today.[3] I found her in good health and good spirits, and she wishes to be remembered to you. I believe she understands the overall strategic situation which Israel faces, and while she has carefully avoided becoming directly involved in the political situation since she left office, my hope is she might prove helpful at some important juncture, if it proves necessary.

---

[3] A memorandum of conversation of the lunch meeting between Meir and Kissinger, which took place on February 14 from 1:10 until 2:50 p.m. at Meir's residence in Ramat Aviv, Israel, is in the Library of Congress, Manuscript Division, Kissinger Papers, CL 163, Memcons, February 1973–February 1975.

135. Memorandum From the President's Deputy Assistant for National Security Affairs (Scowcroft) to President Ford[1]

Washington, February 16, 1975.

Secretary Kissinger asked that I pass the following report to you on his latest observations now that he has completed his Middle Eastern stops.

"Now that I am flying to Europe and have completed all of my Middle Eastern stops, the latest today being talks with King Faisal and his key advisors,[2] I want to share with you my latest observations. There are two principal unanswered questions which concern me as I look ahead to my next mission to the Middle East.

"First, will Prime Minister Rabin and his key advisors take the major strategic decision to withdraw east of the passes and out of the oil fields and bring within reason the kind of quid pro quos they will insist upon from Sadat? I, of course, hope so, and the Israelis have no rational alternative. The formulas developed by Sadat can be built upon if Israel accepts the real situation. But prediction is most uncertain. The public statements being made by Rabin since I left Israel seem unduly rigid and are likely to have the effect of reducing his flexibility once we get into the detailed negotiations in early March.

"Second, is the critical question as to whether Sadat will feel able to move ahead on an agreement without a simultaneous agreement between Israel and Syria on the Golan Heights. What has impressed me is the strength of Asad's expressed intention to cause difficulties for the Egyptians if they go ahead on their own in this next piecemeal step. An added factor is Faisal's view as expressed to me today in which he underscored that he was opposed to the idea of another step by Egypt alone on the grounds that this would split the Arab world and would pose serious problems for Saudi Arabia. Even if we are able to get common ground achieved between Egypt and Israel on the next step, it is altogether possible that the combined pressure from Asad and Faisal that there must be a parallel step on the Golan Heights could become a critical impediment to Sadat's freedom of action.

---

[1] Source: Ford Library, National Security Adviser, Trip Briefing Books of Henry Kissinger, Box 5, February 10–18, 1975, Middle East and Europe, HAK Messages for President, February 16, 1975. Secret; Sensitive. Sent for information. Ford initialed the memorandum.

[2] No memorandum of conversation has been found of a meeting between King Faisal and Kissinger. A memorandum of conversation of Kissinger's meeting with Prince Fahd, February 15 at 3:10 p.m. at the Royal Guest House in Riyadh, is in the Library of Congress, Manuscript Division, Kissinger Papers, CL 208, Geopolitical File, Saudi Arabia, February 5–March 26, 1975, Folder 4.

"In my meeting today with Faisal and his advisors I underscored our determination to make rapid progress towards peace in the area and our desire to cooperate closely with Saudi Arabia on economic matters. I told the King we will be consulting closely with him as we move ahead on the negotiations over the next several weeks and arranged for Under Secretary Robinson to hold immediate follow-up talks with Saudi officials on economic issues.

"On the political side, Faisal wished us well and underscored the need for progress on a very urgent basis. Leading to an overall settlement on the question of resuming the Geneva Conference, he said it would be better not to go to Geneva until we are ready to endorse an overall settlement. He sees the opportunities given to the Soviet Union to exploit any Geneva convention.

"On the economic side, I told Faisal, Fahd and Yamani that we are prepared to work with Saudi Arabia bilaterally as well as multilaterally to cooperate and coordinate in dealing with such questions as preparing for a constructive producer-consumer conference (rather than a chaotic confrontation), a possible long-term agreement on a minimum oil price, and investment of oil revenues in the United States. I also indicated our interest in helping the Saudis develop their economy through the Joint Commission and by increasing their agricultural and fertilizer production.

"The King reacted favorably, saying he wanted to work closely with us to remove obstacles between producers and consumers and to agree to things of mutual interest to both countries.

"Last night I had a good talk with Hussein at Aqaba,[3] reassuring him of continued U.S. support after Rabat. He is against going to Geneva until his problem with the other Arabs and the PLO is resolved. He is also worried about Syria's determination to work with the PLO to forestall a separate Egypt–Israel agreement but believes that while it would be most difficult, Sadat would still be inclined to accept such an agreement if there was no other alternative. Hussein would like to call on you in Washington in late April and I have asked Scowcroft to arrange a date.

"I now go on to Bonn as the first stop in Europe."

---

[3] No memorandum of conversation has been found.

136. Memorandum of Conversation[1]

Washington, February 19, 1975, 4:10–5:40 p.m.

PARTICIPANTS

President Gerald R. Ford
Dr. Henry A. Kissinger, Secretary of State and Assistant to the President for National Security Affairs
Lt. General Brent Scowcroft, Deputy Assistant to the President for National Security Affairs

SUBJECT

Secretary Kissinger's Report on His Trip to the Middle East and Europe

[Omitted here is a brief discussion of the Soviet Union, the President's standing, and France.]

[Kissinger:] The Israeli Government is weak. Rabin is okay but he is afraid to move and he is afraid of Peres. Allon wants to move in the right direction.

I had a two-hour lunch with Golda.[2] She is a peasant and hates to give up the land. I could get her though, if she was the Prime Minister. The Cabinet is unbelievable. Rabin's weakness is shown by the fact that I had to have lunch with the Cabinet to win them over.

Sadat is a big man. If we pull this off, we should get him right over here. He is very worried—but he didn't complain about his troubles.

We had a two-hour talk alone[3] and I said we had to have something for Israel.

If we will give them a letter that Israel won't attack Syria or any of its neighbors, he won't attack Israel.

The President: Would that include Lebanon?

Kissinger: That is a problem—I have to think of that.

On duration, he will extend UNEF a year and agree beforehand to an extension. The Soviet Union could veto it. But he will agree to joint Egyptian-Israeli inspection teams.

The Israelis have agreed to the oil fields but not yet the passes.

The President: Do they want an indemnity?

Kissinger: It will cost us.

---

[1] Source: Ford Library, National Security Adviser, Memoranda of Conversations, Box 9, February 19, 1975, Ford, Kissinger. Secret; Nodis. The meeting was held in the Oval Office at the White House. All brackets, with the exception of ones describing omitted material, are in the original.

[2] See Document 134 and footnote 3 thereto.

[3] For a report to the President of the talk with Sadat, see Document 132.

You can't imagine the monomania, the hysteria in Israel. There is no sense of gratitude. They demand we put our whole policy in hock to them.

The President: Did they raise Matmon B?

Kissinger: I said I wouldn't discuss until we saw what happened. I said we would go to Geneva but we would have to make proposals—that cooled them.

If we go to Geneva with a failure, we must consider whether or not to make an end of it.

The President: Did you see Dayan?

Kissinger: No. The whole Cabinet is opposed. They are vultures. You have to sympathize though, because they have seen their world position deteriorate to just us.

Sadat pleaded for some sort of arms just so he could show his military.

[There was discussion of a list and C–130s.]

The President: Asad?

Kissinger: If Asad could get something on the Golan, you would never hear of Geneva again.

You would like Asad. The Syrians and the Israelis are much alike. Asad's basic problem is he has lost 15,000 men in the war and hasn't gotten an inch. If Egypt makes big progress, he will look like a sucker to his people.

[When Asad and Nixon had their conversation last year,[4] Nixon finally agreed to the '67 borders.]

I asked Asad what he needed. He said "Everything." I said, "What will you give for it?" He said, "Good will." I said you don't get good will for services already rendered.

It is almost impossible to move because of the Israeli villages, but if we could, we would have Geneva off our back for a year. That is what the Soviets are afraid of. I made noises about a simultaneous step, but Asad knew.

Faisal also supported a simultaneous step. If he sticks to it, we can't pull it off. We may have to promise Sadat a follow-on step with Syria.

If Israel had a great leader, they would move jointly with Egypt and Syria and get the PLO off their back. Syria didn't mention the PLO.

If Faisal gets exercised, we have a problem. At a minimum he would need a letter that you would make an effort with Syria. As a du-

---

[4] See Document 92.

plicitous move, we could go to Geneva for a Syrian move and have it fail.

The President: You had been concerned whether Israel was setting us up.

Kissinger: I changed my mind. I think Rabin wants a move. Gur made a good statement that Israeli security didn't depend on any particular topography.

But they are in such a difficult domestic situation they could even prefer to go to Geneva and be raped.

The President: How about Likud?

Kissinger: They just want us to be tough. This is where the Jewish leaders are hurting us. They are leading to anti-Semitism.

The President: Javits told me we should make some statement about discrimination in banking.

Kissinger: That we should do.

The Likud is sort of Fascist. Like Perle.[5] That reminds me—Jackson is making an issue about Romania. He is insisting no MFN without a specific number on emigration. I think we shouldn't buy it—let him kill it.

If I told the Soviet Union we favored a step with both Egypt and Syria, but would only do Egypt separately and do Syria at Geneva, that would get Faisal off our back. To do it ourselves would be a horrible negotiation and a confrontation with Israel.

The President: I don't think we can divert you that long.

[Omitted here is discussion unrelated to the Arab-Israeli dispute.]

---

[5] Richard Perle, an aide to Senator Henry Jackson.

137. Memorandum of Conversation[1]

Washington, February 20, 1975, 7:28–9:30 a.m.

PARTICIPANTS

    President Gerald Ford
    Dr. Henry A. Kissinger, Secretary of State and Assistant to the President for National Security Affairs
    Lt. General Brent Scowcroft, Deputy Assistant to the President for National Security Affairs
    Congressional Leadership

The President: I am happy to have you here.

[He introduced new people.]

I thought the leaders would like to have Secretary Kissinger's observations of his trip to the Middle East. We talked for two hours last night.[2] We face the problem of sorting out the difficulties of a most difficult area of the world. I want to thank you, Henry. The country is very lucky to have you. Would you make some observations?

Kissinger: Let me talk in several categories: (1) The trip; (2) The Soviet Union, (3) The Europeans and energy.

What are we trying to do? Many say that Geneva is an alternative to the step-by-step approach and also that we should cooperate with the Soviet Union. We don't consider either accurate.

Our problem is how to go to Geneva so that it doesn't lead to confrontation and how to cooperate with the Soviet Union in a way that the Soviet Union does not act as the lawyer for radical Arabs.

We know we must go to Geneva soon, but it makes an enormous difference under what conditions we go. If we go under circumstances where the chief moderate—Sadat—has achieved something, it will be known that moderation pays and that only the U.S. can achieve progress. Then we will have some control. But if we go there with Egypt having failed, with pressure from the Soviet Union and the radicals, and the Europeans would be nervous. So it is not a trivial matter how we get to Geneva. And we have to prove to the Soviet Union that if it wants to get into the game it must be on our rules. So the issue is, will Geneva be the prelude to a confrontation or a negotiation?

---

[1] Source: Ford Library, National Security Adviser, Memoranda of Conversations, Box 9, February 20, 1975, Ford, Kissinger, Congressional Leadership. Secret; Nodis. The breakfast meeting was held in the First Floor Private Dining Room at the White House. All brackets, with the exception of ones describing omitted material, are in the original. A list of attendees is in the President's Daily Diary. (Ibid., Staff Secretary's Office Files)

[2] See Document 136.

We are talking now about a withdrawal which is not just token—so it is painful for Israel. So they want reciprocal measures that are hard for Egypt to make publicly. It is even difficult for Egypt to make a separate move at all. So we have to get a quid pro quo in a way that doesn't serve to overthrow Sadat. We are making progress.

Israel's domestic situation is difficult. Also, compared to Israel, American standards of secrecy are extraordinary.

We have a long way to go, but you can see where with luck and perseverance we might make progress on an agreement. The next problem is Syria. Earlier Syria said she wouldn't participate in another partial move. She now wants to, but Israeli settlements are placed so close to the line that any withdrawal is impossible without moving them. So how we manage this is the problem. Egypt wanted us to do this negotiation in one trip because she wanted it done quickly. I wanted two because the Israelis said they needed time. Faisal is now supporting Asad but we don't know how seriously.

The next issue is the Soviet Union. They are like a football team with only one play, which they keep running.

However, they want in but they don't want to contribute. Israel and Egypt don't want them in, nor would Syria if they could get three kilometers withdrawal. We don't want to antagonize them; they could create massive problems—with the radical Arabs and thus with the Europeans and Japanese. Maybe even an embargo.

So we will attempt another stage, then Geneva. I will go back in March and it will be hairy. The Soviets will oppose, but not actively, so long as they think it may succeed. We should keep this quiet because much is riding on this. If we go to Geneva and the Soviet Union puts forward a proposal, we will have to do so. It will be a constant crisis where the Soviet Union, the Europeans, the Japanese beat on us constantly with threats of economic disaster and an embargo.

I think the leaders of Israel understand but they have a massive domestic problem.

[Omitted here is discussion of the Soviet Union and Europe and Cyprus.]

138. Memorandum of Conversation[1]

Washington, February 25, 1975, 3:15–4:05 p.m.

PARTICIPANTS

Max Fisher
Rabbi Israel Miller, Chairman, Conference of Presidents of Major American-Jewish Organizations
Elmer Winter, President, American Jewish Committee
Dr. Arthur Hertzberg, President, American Jewish Congress
Rabbi Alexander Schindler, President of the Union of American Hebrew Congregations
Mrs. Charlotte Jacobson, President of the World Zionist Organization, American Section, Inc.
Yehudah Hellman, Executive Director, Conference of Presidents of Major American-Jewish Organizations
Frank Lautenberg, General Chairman, the United Jewish Appeal
Lewis Cole, President of the National Jewish Community Relations Advisory Council
Mrs. Rose Matzkin, President, Hadassah
Daniel Rose, President, National Jewish Welfare Board
Mordecai Waxman, President, Rabbinical Assembly
Herman Rosenbaum, President, National Council of Young Israel
Dr. Judah J. Shapiro, President, Labor Zionist Alliance
Seymour Graubard, National Chairman, Anti-Defamation League
I. L. Kenen, Chairman, American-Israel Public Affairs Committee

Dr. Henry A. Kissinger, Secretary of State and Assistant to the President for National Security Affairs
Prof. Robert Goldwin, Special Consultant to the President
Peter W. Rodman, NSC Staff

[Mr. Fisher spoke with Secretary Kissinger privately in the Secretary's office for a few minutes. Mr. Fisher then spoke to the group alone in the Conference Room. The Secretary then joined.]

Fisher: Henry, you've met most of the members of this distinguished group. I haven't coordinated this with you, but I wonder if you could give us your impression of your trips, past and prospective.

Kissinger [To Ms. Jacobson]: I kicked you out of the King David Hotel.

Jacobson: Now I know which floor to stay on.

Kissinger: My relations with the King David Hotel are symptomatic of my relations with Israel. [Laughter] The manager of the hotel

---

[1] Source: Library of Congress, Manuscript Division, Kissinger Papers, CL 157, Geopolitical File, Israel, February 12–28, 1975. Confidential. The meeting was held in the Secretary's Conference Room at the Department of State. Brackets are in the original.

came to me saying, "You can't do this to me." I said, "What?" He said, "Move to the Hilton." I said I had no intention of doing it; that just confirmed his suspicions. [Laughter] He said, "Now that you started at the King David, to switch would be aggression." [Laughter] I never even dreamt of it. I've spent more time trying to convince him. I've grown attached to the King David.

I wanted to talk to you about where we stand in the negotiations. I appreciate that we've never had any leaks or any problems with this group, so I'll speak very frankly.

First, before getting into detail, let's get clear what we're trying to do. There is one school of thought that says, let's get the Russians in—George Ball, Nahum Goldmann. Second, some say let's give up the step-by-step approach.

First, on the Soviets, it has to be remembered that we have no option with the Soviets except on Syrian terms. The Soviets have never taken any position other than that of the radical Arabs. If we were going to do that, we could recommend that Israel do it directly with Syria and we'd get some of the benefit. No other terms have ever been available. Under these conditions we have no overwhelming interest in doing it. And there is no advantage in doing it with the Soviets over what we could get if we did it unilaterally.

It is dangerous to start down this road.

On Geneva and the step-by-step—these are not really alternatives. We could have kept the step-by-step going indefinitely had it not been for Rabat.[2] That was a tragedy. If we go to Geneva after a successful step, every progress in the Middle East will be the result of the U.S. and every Arab will know it. Israel will go to Geneva having shown great conciliatoriness. And third, the most moderate Arab will have had a success and the radicals who did Rabat will have got nothing. The Soviets and the Europeans won't be involved.

If the step-by-step breaks down, the Soviets and the Syrians and the radicals will be vindicated. The scenario will be to bring maximum pressure on the United States. It will meet under the threat of war. The Europeans and the Japanese will press us—and Israel, of course. And the domestic situation in America will get very complicated.

The step-by-step is the only way to go to Geneva without the whole world putting pressure on Israel. And so you have to look at this process over time, not every week or every month.

---

[2] See Document 112.

My impression—you can confirm this from your own sources—is that there is no difference in the strategic assessment between the U.S. and Israel.

There are people who say you can't trust Sadat. It doesn't make any difference. If there is an agreement now, objectively an agreement will create an intense discussion, to put it mildly, in the Arab world. Even if the worst happens and Sadat makes new demands in a year, it will be in a different situation.

Let me talk about this negotiation. In the relationship between Egypt and Israel, there is an abstract debate about should there be a quid pro quo? It stands to reason there has to be a quid pro quo. Israel is a democracy; there can be all sorts of agreements, but there have to be visible parts for the Israeli Government to show their people. Secondly, there has to be a return because it's not in our interest that Israel be pushed. Even by the most cynical estimate of our intentions, Israel has to be difficult. It is not in our interest for Israel to be a pushover because then the process will never end. There will be constant demands. We've never told Israel not to put its demands.

How to construct the quid pro quo is a problem. On the last trip I didn't ask for decision on a particular line.

It's in all our interests, if something is agreed, that the Israelis do it with their heads held high. Because—in this country—if it could be said that Israel made a constructive move for peace, it would be very helpful. Dinitz doesn't like me to say this, but—it has nothing to do with Israel—I would not want to have to manage a crisis now. In 1970 we moved a battalion on the autobahn, we moved a plane from a carrier into Tel Aviv, and we wanted it to be picked up. We wanted to create a crisis atmosphere to scare the Russians. Now, could we move a plane into Tel Aviv without starting an impeachment? In 1973 we did 75% of what we did in 1970 and it got out in four hours and I had to spend three weeks explaining it. We recently sent a carrier into the Indian Ocean; it wasn't out of Manila Harbor before we had to explain where it wasn't going. We have to get executive authority reestablished here. And with the anti-Semitic element and Israel, that makes it more difficult.

I hear some people say it's salami tactics. But if we wanted to push Israel to the '67 borders, we'd get lots of takers. It would solve all our problems with the Russians. The Europeans and Japanese would join us. If we were going to do it we would do it head on and get lots of short-term benefits. The Jewish Community has to understand that we've adopted a different strategy, that has to be complex.

On the Syrian side, as I said at the press conference today, it's significant that Asad is now talking about a peace treaty with Israel where when I first came there all Israel to him was "occupied territory."[3] But we recognize the particular concern on the Golan. The Syrians are now trying to block an Egyptian agreement because he lost 15,000 men and the Egyptians seem to be doing all the gaining. The Saudis seem to be leaning toward the Syrians.

Then there are the Soviets. I hope I've done enough to quiet them down. They could upset the applecart. By themselves, they can't, but they can if the Syrians and the Saudis gang up.

I think Egypt will go ahead with it in the face of Syrian and Saudi opposition. This in itself is an achievement for Israel. I'll go on the 7–8th to Aswan, then I go to Damascus—to get that out of the way. It won't be a pleasant visit.

One other point. Every time some Senator says something unpleasant to Israel, there is the theory that I put him up to it. If I want to say something, I'll say it myself. Our whole strategy depends on keeping the PLO out of this. The strategy is to keep the PLO out of it as long as is humanly possible. It's the Europeans who are obsessed with the PLO, not the U.S.—or even the Arabs, strangely enough.

Miller: On the question of keeping Israel strong in this. Every once in a while we get signals that Israel isn't getting what it needs. Where is there a strong Israel in this?

Kissinger: First, the strategy requires a strong Israel. Second, if you look at the balance, Israel is stronger than before October. Every Minister of Defense is never satisfied with what he has. But there are no unfulfilled requests—no requests that give us any problem.

The only question is the amount of aid. I must say it wasn't tactically brilliant to publish the figure in the budget before consulting us. Not tactically brilliant. But that runs up against the mood in the country, not the Administration.

Kenen: We hear Sadat say he's negotiating not with Israel but with the United States. Is there a chance for an agreement between Egypt and Israel? Because otherwise an agreement could collapse.

Kissinger: He has the problem of how he's going to explain what is essentially a separate deal with Israel. It has to be an agreement signed by Egypt and Israel, that's clear. There will be some assurances he'll give to us—that's actually better, because it will involve his stake here, and the weight of his credibility with us. There will be some of both.

Question: Too often we hear of the Suez Canal, that was part of an earlier negotiation. Will we get this again? That he was supposed to do before?

---

[3] In his February 25 press conference, Kissinger commented on President Asad's statement to *Newsweek* magazine that he was willing to sign a peace agreement with Israel. (*New York Times*, February 26, 1975, p. 12)

Kissinger: We have to separate two things. They're putting a lot of money into rebuilding the Canal cities. So the idea of the Canal as a hostage to Israel already exists. Second, as for opening it, we can debate about how much it's in Israel's or our interest to have Soviet ships come in. I think he's using it for the Arab debate, to explain how he couldn't do it with the Israelis so close.

Jacobson: Can you comment on the arms buildup with the Saudis? Doesn't it encourage them to build up for another war?

Kissinger: The Saudi program will be over five years, and the record of the last war shows that the Saudi army is not Israel's biggest problem. They set a record for slow movement and the only people they fought were the Iraqis, by mistake. Last June when we tried to sell a nuclear reactor to Egypt and all hell broke loose.[4] We thought that while it was being built, it would give us eight years of leverage, with safeguards that only we could insist on. Now the French are selling two reactors to Egypt, with no safeguards and no leverage. The Saudi weapons will not be sophisticated; they can't be used because they won't have three weeks of spare parts. There won't be resupply in a war. We're trying to soak up the money and prevent another embargo. Though we're not doing it for economic reasons.

Question: You mentioned the mood of America. What is your impression of it? Is it changing? Why? Is it Arab propaganda?

Kissinger: Dinitz is upset when I say this, but I may be in a better position to pick this up than you.

Question: How?

Kissinger: In the leadership groups in this country.

Question: The Congress?

Kissinger: Yes. But in the establishment groups, there is a feeling that we could get it over with by pressing Israel. Much of the criticism you must remember, is from people who think the progress isn't rapid enough, not that it's too rapid. Then there is the general opposition to foreign aid. Then there is the nihilism in this country. Portugal is going Communist without opposition from the United States; the Congress is more interested in ripping up our intelligence establishment than in preventing this. We're cutting off Turkey—when the major danger of war now in the world is in the Middle East. Asad asks me for political science tutoring once in a while; before, he thought we had overthrown Makarios—which is not true—in order to get a base in the Eastern Mediterranean. That was his theory. He thought he understood. Now he can't figure it out. And Vietnam: To throw the country to the Communists for $300 million is inconceivable. At the press conference they

---

[4] See footnote 5, Document 112.

tried to get me to link the Middle East and Vietnam; I refused. There is a malaise here.

I talked to Senator Humphrey. Israel has no better friend. He's pro-Israel, and said it'll be difficult to get the aid this year. A Congressman who's a friend of Israel—whom I won't name, because it wouldn't be fair—said "We won't take you seriously unless you cut it in half." It's unrelated to any negotiation: it's just a general feeling.

Question: You said you would go to Aswan, then Damascus, then to Jerusalem.

Kissinger: All this is agreed with the Israelis.

Question: All this could be currying favor with the U.S. and a lot of posturing. Are a majority of the Arabs really willing to accept the existence of Israel, or is it a delaying game?

Kissinger: It depends. Jordan genuinely accepts the existence of Israel. Egypt substantially does. Syria does now verbally but not inwardly. The PLO neither verbally nor inwardly.

Miller: The Saudis?

Kissinger: Verbally, not inwardly—but that's a big change. By the way, none of this would change if tomorrow the Arabs signed in blood.

Jacobson: Of course.

Kissinger: Rabin cites a remark I once made jokingly—that wars in the Middle East start among countries who are already at war, unlike India and Pakistan who fight their wars while they are at peace. So even with a peace treaty, Israel will still have the problem of defense.

In the 15 months or so, Syria and Saudi Arabia have moved to verbal acceptance of Israel. Egypt is in a process that must inevitably lead to acceptance of legal peace. So there is progress.

But I told Golda I've never promised an easy course. There will be another crisis inevitably.

Fisher: We read a lot about guarantees . . .

Kissinger: Here is an example of why some confidence is needed on the part of the Jewish Community. Two months ago a *Washington Post* reporter called me after a lunch with Dobrynin and she said the Soviets have offered a joint U.S.-Soviet guarantee and this was a breakthrough. Any Israeli Government would be insane to accept any kind of Soviet guarantee, even a joint one. What does it mean? That if the Syrians attacked in the Golan the Soviets would land in Haifa? It's a constant right of intervention.

But some American guarantee may be necessary. It has to be considered as part of the final settlement. I've never said it can be a substitute for secure boundaries. I said the opposite. I said it at my press conference this morning.

Question: I think that public opinion in the Jewish Community supports your step-by-step. Counterarguments are heard and discounted, but the general trend is supportive, with the usual obstreperousness to get more out of negotiation.

Kissinger: I wouldn't have it otherwise! [Laughter]

Question: You said to us you would go to Geneva.

Kissinger: I won't beat any world records to go to Geneva.

Question: I'm glad to hear it. But you once said the Soviets can always outbid us at Geneva. How do we avoid being there with six to one [against us] and the U.S. having to veto all the demands?

Kissinger: We have to go to Geneva; if we had another step we could postpone it. We could turn it into another European Security Conference, where no one remembers who proposed what to whom. I've educated Faisal; he doesn't even mention Jerusalem. We can go to Geneva and say "our specialty is concrete progress. If you want theory, go to the Europeans." We can turn the Soviets' detailed plans into a trap for them.

Miller: In the leadership groups we don't see that nasty word "erosion" of support.

Graubard: The ADL had a press conference today and we issued a statement about the American businessmen and groups complying with Arab boycotts. We have the material here. [Tab A][5]

Kissinger: Have you given it to the Attorney General?

Graubard: Yes, and with a memorandum of law.

Kissinger: I would appreciate it.

Graubard: We took the position that we don't object to Arab participation in investment but not if there is discrimination against anyone or against a friendly country.

Kissinger: I said something like that at the press conference, though I'm sure not as precisely, and the President tomorrow at his press conference in Miami will make a very strong statement on the same subject.[6]

Question: Suppose the counterpressures expand—you can't give a guarantee that there won't be resupply for the Saudis. The other point is this bigotry problem. We know the people hiring for this Saudi deal are making clear they won't hire Jews.

---

[5] Tab A has not been found.

[6] The President opened his February 26 press conference in Miami with a statement on discriminatory practices in the international banking community. (*Public Papers: Ford, 1975*, Book I, p. 289)

Kissinger: That problem is overt and can be handled. What I would be worried about if I were you is that over time, fewer Jews will get into positions of responsibility in international business firms.

Fisher: I want to say we've been supportive of your step-by-step approach.

Kissinger: That's true.

Fisher: There are some on the far right or far left of the Jewish Community who don't, but we—while we have some differences, and we express them . . .

Kissinger: It's your duty.

Fisher: We don't want you to get the impression we don't support you.

Kissinger: Thank you. I have to go.

[The Secretary went to the Eighth Floor for the swearing-in of Elliot Richardson as Ambassador to the Court of St. James's. After he returned, he conferred for 10 minutes alone with Max Fisher and Rabbi Hertzberg.]

139. Letter From President Ford to Israeli Prime Minister Rabin[1]

Washington, March 7, 1975.

Dear Mr. Prime Minister:

I am writing to express my further thoughts on the terrorist outrage at the Savoy Hotel[2]. I want you to know how deeply I feel about such senseless acts.

I also want you to know how strongly I believe that our progress toward peace must be maintained. We cannot permit this act of terrorism to attain the goal it seeks—the disruption and collapse of our current peace efforts. I, therefore, hope that your Government's re-

---

[1] Source: Library of Congress, Manuscript Division, Kissinger Papers, CL 157, Geopolitical File, Israel, March 1975. No classification marking. A handwritten notation at the top of the page reads, "Delivered by courier to Min. Shalev at 7:00 p.m."

[2] On the night of March 5, eight PLO guerrillas arrived secretly by boat on a beach in Tel Aviv. They entered the Savoy Hotel and forcibly took the hotel guests hostage. On the morning of March 6, an Israeli commando unit stormed the hotel, leading to a brief battle. The fighting left seven of the eight guerrillas dead and five hostages and three Israeli soldiers were killed.

sponse to this tragedy will be consistent with our mutual interest in maintaining momentum toward a settlement.

Please be assured, Mr. Prime Minister, that the people of the United States fully share with you and your countrymen your grief at this tragic and outrageous event. We are determined to do all we can to attain a peace which will put an end to acts of this nature.

Sincerely,

Gerald R. Ford

---

140. **Memorandum From the President's Deputy Assistant for National Security Affairs (Scowcroft) to President Ford**[1]

Washington, March 9, 1975.

Secretary Kissinger asked that I pass the following report of his meeting with President Sadat to you:

"'I hope this round will be fruitful and decisive.' These first words, spoken by Sadat at the opening of seven hours of talks here in Aswan,[2] characterize the mood of hope, expectation and quiet determination which Sadat reflects. He also added at the press conference that 'this will be a hard round'—meaning it will be a tough negotiation.

"I covered in some detail the principal points which Sadat is willing to consider in return for an Israeli withdrawal from the strategic passes and the oil fields. I got him to delete the point on linkage to a Syrian agreement which I knew in advance would result in a very adverse reaction in Israel. A number of the points which Sadat has given me are positive, and while some will not be acceptable to the Israelis, I am bringing enough with me to at least get the negotiations started in a serious way. The most positive element we have received is a willingness by Sadat to in effect agree to a no-war pledge. The form of words in which this is expressed is likely to be haggled over.

"Sadat is having a monumental problem with the military. Significantly he had with him throughout the day, General Gamasy, his Min-

---

[1] Source: Ford Library, National Security Adviser, Kissinger Reports on USSR, China, and Middle East, Box 3, March 7–March 22, 1975, Volume 1.1 (2), Kissinger's Trip. Secret; Sensitive.

[2] The memorandum of conversation of the meeting between Sadat and Kissinger, which took place on March 8 at 11 a.m. at the Presidential Palace in Aswan, is ibid., Volume 1(1), Kissinger's Trip.

ister of Defense, whose support for any agreement is crucial. He brought in Gamasy to give us a full conceptual explanation from a military point of view of the next step as seen by the Egyptians. All of the possibilities discussed by Gamasy would move Egyptian forces east of the passes. I felt that it was essential that I tell Sadat ahead of time when I spoke to him alone afterward that Israel will not accept Egyptian soldiers east of the passes. We discussed as a possible alternative, a possible small advance of Egyptian troops to the present Israeli line which is west of the passes.

"Gamasy said that the agreement should be based on the following principles: (1) any line manned by one side should be secure from the other side's troops; (2) the agreement should not give either side any military advantage; (3) there should be a balance of troops in the Sinai for both sides; (4) the new lines should be a sufficient distance away to give security to the Egyptian people in the cities in the Suez Canal area and to navigation through the Canal; (5) the buffer zone should be wide enough to avoid clashes between the two sides; (6) navigation through the Suez Canal, once opened, would be an obstacle to Egyptian military reaction in event of renewed hostilities, thus making it necessary for Egypt to have more forces in Sinai.

"My plan is to return to Aswan on Wednesday.[3] In the meantime you will have seen that Esenbel has invited me to come to Ankara. I am planning on having talks with the Israelis on Sunday night and Monday a.m.,[4] after which the Israelis will have 24 hours to think over what I have brought from Egypt. During this 24 hour period—Monday afternoon and Tuesday morning—I will be in Ankara to discuss the Cyprus situation with all of the principal Turkish leaders, including Ecevit and Demirel. I will use the occasion to explore possibilities, but will make no moves in this regard without further consultation with you. The principal focus of the discussions will be on what the Turks would be willing to give in return if we are able to get a commitment from the Greek Government to the concept of a bizonal federation.

"I leave Aswan early Sunday morning; I will make a brief five hour stop in Damascus before arriving in Israel Sunday night."

---

[3] March 12.
[4] March 9–10.

141. Memorandum From the President's Deputy Assistant for National Security Affairs (Scowcroft) to President Ford[1]

Washington, March 10, 1975.

Secretary Kissinger asked that I pass you the following report …

"I have just completed a four-hour meeting with Asad,[2] who obviously is deeply suspicious that the Egyptians will go ahead on a separate agreement leaving him on the sideline. I found him edgy, bordering on the prickly a couple of times during the four-hour period.

'I am not optimistic,' Asad said several times. 'A solution cannot come about without another war. That which has been lost by war, must be returned by war.' He made one specific proposal: That the U.S. keep in limbo its present efforts to achieve an Egyptian-Israeli second stage agreement, and start specific discussions with Syria and Israel more or less simultaneously to work something out with respect to the Golan. I sought to reassure him that we are prepared to make as major an effort for one Arab state as for another, but that this could not be done all at one time, and that conditions had to be prepared carefully before such a Syrian-Israeli process could start and offer some hope of success.

It was interesting that during our four-hour session Asad had both high-level civilian and military officials, the reason being to show them he was pressing Syria's insistence on being included in the negotiating process, and that he was taking an unyielding posture towards Israel. As I expected, he is interested in a continuing U.S. role regarding the Golan. He mentioned the Geneva conference only once, to tell me he does not want to go there since there is nothing in it for Syria.

I do not believe he feels completely reassured that a separate agreement between Egypt and Israel will not be achieved. He believes that talks between Egypt and Israel are much further along than they really are. I pointed out that it was for each individual Arab state and the Arabs collectively, to decide whether they wish to proceed step-by-step and what their attitude will be if there is an opportunity for further Israeli withdrawal from Arab territory. I told him it was not our intention to divide the Arabs and isolate Syria.

---

[1] Source: Ford Library, National Security Adviser, Kissinger Reports on USSR, China, and Middle East, Box 3, March 7–March 22, 1975, Volume 1.1 (2), Kissinger's Trip. Secret; Sensitive. Sent for information. Ford initialed the memorandum.

[2] A memorandum of conversation of the meeting between Asad and Kissinger, which took place on March 9 from 3:15 until 7:30 p.m. at the Presidential Palace in Damascus, is ibid.

While Asad remains suspicious, he has adopted a wait-and-see attitude regarding the Egyptian-Israeli negotiations. In a private half hour session alone,[3] he underlined that he does not know how he can justify extending the UN force in May unless something is going on. He did say that even if there should be continuing differences over the step-by-step approach between us, he did not want this to affect adversely the relations between the United States and Syria.

In short, he still has not in his own mind written off the possibility that we might be able to make some move on the Golan within the present time frame of the negotiations, but he has coupled this with more war talk than we have heard before. Moreover, he struck the theme that time is on their side, and they are willing to wait. It is not without interest that he said the U.S. has given up Vietnam, Cambodia, Taiwan, Turkey, and Portugal. Eventually we would let Israel go down too."

Warm Regards

---

[3] No memorandum of conversation has been found.

---

142. Memorandum From the President's Deputy Assistant for National Security Affairs (Scowcroft) to President Ford[1]

Washington, March 10, 1975.

Secretary Kissinger has asked that I pass you the following report of his meeting with Prime Minister Rabin.

"I have just completed a total of about eight hours of discussions with Prime Minister Rabin and his negotiating team which includes Allon, Peres and Chief of Staff Gur.[2] I shared with them my analysis that he has limited room for political maneuver. I also gave them the sense of the mood I found in Damascus, stressing the tough talk about a

---

[1] Source: Ford Library, National Security Adviser, Kissinger Reports on USSR, China, and Middle East, Box 3, March 7–March 22, 1975, Volume 1.1 (4), Kissinger's Trip. Secret; Sensitive. Sent for information. Ford initialed the memorandum.

[2] A memorandum of conversation of the meeting between the Israeli negotiating team and Kissinger, which took place on March 9 from 10:30 until 11:55 p.m. at the Prime Minister's Residence in Jerusalem, is ibid. A memorandum of conversation of a subsequent meeting, which took place on March 10 from 10:02 a.m. until 1 p.m. at the Prime Minister's office in Jerusalem, is ibid., Volume 1.1 (4), Kissinger's Trip.

possible war expressed by Asad, his strong opposition against a separate agreement between Egypt and Israel, and Asad's strong desire that something be achieved in the Sinai and the Golan more or less simultaneously.

"I explained at some length the conceptual approach of the Egyptians to the next-stage agreement, as described to us by Minister of Defense Gamasy.[3] I described the specific Egyptian thinking, all of which would involve from their point of view an Egyptian defense line east of the strategic passes. I informed the Israelis that I had made clear to Sadat that such a substantial withdrawal was out of the question as far as Israel was concerned, and Rabin of course confirmed this fact during our talk.

"Rabin outlined the principal seven considerations from Israel's point of view, emphasizing two that were particularly key.

"(A) An Egyptian commitment not to make war against Israel; and
"(B) the importance attached to the duration of the agreement, including continued insistence that there must be an Egyptian assurance that the UN force could not be removed except by affirmative Security Council action.

"The key statement which was underscored by Rabin and Allon is, to put it in their words: Israel wants an interim agreement, and it also leaves open the option to pursue a Syrian negotiation on a permanent peace.

"As you can imagine, the Israelis cast all sorts of doubts and threw up all sorts of hurdles on specific issues and points, but on the whole their posture and mood is positive, and they seemed to be ready to discuss matters seriously.

"I left it that I would return to Israel Tuesday[4] evening for a further meeting. This will give Rabin and his colleagues 24 hours to reflect on what I have reported, to discuss my report with the Cabinet, and hopefully to come up with some concrete counterproposals which would not be intended as a final Israeli position but be sufficient to keep the negotiations moving. I urged that they be as generous as possible in the belief that this would have a favorable psychological impact on Sadat and in the long run possibly make him more favorably disposed to meet Israel's principal needs. I am trying to get the Israelis to adopt a strategy which is entirely different and new for them: rather than stick rigidly to point after point, that they make a generous counterproposal which could convince Sadat of their seriousness. It will be interesting to see what they come up with for us to consider on Tuesday evening.

---

[3] See Document 140.
[4] March 11.

"In short, I think the process is going just about as one might expect at this stage.

"I now take a 24-hour break from the Arab-Israeli dispute to see whether I can encourage the Turks to take some step that will help get a meaningful negotiation restarted."

---

143. Memorandum From the President's Deputy Assistant for National Security Affairs (Scowcroft) to President Ford[1]

Washington, March 11, 1975.

Secretary Kissinger asked that I pass you the following report of the second round of talks he has had with Prime Minister Rabin and his Cabinet colleagues.

"I have just completed another round of talks with Prime Minister Rabin and his Cabinet colleagues.[2] I can report no decisive change in the Israeli position, because Rabin at this point does not want to put decisions to the Cabinet because he is not confident of their reaction. Rabin himself seems flexible. They have, however, given me some ideas to take back to Sadat—enough to keep the negotiations going. Rabin has a delicate domestic situation, and he is trying to handle it in such a way that when he recommends Israeli withdrawal from passes and the oil fields, he will have enough from Sadat in return to get the agreement through the Cabinet and the Parliament.

"My strategy will be to try to present the Israeli ideas to Sadat in the most positive way and then to return to Israel to see whether we can begin to reflect some of the key points in a document which I then would try out on Sadat in the next round.

"As our discussions become more specific, it is becoming clear that the two most difficult issues that will have to be reconciled in an Israeli-Egyptian agreement are:

---

[1] Source: Ford Library, National Security Adviser, Kissinger Reports on USSR, China, and Middle East, Box 3, March 7–March 22, 1975, Volume 1.1 (5), Kissinger's Trip. Secret; Sensitive. Sent for information. Ford initialed the memorandum.

[2] A memorandum of conversation of the meeting between the Israeli negotiating team and Kissinger, which took place on March 11 from 10:10 until 11:40 p.m. at the Prime Minister's office in Jerusalem, is ibid. They met again on March 12 from 10:13 a.m. until 12:15 p.m. at the Prime Minister's office. (Memorandum of conversation; ibid., Volume 1.1 (6), Kissinger's Trip)

"(A) Israeli insistence that Sadat commit himself publicly in some way that he will never again resort to military action against Israel, which Sadat says he cannot do so long as Israel remains in occupation of Egyptian territory, and

"(B) Israel's desire for an interim agreement to specify a longer duration than Sadat considers politically possible. In addition, the Israeli-Egyptian negotiating process is taking place against a background of uncertainty as to what Asad of Syria may try to do to prevent Sadat from concluding a separate agreement plus King Faisal's support for simultaneous Egyptian and Syrian agreements.

"We had a military briefing this morning which shows that the Egyptian dispositions are such that they could launch a limited military operation aimed at the passes if a decision were taken. General Gur, the Israeli Chief of Staff, also gave us a military evaluation of the Syrian capacity, and it is clear that the Israelis feel that the situation there potentially is more dangerous and that the most likely alternative they would face in circumstances of an unsuccessful negotiation would be a war of attrition designed to bleed Israel for an extended period.

"I also plan on making stops in Damascus and Jordan sometime this coming weekend, largely to try to keep everybody calm."

144. **Memorandum From the President's Deputy Assistant for National Security Affairs (Scowcroft) to President Ford**[1]

Washington, March 13, 1975.

Secretary Kissinger asked that I pass you the following report . . .

"I met with President Sadat and his key advisers, Foreign Minister Fahmi and General Gamasy, for about three hours,[2] to present the points of a political character which the Israelis want included in any agreement in return for Israeli withdrawal from the passes and the oil fields. I explained to Sadat that the key problem is the Israeli domestic situation and that in order for Rabin to get the cabinet to take the decision to withdraw from the passes and the oil fields he must be in a position to show specifically the political quids he has received in return. I

---

[1] Source: Ford Library, National Security Adviser, Kissinger Reports on USSR, China, and Middle East, Box 3, March 7–March 22, 1975, Volume 1.1 (7), Kissinger's Trip. Secret; Sensitive. Sent for information. Ford initialed the memorandum.

[2] A memorandum of conversation of the meeting between Sadat and his advisers and Kissinger, which took place on March 12 in Aswan, is ibid., Volume 1.1 (6), Kissinger's Trip.

stressed that Rabin cannot agree to a purely military withdrawal, but it must be presented to the Israeli people as a tangible step toward peace. Sadat listened intently, commented decisively on points which he felt he could include, and, equally decisively, where he felt that certain Israeli demands were beyond his political capacity.

His two principal advisers, Fahmi and Gamasy, were, not unexpectedly, more cautious, and Sadat intends to review with them each of the points I discussed today and to give me his considered reply sometime tomorrow evening to take back to Israel. I am cautiously hopeful that Sadat will give me enough to maintain the momentum of the negotiations which could bring us in a few days to the beginning of the actual drafting stage. How much I bring back from Aswan will influence Rabin very significantly on whether and when he places before the cabinet a recommendation to withdraw out of the passes and the oil fields. My impression is that Rabin, Allon, and Chief of Staff General Gur have taken a positive attitude towards the agreement and even Peres seems to be coming around.

Sadat continues to reflect confidence that he can manage Syria's opposition to an Egyptian-Israeli agreement, and he would like us to undertake a further effort with Syria once his agreement with Israel is consummated. He wants something started with Syria by the end of April so as to provide Syria with the justification for renewing in May the UN force in the Golan. I said I would consider this, but I made no final commitment. He did not seem perturbed at the prospect that the PLO issue might immobilize a Geneva conference at the outset, and he left this matter for further discussion between us at a later stage.

There was one particularly interesting moment when I talked to Sadat alone. I presented him with a letter from Rabin which I had suggested and in which, in very human terms, Rabin expressed his strong desire to achieve the agreement with Sadat.[3] This letter moved Sadat to tears, and he said, that this was the kind of thing which he had always wanted. I believe this was a good psychological stroke, and I hope that it will have an impact on the considered version which Sadat will convey to me tomorrow night for subsequent presentation to the Israelis.

---

[3] In the March 11 letter, Rabin expressed his hope to Sadat that Israel and Egypt would reach an agreement. He wrote: "I know that no agreement is possible without difficult decisions but I am ready to grapple with them for the sake of the cause of peace between our countries." He continued that in order to convince the Israeli people of the need to make these difficult decisions, he needed to see "that the act of withdrawal marks the real beginning of progress towards peace by deeds and words that demonstrate the intention of peace." (Ibid., Volume 1.1 (5), Kissinger's Trip)

I will go to both Damascus and Amman on Saturday,[4] and return to Israel on Sunday afternoon."
Warm Regards

---

[4] March 15.

---

145. Memorandum From the President's Deputy Assistant for National Security Affairs (Scowcroft) to President Ford[1]

Washington, March 14, 1975.

Secretary Kissinger asked that I pass you the following report . . .

"Now that the first intensive rounds with the Israelis and the Egyptians have been completed, a clearer picture has emerged as to the needs of each side, and how far each is willing to go to meet these needs. I have now finished my talks with Sadat;[2] whether an agreement is achievable remains uncertain. We have made progress on the political aspects, but we have very difficult problems on the military side of the agreement.

"In rather precise terms, Egypt's key demands are: (A) Israeli withdrawal out of the passes and oil fields; (B) Egyptian forces to move eastward to the western entrance of the passes; and (C) agreement on a balance between all Egyptian and Israeli forces in the Sinai.

"In order to meet Israel's needs on the political side, Sadat, while not willing to give a formal declaration of non-belligerency, is willing to include in the agreement: (A) that the interim agreement is a step towards peace; (B) that Egypt is willing to resolve all differences by peaceful means; (C) that Egypt will refrain from the use use of force against Israel; and (D) that as a part of the process towards peace, the agreement would remain valid until superseded by another agreement. In addition, Egypt may be willing to participate jointly with Israel in as-

---

[1] Source: Ford Library, National Security Adviser, Kissinger Reports on USSR, China, and Middle East, Box 3, March 7–March 22, 1975, Volume 1.1 (7), Kissinger's Trip. Secret; Sensitive. Sent for information. Ford initialed the memorandum.
[2] The memorandum of conversation between Sadat and Kissinger of a final March 13 meeting at Aswan is ibid. According to an annotated chronology of the March 13–22 meetings between Kissinger and Sadat and Kissinger and the Israeli negotiating team, entitled "Chronology of the Decisive Phase of the Negotiation," the meeting took place from 6:50 to 9:50 p.m. (Ibid., Volume 1.1 (1), Kissinger's Trip)

sisting the UNEF command in the buffer zone; it agrees to automatic annual review of UNEF; it is willing for Israeli cargoes to go through the canal; it is willing to reduce hostile propaganda emanating from Egyptian controlled media; it will allow free passage through the Straits of Bab al-Mandab; it agrees to freedom of movement through the Sinai and Gaza for Egyptians; and it is willing to undertake quietly and informally, particularly in relation to selected American firms, ways to ease economic boycott practices.

"What are the key problems which emerge from the above compendium of elements.

"First, and fundamental is whether Rabin feels the political quids Sadat is willing to provide are enough to justify putting before the cabinet on Sunday a recommendation for Israeli withdrawal out of the passes and the oil fields.

"Second, the Egyptian proposal, in which they are insisting not only on an Egyptian move of its military forces to the western entrance of the passes, but also an increase in the number of Egyptian forces east of the Suez Canal, lays bare the Egyptian strategic military objective. Its purpose is to give Egypt a stronger military presence numerically but also to extend substantially its zone east of the canal. Moreover Egypt seeks a more equitable balance in the forces in the Sinai. In other words, what the Israelis face in this proposal is not only a drawback from the passes but also a stronger Egyptian military presence east of the canal. I am virtually certain that this will prove unacceptable to Rabin. If the Egyptians stick on this proposal, it could become an issue on which the agreement could break. It might be possible, however, to work out a lesser Egyptian military move forward with limits on the number of forces, which Israel might be able to live with. It might also be possible to balance Egyptian forces at the western end of the passes with Israeli forces at the eastern entrances of the passes.

"Finally, the Israelis are seeking not only a commitment from the Egyptians that they will not use force, but also a commitment that all future issues will be resolved by peaceful means. It is significant that Sadat has agreed to give a commitment not to use force, and that this will be made public. This should prove reassuring as a practical matter to the Israelis; it would also provide the kind of cosmetically feasible practical step towards peace, going beyond the limits of the military disengagement agreement which Rabin needs to convince his cabinet.

"Moreover, the Israelis want assurances against surprise attack. In addition to the commitment against the use of force, Israel is seeking ways to strengthen UNEF, including some role for joint Egyptian/Israeli participation. On the basis of what we know at present, something along these lines may prove feasible.

"I am asking Scowcroft to show you a cable of the intensity of Syrian pressure.[3] The tragedy is that a few kilometers in the Golan would solve the problem.

"I will be meeting with Rabin and his colleagues tomorrow, and we will know a bit more clearly where matters stand. Further adjustments in the positions of both sides will be required if an agreement is to be achieved. Whether each side has enough political room for maneuver still remains in doubt. Nevertheless, we have received enough from each side to give us something to work with. I therefore expect to continue the process in hopes that we will find ways to close the gap on key issues."

Warm Regards

---

[3] Not further identified.

---

146. Memorandum From the President's Deputy Assistant for National Security Affairs (Scowcroft) to President Ford[1]

Washington, March 14, 1975.

Secretary Kissinger asked me to provide you with the following report of his first meeting with Prime Minister Rabin upon arrival back in Jerusalem:

"Immediately after arriving in Jerusalem from Aswan, I met for almost three hours with Prime Minister Rabin and his colleagues[2] to give them a detailed report on the latest elements of the Egyptian position, which I described in some detail in my report to you yesterday from Aswan.[3] The Israelis raised a number of questions for clarification, but withheld any reaction to the Egyptian ideas until they can consult among themselves and report to the Cabinet during its regular meeting this Sunday.[4] This is contrary to some press reports that will be ema-

---

[1] Source: Ford Library, National Security Adviser, Kissinger Reports on USSR, China, and Middle East, Box 3, March 7–March 22, 1975, Volume 1.1 (8), Kissinger's Trip. Secret; Sensitive; Eyes Only.

[2] The memorandum of conversation of the meeting between the Israeli negotiating team and Kissinger, which took place on March 14 from 1:10 until 3:45 p.m. at the Prime Minister's office in Jerusalem, is ibid.

[3] See Document 144.

[4] March 16.

nating from Israel, based on an obtuse backgrounder, by an Israeli spokesman indicating that Israel has rejected what I brought from Aswan.

"From the questions they raised, it is clear that they continue to attach great importance to getting from Sadat the maximum possible commitment to the non-use of force in the future, to specific evidences of movement toward non-belligerency, and to assurances that, once a new Sinai agreement is achieved, its duration will be open-ended and not linked to early movement toward further agreements on the Egyptian or other fronts.

"I gave them my impression that, if agreement can be reached on a new line and balance of forces in the Sinai which meets Egypt's basic strategic requirements, Sadat would go very far in satisfying Israel's concerns about the political content of the agreement. Rabin summed up the key issue succinctly by saying that there are two basic concepts now under consideration: (a) the Israeli concept of creating a large and effective buffer in the area from which Israel withdraws, and (b) the Egyptian concept of advancing its forces to the western entrance of the Sinai passes as Israel withdraws to the eastern entrance to the passes, with a small buffer zone in between and with each side relying for its strategic security on a balance of deterrent forces in the Sinai.

"It remains to be seen whether these concepts can be reconciled. We should have a better idea when we get the Israeli reaction following Sunday's Cabinet meeting, although I may get some indications when I see Rabin at a small private dinner tonight.[5] I gave the Israelis my judgment that it is important to achieve agreement on a strategic framework by the middle of next week and to go to Sadat with concrete proposals for an agreement that will be sufficiently forthcoming to make it possible to move quickly to conclude the negotiations before counterpressures can build up from Syria and probably from Saudi Arabia as well.

"While awaiting the Israeli Cabinet reaction, I will go to Damascus tomorrow and continue my efforts to persuade the Syrians to keep their options open. From Damascus, I will go to Amman tomorrow night to bring Hussein up to date and discuss a number of bilateral and regional security concerns that are on his mind. I will also seek to enlist Hussein's help with Syria, with whom the Jordanians have greatly improved their relations of late. Given King Faisal's key role and the importance of keeping him from lining up with Syria against a Sinai agreement, I have also asked whether Faisal could see me Sunday afternoon before I return that evening to Jerusalem."

---

[5] No memorandum of conversation has been found.

147. Memorandum From the President's Deputy Assistant for National Security Affairs (Scowcroft) to President Ford[1]

Washington, March 15, 1975.

Secretary Kissinger asked me to pass the following message to you:

"I arrived in Damascus shortly after noon today to discover that Foreign Minister Khaddam, who was to have left for Havana for a preparatory meeting for the non-aligned summit conference to be held this July in Peru, had delayed his departure to be present for today's talks. Khaddam, incidentally, had spent most of the night meeting with Algerian Foreign Minister Bouteflika, who stopped in Damascus en route to Tehran where he will be present for the first meeting of the Iranian and Iraqi Foreign Ministers following the recent agreement between their two countries. According to Khaddam, Bouteflika has pledged full political, economic and military support to Syria. It is clear that the Syrians continue their efforts to line up support against a separate Egyptian-Israeli agreement that, they fear, would deal them out of the peacemaking process.

"In a two-hour meeting with President Asad, Khaddam, Deputy Prime Minister Haydar and Air Force Chief (and Deputy Defense Minister) General Jamil, followed by more than two hours alone with Asad,[2] my principal effort was directed at allaying Asad's suspicion and fear of a separate Egyptian agreement. I again reviewed the reasons why we cannot negotiate simultaneous Egyptian and Syrian agreements, stressed that success in the present negotiations would make a better atmosphere for an effort on the Syrian side, and reassured Asad that we would be prepared to make a major effort for Syria once a Sinai agreement is achieved. I also reviewed for Asad why we cannot now establish political contact with the Palestinians, to whose cause he is more genuinely devoted than most other Arab leaders, but told him we would receive any messages the Palestinians may pass through him.

"As a result of my last visit to Jerusalem and a private talk I had with Rabin,[3] I was able to tell Asad that, for the first time, I think there is beginning to be some serious thought given in Israel for the need for

---

[1] Source: Ford Library, National Security Adviser, Kissinger Reports on USSR, China, and Middle East, Box 3, March 7–March 22, 1975, Volume 1.1 (10), Kissinger's Trip. Secret; Sensitive; Exclusively Eyes Only.

[2] A memorandum of conversation of the meeting between Asad and Kissinger, which took place on March 15 in Damascus, is ibid., Volume 1.1 (9), Kissinger's Trip.

[3] See Document 146 and footnote 5 thereto.

movement also on the Syrian front. This was the principal new element I was able to inject into the conversation. I cannot yet judge whether it has been possible sufficiently to allay Asad's concerns that he will not in the end seek to undermine an Egyptian-Israeli agreement and to line up others, including Faisal, in support of such an effort. The atmosphere of today's meeting with Asad was considerably more relaxed than the last meeting,[4] however, and Asad made an impressively eloquent statement in front of his colleagues of why Syria for the first time has said publicly it wants peace—not for Israel's sake but for Syria's. It was in any event a good thing that I made this second visit to Damascus, and I have told Asad I am prepared to come again before returning to Washington to talk with him about how we might then proceed on the Syrian front. I urged that he be thinking about what Syria can do, in return for further Israeli withdrawal, to convince Israel things were moving in the direction of peace and to help foster a transition from a war to a peace psychosis in Israel which would be irreversible.

"I will spend tonight in Amman and, having just had word King Faisal cannot see me tomorrow due to a state visit by the President of Mali, will return directly to Jerusalem tomorrow (Sunday) afternoon and await word of what the Israeli Cabinet has authorized Rabin to say in response to President Sadat's latest ideas."

---

[4] See Document 141.

---

148. Memorandum From the President's Deputy Assistant for National Security Affairs (Scowcroft) to President Ford[1]

Washington, March 16, 1975.

Secretary Kissinger has sent you the following strategic analysis of our negotiating situation:

"After two rounds of intensive discussions in Aswan and Jerusalem and talks with President Asad, I want to share with you my perception of what lies ahead in broad strategic terms and ask your judgment on how to proceed.

---

[1] Source: Ford Library, National Security Adviser, Kissinger Reports on USSR, China, and Middle East, Box 3, March 7–March 22, 1975, Volume II (7), Kissinger's Trip. Secret; Sensitive; Exclusively Eyes Only.

"I have reported to you on where matters stand in my exchange with the Egyptians and Israelis on the basic elements of another Sinai agreement, some of which seem manageable and others of which (such as non-belligerency and the numbers and location of the Egyptian army east of the Suez Canal) are very difficult issues which may or may not be resolved. You know that Syria and the PLO seem determined to block another Sinai agreement because they believe they will be left out. Finally, it is clear that there has been a slow but steady build-up of military preparedness by Syria, Israel and Egypt which has added to the underlying tension in the area.

"Broadly speaking, we have two choices. First, to persist in trying to get an interim Egyptian-Israeli agreement. The second course would be to let events force upon us a return to the broader setting of a Geneva Conference at which an overall settlement would be addressed. The fact is that each of the above courses carry risks with them and neither is entirely satisfactory.

"The advantages to us in achieving the interim Egyptian-Israeli agreement remain impressive, and I have no intention of deviating from our current efforts as long as I judge there is a reasonable hope for success. Success would keep Sadat's moderate course to the fore; it would defuse the Sinai, it would make less likely that Syria will undertake a one-front war; it would limit Soviet opportunities to reassert itself, and the U.S. would remain the central element in future peacemaking efforts. In short, success would improve the situation in the area and maintain our influence, but we must bear in mind that it is unlikely to usher in a period of calm in the area. Differences of interpretation, for example, are inevitable with one side seeing it as a purely military disengagement agreement and the other as primarily a political agreement. Other parts of the Arab world, led by Syria which historically has played the spoiler role in the Mideast, could substantially unite against us, seeing it as a move to split the Arabs. Some form of renewed military action (the most likely Arab strategy is a protracted war of attrition against Israel) or economic action against the U.S. cannot be precluded as a possibility, though it is less likely.

"The way to avoid this is to find some way to assure Asad he will be brought into the negotiating picture. The Israelis will take some strong convincing, and I have begun to lay the groundwork with Rabin—but I am not optimistic on that score. Sadat has been strongly urging this, as has Faisal. But Syrian suspicion is so strong, and Israeli opposition to giving up anything more on the Golan so great, that a stalemate is likely to result. This is why Asad has refused to accept repeated assurances that we will make a major effort for Syria as the next step after Egypt. However, he might relax his opposition to my present efforts, easing the way for rapid conclusion of a Sinai agreement, if we could find a credible way to guarantee him that a Syrian-Israeli negotiation would start (either at Geneva or with the U.S. as a middleman-catalyst) before the implementation phase of any Egypt–Israel agreement begins. But our difficulties in Israel will be monumental requiring great Presidential pressure.

"Another approach, if we judge the resistance to a separate Sinai agreement is too great, would be to suspend the present Sinai effort by using the daily stalemates as an excuse and go to Geneva to discuss an overall settlement. This would not be unpopular in Israel; it would probably buy us some time with Syria; it could be portrayed as a shift to Geneva in deference to strong Arab views against a separate Egyptian-Israeli agreement; and it might help Syria support renewal of the mandate of the UN force. But it would badly strain our relations with Egypt; it would not be long at Geneva before we would be confronted with the Arabs and the USSR on one side and a recalcitrant Israel on the other over such questions as PLO participation and proposals for total Israeli withdrawal from all occupied territory. Such developments would contribute to further radicalization in the area, and would likely bring the area soon to a renewal of hostilities in circumstances of greater Arab unity than we have ever seen before.

"We face a difficult situation. Success in the current negotiation will buy us more time provided we can find some way to engage Syria, but it will not bring the many years of tranquility as the Israelis hope. On the other hand, failure on our part and the likely frustration of Geneva could bring the area to the brink of reality of another war. Nevertheless, my overall conclusion is that a shift to Geneva is not one we should embark upon voluntarily as long as we have a chance to get an interim Egyptian-Israeli agreement which still best serves our interest, despite the risks. If Geneva is forced upon us as a result of our inability to succeed in the present negotiation, we would have to think in terms of bold overall peace plans at the conference to protect our interests and to discourage resort to war. But this is another chapter.

"I would appreciate your direction.

"Warm regards."

149. Memorandum From the President's Deputy Assistant for National Security Affairs (Scowcroft) to President Ford[1]

Washington, March 18, 1975.

Secretary Kissinger asked that I pass you the following report . . .

"The negotiation has reached a critical stage with the strong possibility that the talks could fail in the next 48 hours. I met with President Sadat for about two hours this evening,[2] and I outlined the position which the Israelis authorized me to convey to him in as positive light as possible. I stressed that Rabin wanted an agreement, but faced an extremely difficult domestic situation.

"I stressed also that if Rabin was to get a proposal calling for Israeli withdrawal out of the passes and oil fields through the Knesset, he had to get something substantial in return on the political side. I reported again Israeli insistence for a formulation which the Israelis had given me which reads as follows:

Quote: Egypt and Israel hereby undertake in the relations between themselves not to resort to the use of force and to resolve all disputes between them by negotiations and other peaceful means.
They will refrain from permitting, encouraging, assisting, or participating in any military, paramilitary or hostile actions, from any warlike or hostile acts and any other form of warfare or hostile activity against the other party anywhere. Unquote.

"Sadat's reaction was very much as I expected. He was calm, sober, and determined. He felt the Israeli formulation was an insult in the context of a partial withdrawal, and expressed deep disappointment. Sadat said that the Israeli proposal went beyond nonbelligerency, forcing him to make peace while his territory was occupied. He said he agreed not to use force but if he went further he would be finished. After further discussion and a quiet hour with him alone, I was able to get him to agree to review his own position, and to provide me with something more to permit me to make a last ditch effort with Is-

---

[1] Source: Ford Library, National Security Adviser, Kissinger Reports on USSR, China, and Middle East, Box 3, March 7–March 22, 1975, Volume II (3), Kissinger's Trip. Secret; Sensitive. Sent for information.

[2] The memorandum of conversation of the meeting, which took place on March 17 in Aswan, is ibid., Volume II (2), Kissinger's Trip. According to the annotated chronology of the March meetings, this meeting took place from 7 until 8:45 p.m. (Ibid., Volume 1.1 (1), Kissinger's Trip) The meeting with Sadat was preceded by two meetings between the Israeli negotiating team and Kissinger. The first of these two meetings took place on March 16 from 6:07 until 10:07 p.m. at the Prime Minister's office in Jerusalem. (Memorandum of conversation, March 16; ibid., Volume II (7), Kissinger's Trip) The second meeting took place on March 17 from 10:15 until 11:30 a.m. at the Prime Minister's office in Jerusalem. (Ibid., Volume II (2), Kissinger's Trip)

rael upon my return tomorrow. He agreed to provide me with some additional proposals as a final Egyptian position. He said no matter what happens in the negotiation, it is not their intention to impair U.S.-Egyptian relations. I believe he means this, but I doubt that he will be able to sustain such a position over a period of time if our efforts fail. He will be violently attacked by the radical Arabs and the Soviet Union.

"About an hour after I completed my meeting with Sadat,[3] I received an urgent call to meet with Fahmi and General Gamasy. Fahmi said President Sadat had reacted very badly to what I had brought back from Israel, that Israel was demanding more than Sadat could give. Fahmi expressed great concern that tomorrow after his meeting with me, Sadat would say something publicly which would take him on an irrevocable course. He urged me to talk to Sadat to discourage such a statement in order to allow time for one more effort with Israel. During the course of this meeting, Fahmi showed me some new Egyptian positions which he is going to recommend to President Sadat tomorrow—all of which are helpful, and go further than any previous Arab position. They are prepared to declare:

(A) That the agreement is a major step towards peace,
(B) To renounce the use of force unconditionally,
(C) To have the agreement last in effect indefinitely ('unless superseded by another agreement'),
(D) To extend UNEF automatically every year.

"In addition they are willing to lift the boycott selectively. But it is practically certain that Israel will refuse on the ground that it wants a legal statement of nonbelligerency and a formal permanent status of UNEF. This Sadat could not do if he wanted. It would mean that he would make peace while Israel is still 100 miles inside Egyptian territory; that he would publicly separate from joint Arab projects like the boycott. Sadat is conceding more than I ever thought possible, but if he goes beyond a certain point he will be destroyed. Sadat is operating within certain political limits.

"I intend to make one more all-out effort tomorrow night with the Israeli negotiating team but with little hope of success. In this connection, you should know since last July we have made it endlessly clear to Allon, Peres, and Rabin on more than a dozen occasions that a formal statement of nonbelligerency is politically impossible. The Israelis heard this during the Allon talks in Washington in July, December, and January; they were told this during the missions in October and November; it was reiterated during the negotiations which I undertook a few weeks ago at their behest to help prepare the cabinet to move

---

[3] Not found.

towards the necessary decisions. I regret to say that either by neglect or design the Israeli government strongly encouraged us to engage our full prestige in this exercise and led us to believe that a formula less than nonbelligerency would be acceptable to Israel. It was on this assumption that my latest mission was undertaken. Yet I have discovered that Rabin, as well as Peres and Allon and the entire cabinet are strongly committed, for internal political reasons, to getting nonbelligerency from Egypt.

"The impact on our international situation could not be more serious. From the Shah to Western Europe, from the Soviet Union to Japan it will be hard to explain why the United States failed to move a country of less than three million totally dependent on it in the face of Egyptian proposals which will seem extremely generous to them. It will be considered a sign of U.S. decline and impotence compounding events in Cambodia, South Vietnam, Turkey, and Portugal. Sooner or later a multiplier effect will set in.

"My plan for Tuesday[4] evening's meeting with the Israelis is to try once again to make clear to them the most serious consequences which would result from failure. I intend to make the following points, subject to your approval. Taking as strong a line as I believe will be necessary is likely to have domestic repercussions and I cannot proceed without your approval. But the repercussions of failing for our interests, as well as Israel's, are too great not to do so. The key points I propose to include are as follows:

"A. I have reported fully to President Ford on the details of our last meeting and the position taken by the Israeli government.

"B. The consequences of failure are so serious for both Israel and the U.S. that it is essential that Israel reconsider its position in light of the latest concrete ideas which Egypt has asked me to convey to you. Failure to achieve a second-stage Egyptian-Israeli agreement, four months of arduous preparatory discussions in which the U.S. has been so directly involved, affects the vital interests of the U.S. and of Israel. In the Middle East, there is going to be a sharp swing away from the West and moderation, with radicalism and the USSR the only beneficiaries. The hopeful shift towards peace, even in Syria, will be lost. This will touch such countries as Saudi Arabia. Western Europe, to protect its position in the Arab world, will dissociate from us. Iran will accelerate its own cause. The Soviet Union will reemerge in an increasingly strong position. There will be a very great risk of a costly war of attrition between Israel and its Arab neighbors. I am convinced, after my talks in Syria, Egypt, and Jordan that this is the case.

---

[4] March 18.

"C. Failure of these negotiations will also have an adverse influence going well beyond the Middle East. The economic repercussions for the West could be disastrous, as well as the ensuing political shifts in Western Europe. We are being asked to (garbled) a stalemate threatening our interests in all parts of the world.

"D. All of this is the result because Israel either accidentally or deliberately misled the U.S. and even the moderate Arab states.

"E. Israel's inability to be more responsive to achieve a successful negotiation cannot but have far-reaching repercussions in the U.S. Failure of these negotiations will require an overall reassessment of the policies of the U.S. that have brought us to this point.

"F. I have been asked to make these points with the full authority and approval of President Ford.

"I would appreciate your response by NLT 1100 March 18. If it could include a sentence or two of support that could be read to the cabinet, it would help."

Warm Regards.

150. Telegram From the President's Deputy Assistant for National Security Affairs (Scowcroft) to Secretary of State Kissinger[1]

Washington, March 18, 1975, 1412Z.

Tohak 133/WH 50487. 1. The President has read your latest report.[2] He agrees with every word and would like you to impress upon the Prime Minister and the Cabinet that you are speaking with his full authority and total support. The President is totally and completely behind your current efforts and the strategy which they represent and feels deeply that these efforts have the overwhelming support of the American people.

2. The President also said that we cannot be in a position to isolate ourselves from the rest of the world simply in order to stand behind the intransigence of Israel. He was not specific as to whether or not that particular comment was for attribution. I leave it to your judgement.

---

[1] Source: Library of Congress, Manuscript Division, Kissinger Papers, CL 194, Geopolitical File, Middle East, Peace Negotiations, Shuttle Diplomacy, Chronological File, February–April 1975. Secret; Sensitive.

[2] See Document 149.

3. The President, as always, says that you should speak for him in whatever terms you feel are required for the circumstances at hand.

4. The warmest best wishes from us both in your efforts.

---

151. Memorandum From the President's Deputy Assistant for National Security Affairs (Scowcroft) to President Ford[1]

Washington, March 18, 1975.

Secretary Kissinger asked me to pass the following message to you:

"I completed a two-hour meeting this morning with President Sadat[2] at which he presented me with further Egyptian modifications of their position in order to make a final try with the Israelis. I will now meet with the Israelis this evening underscoring that Sadat, in my judgment, has carried the political concessions, in return for withdrawal, as far as he is able.

"He has committed himself to refrain from the use of force which every man in the street will interpret more or less synonymously as no different than a non-belligerency pledge. He has agreed to renew the UN force mandate annually and has given us a formula which, for all practical purposes, amounts to an indefinite commitment. He has linked the agreement to no other agreement, and therefore, meets the point made by the Israelis that the agreement must stand on its own feet. And finally, by agreeing that the agreement will remain in effect until it is superseded by another agreement, it meets the key Israeli point that it is open-ended.

"The meeting was somber. Sadat said all of this more in sorrow than in anger, repeating often that he was very disappointed in the Israeli reaction, and underscoring that he has lost faith that Israel can be worked with as a peace partner in the future. Time and again, however, as I previously reported to you, he stressed that he would not permit failure of this agreement to affect our relations adversely. I believe this

---

[1] Source: Ford Library, National Security Adviser, Kissinger Reports on USSR, China, and Middle East, Box 3, March 7–March 22, 1975, Volume II (3), Kissinger's Trip. Secret; Sensitive; Exclusively Eyes Only. Ford initialed the memorandum.

[2] A memorandum of conversation of the meeting between Sadat and Kissinger, which took place on March 18 in Aswan, is ibid. According to the annotated chronology of the March meetings, the meeting took place from 11:45 a.m. until 2:30 p.m. (Ibid., Volume 1.1 (1), Kissinger's Trip)

to be his intention, but henceforth events will dictate positions. And on a whole series of issues he will have to side with the radical Arabs. He had a number of laudatory things to say about you which I will wish to report to you personally upon my return.

"I deeply appreciate your prompt response to my message[3] and the go ahead which you have given me in presenting our case strongly and firmly to the Israelis tonight."

[3] See Documents 149 and 150.

152. Memorandum From the President's Deputy Assistant for National Security Affairs (Scowcroft) to President Ford[1]

Washington, March 19, 1975.

Secretary Kissinger asked that I pass you the following report ...

"I met for three hours with Rabin and his negotiating team this evening,[2] presenting in detail the position conveyed to me by Sadat which I described in my last message to you.[3] I gave them my judgment that while some drafting modifications are possible, what Sadat has now offered is the maximum he will be able to do. I also reviewed at some length the reasons why I thought Israel would face a much more dangerous situation if it did not reach an agreement along the lines of the present position, unsatisfactory as it is from Israel's point of view, than if it made an agreement now. I also reminded the Israelis that I have told them consistently since last July that an Egyptian renunciation of belligerency was unachievable in the context of the kind of Israeli withdrawal we are talking about.

"The Israeli team was clearly both disappointed and sobered by what I had to tell them. The most critical was Peres, who pressed very hard the view that, if Israel accepted what Sadat has offered as a basis

[1] Source: Ford Library, National Security Adviser, Kissinger Reports on USSR, China, and Middle East, Box 4, March 7–March 22, 1975, Volume II (5), Kissinger's Trip. Secret; Sensitive. Sent for information.

[2] A memorandum of conversation of the meeting between the Israeli negotiating team and Kissinger, which took place on March 18 from 7:10 until 9:45 p.m. at the Prime Minister's office in Jerusalem, is ibid., Box 3, March 7–22, 1975, Volume II (4), Kissinger's Trip.

[3] See Document 151.

for an agreement, it would be very shortly faced with renewed pressures on all fronts in a less favorable strategic position than it enjoys today. I acknowledged that, with such an agreement, Israel's problems would not be over but gave my judgment that both Israel and the United States would face those problems from a much stronger position than would be the case if the present negotiations failed.

"Following this group meeting, I met alone with Rabin.[4] He is disposed to try to bring the government around to negotiating on the basis of the position I presented tonight, although at the moment he seems to be the only member of the Israeli team prepared to do so. In the circumstances, I concluded that the strong language you authorized me to use was not at this time necessary. Rabin and his colleagues will consider tonight what they can do, and we have agreed to meet early tomorrow morning and again tomorrow evening. In between, I will go to Riyadh for an audience with King Faysal."

Warm Regards

---

[4] No memorandum of conversation has been found.

---

153. Memorandum From the President's Deputy Assistant for National Security Affairs (Scowcroft) to President Ford[1]

Washington, March 20, 1975.

Secretary Kissinger asked me to provide you with the following report of his latest meeting with Prime Minister Rabin:

"Rabin communicated the result of ten hours of Cabinet deliberations yesterday[2] and presented us with a position which in our judgment is substantially unchanged and would lead to a suspension of the negotiations tomorrow. The formulation on no resort to force is what Sadat has already rejected; the withdrawal line would be cut through the middle rather than out of the passes; and they are still insisting on a

---

[1] Source: Ford Library, National Security Adviser, Kissinger Reports on USSR, China, and Middle East, Box 4, March 7–March 22, 1975, Volume II (6), Kissinger's Trip. Secret; Sensitive; Exclusively Eyes Only. A handwritten notation at the top of the page reads, "Pres. has seen."

[2] A memorandum of conversation of the meeting between the Israeli negotiating team and Kissinger, which took place on March 19 from 8:45 until 10:20 a.m. at the Prime Minister's Residence in Jerusalem, is ibid., Volume II (5), Kissinger's Trip.

five-year commitment that they will not be pressed to make any further withdrawals. After I informed the Israeli negotiating team that it was certain to be unacceptable to the Egyptians, Rabin said that he, too, had informed the Cabinet that it was "98 percent certain that Sadat would reject this latest proposal" and that the negotiations would be suspended.

"I then utilized the talking points that you authorized me to make two days ago,[3] pointing out the serious consequences that would ensue. I underscored that we believe the Cabinet position constituted a strategic Israeli decision to go to war in 1975, and to confront the U.S. I said a reassessment of American policy was now inevitable.

"Rabin had previously agreed to report my views to the Cabinet, and the Israeli Cabinet is now in an afternoon session. Rabin has acted extremely well, and he himself wants an agreement. He deeply appreciated the strong statement I made with your approval at this morning's meeting, and will use it to press for reconsideration of the Cabinet decision. He is not sanguine—nor am I—that there will be sufficient change in the Israeli position, particularly on the question of the line, to come up with a position that Sadat will find acceptable. We expect to meet with the negotiating team again later in the day, and I have therefore delayed my departure for Aswan."

---

[3] See Documents 149 and 150.

---

154. Memorandum From the President's Deputy Assistant for National Security Affairs (Scowcroft) to President Ford[1]

Washington, March 20, 1975.

Secretary Kissinger has asked that I provide you with the following report concerning the outcome of the Israeli Government's deliberations:

"The Israeli Government has just completed its deliberations, and we have been given the results by Rabin and his colleagues.[2] There

---

[1] Source: Ford Library, National Security Adviser, Kissinger Reports on USSR, China, and Middle East, Box 4, March 7–March 22, 1975, Volume II (7), Kissinger's Trip. Secret; Sensitive; Eyes Only. Ford initialed the memorandum.

[2] A memorandum of conversation of the meeting between the Israeli negotiating

were some modest modifications from the position that was conveyed to us this morning,[3] which essentially does not change the situation in any substantial way.

"I am now leaving for Aswan to meet later this evening with Sadat. The odds are very much against Sadat accepting what I am bringing with me, and since I feel it is inadequate, I will present the Israeli position without encouraging acceptance on the part of Sadat. I do not, of course, absolutely preclude that Sadat will decide that there is enough in it to continue the negotiations but I think this is unlikely. I will report to you later this evening after I complete my talks with Sadat."

---

team and Kissinger, which took place on March 20 from 5:30 until 6:45 p.m. at the Prime Minister's Office in Jerusalem, is ibid., Volume II (6), Kissinger's Trip.

[3] A memorandum of conversation of the meeting between the Israeli negotiating team and Kissinger, which took place on March 20 from 9:50 a.m. until 12:35 p.m. at the Prime Minister's office in Jerusalem, is ibid.

---

155. Memorandum From the President's Deputy Assistant for National Security Affairs (Scowcroft) to President Ford[1]

Washington, March 21, 1975.

Secretary Kissinger asked that I pass on to you the following report on his meeting with Sadat.

"I have just completed a two hour conversation with Sadat at which I presented the latest Israeli ideas.[2] As I expected, he was strongly insistent that he could not accept the line to be drawn through the middle of the passes and reiterated strongly that the Egyptian forward line must be at the western entrance of the passes while the Israeli line could be at the eastern entrance of the passes. In short, he insists on the principle that neither side will occupy the passes, but that rather they will be supervised by the UN force.

---

[1] Source: Ford Library, National Security Adviser, Kissinger Reports on USSR, China, and Middle East, Box 4, March 7–March 22, 1975, Volume II (7), Kissinger's Trip. Secret; Sensitive. Sent for information.

[2] A memorandum of conversation of the meeting between Sadat and Kissinger, which took place on March 20 in Aswan, is ibid. According to the annotated chronology of the March meetings, the meeting took place from 10 p.m. to midnight. (Ibid., Box 3, March 7–22, 1975, Volume 1.1 (1), Kissinger's Trip)

"As you know, with respect to the oil fields, the Israelis have indicated willingness to provide for an enclave in which presumably there would be some cooperative agreement worked out between Egypt and Israel. Under the Israeli proposal, the oil fields would be totally undefended and be surrounded by Israeli forces. Sadat's counter proposal as conveyed to us this evening would establish a broad United Nations zone in the area of the oil fields in which neither side would maintain armed forces and in which there would only be civilian and ordinary police under Egyptian administration. Moreover, the Egyptians will insist on an increase of the number of forces from the present 7,000 east of the canal, whereas the Israelis will want to maintain this limit.

"These are the key issues in the military aspect of the agreement and I remain very doubtful that these differences can be bridged. I have agreed at Sadat's urging to make a further substantial effort with the Israelis, while reiterating my judgment to him that it is unlikely that the Israelis will agree to the latest proposal on the military aspect of the problem. In this connection, I noted that Gamasy was very happy with Sadat when the latter suggested a UN zone around the oil fields, rather than drawing the line so that there would be Egyptian forces there.

"Another important concession which Sadat made this evening is that he is willing to give me an oral assurance which I may transmit to the Israelis that in the event Syria attacks Israel, and this is confirmed by the UN observers, he would not attack Israel.

"I have sent word to Rabin that I will wish to meet with the negotiating team in the early afternoon on Friday[3] and that I have agreed to stay through next Sunday in order to give him the opportunity to call another Cabinet meeting on the latest Egyptian ideas.

"The basic problem remains that Israel is dealing with this issue largely as a matter of domestic politics. They have nailed themselves to propositions they could not fulfill and are jeopardizing our entire position in the Middle East in the pursuit of entirely marginal points."

---

[3] March 21.

156. Letter From President Ford to Israeli Prime Minister Rabin[1]

Washington, March 21, 1975.

Dear Mr. Prime Minister:

Secretary Kissinger has just reported on the imminent suspension of his mission[2] whose objective was to achieve an interim second-stage agreement between Egypt and Israel.

I am writing to convey my deep disappointment over the position taken by Israel during the course of the negotiations. You know from our conversations, as well as my conversations with the Foreign Minister, the importance I have attached to the success of the efforts of the United States to achieve constructive results, as well as the framework that seemed reasonable to me. Secretary Kissinger's mission, which your government strongly encouraged, involved the vital interests of the United States in the area. The failure to achieve an agreement is bound to have far-reaching effects in the area and on our relations.

I have directed an immediate reassessment of U.S. policy in the area, including our relations with Israel, with a view to assuring that the overall interests of America in the Middle East and globally will be protected.

You will be informed of our decisions.[3]

Sincerely,

Gerald R. Ford

---

[1] Source: Library of Congress, Manuscript Division, Kissinger Papers, CL 157, Geopolitical File, Israel, March 1975. Secret.

[2] See Document 155.

[3] Rabin replied to Ford's letter on March 30, writing that he shared Ford's "deep disappointment over the failure of the negotiations," but that Egypt's desire to make an agreement of "an essentially military character" instead of a political agreement that would end the state of war between Egypt and Israel made it impossible for Israel to conclude an agreement. Rabin argued that Israel had exhausted "every possible avenue for a positive outcome." (Library of Congress, Manuscript Division, Kissinger Papers, TS–29, February 12–December 22, 1975)

157. Memorandum From the President's Deputy Assistant for National Security Affairs (Scowcroft) to President Ford[1]

Washington, March 22, 1975.

Secretary Kissinger asked that I pass you the following report.

"1. The Israeli cabinet completed five hours of discussion today, and we were informed later this evening by Rabin and his colleagues that the cabinet made no new modifications in the Israeli position and reaffirmed the position previously conveyed to us.[2]

2. Your letter arrived before the end of the cabinet meeting,[3] and we understand it was read to the entire cabinet. From my two hours of discussions alone with Rabin, Allon and Peres, it was clear that the letter had shaken them and all three seemed to be beginning to realize the consequences of Israeli intransigence. As a result, Rabin asked that no suspension of the talks be announced, and that they will think matters over tomorrow. We will reconvene again at 6:00 P.M. Israeli time Saturday.[4]

3. My impression continues to be that the three key members of the negotiating team want an agreement, particularly in the aftermath of your letter, but they do not seem to know how to get out of the hole domestically they have dug for themselves. Sadat has given them two options: Egyptian forces would be in the western part of the passes while Israeli forces would be in the eastern part of the passes; or alternatively, the forces of neither side being in the passes with the UN taking it over in its entirety. Israel finds both these proposals unacceptable and has offered a smaller withdrawal largely because they have nailed themselves to such a position domestically. As to the oil fields, Israel is willing to give Egypt a small enclave within Israeli controlled territory. Sadat is equally insistent that the area along the Gulf of Suez, including the Abu Rudeis oil fields, should be a UN buffer zone in which neither side's forces are located. He feels he cannot have Egyptians cross Israeli territory to get to the oil fields. We have not been able to bridge the gap, and I do not expect the Israelis to come up with anything significantly

---

[1] Source: Ford Library, National Security Adviser, Kissinger Reports on USSR, China, and Middle East, Box 4, March 7–March 22, 1975, Volume II (8), Kissinger's Trip. Secret; Sensitive. Ford initialed the memorandum.

[2] A memorandum of conversation of the meeting between the Israeli negotiating team and Kissinger, which took place on March 21 from 10:10 p.m. until 12:10 a.m. at the Prime Minister's office in Jerusalem, is ibid. There is also a memorandum of conversation of a previous meeting that afternoon from 1:45 until 4 p.m. (Ibid., Volume II (7), Kissinger's Trip)

[3] Document 156.

[4] March 22.

new tomorrow night. In the meantime, I am canvassing Sadat again to see whether he has any new suggestions which might help eliminate the deadlock. The tragedy is that Israel knows it must have an agreement and yet is paralyzed by its domestic politics. We may be witnessing the twilight of democracy."

158. Memorandum of Conversation[1]

Jerusalem, March 22, 1975, 6:35–8:15 p.m.

PARTICIPANTS

Yitzhak Rabin, Prime Minister of Israel
Yigal Allon, Deputy Prime Minister and Minister of Foreign Affairs
Shimon Peres, Minister of Defense
Simcha Dinitz, Ambassador to the United States
Lt. Gen. Mordechai Gur, Chief of Staff
Mordechai Gazit, Director General, Prime Minister's Office
Avraham Kidron, Director General, Ministry of Foreign Affairs

Dr. Henry A. Kissinger, Secretary of State and Assistant to the President for National Security Affairs
Amb. Kenneth Keating, U.S. Ambassador to Israel
Joseph J. Sisco, Under Secretary of State for Political Affairs
Alfred L. Atherton, Jr., Assistant Secretary of State for Near Eastern and South Asian Affairs
Harold H. Saunders, Deputy Assistant Secretary of State for Near Eastern and South Asian Affairs
Robert B. Oakley, NSC Staff
Peter W. Rodman, NSC Staff

Rabin: Shimon and I met with the opposition leaders in Tel Aviv this morning.

Do you have anything new from Egypt?

Kissinger: Yes. I sent two messages last night, one about military matters and one about the status of the negotiation. I asked if there were any aspects of the Egyptian position that had not yet been revealed. I referred specifically to retaining an early warning station in

---

[1] Source: Ford Library, National Security Adviser, Kissinger Reports on USSR, China, and Middle East, Box 4, March 7–March 22, 1975, Volume II (9), Kissinger's Trip. Secret. The meeting was held in the Prime Minister's office. Brackets are in the original. The Israeli negotiating team and Kissinger met again from 10:35 p.m. until 12:05 a.m. at the Prime Minister's office in Jerusalem. Their discussion focused on the suspension of the negotiations. (Memorandum of conversation, March 22; ibid.)

the buffer zone and giving Egypt one, in order to get the Israeli line back. Before it was inside the Israeli line; now it would be in the buffer zone. We have received the following reply from Fahmy. [He reads from Aswan 273]:[2]

"There is no change in our position as you knew it before your departure.

"We cannot accept a monitoring station so far as Israel alone is concerned, or even on a reciprocal basis.

"There is no necessity to leave Joe Sisco because if you do not succeed this time, there will be no chance for a future success, and therefore we cannot agree to a suspension.

"The concrete result of a failure will have a tremendous and diversified impact in the Arab world and other circles. And it could not be a mere suspension but will in fact be, as the President and I told you before, an irrevocable and fatal blow to the step-by-step process.

"The new course will then have to be, as you know, the convening of Geneva. The President will have no problem to declare the failure of the step-by-step process and that we will try the second alternative, which is Geneva.

"I am sure you will understand that once there is a failure this time, we will not be bound by any undertakings we have already given thus far during these talks and that our position remains as defined by us and by the Arab world and in particular its latest summit meeting in Rabat.[3]

"You are certainly welcome to come back to Aswan if you feel that you are able to gain progress. If not, in case of your decision to go back to Washington, the President still prefers that in that case you should proceed directly from Tel Aviv to Washington."

Ambassador Eilts talked to Fahmy and expressed concern at the seemingly negative cast of the above. Fahmy said he was writing this at the personal instructions of the President.

"Fahmy expects that the Foreign Ministers' meeting in Cairo will focus on the talks. He also notes that unless there is a marked change in the next 24 hours, the President will probably have to make his long-deferred talk to the People's Assembly in two or three days' time to explain that Egypt has followed the step-by-step course as far as it seemed viable but that now Geneva is the only alternative."

"There is considerable gloom, frustration, and bitterness among the Egyptians. They profess inability to understand how your mission

---

[2] Dated March 22. (National Archives, RG 59, Central Foreign Policy Files, P850014–1602)

[3] See Document 112.

could have been undertaken without a clearer idea about the correlation between the Israeli demands and offers."

This is self-explanatory, but I will add only one additional point.

There is no question that for whatever reason, on the American side there is a conviction similar to what the Egyptians said. We would not have conducted ourselves for the last seven months in the way we did if we knew this would be the final Israeli position. Particularly after Rabat. This accounts for the reaction. But aside from this are the realities that will follow.

None of this was a matter of pressure on Israel. Some of this can be worked out in a matter of the next weeks. But there is a concern about the reality that will now descend upon us. There was a conviction that this process, while it was in the United States' interest, was also in Israel's interest—splitting all the Arabs, keeping the Soviets out, keeping the Europeans and Japanese quiescent—and that this in itself was a quid pro quo for Israel, and for this reason we thought an agreement would be reached.

So whatever goodwill will be lost, we will make an effort to overcome. The real danger is that with the best will in the world, we will now be forced into a series of decisions that will face the U.S. with increasingly difficult dilemmas. This is the reality. This is where the pressure came from. Mr. Prime Minister, if you assigned a team of intelligent and serious people to examine from our point of view the decisions that will now have to be made, you would see the dilemmas we face. It is not possible for a superpower to separate itself totally from the Arab world, to separate ourselves totally from the West, to separate ourselves totally from the Soviet Union.

So let us part on good terms. We will keep in close contact with you. I wanted to say this ahead of time. There will be no pressure from us. We are not forcing Israel to do anything. The pressure we see is inherent in the situation—that we attempted to protect you from, that we attempted to manage. And you will, if you review the record, admit that nothing was done that was not coordinated with you. There will now be enormous pressures to separate us, instead of enabling us to stay together and enabling the U.S. to protect Israel's position.

The decisions to be taken now will be the real tests. This is the only pressure you will feel. All the rest will be worked out one way or another.

Rabin: We all wanted the process to proceed in such a way as to save our interests and your interests. We agreed to give up the oil and we explained the importance of the passes. We see as part of the process for the future the need for practical arrangements by Egypt. We thought the wording—and that there will not be cooperation in supervising and patrols of the demilitarized zone, and that there will be no easing of boycott, and what about other issues that were not discussed—To give the passes and the oil field for this, when they are our best card in the process, is unexpected. This is what caused the misunderstanding.

Our position can be changed but only slightly. The road in the Israeli zone into a UN checkpoint; a move with the line in the North. But there is an enclave for the oil, and our line in the passes. Where do the Egyptians move to, with a new line?

The refusal of the monitoring station is a sign.

Allon: We do need a talk about how the communications broke down. I have checked the minutes of the previous talks, and from what I could read, there was no reason for misunderstanding about our position. And I was disturbed by the language from my counterpart; there seems to be an ultimatum from Fahmy. It sounds like we misunderstood the intentions of the Egyptians. The Egyptian insistence on removing the monitoring installation, even from the buffer zone, serves as a warning that even if we have an agreement, we will have another war or will be subjected to such strong pressures very soon. They may think they can pressure the U.S. to get Israel out of the Sinai for nothing. We agree that the process is worth retaining, but for almost no element of nonbelligerency? We assumed that whatever area we evacuated would be controlled by the UN; we were even willing to give Egypt the buffer zone. They don't want the oil even though their people are starving. We have all this information about their military build-up. And we get this ultimatum to the Secretary of State from Fahmy.

And we wanted an agreement. We thought it would be good for Egypt. We thought it would be good for the U.S. I am sorry to see one of my best friends fail.

Kissinger: That is irrelevant.

Allon: Would it be advisable to go to Aswan to make the announcement?

Kissinger: I cannot go.

Allon: Do they know we are willing to give them free access on the road to the enclave?

Kissinger: I don't want to give little concessions until we get an agreement on the basic points—the passes.

Allon: Let us use only the encouraging sentence in the communiqué of the suspension[4]—that you are going to keep in touch with the

---

[4] Late in the evening of March 22, both the United States and Israel released statements on the suspension of the negotiations. See the *New York Times*, March 23, 1975, p. 18.

parties. After the Passover you can take a new initiative—in a different way.

Kissinger: It is totally out of the question. The U.S. will not again engage—nor will it be able to engage—in bilateral diplomacy again.

Peres: I don't see much reason to go into the past. The dilemma Israel faces is about the future, and we cannot separate from our own shadow.

There were four issues on which the talks concentrated: duration, the passes, the oil, and nonbelligerency. Israel moved on all four, and Egypt did not move at all. We agree that the pressure is inherent in the situation—and it will come again with Syria. So what sort of Israel will face this uncompromising Arab mood? We were more hopeful about the Egyptian mood at the beginning. No nation can take this pressure. We have to choose between confrontation and movement to peace, but we are not met by conciliation on the part of Egypt.

I hope that the friendship of the U.S. and Israel will overcome this test. We and the team tried to bridge the unbridgeable.

Kissinger: In fairness I believe I cannot let pass the proposition that Egypt made no concessions. It is simply not correct. The correct statement may be that both sides made the maximum concessions they were capable of making, and that it wasn't enough. But it is not a trivial matter for an Arab state for the first time to say that there will be no recourse to the use or threat of force; that all conflicts henceforth between you will be settled by peaceful means; that the agreement is open-ended and will last until it is superseded by another agreement; together with an assurance to the United States that if Syria attacks Israel, Egypt will not join; and on duration we could have worked it out with the UNEF to give an assurance that it will be automatically extended indefinitely. So that is the wrong view. I believe the issue has been wrongly defined from the beginning. And I of course would say in Egypt that it would be incorrect to say that you did not make concessions. You made significant concessions.

Incidentally, another concession that is not insignificant is the assurance that would be given to the U.S. that no matter what happened at Geneva, it would not affect the agreement. If nothing that is done at Geneva will affect the agreement, what could break the agreement?

And it would enormously strengthen your position in public opinion in America.

Allon: Their answer on the early warning system is a new element.

Kissinger: They believe it is their territory. This is the problem, not necessarily that they are planning a surprise attack. You could put up another early warning station. It is expensive to replace; it is reasonable to ask—but their refusal is not necessarily evidence of an intention to attack.

Gur: What about the idea of reducing forces on both sides?

Kissinger: I made the point to them—about deployment which gave both sides assurance against a surprise attack. They agree to discuss that—they liked the idea—they agreed to this. I told Sadat that a reduction of the standing army would be reciprocated by a thinning out of Israeli forces or a reduction of the term of service. He said this could be considered. He did not accept it but he did not reject it. The early warning site has been rejected consistently. I put it to him in the context of preventing a surprise attack, that a reduction in the numbers in the standing army in Egypt and a reduction in military service in Israel would mean movement toward peace.

Sisco: I took it up independently with Gamasy, who said he was open-minded about this.

Rabin: So how do you see it?

Kissinger: There has been no change in the Israeli position in the past 24 hours?

Rabin: In the passes and the line, no change. North from the passes and in the road to Abu Rudeis, we are willing to make some change. The opposition leaders believe we are selling out the country. They said that if an agreement like this with Egypt is reached, they will attack us.

Allon: May I ask a question? Is it conceivable that if we agreed that our men in the zone would remain for 5–6 years only?

Rabin: Let's be realistic. They don't think of keeping the present position for 5 years—one or two years maybe.

Kissinger: If we had achieved success, in an atmosphere of cooperation there would have been a real turning toward peace, and we could have achieved a de facto situation which, with skill, would last for four years. I thought certainly it would last more than two—but he can't publicly admit it will last 5 years.

Peres: You once said you could predict only two years.

Kissinger: I did not say two years with no pressure. He will of course make his demands at Geneva. But the American public would have treated an attack on Israel under a non-recourse to force provision as aggression, and would have been behind Israel all the way.

Peres: All our wars in the area—four of them—have been due to the Sinai.

Kissinger: In May you said all the wars were the result of Syria! At this very table I heard it.

Peres: If we could have arranged that Sinai be potential for a period of calm and not for force, could it be theoretically possible one day to put Sinai under Egyptian sovereignty and public administration and only police—and no armies? Can we do this?

Kissinger: It is essential that we have no illusions about the significance of this sequence of events. The Arab leader who banked on the United States is discredited; the Arab leader who attempted to separate himself from the others has failed. We will now see a united Arab front. We will see a greater emphasis on the Palestinians. There will be no propositions about the Sinai separated from propositions about the Golan. The step-by-step process has been throttled, first for Jordan and now for Egypt. The Soviets will step into the area at least as the equals of the United States. So it is senseless to talk about ideas that the United States could arrange. We are losing control over events in the Middle East for the first time since 1969. That is a fact, and we had better adjust ourselves to the reality.

The European Community will now accelerate its relationship with the Arabs.

If the 1971 interim agreement[5] had succeeded, there would have been no war in October 1973. It is the same process here. We are losing control over events in the Middle East. Ideas we might have been able to work out are dead. We have no strategy for the situation ahead. Our past strategy was worked out and agreed to between the U.S. and Israel. Now I don't know what we are going to do.

Events will impose on us a necessity—against our will—which will inevitably lead to a certain dissociation. We will be forced to maneuver with the Soviet Union, with the Arabs, with the Europeans, so as not to be totally isolated. All our strategy which we devoted ourselves to for a year and a half is smashed. Let's not kid ourselves; we've failed. Sadat will say that his desire to have good relations with the U.S. will continue, but events will drive him.

The Prime Minister and I used to talk, when he was in Washington, about such ideas as sovereignty for the Sinai, in 1970. But a long, long period of turmoil will be ahead.

Sisco: It is another lost opportunity. And there is a good possibility there will be another war in the next year.

Allon: Why not start it up again in a few weeks?

Kissinger: Because Sadat has to explain why he did it to protect himself. Because I am no longer the figure who mesmerizes them in the Arab world, because in every area the United States is no longer a country that one has to take so seriously. If the U.S. acts with brutal decisiveness somewhere, in a test of strength, maybe we can again, but I would not count on it, given our domestic situation. And don't misun-

---

[5] See footnote 3, Document 9.

derstand: I am analyzing a situation with friends. One reason my colleagues and I are so exasperated is that we see a friend damaging himself, for reasons which will seem trivial five years from now, like Soviet soldiers across the Canal in 1971.

We should discuss the suspension scenario. We want two hours to notify Washington, and to get messages off to foreign governments, and to notify Aswan. When should we announce it—at 10:00 tonight?

Rabin: Make it 11:00. We want to notify the Cabinet.

Peres: What do we announce?

Rabin: That Dr. Kissinger announces the suspension of the talks.

Peres: We do not want to fight.

Kissinger: We leave Jerusalem at 10:00 tomorrow, and we leave Ben-Gurion at 11:00. We will read the following statement [he reads text of draft statement]:

"We have been seeking, in response to the desires of the parties, to help them achieve an interim agreement as a further step toward a peace settlement. We believe both sides have made a serious effort to reach a successful outcome. Unfortunately, the differences on a number of key issues have proved irreconcilable. We, therefore, believe a period of reassessment is needed so that all concerned can consider how best to proceed toward a just and lasting peace. Secretary Kissinger has accordingly informed the parties that he is returning to Washington to report to the President and the Congress on the present stage of the negotiations. He will remain in close touch with the parties and the co-chairman of the Geneva Conference during the period ahead."

Rabin: If you announce this way, I will have to follow and explain why to the Israeli people.

Kissinger: While I am in this area, I will have to disassociate myself.

Peres: President Ford's letter[6] is an occasion . . .

Rabin: The brutality of the formulation of President Ford's letter upset the Cabinet.

Kissinger: If an argument starts about the letter, it will not be in the interest of Israel or of the Jews in America.

Rabin: It is not a compliment to the Israelis that one can talk like that to Israelis.

Kissinger: I have made it clear to you how the U.S. must react to the objective undermining of our position.

I cannot believe it is in Israel's interest to tackle the President.

---

[6] Document 156.

Allon: Forget about the letter. The other branches of the Administration will put the blame on Israel and Egypt will get full credit.

Rabin: I ask now, what can we say? We have kept silent for two weeks. We must explain the problem. The Egyptians have explained their position all the way through.

Peres: Make it public after another meeting; then we will state our case. There will be no polemics tonight with Egypt or Israel.

Kissinger: Good. Let's suspend for two hours and meet again at 10:00—to discuss how we conduct ourselves in the weeks ahead. We should discuss where we go next. We will not criticize Israel; we will not engage in attacks on Egypt. We will be evenhanded. So to that extent there will be a dissociation. We will say both sides made a serious effort. We will not support either position. We will say both sides made a serious effort and failed. We will inform our Congress.

Rabin: We will meet again at 10:30. I will phone the Cabinet at 10:00.

[The meeting ended, and the group rose from the table.]

It is a Greek tragedy.

Kissinger: It is. That's what makes it worse—that each side, following the laws of its own nature, reaches an outcome that was perfectly foreseeable.

159. Memorandum of Conversation[1]

Washington, March 24, 1975.

PARTICIPANTS

President Ford
Dr. Henry A. Kissinger, Secretary of State and Assistant to the President for National Security Affairs
Lt. General Brent Scowcroft, Deputy Assistant to the President for National Security Affairs

Kissinger: To sacrifice peace for half of the passes—you told Allon the passes were now essential. At Vladivostok[2] you could have sold Geneva for a good price. If they had said this wouldn't work earlier, we could have made other arrangements.

President: We told them that all along.

Kissinger: Sadat is willing to say in several different ways there will be no use of force. He agreed to renewal of the UN force.

President: I am afraid if this gets out, Sadat would be in trouble.

Kissinger: All of my party is outraged at the Israelis. They have decided that to trade territory for assurance, is disastrous.

President: I think the letter shows strength and initiative. I'm not afraid of the letter at all.[3]

Kissinger: I think you should tell the leaders about the letter. Don't release a text, but explain it. The Israelis think they can use it against you.

[Dr. Kissinger then showed the President the chronology of how many times we had said that non-belligerency was impossible and the passes were essential.][4]

President: Your cables indicated that Rabin and Allon are okay.

Kissinger: I am no longer sure. Look at the record—Allon was here in July. Rabin was here in September and you told him progress was es-

---

[1] Source: Library of Congress, Manuscript Division, Kissinger Papers, CL 281, Presidential File, March 1975. Secret; Nodis. The meeting was held in the Oval Office at the White House. All brackets, with the exception of ones describing omitted material, are in the original. The original incorrectly indicates the time of the meeting as from 9:21 to 9:54 a.m., but clearly the discussion took place prior to the meeting with the congressional leadership (see Document 160). According to the President's Daily Diary, President Ford and Kissinger met at 7:58 a.m. in the Oval Office before proceeding to the Cabinet Room. (Ford Library, Staff Secretary's Office Files)

[2] See footnote 4, Document 123.

[3] Document 156. The contents of the letter were leaked in Jerusalem. (*New York Times*, March 24, 1975, p. 14)

[4] The chronology has not been found.

sential. Our fatal mistake was all the equipment we gave them. We did it to strengthen Rabin's position and as a gesture of support and good will.

Allon came over twice and you told him. All this time Sadat has stuck with us. Faisal said he didn't agree with separate settlements. They argue they couldn't get non-belligerency. Sadat said he couldn't do non-belligerency with 180 kilometers of his territory still in Israeli hands. But he gave all the military components of non-belligerency: Cargoes through the Canal, relaxation on the boycott. They got 90% of what they asked. Israel made no serious effort. They kept haggling over details but they showed no serious purposes.

They never showed us a map so we never knew what they meant by the middle of the passes.

[More discussion.]

On oil, Israel agreed first to leave it an Egyptian enclave surrounded by Israel. Sadat said no because it would force his people to go through Israeli control.

The effect on our policy in the Middle East is devastating. The radicals are vindicated; Sadat is jeopardized. He will either go radical or be left. Either way, Israel will say "we told you so."

President: What should we do? I haven't thought it through.

Kissinger: They are sure they can outbest you militarily. But we should say: The F–15 team can't come. Peres shouldn't come. Every Department should put Israeli activities at the bottom of the list. [*1 line not declassified*] I would instruct Schlesinger to slow the LGB and Lance.

President: How about an NSC meeting so I can tell everyone?

Kissinger: I am Jewish. How can I want this? I have never seen such cold-blooded playing with the American national interest. Every Arab was looking to us; we had moved the Soviet Union out of the Middle East; even Iraq was being moved. What they have done is destroy this.

President: What do they think they have gained?

Kissinger: It could be Rabin wanted to do this and couldn't get it through, but the treatment of this letter makes me wonder. They are leaking it so they want a confrontation. Why? Because they see this as a never-ending process—Syria coming next—so they would rather throw down the gauntlet now. They will play the Jackson game with the Soviet threat. If you don't give arms, you weaken an ally; if you give them arms, they get total freedom.

They think they can get from Congress what they want and by-pass you.

But I wouldn't take them on at the meeting. Everything gets right back to them. I could give a rundown without assessing the blame. If we put out facts, we are ahead. At the end, you should say the Middle East is heading towards an explosion and a risk of war and a confrontation, and you have under these circumstances to reassess our policy.

President: And I can mention the letter in this context.

Brent and I talked every day while you were there, and I have no hesitancy to bite the bullet.

Kissinger: This is terribly painful to me. First of all we have to go to Geneva. Second, we have to put forward a global plan, which will inevitably mean close to the '67 borders. Callaghan offered to make a joint effort on his own. Sadat will renew the UNEF only for three months. Asad will renew not at all or only in such a way that both of them expire at once. Sadat will open the Canal but will say it is too dangerous to transit. He will ask for resumption of Geneva. There we will face an immediate and massive problem. The PLO will be the first issue raised and Israel will try to tie us up for months. The Soviet Union will put forth the '67 borders. We can put out ideas about special zones, and so on, but there is no need to do that immediately.

President: We must do that?

Kissinger: We are stopped on the step-by-step. I think there is a high chance of a war before 1976. Israel would rather have a war before 1977.

President: Rabin wasn't as forthcoming?

Kissinger: They weren't forthcoming at all. They couldn't have been under any illusion as to what was needed. If they couldn't give it, they could have said so in October and we could have sold Geneva. If I could have told Sadat in November we couldn't do it because of Rabat, he wouldn't have been happy but he wouldn't have been made a fool.

President: Tomorrow I will open the meeting, turn it to you, then end up with this assessment.[5]

Kissinger: I am truly sorry we couldn't spare you this. But the letter will help you with the Arabs. Fahmy broke down when he announced it.

President: How about your press?

Kissinger: They are in shock. 80% of them are Jewish and they are practically in tears. Marvin Kalb said, "Maybe Israel knows something we don't, but if they don't, it's awful." They have brought the Soviets back in, and could have given the American people a shot in the arm which would have helped them.

---

[5] Possibly a reference to the Cabinet meeting held March 26. (Ford Library, National Security Adviser, Memoranda of Conversations, Box 10, March 26, 1975, Cabinet Meeting)

Rabin, when I talked to him alone, said it was a Greek tragedy. I said his proposals were not unreasonable, but they were disastrous.

You have been very kind to the Israelis; what I have done is beyond description. And they do this to us at a moment when we need this. It is a disaster for the United States. We had it won—the Soviet Union was out of the Middle East. They are bringing the world to the edge of war for three kilometers in the Giddi and 8 kilometers in the Mitla. Sadat even would have given them six to eight months to move.

It is a really sad occasion. All of the people in my party are furious.

President: We won't let the Israelis through their usual apparatus get us into a confrontation with the Soviet Union, the Arabs and the Europeans.

Kissinger: I agree—that is why we need a program near the '67 frontiers.

President: At the NSC we will put the emphasis on the reassessment and planning.

Kissinger: I would say you have ordered a reassessment and a cooling of relations with Israel—which should be friendly, but correct. Each agency should, as if it were on its own, hold back—[*less than 1 line not declassified*].

Brent, have I exaggerated?

Scowcroft: You have bent over backward.

President: Did you ever get the feeling they wanted to settle?

Kissinger: I told Brent it didn't feel right. They just somehow didn't act like they wanted a deal.

President: The papers are talking about an American failure. I want to insure that the leadership has a correct impression.

Kissinger: I can say we went there in good faith and the two sides just couldn't bridge the gap. But that is not fair to Sadat. Sadat tried— Eilts said he had given so much that it was dangerous.

[Omitted here is discussion unrelated to the Arab-Israeli dispute.]

[Kissinger:] What the Israelis have done to us ... First on the trade acts, now on the Middle East. They knew exactly what was needed.

We should say all this is happening as a result of Congress. Asad said you have let Cambodia go, Vietnam, Portugal, Turkey—you will let Israel go also.

President: We went through another with the sub, but this turned out okay.

You have had your problems, but we have too.

Kissinger: You have behaved magnificently. The tragedy is that we had a good foreign policy. This is no reflection on you, but Israel doesn't think they have to be afraid of you.

President: They will find out.

[Omitted here is discussion unrelated to the Arab-Israeli dispute.]

[Kissinger:] The people will look back at the crisis created by eight lousy kilometers in a pass that nobody knows.

President: We made a massive effort I know of, on the invitation of the parties. I spoke to Allon, to Rabin, to Fisher, and to Golda. The sequence and timing was at the request of Israel. At the end, I will lay out the consequences. I should have a copy of the letter.

Kissinger: Step-by-step is dead. We have to consider whether we and the Soviet Union shouldn't make a global approach.

160. Memorandum for the Files[1]

Washington, March 24, 1975, 8 a.m.

SUBJECT

President's Meeting with the Secretary and Congressional Leadership—Monday, March 24, 8:00 a.m.

The President: We are not assessing blame. We want to tell you factually and forthrightly the new sequence of events. Everything that we have done with respect to the Middle East we have done with the consultation of the parties and has been primarily at their request. I had two full meetings with Rabin—another meeting with Allon and Mrs. Meir, as well as a number of Foreign Ministers from the Arab World. Secretary Kissinger went to the Middle East with the full cooperation of the parties. A further agreement did not materialize. We are disappointed and I think we are going to see a situation where tension will develop instead of steady progress towards peace. It is likely that the Geneva Conference will be reconvened with all of its potential dangers. What happened will give the Russians an opportunity to reassert themselves, tend to unify the Arabs, the Europeans are unified, and Geneva is hardly going to be a very happy place to conduct diplomacy. And on top of all of this there is the PLO question.

---

[1] Source: Library of Congress, Manuscript Division, Kissinger Papers, CL 281, Presidential File, March 1975. Secret; Nodis. Brackets are in the original. According to the President's Daily Diary, which includes a list of attendees, the meeting took place in the Cabinet Room and began at 8:03 and ended at 9:20 a.m. (Ford Library, Staff Secretary's Office Files)

Secretary Kissinger: First, let me tell you a little bit about the history. (The Secretary then gave a rundown of how the October war led to the step-by-step strategy which was designed both to help and protect Israel and that it was undertaken with their full knowledge and cooperation and that Israel was the principal beneficiary of that policy.) An approach was designed to reduce Soviet influence and protect the Israelis from having to take final decisions on Jerusalem, borders, the West Bank and Gaza and to give them an opportunity to take decisions on a piece-by-piece basis. For these reasons we always in the past have been very leery of the Geneva Conference.

What is it that we have attempted to do on this trip? We tried Jordan out in August and the Israelis turned it down. They turned it down for their own reasons and then we delayed all the way until the end of the year, even though Egypt wanted another agreement most sooner. The President had to refuse at Vladivostok[2] a Soviet move to Geneva because basically we were pursuing a strategy to the benefit of Israel; that was the whole theme. (The Secretary then outlined the issues during the negotiations.) Basically we couldn't bridge the gap between the two sides.

However, the real reason was that the parties were limited in what they could do politically. The Israeli domestic situation is difficult in that regard and Sadat has a confined political position in the Arab world. The dilemma we faced was that the political situations in which each government had room to maneuver were limited. We went into this mission on the basis of a genuine expectation of the possibilities for peace. There were at least 24 occasions—the records indicated—when we told the Israelis that non-belligerency could not be achieved. Israel had made such a public commitment to the achievement of non-belligerency that they could not take the final step short of that. We had brought Syria and Faisal around on this trip but the fact that the parties could not be brought to the final crunch was inexplicable in terms of the immediate issues that were at hand. Hussein advised us very strongly not to suspend the effort and that what was really needed primarily was the process. This process was much more important than the terms of the negotiation because it made the difference between our managing things and not being able to manage them. A few months from now, a few kilometers are going to appear to be miniscule as compared with the kind of pressure Israel is going to face on the substantive issue of an overall settlement. (The Secretary then described what we face vis-à-vis the Soviet Union and a united Europe.)

The immediate problems are the renewal of UNEF and UNDOF and the increased dangers of war. We are not assessing blame and what

---

[2] See footnote 4, Document 123.

is required is a reassessment of the whole situation in the aftermath of the trip. This policy had the singular support of the Congress; it was bipartisan and it is very important that this continues.

Speaker Albert: Could you be more specific as to what you mean that an overall assessment has to be undertaken?

Secretary Kissinger: Nothing can be ruled out; it would be a broad across-the-board reassessment.

Senator Mansfield: We have no choice but to reassess our policy. (The Senator was highly critical of what he termed the extreme rigidity of the Israeli stance.) It is beginning to look as if they have a death wish.

Speaker Albert: I can speak for the Democratic leadership in Congress. The Secretary of State has outdone himself in this and has their support.

Congressman Mahon: Why can't we reconsider this whole situation in two weeks and go back to the area if the gap is not that large?

Secretary Kissinger: If both sides want us to do this, obviously we would. We are open-minded about it. The Knesset supports Rabin's position; the ministers are meeting today and tomorrow will announce a willingness to move to Geneva. It was probably irretrievable but if both sides want us to do it, we will do it.

Senator Sparkman: Do you see any signs that the Israelis were reluctant to do anything because Israel feels that it has the absolute support of the U.S. no matter what?

Secretary Kissinger: There were a lot of reasons for the positions taken by the Israelis—one was their internal situation. Secondly, it might be related to our domestic situation as well, figuring that they could see it through the next Presidential election.

(The President then described his meeting with the Jewish leaders,[3] how this was done with their full knowledge and cooperation.)

The Vice President: I wonder whether the Israeli position was strictly to buy time and that maybe they were not very serious about getting this thing done. In other words, was this merely a deliberate policy of buying time? (Both the President and the Secretary said the Israelis went into the negotiations in good faith.)

Senator Scott: This is a policy that has had bipartisan support and it is important to continue to have it. We should make statements on it to this effect.

Senator Stennis: The trouble is that the Israelis just assume we will be supporting them no matter what. If the leadership could get the

---

[3] Possibly a reference to the February 25 meeting; see Document 138.

message across that this was not the case, if we made it very clear as to where we stood—it's not only the President and Henry—that we are with the Administration no matter what.

Senator Mansfield: We need united support. Perhaps the Israeli Ambassador should be called in immediately to reflect what we feel is the sense of this entire matter. We here are united. (The Senator's implication was to let the Israelis know that they had not really done everything they needed to do.)

Congressman Rhodes: We have to be careful not to overreact. We don't want to worsen the situation.

(The meeting concluded with the President ordering a reassessment of our overall Mid-East policy. He said that he has no objection to announcing the reassessment publicly provided that the onus is not directed at any one state.)

161. Memorandum of Conversation[1]

Washington, March 24, 1975, 9:20–9:52 a.m.

PARTICIPANTS

    President Gerald Ford
    Vice President Nelson Rockefeller
    Dr. Henry A. Kissinger, Secretary of State and Assistant to the President for National Security Affairs
    Lt. General Brent Scowcroft, Deputy Assistant to the President for National Security Affairs

Kissinger: I think if they had heard this before I left they would have caved. They think that we are too weak to take seriously and that they can get what they want from Congress.[2]

The President: Mike [Mansfield] and Hugh [Scott] will make a joint statement and McClellan will introduce a joint resolution.

Kissinger: I think they have made basic misjudgment. I think Nessen should announce a reassessment.

---

[1] Source: Library of Congress, Manuscript Division, Kissinger Papers, CL 157, Geopolitical File, Israel, March 1975. Secret; Nodis. The meeting was held in the Oval Office at the White House. All brackets, with the exception of ones describing omitted material, are in the original.

[2] Kissinger is referring to Israeli reaction to congressional leaders' criticism of Israel after Ford and Kissinger reviewed the failure of the negotiations. See Document 160.

President: How about calling Dinitz in?

Kissinger: I think it would look like blackmail. The reaction was amazing.

The President: They won't get $2 billion again like the last time.

The Vice President: That is why I asked the question I did—were they leading us along until they got arms?

Kissinger: It's the right question, but we couldn't answer.

The President: I am glad Schlesinger was there. He won't think there is any money to make anymore.

Kissinger: The Israelis' behavior is an outrage. To have received a letter from you[3] and not to change one iota is an indignity to the United States.

President: What do we do?

Kissinger: We should send out a NSSM today. We should have an NSC meeting on Wednesday or Thursday.[4] There should be no visit by Peres, no F–15 mission; we should slow up Lance and LGB. Every Department is to be instructed to end the special relationships. We should know who they see—they should have one special contact in each Department. [*less than 1 line not declassified*] We should work for two–three weeks on a position. We must have a comprehensive plan for Geneva.

The President: It was great when O'Neill asked where the boundary was. Let's get the assessment.

[Omitted here is discussion unrelated to the Arab-Israeli dispute.]

Kissinger: I think you were really in charge. You never know until a crisis where the steel is. Maybe this will pay us.

The President: When you keep Burton quiet—and Cliff Case and Scott. Have we heard from anyone but Fisher?

Kissinger: They will mobilize the Jewish Community against us—no doubt.

[Omitted here is discussion unrelated to the Arab-Israeli dispute.]

[Kissinger:] For the reassessment, you should tell Nessen: This will be a reassessment of our policy toward all the countries in the area. When progress is no longer possible along one direction, it is essential that a reevaluation take place to determine where we are and where we should go.

Don't use the word "failure." If they ask, "Does this mean a cutoff of aid to Israel?", say "Not at all."

---

[3] Document 156.

[4] March 26–27. The meeting was held on March 28; see Document 166.

162. Memorandum of Conversation[1]

Washington, March 26, 1975, 9:22–10:18 a.m.

PARTICIPANTS

    President Ford
    Dr. Henry A. Kissinger, Secretary of State and Assistant to the President for National Security Affairs
    Lt. General Brent Scowcroft, Deputy Assistant to the President for National Security Affairs

[From 9:30–9:34 a.m., Secretary Kissinger stepped out to take a telephone call from Ambassador Eilts.]

Kissinger: Javits came in very threatening. If we went after Israel, he and Ribicoff would come after me. He said our interests were identical with Israel.

He wanted to introduce a resolution in both Houses to urge you to use the waiver on the Turkish issue.

President: That is stupid on the part of Israel.

Kissinger: We are in the position where three million Israelis and three million Greeks are running American foreign policy. We are giving aid to Israel at a rate which would be unbelievable for any other country.

I could keep the Middle East quiet through the '76 election. I did the same in '72, when Israel did the same thing to Rogers in '71. Then I cooperated to keep the Soviet influence out.

On the Middle East, there is an option to let Geneva go on, get it all screwed up and have a stalemate. The other is to force the pace of events. I am afraid that a stalemate will radicalize the Arabs and lead to war. The European Ambassadors told me last night that we did our best and they would cooperate in a settlement.

But the press campaign is that this is just a minor misunderstanding and we can go back to business as usual.

President: We can't do that. We must move comprehensively. Let's get that speech under way.

Kissinger: If we stay steady, Israel may crack and give us something to get things under way.

President: We must stay steady.

---

[1] Source: Ford Library, National Security Adviser, Memoranda of Conversations, Box 10, March 26, 1975, Ford, Kissinger. Secret; Nodis. The meeting was held in the Oval Office at the White House. All brackets, with the exception of ones describing omitted material, are in the original.

Kissinger: They will come after me.

[Omitted here is discussion relating to the United Nations and the Geneva Conference.]

[Kissinger:] At my press conference, I thought I would make a strong statement on Vietnam, I have a statement on Israel.[2] Is it worth doing?

President: I gave a press conference. I said Israel is inflexible.

Kissinger: Good. They will attack you.

President: I know they will hit us, but I kind of enjoy a fight when I know I am right.

Kissinger: It is reaching impossible proportions. First, they ruin our trade relations with the Soviet Union. Rabbi Miller is demanding we hold up MFN to Romania until they agree to 9,000.[3]

President: Did you see the emigration figures?

Kissinger: I will bring Fisher in.

[Omitted here is discussion unrelated to the Arab-Israeli dispute.]

---

[2] Kissinger's opening statement on the Middle East at his March 26 press conference was printed in the *New York Times*, March 27, 1975, p. 17.

[3] A reference to Romania allowing 9,000 Romanian Jews to emigrate.

---

163. National Security Study Memorandum 220[1]

Washington, March 26, 1975.

TO

The Secretary of the Treasury
The Secretary of Defense
The Deputy Secretary of State
The Director of Central Intelligence

SUBJECT

U.S. Policy in the Middle East

The President has directed that a study be conducted of United States interests, objectives, strategy and policy toward the Middle East

---

[1] Source: Ford Library, NSC Institutional Files (H-Files), Box 34, NSSMs, NSSM 220, U.S. Policy in the Middle East, Folder 4. Secret; Sensitive. A copy was sent to the Chairman of the Joint Chiefs of Staff.

in the light of recent developments. The study should address our bilateral relationships with the principal countries in the area as well as the diplomacy of settlement of the Arab-Israeli conflict. It should take into account the impact of our Middle East policy on our relations with countries outside the area.

—The study should reflect consideration of significant changes likely to take place in the region, within individual countries, and in the overall diplomacy of settlement.

—The study should consider the likely policies of outside powers, particularly the USSR, the European Community, Japan and China, with respect to the Middle East over the next several months.

—The study should examine closely the possibility of renewed Arab-Israeli hostilities and should make recommendations for U.S. policy in response to likely scenarios of renewed hostilities.

—The study should focus on developing alternative policies and recommendations for United States bilateral and multilateral relations with the countries of the Middle East, and with other major powers with respect to the Middle East, in the diplomatic, political, economic and military fields.

This study should be carried out by an NSC Ad Hoc Group composed of representatives of the addressees and the NSC staff and chaired by the Under Secretary of State for Political Affairs. It should be conducted on a close-hold basis and submitted not later than April 10 for consideration by the Senior Review Group prior to submission to the President.

Henry A. Kissinger

164. Memorandum of Conversation[1]

Washington, March 27, 1975, 9:30–10:32 a.m.

PARTICIPANTS

President Ford
Dr. Henry A. Kissinger, Secretary of State and Assistant to the President for National Security Affairs
Lt. General Brent Scowcroft, Deputy Assistant to the President for National Security Affairs

Kissinger: I have the uneasy feeling Egypt is ready to cave and we don't want that. Israel would get out of control.

The President: They would claim they were right.

Kissinger: We plan to say the maps Dinitz is putting out are inaccurate.[2]

The President: If it is the truth.

Kissinger: I am glad I read the text of your Hearst interview. You blame them for being inflexible. You should tilt a little against Israel.[3]

The President: That is not hard.

Kissinger: Here are two cables[4] I want to show you. King Hussein despairs of the U.S. and the Middle East—we aren't even prepared publicly to say Israel is to blame. War is inevitable.

In one way our withdrawal is good, because everyone now sees the important role we play.

I think we need psychological warfare against Israel. We may yet get an agreement.

The President: I have had it in the back of my mind that if we play brinkmanship, we may get something. But we shouldn't talk about it. I thought you were too unhappy to entertain it.

Kissinger: Not so much that as the unravelling of our Middle East policy, and Israel has treated us as no other country could.

The President: Should we tell Max[5] that?

---

[1] Source: Ford Library, National Security Adviser, Memoranda of Conversations, Box 10, March 27, 1975, Ford, Kissinger. Secret; Nodis. The meeting was held in the Oval Office at the White House.

[2] On March 26, Ambassador Dinitz gave newsmen maps of the Israeli and Egyptian negotiating positions in the Sinai. They were printed in the *New York Times*, March 27, 1975, p. 17.

[3] President Ford's interview with Hearst Newspapers was published on March 27. See ibid., March 28, 1975, p. 57.

[4] Not further identified.

[5] A reference to Max Fisher.

Kissinger: Max must know. It is not just a friendly misunderstanding. If the Jewish Community comes after us, we will have to go public with the whole record.

Tell the NSC that Israel behaved recklessly. You are trying to create a state of mind in Israel that if we have to run the risks of war for them, they have to run the risks of peace for us.

The President: Did the interview go too far?

Kissinger: Nope. It was a good, strong interview. They will put heat on you anyway, so there is little to lose.

We may yet get an agreement within a couple of months, and it may be a lesson—even to the Arabs.

Tell Max Fisher that Israel misled us. Moynihan said Israel really let the President down, didn't they? They attempted to blow up our Middle East strategy. Now they are dumping on Geneva.

[Omitted here is discussion unrelated to the Arab-Israeli dispute.]

165. Memorandum of Conversation[1]

Washington, March 27, 1975, 3:10 p.m.

PARTICIPANTS

    Mr. Max Fisher
    President Ford
    Dr. Henry A. Kissinger, Secretary of State and Assistant to the President for National Security Affairs
    Lt. General Brent Scowcroft, Deputy Assistant to the President for National Security Affairs

President: I don't think I have ever been so disappointed as when I heard Henry was coming back without a settlement. It was as low as I have been in this office. The impression I had, after my meetings with Allon twice, with Rabin, with Golda, etc., was that we had been working so closely that when the chips were down they would see how deeply this would affect the prestige of the United States. When the final decision was made, their inflexibility has created all sorts of

---

[1] Source: Ford Library, National Security Adviser, Memoranda of Conversations, Box 10, March 27, 1975, Ford, Kissinger, and Max Fisher. Confidential. The meeting was held in the Oval Office at the White House. According to the President's Daily Diary, the meeting ended at 3:50 p.m. (Ford Library, Staff Secretary's Office Files)

problems. When Henry reported to the leadership, they without exception strongly supported our efforts and were quite critical of Israeli actions.[2]

The result is that we have undertaken a reassessment. That doesn't mean we will drop Israel but we have to go on a broader basis. You know me well enough personally and officially—we just can't get led down the primrose path and be rejected.

Kissinger: Max doesn't know that the timing resulted from Israeli insistence.

Fisher: I don't feel any better than you. I had lunch with Dinitz today. I have the transcript of what he said in New York. My first responsibility to you is to keep things cool. That is what I tried to do. I called the president of every community in the U.S. I didn't want sermons coming out on Passover week and the 30th anniversary of the Holocaust.

To make a decision which in their own mind they had to know created a gulf with the U.S.—something must have happened. I just don't know. I think we all have a desire for peace. I agree with your strategy, and I see what could happen at Geneva.

This coming on top of everything else—with a Congress wanting to act like a State Department. But the only one who can settle this is the United States. The Soviet Union can't do it.

Kissinger: That was our policy. But Eban and Peres and a third of the Jews go around saying let's go back to Geneva. You can't undermine us and keep telling us to do it.

Fisher: The Jewish Community is saddened and disturbed by this, but they haven't lost the reservoir of good will. I read Safire today.[3] You have done a tremendous job for the U.S.—don't let a small group get to you. Look at the rank and file of the people. If anything can be salvaged, you can do it.

Kissinger: But the Israelis have to help us if anything can be salvaged. When Eban and Peres say we should go to Geneva, it cuts any other way.

Fisher: I told Dinitz that, tough as it looks, we can't let it go down the drain—and it will. I think there must be some sober realizations in both Israel and Egypt. Geneva will just be a shouting match. I think both sides want peace. How it got off the rail, I don't know. But before we get too far off, I want to suggest ... The reassessment raises too

---

[2] See Document 160.

[3] William Safire, an editorialist for the *New York Times*, wrote an essay entitled, "Henry's Two Faces," in which he criticized Kissinger for privately pressuring Israel while publicly denying it. (*New York Times*, March 27, 1975, p. 25)

many fears. This weakens the hand of what you are doing in diplomacy. I feel that people are having second thoughts, but I can't prove it. I think they may be facing up to it. The blame is never totally on one side. I want to keep things calm and with maximum good will. I owe that to you.

President: Henry and I have spent more time on this than on any other foreign policy issue. We put my credibility on the line and it was a hell of a disappointment. I detect an undercurrent that some in the community are spreading the word I am turning my back on Israel and they made unkind remarks about Henry. We haven't taken one step about Israel. But when people start to attack, the impulse is to lay out the record. We haven't done it because we want a solution, but when we have been led down the primrose path . . .

Fisher: Let me tell you about the things I hear. In my room Sunday[4] I will have ten stalwart people there to tell them what I believe. I will put it on the table. I think Henry is right. You have a tremendous amount of good will. I want to find out what went wrong. I want to get an excuse for going over there to find out. Meanwhile, I will do what I can to hold things calm. Israel has no chance without the U.S. Somehow we have to find a solution. I don't want to go over there on a delegation, as Javits wanted. I don't want to do that.

Kissinger: I didn't encourage him. I don't know what could be done.

President: We see no alternative now to Geneva. We don't like it but I see no choice. We have warned about Geneva for eight months—now the Jews are starting to worry about it.

Fisher: We have to be positive and do what we can.

President: You are a good friend, and I have to tell you on a personal basis that nothing has hit me so hard since I've been in this office. I see no choice but Geneva. Maybe something will turn up, but unless people will sign on the dotted line, I see no alternative.

Fisher: But if you go to Geneva, Israel has to fight on the basis of the '67 frontier.

Kissinger: That's what we have been saying.

Fisher: We have got to try to find a solution. It can't be settled by the Soviet Union; the Europeans. I want to be of service on this.

President: Keep in touch with Henry and Brent. We will keep cool and calm but we must set a steady course. Unless we get a firm commitment, we can make no promises.

Fisher: How do you account for it?

---

[4] March 30.

Kissinger: Frankly, they looked at what happened with Iran and Iraq, and they didn't want to be dependent on Iranian oil; they looked at Southeast Asia; they looked at our domestic weakness. Peres wanted to stick it to Rabin and pick up the pieces. No one had tried to prepare the people. They were paralyzed from the second day. Rabin couldn't carry his Cabinet, I think. He doesn't have the strength of Golda.

President: And whoever is giving them advice on American domestic policy gave them bad advice. If this ends up in a confrontation with the Soviet Union and an oil embargo, there will be a turnaround in this country. I supported Israel because I think it is right. Some of my best friends are Jews because I admire strength and brains. I feel awful to be put in this kind of position.

166. Minutes of National Security Council Meeting[1]

Washington, March 28, 1975, 3:15–5:15 p.m.

SUBJECT

Middle East and Southeast Asia

PRINCIPALS

The President
The Vice President
Secretary of State Henry A. Kissinger
Secretary of the Treasury William Simon
Secretary of Defense James Schlesinger
Chairman, Joint Chiefs of Staff General George S. Brown
Director of Central Intelligence William Colby

OTHER ATTENDEES

State
Deputy Secretary of State Robert Ingersoll (only for Vietnam portion)
Under Secretary of State for Political Affairs, Joseph Sisco

Defense
Deputy Secretary William Clements

WH
Donald Rumsfeld

---

[1] Source: Ford Library, National Security Adviser, Box 1, NSC Meetings File, NSC Meeting, March 28, 1975. Top Secret; Sensitive. The meeting was held in the Cabinet Room at the White House.

NSC
Lt. Gen. Brent Scowcroft
Robert B. Oakley

President: This is the first of the steps, and a very important step, which we must take following the extremely disappointing results of Henry Kissinger's long and arduous trip to the Middle East. I told Rabin that unless there was a settlement, we would have to reassess our policies toward the Middle East, including Israel.[2] I don't know if they understood what I was saying but I think they do now. Since I have been in office, we have worked with Israel to try and get a settlement. We acted in good faith and I assume they did, also, but when the chips were down they showed a lack of flexibility which was needed for an agreement. What I said to the Hearst papers about more Israeli flexibility being in the best interests of peace is true.[3] But there was no flexibility. I will catch flak for my position and Henry is already catching it. The time has come for a good hard look.

I will tell you briefly about my record in Congress where Israel is concerned. It was so close that I had a black reputation with the Arabs. I have always liked and respected the Israeli people. They are intelligent and dedicated to the causes in which they believe. They are dedicated to their religion, their country, their family and their high moral standards. I admire them and respect them. And I have never been so disappointed as to see people I respect unable to see that we are trying to do something for their interest as well as for our own. But in the final analysis our commitment is to the United States.

Vice President: Hear, hear.

President: We could have been together but now I do not know. The reassessment will take place and we will see.[4] We cannot afford to have our position in this country undercut but I must tell you what I think. We will be following a firm policy of reassessment. It will not be

---

[2] See Document 156.

[3] See footnote 3, Document 164.

[4] On March 29, Kissinger informed the Ambassadors to Egypt, Jordan, Syria, and Israel, that the U.S. Government would be making a reassessment of U.S. policy in the Middle East (see Document 163) and instructed them to return to Washington early the following week. (Telegram 71670 to Tel Aviv; Library of Congress, Manuscript Division, Kissinger Papers, CL 157, March 1975; telegram 71673 to Amman; National Archives, RG 59, Central Foreign Policy Files, P840178–1656; telegram 71674 to Damascus; Ford Library, National Security Adviser, Presidential Country Files for Middle East, Box 31, Syria, State Department Telegrams from S/S, Nodis, Folder 4; telegram 71675 to Cairo; National Archives, RG 59, Central Foreign Policy Files, P840178–1651). Kissinger also asked the Ambassadors to pose a set of questions to the leaders of each country: what was that country's view on the next step toward peace, what role did that country see for the United States, and what was that country's view on the Geneva Conference and if it resumed, what did they expect to happen there.

decided today. Everyone will take a close look first. But in the meantime, keep everyone at arm's length.

Henry, do you want to tell us about your mission and where we are now?

Kissinger: Let me describe some of the issues which we will face in the reassessment of a Middle East policy. First, what have we been trying to achieve?

In November 1973 all the Western Europeans, the Japanese and the USSR were solidly united on an immediate Israeli return to the 1967 lines. If the situation had been allowed to continue, given the economic problem in the West, all the pressures would have been on us. And at Geneva everyone would have been united against Israel with the US acting as Israel's lawyer. Our policy helped abort this sort of Geneva Conference, even though we went along with the idea in order to keep the Russians calmed down. We had the willingness of Sadat to play a constructive, cooperative role and the active encouragement of Feisal for the step-by-step approach. This held off the radicals and enabled us to create a situation in which all the Arabs were turning to us, while Israel had a situation which it could handle politically since it had to deal with only a small piece at a time. We also neutralized the Western Europeans and Japanese who are anxious to replace us in the Middle East. Objectively, there is little to distinguish the effect of their policies from those of the Soviets. This process which we instituted proceeded well and met Israel's interests as well as our own. The two were compatible in the step-by-step approach.

So the big issue with Israel during my last trip was not lines on maps. By the way, the leaked maps in the *New York Times* and elsewhere are inaccurate.[5] They only showed us a map after the negotiations were over. But lines are trivial compared to whether or not the moderate Arab leaders are able to say the US has delivered something. And this is fully in line with the survival of Israel, really the best way to ensure Israel's survival. The USSR was completely out of the game and on this last trip Feisal came to the point where he told me he trusted me to proceed as I judged best even though he would have preferred another approach. And Asad told me he wanted separate negotiations with Israel rather than Geneva.

So our disappointment is that Israel did not understand. They could have been shielded and their only friend, literally their only friend in the world, was in control of the process, dealing with the Arabs singly and keeping the USSR out. Even Iraq was beginning to move out of the Kurdish orbit. I do not approve of the brutal way in

---

[5] See footnote 2, Document 164.

which Iran and Iraq disposed of the fate of the Kurds, but it created a situation whereby the Iraqis no longer had such need for the Soviets. I was hoping that in such a situation with all the Arabs turning to us and away from the USSR, someone in the Kremlin would have gotten discouraged and said, "Let's stop pouring so much money and effort down a rat hole." That was the situation we had one week ago.

On the whole, in the negotiations, I think Egypt went further and Israel not as far as I had expected. But our role and the whole strategy we had followed for eighteen months, putting us in the key position, has been disrupted. Now that the parties are face to face with it, they are not so eager for Geneva.

A unilateral US effort now would be a mistake, would make it look as if we were more anxious than the parties. If they came to us, we could think about doing something but there can not be any more shuttles. The pressure on the Arabs is likely to be against cooperating with us. Sadat will have to move toward the other Arabs in order to protect himself and also a bit toward the Soviets and Western Europeans and Geneva. Moreover, tensions in the area will build up. UNEF is due for renewal on April 26 and UNDOF a month later. Sadat told me he would renew UNEF for three months, not six. I would expect UNDOF to be renewed for two months. Both would thus expire simultaneously by the end of July and by August we could have a flash point on both fronts.

Schlesinger: Will the Soviets veto a renewal?

Kissinger: Not if the parties are for it. I expect we will have some violations of the agreement soon. The Egyptians already have some SAM sites across the Canal and there will probably be more. Syria and the PLO will get back in the game, perhaps with guerilla raids from Lebanon. The Secretary General is already in the game, trying to arrange Geneva. I am trying to slow him down a little. If Geneva meets, things will happen. Israel will have to deal with all of its neighbors and all of the final issues at the same time. Up to the present, thanks to our strategy, we and Israel were able to avoid this.

President: When would Geneva meet?

Kissinger: Let's not rush into it. We must act as if we were ready to go all-out to head for Geneva but not actually set a date. That will have a good effect on the parties. I think we can wait until June but we can not appear to stall or hang back. Even though the Soviets are now in a good tactical position, we still have the chips because everyone is still counting on us to move Israel. We can get the benefit of this basic situation if we can deliver. This is true bilaterally or at Geneva. If we do not deliver, the Arabs will conclude that only force can get anything from

Israel. For the moment Egypt and Saudi Arabia still have some confidence in the US, judging from what was said to the Vice President.[6]

Vice President: And also affection for the US and for Henry.

Kissinger: There will now be a more active Soviet role and if the Arabs do not think they can get enough progress they will ask that the UK and France participate at Geneva. We have an interest in the survival of Israel but we also have broader interests with the Western Europeans and Japan and the Arabs. If there is another war we run the risk of antagonizing the Arabs definitively and of pushing them into the arms of the Soviets. We will also risk a direct confrontation with the Soviets. At Geneva we will confront the basic issues of final frontiers and Palestine and guarantees and demilitarization. We may have to draw up a comprehensive US plan for the Middle East so as not to be empty-handed.

A big question is to what degree we will want to coordinate with or dissociate ourselves from Israel. What kind of economic and military aid should we provide and what should the timing be? What kind of military supply policy should we have for the Arabs? As I see it, the only remaining Soviet influence in Egypt is the latter's need for spare parts and other military items from the USSR. What about our energy policy and the Joint Committees? What about the PLO?

Even if we decide to do nothing we must have a policy. We need a diplomatic strategy for Geneva and a strategy for bilateral relations, with the Arab states and Israel, economically and militarily. There are also some tactical questions concerning Geneva: Should we go for a stalemate with a subsequent resumption of our bilateral efforts, or go to Geneva with a US plan and force a settlement? We need a carefully worked-out strategy for another war. The last time we came out very well without an advance strategy but the next time we can not improvise. Another war will produce very heavy casualties—I think Bill Colby's estimate is for 7000 Israeli dead—with more Arab countries joining in and a greater risk of Soviet involvement!

The Soviets will be a much bigger threat than in the past. In 1967 and again in 1973 they stood aside while their Arab allies were humiliated. The cumulative resentment is building up and is likely to push them to be less cautious this time in showing their power. This is all the more true since they see the US as weak and unwilling to stand up for its commitments anywhere in the world.

---

[6] Rockefeller and Sadat met on March 27 in Riyadh where they both attended King Faisal's funeral. Rockefeller described the meeting in the press conference he held when he left Saudi Arabia. (Telegram 8 from Riyadh, March 27; National Archives, RG 59, Central Foreign Policy Files) No memorandum of conversation of the meeting has been found.

That is why we need a total reassessment. Joe Sisco will be in charge of a special working group to consider all of these questions. It should take about three weeks.

We need to keep the immediate situation under control and then recapture control of the long-term situation. We can do this since the Arabs know they still need to come to us to get progress. But we must be absolutely certain that we can deliver progress the next time.

President: Thank you, Henry, what do the others have to say?

Schlesinger: I think Henry's presentation was very accurate. Our position could be one of dignified aloofness. We are in the cat-bird seat. We can go to Geneva, point out we have already done our best but did not succeed, so we will just sit and wait to see what develops.

Vice President: Do you mean aloofness from Israel?

Schlesinger: Yes, I do. There should not be full policy coordination with Israel as in the past. We should look forward, not to the past. United States policy has been frustrated to the extent we hope to be successful in the years ahead. We can not allow Israel to continue its relationship with us as if there were no problems. We can not let them conclude that they can upset the US applecart but the Administration can do nothing about it. The military balance from the Israeli standpoint is much better than the last time we met (in the NSC) to discuss this problem.[7] We overestimated badly the amount of Soviet arms which Egypt had received. So the balance for Israel is reasonably favorable and we need not be concerned over our aloofness.

Simon: What about the Joint Economic Commissions?

President: This is a crucial question. Joe Sisco is coordinating our reassessment. It is not aimed at tilting toward or against Israel or toward or against Arabs. It is aimed at the best interests of the US. Jim (Schlesinger) used a good word, "aloof," and I think this is the posture we should adopt at least during the period of our policy reassessment. As an example of this, it would be better if Peres did not come on his visit as originally planned. And as for the F–15, I think we should hold up the visit by the Israeli team which was coming to make an assessment. Bill (Simon), you should be aloof with the Joint Committee.

Simon: We have Joint Commissions with several countries, including Iran and Saudi Arabia. How shall we handle this?

President: The Iranians and Saudis are in a different category. They were not involved in the negotiations.

Simon: What about Egypt?

President: What are we doing there?

---

[7] See Document 111.

Simon: We have several projects, particularly helping them rebuild the area along the Suez Canal.

President: As I recall, we were slow in getting started with Egypt so we can afford to be more forthcoming than with the Israelis. [2 lines not declassified] There is no pique on our part but we are reassessing so we will be restrained.

Colby: [1 line not declassified]

President: As I recall my own experiences as a Congressman, the Israeli representatives float very freely on Capitol Hill. Now we can't do anything about that with Congress. But I have the impression the Israeli representatives are almost as free in many Departments as they are with Congress. You must try to control that.

Schlesinger: We have both overt and covert Israeli representatives. It is very difficult to handle.

President: Try to do both but concentrate on the overt ones. Channelize the relationships with Israeli representatives. The proper relationship should be business-like but arms-length and aloof. Jim, what did we do about that Israeli shopping list last fall?

Kissinger: The NSC recommended that we give them two out of eight slices but we ended up by giving them four out of eight.[8]

President: I decided to include the Lance and the LGB because I thought they needed it. In retrospect, bearing in mind what I believed we were going to do together and what has actually happened, we were probably too generous. Jim, hold off on delivering those high priority items if there is a way to do it.

Schlesinger: We have a commitment to deliver the Lance.

Vice President: I thought they had a commitment, too, on negotiations.

Clements: We can prolong the Lance training in order to delay delivery.

President: Stay within the guidelines. How you implement it is your business. When we have reassessed, then we can proceed. For the moment, I would like to look at the four slices of arms we gave them and what we have delivered already.

Schlesinger: Haig was here last week complaining about the drawdowns on NATO stocks in Europe. I told him he knew all about it.

President: I would like to see those four slices. Did we go so far as to increase their offensive capability, not only improve their defensive capability? I want to see everything that has been delivered to Israel. I want to be able to show Congress just how much we have done mili-

---

[8] See Document 101.

tarily for Israel. Also, I would like to see what we have delivered to the Arabs in the way of military hardware.

General Brown: There is the question of when the stocks we have drawn down for Israel will be replaced for our own forces. You can use this with Congress.

President: That would be useful. Get me a list of what we have done since I have been President. If challenged, I want the record.

Kissinger: It would also be valuable to know what we have delivered since November 1973 when our major re-equipment program began.

President: That will be useful for background but the stress should be on what has happened since I came to office, so show where the cut-off is. We have drawn down our own capability.

Clements: We have even drawn out of our own stocks.

President: I want to look at the facts. Bill (Colby), do you want to talk?

Colby: A major factor is the increased chance of war. We put out a Special National Intelligence Estimate yesterday.[9] The armies of Egypt, Syria and Israel are all in a state of alert and there is a substantial chance of hostilities breaking out either deliberately or by accident at any time in the next few weeks. If it does not happen quickly, then there will be negotiations at Geneva and if there is no progress there by early summer there are high odds that Egypt and Syria will launch a coordinated attack and even higher odds that Israel will attack first. Israel probably sees war as inevitable and may decide to hit now. Comparatively, they are well off. They can probably beat Egypt and Syria both in 7–10 days.

Kissinger: We told Asad this was our estimate of how the war would develop, not Israel's estimate but our own. Asad told me we did not understand: "We learned in 1973 that Israel can not stand pain. We will lose a lot but we will not give up and we will use the strategy of inflicting casualties and fighting an extended war. We will lose territory and men but bleed Israel and draw the Soviets in."

Schlesinger: If Israel strikes first, they will not behave rationally. They are likely to strike through Lebanon.

Kissinger: They may be able to hit quickly but the Syrians are determined to hold out.

Colby: We project 7,000 Israeli killed, three times as many as in October 1973. But we believe they can punch through.

---

[9] SNIE 30–1–75, March 27, entitled "Next Steps in the Middle East," analyzed various aspects of the long-term trends potentially affecting the Middle East peace process. (Central Intelligence Agency, NIC Files, Job 79–R01012A)

Sisco: The Arabs will not stick their necks out. This is a very critical judgment. It can determine the outcome of the war. The Arabs will fight on the defensive and drag it out as long as possible.

Kissinger: The Arabs think of prolonged war and an early oil embargo.

Schlesinger: Before the US resupplies? That would be crazy. We won't stand for it.

Kissinger: We must think of it. Also, our contingency planning needs to assume higher risk-taking by the Soviets.

President: Did the Soviets go further in 1973 than before?

Schlesinger: They threatened the British and French in 1956 with nuclear attack.[10]

Kissinger: Only after we had dissociated ourselves from our allies and told them to pull back.

Schlesinger: The Soviets were all bluster.

Clements: The priority problem is that Israel may decide their position will worsen so they will preempt. They already had before April 1st enough to preempt and as their situation worsens, they could decide to go now. Also, as we become more aloof, this could aggravate the situation. It could push them to this kind of decision.

Kissinger: We must weigh many factors. I agree with Bill that if there is no progress by summer, there will be war within one year or maybe this year. We have six months to produce something. For Israel to go to war at the known displeasure of the US would be a monumental decision. We must keep the Arabs from becoming too upset but show Israel they can not ignore us. The next time we must be in a position to get results from Israel.

Schlesinger: Maybe the word aloof is not a good one. We can say to the Israelis that we have made an honest effort and our well is temporarily dry. Whether it will be temporary or permanent depends on you. We are here.

President: Rocky, what about your talks with Sadat and the Saudis?

Vice President: Mr. President, your thought of sending someone to the funeral of King Feisal and your letters[11] made a deep impression and I believe really helped the Saudis get through a very difficult period. Saudi Arabia wants to follow the policy of cooperation of King

---

[10] A reference to the 1956 Suez Crisis when the United Kingdom, France, and Israel coordinated an invasion of Egypt's Sinai Peninsula and the Suez Canal.

[11] President Ford and Secretary Kissinger both sent messages of condolence to Crown Prince Khalid. (Telegrams 66828 and 66911, March 25; National Archives, RG 59, Central Foreign Policy Files)

Feisal, judging from my talks with Khalid and Fahd. I told Fahd we want his advice. He said that Feisal had stood up to Nasser on radicalism in the Arab world when it appeared that Saudi Arabia was all alone but by the time of his death Egypt had come around to seeing that Feisal was right. Fahd said, however, that unless there is a "just, equitable and lasting peace within one year"—and those are his exact words—the Soviets will move back in, the radicals will be reinvigorated and rearmed by the Soviets while the moderates will move away from the US and establish a close relationship with Western Europe. The Europeans have arms they want to sell, we have the money to buy and we can learn to fly the planes and drive the tanks. The Arabs will keep building their military strength as long as it takes from the USSR and Western Europe and in time we will crush Israel. That is what Fahd said to me. He is right about the Western Europeans. The French sent their Defense Minister to the funeral with a list of items for sale and models of aircraft and tanks. This offended the Saudis.

Simon: Israel might strike first. Is Egypt fully resupplied? I gather they are not and Israel is militarily superior. They won't allow the Arabs to fight a war of attrition. Also, if there is too much uncertainty about our support, it could lead Israel to conclude it must hit first.

Kissinger: Our problem would be the same if Israel hits soon or later on. Even if Israel destroys the Arab armies, we will face the same problems in our relations with the Arabs, Western Europeans and Soviets. We would be obliged to step in, tell Israel that is enough and impose or try to impose a settlement along the 1967 line. There is a physical limit to what three million people can occupy and sooner or later we will have to stop this process.

President: Exactly. How many miles of territory and how many cities can Israel occupy?

Kissinger: And would the Soviets stand by while that happened?

Colby: We think the Soviets are freer to support the Arabs than they have been before. It would take them only a very few days to fly in defensive support such as SAMs and aircraft. Their airborne troops could probably be beaten by the Israelis because they would only be lightly armed, but they could reinforce the air defense around Cairo and Damascus and other cities.

Kissinger: I am not sure Israel would directly attack Soviet troops.

Brown: When I was reading the Special National Intelligence Estimate, I had the impression of hearing an old record over again. We made a mistake about the Arabs in October 1973. What Sisco had to say is very important. We must keep our minds open.

Schlesinger: Israel will certainly win another round.

Brown: Israel's army is very good. We know that. But don't count out the Arabs.

Vice President: Think what another war would mean for us. The OPEC countries would stick together in an oil embargo, particularly since the Latin Americans are already unhappy with us. This could cause paralysis of the East Coast of the United States.

President: I told Morton to put together a contingency plan on what would be likely to happen if there were another oil embargo, what measures we can take, and what the probable result would be. We need to follow up on this.

[Omitted here is discussion unrelated to the Arab-Israeli dispute.]

167. **Telegram From the Embassy in Lebanon to the Department of State**[1]

Beirut, March 29, 1975, 0040Z.

4044. Eyes only for Secretary Kissinger from Senator McGovern. Secretary please pass to Pat Holt, Chief of Staff Senate Foreign Relation CMTE. Subj: Senator McGovern's Meeting With Yasir 'Arafat.

1. I wish to advise you that I and two staff aides met in Beirut for over one hour evening Mar 28 with PLO Chairman Yasir 'Arafat. Following for your personal information are salient points of our discussions.

2. 'Arafat initially gave long exposition re bases and purposes of Palestinian cause and Fedayeen movement, dwelling heavily on his people's sufferings, etc. and pointing out that despite emotional trauma experienced by Palestinians, PLO leadership has refrained from "overbidding." He said steps PLO leadership has taken have been "realistic" and well as "bold" and "courageous." Traditional Palestinian leaders, he said, used to offer slogans which offended international opinion, but PLO leadership now adopts realistic positions. As example, he noted that Palestine National Council in June 1974 had decided to welcome opportunity to establish national authority over any piece of Palestinian land liberated from Israeli control.

3. 'Arafat said PLO foresees democratic secular state as "vision of future," but it realizes this is "long-term objective" which PLO hopes to achieve through "intellectual transformation" and "political persua-

---

[1] Source: Library of Congress, Manuscript Division, Kissinger Papers, CL 194, Geopolitical File; Middle East, Peace Negotiations, Shuttle Diplomacy, Chronological File, February–April 1975. Secret; Immediate; Nodis; Eyes Only.

sion." When IA asked if territories to form the basis for an independent Palestinian state in context of some overall peace settlement meant West Bank and Gaza, 'Arafat replied "yes." He described his "vision" of democratic secular state as benefitting both Israelis and Palestinians. He believed that if Israelis do not succumb wholly to a masada complex,[2] they will come to accept this concept as their "vision" also and would allow themselves to become "part of our area." He considered this would be commensurate with Israeli interests, since he thought it unlikely that USG would continue forever to provide enormous sums to sustain Israeli intransigence.

4. Discoursing further re strength and durability of Palestinian cause, 'Arafat averred that Palestinians can sustain their struggle for 30–50 years if necessary. He said Palestinian people are not willing to remain as observers on periphery of history, and that their revolution reflects dynamism of Palestinian people. If things do not go well, he said, PLO leadership at some point would be forced to display greater extremism, with leaders emerging who would be "better than us" and perhaps "better for Palestinian people." Current PLO proposals, contended 'Arafat, are "neither violent nor extreme, but realistic." He added that "if Palestinians do not achieve stability, the area will not achieve stability."

5. When IA asked what specific arrangements might cause PLO to agree to be represented at Geneva, 'Arafat said this question was less important at present time than "terms of reference" of PLO participation.

6. Asked again if he would agree to two co-equal states of Israel and Palestine, latter comprising West Bank and Gaza, which would recognize each other's existence, 'Arafat reiterated that official Palestinian National Council position is to establish national authority over any territory that could be made available—"even one village." He then intimated that PLO would accept territorial division based on 1967 lines, but he warned that PLO leadership has had to struggle hard to get Palestinian people to acquiesce in this arrangement. When I asked if extremists might disrupt any ME settlement based on such an arrangement, 'Arafat said it would rpt not because "this is the Palestinian consensus." One of his interjected: "some of the theoreticians are sometimes backward from the historical process."

---

[2] A reference to the Roman siege of the ancient fortress at Masada during the First Jewish-Roman War from 66–70 A.D. According to the ancient Jewish historian Josephus, a group of Jewish extremists known as the Sicarii seized the fortress at the start of the war in 66 A.D. After the Romans conquered Jerusalem in 70 A.D., effectively ending the war, they lay siege to the last bastion of Jewish resistance at Masada. In 72 A.D., with the Romans on the brink of taking the fortress, the leaders of the Sicarii opted to commit suicide rather than surrender to the Romans.

7. I pointed out that terrorist attacks like the Mar 5 raid on Tel Aviv's Savoy Hotel[3] create political difficulties for Americans who sympathize with Palestinian aspiration. In reply, 'Arafat asked why it is that terrorism "by people who live as we do" is condemned, while UN member state which "murders our leaders in their homes" is not accused of similar or worse terrorism.

8. Asked again about PLO representation at Geneva, 'Arafat said Sadat has not raised this issue with him. Asked again if PLO would agree to go to Geneva, he said PLO would await invitation and examine "terms of reference" before deciding. In any case, 'Arafat noted, PLO is not interested in Geneva as cover for further "procrastination."

9. I said that while I could not rpt not speak for Secretary Kissinger, it was my impression that you would be interested in meeting with 'Arafat at some point in future. I told him at least this was my impression prior to recent suspension of your step-by-step peace mission. 'Arafat nodded, and added smilingly: "Dr. Kissinger delivered a meaningful warning to the Israelis when he visited Masada following breakdown of peace talks."

10. I called attention to enormous fear which influences Israelis and many of their American supporters. As friend of Israel and one who believes Israel should and will survive, I said I hoped Israelis would overcome their fear of reaching accommodation with Palestinians. In this connection, 'Arafat noted his UNGA speech[4] had been followed by "orchestrated efforts" by Zionist leaders in US to portray his words as containing "something which was not in them"—i.e., as threat to destroy Israel.

11. 'Arafat said he had asked King Faisal night before he was assassinated[5] how much he thought US had lost through suspension of your peace mission. King reportedly replied: "a great deal."

---

[3] See footnote 2, Document 139.

[4] A reference to Arafat's November 13, 1974 speech to the U.N. General Assembly. A transcript of Arafat's speech is in the *New York Times*, November 14, 1974, p. 22.

[5] King Faisal was assassinated on March 25, 1975, by Faisal bin Musai'id, the son of the king's half brother.

168. Memorandum of Conversation[1]

Washington, March 31, 1975, 11 a.m.

PARTICIPANTS

The Secretary of State
Mr. John Stoessinger
Mr. Elie Wiesel
Mr. Hans Morgenthau
Mr. Max Kampelman
Mr. Jerry Bremer (Notetaker)

Kissinger: Would any of you like coffee or tea? How many is that, then. Three coffee, two tea. I tell you, Hans, it is beyond the competence of this Department to do coffee and tea together. If you all ask for coffee, or if you all ask for tea, we could handle it, but we can't do it when it's mixed.

Morgenthau: I always said the Department operated from a single-minded purpose.

Kissinger: In the 18 months I've been here, there has been no idiocy that I have predicted that has failed to come to pass. Anything which some bureaucracy could conceive, it has conceived.

First, I would like to get straight what basis we are talking on here. On a number of cases, frankly, I have talked to Jewish intellectuals who said they were in anguish over the situation. I told them our position, and then the next thing I know they published reports of our meetings, rarely reflecting what had actually been said or what had had happened. You should know that there is little in this meeting for me. You can help me intellectually, but I don't need the meeting for public relations or for support on the Congress. But I do think, as a Jew, that we are in a critical period in which we will operate either in an atmosphere of trust or in an atmosphere of grave calamity.

Are we meeting as potential antagonists? I am not asking for your support, but I want to explain what happened. The current situation has the making of a disaster. At the end of the Cabinet meeting on the day that we broke up the talks, I said to the Israelis, you are not unreasonable but disastrous.[2] Rabin at the end said it was a Greek tragedy. As you know, in a Greek tragedy what happens is that both sides wind up bringing about the very consequences that they fear most.

---

[1] Source: National Archives, RG 59, Records of Henry Kissinger, 1973–77, Box 22, Classified External Memcons, December 1974 to April 1975, Folder 7. Limited Official Use; Sensitive. The meeting was held in the Secretary's office.

[2] March 22. See Document 158.

Kampelman: Well, I would hope that we could be of some assistance to you, Mr. Secretary.

Kissinger: If you can, that's fine. But if you do nothing, that's up to you also. I know Hans will lascerate me anyway, but I admire him. By the way, your *Encounter* article was very good.

Morgenthau: Well, I said what I thought.

Kampelman: I don't normally write in this area anyway but usually against the press. I am not an expert on the Middle East. As far as I'm concerned this is a confidential, off-the-record exchange of views with the hope that perhaps we can be of help.

Kissinger: Whether you tell the Israelis about this meeting or not is your business. I don't want the Israelis to say that I am trying to organize the Jewish community.

Morgenthau: You used the word disaster. In what way is it a disaster?

Kissinger: Let me explain to you our strategy and why the Israeli decision is a historic disaster. First let me describe the situation in October 1973.

In October 1973, Israel confronted a united, radicalized Arab world, a western Europe on the record as supporting a maximum Arab position, the Soviet Union using military threats, and Japan moving rapidly to the Arab position—all of this without even addressing the question of the Group of 77 position.[3] Israel at that time had one friend in the world to count on. That friend was under tremendous pressures that can only be generated by the close intellectual and cultural intimacy which we had with Europe.

In the Arab world, as a result of our airlift, the U.S. position was negligible. We faced an oil embargo, there was general panic and we faced also Geneva. Geneva could then have one possible outcome which was that Israel would be pushed back to the 1967 borders. Therefore, Israel at Geneva at that time would be totally defensive.

At this point I entered the sequence with a strategy of what we now call the step-by-step approach. Hans has said of it that if it succeeds it will be the greatest feat. I agree because it really should not have succeeded, logically. Hans, everything you said in the *Encounter* article about the pitfalls I faced, I agree with. You know Branch Rickey used to say that luck is the residue of design. Show me a statesman who succeeded without luck.

---

[3] The Group of 77, founded in 1964 by 77 developing nations, sought to enhance its negotiating influence at the United Nations and promote its members' economic interests.

Our strategy was to segment the problem into component parts, to enable Israel to negotiate with the Arab states separately other than on the basis of final frontiers, to maneuver the USSR at the same time since we alone could produce progress for the Arabs; to scare off the Europeans and Japanese by saying that we had something going (this accounts for our strongly stated opposition to any political content in the Euro-Arab dialogue); and finally to induce the Arabs to engage in separate talks with the Israelis. Now some have criticized this as salami tactics. You can make that criticism and argue that we could have gone to Geneva and asked for an immediate final settlement with the enormous uproar that would have accompanied that.

However, I judged that if the process itself went along long enough with individual Arab states, the point would eventually be reached where one Arab state would say "This is enough. It simply is not worth fighting every six months for every 20 kilometers." So my constant refrain with the Israelis (and the Israeli government will tell you) was: don't yield too quickly. Make it hard for the Arabs to get gains. You know I invested a tremendous amount of time to enable the Israelis to look very difficult on these matters. The Soviets might also tire of this process, I judged, since their perception was that they were pouring billions of dollars into the Middle East and yet several countries were operating separately from Soviet control.

For example, Asad, who is really a remarkable man, I met with first for seven hours.[4] He was vicious and violent. He threatened war, even against the United States. I was just as tough. He has the interesting technique of having me meet with him alone first and then he brings in his advisers to hear me repeat the same things I've said so that he's not the sucker, I am. Anyway, the first meeting was the nastiest meeting I think I've had since I've been in office.

I told him and his advisers that if he had a war with the Israelis, he would lose it. If he threatened us with the Soviet Union, we would destroy him. Moreover, the Golan did not appear to be suitable for a disengagement agreement. The decisions were simply too big for Israel, since a withdrawal on the Golan would either be so small that it would insult Asad or big enough to touch the Israeli settlements on the Golan and thereby call in to question Israel's very existence. I told Asad to think about this for a week. The next week, when I went back, he said he was prepared to talk about a Golan withdrawal with the Israelis.[5] Now it is possible that we might have had some kind of principle on the Golan of withdrawing to the '67 borders in stages giving Israel in return some kind of security zone. That might or might not have worked.

---

[4] See footnote 3, Document 19.
[5] See Document 19.

From the Soviet point of view, the point could have been reached, when someone in the USSR, someone in the Politburo says—this is a rathole, everything we pour in there is just going down a rathole.

Thus, our process required progress at stated intervals. Our trump card was always that we alone could get that progress. The essential quid pro quo for the Israelis was that the U.S. was protecting Israel from the international environment. I had even trained Faisal to stop talking publicly about the '67 borders. The last time I saw him he said he would support our approach to progress even though he was not sure it would work.

Now, some people who are attacking me are saying that this would lead to a Czechoslovakia in the Middle East. Maybe, though not while I am Secretary of State. But the worst thing which we could have faced under our former strategy is now the probable outcome. Under our strategy, the 1967 frontiers. Their validity and the manner in which they are reached. If Israel goes to those frontiers all at once, it could very well hurt Israel's self image and self defense.

Let me turn now to the negotiations themselves. Last June we told the Israelis roughly what we could see would be needed for another agreement with Egypt. The Israelis could have said at the time, no, we cannot give that—we don't want that and we will have to move to one grand move towards a settlement. In fact, you could argue that they were honor-bound to tell us that. But they didn't. In June, they said we are a new government and we need a little bit more time.

Now what I'm going to tell you is not generally known but in July, Hussein offered two things.[6] In effect he offered to accept one half of the Allon plan,[7] the concept that the Jordan valley was Israeli. He offered either an Israeli withdrawal of four kilometers there along a straight line (and when I asked King Hussein why would he stop there, he said—I know the Israelis, they don't give up hills) or he offered to accept half of the Allon plan under which the valley would be Israeli but there would be a sausage shaped area under UN control along the West Bank and in Jerusalem so that the Arabs on the West Bank could continue to work in Israel. He would also have civil administration in the big towns such as Nablis and Jericho so that Jordan would be on the

---

[6] No memorandum of conversation has been found. On July 14, King Hussein secretly met with Israeli Prime Minister Rabin to discuss possible solutions concerning Israeli control of the West Bank. (Library of Congress, Manuscript Division, Kissinger Papers, CL 155, Geopolitical File, Israel, July–August 1974)

[7] The Allon Plan was conceived in July 1967 by Israeli Foreign Minister Yigal Allon. It called for Israel to maintain a row of fortified settlements along the Jordan River to provide Israel a security buffer from future Arab attacks, but leave the rest of the West Bank demilitarized. See *Foreign Relations,* 1964–1968, volume XX, Arab-Israeli Dispute, 1967–1968, Document 213, footnote 4.

West Bank. This proposal was rejected by Israel since they said they could not face these issues until 1975. Now if the Israelis had accepted them then, there would have been no Rabat and we wouldn't have this PLO problem now. We have never made an issue of this and we have never even told anyone about it.

It is a fact that on 24 separate occasions since last July, both the President and I have told the Israelis that formal nonbelligerency was unobtainable in our opinion, and on 18 occasions we have told them that Sadat could settle for no less than the passes and the oil fields. Now, they have the right to disagree with our assessment, but we have told them many times that that was our view. In both cases, Israel never told us that they could not accept these positions. When Rabin made his speech on nonbelligerency, I called Allon to ask him what was going on. (At this point the Secretary takes a phone call.)

Kissinger: Sadat told us he had to have something before Rabat and we told him it was not possible. Then, he told us he needed something before the Brezhnev visit and again we were forced to tell him we thought it was not possible.

Anyway, Allon said that I have told Rabin to take this comment out of his speech but he thought he was being helpful by leaving it in. Now, you could agree that there is such a thing as being Talmudically correct and such a thing as being politically correct. In sum, the President and I operated on an assumption that these negotiations would succeed.

Allon came over early this year and said "do the thing in two bites. You should first come for a week and then we will use some time to get the Cabinet aboard, then come out again to finish it off."[8] You know, it is interesting, I told Sisco and Scowcroft before we left on this last trip that something does not smell right about this negotiation. The Israelis are not, if you pardon me, being as obnoxious as they should be and as they have been in the past when they are getting ready to settle something. They are not asking enough, they are not bothering us enough on side issues. Sisco said, that's impossible—it cannot be true.

Let me turn now to the substance of the negotiations. It is absolutely not true that Egypt tried ultimatums on us. Whether Sadat has in the back of his mind that he can somehow separate us from Israel and then kill off Israel more easily, I do not exclude. But Sadat in any case was willing to grant all the military aspects of nonbelligerency. This included the non-use of force during the duration of the agreement. He agreed that the agreement would last until it was superseded. He made a commitment both to Israel and to the U.S. on this so that we would

---

[8] See Document 127.

have a standing in it. He was willing to assure that no matter what happened at Geneva, he would not use it as an excuse for breaking off the disengagement agreement. He agreed to the free circulation of Arabs and to the lifting of the boycott against U.S. firms. He agreed that Israeli cargoes could pass freely through the Canal and he agreed to renew UNEF on an annual basis. He also agreed, for example, that Egypt would tone down the Cairo radio attacks on Israel though he could not agree to tone down the PLO radio.

Kampelman: How did these compare with the 1957 assurances?[9]

Kissinger: These would be public assurances. Finally, Sadat said, if he gave up all aspects of belligerency right now, what was he going to do to recover the other 180 kilometers of Egyptian territory? How would he face the other Arabs? He said to me—You write the formulation on the military side, I will accept it. Now, I admit that it's possible Sadat could be capable of breaking these assurances, but that is true either way. The only thing he didn't give to the Israelis were things that had nothing to do with the security of the line.

Israel's problem was that they were giving up tangible land for assurances and for non-belligerency. I tell you that if this were a negotiation between Spain and France in which the peace of the world were not dependent on the U.S. financing the whole thing, I would say that these were perfectly reasonable statements. Every country has to decide on the balance between their sovereignty and their security. This agreement would have taken six months to complete which would have guaranteed perfect Egyptian behavior in Geneva. Meanwhile, Syria had told me that they would not go to Geneva if Israel made a separate agreement and the Egyptians really had no interest in Geneva. So we would have been in the interesting position of being able to ask for Geneva with the assurance that no one would go there.

Now these terms for Israel involved the tangible giving up of territory. But the disaster of the thing, and here I am not an unbiased observer in this negotiation—they were very painful for me—the danger is that they are in danger of losing control over the process.

Let us assume that our aid is given to the Israelis in undiminished quantities so that we do not retaliate. And we are not talking of retaliating. I must tell you that I have never seen the President so outraged. He feels deceived. Jerry Ford from Grand Rapids, Michigan who thinks that all his life he has liked Jews and has supported Israel, suddenly he

---

[9] On February 11, 1957, Secretary of State Dulles handed to Israeli Ambassador Eban an Aide-Mémoire that provided assurances to Israel after the Suez Crisis. See *Foreign Relations*, 1955–1957, volume XVII, Arab-Israeli Dispute, 1957, Document 78.

is faced with this. In September, we told Rabin what we wanted[10] and we poured in the arms over the Arab protest because we felt it was important that when Israel was ready to move, it did so as a proud nation with a sense of its own security.

The President is outraged and this may or may not pass. But I tell you the loss of confidence among all of the people who were with me on this trip is very great. We simply cannot get over it.

We now face some practical problems. Sadat has extended UNEF for three months and if I know the Syrians, they will extend for two months both to make their expiration coincide with Egypt and to prove that they are tougher than the Egyptians. Then you will see that Sadat is already losing some control of the events because Asad won't renew again when it expires. And at some point, both of these will not be renewed.

What do we say in Geneva?—having demonstrated now our impotence. My thought was to go there and say if you want some progress, you will have to come to us. If you want to have a lot of high-sounding talk, you can go to the Soviets.

You must forget now whether we are angry or whether we are going to retaliate. We will not retaliate. That is a petty for a great power to do.

As a Jew, I must tell you that if the Jewish community starts taking on the President we will have a debacle. I briefed the congressional leaders last week with pedantic accuracy,[11] especially since I know the verbatim transcript goes to the Israeli Embassy before the day is over. I leaned over backwards. The congressional reaction was unanimously hostile. We were talking about the Israeli observation stations in the passes and O'Neill asked—Why shouldn't the Israelis have one there? And I said because it's 180 kilometers from the border.

We can now try to get the talks started again. But I have almost no conviction that it will happen. The Israelis, of course, are saying they want to talk but when we ask them we get the same positions from them. Another alternative now is to go to a bigger forum toward which I now lean. But for that we will need a comprehensive plan and I don't know how far we can deviate from the 1967 borders in the comprehensive plan. Also, the British and the French will certainly want to participate and we can't refuse them. Then we face the PLO question. How can we exclude them now when we have no step-by-step process going? I am sure they will now accept the existence of Israel. We used to

---

[10] Kissinger and Ford met with Rabin on September 10 and September 13. See Documents 99 and 100.

[11] See Document 160.

have intelligence contacts (though no political contacts) with the PLO until the Rabat Conference. Now we don't have that any more. We had hoped that the other Arabs would tire of the Palestinians and finally go to Hussein. Boumediene, who is a smart cookie, said: "I know what you are trying to do. Syria and Egypt will accept some kind of a peace with new borders and the PLO will get nothing."

Hans, you've studied diplomacy a lot and you know all one can do as a diplomat is create options. You cannot guarantee how it will happen. The questions we now face would not have come up for three years if we'd followed my strategy. All of this for 8 kilometers and the passes and nonbelligerency! I'm not saying the Israelis were wrong. But if it were between other states you wouldn't have the same problem; giving up something tangible.

Morgenthau: But a lot depends on what is in Sadat's mind.

Kissinger: I don't dispute that all Arabs, except possibly Hussein, may want to destroy Israel. Sadat I think is a statesman and an Egyptian nationalist. He has had his heroic moment and was beaten so he doesn't want another war. When Asad speaks of other Arabs, I have noticed that he is talking of the same nation. But when Sadat speaks of other Arabs, it is as friendly governments. He doesn't live there.

Morgenthau: But that doesn't answer the question and the point that he cannot exterminate Israel now anyway unless Israel becomes sufficiently weakened.

Kissinger: No, I agree there is no question that Israel should not be so weakened that they need to live ever on the good will of the Arabs.

Morgenthau: Nonbelligerency has a symbolic meaning. If a country says we will end belligerency that has a symbolic value.

Kissinger: The only way to test their will is to return close to the frontier with Egypt I think. Would you, if you were Sadat, give nonbelligerency with 180 kilometers of your land still occupied?

Morgenthau: No.

Kissinger: As I see the diplomacy developing, there will be a certain dissociation between the United States and Israel. This is mathematically certain. We cannot go to Geneva as Israel's lawyers. You can put anyone you want in this job—Laird, Richardson, it doesn't matter. The United States has interests in Western Europe, with the Soviet Union, and with Japan that are different from our interests with Israel.

Quite frankly I fear the possibility of anti-Semitism in this country which I worry about quite a bit. You know I am in the unfortunate position that whenever I predict something, I am then accused of producing it when it comes true just to prove myself right. This is precisely what happened with Turkish aid.

Stoessinger: I can't help but listening here and thinking that if we could make these facts public somehow ...

Kissinger: I'm rather fatalistic since we've given Israel all of their equipment since 1969. This strategy was designed to give Israel the maximum opportunity to survive.

Wiesel: Is Israel's survival at stake?

Kissinger: My honest opinion is yes. Not at this minute, mind you. A few weeks ago in Houston, I saw John Connally.[12] He called on me. He said, you know if I were advising somebody on how to sweep the midwest and the southwest in the next election, I would recommend an anti-Semitic campaign. And this he told me before the negotiations broke down.

If the Jewish community attacks the President you will see for the first time an American President attacking Israel and this could unleash the most profound consequences. If they attack me, the President may come to my support too. I can survive it.

Kampelman: It seems to me that we remain with one important question. We cannot undo yesterdays and this question has domestic and world implications. The worldwide ones come first and speaking as a supporter of your piecemeal negotiations I should say that I appreciated your efforts and I know that your objectives were both pro-U.S. and pro-Israeli.

When Rabin was here last, I had a breakfast with him alone. Simcha was not there. And we talked about you. This was at about the time of the *Commentary* piece and his comment about you was, "I've had long dealings with Henry Kissinger. He has never misled me or never made a commitment that he has not fulfilled. I wish he had made more commitments to me but I understand that he is the United States Secretary of State."

Kissinger: I think if Rabin could have acted like Golda, it might have worked.

Kampelman: I was in Israel when you were there and my impression is if you could have found a way to leave for one week to let the letter[13] wear off ...

Kissinger: The letter had no effect. It was over by that time.

Kampelman: Maybe if a different kind of letter or a different tone.

Kissinger: No, I don't think so. We were going to have a meeting at 7:00 and announce the breakoff. I wired the President because he had to

---

[12] John Connally was Governor of Texas from 1963 until 1969 and Secretary of the Treasury from 1971 until 1972.

[13] Document 156.

know we were going to break up. At 6:45, I called Rabin. Just to talk to him about the timing of the meeting and he said every cabinet member wishes to speak so it will go longer than I thought. I then called Scowcroft and said don't under any circumstances send any Presidential letter. Scowcroft said it had gone just a half an hour ago. I then called Dinitz out of the meeting to say: "For Pete's sake don't let him read the letter." Dinitz said he just read it five minutes ago.

But the letter was not intended to affect the deliberations. It was to tell the Israelis you are now in another ball game and it was to prepare Israel for Geneva.

Kampelman: I think if there is a way to open the piecemeal talks you should do it.

Kissinger: I will tell you I wrote a letter this week to the Israelis and to the Egyptians—this is very secret—asking each of them for any other thoughts saying what would you do now. Egypt gave us a forthcoming reply. This morning I got the Israeli reply and it was verbatim of the Friday evening statement to us when we broke up.[14]

On Friday evening I met alone with Rabin, Allon, and Peres[15] as friends and said look, let's take 24 hours and think about it. In those 24 hours they did nothing but give the Presidential letter to the Likud. They didn't call any meetings, they didn't call any cabinet talks, they did nothing. And I should tell you that this letter was nothing compared to the kind which Nixon sent them. Now Golda when we sent such letters would never read them to the cabinet. She would first ask me what to do about the letters. Sometimes I told her, look, you should take this one very seriously. But she never confronted the President.

I was hoping that they would say we will modify something. Our Ambassador there, who is not a genius, asked what is new here? They said what's new is the old position which we gave you last week. I don't think I'll show this cable to the President.

Kampelman: You discussed the possibility that at the end of this process, the Israeli sovereignty might be recognized. I think that's a new ingredient.

Kissinger: I cannot again stake U.S. prestige on this because they will leak the proposals, they will pocket them to bring them out later.

Stoessinger: Is there any way we can help?

Kissinger: We have two problems. Can the negotiations be rescued? Only if Israel moves in the next two weeks and changes their

---

[14] No letters were found.

[15] No memorandum of conversation has been found for a March 21 meeting between Kissinger and only Rabin, Allon, and Peres. There was a meeting that included the Israeli negotiating team. See footnote 2, Document 157.

tune. Now I understand they are sending teams here to brief. I must tell you that the maps which they leaked to the newspapers are wrong.[16] And if they continue to do it we will have to explain what is right and what is wrong. We are prepared now to keep quiet. Secondly, the Soviets have now approached us on Geneva. I told them it will take us at least three weeks to reassess our position. But I'm sure at some point we will have to say something. Hans, what do you think about the 1967 borders?

Morgenthau: They are inevitable except around Jerusalem which should be outside of artillery range.

Kissinger: Well, artillery range is 20 kilometers. You mean there can be no Arab troops within 20 kilometers?

Morgenthau: Well, there could be demilitarization around that area.

Kissinger: That is a concept.

Stoessinger: Will the PLO negotiate on the basis of 242?[17]

Kissinger: I don't know what Sadat is other than an Egyptian nationalist. I've been to lunch and supper with him. I've seen him, his family and his lifestyle. I think he is an Egyptian bourgeois nationalist. To Asad, Israel is just southern Syria. To the PLO it is the dividing line across their fields. I wouldn't trust the PLO and I wouldn't ask the Israelis to either. Asad however, could be brought to do something and Sadat too.

You know what Sadat said last time? He said: "I miss the old lady." And I think he is right. With Golda, everything would have happened on the first day which happened with us on the last day. We would have had a terrible blow-up on the first day and then later we would have moved on. But if I had talked to her in the kitchen, she would have understood that there is such a thing as historical versus negotiating truth.

Sadat said to Nancy this last time, when we thought things were still going well, "what worries me in the Israelis is their confusion. They've had the shock of the war and they have no confidence in the future. I don't know how we will do it." Now I grant you this could be great showmanship. But I think he's a moderate.

I think the Israelis could get Egypt off their backs by going close to the 1967 borders. If you look at history the Israeli position is inherently desperate. How can Israel with 2½ million people hold off 130 million with the U.S. increasingly losing its own self-confidence? I'm not

---

[16] See footnote 2, Document 164.
[17] See footnote 6, Document 7.

saying we'll see the same thing as what happened in Indochina where after all it didn't happen overnight either.

One misconception the Israelis had was that I needed the agreement for my domestic position. The Israeli press, while I was there, kept saying don't yield to Kissinger because he needs the agreement to solidify his position. My historic position is now established. One agreement now will neither add nor subtract to it. And to say that I would carry out an agreement for my own sake is simply not true. No man in this job can carry out an agreement simply for his own sake. Also, they have forgotten that although if I had gotten an agreement I would be a hero for six weeks, and after six weeks I would be blamed for everything that went wrong. Now there will be a two month uproar and by June the people here will know nothing except the fact that there are tensions in the area. The issues will be forgotten. So even if I get blamed for botching a negotiation now the question is who will be blamed for producing a condition of war.

It is my assessment that there is a 50–50 chance of war. Now let me tell you. What would happen if in a war the Soviet Union lands two airborne divisions in Syria, since they simply cannot afford to have another humiliation in the next war. In the past, we operated from a position of great authority. Suppose the Soviets, this time, say that all they want to do is move the Israelis back to the '67 borders. You know very well the Western Europeans will bend to that and then what will we do.

I ordered the alert in October, 1973.[18] Although at the time all the Russians were going to do was to put a division at the Cairo airport. Simply to teach them that they could not operate far from home. If they put troops in Syria, we will have to put troops in Israel. But I doubt if Congress would approve it. And do you realize that now 40 percent of our troops are negroes. Think of the possible race riots here. Even if Congress approves we will have a real Vietnam-type situation.

Kampelman: I see the real possibility of a serious division within the United States society. To avoid this I think we simply have to eliminate the concept of fault and the President's first interview was not very helpful in that regard.[19]

Kissinger: I didn't even know he was giving the interview until after it was done.

Kampelman: The Jewish community here is now being held back by the Israelis. Many of them are very unhappy about the breakdown and are blaming the Israelis. They identify the possibility that if Israel is

---

[18] A reference to Kissinger's request to President Nixon on October 24, 1973, to put American troops on nuclear alert. See footnote 8, Document 91.

[19] See footnote 3, Document 164.

at fault, we will have an anti-Semitic campaign in the United States. In fact there is a danger of such a campaign whether or not it is correct to blame the Israelis. What is vital now, is to avoid internal domestic divisions on this issue similar to those we had on Vietnam. I know you have tried by saying that we need a bipartisan foreign policy. In my view if you can revive the negotiations we can make some progress.

Kissinger: Well you have to talk to the Israelis about that.

Stoessinger: Should we?

Kissinger: I'm not asking you for anything. I'm telling you scientifically that they have to tell us something new. That might possibly revive the negotiations but it has to be done within the next two weeks.

Kampelman: If that doesn't happen, then it is vital that the different segments on the hill going to people like Humphrey, Jackson, and Goldwater must be brought in on the takeoff so they're not just included on the crash landing.

Kissinger: We have to date deliberately avoided this. But once there's Geneva we will have only three choices. We can try to revive the interim agreement. This we can do only at the Israeli initiative with some kind of a modification of the Israeli position. Even with that however, I have to ask myself if we wouldn't be better off driving right now for a full solution. If we go the other route, I have to tell you that we will wind up very close to what Hans said—something like the 1967 frontiers with demilitarized zones around it. This would be similar to Resolution 242. What would the Jewish community reaction be to that?

Wiesel: That depends on whether Israel accepts it. Do you think they would not accept it, not even for a guarantee of peace?

Kissinger: I doubt it frankly. I don't think they would do it for any frontier. Not even for a formal peace agreement.

Morgenthau: What will they do?

Kissinger: Well for Egypt they would be willing to draw a line from El Arish to Sharm-el-Sheik. On the West Bank I don't know. On the Golan, perhaps half of the Golan.

Morgenthau: Sharm-el-Sheik is vital.

Kissinger: Yes, we could do a lot there but I don't think the government will accept it. Therefore, I've engaged in such torturous negotiations.

Stoessinger: Well, we would like to help any way we can.

Kissinger: Jerry, would you please leave the room now so I can have a few minutes with these men alone.

169. Memorandum of Conversation[1]

Washington, March 31, 1975.

PARTICIPANTS

Dean Rusk
Cyrus Vance
McGeorge Bundy
George Shultz
Douglas Dillon
Averell Harriman
Robert McNamara
David Rockefeller
George Ball
William Scranton
Pete Peterson

David Bruce
John McCloy
Larry Eagleburger
Joseph Sisco
Jerry Bremer (notetaker)

(The meeting had already been underway for an hour and a half.)

Secretary Kissinger: If there is no progress by September, then I think the probability of a war by next spring is very great.

Mr. Bundy: This underlines Shultz's point.

Secretary Kissinger: George, what do you think?

Mr. Ball: I agree.

Secretary Kissinger: I just don't think the Syrians or the Palestinians will hold much longer.

Mr. Ball: I would have thought that given the present state the possibility is greater for hostilities from the Israeli side.

Secretary Kissinger: Our intelligence estimates, for whatever they are worth, are that in another war the Israelis will have no fewer than 8,000 killed.

Mr. Bundy: Does that assume a war without resupply?

Secretary Kissinger: I don't know whether I should give this group anything more with which to attack me. But I should say that we, and others looking for political office, appear to have given the Israelis too much. They now have about three weeks supply.

Mr. Bundy: That is too much.

Secretary Kissinger: The single worst mistake we made was during the Rabin visit to agree to these tranches of military supplies. We felt we had this agreement and that's why the President is now feeling aggrieved.

---

[1] Source: National Archives, RG 59, Records of Henry Kissinger, 1973–77, Box 22, Classified External Memcons, December 1974 to April 1975, Folder 7. Limited Official Use; Sensitive. The meeting was held in the Secretary's office.

Mr. Rusk: Do the Israelis understand that if they bring in any nuclear weapons they lose us?

Secretary Kissinger: That is a good question. We should make that clear to them.

Mr. Rusk: Take a look at my last talk with Eban when I was Secretary.[2]

Secretary Kissinger: When I was trying to keep Syria out of the war, I gave them our intelligence estimate. I said you'd be badly beaten. Asad's reply was interesting. He said, "You don't understand that the lesson we learned in 1973—what we finally understood—was that the Israelis could not stand pain. We won't win the war, but we will keep them fighting for many weeks until they can stand it no longer." The CIA estimates are that the next war would last about 10 days.

Mr. Ball: Jerusalem says five days.

Mr. Sisco: You don't know, they could start in on the Fatah land.

Secretary Kissinger: Well, there's no personal judgment here. But the Israelis are stronger than they were in 1973, and the political consequences of a war are the same, whether it lasts five days or five weeks. Western Europe and Japan would blame us for not preventing it. The Soviet Union would support the Arabs. It is most likely we would have an embargo and the diplomatic problems are the same anyway, even if the Israelis take Damascus and Cairo.

Mr. Scranton: Do you think the Soviets would come in?

Secretary Kissinger: I don't know—the Israelis think they can defeat the Soviets because the Soviets are so badly armed. Anyway, that is totally irrelevant.

Mr. Vance: Why do you think the Israelis took the position they did?

Secretary Kissinger: Because their government is weak and in the hole with the public statements which they had already made. I think Rabin would agree with everything I have said. Either that or he is the most treacherous leader I've ever met. But I don't think he is. My impression is that Rabin wanted the agreement. Secondly, at about the time of our trip, his popularity dropped to 30% while Peres, who opposed the agreement, went up to 67%. Third, we were there at a bad time for us in Indochina and the Israelis had seen what they thought was the Iranian sellout of the Kurds. Also, they have total contempt for our domestic position. Now, Joe (Sisco), you have traveled with many Secretaries of State to the area and as far as I know, never, since Sisco

---

[2] See *Foreign Relations, 1964–1968*, volume XX, Arab-Israeli Dispute, 1967–1968, Document 288.

has been in the area, has a U.S. Secretary of State been treated with such total disdain.

Mr. Sisco: That's right. That's what I told you about it.

Secretary Kissinger: It was a humiliating experience to be there under these circumstances.

Mr. Rusk: I avoided it by simply never going there.

Secretary Kissinger: Joe was there with Bill Rogers. If you can imagine delivering a Presidential message and there being no attempt on the other side to meet any single point in it. When I met Asad, which gets me to the impact of the domestic position on foreign policy, he said he could not understand why Sadat should make any concessions. He said you have let Taiwan go, you have let Korea go, you have let Cambodia go, you have let Vietnam go, you have let Turkey go, you will sooner or later let Israel go. There was a debate between Asad and his Foreign Minister whether or not Portugal fitted into that category. It is not exactly elevating when you are there while they are discussing the extent of your worldwide treachery. Finally, I think the Israelis felt they were stronger than we were domestically.

Mr. Sisco: I agree. And as I told you, I think that they have decided that if they face war, they would prefer to face it this year with the passes when they can manage U.S. policy rather than after the elections.

Mr. Rockefeller: Rabin has as much as said this to me.

Mr. McNamara: I think there is a fifth point to the ones Henry has mentioned, too. And that is that we must begin to get tough with Israel quickly.

Secretary Kissinger: Yes, but only on a bipartisan basis. This cannot be a fight with petulance.

Mr. Bundy: You don't need to tell them or fight it. The Israelis are already perceived as bad boys. This goes back to 1948 when we didn't make clear our position.

Secretary Kissinger: We are now cutting back on our intelligence cooperation, except that intelligence which is relevant to surprise attack. We can't afford to let them be blind. The F–15 will not be coming here and we are slowing down the Lance and laser bomb deliveries. We've also cancelled Defense Minister Peres's visit. This will all lead to some unshirted hell and we won't announce it, but will leave it to Israel to start the fight.

We are not doing this to punish Israel, but to try to get them into a frame of mind where they see that although we have parallel interests, they are not the same as Israel's. We have global interests that they simply do not have. We do not want polarization with the Arabs or the Soviets, and nor do we want to have the Soviets be the lawyer for the

Arabs and us as the lawyer for the Israelis in Geneva. Therefore, we are engaged now in some dissociation from Israel.

They should know that we will act in what we, in our own best judgment, see as our interest and in their best interest. Fahd told the Vice President that we have a year. After that they'd put all of Saudi Arabian resources behind the Arabs totally. Now Faisal never pledged all of his resources. I think he was too much of a Bedouin.

Ambassador Bruce: Do you think the Israeli leaders believe they can go over the heads of the executive branch negotiators and think that we will give them complete support, including U.S. forces, if they have another war?

Secretary Kissinger: The Israeli government is starting a massive propaganda campaign to blame Egypt. Then, if I don't miss my bet, they will begin to say that Geneva is a terrible forum and they will try to force us back to the step-by-step approach. Therefore, they keep saying over and over that the U.S. must stay active and they're sending these teams here to brief. They gave an account to the British of the talks, which was unbelievable. Now we can't be dragged into an argument with the Israelis about the day-by-day description of the negotiations.

Mr. Bundy: The consequences of the last few weeks should not emerge in the talks with Israel. In my experience it always worked better to say that their military situation was better than they say it is. In other words, we should say, look you guys, you are stronger than you say you are.

Secretary Kissinger: That is a good point.

[Omitted here is discussion unrelated to the Arab-Israeli dispute.]

170. Memorandum of Conversation[1]

Washington, April 3, 1975.

SUBJECT

Middle East

PARTICIPANTS

The Secretary of State
Mr. Sisco, Under Secretary of State for Political Affairs
Ambassador Keating, Ambassador to Israel
Ambassador Eilts, Ambassador to Egypt
Ambassador Murphy, Ambassador to Syria
Ambassador Pickering, Ambassador to Jordan
Mr. Atherton, Assistant Secretary of State for Near Eastern and South Asian Affairs
Mr. Saunders, Deputy Assistant Secretary of State for Near Eastern and South Asian Affairs
Mr. Oakley, NSC
Mr. Bremer, Notetaker

Secretary Kissinger: I thought we'd have a preliminary talk now and then a longer one next week on where we stand. The President means business about reassessing our policy. Do your clients understand that, Ken?

Ambassador Keating: I think so. They are forming the feeling in their minds that we mean business.

Secretary Kissinger: They really ripped it with the President this time.

Ambassador Keating: You mean with their "new ideas"?

Secretary Kissinger: In the sense that he feels that they double-crossed him. You know the President. You (Sisco) saw him. He feels that they are making us pay out of proportion to any issue involved during the negotiations. What's the difference between the end or the middle of the passes?

Can you give us two minutes on the mood in Israel, both among the officials and the people?

Ambassador Keating: Well, the officials still look to us and want to be close to us as their only friends.

Secretary Kissinger: But what are they willing to do?

---

[1] Source: Library of Congress, Manuscript Division, Kissinger Papers, CL 346, State Department Memorandum of Conversations, Internal, April–May 1975. Secret; Sensitive. Drafted by Bremer. The meeting was held at the Department of State.

Ambassador Keating: Well, you got my cable.[2] And I would like to stress that the people are behind Rabin. He now has about 90% of the people backing his being firm.

Secretary Kissinger: Oh, there's no question of that. What about Geneva?

Ambassador Keating: Well, they don't want to go. Though they expect to have to go if you don't return. I know you're not planning to. But they expect that something will be worked out. In fact, I have an idea.

Secretary Kissinger: What?

Ambassador Keating: The only part of Allon's talk which had anything new in it was where do we go from here and the fact that Israel is prepared to go very far, in fact all the way for peace and very far for non-belligerency—way beyond the passes.

Secretary Kissinger: I really don't understand them. They make fun of the non-use of force on the grounds that you can't trust the Arabs but if that is true at the passes, then why should you trust the Arabs with non-belligerency 100 kilometers further back?

Ambassador Keating: I don't see either.

Secretary Kissinger: Can Sadat accept non-belligerency?

Ambassador Eilts: I'm not so sure that it isn't the way to get the thing started. If faced with having to make a choice he'll back out of it, but it still cannot be done with non-belligerency without a definition defining the difference between non-belligerency and peace so clear as not to give everything away. The Israelis might have some tendency to look again at the El Arif line with another look at the non-belligerency definition.

Secretary Kissinger: If the Israelis do that, I will really doubt their sanity. If they blew up the talks for 6 kilometers and then go back 80 kilometers for something that's not quite non-belligerency, they must be nuts.

Ambassador Keating: I think we may really have trouble.

Secretary Kissinger: When will we hear from the Israelis? In three weeks we'll be too far down the road. Once the Geneva dates are set, it will be very difficult.

Ambassador Keating: Well, am I authorized to discuss this with them?

Secretary Kissinger: No. They have to come to us. The next round is the round when both sides come and ask us. The time when they

---

[2] Probably a reference to telegram 1834 from Tel Aviv, March 30, which reported on Keating's conversation with Allon. (National Archives, RG 59, Central Foreign Policy Files, P850014–1515)

think I need these negotiations for my domestic position is over. We're not going to go begging. The Egyptians weren't bad. At least they gave us what they could.

Ambassador Keating: How do we get started then?

Secretary Kissinger: It's Israel's choice. We can try to start the talks again or we can go to Geneva and let nature take its course or we can go to Geneva with an American plan.

Mr. Atherton: Could we get the talks started with an American plan now?

Secretary Kissinger: They'll kill us. We have to know what we want. Many of the reasons we wanted the talks have now gone. Geneva seems to me as almost inevitable. It will mean spilling much blood and it may not be worth it, especially if we make Israel accept an American plan and then go to Geneva.

If Israel had accepted even after bitter negotiations then we could have gone to Geneva, though there might not even have been a Geneva, since I doubt if Dick's guys would have come.

Ambassador Murphy: That's right.

Secretary Kissinger: To go to limited talks now and to impose a settlement in six months, I just don't know.

Ambassador Keating: Perhaps we should talk now about a complete settlement.

Secretary Kissinger: By that you mean a settlement on all fronts?

Ambassador Keating: Right.

Secretary Kissinger: That we can undertake either in or out of Geneva.

Ambassador Keating: We are talking about a line East of El Arish-El Tor. I think we would have to move on at least two fronts at the same time.

Secretary Kissinger: Let me understand this. I think there are two problems. The Israelis are talking around that they want us back, but they have never stated what they mean by that. (To Ambassador Murphy) Did you see Asad before you left?

Ambassador Murphy: Yes.

Secretary Kissinger: Was it friendly?

Ambassador Murphy: Yes, very friendly. He very much wants us engaged.

Secretary Kissinger: Well, I share your feeling, Ken, in the last paragraph of your cable. I don't see any new element in the Israeli answer.

There are two possibilities. Either the Israelis tell us that we should complete an interim agreement with a U.S. plan agreed to by the Israelis ahead, this would involve a line east of the passes with a narrow coastal corridor.

(Secretary leaves room to take a phone call.)

Secretary Kissinger: Here is the basic problem. The Israelis keep asking us to get back in but they have no practical proposal. They are putting it out to the media and everyone imploring us without any constructive ideas.

Mr. Sisco: That is one reason why I don't think you can be too rigid about who takes the initiative.

Secretary Kissinger: Suppose we come up with an idea. What is needed is a line east of the passes, even one kilometer. Am I not right?

Ambassador Eilts: Right.

Secretary Kissinger: If the line goes down even with the continuous line with some kind of a corridor . . .

Ambassador Eilts: With civilian administration.

Secretary Kissinger: He doesn't need a wide corridor. You could probably even say that Israeli trucks could use the road, but there is simply no truth to the argument that they need that road as an alternative to the Sharm-el-Sheik road.

Ambassador Eilts: Sadat would probably buy what you're talking about, but I doubt Sadat will offer more.

Secretary Kissinger: Would he accept all three Israeli formulations?

Ambassador Eilts: I would think he would argue that they are redundant.

Secretary Kissinger: But these people are essentially rug merchants. The question is would he accept all three.

Ambassador Eilts: No, I think he would want to play with the language a little bit to eliminate what he sees as redundancy.

Mr. Sisco: My judgment is, on the other hand, that he would accept. I'll go further. I think we can play with the first paragraph.

Secretary Kissinger: The more fundamental question is where are we then. Now had we gotten this Egyptian agreement, Asad wouldn't have gone to Geneva and he would have been willing to have talks with the Israelis. Now he'll insist on going to Geneva.

Ambassador Murphy: He's much more reticent now. Everything is being prepared in detail for Geneva.

Secretary Kissinger: Here is my worry. We would pay such a price in Israel for only a limited agreement. And there are only two ways to get a limited agreement. They can come to us or we can ask them are you prepared to accept a U.S. proposal. They may accept such a proposal, but there will be unshirted hell.

Mr. Sisco: The best would be if the Israelis would come up with something. I feel that we could say procedurally they have already come back to us with something. Our ideas can then be put in diplomatic channels to the Israelis as a discussion without any formal proposal until we get their reactions.

Secretary Kissinger: Yes, but is it worth it?

Mr. Sisco: I assume in Geneva we can do no more than posture and take a public position of dissociation with Israel. I just don't think that between now and 1976 we can get an overall agreement. I think the price of starting up again now is less than the price we would pay if we lost the American role entirely.

Secretary Kissinger: What about Syria?

Mr. Sisco: There are two choices. Either the beginning of a process along the lines which you discussed with Asad or to try to start it up in Geneva.

We need to try to resurrect the negotiations.

Secretary Kissinger: I disagree. Is this coming from Goldberg[3] in any way?

Mr. Sisco: No, it has nothing to do with Goldberg. That's not fair.

Ambassador Keating: We can keep Geneva in the distance.

Secretary Kissinger: There's no way to do that. It will now meet.

Ambassador Keating: That's unfortunate.

Secretary Kissinger: Well, who lectured them on this? Who was giving insolent speeches to us about how eager they were to get there.

Ambassador Eilts: I would like to see the talks resurrected. In the end we may have to go to Geneva, but this would happen in different circumstances if the talks were resurrected. There is certainly some advantage to trying. We can ask a higher price for non-belligerency.

Secretary Kissinger: That is a totally new negotiation. If there is a massive Israeli withdrawal, it must go to El Arish-El Tor. In that case then there must be something for Syria. I doubt Asad could survive a massive move there without something for him.

Ambassador Eilts: I think it will be too much for the Israelis. Then they will fall back to getting both sides out of the passes.

Secretary Kissinger: We should separate the problems. I see no domestic basis for Rabin to make a move. I can see a line that might parallel the passes one kilometer back and then swings maybe out to two kilometers from the coast. I think the Egyptians would accept it.

Ambassador Eilts: For the non-use of force.

---

[3] Arthur J. Goldberg, a former Supreme Court Justice, Ambassador to the United Nations, and President of the American Jewish Committee.

Secretary Kissinger: That's what they told the congressional delegation.

That's one negotiation. On the tactics, I think we must let the Israelis stew for another week and let the Jewish community here get a little more frantic.

Mr. Sisco: I didn't like what you said a while ago about Goldberg, Henry.

Secretary Kissinger: I didn't even know you had met with Goldberg. I thought you would call him. I had a meeting myself with a west coast Jewish group, including Ziffren and Taft Schreiber at breakfast. There is an important difference. They are scared to death of a fight. They can yell and scream, but they are not ready for a fight, because they don't know where a fight will take them.

Almost every Jew I've talked to has wound up saying he'll talk to the Israelis. I think eventually that will seep through. Therefore, our official position is that we don't give a damn.

Dayan, who is always contrary, says we should start with the Syrians. He says until the Israelis bite the bullet on Syria we are wasting our time. He says the Syrians will start a war so it doesn't really matter what the Israelis do with Egypt. And we should not be so eager for step-by-step progress. He doesn't care where the Sinai line is. He said you know, Simcha is explaining on television things Americans simply don't understand. The only question is Syria, and since Syria won't make peace without the Palestinians, you have to make an interim settlement with Syria. I tell you, while he was telling me all this Simcha was dying. I told Simcha that I wanted the record to show that I wasn't asking anything and if you have an idea ok; if not, we go to Geneva.

Let them cook another week.

Mr. Sisco: You may be right about the importance of that last talk in Damascus.[4]

Secretary Kissinger: Here is my concern. If the President wrote Rabin and said for the sake of Israeli-U.S. relations, you must get out of the passes. It just might give us a chance. There's a better than even chance that this might get them out. But where are we then. We have a massive problem with Syria in three months. Therefore, I'm reluctant to put forth a U.S. proposal which would make it look like the Egyptian one is the only important settlement. I think having driven us to this point and having gotten the Jewish community so upset, we should get more for it.

Mr. Sisco: I don't think you can.

---

[4] See Document 147.

Secretary Kissinger: What is Goldberg's view?

Mr. Sisco: He thinks we should pick up the talks again.

Secretary Kissinger: And go where with them?

Mr. Sisco: Well, he has no clear views.

Secretary Kissinger: How does he feel about the '67 borders?

Mr. Sisco: He called Dinitz last night and told them they should get peace for the '67 borders.

Secretary Kissinger: Think of our position in the Arab world. If we can get into a position of peace for the '67 borders while the Jewish community supports us ... I'm not sure we should be so hot for a limited agreement.

Mr. Sisco: But I think we can do that even if we fail in the next try.

Secretary Kissinger: If we fail, it's easy to go to the '67 borders. What I worry about is if we succeeded the next time, we would have our problems. You know my view. I didn't want to reach that point for several years. We could go for this agreement now; it is attainable. And selfishly it would be a great accomplishment, but where are we afterwards? We are in a good psychological position now. The Jews are very nervous, they will go after me, and they'll try to destroy me. But the President is ready, the Leadership is ready, and I just don't think we should give that away for six kilometers in the passes. I have always thought the confrontation was inevitable, but I thought it would happen over Syria. I am deeply worried that in six months we will be much worse off. Now everybody is pleading, but we are under no great pressure yet. When we try to pressure the Israelis, Jackson, et al., that's when it will get rough.

My previous strategy was to do Egypt and then close down the whole thing until after our elections. I was not, quite frankly, going to spill very much blood for Syria. Get it started maybe and then let it drag into 1976. I think Sadat was willing to do that.

Mr. Sisco: In the Syrian discussions, we're not talking about 2 or 3 kilometers—we will need to put forth a peace settlement.

Secretary Kissinger: If you look at all this Jewish community turmoil, it may be that they start saying, talk peace, we will get an interim settlement, and perhaps even more. If we settle too quickly for an interim settlement, we'll pay lots in arms, memoranda of understanding, etc.

Goldberg was close to hysteria. There are no pro-Israeli editorials in all of these weeks in the papers. Did you see the *Baltimore Sun* editorial today?

Mr. Sisco: I think we're all agreed that we're in no hurry.

Secretary Kissinger: There is no gain in pushing them to the edge of the passes. I think Sadat will let go the whole thing until 1977.

Ambassador Eilts: Definitely.

Secretary Kissinger: What about Asad?

Ambassador Murphy: He'll try to wreck it, linking himself more and more to Algeria, the PLO, etc.

Secretary Kissinger: I don't want it said that the U.S. is splitting up the Arabs.

Mr. Sisco: We must remember there is also a difference between Sadat and Fahmy. Sadat is facing the reality that the interim agreement is behind us though Fahmy I think is hopeful.

Secretary Kissinger: There are a number of things we must understand. Suppose I revived the negotiations. I see no possibility that Sadat will put up with another three-week nightmare. He simply can't risk it. He can only risk the talks with a practical assurance that it will work before we start and we'll have to start, therefore, with an agreed line.

Mr. Sisco: You'd have to be very far along before you go out.

Secretary Kissinger: In terms of the U.S. dignity, we will never put up with what we did on this last trip. We might do a one-week trip. Can they focus on that?

Ambassador Keating: Not to that extent—not in a week. I don't think they can do it.

Secretary Kissinger: Well, it must be done in a week. That is just the point. Next time we do it in one week.

Mr. Sisco: Even less.

Ambassador Keating: Are we talking about a big settlement here in a week?

Secretary Kissinger: No, but the minute they talk about the big settlement, they must offer a big settlement to Syria too. Sadat simply can't accept a big one without Syria as well.

Ambassador Eilts: That's right, he cannot. He's safe as long as it's a military agreement only.

Secretary Kissinger: But if you have a big one, he must have some kind of an offer to Syria too.

Ambassador Eilts: He needs the linkage.

Secretary Kissinger: I don't insist that it be a final peace. The Israelis, however, would have to make a big move everywhere. I had a strategy that would have worked. We'd have done what was possible for Syria. And what we failed to achieve we would have taken to Geneva. It would have been stalled until 1977.

This hasn't happened. Our profound disappointment may turn out to be a blessing. It has shaken the Jewish community from their complacency and there must now be forces in Israel to face the nature of peace. It is a U.S. opportunity to really stand for something. Geneva is a matter of stage managing. No one expects anything to happen there. But if it doesn't happen with nothing else going on, we may have a war.

Mr. Sisco: I feel if we go to Geneva without an interim agreement, it won't get off the ground—it will be an impasse, and it is more likely that we will have a war within a year. That is another reason why whatever price we have to pay, we need to get this thing in hand. Asad will be reluctant to start a one-front war against the Israelis and therefore an interim agreement is a deterrent.

Secretary Kissinger: It depends on what we pay for it.

Ambassador Eilts: I'm inclined to share Joe's view. The interim agreement would be a deterrent.

Secretary Kissinger: Ken, what do you make of Rabin's statement about not giving one whit.

Ambassador Keating: Oh, I think that's for public consumption; he's riding very high.

Secretary Kissinger: But how does he get the Egyptians to the end of the passes then?

Ambassador Keating: He's naive. He can talk about a peace settlement more easily than anyone.

Secretary Kissinger: Then we're not talking about an interim agreement. We're talking about a big agreement.

Ambassador Keating: I agree. It is easier for Rabin, now that he didn't give up the passes, to go all the way for a peace settlement.

Secretary Kissinger: Is there a step in between? If one can find a difference between peace and non-belligerency, maybe it will be easier for all of the Arabs.

Ambassador Pickering: We have to keep in mind the Palestinian and West Bank problems. Sadat and Asad will be plunged right into that.

Mr. Oakley: I'm not sure—I think they might wait.

Ambassador Eilts: If you can move fast enough for the Syrians, the Palestinians will wait.

Secretary Kissinger: Suppose the Israelis accepted the '67 frontier in principle. Would the Syrians leave the Israelis on the Golan for ten years?

Ambassador Murphy: No.

Secretary Kissinger: Would they be willing to see a UN force there for 15 years?

Ambassador Murphy: I think so.

Ambassador Keating: May I just say that the UN in Israel is a really bad word. If you can say a force of a specific people, that would be much better.

Secretary Kissinger: What if we said a non-Syrian force?

Ambassador Keating: That's better.

Ambassador Pickering: If you move quickly with Syria, there are Arabs who will say that Asad has moved and forgotten about the Palestinians.

Ambassador Eilts: I have one problem with this strategy. I admit I do not have the sense or feel that you have for the local Jewish community. But if it is so disturbed, and if their reaction is to destroy you, then this effort is gone and we take that very serious risk.

Secretary Kissinger: Well, as DeGaulle said, the graveyards are full of the tombs of the indispensable people. When sanity returns to the Jews here, we will find their options are not that great. It's going to be pretty hard to accuse a Jewish Secretary of State of anti-Semitism, though they will harass me. I am already spending three-quarters of my time with Jews. It's just the price we pay.

I found it damn humiliating on the last trip that they all thought that I needed and that the President needed this agreement for ourselves. And the U.S. desperately needed a success. We are suffering a national disgrace in Vietnam. Having suffered it, we will have to act twice as strong. It is the only way to come out with our self-respect. We'll do what's right now.

I take your concerns seriously, Joe, but we may be in a new period now.

What are our options? A little agreement, a peace settlement, or a semi-permanent interim agreement.

A peace agreement I don't think can be faced. The semi-permanent interim agreement, say of ten years with Syria, I don't exclude. Perhaps along the lines of an El Arif-El Tor line and something between non-belligerency and non-use of force.

The Syrians being in a way more legitimate can make more concessions than the Egyptians. This is the interesting thing. And Asad is a bargainer. He's really my favorite Arab. In a funny way, he's an honorable man, though Sadat is the greater statesman.

Now that we're in a brawl, I think maybe we should go for the bigger interim agreement. Simcha has said Israel is thinking of a big step towards non-belligerency. Let them. Why should we now go only for the passes?

Rather than give up non-belligerency, they might move the line to El-Arish El-Tor. They will of course chisel, but at that point, we should say we cannot do this without the Syrians. Then you have something. If we could do all this this year, then in Geneva we can talk about Jerusalem, Palestine, etc.

If we make an American proposal, we draw a line to the edge of the passes. We won't get much more from the Egyptians and as for the eight elements, there's nothing in there.

Mr. Saunders: There might be for a broader line.

Mr. Atherton: I think the Israelis will want literal non-belligerency.

Secretary Kissinger: There is another thing. Are these guys serious or are they trying to get into another position? Suppose our instinct is right and they have decided not to agree.

Ambassador Keating: I know Sadat may not be able to accept it.

Secretary Kissinger: Non-belligerency without withdrawal, you mean?

Ambassador Eilts: When confronted with it, he might have a lot of trouble.

Secretary Kissinger: Well, let's do the following. Let us plan to meet next Tuesday[5] morning for an hour and a half. I would like to see at that time a plan for a full peace, a plan for an interim agreement of substantial size and a little plan.

Let's discuss it from the point of view of what is right and not what is at this point politically feasible in this country.

---

[5] April 8. See Document 171.

Negotiations and Reassessment   621

171. Memorandum of Conversation[1]

Washington, April 8, 1975, 11 a.m.

SUBJECT

Middle East

PARTICIPANTS

The Secretary of State
Under Secretary Sisco
Ambassador Keating
Ambassador Eilts
Ambassador Pickering
Ambassador Murphy
Mr. Atherton
Mr. Saunders
Mr. Oakley
Mr. Bremer (Notetaker)

Secretary Kissinger: (to Keating) Your clients' version of the talks are getting more fantastic every day.

Ambassador Keating: I'm aware of that. I just hope you haven't seen everything. It's pretty bad.

Secretary Kissinger: I didn't see the Peres briefing.

Ambassador Keating: In addition, you know McGovern was going to a dinner party there by the Israelis and when he gave his press interview and talked about a separate Palestinian state, the Israeli cabinet people all cancelled the dinner.

Secretary Kissinger: Peres has now said the '67 frontiers are not defensible. Therefore, they want to make the interim agreement for less than non-belligerency and won't accept the '67 frontiers. (Kissinger reads cable)[2] How do the Israelis say they got nothing in return?

Ambassador Keating: We don't agree but they will stick to it.

Secretary Kissinger: Do they really think that if passengers could fly from Cairo to Tel Aviv this would mean something?

Ambassador Keating: Yes.

---

[1] Source: Library of Congress, Manuscript Division, Kissinger Papers, CL 346, State Department Memorandum of Conversations, Internal, April–May 1975. Secret; Sensitive. Drafted by Bremer. The meeting took place in the Secretary's office at the Department of State.

[2] Telegram 2051 from Tel Aviv, April 7, reported on Israeli Defense Minister Peres's meeting with a congressional delegation led by Representative O'Neill. Peres expressed Israel's concerns about security and provided Israel's version of the Israeli-Egyptian negotiations. (National Archives, RG 59, Central Foreign Policy Files)

Secretary Kissinger: How can he say it was linked to Syria when we had broken the link?

Mr. Sisco: They are simply telling outright lies. To say that we've gotten just one year renewal on UNEF is a lie. That's what was in the Gwertzman article.[3] Gwertzman told me he got this from Dinitz. I said in the first place, they didn't give us a map until the talks were all over, and Roy followed up with Bernie who said that's what Dinitz told me.

Yesterday Bernie called me to say that the Israelis have made three proposals. One, a peace agreement; two, consider the next step in a broader context; and three, resume the next stage interim agreements.

Secretary Kissinger: Well, that's technically true.

Mr. Sisco: Of course, but the key point is that there is no substantive change in their position. I think that is now reflected in Bernie's article this morning.

Secretary Kissinger: (reading cable) This is a bunch of lies. Everything he says they asked for—they got. Shouldn't we see these congressmen when they get back?

Mr. Sisco: I think we should see O'Neill. He'll raise some specific questions.

Secretary Kissinger: Say that we've seen the account. I shouldn't do it. Ken, you and Joe can do it.

Mr. Sisco: We need to consider how long to keep the Ambassadors here. Maybe Roy and I can do it.

Secretary Kissinger: The thing that worries me now is that the Israelis have their second wind. They will so confuse the issues around here that no one knows what happened, and in three weeks the Egyptians will be the villains.

Mr. Sisco: We're just not in a position to confront them now.

Secretary Kissinger: Why not?

Mr. Sisco: We need to look ahead to our reassessment. It is not worth doing if we do it fast. We have to try to correct these things in the briefings but I'm convinced that the statements they're making are not even remotely linked to the truth.

Secretary Kissinger: I'm seeing Dinitz this afternoon, and mostly for tactical reasons since they're saying I refuse to see them. It really is an unbelievable situation when the Secretary of State sees all these past important people—this establishment group[4]—and is then accused of

---

[3] Bernard Gwertzman's article, "Failure of Kissinger's Mideast Mission Traced to Major Miscalculations," revealed several supposed details that led to the collapse of Egyptian-Israeli negotiations. (*New York Times*, April 7, 1975, p. 12)

[4] See Document 169.

seeing an anti-Semitic group. I've been meeting regularly with them for years. When I see the Jewish Presidents group once a month[5]—and I've seen more Jews in the last week than anything else—it really is unbelievable.

I would just as soon have Goldberg go public. I'd rather have no further discussions with him. After your briefing he's even more outraged, since the differences are so small that he figures that only incompetence or malice could account for our failure. He also offered to mediate.

Mr. Sisco: I know.

Secretary Kissinger: I'm just telling you what his conclusion was.

Mr. Sisco: I wouldn't be too excited about that.

Mr. Oakley: You told them in the talks that the propaganda battle would last two or three months and then would focus on the issues.

Secretary Kissinger: Well, I will have ten minutes alone with Dinitz, then Joe, you can come in for the rest of the meeting. This is not the normal Israeli-U.S. confrontation. The President, the Vice President and I are totally united. Fisher demanded to see the President alone and I want to put them on notice. (Kissinger reads ticker) Does this come from Fisher?

Mr. Sisco: No, I think he's well meaning. There really is no free press in Israel. They're just following the party line under instructions.

Secretary Kissinger: Do you agree, Ken?

Ambassador Keating: It's hard to believe that Fisher said it. The press is generally united, but they feel a need for fine relations with the United States.

Secretary Kissinger: That's how the negotiations started.

The deception of the Israelis started in October when, if they had said under no circumstances would they give up non-belligerency, we could have told Sadat in November and avoided the entire sequence of events. The basic fact is they permitted us to continue on a road we had said would fail and to follow a procedure which humiliated us with the Egyptians.

Ambassador Keating: Allon and Rabin in private talks probably led you to believe they were more flexible.

Secretary Kissinger: I showed the nonuse-of-force formulation to Rabin alone in February.[6] He said, "Don't show it to the Cabinet or I'll

---

[5] The Presidents Group was a group of American Jews who met with President Ford and Secretary Kissinger on issues relating to Israel. See, for example, Documents 36 and 261.

[6] Kissinger met with Rabin and the Israeli negotiating team on February 11 and February 13. See Documents 131 and 134. No memorandum of conversation has been found for a private meeting between Rabin and Kissinger.

have a two-week fight." We had never heard of the line through the middle of the passes until the end. They misled us no matter what they say.

The first time in Aswan[7] I got Sadat to drop conditions on the nonuse-of-force. I brought it to Israel. They never reacted.

Mr. Sisco: They are rewriting the history of the talks.

Ambassador Keating: They've got a lot of big guns coming over here to tell their story.

Mr. Oakley: I have the general impression that people are not that sympathetic to Israel's cause.

Secretary Kissinger: I will tell Dinitz the way I see it developing. I warned them solemnly that we are determined to see it through and even if they win it will do so much damage to the Jewish community here that it may never recover. There can be no wedge or disagreement between me and the President.

Mr. Sisco: Well, you have to bear in mind the next campaign. You should remember that they will try to drive a wedge between you and the President.

Secretary Kissinger: Well it can't be done. With Nixon it was possible.

Ambassador Keating: I saw Percy and Pell at dinner last night. They're pretty solid. I think they see the error in the Israeli point of view.

Mr. Sisco: Unfortunately, they carry no weight.

Secretary Kissinger: Why have a tremendous bloodletting just to get an interim agreement? A lot of the assurances we were previously willing to give them, we simply can't give them.

Mr. Sisco: We can't say anything and Sadat can't either. Therefore, these press stories are just the opposite of what we need.

Secretary Kissinger: Can we now say that nothing happens until 1978? I don't think we can. Faisal is dead now and Fahd may not stand still for it.

Mr. Sisco: What do you think, Hermann?

Ambassador Eilts: It will depend in part on the internal situation in Saudi Arabia. Fahd is not as preoccupied as Faisal. If Fahd is assured of support, for his own internal ambitions, he'll be more reasonable. But something has to happen.

Secretary Kissinger: That's my point. The Israeli strategy now is to wait until 1977. They have enough equipment to survive.

---

[7] See Document 132.

Ambassador Keating: I think the vote on the '76 provisions may be surprising.

Mr. Sisco: Nothing is yet proposed.

Ambassador Keating: I think the Israelis are concerned.

Mr. Sisco: I'm worried about what the traditional supporters of Israel will do. People like Humphrey.

Secretary Kissinger: If the President puts up $750 million will they go to $1½ billion?

Ambassador Keating: An effort should be made to talk to the congressional leaders about these amounts.

Mr. Sisco: We have the Mathias proposal which is to get a negotiated amount.

Secretary Kissinger: Did you brief Inouye?

Mr. Sisco: Yes, Inouye, Ribicoff, and Mathias.

Secretary Kissinger: What about Brooke?

Mr. Sisco: No.

Secretary Kissinger: Let's go back and look at the options again. An interim agreement—there are only three ways to get it. First, the Israelis give us some new proposals. Second, Egypt puts forward a new proposal. Or third, we put forward ours.

On the Israeli proposal, there's just no sign whatsoever.

Ambassador Keating: Right.

Secretary Kissinger: In fact, I do not think that there is any political basis in Israel for it. So that there can't be an Israeli proposal under the present Israeli circumstances. Does anyone disagree?

Now, an Egyptian proposal. I think they would be willing to modify it if they get the passes and an unbroken line.

Ambassador Eilts: Right.

Secretary Kissinger: However, they won't volunteer modifications in their position in the absence of knowing what they will get. Therefore, if the Israelis wanted something in return for one half of the passes, we could get, in my judgment, only a little more from the Egyptians. I don't think we can even get what's in your paper.[8]

Now a U.S. proposal. For the first time in our relations with Israel, this would be done without prior approval by the Israelis. You know, I ask myself, what nation of 2½ million has a right to say to us that we cannot put forward a proposal without their approval.

Basically, the more you analyze the Israeli proposal, the more preposterous it is. Assume the line goes through the middle of the passes

---

[8] Not further identified. Presumably it was a first draft of the response to NSSM 220 (Document 163).

and there is a line of limited armaments of 18 kilometers either side. This puts the Israeli line 18 kilometers back of the passes. Therefore, there is no defense line in the middle of the passes. Since it's a zone of limited armaments how can the 8 kilometers matter? It is a pure political gimmick.

Our proposal line would have to be here. (pointing at map)[9]

Mr. Sisco: According to the CIA, that road next to the Red Sea is not usable.

Ambassador Eilts: Well, why don't we build them a shore road with our AID program?

Secretary Kissinger: Where is that UNEF checkpoint and what does it do? Check that no military aid goes in?

Mr. Sisco: Yes. If you ask that the line go to the east here and limit the Egyptian zone to this place (pointing at map) . . .

Secretary Kissinger: Impossible.

Mr. Sisco: Not if they move east of the passes.

Ambassador Eilts: I thought we had agreed that there would be some Egyptian civil administration in that zone.

Secretary Kissinger: The worst possible position is to put up a proposal which neither side will accept. Sadat has said he will not do it if he has to cross Israeli territory.

Mr. Sisco: I had in my mind a road as the UN zone; then he doesn't have to go through Israeli territory.

Secretary Kissinger: The question is when you have Egyptian administration in UN territory.

Mr. Sisco: My point is if we were able to get a little bit more east of the passes, the Egyptian administration in the enclave and the UN zone, Sadat might be able to buy it.

Ambassador Eilts: I don't think Sadat will buy it.

Secretary Kissinger: I don't either. He can't justify it to the Arabs. It will be difficult to Gamasi. They'll be far from the passes; the Israelis will be at the passes. He might be able to sell this as a demilitarized Egyptian zone with UN supervision but we can't sell three zones. He has to show that Egypt gained something.

The Israeli tragedy is that they won't rest until Sadat is as bad as Asad. He will become their image of Asad. What would he have gotten from all of this? The oil fields plus the east of the passes.

Mr. Sisco: We discussed it yesterday. I don't think our proposal can ask for them to go east of the passes, as that is a fundamentally new

---

[9] Map is not attached.

proposal. A thin UN zone goes beyond what they have already talked about.

Ambassador Eilts: I share your view, Mr. Secretary. A demilitarized zone with a UNEF control and with a symbol of Egyptian civilian administration, he could buy.

Mr. Sisco: I think he could buy a UN zone as long as it was neither Israeli nor Egyptian.

Ambassador Eilts: I don't think he would. A demilitarized zone with nominal Egyptian civilian administration and with UNEF control, he could buy.

Secretary Kissinger: Something similar to the Syrian UNDOF zone, he could buy.

If the Israelis thought about it like statesmen, what would they lose by giving him 10 kilometers of sand?

Mr. Oakley: There are tank traps here (pointing at map).

Secretary Kissinger: But if it's in the UN zone or in the Egyptian zone, the tank traps would have to go.

Mr. Oakley: Well, they could stay if it was the UN zone.

Secretary Kissinger: It's hard for me to see that Egypt would permit the Israeli tank traps to stay on their own territory even if it was a UN zone.

Ambassador Eilts: I agree, I don't think they could permit it.

Secretary Kissinger: Sadat would have to publish a map which the Arabs see. He's gaining next to nothing but Israeli withdrawal. From my talks with Gamasi, I doubt this agreement will help us much with Sadat. He might take it on the theory that he can get the Israelis in the next round.

Israel's biggest opportunity was to turn Sadat away from the United Arab front and towards peace.

Ambassador Eilts: I think they've already turned them towards the United Arab front.

Mr. Sisco: I don't agree. You know, I think we're in the eighth inning here.

Secretary Kissinger: On the other agreements you've put forward I have the most serious questions.

Mr. Sisco: It is a very discouraging exercise since none of our options are good.

Secretary Kissinger: I don't think they will permit tourists to go through the Sinai.

Ambassador Eilts: No, I agree.

Secretary Kissinger: (reading paper) Will they permit direct charter flights?

Ambassador Eilts: No.

Mr. Oakley: I'm not so sure. There are cruise ships that go from Beirut to Israel.

Ambassador Keating: This would be very helpful from an Israeli point of view.

Secretary Kissinger: I think there's a big difference. In this case, the Israelis would trumpet it all over the papers. They'll play it as a great victory. And they'll put Israelis on the cruise ships or make the passengers 80 percent Jewish.

Why put forward a U.S. proposal which will be rejected by the Israelis, and have Sadat throw up his hands saying, "The worst mistake of my life was to deal with the Americans."?

Point five, I think we can get.

Point six is ok, and the rest possible.

I don't think Sadat can sign such a letter here, though. Also, it would not be acceptable to the Israelis.

Ambassador Keating: I seriously doubt it.

Secretary Kissinger: The Israelis will say that Egypt will find that Israel has violated the understandings with Syria.

Ambassador Eilts: I think Egypt will agree to the principle of consultations.

Secretary Kissinger: That won't be good enough for the Israelis. To sum up, the Israelis will not change their position. Is that correct?

Ambassador Keating: I don't think you can totally discount the possibility of some modifications.

Secretary Kissinger: But not enough to get out of the passes or to permit uninterrupted access to the oil fields.

Ambassador Keating: They will consider these great concessions and that they will require Egyptian concessions in return.

Secretary Kissinger: On the eight points, the only place Joe and I disagree is on the cruise ships. If it were possible to get that, is that going to change the Israelis' position?

Ambassador Keating: Probably not.

Secretary Kissinger: Exactly, especially since there are a lot of things Egypt can do but not say. If Sadat is moving to peace, he can do things de facto. But not if they trumpet them before the Knesset as a great victory. Therefore, comparing this with the cruise ships' visits to Lebanon is essentially irrelevant.

The basic point is, do we make a U.S. proposal, since in Ken's judgment no Israeli proposal is coming which frees the passes and gives them access to oil.

Ambassador Keating: Unless a change of attitude has occurred that has not been communicated to us.

Mr. Sisco: I am not in favor of that course of action. I think if we put a proposal together we could call it a working paper and ask for the Israelis' views on it.

Secretary Kissinger: You're beginning to slide back to the Rogers approach for dealing with the Israelis. I want to treat Israel like a friendly country, but they blew up 18 months of U.S. diplomacy and this cannot be free.

Mr. Sisco: It is too dangerous for us to put forward a U.S. proposal without knowing where we stand. That's the reason I don't favor it.

Secretary Kissinger: That means if we go this route, Hermann has to talk to the Egyptians and we have to talk to the Israelis. It gets very tricky. I distrust the Israelis. We could put forward a proposal to the Israelis, and then they could make us take it to the Egyptians, who will turn it down.

Look at the last 24 hours. They had flatly rejected the Egyptian proposal. They asked for another 24 hours and what did they do with it? Nothing, except ask me to send a message to Sadat asking if he'd move. He would have been nuts to have done anything at that point. Therefore, I am really worried about tactics. My instinct is that it is better to start with Egypt and not with Israel.

Mr. Oakley: Egyptians have been more honorable by and large.

Mr. Sisco: Yes, that's true. The danger is if you go to Egypt the Israelis will say that we're colluding with Egypt.

Secretary Kissinger: We'd say we were trying to get Egypt to put forward further ideas and if they bought it we'd have some new concessions.

But, assuming Sadat and Israel agree, we'll have the problem of Syria, we'll have to agree not to use Geneva, the oil supply problem, total unity facing us in Geneva, and total support for the Arabs in the international organizations. Is it really worth it?

I've looked at the transitional agreement and see nothing in it.

Mr. Sisco: We all agree. When we looked at the transitional agreement we injected some ideas from there into the interim one and we tried to find an augmented nonuse-of-force formula.

Secretary Kissinger: I thought the old one was better. No, seriously, the less said the better. If you add to it it gives more escape clauses.

The Israeli negotiating tactic is really unbelievable. Golda, who was a pluperfect pain, would never have thrown away a nonuse-of-force agreement.

Did Rabin want an agreement?

Ambassador Keating: Yes, I think he did.

Mr. Atherton: There was that enormous public opinion swing between your two trips.

Mr. Oakley: I think also he was tricked by Begin into a public position when he went on ABC trying to sell giving up the passes and the oil fields.

Secretary Kissinger: I treated him much too honorably saying that we would use only the negotiating team and not the cabinet. On the interim agreement, I don't think we can get any support for this strategy. It will look like Kissinger trying to save his ass by getting some kind of an agreement and after we get it we are still nowhere. If it had happened, with the Arabs thinking America did it all again, that would have been fine. But that's now gone.

If we put forth the right proposals, it's not even certain the Arabs will buy it. But something involving the '67 borders, demilitarized zone, and the end of the economic boycott—and doing all of this over a five-year period.

Now we're starting to get letters from all of our critics like Brzezinski and Hoffman and those guys. I think we could get to the academics and establish some support now. And if it stalemates, you can still do these other agreements.

Mr. Sisco: The obverse is that there is a greater risk of war because there is a feasible way to constitute practical progress in the next 18 months. We will also confront the Israelis. We will be shot at by both sides and will have many other questions to face.

Secretary Kissinger: If we don't have a position on which to stand, if we can't get an interim agreement it will blow next spring anyway with nothing for us to stand on.

Ambassador Keating: It has the merit of nobody being able to say that we haven't gone all out.

Secretary Kissinger: If we keep on our present line, in three weeks the debate in the U.S. will be whether we support Israel. Then, whatever we do on the F–16 and the Lance will be confused with a misrepresentation of the agreement. It will suddenly be that the Egyptians asked for Tel Aviv in the agreement and the Israelis agreed as long as they were allowed a monitoring station in Haifa.

When the UNEF expires at the end of July, what do you think Sadat will do?

Ambassador Eilts: He'll ask for another three months.

Secretary Kissinger: Ok, so you get three more months but at some point won't he drop it?

Ambassador Eilts: Yes, if nothing happens.

Secretary Kissinger: Well, we have Geneva, we can probably play that for three months. But what do we say there without a program of our own? The parties will put forward incompatible positions, the Soviets will put forward pro-Arab positions. It will be very similar to where we were in 1971, in a much more volatile atmosphere.

Ambassador Keating: Jacobi is supposed to have said that we'll go to the '67 borders for non-belligerency.

Secretary Kissinger: He's a student of mine and with all due respect a horse's ass.

My strategy was to go from this to Syria. The most disquieting thing we told the Israelis was that Asad was going to have private talks with them.

Joe, you and I thought that we could finally see the beginning of a settlement in that last meeting with Asad.

Now, what is the method to get a new interim agreement. We can ask the Israelis conceptually whether they can move out of the passes and the oil fields, then we can go to the Egyptians with something like this proposal, and then go with it as a U.S. proposal to the Israelis. Assuming they accept it. Think of the price we will pay, it will be total U.S. immobility in the Middle East. Is it worth it?

Supposing the President, in mid-May, makes a speech. He says: Our reassessment is complete and we back Israel completely. Now, let's stop the argument about what does Israel really need now. We will analyze the situation. On the other hand, the U.S. has interest in the Arab world, Europe, the Soviet Union, etc. The survival of Israel must be linked to peace. Therefore, before we go to Geneva, we will sketch out something like this. We know it is difficult and may lead to a stalemate but we're willing to support interim steps towards it.

It will give sensible Israelis something to hold on to. We will get some heat, but these people will be at us like flies until we give them complete assurances. Do you know that two Jews went to McNamara, an arch liberal, a Kennedy appointee who attended the meeting with me, and said, "We will penalize you for attending the meeting." I tell you we will be cut to pieces if we don't have a platform on which to stand.

Now can we negotiate it? Absolutely not. It is unobtainable until after the U.S. election. But, will it produce war? This I question. We could say that having presented our program, we could warn both parties. Now if we get an interim step, what next?

Mr. Sisco: The Israelis have said they are willing to negotiate with Asad.

Secretary Kissinger: If we say to Asad, we'll support the '67 lines but you must keep the Syrians back behind the UN, there are two chances out of three that he'd accept. But there is one chance in 10 million that the Israelis would accept.

Asad would accept provided the Israelis accept the principle of the '67 borders. It is barely possible the Egyptians will cede territory to the Israelis, but it is inconceivable that the Syrians will.

Ambassador Eilts: I think we should go for the larger agreement.

Secretary Kissinger: My tendency is to tell the Israelis we'll support a limited agreement but focus on the overall plan.

The Ambassadors here must meet with the President before they go back. Ken, you have the hardest job. We'll give you more business to do and cut back on Dinitz here.

Ambassador Keating: I'll take care of it.

Secretary Kissinger: They are dealing with a very friendly government, but no longer with a brother. They must pay a price.

Ambassador Murphy: I think we should go for the larger one. I'd like to hear more about the war prospects, though.

Secretary Kissinger: The argument is that the Arabs may think they can jump Israel, but we could also argue that the U.S. having put forward its proposal, would make it unmistakably clear that we wouldn't tolerate a war.

When there was magic in the step-by-step approach, it was great. When I left, I suffered and the U.S. suffered a great loss of prestige.

Ambassador Eilts: Well, speaking for Egypt, it may be that the United States government has lost some confidence or prestige, but certainly not you.

Secretary Kissinger: Well, I don't care. The magic is gone. Asad was pleading with me to come back, but I am, if anything now, a negative factor in Israel. The mood has changed. The Israelis on the whole are trying to stonewall to January 1977. There is no basis for support in this country for any interim agreement. It will be a hell of a battle with Israel or the Jews here or we will pay an enormous price.

If Dinitz says we'll give up the passes, we'll take it. He wants to give the impression of normalcy without any price, though, I think.

The overall program may lead to a series of interim agreements. The overall idea will get into an immediate stall but it gives us a chance to hold off the Europeans and the Soviets.

Mr. Saunders: How do you cope with the Israeli argument that you preempt Israel by stating what the U.S. would support?

Secretary Kissinger: Well, that would be true if we weren't supporting Israel with $2.5 billion which itself may prejudice the Arab positions.

Mr. Atherton: The Arabs may hold their fire to see the Israeli reaction.

Secretary Kissinger: What is our alternative? We will be beaten back to total support for Israel. When I told the President about sum plus the inflation factor, he said it's too high. You know Congress will put up $1.2 billion. He can't veto it. If we put $1.2 billion into Israel with no interim or overall program, the Arabs will pressure us through the Europeans and will turn to the Soviets.

Mr. Atherton: Would we put $1.2 billion into Israel if it rejected an overall proposal?

Secretary Kissinger: Probably not. We'd have to say, there's an overall idea and we'll support anything in between.

Mr. Sisco: I'm going to equivocate. I think we should keep our options open over the next few days. Let us put together some ideas.

Secretary Kissinger: I don't want an overall paper going to the Defense Department. For the next meeting, we need to know how to do the interim one. The basic paper is ok. What we don't know is the diplomacy for the overall solution. If I take it, all of the Ambassadors here favor the overall plan. Even you (to Keating).

Ambassador Keating: Especially me.

172. Memorandum of Conversation[1]

Washington, April 12, 1975, 10:56–11:11 a.m.

PARTICIPANTS

Dr. Henry A. Kissinger, Secretary of State and Assistant to the President for National Security Affairs
Amb. Daniel P. Moynihan, U.S. Ambassador to the United Nations
Lt. General Brent Scowcroft, Deputy Assistant to the President for National Security Affairs

Kissinger: One major problem you will have is on Israel. We must dissociate ourselves a bit from Israel—not to destroy them but to prevent them from becoming a Sparta, with only military solutions to every problem. They are desperately looking for a spokesman—and

[1] Source: Library of Congress, Manuscript Division, Kissinger Papers, CL 273, Chronological File, April 1975. Secret; Nodis. The meeting was held in the Secretary's office in the White House. Brackets are in the original.

they will work on you. What Israel did in the last negotiation was unconscionable. We may come out with our own ideas of the elements of a stable peace in the Middle East. We can't afford a crisis in the context of blind support of Israel.

I don't want Israel to get the idea that our UN mission is an extension of theirs. Treat them in a very friendly way, but as a foreign government. On expulsion, give them total support. On UNESCO, I am inclined to think the same. On the PLO, give them total support, at least until they recognize the existence of Israel.

We have to show Israel they don't run us and we can't support massive acquisition of territory. You can't maintain that selling out Vietnam has no impact on Israel—as the Jewish community thinks. It can't be.

We triggered the debacle in Vietnam. [They discussed what happened.] We shouldn't kid ourselves that what we have done does not have catastrophic results. When the Japanese Foreign Minister visits here and demands to put out a statement reaffirming the Security Treaty. You know that in Japan you preserve it by never mentioning it. The President and I are going out in a Churchillian way. The UN is very important in this campaign. You have got to show that we are staying the course.

Moynihan: The American Jews have got to be Americans.

Kissinger: We will probably aim for security essentially within their borders, in total security and for total peace.

This ruthless using of a Communist threat at one moment, and Jewish immigration at another has got to stop. On expulsion we will fight to the death; on UNESCO I am inclined to agree. But Israel must be treated like Great Britain, not like the Department of Treasury.

173. Memorandum of Conversation[1]

Washington, April 14, 1975, 11:15 a.m.–12:50 p.m.

PARTICIPANTS

    President Ford
    Kenneth B. Keating, U.S. Ambassador to Israel
    Hermann F. Eilts, U.S. Ambassador to Egypt
    Thomas R. Pickering, U.S. Ambassador to Jordan
    Richard W. Murphy, U.S. Ambassador to Syria
    Dr. Henry A. Kissinger, Secretary of State and Assistant to the President for National Security Affairs
    Lt. General Brent Scowcroft, Deputy Assistant to the President for National Security Affairs
    Alfred L. Atherton, Jr., Assistant Secretary of State for Near Eastern and South Asian Affairs

Kissinger: Mr. President, I thought I should outline what we have been talking about and then let each of my colleagues say what his dominant impression is. Then any instructions you may have.

We have looked at various choices: One is to resurrect the interim agreement.

Sadat said the setback was a humiliation for the United States. He said they couldn't understand how the United States, which supplies 98% of Israel's equipment, couldn't produce an agreement which was so close to being achieved. The consensus of these four is that if nothing happens, events will get out of control within six months. If there is any disagreement, please speak up.

President: I believe it. I would like to hear the views of each of you.

Kissinger: In a new crisis, the Europeans would back the Arabs, and the Soviet Union; Japan would move away. So, the various approaches are first, to resurrect the interim agreement. It would clearly have to include the passes and a line including the oil fields. Sisco thinks the territory could be in the neutral zone going to the oil fields.

Eilts: I disagree.

President: How long and how wide would it be?

Kissinger: Two to three kilometers—just one road. But they need a map that shows their access to their oil fields.

President: But the passes could be under the UN.

---

[1] Source: Ford Library, National Security Adviser, Memoranda of Conversations, Box 10, April 14, 1975, Ford, U.S. Ambassadors Keating (Israel), Eilts (Egypt), Pickering (Jordan), and Murphy (Syria). Secret; Nodis. The meeting was held in the Oval Office at the White House. Brackets are in the original.

Kissinger: Yes. Probably we could keep the Egyptian advance limited to the edge of the UN zone. These would be bitter pills for Israel. We have seen nothing to indicate a changed position by Israel. Eilts thinks Sadat can offer nothing more; in fact he thinks Sadat has already gone a shade too far. So unless Israel caves—and there is no indication of that—an interim agreement is dead. Also one might have to pay a price of enormous economic aid, no demands for further withdrawal for three years, and we might just sell it in Israel. But it would become public, and that is intolerable in Syria. So I think we would have to do something on the Syrian front.

President: Do you mean a good faith effort, or actually doing something?

Kissinger: Things have changed. Before, I think a good faith effort would have done it, but Sadat has now been placed in a more difficult position, and the Syrians, who would have accepted most anything in March, are now in a stronger position. Therefore our effort would have to be as great as now. A shuttle wouldn't suffice because that has been depreciated now. Asad is under pressure at home for going too far. He told me his domestic situation will be impossible if Sadat gets something and he doesn't. I said the Israeli settlements were so far forward that we could get only a sliver, or else something greater in the context of peace. He said that in the context of peace he could assure there would be no Syrian troops forward of the line looking into Israel. I reported this in Israel as a great achievement, but it was counterproductive because I think the last thing Israel wants is a negotiation with Syria.

Everyone now is telling us to go back to the interim agreement. We could probably do it, with the headaches noted above, but it would buy you maybe six months and further excite the Syrians.

The second idea is, Israel has floated the idea of nonbelligerency in exchange for moving half or two-thirds back in the Sinai. We studied this and tried to examine if there was a difference between nonbelligerency and peace. Sadat opposes giving nonbelligerency because if he gives up the main aspects, he has no bargaining power left to get them the rest of the way out. We could find no difference. Even the Israeli legal guy couldn't find any.

President: Publicly you could make a difference.

Kissinger: But they talk the El Arish line. I am sure they mean west of El Arish. Sadat I think wouldn't buy it, but this would upset Asad even further.

President: Didn't Egypt promise not to support a Syrian attack? Would Syria then attack?

Kissinger: You can't say that publicly. Syria calculates that if it attacked, it could drag the others in.

Eilts: I don't see how Egypt could stay out of a war more than a week. The pressures to save Syria would be overwhelming.

Kissinger: The consensus of this group is that Option Two is the worst because the negotiation would be even tougher, and it doesn't buy any more. I don't think we could get more from Egypt.

Eilts: I don't see how they could offer a great deal more until the final peace discussions. They offered three things in particular that I thought were beyond what they could do: an unconditional pledge to refrain from the use of force; agreement to leave the agreement open-ended in duration; and a commitment not to aid a Syrian attack. I thought these were beyond what was politically wise for him. He can live with the first, but the other two are bad.

President: Why did he just fire his cabinet?

Eilts: His economic problems are enormous. They have 37 million unemployed; the whole infrastructure is in disrepair. Hegazi has no political base. The cabinet hasn't been effective in the economy. Because so little has happened, the new cabinet was designed to assuage the people.

Kissinger: Sadat wanted an agreement to build his prestige and ease the pressure from the domestic side.

Three, probably the best is to come up with a comprehensive plan. It would give us something to stand on with the Arabs. We would be taking on the Israelis, but for something more significant than the line through the passes. It would make the interim stages easier under an overall umbrella. I had better stop here.

Keating: If something isn't done within six months or less ... If the Syrians are smart they will end the UN forces at the same time as Egypt. If they extend again, it would be short. I think it is best to go for an overall agreement. Politically, Rabin jumped from 46% to 92% in popularity for "standing up to the Arabs and the United States." The same poll that by 68% thought that Henry should come back. But this is heady stuff for Rabin. I think he wants an agreement, and do the other negotiation.

President: Do they know I think they were inflexible?

Keating: They do. Economically, they are in serious trouble. Forty percent of their budget goes to defense. Inflation is running 30–40%. They are tightening their belt and actually getting unemployment. They are stronger militarily than in '73. They are on alert and they are well led. They will not be surprised again, but I don't think they plan a preemptive strike. They have made so much at home about giving up only half the passes, that it will be very difficult to give up all the passes.

Kissinger: So much has been put out on the interim agreement, it is difficult to move. Except that Israel has lied so much about the Egyptian position that the real truth would appear a significant concession. They would need three to four years of guaranteed aid, and three to five years of no movement. We can't afford that in the Arab world.

President: We can't come out with $2.6 billion for an interim agreement. Tip O'Neill pointed that out.

Keating: Humphrey and McGovern were good. I don't want to pretend we can sell a comprehensive plan to Israel. But Allon's departure statement leaves the door open. Eban said the same.

Kissinger: These are platitudes all depending on their definition of peace and security. If we don't support the '67 borders, with perhaps minor modifications, we will get no Arab support. Israel wants half the Golan, a third of the Sinai, and a third to a half of the West Bank. If we came up with the '67 frontier, demilitarized zones, limited armaments zones, we still have problems with the Arabs who would demand that they thin out on both sides. We can't keep the Arabs for less than the '67 borders. Jerusalem we should stay away from for now. If we do this, what trouble are we in with Israel?

[General Scowcroft leaves briefly to get a map of the Middle East and then returns.]

Kissinger: Israel, by border rectifications, means the El Arish line back to Sharm el Sheikh. When it gets to military limitations, they will want to keep Egyptian forces off the plain. In the Golan, I would be surprised if they would give up over half the Golan.

Keating: Perhaps some security agreement could be worked out.

Kissinger: The Arabs won't buy a security agreement with Israeli troops inside.

On the West Bank, they would permit a narrow corridor to the Arab population. If you declare you are for the '67 borders with some rational rectification, the Arabs will be back immediately to ask what. You have to decide before going public whether you will support essentially the '67 frontiers. That is the big issue. Dick?

Murphy: This is the bitterest relationship in the area. Asad has opened his country some to the other Arabs. He has turned the country around so they could talk of peace. His price for peace is precisely the '67 frontiers. He has indicated willingness to permit UN control of the areas from which Israel withdraws.

Kissinger: If it would happen when we still control events, we could probably sell half the Golan.

Murphy: He feels the Palestinian issue deeply. He is pleased at Secretary Kissinger's failure in the last shuttle because he feared we were taking Egypt out of the war and he was losing his leverage. He said the United States should stay engaged.

President: Does he want Geneva?

Murphy: Recently there have been the first hesitations. He wants quick agreement on an overall outline.

Kissinger: The dream of Israel is stalemate. Sadat is a bigger problem for Israel than Asad, because he is willing to move to peace. They want peace but aren't willing to pay the price. Tom?

Pickering: Hussein is our best friend. He knows he is knocked out and he has not much chance to go back in unless he's asked. He would insist on self-determination for the West Bank. He thinks he is a lamb among wolves. I can't go back there without something for him on air defense. There are other bilateral issues he will want to discuss with you when he comes.[2] He thinks progress is possible only in steps, but he would buy a compromise now to get things going.

President: If war broke out, why would he be more involved this time?

Pickering: The last time he got in just a little. He doesn't think it would be over quickly this time and he thinks Israel next time would make a pincer through Jordan and Lebanon.

Kissinger: I think Israel would do something surprising next time.

Keating: I think they would go through Lebanon.

President: What is the significance of the disputes in Lebanon?

Kissinger: I think the Lebanese are trying to assert some control over Fatahland. Lebanon has been helpless in the fighting between Israel and the PLO. Lebanon wants a settlement to get rid of the Palestinians. They would be most aggressive if they went to Geneva, because of the Palestinians.

One other problem is that Iraq, freed of the problem of the Kurds, will now exert radical pressure on Syria and Jordan.

President: If we went to Geneva, would we have to have a comprehensive plan?

Kissinger: There are three possibilities: we could do nothing but be an honest broker; we could support the Israeli position; we could put forward a plan of our own. If we support Israel, the Arabs will decide the only way to move is to put enough pressure on what we are brokering. If we put out a plan, Israel will violently oppose. The Arabs may not accept it, but we can rest on it for several months. The Arabs, I think, gradually would come around to our mind.

---

[2] King Hussein visited Washington April 29–31.

Eilts: They would originally look askance at it. But if they see the final outline, they can more easily buy interim steps. That has been the problem with interim steps up to now.

President: Should that be at Geneva?

Eilts: Inside or outside Geneva. I would prepare to do it first before Geneva.

Kissinger: Hermann thinks it would be nice to have an interim agreement before Geneva but it is essential to have a plan.

Pickering: Jordan thinks Geneva would get out of hand if the U.S. goes in without a position.

Eilts: The same with Egypt. He would prefer an interim agreement before, but at least he would hope for some plan.

President: How would Israel react to a comprehensive plan and what could they try to do in the United States?

Keating: We are in trouble with the American Jews whatever we do. If we pursue interim measures I think we will get the same eventual flak as we would with the '67 borders modified.

President: You mean the Jews here would feel as strong about a pressured interim agreement as a comprehensive plan?

Kissinger: The Israelis have been specialists in stating something, which was unattainable, for which they would do something special. First they wanted a signature on a piece of paper. They said it would get us into the same room with the Arabs. We did both and they backed off right away. Now they say they want peace. But by coming out for '67 borders, the Jews will complain we have given away their leverage in advance. Roy, what do you think?

Atherton: I have come grudgingly to a comprehensive move because we can demand more from the Arabs. But Israel has sold the idea for eight years that the '67 borders are insecure.

President: My impression of the public reaction in the U.S. is it would be like the reaction in the leadership meeting when Henry came back.[3] All the focus was on Israel's lack of realization of a different attitude in the United States.

Keating: But Dinitz tells them there is no different attitude. Hamilton will stand with you, but he is doubtful we can hold the line when the pressures come.

Kissinger: If you go the interim route, you can either say you would ask no aid unless there is an agreement. If they do, then you are up the creek with Syria; if not, Congress may pass the aid anyway. If there is a comprehensive plan, you can give aid in that context. Now,

---

[3] See Document 160.

they want peace, they don't want to pay a price, and they think they can get the $2.6 billion anyway.

President: I have a reputation as being pro-Israel. The situation in Congress is totally different now. Until we get progress there will be no request for Israeli aid. If Congress tries to force it, I will veto it.

Keating: They couldn't override a veto.

President: We have to decide which approach to pursue. This has been very helpful.

Kissinger: We think we need a letter to Sadat. Hermann is drafting it. I have told Ken that we would do more business through him and he should deal with as a foreign government—friendly but foreign.

President: That is the way I have told the bureaucracy to behave.

Eilts: It is important that Sadat be kept on a moderate route. The suspension has been a bitter pill. He desperately wants peace with honor. He made courageous moves during the negotiation. He is adrift right now. He will welcome American leadership—he wants to work with us. I must get back before Fahmy leaves for the Soviet Union. We must use him to keep the Arabs from making asses of themselves. He wants to work with us.

174. Minutes of National Security Council Meeting[1]

Washington, May 15, 1975, 5:30 p.m.

SUBJECT

Middle East

PRINCIPALS

The President
The Vice President
Secretary of State Henry A. Kissinger
Secretary of Defense James Schlesinger
Chairman of the Joint Chiefs of Staff Gen. George S. Brown
Director of Central Intelligence William Colby

OTHER ATTENDEES

State
Deputy Secretary Robert Ingersoll
Ellsworth Bunker, Ambassador at Large

Defense
Deputy Secretary of Defense William Clements

WH
Donald Rumsfeld

NSC
Lt. Gen. Brent Scowcroft
Robert B. Oakley

President: This group is familiar with the reasons that I ordered the reassessment of the Middle East on March 28,[2] following the suspension of negotiations and the decision to treat Israel as a friend, correctly but like our other friends and no more. I have no apprehension about the vigor of our commitment to their security but there must be a suspension of certain deliveries and contacts in the interim. I trust my orders on this subject are being carried out.

In the meantime, I have met with a number of people and Henry has met with a number of others. We have told all of them, whether they were Israeli or pro-Israeli or Arab or pro-Arab or independent, the same thing, that we will not tolerate stagnation or stalemate in the Middle East. Momentum is the key word. I plan to meet Sadat and

---

[1] Source: Ford Library, National Security Adviser, Box 1, NSC Meetings File, NSC Meeting, May 15, 1975. Top Secret; Sensitive; Nodis. The meeting was held in the Cabinet Room at the White House. The original is marked "Part III of III." Parts I and II concern the seizure of the ship *Mayaguez* and the Panama Canal negotiations. According to the President's Daily Diary, the meeting ended at 6:09 p.m. (Ford Library, Staff Secretary's Office Files)

[2] See Document 166.

Rabin and at some time subsequent to that we will make a decision on United States policy in the Middle East.

Henry, would you please give us a rundown on the diplomatic options open to us.

But before Henry begins, let us recognize the fact that the professional members of the American Jewish Community have undertaken a certain nationwide campaign to paint the picture that the reassessment is a change of heart toward Israel. First, they are wrong. I reiterate my dedication to the survival of Israel, period. That is the word we use, survival. Second, anyone who knows me, and those who do not shall soon know that inequitable, unfair pressures are exactly the wrong way of trying to change my views. Inequitable, unfair public pressure tactics are the wrong way to convince me. I will tell certain people directly if this continues.

Now, Henry, tell us where we stand diplomatically.

Kissinger: We have made no attempt to move our policy examination to a conclusion. However, all concerned are convinced that within a year of what the Arabs perceive as a stalemate, there will be a war. We are also all convinced that the economic and military consequences would be unacceptable for the U.S. That is why we are trying so hard to get negotiations started again. The fact of our reassessment has bought us some time with the Arabs since they are less frustrated than they would have been had nothing been happening at all. But when it comes time for the next renewal of the UN forces in late July if nothing is going, or at least the clear prospect of progress seen, the situation will be out of control. After that events will move rapidly.

In our reassessment we have identified the several options. First, would be to restart the interim negotiations between Egypt and Israel. In some ways this is the easiest approach but there are two problems. One is that each side is now so dug in publicly as to their positions on the details of this negotiation that it will be extremely difficult for them to make concessions that might have been possible for them before. The other is that there is a different atmosphere now in the Arab world. Feisal had been convinced on the step-by-step approach, a separate negotiation for Egypt, and Asad had no choice but to go along. But now Fahd has taken over and he does not think exactly the same way, he is less liable to support a separate Egyptian negotiation. Moreover, the Egyptians and Syrians are now much closer to each other, with Saudi support. So if we decide to go for another interim agreement for Egypt we will also have to go for another one with Syria or we will create a situation where Syria could easily go to war and ruin everything we have accomplished.

The second option is for Israel to give up a bigger piece of territory for a bigger political concession from Egypt. But this would raise the

Syrian question in an even more acute way, even more dangerous. Also, it could never work because Israel would demand non-belligerency and this is impossible for Egypt except in the context of total or almost total withdrawal.

The third option is a comprehensive proposal at Geneva, either by the U.S. or put forward by someone else. This will happen at Geneva whether we like it or not and we will be forced to take a position on the key elements, anyway. We can go for a comprehensive settlement alone or with the Soviets or start alone and then bring in the Soviets, or try to work it out together with the Israelis. There are many possible variations of the comprehensive approach. But they will all be very difficult for Israel.

The fourth option is to go to Geneva and let a stalemate develop and then try to move back to a U.S. interim agreement. The Soviets may fear this is what we have in mind and that we already have worked at an agreement with Sadat. But a stalemate at Geneva without prior progress outside of Geneva is very dangerous and could lead to war as easily as to an interim agreement. This would be especially true if we were seen to be the obstacle causing the stalemate at Geneva.

Given these options, what we will recommend to the President will depend upon the degree of flexibility the President discovers in his meetings with Sadat and Rabin[3] and what I find about the Soviet position when I see Gromyko.[4] When I meet Gromyko the guidance is not to be specific. This is really an exploration to get their views before meeting Sadat and Rabin. We can probably keep this round of consultations going into the first part of July but not beyond that or the Arabs will conclude we will do nothing. It is also possible that the Israeli strategy is just to sit tight, wait until elections come next year and do nothing.

Schlesinger: It is clear to me that is precisely their strategy, don't you agree?

Kissinger: Yes, I think this is their strategy. Since I left Israel in March there has not been a single substantive message from the Israeli Government capable of enabling progress to be made. Either they repeat their earlier positions and call them new when they are the same, or they are so vague as to be worthless. That is why we must be firm with them and impress upon them the need to come up with some new substantive proposals.

Clements: I want to assure you, Henry, and the President that the Saudis have great confidence in you and the President wanting a just

---

[3] See Documents 177, 178, and 183.
[4] Kissinger and Gromyko met in Vienna May 19–20. See footnote 2, Document 178.

peace in the Middle East. When I was there with George (General Brown), they made this very clear. And they said it is also true of Egypt. They are optimistic that you and the President will pull something out of the hat to keep it going.

Kissinger: They are optimistic because they think we will do it but at this point we have nothing at all to work with.

Schlesinger: Could I say something about using the word survival instead of security? It is a codeword of significance. After October 1973 we took a position on maintaining the security of Israel and working for a just and equitable solution to the Middle East situation. That formula is reassuring to Israel. It means their undiminished survival. This is a sensitive period and it is not advisable to get drawn into semantic disputes.

President: I have used survival and security interchangeably, synonymously. But they have now chosen to make a distinction, not I.[5] I will therefore use survival and I do not want anyone else to paraphrase or explain away what I say. The record of my commitment to Israel is clear. I have before me the major items furnished to Israel by the U.S. since October 1973 and since I became President, up until April of this year.[6] The facts are that Israel is far better off today militarily than prior to October 1973. I am delighted they are in that position since it makes our position very strong in holding off on certain items. If this criticism continues, we may release this information.

Now, we are dedicated to Israel's survival and to the avoidance of stagnation and stalemate. All Departments and Agencies should maintain a correct attitude toward the Israelis. All the parties should be treated with the same correctness. Our position is right and has to be maintained that way. In the meantime, we will make a bona fide reassessment of our policy and announce a final decision after the meeting with Rabin in June. We made a maximum effort in March. We are disappointed it did not succeed. But that is not the reason for our reassessment. We have some critical issues to solve. In the meantime our attitude is one of correct behavior.

Vice President: What about using "survival of Israel as a free and independent state?" That is what I have always used.

President: We want to stick to survival.

---

[5] According to Kissinger's memoirs, Ford made an "off-the-cuff" statement in May that he had always supported Israel's survival and would continue his support. The Israeli Government protested the statement because it objected to the term "survival" instead of the term "security," which had been the standard term used by U.S. officials previously. (*Years of Renewal*, pp. 426–427)

[6] Not attached.

Kissinger: They have said they need the word security because it means expanded frontiers. They want us to endorse that position so they have made it an issue.

Schlesinger: Have they said so?

Kissinger: They have said it in the press and have accused us publicly of trying to get away from supporting their territorial claims.

Schlesinger: In the past we have used the word security.

President: But they have made it an issue and we will not back down.

Vice President: I have used "survival as a free and independent state" for 26 years. I have attended the kick-off dinner of the United Jewish Appeal every year and have a lot of experience in finding just the right words. I have had to be careful. This will avoid the territorial issue which is linked to security.

President: That is okay. Survival or survival as a free and independent state.

[Omitted here is discussion unrelated to the Arab-Israeli dispute.]

---

175. Telegram From the Department of State to Secretary of State Kissinger in Ankara[1]

Washington, May 22, 1975, 1927Z.

Tosec 10221/119886. Subject: Javits and Percy Letters on the Middle East. For the Secretary from McCloskey.

1. Following are texts of Javits' letter, signed by 75 Senators,[2] released today and the Percy letter, which was not rpt not released:

2. Dear Mr. President: You will recall that last December a substantial majority of the Senate wrote you urging a reiteration of our nation's long-standing commitment to Israel's security "by a policy of continued military supplies and diplomatic and economic support."[3]

---

[1] Source: Library of Congress, Manuscript Division, Kissinger Papers, CL 158, Geopolitical File, Israel, May 1975. Confidential; Immediate.

[2] Another Senator signed the letter after its release, bringing the number of signatories to 76.

[3] On December 9, 1974, 71 Senators signed a letter to President Ford, criticizing the United Nations for dealing with the PLO and for UNESCO expulsion of Israel. The Senators' letter urged Ford to "reiterate our nation's long-standing commitment to Israel's security by a policy of continued military supplies and diplomatic and economic support." (*Israel's Foreign Relations: Selected Documents*, volume 3: 1974–1977, Document 53)

3. Since 1967, it has been American policy that the Arab-Israel conflict should be settled on the basis of secure and recognized boundaries that are defensible, and direct negotiations between the nations involved. We believe that this approach continues to offer the best hope for a just and lasting peace.

4. While the suspension of the second-stage negotiations is regrettable, the history of the Arab-Israel conflict demonstrates that any Israeli withdrawal must be accompanied by meaningful steps toward peace by its Arab neighbors.

5. Recent events underscore America's need for reliable allies and the desirability of greater participation by the Congress in the formulation of American foreign policy. Cooperation between the Congress and the President is essential for America's effectiveness in the world. During this time of uncertainty over the future direction of our policy, we support you in strengthening our ties with nations which share our democratic traditions and help to safeguard our national interests. We believe that the special relationship between our country and Israel does not prejudice improved relations with other nations in the region.

6. We believe that a strong Israel constitutes a most reliable barrier to domination of the area by outside parties. Given the recent heavy flow of Soviet weaponry to Arab states, it is imperative that we not permit the military balance to shift against Israel.

7. We believe that preserving the peace requires that Israel obtain a level of military and economic support adequate to deter a renewal of war by Israel's neighbors. Withholding military equipment from Israel would be dangerous, discouraging accommodation by Israel's neighbors and encouraging a resort to force.

8. Within the next several weeks, the Congress expects to receive your foreign aid requests for fiscal year 1976. We trust that your recommendations will be responsive to Israel's urgent military and economic needs. We urge you to make it clear, as we do, that the United States acting in its own national interests stands firmly with Israel in the search for peace in future negotiations, and that this premise is the basis of the current reassessment of U.S. policy in the Middle East.

9. Respectfully yours, *End text*.

10. Percy decided to send his anti-Javits letter as a personal message from him to the President only. Following is text of Percy letter:

11. Dear Mr. President: In view of the letter on the Middle East circulated in the Senate by a number of my distinguished colleagues, I wish to directly express to you my own position.

12. I concur with the co-signers in their profound support for the security and survival of the state of Israel; however, I do not believe that an expression of concern for the interests of only one party to the

conflict is adequate at a time when American good will toward all the parties is required in order to facilitate a fair and equitable settlement.

13. I am interested that the administration has chosen to reassess its policies, and I am heartened that Secretary Kissinger has agreed to consult with the Congress as part of the reassessment. Since the goal of all of us is to promote a just and equitable peace in the region, it is important that those consultations take place in an atmosphere of mutual confidence and with candor. The originators of the above-mentioned letter, who are so knowledgeable about the problems [garble—in the Middle?] East, will have much to contribute to such consultations.

14. In regard to Israel, I believe strongly and without equivocation of any sort, that the United States has an absolute moral obligation to provide diplomatic, political and appropriate levels of economic and military assistance support during the difficult time of negotiation and during the rearrangements following negotiation. With such continuing American support, and with determined efforts by the Government of Israel to achieve a successful negotiation, I believe that Israel can finally achieve the peace, security and the essential recognition of her neighbors which she has long sought and deserved.

15. In regard to the Arab states, I believe strongly and without equivocation that the United States, by continuing diplomatic effort, can build on what has already been accomplished in improving our relations with Arab leaders on the basis of understanding and trust. The progress which has already been achieved gives hope that the Arab states will realize that our approach to peace in the area rests on a basis of concern for all the parties, just as we seek peace and security for all the parties. I have outlined in my recent report to the Senate Foreign Relations Committee the steps that Arab states in my opinion can take to demonstrate their desire for a peaceful and lasting settlement of the Mideast conflict.

16. Obviously, the search for peace will succeed only when the parties directly involved are prepared to make the concessions necessary to a settlement. I deeply believe that the process of accommodation, which is so long in coming, could be accelerated if direct talks would be undertaken.

17. It is my hope that the executive and legislative branches will reach substantial consensus on Middle East policy, as a result of consultation within the context of the reassessment, and that Israel and the Arab states will reach agreement soon on positive steps toward peace in their own mutual interest.

18. Sincerely, Charles H. Percy, United States Senator
End text.

Ingersoll

176. Telegram From Secretary of State Kissinger to the President's Deputy Assistant for National Security Affairs (Scowcroft)[1]

Paris, May 27, 1975, 2155Z.

Hakto 2. Ref: Tel Aviv 3195.[2]

1. Please show reftel to the President at the earliest opportunity but before his departure. Please draw his attention particularly to paragraphs 5, 6, and 7. This provides concrete evidence of Rabin's willingness to treat us as an antagonist and to use the senatorial letter[3] to support his intransigence.

2. You should then call Dinitz to express our extreme outrage over this latest violation of confidence. First of all, he knows that it is simply not true that Allon brought written proposals to Washington.[4] Secondly, we regard it as a matter of great concern that Rabin would reveal what we regard as confidential communications prior to the Sadat meeting. Additionally, you should point out that the tone of Rabin's remarks sounded as if he were not even talking about a friendly government. The final point you should make is that the Israelis should not necessarily count on a realization of the relaxation of tensions which Rabin claims is emerging of the weakness of the administration vis-à-vis the Congress.

3. You should make this a very, very strong protest.

4. Warm regards.

---

[1] Source: Library of Congress, Manuscript Division, Kissinger Papers, CL 158, Geopolitical File, Israel, May 1975. Confidential; Black Patch.

[2] In telegram 3195 from Tel Aviv, May 27, the Embassy reported a local American journalist's May 26 interview with Rabin, which was described as "off the record." Rabin claimed that Allon had brought Israeli proposals "in writing" to Washington in April. He also expressed pleasure with the letter sent by 76 Senators to Ford declaring their "stern" support for Israel. Rabin acknowledged the letter served as a "concrete example of real limitations on administration potential to 'pressure' Israel," and claimed it supported his policy of holding fast in the "face of administration pressure." (Ibid.)

[3] See Document 175.

[4] Allon visited Washington and met with Kissinger on April 21 from 11:45 a.m. until 2:40 p.m. in the Secretary's office and then in the Madison Room at the Department of State. (Memorandum of conversation, April 21; Library of Congress, Manuscript Division, Kissinger Papers, CL 157, Geopolitical File, Israel, April 21–30, 1975)

177. Memorandum of Conversation[1]

Salzburg, June 1, 1975.

PARTICIPANTS

Egypt
Anwar al-Sadat, President
Major General Mubarak, Vice President
Ismail Fahmi, Foreign Minister

United States
The President
The Secretary
Joseph J. Sisco, Under Secretary for Political Affairs

The President: I would like to make two points in particular. First, the importance of the letter signed by 76 Senators[2] is being distorted out of proportion; half of them didn't read it and a quarter didn't understand the letter. Whereas the additional quarter knew very precisely what it was doing. The impact of the letter is negligible. Secondly, I want to tell you that Secretary Kissinger and I have a close personal and professional relationship. There is no more trusted person than Secretary Kissinger that I deal with. He speaks for me. We work closely together. In time my hope is that the Senate will see to it that we work as a team. I am confident that the execution of our policy will be successful.

I was very disappointed in the position taken by Israel last March; the Israelis decided to go off in a direction different than we expected. I want to tell you that as far as we are concerned, stagnation is unacceptable. As you know, we are in the process of a reassessment. It would be helpful to me for you to tell me where you believe we are and any suggestions that you may have on how we can work together in the future towards peace in the Middle East.

President Sadat: Mr. President, I want to thank you for the statement that you have just made and, in particular, what you have said that you will not tolerate stagnation; that is marvelous. These words have made a great impact on me.

As to where we are now, I must say to you that the process of peace has slackened to a certain extent due to problems in the United States.

---

[1] Source: National Archives, RG 59, Records of Henry Kissinger, 1973–77, Box 11, Nodis Memcons, June 1975, Folder 2. Secret; Nodis. Drafted by Sisco on June 7. According to the President's Daily Diary, the meeting took place from 5:05 until 6:46 p.m. (Ford Library, Staff Secretary's Office Files) Ford traveled to Salzburg, Austria, from June 1 to June 3 to meet with Austrian Chancellor Kreisky and President Sadat. He then visited Rome and Vatican City on June 3 to meet with Italian President Leone, Italian Prime Minister Moro, and Pope Paul VI.

[2] See Document 175.

Dr. Kissinger made two visits this year and, as you know, we were quite ready to achieve progress and we went beyond where it might reasonably be expected that we might go. We did this for two reasons: I want to push the peace process; and, secondly, I want you to know that I have been in power since 1952. I have dealt with Secretaries of State since Dulles. The first time I met Henry Kissinger was in November of 1973, and I felt at that time that I could put full confidence in him, that he was a man of trust, and I could rely on his word. This is very essential. We have never felt the small power complex in relationship to big powers. I can recall how we together developed the six principles[3] and then the first disengagement agreement. This brought about a new image of the United States in the area.

Candidly, Mr. President, I felt Nasser had treated the United States unfairly because I recall that in 1956 the United States had ordered Israel, the U.K., and France out of Egypt. The Soviet ultimatum at that time came after the United States had already achieved Israeli withdrawal. Nasser, unfairly in my judgment, attributed the Israeli withdrawal to the Russian ultimatum. The United States' image in the area has been changing completely since the first disengagement agreement. Egypt leads the Arab world. We started promoting better relations with the United States. The United States has all the cards in its hands and Israel should heed the United States. After the failure of the Kissinger mission in March, an angry Egyptian reaction was expected. Yet I told Dr. Kissinger that we would extend the UNEF for three months. I decided that the Suez Canal should be opened.[4] Israel fears peace. It is not capable of making peace, of taking the decisions. You supported Israel during the October War. It received ultra-sophisticated arms from the United States. Syria has replaced its losses by getting weapons from the USSR for the last year and a half. I remain without any replacements. Syria has been stimulating the Palestinians against Egypt in the Arab world. I went to the Arab world and got the embargo lifted after the disengagement agreement. Egypt is key in the Arab world. We have helped promote a new image of America in the Arab world.

Mr. President, this is a moment of decision. Nobody in the Arab world believes that the United States cannot put pressure on Israel. I have said that I am ready for a peace agreement with Israel. I am opening the Canal, even though it inhibits military operations. I am not intending to start military operations. I returned 39 corpses to Israel without conditions. Egypt is different from other Arabs. We have a

---

[3] See footnote 8, Document 5.
[4] The Suez Canal was reopened on June 5 after it had been closed in June 1967 due to the 1967 Arab-Israeli War.

background of patience, of civility and understanding. Millions greeted President Nixon and Secretary Kissinger when they came to Egypt[5] saying we want to be friends with America. The failure of Kissinger's mission has not been taken as a failure of the whole image of the United States. The question that is being asked is whether the United States is unable to achieve peace after all that it gives to Israel. We don't want war again, but I will never submit one inch of my land to Israel. We have patience. The time may come when we will have to liberate our lands.

The Soviets don't lose time to exploit the situation. Israel is undermining the policy of the step-by-step approach which is attacked by the Soviet Union and defended by me. The Egyptian people cannot understand. My people have faith in me and I tell them I have confidence in President Ford and Henry Kissinger. Everyone in Egypt is waiting for the next step. The Soviet Union has stimulated the Syrians and Palestinians against me and against United States' policy. They have given me no military replacements since the October 1973 ceasefire. I have not received over 10 planes from them since last June. The Soviets are sending no ammunition and 44 airplanes is the maximum, including 20 MIG–23's (not Foxbats). They did this when I started attacking them after the failure of negotiations.

Our people want to see a real peace but they will not give up one inch of Arab land.

The prestige of the United States is in balance. I say Israel, not the United States, is responsible for the failure of negotiations. The Soviets can connect U.S. and Israeli policies. The Soviets are trying to undermine me and the entire world. The lastest development is in Libya where there is 2,000 kilometers of sea (?) line, where they have sent a large arsenal of arms; $12 billion worth for 12½ million people. There are no frontiers in Libya. The Soviets are trying to outflank me from Libya. It is against your interest and against the global balance in the Middle East. The Soviets can build anything they want there and no Libyan will see it because there are large areas of empty land. Also the Soviet economic squeeze on me is continuing. They refuse to give me any grace period on loans or sale of arms. Economic cooperation has stopped. They want to paralyze me. The latest act is in Libya. I shall fight it in Libya.

Secretary Kissinger: We will support Egypt in international forums if the Russians do something in Libya.

President Sadat: My people have not lost confidence in Doctor Kissinger. I have been looking forward to this meeting. I want you to

---

[5] See Document 92.

look at me as a friend. If the United States cannot do something, I will not be able to defend the United States again because Israel gets everything it needs from the United States. I want good relations with the United States. I will be very disappointed if nothing can be achieved. Mr. President, we have gone beyond where any Arab has gone in the past. My people will be very disappointed if nothing can be achieved. I want us to make progress; to make a complete peace. And I want the United States only to achieve it, not the Soviet Union, not through a Geneva Conference, where the USSR is sitting. The United States can achieve anything without the Soviet Union.

If a meeting can be achieved, then we have to go to Geneva, even though there are no bright prospects there. I won't be able to defend you at Geneva because you are defending Israel. We will reach stagnation if we try to broaden the participation in Geneva. Israel can blame everything on the PLO issue since I will have to insist upon its participation. Israel wants to gain time until your next election. Israel wants to get rid of Henry Kissinger. Israel wants to cause difficulties with the Congress. They want to wait until your election when Israel can monopolize the situation. I face a confrontation with the Soviet Union this summer. The situation in our relations with them will get worse. All of my arms have come from the USSR and there was no other way for me. The USSR is suspicious. It is clumsy in diplomacy. There is no leadership there. This is the situation there.

The President: I want you to know that the reassessment which I have announced is more than words. It is a bona fide analysis of how we can proceed best as a nation towards peace on a fair and equitable basis. However, we can make a contribution. Our Israeli friends don't believe it. The initial shock and disbelief has sunk in. Israel has reacted in the wrong way. Instead of saying whether they made a mistake, they have reacted to try to convince people that they are right. There has been typical pressure in the Congress. I don't intend to capitulate to this kind of pressure. It could lead to difficulties within our society and a struggle. The Israelis have misjudged American public opinion and me. I want you to know that I have heard nothing but good about you. You are a powerful leader with a broad approach. It is a pleasure to deal with you. I want to work with you to try to help achieve continued progress.

I would like to have any key points from you as to specifics for when I talk to Rabin. When I talk to the Prime Minister, I will lay it on the line. Of course, we have created an impression of going to Geneva with a broad comprehensive approach. The Israelis would not like us to take such a broad approach. You know that at Geneva the prospects for progress are negligible. Yet we might have to do it as the only option we see if there is no progress on the interim agreement. I have impressed Israel on the need to cooperate. The options you know. If Israel takes the same attitude as it took in February and March, I see no hope. They have to hear this from me. They know the pitfalls of Geneva. I can't imagine that they want the Soviet Union involved. It is beyond my comprehension as to why they have taken this view. Israel knows it will be isolated if they stay with their position and if we shift our attitude. Israeli-U.S. relations are good but difficult. I want to assure you that we will exercise as much leadership as we can. Some alternatives are worse than others for Israel. I appreciate your suggestion that there has to be a framework for negotiation soon or we have to go to Geneva. Israel ought to be shrewd enough to see this.

President Sadat: If we can keep complete understanding between the United States and Egypt regarding the efforts that are made before Geneva or at Geneva, if they know that the United States won't be behind them 100 percent at Geneva, all of this would help. I am furious that after all that the United States has done for Israel they could not agree to a second step. I want us to agree on a strategy of our own of course. We can achieve together a lot and we can save the Arab world from Soviet infiltration.

The President: Is there a strong reservation by Qadhafi regarding the Soviets in Libya?

President Sadat: Can you imagine $12 billion? Qadhafi is insane. Therefore, there has been no Arab comment. We got this information from those who actually signed the contract. I put it out publicly myself because I didn't want you to have to get charged by the Soviets that you had done so. The Soviets know that their days are numbered in Egypt. Every ship that leaves Egypt never comes back. Take, for example, the 4 Foxbat planes in Egypt. Last week I received something very queer. I was told by the Soviets that they wanted to replace the 4 Foxbats with 4 others sent in a large transport plane. I refused this. I ordered the 4 planes to be grounded. I said either you deliver 4 planes to us, train us, or get them out. This is a popular issue in the Arab world.

I need help from you in trying to convince those idiots in Israel to come to their senses. I have 270,000 Egyptians in Libya and I can send more. I have all of the training people in Libya. I don't need help in Libya. I can take care of that by my effort. This front has to be kept quiet.

The President: Let me assure you our policies will coincide with your thoughts. It may have repercussions with Israel. If we can talk about specifics, I think it would be helpful to me. To Rabin it is this interim agreement or Geneva. They have to recognize that at Geneva it will not be to their liking. We want the friendship between the United States and Egypt to grow. I don't like pressure. We can work together; we will work together.

Secretary Kissinger: We have spoken frankly. We have outlined the concrete possibilities. The Israeli strategy is to divide our Administration, if not to gain time to drag it into our elections. In the meantime, even President Sadat cannot keep the situation quiet. By that time the Arabs will be anti-American. Israel has said to us resume the interim negotiations. They have also talked in terms of a broader interim agreement. Our approach to this latter proposal is that you can explore it if you want but, in our judgment, it is a trap. And Geneva is the third alternative. What we need is a result this year. President Ford is prepared to go the overall route if necessary. While it would be prolonged and difficult, we are not rejecting it. The other alternative is the resumption of the interim negotiations. We will be accused domestically of trying to impose this—that we will be trying to impose a U.S.-Egyptian solution. If we could find some modification in the Egyptian position on an interim agreement—we know your range is limited for I have told the President that you have gone well beyond anything that was thought possible—if, for example, Egypt could make a move, we could then make an American proposal. If the Israelis then turn down an American proposal, they would be considered wrong by American public opinion. What I am talking about are Egyptian modifications in their position on an interim agreement which would be used as an excuse to put forward an American proposal on an interim agreement. If Israel did refuse, we would be in a better tactical position for moving to a comprehensive plan. You would have to help us in 1976, since we could take a position on an overall settlement at Geneva even though we could not implement it during 1976.

The President: If something could be done in 1975, our overall approach would keep U.S. domestic problems from festering. They can't attack us on peace and war issues.

Secretary Kissinger: If you have time, we can go to the overall approach. If you want something very fast, it would have to be the interim approach. They have said if you change, they will change. We do not intend to communicate anything of substance to Rabin regarding our meeting here. It would be possible for a quick shuttle to be undertaken by Mid-July. The Soviets are very anxious to go to the European Security Conference and they would be terribly disturbed if the President didn't go to Helsinki in July and if there were no conference. You will recall that the Israelis have also talked about a wider interim agreement but they would expect a declaration of non-belligerency. We could try that but I am very uneasy about it. I know that you are insisting on the Israelis getting out of the passes and the oil fields. We noticed that the Israelis now have shifted from non-belligerency to an emphasis on the duration point which they say is the point which most concerns them. There is also a focus on the warning stations and other elements regarding the boycott. I have not discussed these with the President. What we need from you is not anything fundamental but anything which would permit us to say there has been a shift in the Egyptian position and would give us a chance to make an American proposal. A proposal where the line would be drawn east of the passes and you would be given land access to the oil fields. There would be a chance to do it in a month. We have been scaring the Israelis with plans regarding the Geneva Conference. And this has been leaked back to the Israelis. I want to stress, however, if we first go to the interim agreement and then to Geneva, then you will have to be patient. If there was no war and no embargo, we could win and even if it doesn't work in July, we could prove to our public that we have done everything possible. If you can tell us tomorrow what specifically you might be able to do.

President Sadat: In what direction?

Secretary Kissinger: First, the renewal of UNEF for more than a year and afterwards for annual periods. And the question of a warning station perhaps under UN control. You could get a similar one. You might also see whether there is something you can do on the boycott. Maybe you could add some additional firms.

President Sadat: Don't ask this of me. The boycott will raise havoc for me.

Secretary Kissinger: You have agreed selectively to remove some American firms. The boycott could be done bilaterally.

President Sadat: What if they refuse the interim agreement?

The President: We can go to the overall settlement.

President Sadat: In such circumstances you must be with me at Geneva. I have no objections to the United States having good relations with Israel. As far as I am concerned, it can have the full protection of the United States. If we go to Geneva, I shall anticipate we will be working towards an overall solution with the United States taking the initiative.

Secretary Kissinger: We probably can put forward something on borders.

President Sadat: Borders with minor rectifications; demilitarized zones on both sides of the border.

Secretary Kissinger: It is important that the Arabs not start a holy war against us if our overall settlement proposal is not all that you want. If what America puts forward at Geneva is rebuffed by both Arabs and Israelis it would be bad.

President Sadat: I shall be raising hell at Geneva but really agreeing with you.

Secretary Kissinger: Suppose we succeed on an interim agreement in July. Can Syria be managed?

President Sadat: There must be a Syrian disengagement. This must be discussed before Geneva.

The President: If we talk in terms of the 1967 borders isn't that enough to keep the Syrians quiet?

President Sadat: No, there is jealousy. The Soviets will find the basis to cause further difficulties. In any interim agreement there has to be a change of a kilometer or two. And they settle for that. (Conversation had to be terminated at that point because of schedule. It was agreed that the talk would be continued at the next session.)

178. Memorandum of Conversation[1]

Salzburg, June 2, 1975.

PARTICIPANTS

Egypt
Anwar Al-Sadat, President
Major General Mubarak, Vice President
Ismail Fahmi, Foreign Minister

United States
The President
The Secretary
Joseph J. Sisco, Under Secretary for Political Affairs

The President: How would you like to proceed?

President Sadat: As you would like. I have studied the points we discussed. I want you to have something to present to the Israelis despite the fact that they are occupying my lands and despite the fact that they are in a psychological state and confused. We are at a turning point. It seems to me that no one is able to work out peace in Israel. It is too weak a government. The world is waiting for results. I want to push the peace process. I want to move in the direction of agreement. With Dr. Kissinger I indicated that I was willing to renew annually the UNEF Force. I renewed it for three months to July. If we reach agreement, I

---

[1] Source: National Archives, RG 59, Records of Henry Kissinger, 1973–77, Box 11, Nodis Memcons, June 1975, Folder 2. Secret; Nodis. Drafted by Sisco on July 1. The meeting took place at the Residenz in Salzburg. According to the President's Daily Diary, the meeting took place from 3:37 until 3:59 p.m. (Ford Library, Staff Secretary's Office Files)

can agree to renew it annually and to give you another year in writing until July 1977, one year to July 1976, and then an additional year.

The Secretary: President Sadat, that is what we have agreed before. The Israelis will not see this as new.

The President: You mean you would be willing to give me a letter which comprises a two-year commitment?

The Secretary: Let me explain. We have already told the Israelis of the Egyptian intent to renew UNEF annually and the renewal just described by President Sadat will not be considered a new concession by the Israelis. I have already indicated to them your willingness to renew the mandate of UNEF after a one-year period.

The President: It could be renewed annually as long as the process of peace goes on. The written assurances would be for the two-year period until July 1977?

Foreign Minister Fahmi: I want to be realistic.

The Secretary: Candidly, the Israelis think that already based on what we have said. What we need is something beyond this. It has to encourage the Israelis to make progress. It has to avoid the impression of an Egyptian-American proposal or Egyptian-American collusion. You agree in principle to getting something new to them. We need to get some new idea from you. We would take it to Rabin and then he would go back to the Cabinet to report and there would be a several week hiatus. We really need something on duration which is different from what we had in March. There are two aspects to the question of duration. First is what you have agreed to that the agreement will remain in effect until superseded by another agreement. The other aspect relates to UNEF renewal. Would it be possible initially to have a two-year period followed up by a one-year renewal which would give us a total of three years? As to the warning station, maybe the Israelis could hold on to it for the first two years until they had built another one. As to any American plan that would be put down by us, as you know, we believe that the Egyptian line should be east of the passes, Egypt should have continuous access to the oil fields, and the Israelis should be out of the passes.

Foreign Minister Fahmi: The President will give us a letter for whatever length of time but I cannot put it in a UN resolution. This would raise hell with the Arabs. If we put it in the Security Council Resolution everybody will say it is a partial solution.

The Secretary: If you give such a letter the Israelis will leak it.

Foreign Minister Fahmi: Let them leak it.

President Sadat: If we agree to two years and in the letter we include then an additional year, what's the use of going to Geneva if we do this?

The President: Well if I understand your question, the answer is that we would be going to Geneva with an approach to an overall settlement.

President Sadat: The Israelis will not want to go to Geneva.

The Secretary: They have to recognize the price the Russians will ask. If the Israelis insist that the price for an interim agreement is that we will not go to Geneva for the period which an interim agreement lasts, we won't pay that price. We would go to Geneva, perhaps put up a proposal about December but it would have to be understood that it would not be implemented in 1976. Implementation could be considered in 1977. If President Ford wins, we could start implementing it in 1977.

The President: We could meet your concerns if we went to Geneva. We could make a broad comprehensive proposal.

The Secretary: We have worked out the strategy to press for an interim agreement or to go for the overall settlement. The Israelis are getting ready for an interim agreement. We are tactically in a better position to do something unexpected. We hope that President Ford can break the impasse in the Middle East. If we could get an interim agreement, we could then reconvene Geneva in October, let it go for a while and perhaps submit our substantive ideas around December. This would help you. I realize this would produce an explosion in America. The President can fight that battle based on the interim agreement. Moreover, after our elections he will have created a moral basis for a big move in 1977.

President Sadat: I agree to the principle that we should try to hold matters until 1977. I can't put two years in the agreement but we don't differ practically.

The Secretary: In practice it is in our President's interest to do it soon in 1977, that is, in the honeymoon period after his reelection. Anything that we can bring to Rabin which would give us three years would help and it would help avoid a war in 1976.

President Sadat: I can assure you, Mr. President, that I do not want any war. As far as I am concerned, Syria can go to war by itself. I am not intending to start a war. As to the monitoring stations that we discussed, I believe that should be manned by Americans.

The President: Will the Russians agree?

President Sadat: They have no voice in the matter. We have full confidence in you.

The Secretary: It is conceivable that Americans manning such stations would be acceptable at home. It could be characterized as an essential of our surveillance responsibility under the disengagement agreements where we fly U–2, where we analyze the pictures and give them to both sides. We would have to assume that could be a matter of tactical intelligence. Mr. President, you would have to sell this to Congress. Maybe civilians could do the monitoring in the stations.

President Sadat: By radio.

Foreign Minister Fahmi: Take the question of Israeli cargoes going through the Suez Canal. The Israelis leaked it.

The Secretary: As to the UN Force, what happens if the Soviets did veto its extension?

President Sadat: I could ask the nations to stay. I can't say that in a letter but if there is a veto, I can ask the nations to stay on on another basis. They could stay on the basis of an Egyptian request.

Foreign Minister Fahmi: We could go to the General Assembly if the Soviets veto where we will get very broad support for the renewal of the UNEF Force.

The Secretary: You know how important it is to get a longer duration. That must be made to move. We would not give them your proposal. The President would put it strongly and then at some point there would be an American proposal. We have to have some three-year phraseology and an answer to the veto problem.

President Sadat: (Turning to Fahmi.) We should work out the phraseology in this three-year thing and on the veto question there is also the question of the warning stations. We would propose that Americans man the warning stations. This is an important proposal. Americans would be witnesses. It would be a complete guarantee for the Israelis.

The Secretary: We have been dealing with President Sadat for some time as a statesman. I think we can sell these ideas.

President Sadat: I believe that our ideas will give the President some leverage.

The Secretary: If the Israelis think about it carefully, the idea of Americans manning the warning stations is an interesting idea; it is a very novel idea. From the Israeli point of view an American presence is better than a three-year agreement.

President Sadat: I am going to have to pay for all of this.

Foreign Minister Fahmi: The Americans can give us the money.

The Secretary: The idea of the Americans manning the stations engages the United States in a permanent way. It is a better assurance for Israel.

The President: I believe it is very salable with the American public. Moreover, if Israel accepted the proposal, the Israeli supporters would help.

The Secretary: It is very important that this should not be told to Rabin next week. We will indicate to Rabin that you, President Sadat, have indicated a willingness to look at the question of duration. We will also indicate that you are willing to look at the question of the warning stations and then two weeks after the Rabin visit we could go back to them specifically with your creative idea.

President Sadat: The President has said that it is salable in America.

The Secretary: It is important, President Sadat, that you not look eager for an interim agreement. That the indications be that everything is still open, that you are going home to think about what we have talked about. We have a chance if we get tough with Rabin. If we could get agreement by July 5, then it could all get done in a week or so.

President Sadat: An interim agreement would be a big blow to the USSR.

The Secretary: It would be important to do it before the European Security Conference since we have leverage on the Russians and they would not want to cause too much difficulty before that Conference. The United States is the only one they really wanted at the conference. They would have to be very careful not to cause difficulty before then. As to procedure, diplomatic channels are useless. You will have to shake the Israelis. Then we hear from them in ten days and then you could send me out to the area with your proposal.

President Sadat: As to an American proposal, President Ford could adopt the posture of putting pressure on me. He could say that he, President Ford, has insisted that I modify my position.

The Secretary: This would enable us to say that President Ford has broken the impasse. In other words, the warning stations would be manned by Americans, and there would be three-year language in the letter on the UNEF extension.

President Sadat: (Turning to Fahmi.) Work out the language with Henry. As to the Soviets, I tried to tell the Soviets (not) to fly Foxbats on my land.

The Secretary: The interim agreement will not help our relations with the Soviets nor will it help your relations.

President Sadat: You have nothing to fear from the Soviets.

Foreign Minister Fahmi: This will bring a major crisis between Egypt and the Soviets.

President Sadat: It will give the United States the upper hand.

The Secretary: They cannot do anything.

The President: I believe the ideas indicated by President Sadat are salable.

President Sadat: The Soviets reported to us on Henry's last meeting with Gromyko.[2] Gromyko reported complete surrender to Kissinger.

The Secretary: Fahmi knows who gave up what.

Foreign Minister Fahmi: I told Gromyko there would be no more communiqués with him. We write communiqués and he surrendered totally to Kissinger.

President Sadat: The Soviets are clumsy and suspicious.

The Secretary: I believe our approach here ought to be that you are going home to consider what each of us has said and to weigh our conversation. You should not appear too anxious to get an interim agreement. It is still 50–50.

The President: The Israelis are scared to death about going to Geneva.

The Secretary: I have consulted with a lot of Senators on the Hill. As to the press, we could say that we have discussed a number of questions, that the atmosphere was excellent and that both President Ford and President Sadat are going to go back home and think about the substance of the conversations.

President Sadat: I will bear witness to the fact that President Ford and the United States would be responsible for breaking the impasse and achieving the interim agreement.

The Secretary: The Israelis cannot yield to me; they can yield to President Ford.

President Sadat: I would like to say a word, Mr. President, about our economic position. We need a billion and a half dollars, half of which should come from the Arabs. We need long loans with a grace period.

The President: Henry and I have discussed this matter.

The Secretary: Our aim is to put in for $500 million for Egypt for FY '76. As to Egypt's immediate problem, we have talked to a number of countries. We would hope it would be possible to get $250 million from Saudi Arabia and Iran, respectively, and maybe $100 million from Germany and $100 million from Japan, and the United States would put in $250 million. We would try to do this on a long-term basis, perhaps with a five-year grace period. I have talked to Genscher and the Germans have agreed to approach other European countries.

---

[2] According to telegram Secto 1049, May 20, Gromyko, at the May 19–20 meetings in Vienna, emphasized the need to move promptly to convene the Geneva Conference and insisted on Soviet participation in all its phases. He also proposed a joint U.S.–USSR invitation to the PLO to participate in the conference. (National Archives, RG 59, Central Foreign Policy Files)

President Sadat: See if you can get Japan to raise their figure of $100 million.

The President: We will make maximum efforts.

The Secretary: We will also talk to the French. I want to explain, President Sadat, the connection between this and Israeli assistance. As you know, we have been disappointed by the Israelis before and we could be fooled again on this question of an interim agreement. It may prove necessary to hold up on their aid but what you have to understand is if we have to do that, your aid would become hostage to their aid.

President Sadat: I understand this. On the Hill they will try to hold up the whole aid bill until I give Israel what it wants.

President Sadat [*President Ford*?]: I can understand this.

The President: The Israelis believe they can ram down my throat any figure; they are wrong. I could sustain a veto. If we can get an interim agreement, then we could negotiate with the Congress in advance on what the figures might be. This may make time.

President Sadat: I have half of what I need already from the Arabs. I can manage for the remainder of this year if necessary.

The Secretary: If the interim agreement works, they will go to the Congress very early. We will have to [illegible] large sum for Israel. If the interim agreement [illegible] we will go early.

The President: When we went up to the Hill, we did not reduce the amount for Egypt. [illegible] that we had the [illegible].

President Sadat: I would hope that something would be done about the problem of arms for Egypt after the interim agreement is achieved. I am heading for a confrontation with the Soviets. The Soviets have never forgiven me for this—for being close to the United States. I need to buy defensive arms from the United States.

The Secretary: If we can create a real climate for peace this might be possible.

The President: President Sadat, your proposal for the monitoring stations is a very helpful and constructive proposal.

The Secretary: As to the economic consortium, [illegible] be helpful, Mr. President, to keep Saudi Arabia with it because this will help us in encouraging the Europeans.

President Sadat: If I understand, we can persuade the Saudi Arabians to remain included.

The Secretary: We will also be in touch with the Saudi Arabians, as well as the Europeans. As to the question of Syria, we will have to make a maximum effort with Syria to assure that something is going on. In practice Syrian negotiations may have to [illegible] in the context of Geneva.

179. Memorandum of Conversation[1]

Washington, June 5, 1975, 2 p.m.

PARTICIPANTS

> President Ford
> Dr. Henry A. Kissinger, Secretary of State and Assistant to the President for National Security Affairs
> Lt. General Brent Scowcroft, Deputy Assistant to the President for National Security Affairs

President: Pete Dominick said he just couldn't carry on.

Kissinger: The Middle East. I think we can work it. Israel is making noises like they are going to cave.

President: They know they haven't pushed it one inch.

Kissinger: I told Dinitz they had said there were three areas they knew there had to be movement in—duration, warning sites, and boycott. You must be firm because they will try to rattle us. Now they have Joe Kraft[2] saying I shouldn't be the negotiator. That is another ploy.

I think you should hit Rabin between the eyes—your extreme concern over what happened in March, over the leaks, and over their trying to win public opinion here. This will actually give him something to sell at home. Tell him if there is no movement we will go to Geneva with a comprehensive proposal.

President: There are about ten things which related to a comprehensive proposal we would raise at Geneva. I wouldn't tell him what position, just what we needed positions on.

Kissinger: You could suggest that he and I work out something that Israel can support. I will then try to move him toward the Egyptian positions without telling him about them. Then you tell him to go home and see if he can sell it to the Cabinet, and if he can, I will go to Egypt

---

[1] Source: Ford Library, National Security Adviser, Memoranda of Conversations, Box 12, June 5, 1975, Ford, Kissinger. Secret; Nodis. The meeting took place in the Oval Office at the White House.

[2] Joseph Kraft was a *Washington Post* columnist.

to sell it. If you give it as an Egyptian proposal, they will play it as Egyptian-American collusion.

President: This would be while he is here.

Kissinger: In between your meetings with him. I will tell him he has got to go East of the passes and have an unbroken line to the oil fields. I don't know how to work the duration—probably we can bargain. On the warning stations, I would leave the manning of them open. If they offer American manning, we can say we have to run it by the Egyptians. Then he would run this past the Cabinet and I would go out a week later. We'd get it done before the Soviet Union and Syria get set.

I think you have got to show you are determined and won't tolerate a stalemate. My impression from Dinitz—unless they are setting us up . . . I asked Bryce Harlow[3] what kind of flak we would take in a confrontation. He said "Go on television to explain it and you would get overwhelming support." I think you can get an agreement, based on your Salzburg meetings.[4]

President: It would put some meat on the bones.

Kissinger: I think this is the way we can do it.

President: I liked the Gromyko comment about how cumbersome democracy is in foreign policy.

Kissinger: My strong recommendation is to keep the Rabin dinner as much a working dinner as possible—even if it hurts Max Fisher's feelings. The essence of a working dinner is that it's only the Executive Branch plus some from Congress.

President: Okay—about 32. No Jewish leaders.

Kissinger: Rabin will want an assurance that you won't press him on Syria and at Geneva.

President: We can't promise that.

Kissinger: They will say they would be pressed at Geneva anyway, so why make a deal beforehand? You could say we do it to defuse the Soviets . . .

[Omitted here is discussion unrelated to the Arab-Israeli dispute.]

---

[3] Bryce Harlow served as an adviser to President Ford and as a congressional liaison.

[4] See Documents 177 and 178.

180. Memorandum of Conversation[1]

Washington, June 9, 1975, 9:24–10:24 a.m.

PARTICIPANTS

    President Ford
    Dr. Henry A. Kissinger, Secretary of State and Assistant to the President for National Security Affairs
    Lt. General Brent Scowcroft, Deputy Assistant to the President for National Security Affairs

[Omitted here is discussion unrelated to the Arab-Israeli dispute.]

Kissinger: Nahum Goldmann's views are that Israel will never back up under overwhelming pressure. If the Klutznick meeting goes well,[2] you might consider meeting with them. It is quite a group. Goldmann says there is nothing we can do through the Presidents Group.[3] They are too committed.

They are very upset about the letter of the 76 Senators.[4] They thought it was a great mistake. Even Ribicoff thought so.

President: Who started it?

Kissinger: Javits with Dinitz. It was designed to bring pressure on Congressmen like Percy, and you.

I have tried to give you a fair analysis in this package. I don't think you should get into aid. Tell them you can't talk aid until you know whether or not you are supporting a stalemate. They are projecting a conciliatory air. I think you should be very stern—whether you were misled or not you were deeply disappointed. Next, the leaks and proselytizing with Congress and the public here is unacceptable. Then say you must know within two weeks whether or not an interim agreement is possible. We have a window with the Soviets until CSCE and I wouldn't let it drag out.

I think we are in good shape for a comprehensive settlement. Ribicoff says the Jews couldn't stand against you if you went on TV stating an American position. He spoke very highly of you and he thought only Kennedy would have a chance against you. And Kennedy's life is such a mess that it would be a real problem.

---

[1] Source: Ford Library, National Security Adviser, Memoranda of Conversations, Box 12, June 9, 1975, Ford, Kissinger. Secret; Nodis. The meeting was held in the Oval Office at the White House.

[2] See Document 189.

[3] See footnote 5, Document 171.

[4] See Document 175.

President: Some people are prone to mistakes. He can't make good judgments under pressure. He doesn't plan it—it just happens.

Kissinger: It's almost as if he punishes himself.

President: The odds are he will make another public mistake.

Kissinger: Back to the Israelis. Their capacity to misrepresent is so total that it's hard to know how they will hit you. I think they might say they will accommodate if Egypt will change its position. Then they will leak the Egyptian position and we will be in a hassle. We should do it the other way around. Ask them what they want; if they say non-belligerency, say forget it. If it's about duration and warning sites, say he and I should talk about it.

President: How about American manning of the warning sites?

Kissinger: I would leave that to the last, as a major concession. Don't give it during the meeting. They should then send Allon back over with the answers to the questions we need. They shouldn't spend more than a week.

He will also want to tie you down to a figure, and a commitment not to make an overall proposal. That you can't do.

President: How about a move with Syria?

Kissinger: If he is willing to go for a Syrian one, we can avoid a comprehensive proposal. If not, I would say we have to go to Geneva. Don't tell him we would put forward a comprehensive proposal, but just say we would consult with them closely, but keep open the option.

My meeting with the SFRC was an eyeopener. They were very deferential and every few sentences there was a comment about the success of your trip.[5]

The Israeli Cabinet has said it would stick with their March position unless Egypt made some changes in its position.

The first day I would be very tough—say there's no sense talking economics. Rabin's nerves are not that good. He is smart and shy, but he's not all that tough.

On aid, we have a really good paper. The $2.6 figure they gave is phony. With $1.5 they can meet their military purchases and still have a GNP growth of 4%. I think we should keep them on a tight leash and give $1 billion if they come across. If they don't . . .

President: Keep them to the level of this year.

Kissinger: Right.

[Omitted here is discussion unrelated to the Arab-Israeli dispute.]

---

[5] On June 6, Kissinger briefed the Senate Foreign Relations Committee on President Ford's trip to Europe. (*Washington Post*, June 7, 1975, p. A2)

181. Briefing Memorandum From the Assistant Secretary of State for Congressional Relations (McCloskey) to Secretary of State Kissinger[1]

Washington, undated.

Middle East Reappraisal: The Javits Letter

The surprising 76 vote tally which Javits & Co. managed to collect as co-signers to the letter endorsing Israel's request for additional military assistance[2] has frequently been interpreted as a Congressional endorsement of carte blanche for the Israelis. Our conversations with a wide range of Senators (and their staffs) who signed or opposed the letter belie that interpretation. Almost everyone with whom we spoke agreed that, while the 76 total is a sharp reminder of continuing solid support for Israel in the Senate, it does not negate the fact that a sea change has started in Senate attitudes against providing Israel with a blank check this year. In fact, many of the Senators who signed did so reluctantly, including Senator Bentsen whose mail shows a significant decline in support for aid to Israel. Similarly Stevenson's mail is running 9–1 criticizing his having signed the letter.

Background

In the face of your meeting with President Sadat and the increasing perception in Congress that the Middle East reappraisal would include a sharp reduction in military assistance to Israel, Javits and a few of his colleagues felt that it was essential to try and tie your hands or at least delimit your maneuverability. The first draft letter, patterned on last year's (which attracted 71 signatures)[3] was prepared by staff aides, but initiated by the Jewish community. It was a tough, uncompromising endorsement of the Israeli request and entirely partisan in tone. It was circulated to the 18 original co-sponsors. Subsequently, it was softened on several points and the partisan nature of the letter was balanced by the insertion of the sentence expressing support for improved relations with all the nations of the Middle East area. Reportedly, Jackson was responsible for the last change. In doing so, he overrode his zealous staff man Perle who had been responsible for most of the tendentious tone of the first draft.

---

[1] Source: Library of Congress, Manuscript Division, Kissinger Papers, CL 158, Geopolitical File, Israel, June 1–20, 1975. Confidential; Exdis. Drafted by Jenkins on June 3. A handwritten notation at the top of the page reads: "June 10, 1975."

[2] See Document 175.

[3] See footnote 2, Document 175.

Once the corrected draft had been approved by the original co-sponsors, staffers for Jackson and Javits (Perle and Lakeland) and other staffers fanned out to collect co-sponsors, and the Jewish community was mobilized for a phone campaign to elicit support. A counter-initiative by Senator Percy, who was, as you know, reluctant to engage in an all-out effort because he is already a marked man with the Jewish community, failed to get organized. Its sole result was Percy's own letter to the President and McGovern's letter explaining that, although he signed the Javits letter, he still supported a number of anti-Israeli initiatives such as establishment of an independent Palestinian state.

Assessment

Our conversations suggest that, while not all 76 signers would support the full Israeli request of $2.59 billion, there is still widespread reluctance to publicly back down from all-out support for Israel. However, a shift in the Senate attitude toward Israel is underway. It is my judgement that a number of the key members of the 76 would be receptive to negotiating with the Administration on a compromise level which would endorse a reduced amount of assistance for Israel. There is increasing support for an adjustment, but not a radical cutback in our support for Israel.

Sentiment in the House parallels that in the Senate, though no legislative or written initiatives have emerged, as yet. Congressman Murphy of New York is reputed to have tried unsuccessfully to circulate a Javits-type letter.

It is worth noting that an important interest in this process will be Muskie's new Budget Committee which is likely to cast a cold eye on a high figure.

182. Memorandum of Conversation[1]

Washington, June 11, 1975, 9:34–10:06 a.m.

PARTICIPANTS

President Gerald R. Ford
Dr. Henry A. Kissinger
Lt. General Brent Scowcroft

The President: The papers on Rabin and the arms requests are very well done. Really well done. It was an eye opener to me. With all they have gotten, they can never say we are not concerned with their security.

Kissinger: If we ever put these figures out, we could carry the country. If the Kennedy appraisal is correct—and I think he is—you are in good shape. He thinks you will be tough to beat—because you have the center.

I told Rabin you leaned toward an overall agreement.[2] On an interim deal, he is more flexible on giving access to the oil; he is willing to give up the warning station, but he is not ready to move out of the passes. This is a new argument—he says the next line is near the '67 borders.

The President: If he is worried about security, won't those warning stations do it?

Kissinger: He has a point. Their infrastructure is right behind the passes, but why didn't he say that nine months ago? The other point is if he makes an interim deal, what understanding will there be about the next steps? He wants a promise there'll be no more moves. I didn't answer. But you can't commit yourself to anything more than to work in close consultation with them.

Scowcroft: We can't do it. You have consistently warned them that a Syrian move was essential.

Kissinger: He says he can move only a few hundred yards there. We would need at least three kilometers—and that would hit the settlements. He says he can't do it, even for ten years of no movement—only for peace. But if he talks peace with Syria, he can't avoid talking peace with Egypt, and then we would be talking borders.

---

[1] Source: Ford Library, National Security Adviser, Memoranda of Conversations, Box 12, June 11, 1975, Ford, Kissinger. Secret; Nodis. The meeting was held in the Oval Office at the White House. Brackets are in the original.

[2] Kissinger and Rabin met on the morning of June 11 from 8 until 9:25 a.m. at Blair House. (Memorandum of conversation, June 11; National Archives, RG 59, Records of Henry Kissinger, 1973–77, Box 11, Nodis Memcons, June 1975, Folder 2)

The President: Will he push for free access to the Canal?

Kissinger: He didn't raise it—nor aid, but he will. You might begin by raising the point about domestic interference here, and the leaks, and then let him go. It is hard work, but if it doesn't work, I think you should put out an overall plan.

The President: What are the elements of an overall proposal?

Kissinger: Borders, Arab peace commitments, the Palestinians, guarantees.

The President: I thought I would start with him saying how disappointed I was at the failure in March, and the problem of leaking my letter,[3] their interference in our domestic affairs, why I announced the reassessment. I would say I was committed to peace which would guarantee Israel's survival, and I was leaning toward an overall settlement and ask him how he sees it.

Kissinger: I would be tough on leaking—not just the letter, but the Schmidt leak also.

[Describes the Israeli leak to Schmidt about him setting up Israel-Soviet contacts.]

The President: If we talk about the leaking of the letter, that is a gross example.

Kissinger: Yes, but it is not the only thing; it is a pattern.

---

[3] Document 156.

183. Memorandum of Conversation[1]

Washington, June 11, 1975, 10 a.m.–noon.

PARTICIPANTS

Yitzhak Rabin, Prime Minister of Israel
Simcha Dinitz, Ambassador of Israel
Mordechai Gazit, Director General, Prime Minister's Office
Mordechai Shalev, Minister, Embassy of Israel

President Ford
Dr. Henry A. Kissinger, Secretary of State and Assistant to the President for National Security Affairs
Joseph J. Sisco, Under Secretary of State for Political Affairs
Lt. General Brent Scowcroft, Deputy Assistant to the President for National Security Affairs

[The press was admitted for photographs and then dismissed.]

Prime Minister Rabin [pointing out the bust of Truman]: We have very special feelings toward Truman.

The President: He took a big step.

Prime Minister Rabin: Yes. He was instrumental in the establishment of the state of Israel.

Secretary Kissinger: Did you see the play ["Give 'em hell, Harry," with James Whitmore]?

Prime Minister Rabin: No. I heard of it.

The President: There were two hours of monologue. It was a very good portrayal; even Margaret [Truman Daniel] thought so. There were a few bad cracks, but it was really good.

He was the first President I met and served under. I was on the committee on rebuilding or tearing down the White House. [The President described the reasons for rebuilding the White House and how it was done.]

Secretary Kissinger: I met him as an ex-President, when I was a consultant for Kennedy. He asked me what I had learned working in Washington. I said I had learned that the bureaucracy was the fourth branch of government and that even the President couldn't always get his decisions implemented. His reply was "bullshit." It shocked a poor Harvard professor. [Laughter]

The President: It is awfully nice to see you. I have been looking forward to the opportunity to discuss matters with you since the unfortu-

---

[1] Source: National Archives, RG 59, Records of Henry Kissinger, 1973–77, Box 11, Nodis Memcons, June 1975, Folder 2. Secret; Nodis. The meeting was held in the Oval Office at the White House. Brackets are in the original.

nate events of last March. I hope we can be open and frank, as we have in the past. As you know, I operate in this way, being categorical and frank, and I would like to proceed on that basis. I want to be open in order to clear the air, so you and I understand each other and so we don't just hear things from the press. And, if we can do so, it would help us both to work towards what Israel wants and the United States wants.

When I came into office on August 8, one of the first things Henry talked to me about was how to achieve a major step forward to an equitable settlement in the Middle East. You will recall that I met with you and I met with Foreign Minister Allon twice.[2] I wanted to be as helpful as possible and to meet the military requests of Israel, so that Israel would have no feeling of insecurity. You will recall that I had received four options; the Defense Department recommendation was the lowest option, but I went for a higher option. I made an analysis and I wanted you and your Government to feel certain that you had the capability to defend yourself. As you will recall, by April, as a result, you received the urgent items, roughly about $700 million worth.[3] I know there are several items at this time that have not been delivered for one reason or another. I was trying to create the feeling that Israel should have a high degree of security.

But I want to say to you that I am disillusioned, I am disappointed, and disturbed. I am disillusioned over the results of last March. I believe that Israel could have been more frank in the crunch. I was disillusioned over the inflexibility of Israel at the final testing point. I understand your political problems in trying to be more forthcoming, but I have to say to you that I was disappointed, disturbed and disillusioned over the position taken.

A second point relates to the release of my letter of March 21. I was upset over the release of that letter and the inference that was put on it that I was trying to apply pressure on Israel. I tried to be frank with you in that letter. I do not know whether it was a deliberate leak, but it was very bad. There was also the question of the leaking of the conversation with Chancellor Schmidt of the Federal Republic of Germany. It is important that I get these things off my chest. I cannot talk to a friend if there is something gnawing at me.

You and I worked very closely together when you were Ambassador in Washington. You should have no doubt about my attitude regarding Israel, and yet I get reports that political efforts are being made

---

[2] Ford met with Rabin on September 10 and 13, 1974, and with Allon on December 9, 1974, and January 16, 1975. See Documents 99, 100, 123, and 127.

[3] See Document 101.

domestically by Israel and the Embassy. This is not at all helpful—this kind of pressure.

Now let me turn to the substance. I meant what I said when I said we were going to reassess our policy. I meant it. I felt I had made a maximum effort to resolve the problems before, and after the suspension, I had to. So we have begun it. As President I have listened, I have read more, and analyzed more about the Middle East than other Presidents. I have read articles by George Ball, I have talked to Rostow and Goldberg. I have talked to other people and to members of Congress and the Executive Branch to give me their suggestions. The whole process of reassessment is aimed at trying to determine what to do to achieve a fair, equitable and permanent peace. I feel that I have done everything to help assure the survival of Israel, one, with strong military strength and a viable, strong economy.

We have looked at all—not just from State and elsewhere but all the options which in my mind made sense—and my own thoughtful evaluations have been made. And where I come out, even though I have not made any final judgments, where I come out—and I want your assessment as well if I am wrong—I come out on the option of moving to an overall settlement to Geneva, to try to achieve a peace with guarantees, a peace with all of your neighbors that would include agreement on borders. Now, that is where I come out at the moment, and I would appreciate your views and assessment which would help me. My plan would be to make some kind of public announcement this summer, or earlier. However, I have an open mind and I would appreciate your frank assessment and recommendations. They will have a significant impact on what I decide. I feel we have come through three months of agonizing reassessment. This is where I am, but I am saying to you I have not made a firm decision. I want you to be as frank with me.

Prime Minister Rabin: I am glad to have the opportunity to come here at your invitation. It is a meeting which is urgently needed and I hope it will be helpful to you. The only way is for me to talk frankly. Without being frank, all the misunderstanding will come up again.

We in Israel have great admiration for you and we know you are a friend of Israel. As President of the United States, we know that you have to do everything to try to help bring about peace in the Middle East.

We appreciate your generosity in approving all of the arms that have been shipped to Israel. Your action has strengthened Israel. The strength of Israel I believe is one of the elements which might bring peace. We believe we have cooperated in the effort to move towards an interim settlement. We were and are flexible, although perhaps we might not have been flexible enough to meet the Egyptian demands. I feel bad in a way as to how you have put it. I feel we did the best in light of our public opinion. There were limits as to what we could give in response to Egyptian demands.

As to your letter, I brought it to the Cabinet. We do have the problem of leakage. We were disturbed over the leak. Unfortunately it is the plague of most democracies.

The President: We all have our problems.

Prime Minister Rabin: In the future I promise to do everything to prevent this. We will limit the information to a certain number of Cabinet members.

Mr. President, I prefer to go to the problems as I see them. I want to start with this basis: If there is any country eager for peace in the area, it is Israel. Israel has fought many wars and lost many people.

We know we cannot achieve peace by military means; conditions do not allow this. It happened in 1949, in 1956, in 1967, in 1973. We know that force will not bring a political settlement. Clausewitz said that war is the extension of diplomacy by other means, but the objective in war is to destroy the opposing force, to impose one's will. We cannot impose our will. Military means will not solve the problem. We have no interest in war but we have an interest in defending ourselves. Without being able to defend ourselves we will not survive. When we talk of peace, I mean by this our existence as a Jewish state with boundaries we can defend with our defenses—not to depend on others to send their own troops. That would be the end of us.

International guarantees have no meaning whatsoever with us. We have experienced them over many years. We have tried mixed armistice commissions, UNTSO, UNEF. We don't believe in putting our defense in the hands ... To drag a major power into a conflict which is local would be a serious mistake. We have never asked for one American soldier to aid in our defense.

We have tried for peace from 1949 to 1967, without results. There is an accumulation of suspicion, which must be cleared on the way to peace.

We have two specific ways. One is the one you mentioned: we would like to solve all the problems with all of the countries at the same time and bring about a final peace. And even if such a peace could take place it would be first a peace by diplomats and governments and not by people. In order to change attitudes in the area it would take a very long time. Even Sadat does not expect true peace; he distinguishes between the end of belligerency and normalization of relations.

Israel has its position about peace. There are three key issues on which I fear the gap is wide open with respect to an overall settlement and has never been bridged in the past by diplomacy: First, the nature of peace. The Arabs talk about the end of the war, the end of belligerency; for us it is much more. We mean normalization of relations.

Second, the boundaries of peace. The Arabs stress total Israeli withdrawal to the pre-June 1967 lines, which we consider practically indefensible. In the past when they moved their troops, we either had to wait for the attack or preempt. Take Egypt. Their forces have a million to one-and-a-quarter million, without mobilization. This would require total mobilization on our part. A half a million is the most we can mobilize. It is the highest ratio in the world. We mobilized about 400,000 in the 1973 war. We have revised our system to get the utmost. So the problem for Israel as far as an overall settlement is concerned is not to be in a position that in a few years, whenever they move, we have to go to a preemptive war. The real fact that they can move near to our borders means that we would have to mobilize and they then can destroy our economy by requiring total mobilization.

The third issue is the Palestinian issue.

We cannot withdraw to the 1967 borders in the Sinai. We cannot go down from the Golan Heights even in the context of peace. There can be a stationing of forces in Sharm el-Shaykh for example, and there must be a land linkage to it. And on the Golan for example, for a period of say 10 to 20 years, until there is a change of attitudes that occurs with the Arabs. The concept of stationing of forces and changing of attitudes, it is applicable to Egypt as well.

As to the West Bank, it is more complicated. Here there is an issue both of defense as well as the Palestinian issue. What the Arabs say is not new and hasn't changed since Nasser. They say the solution is creation of what is now an Arafat state. When Arafat is asked what he has in mind, he says he has a dream of a secular state, which would eliminate the Jewish state of Israel. It would require the elimination of all Jews who have arrived since 1923 or even 1948. A Palestinian state would mean that with Strela missiles[4] they could shoot down our planes at Tel Aviv airport. Therefore, as we see it, a return to the 1967 borders and the establishment of a Palestinian state means that Israel cannot survive.

I had five meetings with Hussein last year.[5] I said to him, "You have proposed a federation as a solution. If we can reach an agreement on a confederation in which Israel would be involved for about 30 years with open borders, with minimum changes—though there is a complicated problem of Jerusalem—we could also include the bulk of the

---

[4] Strela missiles are portable, shoulder-fired, anti-aircraft missiles.

[5] For further information on these meetings see the detailed list in the Note on Sources.

Gaza Strip. We would be prepared to make an agreement with Hussein on this basis. It was refused by Hussein. We also put to him the Allon plan[6] as a basis for negotiations and this was refused.

Therefore, in terms of the readiness of Israel for a final peace and the needs for Israel's security, the 1967 lines with respect to Egypt and Syria do not allow for security arrangements which are required for a small country of three million people against a composition of states who total 60-to-65 million. We are ready to try to achieve peace, but the gap on these three issues is wide. We have not sensed an Arab readiness to come close to the essentials of peace as we see them from our point of view.

I recall that in 1973 Dr. Kissinger was willing to explore the concept of security and sovereignty. But Sadat had probably decided on a war. I wish that we could have reached an overall peace. That is a real peace. I don't want the Israelis to be like the Christians in Lebanon. The fate of minorities in Arab lands—Christians, Kurds, Jews—is bad. The reason why the French set up the State of Lebanon is that they wanted to save the Christian minority in Syria. Ben-Gurion said Israel can win 20 wars and it will not solve the problem; but the Arabs need to win only once and it would mean the end of Israel.

What I have said is not popular in Israel. There are people who fought three times in the Sinai. Eisenhower, under the threat of the Soviet Union, brought about a withdrawal from the Sinai. And he said he hoped it would bring conditions of peace.

We can consider an overall peace, but we cannot budge from the positions which I have described. If there is a Geneva Conference, we will bring our positions there and we will struggle there, because we believe in our positions.

However, in many realistic appraisals we have concluded that there is another way which is more practical, that is, especially an interim agreement with Egypt. Egypt is the key. I recall that Egypt on its own decided to sign the armistice agreement and the other Arabs then followed.[7] Every war has stemmed from Egypt joining and every war has stopped when Egypt stopped. We hoped that through an interim agreement it can be a step towards peace, not just another military disengagement. An interim agreement which might change the realities on the ground, so that after a prolonged period we would not find ourselves in difficult conditions in the Middle East.

If you decide to move towards an overall settlement, there would be no use of any interim agreement, even though we recognize that an

---

[6] See footnote 7, Document 168.
[7] A reference to the 1949 Armistice Agreements. See footnote 5, Document 123.

overall peace could come by phases. The purpose of an interim is to postpone the overall until the situation becomes more favorable. As we see it, the Sinai is the card to win an overall peace, for in the case of war it gives Israel depth, time and territory against any enemy. I have no emotional attachment to the Sinai and I tell you frankly I see it as a bargaining card to achieve a final peace.

There are three key strategic elements in the Sinai:

1. the southern tip of the Sinai, that is Sharm el-Shaykh;
2. the oil fields (60% of Israel's oil comes from there, making us mostly independent, and it saves about $350 to $400 million); and
3. the strategic passes.

[He takes out a map.][8]

Once we are out of the passes, we have to reestablish a very long defensive line which takes a considerable amount of time. Egypt keeps five divisions and two armored divisions along the Canal. We have to bear in mind that what we give in an interim agreement has to be related to what we hope to achieve in a final peace. We will have to give much more in a final agreement. [He illustrates a final line on the map.]

Secretary Kissinger: In this concept of security and sovereignty, would you want a change in the borders and also a different deployment line?

Prime Minister Rabin: A deployment line [pointing to a map] would be defensible if combined with a political line which would be the final border. We don't claim Sharm el-Shaykh; we just want to be there, until we see a commitment to peace which is solid.

We have to decide in which direction to go. One way is to solve it in one act, or another way is one that tries to change the realities by an interim agreement. We cannot see the relation between an interim agreement and other factors; for example, Syria. We cannot evaluate the agreements in the context of an interim settlement with Syria.

As to the Golan Heights, we have not definitely decided on any line as it relates to an overall settlement but the same idea of security and sovereignty could be applied both to Golan and Egypt. [With the map on the floor he shows as it relates to Egypt a deployment line which was forward of what presumably would be a final political line.] In the Golan the chances are so small. [He shows on a Golan map.] We cannot evacuate settlements in an interim agreement. I am being frank. That is not true in an overall settlement.

---

[8] The Israeli maps are not attached.

Secretary Kissinger: Mr. President, what you should know is that there is no way in which the Israelis can make any kind of a small withdrawal, even of a kilometer or two, without touching the settlements.

Prime Minister Rabin: That is right.

The President: What is the line for an overall settlement?

Prime Minister Rabin: I can't give an exact line. It wouldn't be fair.

Secretary Kissinger: You have the same theory about security and sovereignty as in the Sinai?

Prime Minister Rabin: Yes. I said it publicly.

In 1965 Jordan got tanks on the condition they would not cross the Jordan.[9] They crossed.

All we can do in the Golan would be cosmetic.

Secretary Kissinger: Even three kilometers? How many settlements would you have to move?

Minister Gazit: At least half. About six or seven.

Prime Minister Rabin: It is not only a question of settlements. It is also the destruction of our defensive line which would have to be rebuilt and would take at least two or three years.

Secretary Kissinger: But six or seven settlements are within three kilometers. How many people is that?

Prime Minister Rabin: There are about 100 or 200 people in a settlement. But I will be frank. In the context of an interim settlement it is impossible to move any settlements.

The President: What about an overall settlement?

Prime Minister Rabin: I have said that this would involve both changes of the boundary line, as well as deployment to a defensible border. But I have no Cabinet decision. I would be willing to take something like this to the Cabinet for a decision, even though this would bring about probably an election in Israel.

The President: We have both been getting stronger, I see [referring to recent polls].

Prime Minister Rabin: We appreciate very much the handling of the *Mayaguez* incident by the United States.[10]

Now, what are the problems? One, what will be the relation between the interim agreement to the Syrian issue? Secondly, in terms of duration what does it mean with respect to efforts to achieve an overall peace at Geneva? We need several years to change the realities and the

---

[9] Under the U.S. military assistance program, the Johnson administration provided 50 to 100 Patton tanks to Jordan. (*New York Times*, December 29, 1965, p. 1)

[10] For documentation on the *Mayaguez* incident, see *Foreign Relations*, 1969–1976, volume X, Vietnam, January 1973–July 1975.

environment. I do not know what the United States' position is regarding the Syrian issue. And I do not know what the relationship is between the duration of the interim agreement to the overall settlement. There is no purpose served for Israel to go to an interim and lose one-and-a-half of our three cards and then have a weaker situation for an overall. Why should we give up the passes for nothing and end up negotiating an overall settlement in six months from a weaker position? We have to know what is to be done regarding Syria and Geneva. The defense line based on the passes is very important. Almost everything we have built in the Sinai is attached to the passes here [in the eastern part] and if the passes are not in our hands, then it is not defensible. The UN is no defense.

Secretary Kissinger: Would that situation be changed if you were one kilometer out of the passes?

Prime Minister Rabin: Being one kilometer out of the passes would completely change the situation. It would mean the total disruption of our defense system for two or three years and the need to have to rebuild it.

Secretary Kissinger: How about the Egyptian idea of Egypt being in one end of the pass and Israel in the other?

Prime Minister Rabin: This would be complicated. There would be an argument as to where the western and the eastern end of the passes are. We have to view the Sinai in the context of an overall peace. We want the Sinai to be demilitarized in a final peace.

As to the question of duration, how long is the agreement to last; what is its relationship to the Syrian matter; what is its relationship to the Geneva Conference and an overall settlement? In the previous American plan the time period was too short. It was one year. The Russians are also talking about phases.

Secretary Kissinger: It is conceivable that one could talk about a five- to seven-year period as it relates to an overall agreement but the problem would be, as you know, that the Russians would want to know what the final line was before one talked in terms of a five- to seven-year period to carry out a final agreement. Our approach, as you know, has been that we have sought an interim agreement so as to avoid stating a final position on a final peace.

Prime Minister Rabin: Yes, I know. I need the kind of duration at least between the United States and Israel applicable to Egypt that would give me enough time that there would be no activity undertaken which would be counterproductive.

[There was discussion of various lines on the map on the floor.]

Secretary Kissinger: This map shows various lines that were given to us by Egypt. Actually, if you look at that last line, the Egyptian and the Israeli lines are not too different. The fundamental difference is that Egypt was talking about that line in the context of an interim agreement whereas the Israelis are talking about it in the context of a final agreement.

The President: As to an interim agreement, talking about the duration point, what is your idea?

Prime Minister Rabin: It has two implications: First, the period between the signing of the agreement and the deployment to a new line. This would take somewhere between six to nine months. That is because we would have to move all of our defense positions.

Secretary Kissinger: If Israel were willing to give up the oil fields in the first two months, the six- to nine-month period for the passes might be soluble.

Prime Minister Rabin: The withdrawal from the oil fields could be done sooner than two months. But in terms of the duration of the agreement, we have talked in terms of four years. This is a very complicated problem. Secretary Kissinger said Egypt would never agree. In 1967 the UN was indefinite and the budget was annual. Once Egypt would give you a commitment for a number of years, that is fine with us. There are two options—the interim and the overall—and it is difficult to make these two options one. There are great risks in an interim agreement. We have an émigré coalition of the right and left against the Government that argues that to go to an interim agreement means Israel weakens its bargaining power on an overall settlement.

The President: What you want in an interim agreement is a line plus security.

Prime Minister Rabin: We want something that helps move towards peace. The alternative is stagnation, which we don't want. Also, the problem is in relation to Syria and when we would be expected to deal with an overall settlement.

Secretary Kissinger: Do you have any concrete ideas on these problems?

Prime Minister Rabin: It is probably possible to get talks on an overall settlement.

Secretary Kissinger: The dilemma is what to do or how do you face the problems of an overall agreement with Syria once they begin? The dilemma is that if you decide on talks on an overall settlement with Syria, you cannot avoid talks on an overall settlement with Egypt. Therefore, you in effect face talks on an overall settlement per se.

Prime Minister Rabin: Exactly.

The President: If you can get an interim agreement in which you have security and adequate warning, there would be a problem because we could not say that we will not go to an overall settlement or to say we cannot expect some discussions with Syria on an interim basis.

Prime Minister Rabin: That is the problem. We do not know what the Syrian attitude is. We do not talk to the Syrians.

Secretary Kissinger: Khaddam will not be a reliable indicator when he comes here next week. He is always tougher than Asad.

Prime Minister Rabin: I am not saying that additional diplomatic activity is not necessary. The developments after the suspension were not too bad. I am not saying it can last.

The President: The problem is how much longer can the status quo be maintained without political movement? It is a volatile situation. Either we have an interim settlement in a quick period of time—within two or three weeks—in which there would not be a lot of shuttle back and forth; it would be necessary to firm up things, to move fast, which would give us another span of time. Either we move in this way, or my choice—with all of its pitfalls as you suggest—is to move towards an overall settlement. The only way to bring about continued stability in the Middle East and keep all the parties reasonably satisfied, to give all the parties some hope of a permanent settlement being possible, would be to move in this way. Your thoughts have been helpful. If we were to move in the direction of an interim agreement, we would have to do so rapidly, otherwise we lose that option and I would have no alternative but to go to an overall settlement. Time is of the essence. We would have to work out all of the practical details. Quite candidly, looking at more of these options, they may have some possibilities, but to drag them out is not possible.

Secretary Kissinger: And it has to be worked out before I go there.

Prime Minister Rabin: There can be no attempt at shuttle diplomacy and have it fail again. I agree that unless we can get agreement on the details no new shuttle diplomacy should be undertaken. The purpose of Dr. Kissinger coming should be just to finalize the interim agreement.

Secretary Kissinger: Mr. President, I will be seeing the Prime Minister tomorrow morning. You will see him also. And I wonder if he and I could have a talk and see whether we can find something practical to put to the Egyptians, which the Prime Minister could then put to his Cabinet and we could then put to the Egyptians. Then we could see whether there was any basis for a shuttle.

I don't know if an interim solution is possible on the passes with you remaining there.

Prime Minister Rabin: I think many Israelis would be happy if they hear we are moving toward an overall settlement route.

Secretary Kissinger: They don't know the problem!

Prime Minister Rabin: Recalling the previous position developed by the United States on an overall settlement, the United States could have played a great role if it had not committed itself so specifically. President Johnson had said that the parties to the conflict had to be the parties to the peace.

The President: I want to say to you, Mr. Prime Minister, and I want to make this clear, that for me to make an overall proposal without being specific would be meaningless. I would intend to be more definite and more specific than past Presidents and I understand the difficulties that this might cause with the parties as well as at home domestically. For me to speak in generalities would be meaningless and not worthy of the Oval Office. I am willing to gamble with all of the parties and domestically if I think it would be constructive in holding the situation while we get to Geneva or wherever negotiations would take place. For me to talk platitudes is not my style and I do not believe it would be helpful. I would intend to be specific in what I would announce and that is the option and the other, of course, is the interim agreement.

I believe Henry's suggestion is a good one, to see whether there is anything practical that could be worked out by the two of you.

Prime Minister Rabin [reluctantly]: I'll try.

The President: You have to understand that perhaps an interim agreement is a better gamble but if it can't work, I have to take the other route and I will be specific and not talk in terms of platitudes. I think you ought to see if you and Henry can come closer. I would certainly have to be specific on any overall view we expressed.

Prime Minister Rabin: I still believe, Mr. President, there is more time than you indicate. I agree that the last phase of a negotiation on an interim agreement should not start unless there is prior agreement on the details. And there is the Syrian problem and the relation to the time for an overall settlement. If we do not reach such an understanding, we would find ourselves in a very difficult position. We have got to see the realities and what we are headed for.

Let's talk it over.

The President: Good.

[The President escorted the Prime Minister to his car.]

184. Memorandum of Conversation[1]

Washington, June 12, 1975, 10 a.m.

PARTICIPANTS

The President
Henry A. Kissinger, Secretary of State and Assistant to the President for National Security Affairs
Lt. General Brent Scowcroft, Deputy Assistant to the President for National Security Affairs

Kissinger: I think they are cracking.

President: I went to bed last night thinking there was no give at all.

Kissinger: These guys are the world's worst shits. His performance last night was a disgrace.[2]

President: He shouldn't have been encouraged by the questions—they didn't indicate that the Congress considers that there is an open treasury for Israeli benefit.

Kissinger: [Shows map][3] We are okay on the oil fields. He is prepared to let Egypt station forces in the mouths of the passes forward of the Egyptian line. He mentioned one company in each position, but privately he said we could go to two companies. I saw him alone[4] and floated the idea of the two warning stations with U.S. manning. I thought it was essential that we be covered if the whole negotiation should blow up. His first reaction was very positive but then he asked what it would cost. That means he thinks it is a favor to them and that is the way we should keep it. You should raise it with him alone at the end of the meeting and don't appear too eager.[5]

President: What do they do beyond letting Egypt into the western end of the passes?

---

[1] Source: Ford Library, National Security Adviser, Memoranda of Conversations, Box 12, June 12, 1975, Ford, Kissinger. Secret; Sensitive. The meeting was held in the Oval Office at the White House. Brackets are in the original. According to the President's Daily Diary, the meeting ended at 10:36 a.m. (Ibid., Staff Secretary's Office Files)

[2] No memorandum of conversation of the meeting between Kissinger and Rabin on the night of June 11 has been found.

[3] Map is not attached.

[4] The memorandum of conversation of the meeting between Rabin and Kissinger, which took place from 8 until 9:40 a.m. at Blair House, is in the National Archives, RG 59, Records of Henry Kissinger, 1973–77, Box 11, Nodis Memcons, June 1975, Folder 2.

[5] Ford and Kissinger met with Rabin in the Oval Office immediately after this meeting until 11:56 a.m. A memorandum of conversation is in the Library of Congress, Manuscript Division, Kissinger Papers, CL 164, Geopolitical File, Israel, Memoranda of Conversation, Reference Books, August 1974–September 1975.

Kissinger: They would move their own forces to the eastern end of the passes. I think personally Sadat will refuse the offer. If he does, then there is a 50–50 chance that Rabin will use Sadat's refusal to prove that he has been forthcoming and his offer was refused. Or he may agree to some bulges in the line. That would cause him problems at home. The Israeli Cabinet would die trying to agree to something like that.

He also said they have to have assurances that no further reassessments would take place. They cannot be in a position where they would be faced in a short time with further demands perhaps followed by further reassessments.

President: How about movement with respect to Syria and the comprehensive approach, including Geneva?

Kissinger: I said that the urgency would be somewhat reduced.

Nessen wants to know about the briefings.

President: My reaction is that with all these complications . . .

Kissinger: We could have Sisco, or me, do it for 10 minutes. I would propose saying that we had constructive meetings, that Rabin has to report to the Cabinet and we will be in touch. Perhaps we should not say anything about the Cabinet—that is his problem. We can agree with Rabin what I will say.

[General Scowcroft leaves for map.]

He has offered a few hundred yards in Syria and to give Asad a part of the demilitarized zone.

We could give Sadat these proposals and ask for an answer by 5 July. Then I would go to meet with Gromyko on the 7th and 8th and from there on to the Middle East to finalize the agreement.

On Iranian oil—if we could make a deal at the current market value fixed prices, with a 20 percent discount, it would almost kill a price increase—maybe even crack OPEC. Robinson is negotiating two deals ad ref—one at the fixed prices and one at market prices.

President: Greenspan is terribly worried about an OPEC price increase. If this will stop that, I think he would favor it.

Kissinger: If the interim settlement works, I would write to Khalid that we can't be working with the Arabs for settlement when they are increasing prices.

President: Why don't you talk just to Alan alone?

185. Memorandum of Conversation[1]

Washington, June 13, 1975.

PARTICIPANTS

The President
Dr. Henry A. Kissinger, Secretary of State and Assistant to the President for National Security Affairs
Lt. General Brent Scowcroft, Deputy Assistant to the President for National Security Affairs

SUBJECT

Rabin Visit; FRG-Brazil Nuclear Deal; Turkish Aid; Iranian Oil Deal

Kissinger: They are a bloody minded bunch. There could be some dispute about whether they said they would get out of the passes. There can be no dispute that we have been telling them for months that getting out of the passes was the sine qua non of an agreement. Of that there can be no doubt. [Rockefeller calls]

Kissinger: Then they raise duration and warning stations. We settled duration and I showed them Sadat's letter[2] without saying he had bought it.

President: What was their reaction?

Kissinger: They slobbered. Then we gave them the warning stations. Last night I asked for precision about where they would be in the passes. He said they would be deep into the passes.

President: You tell him I understood they would have the eastern end and Egypt the western end.

Kissinger: I am meeting him again at 5:00.[3] If it turns out we get into another endless haggle ...

On Syria, he said he would consider a unilateral move but he would never do it. Then there is the question of armaments and thinned-out zones—again it was unsuccessful.

President: I thought last night we should start a specific proposal for an overall settlement.

---

[1] Source: Ford Library, National Security Adviser, Memoranda of Conversations, Box 12, June 12, 1975, Ford, Kissinger. Secret; Nodis. The meeting was held in the Oval Office at the White House. All brackets, with the exception of ones describing omitted material, are in the original. According to the President's Daily Diary, the meeting began at 9:50 a.m. and ended when Max Fisher arrived at 10:35 a.m. (Ibid., Staff Secretary's Office Files)

[2] Sadat's letter has not been found.

[3] No memorandum of conversation has been found.

Kissinger: We are well along on that. Let me meet with him and tell him that an interim arrangement won't work.

Scowcroft: [Described the Presidential statement.][4]

Kissinger: There just cannot be an Egyptian arrangement with nothing at all on Syria. We would be beaten to death and I think it would be better not even to go into it.

I don't think Sadat will accept each side being at the respective ends of the passes unless the positions are symmetrical. Much of this is pure Israeli domestic politics. He said publicly in February that he would give up the passes only for nonbelligerency; he can't wriggle off the hook now. I wanted just to have a line at the eastern end without defining it at the end of the pass—so Sadat would say they are out of the pass and Israel would know they weren't, I didn't get that far.

President: Let's refine this, pass it to Sadat, and see his reaction. If it doesn't work, we will go to a comprehensive settlement.

Kissinger: That is probably the best. I think we should not spill too much blood for an interim settlement.

President: One argument is that it looks forthcoming if we put in the manned warning stations than if we go for an overall settlement.

Kissinger: They are almost irrational. It is 90 percent domestic politics.

President: Betty found Mrs. Rabin very demanding and aggressive.

Kissinger: Let's see where we are tonight. If they are close, you might think of making an American proposal, but not before we see Sadat's reaction.

You will see Max Fisher. They are constantly telling me they are getting to you. I say go ahead. They said a leading Jew told you that your place in history depends more on what you do for the Jews than on what you do for the Arabs.

I'll tell Max there has been some progress but there are still some issues on passes. Sadat has made some concessions.

President: Why not say I have ordered a comprehensive plan?

[Omitted here is discussion unrelated to the Arab-Israeli dispute.]

---

[4] Statement not further identified.

186. Memorandum of Conversation[1]

Washington, June 13, 1975, 10–10:15 a.m.

PARTICIPANTS

    President Ford
    Mr. Max Fisher
    Dr. Henry A. Kissinger, Secretary of State and Assistant to the President for National Security Affairs
    Lt. Gen. Brent Scowcroft, Deputy Assistant to the President for National Security Affairs

President: When do you leave? [For Israel].

Fisher: Tonight. I just thought anything you want to tell me would be of help.

President: We have narrowed the differences with Rabin, but we still are at a crunch point. I thought we made more progress, yesterday compared to the first day. There still are some differences, specifically related to the passes. Unless we make more progress it won't work. I was encouraged yesterday, less so today. Henry will meet with Rabin today to see if we can make more progress. Both sides have moved, but if neither moves any further we won't have an agreement. Is that right, Henry?

Kissinger: Yes, except you know the Israeli domestic situation. The Cabinet hasn't approved anything, so the movement is Rabin, not Israel. The President described it precisely. We will have to see if there are still possibilities.

Fisher: The Likud seems to be having problems. It looks to me like the political situation is better, but I'll know better when I get there. But it sounds like you are narrowing the differences.

Kissinger: Yes. But we have no reason to think Egypt will settle for less than the passes. But they have offered more, so it wouldn't be an Israeli cave. So both would appear to have given some.

Fisher: How about duration?

Kissinger: We are working on it. We haven't solved it.

Fisher: The boycott.

Kissinger: We can make some concrete steps. Sadat said he can't invite American companies into Egypt, but if they apply, he won't make the boycott list be a barrier.

---

[1] Source: Ford Library, National Security Adviser, Memoranda of Conversations, Box 12, June 12, 1975, Ford, Kissinger, Max Fisher. Confidential. The meeting was held in the Oval Office at the White House. Brackets are in the original.

Fisher: I think it is important that we make this their work.

Kissinger: Another problem where you could help: The propensity is to drag things out. We have a window with the Soviets to the end of July, so we need to move before then.

President: They want our help on CSCE. So as long as we have that in front of us, we can keep them quiet on the Middle East.

Kissinger: We have told the Israelis this; it is just that you could emphasize it.

President: If we don't get a basic agreement by the middle of July, we lose our leverage, and I will have to go to the overall alternative. I have told State to draw up an overall plan as insurance. I am telling you that—I haven't told the Israelis that, although I am sure they realize. To put all our chips on an interim which fails, and to have no back-up, just won't work.

Fisher: Did this matter of Egyptian arms come up?

Kissinger: There was one story about us selling. That is bunk. Today there was a report about $1 million in arms from Great Britain. I doubt it and it was not confirmed by the British. The British don't have the kind of sophisticated arms Egypt needs. The problem is Egypt has cut itself off from the Soviet Union. We must decide whether we want them to go back to the Soviet Union or whether we will do it. Basically, I don't think it against the American interest for Egypt to buy its arms in the West.

Fisher: How about Syria and Jordan, just for my information?

Kissinger: All we know is what is in the paper. Hussein told the President he wouldn't agree to a joint command.[2] We have to find out. If it is to bring the PLO under control, that is not against out interests. We are looking into it.

President: We have narrowed the gap, but it doesn't help if it is not closed.

Fisher: What can I do?

Kissinger: Emphasize the seriousness of it.

President: We have to have the flexibility if it is to work.

---

[2] See footnote 2, Document 173. On June 12, Syria and Jordan announced that they would form a Joint High Commission to coordinate military, economic, political, and cultural policies. The joint statement also endorsed the decisions of the Rabat summit. (*New York Times*, June 13, 1975, p. 3)

Second Egyptian-Israeli Disengagement Agreement, June 1975–March 1976

187. Memorandum of Conversation[1]

Washington, June 14, 1975.

PARTICIPANTS

    The Secretary
    Mr. Sisco
    Mr. Atherton
    Mr. Saunders
    Gen. Scowcroft
    Jerry Bremer, notetaker

SUBJECT

    The Middle East

The Secretary: Let me sum up where I thought we were in March and where I think we are now. The last Israeli proposition in March was a line in the middle of the passes without definition. Secondly, the Egyptians could use the road under UN supervision to Abu Rudeis though it was never clear which road they had in mind. As I understand it (pointing at the map)[2] there is only one road open the whole way down.

Atherton: That's right, the other one needed repairs.

The Secretary: This road is not now being used, however. I think we should get an exact report on the status of this road if we can, please Hal. I'm trying to define precisely where we are. Has Peter found those quotes by the way?

Scowcroft: They will be here in five minutes.

The Secretary: Could he read them to me do you think?

Scowcroft: Sure.

The Secretary: Whatever anyone can argue about what the Israelis told us in March, there can be no question that we told them before March that we considered the passes and oil fields the Sine qua non. (Kissinger takes phone call to Rodman) I asked Rabin whether the Israeli post could be at Kilometer 1 or Kilometer 5. He said I have to look at a map. I certainly made it clear then what my thinking was. There-

---

[1] Source: Library of Congress, Manuscript Division, Kissinger Papers, CL 346, State Department Memorandum of Conversations, Internal, June 1975. Secret; Sensitive.

[2] Map is not attached.

fore, it is perfectly clear that we were talking about each of the passes. They rationalized that the middle because they had no non-belligerency. Since then we've made it clear that the evacuation of the passes was the problem. The Israelis then raised the problem of duration, warning stations, and the boycott. When we talked to Sadat, there was no point to make concessions for a line that was within the passes.

Sisco: Absolutely, our assumption was that they would leave the oil fields and the passes.

The Secretary: In March Sadat could have had an agreement with the line in the passes and the UN road to Abu Rudeis oilfield on the basis of what he had. Therefore, when we asked for a three-year commitment with U.S. stations, it was on the assumption that the Israelis would leave the passes.

Now, what is the point of the present visit? Rabin told me that if the Israelis could have the eastern end of the passes, the Egyptians could have the western end of the passes. Therefore, I assumed there was to be some symmetry between the Egyptian and the Israeli positions in the passes. In addition, he agreed to turn this road (pointing to map) over to the Egyptians.

Scowcroft: Initially he was fuzzy about which road.

Sisco: He didn't pick the road, but he said it was not a line that was up against the mountains.

The Secretary: (reading papers)[3] I'm talking about what happened at the second breakfast.[4] At any rate, when I briefed the President I was under the same misapprehension as in March—the Israelis accepted the principle of symmetry. Israel would move to the end of the passes. (to Scowcroft) Did you review your notes?

Scowcroft: Yes, that is right.

The Secretary: Do you have close to a verbatim record of it?

Scowcroft: Yes I do.

The Secretary: Well take a look and see how I presented it to the President. Now we have two problems: one of substance and the other of procedure. On procedure, the Israelis had to know that I would not hail as a success their selling for a higher price than what they had been prepared to give us in March.

What is the change in the Israeli position? An Egyptian company here (pointing at Giddi pass). That is Rabin's pencil mark on the map. It's about eight kilometers forward of the present line.

---

[3] Papers not further identified.
[4] See footnote 4, Document 184.

Sisco: But it is dominated by the high ground.

The Secretary: The Israelis would move to the middle of the Giddi pass, they'd give Egypt this position on the Mitla. In other words, they want the slope of the mountain range.

Atherton: What do they want there?

The Secretary: A fortified defense line. In addition, they will give us this road and draw the line north of the road. It's not shown exactly, but it would be here (pointing to map), parallel to this road. In effect, the Israelis are returning the road they were going to keep and giving up a road they're not using.

Sisco: We did ask them to consider having a demilitarized zone.

The Secretary: They are willing to make it all a UN zone.

Atherton: Where do the Israelis want to go to?

The Secretary: (pointing at map) Here to this mountain range. But they would be permitted to use this road. They'll have this road.

The improvement in the Egyptian position compared to March is in these two companies. Since Egypt didn't know where the line would be before, it's hard for us to sell it to them as an improvement.

Scowcroft: But the crests are the key point.

The Secretary: In the Giddi pass, there is no improvement though I suppose you could say there is a slight improvement in the Mitla. They want to be on the down slope of the ridges similar to the position they took on the hills around Kunitra. That's their doctrine. The defensive position is not on top but on the down slope.

Now, I have a number of concerns. When Sadat met with the President,[5] he had every reason to believe that the President would make a monumental effort with Israel which, however, has produced no operational change within the passes—two companies forward of their line. The Giddi one is unsaleable as being inside the pass.

Sisco: It's very difficult.

The Secretary: In the Mitla, they could sell it as being inside the pass.

Atherton: They are forward of where they thought they would be in March.

Sisco: If you're putting the best face on it, that's what you'd emphasize.

Atherton: Plus the road.

---

[5] See Documents 177 and 178.

The Secretary: First of all, I think there is also a psychological problem. I must say that there was again a clear pattern of deception. Joe, you were at both the meetings.

Sisco: I've been to all of them except the first breakfast.

The Secretary: Did you have the impression at any of the meetings that they'd hold a position deep inside the passes?

Sisco: No. At the mouth or at the entrance with the UN inside—that was my impression.

Scowcroft: You presented it to the President that for domestic purposes they had to say they had troops at the entrance of the passes.

The Secretary: When we reviewed it Wednesday night,[6] it was to draw the lines so that you couldn't tell. Now I tell you there's a pattern of deception in Rabin. He's unlike Golda. It was not in our interest to kid ourselves. If I'd have understood it, I could have turned the President the other way. I could have told him that they were reselling the March proposal in return for three years. He'd have gone through the ceiling and we would have had a brutal session Thursday morning.[7] I could have turned him either way. (Secretary's interrupted for a phone call)

First we have this deception. Analytically the objective change is the movement forward of two companies. There is no change in the passes and the change in the road to Abu Rudeis does not change the Israeli position but makes it possible for Egypt to get access. If Sadat is drooling for this agreement and wants the $450 million,[8] he can pretend that the two companies give him what he wants. But, substantively it won't fool him. He's a very bright man on these things. He would feel that a brutal bargain is being produced here.

Scowcroft: And this is the result of a major effort on our part.

The Secretary: It's hard for Egypt to understand how a country who gets everything from us gives this little. This is then coupled with a 3½ year moratorium, two U.S. army stations on Egyptian soil.

I think there's also the possibility that Sadat will react as in the December proposals, he will say it is an insult and an outrage and why even send it to him. Roy, which reaction do you think he'll have?

Atherton: I think he wants the oil revenue pretty badly. But I'm not sure if he needs it badly enough.

---

[6] June 11. See footnote 2, Document 184.
[7] See footnote 4, Document 184.
[8] A reference to the $450 million in U.S. aid promised to Egypt as part of a second disengagement agreement.

Sisco: Let's try it on Hermann. I think you need a commitment from Rabin tomorrow. We've analyzed it but are disappointed. If we decide to present it, we'll do it fairly.

The Secretary: The President has already said that we will only present it and not support it.

Sisco: When we come back to see where we are, we still have the card of our own proposal.

The Secretary: But one problem of the professional negotiators is they become obsessed with negotiations. If we tell Sadat this isn't the last word, he'll reject it. Hermann should present it with no explanation and await Sadat's candid views. This we know we can get now. Get his reaction from it and if he accepts it, OK.

My estimate of Golda and Rabin is different. Golda was tough but honorable. Rabin is basically a chisler and he hasn't played us fairly. For example, in the February breakfast[9] he said "if you do what you want, we'll have to leave this space." (pointing to map) "It will cost you several hundred million. Will you help?" I said, "We'll do our damnedest." In March, I asked Dinitz, "How could he say that?"

I know Rabin is a chisler and he's not honorable. He owed it to us Thursday morning to say what he meant by the middle of the passes. He should have said "It's a line on the far slope of the mountain range." No one cares where the line is; it is the slope of the mountain that matters.

Sisco: Gazit used the phrase "the end of the passes."

The Secretary: Peter just read the quotes of the end of the passes. The east end of the passes is anything that's not the west end of the passes. Now he didn't technically lie.

Have we found anything out about their reports that Allon visited Kiev?

Scowcroft: We're trying to confirm whatever data we have.

The Secretary: I'm going to start tomorrow saying we have what looks like reliable intelligence data that Allon met with Gromyko. Did he? Joe, your wrinkle of having them tell me that this is not their last word is useless.

The President called him last night[10] and said he was extremely disappointed—that it was not his understanding. He said, "I cannot support it with Egypt or with the U.S. people." Rabin said to him, "I can

---

[9] Apparently a reference to a February 11 breakfast meeting between Rabin and Kissinger. See footnote 2, Document 131.

[10] Ford and Rabin spoke on the telephone from 9:35 to 9:57 p.m. (Ford Library, Staff Secretary's Office Files, President's Daily Diary) No transcript of the June 13 telephone conversation has been found.

hold to the agreement you and I made yesterday morning—I won't give up the eastern passes." The President, in other words, is being stonewalled and treated as curtly on the phone as ever. The President asked Brent to send Dinitz a message for Rabin to say, "I want you to know that what you presented to Henry Friday[11] was not my understanding and I consider my phone call a request for a new position from you."

I'm glad he did it because they will report that I had changed his mind and backed the President off it. Tomorrow I think I will start the meeting asking what I can report to the President.

Scowcroft: I'd go a step further and ask them if they have anything further to discuss and if they don't, I wouldn't even have the meeting.

The Secretary: No, I can't do that.

Sisco: No, I don't think that's desirable. It's been announced now.

The Secretary: Yes. It's announced. We can play it cool. Brent just has his Mormon temper up.

Scowcroft: You bet. I really think we've been had.

Sisco: Well, it does shake you.

The Secretary: Joe, let's not forget we left Israel with a bad taste last time in March. We were not treated honorably and we were very much disappointed with the outcome.

This time we acted in good faith. I gave the press conference. I gave a very warm toast Thursday night.[12] Rabin would have let us ride this through until we presented the wrong things to the Egyptians and got caught in some kind of a shuttle. We went through all of the papers on Page 7—this was Thursday night—we had checked everything. We went through all of it and at the end I said, "Can I give you my interpretations? We have to understand that the passes does not mean the middle of the passes, the way it was in March. It has to be different from the March proposal." (Secretary reads from the memcon) You can see I had to drag it out of them. Rabin said, "We'll have to draw on the map." "What I have in mind is the defense line to control the entire eastern ridge." I asked, "Do you mean you want to be on top of the ridge?" Now this is the first time I finally understood it. The reason I'm raising this is an honorable man would have said it earlier. If I had not beaten him back step by step to the meaning of "end of the passes"—if I had quit where he says he means "at the entrance" we'd have been in trouble.

---

[11] Apparently a reference to the 5 p.m. meeting on June 13. See footnote 3, Document 185.

[12] No transcript of Kissinger's toast at a dinner at the Israeli Embassy has been found.

Sisco: What did he say to the President?

The Secretary: Do you have the memcon with you Brent?

Scowcroft: No.

The Secretary: (reading memcon) Here, Thursday morning.[13] "Eastern end" "entrance" Let's look at Wednesday, what did he say then. (reading memcon) There is nothing here.[14]

The fact is it's like saying—get out of the passes. There are two possibilities. One, that Sadat is so hungry for the 450 million and eager that he'll accept this. The counter argument is that he explained the breakdown in March in terms of getting Israel out of the passes. Qadaffi won't let him show he did that. Israel won't let him show it.

Sisco: Oh no, they'll crow all over the place.

The Secretary: I suppose if he's desperate, he could say he got an Egyptian presence in the passes. He can do that.

Scowcroft: We'll pay quite a price with Sadat though.

The Secretary: But even then we're not out of the woods. Israel will say, give us a three year letter. He may be willing to do that since the letter is phony.

Sisco: I think he's rightly cynical about that.

The Secretary: If the Israelis weren't such SOBs we wouldn't have this problem. Supposing Sadat indignantly rejects it, and I think that's a 50–50 possibility. With this agreement, he couldn't sit still and let the Syrians take it. Then we have three choices. When we get his rejection, we can convey it to the Israelis who will move back a kilometer or two or we can try to cut the Gordian knot with the U.S. interim proposal to both of them and make them turn it down or we can give up on the interim and go to the overall.

Sisco: Yes.

The Secretary: The problem of putting up a U.S. plan is if the Israelis accept it—which I don't exclude—we'd be in hock forever to them. Anything that went wrong then would be forever our mistake. The problem with the overall is . . .

Sisco: . . . The possibility of war in 1976. Of course we don't have to answer that right now.

The Secretary: No, but we have to be thinking about it. We will run out of time anyway because I've accepted July 7 and 8 for my meetings with Gromyko and I don't see how we can get the back of this broken by July 7. If we haven't, then we should agree with Gromyko to con-

---

[13] Presumably at the breakfast meeting with Kissinger. See footnote 4, Document 184.

[14] See Document 183.

vene Geneva at some time in the future with an announcement to that effect.

Sisco: You can decide with the President shortly before the Gromyko meeting.

The Secretary: Well, I want everyone here to think about whether we should do a U.S. plan on the interim. Roy, what do you think?

Atherton: I think it's risky. If we do and Sadat accepts it and the Israelis don't, we will look very impotent to Sadat. If they both accept, the price of Israel will be very high.

The Secretary: What about the aid in this sequence? At some point, the President has to put the record of negotiations out and you and I have to brief it. He will have to say that under the circumstances, he can't ask increased aid for Israel and we'll have to put out our full assessment of their military strength.

Scowcroft: They have to be aware of that.

Atherton: Our proposal would have to get the Israelis out of the passes and the Israelis will reject that.

The Secretary: We could put them to the entrance off the slope anyway.

Atherton: I would be surprised if they'd accept that.

The Secretary: The duplicity of it. If they were willing to move out of the passes for non-belligerency, they would certainly do it for non-use of force.

Sisco: Here's the checklist for tonight.

The Secretary: Yes. Is there any disagreement with the analysis?

Sisco: On the U.S. Plan, I really think that's risky but my judgment is that the advantage is, even if it's rejected, we're no more impotent than if this fails. In terms of being held responsible, there's a shade of difference because pushing them off the slope hurts their defense.

The Secretary: What will happen tomorrow is that they will give us a slightly better line than yesterday because they can't afford not to respond to the President, but it won't change the essence.

Scowcroft: I would pay no attention to it if it doesn't get them back off the ridge.

The Secretary: What's your view, Roy?

Atherton: Sadat just might accept it because of the importance of the oil fields but the price down the road is too much.

The Secretary: How will Sadat look in the Arab world with a sliver down the coast? Maybe it's better than nothing.

Atherton: That's our only hope.

188. Memorandum of Conversation[1]

New York, June 15, 1975, 9:15 a.m.

PARTICIPANTS

Israeli Side
Prime Minister Rabin
Ambassador Dinitz
Mordecai Gazit
Minister Shalev

U.S. Side
Secretary Kissinger
Under Secretary Sisco
Ambassador Toon
Deputy Under Secretary Eagleburger

Secretary: Is the press coming in?

Rabin: Yes. Since they already knew of the meeting . . .

Secretary: No, no, That's OK.

I need not ask if you had an active day.

Dinitz: We had a crowd of more than 2,300 people—the largest crowd ever.

Rabin: And whenever I said anything negative—whew!

Secretary: Especially when you said something against our Government.

Dinitz: No, no.

Rabin: Well, let's start. As you know, we had another terrorist attack last night.[2]

Secretary: Yes. I wanted to express our regret.

Rabin: The town was one settled by immigrants from India mainly. They are very nice people. They have done very well. They became very good farmers.

Secretary: Do they look like Indians?

Rabin: Generally, yes they do look like Indians.

---

[1] Source: National Archives, RG 59, Records of Henry Kissinger, 1973–77, Box 8, Nodis Memcons, May 1974, Folder 11. Secret; Sensitive; Nodis. The meeting was held at the Waldorf-Astoria in New York.

[2] In the early morning of June 14, four Palestinian guerrillas crossed into Israel from Lebanon and attacked the town of Kfar Yuval. They fought past the Israelis guarding the entrance to the town and made their way to a farmhouse where they took an Israeli family hostage. Israeli soldiers launched an assault on the house just after 8 a.m. and killed the four Palestinians while losing one Israeli in the raid. (*New York Times*, June 16, 1975, p. 1)

Secretary: Do they act like Indians?

Rabin: No, they act much better than that.

Sisco: Don't you have an Indian orchestra conductor?

Secretary: That's Mehta. He's not Jewish; I know him well and he is a good friend of mine.

Rabin: The terrorists went into a home. The owner was out; there were four terrorists, all were killed. But the father—the man who was out of the house and returned—was killed. One son was killed, too. A woman and a baby were wounded but are not critical.

I want you to know that the village of Shuba, in Lebanon but close to the border, was attacked by some of our planes and artillery because we know there is a concentration of terrorists there.

Can we now go back to the subject at hand.

Secretary: Before we do that, I have one question to ask. We have had reports to which we would otherwise attach considerable importance that Foreign Minister Allon while in Bucharest took a side trip to the Soviet Union or met with Soviet officials.

Rabin: Not to the best of my knowledge. Romania would be the worst place from which to do something like that.

Secretary: We don't object to contacts, but we do have ...

Rabin: As I told you, I met with the Russians. In the meeting I had with them nothing was changed. Perhaps there was a better atmosphere, but except for words, nothing much was different. They gave me a long talk about the role of the Soviet Union in the creation of Israel, Russian support for Israel during its first year, and said that they would support peace in return for our total withdrawal and the creation of a Palestinian state. Admittedly they did say that once we accepted withdrawals, there could be some changes in the lines.

Secretary: Gromyko said that to me, too.

Rabin: They also said they were prepared to give guarantees to the safety of Israel. But they said that it's up to us.

Secretary: Well, we have a lot of collateral intelligence, not clearly related to Allon ... but I accept your assurance. I don't see what's in it for the Soviets either as far as that's concerned.

Rabin: They said they wanted to continue communications through this channel.

Secretary: So, there were no meetings with members of Allon's party; Allon didn't meet with the Soviets, or travel somewhere to meet with the Soviets? I want to make sure that I don't fail to ask the right question.

Rabin: No, nothing.

Secretary: OK. Let's go to our business.

Rabin: As I'm sure you know, I got a telephone call from the President.[3]

Secretary: Yes, he told me.

Rabin: I believe that in response all I can say here is to give you a map, go back to Israel, and talk first with the other two Ministers who are on the negotiating team. There might be, might be, certain slight changes. But in my opinion we can't change the principle.

I understand you wanted two maps. We only have two and I need to take one back with me.

I am not prepared for detailed discussion of a kilometer or kilometer and a half here and there.

All I can do is take the President's word back. I will be home about midnight Monday.[4] Tuesday morning I will have discussions with the team; and Tuesday afternoon there will be a Cabinet meeting; on Wednesday I can notify Simcha and perhaps send him a map.

Secretary: We were planning on sending Eilts back to Cairo on Wednesday afternoon. I plan to see Gromyko on July 7 and 8 and we will set our course by then.

Before I look at it (the map) you have to understand that as a result of our breakfast I briefed the President to the effect that you were prepared to give one end of the passes to Israel and one end to Egypt.[5] His Thursday behavior has to be seen in the context of a belief that there was a substantial change in your position.

Rabin: I believe there is.

Secretary: Then on Thursday evening and Friday I learned that there was not much change in your position on the passes.

Rabin: We made very clear to the President what we wanted.

Secretary: It was not clear to me, it was not clear to Sisco. When we met Thursday afternoon,[6] we on our side started on the basis of the belief that Egypt and Israel would each hold ends of the passes. Whatever your records show, there is no question that we on our side had a different perception. Either you tried to trick us or there was another misunderstanding—we seem to have many of those these days.

---

[3] See footnote 10, Document 187.

[4] June 16.

[5] See Document 184.

[6] The memorandum of conversation of the meeting between Rabin and Kissinger, where they discussed U.S. economic aid and military assistance to Israel, and which took place on June 12 from 1:05 until 2 p.m. in the Monroe–Madison Room at the Department of State, is in the National Archives, RG 59, Records of Henry Kissinger, 1973-77, Box 11, Nodis Memcons, June 1975, Folder 2.

In any event, I want you to understand that the President's meeting with you was geared to a conception which we have now had to change as a result of later discussions with you.

Rabin: We have worked together many years. Never were there so many misunderstandings. I can't recall other misunderstandings.

Secretary: You must ask why should Joe, Brent Scowcroft and I all have so substantial a misunderstanding. You are right. We never used to have misunderstandings with the Israeli Government.

Well, let's look at the map.

(Rabin shows map to the Secretary)

Rabin: The line went here.

Secretary: Where?

Rabin: Here.

Secretary: Well, since we never got a line from you in March, I can't judge that.

Rabin: Let me repeat:

The area of thinning out would be between the Canal and the blue line. Our area would be this one (pointing to map). It is not symmetrical all the way. But there would be the same size of force. There might be some increase in the number of tanks but I cannot agree to any sizable increase of their forces East of the Canal in an interim agreement.

70–75 tanks—this is not an issue.

There is a question of the road. I know they need one. But I can't describe the arrangements in detail. Sometimes there are two roads. We will have to find a solution to that problem.

Secretary: To what problem?

Rabin: I understand the basic principle. They need a road.

Secretary: One not also used by the Israelis.

Rabin: I understand.

Secretary: (looking at map) They will claim you're keeping all of the Gidi.

Rabin: This sector (pointing to southern sector of map) is not separated because we have built a road but in case of war it would be separated.

Our logistical and warning posts are here—here in the center.

And we have our logistics here (pointing to northern sector of map). All of this is backed by a complex here (pointing to center rear of map).

Secretary: There is no line here (pointing to map)?

Rabin: No. We will have to work this out. We don't want misunderstandings on this.

Secretary: How will you get me a map? Will you send someone?

Rabin: Yes.

Sisco: Then we should hold Hermann[7] back.

Is there anything further we should know now?

Rabin: I don't want to say any more now. I have heard the President and have to discuss matters with my Chief of Staff.

Secretary: The forces in these two areas would be symmetrical (pointing to map). In effect there would be about 7,500 in the whole area (southern sector of map).

As the President told you, we will transmit your proposals to the Egyptians without recommendation.

Rabin: He said more; he said it would be transmitted without your support.

Dinitz: That was told us by Scowcroft.

Secretary: Oh, yes. The President went to Ft. Benning;[8] he talked with Brent before he left.

Let me sum up our view:

We will debate forever whether we had reason to believe before March that you might be prepared to leave the passes. I see no purpose to discuss that further.

But there can be no question that we have undeviatingly pointed out that no agreement is possible without Israeli withdrawals from the oil fields and the passes. Our judgment may be wrong—it has been before—but this is the context in which we see it.

Therefore, after the March negotiations, we wrote off the interim agreement route, though we did stall on Geneva independently of you. Then, and I must say never really through any formal communications from you, interest seemed to revive in the interim agreement route.

It was clear when the President talked to Sadat,[9] asking him for a new Egyptian proposal, that there had to be in the President's mind—and admittedly in mine as well—a conviction that something might yet be possible.

But I do not see how anyone can expect to ask the Egyptians that they pay an additional price now beyond what they had been prepared to pay in March for nothing more than this nebulous road which will take a year's work to make passable.

---

[7] Ambassador Eilts.

[8] According to the President's Daily Diary, Ford visited Fort Benning in Georgia on June 14 to attend the 200th anniversary of the U.S. Army and Infantry. (Ford Library, Staff Secretary's Office Files)

[9] Ford met with Sadat on June 1 and June 2. See Documents 177 and 178.

Rabin: The road is being used by us.

Secretary: We may be wrong but our intelligence tells us that it ends halfway down. Also parts of it are unusable and there is no question that it is in difficult topography.

Rabin: That is true.

Secretary: Let's suppose it is usable; it will still be necessary to construct a road from here (pointing to map) to Abu Rudeis.

But that seems to be the new part of the proposal: your offer of a road.

Rabin: And that Egyptian forces would be permitted at what we consider the West end of the passes.

Secretary: But that will be no change for the Egyptians since we only told them the middle of the passes anyway. Also, as to the listening station, they already knew of this so when you proposed it, the Egyptians had to assume that your line was behind it.

To be frank, when Gamasy sees this, I can tell you that it is my estimate he will only believe you put the line where you would have anyway. Once we said to them that you would move to the middle of the passes, we can't argue with the Egyptians that what you now have is a change.

The two companies would be the only other change.

The only other thing is this road which I can't adequately explain.

It is a complex position. Sadat may be desperate enough that he will take these two cosmetic changes and try to make something out of them. But you know that they could not hold out for 15 minutes here if there were a war.

Rabin: True. But this establishes a presence for them.

Secretary: Right. It may be politically and symbolically useful. But it is certainly not militarily useful.

In any event, this doesn't change our position with Sadat. We have had extensive talks with him trying to change his position and now you ask us to get a three to three and a half year commitment, the thing on the boycott, and the warning station—and to do all that for two companies. That is what it comes down to.

If it were our strategy to drive the Soviets out, a very good way to do so would be by frustrating their allies by demonstrating how ineffective they are. The opposite can also be argued—it may well be that we will end up by driving Sadat or his successor in the direction of pushing us out of the Middle East. What we have here is not an impressive performance by the United States if all we can do is get this little bit.

I will tell you what we will do:

We will send this to the Egyptians without comment. That will be my recommendation. We will not support it, recommend it, or argue against it.

If the negotiation fails, we will wash our hands of interim agreements. We cannot support this or argue for it. This is out of the context of our previous conversations but it is essentially the same thing that we had in March.

What happens later we will have to discuss when the time comes. But you should understand that as you said you would protect your interests, so will we protect ours. What I am saying now has been checked with the President and reflects his views.

Rabin: You must bear in mind that an interim agreement is for a limited time. You must believe that we will give the oil fields and withdrawing only in return for time.

Secretary: I know that a non use of force agreement can be violated, but it surely would improve your position then.

Rabin: It won't be violated by Israel. It will be done by the Egyptians, in regard to what will be done after the interim agreement. It will occur over an argument over an over-all agreement and will be linked to a stalemate over those negotiations. No one can foresee today what the circumstances might be.

Therefore, if we go for an interim agreement, we can't be in a position later to negotiate from a position of weakness. We must bear this in mind.

Secretary: You know my view. The fact is that the presentation you made on Wednesday[10] could have been made in September. Then we would not have committed ourselves so far.

It has been our fixed strategy to have a common program with Israel. We always believed we could use agreements to cement the common strategy between us and use the interim agreements to delay a final settlement as long as possible. Then we would work hard for all we can get in a final settlement.

But now I have doubts. If so much blood is necessary for an interim agreement, it is probably not worth it and we should go our own ways and consult our own interests.

Speaking personally, I must say that I no longer have much confidence that the interim route will work.

But we will present this (the Israeli offer), but don't assume that what I earlier said was possible is possible now under current circumstances. I don't believe it is possible.

---

[10] See Document 183.

But perhaps Sadat is so anxious that he will take these two points and trumpet them as a great triumph and make a settlement. So we will present it to him and see what happens.

Rabin: If what we must do is get out of the passes in return for three and a half years, I am sure many Israelis would prefer negotiations for a final settlement, even with all its complications.

I also sense that the President is "tilting" toward an over-all settlement.

Secretary: That's fine with us. But it won't lead to any identity of views between us.

Rabin: We started the interim agreement process with a view that this would have political significance. But what we are in now is nothing more than another disengagement agreement.

Secretary: We've gone through this before. But the position is so fixed in Israel that it's not worth debating. Minds can't be changed. There are too many things mixed into it.

If you conceive this as a process, then you can say that there is political significance in it. I have no doubt that when some distance has been taken from this problem, many of the arguments against this way of proceeding will look short-sighted, but I can't change the arguments now.

Let me say again that my view was when we first talked that you were talking about the Israeli position being at the *end* of the passes. Frankly, I thought you were prepared to let the Egyptians, in small force, at one end of the passes, in return for the Israelis holding a kilometer or two at the other end of the passes.

In my judgment what you want here is a stable situation so that you can concentrate up here (pointing to the northern sector of the map).

Rabin: Exactly.

Secretary: But what is not clear is can't the passes be held from further down?

Rabin: No. Either we are on the ridge or we are not and we cannot hold it from below the ridge.

Secretary: But the Egyptians can't move to the ridge themselves without giving a warning to you.

Rabin: That is no problem. They first have to cross the Canal and then move up. But then we have to mobilize and you must remember that they have not yet violated the line at that point.

Secretary: I once had the idea—which I've not checked with the President—that we could reach some form of agreement that if there were substantial violation of the thinning out zone, we would "understand," or whatever other term we might agree on, if you seized the ridge.

But in any event you concede that they can't take the passes immediately.

Rabin: They have 36 hours on us. We have to mobilize and move.

Secretary: Well you've studied this and I am not going to change any minds now.

You are in no doubt that we won't support your position if this breaks down.

Rabin: That has been made clear to us.

What about Syria?

Secretary: I believe that you have several options:

—you can do nothing;

—you can have disengagement talks;

—you can have overall peace talks;

—you can start disengagement talks followed by unilateral steps as a transition to an overall agreement.

Dinitz: Suppose there were an agreement with Egypt? Can Israel expect support from the U.S. with Syria on (1) an interim agreement with what the Prime Minister said and (2) anything else with Syria only in the context of an overall settlement?

Secretary: Essentially yes. We will not press you on agreements thereafter.

Dinitz: Would there be a principle agreed that we would not be asked to get out of the Golan Heights although the line there might change?

Secretary: We would make a major effort to avoid a repetition of the difficulties of the last few months. As you know there have been major problems presented to the U.S. by Israel in times of difficulties. It is not easy. I cannot overestimate the dangers without an interim agreement.

As to my ideas in regard to Syria, it would seem to me that the best way would be to start disengagement talks through us without me at that stage. We would both understand that they would not be likely to succeed. Then at a time when a stalemate appears near, you would make some cosmetic changes unilaterally as a gesture of good will. Then we would jointly recommend that the negotiations be moved to the overall stage. By that time there would be no compulsion to enter into intensive talks. We would conduct ourselves defensively, aiming at avoiding being isolated.

Certainly with regard to Sadat we could not ask him not to put forward proposals. We would also have to tell him that we don't care how much noise he makes; but he would have to understand that he cannot use the threat of breaking the interim agreement to force an agreement with Syria.

This is our view. You know that whenever you had an understanding with us it has been meticulously kept by our side. But this would have to be a battle of movement. Geneva will be manageable if we don't try to write out everything in advance. There is the one thing, the question of the PLO, which the Arabs can't avoid. Then, of course, there is always Soviet pedantry.

Sisco: If we go to Geneva without a strategy, how do you see the situation of the possibility of a war, say, in 1976?

Secretary: Israel would win.

Rabin: I think we talked with the President about this. If there is an agreement to an interim agreement, then there would be no overall U.S. plan for Geneva.

Secretary: I think it would be better to follow what I said here. There would be general plans, plans of reasonable concreteness. I think that if we had a joint strategy, we could keep the process going and negotiate for a substantial length of time.

Dinitz: Is there a possibility of harmonizing positions for an overall agreement? Then we would not be in confrontation.

Secretary: We could attempt it.

Dinitz: You know our position but we don't know yours.

Secretary: There is a basic reason for this. I am trying to avoid formulating anything; I thought that would be helpful for you.

Dinitz: I understand. But it would also be helpful to know the road we are traveling.

Secretary: If the strategy I'm trying works, I would hope not to be in the government when that time comes.

Dinitz: That's what I'm afraid of.

Secretary: Not if you read Carl Rowan.[11] He had an article yesterday which said that the one thing that all Israelis could agree on was their antagonism for me.

Shalev: He's quite primitive.

Secretary: I know but that makes him a reliable reporter.

Well, let's not waste time on that.

It's easy enough to talk about now and the immediate future and I have described our thoughts on those. But from '78 onward—your objective cannot be realized without time. But the real question is can you

---

[11] Carl Rowan was a syndicated columnist for the *Chicago Sun-Times*.

waste more time in overall negotiations or through the interim approach. I know that's what you're thinking about.

Dinitz: Partly, but we're also thinking about the substance.

Secretary: It cannot be in your overall interest to have a public line drawn between you and this Administration. But I must say that the tendency has been in this direction over the last months. Once that line is drawn, you will win the first battle, perhaps even the first two or three battles, but in the end you will be facing a quite different America. That is what I have long tried to avoid.

In my view Israel cannot pursue its interests from a posture of rigidity. If our aim is for a common strategy, it has to be from a position of less hysteria and better understanding of the facts. And we, on the other hand, have to understand your needs.

That is no answer to your question, I know. We can try. That is the best I can say.

I know what you are trying—it is a process of exhaustion. Let me tell you what Boumedienne told me. He told me that you are trying to get the Egyptians and Syrians so exhausted that they will accept agreement with only minor changes and the Palestinians will be left high and dry.

Rabin: Without the U.S. involved, I doubt the wisdom of the idea of interim agreements.

Secretary: Yes, but then there will be international pressure to force you back.

Rabin: That is meaningless unless the United States is involved. There is no international pressure without the United States.

Dinitz: Can you give us any more ideas with regard to the early alert system?

Secretary: That is a major problem. I have told you that our intention would be to find some solution. I can't give you a final answer yet.

Rabin: There is also the question of bilateral issues.

Secretary: I had the impression that most of those were workable. But open bridges for tourists, that surely is not attainable yet.

Rabin: No.

Secretary: The storage thing we can work out. How to guarantee supply—that we will have to study more. We will have to effect our guarantees through the companies. We can accept the principle of it, but I can't give you the mechanics yet.

Rabin: What about long-range military supply?

Secretary: If there were an agreement we should just start negotiations on it. It would be in our best interests and yours to get an agreement as soon after the interim agreement as possible. It would then be seen by the Arabs as our contribution to that agreement.

Dinitz: What about the scope?

Secretary: I can't tell you yet. Our analysis so far is that $2.6 billion is high and, to be frank, there would probably be some Congressional trouble as well at that level.

We think $2.6 billion is high and that we can take care of the weapons you need and a 3 or 4% growth factor with a lesser figure.

But it is our intention to move substantially toward you. We will meet with your Congressional supporters so that there is no conflict between us. As to a precise figure ... I can give you perhaps an idea within a week or so of what we have in mind. It would be something objectively determined.

Dinitz: The figure was not pulled from the air. $1.5 billion would be for military procurement, as you know.

Secretary: I do not believe it would be in your best interests to put $2.6 billion to the Congress. But our intention is to put a substantial figure to the Congress—a figure that would be considered to be moving substantially to meet your needs.

We would be prepared to move within two or three weeks after an interim agreement—we would want to move fast, certainly before Geneva.

Dinitz: Can CSCE be delayed?

Secretary: We're not pushing it. The only issues outstanding are in regard to confidence-building measures. The Soviets have offered 250 kilometers on maneuvers. The Allies want 300 kilometers. The Soviets have said they want the limit on troops to be 30,000; the Allies say 25,000. This is with regard to notification of maneuvers.

It's all nonsense. We know when they're moving and in the future they won't be able to move anything we don't know about. It's all domestic politics in Europe.

I would like the conference as late as possible. We're not pushing it, certainly. Our instructions to our ambassador are to stay about a half step behind the Europeans. If the Soviets don't yield by the 24th, then the conference would have to go in to September because it will take four weeks to translate the agreement and so forth. The Russians will play to the last day and then yield. Isn't that right, Mac?

Toon: That's right.

Rabin: Did you say June 24th?

Secretary: Yes. I prefer the end of October for the conference.

Gazit: On the military supply issue, did you say the figures could be decided within three weeks?

Secretary: Yes. We'd submit it to the Congress; we want it to be done fast.

Rabin: Now we have the issue of how to handle the press.

Shalev: If I may, Sir. Let me ask that you don't play down our position until the Egyptians reply.

Secretary: I agree. The Gwertzman article today[12] was an outrage. It's our fault. But it is totally against the way I think the issue should be played now. Now we should be avoiding any indication of the distance that separates us.

Rabin: The best position for me to take would be to say that there should be give on both sides.

Secretary: We should all stop talking. The Berger article the other day[13] wasn't helpful either. That was from an Israeli source. That and the Gwertzman article, neither one were helpful. I've given strict instructions that no one is to be debriefed.

Can we say we find some flexibility in both positions?

Rabin: No. Then they will ask what is it in the Egyptian position that's flexible. And I would have to explain that. They would ask me what have we gotten from the U.S. that indicates give from the Egyptians and what flexibility have we Israelis showed.

Secretary: You are right. Let's simply say that we have clarified positions and now have to see what happens.

Dinitz: We need to work to take the edge off the argument that the Israelis have been inflexible. That argument is in the Gwertzman article.

Secretary: It is not in our interests to create that impression.

Sisco: It's a complicated sort of thing.

Secretary: I will instruct our spokesman to be a shade on the optimistic side. But if we get too hopeful, that also is dangerous.

---

[12] A reference to Bernard Gwertzman's article entitled "U.S. Still Unsure of a Sinai Accord after Rabin Talk." (*New York Times*, June 15, 1975, p. 1)

[13] Possibly a reference to Berger's article entitled "U.S. Pushes Interim Pact on Mideast." (*Washington Post*, June 11, 1975, p. A4)

189. Memorandum of Conversation[1]

New York, June 15, 1975, 12:15–2:35 p.m.

PARTICIPANTS

Secretary Kissinger
Marver Bernstein
Edgar Bronfman
Gershon Cohen
Lester Crown
Abraham Feinberg
David Ginsburg
Guido Goldman
John Gutfreund
Walter Haas
Max Karl
Philip Klutznik
David Landes
Fred Lazarus
Morris Leibman
Raymond Nasher
Abraham Pritzker
Henry Rosovsky
Rabbi Alex Schindler
Albert Spiegel
Lawrence Tisch
David Gompert (notetaker)

SUBJECT

Meeting with Jewish Leaders (Philip Klutznik Group)

The Secretary: First of all I want you to know how much I appreciate your taking off on the weekend to come here.

I explained some concerns to Mr. Klutznik about the future of Israel and the Jewish Community in America if we did not behave with wisdom. I am not here to ask you to do anything or to convince you of the wisdom of any particular approach but I would like to explain our approach.

Let me start at the beginning of my term in Washington in early 1969. The '67 war was in the recent past. I personally had nothing to do with Middle East affairs and when I first heard the wording of UN Security Council Resolution 242 I thought that it was impossible when I heard the expression, "just and lasting peace" that policy could be set on the interpretation—the infinite possibilities for interpretation—of each adjective.

I left the Middle East primarily to the State Department and to my predecessor there. But I made clear that my strategy would be to frustrate the Arab-Soviet relationship. Then once the Soviets were frustrated with the Arabs we could begin a process towards peace in the Middle East. During the first term of the Nixon Administration I maintained that our policy was to see the Soviets expelled from Egypt. Therefore, in the various crises that occurred in the Middle East, in the Jordanian crisis and the Suez Missile crisis, we adopted a posture that

---

[1] Source: Library of Congress, Manuscript Division, Kissinger Papers, CL 158, Geopolitical File, Israel, May 1975. No classification marking. The meeting was held in Suite 3111 at the Hotel Pierre in New York.

was very provocative in order to demonstrate the limitations of Soviet influence.

In 1971 Secretary Rogers tried for interim agreements along the Suez Canal. I did not oppose it, but neither did I support it. I am speaking very frankly now. The effort broke down over whether or not 1,000 Egyptian soldiers would be permitted across the Canal. That agreement would have prevented the 1973 war. I must say now that I am sorry that I did not support the Rogers effort more than I did.

Then Sadat threw out the Russians. I must say I never took Sadat seriously before; but then the 1973 war started. The United States saved Israel from collapse at the end of the first week by our arms supply. And even while this was going on, Sadat was sending me notes every day saying that he knew there would have to be talks after the war and that he wanted me to come to Egypt to get the process of peace started as soon as possible. Some have claimed that it was American strategy to produce a stalemate in the 1973 war. This is absolutely wrong. What we wanted was the most massive Arab defeat possible so that it would be clear to the Arabs that they would get nowhere with dependence on the Soviets. What caused the stalemate was the fact that the Israelis were not ready for the war. Also, if anything, the Israelis did not give us sufficient information during the war. Near the end, we did not even know that they were headed south. I even asked them.

We went to Moscow because we wanted to delay Security Council consideration. We didn't go to Moscow to cave. We wanted to delay the Security Council in order to give Israel 72 more hours to fight. Going to Moscow was our way to give Israel more time. If the Israelis had trapped the Third Army during the war it would not have been an American problem and we could have left it alone. But trapping the Third Army after a U.S.-arranged ceasefire was in effect, made it our problem, and even then the United States went on nuclear alert[2] to scare the Soviets out of unilateral action. So this group should understand that stalemate was not our goal.

What is the situation today? Now it is very easy for a group like this to try to say that American and Israeli interests are identical. But this is not exactly so and I think it is wrong for the Jewish community in the United States to get fixed on that concept. The United States has an interest in the survival of Israel; but we, of course, have an interest in the 130 million Arabs that sit athwart the world's oil supplies. Also the Soviets must assume that their problem is that their impotence has been demonstrated in each crisis. Therefore, during the next crisis they may take much greater risks than they have before. Look at our general

---

[2] A reference to President Nixon's decision to order a nuclear alert on October 24, 1973. See footnote 8, Document 91.

domestic situation. Anyone who has had anything to do with sports knows that success involves inches and nuances. This is the same with foreign policy. For example, in October of 1973 what if the Soviets had not caved at noon following the night of our alert? What if they had held on for 36 more hours? Even by noon of the day following the alert everyone was saying this is just a Watergate stunt.

Then look at the Jordanian crisis of 1970; the State Department thought that we should send diplomatic notes to everyone in the world. But we said no; in fact, we told the State Department to discontinue all communications with other countries. Then we sent an armored division down the Autobahn. We flew aircraft from the Sixth Fleet to Lod Airport in order to pick up staging plans. We put the 82nd Airborne on alert. The Syrian tanks turned back. None of this was in the newspapers, in contrast to what happened in October of 1973.

We had to consider the following factors during the '73 war: First, what would be the impact of the oil crisis on Western Europe and Japan? And I must tell you that every European leader that I have seen has told me that under no circumstances will he allow his country to undergo a domestic depression due to an oil embargo. Secondly, our impression is that Israel must be strong, but Israeli strength does not prevent the spread of communism in the Arab world. Israeli strength provides for Israeli security. The best defense against the spread of communism in the Arab world is to strengthen the moderate Arab Governments. So, it is difficult to claim that a strong Israel serves American interests because it prevents the spread of communism in the Arab world. It does not; it provides for the survival of Israel. This was our perception in October of 1973.

What was our strategy in 73? First, we sought to break up the Arab United Front. Also we wanted to ensure that the Europeans and Japanese did not get involved in the diplomacy; and, of course, we wanted to keep the Soviets out of the diplomatic arena. Finally, we sought a situation which would enable Israel to deal separately with each of its neighbors. We told the Arabs they could go to the Europeans if they wanted proclamations, but if they wanted progress toward peace they would have to come to us. Thus, the step-by-step process began.

The step-by-step led to two disengagement agreements; but then we had to make a basic strategic decision: shall we go now for overall settlement or continue the step-by-step? An overall effort has its advantages. Most importantly one can put everything on the table; one can argue the framework of final settlement with full knowledge of the objectives of all sides involved. But the disadvantages are that it would bring all the Arabs together, and when this happens the radical Arabs would have the upper hand. Then the Soviets would always be able to outbid whatever else was on the table and the radical Arabs would, of course, have to opt for what the Soviets had to offer. Of course, the Soviets would not make an offer in the interests of achieving peace but rather in the interest of assuring that there was no progress.

Therefore, we decided to continue with the step-by-step approach. Now the step-by-step approach requires great discipline. There are sharpshooters all over town that say that the step-by-step approach is unsatisfactory and that it is dead. It was inevitable that opposition would develop. For one thing, the overall approach has acquired a certain luster, and it is clear that if Middle East peace is to come the step-by-step approach must eventually merge into a comprehensive framework. But there is one thing you can say for step-by-step, it gives the parties involved a certain degree of confidence in that it is cumulative.

And now a word about the suspended negotiations and here I will be very candid. It is simply not true that there was some personal pique involved in the collapse of the negotiations. In June of 1974 when President Nixon was in Jerusalem[3] we talked with Rabin about the step-by-step versus the overall approach. Rabin affirmed that the step-by-step was preferable as long as Israel did not have to make the first move. His was a new government, and they could not afford politically, he said, to make the first move.

Then Allon came to Washington.[4] He is an old friend of mine and I took him up to Camp David. Allon said that Israel wants to pursue step-by-step, but Israel wanted to have some time first. They wanted no negotiations before December. He even said give us until March; we are a new government and we cannot jump into this. So we gave them some time. The United States went into a protracted stall with the Arabs. I took many trips to the area—with no progress, of course.

At the same time Rabin was asking for U.S. arms. The united bureaucracy came up with an offer which was only ½ of what the Israelis wanted. But due to my efforts we gave him ⁴⁄₇ of what he asked for and we still held back on the diplomacy.

Then Hussein offered to accept what was about ½ of the territory called for in the old Allon Plan. In return for this he said he would agree to end any Jordanian pressure.[5] But the Israelis said no; as a new government they did not feel that they were prepared to accept that. And then we had Rabat.

So you see, you have an Israeli government which says that it won't move at all on the Golan and also that precluded any movement

---

[3] See Document 92.

[4] Kissinger met with Allon on July 31 and August 1, 1974. See Documents 93 and 94.

[5] For further information on the talks with Hussein see the detailed list in the Note on Sources.

on the West Bank by the decision on the Hussein offer and by Rabat.[6] So we were left to try again on the Sinai.

Now the Israelis never tire of dragging out this or that part of the written record about the negotiations. But the man from Grand Rapids does not understand why these legal technicalities are so all important. He assumes if the parties are negotiating about the passes that withdrawal from the passes can in fact be achieved. So Israel cannot really depend on beating the President into submission on legal technicalities.

Speaking very candidly again, I must say that I knew something wasn't right about the March negotiations before they even started. I told Sisco that something smells wrong. I said they are not as obnoxious as they would be if they really wanted an agreement. (Laughter) I told you I was speaking very candidly. Sisco said "impossible."

When I told my deputy at the NSC, Brent Scowcroft, the guy who keeps the State Department in line for me, that the talks were going to be suspended just before it actually happened, he simply could not believe it. Neither could Peter Rodman, who has taken all the notes for me and who is a long-time associate and friend.

We told the Israelis all along that non-belligerency was unattainable. I thought that by non-belligerency they meant non-use of force; and then when Sadat agreed to a conditional non-use of force, I thought we were half way there. I thought that all we would have to do was to remove the conditions on the non-use of force and we would have an agreement. But what the Israelis wanted was complete non-belligerency, that is removal of all the conditions that stand between the present situation and perfectly normal relations, including all the civilian aspects of belligerency.

Well, Sadat's answer to this was, if I have to give up everything just to get them out of the passes what will I have left to give to get back all my land?

Now Sadat did agree that the agreement should have an automatic extension. There was a one-year term for UNEF, but there was a side undertaking that there would be an extension. This was more than I thought we could get. And then to stick the United States out in front like they had, and to say on the last day that we won't leave the passes, well this we cannot regard as a minor matter.

Our first major concern after the talks broke down was to prevent an Arab blowup. The President wrote a letter saying there would be a reassessment,[7] but the Israelis leaked it. Then the President had to

---

[6] See Document 112.
[7] Document 156.

make public the fact that there would be a reassessment. What the reassessment has done is it has kept things cool with the Arabs. The arms that have not been delivered were not scheduled until 1977 anyway, and, of course, they got 200 tanks. So, you can see, we took no punitive action.

Now Israel wants 2.6 billion dollars; but we have to ask for what? Where are we going to go from here? If the United States is seen as financing a Middle East stalemate with 2.6 billion dollars, the Arabs will turn back towards radicalism. Then you will have the Arabs putting oil pressure on the Europeans and the Japanese and eventually on the United States. At first Congress will be very tough. They will say we won't yield to blackmail, but after five years, I ask you, will we be so tough? And when this situation comes and the Jews in America put themselves up as being the spokesmen for Israel, they will have to explain why the United States is in such a state.

Anybody can survive for six months, but the real art to diplomacy is survival over a longer, at least, a medium-term time frame. If we fail now there will be an explosion. I don't know when, but there will be one. And even if Israel takes Damascus, Cairo and Amman the basic political problems will remain. World opinion will turn dramatically against Israel and the United States, and also the Soviets during the next explosion will be willing to take more risks. Now what if they land two battalions in the area and then call for a settlement? I, of course, would be in favor of opposing it but I don't know whether we would get Congressional support to put U.S. Forces in to prevent it.

If there are no chances for the step-by-step to succeed, then we will have to look at the possibility of a comprehensive settlement. And if that comes to pass, world public opinion will certainly favor a '67 borders settlement. When Israel faces such a situation things will be difficult for her, but sooner or later Israel will have to face these questions anyway.

The only thing that is definitely not an option is no progress at all. Any attempt by Israel to organize the American Jewish community against their government, will lead to a disaster. I cannot be expected to solve all this and the American Jewish leaders cannot ask the Secretary of State to represent narrow interests.

So on the whole, we lean toward another interim agreement; but if not, we will go to Geneva because it will be the only way out. And if we go to Geneva the danger of explosion will be very great. We must face the problem of asking ourselves what peace in the Middle East will look like. Mock heroism could lead to the destruction of Israel.

Question: Can you tell us about what happened at Salzburg?[8]

Kissinger: Well Sadat in my judgment is an Egyptian nationalist. If you gave him the '67 borders, you would never hear from him again. He is basically upper-bourgeois. He would like to start the peace process, but he is also an Arab and he must defend his position within the Arab world.

At Salzburg, he told me that he thinks that Israel wants to freeze the situation so that by 1977 some radical Arab will do something wild which will lead the United States to abandon the Arabs.

We told Sadat that Israel needed better terms than in March. And Israel also seems willing to make concessions, but I don't know if they will make the critical move out of the passes. Rabin said he would leave the passes only for non-belligerency. Egypt is willing to turn the passes over to the United Nations. They want the Israelis one kilometer out of the passes. They themselves would be 20 kilometers out of the passes.

I have no interest in achieving an interim agreement if the American Jews are going to think that is the end of history. It will help, but it cannot be seen as the end of the process.

Question: Did the breakdown occur because of failure to achieve Knesset's support?

Kissinger: I have the impression that Rabin did want the agreement, but he had some problem with polls; he was running 30 percent, and Peres according to the polls was up to 68 percent. It doesn't seem to me that Rabin manages his domestic debate with quite the elan that Golda did. Apparently he never told anyone all along how far he had gone in his discussions. Therefore, he probably couldn't have gotten Knesset support. While this may be true the fact remains the United States was way out front for 10 months on this.

Question: (Landes) Has there been any discussion with Sadat or with the Israelis for that matter on just what is meant by the term "legitimate rights of the Palestinians?"

Kissinger: Well, I know Sadat wanted to let Hussein worry about it. That was Sadat's first preference. He wanted the problem to be one of an address, that is if you want to talk about the Palestinians I suggest you write to so and so. Of course, the Palestinians cause similar problems for most of the Arab leaders; namely, they generate domestic radicalism and they also have the assassination problem.

But I have left the Palestinian question alone in order to work on the frontier questions hoping eventually to isolate the Palestinians. And this could work. We could have split the Palestinians from the

---

[8] During Ford and Kissinger's conversations with Sadat; see Documents 177 and 178.

Syrians for only a few more kilometers on the Golan, but the Israelis insisted on moving the settlements right up to the line. My feeling now is that the Syrians will be driven toward even greater radicalism. Israel must realize that it must deal with the Arab governments if it does not want to deal with the Palestinians. But you know, Israel is a lot like Germany before the First World War in that there is this tendency to produce what it most fears.

Question: (Leibman) What is your estimate of the general trends of American foreign policy? Do you see an erosion of American public support?

Kissinger: The United States has had a whole series of shocks since the assassination of Jack Kennedy. Two Presidents have, in effect, been driven from office. We have had a real experience in domestic radicalism and there has been latent isolationism. It seems now that the old isolationists in the Middlewest are the ones who support us the most, whereas the Eastern intellectual establishment tends to be more isolationist.

And we have our Congressional problems. I think the War Powers Act is a calamity. We cannot move any forces anywhere without asking Congress. In January, Hanoi conducted a limited operation which we now see as a test of our reaction.[9] I wanted to move some forces—the 7th Fleet and also in Thailand. It so happened at the same time that a carrier departed Subic destined for the Indian Ocean and, of course, this was all over the television. Everyone was saying that we were sending a carrier to Vietnam. Then we had Congressional demands for an investigation and for more information. Well, we eventually had to call off the whole operation and the carrier wasn't even going to the Tonkin Gulf.

There can be no question that Congressional restrictions would create a problem in another Middle East crisis. The reaction in Congress and probably in the country regarding the use of American forces would be very negative.

Question: I am bothered by one thing. You said that the United States was committed to '67 borders, somewhere down the line.

Kissinger: No I did not say that. I said that somewhere down the line we would have to face the question of what a final peace settlement looks like.

Question: How do you see a final peace settlement in terms of Israeli security?

---

[9] A reference to the January 6 attack by Communist forces against South Vietnamese troops in the provincial capital of Phuoc Binh.

Kissinger: An overall settlement will inevitably have to involve a discussion of the '67 borders. But that is why I have pushed the step-by-step. If necessary, the United States should provide guarantees for the survival of Israel and, of course, some adjustments of the borders might be possible. But at Geneva, events will get ahead of everyone and we will be into these discussions before we want to be.

Question: Do you think that U.S. guarantees would be ratified by the Senate?

Kissinger: You probably couldn't get U.S. guarantees ratified. I think Morrie's question was really the key.

You know, I am being lambasted all over town for holding to a geo-strategic view of the world. The intellectual community attacks me for having these views. And you know these are the only guys writing. So look at what we are doing to Chile now. Look what is happening to the CIA. We are destroying our intelligence establishment. For what? Portugal is seen as a failure of American foreign policy. If so, it is because we have lost our ability to support democratic elements in Portugal. But you all can rest at peace—there are no 40 Committee[10] activities going on in Portugal.

I agree, until we get our people thinking in geo-political terms we are going to be in real trouble. Look at Angola. Now if we don't get in there it will go communist. And yet Jewish intellectuals are saying that the United States is being immoral if it involves itself in Chile and Portugal, but don't give up an inch in Sinai. The Jews in America will suffer if we don't develop some more awareness.

Question: You mean, regarding these geo-political terms?

Kissinger: The strength of Israel is needed for its own survival but not to prevent the spread of communism in the Arab world. So it doesn't necessarily help U. S. global interests as far as the Middle East is concerned. The survival of Israel has sentimental importance to the United States, but believe me it is not easy to maintain this. It would not be wise to push luck to an extreme. $2.6 billion for 3 million people—I don't believe it is in the interests of the Jewish community to push it too hard.

Question: (Cohen) Don't you think there might be some Israeli fear that an assurance from the United States is all that credible due to the War Powers Act, etc? Don't you think Israel sees some American impotence?

---

[10] The 40 Committee reviewed proposed and ongoing covert operations. Founded in 1954 as the NSC 5412 Special Group, then called the 303 Committee, it was renamed the 40 Committee in 1970.

Kissinger: Yes, I agree and the more impotent we look the more the challenges will mount. This, of course, makes the Israeli problem worse. The denouement of Indochina, which was partly our fault, must be seen very anxiously by Israel.

Question: (Tisch) Now what is Rabin's answer to the logic you have presented today?

Kissinger: Well, I think that if we met alone, he would probably agree with 98 percent of what I have said. But you have to remember that advocates of short-term solutions always have the upper hand.

One of the tragedies of history, it seems to me, is that the Jews have been persecuted for having a cosmopolitan outlook. But now it seems that they worry too much about their own particular problem—just that one small part of the world. You see, just now when they really need a Rothschild[11] they have a soldier peasant.

Question: What do you say about Hoffman's[12] argument that if the United States looks impotent then time is not on our side and we should go for an overall agreement, namely through Geneva?

Kissinger: Hoffman thinks that the Europeans and the Japanese will support a reasonable American proposal. I think that will never happen against Arab pressures. Also you have to realize that Soviet pressures at Geneva would have a premium because the Arabs would think to themselves that if the United States cannot accomplish an interim agreement it certainly cannot accomplish something bigger. Now if Geneva were to meet in a less dramatic, more controlled way then maybe the Arabs would try to work through us. But I have not talked about the 1967 borders in any of our discussions.

Question: (Klutznik) Why did Gromyko cool off on the idea of Geneva after he saw you recently?

Kissinger: My personality. (Laughter) No, the Soviets don't have a master plan as far as I can see. Theirs is not a very subtle foreign policy, but they are persistent and you can accomplish much with persistence—especially against an opponent who keeps changing tacks.

But, basically the Soviets are as incapable of anyone of working with the Arabs. Gromyko told me in Vienna[13] as soon as we sat down that he proposed to invite the PLO to Geneva. I told him, alright Mr. Foreign Minister if that is your proposal, I must reject it. Now go ahead and tell the Arabs that you made the proposal and that I rejected it. I

---

[11] A reference to the Rothschild family, a wealthy and politically influential Jewish family in 19th and 20th century Europe.

[12] Apparently a reference to Stanley Hoffman, founder of Harvard University's Center for European Studies.

[13] Kissinger met with Gromyko in Vienna May 19–20. See footnote 2, Document 178.

then immediately told the Arabs that Gromyko had made this proposal and that I had rejected it. That just goes to show the Arabs how little Gromyko is able to accomplish. He then, of course, told all the Arabs that he had made the proposal and that I had rejected it.

I think that Gromyko thinks he is better off waiting to see if we fail. Then he can cooperate to the extent that he wants.

But he also wants CSCE so this gives us a window into July which is when they want the conference. After that, they will become more intransigent.

Question: What can we do?

Kissinger: I don't know and I am not asking you to do anything. But I do hope that you can prevent a Jewish assault on the United States Government. The Jews may win the first battle, but you can be sure that they will lose the war. This must be avoided. On substance, don't just always assume that the Israeli Government is right and the United States Government is wrong. This reflects a basic misperception.

I would be glad to meet periodically with this group.

Question: (Lazarus) I am still not clear on whether you feel that Rabin is going back to Israel convinced that he has got to sell this in Israel.

Kissinger: I think he, personally, will try to maneuver towards a settlement. But don't forget he also wants very much to remain Prime Minister and he has got to be concerned about Allon and Peres. He just won't beat up the Cabinet like Golda did in order to get the Syrian negotiations completed.

Question: (Landes) Henry, what do you tell the Arabs about what they can and cannot do, you know what I mean?

Kissinger: Yes, I know what you mean.

You know, it is now taken for granted that the Arabs look towards Washington. I have never talked to the Arabs on borders. Every time they have attempted to raise it, I have invariably said it is premature and I have always told them that they must think about their commitment to peace. I have told them that they have got to come up with some concrete ideas about how to live with Israel and I think we have convinced at least Sadat that he has got to give some serious thought to how to live with Israel. Why Sadat has said that he would even welcome American guarantees.

We certainly have not whetted the Arab appetite.

Question: Do you, in your geo-political perception, think that we have gone to an extreme in our foreign policy?

Kissinger: Well, the dominant trend, certainly with the press and the intellectual establishment, and one wing, at least, of the Democratic Party has been going away from this geo-political awareness. But I think the public is leaning the other way. And when you have the public going one way the result could very well be populist demagogue who will want to be tough on Russia and soft everywhere else.

We must be careful not to have our overall position eroded to the point that the Soviets don't really have to make a move. Because if our overall position is eroded then some day we will have to face a real challenge.

Question: Can you comment on the question of Soviet Jewry?

Kissinger: When we came into office, Jewish emigration from the Soviet Union was 400 per year. We increased that to 32,000 a year. The President and I never failed, when we talked to the Soviets, to tell them look it would improve the atmosphere if you let some more Jews out.

Then it became a big political issue between Jackson and us. And for what? No country could allow its domestic regulations to be dictated as we were pushing the Soviets to do. So now it is back down to 11,000 and we have also lost the leverage. The Soviets can now get private credits and European credits. I think it was a serious mistake that the Jewish community got hung-up on it.

Question: Would it help if we sought to remove the 300,000 million ceiling on credits?[14]

Kissinger: I cannot say.

Take the question of most favored nation status for Romania. Believe me it will be a real problem if Romania doesn't get most favored nation. First of all, it will help the Soviets at a time when we are trying to split Romania and the Soviet Union. Secondly, it will certainly hurt the Jews in Romania. And finally, it will hurt the President's general credibility in the country—the general problem we were talking about. I think it would be very painful for the American Jewish community to destroy the chances of most favored nation for Romania.

The Romanians simply cannot face a formal commitment to the United States Congress. It would be too embarrassing for them, vis-à-vis the Soviets and, of course, vis-à-vis the Arabs.

Klutznik: Mr. Secretary, thank you very much. I don't think your time has been wasted.

Kissinger: Let's meet again.

---

[14] A reference to the Stevenson amendment to the Export-Import Bank bill, which was signed into law by President Ford on January 4, 1975. The amendment placed a ceiling of $300 million on future credits for exports to the Soviet Union. Although the President could set a higher limit if he deemed it necessary for U.S. national interests, the Congress would still have to approve by concurrent resolution.

190. Memorandum of Conversation[1]

Washington, June 16, 1975, 9:22–10:24 a.m.

PARTICIPANTS

President Gerald R. Ford
Dr. Henry A. Kissinger, Secretary of State and Assistant to the President for National Security Affairs
Lt. General Brent Scowcroft, Deputy Assistant to the President for National Security Affairs

Kissinger: I met with Rabin yesterday in New York.[2] He didn't change his position. He said he couldn't. He can't ignore what you have said. But I think now we shouldn't spill too much blood over an American interim plan. If you have to cram it down their throats, it may be better to go all the way.

President: When will we hear?

Kissinger: They will send someone back from Jerusalem with a map on Wednesday,[3] after they have a Cabinet meeting on Tuesday. Even if they change, I would send the first position to Sadat, unless Filts thinks it would cause a blowup.

[Omitted here is discussion unrelated to the Arab-Israeli dispute.]

President: How did the lunch in New York go?

Kissinger: Extremely well. It's the best meeting with a Jewish group I have had.[4] I told them that Jewish groups take the position that the U.S. is never right and Israel always is, and that is laying the basis for massive anti-Semitism here. I said: "You should be here as Americans, not as Israeli supporters." I think two-thirds of them were enthusiastic. I will meet with them again and maybe you should meet with them.

President: I would like to.

Kissinger: Klutznick—the organizer—is something of a renegade.

[Omitted here is discussion unrelated to the Arab-Israeli dispute.]

---

[1] Source: Ford Library, National Security Adviser, Memoranda of Conversations, Box 12, June 16, 1975, Ford, Kissinger. Secret; Nodis. The meeting was held in the Oval Office at the White House.
[2] See Document 188.
[3] June 18.
[4] See Document 189.

191. Memorandum of Conversation[1]

Washington, June 20, 1975.

PARTICIPANTS

President Ford
Dr. Henry A. Kissinger, Secretary of State and Assistant to the President for National Security Affairs
Lt. Gen. Brent Scowcroft, Deputy Assistant to the President for National Security Affairs

Kissinger: [showing a map:][2] Peres threatened to resign over even this line. So I don't see how you can force an interim settlement on them.

[There was much discussion of the map lines.]

You could tell Sadat you forced them back this far and he can probably get two more kilometers. Any more would force Cabinet resignations and there would be no progress at all. If that is not acceptable, there are the two options: An interim settlement or an overall plan. An interim agreement under these circumstances would cause an explosion as big as an overall agreement. If anything goes wrong with an interim, we are in the soup. But an overall is risky because we would have to ride that for a year and a half. They also want $2.5 billion—even for this line.

The President: Not from me.

Kissinger: They don't want a shuttle before the 13th.

Sadat has three options: To buy the Israeli option, so it would be settled by the middle of August. Or he rejects it and we impose an American interim or overall settlement. If you go to the interim you would have to say they get no aid bill until they accept. We would be stuck with all the consequences. And then the Syrians would demand equal American pressure for them.

I will get all the implications of our interim and overall solutions written up over the weekend. Rabin agreed [almost] to put forward the cosmetic proposal on Golan as a unilateral one. If we could get that

---

[1] Source: Ford Library, National Security Adviser, Memoranda of Conversations, Box 13, June 20, 1975, Ford, Kissinger. Secret; Nodis. The meeting was held in the Oval Office at the White House. According to the President's Daily Diary, it began at 9:44 a.m. (Ibid., Staff Secretary's Office Files) Brackets are in the original.

[2] The map is not attached. For the final agreed map, see Appendix B, map 4. The Israeli proposal and map are attached to a June 20 memorandum of conversation of a meeting between Kissinger and Dinitz, during which Dinitz explained the various issues related to the proposal. (Library of Congress, Manuscript Division, Kissinger Papers, CL 158, Geopolitical File, Israel, June 1–12, 1975)

with a painless interim solution, you could then get through our elections and go for a settlement after the election. The Golan gesture could be about November. Then next year we could put out an overall proposal in general terms—it wouldn't be enough, but it would get us by. That is my ideal scenario. The problem with the overall is what do you do next March. It would be popular right now with everyone but the Jews.

The President: But if we put forward an interim and it is turned down, we could then say we did our best.

Kissinger: Let's think these over over the weekened. I don't see any sense in putting forward an overall one unless you put on aid restrictions until they accept. Restrict them to previous levels—$700 million. Next year is not a good one for you to be in a brawl with the Jews. What Sadat has to understand is what is doable on any of the three options.

With Khaddam, don't put forward the overall idea so forcefully. Say we want progress; we don't want to split the Arabs. On Golan, I would say we won't agree to Israel keeping all the Golan. I have usually said that the Golan should be worked out in a settlement, and I assume Syria wouldn't agree to anything unacceptable. There probably, as a practical matter, will have to be a demilitarization arrangement.

192. Memorandum of Conversation[1]

Washington, June 20, 1975, 10:15–11 a.m.

SUBJECT

Middle East Strategy

PARTICIPANTS

Secretary Kissinger
Ambassador Eilts
Under Secretary Sisco
Assistant Secretary Atherton
Deputy Assistant Secretary Saunders
David Gompert (Notetaker)

Kissinger: Hermann, when you go back do not use the word 'impose' I don't care what the President says. You can see that he is mad though, that should be clear to you.

Sisco: Henry, you know you are to the right of the President on this.

Kissinger: Hermann, you have to get across to Sadat—first, the sense of our determination, and second, a question of management. Can he wait long enough?

The Israelis have put themselves in a position where—Sadat has played this perfectly. No U.S. President has ever been this ready to move on the Israelis. The President figures that an all-out brawl is better now because otherwise they would try to get him out in 1976. If he had to decide in the next half an hour what to do, he would go on television against the Israelis. He would say that there is no more time to horse around and that the United States cannot contribute any longer to the growth of Israeli capabilities.

But don't tell that to Sadat. He would understand, however, that this is farther than last year. The President used to think that Kissinger was a miracle man and that somehow this thing will work out; but now he realizes that he is in a brawl. Sadat should understand this. Then after Sadat has cooled off from his initial exposure, just tell him, look, this is a common problem.

Eilts: O.K. But he is going to ask us what our position is.

Kissinger: Don't pull out the unilateral options.

---

[1] Source: Library of Congress, Manuscript Division, Kissinger Papers, CL 273, Chronological File, June 1975. Secret; Nodis. The meeting was held in the Secretary's office at the White House.

(Hal) Saunders, do a paper (for the President).[2] Explain about the land access to the south.

Hermann, I think you're underestimating the . . .

Eilts: Well, but perhaps the big problem is in the passes.

Kissinger: These guys are determined, but they are underestimating the President. They cannot defeat him. Golda would not have made this mistake. The Jews cannot survive anywhere in the world when they oppose their government.

Sisco: I agree, but I don't think Rabin realizes this.

Kissinger: I know that the Jews cannot survive if they oppose their government. This will bring out centuries of latent hatred.

Sisco: It is horrible to think about.

Kissinger: Hal, lay out the options. Make it cool and analytical. With respect to Egypt, we want to look at several options and sub-options. First of all there is interim versus overall. Then we have to look at whether or not we want a posture of being critical of Israel or a helpful posture. We have to look at a cut in aid versus no cut in aid. We can buy time with the Arabs if we have to by putting forward schemes.

I think he must do it from a posture of criticism of Israel and cut in aid. If he doesn't cut aid we will be in a weaker position when we have to. Now for the question of interim versus overall, if it is to be an interim settlement it can be imposed only on one front, which means that he will buy himself great problems ahead.

Sisco: I disagree. No one expects any movement on the Golan. That could happen in a Geneva context.

Kissinger: An imposed Sinai solution will get them a minimum of two years stand-still in U.S. activity.

Eilts: Syria is the problem. I, therefore, lean towards an imposed interim settlement.

Kissinger: But also give him the overall.

Eilts: In the paper, you should mention the relationship of the options to aid for Egypt.

Kissinger: Explain that to Sadat.

Sisco: The Syrians will also get hurt, which means that they would escalate the Syrian Jew problem.

Kissinger: You tell me what damn business it is of the United States to mess around with the problem of Syrian Jews. Why should the United States risk its relations with a major country over 4,500 Jews? The conditions of the Syrian Jews are no worse than the Biharis in Ban-

---

[2] No such paper has been found.

gladesh, or the untouchables in India. We are not making a fuss about them.

Hal, lay out all the options as cooly as possible.

I am leary about imposing an interim settlement.

Eilts: Something must happen by 1977. If we cannot achieve an interim settlement then something should happen in 1976.

Sisco: I am closer to you Henry on the imposed interim solution.

Kissinger: Look, if we buy 18 months, let's buy it for nothing. If we get tied to three years with American stations, no American plan, then we are stuck.

Sisco: I had not thought of option three. If Rabin says there must be an American proposal, I would say o.k.

Kissinger: You may have to explain option three to Sadat, Hermann, though option three would be harder for him to manage. We would be in Geneva.

Sisco: The unilateral option gives us so much a freer hand.

Eilts: But maybe the price is too high.

Kissinger: The price is only the extension of UNEF. We can still put forward principles without actually putting forward an American proposal.

193. Memorandum of Conversation[1]

Washington, June 20, 1975, 4 p.m.

PARTICIPANTS

    Abd al-Halim Khaddam, Deputy Prime Minister and Minister of Foreign Affairs, Syrian Arab Republic
    Dr. Sabah Kabbani, Syrian Ambassador to the United States
    Sameeh Tawfeek Abou Fares, Ministry of Foreign Affairs (Interpreter)

    The President
    Dr. Henry A. Kissinger, Secretary of State and Assistant to the President for National Security Affairs
    Joseph J. Sisco, Under Secretary of State for Political Affairs
    Amb. Richard W. Murphy, U.S. Ambassador to Syria
    Lt. Gen. Brent Scowcroft, Deputy Assistant to the President for National Security Affairs
    Isa K. Sabbagh, Special Assistant to Amb. Akins, Jidda (Interpreter)

[The press takes photographs and departs.]

President: Mr. Foreign Minister, it is nice to see you again. We are fortunate it is the same week—sort of an anniversary—of the renewal of our relations[2] and the building of better relations between our countries. It is my understanding that you and the Secretary had a lunch and a meeting before.[3] It would be helpful if the Secretary could review for me the discussions thus far.

Khaddam: Mr. President, I am pleased to be here in Washington and am delighted to have the opportunity to meet with you. It is indeed a pleasant occasion to be here on our anniversary and to celebrate the relationship which we hope will become even stronger.

Kissinger: Mr. President, I reviewed for the Foreign Minister the alternatives that we have before us: One is a series of interim settlements eventually leading to an overall settlement and, two, an overall settlement. It is correct to say that Syria didn't declare a day of national mourning last March when the negotiation failed.

The United States is not pushing any particular approach, but you have publicly committed your prestige to producing progress in the Middle East. We have made clear to Israel that any agreement with Egypt would have to be followed by an agreement with Syria. The ad-

---

[1] Source: Ford Library, National Security Adviser, Memoranda of Conversations, Box 13, June 20, 1975, Ford, Kissinger. Secret; Nodis. The meeting was held in the Oval Office at the White House. According to the President's Daily Diary, it ended at 5:25 p.m. (Ibid., Staff Secretary's Office Files) Brackets are in the original.
[2] The United States reestablished diplomatic relations with Syria on June 16, 1974.
[3] No memorandum of conversation has been found.

vantage we saw in this is that the obstacles in the way would be removed, leading to an overall settlement. On the other hand, this is not an American problem, and if the parties can't be brought together, we would support movement to an overall settlement. The Foreign Minister pointed out that an overall settlement need not happen at Geneva and the Foreign Minister would look for other ways than at Geneva through which to work.

God will punish me someday, but I have really developed an affection for the Syrians.

Khaddam: As Secretary Kissinger said, we reviewed the situation in the area. It gives me pleasure to present to you the situation as we see it at the present time.

We in Syria, and the Arabs, greatly appreciate the efforts of the President and Secretary Kissinger to bring peace to the area. We seek peace. We are now before a given situation.

Perhaps it would be useful to go back and review what has happened since I was in Washington last August[4] where we discussed the same subject. If we referred to the minutes of those meetings, we would find that the same discussion we are having now we had then. That is, there has been no progress over the past year, despite the efforts of the United States and the positive attitude of the Arabs.

Despite the alternative approaches, Syria prefers the overall approach. It is difficult, but ignoring the complexities doesn't make them go away. Now is the time to face up to all the problems and see where to go. Especially since we tried the other method. Because we try the overall approach doesn't mean we would not try other avenues to reach the same goal. Therefore, if step-by-step is found to be the only feasible way, it should take account of all the issues on all the fronts together—meaning that any withdrawal should take place on all three fronts simultaneously. Should things turn out different from this, it would be suspect in our minds, not because United States policy doesn't want withdrawal on other fronts, but because of Israeli intransigence. Withdrawal on one front alone wouldn't be conducive to peace.

The Israeli attitude arouses our suspicion—for example, the new settlements and new construction; Israel says they won't withdraw. Even more dangerous would be a map as published by the Labour Party, showing the Golan, Gaza and the West Bank as part of Israel. Labour is not an opposition party—it is the government. And then, it is

---

[4] Ford met with Khaddam in the Oval Office on August 23, 1974, from 10:35 until 11:34 a.m. A memorandum of conversation of the meeting is in the Library of Congress, Manuscript Division, Kissinger Papers, Geopolitical File, Syria, CL 235, August 1974.

softer than the Likud. So what must the attitude of the Likud be? If we were to ignore this in going along with a step-by-step it would give a bad impression in the Arab world. We can't ignore public opinion. Those manifestations of Israeli intransigence concern us about the step-by-step, especially if the steps would be splintered.

Kissinger: But the Foreign Minister was an avid supporter before.

[There is some jesting about using the Kissinger method of analyzing Israel.]

Khaddam: We said that the heavy United States military shipments to Israel would make them more intransigent when others were saying that it would make them more secure and more able to negotiate. Now Rabin is in a position to thumb his nose at the United States. As to what the other methods could be used—Geneva is only one. But if Geneva will turn into an endless conference like the negotiation on Vietnam, we see no use for it. If we agree to Geneva, it would not be for speeches but a serious desire to work for peace. Geneva is the preferred method—the UN called for it. We don't reject Geneva; only that it be turned into an Indochina-type conference. But we want to continue all channels of effort—and American efforts are basic to any progress. The United States has many roles—as Co-chairman, as a great power, and a responsibility for peace and leadership in the world.

We could go back to the Security Council so that it would have to do something for the resolutions that it, itself, had passed. Another method is to increase pressure on Israel by the international community. These are the basic alternative ways of dealing with the subject.

Kissinger: If you want to go one way—say to an overall solution—and if there are explosions, because of failure, a stalemate, etc., then this will be used in the United States to discredit all Arabs so those who supported it would not support other efforts for a while.

Khaddam: We do not want an explosion to occur, especially if we sense that serious efforts are under way in reaching a common and permanent peace. We have now tried for one year, and what do we see? Israel's attitude is more intransigent.

President: Let me assure you that our decision to pursue the step-by-step was made in total good faith. We have maximized our efforts to make progress in that regard. We were disappointed that the negotiations in March did not bring success, and we were happy they were only suspended. Second, I said in March that we were reassessing our policy in the Middle East. In that process we have surveyed all the alternatives and we will decide on the one which offers the best hope for success. That decision may be aimed at resumption of the step-by-step or may take the course of an overall settlement and may include Geneva.

I was interested in your comment that the conference would not take place in Geneva. Where else do you have in mind?

Khaddam: What I meant was that if Geneva turned out like the Indochina negotiation, with just talk, we would go by it to the Security Council.

Kissinger: We don't know until Geneva starts how it will work.

Khaddam: Of course. Even when we followed the step-by-step, we ended up at Geneva. So it doesn't matter whether we end up at Geneva or in the Security Council.

President: Did I understand ...

Khaddam: Given the present circumstances we cannot return to a step-by-step as in the past. Our view of this step-by-step is that we would oppose it if it didn't include all three fronts.

Kissinger: Last year you settled for two. I keep teasing, but Asad and Khaddam have taken—considering the conditions—a very serious view of the problem.

Khaddam: The first method is the past one; the second is Geneva and at the same time step-by-step efforts; and third is Geneva by itself. If these methods—none of them—produce results, then we go back to the Security Council.

President: I have three questions: Would you expect the PLO to be at Geneva?

Khaddam: There are certain facts. One is that the axis on which the whole situation exists, is Palestine. We believe clarity in this will help all to understand. Therefore, I will speak quickly: The basic problem is resolving the Palestinian question. To ignore them would be for a surgeon performing an appendectomy, to find an ulcer but just close the man up after an appendectomy and send him on his way. The Palestinian people exist, as does the PLO. So there are two political alternatives: we acknowledge their existence or we don't. For peace, they should be there. I assure you the Arab world has never been so desirous of peace.

Kissinger: Would the Arabs recognize Israel?

Khaddam: Whatever the Palestinians agree upon, we would accept. That is why we think Secretary Kissinger should meet with the PLO next time.

President: What would the Soviet role be at Geneva?

Khaddam: I can't answer without knowing how the arrangements would be. The Soviet Union is Co-Chairman. The role of the U.S. Government we have discussed, but we have no clear procedure which we think the Soviet Union will follow.

We ought to judge the UN by its experience. We look at it the way it is now—the General Assembly and the Security Council. The General

Assembly could come to certain resolutions which would isolate them and bring certain political and economic pressures. Resolutions by the Security Council would have to take into account the position of the United States.

Kissinger: If everything depends on us, why should we invest our efforts through the UN? It wouldn't bring a result and thus we would pay for having given it to the UN and for its failing.

[General Scowcroft leaves the meeting briefly.]

Kissinger: Supposing the President takes a position. If Israel disagrees with it and all or some of the Arab Governments disagree, we will be in the worst possible position.

Khaddam: As the President and Secretary must be aware, the Syrians and Arabs are anxious that U.S. efforts succeed. Your efforts were greatly appreciated. So when the American decision is announced—which is just in the eyes of the Arabs—we won't pick at it. So we can't say what the Arab attitude would be without knowing the U.S. position.

Kissinger: But you must understand our limiting factors.

Khaddam: Are you hinting that your decision won't be palatable?

Kissinger: No.

Khaddam: I want to assure you both that we are anxious for the efforts to succeed. We discern a new understanding by the President and Secretary Kissinger. The new policy may not be exactly what we want, but we hope it will be different from what existed in the past.

President: Would you be willing to undertake negotiations with Israel on a further step-by-step attempt?

Kissinger: In the case of progress on the Egyptian front?

Khaddam: Our view is that activities should start simultaneously, because otherwise it would leave the impression of favoritism. It is already being said that Israel is adamant about perpetuating their occupation and this map will be used as proof of it. We actually appeal to President Ford and the U.S. Government to consider our attitude. We can't afford to ignore Arab public opinion. If Israel can't ignore the views of a few settlers on the Golan, how can we ignore the views of 100 million Arabs? Every day Israel makes statements about keeping the Golan, the West Bank, and Gaza, etc. If Israel is not dilly-dallying to reach the end of the U.S. elections, how does that jell with the fact that nothing has happened for 10 months? In fact, I repeat my plea—we desire peace, but we are apprehensive because we don't want another year of stalemate.

Kissinger: I will see the Foreign Minister again. As we have told him, there are no decisions, but the President has clearly said there has to be progress toward peace. The President has never confined it to one front. We recognize Syria as the center of the Arab nation.

President: Give President Asad my best. I hope we have a chance to get together very soon.

194. Memorandum of Conversation[1]

Washington, June 21, 1975, 9:15 a.m.

PARTICIPANTS

    President Ford
    Dr. Henry A. Kissinger, Secretary of State and Assistant to the President for National Security Affairs
    Lt. General Brent Scowcroft, Deputy Assistant to the President for National Security Affairs

Kissinger: I got Dinitz in alone and told him it was an outrage. He said Rabin maybe would be willing to give the oil fields unilaterally if we won't put anything forward until 1977. We might be able to do that. But I must say I think they have decided to bring you down. That to me is clear.

President: Dinitz thinks if Sadat turns down the proposal and we write a letter, Rabin may come up with this.

Kissinger: Yes. The advantage to Sadat is he doesn't have to sign anything at all. I didn't want to say anything in front of Eilts.

President: We'll keep this in our hip pocket.

Kissinger: Asad and Fahd are both anxious to see you. We could stop in Vienna and meet with both.

---

[1] Source: Ford Library, National Security Adviser, Memoranda of Conversations, Box 13, June 21, 1975, Ford, Kissinger. Secret; Nodis. The meeting was held in the Oval Office at the White House.

195. Memorandum of Conversation[1]

Washington, June 21, 1975, 9:20–10:22 a.m.

PARTICIPANTS

    President Ford
    Dr. Henry A. Kissinger, Secretary of State and Assistant to the President for National Security Affairs
    Amb. Hermann F. Eilts, U.S. Ambassador to Egypt
    Joseph J. Sisco, Under Secretary of State for Political Affairs
    Lt. Gen. Brent Scowcroft, Deputy Assistant to the President for National Security Affairs

Secretary Kissinger: The Syrian may have seemed tough to you,[2] but he seemed more willing to go along with our strategy, if we have one, than ever. This is the best meeting we have had with them; we all agree. They are anxious for you to meet with Asad. Maybe in Vienna. They prefer Austria, but it can't be Salzburg.

Mr. President, I thought Hermann should give you a frank assessment of what we now face.

Ambassador Eilts: When I saw this map[3] cold, I thought Sadat would be very upset and negative. He has been saying for a year he had to have the passes—and the oil fields, but especially the passes. They are different from the oil because of his military. He is committed to the Army on getting the passes.

In connection with my presentation, I will ask that I speak only to Sadat and Fahmy, but he will probably insist on Vice President Mubarak, who is the Army's eyes and ears.

Sadat will say this is worse than they were offered in March—when they didn't show us a map. The only new elements are the two company positions, but still under Israeli guns. They [the Israelis] are insisting on military positions on the western slope of the passes.

There is even a difference between the two sides on how long the passes are. Egypt considers the Giddi to be nine kilometers long; Israel goes further west. The Mitla Egypt says is 21 kilometers; Israel says it's longer.

At some point, Sadat will explode—or implode, as he does. This is where his heart problem comes in.

---

[1] Source: Ford Library, National Security Adviser, Memoranda of Conversations, Box 13, June 21, 1975, Ford, Kissinger, Ambassador Hermann F. Eilts (Egypt), Joseph Sisco. Secret; Nodis. The meeting was held in the Oval Office at the White House. Brackets are in the original.

[2] A reference to Syrian Foreign Minister Khaddam; see Document 193.

[3] See footnote 2, Document 191.

He will review this in light of Salzburg.[4] He is euphoric about his meetings with you. Now, he will say, "Is this the best the U.S. can bring forth after three weeks? What kind of reliability can we put in the United States?"

The President: What should we do?

Ambassador Eilts: He has been looking to us to present a plan ever since December. We could now ask him whether he would want us to present an interim plan or to go to Geneva with a comprehensive plan, with the understanding that not much can happen for 18 months. I think we must offer to put forward some plan.

Secretary Kissinger: I think if you present a plan, you must accompany it with an aid package not exceeding last year's—$600–$700 million.

The President: I was thinking of this last night. It seemed to me we should submit the aid bill with no more than last year, and whatever we think Egypt needs.

Kissinger: But it all needs to be done together. The only thing the Israelis understand is aid levels—otherwise they will go on debating us forever. Their duplicity is unbelievable. When we were debating my meeting Gromyko on 7–8 July, Rabin knew he was to be in Germany 8–11 July and he said not a word.

Sadat must understand that we can't impose an interim settlement and six months later ask for something on Golan or a comprehensive proposal. An Egyptian-Israeli Agreement would also explicitly be discriminating against Syria. We would, before going that way, have to consult with the Saudis to prevent Arab coalescence over this.

You don't have to decide right now. I am instead thinking that if Sadat rejects it, you should then send a letter to Rabin. We will be drafting one.

I had Dinitz put to Rabin moving the Egyptian line forward to encompass the two company forward positions and Rabin has rejected it.

Here are the talking points I would propose that Hermann use.

[The President reads the Talking Points at Tab A.][5]

The President: If the Israeli Cabinet fell, and they had elections, what would happen?

Kissinger: It would be a mess. It would take nine months to sort out. If Rabin went into the election, he could win overwhelmingly. If he was soft, Peres might become the Prime Minister. As Prime Minister he

---

[4] See Documents 177 and 178.
[5] Tab A, entitled "Talking Points," is attached but not printed.

would be more conciliatory than Rabin. But for nine months your hands would be tied.

The President: What would happen to Dayan?

Kissinger: Dayan in opposition would be a massive problem. As Prime Minister, he would settle. He is the only one who would settle on the Golan. He said in '67 that as long as Israel held the Golan, the conflict with Syria would continue and Israel had to decide whether it wanted war or peace.

Ambassador Eilts: What Sadat can never understand is why the United States, which provides Israel with everything, cannot move them.

Kissinger: Because Israel thinks they can work their way with the Congress. And we must remember this is a carbon copy of the strategy Israel pursued against Rogers in '71.

The President: As I indicated yesterday, unless Sadat accepts this, which I think he will not, we should indicate we will put forth an interim plan. We then are in a better position at home to show we went the last mile. We can show the equipment deliveries last fall, and so on. That protects our flanks and puts us in a better position to go to a comprehensive plan.

Kissinger: I would hold back just for now talking of an imposed American plan. I think maybe it's a better tactic to write formally to Rabin asking for reconsideration. If you take Israel to the mat, it's 55 to 45 they will accept it—but then we are in real trouble with respect to Syria. We couldn't go again on the Golan in a year. Writing Rabin a letter I strongly favor. You could do it in such a way that it is almost an American plan.

Mr. Sisco: You can go back and recite what our presumptions were on the passes and the oil fields.

Kissinger: It puts you in a good position.

The President: The night of the dinner, Dinitz and I got off together and I asked him where their military installations were. The impression I got from him is that the area they are really concerned about is in the vicinity of the airfield, east of the passes.

Kissinger: The Israelis have gotten the whole issue of the passes totally confused. Before Egypt could make an assault, they would have to get across the Canal. By then Israel would have mobilized. They have decided politically not to do it. They have pocketed the American warning station and the non-use of force.

196. Memorandum of Conversation[1]

Washington, June 23, 1975.

PARTICIPANTS

President Ford
Dr. Henry A. Kissinger, Secretary of State and Assistant to the President for National Security Affairs
Lt. General Brent Scowcroft, Deputy Assistant to the President for National Security Affairs

Kissinger: I will be giving a speech in Atlanta tomorrow. Let me read you the part on the Middle East. [He reads it.][2]

President: There is nothing wrong with that. It may be interpreted badly by them.

Kissinger: I think by the end of the year you will have the Jews moving heaven and earth to defeat you.

President: As long as I know what I am doing is right, I will take my chances.

Kissinger: They are unspeakable. They have now published their concessions—making it even less likely that Sadat will agree.

[Omitted here is discussion unrelated to the Arab-Israeli dispute.]

Kissinger: I will have an Israeli-Egyptian option paper. Whichever way you go, you may want a record that they have rejected your request for reconsideration. They have written us off. I never imagined they could ignore a Presidential phone call[3]—they never even acknowledged it. Now they are putting out their offer of a corridor [to Abu Rudeis] designed to show they have been forthcoming.

President: When does Eilts see Sadat?

---

[1] Source: Ford Library, National Security Adviser, Memoranda of Conversations, Box 13, June 23, 1975, Ford, Kissinger. Secret; Nodis. The meeting took place in the White House. All brackets, with the exception of ones describing omitted material, are in the original. According to the President's Daily Diary, the meeting took place from 9:05 until 9:28 a.m. (Ibid., Staff Secretary's Office Files)

[2] Kissinger addressed the Southern Council on International and Public Affairs and the Atlanta Chamber of Commerce. He remarked that the United States "can never lose sight of the fact that U.S. foreign policy must do its utmost to protect all its interests in the Middle East." He also stated that the ultimate goal of the United States was "to find solutions that will take into account the territorial integrity and right to live in security and peace of all states and peoples in the area. To reach that goal will require concessions by all parties. We are determined to persevere in pursuit of what we consider the fundamental national interest of the United States—the security and economic well-being of our country, of our allies and above all of the peoples in the area that demand it." (*Washington Post*, June 24, 1975, p. A1)

[3] Presumably a reference to the June 13 telephone conversation; see footnote 10, Document 187.

Kissinger: Later today. I would be astounded if Sadat accepted, because this will look like pressure on him. It might seriously affect Sadat's perception of our ability—when Israel is totally dependent on us. Maybe give Dinitz a letter on Thursday.[4] Then brief selected Congressmen on all aspects of the negotiations.

President: I think we would have to show them the maps and everything.

Kissinger: I disagree with Eilts about the road. To have an Israeli road within sight and rifle range of the Egyptian road, with the Egyptian road demilitarized and the Israel road not, and with the Egyptian road . . .

[Omitted here is discussion unrelated to the Arab-Israeli dispute.]

---

[4] June 26.

---

197. Memorandum of Conversation[1]

Washington, June 25, 1975, 11:17 a.m.–12:24 p.m.

PARTICIPANTS

President Ford
Dr. Henry A. Kissinger, Secretary of State and Assistant to the President for National Security Affairs
Lt. General Brent Scowcroft, Deputy Assistant to the President for National Security Affairs

[Omitted here is discussion unrelated to the Arab-Israeli dispute.]

Kissinger: That gets us back to our friends. This is one of the most inconceivable things I have ever seen. With their support, with the upturn here, they could put you over the top. Rabin complained to Marquis Childs[2] about our giving things to Jordan and not Israel. We gave them 200 tanks in April—that's more than we give in two years for Jordan.

---

[1] Source: Ford Library, National Security Adviser, Memoranda of Conversations, Box 13, June 25, 1975, Ford, Kissinger. Secret; Nodis. The meeting was held in the Oval Office at the White House. All brackets, with the exception of ones describing omitted material, are in the original.

[2] Marquis Childs, an American journalist.

[He shows the map.][3]

Egypt now can't accept, and this freezes the Israeli position. It makes us look like liars to the Syrians. This is a confrontational position. They are hitting the Jewish community. My children will suffer. They are gambling on being able to take us domestically. Dean Rusk said if what is presented in this country is Semitism, then the only counter is anti-Semitism. If it is true that Israel is not a satellite of the U.S., neither is the U.S. a satellite of Israel. He got tremendous applause.

President: This is a crass effort to undermine our foreign and domestic policy.

Kissinger: Javits is willing to support lifting the Jackson amendment, if they will just give a token increase in emigration. Last year 38,000 wasn't enough. He said he wanted five minutes with you—he said he knows you are mad at him, but he wants to tell you as long as you promise you won't let Israel be destroyed, you can do anything else.

President: Why not show him the map?

Kissinger: I think you shouldn't bargain—these guys know the country isn't with them.

President: But if one of them knows what the Israelis are really doing . . .

Kissinger: I would do it with Ribicoff then. He is more honorable. Javits is too opportunistic. When I was on the ropes he ignored me. I don't trust him. Let him come in; hear him for ten minutes. Tell him you support the existence of Israel but they cannot run our foreign policy.

President: Let's get somebody down here who is Jewish and respected so someone knows the facts.

Kissinger: Javits will want to appear as the moderator. We shouldn't bargain with them.

We have heard from the Egyptians. Their answer is very tough.

[He reads from Eilts' cables.][4]

President: Where does that leave us?

---

[3] Not attached. The Israeli Government released its proposal and an accompanying map on June 24 in Jerusalem. (*New York Times*, June 25, 1975, p. 1)

[4] Not further identified. Eilts's report on his June 23 meeting with Sadat, when he presented the latest Israeli map and proposal, is in telegram 6195 from Cairo, June 23. Sadat was "clearly dismayed," calling the Israeli proposal "totally unacceptable." (National Archives, RG 59, Central Foreign Policy Files) He subsequently wrote to President Ford; see footnote 2, Document 199.

Kissinger: We have drafted a letter to send to the Israelis. I recommend you give it to Dinitz Friday.[5] That would keep it out of the press for a day or so in Israel, and Congress will be out here.

[General Scowcroft left briefly and returned.]

You think about the letter. I don't want to rush it by you. I think we should not give Israel the Egyptian counterproposal;[6] we should not tell him we will ask for reconsideration.

Tell Dinitz he is accredited to the President of the United States. If this continues you will have to take it to the American public. Be icy cold. You have no other choice. I think the tougher you are, the more chance there is to move them. Only you can do it. We have to know by the time I meet Gromyko.[7] I think they will cave.

President: You are more optimistic than I am. I think we have to present them something which they accept or reject.

Kissinger: I think your view is the right one. I think Brent should protest to Dinitz in the sharpest terms today.

President: I should be prepared for a press conference question.

Kissinger: I would be as icy as can be. I would stick to the outline of our policy as I gave it in Atlanta.

[General Scowcroft hands the President a copy of the Atlanta speech.[8] He leaves briefly, and returns.]

President: I would send a letter to Banking, Ways and Means—four committees—saying that shortly after recess we are prepared to move.

Kissinger: We'll do a draft and clear it with Simon. I don't think it is bad to get Simon out ahead on this.

On the letter, I think we need enough of the history in, so if it is leaked it is all there.

President: I agree. We may even have to release the letter.

Kissinger: If Israel had done this gracefully, think what a good position we would now be in.

President: I like the letter. It is firm, not belligerent. I will study it.

Kissinger: Do you agree on having Dinitz in?

President: Let's make it Friday morning.

---

[5] June 27. The letter is attached to Document 200.

[6] Fahmy and Gamasy gave Eilts an Egyptian map and counterproposal in a meeting on June 24. (Telegram 6274 from Cairo, June 25; National Archives, RG 59, Central Foreign Policy Files)

[7] They met in Geneva July 10–11.

[8] See footnote 2, Document 196.

198. Memorandum of Conversation[1]

Washington, June 26, 1975, 10:10–10:25 a.m.

PARTICIPANTS

    President Ford
    Amb. Malcolm Toon, U.S. Ambassador to Israel
    Dr. Henry A. Kissinger, Secretary of State and Assistant to the President for National Security Affairs
    Lt. General Brent Scowcroft, Deputy Assistant to the President for National Security Affairs

The President: When are you actually leaving?

Ambassador Toon: Saturday.[2] I am stopping to pick up my daughter in Rome.

The President: Are you going to straighten out Italian politics?

Ambassador Toon: I'll leave that to Volpe.

The President: We certainly want to maintain a friendly relationship with Israel, but it must be on the proper basis. We are having problems with them. The proper attitude is to keep them at arms length but on a friendly basis. You will have a greater role than some of your predecessors. If we don't get an agreement, we will have difficulty both with Israel and with the Jewish Community here. I am willing to take them on because I think we are right and I am disillusioned with how they have behaved in March and now.

Secretary Kissinger: Are you up to date?

Ambassador Toon: I don't know.

Secretary Kissinger: The map we got was no different from the one we saw here. You saw the letter?[3]

Ambassador Toon: Yes. It was very good. I am in thorough agreement. I read the record and I agree with you on their lack of flexibility. What I don't see is where we go. I think you have to take on the Jewish Community.

---

[1] Source: Ford Library, National Security Adviser, Memoranda of Conversations, Box 13, June 26, 1975, Ford, Kissinger, Ambassador Malcolm Toon (Israel). Secret; Nodis. The meeting was held in the Oval Office at the White House. The previous Ambassador to Israel, Kenneth Keating, died of a heart attack on May 5 and was replaced by Malcolm Toon, who was appointed on June 9.

[2] June 27.

[3] Apparently the letter from Ford to Rabin, presented to Israeli Ambassador Dinitz on June 27; see Tab A, Document 200.

Secretary Kissinger: The Jewish Community is getting very uneasy. Max Fisher and Len Garment, and even Danny Kaye,[4] who is an all-out Israeli supporter but knows nothing about the past.

The President: If the record gets published, the zealots will be shocked. It is a record that our government can be proud of. I hope it doesn't have to take place. If there is a confrontation, your job will be tougher. We recognized this possibility when we picked you.

Ambassador Toon: I appreciate your confidence. I hope I will be kept abreast of everything happening.

Secretary Kissinger: You will know everything they know.

Ambassador Toon: The Hill is getting uneasy. I think you should talk to them.

Secretary Kissinger: We will, it is a matter of timing. We have to know something before I meet with Gromyko on the 10th and 11th of July.

The President: I think Israel is totally misreading the letter from the 76 Senators.[5] Several of them have written qualifications, and it doesn't really commit them to any specific proposals. When it gets to dollars, many of them will have a different attitude.

Secretary Kissinger: If Israel won't agree with the letter, I think there is no choice but to go for an overall settlement.

[Omitted here is discussion unrelated to the Arab-Israeli dispute.]

---

[4] Danny Kaye was an American actor, singer, and comedian who served as an original UNICEF Goodwill Ambassador beginning in 1954.

[5] See Document 175.

---

199. Backchannel Message From Secretary of State Kissinger to the Ambassador to Egypt (Eilts)[1]

Washington, June 27, 1975, 0250Z.

8. 1. You should pass through Fahmy following response from President Ford to President Sadat's latest letter, emphasizing that it

---

[1] Source: Ford Library, National Security Adviser, Backchannel Messages, Box 5, Sandy Circuit, June 1975, Incoming. Secret; Sensitive; Eyes Only; Immediate. Sent with the instruction to deliver at the opening of business.

was sent through same privacy channel you used in transmitting Sadat letter.[2]

2. *Begin text*:

Dear Mr. President:

Ambassador Eilts has conveyed your private letter to me, and I want to respond in the same spirit of personal trust and complete candor.

You know from the Ambassador of my disappointment with the Israeli position, which I nevertheless felt we had to relay to you in order to give you the opportunity to form your own judgment.

After reviewing carefully the conterproposal which Deputy Prime Ministers Fahmy and Gamasy outlined on your behalf to Ambassador Eilts,[3] I have come to the judgment that the best way to proceed is as follows.

I believe that to pass your proposal formally to Israel at this time would in all probability lead to a termination of negotiations. As a next step, I am therefore sending a formal message to Prime Minister Rabin requesting Israel to reconsider its position.[4] I will inform you as soon as I have received Israel's reply, and we can then determine together how best to proceed.

Meanwhile, I am proceeding on your assurance that your Salzburg formulations stand,[5] provided your fundamental requirements of Israeli withdrawal from the passes and the oil fields are met. I appreciate your expressions of confidence, Mr. President, and want to reiterate my determination to achieve early progress, in whatever way proves most feasible, toward peace in your area.

With warm regards and personal good wishes, Gerald R. Ford. End text.

3. *FYI*: In conveying foregoing, if you believe it would be helpful, you may make the point as your personal view that there is a high probability that Egyptian map would be leaked once it was given to Is-

---

[2] The letter was sent in a backchannel message from Eilts to Kissinger, June 25. In the letter to Ford, Sadat complained "that the Israelis are neither willing nor capable, for one reason or another, to move along the long and arduous road to peace." Sadat expressed his belief in Ford's "sincerity and determination" to prevent stagnation in the disengagement negotiations, but he insisted that "the present Israeli attitude is an obvious result of the continuous United States pampering to Israel." Without movement, Sadat would call for the convening of the Geneva Conference "to which all the parties should be invited, including the P.L.O." He concluded that it was "high time for the United States, as a way out, to propose an American map reflecting its proposals in order to avoid a complete and drastic deterioration of the situation." (Ibid.)

[3] See footnote 6, Document 197.

[4] See Tab A, Document 200.

[5] See Documents 177 and 178.

raelis. Given leaks that have already occurred from Israel with respect to the Israeli proposal, this would reveal graphically the present irreconcilability of Israeli and Egyptian positions and make matters much more difficult should we subsequently put forward our own proposal based on what we know the Egyptian position is from Salzburg talks and Sadat's latest letter. *End FYI.*

200. Memorandum of Conversation[1]

Washington, June 27, 1975, 9:58–10:09 a.m.

PARTICIPANTS

    President Ford
    Simcha Dinitz, Ambassador of Israel
    Mordechai Shalev, Minister of the Embassy of Israel
    Dr. Henry A. Kissinger, Secretary of State and Assistant to the President for National Security Affairs
    Lt. Gen. Brent Scowcroft, Deputy Assistant to the President for National Security Affairs

President: As you know, we have sent to Sadat the plan that was submitted to us. I am sure you understand their reaction.[2] Sisco will give you the details. Their reaction is understandable. We submitted it without comment. In brief, they rejected it and the reaction was that they would immediately call for the convening of Geneva.

Henry will meet with Gromyko on July 11. At that meeting we will discuss Geneva, and indicate one way or another whether we will go to Geneva.

I have a letter here [Tab A], which I would like you to transmit to Prime Minister Rabin as soon as possible. It is a frank letter setting forth what has happened since I came into office, and it lays out factually, and I think accurately, what has taken place. I am convinced that if there is to be any chance of success, there has to be movement out of the passes and a better situation in the south. I have looked at the map that was in the *New York Times*,[3] and there is little similarity, either in the

---

[1] Source: Ford Library, National Security Adviser, Memoranda of Conversations, Box 13, June 26, 1975, Ford, Kissinger, Israeli Ambassador Simcha Dinitz. Secret; Nodis. The meeting was held in the Oval Office at the White House. Brackets are in the original.

[2] See footnote 4, Document 197, and footnote 2, Document 199.

[3] See footnote 3, Document 197.

north or south. If we are to progress, the *New York Times* map is more acceptable but for the passes. I want an interim agreement, but we have to get action on the passes and the oilfields.

It is a frank and factual letter. I have tried to be strong in my conviction that we need action in order to continue the relationship we have had in the past. My record in favor of a strong independent Israel is clear. But I think the only way to keep that is to move on an agreement. I want to work with the Prime Minister; I will work with him, but we have to move. I do not think it useful to get into a political confrontation with the Jewish community in the United States. I have dear personal friends in the Jewish community. I want to work with them cooperatively for the goals we both seek. But we must have progress. Any political activity would be very, very unhealthy. It would not be good for your country, for my country and for our relationship. To come back to my point, we can get a settlement. We can get an interim agreement, but there has to be some give.

Dinitz: May I say a few words, Mr. President?

President: Of course, but I don't think we ought to get into a debate on the substance.

Dinitz: I thank you for inviting me in. We never doubt your friendship for Israel. I want to say just a word on *The New York Times* map. It is not our map. On the road to the south, the problem is the topography. We will make the zone as wide as the topography permits. We want to work in harmony, not confrontation, with the United States. I know your many friends. No good can come to Israel by taking a divergent course.

President: It is not good for either of us, or for the peace of the world, for us not to work together. We are concerned about peace in the area and the world.

Tab A

Letter From President Ford to Prime Minister Rabin[4]

Washington, June 27, 1975.

Dear Mr. Prime Minister:

We have now presented to President Sadat the Israeli positions on an interim agreement between your government and Egypt, and we

---

[4] Top Secret. A handwritten notation at the top of the page reads, "Handed to Amb. Dinitz by President Ford at 9:50 a.m., Fri., 6/27/75."

Second Egyptian-Israeli Disengagement Agreement 747

have reported to you separately the Egyptian reaction. This is a time, therefore, to review where matters stand and the choices before us.

I want first to recall the main elements of the strategy which Israel and the United States have pursued together since I became President. In our first conversation last September,[5] you asked that we give the Israeli Government time to consolidate its position in order to pursue an effective peace strategy. You urged that we undertake a maximum military supply effort which would strengthen the Israeli sense of security. I can recall vividly the point you made to the effect that a secure Israel would be a flexible Israel. We acceded to your requests in the spirit of trust and friendship that has grown up between us. We did not urge negotiations for many months—despite very great pressures to do so. I substantially increased the amount of military aid recommended unanimously by all our departments.

From the beginning we made clear two points that would have to be met if an interim agreement between Egypt and Israel were to succeed: (a) It would have to involve Israeli withdrawal from the two strategic passes in the Sinai and the Abu Rudeis oil fields. (b) Egypt could not in such a partial agreement subscribe to a full declaration of non-belligerency. The latter point led to extended discussion between us of the elements of non-belligerency and how those of most concern to Israel could be met in practical ways short of a formal declaration of non-belligerency. Your Government provided us with its own views on alternative ways of dealing with this problem.

Our records show that these points were made either by me or by Secretary Kissinger on numerous occasions. The record is clear that at no time did you or Foreign Minister Allon state that these were unfulfillable conditions. On the contrary, your Government pressed the United States to assist the parties, to undertake several missions to the area within the framework which had been discussed frequently between us. If I had thought that Israel would not accept the context which we had described, I would not have committed the United States to continue the step-by-step approach, and I would not have sent the Secretary of State to the Middle East to conduct negotiations which were foredoomed to failure.

In the course of the negotiations, we have met the Israeli concerns one by one on most of the principal issues. In case of an agreement, Egypt would be prepared to give assurances that it would not use force to resolve the remaining problems between Israel and Egypt. On the question of the duration of the agreement, we believe the formula proposed by Israel—that this agreement would remain in effect until su-

---

[5] See Document 99.

perseded by another agreement—would be accepted. We have also informed your government of an arrangement which we believe would be possible for assuring continuation of the mandate of the UNEF for several years. Several solutions have been suggested to deal with the problem of the Israeli intelligence station which would meet the requirement of early warning and add to the durability of the agreement. As you know, some progress has been made in easing the boycott.

In my recent conversation with you[6] I stated frankly that I was deeply disappointed—indeed disillusioned—with the position taken by the Israeli Government which led to the suspension of the negotiations last March. I presented to you several modifications I thought possible in the Egyptian position following my talks in Salzburg.[7] In light of this, and after the misunderstandings last March, my hope was that as a result of our most recent conversations Israel's position would have evolved further to embrace those minimum requirements of an interim agreement which we have described to your Government over the past year.

As you know, I consider the changes you communicated to me during the recent discussions to be inadequate, and I informed you that I would transmit the Israeli position to President Sadat without recommendation. In our conversations in Washington, there was no essential change in Israel's position on the passes, and the manner in which access to the oil fields was offered presents significant problems. Given his well-known position which we have described to you for a year, the reaction of President Sadat was to be expected.

With the formulation of your latest position and President Sadat's reply, we are now at a point where fundamental decisions must be made.

I do not regard standing still a realistic choice. It runs an unacceptable risk of leading to another war and to a coalescence of the same international forces which Israel faced in 1973 and early 1974. Since such a situation would jeopardize fundamental U.S. interests—most of which are also of deep concern to Israel—the U.S. cannot be expected to underwrite such a course of action.

Our judgment is that Israel's position is forcing the evolution of negotiations toward an outcome which runs counter to the interests of the United States and the world. We therefore want to hold open the opportunity which I presented to you in our telephone conversation[8] to reconsider the Israeli position within the parameters which we have

---

[6] Apparently a reference to Ford's meetings with Rabin in Washington on June 11 and June 12; see Documents 183 and 184.

[7] A reference to Ford's meetings with Sadat; see Documents 177 and 178.

[8] Presumably the telephone conversation of June 13; see footnote 10, Document 187.

discussed with you since last summer—parameters which in our considered judgment pose no threat to the vital interest which Israel and the United States share in the security and well-being of your country. No lesser proposal can now meet the need. If your Government does not feel able to do this, we must reserve our course on next steps, and explain to our people the Administration's appraisal of our national interest in this matter.

Mr. Prime Minister, the matter before us goes to the very core of American-Israeli relationships. It is not a public relations problem; it is not a matter of a difference of view between the Legislative and Executive Branches of our Government since, when all the facts are known, the Congress will support my conclusions as to the national interest. It is a matter of whether our two Governments over the coming months and years will continue to work in common endeavor as we have in the past. I need not add that I hope very much that close cooperation for the future will be the outcome.

Mr. Prime Minister, it is a source of profound regret to me that matters have reached such a point—particularly since the impasse is so unnecessary. I have written this letter with candor, in the spirit of friendship, in understanding of the values we share, and in continuing commitment to the survival of Israel. It is in this spirit that I request a reconsideration of the position of the Israeli Government and an early reply.

Sincerely,[9]

---

[9] Printed from an unsigned copy.

201. Memorandum of Conversation[1]

Washington, June 27, 1975, 10:23–10:45 a.m.

PARTICIPANTS

President Ford
Senator Jacob K. Javits (Republican—New York)
Dr. Henry A. Kissinger, Secretary of State and Assistant to the President for National Security Affairs
Lt. General Brent Scowcroft, Deputy Assistant to the President for National Security Affairs

[Omitted here is discussion unrelated to the Arab-Israeli dispute.]

[Senator Javits:] I told Henry I wanted five minutes to give you the feeling of the American Jewish Community. It is deeply devoted to Israel. Consistent with that, it is deeply devoted to America. If the President would lay it on the line and say this is in the American interest, it would be agonizing. If there is no doubt that we will provide Israel with military equipment immediately. Their worry is we will use military equipment as leverage and undermine what they think they need for their defense. If that is laid to rest, I think the rest is manageable.

At least 15 years ago I was in the office of Chief of Protocol in Israel and they began to talk sensitive matters. I reminded him I was an American Congressman and they shouldn't discuss anything in front of me they wouldn't say before any other Congressman.

President: I think you know the way I have voted and spoken. I am a firm friend of Israel.

Senator Javits: I know.

President: I have hundreds of Jewish friends. I am deeply convinced an interim agreement is the best. But it may fail. The odds are not good because of the problem of the passes. To make certain that Israel is strong unilaterally and secure, I was far more generous than my advisors recommended. The result is that Israel is far more secure than before the war or at any other time. They will tell you that. There has to be flexibility on the passes. Without them, they will be more secure than they were before. There is no question about their military security. I don't understand their lack of flexibility. I don't want to have to go to Geneva but we can't have a stalemate.

I hope our good friends here and in Israel know we think it is in their and our best interests. It is in our mutual interest to get an interim settlement.

---

[1] Source: Ford Library, National Security Adviser, Memoranda of Conversations, Box 13, June 27, 1975, Ford, Kissinger, Senator Jacob Javits. Secret; Nodis. The meeting was held in the Oval Office at the White House.

Senator Javits: Are the Egyptians just sweetening us for the eastern end of the passes?

President: They want our friendship and help. They want to show independence. If they don't get it, they will be forced to go elsewhere.

Kissinger: Remember that Egypt isn't asking for the passes for themselves. They would be UN.

Javits: I assume that all the variables are within your command.

Kissinger: I think we can find a solution. Sadat made some additional concessions at Salzburg to get Israel out of the passes—including electronic surveillance. He now thinks Israel has just pocketed these concessions and not moved.

Javits: The American Jews think Israel is so exposed that they would fall on the Israeli side on anything that Israel thought it needed for its security. You have to be thoughtful on this point. American Jews have thought that Israel was being asked to be given up ground for paper. Israel must be in harmony with the U.S. and American Jews haven't grasped that. They fear that our interest in the Arabs will lead us to ask Israel to make concessions in exchange for an American moral commitment. So there is no pressure from American Jews to push Israel to make concessions relating to security.

President: If we don't get some movement, I have to lay the record out—that is not good.

Javits: Rabin said they would have to reconstruct their whole defense line. Would we help them—give them enough to do that?

President: They would still have their main line.

Kissinger: The side issues have all been sorted out. Their mines, forward lines and logistic installations would have to be moved—but we would support a jog in the line so the logistic installations wouldn't have to move. We would support a six-month transition in the north to give them time to reconstruct the line.

Javits: How long would it last?

Kissinger: There are two aspects. The first is that the agreement would last until it is superseded by another agreement. That Israel knocks aside—and shouldn't. The other is UNEF. We can get three years there.

Javits: The crisis for Israel is the United States. It is extremely desirable to have a settlement and not to go to Geneva. Those are the two real points for American Jews.

Kissinger: Geneva is a lousy way to have to go. You know, it brings all the Arabs together, brings the Soviet Union in, and forces a consideration of all issues comprehensively.

202. Memorandum of Conversation[1]

Virgin Islands, July 1, 1975, 9 p.m.

PARTICIPANTS

Secretary of State Kissinger
Israeli Ambassador Simcha Dinitz
Deputy Under Secretary Eagleburger

Dinitz: The Prime Minister wants to make a serious effort to save the situation and to prevent a crisis. The Israeli Government is facing a difficult decision. It is imperative that we have (a) all the information possible and (b) alternatives which would make it possible for us to avoid the crisis. We believe that a crisis with the United States would have the gravest consequences for Israel, for the U.S. and for the world. The Israeli Government is aware of these consequences.

Everything I will say from now on is from Rabin although it may not be verbatim text.

At the same time the Israeli Government cannot take decisions that will hurt its security dispositions. Also, it should not look as if the Israeli Government is making decisions under pressure.

Secretary: I said that. Then why are you always leaking?

Dinitz: The leaks don't come from us.

Secretary: The Groewald article came from you. Americans wouldn't leak that I was angry with Israel. That line is part of the Israeli campaign.

Dinitz: Mr. Secretary, a part of our relationship has always been faith and trust. I can tell you that only Shalev and I knew what was going on and neither one of us leaked. No one in Israel knew. But when the White House spokesman announced that the President had seen Ambassador Dinitz for eleven minutes,[2] that ought to have made it clear to everybody that there was a difficult situation. Even Scowcroft admitted it was a silly statement.

Secretary: I at first thought the Groewald article came from us and I raised hell with Sisco about it. But Groewald is a White House reporter and the line sounds very much like an Israeli line.

Dinitz: My press spokesman said it was clear to him that it didn't come from the State Department but did come from the White House.

---

[1] Source: National Archives, RG 59, Records of Henry Kissinger, 1973–77, Box 23, Classified External Memcons, May–December 1975, Folder 3. Secret; Nodis. The meeting took place at Caneel Bay in the Virgin Islands. Brackets are in the original.

[2] See Document 200.

Secretary: Yes, but who would say that Kissinger is angry at the Israelis, other than the Israelis? However, if you say it didn't come from you, then I will accept that.

Dinitz: I did not do it.

Secretary: I hope you will remember that I also said that it cannot look as if Israel is doing things under pressure.

Dinitz: When the line started to come out of the White House, Shalev called Larry[3] and I called Scowcroft. We all tried to stop it.

Secretary: Go ahead with what you have.

Dinitz: It is important that the Israeli Government not make decisions under pressure and without sufficient information from you. In the end the risks are up to us. Therefore we must act with full knowledge of the details.

The Israeli Government also accepts that it must do all that it possibly can to avoid a crisis. The U.S., we believe, should also be interested in doing what it can. The crisis could destroy our relationship. Israel would be hurt severely; the U.S. and the prospects for peace would not be better off for it.

Secretary: I agree.

Dinitz: It would be politically and strategically destructive. The Prime Minister therefore has instructed me to explore with you on a personal basis.

He has asked for a clarification of certain items so that we may understand what can be done and what is expected of us.

You will recall that when the two of us met in the last meeting[4] you said there were actually three possibilities: 1) accept the Egyptian proposal made at Salzburg, even though we don't know exactly where the line would be east of the passes; 2) each go his own way; 3) Israel propose suggestions of its own. And finally, of course there must be no pressure.

The Prime Minister feels there is no sense for us . . .

Secretary: There is a fourth possibility. We could propose a line; that the Egyptians urged us to do and I have resisted it. The President would be eager to do it.

Dinitz: The Prime Minister feels there would be no sense in coming to the Cabinet and proposing something on the summit, something to adopt a line in regard to the pass, then bring it to you, and have you say, "Sorry, it's not answering the question." It is imperative that we

---

[3] Larry Eagleburger.
[4] Probably a reference to the meeting in New York on June 15; see Document 188.

have some idea what you would accept—of what the U.S. would find acceptable in order to make an agreement viable.

The Prime Minister fights in the Cabinet and then fails. There would be no sense in that.

Secretary: You're absolutely correct.

Dinitz: There are a number of things the Prime Minister needs to know in order to see if we can arrive at an understanding.

(They look at map)[5]

1) We need to be sure when the Egyptians talk about a military line that it includes the present buffer zone, that is the red line.

2) What is acceptable to the Secretary of State in regard to the passes and the east slope? What is it you have in mind? Do you need several kilometers between us?

3) Is the line south of the passes between the passes and the corridor to the oil fields acceptable to you? You have not commented on that before.

4) If we move the line to the east of the passes, is it possible to have compensation to the north to protect our logistics?

5) What are the requirements for changes of the corridor to Abu Rudeis?

6) Can the early warning system be manned by a combination of Americans and Israelis and American and Egyptian personnel respectively?

7) What does easing of the boycott mean?

8) What does easing of diplomatic conflict mean?

Secretary: Simcha, it is heartbreaking that we weren't talking like this eight months ago. (Discussion now off the record for several minutes). Let's now go back to the ... Incidentally I would like to know the things you say Nixon promised Sadat. Sadat certainly didn't raise any of these with Ford when they were in Salzburg.

Simcha, it was not until that Thursday evening[6] that I understood what Rabin was up to. Once I had a chance to think about it, I recognized that it made strategic sense. In any presentation of the pros and cons, Israel must come out worse. There can be no real quid pro quo because you're giving up territory. Thus my time-wasting strategy.

Dinitz: I understand and I agree. We are afraid that the Egyptians when they have built up their military might will seek to force a solution by military means.

---

[5] Map is not attached, but a final status map is printed in Appendix B, Map 4.
[6] Thursday, June 12. See footnote 5, Document 184.

Secretary: That may well be. Another problem we have is that we must avoid getting into a polarized Middle East situation. If we are not careful, we will ultimately be in another Vietnamese-type problem.

Dinitz: I know.

Secretary: Rabin is by far the best available man to run Israel now.

(Discussion off the record for several minutes).

Dinitz: With regard to our timetable, I have a suggestion. There are two dates that drive us. One is our Government meeting on Sunday.[7] And the second is your meeting with Gromyko.

We are not trying to stall but if we can take some time, it would be better. We want to avert a collision course. The Prime Minister has begged that I tell you that we are not trying to waste time.

Secretary: What I needed was a sense of your strategy, of your strategic problem. One briefing by Gur would have made such a difference.

You know if you move from the assumption that we are not out to hurt Israel, then when our judgment was that the passes were a domestic political issue in Israel and not a military one, then you can understand why we took the position we did.

There was that problem and then the problem of not understanding the distinction between nonbelligerency and non use of force.

Dinitz: Mr. Secretary, I sat next to the President at dinner recently. He at one point said let's talk as friends, not as the President of the United States and the Ambassador of Israel. I said with pleasure, Mr. President. He then said, "What is the bare minimum that you need for an agreement?" I said, "Mr. President, there can be no agreement without leaving us in some part of the passes because it endangers the logistic system in the north." The President said he understood.

Secretary: I thought the Prime Minister was speaking of keeping enough of the passes to keep the Likud off his back. It was not clear that more was involved until that Thursday night.

Dinitz: Also there is the Sisco report of his conversation with Gur.[8] Gur said that under some circumstances we could do without the passes. What he meant, though, was in connection with something like a 20-year treaty with 200 kilometers between us. Then the passes would be neutralized in such a situation. That is still in my opinion doable.

Secretary: It's senseless.

Dinitz: Perhaps. Some day we will come to it though, when the time is right. That's why I don't push for nonbelligerency now. That's

---

[7] July 6.
[8] No record of conversation has been found.

why I've knocked down the proposal for now. I don't see any political sense to it now, though there is some military logic.

Secretary: By the way, I'm not all that eager to get an English translation of the Golan book.[9] Tell Rabin to forget it. The more people who see it, the more likely it is to get out.

All right, let's talk about business.

Dinitz: OK. The Prime Minister wants to know what is acceptable to you before he tries to get anything through his Government. There is no sense in getting something that you then reject.

So let's turn to the clarifications.

The first one is: Can we be sure that the Egyptian military line in the new agreement will be extended to the present U.N. buffer zone. Do they understand this?

Secretary: I thought I made that clear in Salzburg but I've seen no indication of it in their proposals since. There was, of course, the Gamassy proposal to move just east of the passes and have their forward line up to your present main line. But that we told them wouldn't work. We told Sadat that orally and he then told us that he would stick to the Salzburg proposals. Then we sent him a letter and we got an answer on Sunday.[10]

I think it will be a problem but not an issue between us. I cannot give you an ironclad guarantee but it will not be an issue between us.

Dinitz: OK. It's agreed between us; if the Egyptians don't accept, you will support us?

Secretary: I don't want to tie our hands completely. At this point the Salzburg line is at the edge of the U.N. line.

I have to say that everything that has been told to us by the Egyptians since casts doubt on their accepting the idea. But in response to your proposal . . .

Dinitz: We don't want a situation where . . .

Secretary: No. I understand. The only reason I can't give you a flat answer . . . you will recall that during the last disengagement agreement, you made small adjustments. You went back a kilometer or two here or there.

Dinitz: Yes. That was a gesture.

---

[9] Israeli journalist Matti Golan published *The Secret Conversations of Henry Kissinger: Step by Step Diplomacy in the Middle East* in 1975, which included secret conversations between Kissinger and Israeli officials. The Israeli Government initially banned the book for including classified material leaked to Golan by some Israeli officials but later allowed its publication.

[10] Neither letter has been found.

Secretary: Dayan, Elezar and I moved the line back a little bit here and there.

You will recall that during the negotiations there was a time that I asked you to move back. I want to leave room in the negotiations for that kind of adjustment. But essentially I have no passionate feeling on this. It will not lead to a confrontation between us. It's not a major thing.

Dinitz: Now comes the difficult question. What is acceptable from the U.S. point of view with regard to the eastern line on the eastern slopes of the passes, both with regard to the Gidi and the Mitla?

Secretary: I am now a bit confused. You finally have it into my head that there is a military reason for what you're doing. I didn't understand that until Sunday in New York.[11]

Dinitz: The Prime Minister says we cannot go further without losing the summit.

Secretary: I am telling you that without movement to the eastern slopes, we will not get an Egyptian agreement.

Dinitz: Are you saying that as long as we are on the summit, it won't work?

Secretary: I wouldn't recommend it to Rabin. Sadat has so committed himself to the other Arabs on the passes that . . .

I just say that I thought that as long as the passes were not militarily important, you would hold one end of the passes and they the other. This was my idea of a compromise. That is still my view but I cannot decide how deep that means you must go.

I don't want to say where the line should be. The distance from your main line to the summit isn't much. It looks to me that wherever you put yourself on the eastern slope can be presented as substantially out of the passes.

Dinitz: That's true. But it depends on how you measure it. The Prime Minister is afraid to present anything because he doesn't know what would satisfy you.

Secretary: It is a hell of a responsibility for me to indicate something precise.

Dinitz: I understand but we have a problem. Can we militarily defend it?

Secretary: There are two problems. First, what is Sadat up to? It is clear that he wants to weaken your hold on the Sinai. It is also clear that he wants an excuse for a period of peace. Our Ambassador thinks, and

---

[11] See Document 188.

it is my view as well, that how he presents this whole issue to the other Arabs is his big problem.

I would think that if you are well back from the summit, whether 2 or 3 kilometers I can't say, would be enough.

Dinitz: You say 2 or 3 kilometers from the summit.

Secretary: It would have to be on the eastern slopes, something he, the Prime Minister, could present as an exit from the passes, even if it isn't. I would like to be in a position to say to the Egyptians that even if we and they don't agree with everything you've offered, I am firmly convinced that we cannot get more without a monumental fight. That's what we want to be able to tell the Egyptians.

Dinitz: So—I'm not trying to pin you down—

Secretary: I'm in a fix. I consider that even with an Israeli proposal, there could be failure for a number of reasons.

Dinitz: But there would be no break with us.

Secretary: That's right. I think that if you get off of the summits toward the exits, we would try to look at it with sympathy.

Dinitz: Can you give me an estimate with regard to the blue line?

Secretary: (looking at map) This is 698, this 750, this 400, this 500, this 600. Somewhere in here (pointing at map), but don't hold me to it.

Dinitz: I think you've said then 2 or 3 kilometers from the summit.

Secretary: That is right. But the Prime Minister has to be ready to negotiate over it.

Let's turn to your other questions and then the south. That also won't work.

Dinitz: Is the line which we proposed between the passes and the southern corridor acceptable? Is it acceptable to the Egyptians and to you?

Secretary: I have no problem with it. They haven't raised it, but their line is forward of that.

Dinitz: We don't want to be in trouble with you.

Secretary: They didn't take any objection to that but their whole line is forward of it.

Dinitz: Yes, but then they went back.

Secretary: That is right. They went back to their Salzburg position but there was no line given.

Dinitz: I understand. We have no map from them. They do have one from us. That's part of the problem. The real question is, though, are we going to have trouble with you?

Secretary: I have no reason to suppose that it isn't substantially acceptable. I just haven't had any response from them.

The Gamassy map,[12] of course, is senseless to talk from. It's useless, and I told them so.

Dinitz: The Prime Minister doesn't want a situation in which we redraw the line and then you say to us, the Egyptians can't accept, and we're in trouble.

Secretary: There is a difference. For a year we said that the passes and oil fields were necessary. But we were never told in a way we could understand that that wouldn't work. We will be in a difficult situation if it can be said that the Israelis could have gone back 5 kilometers and didn't.

Dinitz: The Prime Minister will have to show the Cabinet a map or say that he can't draw a map sufficient to satisfy the U.S. If we were to draw a map and you then rejected, then he would be out of office in 24 hours. You know there are people in the Cabinet who say that every time you come in and ask for more, we end up giving it to you.

Secretary: I can't decide on these other lines. The Egyptian line was further over (pointing to map).

This is substantially all right. But I want a little flexibility for the actual negotiations. We're not talking about a problem of massive proportions.

My hope is that if we can settle the major issue of the passes, then we could talk about other issues as we did before.

Dinitz: We are now trying to assure your success.

Secretary: A lot depends on how the break comes about. If we are pushed by constantly escalating Egyptian demands for more, then we will tell them that we can only be pushed so far.

But again, the two big problems are the passes and the oil fields. The other lines will not be breaking points for us.

Dinitz: All right. The fourth question: Is it possible, to the extent that there might be a change in our line in the passes, to move the northern line (our blue line) westward in order to protect our northern complex?

Secretary: Anything that is not too visible—anything clearly designed to give strategic protection, I think we can handle, but not 5 or 10 kilometers.

You must also be careful not to let the center begin to look like a narrow pocket. If it begins to look like a question of dominating this road (points to map) that is another thing.

Well, some minor adjustments could be handled, I think.

---

[12] See footnote 6, Document 197.

Dinitz: Good. Question 5: What are the changes that the U.S. sees as needed with regard to the southern corridor to Abu Rudeis?

Secretary: I, frankly, am stumped. I told Sadat in Salzburg that a narrow corridor of a few kilometers was the best I could get. Sadat says parallel roads are out of the question—that is roads next to each other.

Dinitz: Next to each other?

Secretary: Yes. Next to each other—roads side by side. Then there is also the necessity of constructing a road on his own territory so that he can use one road while you use the other. That's also a moral issue.

Dinitz: You know the military significance of this. It is the only connection with Sharm-Al-Sheikh.

Secretary: I can't judge it, frankly. What I can understand is that it is tough for him to have Israeli armored vehicles along the road in full view of the Egyptians on their road—and Egyptians who are not armed at that.

Dinitz: Where we see places where construction can be far away, then, you think we should do it? You recognize that this gives Sadat control over the seacoast while we are dictated by topography.

Secretary: Yes. So I can't give you a good answer, except that you should get back as far as you can. For psychological reasons, I would recommend you move your line into your territory as far as you can.

Dinitz: That means the U.N. line . . .

Secretary: Yes. Now this Haman Faroon radar warning system . . . He would accept Americans in these two stations.

Dinitz: On the roads—Sadat objects to parallelism whenever they are close? You say move as far as we can to make the U.N. zone even wider. Once we do what we can, then are you saying there wouldn't be a breaking point between us?

Secretary: If you can remove some of the egregious things such as roads so close to each other.

Dinitz: Yes. Rabin has seen the area and is pessimistic about your question of the distances being changed.

Secretary: To go to Geneva under conditions of failure is not in our interests.

Dinitz: I understand. You don't need to convince me.

Secretary: For whatever it is worth, Ambassador Eilts thinks that Sadat has a massive problem with his military. He has a problem with the whole concept of a civil administration and then with regard to the very narrow zone along the coast. Our Ambassador believes these are all massive problems for Sadat.

Dinitz: What if there were U.N. personnel between, even when they're only 200 meters apart.

Secretary: I don't know what to say. I don't know enough about the topography. On the Egyptian map, the two positions look irreconcilable. We have never supported the Egyptian map.

If the Haman Faroon station were American instead of Israeli, could we then move that section of the road further inland, or is it a question of topography?

Dinitz: If that issue were solved, then the question of nearness would only occur in two places, right?

Secretary: Yes.

Dinitz: Can the stations be manned by U.S. and Israeli and U.S. and Egyptian personnel respectively?

Secretary: I have no way of knowing. Maybe Americans with Israeli liaison officers. Is that your concept? We can't have mostly Israeli people with 1 or 2 Americans.

Dinitz: I'm sure it would be some of each. Perhaps it's a question of presenting the data.

Secretary: If land lines were built directly from the station; if we automated it; if it were manned by Americans, but you didn't have to wait for the information—would that work?

Dinitz: We want to be in on the gathering process, not just analysis.

Secretary: You would have to be guaranteed instantaneous read-out—you can assure the Prime Minister of that, ironclad assurances. As to Israeli liaison, I'll have to check.

Dinitz: What exactly are the Egyptians prepared to do in the area of economic boycott?

Secretary: Sadat told me that he can't break the boycott formally; Fahmi said that they couldn't invite American firms to Egypt, but any that want to operate in Egypt can.

Dinitz: Will they be taken off the boycott list?

Secretary: I didn't check that.

Dinitz: It's one thing to allow them to operate in Egypt; it is another with regard to being deterred from operating in Israel. The black list keeps them out of Egypt but it also deters them from investing in Israel.

When we talked in March, you said that they were willing to take 3 or 5 off the black list.

Secretary: I don't know. I assumed that they meant that they would permit them to operate in Egypt.

Dinitz: This is not crucial but it would help the Government to sell the agreement to the people. Further clarification would be helpful.

Now the next question: What are the Egyptians prepared to do in the fields of diplomatic and propaganda warfare?

Secretary: Fahmi told me Egypt won't pressure African Governments that want to resume relations with you. They might make pro forma noises, but no pressure. As to propaganda, all but the PLO station in Cairo would stop.

We'd better check for more clarification on that too.

Dinitz: Now, let's go back to a reiteration of the points that were covered when Rabin was here.

First of all on Syria: with regard to Syria, is it clear and understood that an interim agreement with Syria would only constitute cosmetic changes and that to the extent there was no agreement with Syria it would not affect U.S.-Israeli relations in the political, economic or military spheres?

Next, as to the Sisco idea, we would be prepared to consider it at a later stage. The Prime Minister is prepared to consider it, but only at a later stage.

Secretary: That would ease our problem considerably if it could be handled.

Dinitz: I'm saying that the PM is not ruling out unilateral moves, just that he can't OK them now. It hasn't yet been discussed with the Cabinet.

Secretary: Do Peres and Allon know?

Dinitz: Yes. I don't know what their opinion is, however,

On Jordan, is it understood that negotiations with Jordan can only be within the overall settlement framework?

And will the U.S. continue to oppose the PLO?

Secretary: On Jordan, we made a big mistake last summer by not trying to get an interim agreement. Now that is not a live possibility.

On the PLO, there is no problem.

Right now, there is no possibility for an interim *or* an overall agreement with Jordan.

Dinitz: In regard to the Geneva Conference, is it agreed that for the duration of the interim agreement with Egypt, the U.S. will not submit an overall plan for a settlement and will refrain from such plans when they are not made in coordination with Israel? We will, of course, be in constant touch with the U.S. and once we agree on something, then there would be no problem.

Secretary: You did not get a clear-cut answer from the President on that question.

Dinitz: I'm talking in terms of three to three and a half years of the UNEF. We are, of course, willing to discuss an overall agreement but don't want a confrontation with you over this.

Secretary: Will we be putting forward a proposal within a three-year period? It is tough to give such a flat commitment. You know my views. If your prediction is correct and I stay in the next Administration, there will be many ways to handle it.

My basic strategy is to exhaust the parties so that we can move toward a break toward non-belligerency. In this sense I disagree with the President with regard to the wisdom of putting forward an overall plan.

Dinitz: On the Syrian position, can I say that we are agreed, especially if a breakdown in the talks were to be followed by unilateral moves on our part?

Secretary: Yes. But I don't want to read that answer in the newspapers.

Dinitz: Now, a second point on Geneva. We would like consultations with regard to timing and procedures to be followed at Geneva. We want, for example, a ratification of our agreement with Egypt, if we arrive at one.

Secretary: If you want Geneva that quickly. Look, if we get an agreement, we will do our best to waste time through the elections and then we will look at it again. How, I haven't yet thought through.

Dinitz: We don't want any substance at Geneva.

Secretary: Well, there will have to be substance at Geneva. But there doesn't necessarily have to be any resolution. The PLO issue, for example, will take months.

Perhaps there would be no need for Geneva at all if we get an agreement with Egypt. We have no overpowering desire for a Geneva conference.

Dinitz: In any event, we want coordination between us over policies before we go to Geneva.

Secretary: I don't want to give you a veto over our every action. What you want is not to have an open break with us. Isn't that right?

Dinitz: One point the Prime Minister made is that if and when there is a Geneva Conference, one subject we can use to waste time is "Peace." What is it, for example?

Secretary: I agree completely. But there is no point in going through this agony if then we are going to rush into Geneva.

Dinitz: I know. But there is a school of thought, Mr. Secretary, in Israel that we will be seduced into another agreement in the north, into going to Geneva, and other similar actions once we have an agreement with Egypt.

Secretary: Your domestic situation makes things very difficult for you, I know. If you look at history, you will see that great decisions are almost always made by a few people who are not understood by their own contemporaries.

Dinitz: One last point—Geneva and Syria. On an overall agreement with Syria, is it understood that while we may be prepared to change the line on the Golan, we are convinced that we must stay on the Golan?

We believe we must have this understanding anew, now, that the U.S. won't press us to get off the Golan.

Secretary: The way to handle Syria is to get less than an overall settlement with a change in the line.

Dinitz: Three bilateral points: 1) Will economic aid to meet our needs as submitted to you be supplied us? 2) are the arms we submitted via Matmon B[13] going to be supplied us? 3) On oil there are 3 subheadings: a) compensation; b) guaranteed supplies; c) storage in Israel.

Secretary: Certainly we can agree on point (c). On point (b) as I told you we will make every effort. The only problem is I don't know how mechanically we do it. On (a) it is certainly OK in principle. On your general economic needs, I don't know anyone in town who thinks $2.5 billion is necessary.

Dinitz: The $2.5 billion is not so large if you look at what it is made up of. We have asked for $1.8 billion worth of military needs, both grant and sales. And we have asked for $700 million worth of supporting assistance. Now if you want to give us $500 million supporting assistance and $200 million in food, that, of course, can be negotiated.

And if you say you can't give me a commitment to $2.5 billion, then can you give me a commitment to something around $2 to $2.4 billion?

Secretary: I tell you that I cannot give you a figure. I can tell you that it will be something substantial and something that will be done soon after any interim agreement, so that we don't have to pay a high price for it with the Arabs.

Dinitz: Something substantial?

Secretary: Our studies indicate that somewhere between $1.5 billion and $2 billion is about right. But don't hold me to this. I am certain that we can come to an agreement.

Dinitz: On the arms, I think we have no problem here.

Secretary: If we're going to do anything, it should be done quickly.

---

[13] See Document 96.

203. Memorandum of Conversation[1]

Virgin Islands, July 2, 1975, 8:45 a.m.

PARTICIPANTS

    Secretary of State Kissinger
    Israeli Ambassador Simcha Dinitz
    Deputy Under Secretary Eagleburger

(Conversation was already in progress when notes began)

Secretary: In the south I told Sadat that the best attainable would be a narrow corridor. He didn't say Yes.

It's not clear to us that at the point where a warning station would be, a road is possible There's almost a sheer drop.

Dinitz: I understood the following on the south: you accept the idea of two roads but the Egyptians don't like the idea of parallel roads at certain places close together.

Secretary: Precisely. The formal explanation is that they do not like the idea of parallelism. And the second thing is, that they don't like the idea of having to build their own road.

Dinitz: I'm trying to sum up our joint understandings. You accept the necessity of two roads?

Secretary: That's right.

Dinitz: The difference is that there are parallel roads close to each other.

Another point is that at the point where the station is at Haman Faroon, you think a road can't be built on the coast so we will check to see if a road can be built further east.

Secretary: If you give up the mountain, then conceivably a road could go on the other side of it.

Dinitz: A road exists. We want to construct a road here (points to map).

Secretary: The question is can a road be built on the other side.

Dinitz: We would use the existing road; they would build another road.

Secretary: If it's not impossible to construct it—the ridge lines here are sharply down.

---

[1] Source: National Archives, RG 59, Records of Henry Kissinger, 1973–77, Box 23, Classified External Memcons, May–December 1975, Folder 3. Secret; Nodis. The meeting took place at Caneel Bay in the Virgin Islands.

Dinitz: So you are asking if the Egyptian road can be built here (points to map) but then, again, there is a question of the nearness of the roads.

Secretary: Rabin was there. What does he think?

Dinitz: That it would be difficult, but perhaps it can be done.

Secretary: We haven't been told that it can't be done.

Dinitz: There may be space.

I know that the problems in the south can't be solved here. Maybe the Americans have some engineering ideas though.

Secretary: Eilts thinks the Army will prevent Sadat from accepting the offer from Israel as it now stands.

This is not necessarily a soluable problem. Once you say there is a need for a road, the maximum you can do would be helpful.

Dinitz: In those places where the U.N. zone would be widened.

Secretary: I am looking for visual things. For example, here it's flat. It looks like there's about 8 kilometers of flat area here. Near Ras el Suda you could take out that bulge, for example.

In your next proposal you should show as much movement as possible.

Larry, you should tell Sisco when you get back all the questions that were asked.

Dinitz: Now let me go over the timetable. 1) This afternoon when I get back, I will repeat the essence of our conversations to the Prime Minister. 2) I will meet with Sisco tomorrow morning. 3) I will leave Thursday afternoon[2] for Israel. 4) The State Spokesman will say on Thursday that in the course of the clarifications Dinitz came at his request to Caneel Bay for a meeting with the Secretary.

You want an idea of the eastern line, plus more on the south.

Secretary: Yes. I'm trying to tell you that the minimum the Egyptians might accept is the eastern slopes.

Dinitz: I understand.

I'll have to check with the Prime Minister. If we are going to pass an Israeli line to the Egyptians, then maybe we will have to clear it with the Cabinet first. You see, the Prime Minister will say either I am willing to give the Secretary a line and have him tell me whether it is worthwhile to put out in the Cabinet. Or that it won't satisfy the U.S. That's the problem as I see it. You want a final, not a bargaining line. Is that right?

---

[2] July 3.

Secretary: Yes. There is no sense in being driven back kilometer by kilometer.

Dinitz: Basically the question is one of principle rather than the line.

Secretary: In the event that you are prepared to get off the summit, then the specific line is not necessary for discussion right now.

It will be very tough for me with Gromyko. I don't look forward to stalling him for so long. I can't refuse to see him and I can't say yes.

Dinitz: You could say you're still in negotiations.

Secretary: I can't do that. I must keep them confused. He has no interest in a solution.

I don't want him to be able to go to the Arabs and say everything else has failed, now it's up to us.[3]

Dinitz: I think you overestimate the problem on the international level.

Secretary: And July 24 is the UNEF deadline.

My idea now is to send Atherton to Cairo—or Saunders. I don't want too high a profile.

Dinitz: Whatever you decide. When will you send him?

Secretary: As early as possible, perhaps Tuesday night. He could be there on Wednesday night, or, well, Wednesday afternoon. But then he would have to go to Alexandria or wherever Sadat is.

He could then meet me in Germany.

I'll be home on Saturday evening[4] or Sunday noon, in any event.

---

[3] Kissinger sent a message to Fahmy in telegram Secto 6056 from Bonn, July 12, which described his discussion of the Middle East with Gromyko. Gromyko continued to favor conducting negotiations in the framework of the Geneva conference but would not obstruct the current talks. (National Archives, RG 59, Central Foreign Policy Files)

[4] July 5.

204. Memorandum of Conversation[1]

Washington, July 2, 1975, 11:04–11:35 a.m.

PARTICIPANTS

    President Ford
    Senator J. W. Fulbright
    Lt. Gen. Brent Scowcroft, Deputy Assistant to the President for National Security Affairs

Senator Fulbright: I appreciate your giving me the time. I wouldn't take it if I didn't think it was important.

The President: It was a very timely trip to the Middle East. I would appreciate hearing your views, from your vast experience.

Senator Fulbright: Let me leave you this, which is by Jim Symington. [Tab A.][2]

I visited seven countries. I was well received, but they think my views were a reflection of American foreign policy. I think it is imperative that you make a statement about our objectives before the election. The Arabs—except Qaddafi—are the most conciliatory they have ever been. They say that if Israel will go back to the '67 lines, they will recognize Israel. Iraq was not as forthcoming. They didn't indicate they would welcome a settlement, but they would not oppose it. But Iraq is just emerging from its isolation. That is breaking down now, with recent developments with Iran, Saudi Arabia and the Kurds.

In Syria, who I thought didn't like us, the Economic Minister is a graduate of New York University. He gave me two cordial hours.

The President: Henry really likes Asad. All the countries around Israel have a different attitude than they had before.

Senator Fulbright: I used the Percy statement. I tried to explain the 76 Senators' letter.[3]

The President: Those fellows who signed the letter—they may support Israel, but I bet not to the tune of $2.5 billion.

---

[1] Source: Ford Library, National Security Adviser, Memoranda of Conversations, Box 13, July 2, 1975, Ford, Kissinger, Senator J.W. Fulbright. Confidential. The meeting was held in the Oval Office at the White House. Brackets are in the original.

[2] Tab A, attached but not printed, is a *Washington Post* text of remarks Representative James W. Symington of Missouri entered into the *Congressional Record* on February 5, entitled "Toward an American Foreign Policy." He stated that America's national interest should be the focus in the formulation of foreign policy, "so that it might be an American foreign policy with no prefixes denoting an infusion of extra-national bias or sentiment."

[3] See Document 175.

Senator Fulbright: The key to my idea—and I am a politician—is the political angle. Not that you need this advice. I have talked to Laird, Kissinger and Ingersoll, etc. You are in a unique position, as a politician. You want to be reelected. Your political opponents are critical to Israel. The question is: can you win on it? I am convinced you need to make a positive statement. This is in Israel's own interest. They are so paranoid they don't know their interest. The Israeli Government is weak and can do it only if they can say that "the damned President forced us." This is the only way we can be free of the burden which has plagued your presidency.

The President: In the next months or year, we have to lay out a comprehensive plan. Now I think there is an advantage to an interim agreement. The chances are against it, and if there is no interim agreement, we have to go for a comprehensive plan. You know the Jews will attack me, but if we posture it right, we can say we tried an interim and we just couldn't get it. I will have 208 million people with me against 6 million Jews.

You may disagree with what we are trying to do on an interim. But that will put it on the back burner for six months or perhaps through the election.

Senator Fulbright: I would just like to get this burden off you. Implementation could wait until the election. But the Arabs need to know your objective. Arafat, of course, is in a more delicate position. I think he will in fact accept the West Bank and Gaza as a place for the Palestinians to call their own. What they do with it is their problem. In five years, with a settlement, Israel would have recognized borders. We just have to get by this damned war. The Jews are propagandizing and using the underdog strategy. They are sending around brochures. I will send you one.

The President: We have been sending them arms. They are better off than they were before the October war.

Senator Fulbright: They would win a war but that wouldn't help—it would be a disaster.

The President: We have bent over backwards to help them. They do have a weak domestic situation.

Senator Fulbright: The Arabs will be terribly disappointed if nothing happens for 18 months. It doesn't have to be action, but at least not a stalemate. I think you are going to win in '76 and I think they will be reassured. The moderates have to be able to point to some progress—if not, they will be pushed out by the radicals. We have to help the moderates. When we didn't help Khrushchev, he got thrown out. You remember we wouldn't let him visit Disneyland! The same will happen to Brezhnev.

The President: Does Arafat think he can control the PLO?

Senator Fulbright: If we can make some progress, so he can contain the radicals. Publicly Arafat is still for a "secular state," but privately he would settle for the West Bank and Gaza.

The President: Not just the West Bank?

Senator Fulbright: Gaza is just a symbol.

The President: What is your impression of Prince Fahd?

Senator Fulbright: He's a powerful fellow. Khalid is a softer fellow, but he is impressive.

The President: The story is that he is weak-minded.

Senator Fulbright: He is quiet, but not feeble-minded. But they have some good people in their 40's. We have a great position in Saudi Arabia. They want to develop with our cooperation—it's the same in Abu Dhabi—they are just dying to do something. The Sheikh is an interesting fellow. They have the highest per capita income in the world.

The President: What do they do with the money?

Senator Fulbright: They built roads; they have the two finest hotels I have ever seen; ports, and factories. I am trying to get him into solar energy.

The President: Did you go to Kuwait?

Senator Fulbright: No. I went there before. I visited Iraq for my first time. There is a big opportunity for American investment. They have the biggest oil reserves, next to Saudi Arabia. There are two big rivers.

The President: They are fighting with Syria over that.

Senator Fulbright: Yes, the Saudis are trying to settle that and I think they have. The key to this war . . . everyone is apprehensive. If we could get the war settled we would have great business opportunities.

Suppose you made this statement, you could go to the Saudis and say "We stuck our necks out here, so now you help us on oil." Make a deal with them. You can't make a deal when you don't do what they are interested in.

The President: If we did lay out a comprehensive plan, is a guarantee essential?

Senator Fulbright: Israel says they want to rely on themselves, but I think it would help the Jews here. Israel was created by the UN. I think a resolution guaranteeing the borders, and the U.S. and the Soviet Union say "We agree with it and will support it." I would use the UN because they created it. I was surprised the Soviet Union said publicly they would go along. Why not?

I fear that a delay would result in Israel doing something reckless.

The President: They would be unwise to do it. The last war was bloodier than ever. I feel their support in the U.S. isn't as strong as it was before. That is why the letters.

Senator Fulbright: That is puffing, not substance.

I think it is a winning issue. The American people are tired of being whipsawed on this. *The Arkansas Gazette* blasted the 76 Senators' letter for preempting your reassessment.

The President: I appreciate your coming in and giving me this and this material.

We will do something within two or three weeks. And within the next year or so, we must come out with a comprehensive plan.

There is no question after the election. It's just a question of timing.

Senator Fulbright: I think the American people will support you. Only you can do it. Think what it would do in Europe and Japan. You would be acclaimed. Conversely, if there's another embargo and you would be blamed for being able to do something and that you didn't.

It is a great opportunity. I know it is a difficult political problem.

I appreciate the opportunity. I know I am no longer in politics, but I have been following this since the Aswan business.

[Senator Fulbright later sent the President a written report on his trip. Tab B.][4]

---

[4] Tab B, attached but not printed, is a memorandum from Fulbright to Ford, July 27, entitled, "The Middle East—An American Policy." Fulbright's memorandum covered various issues relating to the Arab-Israeli dispute. He concluded by writing: "An American guarantee of an agreed settlement, on the other hand, would clarify an ambiguous commitment, bringing it clearly within the scope of our national interest, and at the same time provide Israel with the greatest possible security under the circumstances which exist in the area."

205. Memorandum of Conversation[1]

Camp David, Maryland, July 5, 1975.

PARTICIPANTS

President Gerald R. Ford
Dr. Henry A. Kissinger, Secretary of State and Assistant to the President for National Security Affairs
Lt. General Brent Scowcroft, Deputy Assistant to the President for National Security Affairs

[Omitted here is discussion of Indonesian President Sukarno.]

Kissinger: Let me tell you about the Israeli thing. Dinitz asked me a series of questions:[2] "Where did we want the line?" I don't think we should give them one because then we are stuck with it. They want American troops in this area—there don't have to be too many. Sisco, Atherton and I are all against it. Once we have combat troops there . . . Geneva will stalemate and down the road Egypt may get restive. If we pull our troops out, we will be accused of starting a war. If we won't, we will be accused of protecting a part of the front. The Israelis think you are softening.

The President: On what grounds?

Kissinger: You had a meeting with some contributors and said to a Jew that you are anxious for a settlement and would delay your departure for Europe to get it.

The President: That is not so at all. I don't even remember his name, but I may have said to him I hope for an agreement. We never talked about the European trip.

Kissinger: This just shows you how the network works. Dinitz knows every conversation I have with a Jew. My concern is, if we go in, what will we say to the Syrians if they want us there? Or if they want Soviet troops? This arrangement would break the back of it, so it is a big decision.

The President: My reaction was it is hazardous and will give us a Congressional problem. Why can't we compromise on the warning stations?

Kissinger: That is my thinking. Perhaps we could increase the number of warning stations. Maybe up to five—not more.

---

[1] Source: Ford Library, National Security Adviser, Memoranda of Conversations, Box 13, July 5, 1975, Ford, Kissinger. Secret; Nodis.

[2] See Document 202.

The President: I don't think we could go for a combat troop presence. It would cause much more of a problem than warning stations.

Kissinger: Should I tell Shalev that we can't agree but we can increase the number of warning stations?

The President: Yes. Could we have them manned by civilians or mostly civilians?

Scowcroft: Probably civilian technicians.

Kissinger: They asked for a line in the east, but I wouldn't give them one. In the south they would draw the line straight down, so it would be a bitter pill for Sadat to accept the Israeli line. The Egyptian line also cuts out the Israeli logistics base.

The President: I think Israel should keep that base.

Kissinger: I would like to call Shalev and tell him there can be no area presence, but there can be warning stations. You are absolutely firm that something has to happen?

The President: Absolutely.

Kissinger: On seeing Rabin, I am not anxious to. I would leave it up to them. We have nothing to say. They asked more questions. On Syria, I said the unilateral gesture might get us through 1976. On aid, I said we could go higher with an agreement than without one. I said I didn't think we could go as high as $2 billion. He said they could go down to $2.3 billion.

The President: That is almost as much as the entire foreign aid program.

Kissinger: They want reimbursement for losing the oil fields and a guarantee of oil supply in case of an embargo. We could use the Iranian oil.

We have a deal with Iran if you want it. I will show you it Monday morning.[3] It is a five-year deal, either at or less than the OPEC price. It is payable in 5-year notes, non-negotiable and non-interest-bearing for the first year. Zarb and Greenspan are afraid that if DOD buys the oil, it would lead to a government purchasing agency. Greenspan is worried about whether you should give the Saudis the same deal. That is a nice kind of problem to have. I would give them the same deal for the same amount but ask for a better deal if they want more. I would wait to see if the Saudis came to us. This would end the charges of cuddling the Shah and the money would be spent only in the United States.

The President: On the Israeli thing—I would tell them there can be no combat personnel, and only civilians in the warning stations. It has

---

[3] July 7.

got to be way down on the eastern slopes. Israel keeps the logistics base, but they've got to widen the line in the south.

Kissinger: What I would like to do—the best Jewish group is the Klutznick one. It is the most responsible, but they are unpopular in Israel. Maybe I should bring them down and briefly have you see them.

[Omitted here is discussion of the Conference on Security and Cooperation in Europe.]

206. Memorandum of Conversation[1]

Washington, July 8, 1975, 10:15–10:55 a.m.

PARTICIPANTS

The President
Dr. Henry A. Kissinger, Secretary of State and Assistant to the President for National Security Affairs
Lt. General Brent Scowcroft, Deputy Assistant to the President for National Security Affairs

[Omitted here is discussion unrelated to the Arab-Israeli dispute.]

Kissinger: Let me show you the Dinitz proposal.[2]

—The line in the south has been changed but it is still not satisfactory.
—The shift in the line north and south of the passes puts the passes in a bag.
—They want the Israelis to be left at Umm Khisheiba.

If they move the line west from what Egypt has already seen, I think it would be hopeless. How would it look to the Egyptian masses? What can Sadat say he got?

The President: I think we have to tell them we can't buy it. If they want to do it, that's it.

Kissinger: I am getting to the point of thinking it can't be done, that we tried and we have to move to a comprehensive proposal.

The President: I think we have to demonstrate we offered the four warning points, to show the American people we made an effort.

---

[1] Source: Library of Congress, Manuscript Division, Kissinger Papers, CL 282, President's File, July 1975, Folder 1. Secret; Nodis. The meeting was held in the Oval Office at the White House.

[2] The proposal is the referenced map in footnote 5, Document 202.

Kissinger: They will say they did everything we asked, got out of the passes, and it still didn't work.

I think you should go on television and lay out the situation. Don't blame Israel. Say we will give military support to Israel, but not enough to sustain them in this position.

The President: Did Dinitz ask about aid?

Kissinger: Yes. I mentioned at Caneel Bay[3] that they could get under $2 billion with a satisfactory settlement. I mentioned maybe $1.7 billion. He said yesterday that was unsatisfactory.

The President: I was thinking in terms of $1 billion.

Kissinger: If there is nothing, I would go with $700 million.

The President: I would say it is unsatisfactory and they must do better.

Kissinger: I will see Rabin on Saturday in Germany.

[Omitted here is discussion unrelated to the Arab-Israeli dispute.]

---

[3] See Document 202.

---

207. Memorandum of Conversation[1]

Washington, July 9, 1975, 10:02–10:40 a.m.

PARTICIPANTS

The President
Dr. Henry A. Kissinger, Secretary of State and Assistant to the President for National Security Affairs
Lt. Gen. Brent Scowcroft, Deputy Assistant to the President for National Security Affairs

[Omitted here is discussion unrelated to the Arab-Israeli dispute.]

[Kissinger:] I would like to go over the Israeli thing. De Borchgrave[2] says we would be better going for an overall agreement. This thing looks like it is developing into something for which we will pay

---

[1] Source: Library of Congress, Manuscript Division, Kissinger Papers, CL 282, President's File, July 1975, Folder 1. Secret; Nodis. The meeting was held in the Oval Office at the White House.

[2] Arnaud de Borchgrave was an American journalist.

an exorbitant price. I don't think we can agree to shifts in the line to put the passes in a bag.

I also don't think we can concur to do nothing for 3–4 years without their agreement.

On the four American points, they can't be checkpoints, but just warning posts, with simple radar.

We also can't promise we won't push them on Syria. Informally we can agree to what you and Rabin discussed.[3] If it blows up, we should not be bitter but just move to an overall.

If Rabin will agree not to bend the lines west, there is a chance. But there is still a problem with the south. If they acted with some generosity toward Sadat, they would have a real chance. For the Egyptians to have a road, with the Israelis on the heights looking down on them . . .

President: Make sure you tell them we will put our people into the warning station, so if we have to go public . . .

Kissinger: If it breaks down I would go on television and say it hasn't worked and we will go for an overall settlement. Don't describe it in detail then. I could the next day give a detailed briefing. Then four to six weeks later we can put out our plan.

[Omitted here is discussion unrelated to the Arab-Israeli dispute.]

[3] See Document 183.

208. Telegram From Secretary of State Kissinger to the Embassy in Egypt[1]

July 12, 1975, 1747Z.

Secto 6062. For the Ambassador from the Secretary. Subject: Meeting With PM Rabin. Please pass the following message from me to Fahmi and Sadat.

[1] Source: National Archives, RG 59, Central Foreign Policy Files. Secret; Immediate; Nodis; Cherokee. Repeated to the Department of State. The telegram was sent from the Secretary's aircraft.

1. Secretary has just completed a three-hour meeting with Rabin,[2] which focused on clarifications which the Israelis have been seeking from us regarding bilateral assurances, the elements of the interim agreement, and how such an agreement relates to the Syrian problem and a Geneva Conference.

2. The principle therein which the Secretary wishes to report is that the tentative position discussed by Rabin with us at today's meeting, while reflecting improvement, fell short of what we believe are the necessary requirements from Egypt's point of view, and we therefore pressed for further changes both with respect to where the Israeli forward line would be drawn as well as on the question of access to the oil fields. After much discussion and firm insistence on our part, Rabin agreed to take into account the considerations which we outlined and he will discuss the matter further with his Cabinet tomorrow.

The Israeli Ambassador to the United States, Simcha Dinitz, will return to Washington by midweek at which time we will then be in a position to brief Ambassador Eilts in detail on where matters stand on the interim agreement so that Hermann can report back to Fahmi and President Sadat fully about Friday.[3]

3. You should assure Fahmi we are very mindful of the fact that President Sadat will be making a major speech on the 23rd and that the question of the UNEF extension is very much to the fore as well. In this connection you should say that it is the Secretary's judgement that President Sadat will be able to make a judgement as to whether the interim agreement is achievable when he receives your full report upon your return from the Washington briefing. In short, our present assessment is that we are hopeful but we are still uncertain at this point that what you will be able to present to him at the end of next week will meet Sadat's principal considerations.

Kissinger

---

[2] The memorandum of conversation of the meeting between Rabin and Kissinger, which took place in Bonn on July 12 from 10:15 a.m. until 1:17 p.m. at Schloss Gymnich, is in the Library of Congress, Manuscript Division, Kissinger Papers, CL 158, Geopolitical File, Israel, July 12–22, 1975.

[3] July 18.

209. Memorandum of Conversation[1]

Washington, July 17, 1975.

PARTICIPANTS

The Secretary
Under Secretary Sisco
Ambassador Eilts
Assistant Secretary Atherton
Deputy Assistant Secretary Saunders
Jerry Bremer, Notetaker

SUBJECT

The Middle East

The Secretary: Have you shown them the map?[2]

Sisco: Just in a preliminary way.

The Secretary: What is your reaction?

Eilts: It's not good enough but it's an improvement.

The Secretary: Which one did you see?

Sisco: I showed them both.

Eilts: This is the first one. (spreading map on table)

The Secretary: They will go beyond the line here to here (pointing to map).

Eilts: That's helpful.

The Secretary: He has told us that he can go back here (pointing to the south).

Sisco: Hermann said he thinks we have a massive problem in the south.

The Secretary: Up in the north, I doubt if we can change.

Sisco: How close can we get to the blue line?

The Secretary: There's no way of knowing but he said they can do better than this.

Eilts: In here? (pointing to map)

The Secretary: Yes. They can show it on the map as Egyptian civilian administration but we could make a private deal with Egypt that

---

[1] Source: Library of Congress, Manuscript Division, Kissinger Papers, CL 346, Department of State Memorandum of Conversations, Internal, July 1975. Secret; Nodis. The meeting was held at the Department of State.

[2] No map is attached, but a final status map is printed in Appendix B, Map 4.

while that is true the UN will not exercise civilian administration there. Since there's no population, there won't be anything to administer and there won't be a problem. It will enable him to show an uninterrupted access to the south.

I think it should be handled as follows. The map they will send us will be this map with this (pointing to line on map) moved back a little. I think we should then draw for you this fallback line and say that when I got the first map I said I wanted more ideas. (By the way, you can't leave at 5:00 tomorrow with the map coming at 2:00). Then we should take the map and draw it with the changes and say Rabin said we would make these changes. In my personal opinion, they can do better here (in the south), but not in the north. Don't say it's agreed to yet. Then he can still get something out of us. You see what I mean?

Eilts: This here is up to them to decide (pointing to map). But it must be in the UN zone.

The Secretary: Tell them we are thinking of some mechanisms we have previously worked with in which tethered balbons could be used.

Saunders: That's not immediate. It would take at least a year.

The Secretary: It takes nearly that long to get an agreement.

Eilts: What happens here (in the south)?

The Secretary: Wouldn't it ease Sadat's mind if we could say "if we can find a road to build, they will agree to move their line to let it be built." That is at least morally more acceptable to Sadat. Then they can use the roads on alternate days. I'm not sure he'll accept it but if it shows some meeting of his concerns. Then he'll be able to show on his maps that he's got a stretch and here in the south. It can be temporary.

Saunders: You still have to build the Egyptian road here (pointing at map).

Sisco: It's physically doable, though it will take two years to do.

The Secretary: You have to raise that with the Israelis.

Atherton: The map seems to show tracks here.

Saunders: We have looked at that. There are 90 kilometers in the wadis but it would be a major job.

Sisco: Most of the access in that area is by water anyway.

The Secretary: What do you think, Hermann?

Eilts: I think we're getting in to the range.

Sisco: Did you want to say a word about the companies, Henry?

The Secretary: There would be no companies if they are out of the passes.

Eilts: But *will* they be out of the passes?

The Secretary: They will be 500 meters from the Parker memorial.[3]

Sisco: What is it?

The Secretary: It's a fountain pen that's in the ground and they've called it the Parker memorial. (laughter)

Eilts: Egypt may argue that their forward line should move.

The Secretary: How far?

Eilts: 5 or 10 kilometers.

The Secretary: That's impossible. We have to be realistic. In the last phase we may beat them into two or three kilometers or, alternatively, into two companies.

Saunders: In practical terms, the single use of the road from here to here will be for an extended period.

The Secretary: Would they want to use the road?

Saunders: I think they will just to assert themselves. That is, the Israelis.

The Secretary: But would Egypt?

Saunders: Yes, it's their only way to the oil fields for people and equipment.

Eilts: They will certainly want to use it.

The Secretary: It will take to 24 months to build it to here as I understand it. How long to here?

Sisco: That part is undoable.

Saunders: (unfolding pictures) Let me show you how difficult it is on these maps.

The Secretary: We still have massive problems then right? (looking at pictures) That I've seen. That's to here isn't it? It's about 50 kilometers?

Sisco: That's what it says.

The Secretary: Where is this?

Saunders: Right in here (pointing at map) where it turns back from the east.

The Secretary: Well I think you should show this to Sadat. Say the problem to here is solved but not below unless we can move the Israelis somewhere below.

Saunders: That's where it's insoluble. There is no way to move back from the coast. They would have to have two roads side by side.

---

[3] According to Kissinger's memoirs, the Parker Memorial was a stone slab dedicated to a British engineer who had built roads in the Sinai during the 19th century. (*Years of Renewal*, p. 452)

The Secretary: But at least with two roads they could use them on alternate days.

Saunders: If you're going to alternate, you might as well only build one road. It's a 24–30 month project with lots of money involved.

The Secretary: The way to present it to Sadat is to give him all three options. (Sisco hands the Secretary a cable)[4] Have we done an answer to this?

Sisco: Yes, we've developed a reply which has to go out tonight.

The Secretary: What is the language of the Presidential letter to Sadat?

Sisco: I haven't pulled it out yet. But I thought it was to make a determined effort to push them out.

The Secretary: You should have seen it, Hermann. Here was Dinitz this morning[5] giving me a long Talmudic explanation of why the Egyptians had not renewed UNEF. I think they just screwed up. I said you know you guys are crazy. These were just a couple of guys in Cairo blowing off steam. Unless you understand that you don't understand the Egyptians.

Sisco: I'll show Hermann the paper.[6]

The Secretary: They said they were trying to establish certain legal principles with UNEF that they could use again etc. etc. I tell you they were just blowing off steam. Fahmy wanted to show he was the brightest guy in class.

Eilts: Although I think Sadat was about ready to do it himself too. They certainly were working on each other.

The Secretary: It's funny to hear them tell these heroic epics about how they've exposed somebody; I've never yet found anyone who knows he was exposed. (Laughter)

Eilts: That exposure weapon is their big weapon.

The Secretary: How often have they said it. They've said they've exposed Asad how many times?

Eilts: Why do they want the six stations?

The Secretary: Because there's a road connecting the two passes in addition to the road between the two passes. And then in case Egyptians might hop over one, they need one on each end of the road connecting the passes. They asked for six and I said four. This will then be

---

[4] Not further identified.

[5] Kissinger met with Dinitz from 10:52 a.m. until 12:30 p.m. (Memorandum of conversation, July 17; Library of Congress, Manuscript Division, Kissinger Papers, CL 158, Geopolitical File, Israel, July 12–22, 1975)

[6] Paper is not further identified.

an epic Rabin victory. These two are on higher ground, while these two are in the passes.

 Atherton: Those poor guys on the post will have nothing to do.

 Eilts: What are we talking about—20 people each?

 The Secretary: In these, maybe as few as five.

 Saunders: You have to give them at least enough for a card game.

 The Secretary: I would think maybe 10 or 15 at the most.

 Sisco: It will cause problems on the Hill.

 The Secretary: You should explain to Sadat that we'll have to put this to Congress and it will cause all kinds of hell. It will be very sobering to the Congress with respect to the Israelis. We will generate a debate on what we should never do and they will be more cautious later on. I think it will flush out lots of concerns.

 You should lead Sadat to know that if he can't accept this in principle, we can't push much further. Within the framework of the negotiations, we can get slight improvements on the line here and there and we can probably get the SAMs up to the canal.

 Eilts: That would help with the military.

 Saunders: Moving the SAMs has a practical effect. It covers their troops.

 The Secretary: Don't tell him it's certain. Just say it's based on a private talk with Rabin and he is not sure he can get it through the Cabinet. It certainly cannot be settled before the shuttle. On the shuttle, either we can move the line a little bit or we can get the two companies. He can count on these yellow areas here and also here and he can do a little better here (on the South).

 Sisco: In the shuttle? Shouldn't we get into it now?

 The Secretary: I want to show it on the map as something Rabin will get later, but not now. This he can get now. For him it's better to show progress during the talks. You should try to see him with Fahmy.

 Eilts: There's no way I can do it without Mubarak if he's in the country.

 The Secretary: All right, tell him I've got Rabin's assurance on this during the shuttle. In addition, I think, but don't have assurances, I can get more down here in the south. We can remove the bulge more and make a massive effort to make this part of the Egyptian Civilian zone. Warn him the Israelis want a station here. We are prepared to show it as U.S. administered with Israeli personnel. We don't have enough personnel to man them. He can have Egyptian personnel in his under U.S. personnel.

 Tell him we discussed this with the Israelis and that we'd also like to give American equipment with this and the Israelis did not object.

Sisco: I understood you to say that we would *not* give American equipment.

The Secretary: No, just that we would not give the most sophisticated equipment. We cannot give the most sophisticated equipment.

Saunders: The easiest thing is for the Egyptians to move in their own equipment since they're not trained on ours anyway.

Eilts: We have to reckon with the fact that Gamassy will see the station as having a limited value.

The Secretary: We have worked with the tethered balloon concept and I asked the Israelis about it.

Saunders: That's why we are in the tethered balloon business. They are the ones who asked us to develop it.

The Secretary: I think we are getting to the point where you have to convince the Egyptians that if the basic concept does not now go, we'll have to go to Geneva.

Eilts: Okay.

The Secretary: I think if he wants to put his romantic qualities to the test he can sell this. There are two areas here which are still troublesome.

Eilts: The pass thing is helpful.

Saunders: This stuff in the north here is really niggardly though.

Sisco: We should avoid supporting it.

The Secretary: It's not a question of supporting it. Say that beyond this we'll require an effort of the magnitude not distinguishable from that needed for an overall agreement. Up here, I think they should go back (pointing to north).

Sisco: I can't believe we can't get them back to the blue line all the way along in the north. I just don't believe that Rabin draws a line loosely like that.

Saunders: There certainly is no military argument.

Sisco: It doesn't touch his installations.

The Secretary: It does touch the installations because it means that there is no heavy equipment ahead of them.

Eilts: It's an improvement taken as a whole.

The Secretary: I would think we could move the thin-out line back here. I don't think they'd move the forward line back to here (pointing to the north on the map).

Saunders: If there's a chance to make an effort, we can get an improvement there.

Sisco: The important thing is in the south.

The Secretary: My worry is that these guys have sold it in the Cabinet on the basis of trading one thing for another. I told him in Bonn[7] that we'd understand the bulge. Do you think, Hermann, the bulge is important enough to go on the barricades for?

Eilts: No, I would make an effort but I wouldn't go on the barricades about it. Other problems exist. The big thing is getting them out of the passes even if it's only 500 meters.

The Secretary: Assuming the Parker memorial is at the end of the passes. Who was Parker anyway? I think the road is further down than the mountains.

There are two choices. Either we go through the same business and tell Rabin it's unacceptable and we're passing it along without a recommendation. I think there's a 50–50 chance the Israelis would say the hell with it. My personal evaluation is that Rabin is the biggest dove in the Cabinet and is doing what he can. Hal, what do you think?

Saunders: I doubt we can get much more.

Sisco: I think Egypt will come back and then we will go back to the Israelis.

The Secretary: Sadat has to decide whether he finds it roughly acceptable. I'd tell Dinitz tomorrow that we will pass it along only with a stronger statement but with the understanding that we need some room for negotiations but not massive changes.

Eilts: Do the Israelis know about Sadat's final map?

The Secretary: No, I was afraid it would leak. They would have used it to prove it was hopeless. I described the first map orally. I never told them about the second one.

Atherton: What if Sadat asks again for an American map?

The Secretary: This is as close to an American map as we'll get since I've told the Israelis what they can do.

Atherton: It's not quite everything.

The Secretary: But we judged that giving an ultimatum would not work.

Saunders: We can't draw them a map.

The Secretary: There's some progress here.

Eilts: I think it's very helpful in the south.

The Secretary: He's three quarters of the way down there. Maybe he has an idea how we can finish it up.

---

[7] See Document 208.

Saunders: What does happen down there? Is there any way to widen the corridor? If they both use the same road perhaps we can eliminate the appearance of a choke point down there some how.

The Secretary: But are the Israelis permitted to move military equipment on the road?

Now I think we should get agreement in principle on what we have got. The Israelis are now sufficiently interested. Once they have gotten agreement in principle they'll be awful. But they will have to sell some of it to the Cabinet. This will take two or three weeks. The shuttle simply can't be done in two or three days.

Sisco: I don't see the shuttle happening in August. I think it's closer to September. He hasn't even surfaced all the text of the bilateral agreements.

The Secretary: Let's not bother with that now. If Sadat doesn't accept this, there's no point in adding the other things.

Sisco: (handing the Secretary a cable)[8] I'd like you to see this reply. I think it has to go.

The Secretary: (reading and changing cable) Did Hermann agree with this?

Eilts: I haven't seen it.

Sisco: It just came in 15 minutes before we came up. I'll show it to Hermann.

The Secretary: Will you see the British please.

Sisco: Sure.

The Secretary: Tell Sadat we won't do any of this until he approves it (referring to cable). We can do it only knowing their reaction. Just say please just let us know immediately.

Sisco: We may want to make a few changes in it.

Saunders: Do I understand we send only one map with Hermann?

The Secretary: The best would be to put it in one of our own maps because our own maps don't show the mountains so crassly.

Atherton: It may look as if it's out of the passes.

Eilts: They have the same map in Arabic and on the same scale. It's that map I sent back—it's the same as this one.

The Secretary: I would present the exact map the Israelis presented us then give him the other map, perhaps on one of ours, showing the yellow areas on a separate map and say, "These are the areas which we obtained as a result of our going back to Rabin." In addition, I have a private belief that in the south they can do better than the yellow area

---

[8] Cable not further identified.

and get this part (pointing to the south). I think it's better to show something beyond what he already has.

Saunders: It would make sense psychologically to put these variations on our map, I think. Then we can say that's our working map.

The Secretary: That's good. You're beginning to think like an Arab, Hal. (laughter) The first map is the Israeli map, the second is our map. We can fix it up later. Do it in bites. No, let's show the real Israeli map. Say the yellow line is approved by the negotiating team but not approved by the Cabinet. Anything beyond that is Rabin's personal view.

Now let's get a cable out tonight to Fahmy. Tell him we met with the Israelis. There's distinct progress. They raised an additional consideration on which I want further progress. Therefore I'm holding Hermann here to get some replies. I think that given their epic minds this will help.

Eilts: I should be there not later than Saturday PM.[9]

The Secretary: There's nothing to hold you until the map arrives at about 4:00 tomorrow. We have to go over it so you could leave Saturday morning.

Eilts: There's really no good way to go.

The Secretary: It's up to you. I doubt you'll make 7:30 tomorrow night. We'll want to go over your talking points too. I don't think you should cut it that close. (reading cable on UNEF) Tell Fahmy nothing we've presented here has been discussed with the Israelis. The three things he wants we can do. Why not tell him we can do it?

Sisco: I'm sending it along these lines: That we need to consult with the Israelis who feel they didn't feed this crisis.

Eilts: The proximate cause, of course, was Rabin's statement.

Atherton: May I raise again the Ford-Asad meeting?

The Secretary: There's just no time for it now.

Atherton: I reviewed the exchange with Asad and I think it will be a severe disappointment.

The Secretary: I know. Khaddam raised it again.[10]

Atherton: Well, let's not underestimate the setback with Asad and the loss of our position. There is a real benefit in linking him with the President.

The Secretary: The only possibility is seeing him before Helsinki.

Sisco: When are you leaving?

---

[9] July 19.
[10] See Document 193.

The Secretary: Saturday. We could leave Friday and do Asad Sunday in Vienna.

Sisco: Do you think you should check with the President?

The Secretary: I'll discuss it with the President. I agree with you. It's a cheap thing to pay and it happens to be a lousy time because we must tell him something. He's too bright to be fobbed off. We could explain the problem with the Japanese.

Saunders: He would ask why not come early.

The Secretary: Would Asad come to Bonn?

Atherton: Probably, yes.

The Secretary: I just wonder why the President should have to move.

Atherton: Khaddam said they could do it any place.

The Secretary: Well he mentioned Vienna.

Atherton: Bonn is a problem because you saw Rabin there.

The Secretary: You know I'm fonder of Asad than Sadat. I have a weak spot for Asad. In his context, he's showing as much courage as Sadat. He has that wild Syrian integrity.

Eilts: No Syrian has integrity

The Secretary: No Egyptian has integrity.

Eilts: I agree.

The Secretary: Though there is a smidgen more in Asad. Sadat is a statesman. Safire got it totally screwed up you know. It's the exact opposite that's true. Fahmy is our friend there, not Sadat.

Eilts: Sadat likes you though.

The Secretary: He likes this President more than Nixon I think.

Eilts: Yes, he finds him more human.

The Secretary: That sounds plausible. (Laughter)

Eilts: When Nixon was there, there were those long awkward silences.

The Secretary: That is also a quality of Sadat though.

Eilts: Well, with Ford he chatted all the time.

210. Memorandum of Conversation[1]

Washington, July 18, 1975, 9:07–10:12 a.m.

PARTICIPANTS

The President
Dr. Henry A. Kissinger, Secretary of State and Assistant to the President for National Security Affairs
Lt. General Brent Scowcroft, Deputy Assistant to the President for National Security Affairs

SUBJECTS

Middle East, Angola; Soviet Grain; SALT; President's Trip

[There was discussion of the new Israeli lines in Sinai]

Kissinger: We will send Eilts back Saturday.[2] This won't help us with Sadat. It's not a big concession after all our table-pounding. He could quit his talk and take it, or tell us to go to hell. If he says no, maybe we should go for an overall settlement.

President: I agree.

Kissinger: The only value of this is it gets us a settlement and a year and a half.

President: If Sadat says no, there is no reason to force more concessions from Israel for an interim, is there?

Kissinger: If you give them an ultimatum, they will do it, but you will pay for it in a confrontation.

My assessment of Israel's situation is that for us to start a showdown for a few changes ... It's better to brawl over a failure.

President: Sadat might buy it; he may want something more. He must understand we can't make a major effort for changes.

Kissinger: We will make an effort, but not a massive one.

President: We will do what we can; if that is not enough we will tell Sadat we will go comprehensive.

Kissinger: That's my judgment. [To Scowcroft:] What do you think?

Scowcroft: I agree.

---

[1] Source: Library of Congress, Manuscript Division, Kissinger Papers, CL 282, President's File, July 1975, Folder 1. Secret; Nodis. The meeting was held in the Oval Office at the White House. All brackets, with the exception of the ones describing omitted material, are in the original.

[2] July 19.

Kissinger: The reason I reluctantly came to an interim agreement is that if you get it, plus a SALT agreement and one or two others, you'll be in good shape in foreign policy.

[Omitted here is discussion unrelated to the Arab-Israeli dispute.]

211. Memorandum of Conversation[1]

Washington, July 23, 1975.

SUBJECT

The Middle East

PARTICIPANTS

The Secretary
Under Secretary Sisco
Assistant Secretary Atherton
Deputy Assistant Secretary Saunders
Jerry Bremer, Notetaker

The Secretary: Actually didn't you think Dinitz's behavior was poor?[2]

Sisco: It was a very bad show. He got very emotional and played the Mr. Negative role.

The Secretary: His attitude was that this is an outrage, that there are no Egyptian concessions at all.

Sisco: It's partly posturing but I must say it was unattractive.

The Secretary: No, I wish it were posturing and didn't reflect their inability to understand the problem.

(Secretary's interrupted for a phone call.)

I thought it was a really revolting performance. To say that the Egyptians didn't do anything.

---

[1] Source: Library of Congress, Manuscript Division, Kissinger Papers, CL 346, State Department Memorandum of Conversations, Internal, July 1975. Secret; Sensitive. The meeting took place in the Department of State. Brackets are in the original.

[2] Kissinger met with Dinitz earlier that day from 11:30 a.m. until 12:45 p.m. to present the Egyptian counterproposal. (Memorandum of conversation, July 23; ibid., CL 158 Geopolitical File, Israel, July 23–31, 1975) On July 20, after his return to Cairo, Eilts met with Sadat, Fahmy, and Gamasy to give them the latest Israeli proposal. In another meeting the next day, Sadat gave Eilts a counterproposal and a second "fallback" proposal. (Telegrams 7122, July 21, and 7171, July 22, from Cairo; National Archives, RG 59, Central Foreign Policy Files)

Sisco: Did he ease off at all with you when you were alone?

The Secretary: He wanted an assurance before he gave the fallback that that's all they wanted. He did say he thought the forward line could go forward a couple of kilometers beyond the UNEF line. Sadat has already accepted their eastern line and the fallback forward line. If they just put it forward.

I'll advise Sadat to move his line halfway towards the UNEF line. That gives him five kilometers and he'll settle for two. Tell him not to propose moving his troops across the canal. I can see it working except for the six stations. We know from the Fahmy cable[3] that they will yield. It is only reasonable that the Egyptians get two stations in the north. What's in the way now is the six U.S. stations. I think they'll sell them for cash. They'll demand military equipment in return. The stations are not in their interest anyway. The only thing I saw in the stations was that they'd force them to go to the Congress. I'm optimistic. I think it may work.

Atherton: If we can work out the memorandum of understanding.

Sisco: We'll buy ourselves to mid-'77 with it.

The Secretary: *You* buy *yourself* to mid-'77. I'll be making $300,000 a year by then.

Sisco: I don't know. Ford will be re-elected and you'll have to reassess your determination by then. He did a good job at breakfast. I don't mind his over-promising.

The Secretary: I'm furious with the Greeks and I think he should raise hell.

Now we must keep the Egyptians calm. Explain to Fahmy that now that I know his fallback, which the Israelis don't, we can move much faster. My tentative idea is to move to the shuttle about August 18 and I have asked Rabin to cancel his trip to Austria. That way we can get it done by the end of August. On the political conditions, my impression is the Israelis won't go beyond what we have said in Salzburg.[4]

Sisco: Say, "I think that they will ask, but we've made clear that the Egyptians cannot go beyond what was discussed in Salzburg." I think we should say also that we are making progress.

The Secretary: I think I can now see a way this can go to a conclusion. Only the six stations are standing between us plus some of that stuff in the south. But if the Israelis agree to that road, the Egyptians

---

[3] The cable is not further identified. Possibly a reference to telegram 7226 from Cairo, July 23. (Ibid.)

[4] See Documents 177 and 178.

will let them use the road and the new one will never get built. (Secretary is interrupted for a phone call to Senator Case.)

Sisco: He (Senator Case) has been just awful. I don't know what's wrong with him.

Atherton: Every conversation we've had with him has been accusatory.

The Secretary: He accused me of misleading the committee, what was it about?

Bremer: On the oil sharing.

The Secretary: That's right. When I testified he accused me of misleading them on the fact that we would under certain almost inconceivable circumstances have to share our domestic oil. Anyway, is Pickering on the way up there?

Atherton: He will go as soon as he gets an appointment. I think it will clear the air a bit.

The Secretary: I think Pickering should take this to the others also.

Sisco: Not a bad idea. (Secretary is interrupted for a phone call.)

The Secretary: Rabin wants to meet the President in Europe. I think the President has to tell him he won't take no for an answer.

Atherton: Undoubtedly he wants to talk about the bilateral commitments.

Saunders: We just got through telling Asad there was no time.

The Secretary: But where would it take place?

Atherton: In Bonn.

The Secretary: It would have to be Bonn.

Saunders: And it is the same weekend that Asad couldn't come.

Atherton: It would certainly not help our credibility with Asad.

The Secretary: The other thought I had was that I might cut out of the trip in Romania and Yugoslavia and drop down to Egypt and Jerusalem for a few days. There would be no shuttle. Just to get the framework established.

Atherton: It would certainly help with the Egyptians. There will be lots of loose ends.

The Secretary: Which is better? (Secretary is interrupted for a phone call.)

I'm a little worried about Rabin meeting the President in Europe. I don't know when or how to get the President ready and how to have the talks without everyone in Europe listening. You might be able to do it in Helsinki. But that's really rubbing the Russians' noses in it. Also, it leaves the Egyptians out. I think it's better if I go to Egypt and Israel for one day each and get the line settled.

Sisco: The objection may be that if the Israelis have a meeting with the President, Sadat won't like the beginning of the shuttle to begin without having it finished.

The Secretary: How about asking Fahmy? Say, to speed up the progress, I could peel off and spend a day in each place.

If this is another Israeli trick, I will be furious. You know Simcha said is it possible for you and Rabin to talk in Europe. I said I'm free on the 30th. If the President sees him, it cannot be until August 8. Then there's no Cabinet meeting before the 12th.

Sisco: That's right and whatever he gives he will give in exchange for the meeting with the President. The President will not be able to give that kind of categoric assurance.

The Secretary: I think we can settle the lines with what we have. The warning stations worry me. He must move the forward line back too.

Sisco: Maybe Sadat can buy two stations. Six is a lot.

The Secretary: He can't buy any.

Sisco: He's worried about the Russian angle perhaps.

Atherton: The Israelis made it clear they want the bilateral assurances pinned down first.

The Secretary: When the President sees Rabin, there will be 500 more newsmen. Any country where he does it will feel he's taking away from his visit there. Therefore, it can only be at the end of the trip which is another ten days.

Atherton: He doesn't need that much time. They could just do an airport meeting.

The Secretary: Oh, come on! He's leaving Belgrade at 6:00 p.m. He has Miki at 10:30 the next morning at the end of an 11-day trip and after 14 hours of flying. You guys have got to be kidding.

Saunders: Can you just say it's physically impossible?

The Secretary: I think I have to say it's out of the question and I'll check with the President on the idea of my going. And anyway, there's no excuse for not putting forward their position. I'll say we want their position.

Sisco: I think you should go easy on your peeling off from the trip.

Atherton: I'd suggest not putting it in a message.

Sisco: I agree. We're basically on course.

The Secretary: If the Israelis will put forward their fallback, we're on course.

Atherton: How was it with Dinitz this morning?

The Secretary: He doubted they could forward anything.

Sisco: He was snotty.

The Secretary: And disrespectful.

212. Memorandum of Conversation[1]

Washington, July 24, 1975, 9:25–10:22 a.m.

PARTICIPANTS
President Ford
Dr. Henry A. Kissinger, Secretary of State and Assistant to the President for National Security Affairs
Lt. General Brent Scowcroft, Deputy Assistant to the President for National Security Affairs

[Omitted here is discussion unrelated to the Arab-Israeli dispute.]

Kissinger: I met with Dinitz yesterday.[2] It was very unpleasant. I think they want to turn the Arabs against us. They liked it between '67 and '73 when we were isolated from the Arabs.

Rabin said publicly that there could be no agreement without direct negotiations. Then he sent a letter saying he didn't mean it.

I turned off having a meeting with you and Rabin on the trip. The only real possibility would be Bonn. To do it in Bucharest would be bad and Helsinki provocative.

President: I would meet only if he would accept the line and settlement we would propose. Under no other conditions.

Kissinger: How about the six stations?

President: Drop them.

Kissinger: I will tell Dinitz. That is a good idea. I think the six stations would be an albatross. The Lavon affair in the '50s was about Israelis blowing up American installations in Cairo and blaming it on the

---

[1] Source: Library of Congress, Manuscript Division, Kissinger Papers, CL 282, President's File, July 1975, Folder 2. Secret; Nodis. The meeting was held in the Oval Office at the White House.

[2] See footnote 2, Document 211.

Arabs.[3] They could do the same with one of these stations and blame it on the PLO.

The outline of a deal is there, if we can get inclusion of the six stations. We can do it in August if the Israelis play ball.

President: The American public won't buy the six stations.

Kissinger: I agree, especially since we have offered to man the other four. Though we may end up with the UN then.

President: But keep offering an American role there. I will meet Rabin if necessary, but it must be predicated on his accepting our best judgment. We must do it in August.

Kissinger: If the negotiations fail, we don't have to blame Israel, but we can say it failed for lack of a common concept.

[Omitted here is discussion unrelated to the Arab-Israeli dispute.]

---

[3] The Lavon affair refers to an Israeli covert operation in 1954. Israeli Defense Minister Pinchas Lavon organized a plan to use Egyptian Jews and undercover Israeli agents to bomb American, British, and Egyptian buildings in Cairo. Lavon's goal was to blame the bombings on Arabs, creating the impression of an anti-Western atmosphere and helping convince the British and Americans of the need to have the British stay in the Suez Canal zone.

213. Memorandum of Conversation[1]

Washington, August 4, 1975.

PARTICIPANTS

President Ford
Dr. Henry A. Kissinger, Secretary of State and Assistant to the President for National Security Affairs
Lt. General Brent Scowcroft, Deputy Assistant to the President for National Security Affairs

Kissinger: This is the old map.[2] Sadat accepts this line but wants it out of the passes. It still leaves them the high ground. Here you must be as ruthless as necessary.

---

[1] Source: Ford Library, National Security Adviser, Memoranda of Conversations, Box 14, August 4, 1975, Ford, Kissinger. Secret; Nodis. The meeting was held in the Oval Office at the White House.

[2] Map is not attached.

President: You mean off the crests?

Kissinger: No, only in the passes themselves.

He accepts the north line but wants a few hundred yards on the curve.

South of the passes he accepts whatever line we can get him. He accepts the whole coast road provided his people don't have to go through Israeli checkpoints. But I am going to block off the two stretches as UN or something so the line is continuous.

Rabin's actions make it look like Israeli-U.S. collusion, which will drive the Egyptians wild. Sadat says he needs a token two kilometers past the UN line. They want two stations in the north. They will give them Umm Khisheiba if we supervise it. They won't let Israel man the south station but they will let the U.S. or UN do it. In the next round I will say that Egypt wants all the stations American and that they rejected all six stations. We could get two stations in the Giddi under the guise of checking access to Umm Khisheiba.

Basically this negotiation is done unless Rabin is setting us up for a fall. Here is his letter.[3] I think we should go back to him and say we won't pursue the matter further; that the European briefings contradict what he says, and that the President promised they would get out of the passes.

I would propose leaving the 18th or 19th, and hope to wrap it up by the 28th or 29th.

We couldn't have done it without you either.

President: We couldn't have done it without your strategy. No one else could have done it.

[Omitted here is discussion unrelated to the Arab-Israeli dispute.]

---

[3] In the letter, Rabin denied American accusations that Israel had made approaches to European governments requesting their involvement in the negotiations with Egypt. (Telegram 4957 fronm Tel Aviv, August 1; National Archives, RG 59, Central Policy Files P850012–1775)

214. Memorandum of Conversation[1]

Vail, Colorado, August 16, 1975.

PARTICIPANTS

President Ford
Dr. Henry A. Kissinger, Secretary of State and Assistant to the President for National Security Affairs
Lt. General Brent Scowcroft, Deputy Assistant to the President for National Security Affairs

[Omitted here is material unrelated to the Arab-Israeli dispute.]

[Kissinger:] On the Middle East. We have a good map coming. [He points out the passes on the map.][2]

I guarantee you the Israelis, once the agreement is signed, will announce that they are not out of the passes.

The passes are one big contested point. The next point is the warning stations. I told Dinitz the worst thing Israel has done is to insist on these stations. We will supervise Umm Khisheiba and can justify one station as needed to check Umm Khisheiba. This issue is pure Israeli domestic politics.

Jackson told Dinitz not to make an interim agreement because it would only help you and me. He said he would vote for the stations but they would damage Israel. I am getting turned off with Jackson. They say he turned on Vietnam; why wouldn't he on Israel?

I will shave some off the Israeli line.

Then there is the problem of moving the Egyptian line forward. In the South, they have agreed to broaden the narrow parts. There will be joint use of the road.

This is not a satisfactory agreement. The Israelis have not been smart to push Egypt this far. It will lead either to peace or another war.

[He reads the Sadat letter to the President.][3]

---

[1] Source: Library of Congress, Manuscript Division, Kissinger Papers, CL 282, President's File, August 1975, Folder 2. Secret; Nodis. All brackets, with the exception of ones describing omitted material, are in the original.

[2] Map is not attached.

[3] In his letter to Ford, Sadat reminded Ford of their common strategy, devised in Salzburg, whereby the United States would ultimately offer "a package deal to solve this chronic and explosive crisis." Sadat also stated that it was "imperative to tackle the Middle East crisis in its entirety, namely, effecting the withdrawal of Israeli forces from all occupied territories and solving the Palestinian problem with a view to restore to the area tranquility and normalcy in a binding form." (Backchannel message, August 14; Ford Library, National Security Adviser, Backchannel Messages, Box 5, Sandy Circuit, August 1975, Incoming)

The problem with this letter is we can't be caught in a position where we look duplicitous, because the Israelis want the opposite. They have given us a 25-page memorandum of what they want from us.[4] I will leave a copy of this with you.

[Reads from the Israeli document.]

They asked us not to make an overall proposal which they haven't approved and any proposals which they haven't cleared.

I would like to reaffirm what you have already said to Rabin—that you will take the Israeli views very seriously.

I would tell Sadat that we will be ready in 1977 for an overall proposal.

[Gives the President a draft letter that Israel wants him to send to Rabin.]

On an agreement, there will be three sets of documents. We will leave a set of everything with Brent and let you know every day where we stand. It will be the most tawdry nitpicking.

There is the basic agreement, a protocol spelling out where the lines are, then a U.S.-Israeli bilateral agreement—that 24-page paper. They want to prevent your doing what you did last Spring—hold up military equipment. [Reads all the military equipment they want.] For now they want just a military figure that we will promise. There are other items. The figure is now $3.2 billion. Those demands—and the *warning* stations—may barely evoke their support for 1977. They want a figure today.

President: I can't, in good conscience, go above $2.1 billion. We had been thinking of 1.6 to 1.8. We have cut back so much on other programs that it really is hard on us. What is the budget figure?

Scowcroft: We haven't given any, but the estimate was at the previous year—$700 million.

President: Tell them $2 billion and not one cent more. Even that will be hard to sell to the Congress.

Kissinger: I think we can explain 2.1 better than 2.0.

President: O.K. But start with 1.6. For 3 million people that is a lot.

[Omitted here is discussion unrelated to the Arab-Israeli dispute.]

---

[4] The 25-page Israeli memorandum has not been found, but an August 12 memorandum of conversation between Dinitz and Sisco includes Dinitz's explanation of a proposed Israeli text of an Israeli-Egyptian agreement and a U.S.-Israeli memorandum of understanding. (Library of Congress, Manuscript Division, Kissinger Papers, CL 159, Geopolitical File, Israel, August 10–18, 1975)

215. Memorandum of Conversation[1]

Washington, August 19, 1975.

PARTICIPANTS

The Secretary
Under Secretary Sisco
Deputy Assistant Secretary Saunders
Assistant Secretary Atherton
Jerry Bremer, Notetaker

SUBJECT

The Middle East

The Secretary: I think the Israelis are setting us up as the guys who are beating them into it.

Sisco: Yes, I agree. Part of it is show for us. That outburst yesterday[2] was because the government has arranged that there be no real debate until after the agreement.

The Secretary: But it is also clear that the government is putting out the word that they're being raped by us.

Sisco: Yes, they're making us the scapegoat. It disturbs me and it doesn't disturb me.

The Secretary: That's because you're not the villain. Why should it disturb you?

Sisco: I don't mean that personally. They will have to say it was done under U.S. pressure. Did you see Gwertzman's analysis today?[3] It is that the U.S. has brought about these concessions, though it is unfair to make you personally the villain.

The Secretary: That they are doing anyway. If they can establish the theory that they're being raped, the agreement cannot last; so, in two or three years we will have to move to the overall.

Sisco: Rabin is justifying it on the grounds of direct benefits to Israel. He has to argue it positively.

The Secretary: The fact is we will have to move to an overall in a foreseeable time. I'm not sure we're not making a mistake.

---

[1] Source: Library of Congress, Manuscript Division, Kissinger Papers, CL 346, State Department Memorandum of Conversations, August–September 1975. Secret; Sensitive. The meeting was held at the Department of State.

[2] The *New York Times* reported on August 18 ("Israel Approves Kissinger Mission") that Israeli opposition leaders stated that Kissinger had "thrust himself" on Rabin's government, which could not refuse Kissinger's offer to come to Israel.

[3] "On Sinai, Pledges and Pressure," *New York Times*, August 19, 1975 p. 10.

Sisco: I agree, but there's no turning around now.

The Secretary: What did Toon scream about yesterday? That was the real screw-up, sending out a draft letter.[4] That was to be a side letter to be done after the agreement, after the President screamed about the first one, we edited it a bit and I said to Brent to get it back to Sisco.

Sisco: I'm disturbed about one thing. In the Sunday meeting they asked for in writing a statement to the effect that the President said for the first 18 months we will put forward no proposal in Geneva and for the next 18 months "trust me."

The Secretary: That of course is almost certainly what happened, but we can't put it in writing.

Sisco: The President didn't even put it that way. He kept open his options, as I remember.

The Secretary: He probably said for 18 months we don't do anything, but whether he writes it or says it are two different things.

Sisco: Secondly, Dinitz says he talked to you on the following: He says 1. There has to be a commitment that the agreement won't be carried forward unless congressional action is completed on the U.S. presence and on the oil.

The Secretary: That I sort of said.

Sisco: The presence we can get through, I think, in a big hurry.

The Secretary: Why did you raise the question?

Sisco: I didn't, he took the initiative.

The Secretary: No, no. You guys told him we might need congressional action on the oil.

Sisco: Yes, that's been part of our analysis for months.

The Secretary: I cannot understand people saying we are not certain we have the authority. Either we have it or we don't.

Saunders: There is legal authority. The question is whether you wanted to exercise it. That's where a feel for Congress comes in.

The Secretary: Therefore, there is authority but whether we want to use it is our business.

Saunders: The question is whether you want any additional authority.

The Secretary: We cannot ask the Israelis to enter into an agreement which Congress can break major parts out of. (Eagleburger enters with ticker and leaves.)

---

[4] In a meeting on Sunday, July 17, Toon read the President's letter to Rabin. Telegram 5370 from Cairo, July 17, reported Rabin's reaction to the letter. (National Archives, RG 59, Central Foreign Policy Files)

Sisco: (looking at ticker) I see the bilateral document is now beginning to leak.

Saunders: There's another major point about Congressional action on the oil supply. The Israelis are seeking security of supply, which they have never had. This is a major new thing for us. The Israelis are looking for something new, the security aspect of oil, which they'd never had before. It really is not relevant to the agreement itself.

Atherton: I wonder if we don't want to ask Congress for explicit approval of both the presence and the oil.

Sisco: I think it would be unwise on the oil. We should exercise our authority on the oil and inform Congress. On the presence I am confident we can get it. What worries me is the oil conditionality.

The Secretary: I'll tell Dinitz I thought there were two separate authorities required.

The other thing that worries me is Fahmy's response.[5] It is totally unsatisfactory. I cannot be the fall guy for everything. Sure it's predictable, but what will I do when those guys start working me over again? I want a cable to Fahmy. I'd rather have the shuttle cancelled than beat my head against the wall when we get out there. It is essential to tell Fahmy that these conditions are essential. We were disappointed to find that he is presenting the old ones in such a grudging way. Also say that there is the Syrian point I want to talk to Sadat about when I get out there. Call his attention to the precise understandings at Salzburg. I'm not asking for an answer. Second, we have to answer the Sadat letter.[6]

Sisco: We sent you a draft reply on Saturday. Also I haven't heard from you on that one on Allon.

The Secretary: You don't think in this madhouse I saw it?

Sisco: We thought it was a good time for the President to remind Sadat that we'd like to have him visit sometime.

Atherton: Here is a copy. (handing the message to the Secretary)

The Secretary: (reading message) No, it speaks too much of an agreed common strategy. Since it will leak, we have to go easy on that.

Sisco: The reason it's in there is that he loves that phrase. His eyes light up when he hears it.

The Secretary: I don't mind saying it once. Just say we both agreed to set some point at the time most promising a comprehensive settlement would have to be addressed. Also that we agreed the U.S. would stay fully engaged and is willing to put forward our own ideas as in the

---

[5] Fahmy's response was transmitted in telegram 8195 from Cairo, August 18. (Ibid.)
[6] See footnote 3, Document 214.

past. Then point out that the agreement has major consequences to Egypt. Basically the critics in Israel have a point. Spell out our idea on the settlement. Strengthen the idea of inviting him. Now get it out today and have it delivered by Wednesday.[7] Get a phrase on the final phase and something about support for Dr. Kissinger—you see what I mean. But be sure the letter can't be pulled out later and be used against us.

Do you think we're doing the right thing or would we have been better off going for an overall?

Atherton: Only if we could have gotten an overall.

Sisco: What is the price the President's willing to pay?

The Secretary: $2.1 billion maximum.

Sisco: I don't think the U.S. people will think that's cheap.

The Secretary: I think the agreement is the beginning of the end of Israel, not because of what's in the agreement, since they are better off strategically than they were before. A jeep cannot move anywhere this side of the canal without being seen. The Egyptians have to cross the canal and move 40 miles against opposition. That's a day-and-a-half operation before they meet any opposition.

Atherton: The air force would take them out by then anyway

The Secretary: If they'd have done that in '67, they'd be impregnable now and the entire coastal corridor they're holding as a hostage.

Sisco: Will they have to do much on the new defense line? Since they are now telling us how much money they have to spend.

Atherton: Yes, they'll have to do alot of bunkering.

The Secretary: But I think when Congress gets the two billion dollar bill at a time when we are cutting domestic programs and at a time when for $180 million we could have saved Cambodia ...

Sisco: Did you see the figures we sent you Saturday which added to $3 billion?

The Secretary: I saw it. But now it's disappeared.

Sisco: I just think the figures are telltale.

The Secretary: Of what?

Sisco: Oh, of the fact that they're just throwing everything in.

Atherton: Here is the list. (handing Secretary the list)[8]

The Secretary: (reading list) Have they seen your $2.6 billion?

---

[7] August 20. The letter to Sadat was sent in telegram 197497 to Cairo, August 20. (National Archives, RG 59, Central Foreign Policy Files)

[8] The list is not attached.

Sisco: God, no. I wrote nothing in here either to make it look like I was recommending $2.6 to you either.

[Omitted here is discussion unrelated to the Arab-Israeli dispute.]

216. Memorandum of Conversation[1]

Jerusalem, August 21, 1975, 7:25–7:50 p.m.

PARTICIPANTS

Dr. Henry A. Kissinger, Secretary of State and Assistant to the President for National Security Affairs
Joseph J. Sisco, Under Secretary of State for Political Affairs
Amb. Malcolm Toon, US Amb. to Israel
Winston Lord, Director, Policy Planning Staff
Alfred L. Atherton, Jr., Assistant Secretary of State for Near Eastern and South Asian Affairs
Harold H. Saunders, Deputy Assistant Secretary for Near Eastern and South Asian Affairs
Robert B. Oakley, NSC Staff
Peter W. Rodman, NSC Staff

SUBJECT

Israeli Political Situation

Kissinger: [Turns on the babbler][2] What is the situation here now?

Toon: Not good. The public is upset, the press is very nasty. Rabin thinks he can do it.

Kissinger: You think there is doubt he can?

Toon: If you are prepared to pay the price.

Kissinger: What price?

Toon: Aid, political commitments you might not be prepared to give.

Kissinger: We offered $2.1 billion, which gets to the outer limit of what we can do. Look, the President now is vetoing milk for feeding

---

[1] Source: Ford Library, National Security Adviser, Kissinger Reports on USSR, China, and Middle East, Box 4, August 21–September 1, 1975, Vol. I (1), Sinai Disengagement Agreement. Secret; Nodis. The meeting was held in the Secretary's Suite (Room 620) at the King David Hotel. Brackets are in the original.

[2] A babbler is an electronic device designed to prevent eavesdropping by producing incoherent fragments of sentences that drown out or overwhelm the voices of those conversing in a room.

mothers. He has been told that once he gets to $2 billion, he gets in trouble.

Toon: But the trouble is, there has been a whole troupe of Congressmen coming here saying they can get it, saying they could get $3.5 billion.

Kissinger: It is not in our interest to give $3.5 billion.

Toon: One figure mentioned was $1.9 billion. Rabin said it was not enough. $2.1 billion might do.

Kissinger: As Joe knows, I have had massive problems with the President. He asked me to offer $1.9 and settle for $2.1 billion. But I don't want to play games.

What do they think they are giving up? If it fails, do they want us to cut it down and go for an overall?

Toon: There is opposition.

Kissinger: Any other Administration would follow the same policy, after one year.

Toon: $1.9 billion is not enough. $2.1 billion is enough.

Kissinger: Maybe he will settle. We didn't mention $1.9 billion.

We should keep Mac better informed. There was a series of meetings. Last week we were overworked.

Dinitz wanted to chisel more on the last day. I was inclined to, but luckily the President didn't. Rabin would have asked for more.

By political commitments, he means from the Egyptians?

One thing the President won't do is to give them a veto over our policy. "Consider seriously," yes.

Sisco: Their negotiating team has no latitude. If a technical team gets together, the document will only get worse.

Kissinger: I am not so eager for everyone to be in the room.

Sisco: There should be a brief checklist of points—in a small group; you and Allon and whoever—and then turn it over to others. The other way would make it worse. The proposal was for a technical team to get together while the Ministerial team is working.

Kissinger: Whatever we sent back, the wise guys here would prove how tough they are.

Sisco: The wise guys are here.

Toon: I didn't like their idea of waiting to discuss the line until they have the political commitments. The political commitments about Geneva.

Sisco: And second, political commitments about the agreement—boycott, propaganda.

Kissinger: I won't leave here tomorrow until I have something from them. It was a mistake not to hold out part of the line. Now all the parts of the line to be changed are something they have to give.

Sisco: We need to settle the line and political commitments.

Kissinger: I don't need everyone in Alexandria. I could leave Roy. What are the issues? We must settle the passes. How far back do you think they will go?

Toon: Some back.

Kissinger: To the Hoskinson position?[3] They said no. It's one kilometer.

Toon: Gur's idea is on the highlands.

Kissinger: How the Egyptians will ever get to that point, I haven't figured out.

Saunders: Here is a checklist. [He hands him the first day's checklist.][4]

Kissinger: On geography—the passes, the southern area to the oil, and the Beta Line. Will we get the Beta Line?

It's ridiculous; if every time they withdraw 30 kilometers and the Egyptians advance one kilometer, then when they're at the 1967 borders the Egyptians have moved six kilometers.

Now I think they are under the necessity of breaking quickly or settling quickly.

Why are they turning everybody out tonight [at the Knesset reception]?

It was one of the warmest receptions at the airport I have seen. [Laughter]

Lord: It reminded me of Peking.

Kissinger: [Laughs] On the first visit! Yes.

To receive the Secretary of State of a country that gives them every screwdriver. No other country would have done this.

Lord: Hanoi maybe.

Kissinger: No, Le Duc Tho[5] was very warm. He practically raped me.

We need the passes, the southern line—whatever maneuvers they will do on the road, and the Beta Line. We need to settle Umm Khisheiba and the stations.

Politically, something on boycott, etc.

Toon: Plus the commitments in a Presidential letter.

---

[3] A reference to Samuel Hoskinson, a CIA expert on the Middle East. According to Kissinger's memoirs, Hoskinson suggested designating the Parker Memorial (see footnote 3, Document 209) as the eastern end of the Israeli line. (*Years of Renewal*, p. 451)

[4] The first day's checklist is not attached.

[5] Le Duc Tho was the chief North Vietnamese negotiator at the Paris Peace Talks.

Kissinger: They won't get it.

Sisco: They want a veto on our policy and secondly, a commitment that they won't be pushed off the Golan.

Kissinger: How can we do it?

Sisco: Henry's been very firm on that.

Kissinger: We really should make Mac the anchor here.

They asked us for a letter saying we don't ask them to go off the Golan. I took it to Vail.[6] The President said absolutely not. I didn't recommend it. I was overworked. That is the reason for the screwup [the sending of a draft to Rabin by mistake].[7] Scowcroft took it out of the meeting and said "This can go." I was going to take it up with Dinitz the next day. He meant back to Sisco. Dinitz called me and said the Prime Minister was outraged.

So those are the issues.

Will there be speeches there tonight?

Toon: Probably.

Give me the text [of the arrival statement]. I will use it again. [Laughter]

Saunders: The fact that you gave a prepared text and read it attracted press attention.

Kissinger: Our press—Barry Schweid—won't understand it until they get the word. And they don't take it from us! How will they brief the press?

Toon: Through Dinitz.

Kissinger: That isn't bad. He is for it.

They say Umm Khisheiba will go to Israel. I have never discussed it. We can't get that without the Beta Line. I told them specifically it wasn't agreed.

Lord: It is in the *Jerusalem Post* today.

Kissinger: Where did they hear that? I never said it. [To Rodman] Did I say it to the Jewish leaders?

Rodman: No, you never got into details.

Kissinger: Great patriots they are. The leaders of the American Jewish Congress, or whatever, were asked by the press "What about the agreement?" They said: "Whatever the Israeli Government thinks." They could have mentioned America once.

Atherton: Actually it was meant as a signal to those who say there should be no agreement.

---

[6] See footnote 4, Document 214.
[7] See footnote 4, Document 215.

Kissinger: Actually Rabbi Miller[8] is a nice one.
Rodman: He's not very bright.
[The meeting broke up.]
Atherton: You need a decision on this [the Hawks for Jordan.][9]
Toon: Why?
Sisco: It goes to the heart of our relationship with Hussein, and it was a Presidential commitment. We got it.
Atherton: No thanks to General Brown.
Toon: It means a lot of them here.
Oakley: We promised 22.
Kissinger: We can't go back on a Presidential commitment.
[The meeting ended.]

---

[8] Rabbi Israel Miller, a leading member of the American Jewish community.
[9] A reference to the U.S. Government plan to sell Hawk missiles to Jordan.

---

217. Memorandum From the President's Deputy Assistant for National Security Affairs (Scowcroft) to President Ford[1]

Washington, August 23, 1975.

Secretary Kissinger asked that the following report of his meeting with Rabin be passed to you:

"I have just completed my first round of talks with Rabin and his negotiating team,[2] including Foreign Minister Allon and Defense Minister Peres lasting five hours. My overall impression is they want to achieve the interim agreement—not because they view it as opening a new chapter in Israeli-Egyptian relations and ushering in new hope for

---

[1] Source: Ford Library, National Security Adviser, Kissinger Reports on USSR, China, and Middle East, Box 4, August 21–September 1, 1975, Volume I (2), Sinai Disengagement Agreement. Secret. Sent for information.

[2] The memorandum of conversation of the meeting between the Israeli negotiating team and Kissinger, which took place on August 22 from 9:50 a.m. until 2:30 p.m. at the Prime Minister's Residence in Jerusalem, is ibid., Vol. I (1), Sinai Disengagement Agreement. This meeting was followed by others over the next two days. There are memoranda of conversation of meetings between the Israeli negotiating team and Kissinger that took place on August 23 from 9:50 until 11:55 p.m. (ibid., Vol. I (4), Sinai Disengagement Agreement) and August 24 from 6:15 until 10:30 p.m. (ibid., Vol. I (5), Sinai Disengagement Agreement).

the future, but rather because the terms they are expecting to get will leave them in a strategic position in the Sinai not significantly inferior to their present position and because an agreement provides the vehicle to ensure continued Israeli military supremacy resulting from the $2.5 billion in aid and the military equipment Rabin seeks and because it will stabilize American-Israeli bilateral relationships.

"In addition, Mr. President, the mood I found in Israel will be of interest to you. The basic attitude of the negotiating team seems dominated by domestic political considerations. Allon has carved out his niche in the Cabinet minutes in the forefront of those insisting that 'there must be more political concessions' from Sadat to show that Israel is getting a piece of peace for withdrawal from the passes and the oil fields. Peres' domestic political strategy combines hawkish public statements with an insistence that there must be an American presence in the passes which will help deter Egyptian attack, add strategic stability, and be credible. To achieve this, he pressed hard for six American posts. Rabin is somewhere in the middle, determining his position on the kind of consensus he can achieve in his coalition on each of the various elements of the agreement. The mood and mode of operation is strikingly different from the negotiations of the 1974 Disengagement Agreement with Meir and Dayan, during which the talks reflected a common framework and assessment, and characteristic close friendly ties. This is not the case with the group—the new generation of Sabral leadership. The talks have taken on more the character of exchanges between adversaries than between friends; more the character of a necessary bargain to be struck with America; something Israel feels it must do, and do in such a way as to assure that at least part of the blame can be placed on the U.S. if something goes wrong in the future. In other words, the mood is grudging not generous, more concerned with finding a scapegoat than a common strategy.

"The public mood is feverish and emotional, partially as a result of months of negative conditioning by the Israeli leadership since last March towards the interim agreement and partly out of genuine concern by other Israelis regarding the future. The demonstrations are from the same groups who demonstrated in 1974 against the disengagement agreement. I get the impression that the government is not making a major effort to halt them using them as a protection against pressures for further concessions. They are obviously taking measures to keep them from getting out of control.

"The principal issues that now remain are:

—The Israeli line in the passes, although we may have made a little progress on that today depending on how other issues come out.
—An advance in the Egyptian main line a kilometer or two east of the present UN buffer zone.

—The arrangements at the Israeli and Egyptian intelligence stations.
—Whether there will be any U.S. stations and, if so, how many.
—The level of U.S. aid.
—Some specific commitments on military equipment.

"In this situation there are two options:

"1. We can continue the negotiations even though the agreement will not be taken by Sadat as a reflection of a genuine desire on the part of Israel to move towards peace. The arguments for this are the same as for the agreement initially—that it will reduce the risk of war, give new momentum to the U.S.-managed diplomatic effort toward peace in the Middle East, keep the Soviets on the sidelines, and avoid pressure to divide us from our allies.

"2. We could break off the negotiations after the first round if we judge that the Israelis will continue to insist on a price that is too high. The main argument for this approach is that the Israelis are plainly using this agreement not as another step toward peace but as a means of strengthening their position to resist efforts to achieve an overall settlement in the long run on any terms the Arabs might accept. This agreement grudgingly achieved will not do what the step-by-step approach was designed to achieve—increase confidence and provide stepping stones toward peace. The tactical argument for breaking the talks off quickly, if that is our judgment, is that what Israel is asking will still be starkly clear.

"It is still a bit early to make this judgment, but I wanted you to have a chance to consider the options. I will make every effort to bring Sadat along, but if the Israelis decide they are going to drag this out, a decision may need to be made by the middle of the week."

218. Memorandum From the President's Deputy Assistant for National Security Affairs (Scowcroft) to President Ford[1]

Washington, August 23, 1975.

Secretary Kissinger asked that the following report of his meeting with President Sadat be passed to you.

---

[1] Source: Ford Library, National Security Adviser, Kissinger Reports on USSR, China, and Middle East, Box 4, August 21–September 1, 1975, Volume I (3), Sinai Disengagement Agreement. Secret. Sent for information. Initialed by Ford.

"Four hours of discussion on Friday evening with President Sadat,[2] joined by Vice President Murabak, Foreign Minister Fahmy and Defense Minister Gamasy, leads me to the judgment that while Sadat feels the Israelis are being ungenerous, he nevertheless is ready to settle—and to settle expeditiously—on the best deal which proves attainable. He took a realistic approach, discussed the principal issues within the present limits of the negotiations, and distinguished between what he wants and what might prove achievable.

"The atmosphere was warm and cordial, Sadat was relaxed, looked well, and he displayed keen appreciation of the domestic pressures on all parties including Israel.

"His principal focus was getting the Israelis clearly out of the Giddi Pass. He accepted the present Israeli line in the Mitla as one which can plausibly be justified as 'out of the pass.' In order to get the Israelis out of Giddi, he has agreed not to insist on moving Egyptian forces forward beyond the present UN zone. He also asks that this concession will also get him a bit more territory along the proposed Israeli forward line.

"Sadat has accepted two American early tactical warning posts and the concept of American managed strategic warning stations operated by Israel and Egypt respectively. He wants his strategic warning station in the north rather than in the passes where General Gamasy feels it would be too vulnerable to the Israelis. Sadat expects, and I agreed in principle, that we will provide some sophisticated equipment and technical advice.

"There are two significant problem areas that will require concentrated effort in the next few days in addition to the territorial aspects described above.

"First, is the corridor area in the south of the Sinai which makes possible direct Egyptian access to the oil fields. Fahmy in particular insisted that this area should be Egyptian territory free of military forces rather than a UN zone under Egyptian civil administration. This is a different concept than one previously indicated by the Egyptians, and it will give the Israelis problems. I will know more clearly how best to deal with this new complication after I have explored Israeli thinking in more detail, and once we know the Egyptian thinking in more detail.

"Another area of concern is that the Israelis feel strongly they need to show more political concessions from Egypt in return for giving up tangibles such as the passes and oil fields. We will make a major effort

---

[2] The memorandum of conversation of the meeting between Sadat and Kissinger, which took place on August 22 at 6:30 p.m. at President Sadat's Guest House in Mamura, Alexandria, is in the National Archives, RG 59, Records of Henry Kissinger, 1973–77, Box 23, Classified External Memcons, May to December 1975, Folder 3.

to use what more we can get from the Egyptians on the question of the boycott, political warfare, and reduction of propaganda on Cairo radio, but my impression is that Sadat's sensitivity and vulnerability to attacks from other parts of the Arab world sharply limit his capacity for further significant concessions.

"Finally, Israel pressed me to seek—and Sadat has agreed—to let an Israeli cargo through the Suez Canal sometime near the end of next week. This will have a very favorable psychological impact in Israel and an equally unfavorable one in various parts of the Arab world.

"I renewed your invitation to Sadat to visit the U.S., and it was obvious from his response that he will be very anxious to do this once and if the agreement has been concluded.

"In short, the negotiations have moved somewhat due to Sadat's position, a bit slowly. Tomorrow I will make a short stop in Damascus to keep Asad calm before returning to Jerusalem in the evening to convey Sadat's latest thought."

---

219. Memorandum of Conversation[1]

Damascus, August 23, 1975.

Tête-à-tête Meeting between President H. Asad and Secretary of State Dr. Henry A. Kissinger (following larger meeting)

[Counselor Isa K. Sabbagh interpreted]

1. U.S.-Syrian Relations

The Secretary humorously reiterated his feeling of disappointment at his quiet but amicable reception in Damascus, as contrasted with what he had had, and would have again later in the evening, in Israel.

President Asad (Also humorously) said similar receptions could be arranged, but for the seriousness of the Syrian character and the true traditions of hospitality.

The Secretary said he realized that; from the President on down, the Syrians have been most hospitable and cordial to the Secretary and his group.

---

[1] Source: Ford Library, National Security Adviser, Kissinger Reports on USSR, China, and Middle East, Box 4, August 21–September 1, 1975, Volume I (3), Sinai Disengagement Agreement. Secret; Nodis. The meeting took place at the Presidential Palace. Brackets are in the original.

President Asad: We always make a distinction between a person and his policy. In the case of Dr. Kissinger, President Asad felt truly sorry at the failure in March '75 of the U.S. peace efforts. But objectively and realistically "we did our bit to make your mission fail!"

The Secretary: You can only do your best! But seriously your timing of doing things seems strange. Just as we were about to reach a positive point with Israel, vis-à-vis the West Bank involving Jordan, you engineer the Rabat Summit stand,[2] making it impossible for Israel to negotiate with the PLO. Now, we have your Syrian-Jordanian declaration of joint commands and councils, etc.[3] Frankly, anybody who could have unison with Jordan and the Palestinians at this juncture is ingenious! But didn't somebody jump the gun by a few months?

President Asad: We know how this latest joint communiqué is going to be interpreted against us. Actually, we have not set up anything jointly yet. We expressed hopes and intentions looking towards the future. I have always told you my views favoring Arab unity. This is no exception. But if you let this development strengthen the hand of those Congressional elements opposed to your carrying out your promise of giving Jordan the 14 rocket battalions, you would be making a grave mistake whose significance would go beyond the borders of Jordan. [Just before the Secretary took his leave, President Asad repeated this thought again—in fact for the fourth time—specifically referring to Saudi Arabia, the Gulf and North Africa as countries whose faith in U.S. promises and policies would be greatly reduced and shaken.]

President Asad continued: "Don't you worry, Jordan will get what it needs: from you, from us or from any other source."

The Secretary: We hope Congress will reverse itself. We do want to give Jordan what we promised King Hussein.

President Asad: You would be well advised to do so. The world is already thinking you have a strange system where more than a dozen loci of power seem to exist. The world is beginning to think that nothing should be surprising coming from the U.S. Congress. Why should Congress be anxious about what happens between Syria and Jordan. Why should U.S.-Arab relations be almost entirely based on Israel's wishes, demands or what have you?

The Secretary: I was disappointed that a meeting between President Asad and President Ford did not take place in Europe as we had hoped. Of course we realize that time was short on both sides. But a

---

[2] See Document 112.

[3] On August 22, Syria and Jordan announced the formation of a supreme command to coordinate and direct military action against Israel. The communiqué was issued at the end of King Hussein's State visit to Damascus. (*New York Times*, August 23, 1975 p. 7)

meeting between the two Presidents would be very useful. For one thing, President Asad would hear the U.S. policy straight from President Ford who is a straightforward man [less complicated than former President Nixon] and a man of his word. "Frankly we cannot tolerate any more a nation of 3 million dictating to U.S. policies which are not necessarily in our best interest." [The Secretary underscored this line more than once.] Secondly, if Presidents Asad and Ford meet, this would be definitely useful to Syria's image in the U.S.

President Asad agreed and hoped a meeting could be arranged in Europe. To meet in the U.S. would be difficult at present, said the Syrian President.

II. The PLO

Secretary Kissinger, responding to President Asad's remark that the U.S. non-recognition of the PLO was a big mistake, said the Syrian President surely appreciated how delicate this point was and how, as in anything else, timing was of the essence. Furthermore, we all know that the Palestinians did not have the untarnished reputation for keeping things quiet, not to mention their "genius" for not agreeing among themselves as to who should represent them.

President Asad emphasized that contacts on a high level should be established with the PLO.

Secretary Kissinger suggested that perhaps George Shultz, former Secretary of the Treasury "who is closely associated with President Ford and me" could visit the area once again and be put in touch with Palestinian elements which the Syrian President might recommend.

President Asad promised to talk to the PLO about this.

[According to news reports, President Asad did receive Yasir Arafat a day or two after Dr. Kissinger's visit to Damascus—IKS]

III. Syria-Israel

Secretary Kissinger emphasized that it is not the U.S. policy to split up the Arabs. "What would we get out of this, save going contrary to the logic of history?"

That's why we hope the Syrian President understands that an Egyptian-Israeli agreement, if it is finalized, would be in the right direction of making the Israelis used to the idea, indeed the necessity of agreements with the Arabs.

The Secretary conceded that an agreement between Israel and Syria would be more difficult than the one on Sinai (the differences between the two being, inter alia, in the terrains, the temperaments of Egypt and Syria!).

President Asad expressed deep doubt that anything would be achieved between Israel and Syria at this rate, and given Israel's continued intransigence and declarations. "What's the use of a few kilometers in the southern Syrian front? No, if Israel remains in Golan, as her actions and strengthening of settlements seem to indicate, then it is absolutely hopeless even to fool our people with any hopeful prospects. What would any Syrian, or any Arab for that matter, feel when he sees Quneitra as a ghost town? What kind of liberation can we call *that* when the Israelis are not only looking down on Quneitra but also building more and more things right on the edge of that city! Are we kidding?!"

Secretary Kissinger promised to give the Syrian President's legitimate pre-occupation serious thought in order hopefully to come up with some kind of a suggestion. Continuing, the Secretary explained how precious time was lost because of Watergate and what happened as a result of this "historic accident" i.e., the resignation of former President Nixon. If this had not happened, the element of continuity in our efforts and in using our influence might very well have solved several of the problems we are still facing.

Now President Ford is beginning noticeably to recoup a lot of prestige which the American presidency had lost. He still has a vocal and pro-Israeli Congress to deal with, especially those 40 members who realize that, no matter what happens, they are not going to be re-elected.

With President Ford elected, and Congress having new faces, the tempo could be quickened in pursuing a solution. President Ford, you would notice when you meet him, has positive views on this problem, not unlike what former President Nixon unfolded before you during his visit to Damascus.[4]

President Asad was glad to hear this about President Ford. He added that the Egyptians had described President Ford as honest, courageous, and straightforward.

Asad asked about President Ford's chances in the coming elections.

Secretary Kissinger was almost completely certain of a Ford victory.

Asked about the Democrats, Secretary Kissinger replied the only Democratic candidate he could see was Kennedy. However even Kennedy has similar views regarding this problem (!) said the Secretary.

The Secretary told Asad that Rabin had said that by mid-October 1975 (if the agreement with Egypt is reached), Israel would be willing to send a representative to Washington for quiet talks about the Syrian front.

---

[4] See Document 92.

"While I am not asking you for a reply now," continued the Secretary to Asad, "I'd venture the thought that, in order to maintain the secrecy and low-key aspect of such discussions," President Asad need not send a representative at the outset to Washington. Either the Syrian Ambassador there, or, more discreetly, our Ambassador to Syria, would be summoned once or twice for consultations. Thus we could start or resume the Syrian-Israeli ball rolling, very quietly and pending this the Secretary would keep President Asad informed of any new developments.

The Secretary also gave a tentative "iffy" promise to go back to Damascus: if necessary, if he had any new thoughts on the Golan step, if his schedule did not lag too far behind, etc.

IV. US Aid to Israel

President Asad asked, in seeming consternation, about the reported $3 billion-plus assistance from the U.S. to Israel!

Secretary Kissinger said the figure was grossly exaggerated. It was much less than that. In any case, added the Secretary, it would not be in the form of a ready check in the whole amount. Rather, the assistance would be proportioned in such a way as to keep us in an effective position of influencing Israel through 1977.

In sum, the Secretary urged President Asad not to upset the apple cart (as he is capable of doing!)—frankly for Syria's own good. We (U.S.A) need time to tide us over until after the elections. This did not mean that we would in the meantime, do nothing. No, we would be resorting to arranging things quietly and in a preparatory way with Congress and with American public opinion. The Israeli-Egyptian agreement, if and when it comes about, should help the process we have in mind.

The Secretary advised, for instance, against the Arabs, and through them the non-aligned nations, insisting on Israel's ouster from the UN. This would prove counter-productive and would certainly be interpreted as Arab unreasonableness. So, let Khaddam have an opportunity (in Lima, Peru) to exercise his famous composure!![5]

Asad, smilingly, said "We were not urging that Israel be chucked out of the UN, but that she be held to the promises stipulated in her birth-certificate, i.e., membership in the UN." The Syrian President added: "If Israel does not, she will receive her punishment: if not this year, then the next, or the next."

The Secretary, conceding President Asad's rare gift of machination, suggested that working for peace required a few other consider-

---

[5] A reference to the Non-Aligned Conference held in Lima August 23–29.

ations to be borne in mind, e.g., clear objectives, the image abroad, timing of steps, increasing friends and supporters and so on.

President Asad said he had always enjoyed exchanging philosophical views with the Secretary. Clearly, he (Asad) appreciates the Secretary's need for more time; but by the same token, the Secretary surely appreciates Syria's unswerving demand for deeper results to show the people that America's intercessional efforts are not just talk or show.

The Secretary said the Syrian President had always been honest, frank and forceful of expression with us. We would do our very best to move expeditiously into the next step on the Syrian front, bearing in mind the President's concerns.

220. Memorandum From the President's Deputy Assistant for National Security Affairs (Scowcroft) to President Ford[1]

Washington, August 26, 1975.

Secretary Kissinger asked that the following report of his August 25 meeting with Sadat be passed to you:

"It has been a long and difficult day, with some further progress, some new difficulties, though not necessarily unresolvable, and a seemingly never ending series of details on which to achieve common ground.

"With Sadat today[2] we came a bit closer on a possible agreed line which would get the Israelis out of the Giddi pass. He accepted the additional slivers of territory Israel has given on both the Egyptian and Israeli lines, and we will try to get agreement from Israel tonight on the location of the Egyptian strategic early warning stations. Sadat has also accepted the American presence in the passes.

"We went over in detail with Fahmy and Gamasy a text of an agreement,[3] a copy of which I am sending. Sadat went further in the direction of the Israeli position than expected. For example, he has not only lived up to his commitment to include in the agreement a non-resort to force clause, but also met the Israeli insistence that

---

[1] Source: Ford Library, National Security Adviser, Kissinger Reports on USSR, China, and Middle East, Box 4, August 21–September 1, 1975, Volume I (6), Sinai Disengagement Agreement. Secret; Sensitive.

[2] No memorandum of conversation has been found.

[3] The final agreement is Document 226.

blockades be barred. Cargoes of a non-strategic character will be allowed to pass through the Suez Canal. The text also keeps the agreement open-ended as Israel wants, and Sadat confirmed he will give us a letter committing Egypt to three annual renewals of the UNEF. There are still difficulties ahead on the precise terms of the zone of limitation, and there is a fundamental difference between Egypt and Israel to resolve over the corridor area leading to the oil fields; Egypt wants sovereignty, Israel's position is that Egypt should exercise civil administration. We also need to work out a tripartite agreement governing our technical surveillance role in the passes.

"I expect a difficult session tonight with Rabin. The technical team I left behind in Israel to work with them on the memorandum of understanding incorporating the U.S. bilateral assurances Israel seeks have reported continuing differences. The Israelis are still pushing to limit our future freedom of action politically on this issue."

221. Memorandum From the President's Deputy Assistant for National Security Affairs (Scowcroft) to President Ford[1]

Washington, August 26, 1975.

Secretary Kissinger has sent you the following report on his August 25 meeting with Prime Minister Rabin:

"Immediately upon returning from Alexandria, I met for 2½ hours this evening to give the Israeli negotiating team a report on my talks today with President Sadat and Foreign Minister Fahmy.[2] With only minor details to be cleared up, I believe we now have agreement on the map. With respect to the text of the agreement itself, while the Israelis want to study it overnight, their reaction to the language we worked out in Alexandria[3]—and in particular the inclusion of references to blockades and the passage of Israeli cargoes through the canal—indicates that the differences have been significantly narrowed.

---

[1] Source: Ford Library, National Security Adviser, Kissinger Reports on USSR, China, and Middle East, Box 4, August 21–September 1, 1975, Volume I (7), Sinai Disengagement Agreement. Secret; Sensitive. Sent for information.

[2] The memorandum of conversation of the meeting between the Israeli negotiating team and Kissinger, which took place on August 25 from 10:02 p.m. until 12:06 a.m. at the Prime Minister's office in Jerusalem, is ibid., Volume I (6), Sinai Disengagement Agreement.

[3] See Document 220.

"I will meet again tomorrow morning with the Israeli negotiating team to get their considered reaction before returning to Alexandria tomorrow afternoon. There is still a great deal of work to do if we are to wrap up the agreement by the end of the week, and there are still possibilities that further hitches can develop although the prospects are clearly better as a result of the decisions taken by Sadat today which I have already reported to you.

"The next immediate tasks facing us are to work out the text of a trilateral agreement governing the stationing of U.S. civilian personnel at the monitoring stations in the vicinity of the Passes and of the bilateral U.S.-Israeli Memorandum of Understanding. We provided drafts of both of these in technical talks held by members of my staff with the Israelis in Jerusalem today[4] while I was in Egypt, and they have promised us their reactions tomorrow. On the Memorandum of Understanding, as you know, the Israelis have been pressing for assurances with regard to economic and military assistance and oil supply as well as diplomatic and political support which in many instances go far beyond what we can or should give them. The draft we gave them cut back sharply on many of these assurances, and I expect some tough bargaining before we reach agreement on this document. They are also still seeking Egyptian political assurances through us which greatly exceed anything Sadat can realistically do, particularly since the Israelis leak virtually everything to the press, and here too there are still some difficult discussions ahead. I should have a better idea after tomorrow morning's meeting about how time-consuming the remaining issues between the U.S. and the Israelis will be. A positive factor is that, now that the pace of negotiation has increased, both Egypt and Israel seem to be caught up in the momentum and feel it desirable to wind matters up as rapidly as possible."

---

[4] No memoranda of conversation of these technical meetings have been found.

222. Memorandum From the President's Deputy Assistant for National Security Affairs (Scowcroft) to President Ford[1]

Washington, August 27, 1975.

Secretary Kissinger asked that I pass you the following report:

"After seven hours today of tedious point by point negotiation with Rabin and his colleagues followed by three hours tonight with Sadat,[2] I can report that we have reduced the gap on most issues, but there are several remaining problems, each of which if not overcome could cause a break.

"The first relates to language in the agreement committing the parties to settle all disputes between them by negotiations or other peaceful means. The Israelis are not satisfied with the present formulation. They want it in two successive paragraphs. Sadat will not go beyond mentioning it once. Sadat shows signs of digging in—perhaps a reflection of increasing criticism of him in the Arab world in light of details leaked by the Israelis. I will make a major effort tomorrow to get a satisfactory formulation.

"Second, is Sadat's resistance to writing letters giving certain private assurances. This too is attributable in large measure to Israeli leaks. Sadat said he cannot give assurances by letter which the other side will leak; they will be used against him in the Arab world. I will make another hard try on this one tomorrow.

"The third and most serious problem raised by Sadat relates to the early warning system in the passes. Egypt and Israel have agreed on the locations of their respective strategic early warning stations and we are agreed on U.S. presence. Israel wants them established by means of a tripartite agreement including Egypt, Israel, and the U.S. Sadat raised a fundamental objection to a tripartite agreement governing the maintenance and operation of the system and defining our role on the ground. He says the Sinai is his territory, and he cannot agree that Israel has the legal right to enter into an agreement with the U.S. along with Egypt regarding the use of Egyptian territory. We are exploring urgently other possible ways to establish a proper legal basis for the

---

[1] Source: Ford Library, National Security Adviser, Trip Briefing Books for Henry Kissinger, Box 12, August 20–September 3, 1975, Middle East, Kissinger Messages to President, August 27, 1975. Secret; Sensitive. Sent for information. An attached handwritten notation reads, "The President has seen."

[2] The memorandum of conversation of the meeting between Rabin and Kissinger, which took place on August 26 from 10:25 a.m. until 4:38 p.m. at the Prime Minister's office in Jerusalem, is ibid., Kissinger Reports on USSR, China, and Middle East, Box 4, August 21–September 1, 1975, Vol. II (1), Sinai Disengagement Agreement. No memorandum of conversation of the meeting between Sadat and Kissinger has been found.

U.S. custodial role of the surveillance system in the passes such as an annex to the agreement coupled with a separate protocol between the U.S. and each of the signatories. My concern is that Peres is locked into the tripartite agreement approach and may well break with Rabin on this issue. Thus the press reports are much too euphoric.

"What I am banking on is that both sides are now so far committed that they will find it most difficult to lose an agreement which is so close to their grasp. Both sides are feeling the pressure—Rabin on the domestic scene and Sadat within the Arab world—and if there is to be an agreement it must come in the next few days."

Warm regards.

223. Memorandum From the President's Deputy Assistant for National Security Affairs (Scowcroft) to President Ford[1]

Washington, August 28, 1975.

Secretary Kissinger asked that I pass you the following report:

"After six hours with Sadat today,[2] I brought to Rabin tonight a clean text of the agreement[3] which in our judgment meets all of the essential points which the Israelis have underscored over the past months. It is a further improvement of the text sent yesterday. However, the reaction was one of caution,[4] and it is clear that when we meet again tomorrow morning, we will be receiving additional suggestions from the Israelis for changes, reflecting the maneuverings which are going on within the power structure, and in particular between Peres and Rabin. There is even a chance that they will turn it down.

---

[1] Source: Ford Library, National Security Adviser, Kissinger Reports on USSR, China, and Middle East, Box 5, August 21–September 1, 1975, Volume II (5), Sinai Disengagement Agreement. Secret; Sensitive. Sent for information. A handwritten notation at the top of the first page reads, "Pres. has seen."

[2] No memorandum of conversation of the meeting between Sadat and Kissinger has been found.

[3] The "clean text" of the draft agreement of August 27 is attached to the memorandum of conversation of the meeting with the Israeli team; see footnote 4 below. An August 26 draft with Kissinger's handwritten revisions is also attached.

[4] The memorandum of conversation of the meeting between the Israeli negotiating team and Kissinger, which took place on August 27 from 9:45 until 11:48 p.m. at the Prime Minister's office in Jerusalem, is in the Ford Library, National Security Adviser, Kissinger Reports on USSR, China, and Middle East, Box 5, August 21–September 1, 1975, Volume II (5), Sinai Disengagement Agreement.

"From the point of view of logic, both sides are so far committed that this agreement should be achievable. I regret to say that this remains uncertain, not because of any particular substantive point, but rather due to a combination of factors on the Israeli side comprised of insecurity, inexperience, and domestic maneuvering. Rabin's statement tonight after we presented the clean text of the agreement, meeting all of Israel's essential points, was that "he was not blaming anyone" but that his expectations were greater than the political returns which he believes they are getting. There is, of course, the point that Israel is giving up something tangible such as the passes and the oil fields in exchange for less tangible, but no less important, political concessions. Our most optimistic assessments never included the possibility that Sadat would be willing to commit himself in a public document, contrary to the mainstream of the Arab world, against blockades and in favor of cargoes going through the Suez Canal—yet he has done so. He has met another principal Israeli demand—namely, an American technical surveillance presence in the passes. We were quite perplexed by Rabin's approach tonight—a deep pessimism, in sharp contrast to euphoric pronouncements to the press by Allon last night. We can only assume that Peres is giving him a difficult time and upping the ante, and that he is not sure he can sell the agreement that is emerging to his cabinet—particularly now that Dayan has spoken out against it.

"However, since we have Sadat's agreement in principle to the American role in the warning stations, we believe Peres' main political thrust has been met. It is he who has made an American presence in the passes a precondition of the agreement. It is equally clear that Rabin does not like, or at most is ambivalent about, the idea of bringing Americans into the situation, and this view apparently was reinforced tonight when he met with some congressmen and some prominent American Jewish leaders, and in the aftermath of negative statements regarding the American presence by Mansfield and Jackson and a neutral one by Senator Humphrey, who over the years has been one of the firmest supporters of Israel.

"I urged tonight that we try to review the text of the agreement tomorrow and if the Israelis have any changes, that they be kept to an absolute minimum on points of substance. We will also be going over our respective concepts of the warning system in the passes; Sadat has agreed to this on the understanding that he would not enter into a tripartite agreement because it would derogate from Egypt's sovereignty in the Sinai, but he would be willing to have the concept put in the form of a U.S. proposal to which he would agree as well as Israel.

"There are many other detailed aspects of the documentation which will be most time-consuming, and if there is to be agreement, the earliest initialing which could now take place would be either Sunday or Monday."[5]

Warm regards.

---

[5] August 31 or September 1.

---

224. Memorandum From the President's Deputy Assistant for National Security Affairs (Scowcroft) to President Ford[1]

Washington, August 28, 1975.

Secretary Kissinger asked that the following message be passed to you:

"After seven hours with Rabin today and three with Sadat[2] here is where we stand:

"First, with the exception of a few very minor non-fundamental points, the text of the agreement is agreed and for all practical purposes frozen. I am sending you a text.[3]

"Secondly, there is agreement on the U.S. technical surveillance early warning station system in the area of the passes. This will be made in the form of a U.S. proposal accepted by both sides. It is this element that will be submitted to the Congress for its approval. There will be three U.S. manned stations.

"Thirdly, the map is set with the exception that we will need to get a slight modification from the Israelis on how they have drawn the line through the Giddi Pass.

"Fourth, there is a remaining, serious problem with the Israelis on the kind of arrangements they have in mind in the corridor leading to

---

[1] Source: Ford Library, National Security Adviser, Kissinger Reports on USSR, China, and Middle East, Box 5, August 21–September 1, 1975, Volume III (2), Sinai Disengagement Agreement. Secret; Sensitive; Exclusively Eyes Only. Sent for information.

[2] The memorandum of conversation of the meeting between the Israeli negotiating team and Kissinger, which took place on August 27 from 10:47 a.m. until 4:25 p.m. is ibid., Box 5, August 21–September 1, 1975, Volume III (1), Sinai Disengagement Agreement. No memorandum of conversation of the meeting between Sadat and Kissinger has been found.

[3] The U.S. and Israeli drafts of the agreement, August 28, and an Israel redraft handed over at the meeting of August 28, are attached to the memorandum of conversation of the meeting with the Israeli team. See footnote 2 above.

the Abu Rudeis oil field. They revealed to us for the first time that they have fortifications right up against a single road which is along the Gulf of Suez. This would mean that when Egyptian traffic is on this road on alternate days it will be facing Israeli guns within eyesight. This is exactly what the Israelis did in Kuneitra in the Syrian agreement which has prevented Asad from ever repopulating the city. I have made clear to the Israelis that the Egyptians will not accept this kind of situation and they are studying the matter overnight to see what can be done about it. This is clearly an issue on which the agreement could break, Mr. President, because it would fundamentally abridge the principle of free access to the oil fields, to which the Israelis have been committed for a very long time.

"Fifth, there is also the large area of private commitments and assurances. Israel wants us to get the kind of written commitments from Egypt which, in the context of the Israeli leaks, Sadat is understandably very reluctant to give. Moreover the price which the Israelis are demanding on the bilateral memorandum of understanding agreement between us would restrict seriously our freedom of political action in the future, unless the Israelis back off.

"In short, Mr. President, while the agreement is not yet certain, we are very close indeed. I am not certain that this agreement will have the hoped for effect of opening a new chapter of relations between Israel and Egypt. This is because of the ungenerous manner in which the Israelis have negotiated this agreement. Nor do I come away from this negotiation with the feeling that the Israelis have dealt with us as a close and intimate ally working together within a concerted strategy. The experience of the last week has not enhanced the confidence of any of us in the team which is at the helm of the Israeli government. I do not come away with the feeling that the achievement of this agreement will strengthen the fabric of U.S.-Israeli relationships as much as I had hoped. Moreover, there is the consideration that some at home, at least, will be concerned over the $2 billion-plus price tag, the guaranty of an oil supply, and the American presence in the passes.

"Nevertheless, I believe that the achievement of this agreement is in the overall national interest. It is still the best way to buy time and reduce the risk of war in the area; it is still the best way for us to remain relevant to the diplomacy of the Middle East; it is still the best way for us to avoid a steady deterioration of our relations in the Arab world; it is still the best way to keep on an even keel with our allies in Europe on this issue; it is still the best way to reduce the influence of the Soviet Union in the Middle East and it will avoid a domestic confrontation which is more likely in circumstances of a seriously strained American-Israeli relationship.

"I appreciated receiving your observations on the Middle Eastern situation contained in your recent cable."

225. Memorandum From the President's Deputy Assistant for National Security Affairs (Scowcroft) to President Ford[1]

Washington, August 29, 1975.

Secretary Kissinger asked that I pass you the following report:

"In the longest session of this shuttle—nine hours of unbroken negotiations with Rabin and his team[2]—we widened the area of agreement and I believe we have broken the back of all major hurdles, subject to further discussions with Sadat tomorrow.[3] The prospects are good that this agreement can be initialed on Monday or Tuesday by the two sides and signed in Geneva about Wednesday.[4]

"We are tentatively planning on a simultaneous announcement by you, Rabin and Sadat, and I will be sending you a recommendation on timing as well as a suggested draft text which you might wish to make on the three major networks.

"Here is a current rundown on the productive results of today's nine-hour session.

"A. A text of the agreement[5] is now agreed with both Egypt and Israel except for one point—Israel's insistence that reference to the right of the parties to self-defense under Article 51 of the Charter be eliminated. The Israelis feel this waters down the Sadat commitment not to

---

[1] Source: Ford Library, National Security Adviser, Kissinger Reports on USSR, China, and Middle East, Box 5, August 21–September 1, 1975, Volume III (5), Sinai Disengagement Agreement. Secret; Sensitive. Sent for information. A handwritten notation at the top of the first page reads, "Pres. has seen."

[2] The memorandum of conversation of the meeting between the Israeli negotiating team and Kissinger, which took place on August 29 from 11:52 a.m. until 6:40 p.m., is ibid., Volume III (3), Sinai Disengagement Agreement. The final negotiations continued over the next three days. Memoranda of conversation of meetings between the Israeli negotiating team and Kissinger took place on August 30 into August 31 from 9 p.m. until 12:27 a.m. (ibid., Volume III (6), Sinai Disengagement Agreement), August 31 from 9:13 a.m. until 12:40 p.m. (ibid., Volume III (7), Sinai Disengagement Agreement), and August 31 into September 1 from 9:50 p.m. until 5:30 a.m. (ibid., Volume III (8), Sinai Disengagement Agreement).

[3] No memoranda of conversation with Sadat were found.

[4] September 1–3.

[5] Text of agreement is attached but not printed.

resort to the use of force and resolve all issues by peaceful means. I will make a major effort with Sadat tomorrow in Alexandria to try to get him to drop it.

"B. We are in full agreement with Israel on the concept and the details of how the early warning system will work. We have an agreed text in the form of a U.S. proposal to which each side will send its acceptance. I expect to get Egypt's final approval to the text tomorrow.

"C. We agreed on a text with the Israelis on an annex which will describe the guidelines and framework for the technical group which will meet in Geneva next week after the signing to work out the detailed implementation of the agreement. The implementation, of course, will be on a phased basis and we are trying to arrange it so that the Egyptian takeover of the oil fields comes in the first month or so after the signing and the passes are turned over within six months of the signing. Rabin has made it very clear that no implementation of the agreement can start without the prior approval of the Congress of the U.S. participation in the warning system in the passes. From here the reaction from the Congress seems to be of a mixed character; however, the Israelis are very anxious to make a major effort along with the Administration to assure overwhelming support of the American presence in the passes. I continue to share your previously expressed judgment that the Congress will support you on this matter.

"D. Finally, we made some progress in the area of bilateral assurances which the Israelis expect from us. I dug in strongly in resisting any far-reaching assurances which would tend to tie our hands politically and diplomatically in what we would expect to do in the future in the Middle East. Moreover, the Israelis have been pressing me to go beyond 2.1 billion on aid, but I have continued to maintain the line at this figure.

"E. I concluded the long negotiating session tonight with a meeting alone with Rabin, Peres and Allon at their request.[6] It was somewhat of a hand-holding, hand-wringing sort of discussion which reflects the unsure leadership at the helm of this country. Rabin did a good job at the meetings today of deflecting numerous inane suggestions of both Peres and Allon. Each in his own way is ambivalent about the agreement, but each equally in his own way sees no better alternative. They seem to have a feel for the disastrous situation which would ensue if this present effort were to fail."

---

[6] No memorandum of conversation has been found.

226. Egyptian-Israeli Disengagement Agreement[1]

Jerusalem, September 1, 1975.

TEXTS OF AGREEMENT AND ANNEX AND U.S. PROPOSAL

Agreement Between Egypt and Israel[2]

The Government of the Arab Republic of Egypt and the Government of Israel have agreed that:

Article I

The conflict between them and in the Middle East shall not be resolved by military force but by peaceful means.

The Agreement concluded by the Parties January 18, 1974, within the framework of the Geneva Peace Conference, constituted a first step towards a just and durable peace according to the provisions of Security Council Resolution 338 of October 22, 1973.

They are determined to reach a final and just peace settlement by means of negotiations called for by Security Council Resolution 338, this Agreement being a significant step towards that end.

Article II

The Parties hereby undertake not to resort to the threat or use of force or military blockade against each other.

Article III

The Parties shall continue scrupulously to observe the ceasefire on land, sea and air and to refrain from all military or para-military actions against each other.

The Parties also confirm that the obligations contained in the Annex and, when concluded, the Protocol shall be an integral part of this Agreement.

---

[1] Source: Department of State *Bulletin*, September 29, 1975, pp. 466–470. The *Bulletin* includes the texts of the annex, which concerns arrangements for the preparation of a protocol for the implementation of the agreemeent, and the U.S. proposal for American civilians to man an early warning system in the Sinai. Only the agreement is printed here. All three were also printed in the *New York Times*, September 2, 1975. President Ford issued a statement on the signing of the agreement on September 1 and had an exchange with reporters the same day; see *Public Papers: Ford, 1975*, Book II, p. 1278 and pp. 1285–1287.

[2] The agreement and annex were initialed on Sept. 1 at Jerusalem by representatives of Israel and at Alexandria by representatives of Egypt and signed at Geneva on Sept. 4. [Footnote in the original.]

Article IV

A. The military forces of the Parties shall be deployed in accordance with the following principles:

(1) All Israeli forces shall be deployed east of the lines designated as Lines J and M on the attached map.[3]

(2) All Egyptian forces shall be deployed west of the line designated as Line E on the attached map.

(3) The area between the lines designated on the attached map as Lines E and F and the area between the lines designated on the attached map as Lines J and K shall be limited in armament and forces.

(4) The limitations on armament and forces in the areas described by paragraph (3) above shall be agreed as described in the attached Annex.

(5) The zone between the lines designated on the attached map as Lines E and J, will be a buffer zone. In this zone the United Nations Emergency Force will continue to perform its functions as under the Egyptian-Israeli Agreement of January 18, 1974.

(6) In the area south from Line E and west from Line M, as defined on the attached map, there will be no military forces, as specified in the attached Annex.

B. The details concerning the new lines, the redeployment of the forces and its timing, the limitation on armaments and forces, aerial reconnaissance, the operation of the early warning and surveillance installations and the use of the roads, the United Nations functions and other arrangements will all be in accordance with the provisions of the Annex and map which are an integral part of this Agreement and of the Protocol which is to result from negotiations pursuant to the Annex and which, when concluded, shall become an integral part of this Agreement.

Article V

The United Nations Emergency Force is essential and shall continue its functions and its mandate shall be extended annually.

Article VI

The Parties hereby establish a Joint Commission for the duration of this Agreement. It will function under the aegis of the Chief Coordinator of the United Nations Peacekeeping Missions in the Middle East in order to consider any problem arising from this Agreement and to assist the United Nations Emergency Force in the execution of its man-

---

[3] The map is not attached, but see the final status map in Appendix B, map 4.

date. The Joint Commission shall function in accordance with procedures established in the Protocol.

Article VII

Non-military cargoes destined for or coming from Israel shall be permitted through the Suez Canal.

Article VIII

This Agreement is regarded by the Parties as a significant step toward a just and lasting peace. It is not a final peace agreement.

The Parties shall continue their efforts to negotiate a final peace agreement within the framework of the Geneva Peace Conference in accordance with Security Council Resolution 338.

Article IX

This Agreement shall enter into force upon signature of the Protocol and remain in force until superseded by a new agreement.

Done at _____ on the _____ 1975, in four original copies.

For the Government of the   For the Government of Israel
Arab Republic of Egypt

Witness

227. Memoranda of Agreement[1]

Jerusalem, September 1, 1975.

MEMORANDUM OF AGREEMENT BETWEEN THE GOVERNMENTS OF ISRAEL AND THE UNITED STATES

The United States recognizes that the Egypt–Israel Agreement initialed on September 1, 1975, (hereinafter referred to as the Agreement), entailing the withdrawal from vital areas in Sinai, constitutes an act of great significance on Israel's part in the pursuit of final peace. That Agreement has full United States support.

United States-Israeli Assurances

1. The United States Government will make every effort to be fully responsive, within the limits of its resources and Congressional authorization and appropriation, on an on-going and long-term basis to Israel's military equipment and other defense requirements, to its energy requirements and to its economic needs. The needs specified in paragraphs 2, 3 and 4 below shall be deemed eligible for inclusion within the annual total to be requested in FY76 and later fiscal years.

2. Israel's long-term military supply needs from the United States shall be the subject of periodic consultations between representatives of the United States and Israeli defense establishments, with agreement reached on specific items to be included in a separate United States-Israeli memorandum. To this end, a joint study by military experts will be undertaken within 3 weeks. In conducting this study, which will include Israel's 1976 needs, the United States will view Israel's requests sympathetically, including its request for advanced and sophisticated weapons.

3. Israel will make its own independent arrangements for oil supply to meet its requirements through normal procedures. In the event Israel is unable to secure its needs in this way, the United States Government, upon notification of this fact by the Government of Israel, will act as follows for five years, at the end of which period either side can terminate this arrangement on one-year's notice.

(a) If the oil Israel needs to meet all its normal requirements for domestic consumption is unavailable for purchase in circumstances where no quantitative restrictions exist on the ability of the United States to procure oil to meet its normal requirements, the United States

---

[1] Source: Library of Congress, Manuscript Division, Kissinger Papers, CL 159, Geopolitical File, Israel, September 1–17, 1975. Secret. The texts of both memoranda were initialed on each page by Kissinger and Allon.

Government will promptly make oil available for purchase by Israel to meet all of the aforementioned normal requirements of Israel. If Israel is unable to secure the necessary means to transport such oil to Israel, the United States Government will make every effort to help Israel secure the necessary means of transport.

(b) If the oil Israel needs to meet all of its normal requirements for domestic consumption is unavailable for purchase in circumstances where quantitative restrictions through embargo or otherwise also prevent the United States from procuring oil to meet its normal requirements, the United States Government will promptly make oil available for purchase by Israel in accordance with the International Energy Agency conservation and allocation formula as applied by the United States Government, in order to meet Israel's essential requirements. If Israel is unable to secure the necessary means to transport such oil to Israel, the United States Government will make every effort to help Israel secure the necessary means of transport.

Israeli and United States experts will meet annually or more frequently at the request of either party, to review Israel's continuing oil requirement.

4. In order to help Israel meet its energy needs, and as part of the overall annual figure in paragraph 1 above, the United States agrees:

(a) In determining the overall annual figure which will be requested from Congress, the United States Government will give special attention to Israel's oil import requirements and, for a period as determined by Article 3 above, will take into account in calculating that figure Israel's additional expenditures for the import of oil to replace that which would have ordinarily come from Abu Rodeis and Ras Sudar (4.5 million tons in 1975).

(b) To ask Congress to make available funds, the amount to be determined by mutual agreement, to the Government of Israel necessary for a project for the construction and stocking of the oil reserves to be stored in Israel, bringing storage reserve capacity and reserve stocks now standing at approximately six months, up to one-year's need at the time of the completion of the project. The project will be implemented within four years. The construction, operation and financing and other relevant questions of the project will be the subject of early and detailed talks between the two Governments.

5. The United States Government will not expect Israel to begin to implement the Agreement before Egypt fulfils its undertaking under the January 1974 Disengagement Agreement to permit passage of all Israeli cargoes to and from Israeli ports through the Suez Canal.

6. The United States Government agrees with Israel that the next agreement with Egypt should be a final peace agreement.

7. In case of an Egyptian violation of any of the provisions of the Agreement, the United States Government is prepared to consult with Israel as to the significance of the violation and possible remedial action by the United States Government.

8. The United States Government will vote against any Security Council resolution which in its judgment affects or alters adversely the Agreement.

9. The United States Government will not join in and will seek to prevent efforts by others to bring about consideration of proposals which it and Israel agree are detrimental to the interests of Israel.

10. In view of the long-standing United States commitment to the survival and security of Israel, the United States Government will view with particular gravity threats to Israel's security or sovereignty by a world power. In support of this objective, the United States Government will in the event of such threat consult promptly with the Government of Israel with respect to what support, diplomatic or otherwise, or assistance it can lend to Israel in accordance with its constitutional practices.

11. The United States Government and the Government of Israel will, at the earliest possible time, and if possible, within two months after the signature of this document, conclude the contingency plan for a military supply operation to Israel in an emergency situation.

12. It is the United States Government's position that Egyptian commitments under the Egypt–Israel Agreement, its implementation, validity and duration are not conditional upon any act or developments between the other Arab states and Israel. The United States Government regards the Agreement as standing on its own.

13. The United States Government shares the Israeli position that under existing political circumstances negotiations with Jordan will be directed toward an overall peace settlement.

14. In accordance with the principle of freedom of navigation on the high seas and free and unimpeded passage through and over straits connecting international waters, the United States Government regards the Straits of Bab-el-Mandeb and the Strait of Gibraltar as international waterways. It will support Israel's right to free and unimpeded passage through such straits. Similarly, the United States Government recognizes Israel's right to freedom of flights over the Red Sea and such straits and will support diplomatically the exercise of that right.

15. In the event that the United Nations Emergency Force or any other United Nations organ is withdrawn without the prior agreement of both Parties to the Egypt–Israel Agreement and the United States before this Agreement is superseded by another agreement, it is the United States view that the Agreement shall remain binding in all its parts.

16. The United States and Israel agree that signature of the Protocol of the Egypt–Israel Agreement and its full entry into effect shall not take place before approval by the United States Congress of the United States role in connection with the surveillance and observation functions described in the Agreement and its Annex. The United States has informed the Government of Israel that it has obtained the Government of Egypt agreement to the above.

Yigal Allon
Deputy Prime Minister and Minister of Foreign Affairs
For the Government of Israel

Henry A. Kissinger[2]
Secretary of State
For the Government of the United States

MEMORANDUM OF AGREEMENT BETWEEN THE GOVERNMENTS OF ISRAEL AND THE UNITED STATES

The Geneva Peace Conference

1. The Geneva Peace Conference will be reconvened at a time coordinated between the United States and Israel.

2. The United States will continue to adhere to its present policy with respect to the Palestine Liberation Organization, whereby it will not recognize or negotiate with the Palestine Liberation Organization so long as the Palestine Liberation Organization does not recognize Israel's right to exist and does not accept Security Council Resolutions 242 and 338. The United States Government will consult fully and seek to concert its position and strategy at the Geneva Peace Conference on this issue with the Government of Israel. Similarly, the United States will consult fully and seek to concert its position and strategy with Israel with regard to the participation of any other additional states. It is understood that the participation at a subsequent phase of the Conference of any possible additional state, group or organization will require the agreement of all the initial participants.

3. The United States will make every effort to ensure at the Conference that all the substantive negotiations will be on a bilateral basis.

4. The United States will oppose and, if necessary, vote against any initiative in the Security Council to alter adversely the terms of reference of the Geneva Peace Conference or to change Resolutions 242 and 338 in ways which are incompatible with their original purpose.

5. The United States will seek to ensure that the role of the co-sponsors will be consistent with what was agreed in the Memorandum

---

[2] Printed from a copy that bears only Allon's signature.

of Understanding between the United States Government and the Government of Israel of December 20, 1973.[3]

6. The United States and Israel will concert action to assure that the Conference will be conducted in a manner consonant with the objectives of this document and with the declared purpose of the Conference, namely the advancement of a negotiated peace between Israel and each one of its neighbors.

Yigal Allon	Henry A. Kissinger[4]
Deputy Prime Minister and Minister of Foreign Affairs	Secretary of State
For the Government of Israel	For the Government of the United States

---

[3] See *Foreign Relations,* 1969–1976, volume XXV, Arab-Israeli Crisis and War, 1973, Document 410.

[4] Printed from a copy that bears only Allon's signature.

---

228. Letter From Secretary of State Kissinger to Israeli Foreign Minister Allon[1]

Jerusalem, September 1, 1975.

Dear Mr. Minister:

In connection with the Agreement initialed on September 1, 1975, between the Governments of Egypt and Israel, I hereby convey the following to you:

1. The United States Government has received an assurance from Egypt that it will not use lack of progress at the Geneva Conference as a pretext for not fulfilling its obligations under the Agreement.

2. The United States Government will transmit a letter to Israel conveying Egypt's undertaking on annual renewals of UNEF's mandate.

---

[1] Source: National Archives, RG 59, Records of Henry Kissinger, 1973–77, Box 15, Miscellaneous, Documents, Telegrams, etc., 1975, Folder 8. Secret.

3. The United States Government has received from Egypt an expression of its intention to reduce hostile propaganda in its government controlled media.[2]

4. The United States Government has received an assurance from Egypt of its willingness to ease the boycott of American companies on a selective basis and that it will not discriminate against any American company that wants to do business in Egypt, regardless of whether this company is on the boycott list.[3] The United States will encourage the Government of Egypt to expand the above to include European and other companies.

5. It is the understanding of the United States Government that Egypt intends to avoid active diplomatic efforts to discourage selected other states from resuming diplomatic relations with Israel.

6. The United States Government will seek to ascertain whether Egypt is willing that ships, aircraft, passengers and crews of either Party in distress will be given assistance by the other and will be permitted to continue on their route.

7. The United States informs Israel that Egypt has informed us that it will maintain the assurances, written and oral, undertaken at the time of the Egyptian-Israeli Agreement on Disengagement of Forces in January 1974 in addition to the provisions of the Agreement.

8. The United States informs Israel that Egypt will not interfere with the flights of any civilian Israeli aircraft in the airspace above the Straits of Bab el-Mandeb leading into the Red Sea.

9. With respect to the reference to "para-military forces" in paragraph 3a of the Annex, the United States understanding of the view of the Government of Egypt is that this phrase includes irregular forces as well.

Respectfully,

Henry A. Kissinger[4]

---

[2] Not found.

[3] This assurance was received in the form of a letter from President Sadat to President Ford. Sadat asserted that Egypt would "permit, gradually and on a selective basis, American firms which are ready to carry on significant business or investment in Egypt for the benefit of the Egyptian people, to establish and conduct business activities in Egypt in conformity with the needs of the Egyptian economy and the priorities of our plans for economic development." Sadat concluded by noting that his letter was intended solely for the U.S. Government and that it should not be shown, leaked, or allowed to leak to any government, organization, or individual. (Ibid.)

[4] The original bears this typed signature.

229. Letter From Secretary of State Kissinger to Egyptian Deputy Prime Minister and Foreign Minister Fahmy[1]

Jerusalem, September 1, 1975.

Dear Ismail:

This is to inform you that with respect to Syria, we have an Israeli assurance that Israel will not initiate military action against Syria.

Warm regards,

Henry A. Kissinger[2]

---

[1] Source: National Archives, RG 59, Records of Henry Kissinger, 1973–77, Box 15, Miscellaneous, Documents, Telegrams, etc., 1975, Folder 8. Secret.

[2] The original bears this typed signature.

---

230. Minute of Record[1]

Jerusalem, September 1, 1975.

1. The United States Government has received assurances from Egypt that in the event of a Syrian attack against Israel or in the event of a war of attrition initiated by Syria, Egypt will not participate in hostilities and will refrain from the use of force.

2. Should Syria initiate military or para-military action against Israel or should Syria undertake or tolerate acts that might threaten the ceasefire, the United States Government will support Israel diplomatically. These acts include the infiltration of terrorists across the Israel–Syria ceasefire lines and the stationing of terrorist groups along the frontiers facing Israel.

3. The United States Government takes Egypt's commitment to refrain from the threat or use of force or from military or para-military action contained in the agreement to remain binding in the event Israel undertakes appropriate countermeasures against terrorist operations. Should Egypt take a contrary view, the USG will support diplomatically the above interpretation.

---

[1] Source: National Archives, RG 59, Records of Henry Kissinger, 1973–77, Box 15, Miscellaneous, Documents, Telegrams, etc., 1975, Folder 8. Top Secret. Joseph Sisco and Simcha Dinitz initialed the bottom-right corner of the page.

4. Should negotiations between Israel and Syria on an interim agreement develop, the USG will not expect Israel to make proposals that go beyond what Prime Minister Rabin outlined to President Ford in Washington in June 1975.[2]

---

[2] See Document 183.

---

231. Letter From Secretary of State Kissinger to Israeli Prime Minister Rabin[1]

Washington, undated.

Dear Mr. Prime Minister:

I have the honor to transmit to you the text which follows of a letter to Your Excellency from the President of the United States:

"Dear Mr. Prime Minister:

I am writing you this letter to inform you of the statement I have received of the position of Egypt on the question of the duration of the second Egyptian-Israeli agreement on the Sinai.[2] The agreement includes language that the agreement shall 'remain in force until superseded by a new agreement.'

With respect to the duration of UNEF, I have been informed of Egypt's undertaking to make every effort to extend the United Nations Emergency Force annually for the duration of the agreement. However, should the Security Council, because of the action of a third state, fail to renew the UNEF mandate to assure continuous operation, I am informed that Egypt undertakes to concert actively with the U.S. to have the General Assembly take appropriate action to bring about annual re-

---

[1] Source: National Archives, RG 59, Records of Henry Kissinger, 1973–77, Box 15, Miscellaneous, Documents, Telegrams, etc., 1975, Folder 8. Secret.

[2] The Egyptian statement came in the form of a letter from President Sadat to President Ford, September 1. Sadat wrote that Egypt would "make every effort to extend the United Nations Emergency Force annually for the duration of the agreement." He continued that "should the Security Council, because of the action of a third state, fail to renew the UNEF mandate to assure continuous operation, Egypt undertakes to concert actively with the U.S. to have the General Assembly take appropriate action to bring about annual renewals for at least two renewals after the first annual mandate goes into effect." Sadat concluded that his letter was "for the United States and should not be passed to another government or publicized. (Ibid.)

newals for at least two renewals after the first annual mandate goes into effect.

In the event such affirmative General Assembly action did not prove possible, I am informed that Egypt will request an augmented UNTSO to continue the supervision responsibilities, and to have the joint Egyptian-Israeli Commission cooperate with it.

This letter is for the United States and should not be passed to another government or publicized.

Sincerely,
Gerald R. Ford
His Excellency
Yitzhak Rabin
Prime Minister of Israel."

The signed original of this letter will be forwarded to you.
Sincerely,

Henry A. Kissinger[3]

---

[3] The original bears this typed signature.

---

232. Letter From Secretary of State Kissinger to Egyptian President Sadat[1]

Washington, undated.

Dear Mr. President:

I have the honor to transmit to you the text which follows of a letter to Your Excellency from the President of the United States:

"Dear Mr. President:

In connection with Article VII of the Agreement between Egypt and Israel, the United States' understanding of the word non-military is that it excludes all types of weapons, weapons systems, ammunition, missiles and armor. It does not exclude economic items such as raw materials, oil and other civilian cargo. The Government of Israel has as-

---

[1] Source: National Archives, RG 59, Records of Henry Kissinger, 1973–77, Box 15, Miscellaneous Documents, Telegrams, etc., 1975, Folder 8. Secret.

sured me that it will carry out this Article in accordance with the above definition.

Sincerely,

Gerald R. Ford

His Excellency

Anwar al-Sadat

President of the Arab Republic of Egypt"

The signed original of this letter will be forwarded to Your Excellency.

Sincerely,

Henry A. Kissinger[2]

---

[2] The original bears this typed signature.

---

233. Letter From President Ford to Egyptian President Sadat[1]

Washington, undated.

Dear Mr. President:

I am writing to you to give you some indication as to our intentions with respect to a number of questions on which Secretary Kissinger was asked to ascertain my views.

The United States intends to make a serious effort to help bring about further negotiations between Syria and Israel, in the first instance through diplomatic channels.

In connection with the peace negotiations, I can reaffirm the intention of the United States to promote a solution of the key issues of a just and lasting peace in the Middle East on the basis of UN Security Council Resolution 338, taking into account the legitimate interests of all the peoples of the area, including the Palestinian people, and respect for the right to independent existence of all states in the area.

---

[1] Source: National Archives, RG 59, Records of Henry Kissinger, 1973–77, Box 15, Miscellaneous, Documents, Telegrams, etc., 1975, Folder 8. Secret.

As I indicated to you in my recent letter[2] the U.S. recognizes the situation following Israeli withdrawal from the passes and the oil fields will not be an acceptable permanent solution. You will recall also what I said to you at Salzburg[3] about moving toward a comprehensive, just and lasting peace in the Middle East and the importance of permitting the realities in the area and internationally to mature to the point where an all-out effort to achieve final peace can be made in circumstances that seem most promising for success and in a deliberate and systematic way. The United States will remain active in the peacemaking process. We recognize that a final peace is importantly a matter to be negotiated by the parties. Nevertheless, we would be prepared to put forward ideas of our own when and if it becomes necessary to do so. We have brought these views to the attention of Israeli leaders.

In the event of an Israeli violation of the Agreement, the United States is prepared to consult with Egypt as to the significance of the violation and possible remedial action by the United States.

The United States will provide technical assistance to Egypt for the Egyptian Early Warning Station.

Sincerely,

Gerald R. Ford[4]

[2] Not further identified.
[3] See Documents 177 and 178.
[4] The original bears this typed signature.

234. Letter From President Ford to Israeli Prime Minister Rabin[1]

Washington, undated.

Dear Mr. Prime Minister:

I wish to inform you that the U.S. recognizes that the Israeli-Egyptian Interim Agreement entailing withdrawal from vital areas in

[1] Source: National Archives, RG 59, Records of Henry Kissinger, 1973–77, Box 15, Miscellaneous, Documents, Telegrams, etc., 1975, Folder 8. Secret.

the Sinai constitutes an act of great significance on Israel's part in the pursuit of final peace and imposes additional heavy military and economic burdens on Israel.

I want to assure you that the U.S. will make every effort to be fully responsive within the limits of its resources and Congressional authorization and appropriation on an ongoing and long-term basis to Israel's military equipment and other defense requirements as well as to Israel's economic aid needs, all of this based on the requests submitted by Israel, joint studies and previous U.S. Presidential undertakings.

Further to those undertakings, it is my resolve to continue to maintain Israel's defensive strength through the supply of advanced types of equipment, such as the F–16 aircraft. The United States Government agrees to an early meeting to undertake a joint study of high technology and sophisticated items, including the Pershing ground-to-ground missiles with conventional warheads, with the view to giving a positive response. The U.S. Administration will submit annually for approval by the U.S. Congress a request for military and economic assistance in order to help meet Israel's economic and military needs. Realizing as I do the importance of the Interim Agreement to the Middle Eastern situation as a whole, the U.S. will make every possible effort to assist in the establishment of conditions in which the Agreement will be observed without being subjected to pressures or deadlines.

In the spirit of the special relationship existing between the United States and Israel and in light of the determination of both sides to avoid a situation in which the U.S. and Israel would pursue divergent courses in peace negotiations, the U.S. will take the position that these are negotiations between the parties. As I indicated to you in our conversation on 12 June 1975, the situation in the aftermath of the Israeli-Egyptian interim agreement will be one in which the overall settlement can be pursued in a systematic and deliberate way and does not require the U.S. to put forward an overall proposal of its own in such circumstances. Should the U.S. desire in the future to put forward proposals of its own, it will make every effort to coordinate with Israel its proposals with a view to refraining from putting forth proposals that Israel would consider unsatisfactory.

The U.S. will support the position that an overall settlement with Syria in the framework of a peace agreement must assure Israel's security from attack from the Golan Heights. The U.S. further supports the position that a just and lasting peace, which remains our objective, must be acceptable to both sides. The U.S. has not developed a final position on the borders. Should it do so it will give great weight to Israel's position that any peace agreement with Syria must be predicated on Israel remaining on the Golan Heights. My view in this regard was stated in our conversation of September 13, 1974.[2]

Sincerely,

Gerald R. Ford[3]

---

[2] See Document 100.

[3] The original bears this typed signature.

---

235. Memorandum of Conversation[1]

Washington, September 4, 1975, 7:45 a.m.

PARTICIPANTS

President Ford
Dr. Henry A. Kissinger, Secretary of State and Assistant to the President for National Security Affairs
Lt. General Brent Scowcroft, Deputy Assistant to the President for National Security Affairs

Kissinger: Here are the two letters I mentioned [to Sadat and Rabin on assurances].[2]

The President: These are the ones you don't think we should put out.

Kissinger: They aren't too bad. The one to Sadat is okay. The one to the Israelis would require some long explaining. Neither of them is something you haven't said before.

The President: [Reads] This Sadat thing we have said many times.

Kissinger: Joe and I really came back with a bad taste about the Israelis. They were treacherous, petty, deceitful—they didn't treat us like allies. Sadat said their strategy is to sell his land to us for arms which they will use to prevent giving up any more of any land.

---

[1] Source: Library of Congress, Manuscript Division, Kissinger Papers, CL 282, President's File, September 1975, Folder 1. Secret; Nodis. The meeting was held in the Oval Office at the White House. All brackets, with the exception of ones describing omitted material, are in the original. According to the President's Daily Diary, the meeting between Ford and Kissinger began at 7:30 a.m. (Ford Library, Staff Secretary's Office Files) Presumably Scowcroft joined them at 7:45 a.m. The meeting was followed by the meeting with the bipartisan congressional leadership; see Document 235.

[2] Documents 233 and 234.

The President: [Reads the Israeli letter.]

Kissinger: This one in effect confirms commitments rather than making new ones. You have told Rabin you wouldn't put something forward in '76 and to trust you in '77. To Sadat you said nothing in '76 but more in '77. They aren't inconsistent but the Jewish community would be upset.

The President: The funds for Israel is for the current year.

Kissinger: Our experts think they will be strapped at under $2.6 billion. But this is an annual thing for the indefinite future. If we put it over $2 billion that will become a benchmark. What will you tell the leaders this morning?

The President: I could say there is some flexibility depending on consultations between their and our technicians.

[Omitted here is discussion unrelated to the Arab-Israeli dispute.]

236. Memorandum of Conversation[1]

Washington, September 4, 1975.

PARTICIPANTS

President Ford
Bipartisan Leadership
Secretary Kissinger
Lt. General Brent Scowcroft

SUBJECT

Middle East—Sinai Agreement

Kissinger: The events of 1973 show us that the Middle East conflict produces a danger of great power conflict, and also enormous economic dislocation. Also, our commitment to Israel produces our involvement in any conflict.

A comprehensive approach would have been easy to devise but it tends to put the radicals in the driver's seat; it gives the Soviet Union a

---

[1] Source: Library of Congress, Manuscript Division, Kissinger Papers, CL 282, President's File, September 1975, Folder 1. Secret; Nodis. The meeting was held in the Cabinet Room at the White House. Brackets are in the original. The original is incorrectly dated September 9. According to the President's Daily Diary, which includes a list of attendees, the meeting began at 7:47 a.m. and ended at 9:43 a.m. (Ford Library, Staff Secretary's Office Files)

strong role, and it forces Israel to make many decisions all at once which it is not equipped to do. So we chose an interim approach.

Egypt is the largest Arab state and the leader of the Arab world. The problem has been to reconcile Egypt's concrete territorial needs as against the intangible political needs of Israel. The March negotiations failed when the gap between these could not be bridged. Both Egypt and Israel preferred that we continue the interim approach.

This is the first agreement between Israel and Egypt except in the aftermath of a war. It makes far-reaching moves toward peace and a new relationship between the two countries.

[He describes the map,[2] the zones of limited armaments, and the surveillance stations].

The Israelis insisted that unless there were purely Americans in the passes, they wouldn't withdraw. Egypt said she couldn't accept unless Israel withdrew, so we reluctantly agreed. The American technicians are in the UN zone. Their function is to reassure the two sides in time of peace. If conflict breaks out, their function is over, so we would have no problem withdrawing them in case of conflict—or on a joint resolution of Congress to do this. Those people shouldn't be compared to Vietnam but to the UN forces in the neutral zone.

Bellmon: How about the danger of attack by terrorists?

Kissinger: It would be about impossible for them to get at them in the zone. It is within the UN zone and is uninhabited. There is more of a danger at their bases in Egypt than on duty, but any American anywhere in the Middle East is a target. It is almost impossible to guard completely against terrorism.

Sadat, himself, is in great jeopardy. He has taken risks for peace. But he is the only one who has thrown over the Soviet Union and the only one who has gained anything from this settlement. If we can make this work, it will be a good object lesson on cooperating with the U.S.

The aid package should not be looked at as payment for the agreement. Israel asked for $2.6 billion before the agreement. The increment resulting from the agreement is slight, even though we will provide less than $2.6 billion. We haven't arrived at a figure for Egypt, but it is important to show the benefits for cooperation with the U.S. It is essential that we show our interest in Egypt's economic development.

---

[2] The map is not attached, but see the final status map in Appendix B, map 4.

237. Telegram From the Department of State to the Embassy in Egypt[1]

Washington, September 10, 1975, 0228Z.

214854. Subject: Message for President Sadat. For the Ambassador.

1. Please deliver following message from President Ford to President Sadat:

Quote: Dear Mr. President: I write to you as a friend, as an admirer of your great statesmanship, of your courage and integrity.

Above all, Mr. President, I am writing to you convinced more than ever that the course we have chosen together is the right one, for Egypt, for all of the Arabs, and for the United States.

The successful conclusion of the second agreement between Egypt and Israel on the Sinai was, as I have said, a historic achievement. It is a decision you took in order to advance toward a just and lasting peace in the Middle East not only, as you said to me, for your country but for the entire area. Now that this agreement has been concluded I want to share with you my views of the current situation and of prospects for the future.

The agreement just concluded has brought tangible benefits to Egypt. Not only will you recover the use of your nation's oil resources in the Sinai, but you have also brought about Israel's withdrawal from the strategic Sinai passes. To have foregone these gains in order to pursue, without laying any groundwork, an all-or-nothing negotiation at Geneva would in my judgment have assured stalemate and a rapid deterioration of the situation to the the benefit of no one country. It was this reality which led us, as it did you, to conclude that a further interim agreement was the only way to make early practical progress. In seizing this opportunity, you have made possible what could become, in your own words, a turning point toward peace with justice not only for Egypt but also for the entire Arab world to which Egypt has so long given leadership. These realities will survive long after the criticism emanating from some quarters has been forgotten.

Here in the United States I believe things are going well. The Congress is showing a sympathetic understanding of the agreement and of the responsibilities which the United States has undertaken in connection with it. I believe that the Congress will shortly give its approval to the U.S. proposal to entrust to American civilian technicians

---

[1] Source: Library of Congress, Manuscript Division, Kissinger Papers, CL 132, Geopolitical File, Egypt, September 10–18, 1975. Secret; Cherokee; Nodis; Immediate. Drafted by Atherton, cleared by Sisco and Borg, and approved by Kissinger.

the early warning system in the Sinai passes, to serve as you so aptly put it, as witnesses to the implementation of the peace agreement.[2] The Congress also appears favorably disposed toward providing the economic assistance to Egypt which we discussed in Salzburg and which Secretary Kissinger further discussed with you in Alexandria. I plan to submit a request to the Congress for dols 700 million in economic assistance for Egypt.

We have also been in touch with a number of other governments to emphasize how important this agreement is as a step toward a just and lasting peace. We have encouraged them to give broad support to you. Despite the predictable criticisms which have come from certain countries, I am convinced that history will show that you are the only Arab leader who has made tangible progress toward a just peace. The world will come to understand that you made your historic decision not just for Egypt but for all Arabs. We will continue to make these points with other governments and to urge them to take concrete actions to demonstrate their support of your policies.

I have noted the public expressions of concern coming from the Middle East that the agreement not freeze the situation diplomatically. I share this view. With particular reference to Syria, Secretary Kissinger has told President Asad that we would make a serious effort to help achieve progress on the Syrian front, and he has assured President Asad that the United States counts on a united Arab world to further the peace process. In our view, division in the Arab world is the danger to future progress. As I have said on numerous occasions, we are committed to the proposition that a lasting peace in the Middle East must involve progress on all fronts and must be based on careful attention to the interests of all its people, including the Palestinians.

With regard to the Soviet Union I want you to know that we have taken a very firm line with General Secretary Brezhnev. The Soviet response, while complaining over the lack of involvement in the negotiations, indicates that they do not intend to play an obstructionist role. I have reason to believe, based on a communication we received within the last twenty-four hours from the Soviets, that they will not make major difficulties. Secretary Kissinger will be meeting Foreign Minister Gromyko next week to discuss the situation, and we will keep you currently informed, as we have throughout, of these exchanges.[3]

---

[2] In a letter of September 2, President Ford sent the U.S. proposal for the early warning system in the Sinai to Congress for its approval. The letter was released on September 3; for text, see *Public Papers: Ford, 1975*, Book II, pp. 1292–1293.

[3] Kissinger sent a message to Sadat describing his discussions with Gromyko. (Telegram 225082 to Cairo, September 20; National Archives, RG 59, Central Foreign Policy Files)

An additional reason for my high sense of gratification at the successful conclusion of this agreement is the prospect that it will now be possible for you and Mrs. Sadat to visit the United States. Your visit is one that Mrs. Ford and I have long looked forward to with great pleasure. I want the American people to get to know you as I do. I am confident that such a visit will reinforce both our official and personal ties and reinforce our mutual efforts to achieve peace in the Middle East. I hope you will plan on both a State visit to Washington as well as allow time to travel to other parts of America. I would like to suggest that you plan your visit starting October 28.

With warm regards to you, Mrs. Sadat, and your family, Sincerely, Gerald R. Ford. *Unquote.*

End message.

2. *FYI:* One million tons of grain under PL 480 is in addition to dollars 700 million mentioned in President's letter. *End FYI.*

Kissinger

238. National Security Study Memorandum 230[1]

Washington, September 15, 1975.

TO

    The Secretary of Defense
    The Deputy Secretary of State
    The Administrator, Agency for International Development
    The Director of Central Intelligence

SUBJECT

    Establishment of U.S. Sinai Support Mission

The President has directed that a study be conducted regarding the establishment of a U.S. Sinai Support Mission pursuant to the U.S. Proposal of September 1, 1975,[2] submitted in connection with the Agreement between Egypt and Israel of the same date. The study should analyze how best to organize and supervise the activities of a Sinai Support

---

[1] Source: Ford Library, National Security Adviser, NSSMs, Box 2, NSSM 230. Secret. Copies were sent to the Chairman of the Joint Chiefs of Staff and Director of the Office of Management and Budget.

[2] See footnote 1, Document 226.

Mission and should develop appropriate recommendations for effecting the provisions of the Proposal.

The study should be carried out by an ad hoc group comprised of representatives of the addressees and chaired by the representative of the Department of State. The study should be submitted to the Assistant to the President for National Security Affairs not later than September 22, 1975, for consideration by the President.[3]

Henry A. Kissinger

---

[3] According to a September memorandum from Oakley to Scowcroft, a preliminary study had been created that "could serve as the basis for a draft study to be circulated for review and comment by the addressees of this NSSM." (Ford Library, NSC Institutional Files, Box 38, NSSM 230) Executive Order 11896, January 13, 1975, established the U.S. Sinai Support Mission.

---

239. Memorandum of Conversation[1]

Washington, September 24, 1975, 8:05–9:50 a.m.

PARTICIPANTS

    President Ford
    Vice President Rockefeller
    Mr. Rogers Morton, Secretary of Commerce
    Republican Congressional Leaders (List Attached)

SUBJECT

    Energy, Arms Embargo on Turkey, Sinai Agreement, and Handling of Intelligence Material in Congress

[Omitted here is discussion unrelated to the Arab-Israeli dispute.]

Turning to the Middle East, the President asked Senator Scott to describe the situation in the Senate.

Senator Scott responded that the Senate Foreign Relations Committee was holding an executive session today to consider the draft resolution approving the U.S. technicians in the Sinai.

---

[1] Source: Library of Congress, Manuscript Division, Kissinger Papers, CL 282, President's File, September 1975, Folder 2. No classification marking. The meeting was held in the Cabinet Room at the White House. Attached but not printed is a list of the persons attending.

Senator Case noted that the subject has not been discussed in the full Committee since the briefings provided by Secretary Kissinger and Under Secretary Sisco two weeks ago. He noted that the Committee's problem is whether it can get some unclassified statement of U.S. undertakings and assurances on the public record so that the American people would know the whole story behind the recent Sinai Agreement. Senator Case observed that if this could be done, the Senate could pass the resolution quickly. If it is not done, there will be a great deal of trouble, and he would be reluctant to go to the floor for a vote if he could not lay out fully the record in some unclassified way. He noted that he was in contact with Secretary Kissinger on this problem.

The President asked Senator Scott when the full Senate would vote.

Senator Scott reported that a vote was unlikely before Tuesday or Wednesday[2] of next week.

Senator Case said that he thought the Hawk problem was settled very nicely. There was a small problem with the King after the agreement was reached, but that appeared to be because the King had not read the standard contract language involved in the sale of the weapons. The King's outburst was somewhat surprising but equally surprising was his sudden retraction. Senator Case said there was no longer any problem in the Congress because it was relying on its confidence in the assurances the President had given in his letter to the Senate and the House.

The President said that in regard to the controversy over the Pershing missiles,[3] one of the first things he was presented when he took office last fall was the Israelis' military shopping list called Matmon B.[4] He noted that it was just a list of all the things the Israelis wanted but no U.S. commitments were involved. The Pershing missile was one of the items on that list. The Pershing request was resubmitted to the U.S. during the most recent round of peace negotiations. The President stressed that we made no commitment on the missile and promised only to study carefully the Israeli request for this missile, which was but one item on a very extensive shopping list.

The President asked John Rhodes where the Middle East Agreement stood in the House.

---

[2] September 30 or October 1.

[3] Secretary of Defense Schlesinger had repotedly taken the position that Israel would have to wait to receive modern weapons, such as the Pershing missile, until U.S. forces were equipped, despite the U.S. assurances in the U.S.-Israeli memorandum of agreement (Document 227). ("U.S. Delays Seen on Arms to Israel," *New York Times*, September 20, 1975, p. 7)

[4] See Document 96.

Congressman Rhodes responded that the House is waiting for the Senate to act.

Congressman Anderson said that he wanted to echo the words of Senator Case. The Congress must put to rest the feeling that there are some secret agreements not yet revealed which commit the United States. Unless this issue can be cleared up for the public record, there will be trouble bringing the resolution to a vote. He noted that some Members of the House are very unhappy over reports that Secretary Kissinger had referred in testimony to the value of something called "constructive ambiguity."

Senator Case said to the President that it would be very helpful if he could act to send up the unclassified summary of the various commitments and assurances. Senator Case went on to say that with all due respect for Henry Kissinger, he does have a reputation on the Hill for "constructive ambiguity."

Senator Scott said the Secretary has a reputation for just plain ambiguity.

[Omitted here is discussion unrelated to the Arab-Israeli dispute.]

240. Memorandum of Conversation[1]

Washington, September 25, 1975, 8–9:15 a.m.

PARTICIPANTS

    President Ford
    Vice President Rockefeller
    Dr. Henry A. Kissinger, Secretary of State and Assistant to the President for National Security Affairs
    Rogers Morton, Secretary of Commerce
    Bipartisan Congressional Leadership (list attached)
    Leslie A. Janka (note taker)

SUBJECT

    Energy, Turkey and the Middle East Agreement

[Omitted here is discussion unrelated to the Arab-Israeli dispute.]

---

[1] Source: Library of Congress, Manuscript Division, Kissinger Papers, CL 282, President's File, September 1975, Folder 2. Administratively Confidential. The meeting was held in the Cabinet Room at the White House. Attached but not printed is the list of participants.

Middle East

The President: Let me turn now to the Sinai Agreement. I want to point out to you that the Israelis have refused to sign the Protocol to the Agreement[2] until Congress approves the U.S. proposal on civilian technicians in the Sinai.

General Scowcroft: That is correct, Mr. President. The Agreement cannot begin to take effect until Congress approves the U.S. proposal.

Speaker Albert: I think the Israelis should have signed immediately. They will build a lot of resentment by trying to pressure Congress in this way.

Senator Scott: We are in executive session today but one group wants public disclosure of all papers. Clifford Case tells me that while there is strong pressure to declassify all of the documents relating to the Agreement, a majority of the Committee would be satisfied with a full disclosure to the Committee members without public release.

Representative O'Neill: The House will probably act next week, but I should tell you that the International Relations Committee is not at all satisfied that it is getting all the answers on U.S. arms commitments to Israel, and they are unhappy that no aid bill has yet been sent up.

The President: I am waiting to send up the aid bill until Congress approves the Sinai Agreement. I am holding up because if the Agreement does not take effect, we will have to totally reconsider our aid to Israel in the context of the absence of an Agreement.

Representative O'Neill: (He read a list of several questions regarding the possibility of the U.S. providing the Pershing missile to Israel. Has it been committed to Israel? How many have been committed? Will it carry a nuclear warhead? Was the Defense Department informed of U.S. plans to provide the missile? etc.)

The President: Tip, let me answer all of those questions for this group. Last September, Rabin came to see me.[3] During his visit he presented Israel's military equipment needs. There were several short-range needs we took care of. They also presented their long-range shopping list, called Matmon B. At that time, we said we could not consider that list. It was premature. After the Sinai Agreement was

---

[2] The protocol, which was negotiated by an Israeli-Egyptian military working group in Geneva, contained details on the new lines, force redeployments, arms limitations, surveillance stations, and other points in the disengagement agreement. The *New York Times* reported that on September 21 the Israelis agreed to initial but not sign the document. (*New York Times*, September 21, 1975, p. 1) After further negotiation, the protocol was signed by both parties on September 22. (Telegram 7254 from Geneva, September 23; National Archives, RG 59, Central Foreign Policy Files)

[3] See Documents 99 and 100.

reached, they resubmitted their list. That list contained the Pershing missile, as did the list presented last year. In our negotiations with Israel on the recent agreement, all we said is that we would study the request for the Pershing. There is absolutely no commitment beyond that.

I think you all recognize that the Israelis are very tough negotiators. They want an awful lot of hardware. We will be make a very detailed study of the Israelis' arms request and the Pershing missile will be very carefully studied.

The Department of Defense saw the Matmon B shopping list last year, and the Pershing missiles were on that list. We also told the Defense Department that we would be studying all the items on the list.

Senator Scott: Whatever we do for Israel, we should not draw down further our active military stocks. This would endanger our own security and would lead to a public outcry.

The President: That's absolutely right, Hugh. Orders have been given in the Administration that we are not to draw down our active stocks to provide equipment to Israel. The Israelis know about this. The United States is now procuring new and sophisticated weapons from our manufacturers but Israel will not be put ahead of the United States on the production line. Israel's needs will not preempt U.S. procurement. They will get what they need from later production after our own needs have been met. The Israelis are very well protected with the weapons they now have. They will not be allowed to jeopardize our security and this has been made very clear to the Israelis.

General Scowcroft: Mr. President, I want to point out that there is some urgency on the approval of the Agreement for two particular reasons. First, the Israelis and the Egyptians hammered out with great difficulty at Geneva a withdrawal timetable. If there is any delay in approving the agreement, this timetable would have to be renegotiated and frankly it may not be possible to do so. Second, Sadat is under great pressure, as you know, from the other Arabs. Further delay by the United States would seriously undercut him because congressional questions about the value of the agreement would make it appear that the Congress agrees with his Arab detractors.

Senator Mansfield: Did you say the military aid request would be delayed?

The President: I will not send up my dollar request until the Sinai Agreement is fully set. It makes a big difference on what figures we send up on whether we have an agreement or not. As I have said, we are taking a gamble on peace, and I feel deeply that our military assistance will be a good investment. I have discussed this with the Jewish leaders and our Jewish Community friends are supportive of the agreement. It is clear to me that the Sinai Agreement is good for the United States as well as for Israel and Egypt.

241. Memorandum of Conversation[1]

Washington, September 26, 1975, 10:56–11:34 a.m.

PARTICIPANTS

President Ford
Dr. Henry A. Kissinger, Secretary of State and Assistant to the President for National Security Affairs
Lt. General Brent Scowcroft, Deputy Assistant to the President for National Security Affairs

Kissinger: We have three different problems with these groups: a deliberate attempt to destroy Executive authority, to destroy our foreign policy, and to knock down every strong man around you.

What they are doing to the Sinai agreement is unbelievable. It is the greatest achievement since the opening to China and all that is happening is they are pissing all over it.

I am so overburdened that mistakes are made. They asked Sisco if these were Executive agreements. Sisco is energetic but has no judgment. He got the Legal Advisor to say they are legally binding Executive agreements.

We are now facing a coalition of the pro-Israelis, who want to freeze these papers into concrete agreements . . .

The President: I am disturbed about your comment that I am not tough enough in foreign policy.

Kissinger: No, I didn't mean you. I meant the impression of those around you. We are dominant in the world and at home we are impotent. Don't misunderstand me, it is not you. But Buchen—let me say the manner in which they talk to the Congress does not inspire respect. Why he has to say we would never withhold a whole document . . .

The President: I didn't say that.

Kissinger: No, you are just fine. There is not an iota of difference between us. But we shouldn't promise sweeping things like this—we don't know what will do.

[He reads from agreement to show that the language leaves an escape clause and there is no binding language.]

If I have to testify on these though, I will have to say either it means nothing or it does mean something. Either one is a disaster.

---

[1] Source: Ford Library, National Security Adviser, Memoranda of Conversations, Box 15, September 26, 1975, Ford, Kissinger. Secret; Nodis. The meeting was held in the Oval Office at the White House. All brackets, with the exception of ones describing omitted material, are in the original.

The President: Both Committees have this?

Kissinger: Completely. And it has been leaked to the *New York Times*. But to publish it officially would create a massive problem with the Arabs.

The President: Were you tough with the Committees?

Kissinger: I did not yield, but they are now using delaying tactics. They want Schlesinger to testify and he will be asked about your statement that we will give military assistance to Egypt. He will convey the impression he has been out of it.

The President: I was strong on the Pershing.

Kissinger: Brent told me you were great. Schlesinger knew about the Pershing. He didn't know about the slip of paper. But he has given away all the easy things now—F–16, tank lasers, accelerating the F–15—leaving you with the sticky issues.

The President: How do we get the Sinai thing through?

Kissinger: They are responding to pressure from home like with Vietnam. And the Jews are trying to knock you off. They want a new guy in the White House in '77.

The President: Should I demand immediate action? I have told them . . .

Kissinger: I would write Sparkman and Morgan that peace in the Middle East requires action by the end of the week.

The President: I would add Scott, Mansfield, Albert and Rhodes.

Kissinger: It's not much help in the Committee. But I am not sure that if we don't win it in a week you maybe should yield.

The President: On my letters?

Kissinger: No. Those are safe. You are a victim of Watergate.

The President: Never before has so much been given to the Congress.

[Omitted here is discussion unrelated to the Arab-Israel dispute.]

242. Letter From President Ford to Senator Michael Mansfield[1]

Washington, September 29, 1975.

Dear Senator Mansfield:

I am writing to emphasize the importance of a Congressional decision in the coming week on U.S. participation in the Early Warning System which is an integral part of the Agreement signed between the Governments of Egypt and Israel on September 4 in Geneva.

Over the past two years, our Government has played an essential role in helping defuse the tensions in the Middle East. We have chosen this course because we recognized, as has every American Administration over the past 30 years, that the issues involved in that troubled area are central to the American national interest.

The September 4 agreement, like the two preceding disengagement agreements, was negotiated with the assistance of the United States. The parties themselves have described it as a significant step towards peace in the Middle East. It will reduce the risks of war, create new opportunities for negotiating peace, and help provide a stable environment in which global economic dislocations can be avoided. This Agreement is in the overall national interest of the United States.

There would have been no Agreement without provision for American participation in the Early Warning System. That System is designed to reduce the danger of surprise attack, and the parties to the Agreement were able to agree to entrust the System only to the United States. The special American role was the only one in which both sides had adequate confidence.

I want to be certain that the leaders of the Congress fully understand the consequences of further delay in acting on this important matter.

The first step in the implementation of the basic Agreement under the timetable negotiated and agreed to by Egypt and Israel in Geneva on September 22 is scheduled to be taken October 5. This process will not begin, however, until the Congress has acted on the proposed United States role in the Early Warning System. Delay in Congressional action will, therefore, delay implementation of the basic Agreement. It will risk causing the lengthy and difficult negotiations on the entire five-month implementing timetable to be reopened. It will prevent a

---

[1] Source: Library of Congress, Manuscript Division, Kissinger Papers, CL 159, Geopolitical File, Israel, September 18–30, 1975. Secret. A handwritten notation at the top of the page reads, "Identical letters to Sparkman, Scott, Case, Albert, Morgan, Rhodes, and Broomfield." The letter, which was released on September 30, is also printed in *Public Papers: Ford, 1975*, Book II, pp. 1543–1545.

lessening of the risks of war. If for any reason the agreement should fail, the responsibility would be heavy indeed.

The issue before the Congress now is whether the Congress will approve acceptance by the United States of the role that has been proposed for it. There are other issues which the Congress must eventually consider in connection with our continuing relations, policies, and programs in the Middle East—particularly our programs of military and economic assistance there. The Congress will want to consider those carefully at the appropriate time, but they are not integral to the implementation of the Agreement between Egypt and Israel. Voting in favor of the U.S. role in the Early Warning System will not commit anyone to take a position one way or another on these issues.

In summary, I met with the leadership three weeks ago to describe what was involved in the new Agreement between Egypt and Israel and to request urgent approval of U.S. participation in its implementation.[2] This question has been under intensive discussion in the Congress for nearly three weeks. All relevant papers and all U.S. commitments related to the Agreement have been submitted to the appropriate committees of the Congress. If action is not completed in the coming week, the United States will be in the position of holding up implementation of an Agreement which two key Middle Eastern countries have signed as a significant step towards peace. The Middle East is an area where American policy has long had broad bipartisan support. The issue presently before the Congress offers an opportunity to reaffirm that tradition and to demonstrate how the Executive and Legislative branches can work together on a foreign policy matter of high importance to the national interest and for the benefit of world peace. I, therefore, urge strongly that action be completed as early as possible and no later than Friday, October 3.[3]

Sincerely,

Gerald R. Ford

---

[2] See Document 236.

[3] On October 9, the Senate approved the stationing of up to 200 American civilian technicians as part of U.S. participation in the early warning system. President Ford signed Public Law 94–110, which implemented the U.S. proposal for an early warning system in the Sinai, on October 13.

243. National Security Study Memorandum 231[1]

Washington, October 7, 1975.

TO
- The Secretary of Defense
- The Deputy Secretary of State
- The Director of Central Intelligence

SUBJECT
- Israeli Military Requests

The President has directed a study of the requests of the Government of Israel for military and intelligence equipment and technology from the United States. The purpose of the study is to review and assess these requests within the broad context of United States strategic, diplomatic and economic interests.

The Study should first determine the impact upon Israeli military capabilities of the response to the Matmon–B Urgent List, made pursuant to NSDM 270, dated September 24, 1974.[2] Starting with this revised assessment of Israeli capabilities as a base, the study should consider, but not be limited to, the following military and economic factors.

A. A comparison of the military capabilities of Israel and the Arab States likely to participate in a future Middle East conflict, as well as the estimated threat to Israel in both worst case and probable case scenarios.

B. The impact on Israel's military capabilities and the strategic balance in the area of the release of all equipment and technology approved prior to March 26, 1975, which had been held by the Department of Defense or Munitions Control during the reassessment process.

C. The additional impact upon Israel's military capabilities and the strategic balance in the area of the provision to or co-production by Israel of all equipment and technology contained in Israel's current overall request list (Matmon–B 1975 (MN–2–92)[3] and subsequent requests), assuming that equipment is made available from production only. The study should identify those items or procedures with regard

---

[1] Ford Library, NSC Institutional Files, NSSMs, Box 38, NSSM 231, Israeli Military Requests, Folder 2. Secret; Sensitive. Copies were sent to the Chairman of the Joint Chiefs of Staff and the Director of the Office of Management and Budget.

[2] Document 101. The Matmon B Urgent List was not found but the Senior Review Group discussed it on August 30, 1974; see Document 98.

[3] Not found.

to which release, co-production or joint research and development would compromise sensitive U.S. technology, or have major political, military, or economic impact within the U.S. In addition, the study should examine existing guidelines for military co-production and joint research and development with Israel and make recommendations for their revision, if warranted.

D. An assessment of the likelihood, in light of recent Israeli arms requests, that Israel will increase the scope of the overall Matmon–B program.

E. The impact upon outstanding U.S. foreign military sales commitments and anticipated commitments of the provision of items requested in the overall Israeli equipment list from production.

F. The impact of sales to Israel of items requested in the overall Israeli equipment list upon future Israeli assistance needs, including the estimated additional annual support costs to Israel of such sales.

In addition to the above military and economic factors, the Study should consider the *political effects* of providing the requested military equipment, in particular:

A. The potential such equipment poses for accelerating the arms race in the Middle East, particularly the stimulation of greater Arab pressure for arms from the U.S. or the U.S.S.R. to match improvements in the Israeli military posture.

B. The effect upon the peace settlement process, including the potential of the provision of such equipment for reducing the incentives by Israel and/or the Arab States to negotiate a settlement.

Based on the assessment of the foregoing military, economic and political factors, the Study should suggest a long-term program of security assistance to Israel providing for an adequate but not destabilizing Israeli force level, if different from the Matmon–B force. Within this force framework, the Study should also suggest at least two alternative responses to the current (1975–1976) Israeli equipment and technology request, including different spacing of delivery schedules. The Study should clearly delineate the advantages and disadvantages of each alternative course of action.

Finally, the Study should review current interagency procedures for processing all arms requests by Israel and other Middle East countries through commercial or FMS channels, as well as current USG–GOI interface procedures on arms procurement and recommend any appropriate improvement in such procedures.

The study should be prepared by an ad hoc group composed of representatives of the addressees and the NSC Staff, and chaired by the representative of the Secretary of Defense. The Study should be completed by November 1, 1975 for consideration by the Senior Review Group, prior to its submission to the President.

This Study should be conducted on a close-hold, need-to-know basis.

Henry A. Kissinger

---

244. Study Prepared by the National Security Council Ad Hoc Group[1]

Washington, undated.

EXECUTIVE SUMMARY/NSSM 231:
ISRAELI MILITARY REQUESTS

This study develops recommendations for (1) a Presidential response on military supply issues during Rabin's visit, and (2) a strategy for handling Israel's medium-term (5-year) requirements.

Conclusions

The principal conclusions of the study are:

—Israel retains the near-term capability of defeating any combination of Arab armies. (Tab A)[2]

—Analysis does not support Israel's need for the force levels projected in Matmon B. (pp 5, 14; Tab D)[3]

—Given the altered political situation in the Middle East and the sharply increased magnitude of our military supply relationship with Israel, changes are required in our procedures for deciding: First, how much new matériel Israel should acquire in a given year; and Second, how much security assistance should be made available to help Israel procure those requirements. (pp 6–8)

—Completion of U.S. deliveries already approved and scheduled, plus production in Israel, will satisfy requirements for major weapons systems considered fully adequate to satisfy Israel's needs in 1980.

---

[1] Source: Ford Library, NSC Institutional Files, NSSMs, Box 38, NSSM 231, Israeli Military Requests, Folder 5. Secret. This study was prepared in response to NSSM 231, Document 243. The study has six attachments and eleven tabs (A–K), all attached but not printed.

[2] Tab A is entitled "Intelligence Estimate."

[3] Tab D is entitled "Medium Term Program of Assistance to Israel."

(Since October 1973, Israel has ordered $3.4 billion in matériel, of which over $2 billion will be delivered during the next two years or so; the FY 76 request is in addition to these previous orders.) (pp 8–9, 14)

Recommendations

The principal recommendations flowing from these conclusions are:

Security Assistance

—We should not release items that would be politically or psychologically destabilizing (e.g., Pershing), technologically compromising (e.g., FLIR), or still in R&D (e.g., CBU–84, an air-delivered land mine). (p. 9; Attachment 2)[4]

—All equipment to be provided from this point should come from production excepting those few cases where it is available from stock without adverse impact on our own forces. (p. 9)

—For most items on the list, Israel should be placed normally in the production queue as Letters of Offer are signed. (An option is provided, although not recommended, which would permit quicker deliveries on certain critical items by special placement for the GOI in the production queue.) (p 10; Attachment 4)[5]

—We should reaffirm to Rabin our continuing commitment to Israel's security and agree to an annual joint review to determine appropriate new agreements for sales of matériel. In other words, by indirection we would indicate that a commitment to fulfilling Matmon B per se on a multi-year basis is out of the question. This annual review process would begin with an examination of the political-military situation, move in a systematic manner to the new equipment required to meet this situation, and the payment flow for this equipment. The USG would then unilaterally arrive at a security assistance level for the next year. A systematic approach on an annual basis is essential to enable the decision process to evaluate changing conditions, to review the flow already in the pipeline, and to make a recommendation that will allow the USG to maintain control over both the security assistance levels and the equipment flow. (pp 18–20)

Logistics Contingency Planning

—We should support a restrained version of the logistics contingency plan proposed by Israel, whereby we would preserve U.S. flexibility regarding the circumstances under which the plan would be exe-

---

[4] Attachment 2 is entitled "Items on Current Year Request List to Which Objections Pertain."

[5] Attachment 4 is entitled "Alternative Delivery Options for Current Year Request List."

cuted. The plan would be based on a 30-day in-country level of supply, with certain critical consumables stockpiled in the U.S. Where possible, Israeli sea-lift or air contract carriers would be used. The plan would be subject to annual review. (pp 28–29)

Research & Development (R&D) and Co-production Cooperation

—Based on our extensive existing agreements for R&D cooperation and co-production, and our conclusion that for the most part agreements in this area result in higher costs and longer development time for Israel, we should continue to offer cooperation on a case-by-case basis rather than agree to sweeping commitments. Our guidelines would preserve both our advanced weapons technology from compromise and our arms exports from direct competition while at the same time helping Israel where appropriate. (pp 33–34)

[Omitted here are the table of contents and the body of the draft study.]

245. Memorandum of Conversation[1]

Washington, October 16, 1975.

PARTICIPANTS

The Secretary, Henry A. Kissinger
Under Secretary for Political Affairs, Mr. Sisco
Amb. Catto, Chief of Protocol
Mr. Atherton, Assistant Secretary for Near Eastern and South Asian Affairs
Mr. Saunders, Deputy Assistant Secretary
Mr. Oakley, NSC
Jerry Bremer—Notetaker

SUBJECT

The Middle East

[Omitted here is discussion relating to Lebanon.]

[The Secretary:] Now on this Sinai force, I do not want it under State if at all possible. I want a plan on how we go about approving these people.[2]

---

[1] Source: Library of Congress, Manuscript Division, Kissinger Papers, CL 346, State Department Memcons, October to November 1975. Secret; Sensitive.

[2] A reference to the American civilian personnel serving as part of the Sinai early warning system.

Sisco: My assessment is that there is only one acceptable instrument and that is the State Department.

The Secretary: That's because we haven't tried others. Why can't we just contract it out?

Sisco: Okay, but it doesn't solve the problem of who backstops it. It can't be anyone but State.

The Secretary: I want us as far removed as possible from this. We have no management capabilities anyway.

Sisco: Well, let's put it up under an inter-Departmental framework.

The Secretary: I want it pushed as far away from State as possible. Someone else should do the recruiting and training, etc.

Oakley: In terms of the policy responsibilities, that's difficult.

The Secretary: I need a concept of who will recruit and train and in the first instance, run it. Maybe it should be something like the NSA–DOD relationship.

Sisco: The man in charge back here would be the special representative of the President within the NSC framework. In the State Department we would have the operational backstopping system. The problems will be political.

Oakley: We will have a paper for you by tomorrow.

The Secretary: I don't want it run out of State. It should run itself and report its findings to us. It is not wise for the Department to have it as an agency of the Department.

Saunders: It would be set up as an autonomous NSC group.

Sisco: In which the Department provides the leadership and policy guidance.

The Secretary: It's going to be nothing but trouble. Maybe we should have somebody like Rand[3] set it up under our guidance so that when there is a reporting problem we don't have to run around all over town. When you guys get through with it, NEA will have someone in your bureau doing it. It will be disastrous since when something goes wrong, it's automatically on our doorstep. There are lots of things to which we give policy guidance without running it. I want it managed as an autonomous entity. I don't want to see all of their activities.

Oakley: One question is whether the top few are government or contract. They may have to make political judgments out there.

The Secretary: No, they are to handle the monitoring and if they have political problems, they can report them back here.

---

[3] A reference to the Rand Corporation.

Sisco: Our idea would be an inter-agency group in the EOB with the manager as the special representative of the President.

The Secretary: No. Supposing you contract the whole thing out to the Rand Corporation—the whole thing—recruitment and the operation and policy guidance from us.

Sisco: It's unrealistic. The U.S. Government cannot avoid direct involvement.

The Secretary: I don't want every dispute between the Egyptians and the Israelis to be State's dispute. I don't mind having it under us giving policy guidance but I don't want us running it. If either side has a technical problem, they should go to the manager.

Atherton: Do you think he should be a private citizen?

The Secretary: He certainly should not be State Department, whatever else. It could be a government body.

Oakley: We could try to find a retired person.

The Secretary: I don't want Case and the Israeli lobby to have the State Department as their target every time an amoured car goes across the Sinai. I want us one step removed but with policy control.

Sisco: Okay, I'll look at it. By the way, Congressman Koch called to suggest Sadat have a meeting in New York with a group of American-Jewish leaders.

The Secretary: He's out of his mind. You could of course try it out on Sadat when he comes, but I think he's crazy.

Sisco: This would be Rabbi Miller and three or four others in New York. I discouraged it.

The Secretary: Well, tell Eilts and see what he says.

Sisco: On nuclear reactors. I would like NEA to try that on Israel, that the safeguards would apply to future Dimona activities.

The Secretary: They won't agree, of course.

Sisco: That's right. My assessment on the Sadat visit and the nuclear reactors is that the mood on the Hill is irrational, so even if we got Israeli-Egyptian agreement, we will be accused of railroading it through. The Congressional reaction in fact may be so strong as to sour the Sadat visit.

The Secretary: But what can come out of the visit that won't be sour?

Sisco: I don't know. We will try it out on the Israelis but my conclusion is that it is not desirable to conclude it while Sadat is here.

The Secretary: Then if they say no to Dimona, the Egyptians will put reactors under our safeguards in the future.

Sisco: That's correct.

The Secretary: So all American reactors will be under international control.

Sisco: That's correct. But you will have a vast explosion on the Hill.

Oakley: I'm not certain the Egyptians will accept that idea.

The Secretary: I said the American reactor would be accepted with all of our safeguards but with the other reactors they would stay open on the safeguards. In other words, if we reject that, since they can buy reactors from the others, even that part of their program which would have been under U.S. safeguards will be lost. That's the end result.

Sisco: If we limit our approach to what we provide, this will be viewed by Israel and the Jewish lobby as a huge opening.

The Secretary: But it gives them an incentive to buy French reactors which would be beyond our control. At least this way, we'd be absorbing those purchases and they would buy them with our safeguards.

Sisco: I know it's illogical. It's completely out of whack. But that is the mood in Congress.

The Secretary: Well, what can we settle? We can't give them arms, we can't give them nuclear reactors, what can we give them? Horse-drawn carts?

Saunders: It boils down to no material stuff. We have aid and our diplomatic support.

The Secretary: What diplomatic support? We're a net liability to him.

Saunders: Well, we did get them their oil fields.

The Secretary: I'm not sure why we can't argue this proposition: if Israel puts Dimona under international controls, Egypt will put all of their reactors under international controls. I agree that the Hill is crazy and we are in a nihilistic period. But I don't argue that we have to bend with it. I'm not sure we shouldn't say "to hell with it" and just knock it out with them. Defend what's right. It is totally irrational now. Suppose they don't do Dimona. The Egyptians are still willing to put our reactor under our controls. If we don't build it, it will be under no controls. I feel I'd like to keep this option open.

Arms now would be total suicide, I agree—even though if the Israelis were rational, they'd beg us to supply Egypt. It has to be in their interest even if we give them arms right back to the '73 level.

Atherton: The best way to prevent a war is to be the supplier to both sides.

Sisco: I have used this argument.

The Secretary: I'm convinced the Jewish lobby is trying to defeat the President and emasculate me too. They're going about it in some very subtle ways.

Sisco: On the nuclear thing, we'll talk to the Israelis and see what they say. We'll do it this afternoon.

[Omitted here is discussion of the logistics of the Sadat visit.]

246. Memorandum of Conversation[1]

Washington, October 27, 1975, noon–12:50 p.m.

PARTICIPANTS

    President Gerald R. Ford
    Dr. Henry A. Kissinger, Secretary of State and Assistant to the President for National Security Affairs
    Mohammed Anwar al-Sadat, President of the Arab Republic of Egypt
    Ismail Fahmy, Deputy Prime Minister and Minister of Foreign Affairs

The President: I am delighted to have you here, Mr. President. I felt that our meetings at Salzburg were personally and substantively the most constructive meetings I have had since I have been President. This is a good opportunity to show our two peoples what our good relations can do. Your visit here I am sure will be an enduring basis for our relations in the future.

President Sadat: I must thank you for the efforts that you made after our meeting at Salzburg. Without these efforts, we could not have achieved this Sinai agreement. I must congratulate you. For the first time, the Israelis hear logic and firmness. It is for the benefit of the Israelis as well as of my [Arab] colleagues—even if neither of them understand it now. Let me thank you for your help. Henry's tireless efforts have been marvelous. I look forward to when you visit us, Mr. President. Let the whole Arab world see our relationship.

The President: I look forward to it.

President Sadat: As we have agreed in Salzburg, it is a long road ahead of us.

The President: You must work with us on the timing. But I can assure you I will be as firm in the future as I have been in the past. There is no sense in taking a number of little steps when we can take a big

---

[1] Source: Library of Congress, Manuscript Division, Kissinger Papers, CL 133, Geopolitical File, Egypt, September 19–30, 1975. Secret; Nodis. The meeting was held in the Oval Office at the White House. Brackets are in the original.

step. That agreement was a terrible strain. We might as well take a broader view.

President Sadat: By your efforts you have made it easier for us to take the final step.

[The President explained the American political situation. He discussed the senselessness of the Turkish aid cut-off.[2] He pointed out that NATO is in good shape.]

President Sadat: Giscard, whom I just met in Paris, has severe flu.

For this visit, I have nothing special. But I would like to raise two points: First is economic help. We would hope that you can change our short-term loans into long-term loans. The economic situation in Egypt appears to be in bad shape, but the combination of reopening the Suez Canal and recovering the oil will give us $700 million. We hope to have your help.

The other point is armament.

[Dr. Kissinger explained the parliamentary situation in the Congress. The thrust was that no formal sale of arms to Egypt could probably be made until March of 1976.][3]

President Sadat: The backbone of our air force is the MIG–17. The Russians have said it is now obsolete. The most agreeable plane to us is the F–5E, which the Saudis and Iran have. I would like to request one squadron of these. We would also want the TOW missile.

Dr. Kissinger: You should know that the embargo on arms sales is about to be lifted from Germany.

After the agreement is fulfilled, then we can talk about it.

President Sadat: The Suez is moving along marvelously.

Asad would not get anything from the USSR undermining the agreement.

[Dr. Kissinger showed him a recent intelligence report on Syrian military preparations. See attached.][4]

---

[2] On February 5, Congress cut off all military aid to Turkey in response to Turkey's occupation of Cyprus following its July 20, 1974, invasion of the island.

[3] On October 30, President Ford wrote to Congress proposing specific amounts for security assistance programs to be included in the FY 1976–1977 foreign assistance legislation. His proposal requested $740 million in security support assistance and $1.5 million in military credits for Israel and $750 million in security support assistance for Egypt. He also recommended a Special Requirements Fund of $50 million to reinforce the Middle East process, especially the cost of deploying American civilian technicians in the Sinai. (*Public Papers: Ford, 1975,* Book II, pp. 1756–1762)

[4] Attached but not printed. The intelligence report, entitled "Syrian Military Movements," reported that Syrian ground forces had been placed on a high alert posture and that reports showed movement of Syrian forces toward the Golan Heights. A handwritten notation at the top of the report reads, "Shown to Sadat, 10/27/75."

President Sadat: I do not think that Syria will go to war. They are doing this mostly for domestic reasons to show how tough they are.

Maybe Lebanon is the cause.

The President: What about Lebanon?

President Sadat: I have been reluctant to speak publicly on this because both sides are to blame. The army is weak. The PLO is a state within a state. Saiqa, in the guise of the PLO, is decisive and mischievous. Armaments and money are pouring into Lebanon from all sides. I see no outlet. What do you think, Ismail?

Fahmy: It needs a big mediation.

Dr. Kissinger: By whom?

Fahmy: I have no clear idea.

President Sadat: Maybe the Secretary General of the Arab League. The PLO is a state within a state. Please make sure, Mr. President, that the Israelis do not intervene. Nobody in the Arab world will believe that there is no coordination.

The joint Egyptian-Syrian command no longer exists. The Syrians have not asked Gamasy to replace Marshal Ismail as head of the Joint Command.

247. Memorandum of Conversation[1]

Washington, October 28, 1975, 10:40–11:50 a.m.

PARTICIPANTS

    President Gerald R. Ford
    Mohammed Anwar al-Sadat, President of the Arab Republic of Egypt
    Dr. Henry A. Kissinger, Secretary of State and Assistant to the President for National Security Affairs
    Ismail Fahmy, Deputy Prime Minister and Minister of Foreign Affairs, Arab Republic of Egypt

President Ford: I want to fill the void. The question is how quickly we can do it. But we will do so.

The next question is how can we work together on a common strategy for the Middle East?

---

[1] Source: Library of Congress, Manuscript Division, Kissinger Papers, CL 133, Geopolitical File, Egypt, September 19–December 31, 1975. Secret; Nodis. The meeting was held in the Oval Office at the White House.

President Sadat: To start with, the main item is the Palestinians. They are very greatly influenced by the Soviets. During March, the Soviets tried to turn the Palestinians. They could at that time be thwarted. Now the danger is great again. I recommend that the United States begin a dialogue with Arafat—openly.

President Ford: Your thought is that we begin unofficial but public talks? When do you think it should be done?

President Sadat: It should be done after the disengagement agreement is completed.

FonMin Fahmy: All you hear from the Palestinians is an attempt to get attention.

During the UN you should get in touch with some of them there.

President Sadat: Regarding the Jordanians. King Hussein is a nice man, but the Prime Minister[2] is unreliable. His present course is full of contradictions between Jordan and Syria and the PLO. Hussein will listen to the advice of the United States. Therefore, the U.S. should make clear to Jordan the suicidal nature of that course.

President Ford: Does Asad understand the suicidal nature of that course?

President Sadat: He understands that in a crisis he has no capability and he doubts that he has Soviet support. Syria is trying to arrange a visit of King Hussein to Moscow. Asad is moderate. He wants to be in touch with the United States. Henry should stay in touch with him.

FonMin Fahmy: You must contact the Palestinians informally and split off the Jordanians. Syria is now dealing with Iraq. But that is another house of cards. Syria will not be subordinate to Iraq or vice versa.

President Sadat: There are 15,000 Russians in Syria. If the U.S. can keep in touch with all the parties, it would be a good step.

UNDOF renewal? Asad has already said that he would renew. I believe Israel can destroy Syria in one hour.

President Ford: Why did Asad join?

President Sadat: Because I forced him to do it.

President Ford: Will there be a joint move in Lebanon?

President Sadat: Everybody is too busy to get involved.

---

[2] Jordanian Prime Minister Zaid Rifai.

248. National Security Decision Memorandum 313[1]

Washington, November 14, 1975.

TO

The Secretary of State
The Secretary of Defense
The Administrator, Agency for International Development
The Director, Arms Control and Disarmament Agency
The Director of Central Intelligence

SUBJECT

Establishment of US Sinai Support Mission

The President has reviewed the response to National Security Study Memorandum 230[2] regarding the establishment of a U.S. Support Mission in the Sinai, pursuant to the U.S. Proposal of September 1, 1975. The President concurs in the first recommendation of the study and has directed that a senior interagency group be established under the auspices of the National Security Council to organize, coordinate and provide overall management for the Mission. The member agencies of the management board will be the Department of State and Defense, the Central Intelligence Agency, the Agency for International Development, and the Arms Control and Disarmament Agency.

The President also concurs in the third and fourth recommendations of the Study. He has directed that the Mission be headed by a Director, who will receive broad policy guidance and report to the President through the Assistant to the President for National Security Affairs. He will be assisted by a small staff in Washington, as well as drawing upon the support of the interagency management board. In the field, the major part of the work will be carried out under private contract with the contractors and their personnel responsible to the Mission Director and his designated representatives. In carrying out his functions, the Director shall hold the additional title of Special Representative of the President.

The President wishes the Sinai Support Mission to be established expeditiously, in order to be in position to carry out effectively its assigned tasks once the Basic Agreement has been fully implemented. Addressees should designate a senior representative to serve on the interagency management board.

---

[1] Source: Ford Library, National Security Adviser, NSDMs, Box 1, NSDM 313. Secret. Copies were sent to the Chairman of the Joint Chiefs of Staff and Director of the Office of Management and Budget.

[2] Document 238.

The President has also directed that there be a comprehensive review of all operations of the Sinai Support Mission one year from the date of this memorandum, with a view to determining the advisability of any changes in the management or organization of the Mission.

Brent Scowcroft

249. Memorandum of Conversation[1]

Washington, November 28, 1975.

PARTICIPANTS

The Secretary
Under Secretary Sisco
Assistant Secretary Atherton
Ambassador Buffum, IO
Jerry Bremer, Notetaker

SUBJECT

The Middle East

The Secretary: Where do we stand?

Sisco: Simcha gave me their position. They want us to veto any resolution with a reference to the PLO or to the UN resolutions.[2] Here is a paper which Moynihan has said that the SYG thinks could work.[3] It would end up with a period after "the Palestinian question." But Malik as Security Council President,[4] would say it was decided that the PLO should be heard in January. If it is said as a Council consensus then ...

The Secretary: We cannot say that.

Sisco: That's right. We cannot agree. Then we could fall back to a minimum that his statement would say that a majority are in favor of it and we'd say we're against.

The Secretary: What does Pat think?

---

[1] Source: Library of Congress, Manuscript Division, Kissinger Papers, CL 346, State Department Memorandum of Conversations, Internal, October–November 1975. Secret; Sensitive. Brackets are in the original.

[2] A reference to UN Security Council Resolutions 242 and 338.

[3] The paper is not further identified.

[4] Soviet Representative Jacob A. Malik was President of the Security Council during November.

Sisco: I've been tough with him. He's good on it. He thinks we should take it without this sentence. There is one other possibility which is the French idea. That is to refer to all relevant resolutions without specifying which resolutions you mean. Moynihan could then say that we consider only 242 and 338 are relevant.

The Secretary: Couldn't Malik just say he wants to call attention to the fact that the participation of others in January is a procedural question and not subject to veto?

Sisco: That's another possibility. He might say that the prevailing or majority view is that. I suggest we tell it to Pat.

The Secretary: Do you think it will work out?

Buffum: Yes.

Sisco: I think so.

The Secretary: Have they begun the debate?

Sisco: Not yet. In January it will be pretty rough though.

Buffum: The Syrians will use this as a major propaganda ploy.

Sisco: Simcha's statement was that in January the U.S. was to resist any effort to change 242, 338 and to object to any changes in Geneva. Also, the U.S. should object to the adoption of a General Assembly resolution at that time which refers to the rights of the Palestinians. I made no comment.

The Secretary: It would be kind if they would ask a super power every now and then what we wanted to do. What happens then?

Sisco: In January?

The Secretary: Yes.

Sisco: Well, we'll have an extended debate. There will be 20 Arabs to speak.

The Secretary: We'll have to veto the resolution.

Sisco: Here's the text of the resolution we will have to vote no on. It will be reflected in the Security Council in January. (handing resolution to the Secretary)[5]

Buffum: Yes, that's the maximum Syrian position.

Sisco: I think this will go on all week.

Buffum: The only question is whether we lobby in capitals.

The Secretary: What's your recommendation?

---

[5] A reference to UN General Assembly Resolution 3414, adopted on December 5, which, among other things, called for an invitation to the PLO to participate in UN consideration of Middle East issues and in the Geneva Conference. The United States voted against the resolution. (*Yearbook of the United Nations, 1975*, pp. 241–242) The Security Council convened on January 12, 1976, to continue the Middle East debate, including the issue of PLO participation.

Buffum: I think we should. We have to look tough on this.

Sisco: Why not send a circular out on it? I'll also ask Moynihan tonight if he feels we're doing everything on this end that we should do.

The Secretary: No! No! No! He is an Ambassador. He will be treated like a regular Ambassador. He's a great folk hero at the moment of the Jews, as Jackson was.

Sisco: Your instinct then, if it boils down to the Palestinian question, is that we should go along?

The Secretary: Yes.

Sisco: Is the French formula also okay?

The Secretary: Yes, if we say 242 and 338 are the relevant ones. What are we going to do with those SOB's in Jerusalem? They will claim we've sold out again.

Buffum: No, they've been pretty appreciative so far of our work.

Sisco: We've been making a good record.[6] Dinitz told me tonight he intends to interpret what you said that we are leaning to support the full Israeli position, particularly on the veto. He's encouraged by what you said.

The Secretary: Now, wait a minute. I said we'll veto a resolution mentioning the General Assembly resolution and the PLO but not one including the Palestinian question. No. I talked to the President. I have said publically the rights of the Palestinians have to be considered. Do you think I went too far?

Sisco: I hope not. You know how Simcha is. No it's probably not too far.

Buffum: My question is whether it is vetoable on procedure.

The Secretary: It's fine with me.

Buffum: If it's construed as a procedural resolution, for example, if it says "takes into consideration."

Atherton: How can we veto part of it?

Sisco: You would have to have a vote by division. Then we would consider the paragraph which calls for the reconvening of the meeting as procedural. But "taking into account" really becomes substantive.

Buffum: I'm not sure we could sustain it. Particularly since the reference to the resolution itself is procedural.

---

[6] The U.S. record included votes against UN General Assembly Resolutions 3375, 3376, and 3379 on November 10. Resolutions 3375 and 3376 concerned the rights of Palestinians and the status of the PLO. Resolution 3379 determined that "zionism is a form of racism and racial discrimination." For text of the three resolutions, see ibid., pp. 247–249 and 599–600. On November 11, both houses of Congress passed resolutions condemning the equation of Zionism with racism and called for a reassessment of the U.S. relationship with the United Nations. (*New York Times*, November 12, 1975, p. 1)

The Secretary: "Taking into consideration" is not badly drafted. We will come to a point where we cannot go on like this. We can't refuse forever to talk to the PLO.

Atherton: We'd have some job trying to explain to the American public that we vetoed the extension of UNDOF over the PLO.

Buffum: Particularly if it leads to a dust-up on the Golan.

The Secretary: Should we send a message to Asad explaining our problem and saying not to push us to the wall? Say it's a procedural question. The PLO can participate but does he want us to veto the UNDOF extension or let it stew for a while?

Sisco: If the tactical situation were not so fluid that might be useful, but I have my doubts now.

The Secretary: Where do we stand now?

Sisco: They're about to reconvene at 7:00 p.m.

Buffum: The Jordanians are pressing us to get going on the West Bank.

The Secretary: How?

Sisco: They are open-minded about the Arab summit, they just wanted to reverse the Rabat decision. It's a sort of inconsistent position.

The Secretary: The Israelis better get me out of office. I'll tell you, the next time I'll finish them. A great power cannot be treated this way. What U.S. national interest is served? We could co-exist with the PLO. It is indeed historically inevitable.

Atherton: The only question now is which PLO. The pragmatic part or the doctrinal part.

The Secretary: It is inevitable. If they'd given part of the West Bank to Jordan last year, we'd have a case. Murphy never got a response from Asad on that. Do you think he tried it?

Atherton: He did. Asad may have wanted to talk to Arafat first about it.

250. Telegram From Secretary of State Kissinger to the Department of State[1]

December 1, 1975, 0059Z.

Secto 23015. Subject: Message to Rabin. For Eagleburger from Secretary.

1. Please arrange to have following message from the President to Rabin conveyed to Israeli Chargé in Washington. Please also have it checked with Buffum and Atherton before delivery to assure consistency with what they know of SC proceedings.

2. *Begin text of message to Rabin.*

Dear Mr. Prime Minister:

I have been following the proceedings on the UNDOF extension in the Security Council,[2] and the results in my judgement are mutually satisfactory. Secretary Kissinger's letter to Foreign Minister Allon[3] detailed the successful efforts of the U.S. in this regard based on close and continuous consultations with the Israeli Government. I authorized an affirmative vote on the resolution in the conviction that the U.S. to have vetoed the six month UNDOF extension would have carried with it the greater risk of beginning a chain reaction which would seriously heighten tensions in the area and could lead to a resumption of hostilities.

In the broader context, I want to make a few added observations in the spirit of the close and intimate relationship which exists between Israel and the United States.

We share your view that there is a substantial effort being made to shift the focus of negotiations on the Arab-Israeli dispute from the Geneva Conference to the Security Council. In part, this arises from the fact that it has not been possible to get a serious negotiating process started in the aftermath of the Egyptian-Israeli Agreement, the implementation of which seems to be proceeding well.

I am keenly aware that the position of the other side and conditions in the area have not been conducive to negotiations and reconcili-

---

[1] Source: Library of Congress, Manuscript Division, Kissinger Papers, CL 160, Geopolitical File, Israel, Dec. 1–12, 1975. Secret; Cherokee; Nodis; Flash. Sent from the aircraft taking President Ford and Secretary Kissinger to Beijing.

[2] The UN Security Council voted to renew the UNDOF for an additional six months on November 30, but Syria and the Soviet Union insisted that the renewal be linked with PLO participation in the UN debate on the Middle East to commence on January 12, 1976. Despite Israeli opposition to the linkage, the United States agreed, resulting in PLO inclusion at the January debate. (*Washington Post*, November 30, 1975, p. A16)

[3] The letter is contained in telegram Secto 23012. (National Archives, RG 59, Central Policy Files, P840084–024)

ation. At the same time, Mr. Prime Minister, I must say in all candor and friendship our task has not been made any easier by the fact that Israel has taken no new initiative to stimulate the negotiating process nor have you taken the kind of unilateral step before the UNDOF renewal which you and I discussed during your last visit to Washington.[4]

The position of those who are seeking to make the Council more predominant has been strengthened because of the diplomatic void which presently exists. We will stick to the agreed strategy despite this. An overall review of where we are and where to go has assumed greater urgency. I look forward to my talks with you at the end of January. In the meantime, if Foreign Minister Allon could find it convenient to come to Washington in early January to concert positions on the Security Council debate this would be desirable.

Sincerely,
Gerald R. Ford

---

[4] See Documents 183–185.

---

251. Memorandum of Conversation[1]

December 6, 1975.

PARTICIPANTS

President Gerald Ford
Dr. Henry A. Kissinger, Secretary of State
Lt. General Brent Scowcroft, Assistant to the President for National Security Affairs

SUBJECTS

SALT Negotiation Procedures; Middle East

[Omitted here is discussion unrelated to the Arab-Israeli dispute.]

Kissinger: We also have a Moynihan problem. The basic problem is we are afraid to impose discipline on anyone because of the leaks. It

---

[1] Source: Library of Congress, Manuscript Division, Kissinger Papers, CL 283, President's File, December 1975, Folder 1. Secret; Nodis. The meeting took place during Ford's Asian trip. According to the President's Daily Diary, Ford was in Jakarta until 11:25 a.m. and in Manila from 4 p.m. (Ford Library, Staff Secretary's Office Files) It is likely the meeting occurred while in transit between the two cities.

is now being said that I prevented a veto in the Security Council of the UNDOF resolution. It is a total lie. You know that whole story.

Now we have a new problem. The Israelis have killed 200 people in a raid in Lebanon[2] and the resolution is coming up. If they put something in the resolution condemning terrorist acts, I don't see how we can veto under these circumstances. This wasn't retaliation. But I am afraid to put it on paper.

There is another horror. If we don't protest the four new settlements they are building on the Golan,[3] we will be blamed for acquiescing. But if we do protest, there will be an outburst.

The President: The question is do we let Israel run our foreign policy?

Kissinger: We got UNDOF extended with virtually no price. Anyone can get a Security Council debate. The Israeli strategy is to defeat you and destroy our foreign policy and credibility, or at least to isolate us and kill our relations with the Arabs.

The President: I think we should protest the four settlements.

Kissinger: It should be done while I'm in the country so I can share the blame.

Your foreign policy is going well. Sadat's visit went very well and this trip is being reported well now.

[Omitted here is discussion unrelated to the Arab-Israeli dispute.]

---

[2] On December 2, Israeli fighter jets bombed Palestinian refugee camps and guerrilla bases in northern and southern Lebanon in retaliation for a November 13 Palestinian bombing in Jerusalem that killed 6 and wounded 46 others. According to the *Washington Post*, Lebanese police officials reported the death toll from the Israeli bombing at 91 killed and 150 wounded. (*Washington Post*, December 3, 1975, p. A1)

[3] Apparently a reference to new Israeli settlements constructed on the Golan Heights.

252. Memorandum of Conversation[1]

Washington, December 12, 1975, 7–7:50 p.m.

PARTICIPANTS

    President Ford
    Max Fisher
    Lt. General Brent Scowcroft, Assistant to the President for National Security Affairs

Fisher: I thought you would like a read-out of my trip. They had called a special conference for world Jewish leaders. The mood of the country is hysterical. All these events like Zionism, the UN Security Council vote, the Sadat visit, put them on the defensive. I have never seen it so bad.

I spent two and a half hours with Rabin. He showed me your letter and Henry's letter.[2] I said I could tell him there was no change in our position on the PLO. I said you wanted the six months extension and the only question is whether we could get it without giving anything. Rabin was most disturbed about the PLO invitation and its effect on the Egyptians.[3] It further undercut them in favor of Syria.

I told him he must have confidence in you. He said he did have. I said he shouldn't stir things up and further isolate Israel. The U.S. is his only friend and he shouldn't go public with complaints.

On the settlements, he said he agreed with our assessment, but he had a public posture to uphold. Begin said the Lebanon raid[4] was the biggest mistake they ever made. But he said an independent Palestine would be a dagger at the heart of Israel, controlled by the Soviet Union. At this conference, Begin said the settlements should be allowed to go forward on the West Bank. Rabin said he would not be compromised and put in a box on the West Bank settlements—they would be right in the midst of Arab settlements. He told me that the right was deliberately stirring this up to embarrass him. He has intense political pressure on him.

The President: We don't anticipate any problems here, except getting the $2.3 billion through the Congress.

---

[1] Ford Library, National Security Adviser, Memoranda of Conversations, Box 17, December 12, 1975, Ford, Max Fisher. Secret; Nodis. The meeting was held in the Oval Office at the White House. Brackets are in the original.

[2] Ford's letter can be found in Document 250. Kissinger's letter has not been found.

[3] On December 4, at the request of Egypt, the UN Security Council invited the PLO to participate in a debate on the December 2 Israeli air strikes against Palestinian refugee camps and guerrilla bases in Lebanon.

[4] See footnote 2, Document 251.

Fisher: He said Henry had sort of given a commitment on the Security Council. I told him that was not so and Dinitz had read something which was not there. I think the key to the whole thing is the Palestinian situation.

The President: Does he have any suggestions? I saw that Cabinet members thought Israel should talk to the Palestinians if they would recognize Israel.

Fisher: They have to face this eventually, but it is probably too much to face overnight. We can't push them into it, but I think it is the most important issue and I think it is being recognized as such more and more. Rabin is much more self-assured now.

The President: I noticed that on his last visit.

Fisher: Begin spoke very highly of you. He had a good impression of his meeting with you.

Anyway, they all felt terribly isolated and upset.

The President: I guess I can see how they might have a different perspective. But we were tough on the Zionism resolution, we did our best on UNDOF, and vetoed the terrorism one.[5] They shouldn't feel isolated.

Fisher: You know how they are—like Henry is as a person. It is a national trait.

In the evolution of the Palestinian issue, speak frankly to Rabin on this issue, in terms of the future. I had a good visit with them and I think I quieted it down.

With respect to the American [Jewish] community, we need to do something too. There is a perception that you have written off the Jewish vote. I have a couple of ideas, but I would think it out more. In '72 the Jewish press came in to the Oval Office for an interview.

The President: I think we can work something out. Propose something.

Fisher: O. K. It can't look contrived, but we have to put things into proper perspective.

---

[5] The Zionism resolution refers to UN General Assembly Resolution 3379; see footnote 6, Document 249. For the renewal of UNDOF, see footnote 2, Document 250. The veto of a terrorism resolution is a reference to a draft resolution introduced in the Security Council that condemned Israel for air strikes in Lebanon on December 2. The United States vetoed on December 8. (*Yearbook of the United Nations, 1975,* pp. 227–229)

253. Telegram From the Department of State to the Embassy in Israel[1]

Washington, January 1, 1976, 0110Z.

170. Subject: Presidential Message to Rabin. For Ambassador.

1. Please transmit the following letter from President Ford to Prime Minister Rabin as soon as possible.

2. *Begin text*:

Dear Mr. Prime Minister:

I appreciate receiving your letter of December 16, 1975.[2] In view of the importance of the UN Security Council deliberations beginning January 12, I believe it is essential for me to have a further exchange with you regarding U.S. policy and strategy. I am sharing some tentative views now so that you and your colleagues can reflect upon them before and in connection with Foreign Minister Allon's meetings with Secretary Kissinger. We do not wish the very difficult Security Council proceedings in January to become a source of misunderstanding between us. As you yourself have often said, Mr. Prime Minister, there is much that is common and parallel in Israeli and U.S. policies, but they have never been and cannot be identical.

We have studied your December 16 letter with great care and understanding. Israel need have no concern regarding an imposed solution.

... A settlement must come as a result of negotiations between the principal parties concerned. We are also keenly aware that Syria is seeking to make the Security Council the primary and more or less permanent instrument of diplomacy. Here, too, you should be assured that we would view such a development as contrary to our mutual interests. We continue to believe strongly and firmly that the Geneva Conference framework is best suited for future diplomacy.

Having said this, Mr. Prime Minister, I know you fully realize that we face a most difficult and delicate situation in the Security Council. Your non-participation will make more difficult an outcome satisfactory to you, but this is a judgment for Israel to make.

Our principal concerns are that the Council proceedings not deepen the stalemate so it becomes unbreakable, that they not destroy

---

[1] Source: Library of Congress, Manuscript Division, Kissinger Papers, CL 160, Geopolitical File, Israel, Dec. 13–31, 1975. Secret; Nodis; Niact Immediate. Drafted by Sidney Sober; cleared by Kuchel and Oakley; and approved by Sober. Repeated to Kissinger who was vacationing in Jamaica.

[2] In the letter, Rabin expressed his concerns about the forthcoming Security Council debate. (Ibid.)

the role of the U.S. in the diplomacy of the Middle East, and therefore dim, if not extinguish, the prospects for progress in the Middle East and bring that area closer to a renewal of hostilities.

In this connection, I want to make clear, so as to avoid any future misunderstanding, that the Israeli position regarding Resolutions 242 and 338, as described in your letter, in which you say "we can tolerate no modification whatsoever in the wording or interpretation of those resolutions . . ." does not accord with our view. We have previously made clear to you that we will oppose and, if necessary, vote against any initiative in the Security Council to alter adversely the terms of reference of the Geneva Peace Conference or to change Resolutions 242 and 338 in any way which is incompatible with their original purpose. I do not cite this to raise semantical points. I merely want to say that whether 242 or 338 is considered to be undermined or altered adversely or changes are considered incompatible with their original purpose will require a judgment on a specific text—a judgment that we feel has to take into account as well the considerations and concerns I have outlined in the previous paragraphs of this letter.

Our ability to get support of others for a satisfactory result in the Security Council will also be influenced by what they believe are the prospects for progress through exercise of various available options outside the Council. There undoubtedly will be an overwhelming SC majority—particularly in the new Security Council composition of 1976—for a resolution which provides for PLO participation at a Geneva Conference. We have thought of a number of formulations which we may face, all of which in greater or lesser degree will seek to inject the Palestinian issue. Some formulations would undoubtedly affect adversely 242 and 338, others may not. For example, what if the U.S. is faced with a simple resolution reaffirming 242 and 338 and adding to this resolution language which the U.S. has used in its policy statements to the effect that a durable and just peace has to take into account "the legitimate interests of the Palestinian people." We believe it important that such formulations be dealt with in such a way in the Council that they not destroy other future negotiating options.

The Palestinian question is difficult for both of us, Mr. Prime Minister. Even if this issue can be dealt with satisfactorily in the Council, it is not one that can be avoided entirely outside the Council proceedings if the negotiating possibilities inherent in a Geneva Conference or in an informal preparatory talk of the kind suggested by Secretary Kissinger in his General Assembly speech[3] are to be further pursued.

---

[3] In his address to the General Assembly on September 22, Kissinger suggested convening informal international meetings to discuss the Middle East. Excerpts of his speech were printed in the *New York Times* on September 23. (*New York Times*, September 23, 1975, p. 16)

I have made no final judgments, Mr. Prime Minister, but I felt it important to share my deep concerns with you and to underscore that when your Foreign Minister comes to Washington, he be prepared to speak specifically and concretely on the difficult issues referred to in this letter.

Finally, Mr. Prime Minister, I know that you are aware that planning is progressing speedily and smoothly for your visit to the United States. It is entirely appropriate, Mr. Prime Minister, that in this bicentennial year, Israel's Prime Minister, representing a free and democratic country that shares fully our ideas and firm dedication to independence, will be the first head of government being received in 1976. Israel and the U.S. have been together through much peril and promise. I know these are difficult issues I am posing in this letter; but I do so as a friend whose firm support for Israel's security and survival remains undiminished.

I wish you, your family, and all of the people of Israel a year of progress and tranquility as the search for peace continues.

Sincerely, Gerald R. Ford. *End text.*

Robinson

254. Minutes of National Security Council Meeting[1]

Washington, January 13, 1976, 10:20 a.m.–noon.

SUBJECT

Israeli Military Requirements

PRINCIPALS

The President
Secretary of State Henry A. Kissinger
Secretary of Defense Donald Rumsfeld
The Director of OMB James Lynn
The Chairman of the Joint Chiefs of Staff General George S. Brown
The Director of Central Intelligence William Colby

---

[1] Source: Ford Library, National Security Adviser, Box 2, NSC Meetings File, NSC Meeting, January 13, 1976. Secret; Nodis. The meeting was held in the Cabinet Room at the White House. All brackets, with the exception of ones describing omitted material, are in the original.

OTHER ATTENDEES

  State
    Under Secretary of State for Political Affairs Joseph J. Sisco
    Counselor Helmut Sonnenfeldt

  Defense
    Deputy Secretary William Clements

  WH
    Richard Cheney

  NSC
    Brent Scowcroft
    William G. Hyland
    Robert B. Oakley

Note: The following are the minutes of that portion of the meeting on Israeli Military Requirements.[2] Minutes reporting the discussion of another topic are identified as Part II of II.

President: Our military relationship with Israel is a very important issue and we must examine it carefully. Bill (Colby), will you start by giving us your assessment?

Colby: [Presented briefing attached at Tab A up to point V on page 12. During the first part of the briefing the President asked if Israel already had the weapons and equipment mentioned on page 2 to counter the Arab SAM threat. Colby replied that they do. The President also asked for clarification of the figures in Chart III of the presentation. Colby explained the force ratios in the "worst case" column of Chart III. [2 *lines not declassified*] The following conversation took place following the first part of Colby's briefing.]

Rumsfeld: What are you carrying for participation by all Arab states combined in your "most likely" estimate column?

Colby: [3½ *lines not declassified*] We include everything for Egypt and Syria with lesser amounts from other Arab countries.

Clements: What do you carry for Iraq? It can be very significant.

Colby: [4½ *lines not declassified*]

President: What about the improvement in the military abilities of the Arab soldiers which was apparent in the October 1973 war?

Colby: There has been some improvement but Israel still has an immense qualitative superiority in the training of its men, their technological abilities and their strategy and tactics. Over the next five years we do not expect this to change although the Arabs will catch up over a longer period of time.

Kissinger: Does your Chart (III) take into account new requests by Israel?

---

[2] See Documents 243 and 244.

Colby: No, the numbers and force ratios on the chart assume that Israel will have everything which has been approved for delivery at the present time, but does not include anything which they are requesting now or expect to request in the future.

President: Have the things we have requested funds for in the FY 76 budget gone into this?

Kissinger: No, this shows what has already been approved. For example, you see the Israeli figure for tanks is 3,250 but there are an additional 180 under consideration in the 75/76 list. If they were approved the total would be at least 3,430; the same is true for APCs where there are 1,000 under consideration which, if approved, would make the Israeli total at least 7,800.

Colby: That is right. New requests are not included and agreeing to these would change the ratios.

President: I am trying to relate this to the budget program. Are the new requests going to come out of the FY 76 or the FY 77 program?

Scowcroft: We are considering the calendar year 1976 increment of Matmon–B but there is a lot more ahead.

Kissinger: There will be similar increments later on, so if the President approves anything at all of what they are requesting today, and we assume there will be further requests approved later on, it would give Israel a better force ratio than those shown on Colby's chart. That is why this chart is somewhat misleading. This chart does not show what Israel is really likely to have in 1980 although it projects a 1980 force ratio.

Clements: On the payments angle, this is only the going-in request. Once you agree then it is like becoming pregnant since you will have an obligation to carry forward with financing it in future budgets.

Scowcroft: The Israeli practice is to make the minimum possible down-payment and then worry about how to pay the other increments later on. Also, if we agree to the entire 1975/76 request it will be seen as a signal that we intend to go ahead with the entire Matmon–B plan.

Kissinger: On the other hand, if we do not it will be seen as a decision not to support the concept of Matmon–B and you might have a couple of unexpected, unwanted callers this year, Mr. President.

Rumsfeld: As I understand it, we are considering today only 180 tanks, not the larger figure in Matmon–B. Any additional deliveries will be added to the figures shown for Israel and for the Arabs, as well, won't they?

Kissinger: The CIA projection already contains foreseeable increases between now and 1980 on the Arab side. The Arab figures are 1980 figures but the Israeli figures are 1975 figures. Israel wants over

1,000 tanks during the next five years. The chart is misleading since Israel is not also calculated on a five-year basis.

President: What exactly does the 3,250 figure for Israeli tanks represent?

Scowcroft: What they have on hand or have approved orders for, not what they plan to get later.

Rumsfeld: We need to organize ourselves better, including a better chart, Bill.

President: Have we funded for the Israeli equipment request or not?

Lynn: Every year we have orders but the payment does not come in the same year. The Israelis will have to pay about $1.6 billion in FY 76 for things they have already had approved, some of which have already been shipped. On the other hand, they have carry-over unspent funds of $550 million so they will have about two billion in FY 76 to pay for the $1.6 billion plus whatever new orders they make. But the new orders will have very little financial effect, as Brent just said.

President: This is crucial. The Congress requires full funding for the Department of Defense and I can see why. But Israel uses partial funding and then we have to find the money somehow later on.

Clements: Exactly. This is creating a commitment which will hit us in coming years.

Colby: The impact of the decision we take in the near term will be more political and psychological than military since Israel already has such great power and the delivery dates for new items are not immediate. Such weapons as the Pershing and the F–16 can have this political impact. [2 lines not declassified] (Colby presented the remainder of the briefing at Tab A, starting with point V on page 12 and continuing through the end of page 16.) [3 lines not declassified]

Rumsfeld: The figures you project would be the equivalent of 500,000 Americans. They were badly hurt in the October war.

Colby: The subject of comparative casualty figures is morbid but interesting. Look at the percent of casualties for the United States in comparison to the number of people in the Armed Services and the total of the population. For World War I we had 2% casualties of the total number in the Armed Services, about .1% of the total population. It was about the same for World War II. Israel suffered less than 1% casualties of those in the Armed Services during the October 1973 war, and about .1% of the total population. Our projections for a future war are about 1.6% casualties of those who serve in the Israeli Armed Forces. This is substantial, but not unusual in wars.

Clements: But it will take place in a very brief period of time.

Colby: Yes, but it will lead to victory. [*4 lines not declassified*] We have increased the percentage of Arab participation we estimate over the October 1973 figures; it is up to 35%. [*2 lines not declassified*] We do not see how they can be transported to the front before the war had ended in an Israeli victory even were there no political differences and were the other Arab Governments willing to deprive themselves of security protection at home. There could be pre-positioning but Israel would detect this and react strongly.

Kissinger: Yet sooner or later the sheer numerical superiority of the Arabs will prevail. Take the historical view and this becomes clear. It may take 25 years but the Arabs will eventually catch up technologically and then Israel will be in the gravest danger.

Colby: Yes. That is why they need to negotiate a settlement while there is still time.

President: I saw a report [*less than 1 line not declassified*] that the U.S. sells $10 billion in arms to the Middle East while all the other states combined sell about $3 million.

Colby: Only the U.S. and the U.S.S.R. have a really major capability for arms production. The others can do it but much more slowly.

President: Brent, do you want to get us started again?

Scowcroft: [*less than 1 line not declassified*] Israel's [*less than 1 line not declassified*] idea of a force level for Matmon–B. It is a plan for forty billion dollars of arms and equipment. Only the first five years has been projected in detail. It calls for 1,000 tanks, 3,000 APCs, 250 F–16s, etc. to be added to the IDF by 1980. They are really talking about a program which will change the entire military and strategic balance in the Middle East, whether or not they admit it. [*less than 1 line not declassified*] Today we are faced with the 1976 increment of Matmon–B which was given to us in February 1975.[3] It is hard to get a handle on this issue but it is important. Essentially we need to decide three things: the level of response to the 75/76 list, the related question of how we respond to the request for 250 F–16s, and the list of thirty-two sensitive items which have been requested. If you take out the F–16s, the basic 1975/76 list is valued at about $2.2 billion. Look at these two charts (Tab B)[4] showing the projections at different levels of future Matmon–B and our projected level of assistance.

President: The deficit on this first chart is the difference between Matmon–B and what we project for security assistance for Israel. They will have to make up the difference.

---

[3] Not found.
[4] The charts, Tab B, have not been found.

Scowcroft: The impact of our accepting the entire 1975/76 request would be seen by Israel as a commitment to the whole of the Matmon program; it would be seen by the Arabs as full U.S. support for Israel, abandoning our role as a mediator. As an alternate, we looked at the idea of a package equal in value to what you have asked from Congress for FY 76, $1.5 billion. The concept behind this would be one of modernization and replacement instead of force expansion. This would lower the numbers and give us the philosophic basis for a lower program. For the basic list we must decide whether to go for the entire amount or a lesser amount such as the one we have examined. On the F–16, we have agreed to supply them to Israel but we have given them no commitment on the quantity or the timing of delivery. There are three ways to handle this issue: we can request Israel to cut the number it is asking for, say to 100; this would reduce the price to about $1.3 billion instead of the $3.2 billion for 250. Or we can put Israel at the end of the production queue; or we can defer the entire issue for a year, if necessary promising Israel they would not lose their place in the production line because of the delay.

Kissinger: They also want to produce them in Israel.

Clements: Not really; only to assemble some sub-sections.

Scowcroft: Deferral would upset the Israelis but granting the full request would really upset the Arabs, coming on top of the F–15 deal.

President: What about the effect on our own forces?

General Brown: If we take the earlier delivery option, it would affect our modernization but if we took the slower option there would be no impact. The F–16 is a very modern high-performance aircraft. It is better for ground attack than the F–14 or F–15 which get more publicity. It is almost as good as the F–15 in air combat except at the very high altitude segment of the envelope. It will make a whale of a difference in the Middle East.

Clements: We will be producing 4,000 by 1990.

Brown: We have a firm commitment to NATO, after we persuaded them to take the F–16 over the French.

Clements: We cannot possibly renege on our commitment to NATO.

Kissinger: We never promised Israel anything on delivery dates.

Scowcroft: No dates and no numbers were promised Israel.

Kissinger: If the President were to decide on the total amount, he could delay on delivery.

Scowcroft: The earliest delivery would be 1981 in any event.

President: What is our commitment to NATO and our own forces?

Brown: The option we can exercise is the production rate. We can go for delayed delivery now and then increase the production rate later.

President: When do we deploy the F–16 to our own forces?

Clements: It will be 1980 before they are deployed to squadrons although some testbed aircraft will be operational in 1979.

President: It could be a question of who goes first.

Brown: Put them in the production queue or give them priority, that is the choice.

Scowcroft: They want a decision now so they can place their orders.

Kissinger: I do not recommend delaying a decision. I recall the problem Rogers had in delaying a decision on the F–4 and we never heard the end of it. You are better off putting them on a slow schedule and then speeding up later.

Scowcroft: We can defuse the Arabs by talking about late delivery and put Israel into the production queue.

Kissinger: When we talked about the F–4, Israel was happy to get two or three a month.

Clements: They are getting the F–15 to tide them over.

Scowcroft: Last September Dinitz and Peres gave us a list of 32 high interest items. Some of them have been resolved but those that remain are problems. I will pass out a list of those (Tab C)[5] There are three kinds of problems: some are still in R & D, there is a special sensitivity for the technology on others such as the EA6Q and the FLIR, and others like the CBU72 are politically sensitive. It is like napalm in terms of sensitivity.

Brown: It is a propane mix which spreads out over a wide area and is then ignited by grenades. It makes a huge explosion with great overpressure. There is a cloud like a tactical nuclear weapon. We used it against that island during the *Mayaguez* incident and there was no more shooting. But it will cause a political problem like napalm has.

Scowcroft: There is also our first-line communications security equipment which Israel wants but the intelligence community is adamant against releasing it.

President: Has Israel asked for all these items?

Scowcroft: Yes, and in the quantities indicated. I understand Defense opposes all of these.

Rumsfeld: There is a general Defense doctrine, as I understand it, opposing the transfer of high technology weapons to other countries, the reduction of U.S. stocks and the release of destabilizing items.

Brown: The last time we discussed this, Mr. President, you told us not to take anything more from stocks or production for the U.S.

---

[5] The lists, Tab C, have not been found.

Armed Forces and we have been holding to this.[6] We are planning ahead on this basis.

Rumsfeld: We should not count items still in R & D. They are not operational so why does Israel want them.

Kissinger: They know all about your R & D so if they like an item you can be sure it has promise. In making decisions on arms for Israel you have several problems: foreign policy, the strategic balance, and the domestic impact as well as on our military assets. Our ability to move Israel when we negotiate in earnest is also a consideration. Let's look at this list and see what we can approve. We can promise some of these R & D items safely since they cannot get them and we lose nothing. The items with moral objections can be considered separately.

President: Is the CBU on the refusal list for moral reasons?

Rumsfeld: For foreign policy reasons, I would say. Henry is picking up some Brademus terminology and I want to stop him. It is really a foreign policy and political problem.

Kissinger: In general we deal with Israel on arms by allowing them to beat up the bureaucracy and pick off items one at a time. But in an election year we are better going to a comprehensive list and settle it once and for all. I have no specific recommendations but we did agree to give sympathetic consideration to high technology items during the Sinai negotiations. We are not committed to any specifics.

Clements: They get things and put them in their pocket without ever looking back. They already have a lot of things.

Kissinger: They got the smart bomb by successive waves of attacks.

Rumsfeld: I would do the same thing if I were Israel and out there alone with the Arabs—no matter what Colby's charts say.

President: Henry did not mention the cost. This is a very important factor.

Lynn: We really have two issues. One is the appropriation level for Israel and the mix. They want additional high technology they do not yet have but this is only a partial list and they already have items approved on the longer list. The other issue is whether or not Israel can afford what they want. I will comment on that after passing around these charts. (Tab D)[7] The left-hand column for each year is what Israel will have to pay and the right-hand column is what they will have from us to pay with. The colored segments are annual payments due for each

---

[6] A reference to a brief discussion of the Israeli military requests at the end of the September 17 NSC meeting. The draft minutes of the meeting are in the Ford Library, NSC Institutional Files, Box 10, Meeting Minutes, NSC Meeting, September 17, 1975.

[7] The charts, Tab D, have not been found.

successive year's increment of Matmon–B. In 1976 they will owe $1.6 billion for orders already placed and will need only an additional $200 million to order $2.2 billion in new equipment. But this mushrooms out in the succeeding years.

Rumsfeld: It is like a chain letter.

Lynn: The second chart is based on $1.5 billion for 1976 and only half a billion thereafter. Still, they will be a bit shy.

President: This is why Congress went to full funding for our own Department of Defense. There is no controlling the cost under the system used by Israel. What would be the effect on Matmon–B of $1.5 billion for FY 76 and $1.0 billion thereafter.

Scowcroft: It would be about ⅓ off what they want.

Clements: We must remember that if they get all of Matmon–B, it will double Israel's forces.

Kissinger: That is right. We need charts for the 1981 projection based on full Matmon–B and the reduced rate. If they get all the APCs they want, they would even have more than all the Arabs by 1981. This chart only shows approved Israeli orders, not projected ones.

President: Such charts would be useful.

Scowcroft: The philosophy behind the lower rate was replacement and modernization.

Kissinger: The F–16 is not in here. It should be.

President: When does Israel need to pay for the F–16? Has NATO paid?

Clements: NATO paid right away. They put money into the production.

Kissinger: We should recall, as Brent said, that we have been holding out on Israel since last March. If we give them alternate #2, we can tell Rabin we can meet that percentage of his needs this year. We do not want to study it any more and give him a chance to accuse us of bad faith. He can decide upon the mix.

Scowcroft: We have cut on the basis of a rationale but it is up to them to set the mix.

Kissinger: We must decide this before Rabin arrives.

President: We told the Israelis we would give them between $2 and $2.3 billion in assistance. What did we give them?

Scowcroft: Just about $2.3 billion.

President: We went with the upper level and now they want a list of hardware.

Kissinger: They want this year's Matmon–B slice of $2.2 billion.

President: It has been suggested that we make them choose their priorities out of $1.5 billion.

Kissinger: They separate payments and hardware, saying give us what we want and then we can worry later about how to pay for it. This is the first time in seven years we have looked at the cost and the hardware together. The Israelis never discuss the financial implications. We have three options for this year's list: tell them yes on all of it and then worry later about the cost; or tell them they get a certain percentage; or tell them we will change their list. I do not recommend the latter. I suggest we give them a percentage corresponding to alternate #2 but tell them they can choose the mix. Give them specific numbers and quantities rather than dollar amounts. They can change the breakdown if they do not like it.

President: Henry says we should not disapprove their concept but they must get into the choice about the length of the program.

Kissinger: Don't debate them on the five-year plan. They will tie us in knots. Cut each category and get to the $1.5 billion level. Then tell them we are flexible.

Rumsfeld: We may want to suggest telling them what we can do with the funds available. Have Jim do a chart starting with $1.3 billion. If you make this commitment to $1.5 you are implicitly committed to going higher than the available funding.

President: And the F–16 is not included.

Lynn: We must get into this kind of review and analysis before the budget process every year rather than afterwards.

Kissinger: We cannot allow them to add the charge of double cross to the other problems we will have with them this year. Let us settle on numbers. Their request is never modest. It is like the going-in position of the Armed Services. They can stand being cut but Rabin needs to go home with something.

Rumsfeld: They will want to know what they can buy.

Kissinger: Give them a recognizable slice of Matmon–B. Put a working group together and agree on figures. Give them a big slug of Matmon–B.

President: That is what we did last year, when we gave them more than we needed to.

Scowcroft: We have already done it this year. We have tried to get a handle on bringing the equipment and the funding together. It is an artificial device but it is a try to get it together. The SRG ought to meet again to go over the high-interest list item by item and come up with a recommendation.

Rumsfeld: Let us agree that from now on there will be a U.S. position on Israeli requests. They will get the same response wherever they go, no more good guys and bad guys.

President: I really hope this will be the case. They exploit the good-guy, bad-guy gambit. I don't want that.

Colby: One of the recommendations is to have our own estimate on the military balance each year. I hope this can be approved. It is very important.

President: I like this. This is the way it should be done. Lay out the readiness and the situation in the area and the payments and look at them all together.

Kissinger: This is the best session since I have been here.

Lynn: We have two issues: how much they can buy and how much we will fund.

Kissinger: If you say the latter, they will find other funds. Let us agree on a percentage of the list. We can justify it with our assessment of the strategic balance and the financial implications.

Lynn: That is good. This has been clarified. Are there any items on the list which would lead to an escalation by the Arabs?

Kissinger: Yes, the Pershing and maybe the F–16 but not the Matmon–B list.

Rumsfeld: We agree on some items they will not get. We can tell Rabin that.

Kissinger: It is a little early to tell Rabin. They know they will not get the Pershing but we do not really want to tell them.

Clements: Do you mean, Mr. President, that this funding is for the present or the future?

President: This year is consistent with our Sinai commitment. We have made no commitment past this year but what we are talking about in numbers and dollars is suitable for the future.

Kissinger: This Israeli Government has a habit of publishing everything they get from us that can work to their advantage concerning assurances or commitments, even earlier ones. In the past we were in the habit of giving the Israelis assurances in writing that their needs for military equipment would receive sympathetic consideration. Johnson and Nixon both did this. We can no longer do this and the best way to meet the need and the problem is with an annual strategic review. Concerning amounts, we are better off when Israel is a bit short than when they are a bit long on what they want.

Clements: We met to discuss the Middle East almost one year ago to the day.[8] In my judgment the total situation now is much more volatile than it was then, due primarily to the situation in Lebanon where a major conflict between Israel and Syria could occur at any moment.

---

[8] Possibly a reference to the WSAG meeting on January 14, 1975; see Document 126.

Kissinger: I agree with you. The situation is very explosive due to the generally mounting frustrations of the Arabs, not only because of Lebanon although that is a serious danger. We cannot throw in our lot completely with the Israelis or we will lose our mediating role and compromise our relations with the Arabs. We must give Israel enough to deter an Arab attack but not so much as to lose our relationship with the Arabs. Excessive rhetoric in New York is already hurting us in this regard.

Clements: The situation in Lebanon is extremely explosive. Any day it could bring about Israeli or Syrian direct intervention and end up in major hostilities between the two and another Arab oil embargo directed against us.

Kissinger: The U.S. must be taken seriously as a major factor in the area.

Colby: Another critical factor for the U.S. in the Middle East is the health of President Sadat, and he is not well.

Kissinger: You are right. Look at the situation now compared to Nasser. Egypt played the key role in the fight over the future of Angola at the recent OAU meeting. With Nasser they would have led the opposition and produced an overwhelming majority against us. They even fought harder than we would have done, opposing citing the name of the U.S. alongside Cuba and South Africa and the U.S.S.R. as intervening in Angola. We finally told them we could accept this, if necessary, to get the resolutions adopted.

President: Egypt, Zambia and Zaire really fought hard.

Kissinger: Plus Idi Amin who is momentarily on our side.

President: He is a paradox. And he wears so many medals.

Kissinger: Not so many as Bokassa who has to wear them on the back as well as on the front.

Rumsfeld: The Israelis tell you they need more military equipment as a deterrent. They say make us stronger and we can manage all alone. This is a critical issue of Israeli internal politics as well as a foreign policy issue. The Israeli behaviour makes negotiations very difficult. What would contribute to making them more conciliatory, to be a little stronger or a little weaker? You can say that if they are strong, they will feel secure at home and therefore will be more willing to make essential concessions. Or you can say that if they are too strong, they will no longer feel any need to negotiate or make concessions. It can come out either way.

Kissinger: We have had a lot of historical experience with this question. Rabin asks for weapons as an encouragement to negotiate and then he gets them and does not negotiate. This happened last year, when we gave them too many arms in September 1974. Then in March

1975 they refused to make the concessions we had been led to expect. You can't get them too strong and you must keep something in reserve to reward them with for negotiating. Last time we gave them twice what we should have, and it caused them to be inflexible.

President: We were too generous. I think we have contributed more financial assistance to Israel on a per capita basis than any other country in the world.

Kissinger: This year it is $700 per individual in U.S. assistance.

President: We should put it on a per capita basis to see what the U.S. taxpayer pays.

General Brown: Whether they come out a little weaker or a little stronger than they plan, [4 lines not declassified].

Colby: This is doctrine for many of them and they make no effort to conceal it.

Kissinger: And what happened the last time (October 1973) gave them an incentive to redress what many regard as psychological imbalance since the Arabs did not lose completely.

Brown: They think that the mistake they made the last time [less than 1 line not declassified] and they are determined not to make that mistake again.

Colby: They could have increased their mobilization but not much else. Starting the war two or three hours earlier would have made no difference.

Kissinger: When they did go, they did not do such a good job. They did not know how to handle the SAMs.

Rumsfeld: The problem is that Lebanon and the Israeli mentality make a dangerous combination.

Kissinger: I agree, many in Israel want an opportunity to preempt.

[Omitted here is Part II of the minutes, unrelated to the Arab-Israeli dispute.]

Tab A

Briefing by Director of Central Intelligence Colby[9]

Washington, January 13, 1976.

ISRAELI MILITARY REQUESTS

I. Mr. President, CIA and DIA reviewed the present Arab-Israeli military balance, and assessed the impact on it through 1980 of those weapons and technology already approved for supply to Israel and of those currently under consideration. [5 lines not declassified]

II. The October 1973 War again demonstrated Israel's combat superiority over the Arabs. Israel won despite serious disadvantages resulting from the surprise Arab attack on two fronts. Since then, the Israeli Defense Forces have continued to increase their military advantage through modernization, added equipment, and correction of most of the organizational deficiencies identified during the war.

A. For example, delivery of some 140 A–4 and F–4 combat aircraft allowed Israel to replace its war losses and expand its air force by two fighter squadrons. The "smart bombs," air-to-ground missiles, and ECM equipment will help Israel counter the Arab SAM threat that hampered ground-support operations in the last war. Israel now has at least 50 percent more tanks, twice as much large-caliber self-propelled artillery, and more than 50 percent more armored personnel carriers than it had prior to the 1973 war. These weapons enabled Israel to expand its armored force by two divisions, and will provide the mechanized infantry support that was lacking in the last war.

B. Overall Israeli combat capabilities have also been improved by increased operational readiness, higher active-duty strength, more intensive training, and the correction of mobilization and intelligence deficiencies. We judge that the Israeli Defense Force retains its substantial qualitative advantages in leadership, tactical flexibility, operational proficiency, and technical competence.

C. On the other hand, we believe that the Arab threat to Israel is relatively less than it was in 1973. Current force levels are shown in this chart.[10]

1. *Egypt* has made major efforts to rebuild its armed forces since the war but has been hampered by poor relations with the Soviets and resulting limitations on the supply of weapons, equipment, and spare

---

[9] Secret.
[10] Table II below.

parts. Thus, although Egypt has obtained additional modern tanks, APCs, aircraft, and air defense missiles, its inventories generally are not larger and in some cases fall short of prewar levels. The air force, in particular, is some 30 percent below its prewar fighter strength.

2. We estimate that Egypt's overall combat strength is slightly less than prior to the 1973 war, although it is still capable of a major offensive of limited duration and of strong defensive action. It could not sustain large-scale military operations, however, without major Soviet resupply.

3. Unlike Egypt, *Syria* has been able to rebuild and even expand inventories through extensive Soviet aid. More tanks, APCs, tactical missiles, air defense weapons, and advanced fighter aircraft have made Syria stronger than in 1973.

  a. Still, significant weaknesses remain. These include poor leadership, lack of tactical flexibility, low technical competence, and an inadequate logistic system.

  b. Although the modern MIG–23 and SU–20 aircraft in the Syrian air force provide an increased tactical strike capability, they lack the overall performance of the Israeli F–4s and A–4s.

4. The *other Arab states* are generally stronger than in 1973 but we estimate that distance and logistical and political problems would limit their contribution in a war with Israel.

III. The impact of U.S. weapons shipped to or approved for Israel since 1 April 1975 is considerable, as shown in the center column of this chart.[11] We believe that this weaponry will maintain and, indeed is likely to increase, Israel's military superiority over the Arabs through 1980.

  A. Any "worst-case" Arab military buildup would seriously test Israeli capabilities, but Israel probably would win, although at a much higher cost. It would hold a decisive advantage over the "most likely" projected Arab threat.

  B. The additional weapons will correct almost all remaining deficiencies in Israeli capabilities discovered in the 1973 war and will enable Israel to further modernize and expand its armed forces. For example:

  —The Israeli air force will be strengthened in both size and quality. The F–15 represents a new generation of combat aircraft with greatly improved performance characteristics. It will be more than a match for any Soviet aircraft through the current decade.

---

[11] Table I below.

—New U.S. tanks and APCs will enable Israel to form an additional armored division and greatly expand its mechanized infantry force. The mobility and combat power of the Israeli ground forces will be improved, especially their ability to cope with anti-tank weapons. The additional air defense weapons will increase ground-force air defense and free the air force for other missions.

—The Lance missile battalion will be an important psychological weapon for the Israelis and will provide them with an alternative to aircraft attacks on heavily defended targets in rear areas.

C. Israel argues that the arms requested will be needed by 1980 to protect against a burgeoning Arab threat. We believe that Israel has exaggerated this threat but that, even as a "worst case," the Israeli estimate is still useful as a standard against which to measure Israel's capabilities in 1980. This chart will help explain what I mean.[12]

1. Comparison of the October 1973 force ratios with those for a worst case in 1980 indicates that a dramatic shift in the Arabs favor would occur only in the number of SAM batteries. But this is a defensive category, and the Arab numerical advantage is offset by the significant increase in Israel's air superiority and capability of suppressing SAMs.

2. Nor will Arab quantitative gains in other categories likely overturn the decisive Israeli advantage in leadership, tactical flexibility, and general competence. The ratios remain generally comparable to those with which Israel won a decisive victory in 1973, even overcoming the disadvantage of surprise.

3. The Arabs almost certainly will achieve some qualitative advances in equipment and training despite the burden of absorbing much new and sophisticated hardware. But the Israelis will retain their relative advantage. They are starting from a more advanced technological position and have a broader base of trained and trainable manpower.

D. A *"more likely"* Arab threat in 1980 can be derived [2 lines not declassified] by reviewing the constraints that are likely to influence Arab military developments.

1. We question [less than 1 line not declassified] that all Arabs are irrevocably committed to a massive military buildup with the object of forcing a final military solution to the Middle East problem. Egypt, for one, has sacrificed Soviet military aid for a more pragmatic diplomatic approach.

2. We can only speculate about the Arab ability to overcome the political disunity that has plagued them in the past, but the present

---

[12] Table III below.

trend is toward less coordination between the front-line Arab states. Egypt, for instance, might today avoid a Sinai offensive if Syria started new, unprovoked hostilities.

3. [*3 lines not declassified*] Considering the past performance of those states, including their political inhibitions and logistical difficulties in supporting a conflict, we believe that they would provide only about 20 percent of the Arab forces.

4. A principal constraint on the Arab capacity to expand and upgrade their military forces will remain a shortage of technically trained personnel. The problem will continue to be acute through the late Seventies.

5. The availability of sources of modern weaponry probably will also constrain the Arabs. The Israeli projection represents both a gross increase in new arms deliveries and a massive replacement of older weapons as well. No Western European arms supplier has the capability of supplying the Middle East on the scale projected without a substantial increase in production capacity, and this requires long lead times. Even existing arms contracts call for extended delivery periods.

6. Barring the U.S., this leaves only the Communist bloc as a major source of Arab arms. But Moscow's continued willingness to provide substantial new weaponry, particularly on soft terms, is by no means certain. Nor is the willingness of the Arab states to continue their heavy dependence on Communist military sources, particularly if funded by the conservative Arab oil states.

IV. Finally, let me address the impact of delivering those weapons for which approval is still pending. Delivery of this equipment, shown at the right of the first chart, would obviously increase Israel's already substantial advantage over the Arabs. It might also be met by an Arab effort to match it. We know, for example, that President Asad has already used this argument in Moscow.

A. Much of the initial impact of such deliveries would be psychological, however, as the greatest increase in military capabilities would actually occur in the early 1980s.

1. The first of the 250 F–16 fighters would not become operational before the early 1980s, but both sides would feel at once the psychological impact of knowing that Israeli air strength would soon make a quantum jump. The effect would be magnified by the availability of additional sophisticated ordnance for the Israeli air force.

2. The ground force would not grow much, but the greater proportion of modern weapons would provide added firepower and mobility.

3. The Pershing missile would have greater psychological impact than any weapon Israel has requested to date. Its range would largely

limit it to targets already in reach of the Israeli air force, but it is a disturbing element because of its association with nuclear weapons.

B. There is little the Arabs can do to counter the effects of Israel's new weapons and technology. Nothing that the Arabs could acquire from Soviet or West European sources would be likely to offset Israel's gains from the latest U.S. weaponry, particularly the combination of F–15 and F–16 aircraft armed with advanced air ordnance.

C. *In summary,* we believe that Israel will retain a decisive margin of military advantage over the Arabs in 1980 regardless of whether the pending requests are approved. Israel would hold the advantage against even its "worst-case" threat, and its superiority would be even greater in a "most likely" situation.

[*92 lines (17 paragraphs) not declassified*]

TABLE I
US Military Aid to Israel

	Shipped 6 October 1973– 1 April 1975	*Shipped or Approved Since 1 April 1975*	*Under Consideration*
Combat Aircraft			
F–15	—	25	—
F–16	—	—	250
F–4 and A–4	143	74	—
Ordnance			
"Smart Bombs"	7,800	1,300	200
Air-to-air missiles	900	—	780
Antitank missiles	5,167	26,843	7,520
Ground Weapons			
Tanks	700	500	180
Armored personnel carriers	1,150	2,580	1,000
Self-propelled artillery	365	23	142
Lance Missile battalions	—	1	—
Pershing missile battalions	—	—	1
SAM batteries	4	3	—
Air defense artillery	2	46	12

TABLE II
The Arab-Israeli Force Balance—1 January 1976

	Egypt/ Syria	Expeditionary Forces	Arab Totals	Israel
Tanks	4,350	1,350	5,700	3,000
APCs	4,200	800	5,000	5,500
Artillery	2,150	450	2,600	810
Combat Aircraft	850	200	1,050	420
SAM Batteries	182	0	182	19

TABLE III
Arab-Israeli Force Ratios

	1973 Arabs	1973 Israel	Combat Ratio	1980 (Worst Case)[13] Arabs	1980 (Worst Case) Israel	Combat Ratio	1980 (Most Likely Case)[14] Arabs	1980 (Most Likely Case) Israel	Combat Ratio
Tanks	4,700	2,000	2.4:1	9,100	3,250	2.8:1	6,700	3,250	2.1:1
Armored Personnel Carriers	5,000	3,450	1.5:1	9,660	6,800	1.4:1	7,100	6,800	1.1
Artillery[15]	3,700	700	5.3:1	5,780	890	6.5:1	5,000	890	5.6:1
Combat Aircraft	1,180	380	3.1:1	2,310	550	4.2:1	1,300	550	2.4:1
SAM Batteries	181	15	12:1	400	22	18:1	265	22	12:1

---

[13] The 1980 worst case compares the Israeli estimate of the Arab force with the current Israeli force augmented by items already approved and domestic production. The 1980 most-likely case compares our estimate of the Arab force Israel would face with the same Israeli force as in the worst case. [Footnote is in original.]

[14] The 1980 worst case compares the Israeli estimate of the Arab force with the current Israeli force augmented by items already approved and domestic production. The 1980 most-likely case compares our estimate of the Arab force Israel would face with the same Israeli force as in the worst case. [Footnote is in original.]

[15] The artillery ratio is inflated because the Arab figure includes artillery over and under 100 mm, multiple rocket launchers, and mortars over 100 mm, whereas the Israeli figure includes only artillery over 100 mm. [Footnote is in original.]

255. Memorandum of Conversation[1]

Washington, January 27, 1976, 9:25–10:15 a.m.

PARTICIPANTS

President Ford
Dr. Henry A. Kissinger, Secretary of State
Lt. General Brent Scowcroft, Assistant to the President for National Security Affairs

[Discussion of Angola letter to Speaker of the House.]

[Discussion of Marianias vote and call to Stennis.]

[Discussion on holding arrival ceremony for Rabin outside in rainy weather.]

Kissinger: We had that veto in the UN of the Middle East resolution.[2] We did the right thing.

President: The interesting thing is that they barely had enough votes.

Kissinger: That's right.

President: [Calls Stennis]

He is leaning against but will do what he can. His problem is that Puerto Rico before World War II voted the wrong way at the national political convention!

Kissinger: Lew Wasserman[3] said the only one who could beat you was Kennedy. He said how you should use spots and saturate the media for three days. He is concerned about the Jews. He says the present course in Israel will lead to massive anti-Semitism here and the power of the institutional Jews must be broken.

I had a session with Harlow and Timmons and Korologos about my problems on the Hill and what to do about it. They said the number one issue was the perception that we are not together. It is contradictory—on substance we are together but I may be too dominant, but on selling we aren't together.

President: That is a curious thing. I . . .

---

[1] Source: Ford Library, National Security Adviser, Memoranda of Conversations, Box 17, January 27, 1976, Ford, Kissinger. Secret; Nodis. The meeting was held in the Oval Office at the White House. All brackets are in the original.

[2] A reference to a draft UN Security Council resolution, which affirmed the right of Palestinians to establish an independent state in Palestine and the right of return for Palestinian refugees, and called for Israel to return to the borders preceding the June 1967 war. On January 26, the United States used its veto to block the resolution from passing. See *Yearbook of the United Nations, 1975*, pp. 229–233.

[3] Lew Wasserman was a Hollywood studio executive.

Kissinger: You might want to talk to Harlow, for what it's worth.

President: I will—this week. We ought to do whatever we can. Golly—you and Betty are the most popular in the country. I am lagging behind.

Kissinger: Did you see the Evans and Novak article that Rumsfeld is joining Simon on Iranian oil?[4]

[Some discussion.]

On Rabin—it is a delicate situation. We stuck with them on the veto but we are running out.

The Israelis blocked any possibility of progress with Jordan program and that led to Rabat. They have blocked any progress with Syria and so Syria is turning to the PLO. Israel can't just continue to stall. They say they want to talk to Hussein but they have been doing it for eight years. Talking to him won't help unless they give him a major proposal.

If they were a big government they would make a big offer—retreat a few miles from the border on all the fronts in exchange for non-belligerency. You could sell this one on a Middle East trip—if you still plan one.

President: I definitely do, depending on the primaries. Should we agree to Geneva without knowing what Israel will do?

Kissinger: They are totally cynical on Geneva. They're for it because they know nothing will happen. The first item of business will be the PLO and they'll bring about an immediate stalemate.

[Discussion of the Moynihan meeting.]

I wouldn't mention the settlements except maybe at dinner.

I would tell him if there is a war we will use it for making a final settlement.

[Discussion of military equipment.]

I think you have to tell him we have to move and just talking to Jordan won't do it.

He wants a tour d'horizon today. I would listen and I'll take him on at breakfast tomorrow if there is to be a blow-up, and then you can reinforce it at tomorrow's meeting. I would be very firm with him that he can't continue this kind of relationship and that you won't play electoral politics with foreign policy.

President: I notice Jordan is going to the Soviets to buy helicopters. What the Congress is doing to us ... The mess we had on Hawk missiles.

---

[4] Rowland Evans and Robert Novak were nationally-syndicated columnists.

256. Memorandum of Conversation[1]

Washington, undated, 10:30 a.m.–noon.

PARTICIPANTS

The President
Secretary Kissinger
Mr. Joseph J. Sisco, P
Mr. Brent Scowcroft, NSC
Ambassador Malcolm Toon (notetaker)

Prime Minister Yitzhak Rabin
Israeli Ambassador Simcha Dinitz
Mr. Eiran
Mr. Bar-On

The President: I would like to welcome you again Mr. Prime Minister to Washington and to tell you that I look forward to continuing the efforts toward peace which we began together in 1975. Before we begin our substantive exchanges I would like to inform you that at the end of our meeting Mr. Scowcroft will turn over to you a list of military equipment which we are prepared to supply Israel.[2] The list contains a number of highly sophisticated items in which I understand you are particularly interested.

You know, of course, that tomorrow you will have breakfast with Secretary Kissinger, and I assume that detailed discussions of the problems that face us will be carried on at that time. At this time, however, I would like to make a few general observations and then ask you Mr. Prime Minister to give me your views on the situation in the Middle East. I feel that our two countries should be proud of the progress we have made over the past year; I have in mind particularly the successful conclusion of the Sinai Agreement last fall. I feel, however, that we should build on this agreement and make further progress toward peace. Meanwhile, it is my understanding that you too are satisfied with the progress we have made so far generally and with the way in which the Sinai Agreement is being implemented.

Rabin: Since we give and they take, we are encountering no problems in the implementation of the agreement.

---

[1] Source: National Archives, RG 59, Records of Henry Kissinger, 1973–77, Box 16, Nodis Memcons, January 1976, Folder 3. Secret; Nodis. Drafted by Toon. The meeting was held at the White House. According to the President's Daily Diary, Ford welcomed Rabin to the White House on January 27 at 10:25 a.m. and met with the Israeli party from 11:15 a.m. until 12:40 p.m. (Ford Library, Staff Secretary's Office Files)

[2] See Document 260.

The President: We must do what we can to make further progress in 1976, either at Geneva or through some other approach. While you are here we should discuss frankly what you are prepared to offer the Jordanians and the Syrians in exchange for nonbelligerency. Perhaps we could have a general exchange of ideas on this theme now with detailed discussions to take place tomorrow between you and Secretary Kissinger.

Rabin: I would like to thank you again Mr. President for your kind invitation to visit the United States. I feel that this is a proper time to assess the present situation in the Middle East and what we might face in the future. I would like also to reiterate my invitation to you to visit Israel whenever you happen to be in the area—an invitation which I extended when we last met.

The President: If the primaries should go well I think a visit might be possible in the late winter or early spring. As you know, I have never been in the Middle East.

Rabin: I am glad to hear, Mr. President, that you have included in the list of weapons which you mentioned sophisticated items since we Israelis feel that access to the latest military technology is vital to our continued security. With regard to the situation in the Middle East, I feel that we will inevitably face in the very near future an increase in terrorist activities. Our evidence is that all groups encompassed by the PLO are now cooperating with each other; for example, in a recent raid across our borders we apprehended a number of terrorists each representing different elements within the Palestinian ranks. I should also tell you of a rather alarming development which was uncovered by cooperative efforts on the part of our and Kenyan intelligence services in Nairobi. We had received a report that two terrorists equipped with two Soviet Streletz missiles (the equivalent of the RedEye) were given the mission of shooting down an El Al plane on its approach to Nairobi. The Kenyan intelligence services on the basis of information supplied by us apprehended the agents with the missiles in their possession. This is simply an example of the sort of thing I think we must face in the near future, and this means that the increase in terrorist activities will take place not only in the Middle East but elsewhere around the world.

The President: We ourselves had a recent serious incident of terrorism at La Guardia airfield, and we are now engaged in a massive effort to discover who was responsible for the incident, and our best lead now is that it was carried out by a "hired hit man" and not an organized group.

Secretary Kissinger: Do we yet know by whom the hit man was hired?

The President: We have not yet ascertained this.

Rabin: You asked for my views Mr. President on the situation in the Middle East. As the Secretary has pointed out many times it was not the detailed provisions of the Sinai Agreement which were of primary significance but the approach and changed attitude which Egyptian accession to the agreement reflected. We had a difficult time in our relations after the March breakdown, but that is past history and the important thing now is that agreement was reached and its provisions are now being carried out in a reasonably satisfactory way. We Israelis are not happy at everything that has happened, with everything that the Egyptians say and do, but generally speaking we are not disappointed with their behavior.

On the negative side, I think we must recognize that the Soviets in their struggle to regain their sphere of influence in the Middle East have launched a concentrated effort to undermine the Sinai II Agreement. It is our belief that the Soviets—working with the Syrians and the PLO—are determined to frustrate and if possible reverse the new trend which was started by Sinai II. So long as the Syrians have the support of the Soviets there is no prospect that they will change their approach. Meanwhile, the PLO is completely under Syrian control with the Palestine Liberation Army headquartered in Damascus.

It is for these reasons that we hope the United States decision to exercise its veto in the Security Council yesterday[3] will give a clear sign to the Arab world that the Syrian approach and tactics will not succeed. It is too early, however, to judge what the Soviet and Syrian reaction to your veto will be.

Meanwhile, it is our view that the Syrians are becoming more extremist as each day goes by, and it seems clear that as they continue to make extremist public statements their behavior is going to be increasingly more committed to extremist action. It is generally regarded in the Arab world that the cease-fire which has been reached in Lebanon is a Syrian achievement, and it seems likely that Syrian stock will rise as a result. We must remember that the Syrians blocked all possible action in Lebanon by other Arab countries, either singly or in combination, and in this way retained their influence over the situation. Their instrument was the PLO, the strongest, best organized force in Lebanon today. The Christians themselves were not well organized and, moreover, lacked courage. All of our efforts with the various Christian groups were thus doomed to failure, and without a political partner in Lebanon there was no possibility of successful military action.

The Soviets have shipped huge quantities of arms to the Syrians and according to evidence available to us are committed to ship even

---

[3] See footnote 2, Document 255.

more. This sort of support simply encourages the Syrians to continue their extremist policies. Our only sensible course of action is to match Syrian increased military power with increments of the most modern weapons to our own arsenal. Only in this way will we be able to minimize the possibility of blackmail by the Syrians in the upcoming renewal of UNDOF.[4] It is clear that the Syrians have no appetite for negotiations, and this will continue to be their attitude so long as they feel they have a chance to make substantial political gains in 1976 with their blackmailing tactics. Their aim is to convince the Arab world that their course is right and that the Egyptian course symbolized by Sinai II is wrong and doomed to failure.

The American veto in the Security Council might provide a new signal to the Syrians, but we can not be sure. Our best strategy is to call now for a reconvened Geneva conference, although we should recognize that the Syrians with their pattern of nonparticipation in past political negotiations are not likely to respond positively to an invitation.

I do hope Mr. President with regard to the supply of arms to my country we can work out a long range projection and not simply rest on the list which you mentioned earlier.

With regard to Jordan, it is our belief that the Jordanians are now in a relatively good position. Their economy is in good shape primarily as a result of the increased world price of phosphates and also because of a shift of business from Lebanon. The Jordanians thus feel that because of their ties with Syria they are no longer isolated, and this plus their good economic situation has persuaded the Jordanians that there is no need to rush into negotiations.

The President: Are you concerned about the closer relations between Jordan and Syria?

Rabin: Jordan obviously has concluded that it is tactically wise to improve its relations with Syria, but King Hussein has not forgotten the past and he will not permit reestablishment of a PLO presence in Jordan. While the Jordanian Army is not irrevocably committed to Syrian command, all the necessary steps have been taken on the infrastructure level to make this possible. Incidentally, Mr. President, we have had reports that a Jordanian military mission will soon travel to Moscow.

Kissinger: The Jordanians are already there.

Rabin: We have also heard that the Syrians will acquire Soviet missiles for the Jordanians, but we are not sure of our information. Returning to the relationship between Jordan and Syria, I think that we should recognize that while King Hussein sees the need to be cautious, the momentum of cooperation may bring him closer to the Syrians than

---

[4] The current UNDOF mandate expired on May 31.

even he would consider healthy. We are informed that in some circles in Jordan the feeling is that now that the Jordanians are respected in Damascus the relationship between Amman and Damascus may be worthwhile; and this may be for the Jordanians a dangerous [illegible].

Concerning Lebanon, the Syrians have full control over political events there and Lebanon's ultimate fate depends on Syrian decision. No other Arab country has any significant influence in Lebanon. Deterrence to a Syrian takeover is provided only by the threat of Israeli intervention. It seems likely that the Syrians do not plan any basic change in the Lebanese political structure, and their aim for the present is primarily to solidify the impression that only their proposals, only their influence, carry weight.

The President: What are the prospects for the Christian elements in Lebanon?

Rabin: The prospects are far from good. The Lebanese Army, which is primarily Christian in composition, has not been permitted to play any significant role. The strongest Christian faction, the Phalangists, have not cooperated with other Christian elements although the situation now in this respect is better than it has been. The civil war has been a disaster for Lebanon; it has resulted in 10,000 deaths, the loss of 40 percent of the national GNP, mass emigration, and the departure of business firms which had their headquarters in Beirut.

Kissinger: Where, according to your information, do the Christian elements get their arms?

Rabin: From Lebanese colonies all over the world. The arms are funneled into Lebanon through a port about 50 kilometers north of Beirut.

Kissinger: Why don't the Palestinians choke off the supply?

Rabin: They have made the effort but it has not been successful. The Christians are not short of arms but they are far less well supplied than the Moslems who have access to sources throughout the Arab world. We should not exclude the possibility that Syria will use Lebanon to increase tension in the Middle East and create an atmosphere not conducive to peace talks. If the cease-fire should not be maintained, for example, the Syrians could then increase their intervention by camouflaging their units as units of the PLA. We think this is a real possibility.

The President: What are the prospects for renewal of UNDOF?

Rabin: It is always difficult to predict Syrian behavior. We are reasonably sure, however, that Syria will not start anything that might lead to an outbreak of war unless they are certain of Egyptian and Jordanian support. Meanwhile the Syrians must be taught that the blackmail route does not pay. This is not easy since they have full Soviet support for almost everything they do or say, primarily because the Soviets attach great importance to maintaining their influence in the Middle East through Syria.

The President: It seems obvious that Syria can control the PLA in Lebanon. Can they also control PLO activities generally in the area?

Rabin: A principal element of the PLO is Saiqa which is completely under the control of the Syrians.

The President: What role does Arafat play?

Rabin: Arafat is head of the PLO and the PLA is under his titular command. But, since the PLA is headquartered in Damascus it is completely under Syrian and not Arafat's control.

The President: If Israel were to offer territorial concessions what would the Syrian reaction be?

Rabin: I don't believe the Syrians would consent to an interim agreement without major territorial gains.

The President: What in your view would be Jordan's attitude toward a reconvened Geneva Conference and an overall settlement?

Rabin: If Jordan could be sure of recovering all of the territory lost in 1967 they would be prepared to enter into a meaningful agreement. It is our view that the Jordanians are not interested in recovering territory with the idea of surrendering it to the PLO, and this is consistent with the current Jordanian policy of not permitting the re-establishment of a PLO presence on its soil.

The President: Has there been any substantial effort by the PLO to infiltrate Jordan?

Rabin: The PLO has tried to use Jordan as an infiltration route into Israel, but the Jordanians have consistently frustrated these efforts.

The President: What are your ideas about a positive approach in the wake of our veto in the Security Council?

Rabin: A call to reconvene the Geneva Conference on the basis of Security Council Resolutions 242 and 338 we feel is the best approach at the present time. We doubt if discussions of an overall settlement can be carried on with Egypt alone; Egypt would consider this unwise and we doubt if the Jordanians would join with Egypt. With the Syrians little can be done.

The President: You mean that the Syrians would oppose Geneva?

Rabin: Yes.

Kissinger: We must be realistic in our approach. We must recognize that reconvening the Geneva Conference is impossible without consenting to a PLO presence. The Soviets have already rejected Geneva without the PLO.

The President: Has there been any change in the PLO attitude toward Israel?

Rabin: The PLO attitude is now a good deal tougher. PLO prestige is now higher, primarily as a result of developments in Lebanon as well as in the United Nations.

The President: What can be gained by calling for a reconvened Geneva Conference without a more flexible attitude?

Rabin: We do not believe that flexibility by our side is wise at a time when the Soviet-Syrian position has hardened.

The President: If we should call for a reconvened Geneva Conference and the Soviets and the Syrians reject this approach, what would happen then in Lebanon and what would happen to the PLO?

Rabin: There would be no change in the PLO's attitude or behavior. As far as the Syrians are concerned, they could move militarily before the end of May, but we feel that the Egyptians and the Jordanians would not support them. Our belief is based on the assumption, of course, that Egypt will not change its basic attitude after the implementation of Sinai II. I should point out particularly, Mr. President, that the role of the United Nations in resolving differences which have cropped up between ourselves and the Egyptians has been outstandingly helpful.

The President: If Geneva should not be possible, the Egyptians will then be under increased pressure from other elements in the Arab world to change their attitude.

Rabin: Sadat has said publicly that he would attend a Geneva Conference even without a prior commitment to PLO participation. He said this at a press conference in Cairo during the visit of the Canadian Foreign Minister. With regard to the Syrian attitude, we should recognize that the main aim of the Syrians is not to gain territory but to change the rules of the game, and they will do everything short of war to bring this about. I would like to emphasize again, Mr. President, that while I am reasonably confident that the Syrians will not invoke hostilities, I cannot be sure of Syrian behavior.

The President: In my view the situation in the Middle East remains extremely explosive.

Rabin: We don't necessarily agree. In any case we doubt if anything can be done with Syria in 1976, primarily because they have been led to believe they can count on Soviet support for anything they do.

The President: Would an attempt to negotiate with the Jordanians be a sensible move tactically and strategically?

Rabin: With the Jordanians we have the sort of relationship which makes it easy to exchange views. But the key question is the Syrian manipulation of the PLO with Soviet support. What we do with Jordan will not affect the Syrian attitude.

The President: Do you anticipate that the Syrians will renew UNDOF in May?

Rabin: It is too early to tell. If the Syrians should conclude that they can gain further political concessions [illegible] the end of UNDOF they will not renew the mandate.

The President: Would you anticipate that May would be a good time to reconvene the Geneva Conference?

Rabin: This would be the best time.

Kissinger: We must be sensible about the idea of reconvening the Geneva Conference. It is perfectly clear that Geneva is impossible without resolving the PLO participation issue. Either we set up procedures for talking with the PLO or we in our letter to Geneva participants indicate that the PLO will be welcome at the Conference. Otherwise the exercise is useless; we gain at the most only two weeks time. This is not something that will take us through 1976.

Sisco: In any case a letter of invitation must come from the co-chairmen and the Soviets have already said publicly that they won't agree to a reconvened Geneva Conference without the PLO.

Kissinger: We must have some concept for getting through 1976. Geneva is not the answer unless we can tell the Soviets and the Arabs what they will gain from the Conference.

Dinitz: You mean you have in mind telling them what they will achieve in return for something?

Kissinger: Of course. But the important thing for us to recognize is that the other side will not agree to a reconvened Geneva Conference without the PLO unless they are promised something in advance. They do not have to have promises of gains from Geneva if we agree to PLO participation. Even in the latter case it is conceivable that the Syrians might not attend. In a word, it is impossible to have a Geneva Conference with the Soviets and Syrians in attendance without PLO participation. In my view the situation will become increasingly dangerous if the Soviets by our failure to act are in a position to dominate the pace and direction of events in the Middle East. This is the sort of thing that the Prime Minister and I must discuss tomorrow.

257. Memorandum of Conversation[1]

Washington, January 28, 1976, 11 a.m.–noon.

PARTICIPANTS

The President
Secretary Kissinger
Mr. Sisco, P
Mr. Scowcroft, NSC
Ambassador Toon

Prime Minister Rabin
Ambassador Dinitz
Mr. Eiran
Mr. Bar-On

The President: I understand that you and Henry had breakfast together[2] and discussed the problems facing us in greater detail than we did yesterday. I have not yet had an opportunity to be briefed on your meeting since I had an urgent meeting this morning with the Congressional leadership. Perhaps Henry can now bring us up to date.

Secretary Kissinger: Most of our discussion at breakfast related to the strategy that we should follow after our veto in the Security Council earlier this week.[3] As I see it and as I told the Prime Minister, there are two basic conceptual approaches. First, a reasonable view of terms on which a consensus might be possible would require dealing with the PLO either through informal contacts or through some other means. Secondly, negotiations leading to an overall settlement which, in my view, means that the consuming problem we must face is that once the PLO is at Geneva the creation of a Palestinian state is almost inevitable.

It has always been my view that the Palestinian issue—in whatever form—should be left to the last in order to avoid radicalization at an early stage. I have always consistently felt that we must have some program permitting us to dominate the debate and the negotiations, and this would include agreement on possible gains in advance of Geneva so that the other side would have some reason for attending the

---

[1] Source: National Archives, RG 59, Records of Henry Kissinger, 1973–77, Box 16, Nodis Memcons, January 1976, Folder 3. Secret; Nodis. According to the President's Daily Diary, the meeting was held in the Oval Office at the White House. (Ford Library, Staff Secretary's Office Files)

[2] The breakfast meeting between Rabin and Kissinger took place on January 28 from 7:48 to 10:10 a.m. at Blair House. Their discussion focused on aid requests, Jordan, Lebanon, and their strategy for the next phase of negotiations. (Memorandum of conversation, January 28; National Archives, RG 59, Records of Henry Kissinger, 1973-77, Box 16, Nodis Memcons, January 1976, Folder 3)

[3] See footnote 2, Document 255.

conference without the PLO. My impression from our discussions at breakfast was that the Prime Minister thought this concept was worth exploring. He feels that it would work well with Egypt and Syria; concerning the latter the removal of some settlements in exchange for nonbelligerency would be conceivable. Regarding Jordan, however, the approach would give rise to serious domestic problems in Israel. This question therefore remains unresolved but we agreed that during the Prime Minister's stay in the United States we would meet again in order to pursue the issue further. Both the Prime Minister and I feel that our objective should be to crystalize a diplomatic initiative within the March–April time frame.

Rabin: The Secretary has accurately described the two options we discussed at breakfast. There is, however, Mr. President a third option which I think should be brought to your attention. This option involves resisting the Syrian attack—I mean resistance in political terms not military terms. The purpose would be to convince the Arab world and others that the Security Council cannot be used to bring about changes in the negotiating ground rules. I doubt that Syria plans to return to the Security Council following your veto, but it is possible that toward the end of May she may pursue this option. If this should be the case, I doubt that Syria would go to Geneva, and as I said yesterday, Syria has not in the past followed the pattern of participation in any political negotiations except for the cease-fire agreement and the Israeli-Syrian interim accord. I doubt that Syria would try to use Lebanon as a pretext for increasing tension, but I can not be sure of this. My feeling is that Lebanon is not seen by the Syrians as an immediate instrument for implementing their strategy. I think that the Syrians would prefer to threaten the end of the UNDOF mandate rather than use Lebanon to increase tension. But I believe it would be a mistake to take this threat seriously since I feel strongly Syria is not prepared to go to war. If the Syrian bluff is called—as I think it should—then Syrian credibility as the spokesman of the Arab world and the protector of basic Arab interests would collapse.

I believe our best course is to reconvene the Geneva conference without the PLO. If we do this then there is no need for us to consider any diplomatic initiative until after the end of May. If the Syrians extend the mandate, this would be evidence that they are powerless to dictate events in the area and this would improve the posture of the more moderate elements in the Arab world.

The Secretary: I would like to stress as I did yesterday that an invitation by the Co-chairman to reconvene the Geneva conference is out of the question since the Soviets won't agree to such an invitation without PLO participation.

Rabin: We still feel that our best option would be to call for a reconvened Geneva conference on the previously agreed basis. As to what the reaction of others might be to this course, Doctor Kissinger's judgment is better than mine. As far as Israel is concerned it is impossible to accept participation of the PLO at Geneva. As Dr. Kissinger has said in the past, this would lead to creation of a third state, radical in outlook and supported by the Soviets. In my view PLO participation at Geneva will directly focus the attention of the conference on the Palestinian issue, and this would result in competition for leadership among the extremist elements and would consequently lead to the defeat of the moderate elements.

If we pursue the conference option we should make clear initially that the purpose of reconvening the Geneva conference is to achieve peace: the purpose cannot be to work out further interim agreements. If this effort should fail then our fallback position should be to work toward an end of the state of war. But this cannot be confined to Jordan and Egypt alone; to pursue this course would simply increase tension in the area since it would invite acceleration and intensification of the Syrian-Soviet-PLO efforts to undermine our initiatives. We must understand that the PLO cannot tolerate any ties with Jordan, and the Syrians if we should focus on Jordan and Egypt alone would feel isolated. I doubt that either Jordan or Egypt would wish to assume the responsibility for isolating Syria. The focus therefore should be on the two key Arab states—Egypt and Syria. This may not be possible in 1976, but perhaps it would be in 1977. Our minimum goal should be the formal end of the state of war with Geneva preferably the forum for negotiations. In exchange for this we would not exclude significant territorial concessions, with one or two exceptions. In this connection, you should know Mr. President, that the most difficult sector for Israel is the West Bank.

The President: This is a more serious problem for you than Golan?

Rabin: Yes, since the West Bank is adjacent to the principal centers of Israeli population.

The Secretary: I am sure the Prime Minister does not mean to infer by his statement that Golan would be easy for the Israelis. (With a smile) We should not mislead the President on this point.

Rabin: Of course Golan would not be easy. For the purpose of clarity, let me restate the Israeli position. We should call publicly for a reconvened Geneva conference for the purpose of achieving peace. If peace is not achievable then we should pursue the alternative route of seeking an end to the state of war. For this it is essential for us to focus on both Egypt and Syria since without Syria nothing can succeed.

The Secretary: The Prime Minister's first option reminds me of a game of chess in which the whole strategy is based on the opening move. Geneva can be reconvened tomorrow with the PLO; alternatively, it is conceivable that the conference can be reconvened if we agree in advance that PLO participation would be the first item of business. The Israelis, however, say no to both options.

Rabin: I beg to disagree with the Secretary. Concerning the second alternative we have never excluded discussion of participation by additional groups as set forth in the original letter of invitation.

The Secretary: We should recognize, however, that if we should reconvene Geneva on this basis we would face precisely the problem before us now—i.e., the question of PLO participation.

Rabin: I continue to favor the option of convening Geneva for the purpose of achieving peace.

The President: In extending such an invitation would it be possible also to state that territorial adjustments would be made in the context of peace?

The Secretary: With all respect Mr. President, this is not the issue. The issue is the participation of the PLO.

Rabin: The Israeli side does not oppose discussion of the Palestinian issue at Geneva; but we do oppose participation of the PLO. I felt it was important to clarify this point.

The Secretary: But the reality is the need for PLO participation. Unless the Arab states have a clear understanding in advance of gains that will be derived from Geneva then they will not accept Geneva without PLO participation. We know that an invitation without the PLO would be rejected by the Soviets and the PLO. It might possibly be accepted by Egypt and Jordan; Syrian acceptance is highly unlikely.

Rabin: The Secretary may be right. I think, however, we should make the effort to reconvene the Geneva conference. If this should fail then we should focus on Egypt and Syria. Jordan must be postponed until 1977.

The President: Let me make one or two observations. It is important that both of our countries adopt a positive approach and this must be done in 1976. I must in all honesty make my position absolutely clear to you. In my approach to foreign policy issues I have consistently done and said what I think is right even though my actions may not be popular and may be politically disadvantageous. This has been our approach to Angola; I think we were right, and I hope that Congress ultimately will realize this. Similarly in the Middle East, as the President I must do what I think is right, and I am prepared to take the consequences of my actions even though these might work to my political disadvantage. It is vital for our two governments to work together regardless of the political ramifications for either you or us for our actions. As unpopular as Angola and other issues may be, I am determined to do what I think is in the basic United States interests. I feel strongly that a positive approach on the Middle East issue is right substantively and right politically. We must create a situation in the Middle East in which progress seems to be under way, since otherwise the area can be potentially explosive. Whatever we decide, our approach must be a positive one and must reflect movement in some form. You, Mr. Prime Minister, and the Secretary should devise a strategy for 1976 and 1977 aimed at this objective. This may require tough decisions by both of our countries—decisions that may have difficult repercussions both domestically and with regard to other relationships—for example, with the Soviet Union. We must convince the world that our strategy involves and is designed to promote forward movement. We must keep the momentum going. In this process Israel and the United States must stay together. Moreover, it is not to our mutual advantage to be isolated from all others. You should understand Mr. Prime Minister that anything we can work out together which is designed to make progress in the area I will back to the hilt even if such a course should have disadvantageous political implications for me. We have made the right decisions in the past; we should be able to do the same in the future. I gather from Dr. Kissinger's report on the breakfast discussion and other remarks made here that we have at least a blueprint for action and we should now focus on fleshing out agreed proposals.

The Secretary: I would like to clarify one point. If we should pursue the option of seeking an end to the state of war in exchange for territorial concessions, this would force us to take on the Soviet Union and others. To do this we cannot confine the option to Syria and Egypt; this would simply be regarded as consummate cynicism.

Rabin: If our main purpose is to prevent an explosion in the Middle East then our best course is to focus on Syria and Egypt.

The Secretary: I agree, but our approach must include Jordan as well.

The President: When can we move on this strategy?

Rabin: I must first discuss the strategy with my colleagues in accordance with the Israeli political process and then resume discussions with the United States.

The Secretary: Nothing that we have discussed this morning must be implemented within the next month or two except for the call to Geneva on which we agree. The process of discussions with individual Arab leaders can extend over many weeks.

Rabin: I wish to make clear Mr. President our position on this option. We feel strongly that the Syrians and the Egyptians must be involved; an approach to the Egyptian and the Jordanians is impossible.

258. Memorandum of Conversation[1]

Washington, January 29, 1976, 9:45 a.m.

PARTICIPANTS

President Ford
Dr. Henry A. Kissinger, Secretary of State
Brent Scowcroft, Assistant to the President

[Omitted here is discussion unrelated to the Arab-Israeli dispute.]

[Kissinger:] I saw Rabin for breakfast. Basically Rabin wants to stalemate, but he will make an offer to Syria and Egypt, but not Jordan. He says that [Jordan] would give him monumental problems. But that is impossible. He can't shut out the PLO and not deal with Jordan either. He said if the U.S. wasn't so weak we could stonewall. I said we couldn't stonewall no matter how strong we were.

President: How do we proceed today?

Kissinger: I could summarize our talk, so you don't have to light into him. Then you could tell him (1) we can't be passive this year; (2) we don't have to have a solution, but we have to show activity; and (3) you will not make decisions based on electoral politics.

Bunny Lasker[2] said things have really turned around—many are joining in.

President: I thought the atmosphere was positive at the dinner last night.

Kissinger: Actors are very sensitive to public opinion. They couldn't come out with positive statements if there were doubts.

Herb Schlosser[3] said the polls are really turning up.

President: What was the reaction about the military equipment?

Kissinger: There is some grumbling but he is happy.

Scowcroft: There is no doubt they are pleased with the list.

Kissinger: I would tell him you overruled most of your advisors to give him what you did.

Our optimum course is to go to the PLO. Any other year I would do it. But maybe we could get by with an offer of massive withdrawals with Syria, Egypt, and Jordan, in exchange for non-belligerency.

---

[1] Source: National Archives, RG 59, Records of Henry Kissinger, 1973–77, Box 16, Nodis Memcons, January 1976, Folder 3. Secret; Nodis. The meeting was held in the Oval Office at the White House. All brackets, with the exception of ones describing omitted material, are in the original.

[2] Bernard J. "Bunny" Lasker was a Republican Party fundraiser.

[3] Herbert Schlosser was President of the National Broadcasting Company.

He doesn't want Sisco and Toon to know, but he is thinking of calling an election. That is not a bad idea. He has promised an election on the West Bank anyway.

He also said he would move some Golan settlements in exchange for non-belligerency.

259. Memorandum of Conversation[1]

Washington, January 29, 1976, 9:45–10:30 a.m.

PARTICIPANTS

The President
Secretary Kissinger
Under Secretary Sisco
Mr. Scowcroft, NSC
Ambassador Toon

Prime Minister Rabin
Ambassador Dinitz
Mr. Eiran
Mr. Bar-On

The President: I have reviewed with Dr. Kissinger the record of our talks over the past two days, and I felt that it would be useful for us to have a third meeting before you leave Washington. I would first like to reaffirm the importance I attach to cooperation between our two countries. We must work together. We have cooperated well in the past, and I feel sure that we can do the same in the future. One of the basic problems we face in 1976 is a difference in judgment as to procedure, not on all objectives. You seem confident that we can get through 1976 without any political movement; our feeling is that no political movement would lead to a stalemate in the area which in turn might carry with it a real danger of a blow-up in the Middle East. I recognize that this is a matter of judgment, and I recognize as well that you have had great experience in the area and your views must be given weight. You should know, because that [illegible] disagree with your assessment.

---

[1] Source: National Archives, RG 59, Records of Henry Kissinger, 1973–77, Box 16, Nodis Memcons, January 1976, Folder 3. Secret; Nodis. Drafted by Toon. According to the President's Daily Diary, the meeting was held in the Oval Office at the White House where Rabin and his party joined the President, Kissinger, and Scowcroft at 9:50 a.m. (Ford Library, Staff Secretary's Office Files)

A call for reconvening the Geneva Conference with an understanding about participation by the Palestinians we feel is one viable course of action. You disagree. A second option would involve a non-belligerency pledge in exchange for territorial concessions. You have strong reservations with regard to this approach. I understand that you would prefer simply to call for a reconvened Geneva Conference, fully recognizing that nothing meaningful would emerge. Our best judgment is that such a course will not produce results and will not give any impression of movement. The result might well be an explosive situation in 1976. I should make clear, Mr. Prime Minister, that we do not suggest alternative courses of action in order to undercut Israel. On the contrary, we feel strongly that the courses of action we propose are in the best interest of Israel as well as the United States. I do hope that you will examine carefully in the coming days what we have suggested, and perhaps you and Dr. Kissinger can resume discussions of the problem when he sees you on the West Coast.

Rabin: I appreciate your taking time out of your busy schedule, Mr. President, to meet with us once more. Let me make clear first of all that we do not intend to delay the process simply for the sake of delaying. Our basic policy is to avoid concessions which we feel are not justified and which may in [illegible] impinge in a damaging way on our vital interests. Concerning the first point you are right, Mr. President, in your conclusion that the Israelis are opposed to participation of the PLO in any negotiations. With regard to the second option, we agree that it is doubtful that peace can be achieved, and we are ready, therefore, to work toward the end of the state of war as a political goal.

The Secretary: While I would not want this view to be aired outside this room, I think it can be argued that neither side is in a position to make the concessions required for peace. Peace creates problems for both sides; among others there is Jerusalem for the Israelis and there is the recognition issue for the Arabs. Thus, peace is perhaps not a viable option and an end to the state of war is conceivably the only plausible course open to us. We must be clear on one fundamental point; this course is possible only if it involves substantial territorial concessions. This is the concept we are trying to pursue and on which we should agree. If we seek an alternative to the PLO, then we must work out some scheme which involves Jordan. All we need agree on now is the concept of an approach to all three countries—i.e. Egypt, Syria and Jordan. There is no need now for us to delineate on a map the territorial concessions which we might envisage.

Rabin: I agree that a final peace is not realizeable now and that, therefore, our alternative goal should be an end to the state of war. I have no objection to the concept of a diplomatic approach to all three countries. My problem, however is that I face serious difficulties in agreeing today on territorial concessions to Jordan. It is impossible for me to say in precise terms what sort of concessions on the West Bank might be acceptable in Israel. I agree, however, to the principle of an approach to all three countries.

The Secretary: There is no need for us to arrive now at a precise definition of the concessions which might be involved. The Prime Minister told me last night after the Dinitz dinner[2] that he will return to Israel, have discussions with his colleagues, and within a week or so after his return he should be in a position to say how far he can go with Jordan. This gives us no problem. All we need agree on now is the conceptual approach; a definition of what might be involved is not now required. If we are in a position to put forward as our proposal an end to the state of war in exchange for territorial concessions to Egypt, Syria and Jordan, this would meet our requirements.

Rabin: The Secretary has accurately reflected our exchange of last evening. I would like to make clear, however, my position with regard to the West Bank in order to avoid any possible misunderstanding. I can make no commitments now with regard to territorial concessions involving the West Bank; I must first discuss the issue in Jerusalem. I would also like to point out that in my view if Syria should reject this conceptual approach the option of dealing with Egypt or Jordan alone will be much more difficult for reasons that I have already set forth.

Dinitz: I would like to add one observation to what the Prime Minister has said. If the Prime Minister is in a position to present to the Cabinet a comprehensive plan for all three countries approval would be easier. To get approval for only Jordan and Egypt would be very difficult indeed since in this case the Cabinet would regard Syria–PLO as a continuing threat.

The Secretary: We should understand that if the Jordan–Egypt option should be pursued all kinds of possibilities open up. For example, the Syrians might be separated from the Soviets. In any case, we can discuss the details of the agreed conceptual approach when we meet again on the West Coast. Mr. President, I must excuse myself now in order to proceed to the Hill where I am scheduled to be tormented by Senator Clark.

Rabin: I am also scheduled to appear on the Hill before the Senate Appropriations Committee.

The Secretary: I am sure that you will be treated better than I.

Rabin: Before leaving, Mr. President, I would like again to thank you for the list of weapons which was handed me by General Scowcroft after our first meeting. I think you should know, however, that in my

---

[2] No memorandum of conversation has been found.

meeting last night with the Secretary of Defense I was not able to pinpoint dates of delivery. I do hope that you will do what you can to alleviate this problem.

The President: I am sure there is no serious problem in regard to delivery dates, and Mr. Scowcroft will discuss the issue with the Defense Department.

The Secretary: Perhaps Mr. President, I can bring final information on delivery dates to the Prime Minister in Los Angeles.

260. National Security Decision Memorandum 315[1]

Washington, January 31, 1976.

TO
    The Secretary of State
    The Secretary of Defense
    The Director of Central Intelligence
    The Director, Office of Management and Budget

SUBJECT
    Military Assistance for Israel

The President has reviewed the NSSM 231 response[2] and the options for military assistance for Israel which were discussed at the National Security Council meeting of January 13, 1976.[3]

The President has decided, in response to Israel's revised request for military equipment from the United States, which was submitted to the Department of Defense on January 8, 1976,[4] that the United States Government should approve the placement of orders by Israel under FMS and commercial procedures for military equipment of a value not exceeding a total of about $2.0 billion, as indicated by the list attached at Tab A.[5] The Government of Israel will be permitted to request revisions in the list, particularly with respect to quantities of specific items,

---

[1] Source: Washington National Records Center, OSD Files: FRC 330–79–0050, Box 2, Israel, 091.3, 1976. Top Secret; Sensitive. A copy was sent to the Chairman of the Joint Chiefs of Staff.

[2] See Documents 243 and 244.

[3] See Document 254.

[4] The Israeli list has not been found.

[5] Tab A is attached but not printed.

provided the revisions are consistent with the overall value and types of equipment on the list.

The President has also made a determination with respect to Israeli requests for certain weapons and equipment of an advanced, sophisticated or politically sensitive nature, as indicated in the list at Tab B.[6]

A Middle East Arms Transfer Panel, composed of representatives of the Department of State, the Department of Defense, the Director of Central Intelligence, and the NSC Staff and chaired by the representative of the Department of Defense, will be constituted within the National Security Council system to control the transfer of arms and equipment under FMS and commercial procedures to Israel and such other countries of the Mideast as may be designated.

The President has also directed that Israeli requests for production and delivery of items contained on the list at Tab A, or any subsequent revision, should be handled in accordance with the standard procedures of the Department of Defense for sales to foreign countries. Any exceptions to standard procedures for arms transfers or amended requests for high sensitivity items should be referred, through the Middle East Arms Transfer Panel, to the Assistant to the President for National Security Affairs.

Israel's needs for the acquisition of weapons and military equipment are to be kept under continuous review. An interagency review will be conducted annually, or more frequently if necessary, by the Middle East Arms Transfer Panel for consideration by the Senior Review Group and, if necessary, the NSC, prior to the OMB submission of budget review materials to the President for the following fiscal year. In preparation for each annual review:

The Director of Central Intelligence will prepare an overall assessment of the Middle East military balance and situation projected over a period of five years. This assessment should include an estimate of both the most likely and the worst-case threats to Israel.

The Department of Defense will prepare an analysis of current Israeli arms requests and future plans for weapons procurement, including the impact of these requests and plans on future fund requirements, on U.S. inventories and procurement and on commitments to other nations for arms transfers, and the early identification of sensitive technology.

The Department of State will assess Israeli requests for military arms, equipment, supplies and technology, and the impact which providing such items would have on the Middle East and world political situation.

---

[6] Tab B is attached but not printed.

The Office of Management and Budget will prepare an assessment of the funding implications of the Israeli requests.

With regard to Israel's desire to conclude an agreed logistic plan for emergency resupply of military equipment and supplies in the event of resumed hostilities in the Middle East, the President has authorized the Department of Defense to continue preliminary talks with the Israeli Ministry of Defense to elicit and to evaluate specific Israeli views, and to make appropriate recommendations, through the Middle East Arms Transfer Panel and the Assistant to the President for National Security Affairs, to the President.

The President has approved the continuation of cooperation between Israel and the United States regarding military co-production, research and development, and technology transfer, under existing Department of Defense procedures and the examination of requests on a case-by-case basis, under the general guidance of the Middle East Arms Transfer Panel.

Brent Scowcroft

261. **Memorandum for the President's File by Robert B. Oakley of the National Security Council Staff**[1]

Washington, March 17, 1976, 3:15–4:45 p.m.

SUBJECT

Meeting with American Jewish Leadership Group, on Wednesday, March 17, 1976, 3:15–4:45 p.m. in Cabinet Room

PARTICIPANTS

Mr. Max M. Fisher
Rabbi Alexander M. Schindler, Chairman, Conference of Presidents of Major American Jewish Organizations and President, Union of American Hebrew Congregations
Mr. David M. Blumberg, President, B'nai B'rith
Mr. Yehuda Hellman, Executive Director, Conference of Presidents of Major American Jewish Organizations
Rabbi Arthur Hertzberg, President, American Jewish Congress

---

[1] Source: Ford Library, National Security Adviser, Memoranda of Conversations, Box 18, March 17, 1976, Ford, Kissinger, American Jewish Leadership Group. Confidential. The meeting was held in the Cabinet Room at the White House.

Mr. Jerold C. Hoffberger, President, Council of Jewish Federations and Welfare Funds
Mr. Harold Jacobs, President, Union of Orthodox Jewish Congregations
Mrs. Charlotte Jacobson, Chairman, World Zionist Organization—American Section
Mr. Frank R. Lautenberg, General Chairman, United Jewish Appeal
Mr. Arthur Levine, President, United Synagogue of America
Mrs. Rose Matzkin, President, Hadassah
Rabbi Israel Miller, Immediate Past Chairman, Conference of Presidents of Major American Jewish Organizations
Mr. Edward Sanders, President, American Israel Public Affairs Committee
Mr. Jacob Sheinkman, President, Jewish Labor Committee
Dr. Joseph P. Sternstein, President, Zionist Organization of America
Mr. Elmer L. Winter, President, American Jewish Committee

The Honorable Gerald R. Ford, President of the United States
The Honorable Henry A. Kissinger, Secretary of State
The Honorable Brent Scowcroft, Assistant to the President for National Security Affairs
Mr. David H. Lissy, Associate Director, Domestic Council
Mr. Robert Goldwin, Special Consultant to the President
Mr. Robert B. Oakley, Area Director for Middle East and South Asian Affairs, National Security Council Staff

Max Fisher: Mr. President, I would like you to meet Rabbi Schindler, the new Chairman of the Conference of Presidents of Major American Jewish Organizations. We all welcome this opportunity for an exchange on the concerns we have.

President: Let me make a few general observations first, then Henry Kissinger and I will deal with specific questions. Let's review the developments in the Middle East since I became President. After the Yom Kippur War the U.S. was helping rebuild Israel, providing large amounts of economic and military assistance. Then in March 1975 the negotiations fell apart and we had a period of uncertainty before they were concluded in September 1975, with the historic Sinai Agreement. Now the U.S. and U.N. observers are in place—I just saw a report on that today—and both sides are carrying out their part of the bargain. It took great courage by both sides to reach this agreement. More recently we have had the visit of my friend, Prime Minister Rabin.[2] We had three meetings and a dinner together and came to an understanding on some ideas of how to proceed in trying to get negotiations started again. This is not easy but the Prime Minister recognized the danger of doing nothing.

It is of great importance to us to secure Israel's survival and security. In the current fiscal year we have requested $1.5 billion in military assistance—50% of it in grants—and $800 million in economic aid for

---

[2] Ford met with Rabin on January 27, 28, and 29. See Documents 256, 257, and 259.

Israel. We have asked about $700 million for Egypt and smaller amounts for other Arabs. In fiscal year 1977 we have requested one billion dollars in military aid for Israel and $780 million in economic aid. There is about $650 million for Egypt. We are working in a constructive way to see that Israel has a military capability adequate to meet any contingencies. That and the favorable developments in Egypt give brighter prospects for the future than in the past.

Sadat has taken a strong position toward the USSR. In his speech he cut off all relations with them.[3] It took a lot of courage and I applaud it. It turns Egypt more our way. We should welcome and support this evolution.

That provides a rough estimate of where we are. Now, I understand that you have some questions about the C–130 propeller aircraft we intend to sell to Egypt. This is fully justified. It provides no offensive military capability. You must look at the total picture of aid to Israel, both military and economic, compared to our aid for Egypt. No one should object to the division of support. The planes should go to Egypt. If you disagree, I want to know why. If you have questions, please ask. I am firmly convinced this is the right move for Israel as well as the U.S.

Now I will ask Henry to give you his ideas.

Kissinger: We must take the strategic view, look at what has been created and where the greatest danger to Israel lies. The greatest danger is a unified Arab front backed by the Europeans and the Soviets, isolating the U.S. and Israel. So we want to disentangle the situation and eliminate this threat. The security of Israel is strategic and not tactical. At the end of the October War everyone was united in opposition to Israel and they were all pressing the U.S. to pressure Israel for an immediate return to the 1967 boundaries. Our desire to maintain a special relationship with Sadat is not naive, but to buy time so we can bring about a better situation. This is why we propose C–130s. Sadat is having a tough time with his army who could throw him out and open the way for a massive influx of Soviet arms. We must remain in control of the diplomatic situation. There is no danger of large-scale U.S. arms sales to Egypt. You must keep in mind the overall strategic considerations.

President: The breach in Egypt's relationship with the USSR followed Soviet pressures. They cut off spare parts and maintenance for Egyptian weapons and equipment.

---

[3] In a March 14 speech to the People's Assembly, Sadat requested abrogation of the 1971 Soviet-Egyptian Friendship Treaty. (Telegram 3287 from Cairo, March 14; National Archives, RG 59, Central Foreign Policy Files)

Kissinger: Egypt's MIGs fly only six hours a month. We want to keep Egypt neutralized but no army can be expected to accept the prospect of no weapons at all.

President: If we cut off Israel's spare parts, their military capability would go down. But selling six C–130s will not affect Egypt's military capability.

Someone mentioned to me your interest in the Sheehan article.[4] Our position is firm and clearly understood by both Sadat and Rabin. We stand by Security Council Resolutions 242 and 338, period. They provide for negotiations and secure and recognized boundaries. We stand for that.

Kissinger: We have a problem. We cannot comment on every book or article that appears. There are so many, and full of distortions. Look at Matty Golan and Admiral Zumwalt.[5] We cannot contradict or correct all the errors but the U.S. position is as the President has stated and we have never deviated from it. The Arabs complain that they are never able to get a commitment from us on the 1967 boundaries. Had we wished to pursue the 1967 boundaries, we could have done it much more easily without any need for ambiguity. We could have joined the EEC in October 1973 and done it directly. Instead we decided upon the step-by-step approach to avoid just this and ease the pressure on Israel. We have always said that the location of secure and recognized boundaries is to be negotiated by the parties. We stand on Security Council Resolutions 242 and 338.

Fisher: Some would say this meeting has a teutonic aspect with Kissinger and Schindler.

Kissinger: I would say it is a Harvard aspect.

Schindler: Mr. President, I want to thank you for receiving us and for your past affection for the Jewish Community. Because we are Americans we also thank you for the way you have conducted yourself in office. And we thank you for the overall thrust of U.S. foreign policy in the Middle East—to separate the moderates and the radicals and to drive out the Soviets. There has been more progress in containing confrontation in the past two years than during the preceding twenty years. So we support your overall policy. We also agree that six C–130 aircraft will not affect the military balance of power. Still we are afraid

---

[4] Apparently a reference to an article in the spring issue of the magazine *Foreign Policy*. Written by Edward R. F. Sheehan, the article included exchanges between Kissinger and Arab and Israeli leaders during Kissinger's negotiations in the Middle East. Some of the printed exchanges included discussion of borders between Israel and its Arab neighbors. (*New York Times*, March 6, 1976, p. 9)

[5] A reference to Admiral Elmo Zumwalt's memoir entitled *On Watch*, which was published in 1976 and included criticisms of Kissinger. On Matty Golan, see footnote 9, Document 202.

and we are apprehensive. We fear it is the beginning of a process. The symbolic aspect scares us. We buy the overall approach of supporting moderates so we support economic aid to Egypt and we do not oppose the nuclear agreement.[6] But we are worried about the six C–130s as being the start of a much larger process. Why does Egypt need arms? Its only enemy is Israel. Israel must fear not only Egypt but all the Arabs. Arms can be transferred from one to another. Last year Israel got $1.3 billion in arms but the Arabs got between $14 and $15 billion worth of arms. There is also a qualitative imbalance, the superiority of American equipment. That is why we do not want American equipment going to Egypt. Israel needs to maintain qualitative superiority with planes like the F–15.

President: Let me comment. If we look back at the four wars Israel has fought and the tragic loss of life, perhaps we can agree that the best way to alleviate the fear of another is to have Egypt dependent upon the U.S. rather than the Soviets or even Western Europe. It is better for us to be able to turn them on and off than for others to be in that position. Also, you cannot dismiss the problem between Libya and Egypt. Egypt is a much better friend of the U.S. than Libya which is getting huge amounts of military assistance from the USSR. That is creating a serious problem for us.

Kissinger: Egypt will not allow itself to be totally disarmed. Either Sadat gets some arms from the U.S. or he will go elsewhere or he will be thrown out. Do not drive him to despair. The problem of more arms for Egypt may come back in a year or two but by then we will have gained time for more peace moves. The President is speaking theoretically when he talks of the U.S. having the ability to control Egypt's supply of arms. There is no plan for a significant supply of U.S. arms. You spoke of the F–15 but we have no intention of supplying sophisticated arms to Egypt. The transfer of equipment is a very difficult question. We have no fixed program except the C–130s and the training of ten to fifteen Egyptian officers at our military schools. If we felt the need to move past this to another phase of arms supply we would be obliged to consult Congress but we do not wish to reach this point. On the other hand, we do not wish to go back to the point we were at in 1969 when we had to talk to the Egyptians through the Soviets. Last year there was an influx of Soviet arms to Egypt prior to the expected visit of Brezhnev but we stopped it by Sinai II.

Rabbi Hertzberg: We are sympathetic to your policy. But you are going from a little bit pregnant to more pregnant. How can you stop the process? Egypt is very hungry for arms. If the military is that strong

---

[6] See Document 92.

within Egypt, it will have to come back again for more arms. If we agree to six C–130s as a symbolic act, then it is the symbol of more, but how much more and when? There is a theory that Israel is so dependent upon the U.S. that it means parameters are set for Israeli policy. But what about U.S. influence on Sadat's policy? What will bring Egypt and the Arab moderates closer to the U.S. and Israel? What will Egypt do in return for the C–130s? What do we get in exchange?

President: One thing has already occurred, the breaking of Egyptian military relations with the Soviets. Closing the port of Alexandria to Soviet naval vessels deprives the Soviet fleet of valuable repair and maintenance facilities. They can go to Libya, maybe, but it is not as good. You cannot develop installations overnight to meet the Soviet needs. There are also two ports in Syria but they are not as good as Egypt. That is already a big dividend.

Kissinger: Another dividend is the peace process. So long as Egypt adheres to its present policy we can withstand Arab/Soviet pressures to move too fast toward peace. With Sadat we can move at a pace Israel can accept. We told Rabin to think about what Israel could do next. He sent us some ideas on non-belligerency. We took them to Sadat but to no other Arab.

Mrs. Matzkin: Mr. President, you want to know what the people think. Well, the question I get all the time is if the U.S. supplies both Israel and Egypt, how do you cut off supplies if there is a war? Does the U.S. take sides? U.S. arms will be tested on the battlefield where we do not want them tested. You asked if Egypt did not deserve a reward. I reply that they have a reward. They have most of the Sinai back, they have the oil fields and they are getting large amounts of economic aid. Egypt has internal problems yet it is spending its money on arms and is not committed to peace.

President: It is our hope that military and economic aid will allow the U.S. to avoid another war. Having both dependent upon the U.S. gives us leverage to preclude it. Although Sadat is an outstanding leader, he does have to contend with military leaders who see the Soviets cut off supplies and look to see what the U.S. will do. There is a theoretical potential of military leaders who might want to take charge in Egypt. We must deal with reality and keep Sadat in office. He has done more than anyone since I have been President to try and find a non-military understanding with Israel.

Kissinger: You talk as if Egypt were to be fully rearmed. If the President made such a decision and Congress approved it, there would still be five years or more needed to replace Egypt's present weapons due to production and training problems. But let's be realistic. We are not interested in replacing Soviet equipment with U.S. equipment. That is not our problem. Our problem is to keep the peace process alive. The situation you describe would probably take ten years to achieve even at top speed. But that is not what we are talking about.

Hoffberger: The President and the Secretary of State mentioned Egyptian military influence and the threat to Sadat. Are you telling us Sadat is in a precarious position?

President: My impression—and Henry can supplement it—is that Sadat is in a strong position. He has given the kind of inspirational leadership Egyptians like. Yet there is a history of military rule in Egypt and the army taking power. This was true of both Nasser and Sadat. We must be alert to contingencies. Egypt has an enormous debt and a huge military supply problem. There are great pressures to do more economically and militarily. We see no immediate threat but we must be realistic as to what could happen if the economy were to collapse or military supplies totally cut off. Then there is the threat of Libya and Qadhafi.

Winter: I have just come from a meeting of the Business Council. I am troubled by what you say. Secretary Kissinger says we will not be the chief suppliers of both sides, so where does Egypt turn for the bulk of its arms? To Europe? So how are we going to get them wholly into our camp without a full military relationship which we do not want?

President: The same delay Henry spoke of about U.S. deliveries applies to Europe. It would take five years or more as Henry stated and this applies to the Europeans. Personally, I agree with you and would prefer to have Egypt dependent upon the U.S. rather than Europe. But we have not made that commitment. Practically, I would prefer this but we have not done it.

Kissinger: I understand the dilemma you pose. There is no good answer. We cannot accept either to supply nothing or to be the chief supplier. If we are either one or the other, it would be too much. So we will find a path in between and try to gain time. I do not think we are in a position to make an absolute decision. We do not want to be the main supplier nor to decide to do nothing more, even than the C–130s. But there is no great speed in doing more. We want to be able to move the peace process along.

Rabbi Miller: Mr. President, we all know of your friendship with the American Jewish Community. So we will speak with candor based on respect and show you the deep worries of that community. We are profoundly worried, not about six lousy planes but about what you and the Secretary here have said. We are concerned about tomorrow. We recognize what you are saying is that the U.S. must gamble, that there is no guarantee. We recognize this since the situation cannot remain static. Our concern is that the U.S. will become a supplier to Egypt which will have a mixed source of supply—from France and others—and Saudi Arabia will have a substantial amount of arms, which it can supply to Egypt. Realistically, in another conflict, Egypt will not stand away and it will have many sources of supply. As to negotiations, your gamble on supplying arms to generate movement will necessarily become a fixed commitment. As negotiations progress, another allocation of more advanced and sophisticated weapons will be requested by Egypt as a price for continuing. You will say, we have gone so far so we must go a bit further to keep negotiations going. The American Jewish Community worries about this scenario. We worry also about the Sheehan article. We worry about the billions and billions of dollars in arms for the Arabs. Where are we going? We worry about what is going to happen tomorrow.

President: You expressed the same concerns a year ago prior to the negotiations in March and then after the March negotiations failed. Yet by developing the trust of both Israel and Egypt we were able to obtain the Sinai II Agreement. It is an achievement of great significance. You were concerned throughout the past year but the movement has been a success so your legitimate fears have been eliminated by the results. I believe in Security Council Resolutions 242 and 338. There must be progress within the confines of these resolutions. We cannot eliminate your concerns and apprehensions. They will always be present. But you must have faith and trust. This is not the ideal world but the real world. We are making headway on getting trust between the U.S. and Egypt and the U.S. and Israel and Egypt and Israel. Lots of progress. It should not be underestimated.

Miller: We are expressing the fears of our people. You all must deal with this and get it across to our people. Mr. Jacobs will talk to you about aid, about the fifth quarter. There are certain ways to explain trust. It is not enough to say "trust us."

Mrs. Jacobson: We appreciate your comments on the Sheehan article. I would like to set the record straight on leaving here by saying that you have told us the U.S. position does not go beyond supporting Resolutions 242 and 338. It seems to me that we need an additional step by Egypt toward peace. Sadat dismissed the Soviets because they were not giving what Egypt wants. It is a golden opportunity to move towards peace. Let us make a new effort with Egypt. A major breakthrough on the Sinai. The word peace is still missing.

President: We are always ready to begin negotiations if Israel and Egypt are ready. It is not up to us. But you cannot make overall headway by concentrating exclusively on Israel and Egypt. We are working with Prime Minister Rabin to find ways of further progress. It is up to Israel and the Arabs but we will continue our mediating role.

Kissinger: The Israeli Government is telling us constantly not to go too fast, not to try for overall peace now. We have an agreed strategy with Israel to try for an end to the state of war. But the gamble of turning back on C–130s for Egypt would be extremely dangerous. We asked Israel to do a bit on the West Bank before Rabat to preclude the PLO, but it did not work. The Israelis are nostalgic for Jordan today. I am not sure your idea would be greeted with joy in Jerusalem since Israel would need to spell out its position on final boundaries if it were to negotiate for peace.

Jacobs: I saw your wife in California, campaigning for you, Mr. President. She makes an excellent impression.

President: I am trying hard to get my votes up to her polls.

Jacobs: What about the fifth quarter funding for Israel, are you going to support it or not?

President: We did not recommend any funds for the 5th quarter. We recommended $2.3 billion for FY 76 and $1.8 billion for FY 77, with $1.0 billion in military aid. Based upon the analyses of all the reports in the U.S. Government, this is plenty to keep up with Israel's modernization needs. It is not as much as their Matmon–B plan, but it is enough. The technicians actually recommended $.5 billion, but I upped it to $1.0 billion. In all honesty, during my talks with Rabin there was no sign they were disappointed. Maybe he tells you something he does not tell me but he said he was content. They had a much longer shopping list but a lot of it was filled.

Now the Senate Appropriations Subcommittee has increased the aid bill by one billion dollars, $500 million of it for Israel for the fifth quarter. I am trying hard to get the budget under control. I am squeezing every Department except Defense. So now you want me to approve another one billion. How can I justify that when people complain about how heartless and cruel I am for cutting food stamps, HEW and other programs. This is a very significant increase for the Middle East, especially when I am told by the technicians in CIA and DOD that $500 million would be enough for Israel. I recommended $1.0 billion. I must relate domestic programs to foreign programs. We must stop the growing deficit and inflationary pressures. I think it is wrong to ask for this and I feel strongly about it.

Fisher: To sum up, the six planes to help Sadat is not really a concern. The concern is over the U.S. eventually becoming a major supplier. This year you have to gamble with six planes. Next year, you may have to gamble again, but if so, you will go before Congress. You do not want the U.S. to be a major supplier. You are playing for time. We understand this.

On aid, I know your problem but what will happen if Congress passes the bill. That is a real problem. There is a lot of sentiment in Congress for an increase across the board for Israel. I would not be frank if I did not tell you of our concern that this be approved.

President: I get bill after bill from Congress, they add $1.2 billion to HEW, $1.0 billion to HUD, more to Interior. Look at the totals and see where this would take us. So I veto. We must get a handle on the rate of growth. If we did not change a law, there would be a $50 billion increase in FY 77 expenditures. This country simply cannot afford it. Look at the projections. Already the Congressional Committees have sent increases to the Budget Committee totalling over $20 billion without the increase for foreign aid. How do I answer those who say I am hard-hearted on domestic programs if I go along with greater foreign aid and military assistance. You need to look at all this in context. My job is a tough one, but I can face it.

My fundamental view is the same today as for twenty years in Congress and it will not change. We will deal with day-to-day problems in a frank and candid way. You need to trust me. My view will be the same in the future as in the past on Israel.

Fisher: Thank you for this meeting, Mr. President.

---

262. Backchannel Message From the President's Assistant for National Security Affairs (Scowcroft) to the Ambassador to Egypt (Eilts)[1]

Washington, March 19, 1976, 1909Z.

WH 60360. The President was very pleased and moved by the courage and statesmanship reflected in President Sadat's decisions of last weekend.[2] He has written to Sadat to express to him his respect and support. The character of the letter and the occasion seemed to present a fitting opportunity for trying out the Sunshine Circuit. Thus, the letter is being sent in that channel concurrent to this message.

Begin text: Message for President Sadat.

Dear Mr. President:

I want to convey to you my admiration for the action you took in your address to the People's Assembly on March 14, with respect to the Soviet Friendship Treaty. My government and the American people have viewed this as a courageous assertion of the self-respect and dig-

---

[1] Source: Ford Library, National Security Adviser, Backchannel Messages, Box 5, Sandy Circuit, March 1976, Outgoing. Secret; Priority.

[2] See footnote 3, Document 261.

nity and nonaligned course of the Egyptian nation. You can count on our strong support. The policy of moderation that you have pursued, with us, through so many difficult periods in recent years will, I am convinced, continue to bear fruit. I look forward to redoubling our joint efforts for a just peace in the Middle East.

I remember with warmth our many meetings together.

Sincerely,

Gerald R. Ford

End text.

Warm regards.

Lebanese Civil War, September 1975–August 1976

263. Memorandum of Conversation[1]

New York, September 30, 1975, 10:15–10:35 a.m.

PARTICIPANTS

Lebanon
Foreign Minister Philippe Takla
Permanent Representative Edouard Ghoora
Ambassador to the U.S., Najati Kabbani

United States
Henry A. Kissinger, Secretary of State and Assistant to the President for National Security Affairs
Alfred L. Atherton, Jr., Assistant Secretary of State for Near Eastern and South Asian Affairs
Robert B. Oakley, NSC Staff
Alec Toumayan, Interpreter

Kissinger: I just finished meeting with another Arab Foreign Minister whose Ambassador to the United States is named Takla.

Takla: I hope it was a good meeting. Syria is very important for us.

Kissinger: It is my impression that they will be tough for several months, but they really have no realistic alternative to further negotiations.

Takla: I appreciate all that you have accomplished in moving toward peace in the Middle East. It is of vital importance for Lebanon and the region that the United States continue its efforts, as you have said you intend to do. It is necessary that the Arabs have the conviction that United States efforts will be successful. The present unrest concerning the Sinai agreement is due to doubts that this will be the case.

Kissinger: I fully agree with the importance for continued forward movement but it is necessary for the Arabs to distinguish between appearance and reality. In the United States our policy has succeeded in creating objective conditions more conducive to achieving an overall settlement than ever before. Therefore, the Arabs should take care not to let their emotions carry them away. Should the Arabs return to their 1967 mentality and devote their energies to attacking one another and

---

[1] Source: Library of Congress, Manuscript Division, Kissinger Papers, CL 274, Chronological File, Israel, September 1975, Folder 3. Secret; Exdis. The meeting was held in the Secretary's Suite at the Waldorf Towers.

the United States, instead of cooperation with us, it would become virtually impossible to sustain the favorable conditions presently existing in this country.

Takla: I agree with your analysis.

Kissinger: It is very important that the Arabs keep things calm during this period, but that is not the Arab forte.

Takla: Dr. Kissinger knows us well. We are Orientals, not Occidentals.

Kissinger: What about the situation in Lebanon?

Takla: There is relative calm today but the intermediate and long-term problems are very difficult. There are three pre-conditions for internal peace in Lebanon: Lebanon must remain united with rumors of partition and division laid to rest; there must be a redistribution of political power within the existing constitutional system; and there must be a reduction of external interference. Renewed civil strife and possible efforts at partition would be dangerous for the entire Middle East and even the U.S., not only Lebanon.

Kissinger: We are prepared to be helpful. (As a first step the Secretary and Takla agreed that the State Department spokesman should make a statement about Lebanon following the meeting). If you wish a further statement from me personally, rather than our spokesman, have your Ambassador let us know. What do you judge the Syrians are up to?

Takla: Lebanon is part of the Arab world and cannot escape this reality. Therefore it is essential for us to have close relations with Syria, which is playing a constructive role in the short-term, a necessary role given the weakness of the Lebanese Government. But we are fully aware that Syria's ambitions for greater influence in Lebanon will create long-term problems. The Syrians have no intention of intervening militarily in Lebanon under present circumstances, but they fear Israeli intervention. The Syrians are not helping us out of love but out of interest, yet they are behaving prudently. Over the long term we have ancestral problems with Syria.

Kissinger: That's true of all of Syria's neighbors.

Takla: The Syrians need a period of calm, especially from Israeli threats.

Kissinger: We can keep Israel under control with respect to Lebanon so long as Syria does not move. But if Syria should intervene militarily, it might well be impossible to restrain the Israelis.

Takla: The Syrians will not move militarily. But why does Allon talk about protecting the Christians of Lebanon? It scares me.

Kissinger: I don't know if the world can withstand the Israeli propensity to comment loudly about every event, even when it does not concern them. We shall speak to them again, and I have already cautioned Peres about Lebanon.

Takla: I am very glad to hear that. Israeli intervention would be too dangerous for Lebanon and the entire region.

Kissinger: We agree. How else can we be helpful?

Takla: Perhaps you could encourage Kuwait and Saudi Arabia to help with Syria and the Palestinians. They have not been at all active, yet they have the potential to help us. Maybe France could be helpful with Iraq, and maybe one could get the Soviets to calm the Lebanese left. But I am making no precise request, merely exposing the situation.

Kissinger: I will talk to the Soviets and to some Arabs. It has been a pleasure talking with you, but now I have another appointment. I will walk to the elevator with you.

264. Minutes of Washington Special Actions Group Meeting[1]

Washington, October 10, 1975, 10:40–11:10 a.m.

SUBJECT

Lebanon

PARTICIPANTS

Chairman
Henry A. Kissinger

State
Joseph Sisco
Harold Saunders

DOD
William Clements
James Noyes

JCS
Lt. Gen. William Y. Smith
Note: Gen. Brown was out of town.

---

[1] Source: Ford Library, NSC Institutional Files, Box 25, Meeting Minutes, WSAG-Originals, October 1975. Top Secret; Codeword. The original is marked "Part I of III." The meeting was held in the White House Situation Room.

CIA
William Colby

NSC
Lt. Gen. Brent Scowcroft
Robert Oakley
Jeanne W. Davis

Secretary Kissinger: I thought we should have a review of the situation in Lebanon, then do some work if we decide we know what we want to do. Bill (Colby), what do you have?

(Mr. Colby briefed from the attached text.[2] The briefing was interrupted from time to time with the following exchanges.)

Secretary Kissinger: Who exactly is fighting whom?

Mr. Colby: The Phalanges (radical Christians) are fighting the radical Fedayeen and the radical Moslem leftists.

Secretary Kissinger: If the Lebanese Army came in, on whose side would they be?

Mr. Colby: The Army is about 50–50 Christian/Moslem, but the commanders are Christian.

Secretary Kissinger: Would the Moslem soldiers obey them?

Mr. Colby: The entry of the Army might provoke the less radical Moslems and Fedayeen. They would assume the Army was pro-Christian.

Secretary Kissinger: Would Moslem soldiers fight Moslem civilians?

Mr. Colby: Some would.

Mr. Clements: I agree. There is a very tough feeling toward the refugees among the Moslems in Lebanon. They resent the refugees as a sore point, causing unrest. They are afraid the refugees might try to take the country.

Secretary Kissinger: (referring to a reported appeal by Lebanese leaders for a joint Arab military force to be sent to Lebanon) A joint military force? That's inconceivable!

Mr. Colby: It's a nutty idea.

Secretary Kissinger: I don't know what the Israelis would do.

Mr. Colby: That's just an idea that has been floated in the press.

Secretary Kissinger: The Israelis would be glad to restore order.

Mr. Colby: They are giving some assistance to the Christians.

Secretary Kissinger: Of course. Some of their best friends are Christians.

---

[2] The text is not attached.

Mr. Colby: Karame went to see Asad yesterday to try to convince him that the situation is grave and that the Lebanese Army should be used to keep the peace. Asad essentially supported him. Then they brought Arafat in, and he agreed to try to help calm things down.

(Mr. Colby completed his briefing.)

Mr. Clements: I have one comment. This isn't as simple as the fall-out from an escalating division between Moslem and Christian.

Mr. Colby: You're right; that's too simplistic. There are lots of factors.

Secretary Kissinger: What factors?

Mr. Clements: There are a lot of purely nationalist elements. I have friends over there whose families have been Christians for 4–500 years, but they are still *Arabs*. This pure Christian-Moslem thing just isn't so.

Mr. Colby: It's Christian-Moslem, but it is also have vs. have-not.

Secretary Kissinger: But you could still have a Christian-Moslem fight.

Mr. Colby: You have a fight between extremist Christians and extremist Moslems. All it takes is one man and one bullet to set it off. If the Sunni Moslems (Karame) and Chamoun and his friends can hold things together in the center . . .

Secretary Kissinger: Joe (Sisco), what do you think?

Mr. Sisco: I agree. We have to involve ourselves along the lines you have already started. The report of Syria and Karame trying to substitute an internal security force for the Lebanese army is encouraging. Arafat is meeting with the PLO today to see if they will go along. As a minimum we should talk to (Lebanese Foreign Minister) Takla and get his latest appreciation of the situation. See if he has any further suggestions. I think we should try to get the Saudis involved.

Mr. Clements: I agree.

Secretary Kissinger: What do we want them to do?

Mr. Sisco: Use the leverage of their money. Make it clear to the Arab extremist elements that they should not cause difficulties.

Secretary Kissinger: Are the Arab extremists causing difficulties?

Mr. Colby: Yes.

Secretary Kissinger: All right, let's go to Takla. And let's go to the Israelis and find out what is happening, whether they are going to act. Don't lecture them. Just tell them we don't want a fait accompli. (to Hal Saunders) Make sure that is done.

Mr. Colby: [1 *line not declassified*]

Secretary Kissinger: [1 *line not declassified*] (to Sisco) Did we send out that cable I disapproved the other night? Let's ask for Israeli views, but make sure there is no fait accompli. They are playing games.

Mr. Colby: Yes, they are playing games. [1 *line not declassified*]

Secretary Kissinger: [1 *line not declassified*]

Mr. Colby: We can't just go back to the past in Lebanon. We have to recognize that there must be a greater position for the Moslems.

Secretary Kissinger: I want to define our own interests. I have no particular interest in Lebanon's internal affairs if they do not involve outside countries. I don't want us involved in their internal affairs. Our concern is to prevent outside interference. Ask Takla what he thinks of our approaching the Saudis. What do we want from the Saudis?

Mr. Sisco: We should also tell the Phalanges to cool it, but we have to be careful. They are the only counter-weight in the situation.

Secretary Kissinger: Our cables didn't hack away at the Phalanges, did they?

Mr. Sisco: No, but the Phalanges have undue expectations of direct U.S. involvement. That worries me. They tend to see the situation in terms of 1958 and that is ridiculous.

Mr. Colby: Exactly.

Mr. Sisco: American Marines will not land in Lebanon.

Mr. Clements: Some of the Saudis have a helluva influence on the Palestine refugees. They're the root of the problem.

Secretary Kissinger: I have come to realize that King Faisal was a really great man. The current Saudi leaders may be more moderate intellectually, but I'm afraid they are going to get involved beyond their depth. I want to know what Takla thinks.

Mr. Sisco: I agree.

Mr. Clements: Absolutely.

Secretary Kissinger: I'm worried about the present Saudi leaders.

Mr. Sisco: They're becoming too broadly involved in the Arab world.

Mr. Clements: If we don't counsel Fahd, the Saudis will be involved.

Secretary Kissinger: We should do a cable to Fahd. But I would like to hear first from Takla and the Israelis.

(to Mr. Saunders) Let's get a little working group together on what would happen if the worst occurs and war breaks out. What if Syria, then Israel goes in? Do you think the Sinai agreement can last?

Mr. Sisco: Yes, I think it can. The Egyptians will try to make it last. Syria would put on its usual pressure. They are concerned about the timing of the Sadat visit.

Secretary Kissinger: What about Jordan?

Mr. Sisco: They have not been involved. They are ambivalent about this situation. To the degree that the Palestinians are involved in Lebanon, they are not on Jordan's back.

Mr. Colby: Jordan still thinks the Palestinians will settle down and stay.

Mr. Sisco: The Lebanese situation could turn to a leftist-radical orientation. This would invite outside intervention and all the work we have done with Egypt, Syria and Jordan could be upset.

Mr. Clements: I agree.

Mr. Colby: The real factor is the realignment of the Moslem-Christian relationship using the moderates on both sides. Squeeze out the extremists.

Mr. Sisco: Franjiyah is a disaster. He has lost control. Everyone recognizes the need for political adjustment but it is very difficult to accomplish. Things have to quiet down first in order to prevent outside intervention and then to create a situation for peaceful adjustment.

Mr. Colby: We should try to get them to reopen their dialogue before the election.

Secretary Kissinger: I don't want us to get in. The internal arrangements in Lebanon are too dicey. Let's have the working group look at the military contingencies and get a paper by Monday (October 13). Let's get a cable to our Embassies in Beirut and Tel Aviv[3] and ask for a reply by Monday. This group can meet again on Monday.

---

[3] Telegram 243260 to Beirut and telegram 243279 to Tel Aviv, both October 11. (National Archives, RG 59, Central Foreign Policy Files)

265. Minutes of Washington Special Actions Group Meeting[1]

Washington, October 13, 1975, 10:40–11:14 a.m.

SUBJECT

Lebanon

PARTICIPANTS

Chairman
Henry A. Kissinger

State
Robert Ingersoll
Roy Atherton

DOD
William Clements
Robert Ellsworth

JCS
Gen. George S. Brown
Lt. Gen. William E. Smith

CIA
William Colby
Sam Hoskinson

NSC
Lt. Gen. Brent Scowcroft
Robert Oakley
Jeanne W. Davis

Secretary Kissinger: Bill (Colby), do you have anything?

(Mr. Colby briefed from the attached text.)[2]

Secretary Kissinger: (commenting on the statement that Asad deserves much of the credit for the current calm) Is that true, that Asad deserves the credit?

Mr. Colby: According to our information he has urged the Palestinians to cooperate and Arafat has gone back to Beirut, at Asad's urging, to meet with Chamoun to discuss joint Christian-Moslem security measures.

(Mr. Colby completed his briefing.)

Secretary Kissinger: (to Ingersoll) Bob, what do you think? Or Roy (Atherton)?

---

[1] Source: Ford Library, NSC Institutional Files, Box 25, Meeting Minutes, WSAG-Originals, October 1975. Top Secret; Codeword. The original is marked "Part I of III." The meeting was held in the White House Situation Room.

[2] The text is not attached.

Mr. Ingersoll: Roy can discuss the paper the working group has put together.

Mr. Atherton: The paper identifies two choices: all-out support for the Christians or encouragement of constructive political intervention looking toward a new political compromise.[3]

Secretary Kissinger: The bureaus always give me two choices: what the bureau wants or all-out nuclear war.

Mr. Atherton: The paper outlines four choices built around support for the Christians in a dominant position or an attempt to work with others to see some change in the basic structure.

Secretary Kissinger: But there are basically only two choices: one, to work for change and the other, all-out support for the Christians, together with the Israelis. The rest are tactics.

Mr. Atherton: That is basically correct.

Secretary Kissinger: I have yet to learn how to defeat the bureaus but at least I have come to understand their methods. I assume you don't want to support the Christians.

Mr. Atherton: I think it is a dead-end.

Secretary Kissinger: Bill (Clements), what do you think?

Mr. Clements: I agree we should work for change, but how do you propose to do it? Would we try to bring about a moderate situation or a true balance? The only way is get the Syrians to lay off and get the refugees to settle down. Intervention by Israel would be disastrous.

Mr. Atherton: But we should not let the Syrians live under any illusion. We should let them know that any move on their part might bring the Israelis in no matter what we do. We shouldn't give them the idea they can move with impunity.

Mr. Clements: (to Kissinger) Did you contact that Foreign Minister you were talking about (Lebanese Foreign Minister Takla)?

Secretary Kissinger: Yes, but he had next to nothing to say. He told us to approach the Soviets. I totally disagreed. We have nothing to gain from that.

Mr. Atherton: The question is whether we should approach the Syrians.

Secretary Kissinger: That's not a bad idea.

Mr. Clements: I agree, but I think the most workable way is through the Saudis. They have the money.

Secretary Kissinger: The Saudis can help us with the PLO. But if we want to know what the Syrians are thinking we should ask the Syrians.

---

[3] The paper is not further identified.

The essential point is how active a role should the U.S. play? If we are the ones who arrange a change in Lebanon, that means we will be blamed by everyone for the outcome. If the situation is tending toward a 50–50 Christian/Moslem solution, maybe we should let nature take its course.

Mr. Atherton: I agree; we should not intervene. But the Phalanges still think we will come to their rescue. We should make it clear to them that that is unrealistic. We should get the message across.

Secretary Kissinger: But that might make them fold completely.

Mr. Atherton: We should talk to them.

Secretary Kissinger: What do you think, George (Brown)?

Gen. Brown: I think we ought to go fishing. The U.S. should not get involved. And we should lean on the Israelis to keep their cool.

Secretary Kissinger: We have done that.

Mr. Atherton: We have no indication that that conversation has taken place yet.

Secretary Kissinger: Why not? We gave our Ambassador his instructions three days ago. Ask him why.

Mr. Colby: [1 line not declassified]

Secretary Kissinger: [2 lines not declassified]

Mr. Colby: [1 line not declassified]

Secretary Kissinger: [2 lines not declassified]

Gen. Brown: We should also continue to work with the Syrians.

Secretary Kissinger: We can tell the Syrians that we are interested in the independence and security of Lebanon but not necessarily in any one specific arrangement. We're open-minded. What is their thinking? It is our judgement that if there is foreign military intervention, Israel may come in. If there is no foreign military intervention, we could probably prevent Israeli intervention.

Mr. Colby: We have to be careful that it doesn't sound like a threat. [1 line not declassified]

Secretary Kissinger: Let's see what answer we get from the Syrians first. We should also ask the Saudis for their view.

Mr. Atherton: We have but we have no answer yet.

Secretary Kissinger: The best way to deal with the Saudis is to have a complete proposal for them to make to someone. They may say they want a "moderate" solution but not know how to get it. I'm seriously worried that the Saudis are going to get in over their depth all over the Arab world. They are more moderate but they do not have the wisdom of Faisal. Fahd is tending to get Saudi Arabia overextended. I believe their internal structure is weaker than we think. As their position has moderated, they have lost that exalted quality of Faisal, and may become just another reactionary country. The King is weak. When I was talking to him, the princes were sitting along the wall holding their own private conversations. They treated him as though he didn't exist. Can you imagine that happening with Faisal? When I was talking to him you could have a heard a pin drop. There was nothing unfriendly about them. Indeed, they were friendlier to us than Faisal was, but I have the eerie feeling that it is not a strong government. Faisal positioned them very carefully; he maintained this almost sacred aura and was able to deal with both the moderates and the radicals. I think these new leaders are beyond their depth.

Mr. Colby: One advantage is that the only real candidates for leadership are all cousins and brothers.

Secretary Kissinger: But they could get in trouble with the Arab world. Look at OPEC.

Mr. Colby: Of course now everyone is chasing a piece of the action.

Secretary Kissinger: Their performance at OPEC was not good for them. They are too vulnerable. Of course, it was in our interest.

Mr. Clements: They were doing what they thought you wanted them to do. For that reason we have some responsibility for them.

Secretary Kissinger: Right. That's why I don't want them overextended.

Mr. Colby: They got a little scared at the OPEC meeting about the overall economic impact.

Secretary Kissinger: I agree. But Faisal wouldn't have done it publicly. He wouldn't have put Yamani on television. He would have worked behind the scenes.

Mr. Clements: This is a changed regime. We have some responsibility for them; they are looking to us for advice and counsel.

Secretary Kissinger: That's right. That's why we have to get them to be moderate. They may get in too deep. We have to advise them. Otherwise, can you imagine a Qadhafi in Saudi Arabia?

Mr. Colby: That would be a nightmare.

Mr. Clements: We have to have someone over there who can advise and counsel them.

Secretary Kissinger: I'm in total agreement.

Mr. Colby: And represent their interests.

Secretary Kissinger: We have a heavier responsibility to them than before. (to Atherton) Let's be more specific with the Saudis.

Mr. Colby: While we try to cool the extremists, we should also strengthen the moderates. We can work through Karami and Chamoun.

Secretary Kissinger: What would we do? In principle, yes. Let's draft something on what we would say to strengthen the moderates. Maybe after we hear from the Syrians we might move in that direction.

Mr. Atherton: Karami mostly listened when we approached him.

Secretary Kissinger: We need some Saudi and Syrian input, then we can go back to Karami. Don't tell the Lebanese whom we are talking to. They will try to concert their responses.

What do we do if the Syrians go in, followed by the Israelis? Or the other way around?

Mr. Colby: The situation may get so serious that we have to go in.

Gen. Brown: I would hope we could be involved with the Soviets so that we both stay out.

Secretary Kissinger: Then the Israelis will clean up.

Gen. Brown: Don't we have some leverage on the Israelis? (to Kissinger) They still want that deal you made.

Secretary Kissinger: There is no deal that has not been in effect for years.

Gen. Brown: What about that military equipment they want to start flowing.

Secretary Kissinger: You have got the equipment lists.

Gen. Brown: But there might not be a continuous flow of U.S. arms to Israel if they go in to Lebanon.

Secretary Kissinger: If that is the decision. Do we want the Israelis out of Lebanon under all circumstances? If the Israelis go in first, without consultation with us, that is one situation. But if they go in second, what do we do? Do we crack down on the Israelis or maintain a neutral attitude?

Mr. Atherton: We would have to assess the Syrian motives in moving first. Do they intend to take over Lebanon?

Secretary Kissinger: If the Syrians go in, there would be a radical change in the balance, whatever reasons the Syrians give. The Israelis would go in, even if the Syrians say they are going in to help the Christians. It's not inconceivable that the Syrians would go in to come up with a moderate solution. Suppose they went in to achieve a 50–50 split? That's not impossible; it would be a basically moderate course. But the Israelis would go in no matter what the Syrians stated as their reasons.

Gen. Brown: I agree. But wouldn't Asad understand that?

Mr. Atherton: The Israelis might not go in right away, but at some point they would.

Mr. Colby: I agree.

Secretary Kissinger: Let's get a specific answer on what the Israeli judgement is of a tolerable level of Syrian activity.

Mr. Clements: We can't just "go fishing." If everything goes to hell in a handbasket, the U.S. will be blamed.

Secretary Kissinger: If we get superactive, we may trigger Arab coalescence.

Gen. Brown: We certainly shouldn't step up our ammunition supplies.

Mr. Clements: Okay.

Mr. Colby: The Russians would love to see us painted as friends of the Israelis and the Christians.

Mr. Atherton: The Kuwaitis have asked us about another statement by a high U.S. official. I think not before the Arab Foreign Ministers meeting on Wednesday.[4]

Secretary Kissinger: Let's get our basic thinking to the Syrians and Saudis in a low key way this afternoon. Ask them if they want another statement.

Mr. Colby: They ought to know we are not supporting the Christians.

Secretary Kissinger: They ought to know that we are holding the Israelis back but not in every contingency. Let's get to the Saudis, the Syrians and (Egyptian Foreign Minister) Fahmi. Ask what they think. Get the cables off this afternoon.[5]

Let's have the working group look at what we should actually do if there is a war. Look at the various ways it could start: a unilateral Israeli or Syrian move, or a confused situation. Let's examine it on a diplomatic, military and intelligence level. Would we move some carriers? Reinforce? Let's get something worked out by close of business tomorrow.

---

[4] October 17.

[5] Telegrams 243488 to Cairo, 243489 to Jidda, and 243490 to Damascus, all Ocober 14. (National Archives, RG 59, Central Foreign Policy Files)

266. Minutes of the Secretary of State's Staff Meeting[1]

Washington, October 28, 1975, 8 a.m.

PARTICIPANTS

The Secretary of State—Henry A. Kissinger
D—Mr. Ingersoll
P—Mr. Sisco
E—Mr. Robinson
T—Mr. Maw
M—Mr. Eagleburger

AF—Ambassador Davis
ARA—Mr. Rogers
EA—Mr. Miller, Acting
EUR—Mr. Hartman
NEA—Mr. Atherton

INR—Mr. Hyland
S/P—Mr. Lord
EB—Mr. Enders
S/PRS—Ambassador Anderson
PM—Mr. Vest
IO—Ambassador Buffum
H—Ambassador McCloskey
L—Mr. Leigh
S/S—Mr. Springsteen
S—Mr. Bremer

PROCEEDINGS

Secretary Kissinger: Bob.

Mr. Ingersoll: Things in Beirut are getting rougher. But Godley thinks that they are not turning on any foreigners yet. A sealift is 72 hours away, but the fleet is in Sicily and could be stepped up if we wanted to.

Secretary Kissinger: Why can't they go out by airlift?

Mr. Ingersoll: They are so far. But if things should really get rough, the airport would probably be closed down. And if it got that bad, you are not sure you could even take off with helicopters. Godley doesn't think it is that bad—although we have a skeleton force in the embassy. They are fighting around there. Roy is watching this very closely. We have a task force. We are trying to separate the kidnap task force from the Lebanese area.

---

[1] Source: National Archives, RG 59, Henry Kissinger Staff Meetings, Box 9. Secret.

Secretary Kissinger: What is the situation on the kidnapping?[2]

Mr. Atherton: The latest report [2 lines not declassified] is that they are looking for a way to quietly release them, and they appreciate it very much that we have kept it low-key.

Secretary Kissinger: Who in fact has them?

Mr. Atherton: It's the PFLP itself, or a group under the control of the PFLP.

Secretary Kissinger: What is the PFLP?

Mr. Atherton: Popular Front for the Liberation of Palestine. It is one of the rejectionist Marxist groups of the PLO, one of the splinter groups of the PLO. But we are actually getting quite a lot of help from Arafat's side of the PLO, to rather quietly get them released without any fuss.

Secretary Kissinger: What is the reason for the latest blow-up in Beirut?

Mr. Atherton: It is just more of the same, Mr. Secretary. The Christian Phalange and the Moslem leftist groups are trying to control as much of the territory of the city as they can. What happened is that the Christian groups have now moved into the area, and there is fighting around the embassy and the hotels where the foreigners stay and are trying to in effect establish bases there from which they can direct fire on the areas held by the Moslems.

Secretary Kissinger: Are the Israelis behind this?

Mr. Atherton: I have no evidence of it. This is just a little civil war between the Moslems and the Christians at this point.

Secretary Kissinger: Then how is it going to end?

Mr. Atherton: I think when they both become exhausted. A lot more blood has been shed. The government speaks every day of the hope of an imminent cease-fire, and nothing happens. There is just no central authority.

Mr. Ingersoll: Arms are still coming in on both sides.

Mr. Atherton: Arms are coming to the Moslems from Syria, even though the Syrians are politically trying to calm things, and the Christians have no problem getting arms from whatever commercial sources, and I presume also probably directly or indirectly from the Israelis. At least there is some evidence that has been the case.

---

[2] On October 22, Charles Gallagher and William Dykes, two employees of USIS, were kidnapped from their car while driving in Beirut, purportedly by members of the PFLP. Both Gallagher and Dykes were released unharmed on February 25, 1976. This marked the second time an American had been kidnapped in Lebanon during the previous four months. In July 1975, members of the PFLP purportedly kidnapped Colonel Ernest P. Morgan. He was released unharmed 13 days later. (*New York Times*, October 23, 1975, p. 5)

Secretary Kissinger: Under those conditions they can't get exhausted, if they both get arms. They are not suffering enough casualties to exhaust them.

Mr. Atherton: I don't see an early denouement. I think it is going to go along in a state of total disorder and deterioration. The foreign community is leaving. Our people are carrying out in effect an evacuation phase, having it low-key publicly. But the embassy is accelerating the departure of the various regional organizations, the Foreign Service Institute and others that have been based in Beirut. The private American community is leaving in large numbers every day. Planes are still coming in and out.

If I could just add one other point. I think the important thing is up to now neither side has been directing itself against the foreign community. There have been foreigners caught in the middle in a few situations. There is no concerted effort to jeopardize or to attack the foreign community.

Secretary Kissinger: I know. But even if there were a cease-fire, the foreigners would not come back right away, would they?

Mr. Atherton: I doubt it.

Mr. Ingersoll. The *Chicago Tribune* claims they deliberately fired on their correspondent. He filed a story, walked down the street, and they shot at him.

Mr. Atherton: I think you are going to get thugs in this. But there is no policy decision on the part of either side.

Secretary Kissinger: But still the nature of Lebanon will now be fundamentally changed, if all the foreigners leave.

Mr. Atherton: I think that is true.

Mr. Sisco: And there has to be a political adjustment between the Moslem and Christian community. That is the one thing that I think has to occur, if stability or at least reasonable quiet is going to be achieved. And that has got to be reflected in the constitutional setup and in the election coming next year.

Mr. Atherton: I think that is true.

Mr. Robinson: Financial activities in Lebanon are very likely to move to Cairo. And I can see this as a fundamental and important change.

Secretary Kissinger: But there isn't anything we can do.

Mr. Sisco: Unfortunately, we just don't know how to influence this situation. You have taken the lead diplomatically. We just cannot seem to influence the situation. I don't think we have the capacity.

[Omitted here is discussion unrelated to Lebanon.]

267. Memorandum of Conversation[1]

Washington, March 15, 1976.

SUBJECT

Lebanese Developments: Message to President Asad

PARTICIPANTS

The Secretary
Alfred L. Atherton, Jr., Assistant Secretary, NEA
Harold Saunders, Director, INR
Arthur R. Day, Deputy Assistant Secretary, NEA
Morris Draper, Country Director, Lebanon, Jordan, Syria, Iraq (NEA/ARN)

The Secretary: What is the problem?

Mr. Atherton: Lebanon. The situation in that country has fallen apart since the January ceasefire.[2] There have been a number of reasons for this. Jumblatt resisted the mediation effort conducted by the Syrians and mobilized a lot of opposition to the political solution among his leftist allies. The hard-line Christian leaders conducted their own form of obstructionism, although the terms of the political solution were basically favorable to the Christian side. Meanwhile, the dissident army groups under Lieutenant Khatib picked up support and contributed to the melting away of the army. The result has been a slippage to the forces of the left, to Muslimization, and to military intervention in the form of the "corrective movement."

Mr. Atherton: Fortunately, our most pressing concern of yesterday—Syrian intervention with their own troops—appears less likely for the moment. Did you see Murphy's report of his talk with Asad?[3]

The Secretary: No. I will need to get control ...

Mr. Atherton: Here it is.

The Secretary: (Reading the message) I have an uneasy feeling about the Israelis. I talked to Dinitz.[4] Were you told what he said to me?

---

[1] Source: National Archives, RG 59, Records of Henry Kissinger, 1973–77, Box 16, Nodis Memcons, March 1976, Folder 2. Secret; Nodis. Drafted by Draper on March 16. The meeting took place at the Department of State.

[2] Between January 20 and January 22, Syria introduced "a controlled and strictly limited movement into Lebanon [of] Syrian-controlled PLA and Sa'iqa units" in an effort to broker a cease-fire, which was agreed to by the major combatants on January 22. (Chronology of Events, April 1976; Ford Library, National Security Adviser, Country Files, Middle East and South Asia, Box 24, Lebanon, Folder 4)

[3] Murphy reported Asad's concern about military coups in Lebanon, but noted that Asad gave no indication of plans to send Syrian regular troops into Lebanon. (Telegram 1483 from Damascus, March 15; National Archives, RG 59, Central Foreign Policy Files)

[4] No memorandum of conversation has been found.

Mr. Atherton: Yes.

The Secretary: Can we get in touch with the factions in Lebanon and use our influence?

Mr. Atherton: Not effectively. Not at this time. The only really effective channel of influence with the Lebanese is Syria, or through Syria.

Mr. Atherton: I should have said before that Khatib's Lebanese Arab Army has been moving up from the south and may be aiming at a confrontation with the President in his Palace. But the PLA—and it may be under instructions from Syria—may try to prevent Khatib from moving on the Palace. This suggests that the Syrians want a peaceful resolution of the presidential question.

The Secretary: Dinitz told me that Syrian regulars were already going into Lebanon.

Mr. Saunders: We have no confirmation of this. The reports that Syrian regulars under the guise of PLA soldiers have entered Lebanon came from two sources: the Phalange clandestine radio station and Reuters. Reuters may have gotten its report from the "rejectionists" and it is of course in their interests to pass on this kind of story. But we do not have any confirmation.

The Secretary: (turning to Mr. Atherton). You should get in touch with Dinitz and tell him that we have no confirmation that Syrian regulars have entered Lebanon. Tell him that I have instructed you to say that, if Israeli military actions are taken as a result, it would raise the most serious problems with us ... or words to that effect.[5] We have to be informed in advance.

Mr. Atherton: The Syrians may feel they have to do something if the situation gets worse. The most immediate question is whether you should send a further signal to Asad.

The Secretary: There is no way—no way—in which the Israelis will sit still while the Syrians send in their troops. I am sure of that.

Mr. Atherton: Maybe the Israelis could put up with limited moves. Toon had a long talk with Allon back in October about this[6] and Allon indicated circumstances under which ...

The Secretary: Allon is a fool. A sweet fool, but a fool all the same. No, I'm afraid that we could never exert enough influence to stop Israel.

---

[5] Atherton met with Dinitz the evening of March 15 to tell him that there were no reports of Syrian troops moving into Lebanon. (Telegram 63758 to Tel Aviv, March 16; ibid.)

[6] Reported in telegram 6750 from Tel Aviv, October 24, 1975. (Ibid.)

Mr. Atherton: There are risks in letting things rush on the way they are.

The Secretary: Why not let things rush on?

Mr. Atherton: There may be a clash building up between the military forces supporting the President in his palace and Khatib's forces and others. This could bring down Frangie.

The Secretary: Why not let Frangie go that way?

Mr. Atherton: It would have a long-term negative effect. It would be harder to develop a political solution. There are other things. The drift is towards partition.

Mr. Day: Asad's prestige—and his position in the Arab world—have been enhanced by his initial success in bringing about a Lebanese solution. He has committed so much that he can hardly afford to let the situation unravel. He has a lot to lose. He gave up his trip to Paris because of the problem in Lebanon.

The Secretary: The introduction of Syrian forces would shift the balance further against the Christians.

Mr. Atherton: That's true. And the Christians have lost some of what had been preserved for them through the Syrian mediation.

The Secretary: We have to go back to Asad. Tell Murphy to get in touch with him. Ask him what he is up to and, if we agree with him, we will do our best to help him. But warn him what he does must be done without the use of Syrian regular forces. In that event, we will guarantee that the Israelis do not interfere. Have him tell us what he thinks will be the outcome of what he is doing, and what he wants as the outcome. Tell him I am optimistic we will be able to guarantee that there will be no Israeli action as long as outside forces are not introduced into Lebanon—not in just those words, but in accord with this view.[7] What do you think?

Mr. Saunders: I agree with you that we can not hold out any expectations to the Syrians that the Israelis will not move if Syrian forces come in.

Mr. Day: There may be a chance that the Israelis would not go in.

The Secretary: No, not at this time. Particularly at this time when Rabin is so weak. He would rather have a confrontation with us than face his opposition. He would move ahead and deal with us when we try to stop him, before he would go back and take on his opponents.

The Secretary: Have Murphy tell Asad separately that I was very pleased about the warmth of his reception to Simon.[8] Tell Asad that, as

---

[7] The instructions were sent in telegram 63334 to Damascus, March 16. (Ibid.)

[8] Secretary of the Treasury William Simon visited Damascus March 13.

was discussed between him and Simon, we will do our best . . . we will proceed along the lines of strengthening our economic relations in all possible ways.

The Secretary: Also have him give Asad my best personal regards.

Mr. Atherton: You may want to think about when to bring Murphy back. I assume you would want him out of town by the time Hussein arrives.

The Secretary: Yes, that's true. I want him to get back and talk to Asad by about the 28th, or when Hussein is here.[9] Perhaps he should come here by mid-week of next week, the 25th or 26th. That would work.

Mr. Atherton: That's fine.

The Secretary: Roy, I would like you to stay behind for a minute.

---

[9] King Hussein arrived in Washington on March 29 for a State visit.

---

268. Memorandum of Conversation[1]

Washington, March 23, 1976, 9:30 p.m.

PARTICIPANTS

The Secretary
Gen. Scowcroft, NSC
Bill Hyland, NSC
Under Secretary Sisco
Deputy Assistant Secretary Day
Ambassador Murphy, Syria
Jock Covey, Notetaker

SUBJECT

Lebanon

The Secretary: Now that we have NEA involved, we probably have 500 State Department officers working on the problem. How are we going to keep it out of the press?

---

[1] Source: Library of Congress, Manuscript Division, Kissinger Papers, CL 347, State Department Memorandum of Conversations, Internal, December 1975–March 1976. Secret; Sensitive.

Day: There are only two officers working on this. Me and Draper—the Lebanon country officer.

The Secretary: We can't very well do this without the country director. Who else has he brought into it?

Day: No one.

The Secretary: All right. Where are we then?

Sisco: We have been greatly encouraged by Khaddam's response.[2] It's obvious to me personally that he is going to wait.

The Secretary: Where is Dinitz?

Scowcroft: He's standing by in his office.

The Secretary: (asks his secretary to have Dinitz come over) What did you and Brent tell him today?

Sisco: Just what you told us to tell him. Just what was in the cable.[3] Here, this is a pretty good summary of what we told him.

The Secretary: Now who did this go to?

Sisco: Only 60 posts (laughter). Actually it went only to Tel Aviv and Damascus.

The Secretary: What was the classification?

Sisco: The highest—that means it will take at least 48 hours to reach the *New York Times*. (laughter)

The Secretary: Who is the Chargé while you are gone?

Murphy: Pelletreau.[4]

The Secretary: Is he a good man?

Murphy: Definitely. He's been there for about a year and ...

The Secretary: What would he have to do for you to admit that he isn't a good man?

Murphy: I'd have to admit that I hadn't picked him myself.

The Secretary: You picked him?

Murphy: Yes. After you took Scotes away, I had my chance to pick whoever I wanted.

Sisco: So far he's doing a very good job.

As I look ahead I personally feel that the first move ought to be to try to get the Syrians to institute some minimal arrangement ...

The Secretary: The first problem is to ask him what he has on his mind.

---

[2] Khaddam's request is in telegram 722 from Damascus, March 23. (National Archives, RG 59, Central Foreign Policy Files, P850107–2570)

[3] See telegram 70097 to Damascus, March 23. (Ibid., P840089–2117)

[4] Robert H. Pelletreau, Jr.

Murphy: We don't know yet whether he's been able to get back to Khaddam.

The Secretary: Well, if he hasn't, tell him to get back in first thing in the morning. It's important to know what they have in mind. There is quite a difference between sending in 2,000 or 20,000 troops. What do you think they have on their mind?

Murphy: More than 2,000 ...

The Secretary: Well, how long do you think they're going to stay? How will we ever get them to leave?

Day: Khaddam said that he really had no clear idea of what sort of numbers they might be dealing with.

Murphy: But it's interesting that Khaddam is concerned about getting the PLO out as soon as possible. He is afraid of the resentment that is building up against them.

The Secretary: But then who would have the forces to hold the situation together?

Murphy: Well, the politicians seem to be coming together. And if that works, then the need for military presence would diminish.

The Secretary: But that's just not realistic. That hasn't worked from the beginning. It's important now to get them to tell us what they have in mind. It's one thing if the Syrians tell us that they will be going in for one week and then withdraw, or even if they intend to go in for a month and we give our own guarantee that they'll withdraw. That's one situation. But it is entirely different if the Syrians go in with no intention of leaving. The Israelis simply won't accept that. What do you think?

Hyland: The Israelis certainly won't accept any sort of permanent presence.

The Secretary: What is your solution?

Sisco: Well, I think personally that what we need is a very modest augmentation of the Syrian forces. Let them bring in a few units on a well-camouflaged basis. I don't think it would pose any great problems for Israel. They would understand that the augmentation groups would pull out the moment a political solution has been arranged. Also, other PLA units could simultaneously concentrate to share the role of separating the forces.

The Secretary: How do you put that to Asad? How do you make that into a proposal?

Sisco: Only with the agreement of Israel.

The Secretary: Yes, but how do you propose to the Syrians that they move troops into Lebanon.

Murphy: That would mean that they would have to pull troops out of hot spots like Tripoli, and that those troops would themselves have to be replaced ... although they could draw on some of those 5,000 Saudis that are in Syria.

The Secretary: Saudis in Syria ... What do they do?

Murphy: Nothing much. They sit around in highly polished trucks. They've been there ever since the war and they could be put where they are needed in order to free some of the other troops.

Sisco: The trouble would be with Egypt.

Scowcroft: Yes, they would believe that we had connived with Syria to allow them to infiltrate troops into Lebanon.

The Secretary: What's your idea?

Hyland: Strategically, it's a real opportunity for Syria. The problem is with Egypt.

The Secretary: The only way this could be made tolerable to Israel would be with an American guarantee. They would only use a Syrian move to justify an attack on Southern Lebanon. And if we tell the Syrians that it's okay for them to move, then I'll be up to my ass in alligators with the Egyptians.

What do you think the Israeli perceptions are?

Scowcroft: What surprises me so much is how relaxed they've been for the last two weeks.

The Secretary: Maybe they think they can move in. Their secret dream for weeks has been that they could move in and clear up Fatah-land. You know I issued a strong warning to both sides while I was in Dallas.[5]

Sisco: Let's go back a little bit. Personally I think we probably ought to hear what Dinitz has to say first. There can't be any augmentation without risks. So we should continue to do what we are doing. You saw the report [*less than 1 line not declassified*] today.

The Secretary: It's beginning to look as if Syria is ready to move.

Hyland: That could be.

The Secretary: What does Kirk think? You have all the information he would have don't you?

Hyland: Yes. You saw the Defense Attaché in Damascus reports that the Syrians are massing just about at exactly the place where they would group if they were going to go in.

The Secretary: What's making me so uneasy—what doesn't make any sense to me, is that Israel is so relaxed. It's just not natural. They must know something that we don't know. For one thing our exchange

---

[5] Kissinger made a speech and held a news conference in Dallas on March 22 and 23.

of information has been completely one sided. We have briefed them, but what have they given us?

By the way, where is Atherton? Is he on his way back?

Sisco: Yes, that was arranged today.

The Secretary: Atherton was briefing them daily at my request. [*2 lines not declassified*]

Hyland: They know everything that we know.

The Secretary: But do we know everything that they know.

Sisco: Well let's just be absolutely accurate. We told them our assessment and they told us their assessment so in that sense it was a two sided exchange of information.

The Secretary: Look, it's just not in their nature to behave this way. Israel will seize on any adverse development and use it to push for more arms or milk us for assistance. And they are not doing it.

Sisco: Just so that we can get it on the record: there are actually two other options that we haven't considered. Number 1, there's the possibility of a mixed Arab force, and number 2, it might be possible to arrange a UN cease-fire, to set up some sort of Waldheim instrumentality ... although that would simply act as a cover for the Syrians ...

The Secretary: Syria would never accept a mixed Arab force.

Murphy: The last time we mentioned it was about two months ago. Their response was quite negative.

Sisco: They viewed it as an anti-Syrian move.

Hyland: What I find so fascinating is that virtually yesterday they were pushing for a political solution, and today they're ready to climb right in.

The Secretary: There's no doubt that Sadat is trying to become the spokesman for all the radicals.

Day: One reason that the Syrians might have got their wind up is that what happened over the weekend was probably seen as a significant victory for their enemies. The PLO and the other radical Arabs scored some substantial gains and the Syrians are of course trying to support the Christians.

Sisco: It's weird. It is truly weird. It only proves how unpredictable it can be to work in the Middle East.

The Secretary: This report from Damascus—I think I could just read it to Dinitz.

Sisco: Yes, I think it is a very calming and reassuring cable. The Syrians are trying very hard to be responsible.

The Secretary: I don't think we need to send anything out to Syria before tomorrow morning. They won't move without hearing from us.

After I see Dinitz, we should meet again to figure out what we are going to say to the Syrians.

Scowcroft: The problem if Syria goes in is how to get them out. There has to be an understanding that they would be replaced within a given period by a mixed force or a UN group ...

The Secretary: Never. You think that if the Syrians go in as a solitary force that they would ever leave only to be replaced by other Arabs?

Murphy: That would mean virtual annexation. I don't think they really want to do that.

But it is interesting that they have come to us this time and that they seem to recognize the risks. Only a week ago Asad seemed to be genuinely—physically—surprised when I explained to him the Israeli factor.[6]

Hyland: It's just strange that they should have been so optimistic and so relaxed, and only five days later be ready to go tearing in. It's true that they came to us, but if they came to us then they must have gone to the Russians, too.

The Secretary: Should we go to the Russians?

Hyland: Not now, I don't think. You know Gromyko is in London?

The Secretary: If Gromyko is in London then we could always ask Callaghan to approach him.

Scowcroft: Would Syria have been talking to the British?

Sisco: No, I don't think so. Khaddam did say that they were also consulting with others but he did not say with whom.

The Secretary: There would be no problem with the Syrians if we discussed this with the British. And the Syrians couldn't object if the British on their own took it to Gromyko.

Sisco: It's still early.

Hyland: If Dinitz says that a move by Syria would be intolerable, where are we then?

The Secretary: First thing is to get some answers to my questions. We need time. Everything hinges on the Syrian response. We need some information—like how many Syrians are they planning to send across? What are they going to do? How long will it take them to do it? If we go back to them for the information we gain at least 24 hours. Rather than say that they should do this or they should do that, we should get some answers to our questions. It will also help to keep the Israelis quiet. Those sons of bitches are awfully eager to give the Syrians a real blow.

---

[6] See footnote 3, Document 267.

(Meeting interrupted for small group discussion with Ambassador Dinitz, and resumes after 30 minutes.)[7]

The Secretary: What is your judgment now if the Syrians move in—if Israel says it will leave only if Syria leaves. Oh, you didn't hear Dinitz' proposal. Le me recap them for you quickly. Their position is that they cannot trust the Syrians. They are not at all sure that the Syrians would leave if they go in, so that if they do go in, the Israelis would then quietly take over strategic points in Southern Lebanon and in effect hold them hostage till the Syrians leave.

Murphy: Did he give you any specifics?

The Secretary: I asked him to get some specific answers to our questions back by tomorrow morning. What he means by "strategic," what he means by "quietly" and so on. I asked Dinitz, what if Syria tells us they intend to go in for three weeks and we provide a United States guarantee that they will get out when they say they will. He told me that the domestic situation in Israel probably would not permit it. I'm inclined to say, screw the domestic situation. That's not our most fundamental problem. Our real problems will be with Egypt.

Day: And there may be other problems with the timing. What if we give our guarantee and it comes time for the Syrians to get out, but the situation is still falling apart and it's obvious that the Syrians are the only ones that can hold it together?

Murphy: It would be fairly easy for the Syrians to tell us how many people they intend to send. But I don't see any way they could tell us how long they expect to be there. And in any event, it's bound to get out that the Israelis are holding Southern Lebanon hostage.

The Secretary: They would announce it.

Sisco: They can't possibly keep it quiet. They would be fighting . . .

The Secretary: With the PLO. For them that would make it all worthwhile. But then again, maybe they would go in there like the U.S., and make a lot of noise without actually making contact . . . send in some F–4's to do figure 8's.

Sisco: Now I finally understand why the Israelis have been so relaxed over the last few days.

The Secretary: They have just been dreaming of an opportunity to go in and clean up Fatahland.

Murphy: But that would only push the Fedayeen north.

The Secretary: That's all right. That means they would be further away from the border.

---

[7] No memorandum of conversation for this meeting has been found.

Hyland: Would that be bad for the U.S.? I don't think it would be worse.

The Secretary: But how can the Syrians tell the Israelis it's all right to run around Southern Lebanon. What would they tell the Egyptians? And what if the Syrians break the agreement?

Day: They can't be a party to any such agreement and still remain leaders in the Arab world.

Murphy: Sadat will say that Asad is a traitor to the Arab cause.

Sisco: Sadat would be sorely tempted to put himself up as the defender of the PLO. I think it's highly significant that they had now come to us. Henry what do you think it says to us about Syrian relations with the Soviets?

Scowcroft: While you were in the back room, Bar-On just casually dropped the fact that they considered going to the UN.

The Secretary: Dinitz also rejected the mixed Arab force idea. That would simply be a 24-hour expedient in any case. Look, they simply want Syria to go ahead and take the north. That means they get Southern Lebanon.

Hyland: That wouldn't be so bad in terms of U.S. interest. Except that the Israelis would then have that part of Lebanon where they would have a guerilla war on their hands.

The Secretary: Listen, there are no guerilla wars where the territory is occupied by a force with no moral compunctions. You remember there was never any guerilla activity in the Korean zone in Vietnam.

Day: I just don't see how we can be a party to any operation that allows Israel to take over part of Lebanon.

The Secretary: No, we wouldn't be a party to any proposal. We have to be able to tell both sides we're opposed. But the first problem is to keep everybody quiet and to force both sides to answer our questions. Right now we have to tell the Syrians that we know. And it's also time to talk to Egypt, because if it comes out later that we knew all of this and never told the Egyptians . . .

All right, let's tell the Syrians that we have to get answers to the following questions: How many troops they want to send and where they want to put them; what guarantees are there that they will leave and when they will get out. We have to tell them that it's essential to have their answers before we can make any judgment as to the best course. But our cable should begin with a statement of the dangers that we see, that the dangers of a move outweigh any foreseeable benefits. Then we can say that it is our judgment that if they move, that Israel will then move into Southern Lebanon—I would not tell them yet that we have discussed the situation with Israel—and we need to know what their reaction would be in that situation.

Sisco: That still sounds an awful lot like a U.S. proposal.

The Secretary: You are right. We should ask him simply to elicit as much as he can about their intentions. To just sound them out about their thinking. It's a pity you're not there because you could go in to see Asad.

Murphy: Just tell him to see Asad.

The Secretary: Can he do that?

Murphy: Yes, by all means.

Sisco: Khaddam so far has been all right. He has been quite reasonable.

The Secretary: Asad is simply much wiser than Khaddam, but let's keep it at the Khaddam level.

All right. Then I better get Dinitz in to say we need answers to our questions to them. And we had better make it clear that we do not acquiesce in their moving into Southern Lebanon. I will not tell Dinitz that I am telling the Syrians about them wanting to move into Southern Lebanon. If they knew that, they might try to pre-empt us. I think that's about all we can do for tonight.

Scowcroft: Well, we should get something out to the Egyptians.

The Secretary: Yes, but let's talk about that after I talk to Dinitz now. (meeting interrupted for small group meeting with Dinitz and resumes after 15 minutes)[8]

The Secretary: Okay, now what do we do with Egypt? My fear is that Syria will tell all of this to some Arab and the talk will go around and get back to Egypt. In fact, this whole thing could by a Syrian ploy to break up our relations with Egypt. We've got to tell the Egyptians something. I think it's important to tell them that the Syrians are thinking seriously of moving into Lebanon and that this presents a high risk of provoking an Israeli response. Then we should ask them if they have any ideas about how this situation should be dealt with.

Sisco: Henry, I just want to point out to you that in a previous cable, the Egyptians made two suggestions about what should be done. First, that we should press the Syrians to get out of Lebanon entirely. Now they obviously won't do that and even if they did it would simply leave the whole country in the hands of the PLO. Second, they demand that Franjieh be pressed for his immediate resignation. Now, that would not get anybody anywhere, and in any case it is already part of the Syrian plan.

Now I just hope that whatever we send to the Egyptians won't cause them to go back over this whole litany. We can't say very much in

---

[8] No memorandum of conversation for the meeting has been found.

any case. It can be a very short cable. In a way I am more concerned about it causing the Egyptians to get themselves involved.

The Secretary: That's okay. That would be one more reason for the Syrians not to go in, and even if they did, then it would be an inter-Arab problem. No, we simply have to warn both sides very strongly. You should add that sentence from Dallas (press conference) about the warning. Tell Eilts to go in to see Fahmy urgently and tell Porter to go to the Saudis to do the same. And we should also send one to Hussein.[9] You know, all we are doing is telling them the truth.

Hyland: It is the literal truth. After all, Franjieh himself has invited them in.

Sisco: Why not mention that, since it's going to come out by tomorrow anyway.

The Secretary: Then we don't have to mention it. It would only complicate it. Let's keep it as it is. Mention to Hussein that based on his experience he can probably see that the Israelis are just looking for an opportunity to make a blow against Syria.

Hyland: So where do you think we come out at the end?

The Secretary: I simply am not very eager to do anything with Syria that would allow them to drive the Egyptians and the PLO out. The only result would be that the Israelis would go in and clear out the PLO, and they would be seen to be doing it in collusion with us. It might be different if we could get an iron-clad guarantee that they would be out in three weeks.

Hyland: It would be very interesting if it worked out that way. It would show that we can get agreements and get people to stick to them.

The Secretary: But we simply can't let the Israelis go in, and yet it would be almost impossible to keep them out.

Scowcroft: Exactly. How in the world could you possibly keep them out?

The Secretary: Then the answer is probably to keep the Syrians out.

---

[9] These instructions were sent in telegram 71006 to Cairo, March 24 (National Archives, RG 59, Central Foreign Policy Files, P840090–2124), telegram 70405 to Jidda, March 24, (ibid., N760002–0551), and telegram 71008 to Amman, March 25 (Ibid., P840090–2126).

269. Memorandum of Conversation[1]

Washington, March 24, 1976, 9:45–10:45 a.m.

PARTICIPANTS

    President Ford
    Dr. Henry A. Kissinger, Secretary of State
    Donald Rumsfeld, Secretary of Defense
    Brent Scowcroft, Assistant to the President for National Security Affairs

SUBJECT

    Lebanon

President: Of highest importance is Lebanon. Henry?

Kissinger: Let me bring you up to date. We sent a message to the Syrians last night asking a series of questions about their possible military action. This was designed to waste time. We also sent cables to Egypt, Jordan and Saudi Arabia[2]—but not saying the information came from Syria. We asked the Syrians what they thought of a UN force or an inter-Arab force, and we said we would help with any political solution.

We told Callaghan to raise it with Gromyko who is in London. We didn't want to do it directly because Syria maybe had not gone to them, and it was not the first time they (Syria) came to us. Callaghan reported back to me that Gromyko hadn't heard anything but said he would check. If it makes them mad and they restrain Syria, that helps.

We have a really bizarre situation in Lebanon. Syria is supporting the conservatives and Christians against the PLO and the Communists. Egypt is supporting the leftists and the PLO against Syria. The Soviet Union should be supporting Syria, but it also supports the PLO. Israel is, of course, against the PLO. We cannot allow Israel to go into South Lebanon. If we don't restrain them, there will be a UN Security Council meeting where we will either have to condemn them or veto—and either one is bad.

President: What about the fighting? They are massacring each other.

Kissinger: Unfortunately, I am afraid that is going to continue.

Kissinger/Rumsfeld/Scowcroft: [Discussion of the numbers of Syrian and Egyptian PLA troops in Lebanon.]

---

[1] Source: Ford Library, National Security Adviser, Memoranda of Conversations, Box 18, March 24, 1976, Ford, Kissinger, Rumsfeld, Scowcroft. Secret; Sensitive. The meeting was held in the Oval Office. Brackets are in the original.

[2] See footnote 9, Document 268.

President: What would the Syrians do about Israel going in?

Kissinger: They would have to oppose Israel taking over any more "holy" Arab land. Even though it might start as an inter-Arab fight, they would all turn on the Israelis.

Rumsfeld: [Describes numbers of potential evacuees and our resources.]

President: What is next? Do we wait to hear from Syria?

Kissinger: Let's look at our objectives. If Syria could go in quickly and clean it out, it would be good. They would leave the PLO in the same condition as in Jordan.

Rumsfeld: That is not reasonable.

Kissinger: The best attainable outcome would be to have no one in. We may not be able to keep them out anyway. Syria's prestige is involved and Egypt would like to humiliate them.

Rumsfeld: Don't the Israelis have a domestic problem if they don't go in?

Kissinger: That is true. We would have to put massive pressure on Israel and say wait three weeks to see whether the Syrians leave again.

[More discussion]

The best would be if they don't go in, but that will be a put down by us and we will pay for it down the pike. My guess is the approach to us is a trial balloon and they would have gone in if we had given them a green light. I think now they may not.

President: What will happen if no one goes in?

Scowcroft: If no one does, the PLO will take over.

[Considerable discussion of our overall policy in the Lebanon situation.]

270. Minutes of Washington Special Actions Group Meeting[1]

Washington, March 24, 1976, 11:10 a.m.

SUBJECT

Lebanon

PARTICIPANTS

Chairman
Henry A. Kissinger

State
Robert Ingersoll

DOD
William Clements

JCS
Gen. George S. Brown

CIA
Lt. Gen. Vernon Walters

NSC Staff
Lt. Gen. Brent Scowcroft
William G. Hyland
Michael Hornblow

Gen. Walters: Read attached situation report.[2]

Secretary Kissinger: We have had some feelers from the Syrians. That information must be closely held. We have also discussed this with the Israelis who would go into southern Lebanon under these conditions. There is a curious lineup here with the Syrians, the anti-PLO people, the Christians on one side. I never thought I would read in a cable that the Syrians want to reduce Communist influence in Lebanon. We asked Callaghan to discuss this indirectly with the Soviets. Gromyko said that he had not been told by the Syrians that they contemplate a move. We have also approached the Saudis, Jordanians and the Egyptians. We have not yet heard back from the Egyptians. They are playing a shortsighted but tricky game by supporting the Communists and the PLO in Lebanon as a way of getting out of the box they were put in by the Sinai Agreement. We have not yet heard back from the Syrians. If they go into Lebanon they may never leave. It might be alright though if they were to go in and put out the PLO and then could be replaced by a UN force.

---

[1] Source: Ford Library, NSC Institutional Files, Box 25, Meeting Minutes, WSAG-Originals, March–April 1976. Top Secret. The original is marked "Part II of II." This meeting was held in the White House Situation Room.

[2] Situation report not attached and not found.

Gen. Brown: If the Syrians go in the Israelis might move further in the Golan and might go all the way to the Latali River.

Secretary Kissinger: Once the Syrians go in they might never go out. There are already 4,000 Syrians in Lebanon. Then if the Israelis go in there would be additional complications and they might not get out and would be discussing old Syrian conquered territory and new Syrian territory.

Mr. Clements: And that area is a hell of a lot more desirable than the Sinai.

Secretary Kissinger: It could lead to a bloody fight.

Mr. Clements: What about the mixed force idea?

Secretary Kissinger: We haven't received an answer from anyone on that except Jordan, and they say it won't work.

Mr. Ingersoll: What about Egypt?

Secretary Kissinger: We have no answer from them. A joint force seems inconceivable.

Gen. Brown: What about the Turks?

Gen. Walters: No that would not work.

Secretary Kissinger: There is the possibility of having a UN force composed mainly of Arabs. The problem is that if Israel goes in then all the other Arab states might enter.

Mr. Clements: Yes and it could also play hell with our getting Saudi Arabian oil.

Secretary Kissinger: I was just with the President and told him the Saudis might cut off oil again.

Gen. Brown: In case of a possible evacuation from Beirut we have moved a small force just off of Greece only 40 hours away from Lebanon. The balance of the 6th fleet is off to the West.

Secretary Kissinger: How many carriers do we now have in the Mediterranean?

Gen. Brown: Two, but not close at all.

Secretary Kissinger: Both in the Mediterranean.

Gen. Brown: Yes.

Secretary Kissinger: What reinforcement capabilities do we have?

Gen. Brown: We have reasonable reinforcement capabilities in Europe. There are 1200 marines in the Mediterranean and Army divisions in Europe and a fair amount of airlift capabilities.

Secretary Kissinger: How would you fly there?

Gen. Brown: We could overfly Austria and Italy.

Secretary Kissinger: If there is a war in the Middle East it could get totally out of control. This is because of foreign perceptions of US policy arising out of the domestic situation. If war breaks out my recommendation to the President would be to pour things into the Mediterranean as fast as possible in case the Soviets decide to make a move. We could not face a two week war now.

Mr. Clements: I agree one hundred percent. Of course the real treasure in the area is those 300 billion barrels of oil in Saudi Arabia. There is no other prize like it in the world.

Gen. Brown: I won't quarrel with that but we don't have any force in the Indian Ocean anymore.

Mr. Clements: There are a lot of people with an eye on that treasure.

Secretary Kissinger: If there is a war we just can't afford to fall on our faces. If in the wake of Angola[3] there is a perception of US indecisiveness it could be disastrous. I don't know if we can put any forces in the Indian Ocean. George and Bill, would you go back and see what forces could be available in a crisis. If there is a war perhaps we should appear to be a little reckless. Iraq can now move in greater forces than previously.

Gen. Walters: Yes, they now have 700 tank transports and that can move two Iraqi divisions.

Secretary Kissinger: Really. I didn't know that. I don't want the fact of the Syrian query to get around town.

Gen. Brown: It is encouraging that they have done this without letting the USSR know about it.

Secretary Kissinger: If we had freedom of action we could perhaps act differently. We could let the Syrians move and break the back of the PLO. In a strange way this is a strategic opportunity which we shall miss. The Syrian approach to us is encouraging and I never thought I would read in a cable that the Syrian foreign minister wants to reduce Communist influence in Lebanon.

Mr. Clements: Our difficulty is that we want to have our cake and eat it too.

Secretary Kissinger: If we could get the Syrians in and out again without the Israelis coming in. . . .

Gen. Walters: It could not be done without the Israelis moving.

Secretary Kissinger: And if the Israelis move into southern Lebanon that would unite the Arabs. Do you all agree?

Mr. Clements: I agree.

Gen. Walters: I agree.

---

[3] See *Foreign Relations, 1969–1976*, volume XXVIII, Southern Africa.

Secretary Kissinger: A UN meeting would not help and could lead to a condemnation of Israel.

Gen. Scowcroft: And there could be an oil embargo.

Gen. Brown: How about putting a US force in southern Lebanon in order to prevent an Israeli move? This could prevent something that could lead into a disaster.

Secretary Kissinger: Why don't you look into that. I am not sure Israel would hold still for that unless it would prevent a guerrilla war with the PLO.

271. Memorandum of Conversation[1]

Washington, March 24, 1976, 2:20 p.m.

PARTICIPANTS

    The Secretary
    Gen. Scowcroft
    Under Secretary Sisco
    Deputy Assistant Secretary Day
    Ambassador Murphy
    Bill Hyland, NSC
    Jock Covey, Notetaker

SUBJECT

    Lebanon

The Secretary: I want to go over this cable from Cairo.[2] There's a phrase in there that sticks in my mind about "Asad's pre-eminent position." And did we ever talk to the Pope . . . ?

Day: We have gone over all of the traffic and have found nothing to support . . .

The Secretary: I just have the uneasy feeling—can we make sure that there isn't someone around here making independent policy?

Day: You know that all along our people in the Vatican . . .

The Secretary: What people in the Vatican?

---

[1] Source: Library of Congress, Manuscript Division, Kissinger Papers, CL 347, Department of State Memorandum of Conversations, Internal, December 1975–March 1976. Secret; Sensitive.

[2] Apparently a reference to telegram 3885 from Cairo, March 24. (National Archives, RG 59, Central Foreign Policy Files, P850107–1780)

Day: That is our people in the Embassy in Rome have been consulting on the Lebanon situation with the Vatican.

The Secretary: Well, there's no doubt that we have encouraged the Syrian role. There's just this one phrase that bothers me because it sounds almost like something we could have said. Well, rather than waste time looking for it, let's talk about where we are now. I am not prepared to risk our Egyptian relationship for the Syrians. If the Egyptians are that much up in arms about it, we are going to have to do our best to keep the Syrians out.

And now I see there's another message from Hussein.[3]

Sisco: Yes, you will see he is saying to you that rather than restrain Asad, we should show him some understanding. In effect he is asking you quite directly, what is Asad to do if the leftists take over. He clearly is using this occasion to defend Asad to us.

The Secretary: It's a god damn good letter. I think we ought to send a message to Hussein saying that we found his letter thoughtful, that we share his concern about restraining the Israelis, and that we want to be cooperative and help bring about a solution to the problems he describes—to avoid a takeover by the radical rejectionists.

Sisco: Except how are you actually going to prevent it.?

The Secretary: I agree we don't know how, but we can say we agree with his analysis—that we haven't identified a means yet to prevent what he is so concerned about. But we also see no way that the Syrians can move in without triggering a response by the Israelis. And we should say to him that we would be interested in anything that he can see that we should do to help achieve his political objectives.

Day: You know we have not really been active in Lebanon for quite some time now and it probably would be a good idea to talk to the factions.

The Secretary: Do we have someone there with brains, or are they all hotshots? I don't know this fellow Lambrakis.[4] Is he a Greek? (laughter)

Sisco: Yes.

Day: He carries out his instructions well, and he is cautious and careful. As a Chargé, when he is given instructions, he follows them carefully.

Scowcroft: You mean as opposed to an Ambassador (laughter).

---

[3] Telegram 1581 from Amman, March 24. (Ford Library, National Security Adviser, Country Files, Middle East and South Asia, Box 23, Department of State Telegrams to the Secretary of State, Jordan, Folder 23)

[4] After Ambassador Godley left Beirut on January 13, Lambrakis served as Chargé of the Embassy.

Day: In talking to the factions we should not take any risks. There should be no bold ventures, but it would be easy enough to contact some of the faction leaders.

The Secretary: What I really want is to hear from Asad and to tell him that we agree with his analysis and are trying to avoid the same outcome that he is. We could tell him that we've heard from Hussein. Although, on second thought, I think we better wait for his reply.

Day: Something that has been bothering me is that we may not get a reply from Asad. He may assume that what we sent him is our response.

The Secretary: No my problem is that I simply have no confidence in the judgment of the people who are there. I don't know them. Even if I did have confidence, what objective would we be pursuing?

If we send a message to Asad, we could repeat some of what Hussein says, indicate we share the assessment and that we want to insure that our Embassy in Beirut is working in parallel with his efforts—not at cross purposes. So if he can give us an idea of what he is trying to do ... But if Asad then shows that to the Egyptians we would be in great trouble.

Sisco: On this idea of trying to do something locally, I personally don't feel that we have anyone there who can do it. It is essentially a job of brokering between the parties and we don't have anyone at a sufficiently high level. I simply don't have the same confidence in Lambrakis. I don't think it would produce anything and I think it would be dangerous.

Day: Well, it's not really a brokering role. In the past, we made ourselves useful convincing the Christians that they should ...

Sisco: Well, of course a specific démarche would be another matter.

The Secretary: I think we ought to ask Asad again what he thinks we can do to encourage the solution that he envisiges.

Sisco: Well, we are still waiting for his answer to our first query.

The Secretary: Okay, but we should ask Hussein what diplomatic steps he recommends to achieve these objectives.

Sisco: He may want to seek Asad's views.

The Secretary: That's okay, but we should not be the ones to suggest that he do it. There's no rush on this. It can wait for a few hours in order to see the cables before they go out.

What is your instinct? Mine is that they won't move and that they won't raise it with the Soviets. I told the British to go to the Soviets and say that they had their own sources that told them the Syrians were seriously contemplating a move into Lebanon. The British were then to ask the Soviets to use their influence to restrain the Syrians. That way the Soviets would share the responsibility for restraining the Syrians.

Murphy: It's my personal feeling that the message last night to Damascus[5] would have been very chilling to the Syrians if they were actually ready to make a move.

The Secretary: But do you think it was sufficiently friendly?

Murphy: Yes, it was warm enough, but where it counted it was firm.

The Secretary: Given the likely Egyptian reaction and the Israeli reaction, allowing the Syrians to go in would just be opening an impossible can of worms. If the Syrians go in, the Israelis would almost certainly go in themselves. They would probably tell us to buzz off—face us down.

Sisco: Can you tell the Secretary how all of this has affected Asad's internal position in Syria?

Murphy: It's the first time in years that he's been so far out in front on such a major loss. The last time I saw him he told me, my people have a lot of relatives in Lebanon and they're asking me why we haven't been able to get a settlement. He is deeply involved.

The Secretary: But the sticky thing is the absolutely unconscionable Israeli behavior. I would risk Egyptian displeasure if we could keep the Israelis out. But we cannot risk a Syrian move, and an Egyptian, and an Israeli reaction. The end result would be exactly what we have worked all these years to avoid: it would create Arab unity. Worse yet, it could lead to a war.

Now if I could design the solution, I would go to Asad and say "if you could move in quickly, and if you could give us an iron clad guarantee that you will get out again quickly and that you will not go south of the river, we will keep the Israelis out." I would tell that to Hussein too. The problem is, under the present circumstances, I don't think we could bring it off. The Egyptian displeasure we could handle. But if Israel goes in, Egypt would lead the charge against Syria and then Syria would be forced to attack Israel. You don't seriously think that Asad could permit Israel to move into Southern Lebanon without attacking it, do you?

Murphy: That's something I've been thinking about quite a bit overnight and I have come to agree with that. I think he would have to attack.

The Secretary: He would have to defend those PLO camps.

---

[5] See footnote 3, Document 268.

Murphy: All he really wants is to maintain his own little kingdom. To keep his relations with the PLO, and Jordan, and Lebanon all in tidy order.

The Secretary: The thing those idiots in Tel Aviv just don't seem to be able to get through their heads is that if they back Asad up to the wall in Lebanon and he survives it, they still have UNDOF to go through.

Scowcroft: But there is still a great deal of danger in doing nothing. There is the effect it would have on Asad, and the fact that the PLO would probably take over.

The Secretary: Let's be realistic. The only plan that would really work is the one we simply cannot do. The penalty for an Israeli move into Southern Lebanon is just intolerable. The ideal of course would be for the Syrians to move rapidly in and out.

Murphy: If you could actually get them to promise that they would get out quickly, would you take it to Israel?

The Secretary: How would we get them to promise that? Mechanically, how? You would have to be approached at a high level. Could Hussein do it?

Sisco: Hussein could do it. But he would have to get specific commitments about the level of augmentation, the precise political objectives, and get him to tell us that he needs exactly this amount of time. If we could get him to lay it all out like that, it's just conceivable that the Israelis might consider it.

The Secretary: They would never consider it unless the President called in Dinitz and told him that if they didn't agree, there would be no more military assistance, that we would speak against them in the United Nations and support sanctions. Anything short of that would have no effect at all. I tried last night to reason with Dinitz.[6] We simply have to be a bit careful. They are so inflamed after that speech at the UN. You know I talked to Sam Lewis and I expected that we would be making a statement basically explaining the veto about an hour before the vote. The next thing I know, we're delivering it 48 hours before the vote.[7]

Sisco: Well, I think that we will have to explain it to Sadat.

The Secretary: I'm not worried about Sadat. So long as he has no fulcrum for his displeasure.

---

[6] Apparently a reference to the short conversation on March 23. See footnote 8, Document 268.

[7] The United States vetoed a draft UN Security Council resolution that deplored Israeli attempts to change the status of Jerusalem and called on Israel to respect the inviolability of the Holy Places and the rights of Arab inhabitants of the occupied territories. See *Yearbook of the United Nations, 1975,* pp. 250–253.

Sisco: I see what you mean. As long as they are in and out quickly.

The Secretary: No, no, so long as there is no Israeli occupation, Sadat has no leverage. Even if he believes that we colluded with the Syrians—he will be unhappy, but after all, we colluded with Sadat too. His displeasure would not be unbearable.

Sisco: Well, then it should be fairly easy to go to them and argue that there simply is no other way to keep the Israelis out. After all, he doesn't want the leftists and the PLO to take the ascendancy ...

The Secretary: But of course he does. If they take over, it would discredit the Syrians and get them off his back. It would probably drive the Jordanians back into the Egyptian camp. And Israel wouldn't mind if the PLO took over because their position would be easier to maintain in American public opinion if they faced the PLO across their border.

Sisco: I can see it would be good for them. It may even protect their position on the West Bank and in the Gaza.

Murphy: If we don't get an answer soon to the message last night to Asad, would you consider escalating it to a message from the President to Asad rather than wait for Hussein's visit. That would mean another six days.

Sisco: No, I think we ought to wait until we see the reply. Give it another couple of days.

Hyland: What possibility do you see that Asad might digest our message, decide that there are no other options, and move anyway.

The Secretary: It's certainly possible but I have always found him to be a cautious man. We have handed him a tough problem.

Hyland: Maybe. But I wonder if it's possible that they might just let Israel come in.

The Secretary: They would never agree to that.

Hyland: No I don't mean agree to it, but just let it happen. They would of course scream and yell but they might just let it come about without attacking.

The Secretary: Egypt would do its absolute utmost to get Asad to attack Israel. He would have to. Unless I completely misjudge the man, he does not want to be known as the man who permitted Fatahland to be destroyed. He is the one who always says to you, I am first and foremost an Arab. Sadat never tells you that.

Murphy: Have the Israelis tipped their hand at all about the points they would want to occupy?

The Secretary: No, no answer whatsoever. Maybe we'll get an answer later today, or maybe not at all.

Murphy: Maybe it would pan out that they would want less than Dinitz described last night.

Scowcroft: That's very unlikely.

The Secretary: We simply have no answer.

Murphy: That's a good answer.

Day: One last thing before we go, would you have any objection to our arranging for Pickering to come back on Saturday?

The Secretary: Rather than ... ?

Day: Rather than coming earlier. That would give you a chance for one good talk before the visit.

The Secretary: Okay.

272. Memorandum of Conversation[1]

Washington, March 24, 1976, 6 p.m.

PARTICIPANTS

The Secretary, Henry A. Kissinger
Under Secretary Joseph Sisco
Assistant Secretary Alfred L. Atherton
Mr. Day, NEA
Assistant Secretary Hal Saunders
Ambassador Murphy, Ambassador to Syria
Jock Covey, Notetaker

SUBJECT

Lebanon

The Secretary: Did you send that message to Egypt?[2]

Atherton: It should be on the way now.

The Secretary: It was taking so long—you were obviously hoping you wouldn't have to send it.

Atherton: No, it had to be redrafted a bit.

Sisco: If you are determined to go forward with this cable, how are you going to reconcile your position with the Egyptians with what you said in the letter that's going up to the Hill?[3]

---

[1] Source: Library of Congress, Manuscript Division, Kissinger Papers, CL 347, Department of State Memorandum of Conversations, Internal, December 1975–March 1976. Secret; Sensitive.

[2] The message is not further identified.

[3] Letter not further identified.

The Secretary: It's not a question of what's in the letters; it's a question of what can be said at the hearings.[4]

Sisco: What's wrong with the letters?

The Secretary: Those guys are looking for a commitment not to sell but that would just be a slap in the face for the Egyptians. It would be better for the Egyptians to say that they're not going to ask us for anything more.

Sisco: Well, that's certainly okay if it works. But you'll almost certainly get hit up about it tomorrow at the hearings.

The Secretary: I don't know why I have to do these hearings. It's just totally self-serving for the bureau. And I certainly don't know why I have to do it on the first day that they ask for.

Sisco: We assumed that Humphrey was a friend of yours and it would be very hard to turn down.

The Secretary: Each bureau has one project which is impossible to turn down. But I am not convinced that they will focus on the C–130's. (referring to cable) If they raise this, I want you to stress the positive aspect but you have to clearly identify it as being just for Eilts' information. Unless you do, he will surely raise it with them. If we could get the Egyptians to buy that I would be very tempted to put it into our letter to the Hill. They would be morally committed to go along.

Atherton: We just have to be a bit careful about not getting involved in things that will require munitions control licenses.

The Secretary: All right. (gives cable to Atherton) What I called you all together about—Defense called me to say they had learned that this armored division has left the area around Damascus.

Sisco: But this precedes the latest Khaddam response,[5] doesn't it?

The Secretary: They could be just trying to fool us.

Sisco: They may be washing their hands of the Lebanese situation.

Murphy: It could also be just a pressure tactic. Or that they can't do anything for the moment in Lebanon and they're just going to leave them on their own.

Atherton: Sort of a "plague on both your houses." They may be feeling a bit bad. They've been taking quite a beating from the Moslems.

---

[4] Kissinger met on March 25 with Senators Javits, Case, and Humphrey about the Ford administration's plan to sell six C–130 transport aircraft to Egypt under the Foreign Military Sales program.

[5] Apparently a reference to telegram 1787 from Damascus, March 24, which was the most recent response from Khaddam. (National Archives, RG 59, Central Foreign Policy Files, P850107–2576)

The Secretary: I am wondering if we shouldn't send a message to the Egyptians saying that we heard that a Syrian division has left Damascus. Maybe we should tell the little King too but it's probably too late for him.

Sisco: What would be the implications for a Syrian move for the Egyptians?

The Secretary: Oh, they would launch into whatever uproar they could get started. Do you really think they would just march on into Lebanon without waiting.

Murphy: No, I think they're waiting to hear from us.

Day: If the reports we've been receiving over the last few days are accurate—if they're backing the Christians, the reports must be so distressing . . .

The Secretary phones Clements

Day: You were saying the Syrians were backing the Christians. Actually it may be sort of the other way around. The Christians are backing Syrian attempts to find a political solution.

Sisco: The Syrians really want to prevent a leftist and PLO takeover. Let's say it gets partitioned . . .

The Secretary: The reason we've got to send something to Egypt is that we want to avoid giving them the impression that we are colluding. I think we have to tell them in confidence that we've received some reports to which we give some credibility. An armored division outside Damascus is moving, but we have no word from the Syrians to indicate any action along these lines—what info do they have about this and do they have any recommendations for us. I think it would be worth waking up Fahmy to give him this.

Sisco: Oh, yes; I think we ought to send this out tonight.[6]

Atherton: You will have seen the message that we brought up earlier.[7]

The Secretary: No, I haven't seen it because it probably hasn't made its way through my staff.

Sisco: It was a very short message.

Atherton: I will have someone send up a copy of it.

Murphy: I can't believe that they would try sending a division into Lebanon at this point.

---

[6] Apparently a reference to telegram 72131 to Damascus, March 25, in which Kissinger asked for the Syrian Government's "ideas and suggestions as to how we could best use our influence effectively to this end." (National Archives, RG 59, Central Foreign Policy Files, P840090–2128)

[7] Not further identified.

The Secretary: Don't we have any intercept on this? (referring to draft cable, Secretary says:) I have told you a thousand times not to say regular forces. And they should not intervene militarily because all information that we have indicates that it would immediately cause an expansion of hostilities.

Sisco: I think personally that it's time for us to be fairly explicit.

The Secretary: Now we should add a third paragraph. We are prepared to support their efforts and can Khaddam tell you what or whom we should be contacting, and what measures we should be taking in order to help. He won't do it, of course, but at least we've asked.

All right. Now that we're in a crisis situation. Can we get this Department to perform? I need first of all to see something every day from you, Hal, giving me the situation and your assessment. Second, I need a map showing the disposition of forces in the area. And, third, can't you get yourself into the intelligence loop so that I don't have to get these reports from Defense? And I want you to work out something so that we can get these cables without them getting lost in the bureaucracy. There must be some way that this Department will react to a crisis.

273. Memorandum of Conversation[1]

Washington, March 25, 1976, 2:45 p.m.

PARTICIPANTS

    The Secretary
    Under Secretary Sisco
    Assistant Secretary Atherton
    Deputy Assistant Secretary Day
    Jock Covey, Notetaker

SUBJECT

    Lebanon

The Secretary: Have you seen the reply from Khaddam? (Damascus 1808)[2] What do you think it means?

---

[1] Source: Library of Congress, Manuscript Division, Kissinger Papers, CL 347, Department of State Memorandum of Conversations, Internal, December 1975–March 1976. Secret; Sensitive.

[2] Telegram 1808 from Damascus, March 25, transmitted Khaddam's replies to the questions posed by the United States in telegram 70097 to Damascus, March 24. (Library of Congress, Manuscript Division, Kissinger Papers, CL 237, Geopolitical File, Syria, March 1976)

Atherton: I think it means they want to try to do it in a way that will avoid a direct confrontation with Israel.

The Secretary: Where is Bekaa?

Atherton: East and north of Beirut.

Sisco: I see that they gave us no real idea of the time frame.

The Secretary: What do you think?

Sisco: I personally think that they are moving very fast now towards some sort of intervention. My own recommendation would be that we tell the Israelis pretty quickly what is going on.

The Secretary: Now all of this is said in the framework of a study being done by the Foreign Minister that has not yet been submitted to the President.

Atherton: I would be very surprised if they moved before they had a response from us.

Sisco: Oh yes, I agree.

Atherton: And I think we should wait to hear from the Israelis before we go back to the Syrians.

The Secretary: We're not going to get a reply very fast.

All right, I think we should get a message back to the Syrians quickly. Tell them we are studying it but repeat our warning against any unilateral move and its consequences. And I guess we might as well tell the Israelis what is going on. (Secretary phones Dinitz)

Do you agree with what I told him?

Atherton: Yes.

The Secretary: Okay, I think we can take our time drafting a reply. There's no need to shoot it right back.

Sisco: I personally see no sense in sending it out before close of business tonight.

The Secretary: But don't tell anybody else about this.

Sisco: Henry, I just want you to know that I am personally coming more and more to Fahmy's view—that is, of involving the United Nations Security Council in this. You have seen his latest cable?[3]

The Secretary: No, of course I haven't seen his latest cable yet because it probably hasn't passed mustering among the geniuses in my outer office.

Sisco: Here, you can read mine. (The Secretary reads cable)

The Secretary: I think we better do a cable to Fahmy telling what the difficulties are in going to the UN Security Council, and I think we should sound out the French.

---

[3] Not further identified.

Sisco: The French are working up an initiative to move the question into the Security Council. Or possibly as a combined French, British, US move. Of course, this would not affect the situation on the ground.

The Secretary: Well, then maybe we should do a message to the French to say that we have had further world that the situation may be getting out of control.

Sisco: You know their man here in Washington would be ideal. He's the former Ambassador to the United Nations.

The Secretary: Except that he is already on his way to Minnesota. Well, perhaps he hasn't actually left yet. (The Secretary asks for call to be put through to Kosciusko-Morizet). After we do up this message I think you should get ahold of Ramsbotham and bring him up to date.

Sisco: How much do you want to tell him?

The Secretary: I think you should give him the gist of the Syrian response. He is the only European who knows about this, however, and I specifically don't want the French to be approached by the UK about the Security Council thing before they get our message.

Sisco: I understand. (The Secretary speaks to Amb. Kosciusko-Morizet)

The Secretary: And I guess we had better tell Dinitz right away. (Speaks to Dinitz)

Atherton: I think we have to keep one thing in mind. This shouldn't look like our idea.

Sisco: Especially since most of the parties will be opposed to it.

The Secretary: Oh we are not proposing it. That's the beauty of it. That means the French have to go around and sell it. Although perhaps I better call the French Ambassador right back and make that clear.

Sisco: I would put it in terms of the great advantage to their doing this alone—not in terms of our preference—otherwise that will make the French cool off. I think you have to tell him, you alone is better because we would be suspect.

274. Memorandum of Conversation[1]

Washington, March 26, 1976, 9:10 a.m.

PARTICIPANTS

The Secretary
Under Secretary Sisco
Assistant Secretary Atherton
Assistant Secretary Saunders
Deputy Assistant Secretary Day
Ambassador Murphy
Jock Covey, Notetaker

SUBJECT

Lebanon

The Secretary: Right. Where do we stand then?

Sisco: Well, I personally think that Roy's assessment at the staff meeting[2] was very full this morning. I think we are seeing the beginning of a Syrian pull-out. And I think the Syrians will get Jumblatt over to Damascus tomorrow and will continue to seek a political solution.

The Secretary: Well, that means the Israelis have again done themselves in. Through their brilliant strategy, we will have succeeded in pushing Syria to the left. What do you think?

Murphy: I think the Christians will be able to hold out.

Atherton: We may end up with partition. The Christians will probably be able to defend the Mt. Lebanon area.

The Secretary: How big is the Mt. Lebanon area?

Atherton: All told, it's about ⅓ of the country.

Day: It includes part of Beirut.

Atherton: They still have the militia, they have weapons, they have a port . . .

Day: And in the meantime, there is trouble brewing at home for Asad.

Atherton: The worst possible outcome is that not only will Asad's policy fail, but that the policy itself will be unpopular.

The Secretary: But why did he pursue this policy?

Murphy: I think he may be afraid that the dispute would slop over into Syria. After all, Syria is a patchwork quilt of small groups . . .

---

[1] Source: National Archives, RG 59, Records of Henry Kissinger, 1973–77, Box 16, Nodis Memcons, March 1976. Secret; Sensitive.

[2] The staff meeting took place on March 26 from 8:12 until 8:56 a.m. (Ibid., Henry Kissinger Staff Meetings, Box 9)

The Secretary: But why wouldn't he have supported the PLO? It would have been more natural.

Day: I think he thought at the beginning that the political solution had a good chance. He had support from both the left and the right—excluding the extremists on both ends. But then as the situation developed, the left started to pull away. But he still remains a major base. He still has his part of the PLO.

Murphy: Yes, that's easy to lose sight of. He still retains considerable support among the Palestinians.

Sisco: You mean the Saiqi? How large a group is the Saiqi in relation to the rejectionists and the rest of the PLO?

Murphy: Oh, the rejectionists are just a miniscule part of the PLO, and the Saiqi is about ¼ the size of the Fatah.

Atherton: I don't think that Asad wants Lebanon to be an extension of the Syrian front.

Murphy: Oh no, he's told me "why should I want to go to Lebanon to fight Israel?"

The Secretary: The thing that's so strange is that his interests and Israel's are parallel. This is just another one of those horrors that Israel has inflicted on the rest of us. If they had only let him move ... and clean out the PLO in the process ...

Murphy: Well, he never would have cleaned out the PLO.

Sisco: The thing is that in Israel, they're not able to make much of a distinction between Asad and the Syrians whom they deeply mistrust and the left wing of the PLO and rejectionists. I don't think Egypt can make the distinction either.

The Secretary: Oh yes, Egypt can make the distinction. Egypt wants only to humiliate Syria. They want chaos in Lebanon.

Saunders: Well, it's myopic in the sense that it could lead to war.

The Secretary: No, because they are convinced they can sit the war out. It would be better to have them fighting—their hatred has reached that point.

Murphy: If the worst case does not come about, and I certainly hope it doesn't, I think it's important to get across in detail some sense of how much we share their concerns and what we did in Israel. I think you're able to see in the messages we got from them a note of gratitude for our efforts.

Saunders: I don't think they would be talking to Jumblatt tomorrow if they had decided to go ahead. Maybe they will turn out to be more open minded about a UN effort.

The Secretary: Well, we don't have to worry about a UN effort any more. Sonnenfeldt has now involved himself. We are now assured that it will grow to crisis proportions.

Sisco: How is he involved?

The Secretary: He is in London sending messages to me, telling me that he needs instructions on what he should be telling the French about the initiative on the UN. I will tell him he should just stay out of this.

Sisco: Yes, I believe that he should just tell them that any comments or suggestions should just be sent directly to Washington.

Day: I agree that if they're seeing Jumblatt tomorrow, they won't move today.

Atherton: And Hussein is in Damascus today. We may see a report sometime tomorrow from him. You know the Jordanian assessment has been right on the mark.

The Secretary: Absolutely.

Saunders: The difficulty is you can't always tell when Arab maneuvers are just tactical. I can't see how pulling back will help them with Jumblatt.

Day: Well, the barrage yesterday was seen as an atrocity, and it may be just beyond toleration.[3]

Saunders: Maybe they're not actually pulling out.

The Secretary: No, I don't think they are.

Saunders: Their pull back may be just to help put the Christians back in.

Day: And that means they're still manipulating the situation.

The Secretary: I think we have to get a message to the Syrians. We have got to give them some essence of what has come about. We should tell them that we are trying to understand the situation. That in the present circumstances, Israel is sorely tempted to try to go in to clean out the PLO. We have made very clear to the Israelis the disastrous consequences of such a move and we think our warnings have stayed their hand. Then we have to make four points. First, if the Syrian military moves into Lebanon, the probability of the Israelis moving in is over-whelming. Second, if the Syrians associate themselves with local forces in a non-overt manor, it may be tolerable. That is, there is a possibility of containing the reaction. But to contain the reaction, we must know the facts. The danger of Israeli action increases if Syrian forces go below the Beirut–Damascus axis. Third, we agree with the Syrian approach. We think our most useful role would be to talk with the Christians. If they can bring Jumblatt around, we think we can help with Franghi. We would even talk to Jumblatt if the Syrians think that would

---

[3] On March 25, Moslem forces led by Jumblatt shelled Beirut, forcing President Frangieh to flee the city. (*New York Times*, March 26, 1976, p. 1)

help. But we do not want to disturb the Syrian efforts, so they've got to tell us what they want us to do. And fourth, we've been approached by various people suggesting a UN session, perhaps called by the French. Ask them what they think.

Now, this should be warm and personal, but should not be a letter from me.

Sisco: An oral message from you?

Murphy: Yes, I think that would be very good, especially since we have to remember that we're looking ahead to UNDOF and we want to be able to demonstrate to them that we've really tried.

Day: Could I make a suggestion for a slight change? Instead of saying that we are prepared to talk with the Christians—we have been saying all along that we are prepared to talk to the Christians and they have been criticising us for not carrying out our promises. Can we just say that we are going to begin talking to the Christians?

The Secretary: Yes, but not until we hear from the Syrians.

Since we are agreed on this approach, I think we should be able to get this out by noon.

Atherton: Actually, we're all delighted. This is exactly what we came in to suggest you do.

275. Memorandum of Conversation[1]

Washington, March 27, 1976, 5:45 p.m.

PARTICIPANTS

    The Secretary
    Assistant Secretary Atherton
    Deputy Assistant Secretary Day
    Ambassador Murphy
    General Scowcroft
    Jock Covey, Notetaker

SUBJECT

    Lebanon

---

[1] Source: Library of Congress, Manuscript Division, Kissinger Papers, CL 347, Department of State Memorandum of Conversations, Internal, December 1975–March 1976. Secret; Sensitive.

(Secretary reads cable Amman 1633)[2]

Covey: Sir, we just received word from the Lebanon Country Officer—who had taken the call that Ambassador Murphy placed to Damascus a few minutes ago—that Pelletreau has not been called in yet, and has in fact received no communications from the Foreign Ministry at all.

The Secretary: They could be bluffing us.

Atherton: They could be bluffing us about the matter of hours but I doubt that they are, overall.

Murphy: The pressures against Asad may be getting worse.

Day: But our intelligence throughout the afternoon has showed a rather static situation.

The Secretary: To bring you up to date (to Scowcroft) we've received a report from the French that says that the Syrians called them in to say that the situation has deteriorated. The Jumblatt talks have failed and that they feel they must move soon. They have received an urgent plea from Franghi and the Christians to intervene and they've asked the French to urge us to withdraw our objections.

Murphy: In fact, there's nothing new in the pleas from Franghi. They've been saying that all along.

The Secretary: What is new is that they want to move now. The French want to talk about international guarantees.

I guess I had better read this cable to Dinitz (places call to Dinitz).

Scowcroft: What sort of international guarantees?

Atherton: No indication.

The Secretary: I'm wondering if we shouldn't call in the French Chargé and say that Israel would move under the following conditions ... (interrupted by call to Dinitz)

Murphy: The only other item that Draper got out of Pelletreau was that as of two hours ago, Jumblatt was still in Damascus. There must be some element of bluff in all of this.

The Secretary: Look, we really mustn't panic about this. Anything that would take Woodward and Bernstein off the front page can't be all bad. (laughter)

Basically, Asad is right. If we were not a second-rate government we would have been telling them to get in there fast and get the job done. But this place is full of mattress mice. How would you like to go into an NSC with Rumsfeld and the others.

---

[2] Dated March 27. (National Archives, RG 59, Central Foreign Policy Files)

Scowcroft: Well, politically it certainly wouldn't hurt anyone to have another *Mayaguez* incident[3] on our hands.

The Secretary: But to make this come off, we need to go to war with American Jews. That certainly would be no *Mayaguez*.

As for right now, if they are bluffing, then we don't need to worry about them moving. If they are not bluffing, then they are going to move in the morning.

Murphy: And that would be about 4 hours from now.

The Secretary: It's just possible that he may be just trying to show his hotheads that there just is no way to move the U.S. But one thing is clear, we cannot allow the Lebanese situation to go on teetering on the brink. We must take a more active role in this. The first thing we should do is to tell the French that on the basis of our present information, first, any intervention by the Syrians would lead almost inevitably to an Israeli action. Second, that our information is based on very firm information . . . and then give them some idea of the parameters. Third, it's possible that the question of international guarantees can add a new dimension. At the moment we are urgently exploring the possibility of developing international guarantees of a kind that would limit the stay of the intervening force to just a few weeks, and would define the forces and the nature of international controls that would avoid a widening of international hostilities.

Atherton: We should add that we are in touch with the Israelis.

The Secretary: Yes, and that it will take 18–24 hours to get a response. Then we should also do a message to Hussein.

Day: We should probably tell him exactly the same thing.

The Secretary: Yes, the first thing is we should tell him that we appreciate his concerns.

I don't think he'll be coming on Monday,[4] do you?

Scowcroft: I don't see how he can come now.

The Secretary: He should tell Asad for us that we have great sympathy for his position and are in agreement with his solution and thirdly, on the basis of our present information, we can only repeat what we have said previously, but we have approached the Israelis to see what can be worked out with respect to the size of the force and the modalities and length of stay that would limit the likelihood of Israeli intervention. He will of course understand that it will take 18–24 hours to get an answer back. In the meantime, could he please explore with

---

[3] See footnote 10, Document 183.
[4] March 29.

Asad the need for filling us in on the details of his plans. Syria has never answered our queries about what we could do to help.

Murphy: Just one question on international guarantees. Do they really need to be international?

The Secretary: Just say guarantees, and for the French leave it so that the guarantees are their idea. That is, if international guarantees can be devised, what can the French work out . . .

---

276. Memorandum of Conversation[1]

Washington, March 27, 1976, 6:50 p.m.

PARTICIPANTS

    The Secretary
    General Scowcroft
    Assistant Secretary Atherton
    Deputy Assistant Secretary Day
    Ambassador Murphy
    Jock Covey, Notetaker

SUBJECT

    Lebanon

The Secretary: (reading cable handed to him for clearance)[2] Let's not get to the public statement. Okay (approves cable)

Scowcroft: On the talking points, wouldn't it be better to avoid saying "run unacceptable risks" and instead say "it would almost certainly result in . . ."

The Secretary: Yes. You see Brent, that shows you something about this building. Those Foreign Service Officers who are not missionaries are actually political science professors. Very few of them are foreign policy practitioners. Do you have any problem with what we are saying to the Jordanians?

Scowcroft: No.

---

[1] Source: Library of Congress, Manuscript Division, Kissinger Papers, CL 347, Department of State Memorandum of Conversations, Internal, December 1975–March 1976. Secret; Sensitive.

[2] Not further identified.

The Secretary: We should add something to the Jordanian thing to the effect that we have exhausted all possibility of getting other Arab forces.

Day: It would certainly take too long to try to arrange that.

Scowcroft: What ever forces go in have to do it fast and be able to fight.

Day: And certainly the Kuwaitis can't do either.

Atherton: That seems pretty certain that Asad has had a knock-down-drag-out fight with Jumblatt.

The Secretary: But he always begins his negotiating sessions by hitting the ceiling. He may just want to demonstrate that by god he was ready to go and that he even pulled in other people to see if he could do it without us.

Day: That certainly is what we thought yesterday.

The Secretary: I better call the Israelis (Places call to Dinitz).

Sisco: Has Dinitz given you any reaction at all so far?

The Secretary: He said we will have to stick to our position. I told him to get them out of bed and see what they can think of by way of international guarantees.

Atherton: If Asad is still trying to argue it out with Jumblatt, this may all be just a ploy to try to back up his position.

The Secretary: You know, this is just another example of how the Israelis have done themselves in. They didn't want Lebanon to be part of the Syrian military system, so by stonewalling on this they will succeed in forcing the PLO to take over. And then they will still have Lebanon as part of the Syrian military system.

Well, you can't win them all. But we haven't lost any countries this year, have we?

Day: Only Angola. Not a real country.

The Secretary: We should add a sentence to the France message (takes call to Dinitz).

Now can you do a cable to the Egyptians—I just want him to know about the French approach and the fact that it appears that the Syrians are becoming ever more serious about moving a division into Lebanon, and that we continue to try to dissuade the Israelis from reacting. We should say that we told them that there is a very high risk of Israeli reaction if they move in. And we've asked for more information. If they have any ideas of what we can do to assist a solution, we would like to hear from them.

Sisco: Instead of high-risk, maybe we just should say it's highly likely.

The Secretary: We should say almost certainly.

Sisco: Oh yes, I agree.

The Secretary: Now, we should tell the Frenchmen that the Israelis simply are not to be persuaded. The only way to move them is by threats which we cannot carry out in the present climate.

You know what will happen if the Syrians move in: The Congressional outburst, the calls for cutting off Syrian aid, the raging about the Soviets. This will certainly be seen as a Soviet inspired maneuver to overcome the defenseless Lebanese people.

If the Syrians move, I will recommend to the President massive pressure against the Israelis to try to get them to stay out. The thing the Israelis just can't seem to understand is that if Syria goes in they will have to beat up on the PLO and that they can't stay in for very long.

Atherton: Asad's position would just be impossible. How can he stay up at the north and be accused of shooting Arabs while the Israelis are down in the South shooting the PLO.

Sisco: I think at this point, it would be a very good idea to do a chronology of exactly what we've been doing so far. A list, just to show all of the diplomatic moves we've made so far.

The Secretary: Yes, that's an excellent idea. Let's get the messages together. But you know, as soon as we do that, and we show it to anybody, then we will have people on our backs screaming, but why didn't you go to Oman? And what about Djibouti?

Do you think we ought to go to the Saudis? On second thought, it's probably not such a good idea. If we told them what's happening now, they'd wet their pants.

Atherton: I don't think we should go to the Saudis.

The Secretary: And we probably should hold up on the Hawk thing.[3]

Atherton: We still don't know if Hussein is going to be coming.

Sisco: I think this will all just wash that out.

The Secretary: I think we ought to hold off until we know whether we know whether he's coming or not. If there's going to be a war I don't think we want to be fighting with the Saudis about financing Hawk missiles for Jordan.

Sisco: I don't think he can possibly leave at this point. But by the same token, his Chief of Staff is still here. I just saw him on Friday.

The Secretary: This can all be one big bluff. You know he's an artist at it. I told him when I was there the last time—he's the only person I know who not only goes to the precipice, but actually jumps over, hoping that he'll find a tree on the way down.

---

[3] A reference to the U.S. Government's proposed sale of Hawk missiles to Jordan.

As I see it right now, there are three possibilities. First, the talks with Jumblatt may have gone so badly that he needs to do this as some sort of a demonstration. To prove to Jumblatt that he really would move. Two, he may be doing it to get control of his own hotheads. They may be pressing him pretty hard so he says Okay—let's bring some others to see if we can do it without the United States. Then after it's all over he'll be able to show them that if they still want to go ahead, they'll have to fight Israel. Three, he may have actually decided to go in and may be using this as a device to set us up.

Murphy: How do you mean set us up?

The Secretary: That is, setting us thinking about how we're going to go about restraining the Israelis.

I personally lean towards number 2. Although he may still go in. It just isn't characteristic of Asad to go balls out this way. I am assuming that the Soviets are also trying to discourage him from this. After all, they will be accused of being responsible for everything that happens. Congress will be all over them and us saying, what about your great détente now?

Sisco: What time does it get light there?

Murphy: About 10:00 our time.

The Secretary: I wonder if the Syrians can find Lebanon. How good are they?

Murphy: Good enough to find Lebanon.

The Secretary: I never will understand how the Egyptians actually got five divisions to the Suez, at the same time, at the same place. All right, would you go ahead and draft those cables, and when you're finished, come back up and we'll go over them.

(meeting adjourns during drafting of cables—reconvenes at 7:25 p.m.)

The Secretary: I would not report this to Tel Aviv unless we can hold it to Toon.

Sisco: We can add a slug to that, just to say for Toon eyes only.

The Secretary: Better give Toon an account of exactly what it is we've told the Israelis. (to Atherton) Can you do that?

Day: (referring to cable just arrived from Amman)[4] I don't think this changes anything really.

---

[4] Apparently telegram 1634 from Amman, March 27. (Ford Library, National Security Adviser, Country Files, Middle East and South Asia, Box 23, Department of State Telegrams to the Secretary of State, Jordan, Folder 24)

Sisco: Well, I don't think you were quite this specific with Dinitz. You never gave him the kind of line that's in the first sentence of the sixth paragraph.[5]

The Secretary: (reads cable) I don't want to tell the Israelis this. Until now I have never said to either side exactly what the military maneuvers of the others are. If I do, and then they do move and stray 100 yards from what they said they were going to do, then the other side will be all over us saying we betrayed them.

---

[5] The first line of paragraph 6 reads, "Rifai says he believes Asad will focus on Beirut and establishing a Syrian corridor from border into Beirut." (Ibid.)

---

277. Memorandum of Conversation[1]

Washington, March 28, 1976, 12:25 p.m.

PARTICIPANTS

The Secretary
Under Secretary Sisco
Deputy Under Secretary Eagleburger
Assistant Secretary Atherton
Assistant Secretary Saunders
Deputy Assistant Secretary Day
Jock Covey, Notetaker

SUBJECT

Lebanon

The Secretary: I'm puzzled how Eilts could have gotten this so confused. I think we ought to rush a cable back to him saying that we have informed Asad of the Israeli position and that as far as we can tell, according to all the information we know is available to him now, it can only be interpreted as not authorizing intervention.

Could Asad have misunderstood this the way that Eilts has?

Murphy: No, I don't think so.

The Secretary: Tell him one interpretation of why it's being done this way is that Asad may feel he can exert more pressure on us, and

---

[1] Source: Library of Congress, Manuscript Division, Kissinger Papers, CL 275, Chronological File, March 1976, Folder 2. Secret; Sensitive.

our Ambassador is not in town, any way. I think we better get that off within the hour.

Atherton: We have a few other things to review.

Day: This is a draft cable to Beirut.

The Secretary: Have we heard anything from the Israelis?

Sisco: No.

The Secretary: Of course they have their regular cabinet meeting which meets on Sunday.

Saunders: That would be over by now.

Atherton: I most certainly hope they didn't discuss this at a regular Cabinet meeting.

The Secretary: This really is outrageous. They get all of the cables we have been getting and they give us nothing. I cannot believe that they are not in touch with anyone in Lebanon. Their intelligence has always been very good before.

Sisco: Of course they're in touch with people in Lebanon.

Day: Information exchange with the Israelis has always been a one way street.

The Secretary: Yeah, but just wait until the next Golan book[2] comes out, and it will be us who betrayed the Israelis.

Now, if we tell Lambrakis that he should move to accommodate the Syrian position, won't we just read about it all in the newspapers the next day?

Atherton: We've got to be careful how we say this.

The Secretary: Can't we avoid the phrase "along Syrian lines."

Sisco: Well, at this point, I think we've just got to be more explicit.

The Secretary: Well, we could spell it out but still avoid flagging the Syrian aspect. Does Lambrakis have the judgment to be given such a free hand?

Atherton: Yes, based on the way he's handled things so far over the last couple of weeks.

Day: But we've just got to expect that as he talks—after all Beirut is a very gossipy town and you can't hide a thing like this. But he certainly can play down the Syrian aspect.

Sisco: But do we want such broad consultations? Why can't we just limit it a bit and authorize him to talk to one Christian and one of the Jumblatt people.

The Secretary: That sounds much better.

---

[2] See footnote 9, Document 202.

Day: It's pretty hard to select just one major Christian.

Sisco: Well, just for example, how about Jamail?

Day: Well, he's only a leader of one of the factions.

Sisco: And Chamoun?

Day: Yes, and maybe Sarkis.

Sisco: Well, then maybe we can limit it to just Chamoun, Sarkis and Jamail and tell him specifically he should not go beyond that.

Murphy: Doesn't that amount to placing our benediction on Sarkis?

Day: Yes, I think maybe we better leave Sarkis out.

The Secretary: Now don't just mumble names. The point is I don't want Lambrakis running all over town with his political scientists imposing their own version of the settlement on these people.

Sisco: Yes, I think we need a limited approach. We don't want to leave them with the impression that this is our own mediation effort. We have to limit our effort to just paralleling the Syrian effort. The major problem of course is Jumblatt, and if we have any influence, moving him is what it's all about.

The Secretary: I just don't want to turn all those Embassy political officers loose so that we become a major bone of contention. We should be seen to be supporting the Syrian effort.

Sisco: Well, I personally think we should limit it to Chamoun and Jumblatt.

The Secretary: Let's just have him to go to Jumblatt first and report immediately and tell him we'll have further instructions after that.

Sisco: Jumblatt will probably tell us to go to hell. But that doesn't matter, we will have at least done it.

The Secretary: What do you think Dick?

Murphy: I see your point.

The Secretary: I just don't want those political officers running loose—just leaving everything up to their imagination.

Murphy: Well, you know that every leader in Lebanon has some sort of axe to grind.

Sisco: Who else do you think we ought to contact? We can go to Chamoun because he came to us.

Day: If we go to Jamail, that should help balance it a bit.

The Secretary: I think we should stick with Chamoun and Jumblatt. After we hear from them, maybe the Embassy will want to suggest others.

Sisco: Yes, they should just report back and we will tell them if there are any other people that they should see. That way they can't get the wrong idea.

Saunders: The main purpose of this was just to be able to say that we didn't talk only to Jumblatt.

The Secretary: Okay, tell him they are authorized to contact Jumblatt and Chamoun.

Atherton: That's just what I was drafting when I was on my way up here (hands the Secretary cable).

The Secretary: That means you'll have to rewrite paragraph five.

Day: Well, the main point of it is the talking points.

Sisco: I don't think it would be a good idea for us to have our people contact the British and the French Ambassadors in Beirut. That word would just spread like wild fire.

The Secretary: I agree.

Should it say in paragraph two that it is a conflict drawing in outside power ... how about if outside powers intervene ... I would say "none of the surrounding countries would accept the partitioned Lebanon."

Sisco: Partition would bring about the same undesirable result. (The Secretary leaves room to take phone call)

The Secretary: We should say that we have been in contact with other countries and we see no possibility of the UN intervening.

Sisco: There's not a ghost of a chance.

The Secretary: That is we should say to the Christians that there's no possibility of U.S. intervention—but don't say that to Jumblatt—and if there's any intervention, it must come from other countries in the area.

I think we should say to the Egyptians that on Monday[3] in the press briefing we will again issue a strong warning against unilateral intervention. Tell them we can't do it on Sunday without creating a major crisis.

Sisco: That's the thing I find so interesting. The newspapers have been very calm about this.

The Secretary: Yes. That way we get no credit for doing anything. But it goes wrong, we get all the blame.

Atherton: We should say that as soon as he's accomplished that, we will tell him what to do about the others. He should tell each of the factions that the Syrian approach is the most feasible.

Atherton: I think it would be a good idea to send a report to Hussein in Madrid.

---

[3] March 29.

The Secretary: I don't think it's a good idea for us to go through Pelletreau. After all, they're not using him. I don't mind him being informed, but I don't think he should go seek out Asad. Particularly since there's nothing in that channel. What sort of fellow is he?

Murphy: Great.

Sisco: You remember two days ago you asked the same question and Murphy said that he had picked him himself.

Murphy: He's a tight-lipped fellow. Very discreet.

The Secretary: I just hate to have all of this cable traffic going back and forth about getting guarantees from Israel. Pretty soon they'll be able to claim that we were colluding. It makes me especially uneasy because there's no word from the Israelis. I think we just have to say that we are in contact with each of the parties to indicate an interest in a solution along Syrian lines. I don't think we have to say anything to Khaddam. I think Asad did it this way so that he could be in contact with us directly.

Atherton: You may be right. After all, Hussein just inserted himself in the middle of this.

(Secretary places call to Dinitz).

The Secretary: You know these Israelis really are shits. But I don't think we ought to tell them that Egypt has now said they won't do anything if Syria intervenes.

Sisco: You know the thing they don't understand is even a week from now, they could still intervene.

The Secretary: If the Syrians do go in, I think it's up to us to spend several days trying to pin them down on a precise time of withdrawal. Only then should the Israelis go in.

Saunders: An Israeli mop up operation would automatically bring a Syrian reaction.

(The Secretary speaks to Dinitz on the telephone)

The Secretary: He just reiterated the same position without any explanation at all. That, Golda would never have done.

Sisco: Did he just reiterate it or did he say that they are still reviewing the situation?

The Secretary: They just don't want to be in a position to have authorized a Syrian move into Lebanon which is the same position we're in. So as I see it, we just have to wait until they move and then face a new reality. Then it's up to us to keep the Israelis out and take the rap. Then it will be us that stopped them from going in. I'm just afraid that if we tell all that to the Syrians now, that they will just go ahead and move.

But if the Israelis could only just say what I just said. But instead they just reiterate their position. You know I have read them every cable that we have gotten and they have given us nothing.

Sisco: I can just see them there sitting around that green colored table.

The Secretary: What green colored table. As I remember it it's wooden. Was it green, Hal?

Saunders: No, as I remember it it was just a plain wooden table.

Atherton: Well, a reiteration may have been the only possible way to answer us. After all, if they had a Cabinet meeting, they would have been split 16 ways. I don't think they would have had a whole Cabinet meeting on this.

Atherton: However many people they had there, the opinion would have been split that many ways.

The Secretary: I wonder if we should send some explanation to the Syrians now just so they can see something going on. Tell them we're talking to Jumblatt and to Chamoun . . .

Atherton: Well, we probably should send a report to Hussein too.

The Secretary: Can we get a report to him?

Atherton: Yes, he's already asked Pickering to get in touch with us by phone today and right now, he's at Torrejon where he will overnight.

The Secretary: Hussein will overnight at Torrejon?

Day: Actually, it's Pickering who overnights at Torrejon. Hussein will be somewhere else nearby.

The Secretary: Tell him we need some answers . . . but I don't think he should be telling all of this to Asad over the phone.

Sisco: Our report really should be pretty minimal.

The Secretary: What can we say? That we've had an Israeli response.

Atherton: I think we have to say that we are still in consultation with the others.

Sisco: I think we have to be more precise. We have to tell Hussein that we can't say there's been any progress but we're still consulting. If we say only that we are still consulting, it comes off much too positive.

The Secretary: I think you're right. We should also say we haven't heard from the French but consultations continue.

Sisco: That's it. That's it exactly.

The Secretary: And we have to get that cable off to Eilts right away.[4] This is how I see the situation developing. At this point we are sympathetic to the Syrian move but we have to be sure that we have in

---

[4] Not further identified.

no way authorized it and we have to find some way to keep the Israelis out.

Atherton: Do you think Asad would move without getting an answer from us? I think he's pretty scared of the Israelis.

Murphy: I think he'll wait to hear from us. We still don't know how that meeting with Arafat went.

Day: The other danger is that he may lose his shirt at home and afterward blame us.

The Secretary: Which is exactly what the Egyptians want.

Day: And the Israelis . . .

The Secretary: The Israeli problem is that they just don't want to make any decisions on this.

Day: Well, if I had that government, I wouldn't want to make any decisions either.

The Secretary: Let me tell you a secret, we have that government (laughter).

Murphy: Do you think it would be possible to get a guarantee of precise timing of withdrawal—say three weeks.

Sisco: You mean afterwards?

Murphy: No, before.

The Secretary: There's no way. Even if they said three days, the Israelis could never accept it. We must think about you having a private talk with Asad and telling him that we cannot guarantee anything. And therefore, we urge him not to do it. But if he absolutely must, then he's got to give us some idea of where he wants to go and how many people it would take, and so on. Even so, we can't guarantee him the whole moon.

Murphy: Well, he's already told us that he doesn't think he'll need very many troops but he doesn't know precisely where they will have to go or exactly how long it will take to do it.

The Secretary: That only shows that he's a responsible man. The Israelis will of course say that any intervention will lead to the Syrianization of Lebanon. The irony of it is that even if they stay out, it will lead to Syrianization of Lebanon.

Sisco: They will be able to reduce their forces only when they find a political solution.

The Secretary: Under present circumstances, their going in will make the solution easier. Just by going in they will weaken someone. And even after they come out, there will be the memory of the intervention and the possibility that they will go back. It will certainly create a new sense of reality in Lebanon.

Murphy: Asad is certainly counting on the shock value of the Syrian uniforms to bring back some of the strays who have gone over to Jumblatt.

Murphy: If I leave tomorrow night, I could be in Damascus Tuesday night.[5] I could probably be called in as soon as I get back. That would be Tuesday afternoon your time.

The Secretary: Then we've got to think about what you would say. I think the best thing we can do is be absolutely realistic and no one can blame us afterwards for not coming clean. I think we should say the preferred solution would come about with his assistance, but without his forces. But if he moves his forces, I simply cannot get a clear answer from the Israelis. But no Israeli government could ever give that kind of assurance in advance. And I think you have to tell him that given the domestic situation in this country, the only possible solution must involve very concrete guarantees of a fixed time, a line below which they would not move, and so on. That could be tied to international guarantees. But do you speak Arabic well enough to get that across?

Murphy: I can do it. But if they move, then you'll know I used the wrong verb. (laughter)

The Secretary: No, but can you do it?

Murphy: I'll work it out in advance on this message.

The Secretary: The only way to navigate through this situation is with perfect honesty.

Sisco: Well, let's just jot that all down and we'll have a fresh look at it in the morning.

The Secretary: I still don't understand what it is you want me to do on these Hawk Missiles with the Saudis. What exactly do we want to get from the Saudis?

Atherton: We want to get them to take another look at the 300 million ceiling.

The Secretary: Do we want to get them up to 400?

Sisco: You just have to be able to say to Hussein that you are raising this with the Saudis.

The Secretary: I don't understand how the 300 million was screwed up so badly.

Atherton: The Jordanians just waited too long. They waited until it was too late to tell the Saudis how much it was going to cost. The hardware alone was 300 million. But when you count in the spares and the training ...

The Secretary: And even 700 million would not be enough?

---

[5] April 1.

Atherton: No, 700 would be fine. And maybe we can even pare it down to 500.

Day: If it's all spread over a matter of years, then 700 million would not be enough because of inflation.

Atherton: But if we can sign now, it's a different story.

The Secretary: Okay.

---

278. Memorandum of Conversation[1]

Washington, March 29, 1976, 8:15 a.m.

PARTICIPANTS

The Secretary
Under Secretary Sisco
Assistant Secretary Atherton
Deputy Under Secretary Eagleburger
Assistant Secretary Saunders
Deputy Assistant Secretary Day
Jock Covey, Notetaker

SUBJECT

Lebanon

The Secretary: Dinitz came to see me with both formal answers and talking points—which I seem to have left at home. The formal answer was that they could never agree to Syrian intervention. The talking points, which were strictly for me, said that they can't understand why I am trying to maneuver them into agreeing before hand to such intervention. Their analysis runs about like this:

1. They don't believe that Jumblatt can actually defeat the Christians.
2. They will make sure they can't defeat the Christians by giving them arms—which I didn't discourage but I didn't encourage it either.
3. That basically what Asad is trying to do is restore Soviet prestige in the Middle East, which in the long run will be bad for Egypt.
4. He does not believe that the radicals can unify in Lebanon.

---

[1] Source: Library of Congress, Manuscript Division, Kissinger Papers, CL 347, Department of State Memorandum of Conversations, Internal, December 1975–March 1976. Secret; Sensitive.

5. If Syria goes in they will definitely tie up with the left, or, at least as soon as they have vassalized Lebanon, they will begin to move to the left to bring in the PLO and the others.

6. Once they are in they will be objectively supported by the Soviets.

Now I can't disagree with that analysis—that is quite an intelligent approach and I told him that we would do everything we could to keep Syria out. But that if we are unable to prevent that we will also do our best to keep Israel out—just so that there were no misunderstandings.

Now I have this concern about the psychedelic way in which we go about business in this Department: does Lambrakis have the idea that he is supposed to go out and browbeat the Christians. There are just too many people who seem to have heard that we want the Christians to yield. What is your perception?

Day: We sent out a cable late last night telling him to just listen.[2]

The Secretary: Did you tell me you sent out a cable?

Day: It was a very straightforward cable just reiterating our previous instructions. He ran into him just by accident.

The Secretary: What I am concerned about is that he is saying that we prefer the Syrian solution. Do you think we ought to get a flash off to him to get him to say that we support the old solution? What is the new solution . . . a new President?

Day: We have been trying to avoid going into specifics in this cable.

The Secretary: Yes, but does he know what the old solution is?

Day: Yes, we have identified it for him specifically.

The Secretary: Yes, well what precisely is it?

Day: Well, basically it is a matter of the parliamentary balance shifting from about 45% to 55%, to a 50–50 balance, and the fact that the President would be selected by the Parliament. The only new thing is a proposed constitutional change concerning the resignation of the President.

The Secretary: I really think we ought to make a statement at the press briefing today saying first that developments in Lebanon have become more acute and second that we think the best basis for a settlement is the Syrian proposal of January 22.[3] You can say that we believe that some of the recent proposals with respect to the recent crisis should be taken seriously by all parties. Third, that we believe that in-

---

[2] Apparently a reference to telegram 74955 to Beirut, March 28. (National Archives, RG 59, Central Foreign Policy Files, P840090–2168)

[3] The January 22 Syrian proposal led to the cease-fire, which held in Lebanon until March. See footnote 2, Document 267.

tervention by any of the parties would pose a great danger. And fourth, that the U.S. is prepared to assist all the parties to find a peaceful solution. You see, I want to give the Syrians a real pat on the back.

Sisco: We only have to be certain that the pat on the back is not seen as aimed only at the Israelis.

The Secretary: Well, emphasize that military intervention from outside of Lebanon means everybody. You know, if Eilts is confused on this—and he even thinks like the Arabs—then what will the Arabs be thinking? We want to make it clear that we understand that the Syrian intervention will cause many more problems than it solves. And tell him that if it does happen, we will do as we said. You know if they do it and don't get out fast, then they will be forced to turn more radical. Then it will be like '67: if they wait two or three weeks, by then the Israelis will be forced to go in. You agree?

Murphy: Can't we pick one of those points to emphasize?

The Secretary: We can say we believe progress has been made on the issue of constitutional succession.

But I don't want Lambrakis breaking Chamoun's will to resist.

Day: I think it would have the opposite effect if they know he has been talking to Jumblatt too.

The Secretary: Does Lambrakis have enough judgment to do this well. What do you think Larry?

Eagleburger: Yes, but with one question mark. We came into the foreign service together and he is very good but has a tendency to take off a bit.

Atherton: Yes, that is exactly how I would describe it.

The Secretary: That is what I gathered from reading his cable.[4]

Eagleburger: But if the reins are held tightly, he is okay.

The Secretary: I have no problem with his talking to Chamoun. If the Christians can keep it at a stalemate, that is a better solution for us than if the Syrians go in.

You know I agree with the Israeli analysis. When the Syrians take over and dominate Lebanon, it will drive it in the direction of the Moslems. They would never be able to tolerate a right-wing nut, but a left-wing nut that they can control would be okay.

Saunders: That presumes that the Christians won't break off and partition the country.

Sisco: But wouldn't they have to stay together just to survive?

---

[4] Not further identified.

Day: I don't think the Syrians are natural allies of the Lebanese left. The Lebanese left is much more an Iraqi element.

The Secretary: Look, if the Syrians go in I will try my best to keep the Israelis out. If even Eilts thinks that we are colluding with the Syrians, what will the other Arabs think? Should we do a cable to the Saudis to say that the risk of the Syrian intervention is increasing, that we believe that a solution can be worked out that will achieve many of the Syrian objectives, but that if the Syrians go in the risk of the thing spreading is much too great, and that our impression is that Israel is looking for an opportunity to clean up the PLO in Lebanon.

Sisco: A political solution would be in Arafat's interest.

The Secretary: Wouldn't Asad be pleased if we praise him?

Sisco: Well, if we give him too much of a pat on the back it would not signify enough disapproval of a military move.

The Secretary: That is why I want to strongly speak out against intervention. (takes phone call) What do you think?

Murphy: On balance, if the message is calibrated to give him both a pat on the back and a sharp jerk on the reins about intervention, I think it will work.

Sisco: When D'oud asks the inevitable question, who is it aimed at, what will we say?

The Secretary: Everybody. He can certainly indicate that although everybody is concerned, certainly the neighboring countries, Syria and Israel, are most concerned.

Saunders: We have already been pretty tough with Syria.

The Secretary: But not overtly, not publicly. You have your talking points?

Murphy: Yes. (hands over talking points).

The Secretary: What do you want to say on this subject to Asad?

Sisco: This is not the first subject you think you should raise with Asad, is it?

The Secretary: I think you have too much on Lebanon here, he will interpret it as saying he can move.

Sisco: He has got to come out clearly and say, you cannot move—you just simply cannot do it.

The Secretary: Yes, say that this is our judgment.

Murphy: If we are making the statement today, would that be too much?

The Secretary: Tell him that maybe it is possible to move people in covertly, but overtly would risk great danger. He must also know that we are making great efforts. The basic issue is how we can help him work towards a solution.

Sisco: I don't think we ought to get so specific.

The Secretary: We can say Hussein is here and will be talking to the President and that we will discuss any fine tuning with Hussein. (to Murphy) This is better for you, otherwise they come to you every six hours saying is this enough, is this enough.

Sisco: Yes, they would try all the pressure tactics.

The Secretary: Better to cut it right off.

Murphy: Do you think our statement might be too hard, too insistent?

Saunders: It is a bit cold.

Murphy: I wonder if we shouldn't just hold it up one day so that I can give Asad the substance of the statement before you give it to the press.

Sisco: The other thing is, how will it play to Hussein who will be here two hours after it is delivered.

The Secretary: I would still rather give the statement.[5] We can send a note to Asad giving him the basic line and saying Murphy will explain the details.

Atherton: We ought to send a copy of it to Damascus so that Pelletreau can give it to him now.

The Secretary: The primary effort is to influence the political process in Lebanon.

Sisco: We can do the cables up right away while you are with the President.

The Secretary: Joe, perhaps when you write your book you can explain why it takes us here at the highest levels of the State Department, an hour and a half to do something that any ordinary desk officer can do in five minutes.

Sisco: Well, you are much more deeply involved than any normal desk officer. Things of policy interest have to be cleared through you, and it all takes time. And besides, I won't have the time to write my book.

The Secretary: In a year you will be back here on your knees.

Sisco: Well, the important thing is, when I am back here on my knees, just take me back.

The Secretary: I guess this is just something you have to get out of your system. The nice thing about working at American University Joe, is that no matter what you do it is going to be an improvement.

---

[5] The Department of State statement, issued on March 29, warned that military intervention in Lebanon "contains great dangers and must be avoided" and offered U.S. help toward a political solution. (*New York Times*, March 30, 1976, p. 65)

Whether you improve it 25% or 500%, the effort is all the same. You can go out there and really put your heart into it. Lay it out on the line, you can say that Washington needs a high prestige university and ...

Sisco: How would you like to be the Vice-President in charge of fund raising.

The Secretary: No, I won't take any part in fund raising, but I am willing to do what I can to help.

Sisco: The President said the other day that if he makes a foreign policy speech—and he has already decided not to—that he wanted to use American University.

The Secretary: But that is only because he is anti-Catholic. (laughter)

Sisco: I even offered him an honorary degree, but he decided not to make the speech anyway.

The Secretary: This is a good set of talking points. You should tell Asad that we really have a high degree of admiration for him here, and we are willing to work hard to move towards his objectives ... You should tell him that if this thing works within two years he would have a substantial part of the Golan and the settlements ... once you go beyond four kilometers, what settlements can they keep ... even if they partition the Golan, he would get almost all of the settlements ... at least he would get ⅔rds to ¾ths of the settlements for an end to the state of war.

Saunders: Except for the cluster of settlements in the south. So I guess that figure of ⅔rds is about right.

The Secretary: We can work out something about a delegation on which both the Syrians and the PLO would sit ... but if he goes the procedural route, then it will take forever ... just tell him we are trying to work with him ... but it is no good if he goes in ... two weeks later the Israelis would go in anyway ... then we would have the worst of everything.

Sisco: Do you think he might take umbrage at our pointing out what his longterm interests are?

The Secretary: No, we can tell him where his interests are.

Atherton: Joe has a good point. We can say that we are concerned that if he makes a move ...

The Secretary: You are right. He will say just let me worry about my own interests.

Murphy: We can just say ... but not so international.

The Secretary: Why try to discuss both at the same time. The first time just discuss Lebanon.

Sisco: Then later go back to discuss the second half.

The Secretary: I wouldn't refer to Rifai. You know he called me yesterday.

Sisco: From Spain?

The Secretary: And don't get in to UNDOF. He will just get into a great "state-of-war" debate.

And point out to him what the problem really is—that he really doesn't want to have a debate with six candidates running for the Presidency here, all of whom would have to get involved in this issue ... what we are talking about is how to prepare American public opinion for the final crunch.

Do you want to go tonight? I think you ought to come over with me to the White House now and I will take you in for five minutes with the President.

Murphy: That's fine. Do you think I ought to do this in two sessions?

The Secretary: Maybe three sessions. Lebanon first. But I leave it to your judgment. Maybe you can do more of it at one time, unless he goes into orbit.[6] It makes me think of that picture in his office, picturing himself as the permanent protector of the remnants of the crusaders. Well, I have to go now or I will be late.

---

[6] Telegram 1985 from Damascus, April 1, reported Murphy's meeting with Asad. (National Archives, RG 59, Central Foreign Policy Files, P850107–2530)

---

279. Memorandum of Conversation[1]

Washington, March 30, 1976, 9:40–10:20 a.m.

PARTICIPANTS

    President Ford
    Dr. Henry A. Kissinger, Secretary of State
    Brent Scowcroft, Assistant to the President for National Security Affairs

[Omitted here is discussion unrelated to Lebanon.]

[President:] How about Hussein?

---

[1] Source: Ford Library, National Security Adviser, Memoranda of Conversations, Box 18, March 30, 1976, Ford, Kissinger. Secret; Sensitive. The meeting was held in the Oval Office at the White House.

Kissinger: If I could just review Lebanon. There are two radical groups: the Jumblatt group and the PLO. There are two moderates: the Christians and moderate Arabs.

Syria has historically wanted to dominate Lebanon. Israel thinks that in the long term Syria in Lebanon would turn to the radicals and support the PLO. Syria feels that if they don't go in, the PLO will take over the country. I think Syria is right in the short run and Israel is right in the long run.

I think the best course of action is to support Syria politically and try to keep them out militarily. Under these circumstances, I think we need a senior guy in Lebanon. It could be Dean Brown or Bill Porter. Brown is associated with the Jordanian action of 1970 when Hussein smashed the PLO. That may be a problem. I would discuss Brown with the King.

I think the King is more worried than Rifai. Rifai is practically a Syrian agent. I wouldn't be surprised if he didn't think the King would be knocked off and he would be President.

President: How about the West Bank troubles?

Kissinger: We have been lucky so far but it is in the interest of all the Arabs to stir things up there.

We won't get much more than Lebanon today. Everything you say will get back to Asad. Say we think highly of Asad. We agree with Asad's analysis. We would like his political solution without military intervention, because we see no way that can be done without arousing an Israeli reaction.

We will help by sending a senior representative. If we can get a ceasefire, then Syria could send in some more surreptitiously.

Israel has told us virtually nothing, while we have shared with them everything we had. But they have said they are in touch with the Christians.

What we need is an assessment as to the staying power of the Christians. If they can hold out and if Asad can split the PLO and Jumblatt, we can do it politically. If, though, the Christians can't make it, we maybe have to acquiesce.

President: How would you start it?

Kissinger: I would thank him for his constructive role. Then ask for his assessment and the outcome. Then say you agree with his solution, but you have the gravest doubts about the method. If we could get a ceasefire, then we could implement the Syrian political situation and Asad could sneak in some more forces. I think the Israelis would accept it under these circumstances.

Asad wants to become the spokesman of the Arab world, so he will work to get the PLO under his control. Of course, Sadat does not want this to happen and is therefore supporting the PLO. So we are better off not letting Syrian troops in unless the Christians are in danger of being wiped out.

You could tell Hussein that the results of intervention would be incalculable and it is not in his interest to have the PLO and Lebanese under Syria and perhaps have an Israeli intervention.

If we finish Lebanon, you know where we are on the negotiations The non-belligerence approach is better than the Geneva approach, because it is a one-stage process rather than two.

[Omitted here is discussion unrelated to Lebanon.]

280. Memorandum of Conversation[1]

Washington, March 31, 1976, 10:45–11:03 a.m.

PARTICIPANTS

    Dr. Henry A. Kissinger, Secretary of State
    Joseph J. Sisco, Under Secretary of State for Political Affairs
    Gen. Brent Scowcroft, Deputy Assistant to the President for National Security Affairs
    Alfred L. Atherton, Jr., Assistant Secretary for Near Eastern and South Asian Affairs
    Harold H. Saunders, Director of Intelligence and Research
    Arthur R. Day, Deputy Assistant Secretary for Near Eastern and South Asian Affairs
    Peter W. Rodman, NSC Staff

Sisco: Arafat didn't stop fighting as we hoped. As to what we tell our Jordanian friends, we should, as we did yesterday, say that we believe now is time for a ceasefire.[2]

---

[1] Source: Library of Congress, Manuscript Division, Kissinger Papers, CL 275, Chronological File, March 1976, Folder 2. Secret; Sensitive. The meeting was held in the General Scowcroft's office at the White House. Brackets are in the original.

[2] President Ford met with King Hussein on March 30. The memorandum of conversation of the meeting is in the Ford Library, National Security Adviser, Memoranda of Conversations, Box 18, March 30, 1976, Ford, Kissinger, Jordanian King Hussein. They met again on March 31 immediately after this meeting. The memorandum of conversation is ibid., March 31, 1976, Ford, Kissinger, Jordanian King Hussein, Prime Minister Zaid Rifai.

Kissinger: We'll talk to them about the peace thing. Then I'll talk to the King at 4:00.[3]

Sisco: On the Security Council?

Kissinger: We should say we don't preclude a meeting of the Security Council and we'll be in touch with the Secretary General.

Have we heard from Murphy yet?[4]

Sisco: No.

Kissinger: When I see the King this afternoon, I'll tell him we've absolutely got to get a ceasefire first. Asad must know that if he moves without these efforts, we can do nothing. If a massive effort fails and the Syrians go in, he has to give absolutely a final terminal date. Three weeks at the most. If he [Hussein] wiped out the PLO in nine days, three weeks should be more than enough. [Laughter]

I'm prepared to work on Israel to prevent them from moving into South Lebanon. I won't tell him that. But the consequences would be too great.

Have we been telling the Egyptians everything we have?

Atherton: We have.

Sisco: Should we tell them everything we've told the King?

Kissinger: Yes, because they'll be happy with it. We are strongly against Syrian intervention, but for a political solution. And we sent a mediator,[5] which was partly their idea.

Scranton says I should go out there. What do you think?

Sisco: You can't mediate this thing. Some weeks later, if it's stable enough, you might go out there for a broader purpose.

Kissinger: I agree. Israel's behavior in this crisis is something no U.S. Government can accept. They must know something. They must be doing something. And they've told us nothing. I've been calling them twice a day.

I want, for the President's understanding, a chronology. All the initiatives we made, all the circuits we've made: to the Syrians, the Jordanians, the Saudis. They all said they didn't want outside help.

---

[3] The memorandum of conversation of the meeting between King Hussein and Kissinger, which took place on March 31 from 4:05 until 5:05 p.m. at Blair House, to discuss the Lebanon situation, Middle East negotiating strategy, and bilateral issues is in the National Archives, RG 59, Records of Henry Kissinger, Box 16, Nodis Memcons, Feb. 1976, Folder 1.

[4] See footnote 6, Document 278.

[5] Ford recalled Ambassador L. Dean Brown from retirement on March 30. At a March 30 staff meeting that included Brown, Kissinger instructed him about his mission in Lebanon. (Memorandum of conversation, March 30; Library of Congress, Manuscript Division, Kissinger Papers, CL 275, Chronological File, March 1976, Folder 2)

Sisco: How will Reagan play this, after this Jackson thing [that we should have sent the Marines]?[6]

Kissinger: He'll say we were characteristically weak.

Saunders: I wonder if we could hit back against Jackson.

Rodman: Make *him* look crazy.

Kissinger: We should say at the briefing: This is a novel approach to put U.S. troops in the middle of guerrilla country. It's unfeasible, to put US Marines in PLO territory. We can't get involved unless the parties want us.

Scowcroft: Well ...

Kissinger: Well, I don't want to say we won't fight. We should say it wasn't feasible and it would have been risky.

Saunders: Keep it in the past tense, as you said.

Kissinger: I want a chronology for the President of what we've done at all stages, and the last ten days.[7] If I may say, we've handled it with some delicacy over the last ten days. To keep the Syrians out for ten days.

[Sisco hands over the draft press statement on Waldheim, which the Secretary edits.]

---

[6] Jackson, who was running for the Democratic Presidential nomination, reportedly made the statement at a news conference in Wisconsin. (*New York Times*, March 31, 1976, p. 21)

[7] A paper entitled "Chronology of U.S. Actions in the Lebanese Civil Conflict, March 1975–March 1976" is in the Library of Congress, Manuscript Division, Kissinger Papers, CL 177, Geopolitical File, Lebanon, Oct. 22, 1975–Dec. 23, 1976.

---

281. Memorandum of Conversation[1]

Washington, April 2, 1976, 9 a.m.

PARTICIPANTS

    The Secretary
    Under Secretary Sisco
    Assistant Secretary Atherton
    Assistant Secretary Saunders

---

[1] Source: Library of Congress, Manuscript Division, Kissinger Papers, CL 275, Chronological File, April 1976, Folder 1. Secret; Sensitive.

Deputy Assistant Secretary Day
Jock Covey, Notetaker

SUBJECT

Lebanon

The Secretary: Okay, where do we stand?

Atherton: The ceasefire went into effect about 4 hours ago and there will be a parliamentary meeting on Monday.[2] I think we can expect a standstill for about 10 days.

The Secretary: And if they have a new President, will that extend it?

Atherton: My concern is that Jumblatt will continue to press for more than the Syrian formula. And if he doesn't get it, then he'll break off the ceasefire.

The Secretary: Dinitz called me this morning to say that the Syrians are moving a commando battalion into the Tripoli area.

Saunders: We don't have any word of that but it certainly is possible. They're observing radio silence in the area right now.

Atherton: That's interesting. That's the first piece of shared information we've had from the Israelis.

Sisco: Was he nervous about it?

The Secretary: He was asking us to do something.

Now have we heard anything from the British or the French or any of the others? You know the way the Israelis are playing this, they've designed it so they can say they asked us for our help but that we would do nothing.

These talking points on Lebanon (for the SFRC appearance today)[3] are outstanding. Who prepared them?

Day: It was a community project.

The Secretary: No, they really are outstanding. They're definitely too complex for the Committee but I will probably send them across to the President when he gets back.

All right. What are our next steps?

Day: We have one procedural problem and you may want Dean Brown's assessment—especially of Asad's position.

The Secretary: (reading news ticker) Here it is again: "U.S. warns Syria three times against intervention." Someone of you should call

---

[2] April 7. A 10-day cease-fire began in Lebanon on April 2.

[3] Kissinger's testimony before the Senate Foreign Relations Committee mostly concerned the sale of C–130 aircraft to Egypt. See the *New York Times*, April 3, 1976, p. 2.

Dinitz and warn him again not to play politics with this. They shouldn't think that they have an open drawing account.

All right, I guess we should do a summary for Asad, but we should not indicate that the Christians favor having the Syrians in.[4]

Atherton: This sort of summary would also be useful for our people.

Day: You may want to send it to Toon.

Sisco: Both Toon and Murphy.

The Secretary: You should also repeat it to Sadat. I think the Egyptians are reasonably well satisfied with this.

Day: I strongly suspect that the question of Syrian intervention will still be a lively one.

The Secretary: I still think that the probable outcome will be Syrian intervention.

Day: There will be no strong power center even after there is a new President, and both sides have some pretty heavy weapons.

Saunders: It would virtually mean they would have to take over because no one else has any power.

The Secretary: But it's important that we make it clear that that is absolutely a last resort, and we cannot be seen to be extracting guarantees from Israel at the same time we have been telling the Syrians that we would not work out any guarantees. I think within a week or two it will blow up again. How long do you think it will hold?

Day: There's a lot of new pressure. I think the negotiations will break down because Jumblatt wants them to.

Sisco: When are you going to Africa?

The Secretary: In the third week of April. Do you think it will break down by then?

Atherton: Sooner than that.

The Secretary: The next time it breaks down, Syria will probably go in.

Day: Yes. If it breaks down this time, then they will not be seeing anything ahead.

Atherton: The alternative is for them to try to shift to the left.

The Secretary: The Israelis will say that from their knowledge of the Christians, they can hold out indefinitely.

Saunders: That is not really the issue.

---

[4] The message to Asad was sent in telegram 80365 to Damascus, April 3, 0309Z. (National Archives, RG 59, Central Foreign Policy Files)

The Secretary: That is the only issue to the Israelis. A divided Lebanon would be the best for them.

Saunders: Not if they look further ahead.

Day: We should do some thinking now—if we have eventual Syrian intervention—on what basis will you want to present our position to the public.

The Secretary: First of all, I think we should keep all of these congressional briefings to a minimum. Otherwise every Congressman will be running to us with his own personal plan.

I just hope the President will not crow too much about the ceasefire in his campaign in Wisconsin.

Sisco: The temptation will be very great.

The Secretary: Do you really think it will blow up.

(conversation interrupted by Larry Eagleburger who reports that two shots were fired into the Soviet Mission in New York. Eagleburger recommends, and the Secretary approves, a very strong statement of outrage and apology.)

These Jewish groups are insane. What are they trying to accomplish?

Sisco: These are just the Jewish Defense League[5] tactics, and they've been the wrong tactics since the beginning. They probably feel they have more legitimacy now that there is some harassment going on in Moscow—even though that harassment in Moscow is due in great part, to what they've been doing in New York.

The Secretary: Right. I think we need cables for Eilts, Toon, and Porter. Can we get a cable from Brown? He should be telling us on what basis the U.S. should be doing whatever is necessary—keeping in mind, of course, that Syrian intervention is absolutely a last resort.

Atherton: On these congressional activities—I think we're better off briefing than not briefing.

The Secretary: We just have to be very careful that we don't seem to be inviting intervention.

Atherton: In my talks with Congressional types, I've always talked in terms of the expected chain reaction.

The Secretary: But by the same token we should not be unreasonable in terms of the real Syrian interests. (interrupted by phone call)

(in reference to shooting incident) Can the Governor do anything?

---

[5] The Jewish Defense League, founded in 1968 by Rabbi Meir Kahane, violently protested the Soviet Union's restrictions on Jewish emigration and conducted terrorist activities aimed at forcing the Soviet Government into loosening its emigration restrictions.

Sisco: It's really a city problem, but it certainly wouldn't hurt to call the Governor.

The Secretary: Who should be called first?

Sisco: The Mayor. Just tell him it's intolerable.

The Secretary: We should tell Toon that in our judgment, another flash point is approaching within a week or so—that we appreciate this analysis and he should keep in mind that this is the direction we will want to go if our efforts fail.[6] But that we should not get involved too early in the debate with the Israelis. But tell him I don't want to read all about it in the Israeli papers. Maybe we should meet again by the end of the day.

Sisco: Henry, I really think you should call the Governor, too. After all, you already told the Soviets you would.

---

[6] Telegram 80366 to Tel Aviv, April 3, 0312Z. (National Archives, RG 59, Central Foreign Policy Files)

---

282. Memorandum of Conversation[1]

Washington, April 3, 1976, 4 p.m.

PARTICIPANTS

    The Secretary
    Assistant Secretary Atherton
    Deputy Assistant Secretary Day
    Jock Covey, Notetaker

SUBJECT

    Lebanon

Atherton: The Soviets have announced that they are concerned that the Sixth Fleet is steaming towards Lebanon.

The Secretary: Okay, this is the note I want to send (hands annotated draft back to Atherton). You should get it over to Voronstov, but just don't send it all over this bloody building.

(reading a draft cable) I wonder if we could be more specific with Asad? We've got to keep it all within context.

---

[1] Source: Library of Congress, Manuscript Division, Kissinger Papers, CL 275, Chronological File, April 1976, Folder 1. Secret; Sensitive.

(reading another draft cable) Just make sure Toon gives this to no one below the rank of Allon and that they know they should protect it. Otherwise it will leak all over that government.

(calls Scowcroft—referring to draft note to Soviets) Have you discussed this now with Hyland?

Atherton: Yes, we discussed it with Hyland and Scowcroft has agreed to it.

The Secretary: (with Scowcroft still listening on phone) Don't you ever tell me that Scowcroft agrees to anything. Even if Scowcroft disagrees, it will go anyway (laughter) but in this case it is okay because we agree totally.

Atherton: Mr. Secretary, you'll see that we did up talking points that you may want to use with Dinitz in response to his note about Chamoun's talk with the Israelis.[2] You know Chamoun really is living in the past.

Day: He's headed directly towards partition.

Atherton: Although I don't know how he expects to do it unless he takes all the Christians to Southern Lebanon.

Day: The strategy of strengthening the Christians is basically good, but he is clearly headed toward partition.

The Secretary: Tell Brown that our contacts with the Christians indicate that they are heading towards partition and that his efforts must be aimed towards a united Lebanon. Tell him that he's got to work around a very fine line between strength and intransigence.

Tell Murphy, too, he should tell the Syrians we only want the Christians strong enough to defend themselves. Maybe we should tell Asad that we are letting some Israeli arms in.

Atherton: Do you think he doesn't know already.

The Secretary: I think he is already tumbled to it.

Atherton: Do you feel under any pressure to get back to Dinitz today on the Chamoun business?

The Secretary: There's plenty of time. I'll get back to him by tomorrow.

---

[2] Dinitz's note has not been found.

283. Memorandum of Conversation[1]

Washington, April 7, 1976, 8:05–9:25 a.m.

PARTICIPANTS

    President Ford
    Vice President Rockefeller
    Dr. Henry A. Kissinger, Secretary of State
    Donald Rumsfeld, Secretary of Defense
    David Matthews, Secretary of Health, Education and Welfare
    Brent Scowcroft, Assistant to the President for National Security Affairs
    Bipartisan Congressional Leadership (list attached)
    Leslie A. Janka (note taker)

SUBJECT

    Swine Flu Immunization Program, the Turkish Base Agreement, Lebanon Strife, and Transition Quarterly Funding in the Security Assistance Bill

[Omitted here is discussion unrelated to Lebanon.]

Secretary Kissinger: Let me turn now to Lebanon. We are facing three issues in the Lebanese crisis—a split between the Christian and Moslem communities, the split between the radical and moderate political views, and the intervention of outside powers.

The Christian-Moslem conflict arises from the constitutional structure of Lebanon which is based upon the proposition that the Lebanese population is equally divided between the Christians and the Moslems. However, it is now estimated that the population is 60 percent Moslem, and this is especially true if you consider the influx of large numbers of Palestinians.

The Moslem community is further split between radical groups supported by the Soviet Union and Libya and what could be considered more moderate factions. Another complication is the fact that the leader of the radical leftists Kamal Jumblatt is a Druze and therefore cannot play any role in a constitutional confessional structure. He is therefore in favor of deconfessionalizing the Lebanese Government.

We also have the Palestinians who are divided into basically three factions. As you can see from this map,[2] the population is divided in such a way that the Christians hold the mountainous areas north of Beirut, while the PLO control territory in the south.

---

[1] Source: Library of Congress, Manuscript Division, Kissinger Papers, CL 283, Presidential File, April 1976. Secret; Sensitive. The meeting was held in the Cabinet Room at the White House. Attached but not printed is the list of bipartisan congressional leaders.

[2] The map is not attached.

The Lebanese crisis began in the Christian-Moslem fighting last fall. From the beginning we were in touch with all parties. As you know, I met with the Lebanese Foreign Minister in September at the UN.[3] However, the fighting worsened. The next phase was a Syrian mediation effort which succeeded in late January.[4]

Today we are faced with the situation where there is no central authority of any kind in Lebanon. From the middle of March we have faced the danger that Syria might intervene. Our concern is based upon the fact that Israel would move into Southern Lebanon should Syria intervene in Lebanon and that would clearly risk a full scale Middle East war.

In this crisis we are facing a strange reversal of roles, with Syria supporting the Christians and fighting the PLO. Syrians are also supporting the moderate wing of the PLO, while cutting supplies to Jumblatt leftists and protecting the Christian areas. The Egyptians on the other hand are supporting the radicals because of their hatred for the Syrians.

The United States would prefer the same political outcome as the Syrians do, and so do the Israelis. But the United States and Israel do not want Syrian military intervention. But the paradox is that without Syrian intervention the PLO may in fact win. Our policy is designed to prevent a Syrian intervention, but to support their political mediation efforts along the lines of the January 22 settlement.

Last week we sent Ambassador Brown, one of our most senior and experienced diplomats, to Beirut in an effort to get communications going among the factions. We are the only country that everyone is talking to. So far, there is general agreement that there will be new elections for a new President and for getting parliament reconvened.

But I repeat the biggest problem is that there is no central authority at all in Lebanon, and even a new government will not have a strong security force to prevent the outbreak of new hostilities which could be started by any Lieutenant; and thus the whole thing would break down. If the cease-fire breaks down, Syrians will move in and Israel will surely move also. And therefore we have a very high potential for a wider Middle East conflict.

We have stopped Syrian intervention three times, so therefore the U.S. role is very important in keeping the parties restrained. We have been lucky and so far we have been making progress. We are now trying to get a security force set up with buffer zones between the fac-

---

[3] See Document 263.
[4] See footnote 2, Document 267.

tions. We are in close touch with all the parties, with the exception of the PLO, and we are in very close and constant touch with the Israelis.

The Lebanese economy is running down very badly. Each faction is surviving on outside support. The economy of Beirut is totally devastated.

Representative O'Neill: How do you explain what the Sixth Fleet is doing off the coast of Lebanon?

Secretary Kissinger: It is there for the possible evacuation of the 1,000 Americans left in Beirut. About 6,000 Americans have already left the country but our ships are not off the coast of Lebanon—they are about 36 hours away.

We recognize that any American force put into Lebanon would have to be prepared to fight all of the parties. We have never had and we have no intention now of putting American forces into Lebanon. The fact is that we could not even get diplomatically active until the Syrian mediation effort failed, simply because any U.S. action would tend to unite all parties against us.

Representative McFall: Can we get Egypt to pull out its support? Can the United States talk to the moderate PLO elements?

Secretary Kissinger: We are talking to the Egyptians now. Egypt will be willing to standdown if the Syrians could be kept out. But we have to recognize that the Egyptian role is really a minor one. On the whole, Syria has emerged as the supporter of the Christians and in opposition to the PLO and the Communists.

With regard to contacts with the PLO, we have had a firm policy of not talking to the PLO on the Middle East because the PLO will not recognize the existence of Israel. But we are now dealing with a Lebanese problem, not the broader Middle East issues. Nevertheless, we have so far not talked to the PLO.

Representative Anderson: Where are the radicals getting their arms from?

Secretary Kissinger: From Libya and Iraq. But the Syrians have acted to interdict the flow of supplies to the radicals by putting in its own troops disguised as Palestinians and by having its Navy patrol the coasts.

However, if Syria achieves the domination of the PLO factions, which is what it wants, then its policy in the Middle East might change. What we are working on is a Syrian political solution without Syrian intervention. Deconfessionalization would mean that the Christians would be made a permanent minority and Lebanon would become a pure Arab and a radical state, which neither Syria nor Israel would want on their borders. We have to recognize that the whole thing in Lebanon could fall apart very easily.

Representative Rhodes: Does Syria have territorial ambitions against Lebanon?

Secretary Kissinger: Syria lost some of the eastern valley territories when France created Lebanon. But more importantly, Syria has always wanted a dominant role in Lebanon. If the Syrians intervene militarily in Lebanon, they would smash the PLO just as the Jordanians did in 1970 and then reconstitute under Syrian domination. The question is what is the best outcome for the U.S. and Israel. We hope to be able to avoid making this difficult choice by achieving an independent Lebanon. Israel has been very restrained in all of this but the situation has very precarious elements in it.

[Omitted here is discussion unrelated to Lebanon.]

284. Minutes of National Security Council Meeting[1]

Washington, April 7, 1976, 2:35–4 p.m.

SUBJECT

Lebanon

Principals

The Vice President
Secretary of State Henry A. Kissinger
Secretary of Defense Donald Rumsfeld
Admiral James Holloway, Chief of Naval Operations (Acting Chairman in Gen. Brown's absence)
Director of Central Intelligence George Bush

OTHER ATTENDEES

Defense
Deputy Secretary of Defense William Clements

WH
Richard Cheney
Brent Scowcroft
William G. Hyland

NSC
Robert B. Oakley

---

[1] Source: Ford Library, National Security Adviser, Box 2, NSC Meetings File, NSC Meeting, April 7, 1976. Top Secret. The meeting was held in the Cabinet Room at the White House. All brackets, with the exception of ones describing omitted material, are in the original.

President: I thought we ought to have a meeting so that everyone on the National Security Council would be up to date on the situation in the Middle East, especially the problems we face in Lebanon. Henry and I have been following the situation on almost a daily basis and analyzing events and taking actions to ensure that restraint is continued by all parties. Last week, in the middle of the visit by King Hussein, we sent Dean Brown to take charge of our Embassy and talk to all the parties in order to impress upon them the importance of maintaining the ceasefire and reaching a moderate solution. He arrived there Friday,[2] I believe. He has seen everyone.

Kissinger: Actually, Mr. President, he arrived Wednesday night. He left right after you approved it, on a special aircraft. He has been running ever since and is doing a very good job.

President: Yes, he has been doing a fine job. The ceasefire is in effect although the situation is unsettled. It is so complex that it defies logic. We have been counselling restraint on both Israel and Syria.

Rumsfeld: The situation particularly defies logic as Henry tried to explain it to the Congressional leadership this morning.[3]

President: They came in confused about the situation, as they usually do.

Scowcroft: And they left still confused but at a higher level.

Kissinger: They need to know just how complex it is and to understand that it is not a simple question of pushing troops into Lebanon. If the President can stand it, I will go over again the briefing I gave this morning.

Basically, there are three interrelated levels which are at work: the strictly domestic struggle to redistribute power, the moderate-radical struggle with the impact of outside powers, and the inter-Arab considerations. The division of internal power is still based on a 1932 census which gives the Christians not only the Presidency but a 6 to 5 ratio for the upper civil service positions and seats in Parliament. Yet the total population is now 10 to 15% Palestinian and the rest is probably 60% Moslem. So this big strain has been building up for a reallocation of power and that is one level of the struggle.

The second level is the moderate-radical struggle within the Moslem camp—the Christians are almost all either moderate or conservative. On the Arab side there is a moderate faction which basically wants the status quo, the present system, preserved. The radical faction wants to secularize the state, thereby depriving the Christians of their position and safeguards. Like Rhodesia and South Africa, the minority

---

[2] April 2.
[3] See Document 283.

sees the surrender of its position as a threat to its very existence. These factions are supported from outside. The Christians are getting arms from Israel, which we do not oppose since it helps maintain the balance. The radical group is strongly supported by Libya and Iraq and the Lebanese Communist Party with some encouragement from the Soviets. They are divided, themselves, into a more moderate group—the PLO if you can call Arafat a moderate. Then there is the Syrian group and then the Jumblatt radicals. Jumblatt is getting help from Libya and Iraq and a bit from the Soviets and to some extent from Egypt because it is so angry at Syria.

The inter-Arab lineup is stranger. Syria by tradition would be on the side of the radicals but the situation has evolved in such a way that Syria is with the Christians and the moderate Moslems, trying to preserve the existing system. If Lebanon goes radical, it could get a larger influx of arms from the USSR and Syria would find itself squeezed between Lebanon and Iran. Asad wants to avoid this threat. Syria also wants to control the PLO thru the Saiqa, to replace Arafat by its man, Mohsen, and increase its power in the Arab world. Jumblatt's natural inclination will be to destroy the Christians. In the short-term, therefore, Syria's role is very constructive and serves our interests. But over the long term the Israeli fear of Syrian intervention has merit because Syria could within a couple of years consolidate its power and achieve the dominant position in an arc stretching from Lebanon through Jordan and pose a major radical threat, in line with its past tradition. Saudi Arabia has been playing a very complex role, by supporting the PLO in order to restrain its excesses but opposing the radicals. It wants to see a Syrian political victory but does not want to see Syria move in militarily. Jordan is apparently totally on the side of the Syrians, at least to judge from what Hussein had to say while he was here.[4] Egypt has a complex role.

President: Hussein told us he supported Syrian intervention. He said Jordan had eliminated the radicals in 1970 and Syria has an excellent opportunity to finish the job now.

Kissinger: For a year or two, this would be a good thing. This would be true with respect to the rejectionists. It would stabilize the entire situation in the area. But later you would get too much Syrian influence and then we would have to contend with a massive problem.

The January 22 settlement which the Syrians had worked out[5] collapsed when the army disintegrated and the Moslems went over to the

---

[4] See footnotes 2 and 3, Document 280.
[5] See footnote 2, Document 267.

side of the radicals. So Syria sent us a formal note[6] a couple of weeks ago requesting our advice about its intervening with regular army units to stop the fighting and restore order. We approached the Israelis who said they would move into South Lebanon if Syrian regular units came in. They said they could tolerate a smaller number—up to the total of a brigade but this was ambiguous—if they stayed north of the Beirut–Damascus road. So if Syria moves in regular troop units, Israel will come in. This will upset the entire Arab balance and force Syria to attack Israel. The Syrians could not stand still and face the charge of partitioning the country to share it with Israel. They would have to attack. The Saudis and Jordanians would have to support the Syrians. With Egypt out of the picture militarily, this would be a calamity since Israel would quickly overrun and smash Syria. The Soviets would then come in and we would face an oil boycott.

That is why we have been supporting the Syrian political plan of January 22, but we are concerned over a Syrian invasion. This gives us the opportunity to develop a relationship of confidence with Syria by helping it meet its minimal needs. Once again we find that we are the only country able to talk to all sides and we have the situation in pretty good shape for the moment, although it is uncertain as to how it will evolve. We have used the Saudis to urge restraint on the PLO and we have not discouraged Israel's resupply of the Christians. We support Syria's cutting off military supplies to the PLO by sea as well as land, and Israel has not objected to the activities of the Syrian patrol boats. We have used our fleet to worry the Soviets. They sent us a note protesting the fleet so we replied that a country which is responsible for supporting a faction involved in the struggle should make all efforts to stop the fighting. We now learn they are urging a ceasefire. We have the ceasefire but it is very fragile. We need to keep it together. Brown is doing a good job. But we can't get too far ahead of the Syrians.

The big need is to establish a central authority, and there are three ways of doing that:

one, that the factions will reach agreement among themselves. This is very doubtful.

second, that the factions agree to supply contingents to a central force and put it under the President. This would require us to talk to the PLO as one of the factions.

third is the seepage of additional Syrian forces into Lebanon, not the open entry of large numbers of regulars. We have had close cooperation thus far from the Syrians. A battalion moved into Tripoli quietly over the weekend. In Tripoli and elsewhere they have cut off the

---

[6] See footnote 2, Document 268.

supply of arms by sea. They are thus blockading arms to the leftists by land and sea. We have not discouraged the Syrian actions, nor have the Israelis. Israel grumbles when additional Syrians enter Lebanon and we take note of it to soothe them. Actually, the Israelis are acquiescing but Syria can't go too far, can't send in regulars in large numbers. Right now the Syrians—regulars, Saiqa and PLA—are one of four factions. The Lebanese left, the PLO and the Christians are the others. So far the situation is not out of control but if the balloon goes up as a result of Syria going in and Israel following with an intervention in the South, we will have an Arab war. Israel will not stop just inside the border but will go the Litani River. And once they go in we will never get them out. It will be like 1967. And if they go in and stay, there is a high probability of a major war. We need to plan for this.

My personal view is that if there is another war we need to overpower it quickly and use it as the point of departure to solve the whole Middle East problem. I believe that in another war, there is a high probability that the Soviets will come in in some form. They can't allow Syria to be smashed again. It would be total humiliation for the Soviets to allow Arab countries they arm and support to be totally defeated for the fourth time. It would probably be the end of Asad. Jordan would probably support Syria militarily and be smashed. Also, Saudi Arabia would support them and there would be an oil embargo. Egypt would be forced to come in. The only way to stop it is to demand a ceasefire in the name of an overall settlement.

Rockefeller: Not only an oil embargo. The Arabs own twenty billion in American assets they could dump. The disruption would be terrible.

Kissinger: Greenspan says the only way the Western Europeans can live within their means is thanks to Arab deposits. If the Saudis and Kuwaitis got out of the British pound, it would collapse. So if Syria goes in, we should make a major effort to keep Israel out. We will have to work out a proposal to keep Syria north of the Beirut–Damascus Road and a timetable for withdrawal. If Syria moves, our interest demands that we try to keep Israel out. But it would be better if we can get a solution and Syria does not move.

To get a solution we may have to ask for your authorization to deal with the PLO, Mr. President. There would be no change in our position toward the PLO on the Middle East question but we have no commitment to Israel not to talk to the PLO exclusively about the situation in Lebanon. This could also help us with the Middle East situation.

President: We have an evacuation group off the coast, don't we Don?

Rumsfeld: Yes, sir. [Hands the President a chart showing location.][7]

Kissinger: We don't need to face the PLO question now but we may need to later on. I will come back to you on this.

Bush: What about the French mediation effort?

Kissinger: They are a bunch of jackals. They came to us at Syria's request to ask us to hold off the Israelis and they suggested the idea of international guarantees. We warned that we could not count on stopping Israel but told them we needed to have specific information about Syria's intentions if we were to have a chance. They told the Syrians we had turned them down and said something entirely different to the Israelis. The Quai[8] is full of Gaullists who practice cheap Machiavellian politics. This is not true of Giscard, but it is of many around him. They have irresponsible Gaullist tendencies.

President: Do we have contingency plans, Don?

Rumsfeld: There is a working group which is meeting to work on these plans.

Scowcroft: The working group has met and all the plans are being updated—military, political, intelligence and economic.

Kissinger: In the event of another war, we will need to pour forces into the Mediterranean to dissuade the Soviets. My estimate is that there is a greater probability of a Soviet move now than ever before.

President: When will the plans be prepared?

Hyland: By Tuesday,[9] Mr. President. We will have the plans updated. Right now we are getting the intelligence inputs. We have contingency plans concerning the evacuation of the Sinai and Lebanon. State is working out political and diplomatic contingency plans but you can't be sure of what the circumstances will be so that cannot be too precise. We also have in being an extensive economic contingency plan covering full and partial oil embargoes and financial problems.[10] CIA has just completed an update on free world oil stocks and non-OAPEC production. We are way ahead of 1973. We have forces in the area. We are alert. Our contingency planning is in pretty good shape.

Scowcroft: We will also have a single coordinated situation report to eliminate the confusion we have had in the past.

---

[7] The chart is not attached.

[8] A reference to the Quai d'Orsay, where the French Ministry of Foreign Affairs is located.

[9] April 13.

[10] Documentation on the contingency plan is scheduled for publication in *Foreign Relations, 1977–1981*, volume XXXVII, Foreign Energy Policy, 1974–1981.

Kissinger: We have also learned a lot. We know that the Syrians are scared of the Israelis so the idea of a Syrian attack can be pretty much ruled out. We exaggerate Israel's eagerness to enter Lebanon but Syria is not about to start a war if it can be avoided. Only if they have to go into Lebanon and Israel also goes in. We have also learned that the Soviets are not eager for a war. They are supporting the Lebanese Communist Party and other local elements, including the PLO, but overall they are a factor of restraint. The Lebanese Communist Party is most helpful but the Soviets seem to be counselling the Syrians against moving. They want to have their cake and eat it, too. The Soviets are not looking for trouble but they will be forced to move rather than lose all their assets in the Middle East, should another war come.

Scowcroft: Egypt is in bad shape. It would probably take them a week to get ready and Syria would be knocked out by then.

President: When does the ceasefire in Lebanon end?

Kissinger: Monday. But things are moving in a good direction so we have maybe two weeks. We must get some sort of a force in being, even a force composed of the major elements, to restore some sort of order. We have explored the idea of a neutral zone, but there are too many undisciplined, criminal elements and there is no one to police them. A buffer zone without a force is no good.

Bush: Do you believe what the Israelis tell us about the Christian military situation?

Kissinger: Brown has talked to the Christian leaders and our Defense Attaché has talked to their military men. We believe that they could hold out for three weeks in case of another attack but there could be a lot of erosion in their position during that period.

Rumsfeld: The Lebanese Defense Attaché has come to us and asked for arms and ammunition. We told him to present the request through diplomatic channels to the Department of State.

Kissinger: Let the Israelis do it. They are already supplying the Christians.

Rumsfeld: We have the carrier *Saratoga* which is between 24 and 36 hours away from Lebanon.

Admiral Holloway: They could provide air support within twelve hours.

Rumsfeld: We also have the *Guadalcanal* which is less than 24 hours from Beirut. Beyond that we can use civilian or military airlift or possibly sealift.

I understand the interagency process is working. Plans are being updated and dusted off. We will see there is no carrier gap in the Mediterranean. After the interagency group has gone over the plans we will take other moves.

Scowcroft: We can have the NSC meet again then.

Rumsfeld: We will have our plans ready for review by next Tuesday. What about the military probabilities? What about the role of Jordan?

Clements: The last time I was out there I felt a pulse beating on the confederacy between Jordan and Syria. There are all sorts of likely indicators. Jordan and Syria are getting very, very close to each other, to the disadvantage of Saudi Arabia.

President: My impression from Hussein was that Jordan and Syria are closer so long as Asad is in charge. If a more radical individual comes to power in Damascus, then Jordan will move away.

Kissinger: Jordan is playing a very dangerous game. They are telling the Syrians everything so we can't tell them as much anymore.

Clements: Henry, you are right. Jordan is playing an extremely dangerous game. They are walking on eggs. If they have a full understanding with Syria on Lebanon, it will be trouble.

Kissinger: That is a minor question. The Soviets are the big question if we move into another conflict. Israel will have no trouble with Syria and Jordan.

Scowcroft: Now Israel can go around the Golan through Lebanon, not having to go over the mountains.

Rumsfeld: There is some question about whether or not our task force should anchor. It makes about 24 hours difference in the time needed to reach Lebanon, since they would have to start the boilers and other things.

Admiral Holloway: There is no real problem now. We can have the helicopters in for evacuation within 24 hours. The task force will need to anchor some time to ease the strain on the personnel, including the Marines, but not right away. It is also true that it costs more to steam than to anchor. There is an anchorage off Turkey, but our Ambassador has been reluctant to ask the Turks for permission and we do not need it now. But bear in mind that an extended period at sea causes some deterioration in readiness. We will put it to the Secretary, if there is a need to use the anchorage.

Rumsfeld: Our plans will be ready by next Tuesday. Shall we meet again next week?

President: What is my schedule? Will I be in town?

Cheney: You will be in Texas this weekend but in town all next week.

President: Let us have another meeting the end of next week.

Rumsfeld: In the October War we had a problem with our NATO allies, who did not want to give us permission to use their territory. In the worst-case scenario we need to be able to use some NATO forces yet when the Defcon 3 alert came they were nervous. We might not be able to count on Italy or Germany next time so in the contingency plan, we may want to assign units not in NATO countries, especially those two.

President: Let us meet no later than Thursday.

Kissinger: I think we have an improved situation and we have done reasonably well in keeping it under control. If Syria does go in, despite our efforts, we should do our best to keep the Israelis out.

President: When Hussein was here, he estimated the Christians could only last for 48 hours. That did not happen.

Kissinger: I do not believe an all-out attack will be made on the Christians. We should keep our same posture—not explaining what E and E means so people will be scared by the presence of the fleet and not talking about the Marines going in or not going in. We sent others a threat as well as giving them an excuse to do or not to do things. The fleet movements have been helpful.

Vice President: Don't we have leverage over Israel? With all we are giving them, why can't we simply tell Israel not to go in.

Kissinger: We want to keep the Israeli threat alive for now. That is healthy. But if Syria moves then we must put our interests first.

Bush: Our judgment is that the Israelis are the source of that story in *Time* about their atomic bombs.

Rumsfeld: [*1 line not declassified*]

Bush: [*3 lines not declassified*]

Scowcroft: Schechter came to me for confirmation. I told him it was hogwash but he waited a couple of days and ran it anyway so they must have had a solid source. It looks as if it were an Israeli story.

[Omitted here is discussion unrelated to Lebanon.]

285. Memorandum of Conversation[1]

Washington, April 13, 1976, 10:04–10:44 a.m.

PARTICIPANTS

President Ford
Dr. Henry A. Kissinger, Secretary of State
Donald Rumsfeld, Secretary of Defense
Brent Scowcroft, Assistant to the President for National Security Affairs

The President: What is happening in Lebanon?

Kissinger: Our big problem now is Egypt wants us to get the Syrians out. [*less than 1 line not declassified*] Arafat is asking Egypt to get the Syrians out.[2]

The President: Arafat was just recently blasting Egypt.

Kissinger: I think we are okay on our present course. I think over the long run the Lebanese developments will help. I think Arafat will lose his influence in favor of Saiqa. This will remove the PLO's veto over the actions of Syria. The danger is that Asad may be overthrown.

The President: But if this works out, won't he be strengthened?

Kissinger: He may be thrown out anyway. He has been in there longer than anyone else. If my prediction is right, we may have a unique peace window next year.

The President: Won't all this help with the renewal of UNDOF?

Kissinger: Asad, we have proved, is scared to death of the Israelis.

The President: How about the Sixth Fleet?

Kissinger: I think we should keep it there until a new Lebanese President is elected.

Rumsfeld: The problem is money for steaming time.

[Omitted here is discussion unrelated to Lebanon.]

---

[1] Source: Library of Congress, Manuscript Division, Kissinger Papers, CL 221, Geopolitical File, Middle East, Donald Rumsfeld, 1975–76. Secret; Nodis. The meeting was held in the Oval Office at the White House.

[2] Syrian troops moved into Lebanese territory early on April 9.

286. Minutes of Washington Special Actions Group Meeting[1]

Washington, April 22, 1976, 8:06–8:50 a.m.

SUBJECT

Lebanon

PARTICIPANTS

Chairman
Henry A. Kissinger

State
Roy Atherton

DOD
Donald Rumsfeld
William Clements

JCS
Gen. George S. Brown

CIA
George Bush

NSC Staff
Brent Scowcroft
William G. Hyland
Michael Hornblow

PART I—LEBANON

Secretary Kissinger: This morning we are going to have a brief review of the Working Group's work.[2] After this there will have to be an NSC meeting on Lebanon and Cuba so that the President can make decisions. (George, do you have a briefing?)

Mr. Bush: I don't believe a briefing is necessary this morning. There is no new intelligence on the current situation. It is rocking back and forth. I can't confirm the withdrawal of any Syrian troops. Their troop presence seems about the same as it was.

Secretary Kissinger: We are everybody's whipping boy. Egypt is accusing us of colluding with Syria. Syria is accusing us of colluding with Egypt. Jumblatt says we're colluding with the Christians. The Christians say we're colluding with the Moslems.

Gen. Brown: I would like to tell you about an incident that happened last week. As you know Pan American had been flying into

---

[1] Source: Ford Library, NSC Institutional Files, Box 25, Meeting Minutes, WSAG-Originals, March–April, 1976. Top Secret. The meeting took place in the White House Situation Room.

[2] The Working Group was updating contingency plans; see Document 284.

Beirut once a week. The flights have been bringing in blood for the hospital, mail and some supplies for the embassy. Last week we had to go in with a 141. We parked on the military side of the airport. An attaché was present. Bandits held up the plane and searched it for weapons. They didn't do any harm, but did steal all the regular mail. I have now told our people that no flights should go into Lebanon without specific authorization from Washington.

Secretary Kissinger: That seems sensible.

Mr. Atherton: If there is a need for a flight it could be checked out in advance with Dean Brown.

Secretary Kissinger: Yes. If Brown knows in advance he could work it out.

General Brown: I heard on the radio this morning that there was gunfire at the Beirut airport.

Secretary Kissinger: Yes, I heard that, too. Let's talk about the Lebanese situation. There's not much to say. It is extremely precarious. George, how many Syrian troops are in there now?

Mr. Bush: We believe there are between 5,000 and 6,000 Syrian troops there now. It is also the Intelligence Community's assessment that the Israelis would resist any Syrian move to the Latani River with mechanized force.

General Scowcroft: I believe the DIA has a slightly different estimate for Syrian troops. Closer to 4,000.

Secretary Kissinger: Is that 5,000 figure in addition to the PLA forces?

Mr. Bush: There are not great differences between our estimate and the DIA estimate. We believe there are about 5,000 Syrian troops in Lebanon.

Secretary Kissinger: Is that in addition to the PLA forces?

Mr. Bush: Yes.

Secretary Kissinger: We are bringing Dean Brown back for consultations. We will then send him out again to Lebanon just before Meloy arrives.

Mr. Clements: Did he see Malik?[3]

Mr. Atherton: No, Malik is out of touch with reality.

Secretary Kissinger: Regarding Lebanon it is to be expected that if no group wins, all the groups will be mad. It is almost inconceivable but Egypt has been complaining to us that Israel hasn't yet moved. We are left holding the bag. Syria is not happy with us because we have

---

[3] Charles Malik, former Lebanese Foreign Minister, was one of the founders of the Front for Freedom and Man in Lebanon, which was renamed the Lebanese Front.

been restraining them from moving in with full force. The Christians also are unhappy with us and it now looks as if Syria may end up dominating the PLO with the result being that the Christians would end up in worse shape than they are now. Let's talk about the military situation if it blows up.

Mr. Hyland: If war starts over Lebanon our initial estimate is that by the end of D–3 or D–4 Israel would be able to mount a successful drive against Syria and be within 15 kilometers of Damascus. Syria would then be in a desperate situation and would ask for Soviet intervention.

Secretary Kissinger: Asad might not want to fight there. His strategy is to bleed the Israelis.

Mr. Hyland: Losses in the air might hurt them more than losses on the ground.

Secretary Kissinger: During the last war they got near Damascus in three or four days.

General Scowcroft: I would like to suggest a new element. The Israelis could move in back of Mount Hebron into Lebanon and really wrap things up.

General Brown: That is really rough territory. There is quite a defile there.

Mr. Hyland: We have looked at the situation. Our interpretation is that the USSR could in three or four days put in 7,000 to 8,000 troops—one airborne division. However, it is more likely that Russian intervention would be with aircraft that would enable them to get there faster and with greater numbers.

Our group looked at possible U.S. moves. The first possibility would be a show of force. We could move an infantry battalion from Europe to Crete. However, there might be a political problem. Can we go to Crete?

Secretary Kissinger: I don't think so. In 1973 Crete let us use their airfields. I don't think we could move ground forces onto Crete.

General Brown: The only flag that can go into Crete is the NATO flag. We have no bilateral agreements with Crete that I am aware of.

Secretary Rumsfeld: So it would not be proper to move in our ground forces.

General Scowcroft: No.

Secretary Rumsfeld: We're not speaking about definite plans are we, these are just contingencies?

Mr. Hyland: Well one of the first movements of our ground forces would be in Cyprus.

Secretary Rumsfeld: What about the *Guadalcanal*?

Mr. Hyland: There's also the 509th from Vincenza.

Secretary Rumsfeld: Wouldn't the Italian Government object?

General Brown: Yes. We could move the 82nd.

Secretary Kissinger: Where?

General Brown: To Israel.

Secretary Kissinger: Let's talk about where we might move American forces.

General Scowcroft: There are three places, Crete, Cyprus, or Israel.

General Brown: We are thinking in terms of Incurlick, Turkey.

Secretary Kissinger: That probably won't be possible—not after Congress gets through.

Mr. Bush: Henry, is that letting up at all?

Secretary Kissinger: No, it's going to turn into a real brawl.

General Brown: We do have a force at sea. We have Marines on the *Guadalcanal*. It is 24 hours away. We do have specific evacuation plans.

General Scowcroft: Shouldn't we look at our objectives?

Mr. Clements: You're right Brent, just why should we move into Israel?

General Brown: What would be the consequences if the Soviets moved into Syria?

Secretary Kissinger: In the previous Middle Eastern crisis we had reinforcements in the Mediterranean before the Soviets did anything.

General Brown: A lot depends on the Soviets.

Secretary Kissinger: Our initial problem is to make sure that the Arabs see us in a position of high readiness in the Mediterranean. Our second problem is to see what we would do if the Soviets moved. In the first phase there would be no U.S. troops sent into Israel. In the first phase we would make clear our intention to stay out as long as the Soviets stay out.

Secretary Rumsfeld: What would the Turks, Italians, Soviets, Germans, and Greeks do in this situation?

Secretary Kissinger: I can tell you the Turks would very likely try to prevent our overflying. The Greeks and the Italians would certainly play up to the Arabs as much as possible. The Germans might close their eyes to some of our troop movements as long as we didn't advertise them.

Secretary Rumsfeld: But don't we want to advertise our movements?

Secretary Kissinger: No, that would not be necessary because the Soviets are well aware of our movements. We better face the fact that we will get no support from Europe. The Europeans would be committed on the Arab side.

Secretary Rumsfeld: Well if that is true, it only leaves us with the *Guadalcanal* or the 72nd Airborne Division.

Secretary Kissinger: We can move troops out of NATO, but we can't earmark 5 divisions.

Secretary Rumsfeld: I would opt to use the troops in NATO or the 82nd.

General Scowcroft: The question is where to land them.

Mr. Clements: If we get concurrence from some Arabs that we should put troops into Lebanon, then the NATO equation changes.

Secretary Kissinger: However, it is quite likely that Lebanon would not permit us to land our forces there, that is, if there is a Lebanese government at the time.

Mr. Clements: Oh I think there will be some form of Lebanese government. If we receive an invitation from the Lebanese government—then Sadat might back it up.

Secretary Kissinger: If there is a war between Syria and Israel it would be a miracle if Sadat stayed out of it. It is inconceivable to me that Sadat would support us if we landed troops in Lebanon.

Mr. Clements: Well, I'm trying to think of one move ahead. U.S. troop, in Lebanon could prevent an Israeli-Syrian war.

Secretary Kissinger: If there is no Syrian-Israeli war it is conceivable that we could move into Lebanon, but it would be a tough and possibly costly move and I'm not at all sure that Egypt could support such a move.

Secretary Rumsfeld: If we did go in, the PLO might not fight us. They're more interested in destroying the other factions.

Secretary Kissinger: We're talking about totally different situations here. If U.S. troops move in as a buffer to separate opposing forces it could well embroil us with the Syrians. The Syrians might then move massively into Lebanon. We might then be faced with protecting the PLO from the Syrians. Once we move in, there is no easy way to get out. Are we really prepared to take on Lebanon?

Secretary Rumsfeld: But aren't we really worried about Beirut not Lebanon? If the Israelis move to the north and we put in U.S. troops, that does us no good vis-à-vis Beirut.

Secretary Kissinger: If the situation gets out of hand in Lebanon, we must ask ourselves what national interests we have there which would lead us to put in our forces.

Secretary Rumsfeld: Our national interest is to try to prevent a Middle Eastern war.

Mr. Clements: That is right.

Gen. Scowcroft: If the Israelis start moving we could put in our Marines near the Litani River.

Secretary Kissinger: We are talking about two totally different situations. If the Israelis move, do we put in U.S. forces? If the Israelis don't move, do we put in U.S. forces? If we move our troops into separate opposing forces along the Litani River, that effectively would halt any Israeli advance. But the Arabs would oppose this and take it as our siding with Israel.

Mr. Clements: I just think I disagree with you there Henry. If it really looked like the Israelis were going to win, then the Arabs could very well support U.S. troop involvement.

General Brown: We could move in before the Israelis move and be in place and let the Israelis try to walk over us. It could be at the old UN line. It is kind of a wild idea.

Secretary Rumsfeld: It would be a tripwire.

Secretary Kissinger: If that happened the Israelis would start swearing that we are in collusion with Syria. The Egyptians would also start screaming but for different reasons.

Mr. Clements: We could easily take care of that in one conversation with Sadat and convince him that this would be in his best interest. As long as we are in there we are perceived to be in cahoots with the Arabs and that could be helpful.

General Brown: Helpful where?

Mr. Clements: With NATO and the Arab world.

Mr. Hyland: The marines would land offshore?

Mr. Clements: They could come in by plane.

General Scowcroft: How—from the *Guadalcanal*?

Secretary Kissinger: How long would it take?

General Brown: It would take 28 hours.

Secretary Kissinger: Israel would not move in that fast if Syria goes in.

General Brown: The only military plans we have are evacuation plans.

Secretary Kissinger: We need to have plans for two contingencies: (1) U.S. forces on the old UN line; (2) U.S. forces on the Litani River.

General Brown: We don't have any plans now. Just some concepts.

Secretary Rumsfeld: What bothers me is that we are talking about the last step of things—military action. But military action should only be taken after political and economic actions.

Secretary Kissinger: We have been active diplomatically but we need to have military plans in case the other things fail.

Secretary Rumsfeld: In this paper[4] there is no focus on political or economic steps we should take.

Secretary Kissinger: We have been doing nothing else in this crisis.

Mr. Clements: I know you have been working hard, Henry. I would like to point out that the whole Arab world is opposed to Syria putting their troops in.

Secretary Kissinger: Jordan might support Syria and so might the Saudis. We have managed to keep Syria out until now. It is hard to know if they will move.

Mr. Atherton: I am not certain Israel would move as quickly as we have been suggesting.

General Scowcroft: The Israelis might not consult with the U.S. before they move. They would anticipate that we would exert strong pressure on them not to move. But they might want us to keep them from moving.

Secretary Kissinger: The Israelis might not be eager to move. They realize that the outcome of a move on their part might be massive pressure on them to return to the 1967 borders. What do we do if the Soviets intervene after Syria gets creamed?

Mr. Clements: By making a move like this we can prevent that from happening. We should get hard at it and discuss the possibility of putting U.S. troops into Lebanon with Sadat.

Secretary Kissinger: I would not discuss that sort of thing with Sadat without the President's authorization.

Mr. Clements: Of course, but we could talk to him on an exploratory basis.

Secretary Kissinger: Where would we put our troops? Would we put them between opposing factions or on the Litani River? Sadat might very well construe such intervention as an invitation for the Soviets to move in.

Gen. Scowcroft: We would only do this if the Syrians move in militarily. But then the U.S. forces would be in direct opposition to the Syrian forces and we don't have enough troops.

Secretary Kissinger: Asad would vehemently oppose this and would threaten to fight. There is a chance he might acquiesce to U.S. forces on the Litani River or the Israeli border. We would then get his support but at the same time lose Sadat's support. Sadat might support a U.S. move into Beirut but that has the highest possibility of combat and we would have to go in with overwhelming force.

Mr. Clements: If we go into Beirut it would get people killed.

---

[4] Presumably a reference to a Working Group paper; it is not attached.

General Scowcroft: The Litani River or the old UN line seems the only useful U.S. contingencies.

Secretary Kissinger: If we do make a preventative move it would get Syria in for sure.

Mr. Clements: That is the difference between us, Henry. I am convinced there is enormous Arab pressure on Syria not to go in. Of course before we move in we would have to do our homework.

Secretary Kissinger: Well so far we have managed to get off of the real danger point. There seems to now be a 52 to 48% chance of a settlement. With all due respect, Defense should not constantly say they cannot make up military plans until the political and economic steps have been taken.

Secretary Rumsfeld: Well just what do you want Henry? Tell us what you want and we will do it. Just put it on a piece of paper.

Secretary Kissinger: I want to know what do we do if the Soviets intervene.

Secretary Rumsfeld: We can provide it. Just put it on a piece of paper.

Secretary Kissinger: I want to know what happens if the Israelis win and then the Soviets intervene.

Mr. Hyland: There is a plan and a schedule of possible movements we could take. A lot of it depends on Cyprus.

Secretary Kissinger: Do we have the right to put in forces there?

Mr. Hyland: No. We would have to approach Callaghan and get his approval. This would be a risky step for the UK because they would be risking an oil embargo.

Secretary Kissinger: Could you move the 82nd division to Israel without using an intermediate staging area.

General Brown: Physically yes but I would like to use Lajes.

Secretary Kissinger: What if you don't get Lajes. We need to have three different plans. (1) U.S. forces on the Litani River; (2) U.S. forces on the Israeli-Syrian border; and (3) The third plan is in two stages. What reinforcements would we need in the Middle East if there is an Israeli-Arab war but without Soviet intervention. The second part is to consider what steps we would take if there is Soviet intervention.

Roy will have to work up a diplomatic scenario for the first two. If we send in the marines what do we have to do beforehand? Is there any more planning?

Mr. Bush: I am going to look into strengthening our intelligence collection capabilities in the area.

287. Memorandum of Conversation[1]

Washington, April 27, 1976, 9:45 a.m.

PARTICIPANTS

President Ford
Ambassador Dean Brown, Special Emissary to Lebanon
Brent Scowcroft, Assistant to the President for National Security Affairs

The President: Despite your trials and tribulations, you look great. I would like to know where we stand, but first of all I would like to thank you on behalf of the American people for the outstanding job you did. We don't have everything we wanted but thanks to you we are in fairly good shape.

Brown: Once we get through this Presidential election[2] we will have a period of uneasy truce, at a tolerable level of violence. A security force that is manipulated by internal and external forces can't do better than that. The problem with this "tolerable level" of violence is that business won't go back in. Every Lebanese with a nickel has moved it out of the country. There are countless groups roaming around looting and killing—they have to be put against the wall and shot. So real security is the basic problem.

The President: Where are we politically?

Brown: Frangieh fiddled for an unconscionable time. He really was afraid he would eventually be brought to trial for his misdeeds. Now there will be an election. These are not just politicians; they are really a group of warlords. And everybody will be buying and selling votes. I hope it will be Sarkis but I am saying publicly we have no candidate, because that would be the kiss of death.

The President: How about Asad?

Brown: The Christians were disappointed that he didn't intervene with his divisions. The leftists were worried that he would. The problem with Lebanon is it is run by the same group of old warlords who have been in power since 1943. Until they die off, there is little hope for any real progress.

The President: How much will the Israelis tolerate?

---

[1] Source: Ford Library, National Security Adviser, Memoranda of Conversations, Box 19, April 27, 1976, Ford, Special Emissary to Lebanon Dean Brown. Secret; Nodis. The meeting was held in the Oval Office at the White House. According to the President's Daily Diary, the meeting began at 10:20 and ended at 10:40 a.m. (Ford Library, Staff Secretary's Office Files)

[2] The Lebanese Presidential election was scheduled for May 6.

Brown: It is hard to know how many Syrian troops there are—they are well disguised.

The President: How about Arafat?

Brown: For a while, he was doing most of the fighting. Because the leftists left it to the PLO. Then Asad told him that was crazy, getting his Palestinians all chopped up.

The President: I noticed a number of Lebanese have moved to Cyprus.

Brown: Yes. They are waiting there to see what happens.

The President: When will you go back?

Brown: I thought I would wait until the election is held so I wouldn't be accused of plotting.

The President: Are the Christians Arabs?

Brown: Yes. But only the Maronites are involved. There are 500,000 more Christians who aren't even involved. The Lebanese problem won't be solved until the Palestinian problem is solved.

The President: Jumblatt isn't a Moslem.

Brown: He is an offshot called Druze. He is crazy.

The President: Again, we thank you. Are we welcomed there by everyone?

Brown: Very much so. They want someone to solve their problems. I think we should help in any way everyone approves—including training their security forces.

288. Memorandum of Conversation[1]

Washington, June 16, 1976, 12:40–1:45 p.m.

PARTICIPANTS

    President Ford
    Vice President Rockefeller
    Dr. Henry A. Kissinger, Secretary of State
    George Bush, Director, Central Intelligence Agency
    William P. Clements, Jr., Deputy Secretary of Defense
    Brent Scowcroft, Assistant to the President for National Security Affairs

---

[1] Source: Ford Library, National Security Adviser, Memoranda of Conversations, Box 19, June 16, 1976, Ford, Rockefeller, Kissinger, Bush, William Clements. Secret; Nodis. The meeting was held in the Oval Office at the White House. Brackets are in the original.

Kissinger: They [Meloy and Waring] may have been killed.[2] They have three bodies but it will be an hour or so before they are identified.

[The President looks at the map of Beirut.][3]

They were on their way to a visit with Sarkis to talk about the Arab force.

President: Who gave us the word?

Kissinger/Bush: It was a member of the ICRC.

President: Have we gotten any messages back?

Kissinger: Not yet. We sent messages to the Soviets, British, France, Syria, Egypt, Libya, Saudi Arabia, Jordan[4] that he had been kidnapped and how seriously we take it.

Our estimate is it was done by a rejectionist group, with the motivation perhaps to provoke a violent American reaction which would unify all the Arabs.

We have Dean Brown standing by to go there, because there isn't a cool head there now.

Clements: But we have to remember that even the organized units are out of control and every SOB has a machine gun.

Kissinger: That reinforces my point.

President: What is your appraisal, Nelson?

Vice President: There is a domestic side. Reagan could jump on this and demand that you take strong action.

Internationally, if this could be used as a vehicle to get the Egyptians behind the Syrians to clean up the mess ... Strong Arab action could get the President off the hook.

Kissinger: I don't think there is anything we can do to get Egypt to give Syria a free hand, and to suggest it may be counterproductive.

Vice President: Ike went in in '58[5] and it was successful.

---

[2] Ambassador to Lebanon Francis Meloy, Jr.; Robert Waring, the Embassy's Economic Counselor; and their driver were kidnapped on June 16 and found shot to death that day. Ambassador Meloy had been appointed on May 1, succeeding G. McMurtrie Godley, who had left post on January 13.

[3] The map of Beirut is not attached.

[4] All messages were sent on June 16. The message to Egypt is in telegram 148551 to Cairo (National Archives, Central Foreign Policy Files, RG 59, D760232–0689); to Syria in telegram 148553 from State (Ibid., D760232–0688); to Saudi Arabia in telegram 148554 to Jidda (Ibid., D760232–0691); and to France and the United Kingdom in telegram 148654 to Paris and London (Ibid., D760232–0834).

[5] On July 15, 1958, President Eisenhower authorized U.S. troops to enter Lebanon in response to Lebanese President Camille Chamoun's call for help. Chamoun's government was under pressure from internal opposition and the United Arab Republic, and Chamoun wanted U.S. forces to protect his government. U.S. troops remained in Lebanon until October 25.

President: What assets do we have there?

Clements: [Described the task forces.] But I think intervention would be a mistake.

[Discussion of the possible methods of evacuation—by aircraft, by sea, or by road to Damascus—and the pros and cons of evacuation.]

President: Regardless of the political consequences, there are several actions to consider:

(1) Have a civilian ship available.
(2) Ease our ships in closer. I recognize the concern.

Vice President: The President has to show he is doing something. If we could get the Egyptians to take strong action . . .

Kissinger: We should issue a statement, saying that our best information is this was done by a small group of terrorists. This is a disgusting, reprehensible act. You should say: I call on all parties to condemn this act and to cooperate to bring the perpetrators to justice.[6]

---

[6] President Ford made a statement on the assassinations at 4:05 p.m. on June 16. The next day, the White House announced that the President had designated Ambassador Brown as his Personal Representative to go to Damascus and accompany Meloy's and Waring's bodies to the United Sates. (*Public Papers: Ford, 1976–77*, Book II, pp. 1885–1886)

---

289. Memorandum of Conversation[1]

Washington, June 18, 1976, 11 a.m.

PARTICIPANTS

President Ford
The Cabinet

President: Ron just announced we are evacuating Americans from Lebanon. We will leave essential people in the Embassy to keep operations going. We began announcements on VOA and BBC because communications in Beirut are so poor. There are about 1400 people in Lebanon but we have no idea how many will want to leave, because it is voluntary. Henry, why don't you describe the situation in Lebanon?

---

[1] Source: Ford Library, National Security Adviser, Memoranda of Conversations, Box 19, June 18, 1976, Cabinet Meeting. Secret; Nodis. The meeting was held in the Cabinet Room at the White House. Brackets are in the original. A list of attendees is in the President's Daily Diary. (Ibid., Staff Secretary's Office Files)

Kissinger: First, the situation about the Meloy killing.[2] He was on his way to meet with the new President Sarkis, to discuss the situation and possible U.S. evacuation.

[He describes the assassination.]

To the best of our information, the killing was done by a splinter group of the rejectionist front. To our best knowledge, it was done without PLO involvement. All the Arabs have condemned the act, unlike the Sudan killings.[3]

We will evacuate tomorrow. We will not announce the route. We have been given adequate assurances and most of the route is through Syrian-held territory. We have made adequate contingency preparations but it is important not to comment on this.

We don't know how many will leave. Many have no other real home, but there is no security in Beirut. But none of the responsible groups has any real interest in killing Americans, because if there was, it could be done quite easily at any time. But there are, of course, totally irresponsible elements. But the overall situation in Lebanon is developing in a way that is not unhelpful to our interests. Lebanon is a tragedy. In U.S. equivalents, four million people have been killed.

In March, the Syrians said they were moving in in 48 hours. The Israelis said they would move in that case. If that happened, we would have united all the Arabs against it. If Israel didn't act and if Syria cleaned it up, we would be accused by Egypt of colluding with the Syrians. But if the Syrians didn't move, the radicals could dominate Lebanon and Syria would then be squeezed between a radical Lebanon and Iraq.

We maneuvered our way through this and governmental changes were made. [He describes the election, etc.] But there was no security so the political changes couldn't take place. So Syria decided to act. [Describes Syrian-held territory.]

It looks now like no one will gain an overwhelming victory. What is likely to emerge is an Arab solution with no one in predominance, with the PLO weakened, but with Egypt relatively content and Syria as well. The end result should be a strategic situation which is favorable to us, because Syria and Egypt probably will get back together. We must remember that we are the only ones who are really in touch with all the parties and the only useful force working with all of them. [Compares with the Soviets] It could blow up, of course, but if it goes on track, that is a likely outcome.

---

[2] See footnote 2, Document 288.

[3] On March 1, 1973, Ambassador to the Sudan Cleo Noel, Deputy Chief of Mission George Moore, and the Belgian Chargé d'Affaires were assassinated by Palestinian guerrillas in Khartoum.

A spectacular Syrian defeat probably would overthrow Assad. With this probable moderate outcome, we are in a good position for peace. If we can keep all the radicals from uniting, or all the Arabs, it looks like a positive aspect to the tragedy of Lebanon.

Secretary Richardson: Why did the Syrians support the Christians and what kept them from a spectacular victory?

Kissinger: The Christians were about to be wiped out and that would have given Lebanon to the radicals who would have squeezed the Syrians. A spectacular Syrian victory in March could have given them a need to prove their Arab nature and turn on the Christians; this would have radicalized Jordan and put pressure on the Saudis and isolated Egypt. They didn't win spectacularly, first because it is an agony for them to be attacking the PLO, and second they underestimated the strength they faced.

[The next item was a campaign update.]

[The next item was our line on busing.]

290. Memorandum of Conversation[1]

Paris, June 22, 1976, 5–7:35 p.m.

PARTICIPANTS

    Dr. Henry A. Kissinger, Secretary of State
    Alfred L. Atherton, Jr., Assistant Secretary for Near Eastern and South Asian Affairs
    Amb. Hermann F. Eilts, Ambassador to Egypt
    Amb. Richard Murphy, Ambassador to Syria
    Amb. Thomas R. Pickering, Ambassador to Jordan
    Amb. William Porter, Ambassador to Saudi Arabia
    Amb. Talcott Seelye, Special Representative-designate to Lebanon
    Peter W. Rodman, NSC Staff

Kissinger: Roy, have you seen that cable, in which Ismail [Fahmy] asks for coordination? [See Cairo 8349, Tab A.][2]

---

[1] Source: Library of Congress, Manuscript Division, Kissinger Papers, CL 347, Department of State Memorandum of Conversations, Internal, April–June, 1976. Secret; Nodis. The meeting was held in the Tank at the American Embassy in Paris. All brackets, with the exception of ones describing omitted material, are in the original.

[2] Tab A, telegram 8349 from Cairo, June 17, is attached but not printed. In it, the Embassy reported that Fahmy expressed Sadat's condolences to Kissinger over the assassination of Ambassador Meloy, and he called for "intensified consultation and coordination between the U.S. and the Egyptian positions."

Atherton: It's the one a few days ago.

Kissinger: I thought it was new.

Atherton: Hermann doesn't think it's a problem.

Kissinger: Let me explain why I called this meeting, which I called before the murder of our Ambassadors [Amb. Meloy and Economic Counselor Waring in Beirut].

I think we're sliding into a situation in which there is danger that we'll be everyone's fall guy; but if we play it right, we can continue to play an important role. I'm afraid we're in a situation where the Egyptians accuse us of colluding with the Syrians, and the Jordanians blame us for Syrian setbacks because we didn't encourage Syria to invade.

Pickering: Because there was "no green light."

Kissinger: Because there was no green light.

So I wanted to ensure that we all said the same thing, that we see what role we can play, and anything else we can discuss. Hermann?

Eilts: You've all seen this message from Ismail [Fahmy]. He's again urging that we do something before the elections. This is Ismail's idea, not Sadat's.

Kissinger: What would he want us to do?

Eilts: Call Geneva before the election.[3]

Kissinger: This would raise the PLO issue.

Eilts: Exactly.

Kissinger: My view is that in the United States anything including the PLO would run us into trouble with the Jews in the maximum conditions for irresponsibility. Carter will use it to get himself in, and the Democrats will lock themselves into a situation they couldn't get out of if they came in. The Israelis will be impossible until the election. My idea is that we declare ourselves vocally for that proposal of the Israelis for an end to the state of war, which after all I never expected would fly. It's still alive.

Seelye: Which is that?

Kissinger: An end of the state of war and substantial territorial concessions. They haven't given us a line. In the Sinai, it could be a line from El-Arish to Ras Mohammed. If they do anything comparable on the Golan and the West Bank, we could have a discussion. The trouble is, the Israelis define the end of the state of war as the relationship between New York and New Jersey, and peace as the relationship which those of us who are happily married have with their wives. [Laughter]

---

[3] A reference to the Geneva Middle East Peace Conference.

The Arabs, I believe, can't really make peace now. But my idea of an end of the state of war is something like what Sadat in fact signed.[4] Since countries can go to war even if they're in a state of peace, it is not so difficult to do so from a position of renunciation of war. But I haven't given up on this proposal. At the worst, we could get Israel's outrageous proposals and use it to surface our own proposals for a comprehensive settlement.

The Jordanians, who have the least to gain, are the toughest on this. The Egyptians could hope for El Arish-to-Ras Mohammed.

Eilts: But that isn't "the last 20 kilometers."

Kissinger: But it's not the final Israeli word either. If it comes to that, we're in a typical haggle.

Eilts: If we play it that way.

Kissinger: If, say, Sadat wants a straight line, it could even be eight kilometers. It's a soluble problem.

For the Jordanians, since they're not recognized as the negotiator, they might as well be tough.

It is interesting that Asad hasn't rejected it.

Murphy: He has, sir, publicly, twice. Once after the Israelis leaked it and last week in Paris, in a toast to Giscard. He said explicitly: "There are some who are trying to divide the Arabs with schemes such as the end of the state of war."

Kissinger: Doesn't he realize it includes him? Giscard told us that Asad told him we were trying to divide the Arabs, not in Lebanon, but in the Sinai Agreement.

Eilts: I hope we're all saying the same thing.

Kissinger: We are. We told them all that a substantial withdrawal would include, on the Golan, most of the settlements.

Murphy: I used what we agreed on. I'm not sure it said "most of the settlements." "Substantial" was the word used.

Kissinger: You should correct it with Daoudi. My idea of "substantial" is 5–10 kilometers, which would include an overwhelming majority of the settlements, except in the south.

Murphy: Unfortunately, the way he's handled Lebanon—with the scrap with the PLO—would make him more rigid on negotiations, where the Palestinians are concerned.

Eilts: This is where "dividing the Arabs" comes in. There is nothing in the proposal for the Palestinians.

---

[4] See Document 230.

Kissinger: If he can make peace between the Fatah and the Jordanians, he can have the Jordanians do some negotiating for the Palestinians.

Murphy: That's some time distant.

Pickering: The PLO is quite worried about it, and has been complaining for weeks that this is what we had in mind.

Kissinger: I'm just trying to understand what he's doing. If he doesn't wipe out the PLO or substantially weaken it, he can't leave. It would leave Lebanon implacably hostile to him.

Murphy: He's not going to leave. He's got 19,000 troops there.

Kissinger: Then he's paralyzed in Israeli diplomacy.

If he destroys the PLO, he can make a political settlement and get out. If he doesn't, the PLO will always be hostile.

Murphy: His public venom against the PLO has diminished; it's now directed against Jumblatt.

Kissinger: With all respect, his action in Lebanon resembles our action in Vietnam—the idea that if you do something incompetently, it takes the moral curse off.

Pickering: He seems to be captured by the restrictions we've put on him, all the signals we gave him to "watch it."

Kissinger: Because the Israelis changed signals on us without telling us.

Atherton: They've defined the "red line" for us—and redefined it several times. They'd have gone to war by now [if they stuck to their original definition of the "red line."].

Kissinger: And they never gave us a different concept.

Eilts: The reason Sadat thinks we're colluding is he thinks Asad is chewing up the PLO for us. If Asad does it, his feeling of collusion will grow.

Kissinger: The fact is, as Dick [Murphy] knows, we didn't know a goddamn thing about what Asad was doing. The fact is, as Roy [Atherton] knows, we never knew a goddamn thing about what Israel was doing.

I wonder if the Israelis aren't, in fact, in touch with the Syrians through Jordan.

Pickering: Not that I know.

Kissinger: Or through the Christians.

Pickering: It could be. We heard one report they were in touch somewhere in Europe.

Kissinger: But all of us know all that you know. This isn't a case where there is something going on in Washington that you don't know about.

While we can continue to take credit with the Arabs for restraining the Israelis, the sad fact is we didn't.

Atherton: They restrained themselves.

Kissinger: They never told us.

Seelye: I've just come from AF, a distinguished bureau. [Laughter] Am I right in assuming they've been restrained for two reasons—because the Syrians may weaken the PLO, and (2) because they see a possibility of partition?

Kissinger: But we told them we wouldn't accept partition. I told them in April—maybe I scared the bejeesus out of them—that we wouldn't stand for another Middle East war, and if there were a war, we wouldn't go through this disengagement again.

Seelye: But they're supporting the Phalangists.

Kissinger: That we've acquiesced in. Because we don't want Jumblatt to be able to knock them over. The Syrians understand this.

Seelye: But this opens up a Pandora's box if the Israelis continue their relationship with the Phalange.

Kissinger: I thought you meant an Israeli-Syrian partition.

Seelye: I was thinking of a Moslem-Christian partition, because this would prove the failure of a unitary state, which could apply to their own state.

Atherton: They use that argument anyway.

Eilts: What's wrong with the Israelis continuing to have a relationship with the Phalangists?

Seelye: There is nothing wrong, to save them from being overrun. But a separate Christian state is against our interests.

Kissinger: I had two worries—one is that the radicals would overrun them, and the second is that the Syrians, having overrun the PLO, would restore their Arab credentials by overrunning the Christians.

Seelye: I don't think they'll do that.

Murphy: But it will result in their raising the PLO flag even higher, to get the monkey off their back.

Kissinger: If that's what they did, they've been acting like fools.

Seelye: They just want to change the PLO leadership.

Kissinger: I think they want to change the PLO leadership to bring them closer to Hussein. He [Asad] can't destroy the PLO as an institution but he can want to so weaken it that it exists as an appendage of Syria.

Eilts: That's why Sadat is against his presence in Lebanon.

Seelye: The Syrians went in when the Christians were on the ropes.

Pickering: The PLO took on Saiqa.

Kissinger: They went in because they couldn't make their political settlement stick, and they were afraid the PLO would become out of control and become an instrument of Iraq and Libya.

Porter: The Saudis are restraining funds from Asad.

Kissinger: Really?

Porter: They're restraining funds.

Kissinger: Do they get kickbacks on their own loans? [Laughter]

Porter: What I'm saying is: Won't this be bad news for the Syrian economy?

Murphy: He's had to cut the budget in half.

Pickering: The Soviets gave him oil yesterday.

Murphy: He's gotten 300,000 tons of oil from the Saudis—three months consumption.

Porter: What happens to his economy in the long term? This is a long process.

Kissinger: He either stays, and weakens himself vis-à-vis Israel, or he withdraws and leaves the PLO in control—which, having faced him down, will be even more intractable.

Porter: Or destroy the PLO.

Kissinger: At least change the leadership. What is he doing?

Murphy: They haven't really moved since June 9. One commander made the mistake—Shihabi told me—of going into the cities. So they're staying out of the cities.

Kissinger: So the PLO can stay in the centers and move out.

Murphy: The Syrians are in Bekaa and Tripoli, but the PLO is in Sidon and Beirut. The Sudanese, Saudis and Libyans will be a security force in Beirut, not the Syrians.

Kissinger: So explain to me what he's achieved?

Eilts: Not a damn thing.

Kissinger: He'll control the whole countryside, 80% as he told Giscard. It's the reverse of us in Vietnam, where we had the cities but not the countryside. If he doesn't withdraw, he's got two divisions tied down. If he leaves, the PLO takes over the country.

Murphy: He's trying to pull the teeth of the Lebanese left.

Kissinger: By the way, couldn't we get Dean Brown to shut up? Does he have to say we can't stop the fighting? It looks like encouragement by us to continue fighting.

Murphy: He's got under 10,000. Asad is trying to get Fatah away from Jumblatt. But his technique is a slow squeeze, but not an assault on the cities.

Pickering: They are blocking the ports and roads.

Murphy: Hermann says Egyptian arms are getting in.

He [Asad] says he'll "reeducate" the Fatah—that they've been misguided. He was surprised by the strength of Arafat's support in the Arab world.

Eilts: I think everything he's done shows miscalculation. He underestimated the strength of Arafat.

Kissinger: And then he didn't chew them up. It's just like Vietnam. He's got himself into an inconclusive situation. If the Arab force protects the cities, he's had it. It doesn't matter who they are, they'll be a shield behind which the PLO will reconstitute itself. In the name of what does he stay?

Seelye: I submit he gave up on Beirut. It can't be like Amman [in 1970]. Amman is a village compared to Beirut. Beirut is a big city.

Kissinger: Then why did he go into Lebanon? We went into the Dominican Republic with 25,000 troops, which I'm sure was five times more than we needed. There was more support for Vietnam than for the Dominican Republic, but we won, and it's over. I just don't see what the evolution can be.

Porter: He's stuck.

Kissinger: He made the same miscalculation we did—that if we just showed up with force, they'd crumble.

Pickering: And he had to worry about the Israelis, just as we had to worry about the Soviet Union and China.

Kissinger: But strength wasn't his problem.

Eilts: Is he afraid if he really lets his forces loose, and they get bloodied, this could unseat him at home?

Murphy: His forces had no training for this.

Porter: He doesn't control the supply routes.

Pickering: No, he thinks he has them. He controls the sea routes too.

Porter: Maybe that's what he thinks he can do. He'll just sit there.

Kissinger: But Fahmy—who doesn't understand the Arabs—can take a multilateral situation and come up with more formulas ... Asad can't just sit there for more than another month. He [Fahmy] will keep it boiling.

Eilts: That's right.

Porter: It's a repeat of our story. We put them in—50,000—and nobody quit.

Pickering: Sadat can't put forces in independently.

Murphy: Maybe if Asad shuts up on the Sinai II, Sadat won't object to it.

Eilts: There will be a PLO component in the force too, and the Egyptians will use it to keep getting supplies to the PLO.

Kissinger: When it turns into straight duplicity, no one can compete with the Egyptians! [Laughter] The Syrians aren't slouches, but the Egyptians have been doing it for 3,000 years.

Eilts: The Egyptians are supplying the PLO by sea.

Seelye: But the thesis is that the Syrians are blocking the airport to keep the PLO from getting supplies.

Eilts/Murphy: That's true.

Eilts: There are ships landing arms at Alexandria.

Kissinger: Maybe they're keeping it for themselves. Spare parts! [Laughter]

Porter: The President praised the PLO yesterday.

Kissinger: He did?

Eilts: Oh yes.

Atherton: Off the cuff, in the Rose Garden. [See President's remarks, Tab B][5]

Seelye: The Lebanese Ambassador, Kabbani, told me last night in Washington that this created a pretty good atmosphere for us.

Kissinger: How will you get in?

Seelye: I don't know yet.

Kissinger: Through Juniya?

Atherton: The PLO doesn't control it.

Seelye: I think the way is to go in through the airport. If it's two to three days, I'll go back to Washington.

Kissinger: Let me explain the way I see the situation and then apply it to each of your countries.

At the end of March, when the Syrians first came to us with the idea of intervention, I was at first extremely attracted, on the basis that the PLO was, at best, a nuisance to us, and at worst, created enormous problems in our country, and for the peace process. Once they're in the peace process, they can radicalize all the others. They'll raise all the issues the Israelis can't handle, and no other Arab can raise any other issues once the PLO is raised. So I felt the PLO issue couldn't be the first, not because I didn't favor the PLO but for this reason. Because the

---

[5] Tab B, "Question and Answer Session with the President," is attached but not printed. For text of Ford's exchange with reporters on June 20, see *Public Papers: Ford, 1976–77*, Book II, pp. 1895–1896. The *New York Times* reported on June 22 that the PLO had provided protection for the evacuation of American, U.K., and other foreign nationals from Beirut. (James M. Markham, "Syrian and Libyan Troops of Arab Peace Force Arrive in Beirut," *New York Times*, June 22, 1976, p. 1)

Egyptians and the Syrians have more flexibility than the PLO. As for the PLO as such, at some point some Palestinian entity will emerge, perhaps in confederation with Jordan.

So I wouldn't have wept any great tears if the PLO had been weakened at the end of March.

I moved away from this idea first because Israeli opposition was too great. Syria couldn't accept the partition of Lebanon between it and Israel, because the position of Asad and Hussein would have been untenable. In spite of Hussein's grandiloquence. It would have been a 1967 war; the Arabs would get into a war they weren't prepared for. They would be wiped out, and turn against us. There would be another embargo, even though the Saudis didn't want to.

I started with the assumption the Syrians would succeed. I forgot the infinite capacity of the Arabs to screw things up. I thought they'd weaken the PLO, make it an appendage of Syria, bring in Jordan, and create a Greater Syria. I still think this is what he has in mind. This would bring pressure on the Saudis and really isolate the Egyptians. This is why the Egyptians reacted so violently.

Eilts: If it went that far.

Kissinger: This is what the Israeli threat to intervene created. You should get into Sadat's head that far from colluding with the Syrians, we kept them from invading for five weeks.

Murphy: That's right. He had other bedrock reasons, but it gave him an excuse and he used it.

Kissinger: We then sent out Dean Brown and got a new election. We then lost control over events.

I told Meloy to be less visible than Brown, which he interpreted as being invisible. He just sent Waring around.

Atherton: But he sent Waring around a lot. Maybe that's all that could have been done.

Kissinger: In any case, we lost control of events.

Maybe we're still in a not too bad strategic position. A big Syrian intervention in March would have brought in the Israelis. Israeli intervention would have soured our relations with all the Arabs.

If anyone disagrees . . . I'm just thinking it through.

The Syrians now can't win, so this eases our Egyptian problem. We did keep the Israelis off their back. I hope you use this line with all your clients.

But this is a transitory phenomenon, until there is some resolution.

Seelye: I have one reservation. We can have some influence over the outside parties with interests in Lebanon, but can we really influence internal events in Lebanon?

Kissinger: I think we shouldn't be the principal one. As Roy knows, I picked Meloy. As I said at the arrival ceremony for his body, I wanted him there. So he was my responsibility. Dean Brown was superactive; Meloy can't be faulted for what he did. Before he moved, he wanted to know more about where the bodies were buried. But if I could have written the script, he would have been more active. An American Ambassador who sits at home is a signal of some kind.

I'm not on the spot. I'm telling you what the role should be, and if you tell me it's not safe, your judgment prevails.

Seelye: It's a security problem now.

Kissinger: Look, Talcott, your safety is overriding. But basically I want you to be less active than Brown and more active than Meloy. I'm the one who cabled him to be more active. So I'm responsible.

Atherton: He had already set up the appointment with Sarkis before your cable.

Eilts: I don't see how Lebanon can be settled at all unless we talk to the Palestinians.

Kissinger: You know my reasons are solely domestic.

Porter: That's right.

Kissinger: First of all, no Arab can keep his mouth shut. The Israelis will beat us all over the head. It's after all, only four months.

Seelye: But we didn't do it before.

Kissinger: We have a strategic problem. They have substantive demands too, which will be extremely difficult to handle. I can see peace with Syria, which will be murderous but still is intellectually conceivable.

Seelye: But what about a dialogue? This doesn't address the substance. You said I could discuss security with them.

Kissinger: This isn't the most helpful moment with the Syrians to launch a dialogue with the PLO. [Laughter] Talking with the Palestinians won't end all our problems. If we walk in and say "Seelye will see the PLO," will your guys [Porter] be happy?

Porter: Yes.

Pickering: Do we have to do it before the elections?

Kissinger: I'd like you to get into your guys' heads that talking to the PLO isn't the obstacle. We've offered 100 times to send someone unofficial, like Charlie Yost.

Murphy: But we never did it, and I've told him twice.

Kissinger: If I went to Charlie Yost, who's advising Carter . . .

Seelye: How about the guy at Harvard who's written about the PLO?

Eilts: Roger Fisher.

Kissinger: He's great at coming up with formulas. He has no judgment and no discretion. In the best tradition of the foreign service he'll talk two hours and put into the mouth of his interlocutor what *he* said.

Murphy: It's unhygienic. [Laughter]

Kissinger: I'm not so eager for Talcott to talk to them. It could be someone else.

Seelye: At the consular level.

Eilts: I've felt in Cairo that we had to wait four months, but they had to feel our heart is in the right place. He suspects we want someone to wipe out the PLO.

Kissinger: Look, Sadat has told me his only use for Arafat is if someone raises the Palestinian issue, he can say "Go see Arafat." And he is using Arafat now to end his own isolation. He's enjoying himself now.

A year from now, when we're in the middle of the peace process, and we're going to the 20-kilometer line—which I think he'll do—and the PLO starts screaming "what about the Palestinians?", Sadat will close all the PLO offices and kick them out. They'll all screw the PLO if they get their piece.

As Dick knows, we had absolutely nothing to do with what the Syrians did. If we wanted to, we'd have done it when Hussein was begging for it in Washington. So I believe we can't create the presumption that the PLO is the key to everything. It's everybody's cop-out. It has to be the end of the process.

When I saw Asad at the end of the Sinai negotiations, if I had said: "By October 1 I can get you a negotiation for five kilometers in a straight line down the Golan Heights and a settlement by December," are you morally certain he'd have said: "Nothing without the PLO!"?

Murphy: He was mad at the Egyptians then.

Kissinger: But if I could guarantee it? He asked: "How much?" I had to say we had to get Rabin to Washington and get token concessions, etc. Then he said: "Why should I? What do I get? For giving up my moral advantage over Sadat?"

Atherton: When it started to blow up in his own country, he turned against it.

Kissinger: Right. The issue is what do you all tell your governments. I want to avoid the impression in Egypt that we're colluding with the Syrians, and I want to give the Syrians a sense that we're sympathetic. We want to help weaken the PLO without losing the PLO.

Porter: Use the President's statement!

Kissinger: The President will start backing off it once the Israeli apparatus starts. I wouldn't wrap yourself in that statement.

At my press conference, I said the PLO was helpful, the Egyptians were very helpful, and the Saudis were, with the Palestinians, and we asked the Egyptians to thank those who were helpful, but we didn't pass any formal messages. Come to think of it, I forgot to mention the Syrians.

Eilts: That helps me!

Kissinger: The danger is that in the next two weeks there will be so many qualifiers that the statement won't be helpful.

Atherton: Mr. Secretary, we put together a set of talking points. [He shows the Secretary Tab C.][6]

Kissinger: [Reads.] How will the Egyptians react to our saying "We want these efforts of reconciliation to succeed"?

Eilts: We can sell it, provided it doesn't mean we're asking Sadat to go back on what he's doing.

Kissinger: It's pretty thin gruel.

Murphy: It's not helpful with the Syrians to say: "We want the peace process to resume." When we say "we want Arab suspicions of each other to end," it improves, except they blame us for creating them!

Pickering: There is nothing we could do before the elections that would help.

Eilts: They don't expect anything.

Kissinger: I may go to Iran in August. Should I go to Saudi Arabia?

Porter: I wish you would.

Kissinger: If I go to all the places, they'll expect big promises of what we'll do after the elections, and they'll leak it. And I'll have to go to Israel. I'd love to see Sadat, but there is no way I could see him without seeing Asad. And I can't go to Saudi Arabia without going to the others.

Eilts: You could stop at [omission in the original] to refuel and he—Khalid—would go. Rusk did it.

Kissinger: Khalid is a moron.

Eilts: But it's only a refueling stop.

Pickering: But this isn't Rusk, and it's all changed since then.

Kissinger: The other problem is the Vice President's trip.

Eilts: Is this still on?

Kissinger: That's what I wanted to ask. The trouble is, he's hell-bent on an overall settlement now, and if he runs through the Arab world, he'll raise expectations we can't fulfill.

---

[6] Tab C, a memorandum from Atherton to the Secretary, is attached but not printed.

Eilts: If he tries to sell an immediate settlement before the election, it won't help in Egypt.

Kissinger: On the other hand, it would have the effect of calming things down. My gut feeling is it's not helpful for me to go.

Eilts: No, not really.

Murphy: They'd expect more from you than from the Vice President.

Kissinger: Right.

Seelye: I've seen him in Tunisia. He makes a tremendous impression. If we can control what he says.

Porter: In Saudi Arabia, I could use it on the oil situation, I'm sure of it, because of their concern about its impact on Western economies, particularly ours.

Kissinger: What would that mean?

Porter: Anything we wanted, even lower prices. If we could give them a statement—to which they'd hold us ... They need something for their Arab audience. But I'm in a soft spot compared to you all, in terms of someone bound up with us.

Kissinger: All of them, except the Jordanians, have conducted themselves well. Even the Syrians haven't harassed us this year.

Pickering: Why the Jordanians?

Kissinger: Rifai's a shit.

Seelye: He's our worst enemy in the Middle East.

Kissinger: He's not really our worst enemy, but he's no friend.

If I come, it drives all expectations. I can't make general statements; from me they'll expect more.

Basically the Vice President is an unguided missile. He's a dear friend of mine. We could write it all out for him.

Atherton: My one experience with him was at the Faisal [funeral] business.[7] He stuck to what we had given him. It was very useful, even perhaps in getting Sinai II revived.

Eilts: Not really.

Pickering: They're all waiting now for the election. They're sitting still. If he goes and makes statements that will haunt us later ...

Kissinger: A settlement now is impossible. The Vice President totally underestimates what it involves in taking on the lobby.

Porter: I once told you that.

Kissinger: They never hit you on the issue; you have to fight ten other issues—your credibility, everything. Next year we'll have to do it.

---

[7] See footnote 6, Document 166.

Eilts: As far as Egypt is concerned, there is no need for him to come. They have confidence.

Kissinger: And we'll succeed, if we do it on our own timing, and if we do it in an all-out Presidential way. When the President really gets into it.

Would it help in Syria?

Murphy: They're prepared to wait until November.

Pickering: In fact, they all believe nothing *can* be done before November. A trip that promises something would only weaken our credibility.

Murphy: Maybe after the Kosygin visit.

Atherton: I favored a Vice-Presidential visit but I didn't really realize it would raise expectations.

Porter: They could wait. But a general statement that we're eager to do something would be welcomed.

Kissinger: But Asad will hit him with the real question—"Will it be the '67 borders or not?" The Vice President doesn't give evasive answers.

Let me think about the Vice President. Maybe we'll send him.

And you all think there is no sense in my going to Saudi Arabia and nowhere else if I go to Iran.

Eilts: It would be bad.

Porter: The Saudis will turn on all the pomp and circumstance. They won't let you go on just a refueling stop.

Eilts: If you go to Saudi Arabia and talk to the King and Cabinet in Taif and don't go to Egypt, it will leave a bad impression.

Kissinger: If I do that, I have to go to Damascus and Amman and Israel.

Atherton: And the Kuwaitis will say you've been promising them for two years!

Pickering: Only if it's a refueling stop. The Saudis would accept it.

Murphy: What is the credibility of a refueling stop in Dhahran if you've just left Tehran?

Kissinger: What can you tell your clients? This [the talking paper] is just pap.

Pickering: We've had less to say in the past. What can we say about after November? That's the meat of it.

Kissinger: You can tell them that after November we're absolutely determined to get the negotiating process started because it's in the national interest of the United States. It's not just to delay until November. But they have to help us with the process because it'll be bloody difficult. I didn't think we could deliver on the proposal so I didn't push it. If Asad gets 80% of the settlements off the Golan, he's nine-tenths of the way home.

Murphy: Asad won't do it without the Palestinians, even with what he's done to the Palestinians.

Kissinger: But we'd do it in a determined way. There could be something on the West Bank.

Pickering: But there are 28 settlements on the River. It's just like the Golan.

Kissinger: But you can tell them that that proposal precludes absolutely nothing.

Pickering: They want it in terms of the '67 lines.

Kissinger: But if it's something short of the '67 lines for an end to the state of war, they still have a claim to the '67 lines in exchange for peace.

Murphy: It's always been in the talking points.

Eilts: I don't know about you guys, but when I get back no one will ask me about the peace process. They'll ask me what we're doing in Lebanon.

Kissinger: You can tell them I'm getting mad at being accused by everyone of colluding with the other. Ask them if the incompetence of everyone didn't create a classic mess.

Eilts: They'll agree to that. But they'll say that if we say we endorsed Syrian political involvement, but no military involvement, it's naive. They see it as the green light.

Kissinger: But the fact is we used it to restrain the Syrians.

Eilts: But we didn't always handle it right. When they said the Syrians are sending thousands of troops in, and at the same time Funseth says, "We don't really know," the Egyptians say to themselves: "If we know, the CIA knows."

Kissinger: But Hermann, we were only told about 2,000 in the north and these were to replace PLA units, and the others were moving further west. Isn't that right, Roy?

Atherton: This was our intelligence.

Kissinger: I don't know if it's better for the Egyptians to think we're incompetent or that we're duplicitous. [Laughter]

Eilts: Good question!

Atherton: Can we do anything with these talking points?

Kissinger: Hermann, I know your relationship with Sadat. You can give him a feel from our discussion.

Porter: I've no problem. They believe us. They don't talk about duplicity.

Kissinger: They're afraid of you! Anyone who can destabilize Canada ... [Laughter]

We have to do it differently in each place.

[To Eilts:] You have to get across to Fahmy and Sadat that we don't always understand the Lebanese situation, but the Arabs have screwed this up royally by themselves. My experience with Sadat is he wants an honest assessment.

Eilts: Sadat never taxes me on it.

Kissinger: Just tell him we can't be accused by everybody. We could, if he wants, send someone like Yost or Percy, which we could disavow.

Murphy: If we're going to do it, we should set the date. Because to ask them doesn't mean anything.

Eilts: We haven't said it before.

Atherton: This isn't the time for it. Except in Beirut.

Kissinger [to Seelye]: You shouldn't do it yourself.

Seelye: I was hoping you'd authorize me to do it personally.

Kissinger: No, let your security officer talk to their security officer.

Eilts: What should we say on the Riyadh meeting?[8]

Kissinger: Tell Sadat the possibility that we'll switch to Syria is an absolute impossibility. We've put our chips on Egypt. All these allusions of Fahmy are absurd. On the other hand, we want his judgment about avoiding a situation where Asad is either overthrown or ties up with the Iraqis. This is more divisive for anything we could do. While we won't switch to Syria, we do feel we need Asad in the next phase for our common strategy.

Eilts: He won't disagree.

Kissinger: On Lebanon, the best we can do is to stay in touch with all the parties, and we don't consider Lebanon our safety valve or want to settle the peace process in Lebanon. Six months ago, the idea of Syria attacking the PLO would have been absurd.

Eilts: How about endorsing the Arab force?

Murphy: We've come close.

Kissinger: All right, as it crystallizes.

Seelye: Keep in mind the Libyans are in it. Ambassador Kabbani ...

Kissinger: Which Kabbani is that?

Seelye: He's the Lebanese Ambassador in Washington. He says the Libyan presence helps win PLO acceptance.

---

[8] The Arab League summit was held in Riyadh on October 16.

Kissinger: I don't want you to lead the Libyan charge there.

Eilts: I've just seen him [Sadat]; I don't have to see him immediately.

Murphy: I'm in a different position. I haven't see him [Asad] for two and a half months.

Kissinger: Whom can you see?

Murphy: It depends on how soon you want it. Asad and Khaddam leave Thursday for Romania and Yugoslavia.

Kissinger: Don't seem too eager. But put in a word to see him on Thursday.[9]

Murphy: He agrees Lebanon is blocking everything.

Kissinger: Tell him the French say he feels we're blocking him. Tell him we need Syria in the next phase. He'll ask about the Palestinians. Tell him we need his help to bring them in somehow. If he has the statesmanship to bring the Palestinians and the Jordanians together, we can make progress. Lebanon blocks everything.

I don't mind if Sadat tells him we told him Egypt was the key. We've told Sadat Syria has to have a role.

Tell him in Lebanon we won't do anything to block him.

Tell him we're sending Seelye there.

Atherton: Tell them we're not for splitting the Arabs.

Kissinger: I'm giving a press conference in Germany. They'll ask about South Africa but also about Lebanon. I'll certainly support the Arab force.

Atherton: And Riyadh.

Kissinger: I'll certainly support that. I'll certainly have a press conference in Washington next week.

You can use this guff [the talking points] as a basis. What I want is to convey that on the peace process, now that we're so close to it, they've got to believe us. We've done nothing inconsistent, to those who've believed us. To those who don't believe us, they have nothing to lose by trusting us. As for the shits like Rifai . . .

Pickering: They have justification for their attitude. I'll stick to the line Dick [Murphy] takes.

Kissinger: Let them play it back. To the Saudis, tell them I've said Egypt we've banked on, and Asad I like personally.

Seelye: I'll say we're against Arab divisions.

Kissinger: Tell Asad we want Riyadh to succeed. Tell him we needed the Sinai to show that the Israeli lobby can't stop even a minor

---

[9] June 24.

advance. What would it have profited him if the Arabs gained nothing last year? By next year, it will be clear Sadat was right.

Eilts: That's what he's counting on.

Kissinger: I can't speak for Carter. If he's smart, he'll tackle it in the first year. He's buying himself an awful mess.

The Israelis now claim in 1969 I promised that any list we approved has to be funded. If that's so, what's the point of the Congressional authorization process? The amounts in 1969 were chicken feed. They've now developed this theory.

You know how ostentatiously I avoided the Middle East problem then.

Seelye: One other practical thing in Lebanon. This no-man's land makes it a security problem to go back and forth to the Christian area. So I'd like to station a political officer in the Christian area, with a scrambler radio.

Kissinger: Good idea.

Seelye: The political problem is that it would look like partition.

Kissinger: That's no problem.

Seelye: My life comes first.

Kissinger: We won't lose another Ambassador.

Seelye: The problem is I had a man picked out and he backed out. If any of you have any suggestions . . .

Kissinger: Do you all think you know what to do?

Murphy: Yes. It isn't much, as you say, but we'll stick to the same line. Tom and I will have the same wording.

Kissinger: I want to talk to Dick a moment.

[Secretary Kissinger and Ambassador Murphy conferred alone from 7:30 to 7:35 p.m., and then the meeting ended.]

291. Memorandum of Conversation[1]

Washington, July 2, 1976, 2 p.m.

PARTICIPANTS

    President Ford
    Max Fisher
    Dr. Henry A. Kissinger, Secretary of State
    Brent Scowcroft, Assistant to the President for National Security Affairs

President: That was a good meeting the other day.[2]

Fisher: Look at this. One of the guys was so touched he stayed overnight to write this. [Hands a paper to the President.][3]

President: This is a helleva fine paper.

Fisher: I am leaving this afternoon. I allowed myself two extra days to get armed and meet with more groups. There is a feeling of the Jewish groups around the world that they want more input into the Israeli policy. This could be very helpful. They want me to set it up. There will be a couple launched from the U.S. and 100 or so from elsewhere.

[There is some talk about the political organization and the campaign.]

What can I do to help in Jerusalem?

President: The most overriding thing is in Lebanon. The Israelis have done exactly the right thing by standing aside. As a result the Syrians are wearing down the PLO.

Kissinger: And without any pressure from us. We came to parallel conclusions—there was absolutely no hint of pressure from us. The Syrians are wearing down the PLO and the Syrians are stuck in Lebanon. They can't pull out without turning it over to the PLO and indicating a botched military operation.

The one thing I see that is dangerous is the possibility of Israeli attacks on Fatah camps as a result of this hijacking.[4]

---

[1] Source: Ford Library, National Security Adviser, Memoranda of Conversations, Box 20, July 2, 1976, Ford, Kissinger, Max Fisher. Secret; Nodis. The meeting was held in the Oval Office at the White House. Brackets are in the original. According to the President's Daily Diary, the meeting ended at 2:45 p.m. (Ford Library, Staff Secretary's Office Files)

[2] The memorandum of conversation of the June 24 meeting between President Ford and a group of Jewish leaders is ibid., June 24, 1976, Ford, Jewish Leaders.

[3] The paper is not attached.

[4] On June 27, an Air France plane was hijacked by Palestinian terrorists and flown to Entebbe, Uganda. The Israel Defense Force mounted an operation on July 4 to rescue the hostages.

President: That could coalesce all the Arabs against Israel.

Kissinger: I tell you it is my personal belief that the French are making a mistake conceding to negotiations with the terrorists. But that is their business.

President: Retaliation would just spark the Arabs to unite.

Kissinger: The problem is these are Yemeni Jews—Sephardic Jews. They are not so tough and they are over 50 percent of the Israeli population. That is the reason for the change.

Fisher: What about the role of the PLO in the Lebanon situation?

[The President and Secretary Kissinger described the thinking process and that there was no change in our policy.]

The TQ thing[5] worked out fine. I want to thank you.

President: Javits was very pleased.

Scowcroft: Humphrey told me he thought it worked out fine.

Fisher: So I just wanted to know what was happening.

Kissinger: Not a Goddamn thing is happening. We have given the Arabs proposals and they haven't responded. We have no reason to press.

Fisher: It looks like the message for me to convey is to stay away from retaliation.

This settlement thing is another problem.

Scowcroft: They just authorized three more.

President: Really? Max, that is a very serious matter.

Kissinger: Israel shouldn't make the same mistake of hitting the refugee camps. The PLO is getting chewed up right now without any help.

Fisher: This George Brown thing is bad.[6] I think something will have to be said. Lissy has drafted something innocuous.

President: I don't see how we can make a statement. What is the occasion?

Fisher: You will get a lot of mail. Maybe in response to this, you can get it out by answering the letters.

President: We will look at it.

---

[5] Transitional Quarter.

[6] A reference to General Brown's reiteration during his confirmation hearings for a second term as JCS Chairman of his 1974 statement that Jewish Americans had too much influence over Congress. See the *New York Times*, June 30, 1976, p. 9.

292. Memorandum of Conversation[1]

Tehran, August 7, 1976, 8–10 a.m.

PARTICIPANTS

> Secretary Kissinger
> Ambassador Richard Helms
> Assistant Secretary Atherton
> Ambassador Hermann Eilts
> Ambassador Thomas Pickering
> Mr. Robert B. Oakley, NSC (notetaker)

SUBJECT

> Guidance for Ambassador Eilts and Pickering

[Omitted here is discussion unrelated to Lebanon.]

Secretary Kissinger: I want to make it clear that a Syrian defeat in Lebanon would be a disaster. I know Egypt does not agree but to leave Asad sandwiched between two radical states if the PLO wins in Lebanon and Syria loses would probably mean the overthrow of Asad. This would be of no benefit to Sadat. I do not know what he thinks he can get out of his policy in Lebanon.

Ambassador Eilts: Sadat has no policy in Lebanon. He has a policy toward Syria. He wants to prevent them from winning since this would give them greater weight as leaders of the Arab world and give them control of the PLO. I believe Sadat would respond if there were a genuine Syrian overture. But that communiqué with the PLO was inexcusable.[2] We need to talk to Asad directly about this.

Secretary Kissinger: The Arabs are marvelous. The Syrians claim they are not attacking the Egyptians but are being restrained whereas the Egyptians are attacking them in a major propaganda campaign. Then you see something like the communiqué.

Ambassador Eilts: If we want better relations between the two we must take it out of the Khaddam-Fahmy channel and back to a dialogue between Sadat and Asad.

Secretary Kissinger: I am not that keen on Egypt and Syria getting together but I do not want Syria to lose in Lebanon. Also, I would prefer to have the PLO under Syrian control than freewheeling since we must deal with Syria anyway and the PLO would be under some

---

[1] Source: National Archives, RG 59, Central Foreign Policy Files, P–860122–0281. Secret. The meeting was held at Ambassador Helms's residence.

[2] A reference to a July 29 agreement between Syria and the PLO to commit to a cease-fire, but without any withdrawal of Syrian troops, which numbered approximately 15,000 at that time. (*New York Times*, July 30, 1976, p. 1)

control. If Lebanon is dominated by the PLO it will give us fits and that includes Sadat. It will eliminate all future freedom of maneuver for him as it did for Asad after Sinai II. If at some stage we wanted to move for a Sinai III for Egypt, Sadat would not be able to do it if he had to contend with the PLO. We are not considering that idea for now but it could happen.

Ambassador Eilts: Sadat thinks about it, too. But we must understand that this would separate Egypt forever from the rest of the Arabs.

Secretary Kissinger: We do not seek this as our objective. Our approach, our strategy is to bring Saudi Arabia, Jordan, Syria and Egypt together and to go for an overall settlement. After the overall attempt, we might end up with a Sinai III but it would only be after starting for an overall and exhausting everything else. I would prefer significant territorial progress on all three fronts, Egypt, the Golan and the West Bank, with Jordan beginning to get back into the West Bank. But the 1967 boundaries are unrealizable in a first stage. This approach would keep the PLO out of negotiations where they would not be helpful, at least at the outset. We need first to get them under control and bring them in only at the end of the process.

Ambassador Eilts: I agree that this is the best approach.

Secretary Kissinger: Hermann, I really have to laugh at Fahmy. Every time you see him he talks about exposing someone yet no one seems to feel too exposed.

Ambassador Eilts: His recent accusations about Syrian meetings with the Israelis in Geneva stung Khaddam.

Secretary Kissinger: They were true.

Ambassador Eilts: It upset the Saudis as well as the Syrians and they are investigating.

Secretary Kissinger: Now that they have made direct contact with the Syrians, the Israelis have decided—against my advice—to approach the Saudis. They have asked me to set up a meeting between Dinitz and Alireza but I refused. Then they went to the Vice President but he also refused. I like this Saudi Ambassador.

Ambassador Eilts: He is a good man.

Secretary Kissinger: Do you know him? I am also impressed with that Prince who was here. I think his name was Abdullah.

Ambassador Eilts: I have known Alireza for thirty years. Did Abdullah stammer?

Secretary Kissinger: All the time with Rumsfeld but very little with me. I calmed him down. Can you imagine the Israelis getting a response from the Saudis? They are busy approaching the Chinese, also.

Ambassador Eilts: No one in the Saudi Government could officially authorize a contact. It would be rejected.

Secretary Kissinger: The first thing they would ask the Saudis for if there were a contact would be Jerusalem and this the Saudis could never give. Now, I want to be sure that Hussein supports Asad. My analysis is that had we given Syria the green light in March they would have defeated first the PLO and then the Christians and would have ended up in total control of Lebanon which would gradually have become radicalized. That would have given Syria too much control. So we encouraged or acquiesced in the strengthening of the Christians. They are now strong enough to resist possible Syrian domination. It would require too much Syrian force and Syria is no longer that strong.

Assistant Secretary Atherton: I agree. Also, the Syrians want a balance in Lebanon. They do not want to eliminate the Christians.

Secretary Kissinger: There is no longer a threat of Syrian domination but the danger now is of a Syrian collapse. A more radical Syria after Asad would take the same line on Sinai II and do something about it rather than just talk. What do you think about the analysis of Kamal Adham?[3]

Ambassador Eilts: It is a good analysis but he never said it to Sadat.

Secretary Kissinger: (laughter) These Arabs are impossible and you are in a somber mood, Hermann.

Ambassador Eilts: I am sorry. But he never did say it. All he talked about was the Libyans supposedly having put the denunciation of Sinai II in the communiqué.

Secretary Kissinger: That is easy. Everyone uses Libya as a whipping boy. But how do you know?

Ambassador Eilts: Fahmy told me.

Secretary Kissinger: He would not lie to you?

Ambassador Eilts: That is possible but in this instance I believe not.

Secretary Kissinger: Can't someone make the analysis to Sadat even if he did not?

Assistant Secretary Atherton: It would be better if it comes through the Saudis.

Ambassador Pickering: If it does it will be veiled and weak.

Ambassador Eilts: The Egyptians think we are in a conspiracy with Syria and Israel to crush the PLO. They put all sorts of little signs together to reach this conclusion.

Secretary Kissinger: Egypt wants to be able to show they can deliver U.S. recognition of the PLO as what they got for Sinai II. This would be good for their position in the Arab world. But it would get us nowhere and create a terrible mess domestically in the U.S. We cannot

---

[3] Adviser to the King of Saudi Arabia and chief of the Saudi intelligence secretariat.

deliver the minimum demands of the PLO so why talk to them. They are a Soviet trojan horse because they would give the Soviets leverage over the negotiations if they got into them prematurely. We can bring them in at the end of the process after the others have been satisfied and the PLO has been weakened. We could talk to them as a cover for the Syrians accepting something for themselves but we have nothing at all to give the Syrians. So why should we get the PLO off Arab backs by recognition and create trouble for ourselves both at home and in the negotiating process? The State Department bureaucracy is marvelous. Only they could transform no contacts with the PLO into something sinister. A simple security contact was blown up into a major political issue because of the way it was handled. How did this happen?

Ambassador Eilts: Why didn't we answer the question and admit at the beginning that we were having security contacts?

Secretary Kissinger: I was out of town when this occurred. The best thing to do is to tell the truth.

Assistant Secretary Atherton: We had guidance admitting the contact but you were not there and no one wanted to take the responsibility for approving it.

Secretary Kissinger: You could have sent the guidance to me for clearance.

Assistant Secretary Atherton: It was badly handled. There is no question about that.

Secretary Kissinger: Anyway, it illustrates the problem we have at home. The Israelis used to lobby for their own interests. Now they are lobbying to change the entire course of our policy to coincide with their own policy rather than our interests. Look at the parallelogram of forces and you can see. Even on Iran, 50 percent of our trouble is the Israeli lobby. They want a carom shot off of Iran onto arms sales for Saudi Arabia and Kuwait. Since we are doing so much for Israel and it is so strong, it is hard to kill arms sales to the Saudis who are much weaker. So the best approach is to attack through Iran and kill the idea of all arms sales to the Gulf, thus blocking the Saudis and Kuwaitis. This is despite the close relationship between Iran and Israel. Look at *Commentary* Magazine and you can tell what is happening. There is a Joe McCarthy-like cold war line so that if we tried to get Israel to give up two kilometers on the Golan it would be made to appear that we were selling out to the Soviets as part of a vast worldwide plot against Israel and the free world. At a time when the power of the Executive Branch is as weak as it will ever be, we cannot afford to make official contact with the PLO. Personally, I buy the Kamal Adham thesis. If the PLO is decimated and Saudi Arabia, Egypt, Syria and Jordan are back together, then Jordan can get back onto the West Bank and at the end we can take the PLO as an appendage to one or all of them. But at the start, they will make impossible demands.

Ambassador Pickering: The PLO will remain an Arab cause no matter what.

Secretary Kissinger: I agree. We must deal with the PLO but keep them two steps behind the Arab Governments. We will talk to the governments about the return of territory when we first contact the PLO. Recognition will come at the very end after the Arab Governments have been satisfied. Sadat wants us to say that we are champions of the Palestinian cause so he can get Arafat off his back. He wants to set up a post office box for the PLO so he will not need to be in the middle.

Ambassador Eilts: I have two points to make about your analysis.

Secretary Kissinger: Your points are that it is wrong.

Ambassador Eilts: That is included in my points. First, you are placing too much hope in Asad. He is not that moderate. He screwed up the peace process after Sinai II and he is screwing things up now.

Secretary Kissinger: Right after Sinai II, Asad was not moralizing as he is now. He asked me how many kilometers I could get for him and whether the line would be straight or crooked. I told him I could not promise him anything at all but that next March we might begin to talk about something vague. I could offer him nothing. Were you there Roy? Didn't you think he was interested in an agreement if we could have delivered?

Assistant Secretary Atherton: Yes, I was there. He did not want to go through a negotiation like Sadat did for just a little territory but he was realistic and would have accepted something if we had been able to produce it.

Secretary Kissinger: But I could not tell him he would get anything at all. I told Sadat before Sinai II that he could get the oilfields and the passes. Asad wanted that kind of promise. I could not even tell him the U.S. would support him all the way.

Ambassador Eilts: Sadat did not get the east side of the passes and he did not even have the entire west side until we made the Israelis redraw the line. Israel played games with him.

Secretary Kissinger: Still, we could give Sadat advance assurance but there was nothing for Asad. He wanted a concrete offer. But let's not pursue this. Let's go back to the subject.

Ambassador Eilts: Okay. Still, your plan will not bring the PLO under control. Egypt and Libya and Iraq are in an unholy alliance to supply the PLO with arms and other support. The PLO will be a factor in the peace process. Sadat agrees with you about no early PLO participation at Geneva but he insists that the principle of later participation be agreed upon at the start.

Secretary Kissinger: You say Sadat does not want them in?

Ambassador Eilts: Not at the beginning but he wants the decision in principle at the beginning.

Secretary Kissinger: We don't want the PLO under Syrian control. That is why I resisted Syrian plans for a quick takeover in March.

Assistant Secretary Atherton: Adham's thesis is that the Arabs must be brought together and only then can they get the PLO under control.

Ambassador Pickering: As long as the PLO can play one Arab off against another, it cannot be controlled.

Secretary Kissinger: I could not get Asad to negotiate as Sadat did without promising him something specific. Who remembers Article III of the Sinai agreement.[4] Sadat is not restricted by it today.

Ambassador Eilts: He is inhibited politically by the non-use of force but basically you are right. Why can't we support the Egyptian thesis of a stand-off in Lebanon. Everyone would be badly mauled and a compromise government would emerge.

Secretary Kissinger: I take it for granted that there will be no victor. The Syrians should have gone all the way once they started.

Ambassador Pickering: They were afraid of the Israelis and the PLO were tougher than they thought. The Syrians got hit hard in Sidon.[5]

Secretary Kissinger: Israel would not have gone in in June but it is true we did not give the Syrians a new signal. However, the Israelis never gave us a changed signal so we were not bluffing the Syrians. They should have seen the situation themselves.

Ambassador Pickering: They also had the Iraqis massing along the border. What were they supposed to do about that?

Secretary Kissinger: Take it from me as a veteran of Vietnam, there are no awards for losing moderately. They should have thrown in two divisions in June and gone balls out to win. But now it is too late and I am worried about the collapse of Asad.

Assistant Secretary Atherton: I am worried about the deterioration of our relations with Syria and Egypt, both of whom suspect us. For now Asad seems to be okay.

Ambassador Eilts: The Egyptian situation is manageable except that they are no longer frank with us about Lebanon. We need to get Egypt and Syria back into détente. Maybe we should go to Asad not

---

[4] See Document 226.

[5] A reference to a failed Syrian military attempt in June to extricate Palestinian and leftist forces in the Lebanese city of Sidon that led to numerous casualties on both sides.

Khaddam, and say stop the propaganda. If you do this, we can get Egypt to stop. This would need to be done very delicately. It would still leave the situation on the ground unchanged but they could then begin to talk to one another.

Secretary Kissinger: I have no problem with the Egyptian idea of a balance in Lebanon but I want to prevent a PLO victory.

Ambassador Helms: The Lebanese Ambassador here, Khalil, is from a leading Shia family in South Lebanon. He is talking of bringing the Lebanese back together against the Palestinians. Some kind of a Lebanese coalition.

Assistant Secretary Atherton: We have seen reports that the Syrians are trying to organize something like this.

Ambassador Pickering: Can we bring Syria and Egypt back together by pushing or do we let Egypt continue to resupply the PLO?

Secretary Kissinger: Can we keep Egypt from supplying the PLO? I do not think they would stop if we asked them to. They would only tell the PLO we had asked and keep on doing it to show the PLO what good friends they are.

Ambassador Eilts: Probably so.

Secretary Kissinger: (to Eilts) Avoid attacking the PLO since this would be counterproductive. We do not want Syria to lose in Lebanon and we want the PLO weakened. Our strategy is to bring the PLO into negotiations at the end, keeping them a step behind Egypt, Syria and Jordan so that they will be manageable. Otherwise, the PLO will disrupt the negotiations by demanding more than the Arab Governments want or can meet. They will have the support of the Soviets. The Israelis will reject the demand and the negotiations will collapse. We have no illusion about Asad but we want to keep Syria split from Libya and Iraq and the USSR. If a radical crescent involving Iraq, Syria, a PLO-controlled Lebanon and Libya comes into being—following the overthrow of Asad—it will be very bad for Egypt. You (Eilts) should see Sadat alone—can you see him alone? (Eilts—yes, particularly since Fahmy will be away when I get back.)—and give him my analysis of the situation. As an old and trusted friend I would like him to know what I think and I would like him to tell me where it is wrong. Egypt is still the key element in our policy but I want his comments on my analysis.

Ambassador Eilts: Fahmy has a strategy of building a new strategic belt. It would include Morocco, Tunisia, Egypt, Iran, Saudi Arabia and the Gulf States.

Secretary Kissinger: We could support that.

Ambassador Pickering: Let us not encourage a belt that would force Asad and Hussein into the arms of the Iraqis and Libyans. They will end up in the radical camp like this.

Secretary Kissinger: (to Pickering) Tell Hussein we have asked Asad to authenticate his messages through Hussein. We have told Asad that we do not hesitate to talk to him through Hussein but we do want to hear from him directly from time to time. And above all we want to hear that Hussein actually speaks for Asad.

Ambassador Helms: Here are the agreed minutes of the Joint Commission meeting.

Secretary Kissinger: What is in them? I will not have time to read them since the meeting is about to begin.

Ambassador Helms: They were just completed this instant.

Ambassador Pickering: Can I give Hussein the elements of our strategy, except tell him that we don't want Syria to be defeated rather than we do not want them to win?

Ambassador Eilts: You can't tell Hussein that. It would get back. I am going to say that we do not want them to win. We should have the same line.

Secretary Kissinger: Tell Sadat we are not working for a Syrian victory but I do not want Syria to fail. You should also tell him of the consequences I foresee of a Syrian defeat. We do not want a radical bloc in the north. We want an eventual reconciliation of Egypt, Syria, Saudi Arabia and Jordan so the peace process can be resumed. My fear is that Syria will have to pull out of Lebanon like it did from Jordan in 1970 and this will lead to the overthrow of Asad and the creation of a radical bloc. If Syria had overwhelmed the PLO in March or had gone all the way in June, it might have gained a decisive victory in Lebanon but that is no longer possible.

Ambassador Pickering: What do we mean by saying we do not want Syria to win?

Ambassador Eilts: It means no Syrian dominance. Sadat fears Syria will sew it all up. He wants instead a settlement among the parties and a Syrian pull-out.

Secretary Kissinger: (to Pickering) You need to find words to strengthen Asad's morale. There is a great danger of a Syrian collapse since Asad's policy is unnatural.

Ambassador Helms: The PLO will get the support of Iraq, the Soviets, Libya, etc.

Secretary Kissinger: (to Pickering) You need to find words for Hussein which will strengthen Asad's morale. There is a great danger of Syrian collapse since Asad's policy of opposing the PLO and the left is unnatural. All the pressures are on Asad and he gets no encouragement. The PLO cannot collapse since they have no place to go. They will fight to the end. There is no hope of an all-out Syrian victory. We want to avoid the creation of a radical bloc. Syria can't win. If Asad should ever succeed in knocking off the PLO—and I think it may be too late for that since it would be so expensive and bloody—there would still be the Christians. Last March they were weak and could have been defeated. Now they are strong enough so that Syria could not defeat them, especially after paying the cost of a victory over the PLO. And if they tried, the Israelis would move in. So a Syrian victory over all of Lebanon is not possible. Tell Sadat this and tell him my great fear is that Asad will be overthrown. We do not want to see a glorious victory and Syrian preeminence. In fact, we have worked against this, starting in March, and it is now not possible. My fear is the collapse of Asad.

Ambassador Eilts: Sadat sees us as supplying the Christians and trying to knock off the PLO. He does not trust us. He fears Syrian control over the PLO and the Maronites.

Secretary Kissinger: You accept my analysis, don't you?

Ambassador Eilts: Yes, but what do we tell Hussein so that we have the same line.

Ambassador Pickering: We have never told Hussein or Asad that we favor Syrian preeminence. We can put the emphasis on that.

Secretary Kissinger: Okay. Let's say to Sadat that we are not working for a Syrian victory. We will tell Hussein that we do not want Syria to lose. Hermann, I may inflict Nancy and my son, David, upon you. Do you think Sadat would send a plane to Amman for them? That way they could go to Israel and cross the bridge. It would be in late August but I will let you know.

Ambassador Eilts: I will be delighted. Just tell me when.

Secretary Kissinger: I now know where the skeletons are buried in the State Department. Give me another two years and I will clean the place up. I want to offer Fahmy a dinner during the General Assembly but I find that the bureaucrats have filled my schedule with every Foreign Minister in the world without any reference to the national interest or any priorities. One of the country directors told Win Lord at dinner the other night that I was the most heartless, insensitive man he had ever met. Win asked if he had ever met me and the FSO said no. His complaint was that I would not take time to see officials from his country, which amounts to nothing. That is the way it goes.

Ambassador Eilts: I am glad you will see Fahmy. He needs badly to talk to you at length. He has a lot to get off his chest and a long talk will be good for him.

Secretary Kissinger: I will get him to Washington to see the President as well as having a dinner in New York, or do you think he would prefer to do it all in Washington? I want him given the full treatment and met in New York at the airport by a senior substantive officer.

Assistant Secretary Atherton: I will go up myself to meet him.

Secretary Kissinger: Also, he will be our guest and get him a good hotel suite in Washington.

Assistant Secretary Atherton: He liked the Watergate even if the suite may also have been one where Khaddam stayed.

Secretary Kissinger: Hermann, you can also tell him that on September 27 the Israeli Philharmonic is giving a concert and he may wish to attend. You know that Admiral Zikry[6] was seated right across from the Israeli Navy Commander for the Bicentennial, and was invited to visit the Israeli ship. He declined. The Pentagon is incredible and the Secretary of the Navy must be the dumbest one alive. For the review of ships on the Bicentennial he decided that the Navy had lost too many helicopters in Vietnam so the diplomatic corps would have to use barges to get to the *Forrestal* for the review. He calculated the traffic would make the trip from La Guardia to the pier in two hours so everyone had to catch the 0600 shuttle from Washington. Naturally it only took fifteen minutes so the diplomats were on the deck of the *Forrestal* by 0745 with nothing to do and not even any coffee until the review began at 1100. At 2:30 the President left, followed by the Admirals but there was no priority for diplomats so, with 5,000 people on board, they did not all get off until late. Then one group was on the bus but it would not leave until the second group arrived from the carrier so it waited for 1½ hours until the diplomats raised so much hell the bus finally went to the airport. Then when they got to Washington, there was a huge traffic jam because of the fireworks. It was after midnight when they finally got home. They were infuriated at such treatment.

Ambassador Helms: If it had happened here everyone would have said this is an underdeveloped country.

Secretary Kissinger: It could not have happened here. They are too civilized.

Assistant Secretary Atherton: Certainly there would have been coffee and tea to drink had it happened here.

Ambassador Helms: We must leave for the Joint Commission meeting.

---

[6] Egyptian Vice Admiral Fuad Abu Zikry.

293. Memorandum From Director of Central Intelligence Bush to Secretary of State Kissinger[1]

Washington, September 7, 1976.

SUBJECT

Additional Information Concerning PLO Desire to Enter Political Negotiations with the United States Government

1. The following provides additional background supplementing my memorandum [1½ lines not declassified]

2. [1 line not declassified] Palestine Liberation Organization (PLO) Chairman Yasir 'Arafat has been thinking for almost a year of attempting to establish a totally secret "pre-dialogue" channel to the United States (U.S.) Government. [less than 1 line not declassified] disillusionment with the Syrian relationship has made the PLO far more ready to compromise than it was in the past. The mood within the PLO leadership is definitely one of trying to resolve its own problems through compromise and to resist exploitation of the PLO by other Arab states for their own purposes.

3. [8 lines not declassified] Nevertheless, [less than 1 line not declassified] 'Arafat has political negotiations with the U.S. very much in mind, if they can be arranged.

4. Finally, [less than 1 line not declassified] 'Arafat is suspicious of the tendency of some Arab states, such as Egypt and Tunisia, to project themselves as intermediaries between the PLO and the U.S. 'Arafat judges that such efforts are patently self-serving and should be avoided.

5. A copy of this memorandum is being sent to the Honorable Brent Scowcroft, Assistant to the President for National Security Affairs. No other dissemination is being made.

George Bush[2]

---

[1] Source: Central Intelligence Agency, Executive Registry, Job 79M00467A, Box 23, Folder 427. Secret; Sensitive. A copy was sent to Scowcroft.

[2] Printed from a copy that indicates Bush signed the original.

Appendix A, Map 1[1]

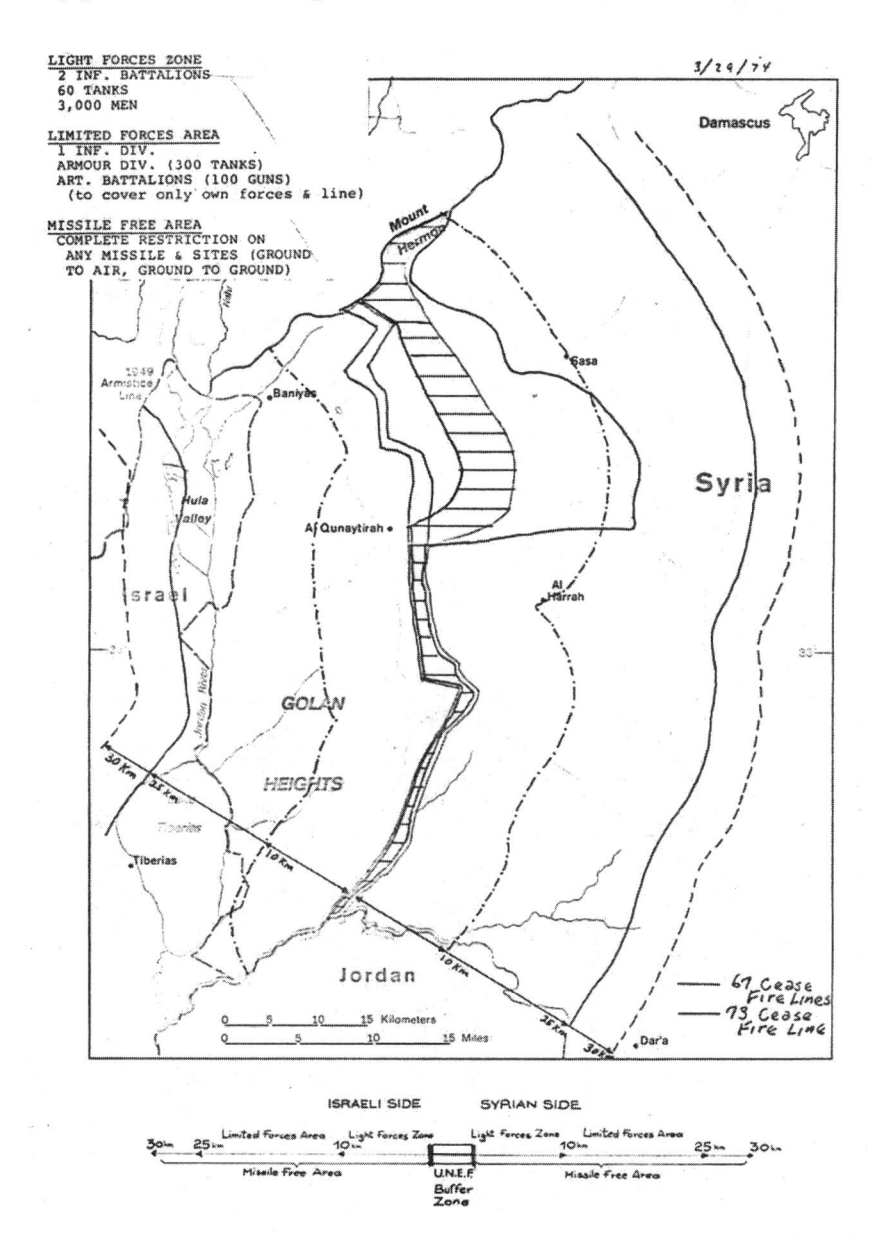

---

[1] Attached to Documents 32 and 35.

Appendix A, Map 2[1]

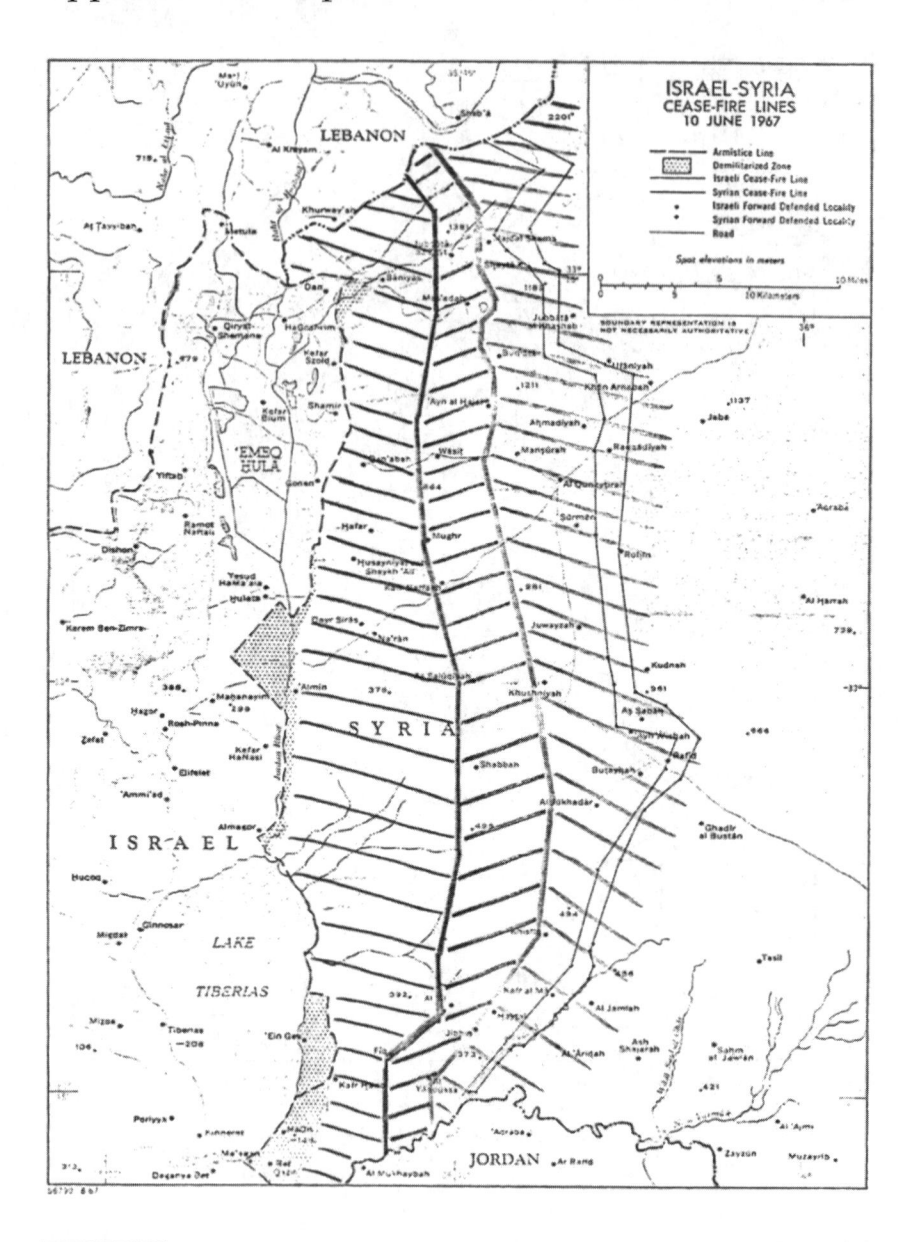

[1] Attached to Document 35.

Appendix A, Map 3[1]

The Israeli-Syrian Disengagement Lines

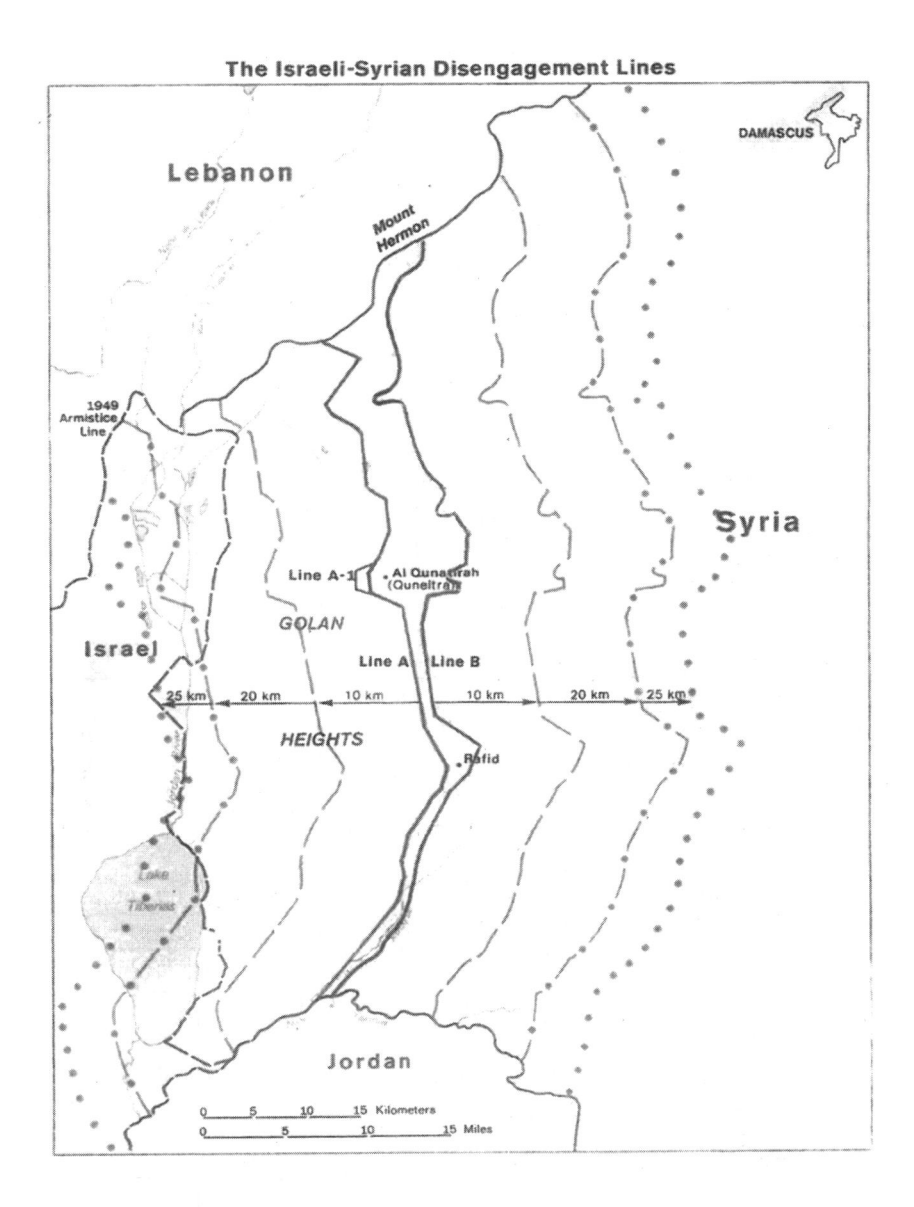

[1] The map is Document 90.

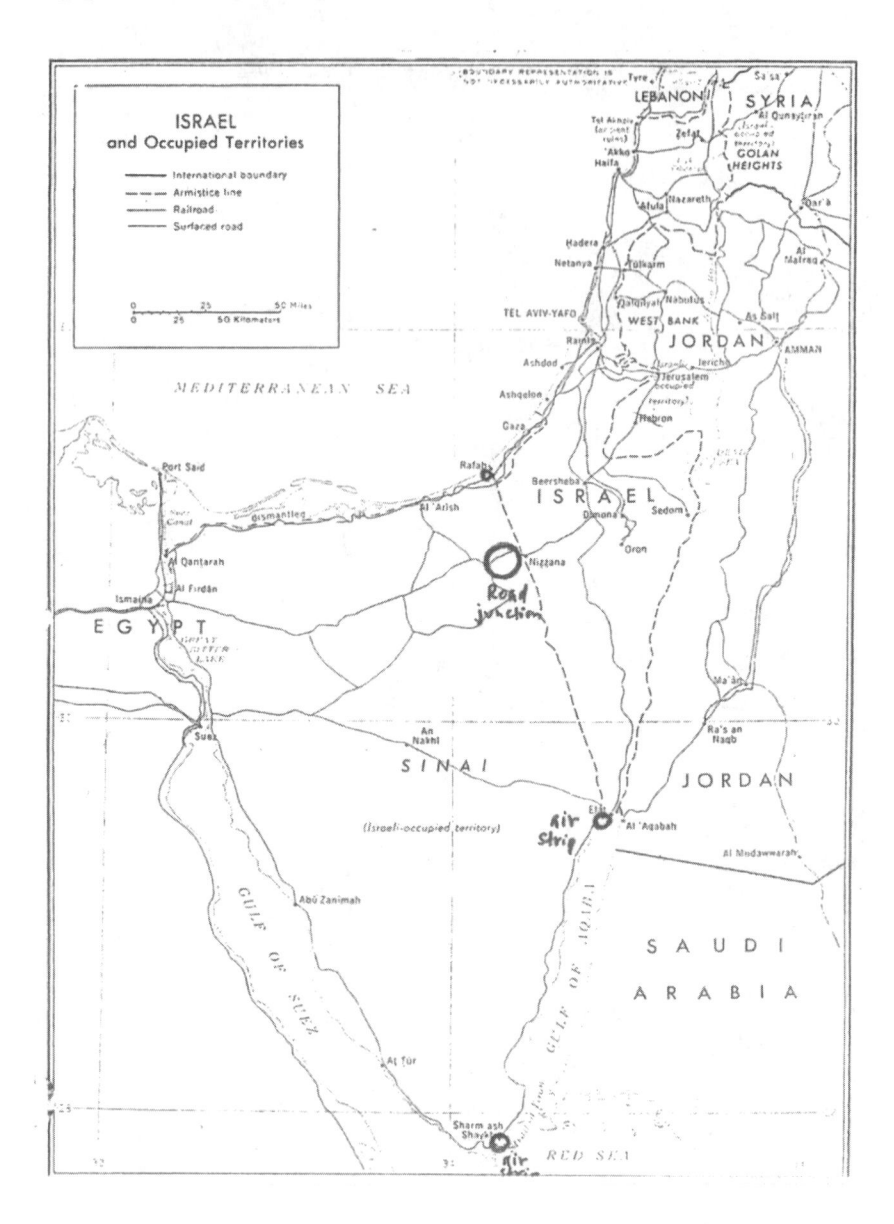

Appendix A, Map 4[1]

---

[1] Attached to Document 94.

Appendix B, Map 1[1]

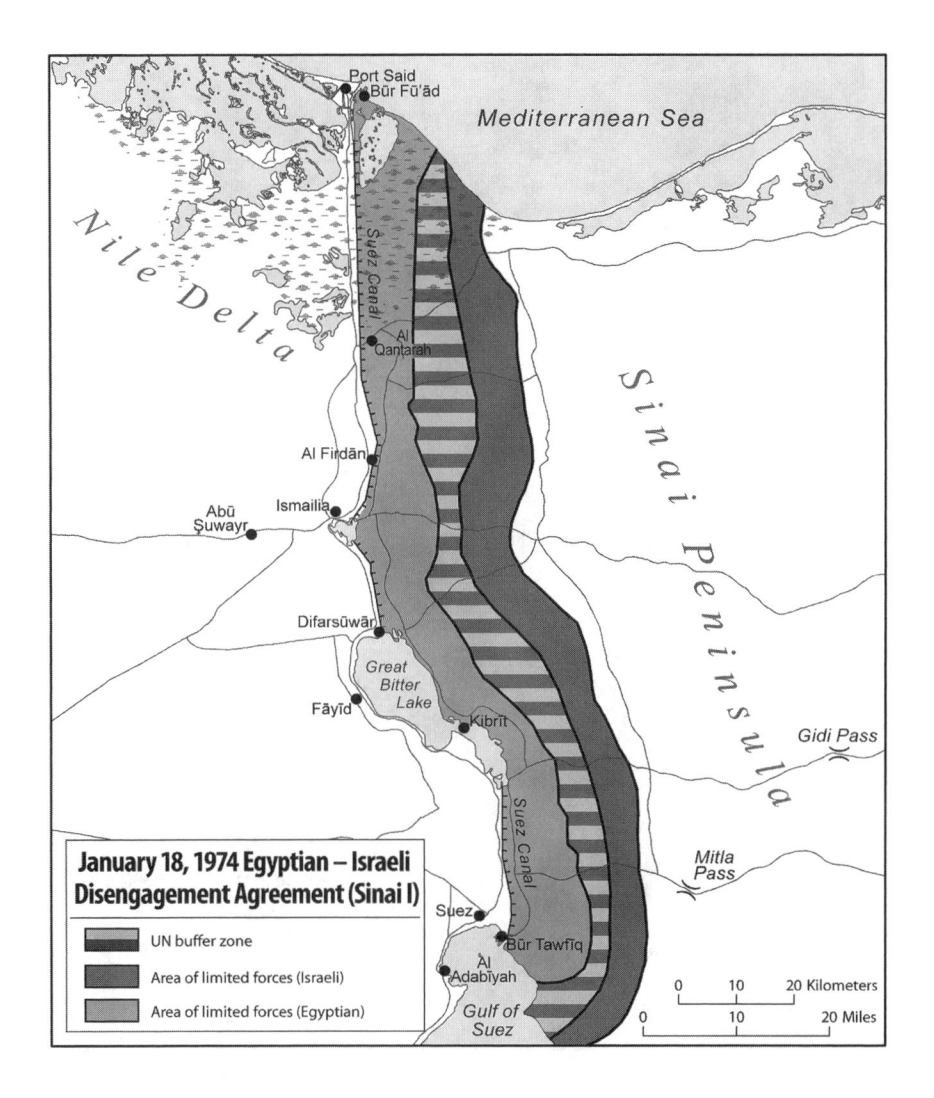

---

[1] Maps provided by the U.S. Department of State's Office of the Geographer.

Appendix B, Map 2[1]

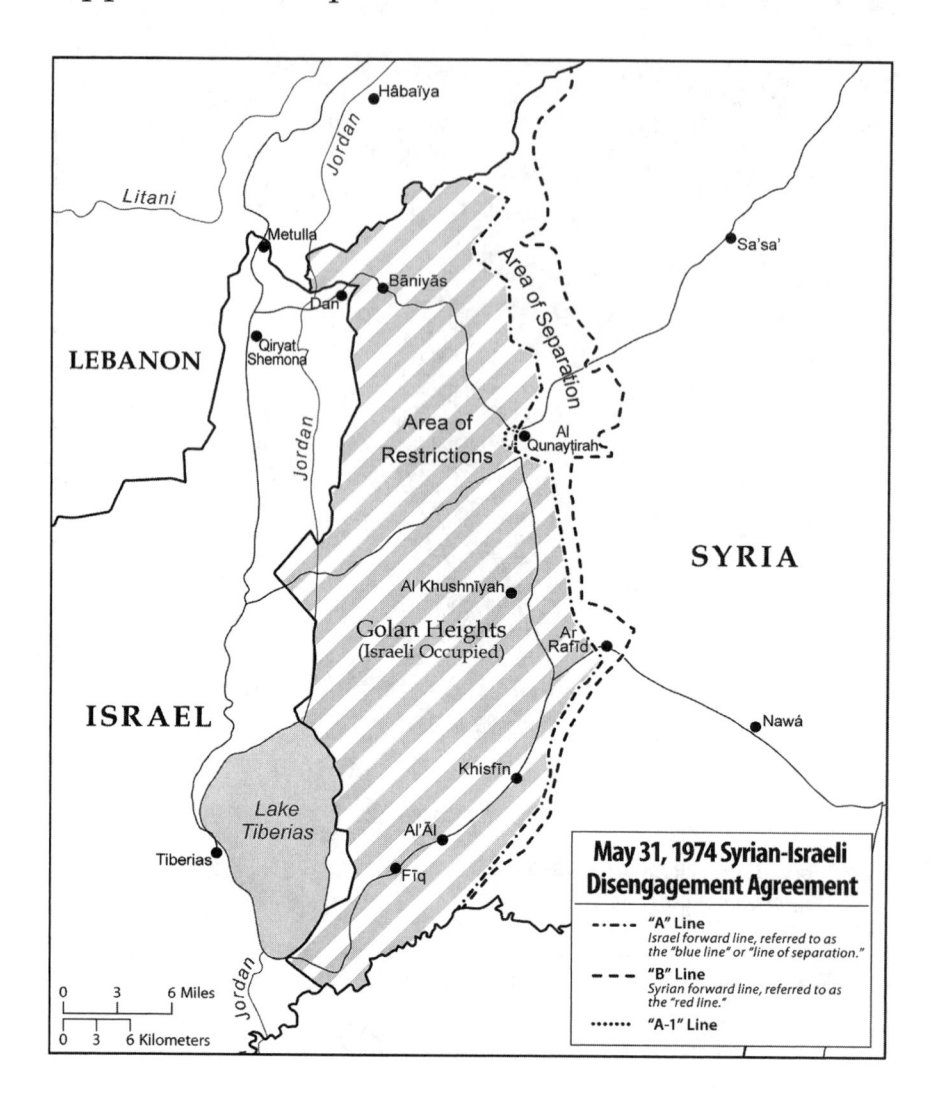

[1] Maps provided by the U.S. Department of State's Office of the Geographer.

Appendix B 1073

Appendix B, Map 3[1]

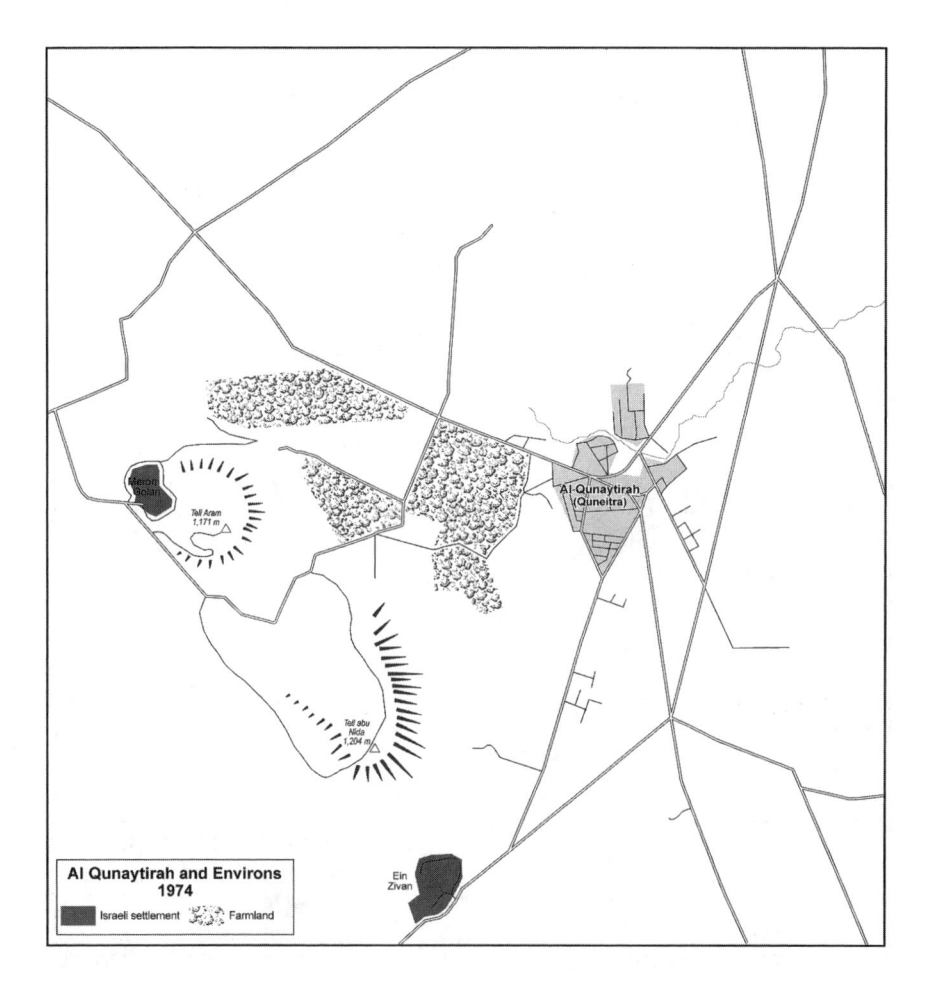

---

[1] Maps provided by the U.S. Department of State's Office of the Geographer.

Appendix B, Map 4[1]

---

[1] Maps provided by the U.S. Department of State's Office of the Geographer.

Index

References are to document numbers

Abou Fares, Sameeh Tawfeek, 193
Abram, Morris, 23
Adan, Gen. Avraham Adan, 16
Adham, Kamal, 46, 292
Ad Hoc National Security Council
 Group, 244
Albert, Carl, 17, 91, 160, 242
Algeria:
 Syrian-Israeli disengagement
  agreement, 36, 43, 44, 45, 46, 47,
  49
 U.S. relations with, 46, 74, 110
Allon, Yigal:
 Egyptian-Israeli disengagement
  agreement, 3, 4, 6, 7, 9
 Lebanese Civil War, 267
 Post-disengagement negotiations,
  113, 123
 Sinai Interim Agreement, 93, 123, 127,
  131, 157, 158, 217, 227, 228
 Syrian-Israeli disengagement
  agreement, 28, 49, 76, 78
 U.S. visits, 93, 94, 120, 123, 127
Allon Plan, 168, 183
American Jewish community groups
 (*see also* Fisher, Max):
 Post-disengagement negotiations,
  138, 261
 Sinai Interim Agreement, 138, 168,
  189, 190, 198, 216
 Syrian-Israeli disengagement
  agreement, 23, 36
 U.S. Middle East policy reassessment,
  168, 174, 180, 181
Anderson, John B., 239, 283
Anderson, Robert, 76, 77, 78, 266
Arab summit (Oct. *1974*). *See* Rabat
 summit.
Arafat, Yassir, 256, 264, 265, 266, 285
Asad, Hafez:
 Lebanese Civil War, 264, 265, 267, 274
 Nixon visit, 92
 Palestinian attacks on Israel, 58, 75
 Post-disengagement negotiations,
  105, 109, 118, 133, 147, 219
 Sinai Interim Agreement, 141, 147
 Syrian-Israeli disengagement
  agreement:
  Gromyko discussions, 29, 77

Asad, Hafez—*Continued*
 Syrian-Israeli disengagement
  agreement—*Continued*
  Kissinger correspondence, 20, 21,
   24
  Kissinger discussions, 19, 25, 26, 29,
   42, 48, 51, 54, 57, 62, 64, 67, 71,
   74, 75, 77, 78
  Nixon correspondence, 80, 81, 82
  U.S.-Soviet discussions, 22
Ash, Roy, 96
Atherton, Alfred L., Jr.:
 Allon U.S. visit, 93
 Egyptian-Israeli disengagement
  agreement, 4, 6, 7, 9
 Lebanese Civil War:
  Ambassadors discussions, 290, 292
  Kissinger-Takla discussions, 263
  Staff discussions, 266, 272, 273, 274,
   275, 276, 277, 278, 280, 281, 282
  Washington Special Actions Group
   discussions, 265, 286
 Palestinians, 249
 Sinai Interim Agreement:
  Ford-Sadat correspondence, 237
  Kissinger-Rabin discussions, 158
  Sinai Support Mission, 245
  Staff discussions, 187, 192, 209, 211,
   215, 216
 Syrian-Israeli disengagement
  agreement:
  Kissinger-Asad correspondence, 20,
   21, 24
  Kissinger-Asad discussions, 29, 77
  Kissinger-Dayan discussions, 32
  Kissinger-Gromyko discussions, 22
  Kissinger-Meir discussions, 28, 49,
   76
  Kissinger-al-Shihabi discussions, 35
 U.S. Middle East policy reassessment,
  170, 171, 173
Avidan, Dan, 5

Bab Al Mandeb Straits, 1, 5, 7, 9, 12, 14,
 94, 145
Ball, George, 169

1075

1076 Index

Barnum, James, 98
Bar-On, Col. Aryeh:
  Egyptian-Israeli disengagement
    agreement, 4, 6, 7, 9
  Rabin U.S. visit, 256, 257, 259
  Syrian-Israeli disengagement
    agreement, 28, 32, 47, 49, 76, 78
Beall, John Glenn, Jr., 31
Begin, Menachem, 252
Bellmon, Henry, 236
Ben-Tsur, Eytan, 4, 7, 28, 93
Berger, Marilyn, 32
Berlin settlement, 23
Bernstein, Marver, 189
Bhutto, Zulfika Ali, 114, 130
Blumberg, David M., 36, 261
Boumediene, Houari, 36, 47, 110, 111
Bouteflika, Abdelaziz, 147
Boycott. *See* Israel boycott.
Bremer, L. Paul:
  Lebanese Civil War, 266
  Palestinians, 249
  Post-disengagement negotiations, 168
  Sinai Interim Agreement, 187, 209,
    211, 215, 245
  U.S. Middle East policy reassessment,
    169, 170, 171
Brezhnev, Leonid, 6, 18, 23, 31, 32, 36,
  48, 74, 97, 111, 115, 119, 120, 123,
  125, 126, 127, 128, 168, 204, 237, 261
Bronfman, Edgar, 189
Broomfield, William, 242
Brown, Gen. George S.:
  Lebanese Civil War, 265, 270, 286
  Middle East war projections, 126
  Sinai Support Mission, 238, 248
  U.S. Middle East policy reassessment,
    163, 166, 174
  U.S. military aid to Israel, 96, 101,
    243, 254, 260
Brown, L. Dean, 280, 284, 287
Bruce, David, 169
Buffum, William B., 249, 266
Bundy, McGeorge, 169
Bunker, Ellsworth:
  Allon U.S. visit, 93
  Egyptian-Israeli disengagement
    agreement, 4, 5, 6, 7, 9
  Syrian-Israeli disengagement
    agreement, 28, 32, 35, 49, 76, 78
  U.S. Middle East policy reassessment,
    174
Burleson, Omar, 31
Burns, Arthur H., 93

Bush, George H.W., 264, 284, 288, 293
Butz, Earl, 97

Callaghan, James, 32
Carter, Jimmy, 290
Case, Clifford P., II, 239, 242
Catto, Henry E., Jr., 245
Ceasefire:
  Kissinger-Meir correspondence, 85
  U.S.-Egyptian discussions, 5
  U.S.-Israeli discussions, 4, 76, 78
  U.S.-Syrian discussions, 42, 75
Chamoun, Camille, 282
Chasin, Eliyahu, 93, 94
Cheney, Richard, 254, 284
Clements, William P., Jr.:
  Lebanese Civil War, 264, 265, 270,
    284, 286, 288
  Middle East war projections, 126
  Post-disengagement negotiations, 111
  U.S. Middle East policy reassessment,
    166, 174
  U.S. military aid to Israel, 98, 254
Cohen, Gershon, 189
Colby, William E.:
  Lebanese Civil War, 264, 265
  Middle East war projections, 126
  Post-disengagement negotiations, 111
  Sinai Support Mission, 238, 248
  U.S. Middle East policy reassessment,
    163, 166, 174
  U.S. military aid to Israel, 96, 243,
    254, 260
Cole, Louis, 36, 138
Congress, U.S.:
  Egyptian-Israeli disengagement
    agreement, 17, 29, 31
  Lebanese Civil War, 281, 283
  Sinai Interim Agreement, 160, 236,
    239, 240, 241, 242
  Syrian-Israeli disengagement
    agreement, 29, 31, 91
  U.S. Middle East policy reassessment,
    159, 160, 161, 162, 166
  Zionism, 249
Covey, Jock, 268, 271, 272, 273, 274, 275,
  276, 277, 278, 280, 281, 282
Crown, Lester, 189

Davis, Nathaniel, 266
Davis, Jeanne W., 126, 264, 265
Dayan, Moshe:
  Egyptian-Israeli disengagement
    agreement, 1, 3, 4, 6, 7, 9

References are to document numbers

Dayan, Moshe—*Continued*
  Political situation, 111
  Syrian-Israeli disengagement
    agreement:
    Kissinger discussions, 32, 40, 53
    Kissinger-Meir discussions, 28, 43, 47, 49, 76, 78
Day, Arthur R., 267, 268, 271, 272, 273, 274, 275, 276, 277, 278, 280, 281, 282
De Borchgrave, Arnaud, 207
Democratic Front for the Liberation of Palestine, 58
Dillon, C. Douglas, 169
Dinitz, Simcha:
  Allon U.S. visit, 93, 94, 127
  Egyptian-Israeli disengagement agreement, 4, 6, 7, 9
  Lebanese Civil War, 273, 275, 276, 278
  Palestinians, 249
  Post-disengagement negotiations, 113, 123
  Rabin U.S. visit, 256, 257, 259
  Sinai Interim Agreement, 127, 158, 188, 200, 202, 203, 230
  Syrian-Israeli disengagement agreement:
    Kissinger-Dayan discussions, 32
    Kissinger-Meir discussions, 28, 46, 47, 49, 76, 78
    U.S.-Israeli Memorandum of Understanding, 84
    U.S. Middle East policy reassessment, 183
    U.S. military aid to Israel, 99, 100, 256
Dobrynin, Anatoliy, 6, 32, 95, 97, 138
Draper, Morris, 267, 275
Duckett, Carl, 111

Eagleburger, Lawrence S.:
  Egyptian-Israeli disengagement agreement, 10
  Lebanese Civil War, 266, 277, 278
  Palestinians, 250
  Post-disengagement negotiations, 113
  Sinai Interim Agreement, 188, 202, 203
  U.S. Middle East policy reassessment, 169
Eban, Abba:
  Egyptian-Israeli disengagement agreement, 4, 6, 7, 9
  Political situation, 36

Eban, Abba—*Continued*
  Syrian-Israeli disengagement agreement, 28, 43, 49, 76, 78, 83
Egypt (*see also* Egyptian-Israeli disengagement agreement; Post-disengagement negotiations; Sadat, Anwar; Sinai Interim Agreement):
  Fahmy U.S. visit, 102
  Kissinger visit (Jan. *1974*), 2, 3
  Lebanese Civil War and:
    Ambassadors discussions, 290, 292
    Ford-Kissinger discussions, 269, 285
    Staff discussions, 268, 271, 272, 274, 276
  Nixon visit (June *1974*), 29, 92
  Political situation, 91, 102, 149
  Sadat U.S. visit, 237
  Soviet military aid, U.S.-Egyptian discussions, 102
  Soviet relations with, 32, 111, 261, 262
  Syrian-Israeli disengagement agreement:
    Kissinger memoranda, 45
    Kissinger-Sadat discussions, 8, 9, 27, 28, 38, 43, 52, 86
    U.S.-Israeli discussions, 49
    U.S.-Israeli Memorandum of Understanding, 84
  U.S. economic aid:
    Ford-Sadat discussions, 246
    Nixon-Sadat accord, 92
  U.S. military aid:
    Ford-American Jewish community group discussions, 261
    Ford-Kissinger discussions, 95, 122
    Ford-Sadat discussions, 246
  U.S. relations with:
    Diplomatic relations, 27
    Nixon-Congressional leadership discussions, 91
    U.S.-Syrian discussions, 74
Egyptian-Israeli disengagement agreement (Jan. *1974*):
  Egyptian-Israeli discussions, 16
  Kissinger Cabinet report, 18
  Kissinger-Dayan discussions, 1
  Kissinger-Israeli cabinet discussions, 3, 4, 6, 7, 9
  Kissinger-Meir discussions, 1, 9
  Kissinger memoranda, 10, 16
  Kissinger-Sadat correspondence, 2
  Kissinger-Sadat discussions, 3, 5, 7

References are to document numbers

Egyptian-Israeli disengagement
    agreement (Jan. 1974)—*Continued*
  Nixon-Congressional leadership
    discussions, 17, 31
  Nixon-Meir correspondence, 11, 12
  Nixon-Sadat correspondence, 11, 13
  Signing, 16
  U.S.-Israeli Memorandum of
    Understanding, 9, 14
Eilts, Hermann F.:
  Lebanese Civil War, 277, 290, 292
  Sinai Interim Agreement, 158, 192,
    195, 199, 209
  Soviet relations with Egypt, 262
  U.S. Middle East policy reassessment,
    170, 171, 173
Eiran, Amos, 256, 257, 259
Elazar, Gen. David, 4, 6, 9, 16, 28
Elias, Asad, 29, 75, 77
Ellsworth, Robert F., 98, 265
Enders, Thomas O., 266
Energy policy, 95, 111
Epstein, Raymond, 36
European allies, 32, 47, 126, 286
European Community (EC), 32
Evron, Ephraim:
  Allon U.S. visit, 93
  Egyptian-Israeli disengagement
    agreement, 4, 6, 7, 9
  Syrian-Israeli disengagement
    agreement, 28, 49, 76, 78

Fahd bin Abdul Aziz al Saud (Prince of
    Saudi Arabia), 51, 166
Fahmy, Ismail:
  Egyptian-Israeli disengagement
    agreement, 5
  Lebanese Civil War, 290
  Palestinians, 247
  Post-disengagement negotiations, 102
  Sinai Interim Agreement:
    Ford-Sadat discussions, 177, 178,
      246
    Kissinger correspondence, 158, 229
    Kissinger discussions, 149
    Kissinger-Sadat correspondence,
      208
    Kissinger-Sadat discussions, 115,
      132, 144, 220
  Syrian-Israeli disengagement
    agreement, 49
  U.S. visit, 102
Faisal ibn Abd al-Aziz al Saud (King of
    Saudi Arabia), 15, 51, 92, 116, 135

Fatah, 29
Fawzy el Ibrashi, 16
Feinberg, Abraham, 189
Fisher, Max:
  Lebanese Civil War, 291
  PLO Security Council debate
    participation, Ford discussions,
    252
  Sinai Interim Agreement, 128, 129,
    138, 186, 198
  U.S. Middle East policy reassessment,
    165, 171
  U.S. military aid to Israel, 261
Ford, Gerald R.:
  Fulbright Middle East trip, 204
  Lebanese Civil War:
    Dean Brown discussions, 287
    Cabinet discussions, 289
    Congressional leadership
      discussions, 283
    Fisher discussions, 291
    Kissinger discussions, 269, 279, 285,
      288
    National Security Council
      discussions, 284
  Palestinians, 139, 183, 193, 247
  PLO Security Council debate
    participation, 250, 251, 252, 253
  Post-disengagement negotiations:
    Allon discussions, 123
    American Jewish community
      group discussions, 261
    Fahmy discussions, 102
    Kissinger-Asad discussions, 105,
      109, 133, 147
    Kissinger-Congressional leadership
      discussions, 137
    Kissinger discussions, 95, 97, 122,
      124, 125, 136, 255, 258
    Kissinger-Faisal discussions, 116
    Kissinger-Israeli cabinet
      discussions, 106, 107
    Kissinger memoranda, 114, 135, 148
    Kissinger-Rabin discussions, 119,
      142
    Kissinger-Sadat discussions, 103,
      104, 108
    National Security Council
      discussions, 111
    Rabat summit and, 112
    Rabin correspondence, 120, 121
    Rabin discussions, 100, 256, 257,
      259
    Shalev discussions, 117

References are to document numbers

Ford, Gerald R.—*Continued*
  Rabin U.S. visit, 256, 257, 259
  Sinai Interim Agreement, 150
    Congressional approval, 241, 242
    Congressional leadership
      discussions, 236, 239, 240
    Dinitz discussions, 200
    Fisher discussions, 128, 129, 186
    Javits discussions, 201
    Kissinger-Asad discussions, 141
    Kissinger discussions, 130, 179, 184,
      185, 190, 191, 194, 196, 197,
      205, 206, 207, 210, 212, 213, 214
    Kissinger-Israeli cabinet
      discussions, 134
    Kissinger memoranda, 145, 223,
      224, 225
    Kissinger-Rabin discussions, 131,
      142, 143, 146, 152, 153, 154,
      157, 217, 221, 222
    Kissinger-Sadat discussions, 115,
      132, 140, 144, 149, 151, 155,
      218, 220
    Rabin correspondence, 156, 158,
      159, 200, 231, 234, 235
    Rabin discussions, 183
    Sadat correspondence, 199, 214,
      228, 232, 233, 235, 237
    Sadat discussions, 177, 178, 246
    Shalev discussions, 117
    Staff discussions, 195
    Talk suspension, 159, 160, 161
    Toon discussions, 198
  Soviet relations with Egypt, 262
  U.S. Middle East policy reassessment:
    Ambassadors discussions, 173
    Congressional leadership
      discussions, 160
    Fisher discussions, 165
    Kissinger discussions, 159, 160, 164,
      182
    National Security Council
      discussions, 166, 174
    Rabin discussions, 183
  U.S. military aid to Israel:
    Allon discussions, 127
    American Jewish community
      group discussions, 261
    Congressional leadership
      discussions, 239, 240
    Khaddam discussions, 193
    Kissinger discussions, 95, 97, 122,
      136, 159, 160, 180

Ford, Gerald R.—*Continued*
  U.S. military aid to Israel—*Continued*
    National Security Council
      discussions, 166, 254
    Rabin correspondence, 234, 235
    Rabin discussions, 99, 100, 256
France (*see also* European allies), 74, 273,
  275, 276
Frangieh, Suleiman, 264, 287
Frelinghuysen, Peter, Jr., 91
Fulbright, J. William, 17, 91, 204

al-Gamasy, Gen. Mohammed Abdel
  Ghani:
  Egyptian-Israeli disengagement
    agreement, 5, 9, 16
  Sinai Interim Agreement, 140, 144,
    149, 155, 220
  Syrian-Israeli disengagement
    agreement, 27
Gammon, Samuel R., III, 24
Garment, Leonard, 36, 198
Gaza Strip, 94
Gazit, Mordechai:
  Egyptian-Israeli disengagement
    agreement, 4, 6, 7, 9
  Sinai Interim Agreement, 158, 188
  Syrian-Israeli disengagement
    agreement, 28, 49, 76, 78
  U.S. Middle East policy reassessment,
    183
  U.S. military aid to Israel, 99
Geneva Conference (*1973*), 3
Geneva Conference resumption:
  Ambassadors discussions, 170, 173
  Ford-Fisher discussions, 165
  Ford-Khaddam discussions, 193
  Ford-Kissinger discussions, 95, 125,
    136
  Ford-Rabin discussions, 256, 257, 259
  Ford-Sadat correspondence, 199
  Ford-Sadat discussions, 177
  Kissinger-American Jewish
    community group discussions,
    23, 138
  Kissinger-Congressional leadership
    discussions, 137
  Kissinger memoranda, 1, 148
  Kissinger-Rabin discussions, 131, 188
  Kissinger-Sadat discussions, 3
  National Security Council
    discussions, 166, 174
  Palestine Liberation Organization
    and, 256, 257

References are to document numbers

1080 Index

Geneva Conference
 resumption—*Continued*
  Sinai Interim Agreement and, 202
  Syrian-Israeli disengagement
   agreement and, 4, 19, 84
  U.S.-Egyptian discussions, 86
  U.S.-Israeli discussions, 4, 76, 93
  U.S.-Soviet discussions, 22, 32
  U.S.-Syrian discussions, 19, 74, 109
Ghoora, Edouard, 263
Ginsburg, David, 189
Ginsburg, Edward, 36
Giscard d'Estaing, Valéry, 47, 246, 284, 290
Godley, G. McMurtrie, 266, 288
Golan Heights (*see also* Syrian-Israeli disengagement agreement), 251
Golan, Matti, 202, 261
Goldberg, Arthur J., 170, 171
Goldman, Guido, 189
Goldmann, Nahum, 180
Goldwin, Robert, 138, 261
Gompert, David, 189, 192
Gorge, Remy, 16
Granger, Col. Clinton, 98
Graubard, Seymour, 138
Great Britain (*see also* European allies), 32, 271, 273
Greenspan, Alan, 184, 204, 284
Groewald, 202
Gromyko, Andrei, 22, 29, 47, 51, 77, 270
Gur, Lt. Gen. Mordechai:
 Post-disengagement negotiations, 106
 Sinai Interim Agreement, 143, 158
 Syrian-Israeli disengagement agreement, 39, 47, 49, 76, 78
Gutfreund, John, 189
Gwertzman, Bernard, 171, 188, 215

Haas, Walter, 189
Haig, Brig. Gen. Alexander M. Jr., 46, 50, 56, 130, 166
Harlow, Bryce, 179
Harriman, Averell, 169
Hartman, Arthur A., 266
Hassan II, 93, 110
Hays, Wayne, 125
Hébert, Felix E., 91
Hellman, Yehudah, 36, 138, 261
Helms, Richard, 292
Hersh, Seymour, 66
Hertzberg, Arthur, 36, 138, 261
Hoffberger, Jerold C., 261
Holloway, Adm. James, 284

Hornblow, Michael, 270, 286
Hoskinson, Samuel, 216, 265
Hussein bin Talal (King of Jordan):
 Lebanese Civil War, 271, 275, 277, 280, 284
 Nixon visit, 92
 Post-disengagement negotiations, 107, 135, 168
Hyland, William G.:
 Lebanese Civil War, 266, 268, 270, 271, 284, 286
 U.S. military aid to Israel, 254

Iklé, Fred, 111, 248
Ingersoll, Robert S.:
 Allon U.S. visit, 93
 Lebanese Civil War, 265, 266, 270
 Middle East war projections, 126
 Post-disengagement negotiations, 111
 Sinai Support Mission, 238
 U.S. Middle East policy reassessment, 163, 174, 175
 U.S. military aid to Israel, 96, 98, 101, 243
Iran, 31, 47, 205, 292
Iran-Iraq dispute, 31, 47
Iraq, 31, 47
Israel (*see also* Egyptian-Israeli disengagement agreement; Israel boycott; Israeli raids on Lebanon; Palestinian attacks on Israel; Post-disengagement negotiations; Syrian-Israeli disengagement agreement):
 Allon U.S. visits, 93, 94, 120, 123
 French military aid, 74
 Lebanese Civil War:
  Ambassadors discussions, 290
  Ford-Kissinger discussions, 269
  Kissinger-Dinitz discussions, 278
  Staff discussions, 267, 268, 273, 274, 275, 276, 277, 280, 281
  Washington Special Actions Group discussions, 270, 286
 Nixon visit (June 1974), 92
 Political situation:
  Kissinger-American Jewish community group discussions, 23, 36, 189
  Kissinger memoranda, 51, 110, 144, 155, 217
  National Security Council discussions, 111

References are to document numbers

Israel—*Continued*
  Political situation—*Continued*
    Nixon-Congressional leadership discussions, 17
    Staff discussions, 195
    U.S.-Syrian discussions, 48
  Rabin U.S. visit, 256, 257, 259
  U.S. economic aid:
    Kissinger-Allon discussions, 93
    Kissinger-American Jewish community group discussions, 36
    Kissinger-Dayan discussions, 32
    Kissinger-Meir discussions, 46
  U.S. military aid:
    Ad Hoc National Security Council Group study, 244
    Ford-Allon discussions, 127
    Ford-American Jewish community group discussions, 261
    Ford-Congressional leadership discussions, 236, 239, 240
    Ford-Khaddam discussions, 193
    Ford-Kissinger discussions, 95, 97, 122, 136, 159, 160, 180
    Ford-Rabin correspondence, 234, 235
    Ford-Rabin discussions, 99, 100, 256, 259
    Javits letter, 175, 176, 177, 180, 181
    Kissinger-Allon discussions, 93
    Kissinger-American Jewish community group discussions, 138, 189
    Kissinger-Asad discussions, 219
    Kissinger-Dinitz discussions, 202
    Kissinger-Israeli cabinet discussions, 8
    Kissinger-Meir discussions, 46
    Kissinger memoranda, 56, 59
    Kissinger-Rabin discussions, 188
    Lebanese Civil War and, 265
    National Security Council discussions, 111, 166, 254
    Nixon-Congressional leadership discussions, 17, 91
    Nixon-Meir correspondence, 87
    NSDM *270*, 101
    NSDM *315*, 260
    NSSM *207*, 96
    NSSM *231*, 243
    Senior Review Group discussions, 98
    Staff discussions, 215, 216

Israel—*Continued*
  U.S. military aid—*Continued*
    U.S.-Saudi discussions, 116
    Washington Special Actions Group discussions, 126
  West Bank/Golan Heights settlements, 251, 252
Israel boycott:
  Kissinger-Allon correspondence, 228
  Kissinger-American Jewish community group discussions, 138, 168
  Kissinger-Dinitz discussions, 202
  Kissinger memoranda, 145, 149
  Kissinger-Rabin discussions, 158
Israeli raids on Lebanon, 34, 36, 37, 251, 252
  PLO Security Council debate participation, 249, 250, 251, 252, 253

Jackson, Henry "Scoop,", 18, 23, 181, 214
Jacobs, Harold, 261
Jacobson, Charlotte, 36, 138, 261
Janka, Leslie A., 240, 283
Javits, Jacob K.:
  Sinai Interim Agreement, 197, 201
  U.S. Middle East policy reassessment, 162, 175, 176, 177, 180, 181
Jewish Defense League, 281
Jones, David C., 111
Jordan (*see also* Palestinian West Bank representation):
  Ford-Sadat discussions, 247
  Kissinger-American Jewish community group discussions, 23
  Lebanese Civil War and, 271, 275, 276, 277, 280, 284
  Nixon visit (June *1974*), 92
  Post-disengagement negotiations, 107, 135, 168
  Syrian relations with, 256
  U.S.-Israeli discussions, 93
  U.S. military aid, 276
Jumblatt, Kamal, 275, 276, 284

Kabbani, Najati, 263
Kabbani, Sabah, 35, 193
Kampelman, Max, 168
Karame, Rashid, 264
Karl, Max, 189

References are to document numbers

Kaye, Danny, 198
Keating, Kenneth B.:
    Death of, 198
    Egyptian-Israeli disengagement agreement, 4, 6, 8
    Post-disengagement negotiations, 123
    Sinai Interim Agreement, 158
    Syrian-Israeli disengagement agreement, 28, 49, 76, 78
    U.S. Middle East policy reassessment, 170, 171, 173
Kenen, I.L., 36, 138
Kennedy, Edward M., 180, 182, 183, 219, 255
Kfar Yuval attack (June 14, 1975), 188
Khaddam, Abdul Halim, 48, 77, 147, 268, 273
Khalid bin Abdul Aziz (King of Saudi Arabia), 166, 184, 204, 290
Kidron, Avraham:
    Egyptian-Israeli disengagement agreement, 4, 6, 7, 9
    Sinai Interim Agreement, 158
    Syrian-Israeli disengagement agreement, 49, 76, 78
Kiryat Shmona massacre (Apr. 11, 1974), 34, 36, 37
Kissinger, Henry A.:
    Allon U.S. visit, 93, 94
    Egyptian-Israeli disengagement agreement, 10, 16
        Cabinet report, 18
        Dayan discussions, 1
        Israeli cabinet discussions, 3, 4, 6, 7, 9, 68
        Meir discussions, 1, 9
        Nixon-Congressional leadership discussions, 17, 31
        Nixon-Sadat correspondence, 13
        Sadat correspondence, 2
        Sadat discussions, 3, 5, 8
    Lebanese Civil War:
        Ambassadors discussions, 290, 292
        Dinitz discussions, 278
        Ford-Cabinet discussions, 289
        Ford discussions, 269, 279, 285, 288
        Ford-Fisher discussions, 291
        Hussein discussions, 280
        National Security Council discussions, 284
        Staff discussions, 266, 267, 268, 271, 272, 273, 274, 275, 276, 277, 278, 280, 281, 282
        Takla discussions, 263

Kissinger, Henry A.—*Continued*
    Lebanese Civil War—*Continued*
        Washington Special Actions Group discussions, 264, 265, 270, 286
    Nixon Middle East trip (June 1974), 29, 32, 38, 66, 74, 75
    Oil embargo:
        American Jewish community group discussions, 23
        Asad correspondence, 21, 24
        Cabinet report, 18
        Nixon-Congressional leadership discussions, 17
        Sadat discussions, 3, 15
    Palestinian attacks on Israel, 58, 75
    Palestinians:
        Allon discussions, 93
        American Jewish community group discussions, 189
        Asad discussions, 29, 74, 75
        Ford-Rabin correspondence, 250
        Ford-Sadat discussions, 247
        Meir discussions, 76, 78
        Sadat discussions, 104, 105, 108
    PLO Security Council debate participation, 249, 251
    Post-disengagement negotiations, 110, 148
        American Jewish community group discussions, 138
        Asad discussions, 105, 109, 118, 133, 147, 219
        Congressional leadership discussions, 137
        Faisal discussions, 116, 135
        Ford-Allon discussions, 123
        Ford-American Jewish community group discussions, 261
        Ford discussions, 95, 97, 122, 124, 125, 136, 255, 258
        Ford-Rabin correspondence, 121
        Ford-Shalev discussions, 117
        Hussein discussions, 135
        Israeli cabinet discussions, 106, 107
        National Security Council discussions, 111
        Rabat summit and, 112, 113, 114, 115, 116
        Rabin discussions, 119, 142
        Sadat discussions, 103, 104, 108, 115
        Rabin U.S. visit, 256, 257, 259
    Sinai Interim Agreement, 145, 223, 224, 225

References are to document numbers

Kissinger, Henry A.—*Continued*
  Sinai Interim Agreement—*Continued*
    Allon correspondence, 228
    Allon discussions, 93
    American Jewish community group discussions, 138
    Asad discussions, 141, 147
    Congressional approval, 241
    Dinitz discussions, 202, 203
    Fahmy correspondence, 158, 229
    Fahmy discussions, 149
    Ford-Allon discussions, 127
    Ford-Congressional leadership discussions, 236, 240
    Ford-Dinitz discussions, 200
    Ford discussions, 130, 179, 184, 185, 190, 191, 194, 196, 197, 205, 206, 207, 210, 212, 213, 214
    Ford-Fisher discussions, 129, 186
    Ford-Javits discussions, 201
    Ford-Khaddam discussions, 193
    Ford memoranda, 150
    Ford-Rabin correspondence, 231, 235
    Ford-Sadat correspondence, 199, 235, 237
    Ford-Sadat discussions, 177, 178, 246
    Ford-Toon discussions, 198
    Israeli cabinet discussions, 107, 134
    Rabin discussions, 131, 142, 143, 146, 152, 153, 154, 157, 158, 188, 208, 217, 221, 222
    Sadat correspondence, 208
    Sadat discussions, 104, 115, 132, 140, 144, 149, 151, 155, 218, 220
    Sinai Support Mission, 238, 245, 248
    Staff discussions, 187, 192, 195, 209, 211, 215, 216
    Talk suspension, 158, 159, 160, 161
    U.S.-Israeli Memorandum of Agreement, 227
  Syrian-Israeli disengagement agreement, 45, 50, 73
    American Jewish community group discussions, 23, 36
    Asad correspondence, 20, 21, 24
    Asad discussions, 19, 25, 26, 29, 42, 48, 51, 54, 57, 62, 64, 67, 71, 74, 75, 77, 78
    Dayan discussions, 32, 40, 53
    Faisal discussions, 51
    Gromyko discussions, 47, 51

Kissinger, Henry A.—*Continued*
  Syrian-Israeli disengagement agreement—*Continued*
    Israeli approval, 79
    Israeli cabinet discussions, 4, 19, 68, 70
    Meir correspondence, 33, 37, 85
    Meir discussions, 26, 28, 29, 39, 40, 43, 44, 46, 47, 49, 53, 54, 55, 60, 62, 63, 65, 72, 76, 78
    Nixon-Asad correspondence, 80, 82
    Nixon-Congressional leadership discussions, 31, 91
    Nixon memoranda, 61, 66
    Sadat discussions, 8, 9, 27, 28, 38, 43, 52, 86
    al-Shihabi discussions, 35
    U.S.-Israeli Memorandum of Understanding, 84
    U.S. military aid to Israel and, 56, 59
    U.S.-Soviet discussions, 22, 32
  U.S. Middle East policy reassessment:
    Ambassadors discussions, 166, 170, 171, 173
    American Jewish community group discussions, 168
    Ford-Congressional leadership discussions, 160
    Ford discussions, 159, 160, 164, 182
    Ford-Fisher discussions, 165
    Ford-Rabin discussions, 183
    McCloskey memoranda, 181
    Moynihan discussions, 172
    National Security Council discussions, 166, 174
    NSSM 220, 163
    Rabin interview, 176
  U.S. military aid to Israel, 56, 59
    Allon discussions, 93
    American Jewish community group discussions, 138, 189
    Asad discussions, 219
    Faisal discussions, 116
    Ford-American Jewish community group discussions, 261
    Ford discussions, 95, 97, 122, 136, 159, 160, 180
    Ford-Rabin discussions, 99, 100, 256
    Lebanese Civil War and, 265
    Meir discussions, 46
    National Security Council discussions, 111, 254

References are to document numbers

1084 Index

Kissinger, Henry A.—*Continued*
  U.S. military aid to Israel—*Continued*
    NSDM 270, 101
    NSDM 315, 260
    NSSM 207, 96
    Rabin discussions, 188
    Senior Review Group discussions, 98
    Washington Special Actions Group discussions, 126
Kissinger shuttle diplomacy. *See* First Egyptian-Israeli disengagement agreement; Sinai Interim Agreement; Syrian-Israeli disengagement agreement.
Klutznik, Philip, 23, 189
Kosygin, Aleksei, 31, 290
Kraft, Joe, 48
Kurdistan, 47
Kuwait, 45, 46

Lambrakis, George B., 277, 278
Landes, David, 189
Lautenberg, Frank R., 138, 261
Lazarus, Fred, 189
Lebanese Civil War:
  Ambassadors discussions, 290, 292
  Egyptian role:
    Ambassadors discussions, 290, 292
    Ford-Kissinger discussions, 269, 285
    Staff discussions, 268, 271, 272, 274, 276
  Ford-Dean Brown discussions, 287
  Ford-Cabinet discussions, 289
  Ford-Congressional leadership discussions, 283
  Ford-Fisher discussions, 291
  Ford-Kissinger discussions, 269, 279, 285, 288
  Israeli role:
    Ambassadors discussions, 290
    Ford-Kissinger discussions, 269
    Kissinger-Dinitz discussions, 278
    Staff discussions, 267, 268, 273, 274, 275, 276, 277, 280, 281
    Washington Special Actions Group discussions, 270, 286
  Kissinger-Hussein discussions, 280
  Kissinger-Takla discussions, 263
  Meloy/Waring assassinations, 288, 289, 290
  Murphy-Asad discussions, 267

Lebanese Civil War—*Continued*
  National Security Council discussions, 284
  Soviet role, 269, 270, 271, 282, 286
  Staff discussions, 266, 268, 271, 272, 273, 274, 275, 276, 277, 278, 280, 281, 282
  Syrian role:
    Ambassadors discussions, 290, 292
    Ford-Cabinet discussions, 289
    Ford-Kissinger discussions, 269, 279
    Ford-Rabin discussions, 256
    National Security Council discussions, 284
    Staff discussions, 267, 268, 271, 272, 273, 274, 275, 276, 278, 281
    Washington Special Actions Group discussions, 265, 270, 286
  U.S. evacuation, 289
  U.S. military intervention, 286
  Washington Special Actions Group discussions, 264, 265, 270
Lebanon (*see also* Israeli raids on Lebanon; Lebanese Civil War):
  Ambassadors discussions, 173
  Palestinian attacks on Israel and, 91
Leibman, Morris, 189
Leigh, Monroe, 266
Leor, Brig. Gen. David, 4, 28, 49, 76, 78
Levine, Arthur, 261
Levran, Col. Aharon, 16
Libya, 290
Lilienthal, Alfred, 23
Linowitz, Sol, 23
Lissy, David H., 261
List, Albert, 23
Lodal, Jan M., 111
Lord, Winston, 28, 216, 266
Lowell, Stanley, 36
Lynn, James T., 238, 243, 248, 254, 260

Ma'alot massacre (May 15, 1974), 58, 59, 60, 61
Mahon, George H., 91, 125, 160
Malik, Yakov A., 249
Mansfield, Michael, 160, 242
Marwan, Ashraf, 46, 47, 49
Matthews, David, 283
Matzkin, Rose, 36, 138, 261
Maw, Carlyle E.:
  Egyptian-Israeli disengagement agreement, 4, 6, 7, 9, 16
  Lebanese Civil War, 266

References are to document numbers

Index 1085

Maw, Carlyle E.—*Continued*
  Syrian-Israeli disengagement
    agreement, 49, 76, 78
McCloskey, Robert J., 28, 76, 78, 181, 266
McCloy, John J., 169
McFall, John J., 283
McGovern, George S., 167
McNamara, Robert S., 169
Meir, Golda:
  Egyptian-Israeli disengagement
    agreement, 1, 3, 6, 11, 12, 9
  Political situation, 36
  Post-disengagement negotiations, 134
  Syrian-Israeli disengagement
    agreement:
      Kissinger correspondence, 33, 37, 85
      Kissinger discussions, 26, 28, 29, 39, 40, 43, 44, 46, 47, 49, 53, 55, 60, 62, 63, 72, 76, 78
      Nixon correspondence, 37, 41, 69
      Protocol text, 89
  U.S. military aid to Israel, 87
Meloy, Francis E., Jr., 288, 289, 290
Middle East war projections:
  Advisors discussions, 169
  Ambassadors discussions, 173
  Kissinger-American Jewish
    community group discussions, 168
  National Security Council
    discussions, 166, 254
  Washington Special Actions Group
    discussions, 126
Miller, Robert H., 266
Miller, Israel, 36, 138, 261
Mizrachi, Eli, 28, 76, 78
Morgan, Thomas E., 242
Morgenthau, Hans, 46, 48, 168
Morton, Rogers B., 239, 240
Moynihan, Daniel P., 172, 249
Mubarak, Hosni, 177, 178
Murphy, Richard W.:
  Lebanese Civil War, 267, 268, 271, 272, 274, 275, 276, 290
  Sinai Interim Agreement, 193
  U.S. Middle East policy reassessment, 170, 171, 173

Nasher, Raymond, 189
Nasser, Gamal Abdel, 17, 31, 166, 177, 183, 254, 261

Nessen, Ronald H., 161, 184
National Security Council (NSC):
  Decision Memoranda:
    NSDM 270, "Military Assistance
      for Israel," 101
    NSDM 313, "Establishment of US
      Sinai Support Mission," 248
    NSDM 315, "Military Assistance
      for Israel," 260
  Meetings:
    Jan. 13, 1976, 254
    Mar. 28, 1975, 166
    May 15, 1975, 174
    Oct. 18, 1974, 111
  Study Memoranda:
    NSSM 207, "Israeli Future Military
      Requirements," 96
    NSSM 220, "U.S. Policy in the
      Middle East," 163
    NSSM 230, "Establishment of U.S.
      Sinai Support Mission," 238
    NSSM 231, "Israeli Military
      Requests," 243
Nixon, Richard M.:
  Egyptian-Israeli disengagement
    agreement, 1, 3, 8
  Congressional leadership
    discussions, 17, 31
  Kissinger Cabinet report, 18
  Meir correspondence, 11, 12
  Sadat correspondence, 11, 13
  Middle East trip (June 1974), 66, 92
  Nixon-Congressional leadership
    discussions, 91
  U.S.-Egyptian discussions, 38
  U.S.-Israeli discussions, 32
  U.S.-Syrian discussions, 29, 74, 75
  Oil embargo, 15, 17, 31
  Resignation of, 95
  Syrian-Israeli disengagement
    agreement, 61, 66
  Asad correspondence, 80, 81, 82
  Congressional leadership
    discussions, 17, 31, 91
  Israeli approval, 79
  Kissinger-Asad discussions, 19, 25, 26, 42, 51, 57, 64, 71
  Kissinger-Faisal discussions, 51
  Kissinger-Israeli cabinet
    discussions, 68, 70
  Kissinger-Meir discussions, 39, 43, 44, 55, 60, 65, 72
  Kissinger memoranda, 45

References are to document numbers

1086　Index

Nixon, Richard M.—*Continued*
　Syrian-Israeli disengagement
　　agreement—*Continued*
　　　Kissinger-Sadat discussions, 27, 38,
　　　　52, 86
　　　Meir correspondence, 37, 41, 69
　　　Protocol text, 89
　　　U.S. military aid to Israel and,
　　　　Kissinger memoranda, 59
　　　U.S. military aid to Israel, 17, 87, 91
North Atlantic Treaty Organization
　(NATO), 23, 286
November 6 Declaration, 32
Nowfel, Camille, 35
Noyes, James H., 98, 264

Oakley, Robert B.:
　Lebanese Civil War, 263, 264, 265,
　　284, 292
　Sinai Interim Agreement, 158, 216,
　　245
　Sinai Support Mission, 238
　U.S. Middle East policy reassessment,
　　166, 170, 171, 174
　U.S. military aid to Israel, 254, 261
October 1973 War, 23, 95, 126
　Security Council Resolution 338, 7,
　　74, 76, 253
Oil embargo:
　Kissinger-American Jewish
　　community group discussions,
　　23
　Kissinger-Asad correspondence, 21,
　　24
　Kissinger Cabinet report, 18
　Nixon-Congressional leadership
　　discussions, 17, 31
　Syrian-Israeli disengagement
　　agreement and, 21, 23
　U.S.-Egyptian discussions, 3, 15
　U.S.-Israeli discussions, 9, 39
　U.S.-Syrian correspondence, 21, 24
O'Neill, Thomas P. "Tip," 91, 283
Organization of Petroleum Exporting
　Countries (OPEC). *See* Oil
　embargo.
Oudjah al-Haffir, 94

Pahlavi, Mohammed Reza, 47, 65, 111,
　114, 126, 129, 149, 205,
Palestine Liberation Organization (PLO)
　(*see also* Lebanese Civil War):
　Ambassadors discussions, 290
　Ford-Rabin discussions, 257, 259

Palestine Liberation Organization
　(PLO)—*Continued*
　Geneva Conference resumption and,
　　256, 257
　Kissinger-American Jewish
　　community group discussions,
　　138, 168
　Kissinger-Asad discussions, 105, 109,
　　118, 219
　Rabat summit on, 112
　Security Council debate participation,
　　249, 250, 251, 252, 253
　Syrian role, Ford-Rabin discussions,
　　256
　UN General Assembly participation
　　vote, 104, 108, 109, 110, 111, 113,
　　123
　U.S.-Israeli discussions, 93, 117, 119
Palestinian attacks on Israel:
　Ford-Rabin correspondence, 139
　Kfar Yuval attack (June 14, 1975), 188
　Kiryat Shmona massacre (Apr. 11,
　　1974), 34, 36, 37
　Kissinger-Asad correspondence, 58
　Kissinger-Asad discussions, 75
　Kissinger-Meir correspondence, 85
　Kissinger-Meir discussions, 76, 78
　Kissinger-Sadat discussions, 86
　Ma'alot massacre (May 15, 1974), 58,
　　59, 60, 61
　Nixon-Congressional leadership
　　discussions, 91
　Nixon memoranda, 61
　Savoy Hotel attack (Mar. 1975), 139
Palestinians (*see also* Palestine
　Liberation Organization;
　Palestinian attacks on Israel;
　Palestinian West Bank
　representation):
　Ford-Khaddam discussions, 193
　Ford-Rabin discussions, 183
　Ford-Sadat discussions, 247
　Kissinger-Allon discussions, 93
　Kissinger-American Jewish
　　community group discussions,
　　189
　Kissinger-Asad discussions, 29, 74, 75
　Kissinger-Meir discussions, 76, 78
　Kissinger-Sadat discussions, 104, 105,
　　108
　Nixon-Congressional leadership
　　discussions, 91
　Rabat summit on, 112
　Staff discussions, 249

References are to document numbers

Palestinians—*Continued*
  UN General Assembly Resolution 3336, 249
  UN General Assembly Resolution 3379, 249, 252
  UN Security Council Resolution 11940, 249, 255, 257
Palestinian West Bank representation:
  Ford-Kissinger discussions, 95
  Kissinger-Allon discussions, 93
  Kissinger-Asad discussions, 74, 105, 109
  Kissinger-Sadat discussions, 108
  National Security Council discussions, 111
  Rabat summit on, 112
  Sisco-Hussein discussions, 107
  U.S.-Israeli discussions, 119
Pauly, Lt. Gen. John W., 98
Pelletreau, Robert H., Jr., 268, 275
Percy, Charles H., 129, 175, 181
Peres, Shimon:
  Post-disengagement negotiations, 106
  Sinai Interim Agreement, 131, 157, 158, 217
  Syrian-Israeli disengagement agreement, 49, 76, 78
Peterson, Pete, 169
Phalanges. *See* Lebanese Civil War.
Pharaon, Rashid, 46
Pickering, Thomas R., 10, 170, 171, 173, 290, 292
Popular Front for the Liberation of Palestine-General Command (PFLP–GC), 34
Popular Front for the Liberation of Palestine (PFLP), 266
Porter, William J., 290
Post-disengagement negotiations (*see also* Geneva Conference resumption; Sinai Interim Agreement; U.S. Middle East policy reassessment):
  Ford-Allon discussions, 123
  Ford-American Jewish community group discussions, 261
  Ford-Congressional leadership discussions, 160
  Ford-Fahmy discussions, 102
  Ford-Kissinger discussions, 95, 97, 122, 124, 125, 136, 255, 258
  Ford-Rabin correspondence, 120, 121
  Ford-Rabin discussions, 100, 256, 257, 259

Post-disengagement negotiations—*Continued*
  Ford-Shalev discussions, 117
  Kissinger-American Jewish community group discussions, 138
  Kissinger-Asad discussions, 105, 109, 118, 133, 147, 219
  Kissinger-Congressional leadership discussions, 137
  Kissinger-Faisal discussions, 116, 135
  Kissinger-Hussein discussions, 135
  Kissinger-Israeli cabinet discussions, 106, 107
  Kissinger memoranda, 110, 114, 135, 148
  Kissinger-Rabin discussions, 119, 142
  Kissinger-Sadat discussions, 103, 104, 108, 115
  National Security Council discussions, 111
  Rabat summit and, 112, 113, 114, 115, 116, 118, 138
  Sisco-Hussein discussions, 107
  Washington Special Actions Group discussions, 126
Prisoners of war (POWs):
  Kissinger-American Jewish community group discussions, 23
  U.S.-Egyptian discussions, 5, 8
  U.S.-Israeli discussions, 4, 6, 7, 9, 28, 76, 78
  U.S.-Syrian correspondence, 21
  U.S.-Syrian discussions, 25, 26, 42, 77
Pritzker, Abraham, 189

al-Qadhafi, Mu'ammar, 177, 261, 265

Rabat summit (Oct. 1974):
  Kissinger-American Jewish community group discussions, 138
  Kissinger-Asad discussions, 105, 109
  Kissinger memoranda, 110, 112, 114
  National Security Council discussions, 111
  U.S.-Egyptian discussions, 104, 108, 115
  U.S.-Israeli discussions, 106
Rabin, Yitzhak:
  Nixon visit, 92
  Palestinian attacks on Israel, 139

References are to document numbers

1088 Index

Rabin, Yitzhak—*Continued*
  PLO Security Council debate participation, 250, 252, 253
  Political situation, 48
  Post-disengagement negotiations:
    Ford correspondence, 120, 121
    Ford discussions, 100, 256, 257, 259
    Kissinger discussions, 119, 142
    Kissinger-Israeli cabinet discussions, 106, 107
  Sinai Interim Agreement:
    Ford correspondence, 156, 158, 159, 200, 231, 234, 235
    Ford discussions, 183
    Kissinger discussions, 131, 134, 142, 143, 146, 152, 153, 154, 157, 158, 188, 208, 217, 221, 222
    Kissinger-Israeli cabinet discussions, 107
    Sadat correspondence, 144
    Talk suspension, 158
  Syrian-Israeli disengagement agreement, 49, 76, 78
  U.S. Middle East policy reassessment, 176, 183
  U.S. military aid to Israel, 99, 100, 234, 235, 256, 259
  U.S. visit, 256, 257, 259
  West Bank/Golan Heights settlements, 252
Raviv, Moshe, 32, 93
Reagan, Ronald, 280, 288,
Rhodes, John, 31, 160, 239, 242, 283
Ribicoff, Abraham A., 162, 180, 197
Richardson, Elliot L., 289
Rifai, Zaid, 247
Rifkind, Simon, 23
Robinson, Charles W., 266
Rockefeller, David, 169
Rockefeller, Nelson:
  Lebanese Civil War, 283, 284, 288
  Post-disengagement negotiations, 127
  Sinai Interim Agreement, 239, 240
  U.S. Middle East policy reassessment, 160, 161, 166, 174
Rodman, Peter W.:
  Allon U.S. visit, 93, 94
  Egyptian-Israeli disengagement agreement, 4, 5, 6, 7, 9
  Lebanese Civil War, 290
  Oil embargo, 23
  Post-disengagement negotiations, 138

Rodman, Peter W.—*Continued*
  Sinai Interim Agreement, 158, 216
  Syrian-Israeli disengagement agreement:
    American Jewish community group discussions, 36
    Kissinger-American Jewish community group discussions, 23
    Kissinger-Asad discussions, 74, 75, 77
    Kissinger-Dayan discussions, 32
    Kissinger-Meir discussions, 46, 47, 76, 78
    Kissinger-al-Shihabi discussions, 35
    U.S.-Israeli discussions, 28, 49
    U.S. military aid to Israel, 87
Rogers, William P., 189, 195, 254
Rose, Daniel, 138
Rosenbaum, Herman, 138
Rosenberg, Herman, 36
Rosenne, Meir, 16
Rosovsky, Henry, 189
Rowan, Carl, 188
Rumsfeld, Donald H.:
  Lebanese Civil War, 269, 283, 284, 285, 286
  Post-disengagement negotiations, 111
  Sinai Interim Agreement, 129, 248
  U.S. Middle East policy reassessment, 166, 174
  U.S. military aid to Israel, 254, 260
Rush, Kenneth, 74
Rusk, Dean, 169, 197

Sabbagh, Isa K.:
  Post-disengagement negotiations, 219
  Sinai Interim Agreement, 193
  Syrian-Israeli disengagement agreement, Kissinger-Asad discussions, 29, 48, 74, 75, 77
Sadat, Anwar:
  Egyptian-Israeli disengagement agreement, 2, 3, 5, 8, 11, 13
  Lebanese Civil War, 290, 292
  Nixon visit, 92
  Oil embargo, 3, 15
  Palestinians, Ford discussions, 247
  Post-disengagement negotiations, Kissinger discussions, 103, 104, 108, 115
  Sinai Interim Agreement:
    Ford correspondence, 199, 214, 228, 232, 233, 235, 237

References are to document numbers

Sadat, Anwar—*Continued*
　Sinai Interim Agreement—*Continued*
　　Ford discussions, 177, 178, 246
　　Kissinger correspondence, 208
　　Kissinger discussions, 104, 115, 132, 140, 144, 149, 151, 155, 218, 220
　　Rabin correspondence, 144
　　Soviet relations with Egypt, 262
　　Syrian-Israeli disengagement agreement, Kissinger discussions, 8, 9, 27, 28, 38, 43, 52, 86
　　U.S. visit, 237
Safire, William, 165
Saiqa:
　Ford-Rabin discussions, 256
　Lebanese Civil War, 274, 284, 285
　U.S.-Syrian discussions, 29, 75
Sanders, Edward, 261
Saqqaf, Omar, 46, 51, 111
Sarkis, Elias, 277, 287, 288, 289, 290
Saudi Arabia:
　Fahd U.S. visit, 51
　Lebanese Civil War and, 264, 265, 292
　Nixon visit (June 1974), 92
　Oil embargo, 15, 21
　Post-disengagement negotiations, 116, 135
　Syrian-Israeli disengagement agreement, 43, 45, 46, 49, 51
　U.S. Middle East policy reassessment, 166
　U.S. military aid, 48, 138
　U.S. relations with, 74, 126, 135
Saunders, Harold H.:
　Allon U.S. visit, 93
　Egyptian-Israeli disengagement agreement, 4, 6, 7, 16
　Lebanese Civil War, 264, 267, 272, 277, 278, 280, 281
　Sinai Interim Agreement, 158, 187, 192, 209, 211, 215, 216, 245
　Syrian-Israeli disengagement agreement:
　　Kissinger-Asad discussions, 48, 77
　　Kissinger-Dayan discussions, 32
　　Kissinger-Meir discussions, 28, 49, 76, 78
　　Kissinger-al-Shihabi discussions, 35
　　U.S.-Algerian discussions, 47
　　U.S.-Saudi discussions, 46
　U.S. Middle East policy reassessment, 170, 171
　U.S. military aid to Israel, 98

Savoy Hotel attack (Mar. *1975*), 139
Scali, John, 17
Schindler, Alexander M., 138, 189, 261
Schlesinger, James R.:
　Post-disengagement negotiations, 111, 127
　Sinai Support Mission, 238
　U.S. Middle East policy reassessment, 163, 166, 174
　U.S. military aid to Israel, 96, 101, 243
Schmidt, Helmut, 47, 127, 182, 183
Scotes, Thomas J., 20, 29, 75
Scott, Hugh D., Jr., 31, 91, 160, 239, 242
Scowcroft, Lt. Gen. Brent:
　Allon U.S. visit, 94
　Egyptian-Israeli disengagement agreement, 3, 8, 17, 31
　Fulbright Middle East trip, 204
　Lebanese Civil War:
　　Ford-Dean Brown discussions, 287
　　Ford-Congressional leadership discussions, 283
　　Ford-Fisher discussions, 291
　　Ford-Kissinger discussions, 269, 285, 288
　　National Security Council discussions, 284
　　Staff discussions, 268, 271, 275, 276, 280, 282
　　Washington Special Actions Group discussions, 264, 265, 270
　Middle East war projections, 126
　Oil embargo, 15
　PLO Security Council debate participation, 251, 252
　Post-disengagement negotiations:
　　Ford-Allon discussions, 123
　　Ford-Kissinger discussions, 95, 124, 125, 136, 255, 258
　　Ford-Rabin correspondence, 120
　　Ford-Rabin discussions, 100, 256, 257
　　Kissinger-Asad discussions, 105, 109, 118, 133, 147
　　Kissinger-Congressional leadership discussions, 137
　　Kissinger-Faisal discussions, 116
　　Kissinger-Israeli cabinet discussions, 106, 107
　　Kissinger memoranda, 110, 114, 135, 148
　　Kissinger-Rabin discussions, 119, 142

References are to document numbers

Scowcroft, Lt. Gen. Brent—*Continued*
 Post-disengagement
  negotiations—*Continued*
  Kissinger-Sadat discussions, 103, 104
  National Security Council discussions, 111
  Rabat summit and, 112
 Rabin U.S. visit, 256, 257, 259
 Sinai Interim Agreement:
  Congressional approval, 241
  Ford-Congressional leadership discussions, 236
  Ford-Dinitz discussions, 200
  Ford-Fisher discussions, 128, 129, 186
  Ford-Javits discussions, 201
  Ford-Khaddam discussions, 193
  Ford-Kissinger discussions, 130, 179, 184, 185, 190, 191, 194, 196, 197, 205, 206, 207, 210, 212, 213, 214
  Ford memoranda, 150
  Ford-Rabin correspondence, 235
  Ford-Sadat correspondence, 235
  Ford-Toon discussions, 198
  Kissinger-Asad discussions, 141
  Kissinger-Israeli cabinet discussions, 134
  Kissinger memoranda, 145
  Kissinger-Rabin discussions, 131, 142, 143, 146, 152, 153, 154, 157
  Kissinger-Sadat discussions, 115, 132, 140, 144, 149, 151, 155
  Sinai Support Mission, 238, 248
  Staff discussions, 187, 195
 Soviet relations with Egypt, 262
 Syrian-Israeli disengagement agreement:
  Israeli approval, 79
  Kissinger-Asad discussions, 19, 25, 26, 42, 51, 54, 57, 62, 64, 67, 71
  Kissinger-Dayan discussions, 32
  Kissinger-Israeli cabinet discussions, 68, 70
  Kissinger-Meir discussions, 39, 40, 43, 44, 53, 54, 55, 60, 62, 63, 65, 72
  Kissinger memoranda, 45, 50, 73
  Kissinger-Sadat discussions, 27, 38, 52, 86
  Nixon-Congressional leadership discussions, 31, 91
  Nixon-Meir correspondence, 69

Scowcroft, Lt. Gen. Brent—*Continued*
 Syrian-Israeli disengagement
  agreement—*Continued*
  Nixon memoranda, 61, 66
  U.S. military aid to Israel and, Kissinger memoranda, 56, 59
 U.S. Middle East policy reassessment:
  Ambassadors discussions, 173
  Ford-Fisher discussions, 165
  Ford-Kissinger discussions, 161, 164, 182
  Ford-Rabin discussions, 183
  Kissinger memoranda, 176
  Kissinger-Moynihan discussions, 172
  National Security Council discussions, 166, 174
  U.S. military aid to Israel, 98, 99, 100, 101, 254, 256, 261
Scranton, William W., 169
Seelye, Talcott W., 290
Senior Review Group, 98
Shafir, Maj. Gen. Herzl, 88, 89
Shakkour, Yusef, 77
Shakkut, Lt. Gen. Youssef, 83
Shalev, Mordechai:
 Allon U.S. visit, 93, 127
 Post-disengagement negotiations, 120, 123
 Sinai Interim Agreement, 117, 120, 188, 200
 Syrian-Israeli disengagement agreement, 32, 41, 69
 U.S. Middle East policy reassessment, 183
 U.S. military aid to Israel, 87
Shapiro, Judah J., 138
Sharm el-Sheikh, 94, 183
Sheehan, Edward R. F., 261
Sheinkman, David, 36
Sheinkman, Jacob, 261
al-Shihabi, Brig. Gen. Hikmat, 35, 46, 48, 77, 88, 89
Shuttle diplomacy. *See* First Egyptian-Israeli disengagement agreement; Sinai Interim Agreement; Syrian-Israeli disengagement agreement.
Siilasvuo, Ensio, 16, 88, 89
Simon, William E., 163, 166
Sinai II. *See* Sinai Interim Agreement.
Sinai Interim Agreement (Sinai II) (Sept. 1, 1975) (*see also* Post-disengagement negotiations; U.S. Middle East policy reassessment):
 Congressional approval, 241, 242

References are to document numbers

Index   1091

Sinai Interim Agreement (Sinai II) (Sept. 1, 1975)—Continued
   Ford-Allon discussions, 123, 127
   Ford-Congressional leadership discussions, 236, 239, 240
   Ford-Dinitz discussions, 200
   Ford-Fisher discussions, 128, 129, 186
   Ford-Javits discussions, 201
   Ford-Kissinger discussions, 130, 179, 184, 185, 190, 191, 194, 196, 197, 205, 206, 207, 210, 212, 213, 214
   Ford memoranda, 150
   Ford-Rabin correspondence, 156, 158, 159, 200, 231, 234, 235
   Ford-Rabin discussions, 183
   Ford-Sadat correspondence, 199, 214, 228, 232, 233, 235, 237
   Ford-Sadat discussions, 177, 178, 246
   Ford-Shalev discussions, 117
   Ford-Toon discussions, 198
   Kissinger-Allon correspondence, 228
   Kissinger-Allon discussions, 93
   Kissinger-American Jewish community group discussions, 138, 168, 189
   Kissinger-Asad discussions, 141, 147
   Kissinger-Dinitz discussions, 202, 203
   Kissinger-Fahmy correspondence, 158, 229
   Kissinger-Fahmy discussions, 149
   Kissinger-Israeli cabinet discussions, 107, 134
   Kissinger memoranda, 145, 223, 224, 225
   Kissinger-Rabin discussions, 131, 142, 143, 146, 152, 153, 154, 157, 158, 188, 208, 217, 221, 222
   Kissinger-Sadat correspondence, 208
   Kissinger-Sadat discussions, 104, 115, 132, 140, 144, 149, 151, 155, 218, 220
   Minute of Record, 230
   National Security Council discussions, 111
   Rabin-Sadat correspondence, 144
   Sinai Support Mission, 238, 245, 248
   Staff discussions, 187, 192, 195, 209, 211, 215, 216
   Talk suspension, 158, 159, 160, 161
   Text, 226
   U.S.-Israeli Memorandum of Agreement, 227
Sinai Separation of Forces Agreement. See Egyptian-Israeli disengagement agreement (Jan. 1974).

Sinai Support Mission, 238, 245, 248
Sion, Col. Dov, 16, 76, 78
Sisco, Joseph J.:
   Allon U.S. visit, 93
   Egyptian-Israeli disengagement agreement, 4, 5, 6, 7, 9
   Lebanese Civil War:
      Staff discussions, 268, 271, 272, 273, 274, 277, 278, 280, 281, 282
      Washington Special Actions Group discussions, 264
   Palestinians, 249
   Post-disengagement negotiations, 107
   Rabin U.S. visit, 256, 257, 259
   Sinai Interim Agreement:
      Ford-Khaddam discussions, 193
      Ford-Sadat correspondence, 237
      Ford-Sadat discussions, 177, 178
      Kissinger-Rabin discussions, 158, 188
      Minute of Record, 230
      Sinai Support Mission, 245
      Staff discussions, 187, 192, 195, 209, 211, 215, 216
   Syrian-Israeli disengagement agreement:
      American Jewish community group discussions, 36
      Kissinger-Asad correspondence, 20, 21
      Kissinger-Asad discussions, 48, 77
      Kissinger-Dayan discussions, 32
      Kissinger-Meir discussions, 28, 49, 76, 78
      Kissinger-al-Shihabi discussions, 35
   U.S. Middle East policy reassessment, 166, 169, 170, 171, 183
   U.S. military aid to Israel, 254
Six-Point Agreement (1973), 5
Smith, Lt. Gen. William Y., 264, 265
Smith, Walter B., 93
Sober, Sidney, 98, 253
Sonnenfeldt, Helmut, 254, 274
Soviet Union:
   Egyptian-Israeli disengagement agreement and, 6, 17, 18
   Egyptian relations with, 32, 111, 261, 262
   Ford-Kissinger discussions, 95
   Ford-Rabin discussions, 256
   Ford-Sadat correspondence, 237
   Geneva Conference resumption, 22, 32, 189

References are to document numbers

1092 Index

Soviet Union—*Continued*
  Kissinger-American Jewish
    community group discussions,
    189
  Lebanese Civil War, 269, 270, 271,
    282, 286
  Middle East war projections, 126
  Military aid to Syria, 48, 74, 256
  Nixon-Congressional leadership
    discussions, 91
  PLO Security Council debate
    participation, 250
  Post-disengagement negotiations,
    Kissinger-Congressional
    leadership discussions, 137
  Syrian-Israeli disengagement
    agreement, 32
    Gromyko-Asad discussions, 29, 77
    Kissinger-American Jewish
      community group discussions,
      23, 36
    Kissinger-Asad discussions, 48, 75
    Kissinger-Gromyko discussions, 22
    Kissinger-Meir discussions, 47
    Kissinger memoranda, 51
    Kissinger-al-Shihabi discussions, 35
    U.S. Middle East policy reassessment
      and, 166, 174
  U.S. relations with:
    Grain deal, 23, 36
    Kissinger-American Jewish
      community group discussions,
      36
    Most-favored nation status, 6, 23,
      31, 126
    Nixon-Congressional leadership
      discussions, 31
    U.S.-Israeli discussions, 49
Sparkman, John J., 160, 242
Special National Intelligence Estimates,
  SNIE 30–1–75, "Next Steps in the
  Middle East," 166
Spiegel, Albert, 189
Springsteen, George S., Jr., 266
Stein, Jacob, 36
Stennis, John C., 91, 160
Sternstein, Joseph P., 261
Stern, Thomas, 98
Stoessinger, John, 168
Suez Canal opening:
  Egyptian-Israeli discussions, 16
  Ford-Kissinger discussions, 95

Suez Canal opening—*Continued*
  Kissinger-American Jewish
    community group discussions,
    36, 138
  U.S.-Egyptian correspondence, 13
  U.S.-Egyptian discussions, 5
  U.S.-Israeli correspondence, 12
  U.S.-Israeli discussions, 1, 7, 9, 93
  U.S.-Israeli Memorandum of
    Understanding, 14
Suez City, 5, 6
Symington, James W., 204
Syria (*see also* Asad, Hafez;
  Post-disengagement negotiations):
  Ford-Sadat correspondence, 237
  Jordanian relations with, 256
  Lebanese Civil War:
    Ambassadors discussions, 290, 292
    Ford-Cabinet discussions, 289
    Ford-Kissinger discussions, 269,
      279
    Ford-Rabin discussions, 256
    National Security Council
      discussions, 284
    Staff discussions, 267, 268, 271, 272,
      273, 274, 275, 276, 278, 281
    Washington Special Actions Group
      discussions, 265, 270, 286
  Nixon visit (June 1974), 29, 92
  PLO Security Council debate
    participation, 250
  Political situation, 46
  Sinai Interim Agreement and:
    Ford-Khaddam discussions, 193
    Kissinger-Asad discussions, 141,
      147
    Kissinger-Dinitz discussions, 202
    Kissinger memoranda, 229
    Kissinger-Rabin discussions, 188
    Minute of Record, 230
    Staff discussions, 209
  Soviet military aid, 48, 74, 256
  U.S. economic aid, 80
  U.S. relations with, 75, 92
  Syrian-Israeli disengagement
    agreement:
    Geneva Conference resumption and,
      4, 19, 84
    Gromyko-Asad discussions, 29, 77
    Israeli approval, 79
    Israeli public protests, 46, 47, 48, 49
    Kissinger-American Jewish
      community group discussions,
      23, 36

Syrian-Israeli disengagement
agreement—*Continued*
Kissinger-Asad correspondence, 20, 21, 24
Kissinger-Asad discussions, 19, 25, 26, 29, 42, 48, 51, 54, 57, 62, 64, 67, 71, 74, 75, 77, 78
Kissinger Cabinet report, 18
Kissinger-Dayan discussions, 32, 40, 53
Kissinger-Faisal discussions, 51
Kissinger-Gromyko discussions, 47, 51
Kissinger-Israeli cabinet discussions, 4, 9, 19, 68, 70
Kissinger-Meir correspondence, 33, 37, 85
Kissinger-Meir discussions, 26, 28, 29, 39, 40, 43, 44, 46, 47, 49, 53, 54, 55, 60, 62, 63, 65, 72, 76, 78
Kissinger memoranda, 45, 50, 56, 59, 73
Kissinger-Sadat discussions, 8, 9, 27, 28, 38, 43, 52, 86
Kissinger-al-Shihabi discussions, 35
Map, 90
Nixon-Asad correspondence, 80, 81, 82
Nixon-Congressional leadership discussions, 17, 31, 91
Nixon-Meir correspondence, 37, 41, 69
Nixon memoranda, 61, 66
Protocol text, 89
Saudi position, 21
Text, 88
U.S.-Israeli Memorandum of Understanding, 84
U.S. military aid to Israel and, 56, 59
U.S. proposal, 83
U.S.-Soviet discussions, 22, 32

Takla, Philippe, 263
Tamil, Gen. Najd, 77
Tisch, Lawrence, 23, 189
Tlas, Gen. Mustafa, 77
Toon, Malcolm "Mac," 188, 198, 216, 256, 257, 259
Toumayan, Alec, 263
Trade Act (*1974*), 126

UN Disengagement Observer Force (UNDOF):
Ford-Fisher discussions, 252

UN Disengagement Observer Force (UNDOF)—*Continued*
Ford-Rabin correspondence, 120, 250
Ford-Rabin discussions, 256
Syrian-Israeli disengagement agreement protocol, 89
U.S.-Israeli discussions, 76, 99
U.S. Middle East policy reassessment and, 166
U.S.-Syrian discussions, 118
UN Emergency Force (UNEF):
Egyptian-Israeli discussions, 16
Egyptian-Israeli disengagement agreement and, 6, 7, 16
Nixon-Congressional leadership discussions, 17
Sinai Interim Agreement and, 145, 149, 220, 231
Syrian-Israeli disengagement agreement and, 71
U.S.-Egyptian discussions, 5, 177, 178
U.S.-Israeli discussions, 1, 6, 7, 9, 32, 71
U.S.-Israeli Memoranda of Understanding, 14, 84
U.S. Middle East policy reassessment and, 166
U.S.-Syrian discussions, 35, 42, 71
United Nations:
General Assembly Resolutions:
No. *3336* (Nov. *10, 1975*), 249
No. *3379* (Zionism) (Nov. *10, 1975*), 249, 252
No. *11898* (Lebanon) (vetoed Dec. *8, 1975*), 252
PLO General Assembly participation, 104, 108, 109, 110, 111, 113, 123
PLO Security Council debate participation, 249, 250, 251, 252, 253
Security Council Resolutions:
No. *242* (Nov. *22, 1967*), 9, 17, 29, 253
No. *338* (Oct. *22, 1973*), 7, 74, 76, 253
No. *347* (Apr. *24, 1974*), 36, 37
No. *11940* (vetoed Jan. *26, 1976*), 249, 255, 257
U.S. Middle East policy reassessment, Kissinger-Moynihan discussions, 172
U.S. Middle East policy reassessment:
Ambassadors discussions, 166, 170, 171

References are to document numbers

U.S. Middle East policy reassessment—*Continued*
  Ford-Congressional leadership discussions, 160
  Ford-Fisher discussions, 165
  Ford-Kissinger discussions, 159, 160, 164, 182
  Ford-Rabin discussions, 183
  Javits letter, 175, 176, 177, 180, 181
  Kissinger-American Jewish community group discussions, 168
  Kissinger memoranda, 176
  Kissinger-Moynihan discussions, 172
  National Security Council discussions, 166, 174
  Rabin interview, 176
  Rockefeller-Fahd discussions, 166
  SNIE 30–1–75, 166
U.S. political situation, 255, 258, 290

Vance, Cyrus, 169
Vatican, 271

Vest, George, 4, 28, 266

Waldheim, Kurt, 249
Walters, Lt. Gen. Vernon A., 98, 270
Waring, Robert, 288
Washington Special Actions Group, 126, 264, 265, 270, 286
Waxman, Mordecai, 138
West Bank (*see also* Palestinian West Bank representation), 252
Wiesel, Elie, 168
Winter, Elmer L., 23, 138, 261

Yamani, Ahmed Z., 135, 265
Yariv, Maj. Gen. Aharon, 5, 23
Yost, Charles W., 290

Zablocki, Clement, 91
Zaira, Gen. Eliahu, 4
Ziegler, Ron, 25, 86
Ziffren, Paul, 23
Zuckerman, Paul, 36
Zumwalt, Adm. Elmo, 261

ISBN 978-0-16-082998-7

References are to document numbers
U.S. GOVERNMENT PRINTING OFFICE: 2012—349-188